LEARN HOW THIS BOOK CAN HELP YOU UNDERSTAND U.S. HISTORY

See pages xxxii–xxxvii.

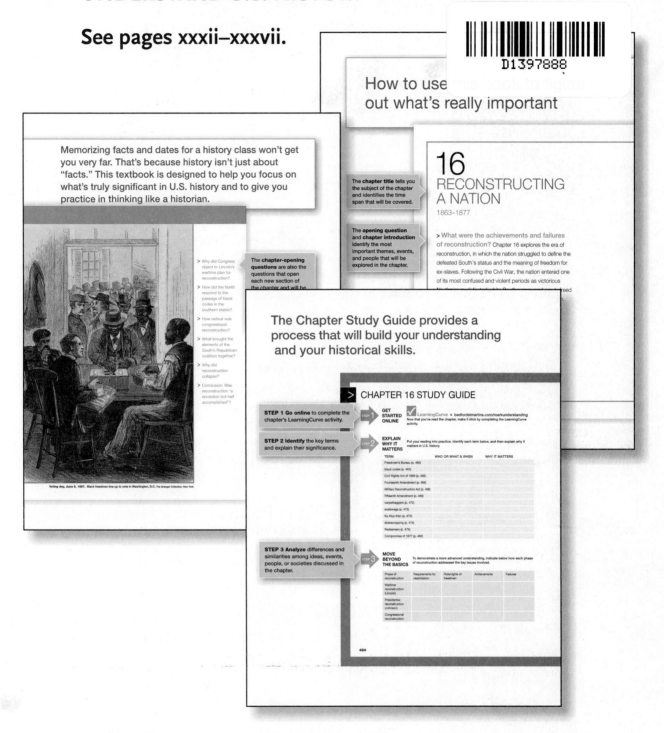

Memorizing facts and dates for a history class won't get you very far. That's because history isn't just about "facts." This textbook is designed to help you focus on what's truly significant in U.S. history and to give you practice in thinking like a historian.

> Why did Congress object to Lincoln's wartime plan for reconstruction?

> How did the North respond to the passage of black codes in the southern states?

> How radical was congressional reconstruction?

> What brought the elements of the South's Republican coalition together?

> Why did reconstruction collapse?

> Conclusion: Was reconstruction "a revolution but half accomplished"?

The **chapter-opening questions** are also the questions that open each new section of the chapter and will be

Voting day, June 5, 1867. Black freedmen line up to vote in Washington, D.C. The Granger Collection, New York.

How to use this book to figure out what's really important

The **chapter title** tells you the subject of the chapter and identifies the time span that will be covered.

The **opening question** and **chapter introduction** identify the most important themes, events, and people that will be explored in the chapter.

16
RECONSTRUCTING A NATION
1863–1877

> What were the achievements and failures of reconstruction? Chapter 16 explores the era of reconstruction, in which the nation struggled to define the defeated South's status and the meaning of freedom for ex-slaves. Following the Civil War, the nation entered one of its most confused and violent periods as victorious

The Chapter Study Guide provides a process that will build your understanding and your historical skills.

> CHAPTER 16 STUDY GUIDE

STEP 1 Go online to complete the chapter's LearningCurve activity.

GET STARTED ONLINE

✓ LearningCurve ■ bedfordstmartins.com/roarkunderstanding
Now that you've read the chapter, make it stick by completing the LearningCurve activity.

STEP 2 Identify the key terms and explain their significance.

EXPLAIN WHY IT MATTERS

Put your reading into practice. Identify each term below, and then explain why it matters in U.S. history.

TERM	WHO OR WHAT & WHEN	WHY IT MATTERS
Freedmen's Bureau (p. 460)		
black codes (p. 463)		
Civil Rights Act of 1866 (p. 465)		
Fourteenth Amendment (p. 466)		
Military Reconstruction Act (p. 468)		
Fifteenth Amendment (p. 468)		
carpetbaggers (p. 472)		
scalawags (p. 472)		
Ku Klux Klan (p. 473)		
sharecropping (p. 474)		
Redeemers (p. 479)		
Compromise of 1877 (p. 482)		

STEP 3 Analyze differences and similarities among ideas, events, people, or societies discussed in the chapter.

MOVE BEYOND THE BASICS

To demonstrate a more advanced understanding, indicate below how each phase of reconstruction addressed the key issues involved.

Phase of reconstruction	Requirements for readmission	Role/rights of freedmen	Achievements	Failures
Wartime reconstruction (Lincoln)				
Presidential reconstruction (Johnson)				
Congressional reconstruction				

464

"The pedagogical tools in *Understanding the American Promise* are superior."
— Tim Myers, Butler Community College

Understanding
the American Promise

A HISTORY

Understanding the American Promise

A HISTORY

SECOND EDITION

James L. Roark
Emory University

Michael P. Johnson
Johns Hopkins University

Patricia Cline Cohen
*University of California,
Santa Barbara*

Sarah Stage
Arizona State University

Susan M. Hartmann
The Ohio State University

Bedford / St. Martin's
Boston • New York

For Bedford/St. Martin's

Publisher for History: Mary V. Dougherty
Executive Editor for History: William J. Lombardo
Director of Development for History: Jane Knetzger
Developmental Editor: Kathryn Abbott
Senior Production Editor: Karen S. Baart
Assistant Production Manager: Joe Ford
Executive Marketing Manager: Sandra McGuire
Associate Editors: Jack Cashman, Jennifer Jovin
Editorial Assistant: Emily DiPietro
Production Assistants: Elise Keller, Kim Lester
Copyeditor: Linda McLatchie
Indexer: Leoni Z. McVey, McVey & Associates, Inc.
Photo Researchers: Pembroke Herbert and Sandi Rygiel, Picture Research Consultants, Inc.
Senior Art Director: Anna Palchik
Text Designer: Cenveo Publisher Services
Cover Designer: Donna Lee Dennison
Cover Art: Winold Reiss, *Father and Two Children, St. Helena.* Mixed media on Whatman board, 1927.
    Fisk University Museum of Art, Nashville, Tennessee.
Cartography: Mapping Specialists, Limited
Composition: Cenveo Publisher Services
Printing and Binding: RR Donnelley and Sons

President, Bedford/St. Martin's: Denise B. Wydra
Director of Marketing: Karen R. Soeltz
Production Director: Susan W. Brown
Director of Rights and Permissions: Hilary Newman

Manufactured in the United States of America.

2 3 4 5 6   17 16 15 14

For information, write: Bedford/St. Martin's, 75 Arlington Street, Boston, MA 02116
(617-399-4000)

ISBN: 978–1–4576–3979–1 (Combined Edition)
ISBN: 978–1–4576–6414–4 (Loose-leaf Edition)
ISBN: 978–1–4576–3980–7 (Volume I)
ISBN: 978–1–4576–6415–1 (Loose-leaf Edition,
    Volume I)

ISBN: 978–1–4576–3982–1 (Volume II)
ISBN: 978–1–4576–6413–7 (Loose-leaf Edition,
    Volume II)
ISBN: 978–1–4576–6255–3 (High School Edition)

Acknowledgments

Page 553: From "Expulsion of the Immigrants" by Huang Zunxian, translated by J. D. Schmidt in *Waiting for the Unicorn: Poems and Lyrics of China's Last Dynasty, 1644–1911* by Irving Yucheng Lo and William Schultz. Copyright © 1986 by William Rudolph Schultz and Irving Yucheng Lo. Reprinted with permission of Indiana University Press.

Pages 704–05: "Pretty Boy Floyd." Lyrics and music by Woody Guthrie. Copyright © 1983 (Renewed 1991) WOODY GUTHRIE PUBLICATIONS (BMI)/Administration by BIG MUSIC. All Rights Reserved. Used by Permission. Reprinted by Permission of Hal Leonard Corporation.

PREFACE: Why This Book This Way

U nderstanding the American Promise grew out of many conversations over the last decade among ourselves and with others about the teaching and learning of history. We knew that instructors wanted a U.S. history text that introduced students to overarching trends and developments but at the same time gave voice to the diverse people who have made American history. We also knew that instructors wanted a text demonstrating that history is a discipline rooted in debate and inquiry. At the same time, we knew that even though many students dutifully read their survey texts, they often come away overwhelmed and confused about what is most important to know. Because of the difficulty many students have understanding the most important concepts when they read a traditional U.S. survey text, a growing number of instructors thought that their students needed a brief text that did not overwhelm them with detail. Instructors also wanted a text that would help students focus as they read, keep their interest in the material, and encourage them to learn historical thinking skills.

With these issues in mind, we took a hard look at the introductory course from a number of different directions. We reflected on the changes in our own classrooms, reviewed state-of-the-art scholarship on effective teaching, consulted learning experts and instructional designers, and talked to students and instructors about their needs. We talked to people who are teaching online and listened to instructors' wish lists for time-saving support materials. *Understanding the American Promise* is a textbook designed to address these wide-ranging concerns. With the second edition, we again combine an abridged narrative with an innovative design and unique pedagogy orchestrated to work together to aid students' understanding of the most important developments while also fostering students' ability to think historically. A number of revisions and additions make the second edition an even better tool for this textbook designed for understanding.

Because, like other instructors, we are eager to ensure students read and assimilate this rich material, we are excited to announce that the second edition of *Understanding the American Promise* comes with **LearningCurve**—an adaptive game-like online learning tool that helps students master content. The second edition also introduces **LaunchPad**, a new robust interactive e-book built into its own course space that makes customizing and assigning the book and its resources easy and efficient. To learn more about the benefits of LearningCurve and LaunchPad, see the "Versions and Supplements" section on page ix.

An Inquiry-based Model Designed for Understanding

By employing innovative pedagogy, we believe that *Understanding the American Promise* helps students not only understand the book's major developments but also begin to grasp the question-driven methodology that is at the heart of the historian's craft. Each chapter opens with a **NEW chapter-opening question** that drives students toward the overarching themes of the chapter, followed by a **brief chapter introduction** that identifies in simple, straightforward terms the most important events and people to be discussed. **Section-opening headings** expressed as questions and **section-ending quick review** questions further model the kinds of questions historians ask and help students engage in inquiry-based reading and understanding.

Chapter Study Guides Designed for Active Learning

At the core of *Understanding the American Promise*'s unique pedagogical features are the revised **Chapter Study Guides** that provide a carefully structured four-step process to help students build deep understanding of the chapter material. In **Step One**, students go online to complete the LearningCurve activity to ensure that they have a grasp of the basic content and concepts of the chapter. In **Step Two**, students not only identify the chapter's key terms but also explain why each matters. In **Step Three**, they begin to apply their understanding of the chapter material through activities that ask them to consider comparison, change-over-time, or cause and effect. In **Step Four**, analytical and synthetic questions require students to engage in higher-order historical thinking. And, finally, in an active recitation exercise, students **answer the chapter-opening question** to fully realize their understanding of the chapter.

Visual Learning Aids

Throughout each chapter, a wide range of visual material keeps students' attention and reinforces important concepts. Some narrative material has been moved into **figures and tables** to call out and organize certain concepts visually and provide an alternative mode of learning. Two **map activities** per chapter engage students in reading maps and making connections and thus enhance geographical literacy. In total, there are over 165 maps in the book. A **visual activity** in each chapter reinforces the role of images as historical evidence. Many of the 300-plus images in the book are historical artifacts that underscore the importance of material culture.

Additional Pedagogical Features

The second edition includes several other helpful learning tools. As mentioned earlier, the **NEW LearningCurve online adaptive activity** is designed to prepare students for class by reinforcing their work reading the textbooks. **Section-based chronologies** of historical developments help students keep events in context as they read. Because students often have difficulty seeing the forest for the trees, innovative **chapter locators** at the foot of the page remind students of where they are in the chapter's larger progression of events and concepts. **Key terms** highlighted in the text and then defined in the margins further remind students of what's most important to know.

Updated Scholarship

In our ongoing effort to offer a comprehensive text that braids all Americans into the national narrative and to frame that narrative in a more global perspective, we updated the second edition in many ways. We have paid particular attention to the most recent scholarship and, as always, appreciated and applied many suggestions from our users that keep the book fresh, accurate, and organized in a way that works best for students.

Volume I draws on exciting new scholarship on Native Americans, leading to enhanced coverage of Pontiac's Rebellion in chapter 6 and more attention to Indians and their roles in the conflict between the British and the colonists in chapter 7. Chapter 9 expands the coverage of American interactions with Indians in the Southwest, adding new material on Creek chief Alexander McGillivray. Chapter 10 greatly increases the coverage of Indians in the West, with a new section devoted to the Osage territory and the powerful Comanche empire known as Comanchería.

Volume II also includes expanded attention to Native Americans—particularly in Chapter 17, where we improved coverage of Indian schools, assimilation techniques used by whites, and Indian resistance strategies. For the second edition, we also provide more coverage of women, African Americans, and the global context of U.S. history. In the narrative, we consider the ways in which the GI Bill disproportionately benefited white men after World War II. Chapter 16 includes new coverage of the Colfax massacre, arguably the single worst incidence of brutality against African Americans during the Reconstruction era. Chapter 27 provides new coverage of civil rights activism in northern states.

Because students live in an increasingly global world and need help making connections with the world outside the United States, we have continued our efforts to incorporate the global context of American history throughout the second edition. This is particularly evident in Volume II, where we have expanded coverage of transnational issues in recent decades, such as the U.S. bombing campaign in Vietnam and U.S. involvement in Afghanistan.

In addition to the many changes noted above, in both volumes we have updated, revised, and improved this second edition in response to both new scholarship and requests from instructors. New and expanded coverage areas include, among others, taxation in the pre-Revolutionary period and the early Republic, the Newburgh Conspiracy of the 1780s, the overbuilding of railroads in the West during the Gilded Age, the 1918–1919 global influenza epidemic, finance reform in the 1930s, post–World War II considerations of universal health care, Latino activism, the economic downturn of the late 2000s, the most recent developments in the Middle East, and the Obama presidency.

Acknowledgments

We gratefully acknowledge all of the helpful suggestions from those who have read or taught from the previous edition of *Understanding the American Promise*, and we hope that our many classroom collaborators will be pleased to see their influence in the second edition. In particular, we wish to thank the talented scholars and teachers who gave generously of their time and knowledge to review this book: Brittany Adams, *Irvine Valley College*; John Bradford Bowers, *Pueblo Community College*; Vincent A. Clark, *Johnson County Community College*; Jane Dabel, *California State University–Long Beach*; Diane Duray, *Howard Community College*; Michael J. Engle, *Pueblo Community College*; Keith A. Erekson, *University of Texas–El Paso*; Josh Fulton, *Valley Community College*; Jessica Gerard, *Ozarks Technical Community College*; Geoffrey R. Hunt, *Community College of Aurora*; Josh Lieser, *MiraCosta College*; Steven Lurenz, *Mesa Community College*; Jeffrey J. Malanson, *Indiana University-Purdue University–Fort Wayne*; Tim

Myers, *Butler Community College*; Marjorie Moss Nash, *Alvin Community College*; Brian D. Page, *Edison State College*; Jessica Patton, *Tarrant County College*; Carmen Reys-Johnson, *Northeast Lakeview College*; Norman Rodriguez, *John Wood Community College*; Mark Roehrs, *Lincoln Land Community College*; Nancy E. Shockley, *Oakland Community College*; Allen N. Smith, Jr., *Ivy Tech Community College*; Adam M. Sowards, *University of Idaho*; Michael A. Sparks, *Ivy Tech Community College*; Danielle J. Swiontek, *Santa Barbara City College*; David Tegeder, *University of Florida*; Joseph Thurman, *Jefferson College*; Kirk Walton, *Black Hawk College*; Laura Westhoff, *University of Missouri–St. Louis*.

A project as complex as this requires the talents of many individuals. First, we would like to acknowledge our families for their support, forbearance, and toleration of our textbook responsibilities. Pembroke Herbert and Sandi Rygiel of Picture Research Consultants, Inc., contributed their unparalleled knowledge, soaring imagination, and diligent research to make possible the extraordinary illustration program.

We would also like to thank the many people at Bedford/St. Martin's who have been crucial to this project. Developmental editor Kathryn Abbott managed the entire revision and supplements program. Her skill, good judgment, and deep commitment to the project are obvious on every page. Thanks also go to associate editor Jack Cashman, who oversaw the development of the supplements, associate editor Jennifer Jovin who assisted in creating some of the reading and study tools, and editorial assistant Emily DiPietro for her help coordinating the pre-revision review and preparing the manuscript. We are also grateful to Jane Knetzger, director of development for history; William J. Lombardo, executive editor for history; and Mary Dougherty, publisher for history, for their support and guidance. For their imaginative and tireless efforts to promote the book, we want to thank John Hunger, Sean Blest, Sandra McGuire, and Alex Kaufman. With great skill and professionalism, senior production editor Karen Baart pulled together the many pieces related to copyediting, design, and composition with the guidance of associate production director Elise Kaiser. Assistant production supervisor Joe Ford oversaw the manufacturing of the book. Designer Carie Keller, copyeditor Linda McLatchie, and proofreaders Kathleen Lafferty and Angela Morrison attended to the myriad details that help make the book shine. Leoni McVey and Associates provided the index. The book's gorgeous covers were designed by Donna Lee Dennison. New media editors Kimberly Hampton and Marissa Zanetti and media producers Rebecca Merrill and Michelle Camisa made sure that *Understanding the American Promise* remains at the forefront of technological support for students and instructors. President of Bedford/St. Martin's Denise Wydra provided helpful advice throughout the course of the project. Finally, Charles H. Christensen, former president, took a personal interest in *The American Promise* from the start, and Joan E. Feinberg, co-president of Macmillan Higher Education, encouraged us through each edition.

James Roark
Michael Johnson
Patricia Cohen
Sarah Stage
Susan Hartmann

VERSIONS AND SUPPLEMENTS

Adopters of *Understanding the American Promise* and their students have access to abundant extra resources, including documents, presentation and testing materials, the acclaimed Bedford Series in History and Culture volumes, and much more. See below for more information, visit the book's catalog site at **bedfordstmartins.com/roarkunderstanding/catalog**, or contact your local Bedford/St. Martin's sales representative.

Get the Right Version for Your Class

To accommodate different course lengths and course budgets, *Understanding the American Promise* is available in several different formats, including three-hole-punched loose-leaf Budget Books versions and e-books, which are available at a substantial discount.

- **Combined edition** (Chapters 1–31)—available in paperback, loose-leaf, and e-book formats
- **Volume 1: To 1877** (Chapters 1–16)—available in paperback, loose-leaf, and e-book formats
- **Volume 2: From 1865** (Chapters 16–31)—available in paperback, loose-leaf, and e-book formats

Any of these volumes can be packaged with additional books for a discount. To get ISBNs for discount packages, see the online catalog at **bedfordstmartins .com/roarkunderstanding/catalog** or contact your Bedford/St. Martin's representative.

▶ **NEW Assign LaunchPad—the online, interactive e-book in a course space enriched with integrated assets.** The new standard in digital history, LaunchPad course tools are so intuitive to use that online, hybrid, and face-to-face courses can be set up in minutes. Even novices will find it's easy to create assignments, track students' work, and access a wealth of relevant learning and teaching resources. It is the ideal learning environment for students to work with the text, maps, documents, video, and assessment. LaunchPad is loaded with the full interactive e-book and the *Reading the American Past* documents collection—plus LearningCurve, additional primary sources, videos, guided reading exercises designed to help students read actively for key concepts, chapter summative quizzes, and more. LaunchPad can be used as is or customized, and it easily integrates with course management systems. And with fast ways to build assignments, rearrange chapters, and add new pages, sections, or links, it lets teachers build the course materials they need and hold students accountable.

▶ **Let students choose their e-book format.** In addition to the LaunchPad e-book, students can purchase the downloadable *Bedford e-Book to Go for Understanding* *the American Promise* from our Web site or find other PDF versions of the e-book at our publishing partners' sites: CourseSmart, Barnes & Noble NookStudy, Kno, CafeScribe, or Chegg.

NEW Assign LearningCurve So You Know What Your Students Know and They Come to Class Prepared

As described in the preface and on the inside front cover, students purchasing new books receive access to LearningCurve for *Understanding the American Promise*. Assigning LearningCurve in place of reading quizzes is easy for instructors, and the reporting features help instructors track overall class trends and spot topics that are giving students trouble so they can adjust their lectures and class activities. This online learning tool is popular with students because it was designed to help them rehearse content at their own pace in a non-threatening, game-like environment. The feedback for wrong answers provides instructional coaching and sends students back to the book for review. Students answer as many questions as necessary to reach a target score, with repeated chances to revisit material they haven't mastered. When LearningCurve is assigned, students come to class better prepared.

Send Students to Free Online Resources

The book's Student Site at **bedfordstmartins.com/roarkunderstanding** gives students a way to read, write, and study by providing plentiful quizzes and activities, study aids, and history research and writing help.

▶ **FREE Online Study Guide.** Available at the Student Site, this popular resource provides students with quizzes and activities for each chapter, including multiple-choice self-tests that focus on important concepts, flashcards that test students' knowledge of key terms, timeline activities that emphasize causal relationships, and map quizzes intended to strengthen students' geography skills. Instructors can monitor students' progress through an online Quiz Gradebook or receive e-mail updates.

▶ **FREE Research, Writing, and Anti-plagiarism Advice.** Available at the Student Site, Bedford's **History Research and Writing Help** includes the textbook authors' **Suggested References** organized by chapter; **History Research and Reference Sources**, with links to history-related databases, indexes, and journals; **Build a Bibliography**, a simple Web-based tool known as The Bedford Bibliographer that generates bibliographies in four commonly used documentation styles; and **Tips on Avoiding Plagiarism**, an online tutorial that reviews the consequences of plagiarism and features exercises to help students practice integrating sources and recognize acceptable summaries.

Take Advantage of Instructor Resources

Bedford/St. Martin's has developed a rich array of teaching resources for this book and for this course. They range from lecture and presentation materials and assessment tools to course management options. Most can be downloaded or ordered at **bedfordstmartins.com/roarkunderstanding/catalog**.

▶ **Instructor's Resource Manual.** The instructor's manual offers both experienced and first-time instructors tools for preparing lectures and running discussions. It includes chapter-review material, teaching strategies, and a guide to chapter-specific supplements available for the text, plus suggestions on how to get the most out of LearningCurve and a survival guide for first-time teaching assistants.

▶ **Guide to Changing Editions.** Designed to facilitate an instructor's transition from the previous edition of *Understanding the American Promise* to the current edition, this guide presents an overview of major changes as well as of changes in each chapter.

▶ **Computerized Test Bank.** The test bank includes a mix of fresh, carefully crafted multiple-choice, short-answer, and essay questions for each chapter. It also contains volume-wide essay questions. All questions appear in Microsoft Word format and in easy-to-use test bank software that allows instructors to add, edit, re-sequence, and print questions and answers. Instructors can also export questions into a variety of formats, including Blackboard, Desire2Learn, and Moodle.

▶ *The Bedford Lecture Kit:* **PowerPoint Maps, Images, Lecture Outlines, and i>clicker Content.** Look good and save time with *The Bedford Lecture Kit*. These presentation materials are downloadable individually from the Instructor Resources tab at **bedfordstmartins.com/roarkunderstanding/catalog** and are available on *The Bedford Lecture Kit* **Instructor's Resource CD-ROM**. They provide ready-made and fully customizable PowerPoint multimedia presentations that include lecture outlines with embedded maps, figures, and selected images from the textbook and extra background for instructors. Also available are maps and selected images in JPEG and PowerPoint formats; content for i>clicker, a classroom response system, in Microsoft Word and PowerPoint formats; the Instructor's Resource Manual in Microsoft Word format; and outline maps in PDF format for quizzing or handing out. All files are suitable for copying onto transparency acetates.

▶ *Reel Teaching: Film Clips for the U.S. History Survey.* This DVD provides a large collection of short video clips for classroom presentation. Designed as engaging "lecture launchers" varying in length from one to fifteen minutes or longer, the fifty-nine documentary clips were carefully chosen for use in both semesters of the U.S. survey course. The clips feature compelling images, archival footage, personal narratives, and commentary by noted historians.

▶ *America in Motion: Video Clips for U.S. History.* Set history in motion with *America in Motion,* an instructor DVD containing dozens of short digital movie files of events in twentieth-century American history. From the wreckage of the battleship *Maine* to FDR's fireside chats to Oliver North testifying before Congress, *America in Motion* engages students with dynamic scenes from key events and challenges them to think critically. All files are classroom-ready, edited for brevity, and easily integrated with PowerPoint or other presentation software for electronic lectures or assignments. An accompanying guide provides each clip's historical context, ideas for use, and suggested questions.

▶ **Videos and Multimedia.** A wide assortment of videos and multimedia CD-ROMs on various topics in U.S. history is available to qualified adopters through your Bedford/St. Martin's sales representative.

Package and Save Your Students Money

For information on free packages and discounts up to 50%, visit **bedfordstmartins .com/roarkunderstanding/catalog** or contact your local Bedford/St. Martin's sales representative. The products that follow all qualify for discount packaging.

▶ *Reading the American Past,* **Fifth Edition.** Edited by Michael P. Johnson, one of the authors of *The American Promise,* and designed to complement the text-book, *Reading the American Past* provides a broad selection of over 150 primary-source documents as well as editorial apparatus to help students understand the sources. Available free when packaged with the print text and included in the LaunchPad e-book. Also available on its own as a downloadable PDF e-book or with the main text's e-Book to Go.

▶ NEW **Bedford Digital Collections @ bedfordstmartins.com/bdc/catalog.** This source collection provides a flexible and affordable online repository of discovery-oriented primary-source projects and single primary sources that you can easily customize and link to from your course management system or Web site. Package discounts are available.

▶ **The Bedford Series in History and Culture.** More than 120 titles in this highly praised series combine first-rate scholarship, historical narrative, and important primary documents for undergraduate courses. Each book is brief, inexpensive, and focused on a specific topic or period. For a complete list of titles, visit **bedfordstmartins.com/history/series.** Package discounts are available.

▶ *Rand McNally Atlas of American History.* This collection of more than eighty full-color maps illustrates key events and eras from early exploration, settlement, expansion, and immigration to U.S. involvement in wars abroad and on U.S. soil. Introductory pages for each section include a brief overview, timelines, graphs, and photos to quickly establish a historical context. Available for $5.00 when packaged with the print text.

▶ *Maps in Context: A Workbook for American History.* Written by historical cartography expert Gerald A. Danzer (University of Illinois at Chicago), this skill-building workbook helps students comprehend essential connections between geographic literacy and historical understanding. Organized to correspond to the typical U.S. history survey course, *Maps in Context* presents a wealth of map-centered projects and convenient pop quizzes that give students hands-on experience working with maps. Available free when packaged with the print text.

▶ *The Bedford Glossary for U.S. History.* This handy supplement for the survey course gives students historically contextualized definitions for hundreds of terms—from *abolitionism* to *zoot suit*—that they will encounter in lectures, reading, and exams. Available free when packaged with the print text.

▶ *U.S. History Matters: A Student Guide to World History Online.* This resource, written by Alan Gevinson, Kelly Schrum, and the late Roy Rosenzweig (all of George Mason University), provides an illustrated and annotated guide to 250 of the most useful Web sites for student research in U.S. history as well as advice on evaluating and using Internet sources. This essential guide is based on the acclaimed "History Matters" Web site developed by the American Social History Project and the Center for History and New Media. Available free when packaged with the print text.

▶ **Trade Books.** Titles published by sister companies Hill and Wang; Farrar, Straus and Giroux; Henry Holt and Company; St. Martin's Press; Picador; and Palgrave Macmillan are available at a 50% discount when packaged with Bedford/St. Martin's textbooks. For more information, visit **bedfordstmartins.com/tradeup**.

▶ *A Pocket Guide to Writing in History.* This portable and affordable reference tool by Mary Lynn Rampolla provides reading, writing, and research advice useful to students in all history courses. Concise yet comprehensive advice on approaching typical history assignments, developing critical reading skills, writing effective history papers, conducting research, using and documenting sources, and avoiding plagiarism—enhanced with practical tips and examples throughout—have made this slim reference a best seller. Package discounts are available.

▶ *A Student's Guide to History.* This complete guide to success in any history course provides the practical help students need to be effective. In addition to introducing students to the nature of the discipline, author Jules Benjamin teaches a wide range of skills, from preparing for exams to approaching common writing assignments, and explains the research and documentation process with plentiful examples. Package discounts are available.

▶ *Going to the Source: The Bedford Reader in American History.* Developed by Victoria Bissell Brown and Timothy J. Shannon, this reader's strong pedagogical framework helps students learn how to ask fruitful questions in order to evaluate documents effectively and develop critical reading skills. The reader's wide variety of chapter topics that complement the survey course and its rich diversity of sources—from personal letters to political cartoons—provoke students' interest as it teaches them the skills they need to successfully interrogate historical sources. Package discounts are available.

▶ *America Firsthand.* With its distinctive focus on ordinary people, this primary documents reader, by Anthony Marcus, John M. Giggie, and David Burner, offers a remarkable range of perspectives on America's history from those who lived it. Popular Points of View sections expose students to different perspectives on a specific event or topic, and Visual Portfolios invite analysis of the visual record. Package discounts are available.

BRIEF CONTENTS

1 | Understanding Ancient America before 1492 2

2 | Europeans Encounter the New World, 1492–1600 28

3 | Founding the Southern Colonies in the Seventeenth Century, 1601–1700 54

4 | Founding the Northern Colonies, 1601–1700 82

5 | The Changing World of Colonial America, 1701–1770 110

6 | The British Empire and the Colonial Crisis, 1754–1775 140

7 | Fighting the American Revolution, 1775–1783 172

8 | Building a Republic, 1775–1789 204

9 | Forming the New Nation, 1789–1800 234

10 | A Maturing Republic, 1800–1824 260

11 | The Expanding Republic, 1815–1840 294

12 | The New West and the Free North, 1840–1860 326

13 | Understanding the Slave South, 1820–1860 358

14 | The House Divided, 1846–1861 390

15 | The Crucible of War, 1861–1865 422

16 | Reconstructing a Nation, 1863–1877 456

17 | Contesting the West, 1865–1900 486

18 | Defining the Gilded Age in Business and Politics, 1865–1900 516

19 The Growth of America's Cities, 1870–1900 *546*

20 Dissent, Depression, and War, 1890–1900 *578*

21 Progressivism from the Grass Roots Up, 1890–1916 *610*

22 The United States and World War I, 1914–1920 *644*

23 From New Era to Great Depression, 1920–1932 *676*

24 Forging the New Deal, 1932–1939 *710*

25 The United States and the Second World War, 1939–1945 *742*

26 Cold War Politics in the Truman Years, 1945–1953 *778*

27 The Politics and Culture of Abundance, 1952–1960 *804*

28 Reform, Rebellion, and Reaction, 1960–1974 *834*

29 Vietnam and the End of the Cold War Consensus, 1961–1975 *868*

30 The Conservative Turn, 1969–1989 *896*

31 Facing the Promises and Challenges of Globalization since 1989 *928*

Appendixes *A-1*
Index *I-1*

CONTENTS

Preface *v*
Versions and Supplements *ix*
Maps, Figures, and Tables *xxviii*
How to Use This Book *xxxii*

1 UNDERSTANDING ANCIENT AMERICA

BEFORE 1492 2

> When and why do historians rely on the work of archaeologists? 4
> How and why did humans migrate into North America? 6
  African and Asian Origins 6
  Paleo-Indian Hunters 8
> Why did Archaic Native Americans shift to foraging and hunting smaller animals? 10
  Great Plains Bison Hunters 12
  Great Basin Cultures 12
  Pacific Coast Cultures 12
  Eastern Woodland Cultures 13
> How did agriculture influence Native American cultures? 15
  Southwestern Cultures 15
  Woodland Burial Mounds and Chiefdoms 17
> What cultural similarities did native peoples of the Western Hemisphere share in the 1490s? 19
  Eastern and Great Plains Peoples 19
  Southwestern and Western Peoples 21
  Cultural Similarities 22
> Why was tribute important in the Mexican empire? 23
> Conclusion: How do we understand the worlds of ancient Americans? 25

✓ **LearningCurve**
bedfordstmartins.com/roarkunderstanding
CHAPTER 1 STUDY GUIDE 26

2 EUROPEANS ENCOUNTER THE NEW WORLD

1492–1600 28

> What factors led to European exploration in the fifteenth century? 30
  Mediterranean Trade and European Expansion 30
  A Century of Portuguese Exploration 32
> What did Spanish explorers discover in the western Atlantic? 34
  The Explorations of Columbus 34
  The Geographic Revolution and the Columbian Exchange 36
> How did Spaniards explore, conquer, and colonize New Spain? 39
  The Conquest of Mexico 39
  The Search for Other Mexicos 41
  Spanish Outposts in Florida and New Mexico 42
  New Spain in the Sixteenth Century 42
  The Toll of Spanish Conquest and Colonization 46
> What impact did Spain's New World endeavors have in Europe? 48
  The Protestant Reformation and the Spanish Response 48
  Europe and the Spanish Example 49
> Conclusion: What promise did the New World offer Europeans? 51

✓ **LearningCurve**
bedfordstmartins.com/roarkunderstanding
CHAPTER 2 STUDY GUIDE 52

3

FOUNDING THE SOUTHERN COLONIES IN THE SEVENTEENTH CENTURY
1601–1700 *54*

> What challenges faced early Chesapeake colonists? 56
  The Fragile Jamestown Settlement 57
  Cooperation and Conflict between Natives and Newcomers 58
  From Private Company to Royal Government 60

> How did Chesapeake tobacco society take shape? 61
  Tobacco Agriculture 61
  A Servant Labor System 63
  The Rigors of Servitude 65
  Cultivating Land and Faith 66

> Why did Chesapeake colonial society change in the late seventeenth century? 68
  Social and Economic Polarization 68
  Government Policies and Political Conflict 70
  Bacon's Rebellion 70

> Why did the southern colonies move toward a slave labor system? 72
  Religion and Revolt in the Spanish Borderland 73
  The West Indies: Sugar and Slavery 73
  Carolina: A West Indian Frontier 76
  Slave Labor Emerges in the Chesapeake 76

> Conclusion: Why were export crops and slave labor important in the growth of the southern colonies? 79

✓ **LearningCurve**
bedfordstmartins.com/roarkunderstanding

CHAPTER 3 STUDY GUIDE 80

4

FOUNDING THE NORTHERN COLONIES
1601–1700 *82*

> Why did the Puritans immigrate to North America? 84
  Puritan Origins: The English Reformation 84
  The Pilgrims and Plymouth Colony 86
  The Founding of Massachusetts Bay Colony 87

> How did New England society change during the seventeenth century? 89
  Church, Covenant, and Conformity 90
  Government by Puritans for Puritanism 91
  The Splintering of Puritanism 92
  Religious Controversies and Economic Changes 94

> What was distinctive about the middle colonies? 98
  From New Netherland to New York 98
  New Jersey and Pennsylvania 100
  Toleration and Diversity in Pennsylvania 100

> What was the connection between the colonies and the English empire? 102
  Royal Regulation of Colonial Trade 102
  King Philip's War and the Consolidation of Royal Authority 104

> Conclusion: Was there an English model of colonization in North America? 107

✓ **LearningCurve**
bedfordstmartins.com/roarkunderstanding

CHAPTER 4 STUDY GUIDE 108

5

THE CHANGING WORLD OF COLONIAL AMERICA
1701–1770 *110*

> How did the North American colonies change in the eighteenth century? 112

> What changed in New England life and culture? 114
  Natural Increase and Land Distribution 114
  Farms, Fish, and Atlantic Trade 115

> What spurred the growth of the middle colonies? 118
  German and Scots-Irish Immigrants 118
  "God Gives All Things to Industry": Urban and Rural Labor 120

> Why did slavery become the defining feature of the southern colonies? 123
  The Atlantic Slave Trade and the Growth of Slavery 123
  Slave Labor and African American Culture 127
  Tobacco, Rice, and Prosperity 128

> What experiences tended to unify the colonists in British North America during the eighteenth century? 130
  Commerce and Consumption 130
  Religion, Enlightenment, and Revival 131
  Trade and Conflict in the North American Borderlands 134
  Colonial Politics in the British Empire 135

> Conclusion: What was the dual identity of British North American colonists? 137

✓ **LearningCurve**
bedfordstmartins.com/roarkunderstanding

CHAPTER 5 STUDY GUIDE 138

6

THE BRITISH EMPIRE AND THE COLONIAL CRISIS

1754–1775 *140*

> How did the Seven Years' War lay the groundwork for colonial crisis? 142
  French-British Rivalry in the Ohio Country 142
  The Albany Congress 144
  The War and Its Consequences 146
  Pontiac's Rebellion and the Proclamation of 1763 148

> Why did the Sugar Act and the Stamp Act draw fierce opposition from colonists? 150
  Grenville's Sugar Act 150
  The Stamp Act 151
  Resistance Strategies and Crowd Politics 152
  Liberty and Property 154

> Why did British authorities send troops to occupy Boston in the fall of 1768? 156
  The Townshend Duties 157
  Nonconsumption and the Daughters of Liberty 157
  Military Occupation and "Massacre" in Boston 159

> Why did Parliament pass the Coercive Acts in 1774? 161
  The Calm before the Storm 161
  Tea in Boston Harbor 162
  The Coercive Acts 163
  Beyond Boston: Rural New England 163
  The First Continental Congress 164

> How did enslaved people in the colonies react to the stirrings of revolution? 166
  Lexington and Concord 166
  Rebelling against Slavery 167

> Conclusion: What changes did the American colonists want in 1775? 169

✓ **LearningCurve**
bedfordstmartins.com/roarkunderstanding

CHAPTER 6 STUDY GUIDE 170

7

FIGHTING THE AMERICAN REVOLUTION

1775–1783 *172*

> Why did Americans wait so long before they declared their independence? 174
  Assuming Political and Military Authority 174
  Pursuing Both War and Peace 175
  Thomas Paine, Abigail Adams, and the Case for Independence 176
  The Declaration of Independence 178

> What initial challenges did the opposing armies face? 180
  The American Military Forces 180
  The British Strategy 181
  Quebec, New York, and New Jersey 182

> What role did the home front play in the war? 185
  Patriotism at the Local Level 185
  The Loyalists 186
  Who Is a Traitor? 187
  Prisoners of War 188
  Financial Instability and Corruption 189

> How were Native Americans and the French involved in the war? 190
  Burgoyne's Army and the Battle of Saratoga 190
  The War in the West: Indian Country 192
  The French Alliance 193

> Why did the British southern strategy ultimately fail? 195
  Georgia and South Carolina 195
  Treason and Guerrilla Warfare 197
  Surrender at Yorktown 198
  The Losers and the Winners 199

> Conclusion: Why did the British lose the American Revolution? 201

✓ **LearningCurve**
bedfordstmartins.com/roarkunderstanding

CHAPTER 7 STUDY GUIDE 202

8

BUILDING A REPUBLIC

1775–1789 *204*

> What kind of government did the Articles of Confederation create? 206
  Confederation and Taxation 206
  The Problem of Western Lands 207
  Running the New Government 209

> How did the states define citizenship and freedom? 210
  The State Constitutions 210
  Who Are "the People"? 211
  Equality and Slavery 212

> Why did the Articles of Confederation fail? 215
  The War Debt and the Newburgh Conspiracy 216
  The Treaty of Fort Stanwix 217
  Land Ordinances and the Northwest Territory 218
  The Requisition of 1785 and Shays's Rebellion, 1786–1787 220

> How did the Constitution change how the nation was governed? 223
  From Annapolis to Philadelphia 223
  The Virginia and New Jersey Plans 224
  Democracy versus Republicanism 225

> What were the objections to ratification of the Constitution? 227
  The Federalists 227
  The Antifederalists 229
  The Big Holdouts: Virginia and New York 230

> Conclusion: What was the "republican remedy"? 231

✓ **LearningCurve**
bedfordstmartins.com/roarkunderstanding

CHAPTER 8 STUDY GUIDE 232

9
FORMING THE NEW NATION

1789–1800 *234*

> What were the sources of political stability in the 1790s? 236
>> Washington Inaugurates the Government 236
>> The Bill of Rights 237
>> The Republican Wife and Mother 238

> What were Hamilton's economic policies? 240
>> Agriculture, Transportation, and Banking 240
>> The Public Debt and Taxes 242
>> The First Bank of the United States and the *Report on Manufactures* 243
>> The Whiskey Rebellion 244

> What external threats did the United States face in the 1790s? 246
>> Creeks in the Southwest 247
>> Ohio Indians in the Northwest 248
>> France and Britain 250
>> The Haitian Revolution 251

> How did partisan rivalries shape the politics of the late 1790s? 253
>> The Election of 1796 253
>> The XYZ Affair 254
>> The Alien and Sedition Acts 255

> Conclusion: Why did the new nation ultimately form political parties? 257

✓ **LearningCurve**
bedfordstmartins.com/roarkunderstanding

CHAPTER 9 STUDY GUIDE 258

10
A MATURING REPUBLIC

1800–1824 *260*

> How did Jefferson attempt to undo the Federalist innovations of earlier administrations? 262
>> Turbulent Times: Election and Rebellion 262
>> The Jeffersonian Vision of Republican Simplicity 264
>> Dangers Overseas: The Barbary Wars 265

> What was the significance of the Louisiana Purchase for the United States? 267
>> The Louisiana Purchase 268
>> The Lewis and Clark Expedition 269
>> Osage and Comanche Indians 270

> Why did Congress declare war on Great Britain in 1812? 272
>> Impressment and Embargo 272
>> Dolley Madison and Social Politics 273
>> Tecumseh and Tippecanoe 274
>> The War of 1812 276
>> Washington City Burns: The British Offensive 278

> How did the civil status of American women and men differ in the early Republic? 280
>> Women and the Law 280
>> Women and Church Governance 281
>> Female Education 282

> Why did partisan conflict increase during the administrations of Monroe and Adams? 284
>> From Property to Democracy 285
>> The Missouri Compromise 286
>> The Monroe Doctrine 287
>> The Election of 1824 288
>> The Adams Administration 290

> Conclusion: How did republican simplicity become complex? 291

✓ **LearningCurve**
bedfordstmartins.com/roarkunderstanding

CHAPTER 10 STUDY GUIDE 292

11
THE EXPANDING REPUBLIC

1815–1840 *294*

> Why did the United States experience a market revolution after 1815? 296
>> Improvements in Transportation 297
>> Factories, Workingwomen, and Wage Labor 299
>> Bankers and Lawyers 300
>> Booms and Busts 301

> Why did Andrew Jackson defeat John Quincy Adams so dramatically in the 1828 election? 303
>> Popular Politics and Partisan Identity 303
>> The Election of 1828 and the Character Issue 304
>> Jackson's Democratic Agenda 305

> What was Andrew Jackson's impact on the presidency? 307
>> Indian Policy and the Trail of Tears 308
>> The Tariff of Abominations and Nullification 310
>> The Bank War and Economic Boom 311

> How did social and cultural life change in the 1830s? 313
>> The Family and Separate Spheres 313
>> The Education and Training of Youths 314
>> The Second Great Awakening 315
>> The Temperance Movement and the Campaign for Moral Reform 316
>> Organizing against Slavery 317

> Why was Martin Van Buren a one-term president? 319
>> The Politics of Slavery 320
>> Elections and Panics 320

> Conclusion: The Age of Jackson or the era of reform? 323

✓ **LearningCurve**
bedfordstmartins.com/roarkunderstanding

CHAPTER 11 STUDY GUIDE 324

12

THE NEW WEST AND THE FREE NORTH

1840–1860 *326*

> What factors contributed to the United States' "industrial evolution"? 328
  Agriculture and Land Policy 329
  Manufacturing and Mechanization 329
  Railroads: Breaking the Bonds of Nature 330
> How did the free-labor ideal account for economic inequality? 332
  The Free-Labor Ideal 333
  Economic Inequality 333
  Immigrants and the Free-Labor Ladder 334
> What factors spurred westward expansion? 336
  Manifest Destiny 336
  Oregon and the Overland Trail 337
  The Mormon Exodus 339
  The Mexican Borderlands 339
> Why did the United States go to war with Mexico? 342
  The Politics of Expansion 342
  The Mexican-American War, 1846–1848 343
  Victory in Mexico 346
  Golden California 347
> How did reform movements change after 1840? 350
  The Pursuit of Perfection: Transcendentalists and Utopians 351
  Woman's Rights Activists 352
  Abolitionists and the American Ideal 353
> Conclusion: How was white freedom in the West and North defined? 355

✓ **LearningCurve**
bedfordstmartins.com/roarkunderstanding

CHAPTER 12 STUDY GUIDE 356

13

UNDERSTANDING THE SLAVE SOUTH

1820–1860 *358*

> Why did the South become so distinctly different from the North? 360
  Cotton Kingdom, Slave Empire 361
  The South in Black and White 362
  The Plantation Economy 365
> What was plantation life like for masters and mistresses? 368
  Paternalism and Male Honor 368
  The Southern Lady and Feminine Virtues 370
> What was plantation life like for slaves? 372
  Work 373
  Family and Religion 374
  Resistance and Rebellion 375
> How did nonslaveholding southern whites work and live? 377
  Plantation-Belt Yeomen 378
  Upcountry Yeomen 378
  Poor Whites 379
  The Culture of the Plain Folk 380
> What place did free blacks occupy in the South? 381
  Precarious Freedom 381
  Achievement despite Restrictions 382
> How did slavery shape southern politics? 384
  The Democratization of the Political Arena 385
  Planter Power 385
> Conclusion: How did slavery come to define the South? 387

✓ **LearningCurve**
bedfordstmartins.com/roarkunderstanding

CHAPTER 13 STUDY GUIDE 388

14

THE HOUSE DIVIDED

1846–1861 *390*

> Why did the acquisition of land from Mexico contribute to sectional tensions? 392
  The Wilmot Proviso and the Expansion of Slavery 392
  The Election of 1848 395
  Debate and Compromise 395
> What factors helped unravel the balance between slave and free states? 398
  The Fugitive Slave Act 398
  Uncle Tom's Cabin 399
  The Kansas-Nebraska Act 400
> How did the party system change in the 1850s? 403
  The Old Parties: Whigs and Democrats 403
  The New Parties: Know-Nothings and Republicans 405
  The Election of 1856 407
> Why did northern fear of the "Slave Power" intensify in the 1850s? 408
  "Bleeding Kansas" 408
  The *Dred Scott* Decision 409
  Prairie Republican: Abraham Lincoln 411
  The Lincoln-Douglas Debates 411
> Why did some southern states secede immediately after Lincoln's election? 413
  John Brown's Raid 414
  Republican Victory in 1860 414
  Secession Winter 417
> Conclusion: Why did political compromise fail? 419

✓ **LearningCurve**
bedfordstmartins.com/roarkunderstanding

CHAPTER 14 STUDY GUIDE 420

15

THE CRUCIBLE OF WAR

1861–1865   *422*

> Why did both the Union and the Confederacy consider control of the border states crucial? 424
  - Attack on Fort Sumter 425
  - The Upper South Chooses Sides 425
> Why did each side expect to win? 427
  - How They Expected to Win 427
  - Lincoln and Davis Mobilize 429
> How did each side fare in the early years of the war? 431
  - Stalemate in the Eastern Theater 431
  - Union Victories in the Western Theater 434
  - The Atlantic Theater 436
  - International Diplomacy 436
> How did the war for union become a fight for black freedom? 438
  - From Slaves to Contraband 438
  - From Contraband to Free People 440
  - The War of Black Liberation 441
> What problems did the Confederacy face at home? 442
  - Revolution from Above 442
  - Hardship Below 443
  - The Disintegration of Slavery 444
> How did the war affect the economy and politics of the North? 445
  - The Government and the Economy 445
  - Women and Work at Home and at War 446
  - Politics and Dissent 447
> How did the Union finally win the war? 448
  - Vicksburg and Gettysburg 448
  - Grant Takes Command 450
  - The Election of 1864 451
  - The Confederacy Collapses 452
> Conclusion: In what ways was the Civil War a "Second American Revolution"? 453

✔ **LearningCurve**
bedfordstmartins.com/roarkunderstanding

CHAPTER 15 STUDY GUIDE 454

16

RECONSTRUCTING A NATION

1863–1877   *456*

> Why did Congress object to Lincoln's wartime plan for reconstruction? 458
  - "To Bind Up the Nation's Wounds" 458
  - Land and Labor 459
  - The African American Quest for Autonomy 460
> How did the North respond to the passage of black codes in the southern states? 462
  - Johnson's Program of Reconciliation 462
  - White Southern Resistance and Black Codes 463
  - Expansion of Federal Authority and Black Rights 464
> How radical was congressional reconstruction? 466
  - The Fourteenth Amendment and Escalating Violence 466
  - Radical Reconstruction and Military Rule 467
  - Impeaching a President 468
  - The Fifteenth Amendment and Women's Demands 469
> What brought the elements of the South's Republican coalition together? 471
  - Freedmen, Yankees, and Yeomen 471
  - Republican Rule 472
  - White Landlords, Black Sharecroppers 474
> Why did reconstruction collapse? 476
  - Grant's Troubled Presidency 476
  - Northern Resolve Withers 478
  - White Supremacy Triumphs 479
  - An Election and a Compromise 481
> Conclusion: Was reconstruction "a revolution but half accomplished"? 483

✔ **LearningCurve**
bedfordstmartins.com/roarkunderstanding

CHAPTER 16 STUDY GUIDE 484

17

CONTESTING THE WEST

1865–1900   *486*

> What did U.S. expansion mean for Native Americans? 488
  - Indian Removal and the Reservation System 490
  - The Decimation of the Great Bison Herds 491
  - Indian Wars and the Collapse of Comanchería 491
  - The Fight for the Black Hills 492
> In what ways did different Indian groups defy and resist colonial rule? 494
  - Indian Schools and the War on Indian Culture 494
  - The Dawes Act and Indian Land Allotment 496
  - Indian Resistance and Survival 496
> How did mining shape American expansion? 500
  - Life on the Comstock Lode 500
  - The Diverse Peoples of the West 503
> How did the fight for land and resources in the West unfold? 506
  - Moving West: Homesteaders and Speculators 507
  - Ranchers and Cowboys 508
  - Tenants, Sharecroppers, and Migrants 510
  - Commercial Farming and Industrial Cowboys 510
> Conclusion: How did the West set the tone for the Gilded Age? 513

✔ **LearningCurve**
bedfordstmartins.com/roarkunderstanding

CHAPTER 17 STUDY GUIDE 514

18

DEFINING THE GILDED AGE IN BUSINESS AND POLITICS

1865–1900 *516*

19

THE GROWTH OF AMERICA'S CITIES

1870–1900 *546*

20

DISSENT, DEPRESSION, AND WAR

1890–1900 *578*

> How did the railroads stimulate big business? 518
>   Railroads: America's First Big Business 519
>   Andrew Carnegie, Steel, and Vertical Integration 521
>   John D. Rockefeller, Standard Oil, and the Trust 522
>   New Inventions: The Telephone and the Telegraph 524

> Why did the ideas of social Darwinism appeal to many Americans in the late nineteenth century? 526
>   J. P. Morgan and Finance Capitalism 527
>   Social Darwinism, Laissez-Faire, and the Supreme Court 527

> What factors influenced political life in the late nineteenth century? 529
>   Political Participation and Party Loyalty 529
>   Sectionalism and the New South 530
>   Gender, Race, and Politics 531
>   Women's Activism 532

> What issues shaped party politics in the late nineteenth century? 534
>   Corruption and Party Strife 534
>   Garfield's Assassination and Civil Service Reform 535
>   Reform and Scandal: The Campaign of 1884 536

> What role did economic issues play in party realignment? 538
>   The Tariff and the Politics of Protection 538
>   Railroads, Trusts, and the Federal Government 540
>   The Fight for Free Silver 541
>   Panic and Depression 542

> Conclusion: Why did business dominate the Gilded Age? 543

✓ **LearningCurve**
bedfordstmartins.com/roarkunderstanding

CHAPTER 18 STUDY GUIDE 544

> Why did American cities experience explosive growth in the late nineteenth century? 548
>   The Urban Explosion: A Global Migration 548
>   Racism and the Cry for Immigration Restriction 552
>   The Social Geography of the City 554

> What kinds of work did people do in industrial America? 556
>   America's Diverse Workers 556
>   The Family Economy: Women and Children 557
>   White-Collar Workers: Managers, "Typewriters," and Salesclerks 558

> Why did the fortunes of the Knights of Labor rise in the late 1870s and decline in the 1890s? 561
>   The Great Railroad Strike of 1877 561
>   The Knights of Labor and the American Federation of Labor 563
>   Haymarket and the Specter of Labor Radicalism 564

> How did urban industrialism shape home life and the world of leisure? 566
>   Domesticity and "Domestics" 566
>   Cheap Amusements 567

> How did municipal governments respond to the challenges of urban expansion? 569
>   Building Cities of Stone and Steel 569
>   City Government and the "Bosses" 571
>   White City or City of Sin? 572

> Conclusion: Who built the cities? 575

✓ **LearningCurve**
bedfordstmartins.com/roarkunderstanding

CHAPTER 19 STUDY GUIDE 576

> Why did American farmers organize alliances in the late nineteenth century? 580
>   The Farmers' Alliance 580
>   The Populist Movement 582

> What led to the labor wars of the 1890s? 584
>   The Homestead Lockout 584
>   The Cripple Creek Miners' Strike of 1894 587
>   Eugene V. Debs and the Pullman Strike 587

> How were women involved in late-nineteenth-century politics? 591
>   Frances Willard and the Woman's Christian Temperance Union 591
>   Elizabeth Cady Stanton, Susan B. Anthony, and the Movement for Woman Suffrage 593

> How did economic problems affect American politics in the 1890s? 594
>   Coxey's Army 595
>   The People's Party and the Election of 1896 595

> Why did the United States largely abandon its isolationist foreign policy in the 1890s? 598
>   Markets and Missionaries 598
>   The Monroe Doctrine and the Open Door Policy 601
>   "A Splendid Little War" 602
>   The Debate over American Imperialism 604

> Conclusion: What was the connection between domestic strife and foreign policy? 607

✓ **LearningCurve**
bedfordstmartins.com/roarkunderstanding

CHAPTER 20 STUDY GUIDE 608

21
PROGRESSIVISM FROM THE GRASS ROOTS UP
1890–1916 *610*

> How did grassroots progressives attack the problems of industrial America? 612
  Civilizing the City 613
  Progressives and the Working Class 614
> What were the key tenets of progressive theory? 617
  Reform Darwinism and Social Engineering 617
  Progressive Government: City and State 618
> How did Theodore Roosevelt advance the progressive agenda? 620
  The Square Deal 621
  Roosevelt the Reformer 622
  Roosevelt and Conservation 624
  The Big Stick 624
  The Troubled Presidency of William Howard Taft 628
> How did progressivism evolve during Woodrow Wilson's first term? 631
  Progressive Insurgency and the Election of 1912 632
  Wilson's Reforms: Tariff, Banking, and the Trusts 633
  Wilson, Reluctant Progressive 634
> What were the limits of progressive reform? 636
  Radical Alternatives 636
  Progressivism for White Men Only 638
> Conclusion: How did the liberal state transform during the Progressive Era? 641

☑ **LearningCurve**
bedfordstmartins.com/roarkunderstanding

CHAPTER 21 STUDY GUIDE 642

22
THE UNITED STATES AND WORLD WAR I
1914–1920 *644*

> What was Woodrow Wilson's foreign policy agenda? 646
  Taming the Americas 647
  The European Crisis 648
  The Ordeal of American Neutrality 649
  The United States Enters the War 651
> What role did the United States play in World War I? 652
  The Call to Arms 652
  The War in France 653
> What impact did the war have on the home front? 656
  The Progressive Stake in the War 656
  Women, War, and the Battle for Suffrage 658
  Rally around the Flag—or Else 659
> What part did Woodrow Wilson play at the Paris peace conference? 662
  Wilson's Fourteen Points 662
  The Paris Peace Conference 663
  The Fight for the Treaty 665
> Why was America's transition from war to peace so turbulent? 667
  Economic Hardship and Labor Upheaval 667
  The Red Scare 668
  The Great Migrations of African Americans and Mexicans 670
  Postwar Politics and the Election of 1920 672
> Conclusion: What was the domestic cost of foreign victory? 673

☑ **LearningCurve**
bedfordstmartins.com/roarkunderstanding

CHAPTER 22 STUDY GUIDE 674

23
FROM NEW ERA TO GREAT DEPRESSION
1920–1932 *676*

> How did big business shape the "New Era" of the 1920s? 678
  A Business Government 679
  Promoting Prosperity and Peace Abroad 680
  Automobiles, Mass Production, and Assembly-Line Progress 680
  Consumer Culture 683
> In what ways did the Roaring Twenties challenge traditional values? 685
  Prohibition 685
  The New Woman 687
  The New Negro 688
  Entertainment for the Masses 690
  The Lost Generation 691
> Why did the relationship between urban and rural America deteriorate in the 1920s? 692
  Rejecting the Undesirables 693
  The Rebirth of the Ku Klux Klan 694
  The Scopes Trial 695
  Al Smith and the Election of 1928 695
> How did President Hoover respond to the economic crash of 1929? 697
  Herbert Hoover: The Great Engineer 698
  The Distorted Economy 698
  The Crash of 1929 699
  Hoover and the Limits of Individualism 700
> What was life like in the early years of the depression? 702
  The Human Toll 702
  Denial and Escape 704
  Working-Class Militancy 705
> Conclusion: Why did the hope of the 1920s turn to despair? 707

☑ **LearningCurve**
bedfordstmartins.com/roarkunderstanding

CHAPTER 23 STUDY GUIDE 708

24

FORGING THE NEW DEAL

1932–1939   710

> How did Franklin D. Roosevelt win the 1932 election? 712
> The Making of a Politician 712
> The Election of 1932 713

> What were the goals and achievements of the first New Deal? 716
> The New Dealers 717
> Banking and Finance Reform 718
> Relief and Conservation Programs 718
> Agricultural Initiatives 721
> Industrial Recovery 721

> Who opposed the New Deal and why? 723
> Resistance to Business Reform 723
> Casualties in the Countryside 724
> Politics on the Fringes 725

> How did the second phase of the New Deal differ from the first? 728
> Relief for the Unemployed 729
> Empowering Labor 729
> Social Security and Tax Reform 730
> Neglected Americans and the New Deal 731

> What major political trends changed during the late 1930s? 734
> The Election of 1936 735
> Court Packing 735
> Reaction and Recession 736
> The Last of the New Deal Reforms 736

> Conclusion: What were the achievements and limitations of the New Deal? 739

☑ LearningCurve
bedfordstmartins.com/roarkunderstanding

CHAPTER 24 STUDY GUIDE 740

25

THE UNITED STATES AND THE SECOND WORLD WAR

1939–1945   742

> How did the United States respond to international developments in the 1930s? 744
> Roosevelt and Reluctant Isolation 745
> The Good Neighbor Policy 745
> The Price of Noninvolvement 746

> How did the outbreak of war affect U.S. foreign policy? 748
> Nazi Aggression and War in Europe 748
> From Neutrality to the Arsenal of Democracy 749
> Japan Attacks America 751

> How did the United States mobilize for war? 755
> Home-Front Security 755
> Building a Citizen Army 756
> Conversion to a War Economy 758

> How did the Allies turn the tide in Europe and the Pacific? 759
> Turning the Tide in the Pacific 759
> The Campaign in Europe 760

> How did the war change life on the American home front? 762
> Women and Families, Guns and Butter 763
> The Double V Campaign 763
> Wartime Politics and the 1944 Election 764
> Reaction to the Holocaust 765

> How did the Allies finally win the war? 767
> From Bombing Raids to Berlin 768
> The Defeat of Japan 771
> Atomic Warfare 773

> Conclusion: Why did the United States emerge as a superpower at the end of the war? 775

☑ LearningCurve
bedfordstmartins.com/roarkunderstanding

CHAPTER 25 STUDY GUIDE 776

26

COLD WAR POLITICS IN THE TRUMAN YEARS

1945–1953   778

> What factors contributed to the Cold War? 780
> The Cold War Begins 780
> The Truman Doctrine and the Marshall Plan 783
> Building a National Security State 785
> Superpower Rivalry around the Globe 787

> Why did Truman have limited success in implementing his domestic agenda? 789
> Reconverting to a Peacetime Economy 789
> Blacks and Mexican Americans Push for Their Civil Rights 792
> The Fair Deal Flounders 794
> The Domestic Chill: McCarthyism 795

> How did U.S. Cold War policy lead to the Korean War? 797
> Korea and the Military Implementation of Containment 797
> From Containment to Rollback to Containment 798
> Korea, Communism, and the 1952 Election 799
> An Armistice and the War's Costs 800

> Conclusion: What were the costs and consequences of the Cold War? 801

☑ LearningCurve
bedfordstmartins.com/roarkunderstanding

CHAPTER 26 STUDY GUIDE 802

27
THE POLITICS AND CULTURE OF ABUNDANCE
1952–1960 *804*

28
REFORM, REBELLION, AND REACTION
1960–1974 *834*

29
VIETNAM AND THE END OF THE COLD WAR CONSENSUS
1961–1975 *868*

> What was Eisenhower's "middle way" on domestic issues? 806
  Modern Republicanism 806
  Termination and Relocation of Native Americans 808
  The 1956 Election and the Second Term 809

> How did Eisenhower's foreign policy differ from Truman's? 811
  The "New Look" in Foreign Policy 812
  Applying Containment to Vietnam 812
  Interventions in Latin America and the Middle East 813
  The Nuclear Arms Race 815

> What fueled the prosperity of the 1950s? 817
  Technology Transforms Agriculture and Industry 817
  Burgeoning Suburbs and Declining Cities 819
  The Rise of the Sun Belt 819
  The Democratization of Higher Education 821

> How did prosperity affect American society and culture? 822
  Consumption Rules the Day 822
  The Revival of Domesticity and Religion 823
  Television Transforms Culture and Politics 824
  Countercurrents 825

> How did African Americans fight for civil rights in the 1950s? 827
  African Americans Challenge the Supreme Court and the President 827
  Montgomery and Mass Protest 829

> Conclusion: What unmet challenges did peace and prosperity mask? 831

✓ LearningCurve
bedfordstmartins.com/roarkunderstanding

CHAPTER 27 STUDY GUIDE 832

> What liberal reforms were advanced during the Kennedy and Johnson administrations? 836
  The Unrealized Promise of Kennedy's New Frontier 836
  Johnson Fulfills the Kennedy Promise 838
  Policymaking for a Great Society 839
  Assessing the Great Society 841
  The Judicial Revolution 842

> How did the civil rights movement evolve in the 1960s? 844
  The Flowering of the Black Freedom Struggle 844
  The Response in Washington 847
  Black Power and Urban Rebellions 848

> What other rights movements emerged in the 1960s? 851
  Native American Protest 852
  Latino Struggles for Justice 852
  Student Rebellion, the New Left, and the Counterculture 854
  Gay Men and Lesbians Organize 855

> What were the goals of the new wave of feminism? 857
  A Multifaceted Movement Emerges 857
  Feminist Gains Spark a Countermovement 859

> How did liberalism fare under President Nixon? 861
  Extending the Welfare State and Regulating the Economy 861
  Responding to Environmental Concerns 862
  Expanding Social Justice 863

> Conclusion: What were the achievements and limitations of liberalism? 865

✓ LearningCurve
bedfordstmartins.com/roarkunderstanding

CHAPTER 28 STUDY GUIDE 866

> How did U.S. foreign policy change under Kennedy? 870
  Meeting the "Hour of Maximum Danger" 870
  New Approaches to the Third World 872
  The Arms Race and the Nuclear Brink 873
  A Growing War in Vietnam 874

> Why did Johnson escalate American involvement in Vietnam? 876
  An All-Out Commitment in Vietnam 876
  Preventing Another Castro in Latin America 878
  The Americanized War 878
  Those Who Served 879

> How did the war in Vietnam polarize the nation? 881
  The Widening War at Home 881
  The Tet Offensive and Johnson's Move toward Peace 882
  The Tumultuous Election of 1968 883

> How did U.S. foreign policy change under Nixon? 886
  Moving toward Détente with the Soviet Union and China 886
  Shoring Up U.S. Interests around the World 887
  Vietnam Becomes Nixon's War 888
  The Peace Accords 890
  The Legacy of Defeat 891

> Conclusion: Was Vietnam an unwinnable war? 893

✓ LearningCurve
bedfordstmartins.com/roarkunderstanding

CHAPTER 29 STUDY GUIDE 894

30

THE CONSERVATIVE TURN

1969–1989 *896*

> How did the Nixon presidency reflect the rise of postwar conservatism? 898
  Emergence of a Grassroots Movement 898
  Nixon Courts the Right 900
  The Election of 1972 901
  Watergate 901
  The Ford Presidency and the 1976 Election 903

> Why did the "outsider" presidency of Jimmy Carter fail to gain broad support? 905
  Retreat from Liberalism 905
  Energy and Environmental Reform 906
  Promoting Human Rights Abroad 909
  The Cold War Intensifies 911

> What conservative goals were realized in the Reagan administration? 913
  Appealing to the New Right and Beyond 914
  Unleashing Free Enterprise 915
  Winners and Losers in a Flourishing Economy 916

> What strategies did liberals use to fight the conservative turn? 918
  Battles in the Courts and Congress 918
  Feminism on the Defensive 919
  The Gay and Lesbian Rights Movement 920

> How did Ronald Reagan's foreign policy affect the Cold War? 921
  Militarization and Interventions Abroad 921
  The Iran-Contra Scandal 923
  A Thaw in Soviet-American Relations 923

> Conclusion: What was the long-term impact of the conservative turn? 925

✔ LearningCurve
bedfordstmartins.com/roarkunderstanding

CHAPTER 30 STUDY GUIDE 926

31

FACING THE PROMISES AND CHALLENGES OF GLOBALIZATION

SINCE 1989 *928*

> How did the United States respond to the end of the Cold War and tensions in the Middle East? 930
  Gridlock in Government 930
  Going to War in Central America and the Persian Gulf 932
  The Cold War Ends 934
  The 1992 Election 936

> How did President Clinton seek a middle ground in American politics? 938
  Clinton's Reforms 938
  Accommodating the Right 940
  Impeaching the President 941
  The Booming Economy of the 1990s 942

> How did President Clinton respond to the challenges of globalization? 944
  Defining America's Place in a New World Order 945
  Debates over Globalization 946
  The Internationalization of the United States 947

> How did President George W. Bush change American politics and foreign policy? 950
  The Disputed Election of 2000 951
  The Domestic Policies of a "Compassionate Conservative" 951
  The Globalization of Terrorism 954
  Unilateralism, Preemption, and the Iraq War 955

> What obstacles stood in the way of President Obama's reform agenda? 958

> Conclusion: How have Americans debated the role of the government? 961

✔ LearningCurve
bedfordstmartins.com/roarkunderstanding

CHAPTER 31 STUDY GUIDE 962

Appendixes A-1
Index I-1
About the Authors *last book page*

MAPS, FIGURES, AND TABLES

CHAPTER 1

MAP 1.1 Continental Drift *7*

SPOT MAP Beringia *7*

FIGURE 1.1 Human Habitation of the World and the Western Hemisphere *8*

MAP 1.2 Native North American Cultures *11*

SPOT MAP Ancient California Peoples *12*

TABLE 1.1 Archaic Indians at a Glance *14*

FIGURE 1.2 Native American Population in North America about 1492 (Estimated) *20*

MAP 1.3 Native North Americans about 1500 *21*

TABLE 1.2 Native North Americans in the 1490s *22*

CHAPTER 2

MAP 2.1 European Trade Routes and Portuguese Exploration in the Fifteenth Century *31*

SPOT MAP Columbus's First Voyage to the New World, 1492–1493 *35*

MAP 2.2 European Exploration in Sixteenth-Century America *37*

SPOT MAP Cortés's Invasion of Tenochtitlán, 1519–1521 *40*

MAP 2.3 Sixteenth-Century European Colonies in the New World *43*

FIGURE 2.1 New World Gold and Silver Imported into Spain during the Sixteenth Century, in Pesos *45*

SPOT MAP Roanoke Settlement, 1587–1590 *50*

TABLE 2.1 France and England Follow Spain to the New World *50*

CHAPTER 3

MAP 3.1 Chesapeake Colonies in the Seventeenth Century *62*

SPOT MAP Settlement Patterns along the James River *67*

MAP 3.2 The West Indies and Carolina in the Seventeenth Century *74*

GLOBAL COMPARISON FIGURE 3.1 Migration to the New World from Europe and Africa, 1492–1700 *75*

CHAPTER 4

TABLE 4.1 Pilgrims and Puritans *86*

MAP 4.1 New England Colonies in the Seventeenth Century *87*

FIGURE 4.1 Population of the English North American Colonies in the Seventeenth Century *95*

MAP 4.2 Middle Colonies in the Seventeenth Century *99*

MAP 4.3 American Colonies at the End of the Seventeenth Century *103*

SPOT MAP King Philip's War, 1675–1676 *104*

CHAPTER 5

MAP 5.1 Europeans and Africans in the Eighteenth Century *113*

MAP 5.2 Atlantic Trade in the Eighteenth Century *116*

SPOT MAP Patterns of Settlement, 1700–1770 *121*

MAP 5.3 The Atlantic Slave Trade *124*

TABLE 5.1 Slave Imports, 1451–1870 *125*

FIGURE 5.1 Colonial Exports, 1768–1772 *132*

MAP 5.4 Zones of Empire in Eastern North America *134*

SPOT MAP Spanish Missions in California *135*

CHAPTER 6

MAP 6.1 European Areas of Influence and the Seven Years' War, 1754–1763 *143*

SPOT MAP Ohio River Valley, 1753 *144*

MAP 6.2 Europe Redraws the Map of North America, 1763 *147*

SPOT MAP Pontiac's Rebellion, 1763 *148*

TABLE 6.1 The Coercive (Intolerable) Acts *163*

MAP 6.3 Lexington and Concord, April 1775 *167*

CHAPTER 7

SPOT MAP Battle of Bunker Hill, 1775 *175*

MAP 7.1 The War in the North, 1775–1778 *183*

MAP 7.2 Loyalist Strength and Rebel Support *187*

SPOT MAP Battle of Saratoga, 1777 *191*

MAP 7.3 The Indian War in the West, 1777–1782 *193*

MAP 7.4 The War in the South, 1780–1781 *196*

SPOT MAP Siege of Yorktown, 1781 *199*

CHAPTER 8

MAP 8.1 Cession of Western Lands, 1782–1802 *208*

SPOT MAP Legal Changes to Slavery, 1777–1804 *214*

SPOT MAP Treaty of Fort Stanwix, 1784 *217*

MAP 8.2 The Northwest Ordinance and the Ordinance of 1785 *219*

SPOT MAP Shays's Rebellion, 1786–1787 *222*

MAP 8.3 Ratification of the Constitution, 1788–1790 *228*

CHAPTER 9

SPOT MAP Major Roads in the 1790s *241*

MAP 9.1 Travel Times from New York City in 1800 *241*

MAP 9.2 Western Expansion and Indian Land Cessions to 1810 *249*

SPOT MAP Haitian Revolution, 1791–1804 *252*

CHAPTER 10

MAP 10.1 The Election of 1800 *263*

MAP 10.2 Jefferson's Expeditions in the West, 1804–1806 *269*

SPOT MAP The *Chesapeake* Incident, June 22, 1807 *273*

SPOT MAP Battle of Tippecanoe, 1811 *276*

MAP 10.3 The War of 1812 *277*

MAP 10.4 The Missouri Compromise, 1820 *287*

MAP 10.5 The Election of 1824 *289*

CHAPTER 11

MAP 11.1 Routes of Transportation in 1840 *297*

SPOT MAP Cotton Textile Industry, ca. 1840 *299*

TABLE 11.1 The Growth of Newspapers, 1820–1840 *304*

MAP 11.2 The Election of 1828 *305*

MAP 11.3 Indian Removal and the Trail of Tears *309*

FIGURE 11.1 Western Land Sales, 1810–1860 *312*

CHAPTER 12

MAP 12.1 Railroads in 1860 *331*

FIGURE 12.1 Antebellum Immigration, 1840–1860 *334*

MAP 12.2 Major Trails West *338*

SPOT MAP Plains Indians and Trails West in the 1840s and 1850s *338*

MAP 12.3 Texas and Mexico in the 1830s *340*

MAP 12.4 The Mexican-American War, 1846–1848 *344*

MAP 12.5 Territorial Expansion by 1860 *347*

CHAPTER 13

MAP 13.1 Cotton Kingdom, Slave Empire: 1820 and 1860 *361*

SPOT MAP The Upper and Lower South *362*

FIGURE 13.1 Black and White Populations in the South, 1860 *363*

MAP 13.2 The Agricultural Economy of the South, 1860 *365*

SPOT MAP Immigrants as a Percentage of State Populations, 1860 *367*

FIGURE 13.2 A Southern Plantation *369*

SPOT MAP The Cotton Belt *378*

SPOT MAP Upcountry of the South *378*

CHAPTER 14

SPOT MAP Mexican Cession, 1848 *393*

MAP 14.1 The Election of 1848 *395*

MAP 14.2 The Compromise of 1850 *396*

SPOT MAP Gadsden Purchase, 1853 *400*

MAP 14.3 The Kansas-Nebraska Act, 1854 *401*

MAP 14.4 Political Realignment, 1848–1860 *404*

FIGURE 14.1 Changing Political Landscape, 1848–1860 *406*

SPOT MAP "Bleeding Kansas," 1850s *409*

MAP 14.5 The Election of 1860 *416*

SPOT MAP Secession of the Lower South, December 1860–February 1861 *418*

CHAPTER 15

MAP 15.1 Secession, 1860–1861 *426*

FIGURE 15.1 Resources of the Union and Confederacy *428*

MAP 15.2 The Civil War, 1861–1862 *432*

SPOT MAP Peninsula Campaign, 1862 *433*

SPOT MAP Battle of Glorieta Pass, 1862 *434*

GLOBAL COMPARISON FIGURE 15.2 European Cotton Imports, 1860–1870 *437*

SPOT MAP Vicksburg Campaign, 1863 *448*

MAP 15.3 The Civil War, 1863–1865 *449*

SPOT MAP Battle of Gettysburg, July 1–3, 1863 *450*

CHAPTER 16

SPOT MAP Reconstruction Military Districts, 1867 *468*

FIGURE 16.1 Southern Congressional Delegations, 1865–1877 *473*

MAP 16.1 A Southern Plantation in 1860 and 1881 *475*

MAP 16.2 The Election of 1868 *476*

MAP 16.3 The Reconstruction of the South *481*

MAP 16.4 The Election of 1876 *482*

CHAPTER 17

MAP 17.1 The Loss of Indian Lands, 1850–1890 *489*

MAP 17.2 Western Mining, 1848–1890 *501*

SPOT MAP Midwestern Settlement before 1862 *507*

SPOT MAP Cattle Trails, 1860–1890 *508*

MAP 17.3 Federal Land Grants to Railroads and the Development of the West, 1850–1900 *509*

FIGURE 17.1 Changes in Rural and Urban Populations, 1870–1900 *511*

CHAPTER 18

MAP 18.1 Railroad Expansion, 1870–1890 *519*

GLOBAL COMPARISON FIGURE 18.1 Railroad Track Mileage, 1890 *520*

FIGURE 18.2 Iron and Steel Production, 1870–1900 *522*

TABLE 18.1 Notable American Inventions, 1865–1899 *524*

MAP 18.2 The Election of 1884 *537*

CHAPTER 19

MAP 19.1 Economic Regions of the World, 1890s *549*

MAP 19.2 The Impact of Immigration, to 1910 *550*

GLOBAL COMPARISON FIGURE 19.1 European Emigration, 1870–1890 *551*

FIGURE 19.2 Women and Work, 1870–1890 *559*

MAP 19.3 The Great Railroad Strike of 1877 *562*

CHAPTER 20

GLOBAL COMPARISON FIGURE 20.1 Share of World Wheat Market, 1860–1900 *581*

FIGURE 20.2 Consumer Prices and Farm Income, 1865–1910 *582*

MAP 20.1 The Election of 1892 *596*

MAP 20.2 The Election of 1896 *597*

FIGURE 20.3 Expansion in U.S. Trade, 1870–1910 *599*

SPOT MAP The Samoan Islands, 1889 *601*

MAP 20.3 The Spanish-American War, 1898 *603*

MAP 20.4 U.S. Overseas Expansion through 1900 *605*

CHAPTER 21

MAP 21.1 National Parks and Forests *625*

MAP 21.2 The Panama Canal, 1914 *627*

SPOT MAP The Roosevelt Corollary in Action *628*

SPOT MAP Taft's "Dollar Diplomacy" *630*

MAP 21.3 The Election of 1912 *633*

CHAPTER 22

MAP 22.1 U.S. Involvement in Latin America and the Caribbean, 1895–1941 *647*

SPOT MAP U.S. Intervention in Mexico, 1916–1917 *648*

MAP 22.2 European Alliances after the Outbreak of World War I *649*

SPOT MAP Sinking of the *Lusitania*, 1915 *650*

MAP 22.3 The American Expeditionary Force, 1918 *654*

FIGURE 22.1 Industrial Wages, 1912–1920 *657*

MAP 22.4 Women's Voting Rights before the Nineteenth Amendment *659*

MAP 22.5 Europe after World War I *664*

MAP 22.6 The Election of 1920 *672*

CHAPTER 23

SPOT MAP Detroit and the Automobile Industry in the 1920s *681*

MAP 23.1 Auto Manufacturing *681*

FIGURE 23.1 Production of Consumer Goods, 1920–1929 *683*

MAP 23.2 The Shift from Rural to Urban Population, 1920–1930 *693*

MAP 23.3 The Election of 1928 *696*

FIGURE 23.2 Manufacturing and Agricultural Income, 1920–1940 *703*

SPOT MAP Harlan County Coal Strike, 1931 *705*

CHAPTER 24

MAP 24.1 The Election of 1932 *714*

MAP 24.2 Electoral Shift, 1928–1932 *714*

FIGURE 24.1 Bank Failures and Farm Foreclosures, 1932–1942 *719*

MAP 24.3 The Tennessee Valley Authority *720*

SPOT MAP The Dust Bowl *725*

GLOBAL COMPARISON FIGURE 24.2 National Populations and Economies, ca. 1938 *737*

CHAPTER 25

SPOT MAP Spanish Civil War, 1936–1939 *746*

MAP 25.1 Axis Aggression through 1941 *750*

MAP 25.2 Japanese Aggression through 1941 *752*

SPOT MAP Bombing of Pearl Harbor, December 7, 1941 *754*

MAP 25.3 Western Relocation Authority Centers *756*

GLOBAL COMPARISON FIGURE 25.1 Weapons Production by the Axis and Allied Powers during World War II *757*

SPOT MAP The Holocaust, 1933–1945 *766*

MAP 25.4 The European Theater of World War II, 1942–1945 *769*

MAP 25.5 The Pacific Theater of World War II, 1941–1945 *772*

CHAPTER 26

MAP 26.1 The Division of Europe after World War II *782*

SPOT MAP Berlin Divided, 1948 *785*

SPOT MAP Israel, 1948 *788*

FIGURE 26.1 Women Workers in Selected Industries, 1940–1950 *790*

MAP 26.2 The Election of 1948 *794*

MAP 26.3 The Korean War, 1950–1953 *798*

CHAPTER 27

MAP 27.1 The Interstate Highway System, 1930 and 1970 *807*

SPOT MAP Major Indian Relocations, 1950–1970 *809*

SPOT MAP Geneva Accords, 1954 *813*

SPOT MAP The Suez Crisis, 1956 *814*

MAP 27.2 The Rise of the Sun Belt, 1940–1980 *820*

FIGURE 27.1 The Postwar Economic Boom: GNP and Per Capita Income, 1945–1970 *823*

GLOBAL COMPARISON FIGURE 27.2 The Baby Boom in International Perspective *824*

CHAPTER 28

MAP 28.1 The Election of 1960 *837*

FIGURE 28.1 Poverty in the United States, 1960–1974 *842*

SPOT MAP Civil Rights Freedom Rides, May 1961 *845*

MAP 28.2 The Rise of the African American Vote, 1940–1976 *848*

MAP 28.3 Urban Uprisings, 1965–1968 *849*

CHAPTER 29

MAP 29.1 U.S. Involvement in Latin America and the Caribbean, 1954–1994 *871*

SPOT MAP Cuban Missile Crisis, 1962 *873*

MAP 29.2 The Vietnam War, 1964–1975 *874*

FIGURE 29.1 U.S. Troops in Vietnam, 1962–1972 *877*

SPOT MAP Chile *887*

SPOT MAP Israeli Territorial Gains in the Six-Day War, 1967 *888*

SPOT MAP U.S. Invasion of Cambodia, 1970 *889*

TABLE 29.1 Vietnam War Casualties *892*

CHAPTER 30

SPOT MAP Integration of Public Schools, 1968 *900*

MAP 30.1 Worldwide Oil Reserves, 1980 *908*

GLOBAL COMPARISON FIGURE 30.1 Energy Consumption per Capita, 1980 *909*

MAP 30.2 The Middle East, 1948–1989 *910*

SPOT MAP The Fight for the Equal Rights Amendment *919*

SPOT MAP El Salvador and Nicaragua *923*

CHAPTER 31

MAP 31.1 Events in the Middle East, 1989–2011 *933*

MAP 31.2 Events in Eastern Europe, 1989–1995 *935*

FIGURE 31.1 The Growth of Inequality: Changes in Family Income, 1969–1998 *943*

SPOT MAP Breakup of Yugoslavia *945*

SPOT MAP Events in Israel since 1989 *946*

MAP 31.3 The Election of 2000 *951*

SPOT MAP Afghanistan *954*

SPOT MAP Iraq *956*

MAP 31.4 The Election of 2012 *960*

How to use this book to figure out what's really important

The **chapter title** tells you the subject of the chapter and identifies the time span that will be covered.

The **opening question** and **chapter introduction** identify the most important themes, events, and people that will be explored in the chapter.

16
RECONSTRUCTING A NATION

1863–1877

> **What were the achievements and failures of reconstruction?** Chapter 16 explores the era of reconstruction, in which the nation struggled to define the defeated South's status and the meaning of freedom for ex-slaves. Following the Civil War, the nation entered one of its most confused and violent periods as victorious Northerners, defeated white Southerners, and newly freed African Americans battled to shape the postwar South.

✓ **LearningCurve**
bedfordstmartins.com/roarkunderstanding
After reading the chapter, use LearningCurve to retain what you've read.

456

Memorizing facts and dates for a history class won't get you very far. That's because history isn't just about "facts." This textbook is designed to help you focus on what's truly significant in U.S. history and to give you practice in thinking like a historian.

> Why did Congress object to Lincoln's wartime plan for reconstruction?

> How did the North respond to the passage of black codes in the southern states?

> How radical was congressional reconstruction?

> What brought the elements of the South's Republican coalition together?

> Why did reconstruction collapse?

> Conclusion: Was reconstruction "a revolution but half accomplished"?

The **chapter-opening questions** are also the questions that open each new section of the chapter and will be addressed in turn on the following pages. You should think about answers to these as you read.

Voting day, June 5, 1867. Black freedmen line up to vote in Washington, D.C. The Granger Collection, New York.

Each section has tools that help you focus on what's important.

The **question in red** asks about the specific topic being discussed in this section. Think about the answer to this question as you read the section.

> ## How did the North respond to the passage of black codes in the southern states?

The Black Codes

Titled "Selling a Freeman to Pay His Fine at Monticello, Florida," this 1867 drawing from a northern magazine equates black codes with the institution of slavery. The ascension of Andrew Johnson to the presidency emboldened many southern states to pass laws severely restricting blacks' freedom. Granger Collection.

ABRAHAM LINCOLN DIED on April 15, 1865, just hours after John Wilkes Booth shot him at a Washington, D.C., theater. Chief Justice Salmon P. Chase immediately administered the oath of office to Vice President Andrew Johnson of Tennessee. Congress had adjourned in March and would not reconvene until December. Throughout the summer and fall, Johnson drew up and executed a plan of reconstruction without congressional advice.

Congress returned to the capital in December to find that, as far as the president and former Confederates were concerned, reconstruction was completed. Most Republicans, however, thought Johnson's plan made far too few demands of ex-rebels. They claimed that Johnson's leniency had acted as midwife to the rebirth of the Old South, that he had achieved political reunification at the cost of black freedom. Republicans in Congress then proceeded to dismantle Johnson's program and substitute a program of their own.

Johnson's Program of Reconciliation

Born in 1808 in Raleigh, North Carolina, Andrew Johnson was the son of illiterate parents. Self-educated and ambitious, Johnson moved to Tennessee, where he built a career in politics championing the South's common white people and assailing its "illegitimate, swaggering, bastard, scrub aristocracy." The only senator from a Confederate state to remain loyal to the Union, Johnson held the planter class responsible for secession.

A Democrat all his life, Johnson occupied the White House only because the Republican Party in 1864 had needed a vice presidential candidate who would

CHAPTER LOCATOR | Why did Congress object to Lincoln's wartime plan for reconstruction? | **How did the North respond to the passage of black codes in the southern states?**

CHAPTER 16
462 RECONSTRUCTING A NATION

The **chapter locator** at the bottom of the page puts this section in the context of the chapter as a whole, so you can see how this section relates to what's coming next.

appeal to loyal, Union-supporting Democrats. Johnson vigorously defended states' rights (but not secession) and opposed Republican efforts to expand the power of the federal government. A steadfast supporter of slavery, Johnson had owned slaves until 1862, when Tennessee rebels, angry at his Unionism, confiscated them. When he grudgingly accepted emancipation, it was more because he hated planters than because he sympathized with slaves. "Damn the negroes," he said. "I am fighting those traitorous aristocrats, their masters." The new president harbored unshakable racist convictions. Africans, Johnson said, were "inferior to the white man in point of intellect — better calculated in physical structure to undergo drudgery and hardship."

Like Lincoln, Johnson stressed the rapid restoration of civil government in the South. Like Lincoln, he promised to pardon most, but not all, ex-rebels. Johnson recognized the state governments created by Lincoln but set out his own requirements for restoring the other rebel states to the Union.

Republican senator Lyman Trumbull of Illinois declared that the president's policy meant that an ex-slave would "be tyrannized over, abused, and virtually reenslaved without some legislation by the nation for his protection." Early in 1866, the moderates produced two bills that strengthened the federal shield. The first, the Freedmen's Bureau bill, prolonged the life of the agency established by the previous Congress. Arguing that the Constitution never contemplated a "system for the support of indigent persons," President Andrew Johnson vetoed the bill. Congress failed by a narrow margin to override the president's veto.

The moderates designed their second measure, what would become the **Civil Rights Act of 1866**, to nullify the black codes by affirming African Americans' rights to "full and equal benefit of all laws and proceedings for the security of person and property as is enjoyed by white citizens." The act required the end of racial discrimination in state laws and represented an extraordinary expansion of black rights and federal authority. The president argued that the civil rights bill amounted to "unconstitutional invasion of states' rights" and vetoed it.

In April 1866, an incensed Republican Party again pushed the civil rights bill through Congress and overrode the presidential veto. In July, it passed another Freedmen's Bureau bill and overrode Johnson's veto. For the first time in American history, Congress had overridden presidential vetoes of major legislation. As a worried South Carolinian observed, Johnson had succeeded in uniting the Republicans and probably touched off "a fight this fall such as has never been seen."

> CHRONOLOGY

1865
– Lincoln is assassinated; Andrew Johnson becomes president.
– Black codes are enacted.
– Thirteenth Amendment becomes part of Constitution.

1866
– Civil Rights Act.

Civil Rights Act of 1866
▶ Legislation passed by Congress in 1866 that nullified the black codes and affirmed that black Americans should have equal benefit of the law. President Andrew Johnson vetoed this expansion of black rights and federal authority, but Congress later overrode his veto.

QUICK REVIEW

When the southern states passed the black codes, how did the U.S. Congress respond?

How radical was congressional reconstruction?

What brought the elements of the South's Republican coalition together?

Why did reconstruction collapse?

Conclusion: Was reconstruction "a revolution but half accomplished"?

✓ LearningCurve
Check what you know.
bedfordstmartins.com
/roarkunderstanding

463

Chronologies for each major section show the sequence of events and underlying developments in the section.

Key terms in the margins give you background on important ideas and events. Use these for reference while you read, but also think about which are emphasized and why they matter.

The quick review helps you check your recall of the section before you resume reading.

The Chapter Study Guide provides a process that will build your understanding and your historical skills.

CHAPTER 16 STUDY GUIDE

STEP 1 Go online to complete the chapter's LearningCurve activity.

GET STARTED ONLINE

 LearningCurve ▪ bedfordstmartins.com/roarkunderstanding

Now that you've read the chapter, make it stick by completing the LearningCurve activity.

STEP 2 Identify the key terms and explain their significance.

EXPLAIN WHY IT MATTERS

Put your reading into practice. Identify each term below, and then explain why it matters in U.S. history.

TERM	WHO OR WHAT & WHEN	WHY IT MATTERS
Freedmen's Bureau (p. 460)		
black codes (p. 463)		
Civil Rights Act of 1866 (p. 465)		
Fourteenth Amendment (p. 466)		
Military Reconstruction Act (p. 468)		
Fifteenth Amendment (p. 469)		
carpetbaggers (p. 472)		
scalawags (p. 472)		
Ku Klux Klan (p. 472)		
sharecropping (p. 474)		
Redeemers (p. 479)		
Compromise of 1877 (p. 482)		

STEP 3 Analyze differences and similarities among ideas, events, people, or societies discussed in the chapter.

MOVE BEYOND THE BASICS

To demonstrate a more advanced understanding, indicate below how each phase of reconstruction addressed the key issues involved.

Phase of reconstruction	Requirements for readmission	Role/rights of freedmen	Achievements	Failures
Wartime reconstruction (Lincoln)				
Presidential reconstruction (Johnson)				
Congressional reconstruction				

STEP 4

PUT IT ALL TOGETHER Now, take a step back and try to explain the big picture. Remember to use specific examples from the chapter in your answers.

STEP 4 Answer the big-picture questions using specific examples or evidence from the chapter.

PRESIDENTIAL AND CONGRESSIONAL RECONSTRUCTION

▶ What role did the black codes play in shaping the course of reconstruction?

▶ What steps did Congress take between 1865 and 1869 to assist ex-slaves in their lives as freedmen? How effective were these actions?

SOUTHERN RECONSTRUCTION IN ACTION

▶ How did white Southerners respond during reconstruction? Consider both Democrats and Republicans in your response.

▶ How did southern African Americans attempt to shape their own lives during reconstruction?

THE END OF RECONSTRUCTION

▶ How and why did the decline of northern support for reconstruction help southern Democrats "redeem" the South?

▶ Why did white supremacy become the foundation of southern politics in the 1870s?

LOOKING BACKWARD, LOOKING AHEAD

▶ How did long-held racial views among whites, in both the South and the North, shape reconstruction?

▶ What were the lasting accomplishments of reconstruction? What were its most important failures?

> **IN YOUR OWN WORDS**

Imagine that you must give an oral report to the class answering the following question: What were the achievements and failures of reconstruction? What would be the most important points to include and why?

ACTIVE RECITATION Explain how you would answer the chapter-opening question in your own words to make sure you have a firm grasp of the most important themes and events of the chapter.

 Do it online at the Student Site ▪ bedfordstmartins.com/roarkunderstanding

Visit the FREE Student Site at **bedfordstmartins.com /roarkunderstanding** to do these steps online.

Understanding
the American Promise

A HISTORY

1

UNDERSTANDING ANCIENT AMERICA

BEFORE 1492

> How did ancient North American peoples shape the history of the continent before the arrival of Europeans in 1492? Chapter 1 charts the history of Native American peoples from their migration out of Asia to the eve of European contact. It explores the development of distinct Native American cultures, as well as their shared characteristics.

 **LearningCurve**

bedfordstmartins.com/roarkunderstanding
After reading the chapter, use LearningCurve to
retain what you've read.

> When and why do historians rely on the work of archaeologists?

> How and why did humans migrate into North America?

> Why did Archaic Native Americans shift to foraging and hunting smaller animals?

> How did agriculture influence Native American cultures?

> What cultural similarities did native peoples of the Western Hemisphere share in the 1490s?

> Why was tribute important in the Mexican empire?

> Conclusion: How do we understand the worlds of ancient Americans?

The Great Tenochtitlán. **Detail of the 1945 fresco by Mexican artist Diego Rivera.** Charles and Josette Lenaris/Corbis.

When and why do historians rely on the work of archaeologists?

Mississippian Wooden Mask

Sometime between AD 1200 and 1350, a Native American among the Mississippian people in what is now central Illinois fashioned this mask from red cedar. Influenced by the culture of Cahokia, the mask was probably used in rituals to depict the face of both worldly and supernatural power. The haunting visage evokes the long history of ancient Americans and their impressive achievements. Mask photograph: © 2002 John Bigelow Taylor, www.johnbigelowtaylor .com. Illinois State Museum, Springfield, Cat. No. 273.

> KEY FACTORS

Archaeologists
– Focus on physical objects such as bones, spear points, and pottery.

Historians
– Tend to focus more on written records.

ARCHAEOLOGISTS AND HISTORIANS share the desire to learn about people who lived in the past, but they usually employ different methods to obtain information. Both archaeologists and historians study artifacts as clues to the activities and ideas of the humans who created them. They concentrate, however, on different kinds of artifacts.

CHAPTER LOCATOR | When and why do historians rely on the work of archaeologists? | How and why did humans migrate into North America?

4   CHAPTER 1
UNDERSTANDING ANCIENT AMERICA

Artifacts That Archaeologists Study	Artifacts That Historians Study
bones	letters
spear points	diaries
pots	laws
baskets	speeches
jewelry/clothing	newspapers
buildings	court cases

The characteristic concentration of historians on writings and of archaeologists on other physical objects denotes a rough cultural and chronological boundary between the human beings studied by the two groups of scholars, a boundary marked by the use of writing.

Writing is defined as a system of symbols that record spoken language. Writing originated among ancient peoples in China, Egypt, and Central America about eight thousand years ago, within the most recent 2 percent of the four hundred millennia that modern human beings have existed. While those who inhabited North America in 1492 possessed many forms of symbolic representation, they did not use writing. Much of what we would like to know about their experiences and those of other ancient Americans remains unknown because they did not write about it.

Archaeologists specialize in learning about people who did not document their history in writing. They study the millions of artifacts these people created. They also scrutinize geological strata, pollen, and other environmental features to reconstruct as much as possible about the world inhabited by ancient peoples. This chapter relies on studies by archaeologists to sketch a brief overview of ancient America, the long first phase of the history of the United States.

Ancient Americans and their descendants resided in North America for thousands of years before Europeans arrived. While they created societies and cultures of remarkable diversity and complexity, their history cannot be reconstructed with the detail and certainty made possible by writing.

QUICK REVIEW

Why must historians rely on the work of archaeologists to write the history of ancient America?

| Why did Archaic Native Americans shift to foraging and hunting smaller animals? | How did agriculture influence Native American cultures? | What cultural similarities did native peoples of the Western Hemisphere share in the 1490s? | Why was tribute important in the Mexican empire? | Conclusion: How do we understand the worlds of ancient Americans? | LearningCurve Check what you know. bedfordstmartins.com /roarkunderstanding |

How and why did humans migrate into North America?

Clovis Spear Straightener

Clovis hunters used this bone spear straightener about 11,000 BP at a campsite in Arizona. Presumably, Clovis hunters stuck their spear shafts through the opening and then grasped the handle of the straightener and moved it back and forth along the length of the shaft to remove imperfections and to make the spear a more effective weapon. Arizona State Museum, University of Arizona.

THE FIRST HUMAN BEINGS to arrive in the Western Hemisphere emigrated from Asia. They brought with them hunting skills, weapon- and tool-making techniques, and other forms of human knowledge developed millennia earlier in Africa, Europe, and Asia. These first Americans hunted large mammals, such as the mammoths they had learned in Europe and Asia to kill, butcher, and process for food, clothing, and building materials. Most likely, these first Americans wandered into the Western Hemisphere more or less accidentally in pursuit of prey.

> CHRONOLOGY

ca. 400,000 BP
- *Homo sapiens* evolve in Africa.

ca. 25,000–14,000 BP
- Glaciation exposes the Beringian land bridge.

ca. 15,000 BP
- Humans arrive in North America.

ca. 13,500–13,000 BP
- Paleo-Indians use Clovis points.

ca. 11,000 BP
- Mammoths become extinct.

NOTE: *BP* is an abbreviation used by archaeologists for "years before the present."

African and Asian Origins

Human beings lived elsewhere in the world for hundreds of thousands of years before they reached the Western Hemisphere. They lacked a way to travel to the Western Hemisphere because millions of years before humans existed anywhere on the globe, North and South America became detached from the gigantic common landmass scientists now call Pangaea. About 240 million years ago, powerful forces deep within the earth fractured Pangaea and slowly pushed continents apart to their present positions (**Map 1.1**). This process of continental drift encircled the land of the Western Hemisphere with large oceans that isolated it from the other continents long before early human beings (*Homo erectus*) first appeared in Africa about two million years ago.

More than 1.5 million years after *Homo erectus* appeared, or about 400,000 BP, modern humans (*Homo sapiens*) evolved in Africa. All human beings throughout the world today are descendants of these ancient Africans. Slowly, over many millennia, *Homo sapiens* migrated out of Africa and into Europe and Asia, which had retained land connections to Africa, allowing ancient humans to migrate on foot. For roughly

CHAPTER LOCATOR | When and why do historians rely on the work of archaeologists? | **How and why did humans migrate into North America?**

6 CHAPTER 1 UNDERSTANDING ANCIENT AMERICA

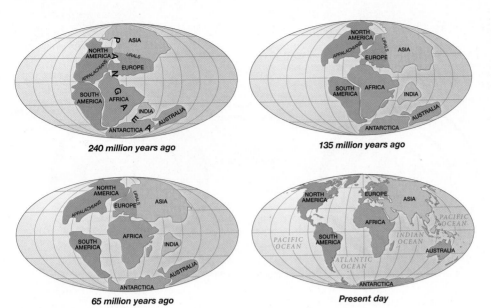

MAP 1.1 ■ Continental Drift

Massive geological forces separated North and South America from other continents eons before human beings evolved in Africa 1.5 million years ago.

> MAP ACTIVITY

READING THE MAP: Which continents separated from Pangaea earliest? Which ones separated from each other last? Which are still closely connected to each other?

240 million years ago

135 million years ago

65 million years ago

Present day

97 percent of the time *Homo sapiens* have been on earth, none migrated across the enormous oceans isolating North and South America from the Eurasian landmass.

Two major developments made it possible for ancient humans to migrate to the Western Hemisphere. First, people successfully adapted to the frigid environment near the Arctic Circle. Second, changes in the earth's climate reconnected North America to Asia.

By about 25,000 BP, *Homo sapiens* had spread from Africa throughout Europe and Asia. People, probably women, had learned to use bone needles to sew animal skins into warm clothing that permitted them to become permanent residents of extremely cold regions such as northeastern Siberia. A few of these ancient Siberians clothed in animal hides walked to North America on land that now lies submerged beneath the sixty miles of water that currently separate easternmost Siberia from westernmost Alaska. A pathway across this watery chasm opened during the last global cold spell—which endured from about 25,000 BP to 14,000 BP—when the sea level dropped and exposed a land bridge hundreds of miles wide called **Beringia** that connected Asian Siberia and American Alaska.

Siberian hunters roamed Beringia for centuries in search of mammoths, bison, and numerous smaller animals. As the hunters ventured farther and farther east, they eventually became pioneers of human life in the Western Hemisphere. Although they did not know it, their migrations revolutionized the history of the world.

Archaeologists refer to these first migrants and their descendants for the next few millennia as **Paleo-Indians**. They speculate that these Siberian

Beringia

Beringia
▶ The land bridge between Siberia and Alaska that was exposed by glaciation, allowing people to migrate into the Western Hemisphere.

Paleo-Indians
▶ Archaeologists' term for the first migrants into North America and their descendants who spread across the Americas between approximately 15,000 BP and 13,500 BP.

| Why did Archaic Native Americans shift to foraging and hunting smaller animals? | How did agriculture influence Native American cultures? | What cultural similarities did native peoples of the Western Hemisphere share in the 1490s? | Why was tribute important in the Mexican empire? | Conclusion: How do we understand the worlds of ancient Americans? | ☑ LearningCurve Check what you know. bedfordstmartins.com /roarkunderstanding |

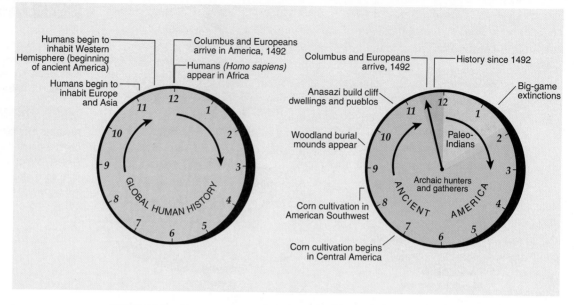

FIGURE 1.1 ■ Human Habitation of the World and the Western Hemisphere

These clock faces illustrate the long global history of modern humans (left) and of human history in the Western Hemisphere since the arrival of the first ancient Americans (right).

hunters traveled in small bands of no more than twenty-five people. How many such bands arrived in North America before Beringia disappeared beneath the sea will never be known.

When the first migrants came is hotly debated by experts. They probably arrived sometime after 15,000 BP. Scattered and inconclusive evidence suggests that they may have arrived several thousand years earlier. Certainly, humans who came from Asia—whose ancestors left Africa hundreds of thousands of years earlier—inhabited the Western Hemisphere by 14,000 BP.

Paleo-Indian Hunters

When humans first arrived in the Western Hemisphere, massive glaciers covered most of present-day Canada. Many archaeologists believe that Paleo-Indians probably migrated along an ice-free passageway on the eastern side of Canada's Rocky Mountains in pursuit of game. Other Paleo-Indians may have traveled along the Pacific coast in small boats, hunting marine life and hopscotching from one desirable landing spot to another. At the southern edge of the glaciers, Paleo-Indians entered a hunters' paradise teeming with wildlife that had never before confronted human predators armed with razor-sharp spears. The abundance of game presumably made hunting relatively easy. Ample food permitted the Paleo-Indian population to grow. Within a thousand years or so, Paleo-Indians had migrated throughout the Western Hemisphere.

Clovis points

▶ Distinctively shaped spearheads used by Paleo-Indians and named for the place in New Mexico where they were first excavated.

Early Paleo-Indians used a distinctively shaped spearhead known as a **Clovis point**, named for the place in New Mexico where it was first excavated. Archaeologists' discovery of abundant Clovis points throughout North and Central America in sites occupied between 13,500 BP and 13,000 BP provides evidence that these nomadic

CHAPTER LOCATOR | When and why do historians rely on the work of archaeologists? | How and why did humans migrate into North America?

8

CHAPTER 1
UNDERSTANDING ANCIENT AMERICA

hunters shared a common ancestry and way of life. At a few isolated sites, archaeologists have found still-controversial evidence of pre-Clovis artifacts that suggest the people who used Clovis spear points may have been preceded by several hundred years by a few non-Clovis pioneers. Paleo-Indians hunted mammoths and bison, but they probably also killed smaller animals. Concentration on large animals, when possible, made sense because just one mammoth could supply meat for months. In addition, mammoths provided Paleo-Indians with hides and bones for clothing, shelter, tools, and much more.

About 11,000 BP, Paleo-Indians confronted a major crisis. The mammoths and other large mammals they hunted became extinct. The extinction was gradual, stretching over several hundred years. Scientists are not completely certain why it occurred, although environmental change probably contributed to it. About this time, the earth's climate warmed, glaciers melted, and sea levels rose. Mammoths and other large mammals probably had difficulty adapting to the warmer climate. Many archaeologists also believe, however, that Paleo-Indians probably contributed to the extinctions in the Western Hemisphere by killing large animals more rapidly than they could reproduce. Whatever the causes, after the extinction of large mammals, Paleo-Indians literally inhabited a new world.

Paleo-Indians adapted to this drastic environmental change by making at least two important changes in their way of life. First, hunters began to prey more intensively on smaller animals. Second, Paleo-Indians devoted more energy to foraging—that is, to collecting wild plant foods such as roots, seeds, nuts, berries, and fruits. When Paleo-Indians made these changes, they replaced the apparent uniformity of the big-game-oriented Clovis culture with great cultural diversity adapted to the many natural environments throughout the hemisphere.

These post-Clovis adaptations to local environments resulted in the astounding variety of Native American cultures that existed when Europeans arrived in AD 1492. By then, more than three hundred major tribes and hundreds of lesser groups inhabited North America alone. Hundreds more lived in Central and South America. Hundreds of other ancient American cultures had disappeared or transformed as their people constantly adapted to environmental and other challenges.

QUICK REVIEW <

Why and how did Paleo-Indians adapt to environmental change?

Why did Archaic Native Americans shift to foraging and hunting smaller animals?

How did agriculture influence Native American cultures?

What cultural similarities did native peoples of the Western Hemisphere share in the 1490s?

Why was tribute important in the Mexican empire?

Conclusion: How do we understand the worlds of ancient Americans?

 LearningCurve
Check what you know.
bedfordstmartins.com
/roarkunderstanding

Why did Archaic Native Americans shift to foraging and hunting smaller animals?

Folsom Point at Wild Horse Arroyo

In 1927, paleontologist J. D. Figgins found this spear point embedded between the fossilized ribs of a bison that had been extinct for ten thousand years. Subsequently named the Folsom point, this discovery stimulated archaeologists to rethink the history of ancient Americans and to uncover fresh evidence of their many cultures.

hunter-gatherer

▶ A way of life that involved hunting game and gathering food from naturally occurring sources, as opposed to engaging in agriculture and animal husbandry. Archaic Indians and their descendants survived in North America for centuries as hunter-gatherers.

Archaic Indians

▶ Hunting and gathering peoples who descended from Paleo-Indians and dominated the Americas from 10,000 BP to between 4000 and 3000 BP.

ARCHAEOLOGISTS use the term *Archaic* to describe the many different hunting and gathering cultures that descended from Paleo-Indians and the long period of time when those cultures dominated the history of ancient America—roughly from 10,000 BP to somewhere between 4000 BP and 3000 BP. The term describes the era in the history of ancient America that followed the Paleo-Indian big-game hunters and preceded the development of agriculture. It denotes a **hunter-gatherer** way of life that persisted in North America long after European colonization.

Like their Paleo-Indian ancestors, **Archaic Indians** hunted with spears, but they also took smaller game with traps, nets, and hooks. Unlike their Paleo-Indian predecessors, most Archaic peoples prepared food from wild plants by using a variety of stone tools. A characteristic Archaic artifact is a grinding stone used to pulverize seeds into edible form. Most Archaic Indians migrated from place to place to harvest plants and hunt animals. They usually did not establish permanent villages, although they often returned to the same river valley or fertile meadow year after year. In regions with especially rich resources—such as present-day California and the Pacific Northwest—they developed permanent settlements. Archaic peoples followed these practices in distinctive ways in the different environmental regions of North America (**Map 1.2**).

CHAPTER LOCATOR | When and why do historians rely on the work of archaeologists? | How and why did humans migrate into North America?

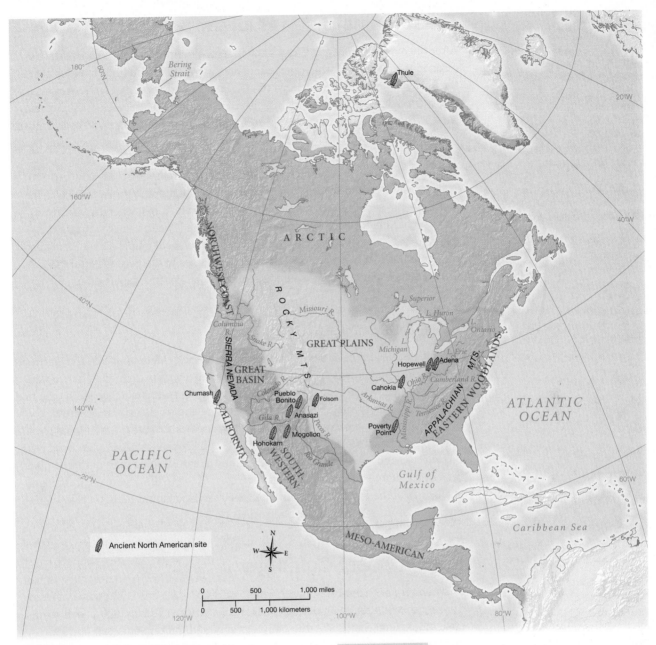

MAP 1.2 ■ Native North American Cultures

Environmental conditions defined the boundaries of the broad zones of cultural similarity among ancient North Americans.

> **MAP ACTIVITY**

READING THE MAP: What crucial environmental features set the boundaries of each cultural region? (The topography indicated on Map 1.3, "Native North Americans about 1500," may be helpful.)

CONNECTIONS: How did environmental factors and variations affect the development of different groups of Native American cultures? Why do you think historians and archaeologists group cultures together by their regional positions?

| Why did Archaic Native Americans shift to foraging and hunting smaller animals? | How did agriculture influence Native American cultures? | What cultural similarities did native peoples of the Western Hemisphere share in the 1490s? | Why was tribute important in the Mexican empire? | Conclusion: How do we understand the worlds of ancient Americans? | ✓ LearningCurve Check what you know. bedfordstmartins.com /roarkunderstanding |

> CHRONOLOGY

ca. 10,000–3000 BP
− Archaic hunter-gatherer cultures dominate ancient America.

ca. 5000 BP
− Chumash culture emerges in southern California.

ca. 4000 BP
− Eastern Woodland peoples practice agriculture and make pottery.

ca. 2500 BP
− Eastern Woodland cultures cultivate corn.

ca. AD 500
− Great Plains hunters begin to use bows and arrows.

Great Plains Bison Hunters

After the extinction of large game animals, some hunters began to concentrate on bison in the huge herds that grazed the plains stretching hundreds of miles east of the Rocky Mountains. For almost a thousand years after the big-game extinctions, Archaic Indians hunted bison with Folsom points, named after a site near Folsom, New Mexico. Like their nomadic predecessors, Folsom hunters moved constantly to maintain contact with their prey. Great Plains hunters often stampeded bison herds over cliffs and then slaughtered the animals that plunged to their deaths.

Bows and arrows reached Great Plains hunters from the north about AD 500. They largely replaced spears, which had been the hunters' weapons of choice for millennia. Bows permitted hunters to wound animals from farther away, arrows made it possible to shoot repeatedly, and arrowheads were easier to make and therefore less costly to lose than the larger, heavier spear points. Great Plains people hunted on foot. After Europeans imported horses in the decades after 1492, Great Plains bison hunters acquired them and soon became expert riders.

Great Basin Cultures

Archaic peoples in the Great Basin between the Rocky Mountains and the Sierra Nevada inhabited a region of great environmental diversity defined largely by the amount of rain. While some lived on the shores of lakes and marshes fed by the rain and ate fish, others hunted deer, antelope, bison, and smaller game. To protect against shortages in fish and game caused by the fickle rainfall, Great Basin Indians relied on plants as their most important food. Unlike meat and fish, plant food could be collected and stored for long periods. Many Great Basin peoples gathered piñon nuts as a dietary staple. Great Basin peoples adapted to the severe environmental challenges of the region and maintained their Archaic hunter-gatherer way of life for centuries after Europeans arrived in AD 1492.

Pacific Coast Cultures

The richness of the natural environment made present-day California the most densely settled area in all of ancient North America. The land and ocean offered such ample food that California peoples remained hunters and gatherers for hundreds of years after AD 1492. The diversity of California's environment also encouraged corresponding variety among native peoples. The mosaic of Archaic settlements in California included about five hundred separate tribes speaking some ninety languages, each with local dialects.

The Chumash, one of the many California cultures, emerged in the region surrounding what is now Santa Barbara about 5000 BP. Comparatively plentiful food resources—especially acorns—permitted Chumash people to establish relatively permanent villages. Although few other California cultures achieved the population density and village settlements of the Chumash, all shared the hunter-gatherer way of life and reliance on acorns as a major food source.

Another rich natural environment lay along the Pacific Northwest coast. Like the Chumash, Northwest peoples built more or less permanent villages. After about

Ancient California Peoples

CHAPTER LOCATOR | When and why do historians rely on the work of archaeologists? | How and why did humans migrate into North America?

5500 BP, they concentrated on catching whales and large quantities of salmon, halibut, and other fish, which they dried to last throughout the year. They also traded with people who lived hundreds of miles from the coast. Fishing freed Northwest peoples to develop sophisticated woodworking skills. They fashioned elaborate wood carvings that denoted wealth and status, as well as huge canoes for fishing, hunting, and conducting warfare against neighboring tribes.

Ozette Whale Effigy

This carving of a whale fin decorated with hundreds of sea otter teeth was discovered along with thousands of other artifacts of daily life at Ozette, an ancient village on the tip of the Olympic Peninsula in present-day Washington that was inundated by a catastrophic mud slide about five hundred years ago. The fin illustrates the importance of whale hunting to the residents of Ozette. Richard Alexander Cooke III.

Eastern Woodland Cultures

East of the Mississippi River, Archaic peoples adapted to a forest environment that included the major river valleys of the Mississippi, Ohio, Tennessee, and Cumberland; the Great Lakes region; and the Atlantic coast (see Map 1.2). Throughout these diverse locales, Archaic peoples pursued similar survival strategies.

Woodland hunters stalked deer as their most important prey. Deer supplied Woodland peoples with food as well as hides and bones that they crafted into clothing, weapons, and many other tools. Like Archaic peoples elsewhere, Woodland Indians gathered edible plants, seeds, and nuts. About 6000 BP, some Woodland groups established more or less permanent settlements of 25 to 150 people, usually near a river or lake that offered a wide variety of plant and animal resources. Woodland burial sites suggest that life expectancy was about eighteen years, a relatively short time to learn all the skills necessary to survive, reproduce, and adapt to change.

Around 4000 BP, Woodland cultures added two important features to their basic hunter-gatherer lifestyles: agriculture and pottery. Trade and migration from Mexico brought gourds and pumpkins to Woodland peoples, who also began to cultivate sunflowers and small quantities of tobacco. Corn, which had been grown in Mexico and South America since about 7000 BP, also traveled north and became a significant food crop among Eastern Woodland peoples around 2500 BP. Most likely, women learned how to plant, grow, and harvest these crops as an outgrowth of their work gathering edible wild plants. Cultivated crops did not alter Woodland peoples' dependence on gathering wild plants, seeds, and nuts.

Like agriculture, pottery probably originated in Mexico. Pots were more durable than baskets for cooking and the storage of food and water, but they were also much heavier and therefore were shunned by nomadic peoples. The permanent settlements of Woodland peoples made the heavy weight of pots much less important than their advantages compared to leaky and fragile baskets. While pottery and agriculture introduced changes in Woodland cultures, ancient Woodland Americans retained the other basic features of their Archaic hunter-gatherer lifestyle until 1492 and beyond.

Why did Archaic Native Americans shift to foraging and hunting smaller animals?

How did agriculture influence Native American cultures?

What cultural similarities did native peoples of the Western Hemisphere share in the 1490s?

Why was tribute important in the Mexican empire?

Conclusion: How do we understand the worlds of ancient Americans?

✔ LearningCurve
Check what you know.
bedfordstmartins.com
/roarkunderstanding

TABLE 1.1 ■ Archaic Indians at a Glance

Great Plains Bison Hunters	
Where they lived	East of the Rocky Mountains, in present-day eastern Colorado, northeastern New Mexico, North Dakota, South Dakota, Nebraska, Kansas, Oklahoma, Texas, Minnesota, Iowa, Missouri, Wisconsin, Michigan, Illinois, Indiana, and southwestern Canada
Lifestyle	Nomadic
How they acquired food	Hunting
What they ate	Bison
Technological developments	Acquired bow and arrow from the north; after Europeans' arrival, used horses to hunt
Great Basin Cultures	
Where they lived	Between the Rocky Mountains and the Sierra Nevada, present-day eastern California, Nevada, Idaho, Utah, Arizona, New Mexico, and Colorado
Lifestyle	Nomadic
How they acquired food	Fishing, hunting, and gathering
What they ate	Fish, deer, antelope, bison, smaller game, plants, and piñon nuts
Technological developments	None
Pacific Coast Cultures: Chumash and Northwest Peoples	
Where they lived	Chumash: around present-day Santa Barbara, California; Northwest peoples: present-day northern California, Oregon, Washington, and the west coast of Canada
Lifestyle	Village settlements
How they acquired food	Chumash: hunting and gathering; Northwest peoples: fishing
What they ate	Chumash: acorns; Northwest peoples: salmon, halibut, and other fish
Technological developments	Northwest peoples: elaborate wood carvings that denoted wealth and status; huge canoes for fishing, hunting, and conducting warfare against neighboring tribes
Eastern Woodland Cultures	
Where they lived	East of the Mississippi River, in the major river valleys of the Mississippi, Ohio, Tennessee, and Cumberland; the Great Lakes region; and the Atlantic coast
Lifestyle	Permanent settlements
How they acquired food	Hunting and gathering
What they ate	Deer, plants, seeds, and nuts
Technological developments	Agriculture and pottery

> **QUICK REVIEW**

Why did Archaic Indians shift from big-game hunting to foraging and smaller-game hunting?

CHAPTER LOCATOR | When and why do historians rely on the work of archaeologists? | How and why did humans migrate into North America?

How did agriculture influence Native American cultures?

Pueblo Bonito, Chaco Canyon, New Mexico About AD 1000, Pueblo Bonito stood at the center of Chacoan culture, which extended over more than 20,000 square miles in the region at the intersection of present-day Utah, Colorado, Arizona, and New Mexico. The numerous circular kivas show the significance of ceremonies and rituals to the people of Chaco Canyon. Richard Alexander Cooke III.

AMONG EASTERN WOODLAND PEOPLES and most other Archaic cultures, agriculture supplemented hunter-gatherer subsistence strategies but did not replace them. Reliance on wild animals and plants required most Archaic groups to remain small and mobile. But beginning about 4000 BP, distinctive southwestern cultures began to depend on agriculture and to build permanent settlements. Later, around 2500 BP, Woodland peoples in the vast Mississippi valley began to construct burial mounds and other earthworks that suggest the existence of social and political hierarchies that archaeologists term *chiefdoms*. Although the hunter-gatherer lifestyle never entirely disappeared, the development of agricultural settlements and chiefdoms represented important innovations to the Archaic way of life.

Southwestern Cultures

Ancient Americans in present-day Arizona, New Mexico, and southern portions of Utah and Colorado developed cultures characterized by agricultural settlements and multiunit dwellings called **pueblos**. All southwestern peoples confronted the challenge of a dry climate and unpredictable fluctuations in rainfall that made the supply of wild plant food very unreliable. These ancient Americans probably adopted agriculture in response to this basic environmental uncertainty.

About 3500 BP, southwestern hunters and gatherers began to cultivate corn, their signature food crop. The demands of corn cultivation encouraged hunter-gatherers to restrict their migratory habits in order to tend the crop. A vital consideration was access to water. Southwestern Indians became irrigation experts, conserving water from streams, springs, and rainfall and distributing it to thirsty crops.

pueblos
▶ Multiunit dwellings, storage spaces, and ceremonial centers — often termed *kivas* — built by ancient Americans in the Southwest for centuries, starting around AD 1000.

| Why did Archaic Native Americans shift to foraging and hunting smaller animals? | How did agriculture influence Native American cultures? | What cultural similarities did native peoples of the Western Hemisphere share in the 1490s? | Why was tribute important in the Mexican empire? | Conclusion: How do we understand the worlds of ancient Americans? | ✔ LearningCurve Check what you know. bedfordstmartins.com /roarkunderstanding |

ca. 3500 BP
- Southwestern cultures cultivate corn.

ca. 2500 BP
- Woodland cultures build burial mounds.

ca. 2500–2100 BP
- Adena culture develops in Ohio.

ca. 2100 BP–AD 400
- Hopewell culture emerges in Ohio and Mississippi valleys.

ca. AD 200–900
- Mogollon culture develops in New Mexico.

ca. AD 500–1400
- Hohokam culture develops in Arizona.

ca. AD 800–1500
- Mississippian culture flourishes in Southeast.

ca. AD 1000–1200
- Anasazi peoples build cliff dwellings and pueblos.

Ancient Agriculture

Dropping seeds into holes punched in cleared ground by a pointed stick known as a "dibble," this ancient American farmer sows a new crop while previously planted seeds — including the corn and beans immediately opposite him — bear fruit for harvest. Created by a sixteenth-century European artist, the drawing misrepresents who did the agricultural work in many ancient American cultures — namely, women rather than men. The Pierpont Morgan Library/Art Resource, NY.

> VISUAL ACTIVITY

READING THE IMAGE: In what ways has this ancient farmer modified and taken advantage of the natural environment?
CONNECTIONS: What were the advantages and disadvantages of agriculture compared to hunting and gathering?

About AD 200, small farming settlements began to appear throughout southern New Mexico, marking the emergence of the Mogollon culture. Typically, a Mogollon settlement included a dozen pit houses, each made by digging out a pit about fifteen feet in diameter and a foot or two deep and then erecting poles to support a roof of branches or dirt. Larger villages usually had one or two bigger pit houses that may have been the predecessors of the circular kivas, the ceremonial rooms that became a characteristic of nearly all southwestern settlements. About AD 900, Mogollon culture began to decline, for reasons that remain obscure.

Around AD 500, while the Mogollon culture prevailed in New Mexico, other ancient people migrated from Mexico to southern Arizona and established the distinctive Hohokam culture. Hohokam settlements used sophisticated grids of irrigation canals to plant and harvest crops twice a year. Hohokam settlements reflected Mexican cultural practices that northbound migrants brought with them, including

Pueblo Bonito

 The largest residential and ceremonial site, containing more than 600 rooms and 35 kivas, in the major Anasazi cultural center of Chaco Canyon in present-day New Mexico.

CHAPTER LOCATOR | When and why do historians rely on the work of archaeologists? | How and why did humans migrate into North America?

CHAPTER 1
16 UNDERSTANDING ANCIENT AMERICA

the building of sizable platform mounds and ball courts. About AD 1400, Hohokam culture declined for reasons that remain a mystery, although the rising salinity of the soil brought about by centuries of irrigation probably caused declining crop yields and growing food shortages.

North of the Hohokam and Mogollon cultures, in a region that encompassed southern Utah and Colorado and northern Arizona and New Mexico, the Anasazi culture began to flourish about AD 100. The early Anasazi built pit houses on mesa tops and used irrigation much as their neighbors did to the south. Beginning around AD 1000, some Anasazi began to move to large, multistory cliff dwellings whose spectacular ruins still exist at Mesa Verde, Colorado, and elsewhere. Other Anasazi communities—like the one known as **Pueblo Bonito**, whose impressive ruins can be visited at Chaco Canyon, New Mexico—erected huge stone-walled pueblos with enough rooms to house everyone in the settlement. Anasazi pueblos and cliff dwellings typically included one or more kivas used for secret ceremonies, restricted to men, that sought to communicate with the supernatural world.

Drought began to plague the region about AD 1130, and it lasted for more than half a century, triggering the disappearance of the Anasazi culture. By AD 1200, the large Anasazi pueblos had been abandoned. Some Anasazi migrated toward regions with more reliable rainfall and settled in Hopi, Zuñi, and Acoma pueblos that their descendants in Arizona and New Mexico have occupied ever since.

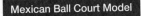

Mexican Ball Court Model

The Mexica and other Mesoamerican peoples commonly built special courts (or playing fields) for their intensely competitive ball games. This rare model of a Mexican ball court, made between 2200 BP and AD 250, shows a game in progress, complete with players and spectators. A few ball courts have been excavated in North America, compelling evidence of the many connections to Mexico. Yale University Art Gallery. Stephen Carlton Clark, B.A. 1903, Fund.

Woodland Burial Mounds and Chiefdoms

No other ancient Americans created dwellings similar to pueblos, but around 2500 BP, Woodland cultures throughout the Mississippi River watershed began to build **burial mounds**. The size of the mounds, the labor and organization required to erect them, and differences in the artifacts buried with certain individuals suggest the existence of a social and political hierarchy that archaeologists term a **chiefdom**. Experts do not know the name of a single chief. But the only way archaeologists can account for the complex and labor-intensive burial mounds is to assume that one person—whom scholars term a *chief*—commanded the labor and obedience of very large numbers of other people, who made up the chief's chiefdom.

Between 2500 BP and 2100 BP, Adena people built hundreds of burial mounds radiating from central Ohio. In the mounds, the Adena usually included grave goods such as spear points and stone pipes as well as thin sheets of mica (a glasslike mineral) crafted into animal or human shapes. Sometimes burial mounds were constructed all at once, but often they were built up slowly over many years.

About 2100 BP, Adena culture evolved into the more elaborate Hopewell culture, which lasted about five hundred years. Centered in Ohio, Hopewell culture extended throughout the enormous drainage of the Ohio and Mississippi rivers. Hopewell people built larger mounds than did their Adena predecessors

burial mounds
▶ Earthen mounds constructed by ancient American peoples, especially throughout the gigantic drainage of the Ohio and Mississippi rivers, after about 2500 BP and often used to bury important leaders and to enact major ceremonies.

chiefdom
▶ Hierarchical social organization headed by a chief. Archaeologists posit that the Woodland cultures were organized into chiefdoms because the construction of their characteristic burial mounds likely required one person having command over the labor of others.

Why did Archaic Native Americans shift to foraging and hunting smaller animals?

How did agriculture influence Native American cultures?

What cultural similarities did native peoples of the Western Hemisphere share in the 1490s?

Why was tribute important in the Mexican empire?

Conclusion: How do we understand the worlds of ancient Americans?

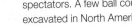 LearningCurve
Check what you know.
bedfordstmartins.com /roarkunderstanding

Cahokia Tablet

This stone tablet, excavated from the largest mound at Cahokia, depicts a bird-man whose sweeping wings and facial features — especially the nose and mouth — resemble a bird. Crafted around AD 1100, the tablet probably played some role in rituals enacted on the mound by Cahokian people. Similar birdlike human forms have been found among other Mississippian cultures. Cahokia Mounds Historic Site.

Cahokia

▶ The largest ceremonial site in ancient North America, located on the eastern bank of the Mississippi River across from present-day St. Louis, where thousands of inhabitants built hundreds of earthen mounds between about AD 800 and AD 1500.

and filled them with more magnificent grave goods. Burial rituals appear to have brought many people together to honor the dead person and to help build the mound. Grave goods at Hopewell sites testify to the high quality of Hopewell crafts and to a thriving trade network that ranged from present-day Wyoming to Florida. Hopewell culture declined about AD 400 for reasons that are obscure. Archaeologists speculate that bows and arrows, along with increasing reliance on agriculture, made small settlements more self-sufficient and therefore less dependent on the central authority of the Hopewell chiefs who were responsible for the burial mounds.

Four hundred years later, another mound-building culture flourished. The Mississippian culture emerged in the floodplains of the major southeastern river systems about AD 800 and lasted until about AD 1500. Major Mississippian sites, such as the one at **Cahokia**, included huge mounds with platforms on top for ceremonies and for the residences of great chiefs. Most likely, the ceremonial mounds and ritual practices derived from Mexican cultural expressions that were brought north by traders and migrants. At Cahokia, skilled farmers supported the large population with ample crops of corn. In addition to mounds, Cahokians erected what archaeologists call woodhenges (after the famous Stonehenge in England)—long wooden poles set upright in the ground and carefully arranged in huge circles. Although the purpose of woodhenges is unknown, experts believe that Cahokians probably built them partly for celestial observations.

Cahokia and other Mississippian cultures dwindled by AD 1500. When Europeans arrived, most of the descendants of Mississippian cultures, like those of the Hopewell culture, lived in small dispersed villages supported by hunting and gathering, supplemented by agriculture. Clearly, the conditions that caused large chiefdoms to emerge—whatever they were—had changed, and chiefs no longer commanded the sweeping powers they had once enjoyed.

> **QUICK REVIEW**

How and why did the societies of the Southwest differ from eastern societies?

CHAPTER LOCATOR | When and why do historians rely on the work of archaeologists? | How and why did humans migrate into North America?

This workbasket of a master weaver illustrates the technology of ancient American textile production. Found in a woman's grave in the Andes dating from one thousand years ago, the workbasket contains tools and thread for every stage of textile production. Weaving — like cooking, hunting, and worship — depended on human knowledge that survived only when passed from an experienced person to a novice. Museum of Fine Arts, Boston. Gift of Charles H. White, 02.680.

What cultural similarities did native peoples of the Western Hemisphere share in the 1490s?

ON THE EVE of European colonization in the 1490s, Native Americans lived throughout North and South America, but their total population is uncertain. Some experts claim that Native Americans inhabiting what is now the United States and Canada numbered 18 million to 20 million, while others place the population at no more than 1 million. A prudent estimate is about 4 million, or about the same as the number of people living on the small island nation of England at that time. The vastness of the territory meant that the overall population density of North America was low, just 60 people per 100 square miles, compared to more than 8,000 in England. Native Americans were spread thin across the land because of their survival strategies of hunting, gathering, and agriculture, but regional populations varied (**Figure 1.2**).

Eastern and Great Plains Peoples

About one-third of native North Americans inhabited the enormous Woodland region east of the Mississippi River; their population density approximated the average for North America as a whole. Eastern Woodland peoples clustered into three broad linguistic and cultural groups: Algonquian, Iroquoian, and Muskogean.

Algonquian tribes inhabited the Atlantic seaboard, the Great Lakes region, and much of the upper Midwest (**Map 1.3**). The relatively mild climate along the Atlantic permitted the coastal Algonquians to grow corn and other crops as well as to hunt and fish. Around the Great Lakes and in northern New England, however, cool summers and severe winters made agriculture impractical. Instead, the Abenaki, Penobscot, Chippewa, and other tribes concentrated on hunting and fishing, using canoes both for transportation and for gathering wild rice.

> **KEY FACTORS**

In 1492, Native Americans populated all of North America:
- One-fifth lived along the Pacific coast.
- One-fourth lived in the Southwest.
- One-third lived east of the Mississippi.
- One-fourth lived in the regions of the Great Plains, the Great Basin, and the Arctic.

Why did Archaic Native Americans shift to foraging and hunting smaller animals?

How did agriculture influence Native American cultures?

What cultural similarities did native peoples of the Western Hemisphere share in the 1490s?

Why was tribute important in the Mexican empire?

Conclusion: How do we understand the worlds of ancient Americans?

✔ LearningCurve
Check what you know.
bedfordstmartins.com /roarkunderstanding

19

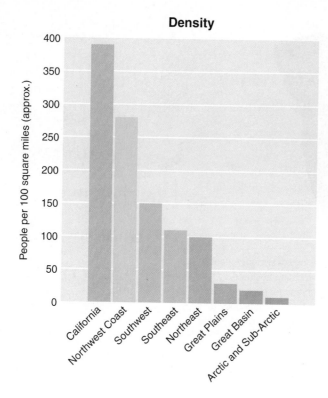

Density

People per 100 square miles (approx.)

(Bar chart showing values for: California ~390, Northwest Coast ~280, Southwest ~150, Southeast ~108, Northeast ~97, Great Plains ~27, Great Basin ~17, Arctic and Sub-Arctic ~7)

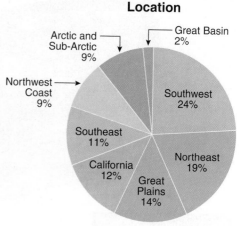

Location

- Arctic and Sub-Arctic 9%
- Great Basin 2%
- Northwest Coast 9%
- Southwest 24%
- Southeast 11%
- California 12%
- Great Plains 14%
- Northeast 19%

FIGURE 1.2 ■ Native American Population in North America about 1492 (Estimated)

Just before Europeans arrived, Native American population density varied widely, depending in large part on the availability of natural resources. The Pacific coast, with its rich marine resources, had the highest concentration of people. Overall, the population density of North America was less than 1 percent that of England, which helps explain why Europeans viewed North America as a relatively empty wilderness.

Inland from the Algonquian region, Iroquoian tribes occupied territories centered in Pennsylvania and upstate New York, as well as the hilly upland regions of the Carolinas and Georgia. Three features distinguished Iroquoian tribes from their neighbors. First, their success in cultivating corn and other crops allowed them to build permanent settlements, usually consisting of several longhouses housing five to ten families. Second, Iroquoian societies adhered to matrilineal rules of descent. Property of all sorts belonged to women. Women headed family clans and even selected the chiefs (normally men) who governed the tribes. Third, for purposes of war and diplomacy, an Iroquoian confederation—including the Seneca, Onondaga, Mohawk, Oneida, and Cayuga tribes—formed the League of Five Nations, which remained powerful well into the eighteenth century.

Muskogean peoples spread throughout the woodlands of the Southeast, south of the Ohio River and east of the Mississippi. Including the Creek, Choctaw, Chickasaw, and Natchez tribes, Muskogeans inhabited a bountiful natural environment that provided abundant food from hunting, gathering, and agriculture. Remnants of the earlier Mississippian culture still existed in Muskogean religion. The Natchez, for example, worshipped the sun and built temple mounds modeled after those of their Mississippian ancestors, including Cahokia.

Great Plains peoples accounted for about one out of seven native North Americans. Inhabiting the huge region west of the Eastern Woodland people and east of the Rocky Mountains, many tribes had migrated to the Great Plains within the century or two

CHAPTER LOCATOR | When and why do historians rely on the work of archaeologists? | How and why did humans migrate into North America?

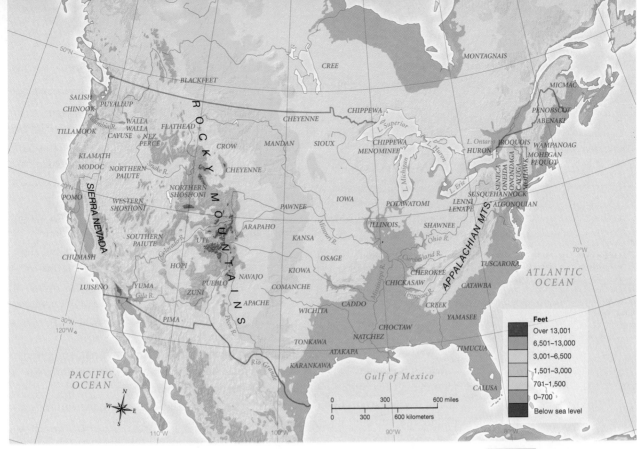

MAP 1.3 ■ Native North Americans about 1500

Distinctive Native American peoples resided throughout the area that, centuries later, became the United States. This map indicates the approximate location of some of the larger tribes about 1500. In the interest of legibility, many other peoples who inhabited North America at the time are omitted from the map.

before the 1490s, forced westward by Iroquoian and Algonquian tribes. Some Great Plains tribes—especially the Mandan and Pawnee—farmed successfully, growing both corn and sunflowers. But the Teton Sioux, Blackfeet, Comanche, Cheyenne, and Crow on the northern plains and the Apache and other nomadic tribes on the southern plains depended on buffalo (American bison) for their subsistence.

Southwestern and Western Peoples

Southwestern cultures included about a quarter of all native North Americans. These descendants of the Mogollon, Hohokam, and Anasazi cultures lived in settled agricultural communities, many of them pueblos. They continued to grow corn, beans, and squash using methods they had refined for centuries.

However, their communities came under attack by a large number of warlike Athapascans who invaded the Southwest beginning around AD 1300. The Athapascans—principally Apache and Navajo—were skillful warriors who preyed on the sedentary pueblo Indians, reaping the fruits of agriculture without the work of farming.

About a fifth of all native North Americans resided along the Pacific coast. In California, abundant acorns and nutritious marine life continued to support high population densities, but this abundance retarded the development of agriculture. Similar dependence on hunting and gathering persisted along the Northwest coast, where fishing reigned supreme.

| Why did Archaic Native Americans shift to foraging and hunting smaller animals? | How did agriculture influence Native American cultures? | **What cultural similarities did native peoples of the Western Hemisphere share in the 1490s?** | Why was tribute important in the Mexican empire? | Conclusion: How do we understand the worlds of ancient Americans? | ☑ LearningCurve Check what you know. bedfordstmartins.com /roarkunderstanding |

TABLE 1.2 ■ Native North Americans in the 1490s

- All native North Americans depended on hunting and gathering for a portion of their food.
- Most practiced agriculture. Agriculture sometimes supplemented hunting and gathering; at other times, hunting and gathering supplemented agriculture.
- All used bows, arrows, and other weapons for hunting and warfare.
- Evidence of artistic expression include drawings on stones, wood, and animal skins; woven patterns in baskets and textiles; designs painted on pottery, crafted into beadwork, or carved in effigies; songs, dances, religious ceremonies, and burial rites.
- Native North Americans did not have a writing system, did not use wheels or sailing ships, and did not have domesticated animals. Metal use was limited to copper.
- Native North Americans were able to adapt to local natural and social environments.

Cultural Similarities

Although North Americans may not have been as technologically advanced in weaponry as were Europeans during the 1490s, it would be a mistake to conclude that native North Americans lived in blissful harmony. Archaeological sites provide ample evidence of violent conflict. Skeletons, like those at Cahokia, bear the marks of wounds as well as of ritualistic human sacrifice. Religious, ethnic, economic, and familial conflicts must have occurred, but they remain in obscurity because they left few archaeological traces. In general, fear and anxiety must have been at least as common among native North Americans as feelings of peace and security.

Native North Americans not only adapted to the natural environment but also changed it in many ways. They built thousands of structures, from small dwellings to massive pueblos and enormous mounds, permanently altering the landscape. Their gathering techniques selected productive and nutritious varieties of plants, thereby shifting the balance of local plants toward useful varieties. The first stages of North American agriculture, for example, probably involved Native Americans gathering wild seeds and then sowing them in a meadow for later harvest. To clear land for planting seeds, native North Americans set fires that burned off thousands of acres of forest.

Native North Americans also used fires for hunting. Hunters often started fires to frighten and force together deer, buffalo, and other animals and make them easy to slaughter. Indians also started fires along the edges of woods to burn off shrubby undergrowth, encouraging the growth of tender young plants that attracted deer and other game, bringing them within convenient range of hunters' weapons. The burns also encouraged the growth of sun-loving food plants that Indians relished, such as blackberries, strawberries, and raspberries.

Because the fires set by native North Americans usually burned until they ran out of fuel or were extinguished by rain or wind, enormous regions of North America were burned over. In the long run, fires created and maintained a diverse and productive natural environment. Fires, like other activities of native North Americans, shaped the landscape of North America long before Europeans arrived in 1492.

> **QUICK REVIEW**

What common characteristics underlay Native American diversity?

CHAPTER LOCATOR | When and why do historians rely on the work of archaeologists? | How and why did humans migrate into North America?

Why was tribute important in the Mexican empire?

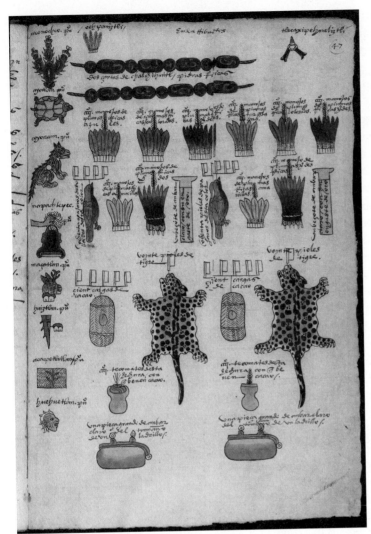

THE VAST MAJORITY of the 80 million people who lived in the Western Hemisphere in the 1490s inhabited Mesoamerica and South America, where the population approximately equaled that of Europe. Like their much less numerous counterparts north of the Rio Grande, these people lived in a natural environment of tremendous diversity. Among all these cultures, the **Mexica** stood out. Their empire stretched from coast to coast across central Mexico, encompassing between 8 million and 25 million people (experts disagree about the total population). Their significance in the history of the New World after 1492 dictates a brief survey of their culture and society.

The Mexica began their rise to prominence about 1325, when small bands settled on a marshy island in Lake Texcoco, the site of the future city of Tenochtitlán, the capital of the Mexican empire. Resourceful, courageous, and

Mexica

▶ A people whose empire stretched from coast to coast across central Mexico and who numbered as many as 25 million. The Mexican culture was characterized by steep hierarchy and devotion to the war god Huitzilopochtli.

Why did Archaic Native Americans shift to foraging and hunting smaller animals?

How did agriculture influence Native American cultures?

What cultural similarities did native peoples of the Western Hemisphere share in the 1490s?

Why was tribute important in the Mexican empire?

Conclusion: How do we understand the worlds of ancient Americans?

✓ **LearningCurve** Check what you know. bedfordstmartins.com /roarkunderstanding

23

c. AD 1325
- Small bands of Mexica settle on a marshy island in Lake Texcoco.

c. 1490
- Mexican empire stretches from coast to coast in central Mexico and encompasses between 8 and 25 million people.

AD 1492
- Christopher Columbus arrives in New World, beginning European colonization.

tribute
▶ The goods the Mexica collected from conquered peoples, from basic food products to candidates for human sacrifice. Tribute engendered resentment among the Mexica's subjects, creating a vulnerability the Spanish would later exploit.

cold-blooded warriors, the Mexica were often hired out as mercenaries for richer, more settled tribes.

The empire exemplified the central values of Mexican society and contributed far more to Mexican society than victims for sacrifice. At the most basic level, the empire functioned as a military and political system that collected **tribute** from subject peoples. The Mexica forced conquered tribes to pay tribute in goods, not money. Tribute redistributed to the Mexica as much as one-third of the goods produced by conquered tribes. It included everything from candidates for human sacrifice to textiles and basic food products as well as exotic luxury items such as gold, turquoise, and rare bird feathers.

Tribute reflected the fundamental relations of power and wealth that pervaded the Mexican empire. The relatively small nobility of Mexican warriors, supported by a still smaller priesthood, possessed the military and religious power to command the obedience of thousands of non-noble Mexicans and of millions of non-Mexicans in subjugated colonies. The Mexican elite exercised their power to obtain tribute and thereby to redistribute wealth from the conquered to the conquerors, from the commoners to the nobility, from the poor to the rich.

On the whole, the Mexica did not interfere much with the internal government of conquered regions. Instead, they usually permitted the traditional ruling elite to stay in power—so long as they paid tribute. Subjugated communities felt exploited by the constant payment of tribute to the Mexica. The high level of discontent among subject peoples constituted the soft, vulnerable underbelly of the Mexican empire, a fact that Spanish intruders exploited after 1492 to conquer the Mexica.

> **The Mexica, at a Glance**

- By the 1490s, the Mexica ruled an empire that covered more land than Spain and Portugal combined and contained almost three times as many people.
- Warriors were the most important members of society. The Mexica worshipped the war god Huitzilopochtli.
- Capturing prisoners in battle was considered the highest act of bravery; prisoners were sacrificed to Huitzilopochtli.
- The Mexica believed that human sacrifice fed the sun's craving for blood, which kept the sun aflame and prevented the fatal descent of everlasting darkness and chaos.
- Wealth collected from conquered peoples gave Mexicans the means with which to build the cities, temples, markets, and luxuriant gardens that so impressed the Spaniards upon their arrival in the New World.

> **QUICK REVIEW**

How did the conquest and creation of an empire exemplify the central values of Mexican society?

CHAPTER LOCATOR | When and why do historians rely on the work of archaeologists? | How and why did humans migrate into North America?

24 CHAPTER 1 UNDERSTANDING ANCIENT AMERICA

Conclusion: How do we understand the worlds of ancient Americans?

ANCIENT AMERICANS SHAPED the history of human beings in the New World for more than thirteen thousand years. They established continuous human habitation in the Western Hemisphere from the time the first big-game hunters crossed Beringia until 1492 and beyond. Much of their history remains lost because they relied on oral rather than written communication. But much can be pieced together from artifacts they left behind at camps, kill sites, and ceremonial and residential centers such as Cahokia and Tenochtitlán, the capital of the Mexican empire. Ancient Americans achieved their success through resourceful adaptation to the hemisphere's many and changing natural environments. They also adapted to social and cultural changes caused by human beings—such as marriages and deaths, as well as political struggles and warfare among chiefdoms. Their creativity and artistry are unmistakably documented in their numerous artifacts. Those material objects sketch the only likenesses of ancient Americans we will ever have—blurred, shadowy images that are indisputably human but forever silent.

When European intruders began arriving in the Western Hemisphere in 1492, their attitudes about the promise of the New World were heavily influenced by the diverse peoples they encountered. Europeans coveted Native Americans' wealth, labor, and land, and Christian missionaries sought to save their souls. Likewise, Native Americans marveled at such European technological novelties as sailing ships, steel weapons, gunpowder, and horses, while often reserving judgment about Europeans' Christian religion.

In the centuries following 1492, as the trickle of European strangers became a flood of newcomers from both Europe and Africa, Native Americans and settlers continued to encounter each other. Peaceful negotiations as well as violent conflicts over both land and trading rights resulted in chronic fear and mistrust. While the era of European colonization marked the beginning of the end of ancient America, the ideas, subsistence strategies, and cultural beliefs of native North Americans remained powerful among their descendants for generations and continue to persist to the present.

Why did Archaic Native Americans shift to foraging and hunting smaller animals?

How did agriculture influence Native American cultures?

What cultural similarities did native peoples of the Western Hemisphere share in the 1490s?

Why was tribute important in the Mexican empire?

Conclusion: How do we understand the worlds of ancient Americans?

☑ LearningCurve
Check what you know.
bedfordstmartins.com
/roarkunderstanding

CHAPTER 1 STUDY GUIDE

STEP 1

GET STARTED ONLINE

✓ **LearningCurve** ■ bedfordstmartins.com/roarkunderstanding
Now that you've read the chapter, make it stick by completing the LearningCurve activity.

STEP 2

EXPLAIN WHY IT MATTERS

Put your reading into practice. Identify each term below, and then explain why it matters in U.S. history.

TERM	WHO OR WHAT & WHEN	WHY IT MATTERS
Beringia (p. 7)		
Paleo-Indians (p. 7)		
Clovis points (p. 8)		
hunter-gatherer (p. 10)		
Archaic Indians (p. 10)		
pueblos (p. 15)		
Pueblo Bonito (p. 17)		
burial mounds (p. 17)		
chiefdom (p. 17)		
Cahokia (p. 18)		
Mexica (p. 23)		
tribute (p. 24)		

STEP 3

MOVE BEYOND THE BASICS

To demonstrate a more advanced understanding, describe the cultural differences of Native American peoples in 1492.

Indian peoples in 1490	Geography and climate	Economy and lifestyle (sources of food and material goods, economic organization, trade)	Social/political organization (religion, family structures, social hierarchy)
Southwestern cultures			
Eastern Woodland cultures			
Pacific coast cultures			
Great Basin cultures			
Great Plains cultures			

PUT IT ALL TOGETHER Now, take a step back and try to explain the big picture. Remember to use specific examples from the chapter in your answers.

THE FIRST AMERICANS

▶ When and how did humans first arrive in the Americas?

▶ Describe the lifestyle of the Paleo-Indians. How did they adapt to the extinction of mammoths and other large mammals around 11,000 BP?

AGRICULTURE AND ADAPTATION

▶ How did Archaic Indians differ from their Paleo-Indian ancestors?

▶ How did the advent of agriculture change the settlement patterns and social organization of some Indian groups?

NATIVE AMERICAN CULTURES IN 1490

▶ What factors shaped population density across North America?

▶ What set the Mexica apart from the other Indian cultures of North America?

LOOKING BACKWARD, LOOKING AHEAD

▶ What accounts for the diversity of Indian peoples on the eve of European contact?

> **IN YOUR OWN WORDS**

Imagine that you must give an oral report to the class answering the following question: **How did ancient North American peoples shape the history of the continent before the arrival of Europeans in 1492?** What would be the most important points to include and why?

 Do it online at the Student Site ■ bedfordstmartins.com/roarkunderstanding

2

EUROPEANS ENCOUNTER THE NEW WORLD

1492–1600

> **What were the most significant effects of European exploration in the sixteenth century?**

Chapter 2 examines the causes, course, and impact of European exploration of parts of the world previously unknown to them. It follows early Portuguese efforts to chart the coast of Africa and the Spanish establishment of a colonial empire in the New World. It then explores the many changes in both the New and Old Worlds that were a result of Europeans' encounters with Native Americans during the sixteenth century.

LearningCurve

bedfordstmartins.com/roarkunderstanding
After reading the chapter, use LearningCurve to
retain what you've read.

> What factors led
  to European
  exploration in the
  fifteenth century?

> What did Spanish
  explorers discover
  in the western
  Atlantic?

> How did Spaniards
  explore, conquer,
  and colonize New
  Spain?

> What impact did
  Spain's New World
  endeavors have in
  Europe?

> Conclusion: What
  promise did the
  New World offer
  Europeans?

Europeans Encountering Indians. Unknown artist, ca. 1700. Private Collection/Picture Research Consultants and Archives.

What factors led to European exploration in the fifteenth century?

> CHRONOLOGY

Mid-fourteenth century
- Black Death kills approximately one-third of Europe's population.

1415–1460
- Portuguese led by Prince Henry the Navigator use new navigational tools and techniques to aid maritime exploration.

1480
- Portuguese ships reach the Congo.

1488
- Bartolomeu Dias rounds Cape of Good Hope.

1498
- Vasco da Gama sails to India.

HISTORICALLY, THE EAST—not the West — attracted Europeans. Wealthy Europeans developed a taste for luxury goods from Asia and Africa, and merchants competed to satisfy that desire. As Europeans traded with the East and with one another, they acquired new information about the world they inhabited. A few people—sailors, merchants, and aristocrats—took the risks of exploring beyond the limits of the world known to Europeans. Those risks could be deadly, but sometimes they paid off in new information, new opportunities, and eventually the discovery of a world entirely new to Europeans.

Mediterranean Trade and European Expansion

From the twelfth through the fifteenth centuries, spices, silk, carpets, ivory, and gold traveled overland from Persia, Asia Minor, India, and Africa and then funneled into continental Europe through Mediterranean trade routes (**Map 2.1**). Dominated primarily by the Italian cities of Venice, Genoa, and Pisa, this lucrative trade enriched Italian merchants and bankers. The vitality of the Mediterranean trade offered merchants few incentives to look for alternatives. New routes to the East and the discovery of new lands were the stuff of fantasy.

Preconditions for turning fantasy into reality developed in fifteenth-century Europe. In the mid-fourteenth century, a catastrophic epidemic of bubonic plague

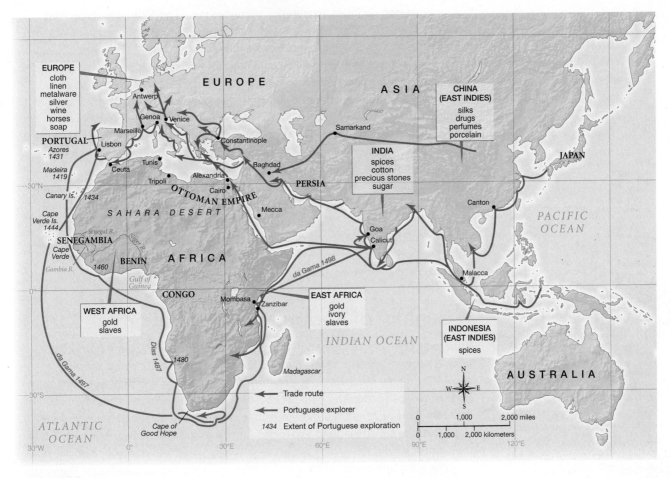

MAP 2.1 ■ European Trade Routes and Portuguese Exploration in the Fifteenth Century

Italian cities' domination of trade from Asia was slowly undermined during the fifteenth century by Portuguese explorers who hopscotched along the coast of Africa and eventually found a sea route that opened the rich trade of the East to Portuguese merchants.

(or the **Black Death**, as it was called) killed about a third of the European population. This devastating pestilence had major long-term consequences. By drastically reducing the population, it made Europe's limited supply of food more plentiful for survivors. Many survivors inherited property from plague victims, giving them new chances for advancement.

Understandably, most Europeans perceived the world as a place of alarming risks where the delicate balance of health, harvests, and peace could quickly be tipped toward disaster by epidemics, famine, and violence. Most people protected themselves from the constant threat of calamity by worshipping the supernatural, by living amid kinfolk and friends, and by maintaining good relations with the rich and powerful. But the insecurity and uncertainty of fifteenth-century European life also encouraged a few people to take greater risks, such as embarking on dangerous sea voyages through uncharted waters to points unknown.

Black Death

▶ An epidemic of bubonic plague that in the mid-fourteenth century killed about a third of the European population and resulted in increased food and resources for the survivors as well as a sense of a world in precarious balance.

What did Spanish explorers discover in the western Atlantic?

How did Spaniards explore, conquer, and colonize New Spain?

What impact did Spain's New World endeavors have in Europe?

Conclusion: What promise did the New World offer Europeans?

☑ LearningCurve
Check what you know.
bedfordstmartins.com
/roarkunderstanding

31

In European societies, exploration promised fame and fortune to those who succeeded, whether they were kings or commoners. Monarchs hoped to enlarge their realms and enrich their dynasties by sponsoring journeys of exploration. More territory meant more subjects who could pay more taxes, provide more soldiers, and participate in more commerce, magnifying the monarch's power and prestige. Voyages of exploration also could stabilize the monarch's regime by diverting unruly noblemen toward distant lands. Some explorers were commoners who hoped to be elevated to the aristocracy as a reward for their daring achievements.

Scientific and technological advances also helped set the stage for exploration. The invention of movable type by Johannes Gutenberg around 1450 in Germany made printing easier and cheaper, stimulating the diffusion of information, including news of discoveries, among literate Europeans. By 1400, crucial navigational aids employed by maritime explorers were already available: compasses; hourglasses; and the astrolabe and quadrant, which were devices for determining latitude. The Portuguese were the first to use these technological advances in a campaign to sail beyond the limits of the world known to Europeans.

A Century of Portuguese Exploration

With only 2 percent of the population of Christian Europe, Portugal devoted far more energy and wealth to the geographic exploration of the world between 1415 and 1460 than all other European countries combined. As a Christian kingdom, Portugal cooperated with Spain in the **Reconquest**, the centuries-long drive to expel the Muslims from the Iberian Peninsula. The religious zeal that propelled the Reconquest also justified expansion into what the Portuguese considered heathen lands.

The most influential advocate of Portuguese exploration was Prince Henry the Navigator, son of the Portuguese king. From 1415 until his death in 1460, Henry collected the latest information about sailing techniques and geography, supported new crusades against the Muslims, sought fresh sources of trade to fatten Portuguese pocketbooks, and pushed explorers to go farther still.

Neither the Portuguese nor anybody else in Europe knew the immensity of Africa or the length of its coastline, which fronted the Atlantic for more than seven thousand miles. At first, Portuguese mariners cautiously hugged the west coast of Africa, seldom venturing beyond sight of land. By 1434, they had reached the northern edge of the Sahara Desert, where they learned to ride strong westerly currents before catching favorable easterly winds that turned them back toward land, which allowed them to reach Cape Verde by 1444.

To stow the supplies necessary for long sea voyages and to withstand the battering of waves in the open ocean, the Portuguese developed the caravel, a fast, sturdy ship that became explorers' vessel of choice. In caravels, Portuguese mariners sailed into and around the Gulf of Guinea and as far south as the Congo by 1480.

Fierce African resistance confined Portuguese expeditions to coastal trading posts, where they bartered successfully for gold, slaves, and ivory. Powerful African kingdoms welcomed Portuguese trading ships loaded with iron goods,

Reconquest
▶ The centuries-long drive to expel Muslims from the Iberian Peninsula undertaken by the Christian kingdoms of Spain and Portugal. The military victories of the Reconquest helped the Portuguese gain greater access to sea routes.

CHAPTER LOCATOR | What factors led to European exploration in the fifteenth century?

32 CHAPTER 2
EUROPEANS ENCOUNTER THE NEW WORLD

weapons, textiles, and ornamental shells. Portuguese merchants learned that establishing relatively peaceful trading posts on the coast offered more profit than attempting violent conquest and colonization of inland regions. In the 1460s, the Portuguese used African slaves to develop sugar plantations on the Cape Verde Islands, inaugurating an association between enslaved Africans and plantation labor that would be transplanted to the New World in the centuries to come.

About 1480, Portuguese explorers, eager to bypass the Mediterranean merchants, began a conscious search for a sea route to Asia. In 1488, Bartolomeu Dias sailed around the Cape of Good Hope at the southern tip of Africa and hurried back to Lisbon with the exciting news that it appeared to be possible to sail on to India and China. In 1498, after ten years of careful preparation, Vasco da Gama commanded the first Portuguese fleet to sail to India. Portugal quickly capitalized on the commercial potential of da Gama's new sea route. By the early sixteenth century, the Portuguese controlled a far-flung commercial empire in India, Indonesia, and China (collectively referred to as the East Indies). Their new sea route to the East eliminated overland travel and allowed Portuguese merchants to charge much lower prices for the Eastern goods they imported.

Portugal's African explorations during the fifteenth century broke the monopoly of the old Mediterranean trade with the East, dramatically expanded the world known to Europeans, established a network of Portuguese outposts in Africa and Asia, and developed methods of sailing the high seas.

QUICK REVIEW <

Why did European exploration expand dramatically in the fifteenth century?

What did Spanish explorers discover in the western Atlantic?

How did Spaniards explore, conquer, and colonize New Spain?

What impact did Spain's New World endeavors have in Europe?

Conclusion: What promise did the New World offer Europeans?

LearningCurve
Check what you know.
bedfordstmartins.com
/roarkunderstanding

> What did Spanish explorers discover in the western Atlantic?

Spanish Tapestry This detail from a lavish sixteenth-century tapestry depicts Columbus (kneeling) receiving a box of jewels from Queen Isabella (whose husband, King Ferdinand, stands slightly behind her) in appreciation for his voyages to the New World. © Julio Conoso/Corbis Sygma.

> CHRONOLOGY

1492
- Christopher Columbus lands in the Caribbean and encounters the Tainos.
- Columbian exchange begins.

1493
- Columbus makes second voyage to the New World.

1494
- Portugal and Spain sign the Treaty of Tordesillas.

1497
- John Cabot searches for the Northwest Passage.

1513
- Vasco Núñez de Balboa crosses the Isthmus of Panama.

1519
- Ferdinand Magellan sets out to sail around the world.

THE PORTUGUESE AND OTHER experts believed that sailing west across the Atlantic to Asia was literally impossible. The European discovery of America required someone bold enough to believe that the experts were wrong. That person was Christopher Columbus. His explorations inaugurated a geographic revolution that forever altered Europeans' understanding of the world and its peoples, including themselves. Columbus's landfall in the Caribbean initiated a thriving exchange between the people, ideas, cultures, and institutions of the Old and New Worlds that continues to this day.

The Explorations of Columbus

Columbus went to sea when he was about fourteen and eventually made his way to Lisbon, where he gained access to maps and information about the tricky currents and winds in the Atlantic. Like other educated Europeans, Columbus

CHAPTER LOCATOR | What factors led to European exploration in the fifteenth century?

believed that the earth was a sphere and that theoretically it was possible to reach the East Indies by sailing west. With flawed calculations, he estimated that Asia was only about 2,500 miles away, a shorter distance than Portuguese ships routinely sailed between Lisbon and the Congo. In fact, the shortest distance to Japan from Europe's jumping-off point was nearly 11,000 miles. Convinced by his erroneous calculations, Columbus became obsessed with a scheme to prove he was right.

In 1492, after years of unsuccessful lobbying in Portugal, Spain, England, and France, Columbus finally won financing for his journey from the Spanish monarchs, Queen Isabella and King Ferdinand. They saw Columbus's venture as an inexpensive gamble: The potential loss was small, but the potential gain was huge.

After frantic preparation, Columbus and his small fleet—the *Niña* and the *Pinta*, both caravels, and the *Santa María*, a larger merchant vessel—headed west. Six weeks after leaving the Canary Islands, Columbus landed on a tiny Caribbean island about three hundred miles north of the eastern tip of Cuba.

Columbus claimed possession of the island for Spain and named it San Salvador, in honor of the Savior, Jesus Christ. He called the islanders "Indians," assuming that they inhabited the East Indies somewhere near Japan or China. The islanders called themselves **Tainos**, which in their language meant "good" or "noble." An agricultural people, the Tainos grew cassava, corn, cotton, tobacco, and other crops. Instead of dressing in the finery Columbus had expected to find in the East Indies, the Tainos "all . . . go around as naked as their mothers bore them," Columbus wrote. Although Columbus concluded that the Tainos "had no religion," in reality they worshipped gods they called zemis, ancestral spirits who inhabited natural objects such as trees and stones. The Tainos had no riches. "It seemed to me that they were a people very poor in everything," Columbus wrote.

What the Tainos thought about Columbus and his sailors we can only surmise, since they left no written documents. At first, Columbus got the impression that the Tainos believed the Spaniards came from heaven. But after six weeks of encounters, Columbus decided that "the people of these lands do not understand me nor do I, nor anyone else that I have with me, [understand] them." The confused communication between the Spaniards and the Tainos suggests how strange each group seemed to the other. Columbus's perceptions of the Tainos were shaped by European attitudes, ideas, and expectations, just as the Tainos' perceptions of the Europeans were no doubt colored by their own culture.

Columbus and his men understood that they had made a momentous discovery. In 1493, when Queen Isabella and King Ferdinand learned Columbus's news, they were overjoyed. With a voyage that had lasted barely eight months, Columbus appeared to have catapulted Spain into a serious challenger to Portugal, whose explorers had not yet sailed to India or China.

Columbus's First Voyage to the New World, 1492–1493

Tainos

▶ The Indians who inhabited San Salvador and many Caribbean islands and who were the first people Columbus encountered after making landfall in the New World.

Taino Zemi Basket

Crafted sometime between 1492 and about 1520, this basket is an example of the effigies Tainos made to represent zemis, or deities. The basket maker used African ivory and European mirrors as well as Native American fibers, dyes, and designs. Archivio Fotografico del Museo Preistorico Etnografico L. Pigorini, Roma.

What did Spanish explorers discover in the western Atlantic?

How did Spaniards explore, conquer, and colonize New Spain?

What impact did Spain's New World endeavors have in Europe?

Conclusion: What promise did the New World offer Europeans?

☑ LearningCurve
Check what you know.
bedfordstmartins.com
/roarkunderstanding

Soon after Columbus returned to Spain, the Spanish monarchs rushed to obtain the pope's support for their claim to the new lands in the West. When the pope, a Spaniard, complied, the Portuguese feared that their own claims to recently discovered territories were in jeopardy. To protect their claims, the Portuguese and Spanish monarchs negotiated the **Treaty of Tordesillas** in 1494. The treaty drew an imaginary line eleven hundred miles west of the Canary Islands (**Map 2.2**). Land discovered west of the line (namely, the islands that Columbus discovered and any additional land that might be found) belonged to Spain; Portugal claimed land to the east (namely, its African and East Indian trading empire).

Isabella and Ferdinand moved quickly to realize the promise of their new claims. In the fall of 1493, they dispatched Columbus once again, this time with a fleet of seventeen ships and more than a thousand men who planned to locate the Asian mainland, find gold, and get rich. Before Columbus died in 1506, he returned to the New World two more times (in 1498 and 1502) without relinquishing his belief that the East Indies were there, someplace. Other explorers continued to search for a passage to the East or some other source of profit. Before long, however, prospects of beating the Portuguese to Asia began to dim along with the hope of finding vast hoards of gold.

Nonetheless, Columbus's discoveries forced sixteenth-century Europeans to think about the world in new ways. He proved it was possible to sail from Europe to the western rim of the Atlantic and return to Europe. Most important, Columbus's voyages demonstrated that lands and peoples entirely unknown to Europeans lay across the Atlantic.

Treaty of Tordesillas

▶ The treaty negotiated in 1494 to delineate land claims in the New World. The treaty drew an imaginary line west of the Canary Islands; land discovered west of the line belonged to Spain, and land to the east belonged to Portugal.

The Geographic Revolution and the Columbian Exchange

Within thirty years of Columbus's initial discovery, Europeans' understanding of world geography underwent a revolution. An elite of perhaps twenty thousand people with access to Europe's royal courts and trading centers learned the exciting news about global geography. But it took a generation of additional exploration before they could comprehend the larger contours of Columbus's discoveries.

By 1500, European experts knew that several large chunks of land cluttered the western Atlantic. A few cartographers speculated that these chunks were connected to one another in a landmass that was not Asia. In 1507, Martin Waldseemüller, a German cartographer, published the first map that showed the New World separate from Asia; he named the land America, in honor of Amerigo Vespucci.

> Early Voyages to the Americas

Explorer	Voyage
John Cabot	Reached Newfoundland in 1497 while searching for a Northwest Passage to Asia.
Amerigo Vespucci	Participated in a Spanish expedition that landed on the northern coast of South America in 1499.
Pedro Álvars Cabral	Commanded a Portuguese fleet bound for the Indian Ocean that accidentally made landfall on the coast of Brazil.

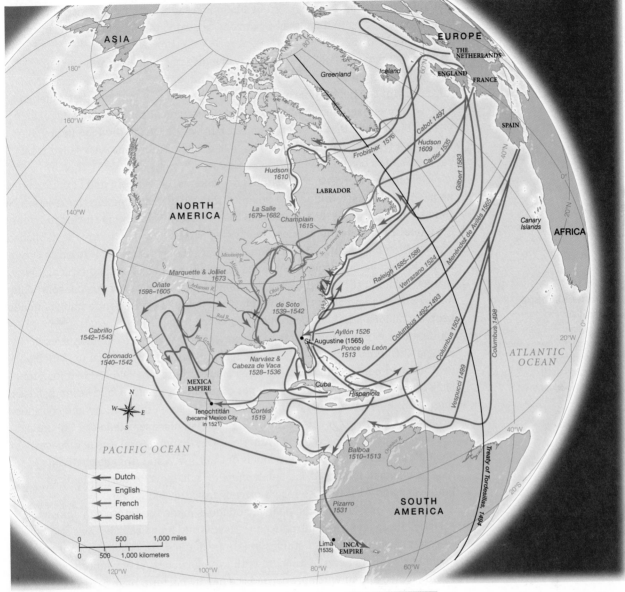

MAP 2.2 ■ **European Exploration in Sixteenth-Century America**

This map illustrates the approximate routes of early European explorations of the New World.

> **MAP ACTIVITY**

READING THE MAP: Which countries were most actively exploring the New World? Which countries were exploring later than others?

CONNECTIONS: What were the motivations behind the explorations? What were the motivations for colonization?

Two additional discoveries confirmed Waldseemüller's speculation. In 1513, Vasco Núñez de Balboa crossed the Isthmus of Panama and reached the Pacific Ocean. Clearly, more water lay between the New World and Asia. Ferdinand Magellan discovered just how much water when he led an expedition to circumnavigate the globe in 1519. Sponsored by Spain, Magellan's voyage took him first to the New World, around the southern tip of South America, and into the Pacific. Crossing the Pacific took almost four months, decimating his crew with hunger and

| What did Spanish explorers discover in the western Atlantic? | How did Spaniards explore, conquer, and colonize New Spain? | What impact did Spain's New World endeavors have in Europe? | Conclusion: What promise did the New World offer Europeans? | ✓LearningCurve Check what you know. bedfordstmartins.com /roarkunderstanding |

thirst. Magellan himself was killed by Philippine tribesmen. A remnant of his expedition continued on to the Indian Ocean and managed to transport a cargo of spices back to Spain in 1522.

In most ways, Magellan's voyage was a disaster. One ship and 18 men crawled back from an expedition that had begun with five ships and more than 250 men. But the geographic information it provided left no doubt that America was a continent separated from Asia by the enormous Pacific Ocean. Magellan's voyage made clear that it was possible to sail west to reach the East Indies, but that was a terrible way to go. After Magellan, most Europeans who sailed west set their sights on the New World, not on Asia.

Columbus's arrival in the Caribbean anchored the western end of what might be imagined as a sea bridge that spanned the Atlantic, connecting the Western Hemisphere to Europe. Somewhat like the Beringian land bridge traversed by the first Americans millennia earlier (see chapter 1), the new sea bridge reestablished a connection between the Eastern and Western Hemispheres. The Atlantic Ocean, which had previously isolated America from Europe, became an aquatic highway, thanks to sailing technology, intrepid seamen, and their European sponsors. This new sea bridge launched the **Columbian exchange**, a transatlantic trade of goods, people, and ideas that has continued ever since.

Spaniards brought novelties to the New World that were commonplace in Europe, including Christianity, iron technology, sailing ships, firearms, wheeled vehicles, and horses. Unknowingly, they also carried many Old World microorganisms that caused devastating epidemics of smallpox, measles, and other diseases that killed the vast majority of Indians during the sixteenth century and continued to decimate survivors in later centuries. European diseases made the Columbian exchange catastrophic for Native Americans. In the long term, these diseases helped transform the dominant peoples of the New World from descendants of Asians, who had inhabited the hemisphere for millennia, to descendants of Europeans and Africans, the recent arrivals from the Old World.

Ancient American goods, people, and ideas made the return trip across the Atlantic. Europeans were introduced to New World foods such as corn and potatoes that became important staples in European diets, especially for poor people. Columbus's sailors became infected with syphilis in sexual encounters with New World women and unwittingly carried the deadly bacteria back to Europe. New World tobacco created a European fashion for smoking that ignited quickly and has yet to be extinguished. But for almost a generation after 1492, this Columbian exchange did not reward the Spaniards with the riches they yearned to find.

Columbian exchange
▶ The transatlantic exchange of goods, people, and ideas that began when Columbus arrived in the Caribbean, ending the age-old separation of the Eastern and Western Hemispheres.

> **QUICK REVIEW**

How did Columbus's discoveries help revolutionize Europeans' understanding of global geography?

CHAPTER LOCATOR | What factors led to European exploration in the fifteenth century?

38 CHAPTER 2
EUROPEANS ENCOUNTER THE NEW WORLD

Cortés Arrives in Tenochtitlán This portrayal of the arrival of Cortés and his army in the Mexican capital illustrates the Spaniards' military advantages of horses, armor, and Indian supporters.
Bibliothèque Nationale de France.

> CHRONOLOGY

1519
– Hernán Cortés searches for wealth in Mexico.

1520
– Mexica in Tenochtitlán revolt against the Spaniards.

1521
– Cortés conquers the Mexica.

1532
– Francisco Pizarro begins the conquest of Peru.

1539
– Hernando de Soto explores southeastern North America.

1540
– Francisco Vásquez de Coronado starts to explore the Southwest and Great Plains.

1542
– Juan Rodríguez Cabrillo explores the California coast

1549
– Repartimiento reforms replace encomienda.

1565
– St. Augustine, Florida, is settled.

1598
– Juan de Oñate explores New Mexico.

1599
– Acoma pueblos revolt against Oñate.

DURING THE SIXTEENTH CENTURY, the New World helped Spain become the most powerful monarchy in both Europe and the Americas. Initially, Spaniards enslaved Caribbean tribes and put them to work growing crops and mining gold. But the profits from these early ventures barely covered the costs of maintaining the settlers. After almost thirty years of exploration, the promise of Columbus's discovery seemed illusory.

In 1519, however, that promise was spectacularly fulfilled by Hernán Cortés's march into Mexico. By about 1545, Spanish conquests extended from northern Mexico to southern Chile, and New World riches filled Spanish treasure chests. Cortés's expedition served as the model for Spaniards' and other Europeans' expectations that the New World could yield bonanza profits for its conquerors while forced labor and deadly epidemics decimated native populations.

The Conquest of Mexico

Hernán Cortés, an obscure nineteen-year-old Spaniard, arrived in the New World in 1504. Throughout his twenties, he fought in the conquest of Cuba and elsewhere in the Caribbean. In 1519, the governor of Cuba authorized Cortés to organize an expedition of about six hundred men and eleven ships to investigate rumors of a fabulously wealthy kingdom somewhere in the interior of the mainland.

A charismatic and confident man, Cortés could not speak any Native American language. Landing first on the Yucatán peninsula with his ragtag army,

| What did Spanish explorers discover in the western Atlantic? | **How did Spaniards explore, conquer, and colonize New Spain?** | What impact did Spain's New World endeavors have in Europe? | Conclusion: What promise did the New World offer Europeans? | ✔ LearningCurve Check what you know. bedfordstmartins.com /roarkunderstanding |

39

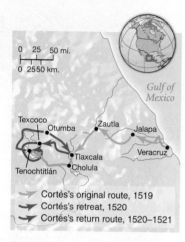

Cortés's Invasion of Tenochtitlán, 1519–1521

he had the good fortune to receive from a local chief the gift of a young girl named Malinali. She spoke several native languages, including Nahuatl, the language of the Mexica, the most powerful people in what is now Mexico and Central America (see chapter 1). Malinali, whom the Spaniards called Marina, soon learned Spanish and became Cortés's interpreter. "Without her help," wrote one of the Spaniards who accompanied Cortés, "we would not have understood the language of New Spain and Mexico."

In Tenochtitlán, the capital of the Mexican empire, the emperor Montezuma heard about some strange creatures sighted along the coast. The emperor sent representatives to bring the strangers large quantities of food. But along with the food, the Mexica also brought the Spaniards another gift, a "disk in the shape of a sun, as big as a cartwheel and made of very fine gold," as a Mexican recalled. Here was conclusive evidence that the rumors of fabulous riches heard by Cortés had some basis in fact.

In August 1519, Cortés marched inland to find Montezuma. Leading about 350 men, Cortés had to live off the land, establishing peaceful relations with indigenous tribes when he could and killing them when he thought it necessary. On November 8, 1519, Cortés reached Tenochtitlán, where Montezuma welcomed him and showered the Spaniards with lavish hospitality. Quickly, Cortés took Montezuma hostage and held him under house arrest, hoping to make him a puppet through whom the Spaniards could rule the Mexican empire. This uneasy peace existed for several months until one of Cortés's men led a brutal massacre of many Mexican nobles, causing the people of Tenochtitlán to revolt. Montezuma was killed, and the Mexica mounted a ferocious assault on the Spaniards. On June 30, 1520, Cortés and about a hundred other Spaniards fought their way out of Tenochtitlán and retreated about one hundred miles to Tlaxcala, a stronghold of bitter enemies of the Mexica. The Tlaxcalans—who had long resented Mexican power—allowed Cortés to regroup, obtain reinforcements, and plan a strategy to conquer Tenochtitlán.

In the spring of 1521, Cortés and thousands of Indian allies laid siege to the Mexican capital. With a relentless, scorched-earth strategy, Cortés finally defeated the last Mexican defenders on August 13, 1521. The great capital of the Mexican empire "looked as if it had been ploughed up," one of Cortés's soldiers remembered.

How did a few hundred Spaniards so far away from home defeat millions of Indians fighting on their home turf? For one thing, the Spaniards had superior military technology that partially offset the Mexicans' numerical advantages. They fought with weapons of iron and steel against the Mexicans' stone, wood, and copper. The muscles of Mexican warriors could not match the power of cannons and muskets fueled by gunpowder.

European viruses proved to be even more powerful weapons. Smallpox arrived in Mexico with Cortés, and in the ensuing epidemic thousands of Mexicans died and many others became too sick to fight. The sickness spread along the network of trade and tribute feeding Tenochtitlán, causing many to fear that their gods had abandoned them. "Cut us loose," one Mexican pleaded, "because the gods have died."

The Spaniards' concept of war also favored them. Mexicans tended to consider war a way to impose their tribute system on conquered people and to take captives for sacrifice. They believed that the high cost of continuing to fight would cause

40   CHAPTER 2
EUROPEANS ENCOUNTER THE NEW WORLD

CHAPTER LOCATOR | What factors led to European exploration in the fifteenth century?

their adversaries to surrender and pay tribute. In contrast, Spaniards sought total victory by destroying their enemy's ability to fight.

Politics proved decisive in Cortés's victory over the Mexicans. Cortés shrewdly exploited the tensions between the Mexica and the people they ruled in their empire (see chapter 1). Cortés reinforced his small army with thousands of Indian allies who were eager to seek revenge against the Mexica. Hundreds of thousands of other Indians aided Cortés by failing to come to the Mexicans' defense. In the end, the political tensions created by the Mexican empire proved to be its crippling weakness.

The Search for Other Mexicos

Lured by their insatiable appetite for gold, Spanish **conquistadors** (soldiers who fought in conquests) quickly fanned out from Tenochtitlán in search of other sources of treasure. The most spectacular prize fell to Francisco Pizarro, who conquered the **Incan empire** in Peru. The Incas controlled a vast, complex region that contained more than nine million people and stretched along the western coast of South America for more than two thousand miles. In 1532, Pizarro and his army of fewer than two hundred men captured the Incan emperor Atahualpa and held him hostage. As ransom, the Incas gave Pizarro the largest treasure yet produced by the

conquistadors
▶ Term (literally meaning "conquerors") that refers to the Spanish explorers and soldiers who conquered lands in the New World.

Incan empire
▶ A region under the control of the Incas and their emperor, Atahualpa, that stretched along the western coast of South America and contained more than nine million people and a wealth in gold and silver.

> Unsuccessful Attempts to Secure New World Riches

Conquistador	Mission
Juan Ponce de León	Sailed to Florida in 1521 to find riches, only to be killed in battle with Calusa Indians.
Lucas Vázquez de Ayllón	Explored the Atlantic coast north of Florida to present-day South Carolina; in 1526, established a small settlement on the Georgia coast named San Miguel de Gualdape, the first Spanish attempt to establish a foothold in what is now the United States. Sickness and hostile Indians destroyed the settlement.
Pánfilo de Narváez	Surveyed the Gulf coast from Florida to Texas in 1528. The expedition ended disastrously with a shipwreck near present-day Galveston, Texas.
Hernando de Soto	Searched for another Peru in southeastern North America in 1539. After his death in 1542, de Soto's men returned to Mexico.
Francisco Vásquez de Coronado	Starting in 1540, searched the Southwest and Great Plains of North America for the mythical Seven Cities of Cíbola, which turned out to be a small Zuñi pueblo. After two years, Coronado gave up searching for the riches that eluded him.
Juan Rodríguez Coronado	Sought wealth along the coast of California in 1542; died on Santa Catalina Island, offshore from present-day Los Angeles. His men sailed on to Oregon, where a ferocious storm forced them to turn back toward Mexico.

What did Spanish explorers discover in the western Atlantic?　|　**How did Spaniards explore, conquer, and colonize New Spain?**　|　What impact did Spain's New World endeavors have in Europe?　|　Conclusion: What promise did the New World offer Europeans?　|　✓ LearningCurve Check what you know. bedfordstmartins.com /roarkunderstanding

41

conquests: gold and silver equivalent to half a century's worth of precious-metal production in Europe. With the ransom safely in their hands, the Spaniards murdered Atahualpa. The Incan treasure proved that at least one other Mexico did indeed exist, and it spurred the Spaniards' search for others.

The probes into North America by de Soto, Coronado, and Cabrillo persuaded other Spaniards that although enormous territories stretched northward from Mexico, their inhabitants had little to loot or exploit. After a generation of vigorous exploration, the Spaniards concluded that there was only one Mexico and one Peru.

Spanish Outposts in Florida and New Mexico

Disappointed by the explorers' failure to discover riches in North America, the Spanish monarchy insisted that a few settlements be established in Florida and New Mexico to give a token of reality to its territorial claims. Settlements in Florida would have the additional benefit of protecting Spanish ships from pirates and privateers who lurked along the southeastern coast, waiting for the Spanish treasure fleet sailing toward Spain.

In 1565, the Spanish king sent Pedro Menéndez de Avilés to found St. Augustine in Florida, the first permanent European settlement within what became the United States. By 1600, St. Augustine had a population of about five hundred, the only remaining Spanish beachhead on North America's vast Atlantic shoreline.

More than sixteen hundred miles west of St. Augustine, the Spaniards founded another outpost in 1598. Juan de Oñate led an expedition of about five hundred people to settle northern Mexico, now called New Mexico, and claim the booty rumored to exist there. When Oñate and his companions reached pueblos near present-day Albuquerque and Santa Fe, he sent out scouting parties to find the legendary treasures of the region. Meanwhile, many of his soldiers planned to mutiny, and relations with the Indians deteriorated. When Indians in the Acoma pueblo revolted against the Spaniards in 1599, Oñate ruthlessly suppressed the uprising, killing eight hundred men, women, and children. Although Oñate's response to the **Acoma pueblo revolt** reconfirmed the Spaniards' military superiority, he did not bring peace or stability to the region. After another pueblo revolt occurred in the same year, many of Oñate's settlers returned to Mexico, leaving New Mexico a small, dusty assertion of Spanish claims to the North American Southwest.

Acoma pueblo revolt
▶ Revolt against the Spanish by Indians living at the Acoma pueblo in 1599. Juan de Oñate violently suppressed the uprising, but the Indians revolted again later that year, after which many Spanish settlers returned to Mexico.

New Spain in the Sixteenth Century

For all practical purposes, Spain was the dominant European power in the Western Hemisphere during the sixteenth century (**Map 2.3**). Portugal claimed the giant territory of Brazil under the Tordesillas treaty but was far more concerned with exploiting its hard-won trade with the East Indies than with colonizing the

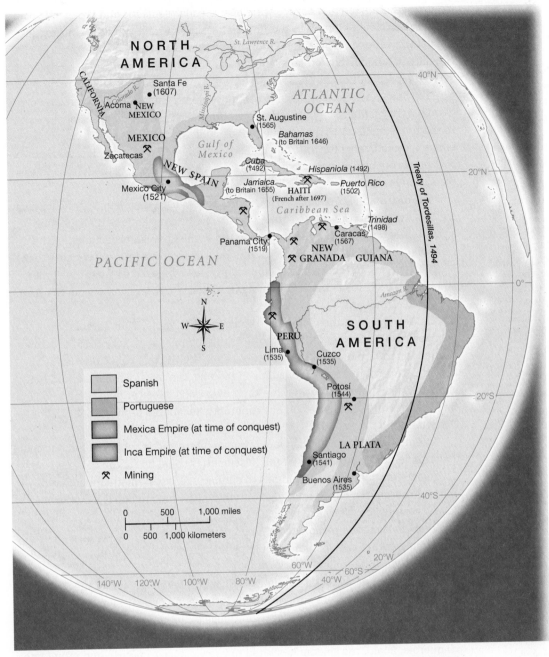

NORTH AMERICA

CALIFORNIA

Santa Fe (1607)

Acoma • NEW MEXICO

Colorado R.

Mississippi R.

St. Lawrence R.

ATLANTIC OCEAN

40°N

St. Augustine (1565)

Bahamas (to Britain 1646)

MEXICO

Gulf of Mexico

Zacatecas ⚒

NEW SPAIN

Cuba (1492)

Hispaniola (1492)

20°N

Mexico City (1521)

Jamaica (to Britain 1655)

HAITI (French after 1697)

Puerto Rico (1502)

Caribbean Sea

Trinidad (1498)

⚒ Caracas (1567)

Treaty of Tordesillas, 1494

Panama City (1519)

NEW ⚒ GRANADA

GUIANA

PACIFIC OCEAN

Amazon R.

0°

SOUTH AMERICA

⚒ PERU

Lima (1535)

Cuzco (1535)

Spanish

Potosí (1544) ⚒

Portuguese

20°S

Mexica Empire (at time of conquest)

Inca Empire (at time of conquest)

LA PLATA

⚒ Mining

Santiago (1541)

Buenos Aires (1535)

40°S

0   500   1,000 miles

0 500 1,000 kilometers

20°W

60°W   60°S

140°W   120°W   100°W   80°W   40°W

MAP 2.3 ■ Sixteenth-Century European Colonies in the New World

Spanish control spread throughout Central and South America during the sixteenth century, with the important exception of Portuguese Brazil. North America, though claimed by Spain under the Treaty of Tordesillas, remained peripheral to Spain's New World empire.

> MAP ACTIVITY

READING THE MAP: Track Spain's efforts at colonization by date. How did political holdings, the physical layout of the land, and natural resources influence where the Spaniards directed their energies?

CONNECTIONS: What was the purpose of the Treaty of Tordesillas? How might the location of silver and gold mines have affected Spain's desire to assert its claims over regions still held by Portugal after 1494 as well as Spain's interest in California, New Mexico, and Florida?

| What did Spanish explorers discover in the western Atlantic? | **How did Spaniards explore, conquer, and colonize New Spain?** | What impact did Spain's New World endeavors have in Europe? | Conclusion: What promise did the New World offer Europeans? | ✓ LearningCurve Check what you know. bedfordstmartins.com /roarkunderstanding |

New Spain

▶ Land in the New World held by the Spanish crown. Spain pioneered techniques of using New World colonies to strengthen the kingdom in Europe. Spain's colonial system would become a model for other European nations.

encomienda

▶ A system for governing used during the Reconquest and in New Spain. It allowed the Spanish encomendero (the "owner" of a town) to collect tribute from the town in return for providing law and order and encouraging "his" Indians to convert to Christianity.

New World. England and France were absorbed by domestic and diplomatic concerns in Europe and largely lost interest in America until late in the century. In the decades after 1519, the Spaniards created the distinctive colonial society of **New Spain**, which showed other Europeans how the New World could be made to serve the purposes of the Old.

The Spanish monarchy gave the conquistadors permission to explore and plunder what they found. The crown took one-fifth, called the "royal fifth," of any loot confiscated and allowed the conquerors to divide the rest. In the end, most conquistadors received very little after the plunder was divided among leaders such as Cortés and his favorite officers. To compensate his disappointed, battle-hardened soldiers, Cortés gave them towns the Spaniards had subdued.

The distribution of conquered towns institutionalized the system of **encomienda**, which empowered the conquistadors to rule the Indians and the lands in and around their towns. Encomienda transferred to the Spanish encomendero (the man who "owned" the town) the tribute that the town had previously paid to the Mexican empire. In theory, the encomendero was supposed to guarantee order and justice, be responsible for the Indians' material welfare, and encourage them to become Christians.

Catholic missionaries worked to convert the Indians. They fervently believed that God expected them to save the Indians' souls by convincing them to abandon their old sinful beliefs and to embrace the one true Christian faith. But after baptizing tens of thousands of Indians, the missionaries learned that many Indians continued to worship their own gods. Most priests came to believe that the Indians were lesser beings inherently incapable of fully understanding Christianity.

In practice, encomenderos were far more interested in what the Indians could do for them than in what they or the missionaries could do for the Indians. Encomenderos subjected the Indians to chronic overwork, mistreatment, and abuse. According to one Spaniard, "Everything [the Indians] do is slowly done and by compulsion. They are malicious, lying, [and] thievish." Economically, however, encomienda recognized a fundamental reality of New Spain: The most important treasure the Spaniards could plunder from the New World was not gold but uncompensated Indian labor.

The practice of coerced labor in New Spain grew directly out of the Spaniards' assumption that they were superior to the Indians. As one missionary put it, the Indians "are more stupid than asses and refuse to improve in anything." Therefore, most Spaniards assumed, Indians' labor should be organized by and for their conquerors. Spaniards seldom hesitated to use violence to punish and intimidate recalcitrant Indians.

Encomienda engendered two groups of influential critics. A few missionaries were horrified at the brutal mistreatment of the Indians. "What will [the Indians] think about the God of the Christians," Friar Bartolomé de Las Casas asked, when they see their friends "with their heads split, their hands amputated, their intestines torn open? . . . Would they want to come to Christ's sheepfold after their homes had been destroyed, their children imprisoned, their wives raped, their cities devastated, their maidens deflowered, and their provinces laid waste?" Las Casas and other outspoken missionaries softened few hearts among the encomenderos, but they did win some sympathy for the

CHAPTER LOCATOR | What factors led to European exploration in the fifteenth century?

44 CHAPTER 2 EUROPEANS ENCOUNTER THE NEW WORLD

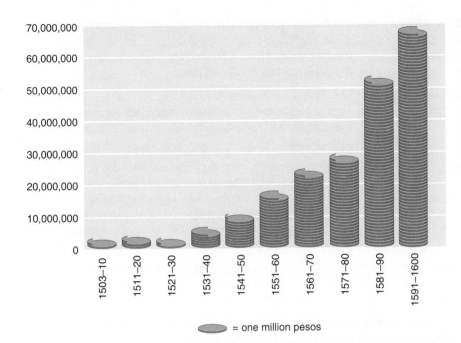

FIGURE 2.1 ■ New World Gold and Silver Imported into Spain during the Sixteenth Century, in Pesos

Spain imported more gold than silver during the first three decades of the sixteenth century, but the total value of this treasure was quickly eclipsed during the 1530s and 1540s, when rich silver mines were developed. Silver accounted for most of the enormous growth in Spain's precious-metal imports from the New World.

= one million pesos

Indians from the Spanish monarchy and royal bureaucracy. The Spanish monarchy moved to abolish encomienda in an effort to replace swashbuckling old conquistadors with royal bureaucrats as the rulers of New Spain.

In 1549, a reform called the *repartimiento* began to replace encomienda. It limited the labor an encomendero could command from his Indians to forty-five days per year from each adult male. The repartimiento, however, did not challenge the principle of forced labor, nor did it prevent encomenderos from continuing to cheat, mistreat, and overwork their Indians. Many Indians were put to work in silver mines. Mining was grueling and dangerous for the workers, but very profitable for the Spaniards who supervised them: During the entire sixteenth century, precious-metal exports from New Spain to Spain were worth twenty-five times more than the next most important export, leather hides **(Figure 2.1)**.

For Spaniards, life in New Spain after the conquests was relatively easy. As one colonist wrote to his brother in Spain, "Don't hesitate [to come]. . . . This land [New Spain] is as good as ours [in Spain], for God has given us more here than there, and we shall be better off." During the century after 1492, about 225,000 Spaniards settled in the colonies. Virtually all of them were poor young men of common (non-noble) lineage who came directly from Spain. Laborers and artisans made up the largest proportion, but soldiers and sailors were also numerous. Men vastly outnumbered women.

The gender and number of Spanish settlers shaped two fundamental features of the society of New Spain. First, Europeans never made up more than 1 or 2 percent of the total population. Although Spaniards ruled New Spain, the population was almost wholly Indian. Second, the shortage of Spanish women meant that Spanish men frequently married Indian women or used them as concubines. The relatively few women from Spain usually married Spanish men, contributing to a tiny elite defined by European origins.

What did Spanish explorers discover in the western Atlantic?

How did Spaniards explore, conquer, and colonize New Spain?

What impact did Spain's New World endeavors have in Europe?

Conclusion: What promise did the New World offer Europeans?

☑ LearningCurve
Check what you know.
bedfordstmartins.com
/roarkunderstanding

45

> Social and Racial Hierarchy in New Spain

Peninsulares	People born on the Iberian Peninsula. They enjoyed the highest social status in New Spain.
Creoles	Children born in the New World to Spanish men and women. They ranked below peninsulares but were still within the white elite. Creoles and peninsulares made up barely 1 or 2 percent of the population.
Mestizos	Offspring of Spanish men and Indian women, who accounted for 4 or 5 percent of the population. Some worked as artisans and labor overseers and lived well, and a few rose into the ranks of the elite, especially if their Indian ancestry was not obvious from their skin color. Most, though, were categorized with Indians.
Indians	At the bottom of the social pyramid were Indians.

creoles

▶ Children born to Spanish parents in the New World who, with the peninsulares, made up the tiny portion of the population at the top of the colonial social hierarchy.

The small number of Spaniards, the masses of Indians, and the frequency of intermarriage created a steep social hierarchy defined by perceptions of national origin and race. The society of New Spain, with *peninsulares* and **creoles** enjoying the highest status, established the precedent for what would become a pronounced pattern in the European colonies of the New World: a society stratified sharply by social origin and race. All Europeans of whatever social origin considered themselves superior to Native Americans; in New Spain, they were a dominant minority in both power and status.

The Toll of Spanish Conquest and Colonization

By 1560, the major centers of Indian civilization had been conquered, their leaders overthrown, their religion held in contempt, and their people forced to work for the Spaniards. Profound demoralization pervaded Indian society.

Adding to the culture shock of conquest and colonization was the deadly toll of European diseases. As conquest spread, the Indians succumbed to epidemics of measles, smallpox, and respiratory illnesses. They had no immunity to these diseases because they had not been exposed to them before the arrival of Europeans. By 1570, the Indian population of New Spain had fallen about 90 percent from what it had been when Columbus arrived, a catastrophe unequaled in human history.

For the Spaniards, Indian deaths meant that the most valuable resource of New Spain—Indian labor—dwindled rapidly. By the last quarter of the sixteenth century, Spanish colonists began to import African slaves. In the years before 1550, while Indian labor was still adequate, only 15,000 slaves were imported from Africa. The relatively high cost of African slaves kept imports low, totaling approximately 36,000 from 1550 to the end of the century. During the sixteenth century, New Spain continued to rely primarily on a shrinking number of Indians.

CHAPTER LOCATOR | What factors led to European exploration in the fifteenth century?

46 CHAPTER 2 EUROPEANS ENCOUNTER THE NEW WORLD

Español con India,
Mestizo.

Mestizo con Española,
Castizo.

Castizo con Española,
Español.

Español con Mora,
Mulato.

Mulato con Española,
Morisco.

Morisco con Española,
Chino.

Chino con India,
Salta atras.

Salta atras con Mulata,
Lobo.

Mixed Races

These eighteenth-century paintings illustrate forms of racial mixture common in sixteenth-century New Spain. In the first painting, a Spanish man and an Indian woman have a mestizo son; in the fourth, a Spanish man and a woman of African descent have a mulatto son. Can you detect any meanings of racial categories in the clothing? Bob Schalkwijk/INAH.

> VISUAL ACTIVITY

READING THE IMAGE: What do these paintings reveal about social status in New Spain?

CONNECTIONS: How do these paintings illustrate the power the Spaniards exercised in their New World colonies? What were some other aspects of colonial society that demonstrated Spanish domination?

QUICK REVIEW

How did New Spain's distinctive colonial population shape its economy and society?

| What did Spanish explorers discover in the western Atlantic? | **How did Spaniards explore, conquer, and colonize New Spain?** | What impact did Spain's New World endeavors have in Europe? | Conclusion: What promise did the New World offer Europeans? | ✓ **LearningCurve** Check what you know. bedfordstmartins.com /roarkunderstanding |

47

What impact did Spain's New World endeavors have in Europe?

Algonquian Ceremonial Dance

When English artist John White visited the coast of present-day North Carolina in 1585 as part of Raleigh's expedition, he painted this Algonquian ceremonial dance. This is one of the only likenesses of sixteenth-century North American Indians that were drawn from direct observation. Copyright © The British Museum.

THE RICHES OF NEW SPAIN HELPED make the sixteenth century the Golden Age of Spain. After Queen Isabella and King Ferdinand died, their sixteen-year-old grandson became King Charles I of Spain in 1516. Three years later, in 1519, just as Cortés ventured into Mexico, King Charles became Holy Roman Emperor Charles V. His empire encompassed more territory than that of any other European monarch. He used the wealth of New Spain to promote his interests in sixteenth-century Europe. He also sought to defend orthodox Christianity from the insurgent heresy of the Protestant Reformation. The power of the Spanish monarchy spread the message throughout sixteenth-century Europe that a New World empire could bankroll Old World ambitions.

The Protestant Reformation and the Spanish Response

In 1517, Martin Luther, an obscure Catholic priest in central Germany, initiated the **Protestant Reformation** by publicizing his criticisms of the Catholic Church. Luther's ideas won the sympathy of many Catholics, but they were considered

Protestant Reformation

▶ The reform movement that began in 1517 with Martin Luther's critiques of the Roman Catholic Church. The Protestant Reformation precipitated an enduring schism that divided Protestants from Catholics.

CHAPTER LOCATOR | What factors led to European exploration in the fifteenth century?

extremely dangerous by church officials and by monarchs such as Charles V, who believed that just as the church spoke for God, they ruled for God.

Luther preached a doctrine known as "justification by faith": Individual Christians could obtain salvation and life everlasting only by having faith that God would save them. Giving monetary offerings to the church, following the orders of priests, or participating in church rituals would not bring believers closer to heaven. The only true source of information about God's will was the Bible, not the church. By reading the Bible, any Christian could learn as much about God's commandments as any priest. Indeed, Luther called for a "priesthood of all believers."

In effect, Luther charged that the Catholic Church was in many respects fraudulent. Luther declared that the church had neglected its true purpose of helping individual Christians understand the spiritual realm revealed in the Bible and had wasted its resources in worldly conflicts of politics and wars. Luther hoped his ideas would reform the Catholic Church, but instead they ruptured forever the unity of Christianity in western Europe.

Charles V pledged to exterminate Luther's Protestant heresies. The wealth pouring into Spain from the New World fueled his efforts to defend the orthodox Catholic faith against Protestants, as well as against any other challenge to Spain's supremacy. As the most powerful monarch in Europe, Charles V, followed by his son and successor Philip II, assumed responsibility for upholding the existing order of sixteenth-century Europe.

American wealth, particularly Mexican silver, fueled Spanish ambitions, but Charles V's and Philip II's expenses for constant warfare far outstripped the revenues arriving from New Spain. The monarchy's ambitions impoverished the vast majority of Spain's population and brought the nation to the brink of bankruptcy. By the end of the sixteenth century, interest payments on royal debts swallowed two-thirds of the crown's annual revenues. In retrospect, the riches from New Spain proved a short-term blessing but a long-term curse.

Most Spaniards, however, looked upon New Spain as a glorious national achievement that displayed Spain's superiority over Native Americans and other Europeans. They had added enormously to their own knowledge and wealth. They had built mines, cities, Catholic churches, and even universities on the other side of the Atlantic. These military, religious, and economic achievements gave them great pride and confidence.

Europe and the Spanish Example

The lessons of sixteenth-century Spain were not lost on Spain's European rivals. Spain proudly displayed the fruits of its New World conquests. In 1520, for example, the German artist Albrecht Dürer wrote in his diary that he "marveled over the subtle ingenuity of the men in these distant lands [of New Spain]" who created such things as "a sun entirely of gold, a whole fathom [six feet] broad." But

> CHRONOLOGY

1517
– Protestant Reformation begins in Germany.

1519
– Charles I of Spain becomes the Holy Roman Emperor Charles V.

1524
– Giovanni da Verrazano explores the Atlantic coast of North America for France.

1535
– Jacques Cartier explores the St. Lawrence River.

1576
– Martin Frobisher explores northern Canadian waters.

1578/1583
– Sir Humphrey Gilbert leads expeditions to Newfoundland.

1585
– Sir Walter Raleigh organizes expedition to settle Roanoke Island.

| What did Spanish explorers discover in the western Atlantic? | How did Spaniards explore, conquer, and colonize New Spain? | **What impact did Spain's New World endeavors have in Europe?** | Conclusion: What promise did the New World offer Europeans? | ✓ LearningCurve Check what you know. bedfordstmartins.com /roarkunderstanding |

49

Roanoke Settlement, 1587–1590

the most exciting news about "the men in these distant lands" was that they could serve the interests of Europeans, as Spain had shown. With a few notable exceptions, Europeans saw the New World as a place for the expansion of European influence, a place where, as one Spaniard wrote, Europeans could "give to those strange lands the form of our own."

France and England tried to follow Spain's example. Both nations warred with Spain in Europe, preyed on Spanish treasure fleets, and ventured to the New World, where they too hoped to find an undiscovered passageway to the East Indies or another Mexico or Peru. By the end of the century, however, England had failed to secure a New World beachhead.

TABLE 2.1 ▪ France and England Follow Spain to the New World

Explorer (sponsoring country)	Destination and result
Giovanni da Verrazano (France)	The Atlantic coast of North America from North Carolina to Canada, to search for a Northwest Passage, 1524. Unsuccessful.
Jacques Cartier (France)	St. Lawrence River, 1535. Established colony in 1541, but it did not succeed.
Martin Frobisher (England)	In 1576, in another attempt to find a Northwest Passage, sailed to northern Canada, where he retrieved worthless "ore" that he thought was gold, causing the English to lose interest in the region and explore farther south.
Sir Humphrey Gilbert (England)	Led expeditions to Newfoundland in 1578 and 1583 to found colonies; vanished at sea.
Sir Walter Raleigh (England)	Organized expedition in 1585 to settle Roanoke Island off the coast of present-day North Carolina. More than one hundred settlers were sent to colonize Roanoke in 1587. The colonists disappeared between 1587 and 1590, leaving only the word *Croatoan* (whose meaning is unknown) carved in a tree.

> QUICK REVIEW

How did Spain's conquests in the New World shape Spanish influence in Europe?

CHAPTER LOCATOR | What factors led to European exploration in the fifteenth century?

Conclusion: What promise did the New World offer Europeans?

THE SIXTEENTH CENTURY in the New World belonged to the Spaniards who employed Columbus and to the Indians who greeted him as he stepped ashore. The Portuguese, whose voyages to Africa and Asia set the stage for Columbus's voyages, won the important consolation prize of Brazil, but Spain hit the jackpot. Isabella of Spain helped initiate the Columbian exchange between the New World and the Old, which massively benefited first Spain and later other Europeans and which continues to this day. The exchange also subjected Native Americans to the ravages of European diseases and Spanish conquest. Spanish explorers, conquistadors, and colonists forced the Indians to serve the interests of Spanish settlers and the Spanish monarchy. The exchange illustrated one of the most important lessons of the sixteenth century: After millions of years, the Atlantic no longer was an impermeable barrier separating the Eastern and Western Hemispheres. After the voyages of Columbus, European sailing ships regularly bridged the Atlantic and carried people, products, diseases, and ideas from one shore to the other.

No European monarch could forget the seductive lesson taught by Spain's example: The New World could vastly enrich the Old. Spain remained a New World power for almost four centuries, and its language, religion, culture, and institutions left a permanent imprint. By the end of the sixteenth century, however, other European monarchies had begun to contest Spain's dominion in Europe and to make forays into the northern fringes of Spain's New World preserve. To reap the benefits the Spaniards enjoyed from their New World domain, the others had to learn a difficult lesson: how to deviate from Spain's example. That discovery lay ahead.

While England's rulers eyed the huge North American hinterland of New Spain, they realized that it lacked the two main attractions of Mexico and Peru: incredible material wealth and large populations of Indians to use as workers. In the absence of gold and silver booty and plentiful native labor in North America, England would need to find some way to attract colonizers to a region that—compared to New Spain—did not appear very promising. During the next century, England's leaders overcame these dilemmas by developing a distinctive colonial model, one that encouraged land-hungry settlers from England and Europe to engage in agriculture and that depended on other sources of unfree labor: indentured servants from Europe and slaves from Africa.

What did Spanish explorers discover in the western Atlantic?

How did Spaniards explore, conquer, and colonize New Spain?

What impact did Spain's New World endeavors have in Europe?

Conclusion: What promise did the New World offer Europeans?

☑ LearningCurve
Check what you know.
bedfordstmartins.com
/roarkunderstanding

51

CHAPTER 2 STUDY GUIDE

STEP 1

GET STARTED ONLINE

✓ LearningCurve ■ bedfordstmartins.com/roarkunderstanding

Now that you've read the chapter, make it stick by completing the LearningCurve activity.

STEP 2

EXPLAIN WHY IT MATTERS

Put your reading into practice. Identify each term below, and then explain why it matters in U.S. history.

TERM	WHO OR WHAT & WHEN	WHY IT MATTERS
Black Death (p. 31)		
Reconquest (p. 32)		
Tainos (p. 35)		
Treaty of Tordesillas (p. 36)		
Columbian exchange (p. 38)		
conquistadors (p. 41)		
Incan empire (p. 41)		
Acoma pueblo revolt (p. 42)		
New Spain (p. 44)		
encomienda (p. 44)		
creoles (p. 46)		
Protestant Reformation (p. 48)		

STEP 3

MOVE BEYOND THE BASICS

To demonstrate a more advanced understanding, consider the similarities and differences in the exploration and conquest of two explorers for Spain — Christopher Columbus and Hernán Cortés. What were the motivations behind each man's expeditions? How did these expeditions affect the peoples each encountered?

Explorer	Motivations	Impact on New World peoples	Benefits for Spain
Christopher Columbus			
Hernán Cortés			

PUT IT ALL TOGETHER

Now, take a step back and try to explain the big picture. Remember to use specific examples from the chapter in your answers.

EXPANSION AND EXPLORATION

▶ Why was Portuguese maritime exploration focused on the west coast of Africa? What did Portugal hope to gain from such journeys?

▶ What was the Columbian exchange, and what were its consequences for both the peoples of the Americas and those from the Old World?

CONQUEST AND COLONIZATION

▶ Describe the government and society of New Spain. How did New Spain reflect the values, beliefs, and goals of the Spanish conquerors?

▶ How did Spanish conquest and colonization affect the peoples of the Americas?

THE IMPACT OF DISCOVERY IN EUROPE

▶ What role did New World wealth play in the clash between Protestants and Catholics in sixteenth-century Europe?

▶ What lessons did other European powers draw from Spain's experience in the New World?

LOOKING BACKWARD, LOOKING AHEAD

▶ How did the isolation of the peoples of the Americas before 1492 affect the course and consequences of European expansion in the New World?

▶ How did Spanish success in the New World influence European competition for control of the Americas?

> IN YOUR OWN WORDS

Imagine that you must give an oral report to the class answering the following question: **What were the most significant effects of European exploration in the sixteenth century?** What would be the most important points to include and why?

> **Do it online at the Student Site ▪ bedfordstmartins.com/roarkunderstanding**

3

FOUNDING THE SOUTHERN COLONIES IN THE SEVENTEENTH CENTURY

1601–1700

> **What were the most important factors that shaped England's southern colonies in the seventeenth century?** Chapter 3 examines the establishment and growth of England's southern mainland colonies in North America over the course of the seventeenth century. It explores the early years of the Virginia colony, the rise of tobacco culture in the Chesapeake and its impact on the region's social and political environment, colonial relations among different groups of people, and the development of African slavery as the dominant labor force in the south.

LearningCurve
bedfordstmartins.com/roarkunderstanding
After reading the chapter, use LearningCurve to retain what you've read.

the people differ very little from them of Powhatan in
..serted those figures in this place because of the convenien...

> What challenges
  faced early
  Chesapeake
  colonists?

> How did
  Chesapeake
  tobacco society
  take shape?

> Why did
  Chesapeake
  colonial society
  change in the late
  seventeenth
  century?

> Why did the
  southern colonies
  move toward a
  slave labor
  system?

> Conclusion: Why
  were export crops
  and slave labor
  important in the
  growth of the
  southern colonies?

King Powhatan comands C. Smith to be flaine,
daughter Pokahontas beggs his life his thankfull

Scene from Captain John Smith, *A Generall Historie of Virginia* (1624), in which Pocahontas "saves"
Smith's life. Bridgeman.

What challenges faced early Chesapeake colonists?

Secotan Village

This engraving was copied from an original drawing John White made in 1585 when he visited the village of Secotan on the coast of present-day North Carolina. The drawing shows daily life in the village, which may have resembled one of Powhatan's settlements. This drawing conveys the message that Secotan was orderly, settled, religious, harmonious, and peaceful—and very different from English villages. Princeton University Libraries, Department of Rare Books and Special Collections.

> VISUAL ACTIVITY

READING THE IMAGE: What does this image say about Indian life in Secotan?

CONNECTIONS: How did Indian society differ from the English tobacco society that emerged later?

IN 1606, England's King James I granted the Virginia Company more than six million acres in North America in hopes of establishing the English equivalent of Spain's New World empire. Enthusiastic reports from the Roanoke voyages twenty years earlier (see chapter 2) claimed that in Virginia "the earth bringeth foorth all things in aboundance . . . without toile or labour." Investors hoped to profit by growing some valuable exotic crop, finding gold or silver, or raiding

CHAPTER LOCATOR | What challenges faced early Chesapeake colonists?

Spanish treasure ships. Their hopes failed to confront the difficulties of adapting English desires and expectations to the New World already inhabited by Native Americans. The Jamestown settlement struggled to survive for nearly two decades, until the royal government replaced the private Virginia Company, which never earned a profit for its investors.

The Fragile Jamestown Settlement

Although Spain claimed all of North America under the 1494 Treaty of Tordesillas (see chapter 2), King James believed that England could encroach on the outskirts of Spain's New World empire. In effect, his land grant to the **Virginia Company**, a joint-stock company, was a royal license to poach on both Spanish claims and the chiefdom of Powhatan, the supreme chief of the **Algonquian Indians** who inhabited the coastal plain of present-day Virginia.

English merchants had pooled their capital and shared risks for many years by using joint-stock companies for trading voyages to Europe, Asia, and Africa. The London investors of the Virginia Company, however, had larger ambitions: They hoped to found an empire that would strengthen England both overseas and at home. Richard Hakluyt, a strong proponent of colonization, claimed that a colony would provide work for swarms of poor "valiant youths rusting and hurtfull by lack of employment" in England. Colonists could buy English goods and supply products that England now had to import from other nations.

In December 1606, the ships *Susan Constant*, *Discovery*, and *Godspeed* carried 144 Englishmen toward Virginia. A few weeks after they arrived at the mouth of Chesapeake Bay on April 26, 1607, they went ashore on a small peninsula in the midst of the territory ruled by Powhatan and quickly built a fort, the first building in **Jamestown**. The fort showed the colonists' awareness that they needed to protect themselves. For weeks, the settlers and Algonquian warriors under the leadership of Powhatan skirmished repeatedly.

The settlers soon confronted dangerous, invisible threats: disease and starvation. During the summer, many of the Englishmen lay "night and day groaning in every corner of the Fort most pittiful to heare," wrote George Percy, one of the settlers. The colonists increased their misery by bickering among themselves, leaving crops unplanted and food supplies shrinking. "For the most part [the settlers] died of meere famine," Percy wrote; "there were never Englishmen left in a forreigne Countrey in such miserie as wee were in this new discovered Virginia."

Powhatan's people came to the rescue of the weakened and demoralized Englishmen. Early in September 1607, they began to bring corn to the colony for barter. Accustomed to eating food derived from wheat, English people considered corn the food "of the barbarous Indians which know no better." The famished colonists soon overcame their prejudice against corn. Indians' corn acquired by both trade and plunder managed to keep 38 of the original settlers alive until a fresh supply of food and 120 more colonists arrived from England in January 1608.

It is difficult to exaggerate the fragility of the early Jamestown settlement. One colonist lamented that "this place [is] a meere plantacion of sorrowes and Cropp of trobles, having been plentifull in nothing but want and wanting nothing but plenty." The Virginia Company sent hundreds of new settlers to Jamestown

> CHRONOLOGY

1606
– Virginia Company receives royal charter.

1607
– English colonists found Jamestown; Pocahontas "rescues" John Smith.

1617
– Pocahontas dies in England.

1618
– Powhatan dies; Opechancanough becomes Algonquian chief.

1619
– House of Burgesses begins to meet in Virginia.

1622
– Opechancanough launches an assault on English settlers in Virginia.

1624
– Virginia becomes a royal colony.

Virginia Company
▶ A joint-stock company organized by London investors in 1606 that received a land grant from King James I in order to establish English colonies in North America. Investors hoped to enrich themselves and strengthen England economically and politically.

Algonquian Indians
▶ People who inhabited the coastal plain of present-day Virginia, near Chesapeake Bay, when English colonists first settled the region.

Jamestown
▶ The first permanent English settlement in North America, established in 1607 by colonists sponsored by the Virginia Company.

How did Chesapeake tobacco society take shape?

Why did Chesapeake colonial society change in the late seventeenth century?

Why did the southern colonies move toward a slave labor system?

Conclusion: Why were export crops and slave labor important in the growth of the southern colonies?

✓ LearningCurve
Check what you know.
bedfordstmartins.com /roarkunderstanding

each year, each of them eager to find the paradise promised by the company. But most settlers went instead to early graves.

Cooperation and Conflict between Natives and Newcomers

Powhatan's people stayed in contact with the English settlers but maintained their distance. The Virginia Company boasted that the settlers bought from the Indians "the pearles of earth [corn] and [sold] to them the pearles of heaven [Christianity]." In fact, few Indians converted to Christianity, and the English devoted scant effort to proselytizing. Marriage between Indian women and English men also was rare, despite the acute shortage of English women in Virginia in the early years. Few settlers bothered to learn the Indians' language.

The miscommunication and misunderstandings between the settlers and Powhatan's people are illustrated by the story of the capture and release of Captain John Smith. In December 1607, Smith was captured by warriors of Powhatan. According to Smith, Powhatan "feasted him after their best barbarous manner." Then, Smith recalled, "two great stones were brought before Powhatan: then as many [Indians] as could layd hands on [Smith], dragged him to [the stones], and thereon laid his head, and being ready with their clubs, to beate out his braines."

Ætatis suæ 21. Aº. 1616.

Matoaks als Rebecka daughter to the mighty Prince
Powhatan Emperour of Attanoughkomouck als Virginia
converted and baptized in the Christian faith, and
Wife to the wor". M". Tho: Rolff.

At that moment, Pocahontas, Powhatan's eleven-year-old daughter, rushed forward and "got [Smith's] head in her armes, and laid her owne upon his to save him from death." Pocahontas, Smith wrote, "hazarded the beating out of her owne braines to save mine, and . . . so prevailed with her father, that I was safely conducted [back] to James towne."

Historians believe that this episode happened more or less as Smith described it. But Smith did not understand why Pocahontas acted as she did. Most likely, what Smith interpreted as Pocahontas's saving him from certain death was instead a ritual enacting Powhatan's willingness to incorporate Smith and the white strangers at

Pocahontas in England

Shortly after Pocahontas and her husband, John Rolfe, arrived in England in 1616, she posed for this portrait dressed in English clothing. The portrait captures the dual novelty of England for Pocahontas and of Pocahontas for the English. The mutability of Pocahontas's identity is displayed in the identification of her as "Matoaks" or "Rebecka." National Portrait Gallery, Smithsonian Institution/Art Resource, NY.

CHAPTER LOCATOR | What challenges faced early Chesapeake colonists?

Jamestown into Powhatan's empire. By appearing to save Smith, Pocahontas was probably acting out Smith's new status as an adopted member of Powhatan's extended family.

After Smith returned to England about two years later, relations between Powhatan and the English colonists deteriorated into bloody raids. In 1613, the colonists captured Pocahontas and held her hostage at Jamestown. Within a year, she converted to Christianity and married a colonist named John Rolfe. After giving birth to a son named Thomas, Pocahontas, her husband, and the new baby sailed for England in the spring of 1616. There, promoters of the Virginia colony dressed her as a proper Englishwoman and arranged for her to go to a ball attended by the king and queen. Pocahontas died in England in 1617. Her son, Thomas, ultimately returned to Virginia.

Events like the capture of Pocahontas gave Powhatan's people good reason to regard the English with suspicion. Although the settlers often made friendly overtures to the Indians, they did not hesitate to use their guns and swords to enforce English notions of proper Indian behavior. When Indians refused to trade their corn to the settlers, the English pillaged their villages and confiscated their corn.

The Indians retaliated against English violence, but for fifteen years they did not organize an all-out assault on the European intruders, probably for several reasons. Although Christianity held few attractions for the Indians, the power of the settlers' God impressed them. One chief told John Smith that "he did believe that our [English] God as much exceeded theirs as our guns did their bows and arrows." Powhatan probably concluded that these powerful strangers would make better allies than enemies.

The English also traded with his people, usually exchanging European goods for corn. Native Virginians quickly recognized the superiority of the intruders' iron and steel knives, axes, and pots, and they eagerly traded corn for them.

But why were the settlers unable to feed themselves for more than a decade? First, as the staggering death rate suggests, many settlers were too sick to be productive. Second, very few farmers came to Virginia in the early years. Instead, most of the newcomers were gentlemen and their servants who, in John Smith's words, "never did know what a day's work was." Smith declared repeatedly that in Virginia "there is no country to pillage [as in New Spain]. . . . All you can expect from [Virginia] must be by labor."

The persistence of the Virginia colony created difficulties for Powhatan's chiefdom. Steady contact between natives and newcomers spread European diseases among the Indians, who suffered deadly epidemics. To produce enough corn for trade with the English required the Indian women to spend more time and effort growing crops. But from the Indians' viewpoint, the most important fact about the always-hungry English colonists was that they were not going away.

Powhatan died in 1618, and his brother Opechancanough replaced him as supreme chief. In 1622, Opechancanough organized an all-out assault on the English settlers. As an English colonist observed, "the savages . . . fell upon us murdering and killing everybody they could reach[,] sparing neither women nor children." In all, the Indians killed 347 colonists, nearly a third of the English population. But the attack failed to dislodge the colonists. Instead, in the years to come the settlers unleashed a murderous campaign of Indian extermination that

| How did Chesapeake tobacco society take shape? | Why did Chesapeake colonial society change in the late seventeenth century? | Why did the southern colonies move toward a slave labor system? | Conclusion: Why were export crops and slave labor important in the growth of the southern colonies? | ☑ LearningCurve Check what you know. bedfordstmartins.com /roarkunderstanding |

59

pushed the Indians beyond the small circumference of white settlement. After 1622, most colonists considered Indians their perpetual enemies.

From Private Company to Royal Government

In the immediate aftermath of the 1622 uprising, the survivors became demoralized because, as one explained, the "massacre killed all our Countrie . . . [and] burst the heart of all the rest." The disaster prompted a royal investigation of affairs in Virginia. The investigators discovered that the appalling mortality among the colonists was caused more by disease and mismanagement than by Indian raids. In 1624, King James revoked the charter of the Virginia Company and made Virginia a **royal colony**, subject to the direction of the royal government rather than of the company's private investors, an arrangement that lasted until 1776.

The king now appointed the governor of Virginia and his council, but most other features of local government established under the Virginia Company remained intact. In 1619, for example, the company had inaugurated the **House of Burgesses**, an assembly of representatives (called burgesses) elected by the colony's male voters. Under the new royal government, laws passed by the burgesses had to be approved by the king's bureaucrats in England rather than by the company. Otherwise, the House of Burgesses continued as before, acquiring distinction as the oldest representative legislative assembly in the English colonies. Under the new royal government, all free adult men in Virginia could vote for the House of Burgesses, giving it a far broader and more representative constituency than the English House of Commons had.

The demise of the Virginia Company marked the end of the first phase of colonization of the Chesapeake region. From the first 105 adventurers in 1607, the population had grown to about 1,200 by 1624. Despite mortality rates higher than during the worst epidemics in London, new settlers still came. Their arrival and King James's willingness to take over the struggling colony reflected a fundamental change in Virginia. After years of fruitless experimentation, it was becoming clear that English settlers could make a fortune in Virginia by growing tobacco.

royal colony

▶ A colony ruled by a king or queen and governed by officials appointed to serve the monarchy and represent its interests.

House of Burgesses

▶ An organ of government in colonial Virginia made up of an assembly of representatives elected by the colony's male voters. It was established by the Virginia Company and continued by the crown after Virginia was made a royal colony.

> **QUICK REVIEW**

Why did Powhatan behave as he did toward the English colonists?

CHAPTER LOCATOR | What challenges faced early Chesapeake colonists?

How did Chesapeake tobacco society take shape?

Smoking Club In Europe, tobacco smokers congregated in clubs to enjoy the intoxicating weed. This seventeenth-century print satirizes smokers' gatherings of fashionable men, women, and children who indulged their taste for tobacco. Emblems of the tobacco trade adorn the wall; pipes, spittoons, and other smoking implements are close at hand; and the dog cleans up after those who cannot hold their smoke. Koninklijke Bibliotheek, The Hague.

TOBACCO GREW WILD IN THE NEW WORLD, and Native Americans had used it for thousands of years before Europeans arrived. Many sixteenth-century European explorers noticed the Indians' habit of "drinking smoke." During the sixteenth century, tobacco was an expensive luxury used sparingly by a few in Europe. During the next century, English colonists in North America sent so much tobacco to European markets that it became an affordable indulgence used often by many people.

By 1700, nearly 100,000 colonists lived in the Chesapeake region, encompassing Virginia, Maryland, and northern North Carolina (**Map 3.1**). Although they differed in wealth, landholding, access to labor, and religion, they shared a dedication to growing tobacco. They exported more than 35 million pounds of tobacco in 1700, a fivefold increase in per capita production since 1620. Settlers lived by the rhythms of tobacco agriculture, and their endless need for labor attracted droves of English indentured servants to grueling work in tobacco fields.

Tobacco Agriculture

Initially, the Virginia Company had no plans to grow and sell tobacco. John Rolfe—future husband of Pocahontas—planted West Indian tobacco seeds in 1612 and learned that they flourished in Virginia. By 1617, the colonists had grown enough tobacco to send the first commercial shipment to England, where

> CHRONOLOGY

1612
– John Rolfe begins to plant tobacco in Virginia.

1617
– Colonists send the first commercial tobacco shipment to England.

1619
– First Africans arrive in Virginia.

1632
– King Charles I grants land for the colony of Maryland.

1634
– Colonists begin to arrive in Maryland.

| How did Chesapeake tobacco society take shape? | Why did Chesapeake colonial society change in the late seventeenth century? | Why did the southern colonies move toward a slave labor system? | Conclusion: Why were export crops and slave labor important in the growth of the southern colonies? | ☑ LearningCurve Check what you know. bedfordstmartins.com /roarkunderstanding |

MAP 3.1 ■ Chesapeake Colonies in the Seventeenth Century

This map illustrates the intimate association between land and water in the settlement of the Chesapeake in the seventeenth century. The fall line indicates the limit of navigable water, where rapids and falls prevented travel farther upstream.

> MAP ACTIVITY

READING THE MAP: Using the notations on the map, create a chronology of the establishment of towns and settlements. What physical features correspond to the earliest habitation by English settlers?

CONNECTIONS: Why was access to navigable water so important? Given the settlers' need for defense against native tribes, what explains the distance between settlements?

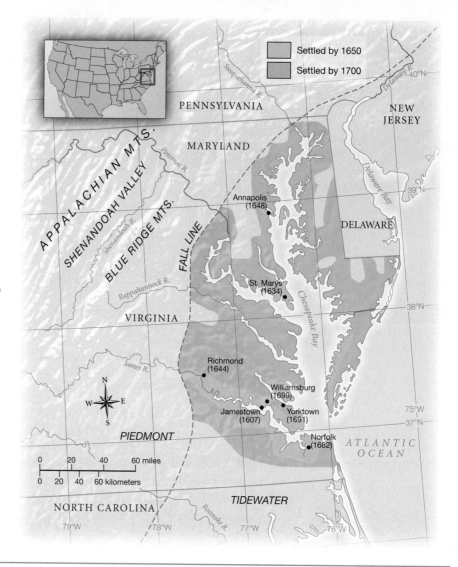

it sold for a high price. After that, Virginia pivoted from a colony of rather aimless adventurers to a society of dedicated tobacco planters.

A demanding crop, tobacco required close attention and a great deal of hand labor year-round. Like the Indians, the colonists "cleared" fields by cutting a ring of bark from each tree (a procedure known as "girdling"), thereby killing the tree. Girdling brought sunlight to clearings but left fields studded with tree stumps, requiring colonists to use heavy hoes to till their tobacco fields. To plant, a visitor observed, they "just make holes [with a stick] into which they drop the seeds," much as the Indians did.

The English settlers worked hard because their labor promised greater rewards in the Chesapeake region than in England. One colonist proclaimed that "the dirt of this Province affords as great a profit to the general Inhabitant, as the Gold of Peru doth to . . . the Spaniard." Although he exaggerated, it was true that

CHAPTER LOCATOR | What challenges faced early Chesapeake colonists?

Tobacco Plantation This print illustrates the processing of tobacco on a seventeenth-century plantation. Workers cut the mature plants and put the leaves in piles to wilt (left foreground). After the leaves dried somewhat, they were suspended from poles in a drying barn (right foreground), where they were seasoned before being packed in casks for shipping. From "About Tobacco," Lehman Brothers.

a hired man could expect to earn two or three times more in Virginia's tobacco fields than in England. Better still, in Virginia land was so abundant that it was extremely cheap compared with land in England.

By the mid-seventeenth century, common laborers could buy a hundred acres for less than their annual wages—an impossibility in England. New settlers who paid their own transportation to the Chesapeake received a grant of fifty acres of free land (termed a **headright**). The Virginia Company granted headrights to encourage settlement, and the royal government continued them for the same reason.

A Servant Labor System

Headrights, cheap land, and high wages gave poor English folk powerful incentives to immigrate to the New World. Yet many potential immigrants could not scrape together the money to pay for a trip across the Atlantic. Their poverty and the colonists' crying need for labor formed the basic context for the creation of a servant labor system.

About 80 percent of the immigrants to the Chesapeake during the seventeenth century came as **indentured servants**. Instead of a slave society, the

headright
▶ Fifty acres of free land granted by the Virginia Company to new settlers who paid their own transportation to the Chesapeake and to planters for each indentured servant they purchased.

indentured servants
▶ Poor immigrants who signed contracts known as indentures, in which they committed to four to seven years of labor in North America in exchange for transportation from England, as well as food and shelter after they arrived in the colony.

| How did Chesapeake tobacco society take shape? | Why did Chesapeake colonial society change in the late seventeenth century? | Why did the southern colonies move toward a slave labor system? | Conclusion: Why were export crops and slave labor important in the growth of the southern colonies? | ✓ LearningCurve Check what you know. bedfordstmartins.com /roarkunderstanding |

seventeenth-century Chesapeake region was fundamentally a society of white servants and ex-servants.

Relatively few African slaves were brought to the Chesapeake in the first half century after settlement. The first known Africans arrived in Virginia in 1619. The "20. And odd Negroes," as John Rolfe called them, were slaves captured in Angola in west-central Africa. A few more slaves trickled into the Chesapeake region during the next several decades. Men and women of African descent occasionally became indentured servants, served out their terms of servitude, and became free. A few slaves purchased their way out of bondage and lived as free people. These people were exceptions, however. Almost all people of African descent were slaves and remained enslaved for life.

Ideally, indentures allowed poor immigrants to trade their most valuable assets—their freedom and their ability to work—for a trip to the New World and a period of servitude followed by freedom in a land of opportunity. Planters

Bristol Docks This painting of the docks in Bristol, England, portrays a scene common at ports throughout the seventeenth-century Atlantic world. Tobacco flooded into Bristol in the seventeenth century while Bristol merchants also became active in the African slave trade, trading English goods on the West African coast for slaves, who were then taken to the New World to be sold to eager sugar and tobacco planters. © Bristol City Museum and Art Gallery/UK Bridgeman Art Library.

CHAPTER LOCATOR | What challenges faced early Chesapeake colonists?

reaped more immediate benefits. Servants meant more hands to grow more tobacco. A planter expected a servant to grow enough tobacco in one year to cover the price the planter had paid for the indenture. Servants' labor during the remaining three to six years of the indenture promised a handsome profit for the planter. Planters also profited because they received a headright of fifty acres of land from the colonial government for every newly purchased servant.

> ### > Features of Indentured Servitude in the Chesapeake

- The majority of indentured servants were white immigrants from England.
- Immigrants borrowed the costs of transportation from a merchant or ship captain in England in exchange for four to seven years of work in North America.
- Immigrants' labor was sold to planters upon arrival in the colonies. Planters paid twice the cost of transportation and agreed to provide food and shelter.
- At the end of the indenture, former servants received "freedom dues," usually a few barrels of corn and a suit of clothes.

About three out of four servants were young men between the ages of fifteen and twenty-five when they arrived in the Chesapeake. Typically, they shared the desperation of sixteen-year-old Francis Haires, who indentured himself for seven years because, according to his contract, "his father and mother and All friends [are] dead and he [is] a miserable wandering boy." Like Francis, most servants had no special training or skills, although the majority had some experience with agricultural work. A skilled craftsman could obtain a shorter indenture, but few risked coming to the colonies since their prospects were better in England.

Women were almost as rare as skilled craftsmen in the Chesapeake and more ardently desired. In the early days of the tobacco boom, the Virginia Company shipped young single women servants to the colony as prospective wives for male settlers willing to pay "120 weight [pounds] of the best leaf tobacco for each of them," in effect getting both a wife and a servant. The company reasoned that, as one official wrote in 1622, "the plantation can never flourish till families be planted, and the respect of wives and children fix the people on the soil." Nonetheless, women remained a small minority of the Chesapeake population until late in the seventeenth century.

The servant labor system perpetuated the gender imbalance. Although female servants cost about the same as males and generally served for the same length of time, planters preferred male servants, as one explained, because they were "the mor[e] excellent and yousefull Cretuers," especially for field work. Although many servant women hoed and harvested tobacco fields, most also did household chores such as cooking, washing, cleaning, gardening, and milking.

The Rigors of Servitude

Servants—whether men or women, white or black, English or African—tended to work together and socialize together. During the first half century of settlement, racial intermingling occurred, although the small number of blacks made it infrequent. In general, the commonalities of servitude caused servants—regardless of

| How did Chesapeake tobacco society take shape? | Why did Chesapeake colonial society change in the late seventeenth century? | Why did the southern colonies move toward a slave labor system? | Conclusion: Why were export crops and slave labor important in the growth of the southern colonies? | ✓ LearningCurve Check what you know. bedfordstmartins.com /roarkunderstanding |

65

their race and gender—to consider themselves apart from free people, whose ranks they longed to join eventually.

Servant life was harsh by the standards of seventeenth-century England and even by the frontier standards of the Chesapeake. Unlike servants in England, Chesapeake servants had no control over who purchased their labor—and thus them—for the period of their indenture. They were "sold here upp and downe like horses," one observer reported. But tobacco planters' need for labor muffled complaints about treating servants as property.

For servants, the promise of indentured servitude in the Chesapeake often withered when they confronted the rigors of labor in the tobacco fields. Severe laws aimed to keep servants in their place. Punishments for petty crimes stretched servitude far beyond the original terms of indenture. After midcentury, the Virginia legislature added three or more years to the indentures of most servants by requiring them to serve until they were twenty-four years old.

Women servants were subject to special restrictions and risks. They were prohibited from marrying until their servitude had expired. A servant woman, the law assumed, could not serve two masters at the same time: one who owned her indentured labor and another who was her husband. As a rule, if a woman servant gave birth to a child, she had to serve two extra years and pay a fine.

Harsh punishments reflected four fundamental realities of the servant labor system. First, planters' hunger for labor caused them to demand as much labor as they could get from their servants. Second, servants hoped to survive their servitude and use their freedom to obtain land and start a family. Third, since servants saw themselves as free people in a temporary status of servitude, they often made grudging, halfhearted workers. Finally, planters put up with this contentious arrangement because the alternatives were less desirable.

Planters could not easily hire free men and women because land was readily available and free people preferred to work for themselves on their own land. Nor could planters depend on much labor from family members because families were few, were started late, and thus had few children. And, until the 1680s and 1690s, slaves were expensive and hard to come by. Before then, masters who wanted to grow more tobacco had few alternatives to buying indentured servants.

Cultivating Land and Faith

Villages and small towns dotted the rural landscape of seventeenth-century England, but in the Chesapeake towns were few and far between. Instead, tobacco farms occupied small clearings surrounded by hundreds of acres of wilderness. Since tobacco was a labor-intensive crop that quickly exhausted the fertility of the soil, each farmer cultivated only 5 or 10 percent of his land at any one time. Tobacco planters sought land that fronted a navigable river in order to minimize the work of transporting the heavy barrels of tobacco onto ships. A settled region thus resembled a lacework of farms stitched around waterways.

Most Chesapeake colonists were nominally Protestants. Attendance at Sunday services and conformity to the doctrines of the Church of England were required of all English men and women. Few clergymen migrated to the

Chesapeake, however, and too few of those who did were models of piety. Certainly, some colonists took their religion seriously. But on the whole, religion did not awaken the zeal of Chesapeake settlers, certainly not as it did the zeal of New England settlers in these same years (as discussed in chapter 4). The religion of the Chesapeake colonists was Anglican, but their faith lay in the turbulent, competitive, high-stakes gamble of survival as tobacco planters.

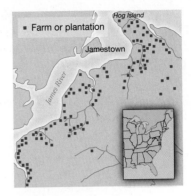

Settlement Patterns along the James River

The situation was similar in the Catholic colony of Maryland. In 1632, England's King Charles I granted his Catholic friend Lord Baltimore about 6.5 million acres in the northern Chesapeake region. Lord Baltimore intended to create a refuge for Catholics, who suffered severe discrimination in England. He fitted out two ships, the *Ark* and the *Dove*; gathered about 150 settlers; and sent them to the new colony, where they arrived on March 25, 1634. However, Maryland failed to live up to Lord Baltimore's hopes. The colony's population grew very slowly for twenty years, and most settlers were Protestants rather than Catholics. The religious turmoil of the Puritan Revolution in England (discussed in chapter 4) spilled across the Atlantic, creating conflict between Maryland's few Catholics—most of them wealthy and prominent—and the Protestant majority, most of them neither wealthy nor prominent. During the 1660s, Maryland began to attract settlers, mostly Protestants, as readily as Virginia. Although Catholics and the Catholic faith continued to exert influence in Maryland, the colony's society, economy, politics, and culture became nearly indistinguishable from Virginia's. Both colonies shared a devotion to tobacco, the true faith of the Chesapeake.

QUICK REVIEW

Why did the vast majority of European immigrants to the Chesapeake come as indentured servants?

How did Chesapeake tobacco society take shape?

Why did Chesapeake colonial society change in the late seventeenth century?

Why did the southern colonies move toward a slave labor system?

Conclusion: Why were export crops and slave labor important in the growth of the southern colonies?

☑ LearningCurve
Check what you know.
bedfordstmartins.com
/roarkunderstanding

Why did Chesapeake colonial society change in the late seventeenth century?

Jamestown Church Tower

This modern-day photograph shows the remains of the tower of the Anglican church that colonists constructed in Jamestown beginning in 1639. Nearby is the foundation of an older church, built in 1617, that also served as the site of the first meeting of the Virginia general assembly or House of Burgesses, the first representative legislative body in English North America. The churches illustrate the importance that Virginia's leaders attached to maintaining the central English institution of worship and spiritual order in the fledgling colony. Courtesy of Preservation Virginia.

THE SYSTEM OF INDENTURED SERVITUDE sharpened inequality in Chesapeake society by the mid-seventeenth century, propelling social and political polarization that culminated in 1676 with Bacon's Rebellion. The rebellion prompted reforms that stabilized relations between elite planters and their lesser neighbors and paved the way for a social hierarchy that muted differences of landholding and wealth and amplified racial differences. Amid this social and political evolution, Chesapeake colonists' dedication to growing tobacco did not change.

Social and Economic Polarization

The first half of the seventeenth century in the Chesapeake was the era of the yeoman—a farmer who owned a small plot of land sufficient to support a family and tilled largely by servants and a few family members. A small number of elite planters had larger estates and commanded ten or more servants. But for the first several decades, few men lived long enough to accumulate fortunes sufficient to set them much apart from their neighbors.

Until midcentury, the principal division in Chesapeake society was less between rich and poor planters than between free farmers and unfree servants. Although these two groups contrasted sharply in their legal and economic status, their daily lives had many similarities. Servants looked forward to the time when their indentures would expire and they would become free and eventually own land.

Three major developments splintered this rough frontier equality during the third quarter of the century. First, as planters grew more and more tobacco, the ample supply depressed tobacco prices in European markets. Cheap tobacco reduced planters' profits and made saving enough to become landowners more difficult for freed servants. Second, because the mortality rate in the Chesapeake colonies declined, more and more servants survived their indentures, and landless freemen became more numerous and grew more discontented. Third, declining mortality also encouraged the formation of a planter elite. By living longer, the most successful planters compounded their success. The wealthiest planters also began to buy slaves as well as to serve as merchants.

By the 1670s, the society of the Chesapeake had become polarized. Landowners—the planter elite and the more numerous yeoman planters—clustered around one pole. Landless colonists, mainly freed servants, gathered at the other. Each group eyed the other with suspicion and mistrust. For the most part, planters saw landless freemen as a dangerous rabble rather than as fellow colonists with legitimate grievances. Governor William Berkeley feared the political threat to the governing elite posed by "six parts in seven [of Virginia colonists who] . . . are poor, indebted, discontented, and armed."

> **CHRONOLOGY**

ca. 1600–1650
- Yeoman farmers predominate in the Chesapeake region.

1644
- Opechancanough leads second uprising.

1660
- Navigation Act requires that colonial products be shipped only to English ports.

1661–1676
- No elections are called in the House of Burgesses.

1670
- House of Burgesses outlaws voting by poor men.

1676
- Bacon's Rebellion.

Governor William Berkeley

This portrait illustrates the distance that separated Governor Berkeley and the other Chesapeake grandees from poor planters, landless freemen, servants, and slaves. His haughty, satisfied demeanor suggests his lack of sympathy for poor Virginians, who, he was certain, deserved their lot. Courtesy of Berkeley Castle Charitable Trust, Gloucestershire.

How did Chesapeake tobacco society take shape?

Why did Chesapeake colonial society change in the late seventeenth century?

Why did the southern colonies move toward a slave labor system?

Conclusion: Why were export crops and slave labor important in the growth of the southern colonies?

✓ **LearningCurve**
Check what you know.
bedfordstmartins.com /roarkunderstanding

Government Policies and Political Conflict

In general, government enforced the distinction separating servants and masters with an iron fist. Poor men complained that "nether the Governor nor Counsell could or would doe any poore men right, but that they would shew favor to great men and wronge the poore." Most Chesapeake colonists, like most Europeans, assumed that "great men" should bear the responsibilities of government. Until 1670, all freemen could vote, and they routinely elected prosperous planters to the legislature. No former servant served in either the governor's council or the House of Burgesses after 1640. Yet poor Virginians believed that the "great men" used their government offices to promote their selfish personal interests rather than governing impartially.

As discontent mounted among the poor during the 1660s and 1670s, colonial officials tried to keep political power in safe hands. Beginning in 1661, for example, Governor William Berkeley did not call an election for the House of Burgesses for fifteen years. In 1670, the House of Burgesses outlawed voting by poor men, permitting only men who headed households and were landowners to vote.

The king also began to tighten the royal government's control of trade and to collect substantial revenue from the Chesapeake colonies. A series of English laws funneled the colonial trade exclusively into the hands of English merchants and shippers. The **Navigation Acts** of 1650 and 1651 specified that colonial goods had to be transported in English ships with predominantly English crews. A 1660 act required colonial products to be sent only to English ports, and a 1663 law stipulated further that all goods sent to the colonies must pass through English ports and be carried on English ships manned by English sailors. Taken together, these navigation acts reflected the English government's mercantilist assumption that what was good for England should determine colonial policy.

Assumptions about mercantilism also underlay the import duty on tobacco inaugurated by the Navigation Act of 1660. The law assessed an import tax of two pence on every pound of colonial tobacco brought into England, about the price a Chesapeake tobacco farmer received. The tax gave the king a major financial interest in the size of the tobacco crop, which yielded about a quarter of all English customs revenues during the 1660s.

Navigation Acts
▶ English laws passed in the 1650s and 1660s requiring that English colonial goods be shipped through English ports on English ships with English sailors in order to benefit English merchants, shippers, and seamen.

Bacon's Rebellion

Colonists, like residents of European monarchies, accepted class divisions and inequality as long as they believed that government officials ruled for the general good. When rulers violated that precept, ordinary people felt justified in rebelling. In 1676, **Bacon's Rebellion** erupted as a dispute over Virginia's Indian policy. Before it was over, the rebellion convulsed Chesapeake politics and society, leaving in its wake death, destruction, and a legacy of hostility between the great planters and their poorer neighbors.

In June 1676, the new legislature passed a series of reform measures known as Bacon's Laws. Among other changes, the laws gave local settlers a voice in setting tax levies, forbade officeholders from demanding bribes or other extra fees

Bacon's Rebellion
▶ An unsuccessful rebellion against the colonial government in 1676, led by frontier settler Nathaniel Bacon.

CHAPTER LOCATOR | What challenges faced early Chesapeake colonists?

for carrying out their duties, placed limits on holding multiple offices, and restored the vote to all freemen. But elite planters soon convinced Governor Berkeley that Nathanial Bacon and his supporters among small planters and frontiersmen were a greater threat than the Indians.

When Bacon learned that Berkeley had branded him a traitor, he declared war against Berkeley and the other grandees. For three months, Bacon's forces fought the Indians, sacked the grandees' plantations, and attacked Jamestown. Berkeley's loyalists retaliated by plundering the homes of Bacon's supporters. The fighting continued until Bacon unexpectedly died, most likely from dysentery, and several English ships arrived to bolster Berkeley's strength.

The rebellion did nothing to dislodge the grandees from their positions of power. If anything, it strengthened them. When the king learned of the turmoil in the Chesapeake and its devastating effect on tobacco exports and customs duties, he ordered an investigation. Royal officials replaced Berkeley with a governor more attentive to the king's interests, nullified Bacon's Laws, and instituted an export tax on tobacco as a way of paying the expenses of government without having to obtain the consent of the tightfisted House of Burgesses.

In the aftermath of Bacon's Rebellion, tensions between great planters and small farmers moderated. Bacon's Rebellion showed, a governor of Virginia said, that it was necessary "to steer between . . . either an Indian or a civil war." The ruling elite concluded that it was safer for the colonists to fight the Indians than to fight each other, and the government made little effort to restrict settlers' encroachment on Indian land. Tax cuts also were welcomed by all freemen. The export duty on tobacco imposed by the king allowed the colonial government to reduce taxes by 75 percent between 1660 and 1700. In the long run, however, the most important contribution to political stability was the declining importance of the servant labor system. During the 1680s and 1690s, fewer servants arrived in the Chesapeake, partly because of improving economic conditions in England. Accordingly, the number of poor, newly freed servants also declined, reducing the size of the lowest stratum of free society. In 1700, when about one-third of the free colonists still worked as tenants on land owned by others, the Chesapeake was in the midst of transitioning to a slave labor system that minimized the differences between poor farmers and rich planters and magnified the differences between whites and blacks.

QUICK REVIEW <

Why did Chesapeake colonial society become increasingly polarized between 1650 and 1670?

How did Chesapeake tobacco society take shape?

Why did Chesapeake colonial society change in the late seventeenth century?

Why did the southern colonies move toward a slave labor system?

Conclusion: Why were export crops and slave labor important in the growth of the southern colonies?

☑ LearningCurve
Check what you know.
bedfordstmartins.com
/roarkunderstanding

Why did the southern colonies move toward a slave labor system?

Sugar Plantation This portrait of a Brazilian sugar plantation shows cartloads of sugarcane being hauled to the mill, which is powered by a waterwheel (far right), where the cane will be squeezed between rollers to extract the sugary juice. The juice will then be distilled over a fire tended by the slaves until it has the desired consistency and purity. Courtesy of the John Carter Brown Library at Brown University.

slavery
▶ Coerced labor. African slavery became the most important form of coerced labor in the New World in the seventeenth century.

ALTHOUGH FORCED NATIVE LABOR was common practice in New Spain, English colonists were unsuccessful in conscripting Indian labor. They looked instead to another source of workers used by the Spaniards and Portuguese: enslaved Africans. On this foundation, European colonizers built African **slavery** into the most important form of coerced labor in the New World.

During the seventeenth century, English colonies in the West Indies followed the Spanish and Portuguese examples and developed sugar plantations with slave labor. In the English North American colonies, however, a slave labor system did not emerge until the last quarter of the seventeenth century. During the 1670s, settlers from Barbados brought slavery to the new English mainland colony of Carolina, where the imprint of the West Indies remained strong for decades. In Chesapeake tobacco fields at about the same time, slave labor began to replace servant labor, marking the transition toward a society of freedom for whites and slavery for Africans.

CHAPTER LOCATOR | What challenges faced early Chesapeake colonists?

Religion and Revolt in the Spanish Borderland

While English colonies in the Chesapeake grew and prospered with the tobacco trade, the northern outposts of the Spanish empire in New Mexico and Florida stagnated. Only about fifteen hundred Spaniards lived in Florida, and roughly twice as many inhabited New Mexico, yet both colonies required regular deliveries of goods and large subsidies. One royal governor complained that "no [Spaniard] comes . . . to plow and sow [crops], but only to eat and loaf."

Instead of attracting settlers and growing crops for export, New Mexico and Florida appealed to Spanish missionaries seeking to convert Indians to Christianity. In both colonies, Indians outnumbered Spaniards ten or twenty to one. Royal officials hoped that the missionaries' efforts would pacify the Indians and be a relatively cheap way to preserve Spanish footholds in North America. The missionaries baptized thousands of Indians in Spanish North America during the seventeenth century, but they also planted the seeds of Indian uprisings against Spanish rule.

The missionaries followed royal instructions that Indians should be taught "to live in a civilized manner, clothed and wearing shoes . . . [and] given the use of . . . bread, linen, horses, cattle, tools, and weapons, and all the rest that Spain has had." In effect, the missionaries sought to convert the Indians not just into Christians but also into surrogate Spaniards.

The missionaries supervised the building of scores of Catholic churches across Florida and New Mexico. Adopting practices common elsewhere in New Spain, they forced the Indians both to construct these churches and to pay tribute in the form of food, blankets, and other goods. Although the missionaries congratulated themselves on the many Indians they converted, their coercive methods subverted their goals. A missionary reported that an Indian in New Mexico asked him, "If we [missionaries] who are Christians caused so much harm and violence [to Indians], why should they become Christians?"

The Indians retaliated repeatedly against Spanish exploitation, but the Spaniards suppressed the violent uprisings by taking advantage of the disunity among the Indians, much as Cortés did in the conquest of Mexico (see chapter 2). In 1680, however, the native leader Popé organized the **Pueblo Revolt**, ordering his followers, as one recounted, to "break up and burn the images of the holy Christ, the Virgin Mary, and the other saints, the crosses, and everything pertaining to Christianity." During the revolt, Indians desecrated churches, killed two-thirds of the Spanish missionaries, and drove the Spaniards out of New Mexico to present-day El Paso, Texas. The Spaniards managed to return to New Mexico by the end of the seventeenth century, but only by curtailing the missionaries and reducing labor exploitation. Florida Indians never mounted a unified attack on Spanish rule, but they too organized sporadic uprisings and resisted conversion.

The West Indies: Sugar and Slavery

The most profitable part of the English New World empire in the seventeenth century lay in the Caribbean (**Map 3.2**). The tiny island of **Barbados**, colonized in the

> **CHRONOLOGY**

1640s
– Colonists in Barbados begin to grow sugarcane with the labor of African slaves.

1663
– Royal charter is granted for the Carolina colony.

1670
– Charles Towne, South Carolina, is founded.

1670–1700
– Slave labor system emerges in Carolina and Chesapeake colonies.

1680
– Popé leads the Pueblo Revolt.

Pueblo Revolt
▶ An effective revolt of Pueblo Indians in New Mexico, under the leadership of Popé, against the Spaniards in 1680. Particularly targeting symbols of Christianity, the Pueblo Indians succeeded in killing two-thirds of the Spanish missionaries and driving the Spaniards out of New Mexico.

Barbados
▶ An island in the British West Indies. Colonized in the 1630s, Barbados became an enormous sugar producer and a source of wealth for England. The island's African slaves quickly became a majority of the island's population despite the deadliness of their work.

| How did Chesapeake tobacco society take shape? | Why did Chesapeake colonial society change in the late seventeenth century? | **Why did the southern colonies move toward a slave labor system?** | Conclusion: Why were export crops and slave labor important in the growth of the southern colonies? | ✓ **LearningCurve** Check what you know. bedfordstmartins.com /roarkunderstanding |

73

1630s, was the jewel of the English West Indies. During the 1640s, a colonial official proclaimed Barbados "the most flourishing Island in all those American parts,
and I verily believe in all the world for the production of sugar." Sugar commanded high prices in England, and planters rushed to grow as much as they
could. By midcentury, annual sugar exports from the English Caribbean totaled
about 150,000 pounds; by 1700, exports reached nearly 50 million pounds.

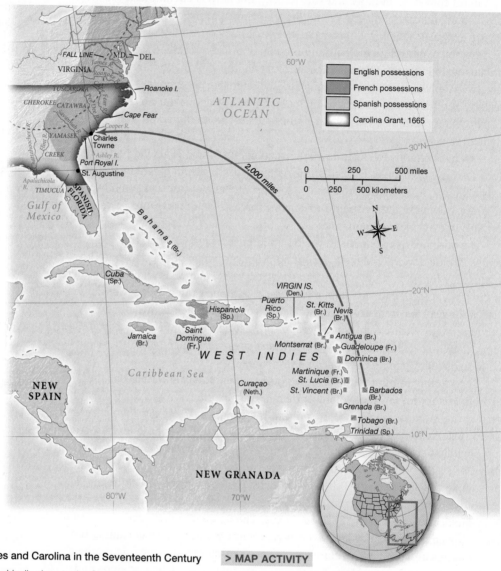

MAP 3.2 ■ The West Indies and Carolina in the Seventeenth Century

Although Carolina was geographically close to the Chesapeake colonies, it
was culturally closer to the West Indies in the seventeenth century because
its early settlers — both blacks and whites — came from Barbados. South
Carolina maintained strong ties to the West Indies for more than a century.

> **MAP ACTIVITY**

READING THE MAP: Locate English colonies in America and
English holdings in the Caribbean. Which European country
controlled most of the mainland bordering the Caribbean?
Where was the closest mainland English territory?

CONNECTIONS: Why were colonists in Carolina so interested
in Barbados? What goods did they export? Describe the
relationship between Carolina and Barbados in 1700.

Sugar transformed Barbados and other West Indian islands. Poor farmers could not afford the expensive machinery that extracted and refined sugarcane juice, but planters with enough capital to grow sugar got rich. By 1680, the wealthiest Barbadian sugar planters were, on average, four times richer than tobacco grandees in the Chesapeake. The sugar grandees differed from their Chesapeake counterparts in another crucial way: The average sugar baron in Barbados owned 115 slaves in 1680.

African slaves planted, cultivated, and harvested the sugarcane that made West Indian planters wealthy. Beginning in the 1640s, Barbadian planters purchased thousands of slaves to work their plantations, and the African population on the island mushroomed. During the 1650s, when blacks made up only 3 percent of the Chesapeake population, they had already become the majority in Barbados. By 1700, slaves constituted more than three-fourths of the island's population (**Figure 3.1**).

For slaves, work on a sugar plantation was a life sentence to brutal, unremitting labor. Slaves suffered high death rates. Since slave men outnumbered slave women two to one, few slaves could form families and have children. These grim

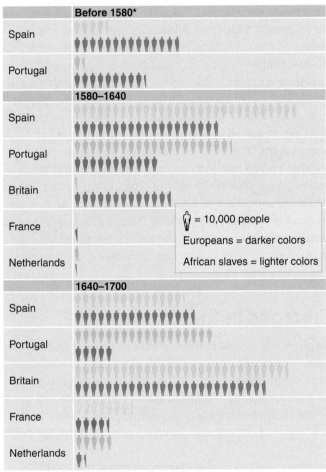

*Note: Before 1580, migration from Britain, France, and the Netherlands was negligible.

> **GLOBAL COMPARISON**

FIGURE 3.1 ■ Migration to the New World from Europe and Africa, 1492–1700

Before 1640, Spain and Portugal sent four out of five European migrants to the New World, virtually all of them bound for New Spain or Brazil. But from 1640 to 1700, nearly as many migrants came from England as from other European nations combined, a measure of the growing significance of England's colonies. From 1492 to 1700, more enslaved Africans than Europeans arrived in the New World. What might explain the shifts in the destinations of enslaved Africans? Were those shifts comparable to shifts among European immigrants?

| How did Chesapeake tobacco society take shape? | Why did Chesapeake colonial society change in the late seventeenth century? | Why did the southern colonies move toward a slave labor system? | Conclusion: Why were export crops and slave labor important in the growth of the southern colonies? | ✓ LearningCurve Check what you know. bedfordstmartins.com /roarkunderstanding |

realities meant that in Barbados and elsewhere in the West Indies, the slave population did not grow by natural reproduction. Instead, planters continually purchased enslaved Africans. Although sugar plantations did not gain a foothold in North America in the seventeenth century, the West Indies nonetheless exerted a powerful influence on the development of slavery in the mainland colonies.

Carolina: A West Indian Frontier

The early settlers of what became South Carolina were immigrants from Barbados. In 1663, a Barbadian planter named John Colleton and a group of seven other men obtained a charter from England's King Charles II to establish a colony north of the Spanish territories in Florida. The men, known as "proprietors," hoped to siphon settlers from Barbados and other colonies and encourage them to develop a profitable export crop comparable to West Indian sugar and Chesapeake tobacco. The proprietors enlisted the English philosopher John Locke to help draft the Fundamental Constitutions of Carolina, which provided for religious liberty and political rights for small property holders while envisioning a landed aristocracy supported by bound laborers and slaves. Following the Chesapeake example, the proprietors also offered headrights of up to 150 acres of land for each settler, a provision that eventually undermined the Constitutions' goal of a titled aristocracy. In 1670, the proprietors established the colony's first permanent English settlement, Charles Towne, later spelled Charleston (see Map 3.2).

As the proprietors had planned, most of the early settlers were from Barbados. The Barbadian immigrants brought their slaves with them. More than one-quarter of the early settlers were slaves, and by 1700 slaves made up about half the Carolina population. The Carolinians experimented unsuccessfully to match their semitropical climate with profitable export crops of tobacco, cotton, indigo, and olives. In the mid-1690s, colonists identified a hardy strain of rice and took advantage of the knowledge of rice cultivation among their many African slaves to build rice plantations. Settlers also sold livestock and timber to the West Indies, as well as another "natural resource": They captured and enslaved several thousand local Indians and sold them to Caribbean planters. Both economically and socially, seventeenth-century Carolina was a frontier outpost of the West Indian sugar economy.

Slave Labor Emerges in the Chesapeake

By 1700, more than eight out of ten people in the southern colonies of English North America lived in the Chesapeake. Until the 1670s, almost all Chesapeake colonists were white people from England. By 1700, however, one out of eight people in the region was a black person from Africa. A few black people had lived in the Chesapeake since the 1620s, but the black population grew fivefold between 1670 and 1700 as hundreds of tobacco planters made the transition from servant to slave labor.

Planters saw several advantages to purchasing slaves rather than servants. Although slaves cost three to five times more than servants, slaves never became

Tobacco Wrapper

This wrapper labeled a container of tobacco from the English colonies sold at Reighly's shop in Essex. The wrapper was much like a brand, promising consumers consistency in quality and taste. The wrapper illustrates tobacco growing in a field and harvested leaves ready to be packed into a barrel, ferried to the ships waiting offshore, and transported to Reighly's and other tobacconists in England. The Granger Collection, New York.

free. Because the mortality rate had declined by the 1680s, planters could reasonably expect a slave to live longer than a servant's period of indenture. Slaves also promised to be a perpetual labor force, since children of slave mothers inherited the status of slavery. And unlike servants, they could be controlled politically. A slave labor system promised to avoid the political problems such as Bacon's Rebellion caused by the servant labor system. Slavery kept discontented laborers in permanent servitude, and their color was a badge of their bondage.

The slave labor system polarized Chesapeake society along lines of race and status: All slaves were black, and nearly all blacks were slaves; almost all free people were white, and all whites were free or only temporarily bound in indentured servitude. Unlike Barbados, however, the Chesapeake retained a vast white majority. Among whites, huge differences of wealth and status still existed. By 1700, more than three-quarters of white families had neither servants nor slaves. Nonetheless, poor white farmers enjoyed the privileges of free status. They could own property, get married, have families, and bequeath their property and their freedom to their descendants; they could move when and where they wanted; they could associate freely with other people; they could serve on juries, vote, and hold political office; and they could work, loaf, and sleep as they chose. These

How did Chesapeake tobacco society take shape?

Why did Chesapeake colonial society change in the late seventeenth century?

Why did the southern colonies move toward a slave labor system?

Conclusion: Why were export crops and slave labor important in the growth of the southern colonies?

✓ **LearningCurve**
Check what you know.
bedfordstmartins.com
/roarkunderstanding

privileges of freedom—none of them possessed by slaves—made lesser white folk feel they had a genuine stake in the existence of slavery, even if they did not own a single slave. By emphasizing the privileges of freedom shared by all white people, the slave labor system reduced the tensions between poor folk and grandees that had plagued the Chesapeake region in the 1670s.

In contrast to slaves in Barbados, most slaves in the seventeenth-century Chesapeake colonies had frequent and close contact with white people. Slaves and white servants performed the same tasks on tobacco plantations, often working side by side in the fields. Slaves took advantage of every opportunity to slip away from white supervision and seek out the company of other slaves. Planters often feared that slaves would turn such seemingly innocent social pleasures to political ends, either to run away or to conspire to strike against their masters. Slaves often did run away, but they were usually captured or returned after a brief absence. Despite planters' nightmares, slave insurrections did not occur.

Although slavery resolved the political unrest caused by the servant labor system, it created new political problems. By 1700, the bedrock political issue in the southern colonies was keeping slaves in their place, at the end of a hoe. The slave labor system in the southern colonies stood roughly midway between the sugar plantations and black majority of Barbados to the south and the small farms and homogeneous villages that developed in seventeenth-century New England to the north (as discussed in chapter 4).

> ## QUICK REVIEW

Why had slave labor largely displaced indentured servant labor by 1700 in Chesapeake tobacco production?

Conclusion: Why were export crops and slave labor important in the growth of the southern colonies?

BY 1700, the colonies of Virginia, Maryland, and Carolina were firmly established. The staple crops they grew for export provided a livelihood for many, a fortune for a few, and valuable revenues for shippers, merchants, and the English monarchy. Their societies differed markedly from English society in most respects, yet the colonists considered themselves English people who happened to live in North America. They claimed the same rights and privileges as English men and women, while they denied those rights and privileges to Native Americans and African slaves.

The English colonies also differed from the example of New Spain. Settlers and servants flocked to English colonies, in contrast to the Spaniards who trickled into New Spain. Few English missionaries sought to convert Indians to Protestant Christianity, unlike the numerous Catholic missionaries in the Spanish settlements in New Mexico and Florida. Large quantities of gold and silver never materialized in English North America. English colonists never adopted the system of encomienda (see chapter 2). Yet important forms of coerced labor and racial distinction that developed in New Spain had North American counterparts, as English colonists employed servants and slaves and defined themselves as superior to Indians and Africans.

By 1700, the remnants of Powhatan's people still survived. As English settlement pushed north, west, and south of Chesapeake Bay, the Indians faced the new colonial world that Powhatan and Pocahontas had encountered when John Smith and the first colonists had arrived at Jamestown. By 1700, the many descendants of Pocahontas's son, Thomas, as well as other colonists and Native Americans, understood that the English had come to stay.

Economically, the southern colonies developed during the seventeenth century from the struggling Jamestown settlement that could not feed itself into a major source of profits for England. The European fashion for tobacco provided livelihoods for numerous white families and riches for elite planters. But after 1700, enslaved Africans were conscripted in growing numbers to grow tobacco in the Chesapeake and rice in Carolina. The slave society that dominated the eighteenth-century southern colonies was firmly rooted in the developments of the seventeenth century.

A desire for land, a hope for profit, and a dream for security motivated southern white colonists. Realizing these aspirations involved great risks, considerable suffering, and frequent disappointment, as well as seizing Indian lands and coercing labor from servants and slaves. By 1700, despite huge disparities in individual colonists' success in achieving their goals, tens of thousands of white colonists who were immigrants or descendants of immigrants now considered the southern colonies their home, shaping the history of the region and of the nation as a whole for centuries to come.

How did Chesapeake tobacco society take shape?

Why did Chesapeake colonial society change in the late seventeenth century?

Why did the southern colonies move toward a slave labor system?

Conclusion: Why were export crops and slave labor important in the growth of the southern colonies?

☑ LearningCurve
Check what you know.
bedfordstmartins.com
/roarkunderstanding

CHAPTER 3 STUDY GUIDE

STEP 1 — GET STARTED ONLINE

✓ LearningCurve ▪ bedfordstmartins.com/roarkunderstanding

Now that you've read the chapter, make it stick by completing the LearningCurve activity.

STEP 2 — EXPLAIN WHY IT MATTERS

Put your reading into practice. Identify each term below, and then explain why it matters in U.S. history.

TERM	WHO OR WHAT & WHEN	WHY IT MATTERS
Virginia Company (p. 57)		
Algonquian Indians (p. 57)		
Jamestown (p. 57)		
royal colony (p. 60)		
House of Burgesses (p. 60)		
headright (p. 63)		
indentured servants (p. 63)		
Navigation Acts (p. 70)		
Bacon's Rebellion (p. 70)		
slavery (p. 72)		
Pueblo Revolt (p. 73)		
Barbados (p. 73)		

STEP 3 — MOVE BEYOND THE BASICS

To demonstrate a more advanced understanding, detail the demographics (who lived in the Chesapeake colonies), economic structures (how people survived and thrived), the major political and sociocultural divisions within colonial Chesapeake society, and the causes of these divisions.

Date	Demographics	Economy	Political/social divisions within colonial society	Reasons for conflicts
1607				
1620				
1650				
1700				

JAMESTOWN AND THE CHESAPEAKE

▶ How did interactions with the Algonquians shape the Jamestown colony's early history?

▶ How did the development of tobacco cultivation transform the Chesapeake?

INDENTURED SERVITUDE AND BACON'S REBELLION

▶ What role did indentured servants play in the transformation of the Chesapeake in the early seventeenth century?

▶ What events led to Bacon's Rebellion, and why did Virginia erupt into violence in 1676?

SLAVERY

▶ What role did sugar play in the development of African slavery in the New World?

▶ How did the introduction of African slaves affect the development of Chesapeake society?

LOOKING BACKWARD, LOOKING AHEAD

▶ How did the seventeenth-century English colonies differ from their sixteenth-century Spanish counterparts?

▶ How did the introduction of African slaves contribute to the emergence of a distinct southern colonial society?

> **IN YOUR OWN WORDS**

Imagine that you must give an oral report to the class answering the following question: What were the most important factors that shaped England's southern colonies in the seventeenth century? What would be the most important points to include and why?

 Do it online at the Student Site ▪ bedfordstmartins.com/roarkunderstanding

4

FOUNDING THE NORTHERN COLONIES

1601–1700

> How did religious dissidents from England come to establish colonies in northern North America? Chapter 4 explores the development of the northern colonies in the seventeenth century, examining the factors that gave each colony its unique character. It pays particular attention to the importance of religion in the evolution of New England and to England's attempts to control colonial trade.

 **LearningCurve**

bedfordstmartins.com/roarkunderstanding
After reading the chapter, use LearningCurve to retain what you've read.

> Why did the
> Puritans immigrate
> to North America?

> How did New
> England society
> change during the
> seventeenth
> century?

> What was
> distinctive about
> the middle
> colonies?

> What was the
> connection
> between the
> colonies and the
> English empire?

> Conclusion: Was
> there an English
> model of
> colonization in
> North America?

Thomas Smith, a New England mariner, created colonial America's oldest known self-portrait around 1680. Worcester Art Museum.

Why did the Puritans immigrate to North America?

In 1629, the Massachusetts Bay Company designed this seal depicting an Indian man inviting English settlers to "come over and help us." Of course, such an invitation was never issued. The seal was an attempt to lend an aura of altruism to the Massachusetts Bay Company's colonization efforts. What does the seal suggest about English views of Indians? Courtesy of Massachusetts Archives.

Puritans

▶ Dissenters from the Church of England who wanted a genuine Reformation rather than the partial Reformation sought by Henry VIII. The Puritans' religious principles emphasized the importance of an individual's relationship with God, developed through Bible study, prayer, and introspection.

English Reformation

▶ Reform effort initiated by King Henry VIII that included banning the Catholic Church and declaring the English monarch head of the new Church of England but little change in doctrine. Henry's primary concern was consolidating his political power.

PURITANS WHO IMMIGRATED to North America aspired to escape the turmoil and persecution they suffered in England, a long-term consequence of the English Reformation. They also sought to build a new, orderly, Puritan version of England. Puritans established the first small settlement in New England in 1620, followed a few years later by additional settlements by the Massachusetts Bay Company. Allowed self-government through royal charter, these Puritans were in a unique position to direct the new colonies according to their faith. Although many New England colonists were not Puritans, Puritanism remained a paramount influence in New England's religion, politics, and community life during the seventeenth century.

Puritan Origins: The English Reformation

The religious roots of the **Puritans** who founded New England reached back to the Protestant Reformation, which arose in Germany in 1517 (see chapter 2). The English church initially remained within the Catholic fold. Henry VIII, who reigned from 1509 to 1547, saw that the Reformation offered him an opportunity to break with Rome and take control of the church in England. In 1534, Henry formally initiated the **English Reformation**. At his insistence, Parliament outlawed the Catholic Church and proclaimed the king "the only supreme head on earth of the Church of England." Henry seized the vast properties of the Catholic Church in England as well as the privilege of appointing bishops and others in the church hierarchy.

CHAPTER LOCATOR | Why did the Puritans immigrate to North America?

Queen Elizabeth This sixteenth-century portrait of Queen Elizabeth celebrates the English victory over the Spanish Armada in 1588 (shown in the panels on either side of Elizabeth's head), which resulted in England's empire reaching North America (notice her right hand covering North America on the globe). © Bettmann/Corbis.

> **CHRONOLOGY**

1534
– English Reformation begins.

1558–1603
– Reign of Elizabeth I in England.

1603–1625
– Reign of James I in England.

1620
– Plymouth colony is founded by Pilgrims.

1629
– Massachusetts Bay Company receives a royal charter.

1630
– John Winthrop leads Puritan settlers to Massachusetts Bay.

The fate of Protestantism waxed and waned under the monarchs who succeeded Henry VIII. In 1558, Elizabeth I, the daughter of Henry and his second wife, Anne Boleyn, became queen. During her long reign, Elizabeth reaffirmed the English Reformation and tried to position the English church between the extremes of Catholicism and Puritanism. Like her father, she desired a church that would strengthen the monarchy and the nation. By the time Elizabeth died in 1603, many people in England looked on Protestantism as a defining feature of national identity.

> **The English Reformation and Puritanism**

- Henry VIII took advantage of the Protestant Reformation in Europe to break with Rome and take control of the Church of England.
- Reformation brought political and religious turmoil to England; many English Catholics wanted to revoke the English Reformation, while other English people wanted a thorough Reformation.
- The Puritans wanted to eliminate what they considered the offensive features of Catholicism that remained in the religious doctrines and practices of the Church of England.
- Puritans wanted to do away with the rituals of Catholic worship and instead emphasize an individual's relationship with God, developed through Bible study, prayer, and introspection.
- All Puritans shared a desire to make the English church thoroughly Protestant.

How did New England society change during the seventeenth century?	What was distinctive about the middle colonies?	What was the connection between the colonies and the English empire?	Conclusion: Was there an English model of colonization in North America?	✔ LearningCurve Check what you know. bedfordstmartins.com /roarkunderstanding

When Elizabeth's successor, James I, became king, English Puritans petitioned for further reform of the Church of England. James authorized a new translation of the Bible, known ever since as the King James Version. However, neither James I nor his son Charles I, who became king in 1625, was receptive to the ideas of Puritan reformers. James and Charles moved the Church of England away from Puritanism. They enforced conformity to the Church of England and punished dissenters. In 1629, Charles I dissolved Parliament—where Puritans were well represented—and initiated aggressive anti-Puritan policies. Many Puritans despaired about continuing to defend their faith in England and made plans to emigrate to Europe, the West Indies, or America.

The Pilgrims and Plymouth Colony

Separatists

▶ Protestants who sought withdrawal from the Church of England. The Pilgrims were Separatists.

One of the first Protestant groups to emigrate, later known as Pilgrims, professed an unorthodox view known as separatism. These **Separatists** sought to withdraw—or separate—from the Church of England, which they considered hopelessly corrupt. William Bradford, a leader of the Separatists, believed that America promised to better protect and preserve their community. Separatists obtained permission to settle in the extensive territory granted to the Virginia Company (see chapter 3). In August 1620, the Pilgrim families boarded the *Mayflower*, and after eleven weeks at sea all but one of the 102 immigrants arrived in present-day Massachusetts.

The Pilgrims drew up the Mayflower Compact on the day they arrived. They pledged to "covenant and combine ourselves together into a civil Body Politick, for our better Ordering and Preservation." The signers (all men) agreed to enact and obey necessary and just laws.

The Pilgrims settled at Plymouth and elected William Bradford their governor. That first winter, which they spent aboard their ship, "was most sad and lamentable," Bradford wrote later. "In two or three months' time half of [our] company died."

In the spring, Indians rescued the floundering Plymouth settlement. First Samoset and then Squanto befriended the settlers. Samoset arranged for the Pilgrims to meet and establish good relations with Massasoit, the chief of the Wampanoag Indians, whose territory included Plymouth. With the Indians' guidance, the Pilgrims managed to harvest enough food to guarantee their survival through the coming winter, an occasion they celebrated in the fall of 1621 with a feast of thanksgiving attended by Massasoit and other Wampanoags.

The Pilgrims persisted, living simply and coexisting in relative peace with the Indians. By 1630, Plymouth had become a small permanent settlement, but it failed to attract many other English Puritans.

TABLE 4.1 ■ Pilgrims and Puritans

Pilgrims	Puritans
Wanted to separate from the Church of England; called Separatists	Wanted to reform the Church of England
Settled in Plymouth in 1620	Settled in Boston in 1630
Led by William Bradford	Led by John Winthrop

CHAPTER LOCATOR | Why did the Puritans immigrate to North America?

86 CHAPTER 4 FOUNDING THE NORTHERN COLONIES

The Founding of Massachusetts Bay Colony

In 1629, shortly before Charles I dissolved Parliament, a group of Puritans obtained a royal charter for the Massachusetts Bay Company. The charter provided the usual privileges granted to joint-stock companies, including land for colonization that spanned present-day Massachusetts, New Hampshire, Vermont, Maine, and upstate New York. A unique provision of the charter permitted the government of the Massachusetts Bay Company to be located in the colony rather than in England. This provision allowed Puritans to exchange their status as a harassed minority in England for self-government in Massachusetts.

To lead the emigrants, the Massachusetts Bay Company selected John Winthrop, a prosperous lawyer and landowner, to serve as governor. In March 1630, eleven ships crammed with seven hundred passengers sailed for Massachusetts; six more ships and another five hundred emigrants followed a few months later. Winthrop and a small group chose to settle on the peninsula that became Boston, and other settlers clustered at promising locations nearby (**Map 4.1**).

In a sermon to his companions aboard the *Arbella* while they were still at sea—probably the most famous sermon in American history—Winthrop proclaimed the cosmic significance of their journey. The Puritans had "entered into a covenant" with God to "work out our salvation under the power and purity of his holy ordinances," Winthrop declared. This sanctified agreement with God meant that the Puritans had to make "extraordinary" efforts to "bring into familiar and constant practice" religious principles that most people in England merely preached. To achieve their pious goals, the Puritans had to subordinate their individual interests to the common good. "We must be knit together in this work as

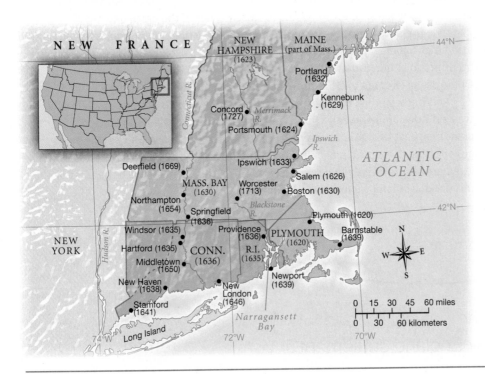

MAP 4.1 ■ **New England Colonies in the Seventeenth Century**

New Englanders spread across the landscape town by town during the seventeenth century. (For the sake of legibility, only a few of the more important towns are shown on the map.)

> MAP ACTIVITY

READING THE MAP: Using the dates on the map, create a chronology of the establishment of towns in New England. What physical features correspond to the earliest habitation by English settlers?

CONNECTIONS: Why were towns so much more a feature of seventeenth-century New England than of the Chesapeake (see also chapter 3)? How did Puritan dissent influence the settlement of New England colonies?

| How did New England society change during the seventeenth century? | What was distinctive about the middle colonies? | What was the connection between the colonies and the English empire? | Conclusion: Was there an English model of colonization in North America? | ✓ LearningCurve Check what you know. bedfordstmartins.com /roarkunderstanding |

one man," Winthrop preached. "We must delight in each other, make others' conditions our own, rejoice together, mourn together, labor and suffer together." The stakes could not be higher, Winthrop told his listeners: "We must consider that we shall be as a city upon a hill. The eyes of all people are upon us."

That belief shaped seventeenth-century New England as profoundly as tobacco shaped the Chesapeake. Winthrop's vision of a city on a hill fired the Puritans' fierce determination to keep their covenant and live according to God's laws, unlike the backsliders and compromisers who accommodated to the Church of England. Their resolve to adhere strictly to God's plan charged nearly every feature of life in seventeenth-century New England with a distinctive, high-voltage piety.

Unlike the early Chesapeake settlers, the first Massachusetts Bay colonists encountered few Indians because the local population had been almost entirely exterminated by an epidemic. And each year from 1630 to 1640, ship after ship followed in the wake of Winthrop's fleet, bringing more than twenty thousand new settlers.

Often, when the Church of England cracked down on a Puritan minister in England, he and many of his followers moved together to New England. By 1640, New England had one of the highest ratios of preachers to population in all of Christendom. Several ministers sought to carry the message of Christianity to the Indians and established "praying towns" to encourage Indians to adopt English ways. But the colonists focused far less on saving Indians' souls than on saving their own.

The occupations of New England immigrants reflected the social origins of English Puritans. On the whole, the immigrants came from the middle ranks of English society. The vast majority were either farmers or tradesmen. Indentured servants, whose numbers dominated the Chesapeake settlers, accounted for only about a fifth of those headed for New England. Most New England immigrants paid their way to Massachusetts. They were encouraged by the promise of bounty in New England reported in Winthrop's letter to his son: "Here can be no want of anything to those who bring means to raise [it] out of the earth and sea."

In contrast to Chesapeake newcomers, New England immigrants usually arrived as families. In fact, more Puritans came with family members than did any other group of immigrants in all of American history. Unlike immigrants to the Chesapeake, women and children made up a solid majority in New England.

As Winthrop reminded the first settlers in his *Arbella* sermon, each family was a "little commonwealth" that mirrored the hierarchy among all God's creatures. Just as humankind was subordinate to God, so young people were subordinate to their elders, children to their parents, and wives to their husbands. The immigrants' family ties reinforced their religious beliefs with the interlocking institutions of family, church, and community.

> **QUICK REVIEW**

What was a "little commonwealth," and why was it so important to New England settlement?

CHAPTER LOCATOR | Why did the Puritans immigrate to North America?

88 CHAPTER 4
FOUNDING THE NORTHERN COLONIES

David, Joanna, and Abigail Mason

In this 1670 painting, which depicts the children of Bostonians Joanna and Anthony Mason, the artist lavished attention on the young subjects' elaborate clothing and adornments: fashionable slashed sleeves, fancy lace, silver-studded shoes, necklaces for the girls, and a silver-headed cane for the boy. The portrait expresses the growing respect for wealth and its worldly rewards in seventeenth-century New England. Fine Arts Museums of San Francisco. Gift of Mr. and Mrs. John D. Rockefeller III.

How did New England society change during the seventeenth century?

> **CHRONOLOGY**

1636
- Rhode Island colony is established.
- Connecticut colony is founded.

1638
- Anne Hutchinson is excommunicated.

1642
- Puritan Revolution inflames England.

1649
- English Puritans win the civil war.

1656
- Quakers arrive in Massachusetts and are persecuted.

1662
- Many Puritan congregations adopt the Halfway Covenant.

1692
- Salem witch trials.

THE NEW ENGLAND COLONISTS, unlike their counterparts in the Chesapeake, settled in small towns, usually located on the coast or by a river (see Map 4.1). Massachusetts Bay colonists founded 133 towns during the seventeenth century, each with one or more churches. Church members' fervent piety, buttressed by the institutions of local government, enforced remarkable religious and social conformity in the small New England settlements. During the century, tensions within the Puritan faith and changes in New England communities splintered religious orthodoxy and weakened Puritan zeal. By 1700, however, Puritanism retained a distinctive influence in New England.

| How did New England society change during the seventeenth century? | What was distinctive about the middle colonies? | What was the connection between the colonies and the English empire? | Conclusion: Was there an English model of colonization in North America? | ✓ LearningCurve Check what you know. bedfordstmartins.com /roarkunderstanding |

89

Church, Covenant, and Conformity

Puritans believed that a church consisted of men and women who had entered a solemn covenant with one another and with God. Each new member of the covenant had to persuade existing members that she or he had fully experienced conversion.

Puritans embraced a distinctive version of Protestantism derived from **Calvinism**, the doctrines of John Calvin, who insisted that Christians strictly discipline their behavior to conform to God's commandments announced in the Bible. Like Calvin, Puritans believed in **predestination**—the idea that the all-powerful God, before the creation of the world, decided which few human souls would receive eternal life. Only God knows the identity of these fortunate predestined individuals—the "elect" or "saints." Nothing a person did in his or her lifetime could alter God's choice or provide assurance that the person was predestined for salvation with the elect or damned to hell with the doomed multitude.

Despite the looming uncertainty about God's choice of the elect, Puritans believed that if a person lived a rigorously godly life—constantly winning the daily battle against sin—his or her behavior was likely to be a hint, a visible sign, that he or she was one of God's chosen few. Puritans thought that "sainthood" would become visible in individuals' behavior, especially if they were privileged to know God's Word as revealed in the Bible.

The connection between sainthood and saintly behavior, however, was far from certain. Some members of the elect, Puritans believed, had not heard God's Word. One reason Puritans required all town residents to attend church services was to enlighten anyone who was ignorant of God's Truth. The slippery relationship between saintly behavior and God's predestined election caused Puritans to worry constantly that individuals who acted like saints were fooling themselves and others. Nevertheless, Puritans thought that **visible saints**—persons who passed the Puritans' demanding tests of conversion and church membership—probably were among God's elect.

Members of Puritan churches ardently hoped that God had chosen them to receive eternal life and tried to demonstrate saintly behavior. Their covenant bound them to help one another attain salvation and to discipline the entire community by saintly standards. Church members kept an eye on the behavior of everybody in town. By overseeing every aspect of life, the visible saints enforced a remarkable degree of righteous conformity in Puritan communities. Total conformity, however, was never achieved. Ardent Puritans differed among themselves, and non-Puritans shirked orthodox rules, such as the Roxbury servant who declared that "if hell were ten times hotter, [I] would rather be there than [I] would serve [my] master."

Despite the central importance of religion, churches played no direct role in the civil government of New England communities. Puritans did not want to mimic the Church of England, which they considered a puppet of the king rather than an independent body that served the Lord. They were determined to insulate New England churches from the contaminating influence of the civil state and its merely human laws. Ministers were prohibited from holding government office.

Puritans had no qualms, however, about their religious beliefs influencing New England governments. As much as possible, the Puritans tried to bring

Calvinism

▶ Christian doctrine of the Swiss Protestant theologian John Calvin. Its chief tenet was predestination, the idea that God had determined which human souls would receive eternal salvation. Despite this doctrine, Calvinism promoted strict discipline in daily and religious life.

predestination

▶ A doctrine stating that God determined whether individuals were destined for salvation or damnation before their birth. According to the doctrine, nothing an individual did during his or her lifetime could affect that person's fate.

visible saints

▶ Puritans who had passed the tests of conversion and church membership and were therefore thought to be among God's elect.

CHAPTER LOCATOR | Why did the Puritans immigrate to North America?

90 CHAPTER 4 FOUNDING THE NORTHERN COLONIES

public life into conformity with their view of God's law. For example, fines were issued for Sabbath-breaking activities such as working, traveling, playing a flute, smoking a pipe, and visiting neighbors.

Puritans mandated other purifications of what they considered corrupt English practices. They refused to celebrate Christmas or Easter because the Bible did not mention either one. They outlawed religious wedding ceremonies; couples were married by a magistrate in a civil ceremony. They banned cards, dice, shuffleboard, and other games of chance, as well as music and dancing. "Mixt or Promiscuous Dancing . . . of Men and Women" could not be tolerated since "the unchaste Touches and Gesticulations used by Dancers have a palpable tendency to that which is evil."

Government by Puritans for Puritanism

It is only a slight exaggeration to say that seventeenth-century New England was governed by Puritans for Puritanism. The charter of the Massachusetts Bay Company empowered the company's stockholders, known as freemen, to meet as a body known as the General Court and make the laws needed to govern the company's affairs. The colonists transformed this arrangement for running a joint-stock company into a structure for governing the colony. Hoping to ensure that godly men would decide government policies, the General Court expanded the number of freemen in 1631 to include all male church members. Only freemen had the right to vote for governor and other officials. When the size of the General Court grew too large to meet conveniently, the freemen agreed in 1634 that each town would send two deputies to the General Court to act as the colony's

How did New England society change during the seventeenth century? | What was distinctive about the middle colonies? | What was the connection between the colonies and the English empire? | Conclusion: Was there an English model of colonization in North America? | ✓ LearningCurve Check what you know. bedfordstmartins.com /roarkunderstanding

91

legislative assembly. All other men were classified as "inhabitants," who had the right to vote, hold office, and participate fully in town government.

A "town meeting," composed of a town's inhabitants and freemen, chose the selectmen who administered local affairs. New England town meetings routinely practiced a level of popular participation in political life that was unprecedented elsewhere in the world during the seventeenth century. Almost every adult man could speak out and vote in town meetings, but all women—even church members—were prohibited from voting. This widespread political participation tended to reinforce conformity to Puritan ideals.

The General Court granted land for town sites to pious petitioners, once the Indians agreed to relinquish their claim to the land, usually in exchange for manufactured goods. Town founders then apportioned land among themselves and any newcomers they approved. Most family plots clustered between roughly fifty to one hundred acres, resulting in a more nearly equal distribution of land in New England than in the Chesapeake.

The physical layout of New England towns encouraged settlers to look inward toward their neighbors, multiplying the opportunities for godly vigilance. Most people considered the forest that lay just beyond every settler's house an alien environment. Footpaths connecting one town to another were so rudimentary that even John Winthrop once got lost and spent a sleepless night in the forest only half a mile from his house.

The Splintering of Puritanism

Almost from the beginning, John Winthrop and other leaders had difficulty enforcing their views of Puritan orthodoxy. In England, persecution as a dissenting minority had unified Puritan voices in opposition to the Church of England. In New England, the promise of a godly society and the Puritans' emphasis on individual Bible study led toward different visions of godliness. Puritan leaders, however, interpreted dissent as an error caused either by a misguided believer or by the malevolent power of Satan. As one Puritan minister proclaimed, "The Scripture saith . . . there is no Truth but one."

The case of Roger Williams provides an example of dissent and its consequences. In 1633, Williams became the minister of the church in Salem, Massachusetts, and stated his belief that the Bible shrouded the Word of God in "mist and fog." That observation led him to denounce the emerging New England order as impure, ungodly, and tyrannical. He disagreed with the New England government's requirement that everyone attend church services. He argued that forcing people who were not Christians to attend church was "False Worshipping" that only promoted "spiritual drunkenness and whoredom." He believed that to regulate religious behavior would be "spiritual rape" and that governments should tolerate all religious beliefs because only God knows the Truth. "I commend that man," Williams wrote, "whether Jew, or Turk, or Papist, or whoever, that steers no otherwise than his conscience dares."

New England's leaders denounced Williams's arguments and banished him for his "extreme and dangerous" opinions. In January 1636, he fled south to Narragansett Bay, where he and his followers established the colony of Rhode

Island, which enshrined "Liberty of Conscience" as a fundamental ideal and became a refuge for other dissenters.

Shortly after banishing Roger Williams, Winthrop confronted another dissenter, this time a devout Puritan woman steeped in Scripture and absorbed by religious questions: Anne Hutchinson. The mother of fourteen children, Hutchinson served her neighbors as a midwife and in 1634 began to give weekly lectures on recent sermons attended by women who gathered at her home. Hutchinson lectured on the "covenant of grace"—the idea that individuals could be saved only by God's grace in choosing them to be members of the elect. This familiar Puritan doctrine contrasted with the covenant of works, the erroneous belief that a person's behavior—one's works—could win God's favor and ultimately earn a person salvation.

The meetings at Hutchinson's house alarmed her nearest neighbor, Governor John Winthrop, who believed that she was subverting the good order of the colony. In 1637, Winthrop had formal charges brought against Hutchinson and denounced her lectures as "not tolerable nor comely in the sight of God nor fitting for your sex." He told her, "You have stept out of your place, you have rather bine a Husband than a Wife and a preacher than a Hearer; and a Magistrate than a Subject."

Winthrop and other Puritan elders referred to Hutchinson and her followers as **antinomians**, people who believed that Christians could be saved by faith alone and did not need to act in accordance with God's law as set forth in the Bible and as interpreted by the colony's leaders. Hutchinson nimbly defended herself against the accusation of antinomianism. Yes, she acknowledged, she believed that men and women were saved by faith alone; but no, she did not deny the need to obey God's law. "The Lord hath let me see which was the clear ministry and which the wrong," she said. How could she tell, Winthrop asked, which ministry was which? "By an immediate revelation," she replied, "by the voice of [God's] own spirit to my soul." Winthrop seized this statement as the

antinomians

▶ Individuals who believed that Christians could be saved by faith alone and did not need to act in accordance with God's law as set forth in the Bible. Puritan leaders considered this belief to be heresy.

How did New England society change during the seventeenth century?

What was distinctive about the middle colonies?

What was the connection between the colonies and the English empire?

Conclusion: Was there an English model of colonization in North America?

☑ LearningCurve
Check what you know.
bedfordstmartins.com /roarkunderstanding

93

heresy of prophecy, the view that God revealed his will directly to a believer instead of exclusively through the Bible, as every right-minded Puritan knew.

In 1638, the Boston church formally excommunicated Hutchinson. The minister decreed, "I doe cast you out and . . . deliver you up to Satan." Banished, Hutchinson and her family moved first to Roger Williams's Rhode Island and then to present-day New York, where she and most of her family were killed by Indians.

The strains within Puritanism exemplified by Anne Hutchinson and Roger Williams caused communities to splinter repeatedly during the seventeenth century. Thomas Hooker, a prominent minister, clashed with Winthrop and other leaders over the composition of the church. Hooker argued that men and women who lived godly lives should be admitted to church membership even if they had not experienced conversion. In 1636, Hooker led an exodus of more than eight hundred colonists from Massachusetts to the Connecticut River valley, where they founded Hartford and neighboring towns. In 1639, the towns adopted the Fundamental Orders of Connecticut, a quasi-constitution that could be altered by the vote of freemen, who did not have to be church members, though nearly all of them were.

Other Puritan churches divided and subdivided throughout the seventeenth century as acrimony developed over doctrine and church government. Sometimes churches split over the appointment of a controversial minister. These schisms arose from ambiguities and tensions within Puritan belief. As the colonies matured, other tensions developed as well.

Religious Controversies and Economic Changes

A revolutionary transformation in the fortunes of Puritans in England had profound consequences in New England. Disputes between King Charles I and Parliament, which was dominated by Puritans, escalated in 1642 to civil war in England, a conflict known as the **Puritan Revolution**. Parliamentary forces led by the staunch Puritan Oliver Cromwell were victorious, executing Charles I in 1649 and proclaiming England a Puritan republic. From 1649 to 1660, England's rulers were not monarchs who suppressed Puritanism but believers who championed it.

When the Puritan Revolution began, the stream of immigrants to New England dwindled to a trickle, creating hard times for the colonists. They could no longer consider themselves a city on a hill setting a godly example for humankind. Puritans in England, not New England, were reforming English society. Furthermore, when immigrant ships became rare, the colonists faced sky-high prices for scarce English goods and few customers for their own colonial products. As they searched to find new products and markets, they established the enduring patterns of New England's economy.

New England's rocky soil and short growing season ruled out cultivating the southern colonies' crops of tobacco and rice that found ready markets in Atlantic ports. Exports that New Englanders could not get from the soil they took instead from the forest and the sea. By the 1640s, furbearing animals had become scarce unless traders ventured far beyond the frontiers of English settlement. Trees from the seemingly limitless forests of New England proved a longer-lasting resource.

Puritan Revolution
▶ English civil war that arose out of disputes between King Charles I and Parliament, which was dominated by Puritans. The conflict began in 1642 and ended with the execution of Charles I in 1649, resulting in Puritan rule in England until 1660.

Masts for ships and staves for barrels of Spanish wine and West Indian sugar were crafted from New England timber.

The most important New England export was fish. Dried, salted codfish from the rich North Atlantic fishing grounds found markets in southern Europe and the West Indies. The fish trade also stimulated colonial shipbuilding and trained generations of fishermen, sailors, and merchants. But the lives of most New England colonists revolved around their farms, churches, and families.

Although immigration came to a standstill in the 1640s, the population continued to boom, doubling every twenty years. In New England, almost everyone married, and women often had eight or nine children. Long, cold winters minimized the presence of warm-weather ailments such as malaria and yellow fever, so the mortality rate was lower than in the South.

During the second half of the seventeenth century, under the pressures of steady population growth (**Figure 4.1**) and integration into the Atlantic economy, the red-hot piety of the founders cooled. After 1640, the population grew faster than church membership. Boston's churches in 1650 could house only about a third of the city's residents. By the 1680s, women were the majority of church members throughout New England. In some towns, only 15 percent of the adult men were members. This slackening of piety led the Puritan minister Michael Wigglesworth to ask, in verse:

> How is it that
> I find In stead of holiness Carnality;
> In stead of heavenly frames an Earthly mind,
> For burning zeal luke-warm Indifferency,
> For flaming love, key-cold Dead-heartedness. . . .
> Whence cometh it . . .
> that an honest man can hardly
> Trust his Brother?

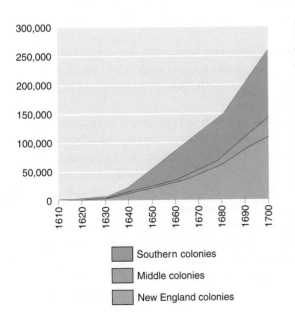

FIGURE 4.1 ■ Population of the English North American Colonies in the Seventeenth Century

The colonial population grew at a steadily accelerating rate during the seventeenth century. New England and the southern colonies each accounted for about half the total colonial population until after 1680, when growth in Pennsylvania and New York contributed to a surge in the population of the middle colonies.

☐	Southern colonies	
☐	Middle colonies	
☐	New England colonies	

How did New England society change during the seventeenth century?

What was distinctive about the middle colonies?

What was the connection between the colonies and the English empire?

Conclusion: Was there an English model of colonization in North America?

☑ **LearningCurve**
Check what you know.
bedfordstmartins.com
/roarkunderstanding

Most alarming to Puritan leaders, many of the children of the visible saints of Winthrop's generation failed to experience conversion and attain full church membership. Puritans tended to assume that sainthood was inherited—that the children of visible saints were probably also among the elect. As these children grew up during the 1640s and 1650s, however, they seldom experienced the inward transformation that signaled conversion and qualification for church membership. The problem of declining church membership and the watering-down of Puritan orthodoxy became urgent during the 1650s when the children of saints, who had grown to adulthood in New England but had not experienced conversion, began to have children themselves. Their sons and daughters—the grandchildren of the founders of the colony—could not receive the protection that baptism afforded against the terrors of death because their parents had not experienced conversion.

Puritan churches debated what to do. To allow anyone, even the child of a saint, to become a church member without conversion was an unthinkable retreat from fundamental Puritan doctrine. In 1662, a synod of Massachusetts ministers reached a compromise known as the **Halfway Covenant**. Unconverted children of saints would be permitted to become "halfway" church members. Like regular church members, they could baptize their infants. But unlike full church members, they could not participate in communion or have the voting privileges of church membership. The Halfway Covenant generated a controversy that sputtered through Puritan churches for the remainder of the century. With the Halfway Covenant, Puritan churches came to terms with the lukewarm piety that had replaced the founders' burning zeal.

Nonetheless, New England communities continued to enforce piety with holy rigor. Beginning in 1656, small bands of **Quakers**—members of the Society of Friends, as they called themselves—began to arrive in Massachusetts. Quakers believed that God spoke directly to each individual through an "inner light" and that individuals needed neither a preacher nor the Bible to discover God's Word. Maintaining that all human beings were equal in God's eyes, Quakers refused to conform to mere temporal powers such as laws and governments unless God requested otherwise. Women often took a leading role in Quaker meetings, in contrast to Puritan congregations, where women usually outnumbered men but remained subordinate.

New England communities treated Quakers with ruthless severity. Some Quakers were branded on the face "with a red-hot iron with [an] H. for heresie." When Quakers refused to leave Massachusetts, Boston officials hanged four of them between 1659 and 1661.

New Englanders' partial success in realizing the promise of a godly society ultimately undermined the intense appeal of Puritanism. In the pious Puritan communities of New England, leaders tried to eliminate sin. In the process, they diminished the sense of utter human depravity that was the wellspring of Puritanism. By 1700, New Englanders did not doubt that human beings sinned, but they were more concerned with the sins of others than with their own.

Witch trials held in Salem, Massachusetts, signaled the erosion of religious confidence and assurance. From the beginning of English settlement in the New World, more than 95 percent of all legal accusations of witchcraft occurred in New England, a hint of the Puritans' preoccupation with sin and evil. The most notorious witchcraft trials took place in Salem in 1692, when witnesses accused more

Halfway Covenant

▶ A Puritan compromise established in Massachusetts in 1662 that allowed the unconverted children of the "visible saints" to become "halfway" members of the church and to baptize their own children even though they were not full members of the church themselves.

Quakers

▶ Epithet for members of the Society of Friends. Their belief that God spoke directly to each individual through an "inner light" and that neither ministers nor the Bible was essential to discovering God's Word put them in conflict with orthodox Puritans.

CHAPTER LOCATOR | Why did the Puritans immigrate to North America?

96 CHAPTER 4
FOUNDING THE NORTHERN COLONIES

than one hundred people of witchcraft, a capital crime. Bewitched young girls shrieked in pain, their limbs twisted into strange contortions, as they pointed out the witches who tortured them. According to the trial court record, the bewitched girls declared that "the shape of [one accused witch] did oftentimes very grievously pinch them, choke them, bite them, and afflict them; urging them to write their names in a book" — the devil's book. Most of the accused witches were older women, and virtually all of them were well known to their accusers. The Salem court hanged nineteen accused witches and pressed one to death, signaling enduring belief in the supernatural origins of evil and gnawing doubt about the strength of Puritan New Englanders' faith. Why else, after all, had so many New Englanders succumbed to what their accusers and the judges believed were the temptations of Satan?

QUICK REVIEW ◁

Why did Massachusetts Puritans adopt the Halfway Covenant?

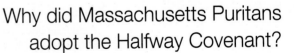

| How did New England society change during the seventeenth century? | What was distinctive about the middle colonies? | What was the connection between the colonies and the English empire? | Conclusion: Was there an English model of colonization in North America? | ☑ **LearningCurve** Check what you know. bedfordstmartins.com /roarkunderstanding |

> What was distinctive about the middle colonies?

SOUTH OF NEW ENGLAND and north of the Chesapeake, a group of middle colonies were founded in the last third of the seventeenth century. Before the 1670s, few Europeans settled in the region. For the first two-thirds of the seventeenth century, the most important European outpost in the area was the relatively small Dutch colony of New Netherland. By 1700, however, the English monarchy had seized New Netherland, renamed it New York, and encouraged the creation of a Quaker colony in Pennsylvania led by William Penn. Unlike the New England colonies, the middle colonies of New York, New Jersey, and Pennsylvania originated as land grants by the English monarch to one or more proprietors, who then possessed both the land and the extensive, almost monarchical, powers of government (**Map 4.2**). These middle colonies attracted settlers of more diverse European origins and religious faiths than were found in New England.

From New Netherland to New York

In 1609, the Dutch East India Company dispatched Henry Hudson to search for a Northwest Passage to the Orient. Hudson ventured up the large river that now bears his name until it dwindled to a stream that obviously did not lead to China. A decade later, the Dutch government granted the West India Company—a group of Dutch merchants and shippers—exclusive rights to trade with the Western Hemisphere. In 1626, Peter Minuit, the resident director of the company, purchased Manhattan Island from the Manhate Indians for trade goods worth the equivalent

CHAPTER LOCATOR | Why did the Puritans immigrate to North America?

98 CHAPTER 4 FOUNDING THE NORTHERN COLONIES

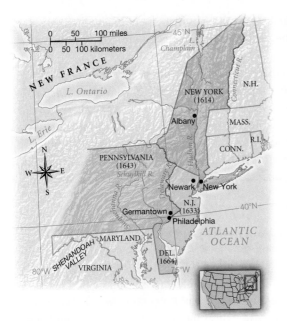

MAP 4.2 ■ **Middle Colonies in the Seventeenth Century**

For the most part, settlers in the middle colonies in the seventeenth century clustered along the Hudson and Delaware rivers. The geographic extent of the colonies shown in this map reflects land grants authorized in England. Most of this area was inhabited by Native Americans rather than colonists.

> **CHRONOLOGY**

1609
– Henry Hudson searches for a Northwest Passage.

1626
– Peter Minuit purchases Manhattan Island for the Dutch; New Amsterdam is founded.

1664
– English seize New Amsterdam and rename it New York.
– Colony of New Jersey is created.

1681
– Colony of Pennsylvania is founded.

New Netherland
▶ Dutch colony in present-day New York. New Amsterdam on Manhattan Island was its capital and colony headquarters.

of a dozen beaver pelts. New Amsterdam, the small settlement established at the southern tip of Manhattan Island, became the principal trading center in **New Netherland** and the colony's headquarters.

Unlike the English colonies, New Netherland did not attract many European immigrants. Like New England and the Chesapeake colonies, New Netherland never realized its sponsors' dreams of great profits. The company tried to stimulate immigration by granting patroonships—allotments of eighteen miles of land along the Hudson River—to wealthy stockholders who would bring fifty families to the colony and settle them as serflike tenants on their huge domains. Only one patroonship succeeded; the others failed to attract settlers, and the company eventually recovered much of the land.

Though few in number, New Netherlanders were remarkably diverse, especially compared with the homogeneous English settlers to the north and south. Religious dissenters and immigrants from Holland, Sweden, France, Germany, and elsewhere made their way to the colony. A minister of the Dutch Reformed Church complained to his superiors in Holland that several groups of Jews had recently arrived, adding to the religious mixture of "Papists, Mennonites and Lutherans among the Dutch [and] many Puritans . . . and many other atheists . . . who conceal themselves under the name of Christians."

The West India Company struggled to govern the motley colonists. Peter Stuyvesant, governor from 1647 to 1664, tried to enforce conformity to the Dutch Reformed Church, but the company declared that "the consciences of men should be free and unshackled," making a virtue of New Netherland necessity. The company never permitted the colony's settlers to form a representative government. Instead, the company appointed government officials who established policies, including taxes, that many colonists deeply resented.

In 1664, New Netherland became New York. Charles II, who became king of England in 1660 when Parliament restored the monarchy, gave his brother James, the Duke of York, an enormous grant of land that included New Netherland. The

How did New England society change during the seventeenth century?

What was distinctive about the middle colonies?

What was the connection between the colonies and the English empire?

Conclusion: Was there an English model of colonization in North America?

✓ LearningCurve
Check what you know.
bedfordstmartins.com/roarkunderstanding

99

duke quickly organized a small fleet of warships, which appeared off Manhattan Island in late summer 1664, and demanded that Stuyvesant surrender. With little choice, he did.

As the new proprietor of the colony, the Duke of York exercised almost the same unlimited authority over the colony as had the West India Company. Like the Dutch, the duke permitted "all persons of what Religion soever, quietly to inhabit . . . provided they give no disturbance to the publique peace, nor doe molest or disquiet others in the free exercise of their religion." This policy of religious toleration was less an affirmation of liberty of conscience than a recognition of the reality of the most heterogeneous colony in seventeenth-century North America.

New Jersey and Pennsylvania

The creation of New York led indirectly to the founding of two other middle colonies, New Jersey and Pennsylvania. In 1664, the Duke of York subdivided his grant and gave the portion between the Hudson and Delaware rivers to two of his friends. The proprietors of this new colony, New Jersey, quarreled and called in a prominent English Quaker, William Penn, to arbitrate their dispute. Penn eventually worked out a settlement that continued New Jersey's proprietary government. In the process, Penn became intensely interested in what he termed a "holy experiment" of establishing a genuinely Quaker colony in America.

Unlike most Quakers, William Penn came from an eminent family. Born in 1644, Penn trained for a military career, but the ideas of dissenters from the reestablished Church of England appealed to him, and he became a devout Quaker.

Despite his many run-ins with the government (he was jailed four times for his Quaker practices), Penn remained on good terms with Charles II. Partly to rid England of the troublesome Quakers, in 1681 Charles made Penn the proprietor of a new colony of some 45,000 square miles called Pennsylvania.

> Quakers in the New World

- Quakers believed in an open, generous God who made his love equally available to all people.
- Quaker leaders were ordinary men and women, not specially trained preachers; women were allowed to hold positions of religious leadership. They considered social hierarchy false and evil.
- Nearly eight thousand Quaker immigrants from England, Ireland, and Wales arrived in Pennsylvania between 1682 and 1685.
- Immigrants represented a cross section of the artisans, farmers, and laborers who predominated among English Quakers.

Toleration and Diversity in Pennsylvania

Quaker missionaries encouraged immigrants from the European continent, and many came, giving Pennsylvania greater ethnic diversity than any other English colony except New York. The Quaker colony prospered, and the capital city,

CHAPTER LOCATOR | Why did the Puritans immigrate to North America?

Philadelphia, soon rivaled New York as a center of commerce. By 1700, the city's five thousand inhabitants participated in a thriving trade exporting flour and other food products to the West Indies and importing English textiles and manufactured goods.

Penn was determined to live in peace with the Indians who inhabited the region. His Indian policy expressed his Quaker ideals and contrasted sharply with the hostile policies of the other English colonies. As he explained to the chief of the Lenni Lenape (Delaware) Indians, "God has written his law in our hearts, by which we are taught and commanded to love and help and do good to one another . . . [and] I desire to enjoy [Pennsylvania lands] with your love and consent." Penn instructed his agents to obtain the Indians' consent by purchasing their land, respecting their claims, and dealing with them fairly.

Penn declared that the first principle of government was that every settler would "enjoy the free possession of his or her faith and exercise of worship towards God." Accordingly, Pennsylvania tolerated Protestant sects of all kinds as well as Roman Catholicism. All voters and officeholders had to be Christians, but the government did not compel settlers to attend religious services, as in Massachusetts, or to pay taxes to maintain a state-supported church, as in Virginia.

Despite its toleration and diversity, Pennsylvania was as much a Quaker colony as New England was a stronghold of Puritanism. Penn had no hesitation about using civil government to enforce religious morality. One of the colony's first laws provided severe punishment for "all such offenses against God, as swearing, cursing, lying, profane talking, [and] drunkenness . . . which excite the people to rudeness, cruelty, looseness, and irreligion."

As proprietor, Penn had extensive powers subject only to review by the king. He appointed a governor, who maintained the proprietor's power to veto any laws passed by the colonial council, which was elected by property owners who possessed at least one hundred acres of land or who paid taxes. The council had the power to originate laws and administer all the affairs of government. A popularly elected assembly served as a check on the council; its members had the authority to reject or approve laws framed by the council.

Penn stressed that the exact form of government mattered less than the men who served in it. In Penn's eyes, "good men" staffed Pennsylvania's government because Quakers dominated elective and appointive offices. Quakers, of course, differed among themselves. Members of the assembly struggled to win the right to debate and amend laws, especially tax laws. They finally won the battle in 1701 when a new Charter of Privileges gave the proprietor the power to appoint the council and in turn stripped the council of all its former powers and gave them to the assembly, which became the only single-house legislature in all the English colonies.

QUICK REVIEW <

How did Quaker ideals shape
the colony of Pennsylvania?

How did New England society change during the seventeenth century?

What was distinctive about the middle colonies?

What was the connection between the colonies and the English empire?

Conclusion: Was there an English model of colonization in North America?

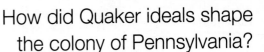

LearningCurve
Check what you know.
bedfordstmartins.com
/roarkunderstanding

What was the connection between the colonies and the English empire?

Pine Tree Shilling

In violation of English rules that forbade colonies from issuing their own currency, John Hull, a wealthy Boston merchant and shipowner, began to mint coins in 1652. Shown here is one of his pine tree shillings, both sides boldly announcing its origins. Courtesy of the Museum of the American Numismatic Association.

> CHRONOLOGY

1636–1637
– Pequot War.

1675–1676
– King Philip's War.

1686
– Dominion of New England is created.

1688
– England's Glorious Revolution.

1689–1697
– King William's War.

PROPRIETARY GRANTS TO FARAWAY lands were a cheap way for the king to reward friends. As the colonies grew, however, the grants became more valuable. After 1660, the king took initiatives to channel colonial trade through English hands and to consolidate royal authority over colonial governments. Occasioned by such economic and political considerations and triggered by King Philip's War between colonists and Native Americans, these initiatives defined the basic relationship between the colonies and England that endured until the American Revolution (**Map 4.3**).

Royal Regulation of Colonial Trade

English economic policies toward the colonies were designed to yield customs revenues for the monarchy and profitable business for English merchants and shippers. Also, the policies were intended to divert the colonies' trade from England's enemies, especially the Dutch and the French.

The Navigation Acts of 1650, 1651, 1660, and 1663 (see chapter 3) set forth two fundamental rules governing colonial trade. First, goods shipped to and from the colonies had to be transported in English ships using primarily English crews. Second, the Navigation Acts listed colonial products that could be shipped only to England or to other English colonies. While these regulations prevented Chesapeake planters from shipping their tobacco directly to the European

CHAPTER LOCATOR | Why did the Puritans immigrate to North America?

102   CHAPTER 4
FOUNDING THE NORTHERN COLONIES

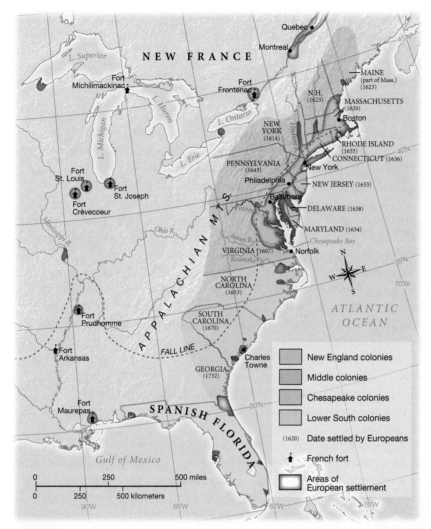

MAP 4.3 ■ **American Colonies at the End of the Seventeenth Century**

By the end of the seventeenth century, settlers inhabited a narrow band of land that stretched from Boston to Norfolk, with pockets of settlement farther south. The colonies' claims to enormous tracts of land to the west were contested by Native Americans as well as by France and Spain.

> **MAP ACTIVITY**

READING THE MAP: What geographic feature acted as the western boundary for colonial territorial claims? Which colonies were the most settled and which the least?
CONNECTIONS: The map divides the colonies into four regions. Can you think of an alternative organization? On what criteria would it be based?

continent, they interfered less with the commerce of New England and the middle colonies, whose principal exports—fish, lumber, and flour—could legally be sent directly to their most important markets in the West Indies.

By the end of the seventeenth century, colonial commerce was defined by regulations that subjected merchants and shippers to royal supervision and gave them access to markets throughout the English empire. In addition, colonial commerce received protection from the English navy. By 1700, colonial goods (including those from the West Indies) accounted for one-fifth of all English imports and for two-thirds of all goods re-exported from England to the European continent. In turn, the

How did New England society change during the seventeenth century?

What was distinctive about the middle colonies?

What was the connection between the colonies and the English empire?

Conclusion: Was there an English model of colonization in North America?

✓ **LearningCurve**
Check what you know.
bedfordstmartins.com
/roarkunderstanding

103

colonies absorbed more than one-tenth of English exports. The commercial regulations gave economic value to England's proprietorship of the American colonies.

King Philip's War and the Consolidation of Royal Authority

The monarchy also took steps to exercise greater control over colonial governments. Virginia had been a royal colony since 1624; Maryland, South Carolina, and the middle colonies were proprietary colonies with close ties to the crown. The New England colonies possessed royal charters, but they had developed their own distinctively Puritan governments. Charles II, whose father, Charles I, had been executed by Puritans in England, took a particular interest in harnessing the New England colonies more firmly to the English empire. The occasion was a royal investigation following **King Philip's War**.

A series of skirmishes in the Connecticut River valley between 1636 and 1637 culminated in the Pequot War when colonists massacred hundreds of Pequot Indians. In the decades that followed, New Englanders established relatively peaceful relations with the more potent Wampanoags, but they steadily encroached on Indian land. In 1642, a native leader urged warring tribes to band together against the English. "We [must] be one as they [the English] are," he said; "otherwise we shall be gone shortly, for . . . these English having gotten our land, they with scythes cut down the grass, and with axes fell the trees, and their cows and horses eat the grass, and their hogs spoil our clam banks, and we shall all be starved."

Such grievances accumulated until 1675, when the Wampanoags, led by their chief Metacomet (whom the colonists called King Philip), attacked English settlements in western Massachusetts. Militias from Massachusetts and other New England colonies counterattacked the Wampanoags, Nipmucks, and Narragansetts in a deadly sequence of battles that killed more than a thousand colonists and thousands more Indians. The Indians destroyed thirteen English settlements and partially burned another half dozen. Mary Rowlandson, a minister's wife in Lancaster, Massachusetts, who was captured by Indians, recalled later that it was a "solemn sight to see so many Christians lying in their blood . . . like a company of sheep torn by wolves."

By the spring of 1676, Indian warriors ranged freely within seventeen miles of Boston. The colonists finally defeated the Indians, principally with a scorched-earth policy of burning their food supplies. But King Philip's War left the New England colonists with a large war debt, a devastated frontier, and an enduring hatred of Indians. "A Swarm of Flies, they may arise, a Nation to Annoy," a colonial officer wrote in justification of destroying the Indians; "Yea Rats and Mice, or Swarms of Lice a Nation may destroy."

In 1676, an agent of the king arrived to investigate whether New England was abiding by English laws. Not surprisingly, the king's agent found all sorts of deviations from English rules, and the monarchy decided to govern New England more directly. In 1684, an

King Philip's War

▶ War begun by Metacomet (King Philip), in which the Wampanoag Indians attacked colonial settlements in western Massachusetts in 1675. Colonists responded by attacking the Wampanoags and other tribes they believed conspired with them. The colonists prevailed in the brutal war.

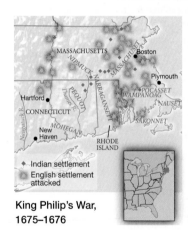

King Philip's War, 1675–1676

Indian settlement

English settlement attacked

CHAPTER LOCATOR | Why did the Puritans immigrate to North America?

CHAPTER 4

104   FOUNDING THE NORTHERN COLONIES

Wampanoag War Club This seventeenth-century war club was used to kill King Philip, according to the Anglican missionary who obtained it from Indians early in the eighteenth century. Although the tale is probably a legend, the club is certainly a seventeenth-century Wampanoag weapon that could have been used in King Philip's War. The heavy ball carved into the head of the club could deliver a fatal blow. Courtesy of the Fruitlands Museums, Harvard, Massachusetts.

English court revoked the Massachusetts charter, the foundation of the distinctive Puritan government. Two years later, in 1686, royal officials incorporated Massachusetts and the other colonies north of Maryland into the Dominion of New England. To govern the dominion, the English sent Sir Edmund Andros to Boston. Some New England merchants cooperated with Andros, but most colonists were offended by his flagrant disregard of such Puritan traditions as keeping the Sabbath. Worst of all, the Dominion of New England invalidated all land titles, confronting every landowner in New England with the horrifying prospect of losing his or her land.

Events in England, however, permitted Massachusetts colonists to overthrow Andros and retain title to their property. When Charles II died in 1685, he was succeeded by his brother James II, a zealous Catholic. James's aggressive campaign to appoint Catholics to government posts engendered such unrest that in 1688 a group of Protestant noblemen in Parliament invited the Dutch ruler William III of Orange, James's son-in-law, to claim the English throne.

When William III landed in England at the head of a large army, James fled to France, and William III and his wife, Mary II (James's daughter), became corulers in the relatively bloodless "Glorious Revolution," reasserting Protestant influence in England and its empire. Rumors of the revolution raced across the Atlantic and emboldened colonial uprisings against royal authority in Massachusetts, New York, and Maryland.

In Boston in 1689, rebels tossed Andros and other English officials in jail, destroyed the Dominion of New England, and reestablished the former charter government. New Yorkers followed the Massachusetts example. Under the leadership of Jacob Leisler, rebels seized the royal governor in 1689 and ruled the colony for more than a year. That same year in Maryland, the Protestant Association, led by John Coode, overthrew the colony's pro-Catholic government, fearing it would not recognize the new Protestant king.

But these rebel governments did not last. When King William III's governor of New York arrived in 1691, he executed Leisler for treason. Coode's men ruled Maryland until the new royal governor arrived in 1692 and ended both Coode's rebellion and Lord Baltimore's proprietary government. In Massachusetts, John

How did New England society change during the seventeenth century?

What was distinctive about the middle colonies?

What was the connection between the colonies and the English empire?

Conclusion: Was there an English model of colonization in North America?

✓ LearningCurve
Check what you know.
bedfordstmartins.com
/roarkunderstanding

105

Winthrop's city on a hill became another royal colony in 1691. The new charter said that the governor of the colony would be appointed by the king rather than elected by the colonists' representatives. But perhaps the most unsettling change was the new qualification for voting. Possession of property replaced church membership as a prerequisite for voting in colony-wide elections. Wealth replaced God's grace as the defining characteristic of Massachusetts citizenship.

Much as colonists chafed under increasing royal control, they still valued English protection from hostile neighbors. Colonists worried that the Catholic colony of New France to the north menaced frontier regions by encouraging Indian raids and by competing for the lucrative fur trade. Although French leaders tried to buttress the military strength of New France during the last third of the seventeenth century to block the expansion of the English colonies, most of the military efforts mustered by New France focused on defending against attacks by the powerful Iroquois. However, when the English colonies were distracted by the Glorious Revolution, French forces from the fur-trading regions along the Great Lakes and in Canada attacked villages in New England and New York. Known as King William's War, the conflict with the French was a colonial outgrowth of William's war against France in Europe. The war dragged on from 1689 until 1697 and ended inconclusively in both Europe and the colonies. But it made clear to many colonists that along with English royal government came a welcome measure of military security.

> **QUICK REVIEW**

Why did the Glorious Revolution in England lead to uprisings in the American colonies?

Conclusion: Was there an English model of colonization in North America?

BY 1700, THE NORTHERN ENGLISH colonies of North America had developed along lines quite different from the example set by their southern counterparts. Emigrants came with their families and created settlements unlike the scattered plantations and largely male environment of early Virginia. Puritans in New England built towns and governments around their churches and placed worship of God, not tobacco, at the center of their society. They depended chiefly on the labor of family members rather than on that of servants and slaves.

The convictions of Puritanism that motivated John Winthrop and others to reinvent England in the colonies became muted, however, as New England matured and dissenters such as Roger Williams multiplied. Catholics, Quakers, Anglicans (members of the Church of England), Jews, and others settled in the middle and southern colonies, creating considerable religious toleration, especially in Pennsylvania and New York. At the same time, northern colonists, like their southern counterparts, developed an ever-increasing need for land that inevitably led to bloody conflict with the Indians who were displaced. By the closing years of the seventeenth century, the royal government in England intervened to try to moderate those conflicts and to govern the colonies more directly for the benefit of the monarchy. Assertions of royal control triggered colonial resistance that was ultimately suppressed, resulting in Massachusetts losing its special charter status and becoming a royal colony much like the other English North American colonies.

During the next century, the English colonial world would undergo surprising new developments built on the achievements of the seventeenth century. Immigrants from Scotland, Ireland, and Germany streamed into North America, and unprecedented numbers of African slaves poured into the southern colonies. On average, white colonists attained a relatively comfortable standard of living, especially compared with most people in England and continental Europe. While religion remained important, the intensity of religious concern that characterized the seventeenth century waned during the eighteenth century. Colonists worried more about prosperity than about providence, and their societies grew increasingly secular, worldly, and diverse.

How did New England society change during the seventeenth century? | What was distinctive about the middle colonies? | What was the connection between the colonies and the English empire? | Conclusion: Was there an English model of colonization in North America? | ✓ LearningCurve Check what you know. bedfordstmartins.com /roarkunderstanding

107

CHAPTER 4 STUDY GUIDE

STEP 1 GET STARTED ONLINE

☑ LearningCurve ■ bedfordstmartins.com/roarkunderstanding
Now that you've read the chapter, make it stick by completing the LearningCurve activity.

STEP 2 EXPLAIN WHY IT MATTERS

Put your reading into practice. Identify each term below, and then explain why it matters in U.S. history.

TERM	WHO OR WHAT & WHEN	WHY IT MATTERS
Puritans (p. 84)		
English Reformation (p. 84)		
Separatists (p. 86)		
Calvinism (p. 90)		
predestination (p. 90)		
visible saints (p. 90)		
antinomians (p. 93)		
Puritan Revolution (p. 94)		
Halfway Covenant (p. 96)		
Quakers (p. 96)		
New Netherland (p. 99)		
King Philip's War (p. 104)		

STEP 3 MOVE BEYOND THE BASICS

To demonstrate a more advanced understanding, compare and contrast the northern colonies—why they were settled, sociopolitical structures, and economic organization.

Colony	Reasons for settlement	Social/political structures (religion, family, legal system)	Economics (land use and distribution, industry, income, labor)
Plymouth			
Massachusetts Bay			
Rhode Island			
New Netherland/ New York			
Pennsylvania			

PUT IT ALL TOGETHER

Now, take a step back and try to explain the big picture. Remember to use specific examples from the chapter in your answers.

NEW ENGLAND

▶ What kind of society did the early settlers of New England hope to create?

▶ What forces challenged Puritan domination of New England?

THE MIDDLE COLONIES

▶ How did the settlement of the middle colonies differ from that of New England?

▶ What explains the religious and ethnic diversity of the middle colonies?

THE EMPIRE

▶ How did the English crown seek to regulate colonial trade?

▶ How did the colonists respond to the English crown's efforts to assert political authority?

LOOKING BACKWARD, LOOKING AHEAD

▶ How did European colonization of the Americas in the seventeenth century differ from Spanish colonization in the previous century?

▶ How did the growth and development of English colonies in the seventeenth century set the stage for conflict between England and its colonies in the eighteenth century?

> ## IN YOUR OWN WORDS

Imagine that you must give an oral report to the class answering the following question: **How did religious dissidents from England come to establish colonies in northern North America?** What would be the most important points to include and why?

 Do it online at the Student Site ▪ bedfordstmartins.com/roarkunderstanding

5

THE CHANGING WORLD OF COLONIAL AMERICA

1701–1770

> **What were the most important changes in colonial North America between 1701 and 1770?** Chapter 5 examines the factors that resulted in regional differences in colonial North America, as well as the common experiences, assumptions, and attitudes that contributed to a growing sense of unity among British American colonists. These unifying trends helped prepare the foundation for what would become the United States of America in 1776.

LearningCurve

bedfordstmartins.com/roarkunderstanding
After reading the chapter, use LearningCurve to retain what you've read.

> How did the North American colonies change in the eighteenth century?

> What changed in New England life and culture?

> What spurred the growth of the middle colonies?

> Why did slavery become the defining feature of the southern colonies?

> What experiences tended to unify the colonists in British North America during the eighteenth century?

> Conclusion: What was the dual identity of British North American colonists?

Chandler wedding tapestry. New England, artist unknown, 1756. Courtesy, American Antiquarian Society.

How did the North American colonies change in the eighteenth century?

New York City Street This painting depicts John Street, a residential neighborhood of New York City, in 1768, as recalled by the artist Joseph B. Smith in the early nineteenth century. Notice that fences separate house yards from the street, rather than houses from one another, hinting of friendly relations among neighbors. Old John Street United Methodist Church.

THE MOST IMPORTANT FACT about eighteenth-century British America is its phenomenal population growth: from about 250,000 in 1700 to over two million by 1770. The eightfold growth of the colonial population signaled the maturation of a distinctive colonial society. Colonists of different ethnic groups, races, and religions lived in varied environments under thirteen different colonial governments, all of them part of the British empire.

In general, the growth and diversity of the eighteenth-century colonial population derived from two sources: immigration and **natural increase** (growth through reproduction). Natural increase contributed about three-fourths of the population growth, immigration about one-fourth. Immigration shifted the ethnic and racial balance among the colonists, making them by 1770 less English and less white than ever before. Fewer than 10 percent of eighteenth-century immigrants came from England; about 36 percent were Scots-Irish, mostly from northern Ireland; 33 percent arrived from Africa, almost all of them slaves; nearly 15 percent had emigrated from the many German-language principalities (the nation of Germany did not exist until 1871); and almost 10 percent came from Scotland. In 1670, more than 9 out of 10 colonists were of English ancestry, and only 1 out of 25 was of African ancestry. By 1770, only about half of the colonists were of English descent, while more than 20 percent descended from Africans. Thus, by 1770, the people of the colonies had a distinctive colonial—rather than English—profile (**Map 5.1**).

natural increase

▶ The growth of population through reproduction, as opposed to immigration. In the eighteenth century, natural increase accounted for about three-fourths of the American colonies' population growth.

CHAPTER LOCATOR | How did the North American colonies change in the eighteenth century? | What changed in New England life and culture?

112 CHAPTER 5 THE CHANGING WORLD OF COLONIAL AMERICA

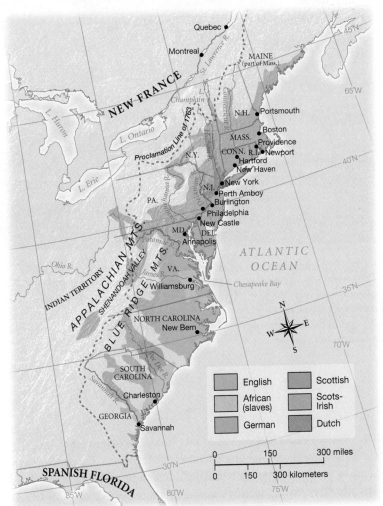

In 1770
- Colonial population had grown to two million, compared with 250,000 in 1700.
- About half of American colonists were of English descent, while more than 20 percent were of African descent.

MAP 5.1 ■ Europeans and Africans in the Eighteenth Century

This map illustrates regions where Africans and certain immigrant groups clustered. It is important to avoid misreading the map. Predominantly English and German regions, for example, also contained colonists from other places. Likewise, regions where African slaves resided in large numbers also included many whites, slave masters among them. The map suggests the diversity of eighteenth-century colonial society.

The booming population of the colonies hints at a second major feature of eighteenth-century colonial society: an expanding economy. The nearly limitless wilderness stretching westward made land relatively cheap compared with its price in the Old World. The abundance of land made labor precious, and the colonists always needed more. The insatiable demand for labor was the fundamental economic environment that sustained the mushrooming population. Economic historians estimate that free colonists (those who were not indentured servants or slaves) had a higher standard of living than the majority of people elsewhere in the Atlantic world.

QUICK REVIEW

How did the North American colonies achieve the remarkable population growth of the eighteenth century?

| What spurred the growth of the middle colonies? | Why did slavery become the defining feature of the southern colonies? | What experiences tended to unify colonists in British North America? | Conclusion: What was the dual identity of British North American colonists? | ✓ LearningCurve Check what you know. bedfordstmartins.com /roarkunderstanding |

What changed in New England life and culture?

Boston Common in Needlework

Hannah Otis embroidered this exquisite needlework portrait of Boston Common in 1750, when she was eighteen years old. From the perspective of the twenty-first century, the scene gives few hints of city life. Otis populated the cityscape with more animals than people and more plants than paving stones. What features of this portrait would suggest a city to an eighteenth-century viewer? Photograph © 2012 Museum of Fine Arts, Boston.

> KEY FACTORS

In 1770
- New England's growth lagged behind that of other colonies.
- Governments in New England stopped granting land to towns.
- New England colonists had only one-fourth as much wealth per capita as free colonists in the South.
- Fish accounted for more than a third of New England's exports.
- The richest 5 percent of Bostonians owned about half the city's wealth.
- The poorest two-thirds of Bostonians owned less than 10 percent of the city's wealth.
- New England's population was 97 percent white.

THE NEW ENGLAND POPULATION grew sixfold during the eighteenth century but lagged behind the growth in the other colonies. Most immigrants chose other destinations because of New England's relatively densely settled land and because Puritan orthodoxy made these colonies comparatively inhospitable to those of other faiths and those indifferent to religion. As the population grew, many settlers in search of farmland dispersed from towns, and Puritan communities lost much of their cohesion. Nonetheless, networks of economic exchange laced New Englanders to their neighbors, to Boston merchants, and to the broad currents of Atlantic commerce. In many ways, trade became a faith that competed strongly with the traditions of Puritanism.

Natural Increase and Land Distribution

New England's population grew mostly by natural increase, much as it had during the seventeenth century. The perils of childbirth gave wives a shorter life expectancy than husbands, but wives often lived to have six, seven, or eight babies. The growing New England population pressed against a limited amount of land (see Map 5.1). Moreover, as the northernmost group of British colonies, New England had contested frontiers where powerful Native Americans, especially the Iroquois and Mahicans, jealously guarded their territory. The French (and Catholic) colony of New France also menaced the British (and mostly Protestant) New England colonies when provoked by colonial or European disputes.

CHAPTER LOCATOR | How did the North American colonies change in the eighteenth century? | What changed in New England life and culture?

114   CHAPTER 5   THE CHANGING WORLD OF COLONIAL AMERICA

During the seventeenth century, New England towns parceled out land to individual families. In most cases, the original settlers practiced **partible inheritance**—that is, they subdivided land more or less equally among sons. By the eighteenth century, the original land allotments had to be further subdivided, and many plots of land became too small to support a family. Sons who could not hope to inherit sufficient land had to move away from the town where they were born.

During the eighteenth century, colonial governments in New England abandoned the seventeenth-century policy of granting land to towns. Needing revenue, the governments of both Connecticut and Massachusetts sold land directly to individuals, including speculators. Now money, rather than membership in a community bound by a church covenant, determined whether a person could obtain land. The new land policy eroded the seventeenth-century pattern of settlement. As colonists spread north and west, they tended to settle on individual farms rather than in the towns and villages that characterized the seventeenth century. Far more than in the seventeenth century, eighteenth-century New Englanders regulated their behavior by their own individual choices.

partible inheritance

▶ A system of inheritance in which land was divided equally among sons. By the eighteenth century, this practice in Massachusetts had subdivided plots of land into units too small for subsistence, forcing children to move away to find sufficient farmland.

Farms, Fish, and Atlantic Trade

A New England farm was a place to get by, not to get rich. New England farmers grew food for their families, but their fields did not produce huge marketable surpluses. Instead of one big crop, a farmer grew many small ones. If farmers had extra, they sold to or traded with neighbors. Poor roads made travel difficult, time-consuming, and expensive, especially with bulky and heavy agricultural goods. The one major agricultural product the New England colonies exported—livestock—walked to market on its own legs. By 1770, New Englanders had only one-fourth as much wealth per capita as free colonists in the southern colonies.

As consumers, New England farmers participated in a diversified commercial economy that linked remote farms to markets throughout the Atlantic world. Merchants large and small stocked imported goods—British textiles, ceramics, and metal goods; Chinese tea; West Indian sugar; and Chesapeake tobacco. Farmers' needs supported local shoemakers, tailors, wheelwrights, and carpenters. Larger towns, especially Boston, housed skilled tradesmen such as cabinetmakers, silversmiths, and printers. Shipbuilders were among the many New Englanders who made their fortunes at sea.

Fish accounted for more than a third of New England's eighteenth-century exports; livestock and timber made up another third. The West Indies absorbed two-thirds of all New England's exports. Almost all the rest of New England's exports went to Britain and continental Europe (**Map 5.2**). This Atlantic commerce benefited the entire New England economy, providing jobs for laborers and tradesmen as well as for ship captains, clerks, merchants, and sailors.

Merchants dominated Atlantic commerce. The largest and most successful New England merchants lived in Boston at the hub of trade between local folk and the international market. The magnificence of a wealthy Boston merchant's home

| What spurred the growth of the middle colonies? | Why did slavery become the defining feature of the southern colonies? | What experiences tended to unify colonists in British North America? | Conclusion: What was the dual identity of British North American colonists? | ✓ **LearningCurve** Check what you know. bedfordstmartins.com /roarkunderstanding |

115

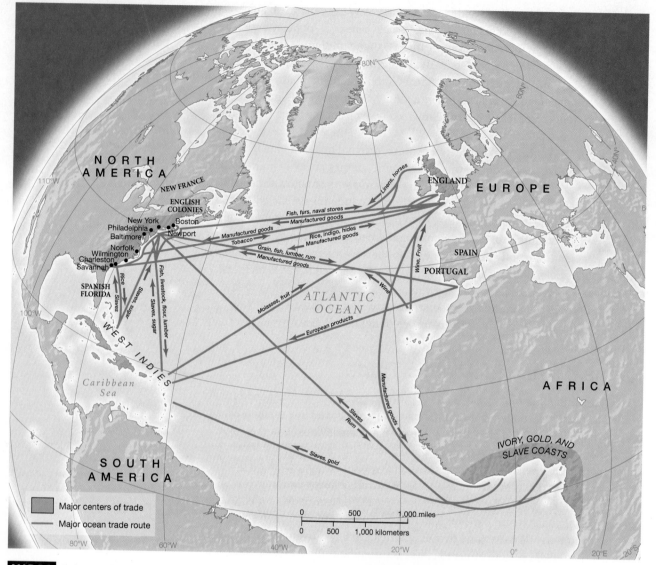

MAP 5.2 ■ Atlantic Trade in the Eighteenth Century

This map illustrates the economic outlook of the colonies in the eighteenth century—east toward the Atlantic world rather than west toward the interior of North America. The long distances involved in the Atlantic trade and the uncertainties of ocean travel suggest the difficulties Britain experienced governing the colonies and regulating colonial commerce.

> MAP ACTIVITY

READING THE MAP: What were the major markets for trade coming out of Europe? What goods did the British colonies import and export?

CONNECTIONS: In what ways did the flow of raw materials from the colonies affect British industry? How did British colonial trade policies influence the Atlantic trade?

CHAPTER LOCATOR | How did the North American colonies change in the eighteenth century? | What changed in New England life and culture?

116 CHAPTER 5
THE CHANGING WORLD OF COLONIAL AMERICA

stunned John Adams, who termed it a house that seemed fit "for a noble Man, a Prince." Such luxurious Boston homes contrasted with the modest dwellings of Adams and other New Englanders, a measure of the polarization of wealth that developed in Boston and other seaports during the eighteenth century.

By 1770, the richest 5 percent of Bostonians owned about half the city's wealth; the poorest two-thirds of the population owned less than one-tenth. Still, the incidence of genuine poverty did not change much. About 5 percent of New Englanders qualified for poor relief throughout the eighteenth century. Overall, colonists were better off than most people in England.

New England was more homogeneously English than any other colonial region. People of African ancestry (almost all of them slaves) numbered more than fifteen thousand by 1770, but they barely diversified the region's 97 percent white majority. Most New Englanders had little use for slaves on their family farms. Instead, the few slaves concentrated in towns, especially Boston, where most of them worked as domestic servants and laborers.

By 1770, the population, wealth, and commercial activity of New England differed from what they had been in 1700. Ministers still enjoyed high status, but Yankee traders had replaced Puritan saints as the symbolic New Englanders. Atlantic commerce competed with religious convictions in ordering New Englanders' daily lives.

QUICK REVIEW <

Why did settlement patterns in New England change from the seventeenth to the eighteenth century?

| What spurred the growth of the middle colonies? | Why did slavery become the defining feature of the southern colonies? | What experiences tended to unify colonists in British North America? | Conclusion: What was the dual identity of British North American colonists? | ☑ LearningCurve Check what you know. bedfordstmartins.com /roarkunderstanding |

> What spurred the growth of the middle colonies?

Bethlehem, Pennsylvania

This view of Bethlehem, Pennsylvania, in 1757 dramatizes the profound transformation of the natural landscape humans wrought in the eighteenth century by highly motivated human labor. Founded by Moravian immigrants in 1740, in less than twenty years Bethlehem featured precisely laid-out orchards and fields in place of forests and glades. By carefully penning their livestock (lower center right) and fencing their fields (lower left), farmers safeguarded their livelihoods from the risks and disorders of untamed nature. Individual farmsteads (lower center) and brick town buildings (upper center) integrated the bounty of the land with community life. Few eighteenth-century communities were as orderly as Bethlehem, but many effected a comparable transformation of the environment. Print Collection, Miriam and Ira D. Wallack Division of Art, Prints, and Photographs, The New York Public Library. Astor, Lenox, and Tilden Foundations.

> VISUAL ACTIVITY

READING THE IMAGE: What does this painting indicate about the colonists' priorities?

CONNECTIONS: Why might Pennsylvanians have been so concerned about maintaining order?

IN 1700, THE MIDDLE COLONIES of Pennsylvania, New York, New Jersey, and Delaware had only half the population of New England. But by 1770, the population of the middle colonies had multiplied tenfold and nearly equaled the population of New England. Immigrants—mainly German, Irish, and Scottish—made the middle colonies a uniquely diverse society. By 1800, barely one-third of Pennsylvanians and less than half the total population of the middle colonies traced their ancestry to England. New white settlers, both free and in servitude, poured into the middle colonies because they perceived unparalleled opportunities.

German and Scots-Irish Immigrants

Germans made up the largest contingent of migrants from the European continent to the middle colonies. By 1770, about 85,000 Germans had arrived in the colonies. Their fellow colonists often referred to them as **Pennsylvania Dutch**, an English corruption of *Deutsch*, the word the immigrants used to describe themselves.

Pennsylvania Dutch

▶ The name given by other colonists to German immigrants to the middle colonies; an English corruption of the German term *Deutsch*. Germans made up the largest contingent of migrants from continental Europe to the middle colonies in the eighteenth century.

CHAPTER LOCATOR | How did the North American colonies change in the eighteenth century? | What changed in New England life and culture?

118 CHAPTER 5 THE CHANGING WORLD OF COLONIAL AMERICA

Most German immigrants came from what is now southwestern Germany, where, one observer noted, peasants were "not as well off as cattle elsewhere." German immigrants included numerous artisans and a few merchants, but the great majority were farmers and laborers. Economically, they represented "middling folk," neither the poorest (who could not afford the trip) nor the better-off (who did not want to leave).

By the 1720s, Germans who had established themselves in the colonies wrote back to their friends and relatives, as one reported, "of the civil and religious liberties [and] privileges, and of all the goodness I have heard and seen." Such letters prompted still more Germans to pull up stakes and embark for the middle colonies.

Similar motives propelled the **Scots-Irish**, who considerably outnumbered German immigrants. The "Scots-Irish" actually hailed from northern Ireland, Scotland, and northern England. Like the Germans, the Scots-Irish were Protestants, but with a difference. Most German immigrants worshipped in Lutheran or German Reformed churches; many others belonged to dissenting sects such as the Mennonites, Moravians, and Amish, whose adherents sought relief from the persecution they had suffered in Europe for their refusal to bear arms and to swear oaths, practices they shared with the Quakers. By contrast, the Scots-Irish tended to be militant Presbyterians who seldom hesitated to bear arms or swear oaths. Like German settlers, however, Scots-Irish immigrants were clannish, residing when they could among relatives or neighbors from the old country.

In the eighteenth century, wave after wave of Scots-Irish immigrants arrived, culminating in a flood of immigration in the years just before the American Revolution. Deteriorating economic conditions in northern Ireland, Scotland, and England pushed many toward America. Most of the immigrants were farm laborers or tenant farmers fleeing droughts, crop failures, high food prices, or rising rents. They came, they told British officials, because of "poverty," the "tyranny of landlords," and their desire to "do better in America."

Both Scots-Irish and Germans probably heard the common saying "Pennsylvania is heaven for farmers [and] paradise for artisans," but they almost certainly did not fully understand the risks of their decision to leave their native lands. Ship captains, aware of the hunger for labor in the colonies, eagerly signed up the penniless German emigrants as **redemptioners**, a variant of indentured servants. A captain would agree to provide transportation to Philadelphia, where redemptioners would obtain the money to pay for their passage by borrowing it from a friend or relative who was already in the colonies or, as most did, by selling themselves as servants. Many redemptioners traveled in family groups, unlike impoverished Scots-Irish emigrants, who usually traveled alone and paid for their passage by contracting as indentured servants before they sailed to the colonies.

Redemptioners and indentured servants were packed aboard ships "as closely as herring," one migrant observed. Seasickness compounded by exhaustion, poverty, poor food, bad water, inadequate sanitation, and tight quarters encouraged the spread of disease. Unlike indentured servants, redemptioners negotiated independently with their purchasers about their period of servitude. Typically, a healthy adult redemptioner agreed to four years of labor. Indentured servants commonly served five, six, or seven years.

> **CHRONOLOGY**

1733
- Benjamin Franklin begins publication of *Poor Richard's Almanack*.

1770
- The population of the colonies of Pennsylvania, New York, New Jersey, and Delaware has increased tenfold since 1700, largely the result of immigration.
- Germans make up the largest percentage of migrants from the European continent.
- The middle colonies' per capita consumption of imported goods from Britain has more than doubled since 1720.

Scots-Irish
▶ Protestant immigrants from northern Ireland, Scotland, and northern England. Deteriorating economic conditions in their European homelands contributed to increasing migration to the colonies in the eighteenth century.

redemptioners
▶ A kind of indentured servant. In this system, a captain agreed to provide passage to Philadelphia, where redemptioners would obtain money to pay for their transportation, usually by selling themselves as a servant.

| What spurred the growth of the middle colonies? | Why did slavery become the defining feature of the southern colonies? | What experiences tended to unify colonists in British North America? | Conclusion: What was the dual identity of British North American colonists? | ✓ LearningCurve Check what you know. bedfordstmartins.com /roarkunderstanding |

119

"God Gives All Things to Industry": Urban and Rural Labor

An indentured servant in 1743 wrote that Pennsylvania was "the best poor Man's Country in the World." Although the servant reported that "the Condition of bought Servants is very hard" and that masters often failed to live up to their promise to provide decent food and clothing, opportunity abounded in the middle colonies because there was more work to be done than workers to do it.

Most servants toiled in Philadelphia, New York City, or one of the smaller towns or villages. Artisans, small manufacturers, and shopkeepers prized the labor of male servants. Female servants made valuable additions to households, where nearly all of them cleaned, washed, cooked, or minded children. From the masters' viewpoint, servants were a bargain. A master could purchase five or six years of a servant's labor for approximately the wages a common laborer would earn in four months.

Since a slave cost at least three times as much as a servant, only affluent colonists could afford the long-term investment in slave labor. Most farmers in the middle colonies used family labor, not slaves. Wheat, the most widely grown crop, did not require more labor than farmers could typically muster from relatives, neighbors, and a hired hand or two. Consequently, although people of African ancestry (almost all slaves) increased to more than thirty thousand in the middle colonies by 1770, they accounted for only about 7 percent of the total population and much less outside the cities.

Most slaves came to the middle colonies and New England after a stopover in the West Indies. Very few came directly from Africa. Slaves—unlike servants—could not charge masters with violating the terms of their contracts. A master's commands, not a written contract, set the terms of a slave's bondage. Small numbers of slaves managed to obtain their freedom, but no African Americans escaped whites' firm convictions about black inferiority.

Whites' racism and blacks' lowly social status made African Americans scapegoats for European Americans' suspicions and anxieties. In 1741, when arson and several unexplained thefts plagued New York City, officials suspected a murderous slave conspiracy and executed thirty-one slaves. Although slaves were certifiably impoverished, they were not among the poor for whom the middle colonies were reputed to be the best country in the world.

Immigrants swarmed to the middle colonies because of the availability of land. The Penn family (see chapter 4) encouraged immigration to bring in potential buyers for their enormous tracts of land in Pennsylvania. From the beginning, Pennsylvania followed a policy of negotiating with Indian tribes to purchase additional land. This policy reduced the violent frontier clashes more common elsewhere in the colonies. Few colonists drifted beyond the northern boundaries of Pennsylvania. Owners of the huge estates in New York's Hudson valley preferred to rent rather than sell their land, and therefore they attracted fewer immigrants. The Iroquois Indians dominated the lucrative fur trade of the St. Lawrence valley and eastern Great Lakes, and they vigorously defended their territory from colonial encroachment, causing most settlers to prefer the comparatively safe environs of Pennsylvania.

CHAPTER LOCATOR | How did the North American colonies change in the eighteenth century? | What changed in New England life and culture?

120 CHAPTER 5
THE CHANGING WORLD OF COLONIAL AMERICA

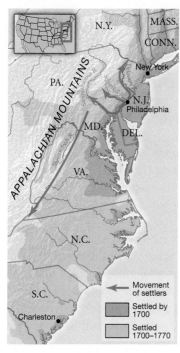

Patterns of Settlement, 1700–1770

Since the cheapest land always lay at the margin of settlement, would-be farmers tended to migrate to promising areas just beyond already improved farms. By midcentury, settlement had reached the eastern slopes of the Appalachian Mountains, and newcomers spilled south down the fertile valley of the Shenandoah River into western Virginia and the Carolinas. Thousands of settlers migrated from the middle colonies through this back door to the South.

Farmers made the middle colonies the breadbasket of North America. They planted a wide variety of crops to feed their families, but they grew wheat in abundance. Flour milling was the number one industry and flour the number one export, constituting nearly three-fourths of all exports from the middle colonies. Because farmers profited from the grain market in the Atlantic world with the steady rise of grain prices after 1720, the standard of living in rural Pennsylvania was probably higher than in any other agricultural region of the eighteenth-century world. The comparatively widespread prosperity of all the middle colonies permitted residents to indulge in a half-century shopping spree for British imports. The middle colonies' per capita consumption of imported goods from Britain more than doubled between 1720 and 1770, far outstripping the per capita consumption of British goods in New England and the southern colonies.

Marten Van Bergen Farm

This detail from a rare 1730s painting depicts the home of Marten and Catarina Van Bergen, prosperous Dutch colonists in New York's Hudson valley. The full-size painting, commissioned by the Van Bergens to hang over their fireplace mantel, is a panorama portraying the farm as a peaceable, small-scale kingdom governed by the couple and populated by their seven children, their slaves and indentured servants, and neighboring Native Americans. Rather than a place of fields and crops, which are absent from the painting, the farm is the locus of a happy, orderly family. Copyright © New York State Historical Association, Cooperstown, NY.

What spurred the growth of the middle colonies?

Why did slavery become the defining feature of the southern colonies?

What experiences tended to unify colonists in British North America?

Conclusion: What was the dual identity of British North American colonists?

✓ LearningCurve
Check what you know.
bedfordstmartins.com/roarkunderstanding

Philadelphia stood at the crossroads of trade in wheat exports and British imports. Merchants occupied the top stratum of Philadelphia society. In a city where only 2 percent of the residents owned enough property to qualify to vote, merchants built grand homes and dominated local government. Many of Philadelphia's wealthiest merchants were Quakers. Quaker traits of industry, thrift, honesty, and sobriety encouraged the accumulation of wealth.

The lower ranks of merchants included aspiring tradesmen such as Benjamin Franklin. In 1733, Benjamin Franklin began to publish *Poor Richard's Almanack*, which preached the likelihood of long-term rewards for tireless labor and quickly became Franklin's most profitable product. The popularity of *Poor Richard's Almanack* suggests that many Pennsylvanians thought less about the pearly gates of heaven than about their pocketbooks. Poor Richard's advice that "God gives all Things to Industry" might be considered the motto for the middle colonies. The promise of a worldly payoff made work a secular faith. Quakers remained influential, but Franklin spoke for most colonists with his aphorisms of work, discipline, and thrift that celebrated the spark of ambition and the promise of gain.

> **QUICK REVIEW**

Why did immigrants flood into Pennsylvania during the eighteenth century?

CHAPTER LOCATOR | How did the North American colonies change in the eighteenth century? | What changed in New England life and culture?

CHAPTER 5
122   THE CHANGING WORLD OF COLONIAL AMERICA

Charleston Harbor
This 1730s painting of Charleston, South Carolina, depicts the intersecting currents of international trade and local commerce in the variety of vessels conveying goods and people between ship and shore. More African slaves arrived in Charleston than in any other North American port, yet no slaves appear in this painting. Colonial Williamsburg Foundation.

BETWEEN 1700 AND 1770, the population of the southern colonies of Virginia, Maryland, North Carolina, South Carolina, and Georgia grew almost ninefold. By 1770, about twice as many people lived in the South as in either the middle colonies or New England. As elsewhere, natural increase and immigration accounted for the rapid population growth. Many Scots-Irish and German immigrants funneled from the middle colonies into the southern backcountry. Other immigrants were indentured servants (mostly English and Scots-Irish). But slaves made the most striking contribution to the booming southern colonies, transforming the racial composition of the population. Slavery became the defining characteristic of the southern colonies during the eighteenth century, shaping the region's economy, society, and politics.

The Atlantic Slave Trade and the Growth of Slavery

The number of southerners of African ancestry (nearly all of them slaves) rocketed from just over 20,000 in 1700 to well over 400,000 in 1770. The black population increased nearly three times faster than the South's briskly growing white population. Consequently, the proportion of southerners of African ancestry grew from 20 percent in 1700 to 40 percent in 1770.

Southern colonists clustered into two distinct geographic and agricultural zones. The colonies in the upper South, surrounding the Chesapeake Bay, specialized in growing tobacco, as they had since the early seventeenth century. Throughout the eighteenth century, nine out of ten southern whites and eight out

> CHRONOLOGY

1711
– North Carolina is founded.

1732
– Georgia is founded.

1739
– Stono Rebellion, an uprising by slaves in South Carolina.

1770
– The southern colonies supply 90 percent of all North American exports to Britain.

What spurred the growth of the middle colonies? | **Why did slavery become the defining feature of the southern colonies?** | What experiences tended to unify colonists in British North America? | Conclusion: What was the dual identity of British North American colonists? | ✓ LearningCurve Check what you know. bedfordstmartins.com /roarkunderstanding

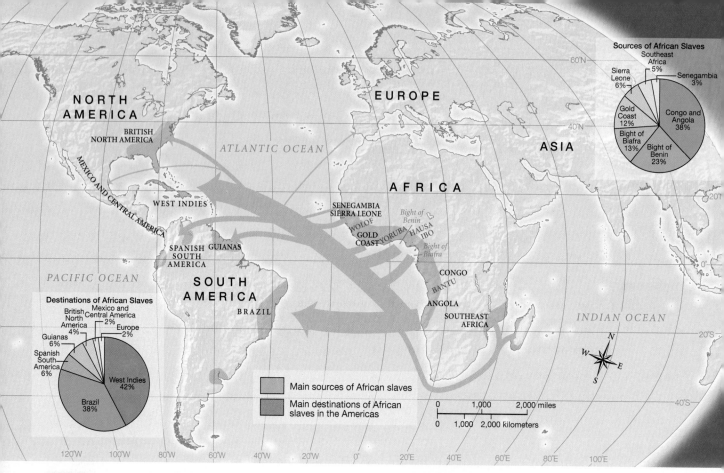

MAP 5.3 ■ The Atlantic Slave Trade

Although the Atlantic slave trade lasted from about 1450 to 1870, it peaked during the eighteenth century, when more than six million African slaves were imported to the New World. Only a small fraction of these slaves were taken to British North America. Most went to sugar plantations in Brazil and the Caribbean.

> **MAP ACTIVITY**

READING THE MAP: Where in Africa did most slaves originate? Approximately how far was the trip from the busiest ports of origin to the two most common New World destinations?

CONNECTIONS: Why were so many more African slaves sent to the West Indies and Brazil than to British North America?

---

of ten southern blacks lived in the Chesapeake region. The upper South retained a white majority during the eighteenth century.

In the lower South, a much smaller cluster of colonists inhabited the coastal region and specialized in the production of rice and indigo (a plant used to make blue dye). Lower South colonists made up only 5 percent of the total population of the southern colonies in 1700 but inched upward to 15 percent by 1770. South Carolina was the sole British colony along the southern Atlantic coast until 1732. (North Carolina, founded in 1711, was largely an extension of the Chesapeake region.) Georgia was founded in 1732 as a refuge for poor people from England. Georgia's leaders banned slaves from 1735 to 1750, but few settlers arrived until after 1750, when the prohibition on slavery was lifted and slaves flooded in. In South Carolina, in contrast to Georgia and every other British mainland colony, slaves outnumbered whites almost two to one; in some low-country districts, the ratio of blacks to whites exceeded ten to one.

CHAPTER LOCATOR | How did the North American colonies change in the eighteenth century? | What changed in New England life and culture?

124 CHAPTER 5
THE CHANGING WORLD OF COLONIAL AMERICA

TABLE 5.1 ■ Slave Imports, 1451–1870

Estimated Slave Imports to the Western Hemisphere	
1451–1600	275,000
1601–1700	1,341,000
1701–1810	6,100,000
1811–1870	1,900,000

The enormous growth in the South's slave population occurred through natural increase and the flourishing Atlantic slave trade (**Map 5.3** and **Table 5.1**). Slave ships brought almost 300,000 Africans to British North America between 1619 and 1780. Of these Africans, 95 percent arrived in the South and 96 percent arrived during the eighteenth century. Unlike indentured servants and redemptioners, these Africans did not choose to come to the colonies. Most of them had been born into free families in villages located within a few hundred miles of the West African coast.

Although they shared African origins, they came from many different cultures. They spoke different languages, worshipped different deities, observed different rules of kinship, grew different crops, and recognized different rulers. The most important experience they had in common was enslavement.

Captured in war, kidnapped, or sold into slavery by other Africans, they were brought to the coast, sold to African traders who assembled slaves for resale, and sold again to European or colonial slave traders or ship captains, who packed two hundred to three hundred or more aboard ships that carried them on the **Middle Passage** across the Atlantic and then sold them yet again to colonial slave merchants or southern planters.

Olaudah Equiano published an account of his enslavement that hints at the common experiences of millions of other Africans swept up in the slave trade. When he was eleven years old, Equiano was kidnapped by Africans in what is now Nigeria, who sold him to other Africans, who in turn eventually sold him to a slave ship on the coast. Equiano feared that he was "going to be killed" and "eaten by those white men with horrible looks, red faces, and loose hair." Once the ship set sail, many of the slaves, crowded together in suffocating heat fouled by filth of all descriptions, died from sickness. "The shrieks of the women and the groans of the dying rendered the whole a scene of horror almost inconceivable," Equiano recalled. Most of the slaves on the ship were sold in Barbados, but Equiano and some others were shipped off to Virginia, where he "saw few or none of our native Africans and not one soul who could talk to me." Equiano felt isolated and "exceedingly miserable"

Middle Passage

▶ The crossing of the Atlantic by slave ships traveling from West Africa to the Americas. Slaves were crowded together in extremely unhealthful circumstances, and mortality rates were high.

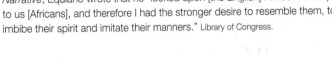

Olaudah Equiano

Created after he had bought his freedom, this portrait evokes Equiano's successful acculturation to eighteenth-century English customs. In his *Interesting Narrative*, Equiano wrote that he "looked upon [the English] . . . as men superior to us [Africans], and therefore I had the stronger desire to resemble them, to imbibe their spirit and imitate their manners." Library of Congress.

What spurred the growth of the middle colonies?	Why did slavery become the defining feature of the southern colonies?	What experiences tended to unify colonists in British North America?	Conclusion: What was the dual identity of British North American colonists?	✓ LearningCurve Check what you know. bedfordstmartins.com /roarkunderstanding

because he "had no person to speak to that I could understand." Finally, the captain of a tobacco ship bound for England purchased Equiano, and he traveled as a slave between North America, England, and the West Indies for ten years until he succeeded in buying his freedom in 1766.

> The Deadly Middle Passage

- Eighty-five percent of slaves to the southern colonies came directly from Africa.
- Mortality during the Middle Passage varied considerably from ship to ship.
- On average, about 15 percent of the slaves died.
- In general, the longer the voyage lasted, the more people died.
- Smallpox, dysentery, and acute dehydration were leading causes of death.
- Men outnumbered women two to one.
- Children usually accounted for no more than 10 to 15 percent of the cargo.

new Negroes

▶ Term given to newly arrived African slaves in the colonies. Planters usually maintained only a small number of recent arrivals among their slaves at any given time in order to accelerate their acculturation to their new circumstances.

Normally, an individual planter purchased at any one time a relatively small number of newly arrived Africans, or **new Negroes**, as they were called. New Negroes were often profoundly depressed, demoralized, and disoriented. Planters expected their other slaves — either those born into slavery in the colonies (often called country-born or creole slaves) or Africans who had arrived earlier — to help new Negroes become accustomed to their strange new surroundings. Although slaves spoke many different languages, enough linguistic and cultural similarities existed that they could usually communicate with other Africans from the same region.

New Africans had to adjust to the physical as well as the cultural environment of the southern colonies. Slaves who had just endured the Middle Passage were poorly nourished, weak, and sick. In this vulnerable state, they encountered the alien diseases of North America without having developed a biological arsenal of acquired immunities. As many as 10 to 15 percent of newly arrived Africans died during their first year in the southern colonies. Nonetheless, the large number of newly enslaved Africans made the influence of African culture in the South stronger in the eighteenth century than ever before — or since.

While newly enslaved Africans poured into the southern colonies, slave mothers bore children, which caused the slave population in the South to grow rapidly. Slave owners encouraged these births. Thomas Jefferson explained, "I consider the labor of a breeding [slave] woman as no object, that a [slave] child raised every 2 years is of more profit than the crop of the best laboring [slave] man." Although slave mothers loved and nurtured their children, the mortality rate among slave children was high, and the ever-present risk of being separated by sale brought grief to many slave families. Nonetheless, the growing number of slave babies set the southern colonies apart from other New World slave societies, where mortality rates were so high that deaths exceeded births. The high rate of natural increase in the southern colonies meant that by the 1740s the majority of southern slaves were country-born.

CHAPTER LOCATOR | How did the North American colonies change in the eighteenth century? | What changed in New England life and culture?

126 CHAPTER 5
THE CHANGING WORLD OF COLONIAL AMERICA

Slave Labor and African American Culture

Southern planters expected slaves to work from sunup to sundown and beyond. George Washington wrote that his slaves should "be at their work as soon as it is light, work til it is dark, and be diligent while they are at it." The conflict between the masters' desire for maximum labor and the slaves' reluctance to do more than necessary made the threat of physical punishment a constant for eighteenth-century slaves. Masters preferred black slaves to white indentured servants, not just because slaves served for life but also because colonial laws did not limit the force masters could use against slaves. Slaves often resisted their masters' demands, one traveler noted, because of their "greatness of soul" —their stubborn unwillingness to conform to their masters' definition of them as merely slaves.

Some slaves escalated their acts of resistance to direct physical confrontation with the master, the mistress, or an overseer. But a hoe raised in anger, a punch in the face, or a desperate swipe with a knife led to swift and predictable retaliation by whites. Throughout the southern colonies, the balance of physical power rested securely in the hands of whites.

Rebellion occurred, however, at Stono, South Carolina, in 1739. A group of about twenty slaves attacked a country store, killed the two storekeepers, and confiscated the store's guns, ammunition, and powder. Enticing other slaves to join, the group plundered and burned more than half a dozen plantations and killed more than twenty white men, women, and children. A mounted force of whites quickly suppressed the rebellion. The **Stono Rebellion** illustrated that eighteenth-century slaves had no chance of overturning slavery and very little chance of defending themselves in any bold strike for freedom. No other similar uprisings occurred during the colonial period.

Slaves maneuvered constantly to protect themselves and to gain a measure of autonomy within the boundaries of slavery. In Chesapeake tobacco fields, most slaves were subject to close supervision by whites. In the lower South, the **task system** gave slaves some control over the pace of their work and some discretion in the use of the rest of their time. A "task" was typically defined as a certain area of ground to be cultivated or a specific job to be completed. A slave who completed the assigned task might use the remainder of the day, if any, to work in a garden, fish, hunt, spin, weave, sew, or cook. When masters sought to boost productivity by increasing tasks, slaves did what they could to defend their customary work assignments.

Eighteenth-century slaves also planted the roots of African American lineages that branch out to the present. Slaves valued family ties, and, as in West African societies, kinship structured slaves' relations with one another. Slave parents often gave a child the name of a grandparent, an aunt, or an uncle. In West Africa, kinship identified a person's place among living relatives and linked the person to ancestors in the past and to descendants in the future. Newly imported African slaves usually arrived alone, like Equiano, without kin. Often slaves who had traversed the Middle Passage on the same ship adopted one another as "brothers" and "sisters." Likewise, as new Negroes were seasoned and incorporated into existing slave communities, established families often adopted them as fictive kin.

Stono Rebellion

▶ Slave uprising in Stono, South Carolina, in 1739 in which a group of slaves armed themselves, plundered six plantations, and killed more than twenty whites. Whites quickly suppressed the rebellion.

task system

▶ A system of labor in which a slave was assigned a daily task to complete and allowed to do as he or she wished upon its completion. This system offered more freedom than the carefully supervised gang-labor system.

What spurred the growth of the middle colonies? | Why did slavery become the defining feature of the southern colonies? | What experiences tended to unify colonists in British North America? | Conclusion: What was the dual identity of British North American colonists?

✓ LearningCurve
Check what you know.
bedfordstmartins.com
/roarkunderstanding

An African in Virginia made this drum sometime around the beginning of the eighteenth century. The drum combines deerskin and cedarwood from North America with African workmanship and designs. During rare moments of respite from their work, slaves played drums to accompany dances learned in Africa. They also drummed out messages from plantation to plantation. © The Trustees of the British Museum.

When possible, slaves expressed many other features of their West African origins in their lives on New World plantations. They gave their children traditional dolls and African names such as Cudjo, Quash, Minda, or Fuladi. They grew food crops they had known in Africa, such as yams and okra. They constructed huts with mud walls and thatched roofs similar to African residences. They fashioned banjos, drums, and other musical instruments, held dances, and observed funeral rites that echoed African practices. In these and many other ways, slaves drew upon their African heritages as much as the oppressive circumstances of slavery permitted.

Tobacco, Rice, and Prosperity

Slaves' labor bestowed prosperity on their masters, British merchants, and the monarchy. Slavery was so important and valuable that one minister claimed in 1757 that "to live in Virginia without slaves is morally impossible." The southern colonies supplied 90 percent of all North American exports to Britain. Rice exports from the lower South exploded from less than half a million pounds in 1700 to eighty million pounds in 1770, nearly all of it grown by slaves. Exports of indigo also boomed. Together, rice and indigo made up three-fourths of lower South exports, nearly two-thirds of them going to Britain and most of the rest to the West Indies, where sugar-growing slaves ate slave-grown rice.

Tobacco was by far the most important export from British North America; by 1770, it represented almost one-third of all colonial exports and three-fourths of all Chesapeake exports. Under the provisions of the Navigation Acts (see chapter 4), nearly all of the exported tobacco went to Britain, where the monarchy collected a lucrative tax on each pound. British merchants then re-exported more than 80 percent of the tobacco to the European continent, pocketing a nice markup for their troubles.

These products of slave labor made the southern colonies by far the richest in North America. The per capita wealth of free whites in the South was four times greater than that in New England and three times that in the middle colonies. At the top of the wealth pyramid stood the rice grandees of the lower South and the tobacco gentry of the Chesapeake. These elite families commonly resided on large estates in handsome mansions adorned by luxurious gardens, all maintained and supported by slaves.

CHAPTER LOCATOR | How did the North American colonies change in the eighteenth century? | What changed in New England life and culture?

128 CHAPTER 5
THE CHANGING WORLD OF COLONIAL AMERICA

The vast differences in wealth among white southerners engendered envy and occasional tension between rich and poor, but remarkably little open hostility. In private, the planter elite spoke disparagingly of humble whites, but in public the planters acknowledged their lesser neighbors as equals, at least in belonging to the superior—in their minds—white race. Looking upward, white yeomen and tenants (who owned neither land nor slaves) sensed the gentry's condescension and veiled contempt. But they also appreciated the gentry for granting favors, upholding white supremacy, and keeping slaves in their place. Although racial slavery made a few whites much richer than others, it also gave those who did not get rich a powerful reason to feel similar (in race) to those who were so different (in wealth).

The slaveholding gentry dominated the politics and economy of the southern colonies. In Virginia, only adult white men who owned at least one hundred acres of unimproved land or twenty-five acres of land with a house could vote. This property-holding requirement prevented about 40 percent of white men in Virginia from voting for representatives to the House of Burgesses. In South Carolina, the property requirement was only fifty acres of land, and therefore most adult white men qualified to vote. In both colonies, voters elected members of the gentry to serve in the colonial legislature. The gentry passed elected political offices from generation to generation, almost as if they were hereditary. Politically, the gentry built a self-perpetuating oligarchy—rule by the elite few—with the votes of their many humble neighbors.

The gentry also set the cultural standard in the southern colonies. They entertained lavishly, gambled regularly, and attended Anglican (Church of England) services more for social than for religious reasons. Above all, they cultivated the leisurely pursuit of happiness. They did not condone idleness, however. Their many pleasures and responsibilities as plantation owners kept them busy. Thomas Jefferson, a phenomenally productive member of the gentry, recalled that his earliest childhood memory was of being carried on a pillow by a family slave—a powerful image of the slave hands supporting the gentry's leisure and achievement.

QUICK REVIEW <

How did slavery influence the society and economy of the southern colonies?

What spurred the growth of the middle colonies? | **Why did slavery become the defining feature of the southern colonies?** | What experiences tended to unify colonists in British North America? | Conclusion: What was the dual identity of British North American colonists? | ✓ **LearningCurve** Check what you know. bedfordstmartins.com /roarkunderstanding

129

What experiences tended to unify the colonists in British North America during the eighteenth century?

An anonymous artist portrayed George Whitefield preaching, emphasizing the power of his sermons to transport his audience to a revived awareness of divine spirituality. The woman below his hands appears transfixed. Her eyes and Whitefield's do not meet, yet the artist's use of light suggests that she and Whitefield see the same core of holy Truth. National Portrait Gallery, London.

THE SOCIETIES OF NEW ENGLAND, the middle colonies, and the southern colonies became more sharply differentiated during the eighteenth century, but colonists throughout British North America also shared unifying experiences that eluded settlers in the Spanish and French colonies.

> Unifying Experiences in British North America

- All three British colonial regions had their economic roots in agriculture.
- Religion had declined in importance by the eighteenth century.
- White inhabitants throughout British North America became aware that they shared a distinctive identity as *British* colonists. They asserted their prerogatives as British subjects to defend their special colonial interests.
- The consumption of British exports built a certain material uniformity across region, religion, class, and status.

Commerce and Consumption

Eighteenth-century commerce whetted colonists' appetites to consume. Colonial products spurred the development of mass markets throughout the Atlantic world. Huge increases in the supply of colonial tobacco and sugar brought the price of

CHAPTER LOCATOR | How did the North American colonies change in the eighteenth century? | What changed in New England life and culture?

130 CHAPTER 5
THE CHANGING WORLD OF COLONIAL AMERICA

these small luxuries within the reach of most free whites. Colonial goods brought into focus an important lesson of eighteenth-century commerce: Ordinary people, not just the wealthy elite, would buy the things that they desired in addition to what they absolutely needed. Even news, formerly restricted mostly to a few people through face-to-face conversations or private letters, became an object of public consumption through the innovation of newspapers and the rise in literacy among whites. With the appropriate stimulus, market demand seemed unlimited (**Figure 5.1**).

The Atlantic commerce that took colonial goods to markets in Britain brought objects of consumer desire back to the colonies. British merchants and manufacturers recognized that colonists made excellent customers, and the Navigation Acts gave British exporters privileged access to the colonial market. By midcentury, export-oriented industries in Britain were growing ten times faster than firms attuned to the home market. When the colonists' eagerness to consume exceeded their ability to pay, British exporters willingly extended credit, and colonial debts soared. Imported mirrors, silver plates, spices, bed and table linens, clocks, tea services, wigs, books, and more infiltrated parlors, kitchens, and bedrooms throughout the colonies.

The dazzling variety of imported consumer goods presented women and men with a novel array of choices. In many respects, the choices might appear trivial: whether to buy knives and forks, teacups, a mirror, or a clock. But such small choices confronted eighteenth-century consumers with a big question: What do you want? As colonial consumers defined and expressed their desires with greater frequency during the eighteenth century, they became accustomed to thinking of themselves as individuals who had the power to make decisions that influenced the quality of their lives.

Religion, Enlightenment, and Revival

Eighteenth-century colonists could choose from almost as many religions as consumer goods. Virtually all of the many religious denominations represented some form of Christianity, almost all of them Protestant. Slaves made up the largest group of non-Christians. A few slaves converted to Christianity in Africa or after they arrived in North America, but most continued to embrace elements of indigenous African religions. Roman Catholics concentrated in Maryland as they had since the seventeenth century, but even there they were far outnumbered by Protestants.

The varieties of Protestant faith and practice ranged across a broad spectrum. The middle colonies and the southern backcountry included militant Baptists and Presbyterians. Huguenots, French Protestants who had fled persecution in Catholic France, peopled congregations in several cities. In New England, old-style Puritanism splintered into strands of Congregationalism that differed over fine points of theological doctrine. The Congregational Church was the official established church in New England, and all residents paid taxes for its support. Throughout the plantation South and in urban centers such as Charleston, New York, and Philadelphia, prominent colonists belonged to the Anglican Church, which received tax support in the South. But dissenting faiths grew everywhere, and in most colonies their adherents won the right to worship publicly, although the established churches retained official support.

Many educated colonists became deists, looking for God's plan in nature more than in the Bible. Deism shared the ideas of eighteenth-century European

> **CHRONOLOGY**

1730s
- Jonathan Edwards promotes the religious movement known as the Great Awakening.

1740s
- George Whitefield preaches religious revival in North America.

1754
- Seven Years' War begins.

1769
- American Philosophical Society is founded.
- First Spanish mission in California, San Diego de Alcalá, is established.

1770
- Spanish mission and presidio are established at Monterey, California.

What spurred the growth of the middle colonies? | Why did slavery become the defining feature of the southern colonies? | **What experiences tended to unify colonists in British North America?** | Conclusion: What was the dual identity of British North American colonists? | ✔ LearningCurve Check what you know. bedfordstmartins.com /roarkunderstanding

131

FIGURE 5.1 ■ Colonial Exports, 1768–1772

These pie charts provide an overview of the colonial export economy of the 1760s. The first two show that almost two-thirds of colonial exports came from the South and that the majority of the colonies' exports went to Great Britain. The remaining charts illustrate the distinctive patterns of exports in each colonial region. What do these patterns reveal about regional variations in Britain's North American colonies? What do they suggest about Britain's economic interest in the colonies?

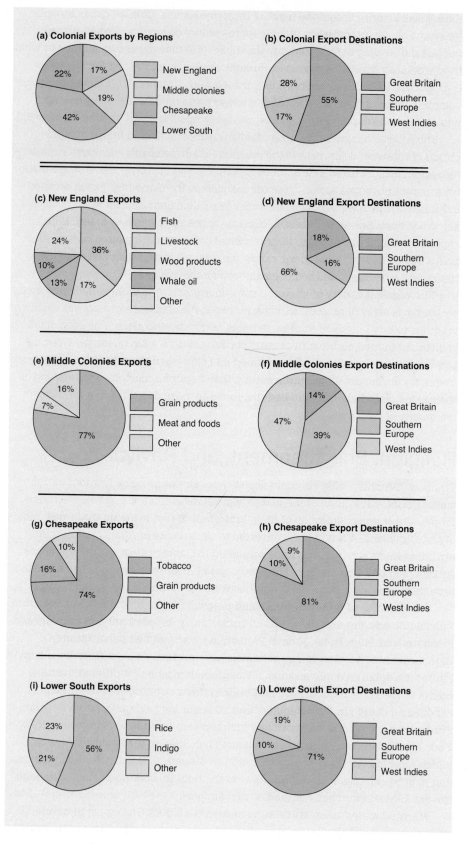

(a) Colonial Exports by Regions
- New England — 17%
- Middle colonies — 19%
- Chesapeake — 42%
- Lower South — 22%

(b) Colonial Export Destinations
- Great Britain — 55%
- Southern Europe — 17%
- West Indies — 28%

(c) New England Exports
- Fish — 36%
- Livestock — 17%
- Wood products — 13%
- Whale oil — 10%
- Other — 24%

(d) New England Export Destinations
- Great Britain — 18%
- Southern Europe — 16%
- West Indies — 66%

(e) Middle Colonies Exports
- Grain products — 77%
- Meat and foods — 7%
- Other — 16%

(f) Middle Colonies Export Destinations
- Great Britain — 14%
- Southern Europe — 39%
- West Indies — 47%

(g) Chesapeake Exports
- Tobacco — 74%
- Grain products — 16%
- Other — 10%

(h) Chesapeake Export Destinations
- Great Britain — 81%
- Southern Europe — 10%
- West Indies — 9%

(i) Lower South Exports
- Rice — 56%
- Indigo — 21%
- Other — 23%

(j) Lower South Export Destinations
- Great Britain — 71%
- Southern Europe — 10%
- West Indies — 19%

CHAPTER LOCATOR | How did the North American colonies change in the eighteenth century? | What changed in New England life and culture?

CHAPTER 5
132 THE CHANGING WORLD OF COLONIAL AMERICA

Enlightenment thinkers, who tended to agree that science and reason could disclose God's laws in the natural order. In the colonies as well as in Europe, Enlightenment ideas encouraged people to study the world around them, to think for themselves, and to ask whether the disorderly appearance of things masked the principles of a deeper, more profound natural order. Leading colonial thinkers such as Benjamin Franklin and Thomas Jefferson communicated with each other as they sought both to understand nature and to find ways to improve society.

Most eighteenth-century colonists went to church seldom or not at all, although they probably considered themselves Christians. A minister in Charleston observed that on the Sabbath "the Taverns have more Visitants than the Churches." In the leading colonial cities, church members were a small minority. Anglican parishes in the South rarely claimed more than one-fifth of adults as members. In some regions of rural New England and the middle colonies, church membership embraced two-thirds of adults, while in other areas only one-quarter of the residents belonged to a church. The dominant faith overall was religious indifference. As a late-eighteenth-century traveler observed, "Religious indifference is imperceptibly disseminated from one end of the continent to the other."

The spread of religious indifference, of deism, of denominational rivalry, and of comfortable backsliding profoundly concerned many Christians. A few despaired that, as one wrote, "religion . . . lay a-dying and ready to expire its last breath of life." To combat what one preacher called the "dead formality" of church services, some ministers set out to convert nonbelievers and to revive the piety of the faithful with a new style of preaching that appealed more to the heart than to the head. Historians have termed this wave of revivals the **Great Awakening**. In Massachusetts during the mid-1730s, the fiery Puritan minister Jonathan Edwards reaped a harvest of souls by reemphasizing traditional Puritan doctrines of humanity's utter depravity and God's vengeful omnipotence. In Pennsylvania and New Jersey, William Tennent led revivals that dramatized spiritual rebirth with accounts of God's miraculous powers.

The most famous revivalist in the eighteenth-century Atlantic world was George Whitefield. An Anglican, Whitefield preached well-worn messages of sin and salvation to large audiences in England using his spellbinding, unforgettable voice. Whitefield visited the North American colonies seven times, staying for more than three years during the mid-1740s and attracting tens of thousands to his sermons, including Benjamin Franklin and Olaudah Equiano. Whitefield's preaching transported many in his audience to emotion-choked states of religious ecstasy, as he wrote, with "most lifting their eyes to heaven, and crying to God for mercy."

The revivals awakened and refreshed the spiritual energies of thousands of colonists struggling with the uncertainties and anxieties of eighteenth-century America. The conversions at revivals did not substantially boost the total number of church members, however. After the revivalists moved on, the routines and pressures of everyday existence reasserted their primacy in the lives of many converts. But the revivals communicated the important message that every soul mattered, that men and women could choose to be saved, that individuals had the power to make a decision for everlasting life or death. Colonial revivals expressed in religious terms many of the same democratic and egalitarian values expressed in economic terms by colonists' patterns of consumption. One colonist noted the analogy by referring to itinerant revivalists as "Pedlars in divinity." Like consumption,

Enlightenment

▶ An eighteenth-century philosophical movement that emphasized the use of reason to reevaluate previously accepted doctrines and traditions. Enlightenment ideas encouraged examination of the world and independence of mind.

Great Awakening

▶ A wave of religious revivals that began in Massachusetts and spread through the colonies in the 1730s and 1740s. The movement emphasized vital religious faith and personal choice. It was characterized by large, open-air meetings at which emotional sermons were given by itinerant preachers.

What spurred the growth of the middle colonies? | Why did slavery become the defining feature of the southern colonies? | **What experiences tended to unify colonists in British North America?** | Conclusion: What was the dual identity of British North American colonists? | ✓ **LearningCurve** Check what you know. bedfordstmartins.com /roarkunderstanding

133

MAP 5.4 ■ Zones of Empire in Eastern North America

The British zone, extending west from the Atlantic coast, was much more densely settled than the zones under French, Spanish, and Indian control. The comparatively large number of British colonists made them more secure than the relatively few colonists in the vast regions claimed by France and Spain or the settlers living among the many Indian peoples in the huge area between the Mississippi River and the Appalachian Mountains. Yet the British colonists were not powerful enough to dominate the French, Spaniards, or Indians. Instead, they had to guard against attacks by powerful Indian groups allied with the French or Spaniards.

revivals contributed to a set of common experiences that bridged colonial divides of faith, region, class, and status.

Trade and Conflict in the North American Borderlands

British power defended the diverse inhabitants of its colonies from Indian, French, and Spanish enemies on their borders—as well as from foreign powers abroad. Royal officials warily eyed the small North American settlements of New France and New Spain for signs of threats to the colonies.

Alone, neither New France nor New Spain jeopardized British North America, but with Indian allies they could become a potent force that kept colonists on their guard (**Map 5.4**). Native Americans' impulse to defend their territory from colonial incursions competed with their desire for trade, which tugged them toward the settlers. As a colonial official observed in 1761, "A modern Indian cannot subsist without Europeans. . . . [The European goods that were] only conveniency at first [have] now become necessity." To obtain such necessities as guns, ammunition, clothing, and sewing utensils manufactured largely by the British, Indians trapped beavers, deer, and other furbearing animals. British, French, Spanish, and Dutch officials competed for the fur trade. Indians took advantage of this competition to improve their own prospects, playing one trader and empire off another. Indian tribes and confederacies also competed among themselves for favored trading rights with one colony or another, a competition colonists encouraged. The shifting alliances and complex dynamics of the fur trade struck a fragile balance along the frontier. The threat of violence from all sides was ever present, and the threat became reality often enough for all parties to be prepared for the worst.

Relations between Indians and colonists differed from colony to colony and from year to year. But the British colonists' nagging perceptions of menace on the frontier kept them continually hoping for help from the British to keep the Indians at bay and to maintain the essential flow of trade. In 1754, the British colonists' endemic competition with the French flared into the Seven Years' War (also known as the French and Indian War), which would inflame the frontier for years (as discussed in chapter 6). Colonists agreed that Indians made deadly enemies, profitable trading partners, and powerful allies.

CHAPTER LOCATOR | How did the North American colonies change in the eighteenth century? | What changed in New England life and culture?

134 CHAPTER 5 THE CHANGING WORLD OF COLONIAL AMERICA

The Spanish kept an eye on the Pacific coast, where Russian hunters in search of seals and sea otters threatened to become a permanent presence on New Spain's northern frontier. To block Russian access to present-day California, officials in New Spain mounted a campaign to build forts (called **presidios**) and missions there. In 1769, an expedition headed by a military man, Gaspar de Portolá, and a Catholic priest, Junípero Serra, traveled north from Mexico to present-day San Diego, where they founded the first California mission, San Diego de Alcalá. They soon journeyed all the way to Monterey, which became the capital of Spanish California. There Portolá established a presidio in 1770 "to defend us from attacks by the Russians," he wrote. The same year, Serra founded Mission San Carlos Borroméo de Carmelo in Monterey to convert the Indians and recruit them to work to support the soldiers and other Spaniards in the presidio. By 1772, Serra had founded other missions along the path from San Diego to Monterey.

One Spanish soldier praised the work of the missionaries, writing that "with flattery and presents [the missionaries] attract the savage Indians and persuade them to adhere to life in society and to receive instruction for a knowledge of the Catholic faith, the cultivation of the land, and the arts necessary for making the instruments most needed for farming." Yet for the Indians, the Spaniards' California missions had horrendous consequences, as they had elsewhere in the Spanish borderlands. European diseases decimated Indian populations, Spanish soldiers raped Indian women, and missionaries beat Indians and subjected them to near slavery. Indian uprisings against the Spaniards occurred repeatedly, but the presidios and missions endured as feeble projections of the Spanish empire along the Pacific coast.

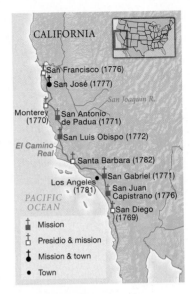

Spanish Missions in California

presidios
▶ Spanish forts built to block Russian access to California.

Colonial Politics in the British Empire

The plurality of peoples, faiths, and communities that characterized the North American colonies arose from the somewhat haphazard policies of the eighteenth-century British empire. Unlike Spain and France—whose policies of excluding Protestants and foreigners kept the population of their North American colonial territories tiny—Britain kept the door to its colonies open to anyone, and tens of thousands of non-British immigrants settled in the North American colonies and raised families. The open door did not extend to trade, however, as the seventeenth-century Navigation Acts restricted colonial trade to British ships and traders. These policies evolved because they served the interests of the monarchy and of influential groups in Britain and the colonies. The policies also gave the colonists a common framework of political expectations and experiences.

Mission Carmel

This eighteenth-century drawing portrays a reception for a Spanish visitor at Mission Carmel in what is now Carmel, California. Lines of mission Indians dressed in robes flank the entrance to the chapel where a priest and his assistants await the visitor. The reception ritual dramatized the strict hierarchy that governed relations among Spanish missionaries, ruling officials, and the subordinate Indians. University of California at Berkeley, Bancroft Library.

What spurred the growth of the middle colonies?

Why did slavery become the defining feature of the southern colonies?

What experiences tended to unify colonists in British North America?

Conclusion: What was the dual identity of British North American colonists?

✔ LearningCurve
Check what you know.
bedfordstmartins.com
/roarkunderstanding

British attempts to exercise political power in their colonial governments met with success so long as British officials were on or very near the sea. Colonists acknowledged—although they did not always readily comply with—British authority to collect customs duties, inspect cargoes, and enforce trade regulations. But when royal officials tried to wield their authority in the internal affairs of the colonies on land, they invariably encountered colonial resistance. A governor appointed by the king in each of the nine royal colonies (Rhode Island and Connecticut selected their own governors) or by the proprietors in Maryland and Pennsylvania headed the government of each colony. The British envisioned colonial governors as mini-monarchs able to exert influence in the colonies much as the king did in Britain. But colonial governors were not kings, and the colonies were not Britain.

Even the best-intentioned colonial governors had difficulty developing relations of trust and respect with influential colonists because their terms of office averaged just five years and could be terminated at any time. Colonial governors controlled few patronage positions to secure political friendships in the colonies. Obedient and loyal to their superiors in Britain, colonial governors fought incessantly with the colonists' assemblies. They battled over issues such as governors' vetoes of colonial legislation, removal of colonial judges, and dismissal of the representative assemblies. But during the eighteenth century, the assemblies gained the upper hand.

Since British policies did not clearly define the colonists' legal powers, colonial assemblies seized the opportunity to make their own rules. Gradually, the assemblies established a strong tradition of representative government analogous, in their eyes, to the British Parliament. Voters often returned the same representatives to the assemblies year after year, building continuity in power and leadership that far exceeded that of the governor.

By 1720, colonial assemblies had won the power to initiate legislation, including tax laws and authorizations to spend public funds. Although all laws passed by the assemblies (except in Maryland, Rhode Island, and Connecticut) had to be approved by the governor and then by the Board of Trade in Britain, the difficulties in communication about complex subjects over long distances effectively ratified the assemblies' decisions. Years often passed before colonial laws were repealed by British authorities, and in the meantime the assemblies' laws prevailed.

The heated political struggles between royal governors and colonial assemblies that occurred throughout the eighteenth century taught colonists a common set of political lessons. They learned to employ traditionally British ideas of representative government to defend their own colonial interests. More important, they learned that power in the British colonies rarely belonged to the British government.

> **QUICK REVIEW**

How did culture, commerce, and consumption shape the collective identity of Britain's North American colonists in the eighteenth century?

CHAPTER LOCATOR | How did the North American colonies change in the eighteenth century? | What changed in New England life and culture?

136 CHAPTER 5
THE CHANGING WORLD OF COLONIAL AMERICA

Conclusion: What was the dual identity of British North American colonists?

<

DURING THE EIGHTEENTH CENTURY, a society that was both distinctively colonial and distinctively British emerged in British North America. Tens of thousands of immigrants and slaves gave the colonies an unmistakably colonial complexion and contributed to the colonies' growing population and expanding economy. People of different ethnicities and faiths sought their fortunes in the colonies, where land was cheap, labor was dear, and work promised to be rewarding. Indentured servants and redemptioners risked temporary periods of bondage for the potential reward of better opportunities in the colonies than in Europe. Slaves arrived in unprecedented numbers and endured lifelong servitude, which they neither chose nor desired but from which their masters greatly benefited.

None of the European colonies could claim complete dominance of North America. The desire to expand and defend their current claims meant that the English, French, and Spanish colonies were drawn into regular conflict with one another, as well as with the Indians upon whose land they encroached. In varying degrees, all sought control of the Native Americans and their land, their military power, their trade, and even their souls. Spanish missionaries and soldiers sought to convert Indians on the West Coast and exploit their labor; French alliances with Indian tribes posed a formidable barrier to westward expansion of the British empire.

Yet despite their attempts to tame their New World holdings, Spanish and French colonists did not develop societies that began to rival the European empires that sponsored and supported them. They did not participate in the cultural, economic, social, and religious changes experienced by their counterparts in British North America, nor did they share in the emerging political identity of the British colonists.

Identifiably colonial products from New England, the middle colonies, and the southern colonies flowed to the West Indies and across the Atlantic. Back came unquestionably British consumer goods along with fashions in ideas, faith, and politics. The bonds of the British empire required colonists to think of themselves as British subjects and, at the same time, encouraged them to consider their status as colonists. By 1750, British colonists in North America could not imagine that their distinctively dual identity—as British and as colonists—would soon become a source of intense conflict.

| What spurred the growth of the middle colonies? | Why did slavery become the defining feature of the southern colonies? | What experiences tended to unify colonists in British North America? | Conclusion: What was the dual identity of British North American colonists? | ✓ LearningCurve Check what you know. bedfordstmartins.com /roarkunderstanding |

137
<

CHAPTER 5 STUDY GUIDE

STEP 1 **GET STARTED ONLINE**

✓ **LearningCurve** ■ bedfordstmartins.com/roarkunderstanding
Now that you've read the chapter, make it stick by completing the LearningCurve activity.

STEP 2 **EXPLAIN WHY IT MATTERS**

Put your reading into practice. Identify each term below, and then explain why it matters in U.S. history.

TERM	WHO OR WHAT & WHEN	WHY IT MATTERS
natural increase (p. 112)		
partible inheritance (p. 115)		
Pennsylvania Dutch (p. 118)		
Scots-Irish (p. 119)		
redemptioners (p. 119)		
Middle Passage (p. 125)		
new Negroes (p. 126)		
Stono Rebellion (p. 127)		
task system (p. 127)		
Enlightenment (p. 133)		
Great Awakening (p. 133)		
presidios (p. 135)		

STEP 3 **MOVE BEYOND THE BASICS**

To demonstrate a more advanced understanding, consider the economy, society, culture, and politics of the major regions of British North America in 1700 and 1770. What accounts for regional divergence?

Region	Economy (imports and exports, jobs, wealth)	Population (ethnicity, race, class)	Culture — ways of life, values (including religious beliefs)	Colonial Politics
New England in 1700				
New England in 1770				
Middle Colonies in 1700				
Middle Colonies in 1770				
Southern Colonies in 1700				
Southern Colonies in 1770				

STEP 4 PUT IT ALL TOGETHER Now, take a step back and try to explain the big picture. Remember to use specific examples from the chapter in your answers.

NEW ENGLAND

► How did the economy of New England differ from that of other regions?

► Why did New England not attract as many immigrants as other areas did? How did that affect the social structure of the region?

THE MIDDLE COLONIES

► How did immigration shape the religious and ethnic diversity of the middle colonies? What factors led immigrants to settle in the middle colonies?

► How did Atlantic commerce, particularly colonial consumption, affect the middle colonies?

THE SOUTHERN COLONIES AND SPANISH CALIFORNIA

► What role did slavery play in the social and economic development of the South?

► How did slaves attempt to maintain their own culture and gain some control within the limits of slavery?

► Why did New Spain establish presidios and missions, and what were their consequences for Native Americans?

LOOKING BACKWARD, LOOKING AHEAD

► How did the relationship between the colonies and Britain in the eighteenth century differ from that of the seventeenth century?

► What were the most pressing sources of potential conflict between the colonies and Britain in 1770? What were the most important sources of cooperation and mutual dependence?

> **IN YOUR OWN WORDS**

Imagine that you must give an oral report to the class answering the following question: What were the most important changes in colonial North America between 1701 and 1770? What would be the most important points to include and why?

> **Do it online at the Student Site ■ bedfordstmartins.com/roarkunderstanding**

6

THE BRITISH EMPIRE AND THE COLONIAL CRISIS

1754–1775

> **What were the most significant factors contributing to deteriorating relations between Britain and its North American colonies?** Chapter 6 explores the efforts of the British government to tax and control the colonies in the aftermath of the Seven Years' War and traces the escalating colonial responses to these efforts, from political protest, to open resistance, and—ultimately—to war.

LearningCurve

bedfordstmartins.com/roarkunderstanding
After reading the chapter, use LearningCurve to
retain what you've read.

Resistance to the Stamp Act. This contemporary engraving (ca. 1765) depicts an angry Boston crowd burning a pile of stamps in protest of the Stamp Act. Picture Research Consultants & Archives.

> How did the Seven Years' War lay the groundwork for colonial crisis?

> Why did the Sugar Act and the Stamp Act draw fierce opposition from colonists?

> Why did British authorities send troops to occupy Boston in the fall of 1768?

> Why did Parliament pass the Coercive Acts in 1774?

> How did enslaved people in the colonies react to the stirrings of revolution?

> Conclusion: What changes did the American colonists want in 1775?

How did the Seven Years' War lay the groundwork for colonial crisis?

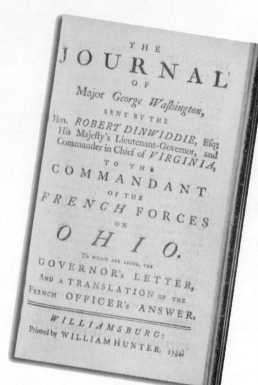

FOR THE FIRST HALF OF THE EIGHTEENTH CENTURY, Britain was at war intermittently with France or Spain. Often the colonists in America experienced reverberations from these conflicts, most acutely along the frontier of New France in northern New England. In 1754, international tensions returned, this time sparked by events in America's Ohio Valley. The land — variously claimed by Virginians, Pennsylvanians, and the French — was actually inhabited by more than a dozen Indian tribes. The result was the costly **Seven Years' War** (its British name — Americans called it the French and Indian War), which spread in 1756 to encompass much of Europe, the Caribbean, and even India. The British and their colonial allies won the war, but the immense costs of the conflict — in money, death, and desire for revenge by losers and even winners — laid the groundwork for the imperial crisis of the 1760s between the British and Americans.

Seven Years' War

▶ War (1754–1762) between Britain and France that ended with British domination of North America; known in America as the French and Indian War. Its high expense laid the foundation for conflict that would lead to the American Revolution.

French-British Rivalry in the Ohio Country

For several decades, French traders had cultivated alliances with the Indian tribes in the Ohio Country, a frontier region they regarded as part of New France, establishing a profitable exchange of manufactured goods for beaver furs (**Map 6.1**). But in the 1740s, aggressive Pennsylvania traders began to infringe on the territory. Adding to the tensions, a group of enterprising Virginians, including the brothers Lawrence and Augustine Washington, formed the Ohio Company in 1747 and advanced on the same land. Their hope for profit lay not in the fur trade but in land speculation, fueled by American population expansion.

CHAPTER LOCATOR | How did the Seven Years' War lay the groundwork for colonial crisis? | Why did the Sugar Act and the Stamp Act draw fierce opposition from colonists?

142 CHAPTER 6 THE BRITISH EMPIRE AND THE COLONIAL CRISIS

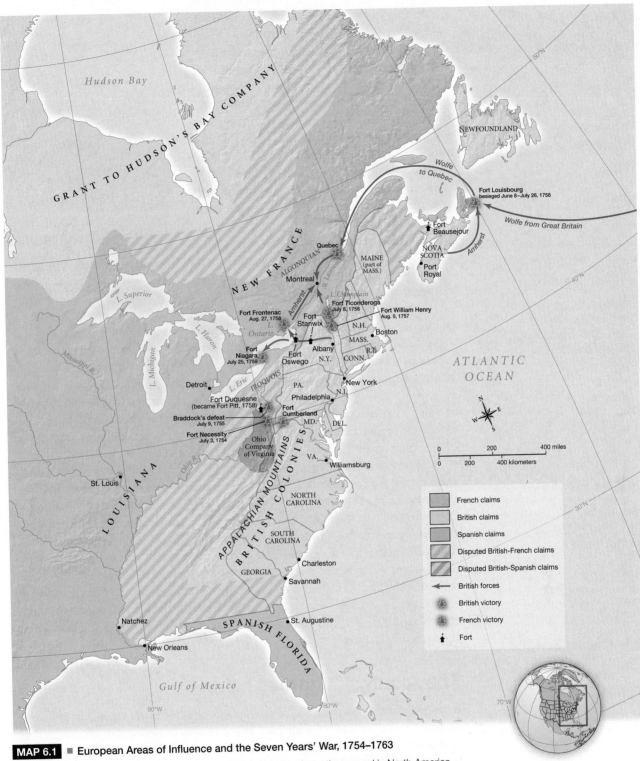

MAP 6.1 ■ European Areas of Influence and the Seven Years' War, 1754–1763

In 1750, the French and Spanish empires had relatively few people on the ground in North America, compared with the exploding population of the Anglo-American colonies. The disputed lands shown here, contested by the imperial powers, were inhabited by a variety of Native American tribes.

Legend:
- French claims
- British claims
- Spanish claims
- Disputed British-French claims
- Disputed British-Spanish claims
- British forces
- British victory
- French victory
- Fort

Why did British authorities send troops to occupy Boston in the fall of 1768?

Why did Parliament pass the Coercive Acts in 1774?

How did enslaved people in the colonies react to the stirrings of revolution?

Conclusion: What changes did the American colonists want in 1775?

✓ LearningCurve
Check what you know.
bedfordstmartins.com
/roarkunderstanding

> CHRONOLOGY

1754
– Seven Years' War begins.
– Albany Congress.

1755
– General Braddock is defeated in western Pennsylvania.

1757
– William Pitt fully commits to war.

1760
– Montreal falls to British.

1763
– Treaty of Paris ends Seven Years' War.
– Pontiac's Rebellion.
– Proclamation of 1763.
– Paxton Boys massacre friendly Indians.

In response to these incursions, the French sent soldiers to build a series of military forts to secure their trade routes and to create a western barrier to American expansion. In 1753, the royal governor of Virginia, Robert Dinwiddie, himself a shareholder in the Ohio Company, dispatched a messenger to warn the French that they were trespassing on Virginia land. That messenger was twenty-one-year-old George Washington, half-brother of the Ohio Company leaders, who did not disappoint. Washington returned with crucial intelligence confirming French military intentions. Impressed, Dinwiddie appointed the youth to lead a small military expedition west to assert Virginia's claim and chase the French away — but without attacking them.

Ohio River Valley, 1753

In the spring of 1754, Washington set out with 160 Virginians and a small contingent of Mingo Indians equally concerned about the French military presence in the Ohio Country. Early one morning, the Mingo chief Tanaghrisson led a detachment of Washington's soldiers to a small French encampment in the woods. Who fired first was in dispute, but fourteen Frenchmen (and no Virginians) were wounded. While Washington, lacking a translator, struggled to communicate with the injured French commander, Tanaghrisson and his men intervened to kill and then scalp the wounded soldiers, including the commander, probably with the aim of inflaming hostilities between the French and the colonists.

This sudden massacre violated Dinwiddie's instructions to Washington and raised the stakes considerably. Fearing retaliation, Washington ordered his men to throw together a makeshift "Fort Necessity." Several hundred Virginia reinforcements arrived, but the Mingos, sensing disaster and displeased by Washington's style of command, fled. (Tanaghrisson later said, "The Colonel was a good-natured man, but had no experience; he took upon him to command the Indians as his slaves, [and] would by no means take advice from the Indians.") Retaliation arrived in the form of six hundred French soldiers aided by one hundred Shawnee and Delaware warriors, who attacked Fort Necessity, killing or wounding a third of Washington's men. The message was clear: The French would not depart from the disputed territory.

The Albany Congress

British imperial leaders hoped to prevent the conflict in the Ohio Country from leading to a larger war. One obvious strategy was to strengthen an old partnership with the Mohawks of New York's Iroquois Confederacy, who since 1692 had joined with New York fur merchants in an alliance called the Covenant Chain. Yet unsavory land speculators caused the Mohawks to doubt British friendship. Authorities in London directed New York's royal governor to convene a colonial conference to repair trade relations and secure the Indians' help — or at least their neutrality — against the looming French threat. The

CHAPTER LOCATOR | How did the Seven Years' War lay the groundwork for colonial crisis? | Why did the Sugar Act and the Stamp Act draw fierce opposition from colonists?

CHAPTER 6
144 THE BRITISH EMPIRE AND THE COLONIAL CRISIS

Chief Hendrick and John Caldwell These two images convey versions of cross-cultural dressing. The aged Mohawk Chief Hendrick (left) appears in fine British clothing, while John Caldwell, a titled Irishman who served with the British army, sports colorful elements of Indian dress. Hendrick: Courtesy of the John Carter Brown Library at Brown University; Caldwell: © Walker Art Gallery, National Museums Liverpool/The Bridgeman Art Library.

conference convened at Albany, in June and July 1754. All six tribes of the Iroquois Confederacy attended, along with twenty-four delegates from seven colonies, making this an unprecedented pan-colony gathering. The elderly Mohawk chief Hendrick gave a powerful and widely reprinted speech, asserting that recent British neglect would inevitably reorient Indian trade relations to the French. "Look at the French, they are men; they are fortifying every where; but we are ashamed to say it; you are like women, bare and open, without any fortifications." Hendrick urged the assembled colonists to prepare for defense against the French.

Delegates Benjamin Franklin of Pennsylvania and Thomas Hutchinson of Massachusetts had their own ambitious plan. They coauthored the Albany Plan of Union, a proposal for a unified colonial government to exercise sole authority over questions of war, peace, and trade with the Indians. Delegates at the Albany Congress, alarmed by news of the defeat of the Virginians at Fort Necessity, agreed to present the plan to their respective assemblies.

To Franklin's surprise, not a single colony approved the Albany Plan. The Massachusetts assembly feared it was "a Design of gaining power over the Colonies," especially the power of taxation. Others objected that it would be impossible to agree on unified policies toward scores of quite different Indian tribes. The British government never backed the Albany Plan either; instead, it appointed two superintendents of Indian affairs, one for the northern and another for the southern colonies, each with exclusive powers to negotiate treaties, trade, and land sales with all tribes.

Why did British authorities send troops to occupy Boston in the fall of 1768?

Why did Parliament pass the Coercive Acts in 1774?

How did enslaved people in the colonies react to the stirrings of revolution?

Conclusion: What changes did the American colonists want in 1775?

LearningCurve
Check what you know.
bedfordstmartins.com
/roarkunderstanding

145

The Indians at the Albany Congress were not impressed with the Albany Plan either. The Covenant Chain alliance with the Mohawk tribe was reaffirmed, but the other Indian nations left without pledging to help the British battle the French. Some of the Iroquois figured that the French military presence around the Great Lakes would discourage the westward push of American colonists and therefore better serve their interests.

The War and Its Consequences

By 1755, George Washington's frontier skirmish had turned into a major war. The British expected quick victories on three fronts. General Edward Braddock, recently arrived from England, marched his army toward Fort Duquesne in western Pennsylvania. Farther north, British troops moved toward Fort Niagara, critically located between Lakes Erie and Ontario. And William Johnson, a New Yorker recently appointed superintendent of northern Indian affairs, led forces north toward Lake Champlain, intending to defend the border against the French in Canada (see Map 6.1).

Unfortunately for the British, the French were prepared to fight and had enlisted many Indian tribes in their cause. When Braddock's army of 2,000 British soldiers marched west toward Fort Duquesne, a mere 8 Oneida warriors came as guides. They were ambushed by 250 French soldiers joined by 640 Indian warriors. In the bloody battle, nearly a thousand on the British side were killed (including General Braddock) or wounded.

For the next two years, British leaders stumbled badly, deploying inadequate numbers of undersupplied troops. What finally turned the war around was the rise to power in 1757 of William Pitt, Britain's prime minister, a man ready to commit massive resources to fight France and Spain worldwide. In America, British troops aided by American provincial soldiers finally captured Forts Duquesne, Niagara, and Ticonderoga, followed by the French cities of Quebec and finally Montreal, all from 1758 to 1760. By 1761, the war subsided in America but expanded globally, with battles in the Caribbean, Austria, Prussia, and India. The British captured the French sugar islands Martinique and Guadeloupe and then invaded Spanish Cuba with an army of some four thousand provincial soldiers from New York and New England. By the end of 1762, France and Spain capitulated, and the Treaty of Paris was signed in 1763.

In the complex peace negotiations that followed, Britain gained control of Canada, eliminating the French threat from the north. British and American title to the eastern half of North America was confirmed. But French territory west of the Mississippi River, including New Orleans, was transferred to Spain as compensation for Spain's assistance during the war. Strangely, Cuba was returned to Spain, and Martinique and Guadeloupe were returned to France (**Map 6.2**).

The British credited their army for their victory and criticized the colonists for inadequate support. William Pitt was convinced that colonial smuggling — beaver pelts from French fur traders and illegal molasses in the French Caribbean — "principally, if not alone, enabled France to sustain and protract this long and expensive war."

Colonists read the lessons of the war differently. American soldiers had turned out in force, they claimed, but had been relegated to grunt work by British commanders and subjected to harsh military discipline, including floggings and

CHAPTER LOCATOR | How did the Seven Years' War lay the groundwork for colonial crisis? | Why did the Sugar Act and the Stamp Act draw fierce opposition from colonists?

146 CHAPTER 6
THE BRITISH EMPIRE AND THE COLONIAL CRISIS

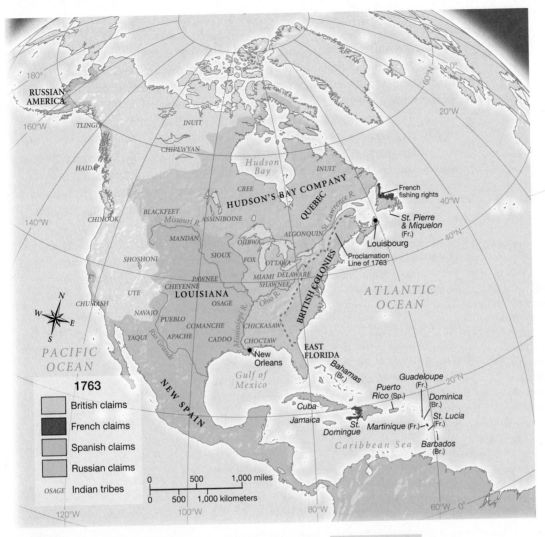

1763

- British claims
- French claims
- Spanish claims
- Russian claims

OSAGE Indian tribes

0   500   1,000 miles
0   500   1,000 kilometers

MAP 6.2 ■ Europe Redraws the Map of North America, 1763

In 1763, France ceded to Britain its interior territory from Quebec to New Orleans, retaining fishing rights in the north and sugar islands in the Caribbean. France transferred to Spain its claim to extensive territory west of the Mississippi River.

> MAP ACTIVITY

READING THE MAP: Who actually lived on and controlled the lands ceded by France? In what sense, if any, did Britain or Spain own these large territories?

CONNECTIONS: What was the goal of the Proclamation of 1763? (See page 148.) Could it ever have worked?

executions. They bristled at British arrogance, as when Benjamin Franklin heard General Braddock brag that "these savages may, indeed, be a formidable enemy to your raw American militia, but upon the king's regular and disciplined troops, sir, it is impossible they should make any impression." Braddock's crushing defeat "gave us Americans," Franklin wrote, "the first suspicion that our exalted ideas of the prowess of British regulars had not been well founded."

Perhaps most important, the enormous expense of the war cast a huge shadow over the victory. By 1763, Britain's national debt, double what it had been when Pitt took office, posed a formidable challenge to the next decade of leadership in Britain.

Why did British authorities send troops to occupy Boston in the fall of 1768?

Why did Parliament pass the Coercive Acts in 1774?

How did enslaved people in the colonies react to the stirrings of revolution?

Conclusion: What changes did the American colonists want in 1775?

✓ **LearningCurve**
Check what you know.
bedfordstmartins.com /roarkunderstanding

Pontiac's Rebellion and the Proclamation of 1763

One glaring omission marred the Treaty of Paris: The major powers at the treaty table failed to include or consult the Indians. Minavavana, an Ojibwa chief of the Great Lakes region, put it succinctly to an English trader: "Englishman, although you have conquered the French, you have not yet conquered us! We are not your slaves. These lakes, these woods and mountains were left to us by our ancestors . . . ; and we will part with them to none."

Indians north of the Ohio River had cause for concern. Old French trading posts all over the Northwest were beefed up by the British into military bases. Fort Duquesne, renamed Fort Pitt to honor the victorious leader, gained new walls sixty feet thick at their base, announcing that this was no fur trading post. Tensions between the British and the Indians in this area ran high.

A religious revival among the Indians magnified feelings of antagonism toward the British. In 1763, the renewal of commitment to Indian ways and the formation of tribal alliances led to open warfare, which the British called **Pontiac's Rebellion**, named for the chief of the Ottawas. In mid-May, Ottawa, Potawatomi, and Huron warriors attacked Fort Detroit. Six more attacks on forts followed within weeks, and frontier settlements were raided by tribes from western New York, the Ohio Valley, and the Great Lakes region. By fall, Indians had captured every fort west of Detroit. More than four hundred British soldiers were dead and another two thousand colonists killed or taken captive.

Some Americans exacted revenge. The worst violent aggression occurred in late 1763, when some fifty Pennsylvania vigilantes known as the Paxton Boys descended on a peaceful village of friendly Conestoga Indians, murdering twenty. The vigilantes, now numbering five hundred, marched on Philadelphia to try to capture and murder some Christian Indians held in protective custody there. British troops prevented

Pontiac's Rebellion

▶ A coordinated uprising of Native American tribes in 1763 in the Northwest after the end of the Seven Years' War. The rebellion heightened Britain's determination to create a boundary between Americans and Indians, embodied in the Proclamation of 1763.

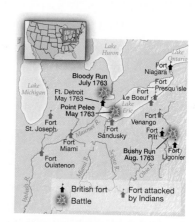

Pontiac's Rebellion, 1763

> The Proclamation of 1763

- Colonists were forbidden to settle west of the Appalachian Mountains.

- The Proclamation offered assurances that Indian territory would be respected. It limited trade with Indians to traders licensed by colonial governors, and it forbade private sales of Indian land.

- Western lands were referred to not as the Indians' land, but as lands that "are reserved to [Indians], as their Hunting Grounds."

- American and French colonists in Canada were British subjects entitled to English rights and privileges.

- Indians were not British subjects and were instead referred to as "Tribes of Indians with whom We are connected."

CHAPTER LOCATOR | How did the Seven Years' War lay the groundwork for colonial crisis? | Why did the Sugar Act and the Stamp Act draw fierce opposition from colonists?

CHAPTER 6
148 THE BRITISH EMPIRE AND THE COLONIAL CRISIS

that, but the Paxton Boys escaped punishment for their murderous attack on the Conestoga village. To minimize violence, the British government issued the Proclamation of 1763, which chiefly aimed to separate Indians and settlers, with added restrictions on trade and land sales.

The Indian uprising had faded by early 1764, but the 1763 boundary was a further provocation to American settlers and also to land speculators who had already staked claims to huge tracts of western lands in hopes of profitable resale. Yet the boundary proved impossible to enforce. Surging population growth had already sent many hundreds of settlers, many of them squatters, west of the Appalachians. Periodic bloodshed continued and left the settlers fearful, uncertain about their future, and increasingly wary of British claims to be a protective mother country.

QUICK REVIEW

How did the Seven Years' War erode relations between colonists and British authorities?

| Why did British authorities send troops to occupy Boston in the fall of 1768? | Why did Parliament pass the Coercive Acts in 1774? | How did enslaved people in the colonies react to the stirrings of revolution? | Conclusion: What changes did the American colonists want in 1775? | ☑ LearningCurve Check what you know. bedfordstmartins.com /roarkunderstanding |

149

Why did the Sugar Act and the Stamp Act draw fierce opposition from colonists?

George Grenville, Prime Minister, 1763–1765

George Grenville became prime minister in 1763, but King George III found him irksome: "When he has wearied me for two hours, he looks at his watch, to see if he may not tire me for an hour more," the king said, and sacked him in July 1765 for being insolent, not for his controversial colonial policies. The Earl of Halifax, Garrowby, Yorkshire.

> CHRONOLOGY

1760
- George III becomes British king.

1764
- Parliament enacts Sugar Act.

1765
- Parliament enacts Stamp Act.
- Virginia Resolves challenge Stamp Act.
- Sons of Liberty stage crowd actions.
- Stamp Act Congress meets.

1766
- Parliament repeals Stamp Act, passes Declaratory Act.

IN 1760, GEORGE III, twenty-two years old, became king of England. Timid and insecure, George struggled to gain his footing in his new job. He rotated through a succession of leaders, searching for a prime minister he could trust. A half dozen ministers in seven years took turns dealing with one basic, underlying British reality: A huge war debt needed to be serviced, and the colonists, as British subjects, should help pay it off. To many Americans, however, that proposition seemed in deep violation of what they perceived to be their rights and liberties as British subjects, and it created resentment that eventually erupted in large-scale street protests. The first provocative revenue acts were the work of Sir George Grenville, prime minister from 1763 to 1765.

Grenville's Sugar Act

To find revenue, George Grenville scrutinized the customs service, which monitored the shipping trade and collected all import and export duties. Grenville found that the salaries of customs officers cost the government four times what was collected in revenue. The shortfall was due in part to bribery and smuggling, so Grenville began to insist on rigorous attention to paperwork and a strict accounting of collected duties. The hardest duty to enforce was the one imposed

CHAPTER LOCATOR

How did the Seven Years' War lay the groundwork for colonial crisis?

Why did the Sugar Act and the Stamp Act draw fierce opposition from colonists?

150 CHAPTER 6 THE BRITISH EMPIRE AND THE COLONIAL CRISIS

by the Molasses Act of 1733 — a stiff tax of six pence per gallon on any molasses (a key ingredient in rum) imported to British colonies from non-British sources. Rum-loving Americans, however, were eager to buy molasses from French Caribbean islands, and they had ignored the tax law for decades.

Grenville's inspired solution was the **Revenue Act** of 1764, popularly dubbed the **Sugar Act**. It lowered the duty on French molasses to three pence, making it more attractive for shippers to obey the law, and at the same time raised penalties for smuggling. The act appeared to be in the tradition of navigation acts meant to regulate trade (see chapter 4), but Grenville's actual intent was to raise revenue. The Sugar Act toughened enforcement policies. From now on, all British naval crews could act as impromptu customs officers, boarding suspicious ships and seizing cargoes found to be in violation. Smugglers caught without proper paperwork would be prosecuted, not in a local court with a friendly jury but in a vice-admiralty court located in Nova Scotia, where a crown judge presided. The implication was that justice would be sure and severe. Grenville's hopes for the Sugar Act did not materialize. The small decrease in duty did not offset the attractions of smuggling, while the increased vigilance in enforcement led to several ugly confrontations in port cities. Reaction to the Sugar Act foreshadowed questions about Britain's right to tax Americans, but in 1764 objections to the act came principally from the small number of Americans engaged in the shipping trades. From the British point of view, the Proclamation of 1763 and the Sugar Act seemed to be reasonable efforts to administer the colonies. To Americans, however, the British supervision appeared to be a disturbing intrusion into colonial practices of self-taxation by elected colonial assemblies. Benjamin Franklin, Pennsylvania's lobbyist in London, warned that "two distinct Jurisdictions or Powers of Taxing cannot well subsist together in the same country."

The Stamp Act

In February 1765, Grenville escalated his revenue program with the **Stamp Act**, precipitating a major conflict between Britain and the colonies over Parliament's right to tax. The Stamp Act imposed a tax on all paper used for official documents — newspapers, pamphlets, court documents, licenses, wills, ships' cargo lists — and required an affixed stamp as proof that the tax had been paid. Unlike the Sugar Act, which regulated trade, the Stamp Act was designed plainly and simply to raise money. It affected nearly everyone who used any taxed paper but, most of all, users of official documents in the business and legal communities. Anticipating that the stamp tax would be unpopular — Thomas Hutchinson had forewarned him — Grenville delegated the administration of the act to Americans to avoid taxpayer hostility toward British enforcers. In each colony, local stamp distributors would be hired at a handsome salary of 8 percent of the revenue collected. English tradition held that taxes were a gift of the people to their monarch, granted by the people's representatives. This view of taxes as a freely given gift preserved an essential concept of English political theory: the idea that citizens have the liberty to enjoy and use their property without fear of confiscation. The king could not demand money; only the House of Commons could grant it. Grenville agreed with the notion of taxation by consent, but he argued that the colonists were already "virtually" represented in Parliament. The House of Commons, he insisted, represented all British subjects, wherever they were. Colonial leaders emphatically rejected this view, arguing that

Sugar (Revenue) Act
▶ 1764 British law that decreased the duty on French molasses, making it more attractive for shippers to obey the law, and at the same time raised penalties for smuggling. The Sugar Act regulated trade, but its primary purpose was to raise revenue.

Stamp Act
▶ 1765 British law imposing a tax on all paper used for official documents, for the purpose of raising revenue. Widespread resistance to the Stamp Act led to its repeal in 1766.

Why did British authorities send troops to occupy Boston in the fall of 1768?

Why did Parliament pass the Coercive Acts in 1774?

How did enslaved people in the colonies react to the stirrings of revolution?

Conclusion: What changes did the American colonists want in 1775?

✓ LearningCurve
Check what you know.
bedfordstmartins.com
/roarkunderstanding

151

virtual representation could not withstand the stretch across the Atlantic. Colonists willingly paid local and provincial taxes, levied by their town, county, or colonial assemblies, to fund government administrative expenses and shared necessities like local roads, schools, and poor relief. By contrast, the stamp tax was a clear departure as a fee-per-document tax, levied by a distant Parliament on unwilling colonies.

Resistance Strategies and Crowd Politics

News of the Stamp Act arrived in the colonies in April 1765, seven months before it was to take effect. There was time, therefore, to object. Governors were unlikely to challenge the law, for most of them owed their office to the king. Instead, the colonial assemblies took the lead; eight of them held discussions on the Stamp Act.

Virginia's assembly, the House of Burgesses, was the first. At the end of its May session, after two-thirds of the members had left, Patrick Henry, a young political newcomer, presented a series of resolutions on the Stamp Act that were debated and passed, one by one. They became known as the Virginia Resolves. Henry's resolutions inched the assembly toward radical opposition to the Stamp Act.

> The Virginia Resolves

1. Virginians were British citizens.
2. Virginians enjoyed the same rights and privileges as Britons.
3. As British citizens, Virginians had the right to tax themselves.
4. Virginians had always taxed themselves, through their representatives in the House of Burgesses.
5. The Virginia assembly alone had the right to tax Virginians.
6. Any tax law originating from outside Virginia was not legitimate.
7. Anyone who disagreed with these propositions was an enemy of Virginia.

The final two propositions were too much for the majority of the representatives in the assembly. They voted down resolutions six and seven and later rescinded their vote on number five as well. Their caution hardly mattered, however, because newspapers in other colonies printed all seven Virginia Resolves, creating the impression that a daring first challenge to the Stamp Act had occurred. Consequently, other assemblies were willing to consider even more radical questions, such as this: By what authority could Parliament legislate for the colonies without also taxing them? No one disagreed, in 1765, that Parliament had legislative power over the colonists, who were, after all, British subjects. Several assemblies advanced the argument that there was a distinction between *external* taxes, imposed to regulate trade, and *internal* taxes, such as a stamp tax or a property tax, which could only be self-imposed.

Reaction to the Stamp Act ran far deeper than political debate in assemblies. Every person whose livelihood required official paper had to decide whether to comply with the act. The first organized resistance to the Stamp Act began in Boston in August 1765 under the direction of town leaders, chief among them Samuel Adams, John Hancock, and Ebenezer Mackintosh. Many other artisans,

CHAPTER LOCATOR | How did the Seven Years' War lay the groundwork for colonial crisis? | Why did the Sugar Act and the Stamp Act draw fierce opposition from colonists?

152 CHAPTER 6 THE BRITISH EMPIRE AND THE COLONIAL CRISIS

Newspapers Protest the Stamp Act

The Stamp Act affected newspaper publishers more than any other businessmen. From New Hampshire to South Carolina, papers issued on October 31, 1765, used dark black mourning lines and funereal language to herald the date the Stamp Act went into effect. A New Hampshire editor dramatically declared, "I must Die, or Submit to that which is worse than Death, Be Stamped, and lose my Freedom." All colonial newspapers resumed publication within a week or two, defiantly operating without stamps. Library of Congress.

tradesmen, printers, tavern keepers, dockworkers, and sailors — the middling and lower orders — mobilized to oppose the Stamp Act, taking the name "Sons of Liberty."

The plan hatched in Boston called for a large street demonstration highlighting a mock execution designed to convince Andrew Oliver, the designated stamp distributor, to resign. On August 14, 1765, a crowd of two thousand to three thousand demonstrators, led by the young shoemaker Mackintosh, hung an effigy of Oliver in a tree and then paraded it around town before finally beheading and burning it. In hopes of calming tensions, the royal governor Francis Bernard took no action. The next day Oliver resigned his office in a well-publicized announcement.

The demonstration provided lessons for everyone. Oliver learned that stamp distributors would be very unpopular people. Governor Bernard, with no police force to call on, learned the limitations of his power to govern. The demonstration's leaders learned that street action was effective. And hundreds of ordinary men not only learned what the Stamp Act was all about but also gained pride in their ability to have a decisive impact on politics. Twelve days later, a second crowd action showed how well these lessons had been learned. On August 26, a crowd visited the houses of three detested customs and court officials, breaking windows and raiding wine cellars. A fourth target was the finest dwelling in Massachusetts, owned by Thomas Hutchinson, lieutenant governor of Massachusetts and the chief justice of the colony's highest court. Rumors abounded that Hutchinson had urged Grenville to adopt the Stamp Act. Although he had actually done the opposite, Hutchinson refused to set the record straight, saying curtly, "I am not obliged to give an answer to all the questions that may be put me by every lawless person." The crowd attacked his house, and by daybreak only the exterior walls were standing. Governor Bernard gave orders to call out the militia, but he was told that many militiamen were among the crowd.

The destruction of Hutchinson's house brought a temporary halt to protest activities in Boston. The town meeting issued a statement of sympathy for Hutchinson, but a large reward for the arrest and conviction of rioters failed to produce a single lead. Essentially, the opponents of the Stamp Act in Boston had triumphed; no one replaced Oliver as distributor. When the act took effect on

Why did British authorities send troops to occupy Boston in the fall of 1768?

Why did Parliament pass the Coercive Acts in 1774?

How did enslaved people in the colonies react to the stirrings of revolution?

Conclusion: What changes did the American colonists want in 1775?

LearningCurve Check what you know. bedfordstmartins.com /roarkunderstanding

November 1, ships without stamped permits continued to clear the harbor. Since he could not bring the lawbreakers to court, Hutchinson, ever principled, felt obliged to resign his office as chief justice. He remained lieutenant governor, however, and within five years he became the royal governor.

Liberty and Property

Boston's crowd actions of August sparked similar eruptions by groups calling themselves Sons of Liberty in nearly fifty towns throughout the colonies, and stamp distributors everywhere hastened to resign. A crowd forced one Connecticut distributor to throw his hat and powdered wig in the air while shouting a cheer for "Liberty and property!" This man fared better than another Connecticut stamp agent who was nearly buried alive by Sons of Liberty. Only when the thuds of dirt sounded on his coffin did he have a sudden change of heart, shouting out his resignation to the crowd above. Luckily, he was heard. In Charleston, South Carolina, the stamp distributor resigned after crowds burned effigies and chanted "Liberty! Liberty!"

Some colonial leaders, disturbed by the riots, sought a more moderate challenge to parliamentary authority. In October 1765, twenty-seven delegates representing nine colonial assemblies met in New York City as the Stamp Act Congress. For two weeks, the men hammered out a petition about taxation addressed to the king and Parliament. Their statement closely resembled the first five Virginia Resolves, claiming that taxes were "free gifts of the people," which only the people's representatives could give. They dismissed virtual representation: "The people of these colonies are not, and from their local circumstances, cannot be represented in the House of Commons." At the same time, the delegates carefully affirmed their subordination to Parliament and monarch in deferential language.

Nevertheless, the Stamp Act Congress, by the mere fact of its meeting, advanced a radical potential — the notion of intercolonial political action. The rallying cry of "Liberty and property" made perfect sense to many white Americans of all social ranks, who feared that the Stamp Act threatened their traditional right to liberty as British subjects. The liberty in question was the right to be taxed only by representative government. "Liberty and property" came from a trinity of concepts — "life, liberty, property" — that had come to be regarded as the birthright of freeborn British subjects since at least the seventeenth century. A powerful tradition of British political thought invested representative government with the duty to protect individual lives, liberties, and property against potential abuse by royal authority. Up to 1765, Americans had consented to accept Parliament as a body that represented them. But now, in this matter of taxation via stamps, Parliament seemed a distant body that had failed to protect Americans' liberty and property against royal authority.

Alarmed, some Americans began to speak and write about a plot by British leaders to enslave them. A Maryland writer warned that if the colonies lost "the right of exemption from all taxes without their consent," that loss would "deprive them of every privilege distinguishing freemen from slaves." In Virginia, a group of planters headed by Richard Henry Lee issued a document called the Westmoreland Resolves, claiming that the Stamp Act was an attempt

CHAPTER LOCATOR | How did the Seven Years' War lay the groundwork for colonial crisis? | Why did the Sugar Act and the Stamp Act draw fierce opposition from colonists?

154 CHAPTER 6 THE BRITISH EMPIRE AND THE COLONIAL CRISIS

"to reduce the people of this country to a state of abject and detestable slavery." The opposite meanings of *liberty* and *slavery* were utterly clear to white Americans, but they stopped short of applying similar logic to the half million black Americans they held in bondage. Many blacks, however, could see the contradiction. When a crowd of Charleston blacks paraded with shouts of "Liberty!" just a few months after white Sons of Liberty had done the same, the town militia turned out to break up the demonstration.

Politicians and merchants in Britain reacted with distress to the American demonstrations and petitions. Merchants particularly feared trade disruptions and pressured Parliament to repeal the Stamp Act. By late 1765, yet another new minister, the Marquess of Rockingham, headed the king's cabinet and sought a way to repeal the act without losing face. The solution came in March 1766: The Stamp Act was repealed, but with the repeal came the **Declaratory Act**, which asserted Parliament's right to legislate for the colonies "in all cases whatsoever." Perhaps the stamp tax had been inexpedient, but the power to tax — one prime case of a legislative power — was stoutly upheld.

Declaratory Act
▶ 1766 law issued by Parliament to assert Parliament's unassailable right to legislate for British colonies "in all cases whatsoever," putting Americans on notice that the simultaneous repeal of the Stamp Act changed nothing in the imperial powers of Britain.

QUICK REVIEW

What rights did many Americans feel were challenged by the Sugar Act and the Stamp Act? How did they express their disapproval of the acts?

Why did British authorities send troops to occupy Boston in the fall of 1768?

Why did Parliament pass the Coercive Acts in 1774?

How did enslaved people in the colonies react to the stirrings of revolution?

Conclusion: What changes did the American colonists want in 1775?

✓ **LearningCurve**
Check what you know.
bedfordstmartins.com
/roarkunderstanding

Why did British authorities send troops to occupy Boston in the fall of 1768?

Edenton Tea Ladies

Patriotic women in Edenton, North Carolina, pledged to renounce British tea and were satirized in this British cartoon, which shows brazen women shedding traditional notions of femininity. Neglected babies, urinating dogs, wanton sexuality, and mean-looking women were the consequences of meddling in politics, according to the artist. The cartoon was humorous to the British because of the gender reversals it predicts and because of the insult it directs at American men. Library of Congress.

ROCKINGHAM DID NOT LAST LONG as prime minister. By the summer of 1766, George III had persuaded William Pitt to resume that position. Pitt appointed Charles Townshend to be chancellor of the exchequer, the chief financial minister. Facing both the old war debt and the cost of the British troops in America, Townshend turned again to taxation, but his plan to raise revenue touched off coordinated boycotts of British goods in 1768 and 1769. Even women were politicized as self-styled "Daughters of Liberty." Boston led the uproar, causing the British to send peacekeeping soldiers to assist the royal governor. The stage was thus set for the first fatalities in the brewing revolution.

CHAPTER LOCATOR

How did the Seven Years' War lay the groundwork for colonial crisis?

Why did the Sugar Act and the Stamp Act draw fierce opposition from colonists?

156 CHAPTER 6
THE BRITISH EMPIRE AND THE COLONIAL CRISIS

The Townshend Duties

Townshend proposed new taxes in the old form of a navigation act. Officially called the Revenue Act of 1767, it established new duties on tea, glass, lead, paper, and painters' colors imported into the colonies, to be paid by the importer but passed on to consumers in the retail price. A recent further reduction in the duty on French molasses had persuaded some American shippers to quit smuggling, and finally Britain was deriving a moderate revenue stream from its colonies. Townshend naively concluded that Americans accepted external taxes. The **Townshend duties** were not especially burdensome, but the principle they embodied — taxation through trade duties — looked different to the colonists in the wake of the Stamp Act crisis. Although Americans once distinguished between external and internal taxes, accepting external duties as a means to direct the flow of trade, that distinction was wiped out by an external tax meant only to raise money. John Dickinson, a Philadelphia lawyer, articulated this view in an essay titled *Letters from a Farmer in Pennsylvania*, widely circulated in late 1767. "We are taxed without our consent. . . . We are therefore — SLAVES," Dickinson wrote, calling for "a total denial of the power of Parliament to lay upon these colonies any 'tax' whatever." A controversial provision of the Townshend duties directed that some of the revenue generated would pay the salaries of royal governors. Before 1767, local assemblies set the salaries of their own officials, giving them significant influence over crown-appointed officeholders. Through his new provision, Townshend aimed to strengthen the governors' position as well as to curb what he perceived to be the growing independence of the assemblies. Massachusetts again took the lead in protesting the Townshend duties. Samuel Adams, now an elected member of the provincial assembly, argued that any form of parliamentary taxation was unjust because Americans were not represented in Parliament. Further, he argued that the new way to pay governors' salaries subverted the proper relationship between the people and their rulers. The assembly circulated a letter with Adams's arguments to other colonial assemblies for their endorsement. As with the Stamp Act Congress of 1765, colonial assemblies were starting to coordinate their protests.

In response to Adams's letter, Lord Hillsborough, the new man in charge of colonial affairs in Britain, instructed Massachusetts governor Francis Bernard to dissolve the assembly if it refused to repudiate the letter. The assembly refused, by a vote of 92 to 17, and Bernard carried out his instruction. In the summer of 1768, Boston was in an uproar.

Nonconsumption and the Daughters of Liberty

The Boston town meeting led the way with nonconsumption agreements, calling for a boycott of all British-made goods. Dozens of other towns passed similar resolutions in 1767 and 1768. For example, prohibited purchases in the town of New Haven, Connecticut, included carriages, furniture, hats, clothing, lace, clocks, and textiles. The idea was to encourage home manufacture and to hurt trade, causing London merchants to pressure Parliament for repeal of the Townshend duties. Nonconsumption agreements were very hard to enforce.

Townshend duties

▶ New duties (established by the Revenue Act of 1767) on tea, glass, lead, paper, and painters' colors imported into the colonies. The Townshend duties led to boycotts and heightened tensions between Britain and the American colonies.

> CHRONOLOGY

1767
– Parliament enacts Townshend duties.

1768
– British station troops in Boston.

1768–1769
– Merchants sign nonimportation agreements.

1770
– Boston Massacre.

Why did British authorities send troops to occupy Boston in the fall of 1768? | Why did Parliament pass the Coercive Acts in 1774? | How did enslaved people in the colonies react to the stirrings of revolution? | Conclusion: What changes did the American colonists want in 1775? | ✓ LearningCurve Check what you know. bedfordstmartins.com /roarkunderstanding

With the Stamp Act, there was one hated item, a stamp, and a limited number of official distributors. By contrast, an agreement to boycott all British goods required serious personal sacrifice, which not everyone was prepared to make. A more direct blow to trade came from nonimportation agreements, but getting merchants to agree to these proved more difficult, because of fears that merchants in other colonies might continue to import goods and make handsome profits. Not until late 1768 could Boston merchants agree to suspend trade through a nonimportation agreement lasting one year starting January 1, 1769. Sixty signed the agreement. New York merchants soon followed suit, as did Philadelphia and Charleston merchants in 1769.

Many of the British products specified in nonconsumption agreements were household goods traditionally under the control of the "ladies." By 1769, male leaders in the patriot cause clearly understood that women's cooperation in nonconsumption and home manufacture was beneficial to their cause. The Townshend duties thus provided an unparalleled opportunity for encouraging female patriotism. During the Stamp Act crisis, Sons of Liberty took to the streets in protest. During the difficulties of 1768 and 1769, the concept of Daughters of Liberty emerged to give shape to a new idea — that women might play a role in public affairs. Any woman could express affiliation with the colonial protest through conspicuous boycotts of British-made goods. In Boston, more than three hundred women signed a petition to abstain from tea, "sickness excepted," in order to "save this abused Country from Ruin and Slavery."

Homespun cloth became a prominent symbol of patriotism. A young Boston girl learning to spin called herself "a daughter of liberty," noting that "I chuse to wear as much of our own manufactory as pocible." In the boycott period of 1768 to 1770, newspapers reported on spinning matches, or bees, in some sixty New England towns, in which women came together in public to make yarn. Newspaper accounts variously called the spinners "Daughters of Liberty" or "Daughters of Industry."

This surge of public spinning was related to the politics of the boycott, which infused traditional women's work with new political purpose. But the women spinners were not equivalents of the Sons of Liberty. The Sons marched in streets, burned effigies, threatened hated officials, and celebrated anniversaries of their successes with raucous drinking in taverns. The Daughters manifested their patriotism quietly, in ways marked by piety, industry, and charity. The difference was due in part to cultural ideals of gender, which prized masculine self-assertion and feminine selflessness. It also was due to class. The Sons were a cross-class alliance, with leaders from the middling orders reliant on men and boys of the lower ranks to fuel their crowds. The Daughters were genteel ladies accustomed to buying British goods. The difference between the Sons and the Daughters also speaks to two views of how best to challenge authority: violent threats and street actions, or the self-disciplined, self-sacrificing boycott of goods?

On the whole, the anti-British boycotts were a success. Imports fell by more than 40 percent; British merchants felt the pinch and let Parliament know it. In Boston, the extended Hutchinson family — whose fortune rested on British trade — also endured losses, but even more alarming to the lieutenant governor, Boston

CHAPTER LOCATOR | How did the Seven Years' War lay the groundwork for colonial crisis? | Why did the Sugar Act and the Stamp Act draw fierce opposition from colonists?

CHAPTER 6

158 THE BRITISH EMPIRE AND THE COLONIAL CRISIS

seemed overrun with anti-British sentiment. The Sons of Liberty staged rollicking annual celebrations of the Stamp Act riot, and both Hutchinson and Governor Bernard concluded that British troops were necessary to restore order.

Military Occupation and "Massacre" in Boston

In the fall of 1768, three thousand uniformed troops arrived to occupy Boston. Although the situation was frequently tense, no major troubles occurred that winter and through most of 1769. But as January 1, 1770, approached, marking the end of the nonimportation agreement, it was clear that some merchants — such as Thomas Hutchinson's two sons, both importers — were ready to break the boycott.

Trouble began in January, when a crowd smeared the door of the Hutchinson brothers' shop with excrement. In February, a crowd surrounded the house of a confrontational customs official who panicked and fired a musket,

The Bloody Massacre Perpetrated in King Street, Boston, on March 5, 1770

Paul Revere's mass-produced engraving shows the patriot version of events. Soldiers appear as a firing squad, shooting simultaneously at an unarmed and bewigged crowd; more likely the shooting was chaotic, and the fatalities were from lower classes who rarely wore wigs. Crispus Attucks, an African-Indian dockworker, was killed, but Revere depicts only whites among the injured.
Anne S. K. Brown Military Collection, Providence, Rhode Island.

> **VISUAL ACTIVITY**

READING THE IMAGE: How does this picture attempt to enlist its viewers' sympathies?

CONNECTIONS: Does this picture accurately represent the events of the Boston Massacre? What might account for its biases?

| Why did British authorities send troops to occupy Boston in the fall of 1768? | Why did Parliament pass the Coercive Acts in 1774? | How did enslaved people in the colonies react to the stirrings of revolution? | Conclusion: What changes did the American colonists want in 1775? | ✓ LearningCurve Check what you know. bedfordstmartins.com /roarkunderstanding |

accidentally killing a young boy passing on the street. The Sons of Liberty mounted a massive funeral procession to mark this first instance of violent death in the struggle with Britain.

For the next week, tension gripped Boston. The climax came on Monday evening, March 5, 1770, when a crowd taunted eight British soldiers guarding the customs house. Onlookers threw snowballs and rocks and dared the soldiers to fire; finally one did. After a short pause, someone yelled "Fire!" and the other soldiers shot into the crowd, hitting eleven men, killing five of them.

The **Boston Massacre**, as the event was quickly labeled, was over in minutes. Hutchinson, now acting governor of the colony, immediately removed the regiments to an island in the harbor to prevent further bloodshed, and he jailed Captain Thomas Preston and his eight soldiers for their own protection, promising they would be held for trial.

The Sons of Liberty staged elaborate martyrs' funerals for the five victims. Significantly, the one nonwhite victim shared equally in the public's veneration. Crispus Attucks, a sailor and rope maker in his forties, was the son of an African man and a Natick Indian woman. A slave in his youth, he was at the time of his death a free laborer at the Boston docks. Attucks was one of the first American partisans to die in the revolutionary struggle with Britain, and certainly the first African American.

At trial in the fall of 1770, the eight soldiers were ably defended by two Boston attorneys, John Adams and Josiah Quincy. While both had direct ties to the leadership of the Sons of Liberty, Adams was deeply committed to the principle that even unpopular defendants deserved a fair trial. The five-day trial resulted in acquittal for Preston and for all but two of the soldiers, who were convicted of manslaughter, branded on the thumbs, and released.

Boston Massacre

▶ March 1770 incident in Boston in which British soldiers fired on an American crowd, killing five. The Boston Massacre became a rallying point for colonists who increasingly saw the British government as tyrannical and illegitimate.

> **QUICK REVIEW**

Why were Boston's resistance to British policies and British reaction to the resistance so pronounced?

CHAPTER LOCATOR | How did the Seven Years' War lay the groundwork for colonial crisis? | Why did the Sugar Act and the Stamp Act draw fierce opposition from colonists?

CHAPTER 6
160   THE BRITISH EMPIRE AND THE COLONIAL CRISIS

Tossing the Tea This colored engraving appeared in an English book published in 1789 recounting the history of North America from its earliest settlement to "becoming united, free, and independent states." This event was not dubbed the "Tea Party" until the 1830s, when a later generation celebrated the illegal destruction of the tea and made heroes out of the few surviving participants, by then in their eighties and nineties. Library of Congress.

IN THE SAME WEEK as the Boston Massacre, yet another new British prime minister, Frederick North, acknowledged the harmful impact of the boycott on trade and recommended repeal of the Townshend duties. Seeking peace with the colonies and prosperity for British merchants, Lord North persuaded Parliament to remove all the duties except the tax on tea, kept as a symbol of Parliament's power. For nearly two years following repeal of the Townshend duties, peace seemed possible, but tense incidents in 1772, followed by a renewed struggle over the tea tax in 1773, precipitated a full-scale crisis in the summer and fall of 1774. In response, men from nearly all the colonies came together in a special "Continental Congress" to debate the crisis.

The Calm before the Storm

Repeal of the Townshend duties brought an end to nonimportation. Trade boomed in 1770 and 1771, driven by pent-up demand. Moreover, the leaders of the popular movement seemed to be losing their power. Samuel Adams, for example, ran for a minor local office and lost to a conservative merchant. Then in 1772, several incidents again brought the conflict with Britain into sharp focus. One was the burning of the *Gaspée,* a Royal Navy ship pursuing suspected smugglers near Rhode Island. A British investigating commission failed to arrest anyone but announced that it would send suspects, if any were found, to Britain for trial on charges of high treason. This ruling seemed to fly in the face of the traditional English right to trial by a jury of one's peers.

> **CHRONOLOGY**

1770
– Parliament repeals Townshend duties.

1772
– British navy ship *Gaspée* is burned.
– Committees of correspondence begin forming.

1773
– Parliament passes Tea Act.
– Tea is dumped in Boston harbor.

1774
– Parliament passes Coercive Acts.
– Powder Alarm shows colonists' readiness.
– First Continental Congress meets.

Why did British authorities send troops to occupy Boston in the fall of 1768?	Why did Parliament pass the Coercive Acts in 1774?	How did enslaved people in the colonies react to the stirrings of revolution?	Conclusion: What changes did the American colonists want in 1775?	✓ **LearningCurve** Check what you know. bedfordstmartins.com /roarkunderstanding

When news of the *Gaspée* investigation spread, it was greeted with disbelief in other colonies. Patrick Henry, Thomas Jefferson, and Richard Henry Lee in the Virginia House of Burgesses proposed that a network of standing committees be established to link the colonies and pass along alarming news. By mid-1773, all but one colonial assembly had set up a "committee of correspondence."

Massachusetts, the continuing hotspot of the conflict, developed its own rapid communications network, with urgency provided by a new proposal by Lord North to pay the salaries of county court justices out of the tea revenue, reminiscent of Townshend's plan for paying royal governors. By the spring of 1773, more than half the towns in Massachusetts had set up **committees of correspondence** to receive, discuss, distribute, and act on political news. The first message to circulate came from Boston. It framed North's salary plan for judges as the latest proof of a British conspiracy to undermine traditional liberties: first taxation without consent, then military occupation and a massacre, and now a plot to subvert the justice system. Express riders swiftly distributed the message, which sparked ordinary townspeople to embrace a revolutionary language of rights and constitutional duties. Eventually the committees of correspondence would foster rapid mobilization to defend a countryside feeling under literal attack.

The paramount incident shattering the relative calm of the early 1770s was the **Tea Act of 1773**. Americans had resumed buying the taxed British tea, but they were also smuggling large quantities of Dutch tea, cutting into the sales of Britain's East India Company. So Lord North proposed legislation giving favored status to the East India Company, allowing it to sell tea directly to a few selected merchants in four colonial cities, cutting out British middlemen. The hope was to lower the price of the East India tea, including the duty, below that of smuggled Dutch tea, thus motivating Americans to obey the law.

Tea in Boston Harbor

In the fall of 1773, news of the Tea Act reached the colonies. Parliamentary legislation to make tea inexpensive struck many colonists as an insidious plot to trick Americans into buying the dutied tea. The real goal, some argued, was the increased revenue that would pay the salaries of royal governors and judges.

But how to resist the Tea Act? Nonimportation was not viable, because the tea trade was too lucrative to expect merchants to give it up willingly. Consumer boycotts seemed ineffective, because it was impossible to distinguish between duttied tea and smuggled tea once it was in the teapot. The appointment of official tea agents, parallel to the Stamp Act distributors, suggested one solution. In every port city, revived Sons of Liberty pressured tea agents to resign. Without agents, governors yielded, and tea cargoes either landed duty-free or were sent home.

Governor Hutchinson, however, would not bend any rules. Three ships bearing tea arrived in Boston in November 1773. The ships cleared customs, and the crews, sensing the town's extreme tension, unloaded all cargo except the tea. Picking up on the tension in Boston, the captains wished to return to England, but Hutchinson would not grant them clearance to leave without paying the tea duty. He gave them twenty days to pay, after which time the tea would be confiscated.

committees of correspondence

▶ A communications network established among towns in Massachusetts and also among colonial capital towns in 1772–1773 to provide for rapid dissemination of news about important political developments. These committees politicized ordinary townspeople, sparking a revolutionary language of rights and duties.

Tea Act of 1773

▶ British act that lowered the existing tax on tea to entice boycotting Americans to buy it. Resistance to the Tea Act led to the passage of the Coercive Acts and imposition of military rule in Massachusetts.

CHAPTER LOCATOR

How did the Seven Years' War lay the groundwork for colonial crisis?

Why did the Sugar Act and the Stamp Act draw fierce opposition from colonists?

162   CHAPTER 6
THE BRITISH EMPIRE AND THE COLONIAL CRISIS

TABLE 6.1 ■ The Coercive (Intolerable) Acts

1. Boston Port Act	Closed Boston harbor to all shipping as of June 1, 1774, until the destroyed tea was paid for. Britain's objective was to halt the commercial life of the city.
2. Massachusetts Government Act	Augmented the royal governor's powers. The governor could appoint the Massachusetts council, which before was elected. He could appoint and remove all judges, sheriffs, and officers of the court. Going forward, town meetings could be held only with the governor's approval.
3. Impartial Administration of Justice Act	Stipulated that any royal official accused of a capital crime would be tried in Britain. The act implied that there would be further violent confrontations between British soldiers and colonists.
4. Quartering Act	Permitted military commanders to lodge soldiers wherever necessary, even in private households, a step toward military rule in Massachusetts.
5. Quebec Act	Not directly related to the Coercive Acts, it gave control of disputed land throughout the Ohio Valley to Quebec.

For the full twenty days, crowds swelled by concerned people from surrounding towns kept the pressure high. On the final day, December 16, a large crowd gathered at Old South Church to debate a course of action. No solution emerged at that meeting, but immediately after, 100 to 150 men disguised as Indians boarded the three ships and dumped thousands of pounds of tea into the harbor while a crowd of 2,000 watched. In admiration, John Adams wrote: "This Destruction of the Tea is so bold, so daring, so firm, intrepid and inflexible, and it must have so important Consequences."

The Coercive Acts

Lord North's response was swift and stern: In 1774, he persuaded Parliament to issue the **Coercive Acts**, four laws meant to punish Massachusetts. In America, those laws, along with a fifth one, the Quebec Act, were soon known as the **Intolerable Acts** (Table 6.1). In a related move, Lord North appointed General Thomas Gage, commander of the Royal Army in New York, governor of Massachusetts, replacing Thomas Hutchinson.

These five acts spread alarm in all the colonies. If Britain could squelch Massachusetts — change its charter, suspend local government, inaugurate military rule, and on top of that give Ohio to Catholic Quebec — what liberties were secure? Fearful royal governors in a half dozen colonies dismissed the sitting assemblies, adding to the sense of urgency. A few of the assemblies defiantly continued to meet in new locations. Via the committees of correspondence, colonial leaders arranged to convene in Philadelphia in September 1774 to respond to the crisis.

Beyond Boston: Rural New England

The Coercive Acts fired up all of New England to open insubordination. With a British general occupying the Massachusetts governorship and some three

Coercive (Intolerable) Acts
▶ Four British acts of 1774 meant to punish Massachusetts for the destruction of three shiploads of tea. Known in America as the Intolerable Acts, they led to open rebellion in the northern colonies.

| Why did British authorities send troops to occupy Boston in the fall of 1768? | Why did Parliament pass the Coercive Acts in 1774? | How did enslaved people in the colonies react to the stirrings of revolution? | Conclusion: What changes did the American colonists want in 1775? | ✔ LearningCurve Check what you know. bedfordstmartins.com /roarkunderstanding |

163

thousand troops controlling Boston, the revolutionary momentum shifted from urban radicals to rural farmers who protested in dozens of spontaneous, dramatic showdowns. Some towns found creative ways to get around the prohibition on new town meetings, and others just ignored the law. Governor Gage's call for elections for a new provincial assembly under his control sparked the formation of a competing unauthorized assembly that met in defiance of his orders. In all Massachusetts counties outside Boston, crowds of thousands of armed men converged to prevent the opening of county courts run by crown-appointed jurists. By August 1774, farmers and artisans all over Massachusetts had effectively taken full control of their local institutions.

Gage was especially distressed by the military preparations of citizen militias, drilling on village greens to gain proficiency with muskets. The governor wrote London begging for troop reinforcements, and he beefed up fortifications around Boston. But without more soldiers, his options were limited. Seizing stockpiles of gunpowder was his best move.

The Powder Alarm of September 1 showed just how ready the defiant Americans were to take up arms against Britain. Gage sent troops to a town just outside Boston reported to have a hidden powder storehouse, and in the surprise and scramble of the attack, false news spread that the troops had fired on men defending the powder, killing six. Within twenty-four hours, several thousand armed men from Massachusetts, New Hampshire, and Connecticut streamed on foot to Boston to avenge the first blood spilled. At this moment, ordinary men became insurgents, willing to kill or be killed in the face of the British clampdown. Once the error was corrected and the crisis defused, the men returned home peaceably. But Gage could no longer doubt the speed and determination of the rebellious subjects.

All this had occurred without orchestration by Boston radicals, Gage reported. But British leaders found it hard to believe, as one put it, that "a tumultuous Rabble, without any Appearance of general Concert, or without any Head to advise, or Leader to conduct" could pull off such effective resistance. Repeatedly in the years to come, the British would seriously underestimate their opponents.

The First Continental Congress

Every colony except Georgia sent delegates to Philadelphia in September 1774 to discuss the looming crisis at the **First Continental Congress**. Delegates sought to articulate their liberties as British subjects and the powers Parliament held over them, and they debated possible responses to the Coercive Acts. Some wanted a total ban on trade with Britain to force repeal, while others, especially southerners dependent on tobacco and rice exports, opposed halting trade. Samuel Adams and Patrick Henry were eager for a ringing denunciation of all parliamentary control. The conservative Joseph Galloway of Pennsylvania proposed a plan (quickly defeated) to create a secondary parliament in America to assist the British Parliament in ruling the colonies.

The congress met for seven weeks and produced a declaration of rights couched in traditional language: "We ask only for peace, liberty and security. We wish no diminution of royal prerogatives, we demand no new rights." But from Britain's point of view, the rights assumed already to exist were radical. Chief

First Continental Congress

▶ September 1774 gathering of colonial delegates in Philadelphia to discuss the crisis precipitated by the Coercive Acts. The congress produced a declaration of rights and an agreement to impose a limited boycott of trade with Britain.

CHAPTER LOCATOR | How did the Seven Years' War lay the groundwork for colonial crisis? | Why did the Sugar Act and the Stamp Act draw fierce opposition from colonists?

CHAPTER 6
164   THE BRITISH EMPIRE AND THE COLONIAL CRISIS

among them was the claim that because Americans were not represented in Parliament, each colonial government had the sole right to govern and tax its own people. To put pressure on Britain, the delegates agreed to a staggered and limited boycott of trade: imports prohibited this year, exports the following, and rice totally exempted (to keep South Carolinians happy). To enforce the boycott, they called for a Continental Association, with chapters in each town variously called committees of public safety or of inspection, to monitor all commerce and punish suspected violators of the boycott. Its work done in a month, the congress disbanded with an agreement to reconvene in May.

The committees of public safety, the committees of correspondence, the regrouped colonial assemblies, and the Continental Congress were all political bodies functioning defiantly without any constitutional authority. British officials did not recognize them as legitimate, but many Americans who supported the patriot cause instantly accepted them. A key reason for the stability of such unauthorized governing bodies was that they were composed of many of the same men who had held elective office before.

Britain's severe reaction to Boston's destruction of the tea finally succeeded in making many colonists from New Hampshire to Georgia realize that the problems of British rule went far beyond questions of nonconsensual taxation. The Coercive Acts infringed on liberty and denied self-government; they could not be ignored. With one colony already subordinated to military rule and a British army camped in Boston, the threat of a general war was very real.

QUICK REVIEW <

In what ways did colonial responses to British actions change after 1772?

Why did British authorities send troops to occupy Boston in the fall of 1768?

Why did Parliament pass the Coercive Acts in 1774?

How did enslaved people in the colonies react to the stirrings of revolution?

Conclusion: What changes did the American colonists want in 1775?

☑ **LearningCurve**
Check what you know.
bedfordstmartins.com
/roarkunderstanding

> How did enslaved people in the colonies react to the stirrings of revolution?

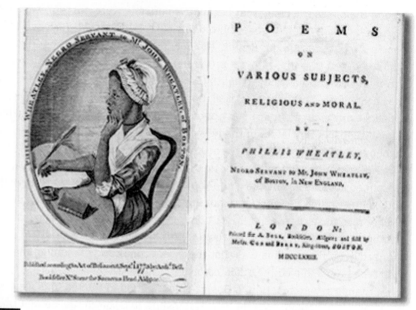

Phillis, born in Africa, was sold into slavery to John Wheatley of Boston at age seven. She published her first poem at age twelve, in 1766. In 1773, her master took her to London, where *Poems on Various Subjects, Religious and Moral* was published, gaining her great literary notice. Library of Congress.

BEFORE THE SECOND CONTINENTAL CONGRESS could meet, violence and bloodshed came to Massachusetts in the towns of Lexington and Concord. Fearing domestic insurrection, General Thomas Gage sent his soldiers there to capture an ammunition depot, but New England farmers mobilized against an intrusive power they feared would enslave them. To the south, a different and inverted version of the same story began to unfold, as thousands of enslaved black men and women seized an unprecedented opportunity to mount a different kind of insurrection — against planter-patriots who looked over their shoulders uneasily whenever they called out for liberty from the British.

Lexington and Concord

During the winter of 1774–75, Americans pressed on with boycotts. Optimists hoped to effect a repeal of the Coercive Acts; pessimists stockpiled arms and ammunition. In Massachusetts, militia units known as minutemen prepared to respond at a minute's notice to any threat from the British troops in Boston.

Thomas Gage realized how desperate the British position was. The people, Gage wrote Lord North, were "numerous, worked up to a fury, and not a Boston rabble but the freeholders and farmers of the country." Gage requested twenty thousand reinforcements. He also strongly advised repeal of the Coercive Acts, but leaders in Britain could not admit failure. Instead, in mid-April 1775, they ordered Gage to arrest the troublemakers.

> CHRONOLOGY

1773
- Phillis Wheatley's *Poems on Various Subjects, Religious and Moral* is published in London.

1775
- Battles of Lexington and Concord.
- Lord Dunmore promises freedom to defecting slaves.

CHAPTER LOCATOR | How did the Seven Years' War lay the groundwork for colonial crisis? | Why did the Sugar Act and the Stamp Act draw fierce opposition from colonists?

166 CHAPTER 6 THE BRITISH EMPIRE AND THE COLONIAL CRISIS

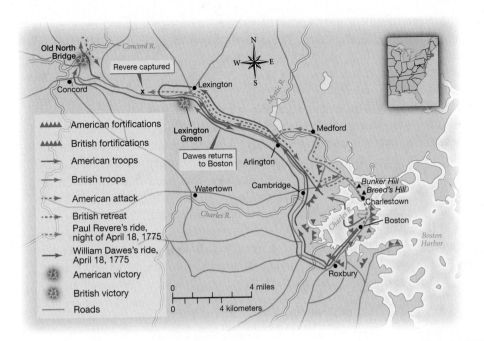

MAP 6.3 ■ Lexington and Concord, April 1775

Two Americans slipped out of Boston to warn of a surprise British attack on Concord. Paul Revere went by boat to Charlestown and then by horse to Lexington, while William Dawes casually rode past British sentries and then galloped at full speed through Lexington to Concord.

> **MAP ACTIVITY**

READING THE MAP: How did Dawes's route differ from Revere's? What kinds of terrain and potential dangers did each man face during his ride, according to the map?
CONNECTIONS: Why send two men on the same mission? Why not send four or more?

Gage quickly planned a surprise attack on a suspected ammunition storage site at Concord, a village eighteen miles west of Boston (**Map 6.3**). Near midnight on April 18, British soldiers moved west across the Charles River. Paul Revere and William Dawes raced ahead to alert the minutemen. When the British soldiers got to Lexington, five miles east of Concord, they were met by some seventy armed men. The British commander barked out, "Lay down your arms, you damned rebels, and disperse." The militiamen hesitated and began to comply, but then someone — nobody knows who — fired. Within two minutes, eight Americans were dead and ten were wounded.

The British units continued their march to Concord, any pretense of surprise gone. Three companies of minutemen nervously occupied the town center but offered no challenge to the British as they searched in vain for the ammunition. Finally, at Old North Bridge in Concord, British troops and minutemen exchanged shots, killing two Americans and three British soldiers. As the British returned to Boston, militia units ambushed them, bringing the bloodiest fighting of the day. In the end, 273 British soldiers were wounded or dead; the toll for the Americans stood at about 95. It was April 19, 1775, and the war had begun.

Rebelling against Slavery

News of the battles of Lexington and Concord spread within days. In Virginia, Thomas Jefferson observed that "a phrenzy of revenge seems to have seized all ranks of people," causing the royal governor of Virginia, Lord Dunmore, to remove all gunpowder from the Williamsburg powder house to a ship, out of reach of angry Virginians. Dunmore also threatened to arm slaves, if necessary, to ward off attacks by colonists. This proved effective for several months.

Why did British authorities send troops to occupy Boston in the fall of 1768?

Why did Parliament pass the Coercive Acts in 1774?

How did enslaved people in the colonies react to the stirrings of revolution?

Conclusion: What changes did the American colonists want in 1775?

LearningCurve
Check what you know.
bedfordstmartins.com
/roarkunderstanding

In November 1775, as the crisis deepened, Dunmore issued an official proclamation promising freedom to defecting able-bodied slaves who would fight for the British. He had no intention of liberating all slaves, and astute blacks noticed that Dunmore neglected to free his own slaves. A Virginia barber named Caesar declared that "he did not know any one foolish enough to believe him [Dunmore], for if he intended to do so, he ought first to set his own free." Within a month, some fifteen hundred slaves had joined Dunmore's "Ethiopian Regiment." Camp diseases quickly set in: dysentery, typhoid fever, and smallpox. When Dunmore sailed for England in mid-1776, he took three hundred black survivors with him. But the association of freedom with the British authorities had been established, and throughout the war thousands more southern slaves fled their masters whenever the British army was close enough to offer safe refuge.

In the northern colonies as well, slaves clearly recognized the evolving political struggle with Britain as an ideal moment to bid for freedom. A twenty-one-year-old Boston domestic slave employed biting sarcasm in a 1774 newspaper essay to call attention to the hypocrisy of local slave owners: "How well the Cry for Liberty, and the reverse Disposition for exercise of oppressive Power over others agree, — I humbly think it does not require the Penetration of a Philosopher to Determine." This extraordinary young woman, Phillis Wheatley, had already gained international recognition through a book of poems published in London in 1773. Wheatley's poems spoke of "Fair Freedom" as the "Goddess long desir'd" by Africans enslaved in America. Wheatley's master freed the young poet in 1775.

From north to south, groups of slaves pressed their case. Several Boston blacks offered to fight for the British in exchange for freedom, but General Gage turned them down. In Maryland, a planter complained that blacks impatient for freedom had to be disarmed of about eighty guns along with some swords. In North Carolina, white suspicions about a planned slave uprising led to the arrest of scores of African Americans who were ordered to be whipped by the revolutionary committee of public safety.

By 1783, when the Revolutionary War ended, as many as twenty thousand blacks had voted against slavery with their feet by seeking refuge with the British army. About half failed to achieve the liberation they were seeking, instead succumbing to disease, especially smallpox, in refuge camps. But some eight thousand to ten thousand persisted through the war and later, under the protection of the British army, left America to start new lives of freedom in Canada's Nova Scotia or Africa's Sierra Leone.

> ## QUICK REVIEW

What was the connection between rebelling against slavery and rebelling against the British?

CHAPTER LOCATOR | How did the Seven Years' War lay the groundwork for colonial crisis? | Why did the Sugar Act and the Stamp Act draw fierce opposition from colonists?

CHAPTER 6
168 THE BRITISH EMPIRE AND THE COLONIAL CRISIS

Conclusion: What changes did the American colonists want in 1775?

IN THE AFTERMATH of the Seven Years' War, neither losers nor victors came away satisfied. France lost vast amounts of North American land claims, and Indian land rights were increasingly violated or ignored. Britain's huge war debt and subsequent revenue-generating policies distressed Americans and set the stage for the imperial crisis of the 1760s and 1770s. The years 1763 to 1775 brought repeated attempts by the British government to subordinate the colonies into contributing partners in the larger scheme of empire.

American resistance to British policies grew slowly but steadily. In 1765, both loyalist Thomas Hutchinson and patriot Samuel Adams agreed that it was unwise for Britain to assert a right to taxation because Parliament did not adequately represent Americans. As a royal official, Hutchinson was obliged to uphold policy, while Adams protested and made political activists out of thousands in the process.

By 1775, events propelled many Americans to the conclusion that a concerted effort was afoot to deprive them of all their liberties, the most important of which were the right to self-rule and the right to live free of an occupying army. Prepared to die for those liberties, hundreds of minutemen converged on Concord. April 19 marked the start of their rebellion. Another rebellion under way in 1775 was doomed to be short-circuited. Black Americans who had experienced actual slavery listened to shouts of "Liberty!" from white crowds and appropriated the language of revolution to their own circumstances. Defiance of authority was indeed contagious.

Despite the military conflict at the battles of Lexington and Concord, a war with Britain seemed far from inevitable to colonists outside New England. In the months ahead, American colonial leaders pursued peaceful as well as military solutions to the question of who actually had authority over them. By the end of 1775, however, reconciliation with the crown would be unattainable.

| Why did British authorities send troops to occupy Boston in the fall of 1768? | Why did Parliament pass the Coercive Acts in 1774? | How did enslaved people in the colonies react to the stirrings of revolution? | Conclusion: What changes did the American colonists want in 1775? | ☑ LearningCurve Check what you know. bedfordstmartins.com /roarkunderstanding |

169

CHAPTER 6 STUDY GUIDE

STEP 1

GET STARTED ONLINE

 LearningCurve ■ bedfordstmartins.com/roarkunderstanding
Now that you've read the chapter, make it stick by completing the LearningCurve activity.

STEP 2

EXPLAIN WHY IT MATTERS

Put your reading into practice. Identify each term below, and then explain why it matters in U.S. history.

TERM	WHO OR WHAT & WHEN	WHY IT MATTERS
Seven Years' War (p. 142)		
Pontiac's Rebellion (p. 148)		
Sugar (Revenue) Act (p. 151)		
Stamp Act (p. 151)		
virtual representation (p. 152)		
Declaratory Act (p. 155)		
Townshend duties (p. 157)		
Boston Massacre (p. 160)		
committees of correspondence (p. 162)		
Tea Act of 1773 (p. 162)		
Coercive (Intolerable) Acts (p. 163)		
First Continental Congress (p. 164)		

STEP 3

MOVE BEYOND THE BASICS

To demonstrate a more advanced understanding, describe the key pieces of British legislation aimed at the colonies between 1763 and 1774, the British rationale, and the colonial response.

Legislation	Provisions	British rationale	Colonial response
Proclamation of 1763			
Sugar (Revenue) Act			
Stamp Act			
Townshend duties			
Tea Act of 1773			
Coercive (Intolerable) Acts			

PUT IT ALL TOGETHER Now, take a step back and try to explain the big picture. Remember to use specific examples from the chapter in your answers.

THE SEVEN YEARS' WAR

▶ How did the outcome of the Seven Years' War change the European balance of power in North America?

▶ How did British and colonial views of the war and its consequences differ?

TAXING THE COLONIES

▶ Why did some colonists see British efforts to tax the colonies as illegitimate? How did the British justify their efforts to raise revenue?

▶ What different groups, both in the colonies and in Great Britain, encouraged Parliament to repeal various taxes? What were their motives?

THE ESCALATION OF THE CONFLICT

▶ Why was the Tea Act so provocative? How did some colonists protest its passage?

▶ How did the British response to these protests, and the colonial reaction, help put Britain and the colonies on the path toward war?

LOOKING BACKWARD, LOOKING AHEAD

▶ How did the relationship between Britain and its North American colonies before 1763 differ from the relationship after 1763?

▶ Was war between Britain and the colonies inevitable after 1774? Why or why not?

> **IN YOUR OWN WORDS** Imagine that you must give an oral report to the class answering the following question: What were the most significant factors contributing to deteriorating relations between Britain and its North American colonies? What would be the most important points to include and why?

 Do it online at the Student Site ■ bedfordstmartins.com/roarkunderstanding

7

FIGHTING THE AMERICAN REVOLUTION

1775–1783

> How were the North American colonists able to successfully gain their independence from Great Britain in 1783? Chapter 7 follows the course of the American Revolution from the Declaration of Independence in 1776 to the Treaty of Paris in 1783. It examines the events leading up to the signing of the Declaration of Independence, the military strategies of both sides, the experience of war on the home front, the role of Native Americans and the French, and the ultimate defeat of the British against seemingly improbable odds.

LearningCurve
bedfordstmartins.com/roarkunderstanding
After reading the chapter, use LearningCurve to
retain what you've read.

> Why did Americans wait so long before they declared their independence?

> What initial challenges did the opposing armies face?

> What role did the home front play in the war?

> How were Native Americans and the French involved in the war?

> Why did the British southern strategy ultimately fail?

> Conclusion: Why did the British lose the American Revolution?

Grosvenor and Salem, 1775. Lieutenant Thomas Grosvenor (1744–1825) and his servant Peter Salem at the Battle of Bunker Hill, 17 June 1775. Detail of an oil painting on canvas, 1786, by John Trumbull. The Granger Collection.

> Why did Americans wait so long before they declared their independence?

Declaration of Independence Read to a Crowd

Printed copies of the Declaration of Independence were read aloud in public places throughout America in the week after July 4, 1776. Library of Congress.

Second Continental Congress

▶ Legislative body that governed the United States from May 1775 through the war's duration. It established an army, created its own money, and declared independence once all hope for a peaceful reconciliation with Britain was gone.

ON MAY 10, 1775, nearly one month after the fighting at Lexington and Concord, the **Second Continental Congress** assembled in Philadelphia. The congress immediately set to work on two crucial but contradictory tasks: to raise and supply an army and to explore reconciliation with Britain. To raise an army, they needed soldiers and a commander, they needed money, and they needed to work out a declaration of war. To reconcile with Britain, they needed diplomacy to approach the king. But King George III was not receptive, and by 1776, as the war progressed and hopes of reconciliation faded, delegates at the congress began to ponder the treasonous act of declaring independence.

Assuming Political and Military Authority

The delegates to the Second Continental Congress were prominent figures at home, but they now had to learn to know and trust one another. Moreover, they did not always agree. The Adams cousins John and Samuel defined the radical end of the spectrum, favoring independence. John Dickinson of Pennsylvania,

CHAPTER LOCATOR | Why did Americans wait so long before they declared their independence? | What initial challenges did the opposing armies face?

174 CHAPTER 7
FIGHTING THE AMERICAN REVOLUTION

who in 1767 critiqued British tax policy in *Letters from a Farmer*, was now a moderate, seeking reconciliation with Britain. Benjamin Franklin, fresh off a ship from an eleven-year residence in London, was feared by some to be a British spy. Mutual suspicions flourished easily when the undertaking was so dangerous, opinions were so varied, and a misstep could spell disaster.

Most of the delegates were not yet prepared to break with Britain. Some felt that government without a king was unworkable, while others feared it might be suicidal to lose Britain's protection against its traditional enemies, France and Spain. Colonies that traded actively with Britain feared undermining their economies. Probably the vast majority of ordinary Americans were unable to envision complete independence from the monarchy.

The few men at the Continental Congress who did think that independence was desirable were, not surprisingly, from Massachusetts, the target of the Coercive Acts. Even so, those men knew that it was premature to push for a break with Britain. John Adams wrote his wife, Abigail, in June 1775: "America is a great, unwieldy body. Its progress must be slow. It is like a large fleet sailing under convoy. The fleetest sailors must wait for the dullest and slowest."

Yet swift action was needed, for the Massachusetts countryside was under threat of further attack. Even the hesitant moderates in the congress agreed that a military buildup was necessary. Around the country, militia units from New York to Georgia collected arms and trained on village greens in anticipation. On June 14, the congress voted to create the **Continental army**, choosing a Virginian, George Washington, as commander in chief. This sent the clear message that there was widespread commitment to war beyond New England.

Next the congress drew up a document titled "A Declaration on the Causes and Necessity of Taking Up Arms," which rehearsed familiar arguments about the tyranny of Parliament and the need to defend English liberties. This declaration was first drafted by a young Virginia planter, Thomas Jefferson, a radical on the question of independence. The moderate John Dickinson, fearing that the declaration would offend Britain, was allowed to rewrite it. However, he left intact much of Jefferson's highly charged language about choosing "to die freemen rather than to live slaves."

To pay for the military buildup, the congress authorized a currency issue of $2 million. The Continental dollars were merely paper; they were not backed by gold or silver. The delegates somewhat naively expected that the currency would be accepted as valuable on trust as it spread in the population through the hands of soldiers, farmers, munitions suppliers, and beyond.

In just two months, the Second Continental Congress had created an army, declared war, and issued its own currency. It had taken on the major functions of a legitimate government, both military and financial, without any legal basis for its authority, for it had not yet declared independence from the king.

Pursuing Both War and Peace

The second battle of the Revolution occurred on June 16, 1775, in Boston. New England militia units had fortified the hilly terrain of the peninsula of Charlestown, which faced the city, and Thomas Gage, still commander in Boston, prepared to attack, aided by the arrival of new troops and three talented generals, William Howe, John Burgoyne, and Henry Clinton.

> CHRONOLOGY

1775
– Second Continental Congress convenes.
– Battle of Bunker Hill.
– Olive Branch Petition.

1776
– *Common Sense* is published.
– British evacuate Boston.
– Declaration of Independence.

Continental army

▶ The army created in June 1775 by the Second Continental Congress to oppose the British. Virginian George Washington, commander in chief, had the task of turning local militias and untrained volunteers into a disciplined army.

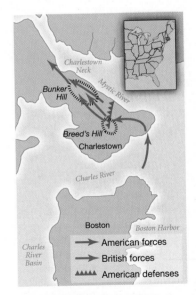

Battle of Bunker Hill, 1775

What role did the home front play in the war?

How were Native Americans and the French involved in the war?

Why did the British southern strategy ultimately fail?

Conclusion: Why did the British lose the American Revolution?

☑ LearningCurve
Check what you know.
bedfordstmartins.com
/roarkunderstanding

General William Howe insisted on a bold frontal assault, sending 2,500 soldiers across the water and up Bunker Hill in an intimidating but potentially costly attack. Three bloody assaults were needed before the British took the hill, the third succeeding mainly because the American ammunition supply gave out, and the defenders quickly retreated. The **battle of Bunker Hill** was thus a British victory, but an expensive one. The dead numbered 226 on the British side, with more than 800 wounded; the Americans suffered 140 dead, 271 wounded, and 30 captured.

battle of Bunker Hill

▶ Second battle of the war, on June 16, 1775, involving a massive British attack on New England militia units on a hill facing Boston. The militiamen finally yielded the hill, but not before inflicting heavy casualties on the British.

Instead of pursuing the fleeing Americans, Howe retreated to Boston, unwilling to risk more raids into the countryside. If the British had had any grasp of the basic instability of the American units around Boston, they might have decisively defeated the Continental army in its infancy. Instead, they lingered in Boston, abandoning it without a fight nine months later.

Howe used the time in Boston to inoculate his army against smallpox because a new epidemic of the deadly disease was spreading in port cities along the Atlantic. Inoculation worked by producing a mild but real (and therefore risky) case of smallpox, followed by lifelong immunity. Howe's instinct was right: During the American Revolution, some 130,000 people on the American continent, most of them Indians, died of smallpox.

A week after Bunker Hill, when General Washington arrived to take charge of the new Continental army, he found enthusiastic but undisciplined troops. Sanitation was an unknown concept, with inadequate latrines fouling the campground. Washington attributed the disarray to the New England custom of letting militia units elect their own officers, which he felt undermined deference. Washington spotted a militia captain, a barber in civilian life, shaving an ordinary soldier, and he moved quickly to impose more hierarchy and authority. "Be easy," he advised his newly appointed officers, "but not too familiar, lest you subject yourself to a want of that respect, which is necessary to support a proper command."

While military plans moved forward, the Second Continental Congress pursued its contradictory objective: reconciliation with Britain. Delegates from the middle colonies (Pennsylvania, Delaware, and New York), whose merchants depended on trade with Britain, urged that channels for negotiation remain open. In July 1775, congressional moderates led by John Dickinson engineered an appeal to the king called the Olive Branch Petition, affirming loyalty to the monarchy and blaming all the troubles on the king's ministers and on Parliament. It proposed that the American colonial assemblies be recognized as individual parliaments under the umbrella of the monarchy. King George III rejected the Olive Branch Petition and heatedly condemned the Americans as traitors.

Common Sense

▶ A pamphlet written by Thomas Paine in 1776 that laid out the case for independence. In it, Paine rejected monarchy, advocating its replacement with republican government based on the consent of the people. The pamphlet influenced public opinion throughout the colonies.

Thomas Paine, Abigail Adams, and the Case for Independence

Pressure for independence started to mount in January 1776, when a pamphlet titled *Common Sense* appeared in Philadelphia. Thomas Paine, its author, was an English artisan and coffeehouse intellectual who had come to America in the fall of 1774. With the encouragement of members of the Second Continental Congress, he wrote *Common Sense* to justify independence.

CHAPTER LOCATOR | Why did Americans wait so long before they declared their independence? | What initial challenges did the opposing armies face?

176   CHAPTER 7
FIGHTING THE AMERICAN REVOLUTION

An Exact View of the Late Battle at Charlestown, June 17th 1775

This engraving was for sale within weeks of the battle of Bunker Hill. British and American soldiers in fixed formation fire muskets at each other, while Charlestown is in flames in the background. Who would buy this picture? Technically, the British won the battle by taking the hill. Is that the story being told here? Colonial Williamsburg Foundation.

In simple yet forceful language, Paine elaborated on the absurdities of the British monarchy. Why should one man, by accident of birth, claim extensive power over others? he asked. A king might be foolish or wicked. "One of the strongest natural proofs of the folly of hereditary right in kings," Paine wrote, "is that nature disapproves it; otherwise she would not so frequently turn it into ridicule by giving mankind *an ass for a lion.*" To replace monarchy, Paine advocated republican government based on the consent of the people. Rulers, according to Paine, were only representatives of the people, and the best form of government relied on frequent elections to achieve the most direct democracy possible.

Paine's pamphlet sold more than 150,000 copies in a matter of weeks. Newspapers reprinted it; men read it aloud in taverns and coffeehouses; John Adams sent a copy to his wife, Abigail, who passed it around to neighbors in Braintree, Massachusetts. New Englanders desired independence, but other colonies, under no immediate threat of violence, remained cautious.

Abigail Adams was impatient not only for independence but also for other legal changes that would revolutionize the new country. In a series of astute letters to her husband, she outlined obstacles and gave advice. She worried that southern slave owners might shrink from a war in the name of liberty: "I have

What role did the home front play in the war? | How were Native Americans and the French involved in the war? | Why did the British southern strategy ultimately fail? | Conclusion: Why did the British lose the American Revolution? | ✔ LearningCurve Check what you know. bedfordstmartins.com /roarkunderstanding

177

sometimes been ready to think that the passion for Liberty cannot be Equally strong in the Breasts of those who have been accustomed to deprive their fellow Creatures of theirs." And in March 1776, she expressed her hope that women's legal status would improve under the new government: "In the new Code of Laws which I suppose it will be necessary for you to make I desire you would Remember the Ladies, and be more generous and favourable to them than your ancestors." John Adams dismissed his wife's concerns. But to a male politician, John privately rehearsed the reasons why women (and men who were free blacks, or young, or propertyless) should remain excluded from political participation. Even though he concluded that nothing should change, at least Abigail's letter had forced him to ponder the exclusion, something few men — or women — did in 1776. Urgent talk of political independence was as radical as most could imagine.

The Declaration of Independence

In addition to Paine's *Common Sense*, another factor hastening independence was the prospect of an alliance with France, Britain's archrival. France was willing to provide military supplies and naval power only if assured that the Americans would separate from Britain. News that the British were negotiating to hire German mercenary soldiers further solidified support for independence. By May 1776, all but four colonies were agitating for a declaration. The holdouts were Pennsylvania, Maryland, New York, and South Carolina, the latter two containing large loyalist populations. An exasperated Virginian wrote to his friend in the congress, "For God's sake, why do you dawdle in the Congress so strangely? Why do you not at once declare yourself a separate independent state?"

In early June, the Virginia delegation introduced a resolution calling for independence. The moderates still commanded enough support to postpone a vote on the measure until July. In the meantime, the congress appointed a committee,

CHAPTER LOCATOR | **Why did Americans wait so long before they declared their independence?** | What initial challenges did the opposing armies face?

CHAPTER 7
178 FIGHTING THE AMERICAN REVOLUTION

with Thomas Jefferson and others, to draft a longer document setting out the case for independence.

On July 2, after intense politicking, all but one state voted for independence; New York abstained. The congress then turned to the document drafted by Jefferson and his committee. Jefferson began with a preamble that articulated philosophical principles about natural rights, equality, the right of revolution, and the consent of the governed as the only true basis for government. He then listed more than two dozen specific grievances against King George. The congress passed over the preamble with little comment, and instead wrangled over the list of grievances, especially the issue of slavery. Jefferson had included an impassioned statement blaming the king for slavery, which delegates from Georgia and South Carolina struck out, not wishing to denounce their labor system. But the congress let stand another of Jefferson's grievances, blaming the king for mobilizing "the merciless Indian Savages" into bloody frontier warfare, a reference to Pontiac's Rebellion (see chapter 6).

On July 4, the amendments to Jefferson's text were complete, and the congress formally adopted the **Declaration of Independence**. A month later, the delegates gathered to sign the official parchment copy. Four men, including John Dickinson, declined to sign; several others "signed with regret . . . and with many doubts," according to John Adams. The document was then printed, widely distributed, and read aloud in celebrations everywhere. (Printed copies did not include the signers' names, for they had committed treason, a crime punishable by death.) On July 15, the New York delegation came on board, making the vote on independence unanimous.

Declaration of Independence
▶ A document containing philosophical principles and a list of grievances that declared separation from Britain. The Second Continental Congress adopted the Declaration on July 4, 1776, ending a period of intense debate with moderates still hoping to reconcile with Britain.

QUICK REVIEW <

Why were many Americans initially reluctant to pursue independence from Britain?

| What role did the home front play in the war? | How were Native Americans and the French involved in the war? | Why did the British southern strategy ultimately fail? | Conclusion: Why did the British lose the American Revolution? | ☑ LearningCurve Check what you know. bedfordstmartins.com /roarkunderstanding |

What initial challenges did the opposing armies face?

Backcountry Riflemen

A German officer with the British army drew this sketch of two American riflemen, dressed in rustic hunting shirts and leggings. One wears moccasins; the other is barefoot. Their celebrated ability to hit small targets at great distances and their willingness to snipe from behind trees and aim particularly at officers made them a terror to the British. Ten companies of riflemen were recruited in 1775 from western Pennsylvania and Virginia. General Washington worried that they were too undisciplined to make good soldiers, but others suggested that the trademark hunting shirt should become the Continental army uniform for all soldiers, just for the fear it provoked in the enemy. Anne S. K. Brown Military College, Brown University Library.

BOTH SIDES APPROACHED the war for America with uneasiness. The Americans, with inexperienced militias, were opposing the mightiest military power in the world. Also, their country was not unified; many people remained loyal to Britain. The British faced serious obstacles as well. Their disdain for the fighting abilities of the Americans required reassessment in light of the Bunker Hill battle. The logistics of supplying an army with food across three thousand miles of water were daunting. And since the British goal was to regain allegiance, not to destroy and conquer, the army was often constrained in its actions.

The American Military Forces

Americans claimed that the initial months of the war were purely defensive, triggered by the British invasion. But the war also quickly became a rebellion, an overthrowing of long-established authority. As both defenders and rebels, many Americans were highly motivated to fight, and the potential manpower that could be mobilized was, in theory, very great.

CHAPTER LOCATOR | Why did Americans wait so long before they declared their independence? | **What initial challenges did the opposing armies face?**

180 CHAPTER 7 FIGHTING THE AMERICAN REVOLUTION

Local defense in the colonies had long rested with a militia composed of all able-bodied men over age sixteen. Militias, however, were best suited for local and limited engagements, responding to conflict with Indians or slave rebellions. In forming the Continental army, the congress set enlistment at one year, which proved inadequate as the war progressed. Incentives produced longer commitments: a $20 bonus for three years of service, a hundred acres of land for enlistment for the duration of the war. Over the course of the war, some 230,000 men enlisted, about one-quarter of the white male adult population.

Women also served in the Continental army, cooking, washing, and nursing the wounded. Close to 20,000 "camp followers," as they were called, served during the war, many of them wives of men in service. Some 12,000 children also tagged along, and babies were born in the camps. Some women helped during battles, supplying drinking water or ammunition to soldiers.

Black Americans at first were excluded from the Continental army. But as manpower needs increased, northern states welcomed free blacks into service; slaves in some states could serve with their masters' permission. About 5,000 black men served in the Revolutionary War on the rebel side, nearly all from the northern states. Black soldiers sometimes were segregated into separate units, and while some of these men were draftees, others were clearly inspired by ideals of freedom in a war against tyranny. For example, twenty-three blacks gave "Liberty," "Freedom," and "Freeman" as their surnames at the time of enlistment.

The American army was at times raw and inexperienced, and often woefully undermanned. It never had the precision and discipline of European professional armies. But it was never as bad as the British continually assumed. The British would learn that it was a serious mistake to underrate the enemy.

Flute-Playing African American

This musician is thought to be Barzillai Lew of Groton, Massachusetts. As a boy, Lew served as a fifer in the Seven Years' War, and in 1775 he again was a fifer in the Revolution through three enlistments, seeing action at Bunker Hill and Fort Ticonderoga. Fife and drum music supplied rhythm and mood for military marches, so fifing was an essential job. Courtesy of Mae Theresa Bonitto; photograph courtesy of the *Boston Globe*.

The British Strategy

The American strategy was straightforward — to repulse and defeat an invading army. The British strategy was not as clear. Britain wanted to put down a rebellion and restore monarchical power in the colonies, but the question was how to accomplish this. A decisive defeat of the Continental army was essential but not sufficient to end the rebellion, for the British would still have to contend with an armed and motivated insurgent population. Furthermore, there was no single political nerve center whose capture would spell certain victory. The Continental Congress moved from place to place, staying just out of reach of the British. During the course of the war, the British captured and occupied every major port city, but that brought no serious loss to the Americans, 95 percent of whom lived in the countryside.

> CHRONOLOGY

1775
– Battle of Quebec.

1776
– Battle of Long Island.
– Washington captures German troops along the Delaware River.

What role did the home front play in the war? | How were Native Americans and the French involved in the war? | Why did the British southern strategy ultimately fail? | Conclusion: Why did the British lose the American Revolution? | ✓ LearningCurve Check what you know. bedfordstmartins.com /roarkunderstanding

Britain's delicate task was to restore the old governments, not to destroy an enemy country. British generals were at first reluctant to ravage the countryside, confiscate food, or burn villages. There were thirteen distinct political entities to capture, pacify, and then restore to the crown, and they stretched in a long line from New Hampshire to Georgia. Clearly, a large land army was required for the job. Without the willingness to seize food from the locals, the British needed hundreds of supply ships — hence their desire to capture the ports. The British strategy also assumed that many Americans remained loyal to the king and would come to their aid.

The overall British plan was a divide-and-conquer approach, focusing first on New York, the state judged to have the greatest number of loyal subjects. New York offered a geographic advantage as well: Control of the Hudson River would allow the British to isolate New England. British armies could descend from Canada and move north from New York City along the Hudson River. Squeezed between a naval blockade on the eastern coast and army raids in the west, Massachusetts could be driven to surrender. New Jersey and Pennsylvania would fall in line, the British thought, because of loyalist strength. Virginia was a problem, like Massachusetts, but the British were confident that the Carolinas would help them isolate and subdue Virginia.

Quebec, New York, and New Jersey

In late 1775, an American expedition was launched to capture the cities of Montreal and Quebec before British reinforcements could arrive (**Map 7.1**). This offensive was a clear sign that the war was not purely a reaction to the invasion of Massachusetts. A force of New York Continentals commanded by General Richard Montgomery took Montreal easily in September 1775 and then advanced on Quebec. Meanwhile, a second contingent of Continentals led by Colonel Benedict Arnold moved north through Maine to Quebec, a punishing trek through freezing rain with woefully inadequate supplies. Arnold and Montgomery jointly attacked Quebec in December but failed to take the city. Worse yet, they encountered smallpox, which killed more men than had the battle for Quebec.

The main action of the first year of the war came not in Canada, however, but in New York. In August 1776, some 45,000 British troops (including 8,000 German mercenaries, called Hessians) under the command of General Howe landed south of New York City. General Washington had anticipated this move and had relocated his army of 20,000 south from Massachusetts. The **battle of Long Island** in late August pitted the well-trained British "redcoats" (slang referring to their red uniforms) against a very green Continental army. Howe attacked, inflicting many casualties and taking a thousand prisoners. A British general crowed, "If a good bleeding can bring those Bible-faced Yankees to their senses, the fever of independency should soon abate." Howe failed to press forward, however, perhaps remembering the costly victory of Bunker Hill, and Washington evacuated his troops to Manhattan Island.

Washington knew it would be hard to hold Manhattan, so he withdrew farther north to two forts on either side of the Hudson River. For two months, the armies engaged in limited skirmishing, but in November Howe finally captured

battle of Long Island
▶ First major engagement of the new Continental army, defending against 45,000 British troops newly arrived on western Long Island (today Brooklyn). The Continentals retreated, with high casualties and many taken prisoner.

CHAPTER LOCATOR | Why did Americans wait so long before they declared their independence? | What initial challenges did the opposing armies face?

182 CHAPTER 7 FIGHTING THE AMERICAN REVOLUTION

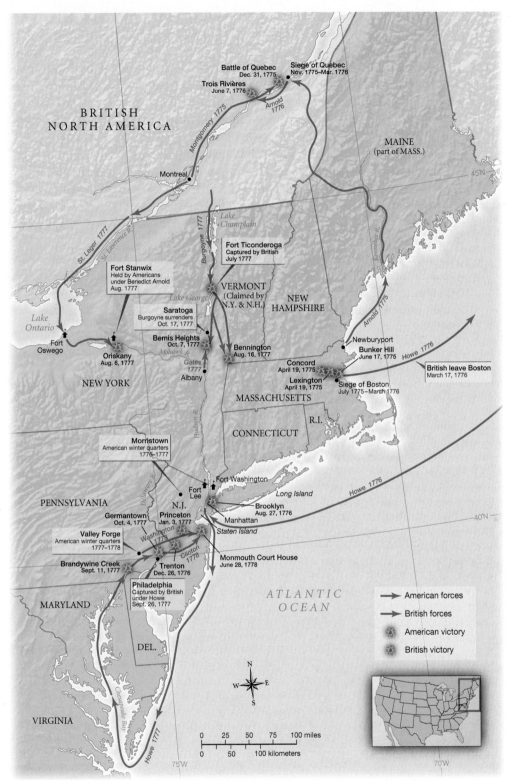

MAP 7.1 ■ **The War in the North, 1775–1778**

After battles in Massachusetts in 1775, rebel forces invaded Canada but failed to capture Quebec. The British army landed in New York in 1776, causing turmoil in New Jersey in 1777 and 1778. Burgoyne attempted to isolate New England, but he was stopped at Saratoga in 1777 in the decisive battle of the early war.

> **MAP ACTIVITY**

READING THE MAP: Which general's troops traveled the farthest in each of these years: 1775, 1776, and 1777? How did the availability of water routes affect British and American strategy?

CONNECTIONS: Why did the French wait until early 1778 to join American forces against the British? What did France hope to gain from participating in the war?

Map labels:

BRITISH NORTH AMERICA

Battle of Quebec
Dec. 31, 1775

Siege of Quebec
Nov. 1775–Mar. 1776

Trois Rivières
June 7, 1776

Montgomery 1775

Arnold 1776

MAINE
(part of MASS.)

45N

Montreal

Lake Champlain

Burgoyne 1777

St. Leger 1777

St. Lawrence R.

Fort Ticonderoga
Captured by British
July 1777

Fort Stanwix
Held by Americans
under Benedict Arnold
Aug. 1777

VERMONT
(Claimed by
N.Y. & N.H.)

NEW HAMPSHIRE

Lake George

Lake Ontario

Fort Oswego

Oriskany
Aug. 6, 1777

Saratoga
Burgoyne surrenders
Oct. 17, 1777

Bemis Heights
Oct. 7, 1777

Mohawk R.

Gates 1777

Albany

Bennington
Aug. 16, 1777

Newburyport

Bunker Hill
June 17, 1775

Concord
April 19, 1775

Lexington
April 19, 1775

Siege of Boston
July 1775–March 1776

Arnold 1775

Kennebec R.

Howe 1776

British leave Boston
March 17, 1776

NEW YORK

MASSACHUSETTS

R.I.

CONNECTICUT

Hudson R.

Morristown
American winter quarters
1776–1777

Fort Washington

Fort Lee

N.J.

Germantown
Oct. 4, 1777

Princeton
Jan. 3, 1777

Manhattan

Long Island

Brooklyn
Aug. 27, 1776

Howe 1776

Staten Island

PENNSYLVANIA

Delaware R.

Washington 1776

Valley Forge
American winter quarters
1777–1778

Clinton 1778

Monmouth Court House
June 28, 1778

Brandywine Creek
Sept. 11, 1777

Trenton
Dec. 26, 1776

Philadelphia
Captured by British
under Howe
Sept. 26, 1777

MARYLAND

DEL.

ATLANTIC OCEAN

40N

Chesapeake Bay

Howe 1777

VIRGINIA

75W

0   25   50   75   100 miles
0   50   100 kilometers

70W

→ American forces
→ British forces
✳ American victory
✳ British victory

What role did the home front play in the war?	How were Native Americans and the French involved in the war?	Why did the British southern strategy ultimately fail?	Conclusion: Why did the British lose the American Revolution?	✓ LearningCurve Check what you know. bedfordstmartins.com /roarkunderstanding

183

Fort Washington and Fort Lee, taking another 3,000 prisoners. Washington retreated quickly across New Jersey into Pennsylvania. Again Howe unaccountably failed to press his advantage. Instead, he parked his German troops in winter quarters along the Delaware River. Perhaps he knew that many of the Continental soldiers' enlistment periods ended on December 31, making him confident that the Americans would not attack him. He was wrong.

On December 25, in an icy rain, Washington stealthily moved his army across the Delaware River and at dawn made a quick capture of the unsuspecting German soldiers. This impressive victory lifted the sagging morale of the patriot side. For the next two weeks, Washington remained on the offensive, capturing supplies in a clever attack on British units at Princeton. Soon he was safe in Morristown, in northern New Jersey, where he settled his army for the winter. Washington finally had time to administer mass smallpox inoculations and see his men through the abbreviated course of the disease.

All in all, in the first year of declared war, the rebellious Americans had a few proud moments but also many worries. The inexperienced Continental army had barely hung on in the New York campaign. Washington had shown exceptional daring and admirable restraint, but what really saved the Americans was the repeated reluctance of the British to follow through militarily when they had the advantage.

> **QUICK REVIEW**

Why did the British initially exercise restraint in their efforts to defeat the rebellious colonies?

CHAPTER LOCATOR | Why did Americans wait so long before they declared their independence? | What initial challenges did the opposing armies face?

184 CHAPTER 7
FIGHTING THE AMERICAN REVOLUTION

[SATURDAY, OCTOBER 25, 1777.]   RIVINGTON's NEW YORK LOYAL GAZETTE.   [No. 140.]

Rivington's New York Loyal Gazette Not all newspaper editors supported the Revolution. James Rivington of New York City heaped abuse on Washington and others and earned a reputation for mean-spirited polemics. When New York City became British headquarters, Rivington curried favor with the British command. Yet it appears now that long-standing rumors about his duplicity are likely true. Evidence suggests that by 1781 he was passing codes to George Washington about British military plans. Courtesy, American Antiquarian Society.

BATTLEFIELDS ALONE DID not determine the outcome of the war. Struggles on the home front were equally important. Men who joined the army often left wives to manage on their own. Some men did not join because they were loyal to Britain and did not welcome war, and many others were undecided about independence. In many communities, both persuasion and force were used to gain the allegiance of the many neutrals. A major factor pushing neutrals to side with the Revolution was the harsh treatment of prisoners of war by the British. Adding to the turbulence of the times was a very shaky wartime economy. The creative financing of the fledgling government brought hardships as well as opportunities, forcing Americans to confront new manifestations of virtue and corruption.

Patriotism at the Local Level

Committees of correspondence, of public safety, and of inspection dominated the political landscape in patriot communities. These committees took on more than customary local governance; they enforced boycotts, picked army draftees, and policed suspected traitors. They sometimes invaded homes to search for contraband goods such as British tea or textiles.

Loyalists were dismayed by the increasing show of power by patriots. A man in Westchester, New York, described his response to intrusions by committees: "Choose your committee or suffer it to be chosen by a half dozen fools in your neighborhood — open your doors to them — let them examine your tea-cannisters and molasses-jugs, and your wives' and daughters' petty coats — bow and cringe and tremble and quake — fall down and worship our sovereign lord the mob. . . .

> **CHRONOLOGY**

1775
- **June.** The Second Continental Congress declares all loyalists traitors.
- Mohawk leader Joseph Brant travels to England to pledge support for the British side.

1776
- In New York City, loyalists sign "A Declaration of Dependence."

1777
- British Parliament suspends habeas corpus.

1778
- Colonial committees of public safety fix prices on essential commodities.

1780
- Philadelphia Ladies Association raises money for soldiers.

| What role did the home front play in the war? | How were Native Americans and the French involved in the war? | Why did the British southern strategy ultimately fail? | Conclusion: Why did the British lose the American Revolution? | ☑ LearningCurve Check what you know. bedfordstmartins.com /roarkunderstanding |

Should any pragmatical committee-gentleman come to my house and give himself airs, I shall show him the door." Oppressive or not, the local committees were rarely challenged. Their persuasive powers convinced many middle-of-the-road citizens that neutrality was not a comfortable option.

Another group new to political life — white women — increasingly demonstrated a capacity for patriotism as wartime hardships dramatically altered their work routines. Many wives whose husbands were away on military or political service took on masculine duties. Their competence to manage farms and make business decisions encouraged some to assert interest in politics as well, as Abigail Adams did while John Adams served in the Continental Congress in Philadelphia. Eliza Wilkinson managed a South Carolina plantation and talked revolutionary politics with women friends. "None were greater politicians than the several knots of ladies who met together," she remarked, alert to the unusual turn female conversations had taken.

Women from prominent Philadelphia families took more direct action, forming the **Ladies Association** in 1780 to collect money for Continental soldiers. A published broadside, "The Sentiments of an American Woman," defended their female patriotism: "The time is arrived to display the same sentiments which animated us at the beginning of the Revolution, when we renounced the use of teas [and] when our republican and laborious hands spun the flax."

The Loyalists

Around one-fifth of the American population remained loyal to the crown in 1776, and another two-fifths tried to stay neutral, providing a strong base for the British. In general, **loyalists** believed that social stability depended on a government anchored by monarchy and aristocracy. They feared that democratic tyranny was emergent among the self-styled patriots who appeared to be unscrupulous, violent men grabbing power for themselves. Pockets of loyalism thus existed everywhere (**Map 7.2**).

> **Who Were the Loyalists?**

- Royal officials, such as governors, local judges, and customs officers
- Wealthy merchants
- Conservative urban lawyers
- People who already disliked pro-Revolution citizens, such as many backcountry Carolina farmers who resented the power of the pro-Revolution gentry
- Southern slaves who looked to Britain in hope of freedom
- Many Indian tribes

Even New England towns at the heart of the turmoil, such as Concord, Massachusetts, had a small and increasingly silenced core of loyalists. On occasion, husbands and wives, fathers and sons disagreed completely on the war.

Many Indian tribes chose neutrality at the war's start, seeing the conflict as a civil war between the English and the Americans. Eventually, however, they were drawn in, most taking the British side. One young Mohawk leader, Thayendanegea (known also by his English name, Joseph Brant), traveled to England in 1775 to

Ladies Association

▶ A women's organization in Philadelphia that collected substantial money donations in 1780 to give to the Continental troops as a token of the citizens' appreciation. A woman leader authored a declaration, "The Sentiments of an American Woman," to justify women's unexpected entry into political life.

loyalists

▶ Colonists who remained loyal to Britain during the Revolutionary War, probably numbering around one-fifth of the population in 1776. Colonists remained loyal to Britain for many reasons, and loyalists could be found in every region of the country.

CHAPTER LOCATOR

Why did Americans wait so long before they declared their independence?

What initial challenges did the opposing armies face?

186 CHAPTER 7 FIGHTING THE AMERICAN REVOLUTION

complain to King George about land-hungry New York settlers. "It is very hard when we have let the King's subjects have so much of our lands for so little value," he wrote; "they should want to cheat us in this manner of the small spots we have left for our women and children to live on." Brant pledged Indian support for the king in exchange for protection from encroaching settlers. In the Ohio Country, parts of the Shawnee and Delaware tribes started out pro-American but shifted to the British side by 1779 in the face of repeated betrayals by American settlers and soldiers.

Loyalists were most vocal between 1774 and 1776, when the possibility of a full-scale rebellion against Britain was still uncertain. They challenged the emerging patriot side in pamphlets and newspapers. In 1776 in New York City, 547 loyalists signed and circulated a broadside titled "A Declaration of Dependence" in rebuttal to the congress's July 4 declaration, denouncing the "most unnatural, unprovoked Rebellion that ever disgraced the annals of Time."

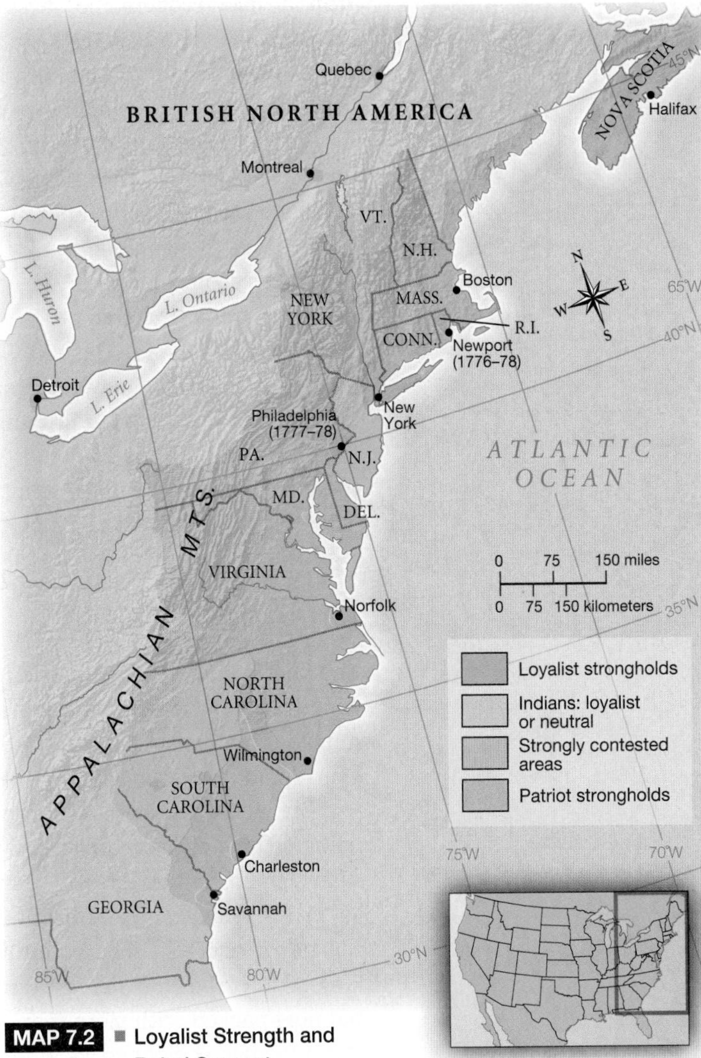

Who Is a Traitor?

In June 1775, the Second Continental Congress declared all loyalists to be traitors. Over the next year, state laws defined as treason acts such as provisioning the British army, saying anything that undermined patriot morale, and discouraging men from enlisting in the Continental army. Punishments ranged from house arrest and suspension of voting privileges to confiscation of property and deportation. Sometimes self-appointed committees of Tory-hunters bypassed the judicial niceties and terrorized loyalists, raiding their houses or tarring and feathering them.

Were wives of loyalists also traitors? When loyalist families fled the country, their property was typically confiscated. But if the wife stayed, courts usually allowed her to keep one-third of the property, the amount due her if widowed, and confiscated the rest. Yet a wife who fled with her husband might have little choice in the matter. After the Revolution, descendants of refugee loyalists filed several lawsuits to regain property that had entered the family through the mother's inheritance. In 1805, the American son of loyalist refugee

MAP 7.2 ■ Loyalist Strength and Rebel Support

The exact number of loyalists can never be known. No one could have made an accurate count at the time, and political allegiance often shifted with the wind. This map shows the regions of loyalist strength on which the British relied — most significantly, the lower Hudson valley and the Carolina Piedmont.

> MAP ACTIVITY

READING THE MAP: Which forces were stronger, those loyal to Britain or those rebelling? (Consider the size of their respective areas, centers of population, and vital port locations.) What areas were contested? If the contested areas ultimately had sided with the British, how would the balance of power have changed?

CONNECTIONS: Who was more likely to be a loyalist and why? How many loyalists left the United States? Where did they go?

| What role did the home front play in the war? | How were Native Americans and the French involved in the war? | Why did the British southern strategy ultimately fail? | Conclusion: Why did the British lose the American Revolution? | ✓ LearningCurve Check what you know. bedfordstmartins.com /roarkunderstanding |

187

Anna Martin recovered her dowry property on the grounds that she had no independent will to be a loyalist.

Tarring and feathering, property confiscation, deportation, terrorism — to the loyalists, such denials of liberty of conscience and of freedom to own private property proved that democratic tyranny was more to be feared than the monarchical variety. A Boston loyalist named Mather Byles aptly expressed this point: "They call me a brainless Tory, but tell me . . . which is better — to be ruled by one tyrant three thousand miles away, or by three thousand tyrants not a mile away?" Byles was soon sentenced to deportation.

Throughout the war, probably 7,000 to 8,000 loyalists fled to England, and 28,000 found haven in Canada. Many stayed put while the war's outcome was unknown. In New Jersey, for example, 3,000 Jerseyites felt protected (or scared) enough by the occupying British army in 1776 to swear an oath of allegiance to the king. But then the British drew back to New York City, leaving the loyalists at the mercy of local patriot committees. Despite the staunch backing of loyalists in 1776, the British found it difficult to build a winning strategy on their support.

Prisoners of War

The poor handling of loyalists as traitors paled in comparison to the handling of American prisoners of war by the British. Among European military powers, humane treatment of captured soldiers was the custom, including adequate provisions (paid for by the captives' own government) and the possibility of prisoner exchanges. But British leaders refused to see American captives as foot soldiers employed by a sovereign nation. Instead, they were traitors, to be treated worse than common criminals.

The 4,000 American prisoners taken in the fall of 1776 were crowded onto two dozen vessels anchored in the river between Manhattan and Brooklyn. The largest ship, the HMS *Jersey*, was a broken-down hull built to house a crew of 400 but now packed with more than 1,100 prisoners. Survivors described the dark, stinking space below decks where more than half a dozen men died daily. A twenty-year-old captive seaman described his first view of the hold: "Here was a motley crew, covered with rags and filth; visages pallid with disease, emaciated with hunger and anxiety, . . . and surrounded with the horrors of sickness and death." The Continental Congress sent food to the prisoners, but most was diverted to British use, leaving General Washington fuming.

Treating the captives as criminals potentially triggered the Anglo-American right of habeas corpus, a thirteenth-century British liberty that guaranteed every prisoner the right to challenge his detention before a judge and to learn the charges against him. To remove that possibility, Parliament voted in early 1777 to suspend habeas corpus specifically for "persons taken in the act of high treason" in any of the colonies.

Despite the prison-ship horrors, Washington insisted that captured British soldiers be treated humanely. From the initial group of Hessians taken on Christmas of 1776 to the several thousand more soldiers captured in American victories by 1778, America's prisoners of war were gathered in rural encampments. Guarded by local townsmen, the captives typically could cultivate small gardens, move about freely during the day, and even hire themselves out to farmers suffering wartime labor shortages. Officers with money could purchase lodging with local families and mix socially with Americans. Many officers were even allowed to keep their guns as they waited for prisoner exchanges to release them.

Such exchanges were negotiated when the British became desperate to regain valued officers and thus freed American officers. Death was the most common fate of ordinary American soldiers and seamen. More than 15,000 men endured captivity in the prison ships, and two-thirds of them died, a larger number than those who died in battle (estimated to be around 5,000). News of the horrors of the British death ships increased the revolutionaries' resolve and convinced some neutrals of the necessity of the war.

Financial Instability and Corruption

Wars cost money — for arms and ammunition, for food and uniforms, for soldiers' pay, for provisions for prisoners. The Continental Congress printed money, but its value quickly deteriorated because the congress held no precious metals to back the currency. The dollar eventually bottomed out at one-fortieth of its face value. States, too, were printing paper money to pay for wartime expenses, further complicating the economy.

As the currency depreciated, the congress turned to other means to procure supplies and labor. One method was to borrow hard money (gold or silver coins) from wealthy men in exchange for certificates of debt (public securities) promising repayment with interest. The certificates of debt were similar to present-day government bonds. To pay soldiers, the congress issued land grant certificates, written promises of acreage usually located in frontier areas such as central Maine or eastern Ohio. Both the public securities and the land grant certificates quickly became forms of negotiable currency, but they too soon depreciated.

Depreciating currency inevitably led to rising prices, as sellers compensated for the falling value of the money. The wartime economy of the late 1770s, with its unreliable currency and price inflation, was extremely demoralizing to Americans everywhere. In 1778, in an effort to impose stability, local committees of public safety began to fix prices on essential goods such as flour. Inevitably, some turned this unstable situation to their advantage. Money that fell fast in value needed to be spent quickly; being in debt was suddenly advantageous because the debt could be repaid in devalued currency. A brisk black market sprang up in prohibited luxury imports, such as tea, sugar, textiles, and wines, even though these items came from Britain. A New Hampshire delegate to the Continental Congress denounced the trade: "We are a crooked and perverse generation, longing for the fineries and follies of those Egyptian task masters from whom we have so lately freed ourselves."

QUICK REVIEW <

How did the patriots promote support for their cause in the colonies?

| What role did the home front play in the war? | How were Native Americans and the French involved in the war? | Why did the British southern strategy ultimately fail? | Conclusion: Why did the British lose the American Revolution? | **LearningCurve** Check what you know. bedfordstmartins.com /roarkunderstanding |

How were Native Americans and the French involved in the war?

Death of Jane McCrea

Jane McCrea, a patriot's daughter in love with a loyalist in Burgoyne's army, gained fame as a martyr in 1777. She met death on her way to join her fiancé — either shot in the crossfire of battle (the British claim) or murdered by Indians (the patriots' version). American leaders used the story of the vulnerable young woman as propaganda to inspire the American drive for victory at Saratoga. Wadsworth Athenaeum Museum of Art, Hartford/Art Resource, NY.

IN EARLY 1777, the Continental army faced bleak choices. General Washington had skillfully avoided defeat, but the minor victories in New Jersey lent only faint optimism to the American side. Meanwhile, British troops moved south from Quebec, aiming to isolate New England by taking control of the Hudson River. Their presence drew the Continental army up into central New York, polarizing tribes of the Iroquois Nation and turning the Mohawk Valley into a bloody war zone. By 1779, tribes in western New York and in Indian country in the Ohio Valley were fully involved in the Revolutionary War. Despite an important patriot victory at Saratoga, the involvement of Indians and the continuing strength of the British forced the American government to look to France for help.

Burgoyne's Army and the Battle of Saratoga

In 1777, British general John Burgoyne, commanding a considerable army, began the northern squeeze on the Hudson River valley. Coming from Canada, he marched south hoping to capture Albany, near the intersection of the Hudson and Mohawk rivers. Accompanied by 1,000 "camp followers" (cooks, laundresses, musicians) and some 400 Indian warriors, Burgoyne's army of 7,800 men did not travel light. Food had to be packed in, not only for people but also for 400 horses hauling heavy artillery. Primitive roads through dense forests slowed their progress to a crawl.

CHAPTER LOCATOR | Why did Americans wait so long before they declared their independence? | What initial challenges did the opposing armies face?

190 CHAPTER 7
FIGHTING THE AMERICAN REVOLUTION

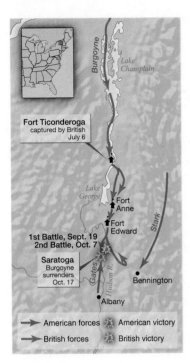

Battle of Saratoga, 1777

Fort Ticonderoga
captured by British
July 6

1st Battle, Sept. 19
2nd Battle, Oct. 7
Saratoga
Burgoyne
surrenders
Oct. 17

Fort Anne
Fort Edward
Bennington
Albany

→ American forces ✕ American victory
→ British forces   ✕ British victory

The logical second step in isolating New England should have been to advance troops up the Hudson from New York City to meet Burgoyne. American surveillance indicated that General Howe in Manhattan was readying his men for a major move in August 1777. But Howe surprised everyone by sailing south to attack Philadelphia.

To reinforce Burgoyne, British and Hessian troops from Montreal came from the east along the Mohawk River, aided by Mohawks and Senecas of the Iroquois Confederacy. The British were counting on loyalism among the numerous German colonists living in the Mohawk Valley. A hundred miles west of Albany, they encountered American Continental soldiers at Fort Stanwix and laid siege, causing local German militiamen and a small number of Oneida Indians to rush to the Continentals' support. Mohawk chief Joseph Brant led the Senecas and Mohawks in an ambush on the German Americans and the Oneidas in a narrow ravine called Oriskany, killing nearly 500 out of 840 of them. On Brant's side, some 90 warriors were killed. The defenders of Fort Stanwix ultimately repelled their attackers. These deadly battles of **Oriskany** and Fort Stanwix were also complexly multiethnic, pitting Indians against Indians, German Americans against German mercenaries, New York patriots against New York loyalists, and English Americans against British soldiers.

The British retreat at Fort Stanwix deprived General Burgoyne of the additional troops he expected. Camped at a small village called Saratoga, he was isolated, with food supplies dwindling and men deserting. His adversary at Albany, General Horatio Gates, began moving his army toward Saratoga. Burgoyne decided to attack first, and the British prevailed, but at the great cost of 600 dead or wounded. Three weeks later, an American attack on Burgoyne's forces in the second stage of the **battle of Saratoga** cost the British another 600 men and most of their cannons. General Burgoyne finally surrendered to the American forces on October 17, 1777.

General Howe, meanwhile, had succeeded in occupying Philadelphia in September 1777. Figuring that the Saratoga loss was balanced by the capture of Philadelphia, the British government proposed a negotiated settlement — not including independence — to end the war. The American side refused.

But supplies of arms and food ran precariously low. Washington moved his troops into winter quarters at Valley Forge, just west of Philadelphia. Quartered in drafty huts, the men lacked blankets, boots, stockings, and food. Some 2,000 men at Valley Forge died of disease; another 2,000 deserted over the bitter six-month encampment.

Washington blamed the citizenry for lack of support; indeed, evidence of corruption and profiteering was abundant. Army suppliers too often provided defective food, clothing, and gunpowder. One shipment of bedding arrived with

> CHRONOLOGY

1777
– Ambush at Oriskany; Americans hold Fort Stanwix.
– British occupy Philadelphia.
– British surrender at Saratoga.

1777–1778
– Continental army winters at Valley Forge.

1778
– France signs treaty with America.

1779
– Americans destroy Iroquois villages in New York.
– Militias attack Cherokee settlements in North Carolina.
– Americans take Forts Kaskaskia and Vincennes.

battle of Oriskany
▶ A punishing defeat for Americans in a ravine named Oriskany near Fort Stanwix in New York in August 1777. Mohawk and Seneca Indians ambushed German American militiamen aided by allied Oneida warriors, and 500 on the Revolutionary side were killed.

battle of Saratoga
▶ A two-stage battle in New York ending with the decisive defeat and surrender of British general John Burgoyne on October 17, 1777. This victory convinced France to throw its official support to the American side in the war.

What role did the home front play in the war?

How were Native Americans and the French involved in the war?

Why did the British southern strategy ultimately fail?

Conclusion: Why did the British lose the American Revolution?

✓ LearningCurve
Check what you know.
bedfordstmartins.com
/roarkunderstanding

191

blankets one-quarter their customary size. Food supplies arrived rotten. As one Continental officer said, "The people at home are destroying the Army by their conduct much faster than Howe and all his army can possibly do by fighting us."

The War in the West: Indian Country

Between the fall of 1777 and the summer of 1778, the fighting on the Atlantic coast slowed. But in the interior western areas — the Mohawk Valley, the Ohio Valley, and Kentucky — the war of Indians against the American rebels heated up.

The ambush and slaughter at Oriskany in August 1777 marked the beginning of three years of terror for the inhabitants of the Mohawk Valley. Loyalists and Indians engaged in many raids throughout 1778, capturing or killing inhabitants. In retaliation, American militiamen destroyed Joseph Brant's village, killing several children. A month later, Brant's warriors attacked the town of Cherry Valley, killing 16 soldiers and 32 civilians.

The following summer, General Washington authorized a campaign to wreak "total destruction and devastation" on all the Iroquois villages of central New York. Some 4,500 troops commanded by General John Sullivan implemented a campaign of terror in the fall of 1779. Forty Indian towns met with total obliteration; the soldiers torched dwellings, cornfields, and orchards. In a few towns, women and children were slaughtered, but in most, the inhabitants managed to escape, fleeing to the British at Fort Niagara. Thousands of Indian refugees, sick and starving, camped around the fort in one of the most miserable winters on record.

Much farther to the west, beyond Fort Pitt, another complex story of alliances and betrayals between American militiamen and Indians unfolded. Some 150,000 native people lived between the Appalachian Mountains and the Mississippi River. Most sided with the British, but a portion of the Shawnee and Delaware at first sought peace with the Americans. In mid-1778, the Delaware chief White Eyes negotiated a treaty at Fort Pitt, pledging Indian support for the Americans in exchange for supplies and trade goods. But escalating violence undermined the agreement. That fall, when American soldiers killed two friendly Shawnee chiefs, Cornstalk and Red Hawk, the Continental Congress hastened to apologize, as did the governors of Pennsylvania and Virginia, but the soldiers who stood trial for the murders were acquitted. Two months later, White Eyes died under mysterious circumstances, almost certainly murdered by militiamen, who repeatedly had trouble honoring distinctions between allied and enemy Indians.

West of North Carolina (today's Tennessee), militias attacked Cherokee settlements in 1779, destroying thirty-six villages, while Indian raiders repeatedly attacked white settlements such as Boonesborough (in present-day Kentucky) (**Map 7.3**). In retaliation, a young Virginian, George Rogers Clark, led Kentucky militiamen into what is now Illinois, attacking and taking the British fort at Kaskaskia. Clark's men wore native clothing — hunting shirts and breechcloths — but their dress was not a sign of solidarity with the Indians. When they attacked British-held Fort Vincennes in 1779, Clark's troops tomahawked Indian captives and threw their still-live bodies into the river in a gory spectacle witnessed by the redcoats. "To excel them in barbarity is the only way to make war upon Indians," Clark announced.

By 1780, very few Indians remained neutral. Violent raids by Americans drove Indians into the arms of the British at Forts Detroit and Niagara, or into the arms of

CHAPTER LOCATOR | Why did Americans wait so long before they declared their independence? | What initial challenges did the opposing armies face?

192 CHAPTER 7 FIGHTING THE AMERICAN REVOLUTION

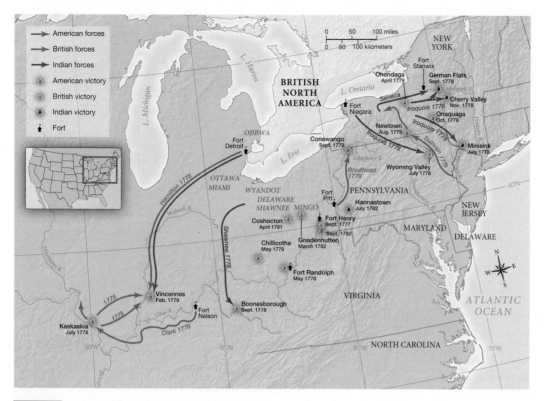

MAP 7.3 ■ The Indian War in the West, 1777–1782

Most Indian tribes supported the British. Iroquois Indians attacked New York's Mohawk Valley throughout 1778, causing the Continental army to destroy Iroquois villages throughout central New York. Shawnee and Delaware Indians in western Pennsylvania tangled with American militiamen in 1779, while tribes near Fort Detroit conducted raids on Kentucky settlers. Sporadic frontier fighting continued through 1782.

the Spaniards, west of the Mississippi River. Said one officer on the Sullivan campaign, "Their nests are destroyed but the birds are still on the wing." For those who stayed near their native lands, chaos and confusion prevailed. Rare as it was, Indian support for the American side occasionally emerged out of a strategic sense that the Americans were unstoppable in their westward pressure and that it was better to work out an alliance than to lose in a war. But American treatment of even friendly Indians showed that there was no winning strategy for them.

The French Alliance

On their own, the Americans could not have defeated Britain, especially as pressure from hostile Indians increased. Essential help arrived as a result of the victory at Saratoga, which convinced the French to enter the war; a formal alliance was signed in February 1778. France recognized the United States as an independent nation and promised full military and commercial support. Most crucial was the French navy, which could challenge British supplies and troops at sea and aid the Americans in taking and holding prisoners of war.

What role did the home front play in the war?

How were Native Americans and the French involved in the war?

Why did the British southern strategy ultimately fail?

Conclusion: Why did the British lose the American Revolution?

✓ LearningCurve
Check what you know.
bedfordstmartins.com
/roarkunderstanding

193

"The Ballance of Power," 1780

This English cartoon mocks the alliance of Spain and the Netherlands with France in support of the American war. On the left, the female figure Britannia cannot be moved by all the lightweights on the right. France and Spain embrace while a Dutch boy hops on, saying, "I'll do anything for Money." The forlorn Indian woman, representing America, wails, "My Ingratitude is Justly punished." Print Collection, Miriam and Ira D. Wallach Division of Art, Prints, and Photographs, The New York Public Library. Astor, Lenox, and Tilden Foundations.

> **VISUAL ACTIVITY**

READING THE IMAGE: What does this cartoon reveal about British perceptions of the American Revolution?
CONNECTIONS: How did British attitudes toward the colonies contribute to the British defeat in the war?

Well before 1778, however, the French had been covertly providing cannons, muskets, gunpowder, and highly trained military advisers to the Americans. From the French perspective, the main attraction of an alliance was the opportunity it provided to defeat archrival Britain. A victory would also open pathways to trade and perhaps result in France's acquiring the coveted British West Indies. Even an American defeat would not be a disaster for France if the war lasted many years and drained Britain of men and money.

French support would prove indispensable to the American cause in 1780 and 1781, but the alliance's first months brought no dramatic changes, and some Americans grumbled that the partnership would prove worthless.

> **QUICK REVIEW**

Why did the Americans need assistance from the French to ensure victory?

CHAPTER LOCATOR | Why did Americans wait so long before they declared their independence? | What initial challenges did the opposing armies face?

194 CHAPTER 7 FIGHTING THE AMERICAN REVOLUTION

Why did the British southern strategy ultimately fail?

Lafayette at Yorktown

An enthusiast for American liberty, the young French nobleman Lafayette came to the United States in 1777 at age twenty to volunteer his services to General Washington. After proving his leadership in several northern campaigns, he went to Virginia in 1781 to fight Cornwallis. Near Richmond, he met James, a slave belonging to William Armistead, who loaned him to Lafayette. At the siege of Yorktown, James, pretending to be an escaped slave, infiltrated the British command, giving them misinformation and bringing crucial intelligence back to Lafayette. James obtained his freedom in 1786 after Lafayette wrote a letter on his behalf to the Virginia assembly. Art Gallery, Williams Center, Lafayette College.

WHEN FRANCE JOINED the war, some British officials favored abandoning the war. As one troop commander shrewdly observed, "We are far from an anticipated peace, because the bitterness of the rebels is too widespread, and in regions where we are masters the rebellious spirit is still in them. The land is too large, and there are too many people. The more land we win, the weaker our army gets in the field." The commander of the British navy agreed, as did Lord North, the prime minister. But the king was determined to crush the rebellion, and he encouraged a new strategy for victory focusing on the southern colonies, thought to be more persuadably loyalist. It was a brilliant but desperate plan, and ultimately unsuccessful.

Georgia and South Carolina

The new strategy called for British forces to abandon New England and focus on the South, with its valuable crops and its large slave population, a destabilizing factor that might keep rebellious white southerners in line. Georgia and the Carolinas appeared to hold large numbers of loyalists, providing a base for the British to recapture the southern colonies one by one, before moving north to the more problematic middle colonies and New England.

What role did the home front play in the war?

How were Native Americans and the French involved in the war?

Why did the British southern strategy ultimately fail?

Conclusion: Why did the British lose the American Revolution?

✔ **LearningCurve**
Check what you know.
bedfordstmartins.com
/roarkunderstanding

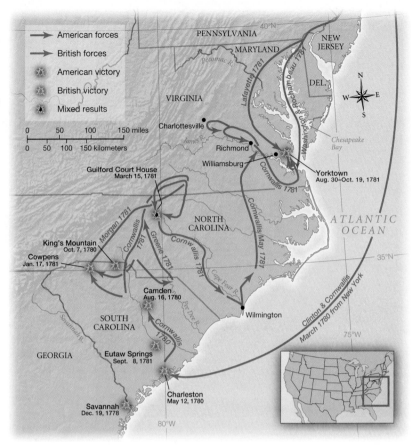

MAP 7.4 ■ The War in the South, 1780–1781

After taking Charleston in May 1780, the British advanced into South and North Carolina, touching off a bloody civil war. An American loss at Camden was followed by victories at King's Mountain and Cowpens. The British next invaded Virginia but were ultimately trapped and overpowered at Yorktown in the fall of 1781.

> CHRONOLOGY

1778
– British take Savannah, Georgia.

1780
– Siege of Charleston, South Carolina.
– French army arrives in Newport, Rhode Island.
– British win battle of Camden.
– Benedict Arnold is exposed as a traitor.
– Americans win battle of King's Mountain.

1781
– British forces invade Virginia.
– French blockade Chesapeake Bay.
– Cornwallis surrenders at Yorktown.

1783
– Treaty of Paris ends war.

Georgia, the first target, fell at the end of December 1778 (**Map 7.4**). A small army of British soldiers occupied Savannah and Augusta, and a new royal governor and loyalist assembly were quickly installed. The British quickly organized twenty loyal militia units, and 1,400 Georgians swore an oath of allegiance to the king. So far, the southern strategy looked as if it might work.

Next came South Carolina. The Continental army put ten regiments into the port city of Charleston to defend it from attack by British troops shipped south from New York under the command of General Henry Clinton, Howe's replacement as commander in chief. For five weeks in early 1780, the British laid siege to the city and took it in May 1780, capturing 3,300 American soldiers.

Clinton next announced that slaves owned by rebel masters were welcome to seek refuge with his army, and several thousand escaped to the coastal city. Untrained in formal warfare, they were of use to the British as knowledgeable guides to the countryside and as laborers building defensive fortifications. Escaped slaves with boat-piloting skills were particularly valuable for crucial aid in navigating the inland rivers of the southern colonies.

Clinton returned to New York, leaving the task of pacifying the rest of South Carolina to General Charles Cornwallis and 4,000 troops. A bold commander, Lord Cornwallis quickly chased out the remaining Continentals and established military rule of South Carolina by midsummer. He purged rebels from government

CHAPTER LOCATOR | Why did Americans wait so long before they declared their independence? | What initial challenges did the opposing armies face?

office and disarmed rebel militias. Exports of rice, South Carolina's main crop, resumed, and pardons were offered to Carolinians willing to prove their loyalty by taking up arms for the British.

By August, American troops arrived from the North to strike back at Cornwallis. General Gates, the hero of Saratoga, led 3,000 troops, many of them newly recruited militiamen, into battle against Cornwallis at Camden, South Carolina, on August 16 (see Map 7.4). The militiamen panicked at the sight of the approaching British cavalry, however, and fled. When regiment leaders tried to regroup the next day, only 700 soldiers showed up. The battle of Camden was a devastating defeat, the worst of the entire war, and prospects seemed very grim for the Americans.

Treason and Guerrilla Warfare

Britain's southern strategy succeeded in 1780 in part because of information about American troop movements secretly conveyed by an American officer, Benedict Arnold. The hero of several American battles, Arnold was a deeply insecure man who never felt he got his due. Sometime in 1779, he opened secret negotiations with General Clinton in New York, trading information for money and hinting that he could deliver far more of value. When General Washington made him commander of West Point, a new fort on the Hudson River sixty miles north of New York City, Arnold's plan crystallized. West Point controlled the Hudson; its capture might well have meant victory in the war.

Arnold's plot to sell a West Point victory to the British was foiled in the fall of 1780 when Americans captured the man carrying plans of the fort's defense from Arnold to Clinton. News of Arnold's treason created shock waves. Arnold

A Shaming Ritual Targeting the Great Traitor In late 1780, Philadelphians staged a ritual humiliation of Benedict Arnold, represented by a two-faced effigy. Behind him stands the devil, prodding him with a pitchfork and shaking a bag of coins near his ear, reminding all that Arnold sold out for money. Library of Congress.

What role did the home front play in the war?

How were Native Americans and the French involved in the war?

Why did the British southern strategy ultimately fail?

Conclusion: Why did the British lose the American Revolution?

✓ LearningCurve
Check what you know.
bedfordstmartins.com
/roarkunderstanding

represented all of the patriots' worst fears about themselves: greedy self-interest, like that of the war profiteers; the unprincipled abandonment of war aims, like that of turncoat southern Tories; panic, like that of the terrified soldiers at Camden. But instead of demoralizing the Americans, Arnold's treachery revived their commitment to the patriot cause. Vilifying Arnold allowed Americans to stake out a wide distance between themselves and dastardly conduct. It inspired a renewal of patriotism at a particularly low moment.

Shock over Gates's defeat at Camden and Arnold's treason revitalized rebel support in western South Carolina, an area that Cornwallis thought was pacified and loyal. The backcountry of the South soon became the site of guerrilla warfare. In hit-and-run attacks, both sides burned and ravaged not only opponents' property but also the property of anyone claiming to be neutral. Loyalist militia units organized by the British were met by fierce rebel militia units. In South Carolina, some 6,000 rebels met loyalist units in engagements. Guerrilla warfare soon spread to Georgia and North Carolina. Both sides committed atrocities and plundered property, clear deviations from standard military practice.

The British southern strategy depended on sufficient loyalist strength to hold reconquered territory as Cornwallis's army moved north. The backcountry civil war proved this assumption false. The Americans won few major battles in the South, but they ultimately succeeded by harassing the British forces and preventing them from foraging for food. Cornwallis moved the war into North Carolina in the fall of 1780 because the North Carolinians were supplying the South Carolina rebels with arms and men (see Map 7.4). Then news of a massacre of loyalist units by 1,400 frontier riflemen at the battle of King's Mountain, in western South Carolina, sent him hurrying back. The British were stretched too thin to hold even two colonies.

Surrender at Yorktown

By early 1781, the war was going very badly for the British. Their defeat at King's Mountain was quickly followed by a second major defeat at the battle of Cowpens in South Carolina in January 1781. Cornwallis retreated to North Carolina and thence to Virginia, where he captured Williamsburg in June. A raiding party proceeded to Charlottesville, the seat of government, capturing members of the Virginia assembly but not Governor Thomas Jefferson, who escaped the soldiers by a mere ten minutes. These minor victories allowed Cornwallis to imagine he was succeeding in Virginia. His army, now swelled by some 4,000 escaped slaves, marched to Yorktown, near the Chesapeake Bay area. As the general waited for backup troops by ship from British headquarters in New York City, smallpox and typhus began to set in among the black recruits.

At this juncture, the French-American alliance came into play. French regiments commanded by the Comte de Rochambeau had joined General Washington in Newport, Rhode Island, in mid-1780, and in early 1781 warships under the Comte de Grasse had sailed from France to the West Indies. Washington, Rochambeau, and de Grasse now fixed their attention on Chesapeake Bay. The French fleet got there ahead of the British troop ships from New York; a five-day naval battle left the French navy in clear control of the Virginia coast. This proved

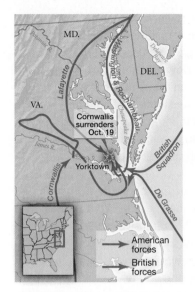

Siege of Yorktown, 1781

to be the decisive factor in ending the war, because the French ships prevented any rescue of Cornwallis's army.

On land, General Cornwallis and his 7,500 troops faced a combined French and American army of 16,000. For twelve days, the Americans and French bombarded the British fortifications at Yorktown; Cornwallis ran low on food and ammunition. He also began to expel the black recruits, some of them sick and dying. A Hessian officer serving under Cornwallis later criticized this British action as disgraceful: "We had used them to good advantage, and set them free, and now, with fear and trembling, they had to face the reward of their cruel masters." The twelve-day siege brought Cornwallis to the realization that neither victory nor escape was possible. He surrendered on October 19, 1781.

What began as a promising southern strategy in 1778 had turned into a discouraging defeat. British attacks in the South had energized American resistance, as did the timely exposure of Benedict Arnold's treason. The arrival of the French fleet sealed the fate of Cornwallis at the **battle of Yorktown**, and major military operations came to a halt.

The Losers and the Winners

The surrender at Yorktown spelled the end for the British, but two more years of skirmishes ensued. Frontier areas in Kentucky, Ohio, and Illinois blazed with battles pitting Americans against various Indian tribes. The British army still occupied three coastal cities, including New York, and in response, an augmented Continental army stayed at the ready, north of New York City.

The **Treaty of Paris**, also called the **Peace of Paris**, was two years in the making. Commissioners from America and Britain worked out the ten articles of peace, while a side treaty signed by Britain, France, Spain, and the Netherlands sealed related deals. The first article went to the heart of the matter: "His Britannic Majesty acknowledges the said United States to be free Sovereign and independent States." Other articles set the western boundary at the Mississippi River and guaranteed that creditors on both sides would be paid in sterling money, a provision important to British merchants. Britain agreed to withdraw its troops quickly, but more than a decade later this promise still had not been fully kept. Another agreement prohibited the British from "carrying away any Negroes or other property of the American inhabitants." The treaty was signed on September 3, 1783.

News of the treaty signing was cause for celebration among most Americans, but not among the thousands of self-liberated blacks who had joined the British under the promise of freedom. South Carolinian Boston King, a refugee in New York City, recalled that the provision prohibiting evacuation of black refugees "filled us with inexpressible anguish and terror." King and others pressed the

battle of Yorktown

▶ October 1781 battle that sealed American victory in the Revolutionary War. American troops and a French fleet trapped the British army under the command of General Charles Cornwallis at Yorktown, Virginia.

Treaty (Peace) of Paris, 1783

▶ September 3, 1783, treaty that ended the Revolutionary War. The treaty acknowledged America's independence, set its boundaries, and promised the quick withdrawal of British troops from American soil. It failed to recognize Indians as players in the conflict.

What role did the home front play in the war?

How were Native Americans and the French involved in the war?

Why did the British southern strategy ultimately fail?

Conclusion: Why did the British lose the American Revolution?

✓ LearningCurve
Check what you know.
bedfordstmartins.com
/roarkunderstanding

199

British commander in New York, Sir Guy Carleton, to honor pre-treaty British promises. Carleton obliged: For all refugees under British protection for more than a year, he issued certificates of freedom — making them no longer "property" to be returned. More than 4,000 blacks sailed out of New York for Nova Scotia, Boston King and his family among them. As Carleton coolly explained to a protesting George Washington, "The Negroes in question . . . I found free when I arrived at New York, I had therefore no right, as I thought, to prevent their going to any part of the world they thought proper." British commanders in Savannah and Charleston followed Carleton's lead and aided the exit of perhaps 10,000 blacks from the United States.

The Treaty of Paris had nothing to say about the Indian participants in the Revolutionary War. As one American told the Shawnee people, "Your Fathers the English have made Peace with us for themselves, but forgot you their Children, who Fought with them, and neglected you like Bastards." Indian lands were assigned to the victors as though they were uninhabited. Some Indian refugees fled west into present-day Missouri and Arkansas, and others, such as Joseph Brant's Mohawks, relocated to Canada. But significant numbers remained within the new United States, occupying their traditional homelands in areas west and north of the Ohio River. For them, the Treaty of Paris brought no peace at all; their longer war against the Americans would extend at least until 1795 and for some until 1813. Their ally, Britain, conceded defeat, but the Indians did not.

With the treaty finally signed, the British began their evacuation of New York, Charleston, and Savannah, a process complicated by the sheer numbers involved — soldiers, fearful loyalists, and refugees from slavery by the thousands. In New York City, more than 27,000 soldiers and 30,000 loyalists sailed on hundreds of ships for England in the late fall of 1783. In a final act of mischief, on the November day when the last ships left, the losing side raised the British flag at the southern tip of Manhattan, cut away the ropes used to hoist it, and greased the flagpole.

> **QUICK REVIEW**

What missteps led to the failure of British strategy in the South?

CHAPTER LOCATOR | Why did Americans wait so long before they declared their independence? | What initial challenges did the opposing armies face?

CHAPTER 7
200 FIGHTING THE AMERICAN REVOLUTION

THE BRITISH BEGAN the war for America convinced that they could not lose. They had the best-trained army and navy in the world, they were familiar with the landscape from the Seven Years' War, they had the willing warrior-power of most of the native tribes of the backcountry, and they easily captured every port city of consequence in America. A majority of colonists were either neutral or loyal to the crown. Why, then, did the British lose?

One continuing problem the British faced was the uncertainty of supplies. The army depended on a steady stream of supply ships from home, and insecurity about food helps explain their reluctance to pursue the Continental army aggressively. A further obstacle was their continual misuse of loyalist energies. Any plan to repacify the colonies required the cooperation of the loyalists, but the British repeatedly left them to the mercy of vengeful rebels. French aid also helps explain the British defeat. Even before the formal alliance, French artillery and ammunition proved vital to the Continental army. After 1780, the French army fought alongside the Americans, and the French navy made the Yorktown victory possible. Finally, the British abdicated civil power in the colonies in 1775 and 1776, when royal officials fled to safety, and they never really regained it. The basic British goal — to turn back the clock to imperial rule — receded into impossibility as the war dragged on.

The Revolution profoundly disrupted the lives of Americans everywhere. It was a war for independence from Britain, but it was more. It was a war that required men and women to think about politics and the legitimacy of authority. The rhetoric employed to justify the revolution against Britain put the words *liberty*, *tyranny*, *slavery*, *independence*, and *equality* into common usage. These words carried far deeper meanings than a mere complaint over taxation without representation. The Revolution unleashed a dynamic of equality and liberty that was largely unintended and unwanted by many of the political leaders of 1776. But that dynamic emerged as a potent force in American life in the decades to come.

| What role did the home front play in the war? | How were Native Americans and the French involved in the war? | Why did the British southern strategy ultimately fail? | Conclusion: Why did the British lose the American Revolution? | ✔ LearningCurve Check what you know. bedfordstmartins.com /roarkunderstanding |

201

CHAPTER 7 STUDY GUIDE

STEP 1

GET STARTED ONLINE

✓ LearningCurve ▪ bedfordstmartins.com/roarkunderstanding
Now that you've read the chapter, make it stick by completing the LearningCurve activity.

STEP 2

EXPLAIN WHY IT MATTERS

Put your reading into practice. Identify each term below, and then explain why it matters in U.S. history.

TERM	WHO OR WHAT & WHEN	WHY IT MATTERS
Second Continental Congress (p. 174)		
Continental army (p. 175)		
battle of Bunker Hill (p. 176)		
Common Sense (p. 176)		
Declaration of Independence (p. 179)		
battle of Long Island (p. 182)		
Ladies Association (p. 186)		
loyalists (p. 186)		
battle of Oriskany (p. 191)		
battle of Saratoga (p. 191)		
battle of Yorktown (p. 199)		
Treaty (Peace) of Paris, 1783 (p. 199)		

STEP 3

MOVE BEYOND THE BASICS

To demonstrate a more advanced understanding, provide the detail of the American strategy, the British strategy, key events, and major battles. Why were the Americans ultimately victorious?

Period	American strategy	British strategy	Key events	Major battles/victor
June 1775–December 1776				
January 1777–February 1778				
March 1778–September 1783				

Now, take a step back and try to explain the big picture. Remember to use specific examples from the chapter in your answers.

DECLARING INDEPENDENCE

▶ Why were so many Americans divided about the question of independence from Britain?

▶ What factors contributed to the decision by the Continental Congress to declare independence in July 1776?

THE FIRST TWO YEARS OF WAR

▶ What challenges did the Americans face in the first year of the war? How successful were they in meeting them?

▶ What impact did other European powers and Indian peoples have on the course of the war?

AMERICAN VICTORY

▶ Why did the British switch to the southern strategy? Why did it fail?

▶ Is it more accurate to say that the Americans won the Revolutionary War or that the British lost it? Why?

LOOKING BACKWARD, LOOKING AHEAD

▶ When did the chain of events that culminated in the establishment of an independent United States begin? In 1763? In 1776? In 1783? At another date? Present evidence to support your answer.

▶ What challenges did the United States face as it emerged victorious from the Revolutionary War?

> ### IN YOUR OWN WORDS

Imagine that you must give an oral report to the class answering the following question: How were the North American colonists able to successfully gain their independence from Great Britain in 1783? What would be the most important points to include and why?

 Do it online at the Student Site ■ **bedfordstmartins.com/roarkunderstanding**

8

BUILDING A REPUBLIC

1775–1789

> **What were the most significant events that led to the formulation and ratification of the U.S. Constitution?** Chapter 8 examines the challenges America faced in the 1780s, the efforts of the states to define freedom and citizenship, and the process that led to the abandonment of the Articles of Confederation and the adoption of the Constitution.

 **LearningCurve**

bedfordstmartins.com/roarkunderstanding
After reading the chapter, use LearningCurve to retain what you've read.

> What kind of government did the Articles of Confederation create?

> How did the states define citizenship and freedom?

> Why did the Articles of Confederation fail?

> How did the Constitution change how the nation was governed?

> What were the objections to ratification of the Constitution?

> Conclusion: What was the "republican remedy"?

George Washington presides over the constitutional convention. **Philadelphia, 1787.** The Granger Collection, New York.

What kind of government did the Articles of Confederation create?

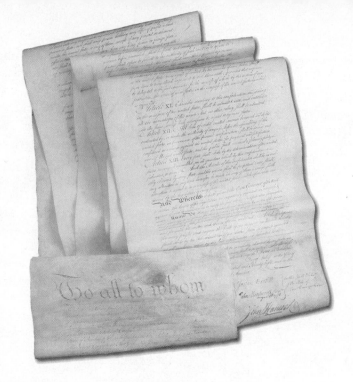

Articles of Confederation Delegates to the Second Continental Congress hammered out the Articles of Confederation over many months in 1776 and 1777. Once the congress agreed on it, the plan was printed and distributed to state legislatures for ratification, a process that took nearly five years because it required the assent of thirteen states. National Archives.

Articles of Confederation

▶ The written document defining the structure of the government from 1781 to 1788. Under the Articles, the Union was a confederation of equal states, with no executive (president) and with limited powers, existing mainly to foster a common defense.

CREATING AND APPROVING A WRITTEN plan of government for the new confederation took five years, as delegates and states sought agreement on fundamental principles. With monarchy gone, where would sovereignty lie? What would be the nature of representation? Who would hold the power of taxation? The resulting plan, called the **Articles of Confederation**, proved to be surprisingly difficult to implement, mainly because the thirteen states disagreed over boundaries in the land to the west of the states. Once the Articles were ratified and the active phase of the war had drawn to a close, the Continental Congress faded in importance compared with politics in the individual states.

Confederation and Taxation

Only after declaring independence did the Continental Congress turn its attention to creating a written document that would specify what powers the congress had and by what authority it existed. There was widespread agreement on key government powers: pursuing war and peace, conducting foreign relations, regulating trade, and running a postal service. By late 1777, congressmen reached agreement on the Articles of Confederation, defining the Union as a loose confederation of states existing mainly to foster a common defense. Much like the existing Continental Congress, there was no national executive (that is, no president) and no judiciary.

CHAPTER LOCATOR | **What kind of government did the Articles of Confederation create?** | How did the states define citizenship and freedom?

Anywhere from two to seven delegates could represent each state, with each delegation casting a single vote. Routine decisions required a simple majority of seven states, whereas momentous decisions, such as declaring war, required nine. To approve or amend the Articles required the unanimous consent both of the thirteen state delegations and of the thirteen state legislatures—giving any state a crippling veto power. Most crucially, the Articles gave the national government no power of direct taxation.

Yet taxation was a necessity, since all governments require money. To finance the Revolutionary War, the confederation congress issued interest-bearing bonds purchased by French and Dutch bankers as well as middling to wealthy Americans, and revenue was necessary to repay these loans. Other routine government functions required money: Trade regulation required salaried customs officers; a postal system required postmen, horses and wagons, and well-maintained postal roads; the western lands required surveyors; and Indian diplomacy (or war) added further large costs. Article 8 of the confederation document declared that taxes were needed to support "the common defence or general welfare" of the country, yet the congress also had to be sensitive to the rhetoric of the Revolution, which denounced taxation by a nonrepresentative power.

The Articles of Confederation posed a delicate two-step solution. The congress would requisition (that is, request) money to be paid into the common treasury, and each state legislature would then levy taxes within its borders to pay the requisition. The Articles called for state contributions assessed in proportion to the improved property value of the state's land, so that populous states paid more than did sparsely populated states. Requiring that the actual tax bill be passed by the state legislatures preserved the Revolution's principle of taxation only by direct representation. However, no mechanism compelled states to pay.

The lack of authority in the confederation government was exactly what many state leaders wanted in the late 1770s. A league of states with rotating personnel, no executive branch, no power of direct taxation, and a requirement of unanimity for any major change seemed to be a good way to keep government in check. The catch was that ratification of the Articles required unanimous agreement, and that proved difficult to secure.

The Problem of Western Lands

The most serious disagreement delaying ratification of the Articles concerned the absence of any plan for the lands to the west of the thirteen original states. This absence was deliberate: Virginia and Connecticut had old colonial charters that located their western boundaries at the Mississippi River, and six other states also claimed parts of that land. But five states without extensive land claims insisted on redrawing those colonial boundaries to create a national domain to be sold to settlers (**Map 8.1**). As one Rhode Island delegate put it, "The western world opens an amazing prospect as a national fund; it is equal to our debt."

The eight land-claiming states were ready to sign the Articles of Confederation in 1777, since it protected their interests. Three states without claims—Rhode Island, Pennsylvania, and New Jersey—eventually capitulated and signed, "not from a Conviction of the Equality and Justness of it," said a New Jersey

> CHRONOLOGY

1777
– Articles of Confederation are sent to states.

1781
– Articles of Confederation are ratified.
– Creation of executive departments.

| Why did the Articles of Confederation fail? | How did the Constitution change how the nation was governed? | What were the objections to ratification of the Constitution? | Conclusion: What was the "republican remedy"? | ✓ LearningCurve Check what you know. bedfordstmartins.com /roarkunderstanding |

207

delegate, "but merely from an absolute Necessity there was of complying to save the Continent." But Delaware and Maryland continued to hold out, insisting on a national domain policy. In 1779, the disputants finally compromised: Any land a state volunteered to relinquish would become the national domain. When Virginia representatives James Madison and Thomas Jefferson ceded Virginia's huge land claim in 1781, the Articles of Confederation were at last unanimously approved.

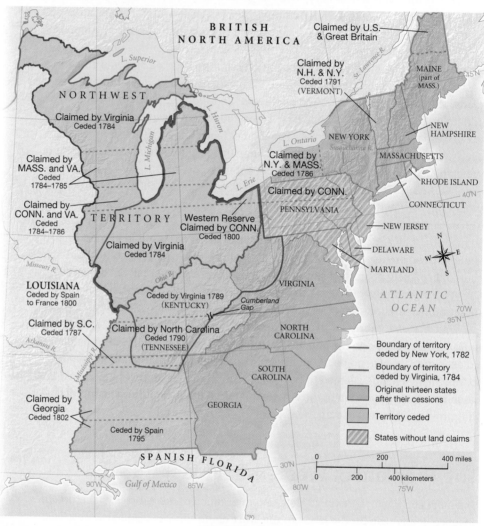

MAP 8.1 ■ Cession of Western Lands, 1782–1802

The thirteen new states found it hard to ratify the Articles of Confederation without settling their conflicting land claims in the West, a vast area occupied by Indian tribes. The five states objecting to the Articles' silence over western land policy were Maryland, Delaware, New Jersey, Rhode Island, and Pennsylvania.

> **MAP ACTIVITY**

READING THE MAP: Which state had the largest claims on western territory?

CONNECTIONS: In what context did the first dispute regarding western lands arise? How was it resolved? Does the map suggest a reason why Pennsylvania, a large state, joined the four much smaller states on this issue?

CHAPTER LOCATOR | What kind of government did the Articles of Confederation create? | How did the states define citizenship and freedom?

208 CHAPTER 8 BUILDING A REPUBLIC

The western land issue demonstrated that powerful interests divided the thirteen new states. The apparent unity of purpose inspired by fighting the war against Britain papered over sizable cracks in the new confederation.

Running the New Government

No fanfare greeted the long-awaited inauguration of the new government in 1781. The congress continued to sputter along, its problems far from solved by the signing of the Articles. Lack of a quorum, defined as two men from seven states, often hampered day-to-day activities. State legislatures were slow to select delegates, and many politicians preferred to devote their energies to state governments, especially when the congress seemed deadlocked or, worse, irrelevant.

It did not help that the congress had no permanent home. During the war, when the British army threatened Philadelphia, the congress relocated to small Pennsylvania towns such as Lancaster and York and then to Baltimore. After hostilities ceased, the congress moved from Trenton to Princeton to Annapolis to New York City. Many delegates were reluctant to travel far from home, especially if they had wives and children. Consequently, some of the most committed delegates were young bachelors, such as James Madison, and men in their fifties and sixties whose families were grown, such as Samuel Adams.

To address the difficulties of an inefficient congress, executive departments of war, finance, and foreign affairs were created in 1781 to handle purely administrative functions. When the department heads were ambitious—as was Robert Morris, a wealthy Philadelphia merchant who served as superintendent of finance—they could exercise considerable executive power. The Articles of Confederation had deliberately refrained from setting up an executive branch, but a modest one was being invented by necessity.

QUICK REVIEW <

Why was the confederation government's
authority so limited?

Why did the Articles of Confederation fail?

How did the Constitution change how the nation was governed?

What were the objections to ratification of the Constitution?

Conclusion: What was the "republican remedy"?

☑ LearningCurve
Check what you know.
bedfordstmartins.com
/roarkunderstanding

How did the states define citizenship and freedom?

Widow from Essex County

Mrs. Elizabeth Alexander Stevens was married to John Stevens, a New Jersey delegate to the Continental Congress in 1783. Widowed in 1792, she would have then been eligible to vote in state elections according to New Jersey's unique enfranchisement of property-holding women. The widow Stevens died in 1799, before suffrage was redefined to be the exclusive right of males. New Jersey Historical Society.

IN THE FIRST DECADE OF INDEPENDENCE, the states were sovereign and all-powerful. Only a few functions, such as declaring war and peace, had been transferred to the confederation government. Familiar and close to home, state governments claimed the allegiance of citizens and became the arena in which the Revolution's innovations would first be tried. Each state implemented a constitution and determined voter qualifications, and many states grappled with the issue of squaring slavery with Revolutionary ideals, with varying outcomes.

The State Constitutions

In May 1776, the congress recommended that all states draw up constitutions based on "the authority of the people." By 1778, ten states had done so, and three more (Connecticut, Massachusetts, and Rhode Island) had adopted and updated their original colonial charters. A shared feature of all the state constitutions was the conviction that government ultimately rests on the consent of the governed. Political writers in the late 1770s embraced the concept of **republicanism** as the underpinning of the new governments. Republicanism meant more than popular

republicanism

▶ A social philosophy that embraced representative institutions (as opposed to monarchy), a citizenry attuned to civic values above private interests, and a virtuous community in which individuals work to promote the public good.

CHAPTER LOCATOR | What kind of government did the Articles of Confederation create? | How did the states define citizenship and freedom?

CHAPTER 8
210   BUILDING A REPUBLIC

elections and representative institutions. For some, republicanism stood for leaders who were autonomous, virtuous citizens putting civic values above private interests. For others, it suggested direct democracy, with nothing standing in the way of the will of the people. For all, it meant government that promoted the people's welfare.

Widespread agreement about the virtues of republicanism went hand in hand with the idea that republics could succeed only in relatively small units, where people could make sure their interests were being served. Eleven states continued the colonial practice of a two-chamber assembly but greatly augmented the powers of the lower house. Pennsylvania and Georgia abolished the more elite upper house altogether, and most states severely limited the powers of the governor. Real power thus resided with the lower houses, responsive to popular majorities due to annual elections and guaranteed rotation in office (term limits).

Six of the state constitutions included bills of rights—lists of individual liberties that government could not abridge. Virginia's bill was the first. Passed in June 1776, it asserted "That all men are by nature equally free and independent, and have certain inherent rights, of which, when they enter into a state of society, they cannot by any compact deprive or divest their posterity; namely, the enjoyment of life and liberty, with the means of acquiring and possessing property, and pursuing and obtaining happiness and safety." Along with these inherent rights went more specific rights to freedom of speech, freedom of the press, and trial by jury.

Who Are "the People"?

When the Continental Congress called for state constitutions based on "the authority of the people," and when the Virginia bill of rights granted "all men" certain rights, who was meant by "the people"? Who exactly were the citizens of this new country, and how far would the principle of democratic government extend? Different people answered these questions differently, but in the 1770s certain limits to political participation were widely agreed upon.

One limit was defined by property. In nearly every state, voters and political candidates had to meet varying property qualifications. Only property owners were presumed to possess the necessary independence of mind to make wise political choices. Are not propertyless men, asked John Adams, "too little acquainted with public affairs to form a right judgment, and too dependent upon other men to have a will of their own?" Property qualifications probably disfranchised from one-quarter to one-half of adult white males in all the states. Not all of them took their nonvoter status quietly. One Maryland man wondered what was so special about being worth £30, his state's threshold for voting: "Every poor man has a life, a personal liberty, and a right to his earnings; and is in danger of being injured by government in a variety of ways." Others noted that propertyless men were fighting and dying in the Revolutionary War; surely they had legitimate political concerns. A few radical voices challenged the notion that wealth was correlated with good citizenship; maybe the opposite was true. But ideas like this were outside the mainstream. The writers of the new constitutions, themselves men of property, viewed the right to own and preserve property as a central principle of the Revolution.

1776
- Declaration of Independence is adopted.
- Virginia adopts state bill of rights.

1778
- State constitutions are completed.

1780
- Pennsylvania institutes gradual emancipation.

1781
- Several Massachusetts slaves sue for freedom.

1783
- Massachusetts enfranchises taxpaying free blacks.

1784
- Gradual emancipation laws are passed in Rhode Island and Connecticut.

1799
- Gradual emancipation law is passed in New York.

1804
- Gradual emancipation law is passed in New Jersey.

| Why did the Articles of Confederation fail? | How did the Constitution change how the nation was governed? | What were the objections to ratification of the Constitution? | Conclusion: What was the "republican remedy"? | ✓ LearningCurve Check what you know. bedfordstmartins.com /roarkunderstanding |

211

Another exclusion from voting—women—was so ingrained that few stopped to question it. Yet the logic of allowing propertied females to vote did occur to a handful of well-placed women. Abigail Adams wrote to her husband, John, in 1782, "Even in the freest countrys our property is subject to the controul and disposal of our partners, to whom the Laws have given a sovereign Authority. Deprived of a voice in Legislation, obliged to submit to those Laws which are imposed upon us, is it not sufficient to make us indifferent to the publick Welfare?"

Only three states specified that voters had to be male, so powerful was the unspoken assumption that only men could vote. Yet in New Jersey, small numbers of women began to go to the polls in the 1780s. The state's constitution of 1776 enfranchised all free inhabitants worth more than £50, language that in theory opened the door to free blacks and unmarried women who met the property requirement. (Married women owned no property, for by law their husbands held title to everything.)

In 1790, only about 1,000 free black adults of both sexes lived in New Jersey, a state with a population of 184,000. The number of unmarried adult white women was probably also small and comprised mainly widows. In view of the property requirement, the voter blocs enfranchised under this law were minuscule. Still, this highly unusual situation lasted until 1807, when a new state law specifically disfranchised both blacks and women. Henceforth, independence of mind, held to be essential for voting, was redefined to be sex- and race-specific.

In the 1780s, voting everywhere was class-specific because of property restrictions. John Adams urged the framers of the Massachusetts constitution to stick with traditional property qualifications. If suffrage is brought up for debate, he warned, "there will be no end of it. New claims will arise; women will demand a vote; lads from twelve to twenty-one will think their rights not enough attended to; and every man who has not a farthing, will demand an equal voice with any other."

Equality and Slavery

Restrictions on political participation did not mean that propertyless people enjoyed no civil rights and liberties. The various state bills of rights applied to all individuals who were free; unfree people were another matter.

The author of the Virginia bill of rights was George Mason, a planter who owned 118 slaves. When he wrote that "all men are by nature equally free and independent," Mason did not have slaves in mind; he instead was asserting that white Americans were the equals of the British and entitled to equal liberties. Other Virginia legislators, worried about misinterpretations, added a qualifying clause: that all men "when they enter into a state of society" have inherent rights. As one legislator wrote, with relief, "Slaves, not being constituent members of our society, could never pretend to any benefit from such a maxim."

One month later, the Declaration of Independence used essentially the same phrase about equality, this time without the modifying clause about entering society. Two state constitutions, Pennsylvania and Massachusetts, also picked it up. In Massachusetts, one town suggested rewording the draft constitution to

CHAPTER LOCATOR | What kind of government did the Articles of Confederation create? | How did the states define citizenship and freedom?

CHAPTER 8
212   BUILDING A REPUBLIC

read "All men, whites and blacks, are born free and equal." The suggestion was not implemented.

Nevertheless, after 1776, the ideals of the Revolution about natural equality and liberty began to erode the institution of slavery. Often, enslaved blacks led the challenge. In 1777, several Massachusetts slaves petitioned for their "natural & unalienable right to that freedom which the great Parent of the Universe hath bestowed equally on all mankind." They modestly asked for freedom for their children at age twenty-one and were turned down. In 1779, similar petitions in Connecticut and New Hampshire met with no success. Seven Massachusetts free men, including the mariner brothers Paul and John Cuffe, refused to pay taxes on the grounds that they could not vote and so were not represented. The Cuffe brothers landed in jail in 1780 for tax evasion, but their petition to the Massachusetts legislature spurred the extension of suffrage to taxpaying free blacks in 1783.

Another way to bring the issue before lawmakers was to sue in court. In 1781, a woman called Elizabeth Freeman (Mum Bett) was the first to win freedom in a Massachusetts court, basing her case on the just-passed state constitution that declared "all men are born free and equal." Another Massachusetts slave, Quok Walker, charged his master with assault and battery, arguing that he was a freeman under that same constitutional phrase. Walker won and was set free, a decision confirmed in an appeal to the state's superior court in 1783. Several similar cases followed, and by 1789 slavery had been effectively abolished by a series of judicial decisions in Massachusetts.

State legislatures acted more slowly. Pennsylvania enacted a **gradual emancipation** law in 1780, providing that infants born to a slave mother on or after March 1, 1780, would be freed at age twenty-eight. Not until 1847 did Pennsylvania fully abolish slavery, but slaves did not wait for such slow implementation. Untold numbers in Pennsylvania simply ran away and asserted their freedom. One estimate holds that more than half of young slave men in Philadelphia joined the ranks of free blacks, and by 1790, free blacks outnumbered slaves in Pennsylvania two to one.

Rhode Island and Connecticut adopted gradual emancipation laws in 1784; New York waited until 1799 and New Jersey until 1804 to enact theirs. These last were the two northern states with the largest number of slaves—New York with 20,000 in 1800, New Jersey with more than 12,000—whereas Pennsylvania had just 1,700. Gradual emancipation illustrates the tension between radical and conservative implications of republican ideology. Republican government protected people's liberties and property, yet slaves were both people and property. Gradual emancipation balanced the civil rights of blacks and the property rights of their owners by promising delayed freedom.

South of Pennsylvania, in Delaware, Maryland, and Virginia, where slavery was critical to the economy, emancipation bills were rejected. All three states,

Elizabeth Freeman in 1811

After suing for her freedom in court, Elizabeth Freeman ("Mum Bett") found secure employment with the family of her lawyer, Theodore Sedgwick. A Sedgwick son later wrote: "If there could be a practical refutation of the imagined superiority of our race to hers, the life and character of this woman would afford that refutation. . . . She had, when occasion required it, an air of command which conferred a degree of dignity." Massachusetts Historical Society.

gradual emancipation
▶ Laws passed in five northern states that balanced slaves' civil rights against slaveholders' property rights by providing a multistage process for freeing slaves, distinguishing persons already alive from those not yet born and providing benchmark dates when freedom would arrive for each group.

Why did the Articles of Confederation fail?

How did the Constitution change how the nation was governed?

What were the objections to ratification of the Constitution?

Conclusion: What was the "republican remedy"?

☑ **LearningCurve**
Check what you know. bedfordstmartins.com /roarkunderstanding

Legal Changes to Slavery,
1777–1804

however, eased legal restrictions and allowed individual acts of emancipation for adult slaves below the age of forty-five under new manumission laws. By 1790, close to 10,000 newly freed Virginia slaves had formed local free black communities complete with schools and churches.

In the deep South—the Carolinas and Georgia—freedom for slaves was unthinkable among whites. Yet several thousand slaves had defected to the British during the war, and between 3,000 and 4,000 left with the British at the war's conclusion. Adding northern blacks evacuated from New York City in 1783, the probable total of emancipated blacks who left the United States was between 8,000 and 10,000. Some went to Canada, some to England, and some to Sierra Leone on the west coast of Africa. Many hundreds took refuge with the Seminole and Creek Indians, becoming permanent members of their communities in Spanish Florida and western Georgia.

Although all these instances of emancipation were gradual, small, and certainly incomplete, their symbolic importance was enormous. Every state from Pennsylvania north acknowledged that slavery was fundamentally inconsistent with Revolutionary ideology; "all men are created equal" was beginning to acquire real force as a basic principle.

> **QUICK REVIEW**

What were the limits of citizenship, rights, and freedom within the various states?

CHAPTER LOCATOR | What kind of government did the Articles of Confederation create? | How did the states define citizenship and freedom?

214 CHAPTER 8
BUILDING A REPUBLIC

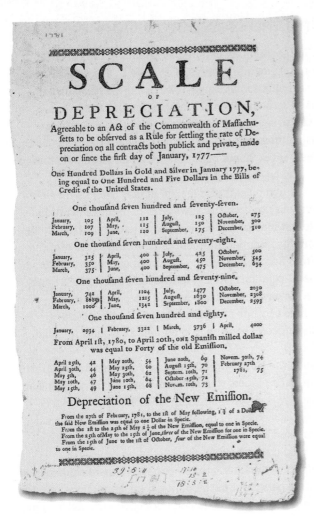

Scale of Depreciation

This chart shows the declining monthly value of two emissions of paper dollars from January 1777 to October 1781 as stipulated by the government of Massachusetts. In January 1777, 105 paper dollars were equal in buying power to $100 in silver or gold. In April 1780, 4,000 paper dollars were needed to equal the buying power of $100 in gold or silver. Such a chart was needed when debtors and creditors settled accounts contracted at one time and paid off later in greatly depreciated dollars. Courtesy, American Antiquarian Society.

Why did the Articles of Confederation fail?

IN 1783, THE CONFEDERATION government faced three interrelated concerns: paying down the large war debt, making formal peace with the Indians, and dealing with western settlement. Lacking the power to enforce its tax requisitions, the congress faced added debt pressures when army officers suddenly demanded secure pensions. Revenue from sales of western lands seemed to be a promising solution, but Indian inhabitants of those lands had different ideas.

From 1784 to 1786, the congress struggled mightily with these three issues. Some leaders were gripped by a sense of crisis, fearing that the Articles of Confederation were too weak. Others defended the Articles as the best guarantee of liberty because real governance occurred at the state level, closer to the people. A major outbreak of civil disorder in western Massachusetts quickly crystallized the debate and propelled the critics of the Articles into decisive and far-reaching action.

Why did the Articles of Confederation fail?

How did the Constitution change how the nation was governed?

What were the objections to ratification of the Constitution?

Conclusion: What was the "republican remedy"?

✓ LearningCurve
Check what you know.
bedfordstmartins.com
/roarkunderstanding

215

> CHRONOLOGY

1783
- Newburgh Conspiracy.

1784
- Treaty of Fort Stanwix.

1785
- Ordinance of 1785.
- Treaty of Fort McIntosh.
- Congress calls for large requisition.

1786
- Shays's Rebellion begins.

1787
- Shays's Rebellion is crushed.
- Northwest Ordinance.

Newburgh Conspiracy

▶ A bogus threatened coup staged by Continental army officers and leaders in the Continental Congress in 1782–1783. They hoped that a forceful demand for military back pay and pensions would create pressure for stronger taxation powers. General Washington defused the threat.

The War Debt and the Newburgh Conspiracy

For nearly two years, the Continental army camped at Newburgh, north of the British-occupied city of New York, awaiting news of a peace treaty. The soldiers were bored, restless, and upset about military payrolls that were far in arrears. An earlier promise to officers of generous pensions (half pay for life), made in 1780 in a desperate effort to retain them, seemed unlikely to be honored. In December 1782, officers petitioned the congress for immediate back pay for their men so that when peace arrived, no one would go home penniless. The petition darkly hinted that failure to pay the men "may have fatal effects."

Instead of rejecting the petition outright for lack of money, several members of the congress saw an opportunity to pressure the states to approve taxation powers. One of these was Robert Morris, a Philadelphia merchant with a gift for financial dealings. As the congress's superintendent of finance, Morris kept the books and wheedled loans from European bankers using his own substantial fortune as collateral. To forestall total insolvency, Morris led efforts in 1781 and again in 1786 to amend the Articles to allow collection of a 5 percent impost (an import tax). Each time it failed by one vote, illustrating the difficulties of achieving unanimity. Now the officers' petition offered new prospects to make the case for taxation.

The result was a plot called the **Newburgh Conspiracy**. Morris and several other congressmen encouraged the officers to march the army on the congress to demand its pay. No actual coup was envisioned; both sides shared the goal of wanting to augment the congress's power of taxation. Yet the risks were great, for not everyone would understand that this was a ruse. What if the soldiers, incited by their grievances, could not be held in check?

General George Washington, sympathetic to the plight of unpaid soldiers and officers, had approved the initial petition. But the plotters, knowing of his reputation for integrity, did not inform him of their collusion with congressional leaders. In March 1783, when the general learned of these developments, he delivered an emotional speech to a meeting of five hundred officers, reminding them in stirring language of honor, heroism, and sacrifice. He urged them to put their faith in the congress, and he denounced the plotters as "subversive of all order and discipline." His audience was left speechless and tearful, and the plot was immediately defused.

Morris continued to work to find money to pay the soldiers, but in the end, a trickle of money from a few states was too little and too late, coming after the army had begun to disband. For its part, the congress voted to endorse a plan to commute, or transform, the lifetime pension promised the officers into a lump-sum payment of full pay for five years. But no lump sum of money was available. Instead, the officers were issued "commutation certificates," promising future payment with interest, which quickly depreciated in value.

In 1783, the soldiers' pay and officers' pensions added some $5 million to the rising public debt, forcing the congress to press for larger requisitions from the states. The confederation, however, had one new source of enormous untapped wealth: the extensive western territories, attractive to the fast-growing white population but currently inhabited by Indians.

CHAPTER LOCATOR | What kind of government did the Articles of Confederation create? | How did the states define citizenship and freedom?

216 CHAPTER 8
BUILDING A REPUBLIC

The Treaty of Fort Stanwix

Since the Indians had not participated in the Treaty of Paris of 1783, the confederation government hoped to formalize treaties ending ongoing hostilities between Indians and settlers and securing land cessions. The most pressing problem was the land inhabited by the Iroquois Confederacy, a league of six tribes, now claimed by the states of New York and Massachusetts based on their colonial charters (see Map 8.1).

Treaty of Fort Stanwix, 1784

At issue was the revenue stream that land sales would generate: Which government would get it? The congress summoned the Iroquois to a meeting in October 1784 at Fort Stanwix, on the upper Mohawk River. The Articles of Confederation gave the congress (as opposed to individual states) the right to manage diplomacy, war, and "all affairs with the Indians, not members of any of the States." But New York's governor seized on that ambiguous language, claiming that the Iroquois were in fact "members" of his state, and called his own meeting at Fort Stanwix in September. Suspecting that New York's claim to authority might be superseded by the congress, the most important chiefs declined to come and instead sent deputies without authority to negotiate. The Mohawk leader Joseph Brant shrewdly identified the problem of divided authority that afflicted the confederation government: "Here lies some Difficulty in our Minds, that there should be two separate bodies to manage these Affairs." No deal was struck with New York.

Three weeks later, U.S. commissioners opened proceedings at Fort Stanwix with the Seneca chief Cornplanter and Captain Aaron Hill, a Mohawk leader, accompanied by six hundred Iroquois. The Americans demanded a return of prisoners of war; recognition of the confederation's (and not states') authority to negotiate; and an all-important cession of a strip of land from Fort Niagara due south, which established U.S.-held territory adjacent to the border with Canada. This cession of territory would enclose the Iroquois land within the United States and would make it impossible for the Indians to claim to be between the United States and Canada. When the tribal leaders balked, one of the commissioners sternly replied, "You are mistaken in supposing that, having been excluded from the treaty between the United States and the King of England, you are become a free and independent nation and may make what terms you please. It is not so. You are a subdued people."

In the end, the treaty was signed, gifts were given, and six high-level Indian hostages were kept at the fort awaiting the release of the American prisoners taken during the Revolutionary War, mostly women and children. In addition, a significant side deal sealed the release of much of the Seneca tribe's claim to the Ohio Valley to the United States. This move was a major surprise to the Delaware, Mingo, and Shawnee Indians who lived there. In the months to come, tribes not at the meeting tried to disavow the **Treaty of Fort Stanwix** as a document signed under coercion by virtual hostages. But the confederation government ignored those complaints and made plans to survey and develop the Ohio Territory.

New York's governor astutely figured that the congress's power to implement the treaty terms was limited. So New York quietly began surveying and then selling the very land it had failed to secure by treaty with the Iroquois. As that fact became generally known, it pointed up the weakness of the confederation government. One Connecticut leader wondered, "What is to defend us from the ambition and rapacity of New York, when she has spread over that vast territory, which she claims and holds?"

Treaty of Fort Stanwix

▶1784 treaty with the Iroquois Confederacy that established the primacy of the American confederation (and not states) to negotiate with Indians and that resulted in large land cessions in the Ohio Country (northwestern Pennsylvania). Tribes not present at Fort Stanwix disavowed the treaty.

| Why did the Articles of Confederation fail? | How did the Constitution change how the nation was governed? | What were the objections to ratification of the Constitution? | Conclusion: What was the "republican remedy"? | ☑ LearningCurve Check what you know. bedfordstmartins.com /roarkunderstanding |

217

Land Ordinances and the Northwest Territory

The congress ignored western New York and turned instead to the Ohio Valley to make good on the promise of western expansion. Congressman Thomas Jefferson, charged with drafting a policy, proposed dividing the territory north of the Ohio River and east of the Mississippi—the Northwest Territory—into nine new states with evenly spaced east-west boundaries and townships ten miles square. He even advocated giving, not selling, the land to settlers, because future property taxes on the improved land would be payment enough. Jefferson's aim was to encourage rapid and democratic settlement and to discourage land speculation. Jefferson projected representative governments in the new states; they would not become colonies of the older states. Finally, Jefferson's draft prohibited slavery in the nine new states.

The congress adopted parts of Jefferson's plan in the Ordinance of 1784: the rectangular grid, the nine states, and the guarantee of self-government and eventual statehood. What the congress found too radical was the proposal to give away the land; it badly needed immediate revenue. The slavery prohibition also failed, by a vote of seven to six states.

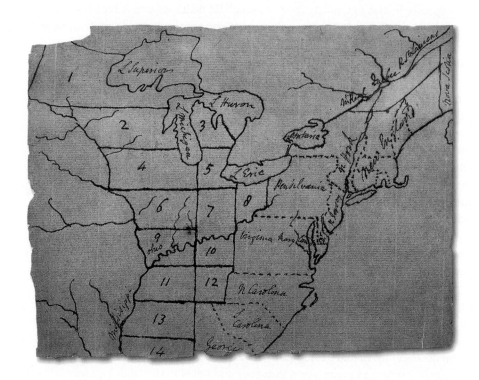

Jefferson's Map of the Northwest Territory

Thomas Jefferson proposed nine states in his initial plan for the Northwest Territory in 1784. Straight lines and right angles held a strong appeal for him. But such regularity ignored inconvenient geographic features such as rivers and even more inconvenient political facts such as Indian territorial claims. William L. Clements Library.

> VISUAL ACTIVITY

READING THE IMAGE: What does this map indicate about Jefferson's vision of the Northwest Territory?
CONNECTIONS: What were the problems with Jefferson's design for the division of the territory? Why did the congress alter it in the land ordinances of 1784, 1785, and 1787?

CHAPTER LOCATOR | What kind of government did the Articles of Confederation create? | How did the states define citizenship and freedom?

CHAPTER 8
BUILDING A REPUBLIC
218

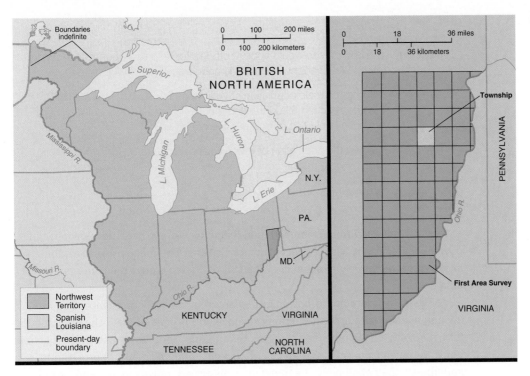

MAP 8.2 ■ The Northwest Ordinance and the Ordinance of 1785

Surveyors mapping the Northwest Territory followed the Ordinance of 1785, using the stars as well as poles and chains (standard surveying equipment) to run boundary lines. The result was a blanket of six-mile-square townships, subdivided into one-mile squares each containing sixteen 40-acre farms.

A year later, the congress revised the legislation with procedures for mapping and selling the land. The Ordinance of 1785 called for three to five states, divided into townships six miles square, further divided into thirty-six sections of 640 acres, each section enough for four family farms. Reduced to easily mappable squares, the land would be sold at public auction for a minimum of one dollar an acre, with highly desirable land bid up for more (**Map 8.2**). Two further restrictions applied: The minimum purchase was 640 acres, and payment had to be in hard money or in certificates of debt from Revolutionary days. This effectively meant that the land's first owners would be prosperous speculators, many of whom never set foot on the acreage. The commodification of land had been taken to a new level.

Speculators who held the land for resale avoided direct contact with the most serious obstacle to settlement: the dozens of Indian tribes that claimed the land as their own. The treaty signed at Fort Stanwix in 1784 was followed in 1785 by the Treaty of Fort McIntosh, which similarly coerced partial cessions of land from the Delaware, Wyandot, Chippewa, and Ottawa tribes. Finally, in 1786, a united Indian meeting near Detroit issued an ultimatum: No cession would be valid without the unanimous consent of the tribes. For two more decades, violent Indian wars in Ohio and Indiana would continue to impede white settlement (as discussed in chapter 9).

A third land act, called the **Northwest Ordinance** of 1787, set forth a three-stage process by which settled territories would advance to statehood. At all three territorial stages, the inhabitants were subject to taxation to support the Union, in the same manner as were the original states.

The Northwest Ordinance of 1787 was perhaps the most important legislation passed by the confederation government. It ensured that the new United States,

Northwest Ordinance

▶ Land act of 1787 that established a three-stage process by which settled territories would become states. It also banned slavery in the Northwest Territory. The ordinance guaranteed that western lands with white populations would not become colonial dependencies.

Why did the Articles of Confederation fail?

How did the Constitution change how the nation was governed?

What were the objections to ratification of the Constitution?

Conclusion: What was the "republican remedy"?

✔ LearningCurve
Check what you know.
bedfordstmartins.com /roarkunderstanding

219

> The Northwest Ordinance of 1787 and the Path to Statehood	
Phase One	The congress would appoint officials for a sparsely populated territory who would adopt a legal code and appoint local magistrates.
Phase Two	When the male population of voting age and landowning status (fifty acres) reached 5,000, the territory could elect its own legislature and send a nonvoting delegate to the congress.
Phase Three	When the population of voting citizens reached 60,000, the territory could write a state constitution and apply for full admission to the Union.

so recently released from colonial dependency, would not itself become a colonial power—at least not with respect to white citizens. The mechanism it established allowed for the orderly expansion of the United States across the continent in the next century.

Nonwhites were not forgotten or neglected in the 1787 ordinance. The brief document acknowledged the Indian presence and promised that "the utmost good faith shall always be observed towards the Indians; their lands and property shall never be taken from them without their consent; and, in their property, rights, and liberty, they shall never be invaded or disturbed, unless in just and lawful wars authorized by Congress." The 1787 ordinance further pledged that "laws founded in justice and humanity, shall from time to time be made for preventing wrongs being done to them." Such promises indicated noble intentions, but they were not generally honored in the decades to come.

Jefferson's original and remarkable suggestion to prohibit slavery in the Northwest Territory resurfaced in the 1787 ordinance, passing this time without any debate. Probably the addition of a fugitive slave provision in the act set southern congressmen at ease: Escaped slaves caught north of the Ohio River would be returned south. Also, abundant territory south of the Ohio remained available for the spread of slavery. The ordinance thus acknowledged and supported slavery even as it barred it from one region. Still, the prohibition of slavery in the Northwest Territory perpetuated the dynamic of gradual emancipation in the North. North-South sectionalism based on slavery was slowly taking shape.

The Requisition of 1785 and Shays's Rebellion, 1786–1787

Without an impost amendment and with public land sales projected but not yet realized, the confederation again requisitioned the states to contribute revenue. In 1785, the amount requested was $3 million, four times larger than the previous year's levy. Of this sum, 30 percent was needed for the government's operating costs, and another 30 percent was earmarked to pay debts owed to foreign lenders. The remaining 40 percent was to go to Americans who owned government bonds, the IOUs of the Revolutionary years. A significant slice of that 40 percent represented the interest owed to army officers for their recently issued "commutation certificates." This was a tax that, if collected, was going to hurt.

CHAPTER LOCATOR | What kind of government did the Articles of Confederation create? | How did the states define citizenship and freedom?

CHAPTER 8
220 BUILDING A REPUBLIC

At this time, states were struggling under state tax levies. Several states without major ports (and the import duties that ports generated) were already pressing their farmer citizens in order to retire state debts from the Revolution. New Jersey and Connecticut fit this profile, and both state legislatures voted to ignore the confederation's requisition. In New Hampshire, town meetings voted to refuse to pay, because they could not. In 1786, two hundred armed insurgents surrounded the New Hampshire capitol to protest the taxes but were driven off by an armed militia. The shocked assemblymen backed off from an earlier order to haul delinquent taxpayers into courts. Rhode Island, North Carolina, and Georgia responded to their constituents' protests by issuing abundant amounts of paper money and allowing taxes to be paid in greatly depreciated currency.

Nowhere were the tensions so extreme as in Massachusetts. For four years in a row, a fiscally conservative legislature, dominated by the coastal commercial centers, had passed tough tax laws to pay state creditors who required payment in hard money, not cheap paper. Then in March 1786, the legislature in Boston loaded the federal requisition onto the bill. In June, farmers in southeastern Massachusetts marched on a courthouse in an effort to close it down, and petitions of complaint about oppressive taxation poured in from the western two-thirds of the state. In July 1786, when the legislature adjourned, having yet again ignored their complaints, dissidents held a series of conventions and called for revisions to the state constitution to promote democracy, eliminate the elite upper house, and move the capital farther west in the state.

Still unheard in Boston, the dissidents targeted the county courts, the local symbol of state authority. In the fall of 1786, several thousand armed men shut down courthouses in six counties; sympathetic local militias did not intervene. The insurgents were not predominantly poor or debt-ridden farmers; they

Daniel Shays and Job Shattuck

A Boston almanac of 1787 yields the only rough depiction of Daniel Shays in existence. Shays is standing with another rebel leader, Job Shattuck, from the town of Groton. This particular almanac series was quite pro-Constitution in 1788, so very likely this picture was intended to mock the rebels by showing them in fancy uniforms and armed with swords, trappings beyond their presumed lowly means. National Portrait Gallery, Smithsonian Institution/Art Resource, NY.

Why did the Articles of Confederation fail?

How did the Constitution change how the nation was governed?

What were the objections to ratification of the Constitution?

Conclusion: What was the "republican remedy"?

LearningCurve
Check what you know.
bedfordstmartins.com
/roarkunderstanding

included veteran soldiers and officers in the Continental army as well as town leaders. One was a farmer and onetime army captain, Daniel Shays.

The governor of Massachusetts, James Bowdoin, once a protester against British taxes, now characterized the western dissidents as illegal rebels. He vilified Shays as the chief leader, and a Boston newspaper claimed that Shays planned to burn Boston to the ground and overthrow the government. Another former radical, Samuel Adams, took the extreme position that "the man who dares rebel against the laws of a republic ought to suffer death." The dissidents challenged the aging revolutionaries' assumption that popularly elected governments would always be fair and just.

Members of the Continental Congress had much to worry about. In nearly every state, the requisition of 1785 spawned some combination of crowd protests, demands for inflationary paper money, and anger at state authorities and alleged money speculators. The Massachusetts insurgency was the worst episode, and it seemed to be spinning out of control. In October, the congress attempted to triple the size of the federal army, but fewer than 100 men enlisted. So Governor Bowdoin raised a private army, gaining the services of some 3,000 men with pay provided by wealthy and fearful Boston merchants.

In January 1787, the insurgents learned of the private army marching west from Boston, and 1,500 of them moved swiftly to capture a federal armory in Springfield to obtain weapons. But a militia band loyal to the state government beat them to the weapons facility and met their attack with gunfire; 4 rebels were killed and another 20 wounded. The final and bloodless encounter came at Petersham, where Bowdoin's army surprised the rebels and took several hundred of them prisoner. In the end, 2 men were executed for rebellion; 16 more who were sentenced to hang were reprieved at the last moment on the gallows. Some 4,000 men obtained leniency by confessing their misconduct and swearing an oath of allegiance to the state.

Shays's Rebellion caused leaders throughout the country to worry about the confederation's ability to handle civil disorder. Inflammatory Massachusetts newspapers wrote about bloody mob rule spreading to other states. New York lawyer John Jay wrote to George Washington, "Our affairs seem to lead to some crisis, some revolution—something I cannot foresee or conjecture. I am uneasy and apprehensive; more so than during the war." Benjamin Franklin, in his eighties, shrewdly observed that in 1776 Americans had feared "an excess of power in the rulers" but now the problem was perhaps "a defect of obedience" in the subjects. Among such leaders, the sense of crisis in the confederation had greatly deepened.

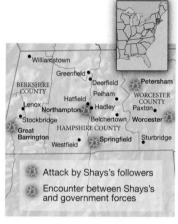

Shays's Rebellion, 1786–1787

Shays's Rebellion

▶ Uprising (1786–1787) led by farmers centered in western Massachusetts. Dissidents protested taxation policies of the eastern elites who controlled the state's government. Shays's Rebellion caused leaders throughout the country to worry about the confederation's ability to handle civil disorder.

> **QUICK REVIEW**

What were the most important factors in the failure of the Articles of Confederation?

CHAPTER LOCATOR | What kind of government did the Articles of Confederation create? | How did the states define citizenship and freedom?

222 CHAPTER 8 BUILDING A REPUBLIC

The constitutional convention assembled at the Pennsylvania statehouse in the summer of 1787. Despite the heat, the delegates nailed the windows shut to eliminate the chance of being heard by eavesdroppers, so intent were they on secrecy. The building is now called Independence Hall in honor of the signing of the Declaration of Independence there in 1776. Historical Society of Pennsylvania.

How did the Constitution change how the nation was governed?

SHAYS'S REBELLION PROVOKED an odd mixture of fear and hope that the government under the Articles of Confederation was losing its grip on power. A small circle of Virginians decided to try one last time to augment the powers granted to the government by the Articles. Their innocuous call for a meeting to discuss trade regulation led within a year to a total reworking of the national government, one with extensive powers and multiple branches based on differing constituencies.

From Annapolis to Philadelphia

The Virginians, led by James Madison, convinced the confederation congress to allow a September 1786 meeting of delegates at Annapolis, Maryland, to try again to revise the trade regulation powers of the Articles. Only five states participated, and the delegates planned a second meeting for Philadelphia in May 1787. The congress reluctantly endorsed the Philadelphia meeting and limited its scope to "the sole and express purpose of revising the Articles of Confederation." But a few leaders, such as Alexander Hamilton of New York, had far more ambitious plans.

The fifty-five men who assembled at Philadelphia in May 1787 for the constitutional convention were generally those who had already concluded that there

Why did the Articles of Confederation fail?

How did the Constitution change how the nation was governed?

What were the objections to ratification of the Constitution?

Conclusion: What was the "republican remedy"?

☑ LearningCurve Check what you know. bedfordstmartins.com /roarkunderstanding

223

The Constitutional Convention of 1787

- Rhode Island refused to send a single representative.
- Most delegates were from the wealthier classes.
- Convention established the three-fifths clause in counting slaves for the apportionment of representation.
- All but three delegates signed the Constitution produced by the convention.

Virginia Plan

▶ Plan drafted by James Madison and presented at the opening of the Philadelphia constitutional convention. Proposing a powerful three-branch government, with representation in both houses of the congress tied to population, this plan eclipsed the voice of small states in national government.

New Jersey Plan

▶ Alternative plan drafted by delegates from small states, retaining the confederation's single-house congress with one vote per state. But like the Virginia Plan, it proposed enhanced congressional powers, including the right to tax, regulate trade, and use force on unruly state governments.

were weaknesses in the Articles of Confederation. Patrick Henry, author of the Virginia Resolves in 1765 and more recently state governor, refused to go to the convention, saying he "smelled a rat." Rhode Island declined to send delegates. Two men sent by New York's legislature to check the influence of fellow delegate Alexander Hamilton left in dismay in the middle of the convention, leaving Hamilton as the sole representative of the state.

This gathering of white men included no artisans, day laborers, or ordinary farmers. Two-thirds of the delegates were lawyers. Half had been officers in the Continental army. The majority had served in the confederation congress and knew its strengths and weaknesses. Seven men had been governors of their states and knew firsthand the frustrations of thwarted executive power. A few elder statesmen attended, such as Benjamin Franklin and George Washington, but on the whole the delegates were young, like Madison and Hamilton.

The Virginia and New Jersey Plans

The convention worked in secrecy, which enabled the men to freely explore alternatives without fear that their honest opinions would come back to haunt them. The Virginia delegation first laid out a fifteen-point plan, known as the **Virginia Plan**, that repudiated the principle of a confederation of states. Largely the work of Madison, the Virginia Plan set out a three-branch government composed of a two-chamber legislature, a powerful executive, and a judiciary. It practically eliminated the voices of the smaller states by pegging representation in both houses of the congress to population. The theory was that government operated directly on people, not on states. Among the breathtaking powers assigned to the congress were the rights to veto state legislation and to coerce states militarily to obey national laws. To prevent the congress from having absolute power, the executive and judiciary could jointly veto its actions.

In mid-June, delegates from New Jersey, Connecticut, Delaware, and New Hampshire—all small states—unveiled an alternative proposal called the **New Jersey Plan**. The New Jersey Plan retained the existing single-house congress of the Articles of Confederation in which each state had one vote. Acknowledging the need for an executive, the plan created a plural presidency to be shared by three men elected by the congress from among its membership. Where it sharply departed from the existing government was in the sweeping powers it gave to the new congress: the right to tax, regulate trade, and use force on unruly state governments. In favoring national power over states' rights, it aligned itself with the Virginia Plan. But the New Jersey Plan retained the confederation principle that the national government was to be an assembly of states, not of people. For two weeks, delegates debated the two plans, focusing on the key issue of representation. The small-state delegates conceded that one house in a two-house legislature could be apportioned by population, but they would never agree that both houses could be. Madison was equally vehement about bypassing representation by state, which he viewed as the fundamental flaw in the Articles.

The debate seemed deadlocked, and for a while the convention was "on the verge of dissolution, scarce held together by the strength of a hair," according to one delegate. Only in mid-July did the so-called Great Compromise break the

CHAPTER LOCATOR | What kind of government did the Articles of Confederation create? | How did the states define citizenship and freedom?

224 CHAPTER 8
BUILDING A REPUBLIC

stalemate and produce the basic structural features of the emerging United States Constitution. Proponents of the competing plans agreed on a bicameral legislature. Representation in the lower house, the House of Representatives, would be apportioned by population, and representation in the upper house, the Senate, would come from all the states equally, with each state represented by two independently voting senators.

Representation by population turned out to be an ambiguous concept once it was subjected to rigorous discussion. Who counted? Were slaves, for example, people or property? As people, they would add weight to the southern delegations in the House of Representatives, but as property they would add to the tax burdens of those states. What emerged was the compromise known as the **three-fifths clause**: All free persons plus "three-fifths of all other Persons" constituted the numerical base for the apportionment of representatives.

Using "all other Persons" as a substitute for "slaves" indicates the discomfort delegates felt in acknowledging in the Constitution the existence of slavery. But though slavery was nowhere named, nonetheless it was recognized, protected, and thereby perpetuated by the U.S. Constitution.

three-fifths clause
▶ A clause in the Constitution stipulating that all free persons plus "three-fifths of all other Persons" would constitute the numerical base for apportioning both representation and taxation. The clause tacitly acknowledged the existence of slavery in the United States.

Democracy versus Republicanism

The delegates in Philadelphia made a distinction between democracy and republicanism new to the American political vocabulary. Pure democracy was now taken to be a dangerous thing. As a Massachusetts delegate put it, "The evils we experience flow from the excess of democracy." The delegates still favored republican institutions, but they created a government that gave direct voice to the people only in the House and that granted a check on that voice to the Senate, a body of men elected not by direct popular vote but by the state legislatures. Senators served for six years, with no limit on reelection; they were protected from the whims of democratic majorities, and their long terms fostered experience and maturity in office.

Similarly, the presidency evolved into a powerful office out of the reach of direct democracy. The delegates devised an electoral college whose only function was to elect the president and vice president. Each state's legislature would choose the electors, whose number was the sum of representatives and senators for the state, an interesting blending of the two principles of representation. The president thus would owe his office not to the Congress, the states, or the people, but to a temporary assemblage of distinguished citizens who could vote their own judgment on the candidates. His term of office was four years, but he could be reelected without limitation.

The framers had developed a far more complex form of federal government than that provided by the Articles of Confederation. To curb the excesses of democracy, they devised a government with limits and checks on all three of its branches. They set forth a powerful president who could veto legislation passed in Congress, but they gave Congress the power to override presidential vetoes. They set up a national judiciary to settle disputes between states and citizens of different states. The framers separated the branches of government not only by functions and reciprocal checks but also by deliberately basing the election of

Why did the Articles of Confederation fail? | **How did the Constitution change how the nation was governed?** | What were the objections to ratification of the Constitution? | Conclusion: What was the "republican remedy"? | ✔ LearningCurve Check what you know. bedfordstmartins.com /roarkunderstanding

225

the legislative and executive branches on different universes of voters—voting citizens (the House), state legislators (the Senate), and the electoral college (the presidency).

The convention carefully listed the powers of the president and of Congress. The president could initiate policy, propose legislation, and veto acts of Congress; he could command the military and direct foreign policy; and he could appoint the entire judiciary, subject to Senate approval. Congress held the purse strings: the power to levy taxes, to regulate trade, and to coin money and control the currency. States were expressly forbidden to issue paper money. Two more powers of Congress—to "provide for the common defence and general Welfare" of the country and "to make all laws which shall be necessary and proper" for carrying out its powers—provided elastic language that came closest to Madison's wish to grant sweeping powers to the new government.

While no one was entirely satisfied with every line of the Constitution, only three dissenters refused to sign the document. The Constitution specified a mechanism for ratification that avoided the dilemma faced earlier by the confederation government: Nine states, not all thirteen, had to ratify it, and special ratifying conventions elected only for that purpose, not state legislatures, would make the crucial decision.

> **QUICK REVIEW**

Why did the Constitution proposed by the Philadelphia convention devise multiple checks on the branches of the government?

CHAPTER LOCATOR | What kind of government did the Articles of Confederation create? | How did the states define citizenship and freedom?

226 CHAPTER 8
BUILDING A REPUBLIC

What were the objections to ratification of the Constitution?

This pro-Federalist cartoon depicts the debate over the ratification of the Constitution. On the left, Federalists pull a stuck cart toward the shining sun. To the right, Antifederalists pull it toward stormy skies. Library of Congress.

THE PROCESS OF RATIFYING the Constitution was highly contentious. In the three most populous states — Virginia, Massachusetts, and New York — substantial majorities opposed a powerful new national government. North Carolina and Rhode Island refused to call ratifying conventions. Seven of the eight remaining states were easy victories for the Constitution, but securing the approval of the ninth proved difficult. Pro-Constitution forces, called Federalists, had to strategize very shrewdly to defeat anti-Constitution forces, called Antifederalists.

The Federalists

Proponents of the Constitution moved swiftly into action. They first secured agreement from an uneasy confederation congress to defer a vote and instead send the Constitution to the states for their consideration. The pro-Constitution forces next called themselves **Federalists**, a word that implied endorsement of a confederated government. Their opponents thus became known as Antifederalists, a label that made them sound defensive and negative, lacking a program of their own.

To gain momentum, the Federalists targeted the states most likely to ratify quickly. Delaware ratified in early December, before the Antifederalists had even begun to campaign. Pennsylvania, New Jersey, and Georgia followed within a month (**Map 8.3**). Delaware and New Jersey were small states surrounded by more powerful neighbors; a government that would regulate trade and set taxes according to population was an attractive proposition. Georgia sought the

Federalists

▶ Originally the term for the supporters of the ratification of the U.S. Constitution in 1787–1788. In the 1790s, it became the name for one of the two dominant political groups that emerged during that decade. Federalist leaders of the 1790s supported Britain in foreign policy and commercial interests at home. Prominent Federalists included George Washington, Alexander Hamilton, and John Adams.

Why did the Articles of Confederation fail? | How did the Constitution change how the nation was governed? | **What were the objections to ratification of the Constitution?** | Conclusion: What was the "republican remedy"? | ✓ LearningCurve Check what you know. bedfordstmartins.com /roarkunderstanding

227

MAP 8.3 ■ Ratification of the Constitution, 1788–1790

Populated areas cast votes for delegates to state ratification conventions. This map shows Antifederalist strength generally concentrated in backcountry, noncoastal, and non-urban areas, but with significant exceptions (for example, Rhode Island).

> **MAP ACTIVITY**

READING THE MAP: Where was Federalist strength concentrated? How did the distribution of Federalist and Antifederalist sentiment affect the order of state ratifications of the Constitution?

CONNECTIONS: What objections did Antifederalists have to the new U.S. Constitution? How did their locations affect their view of the Federalist argument?

NEW HAMPSHIRE
9th
June 21, 1788

MAINE
(part of MASS.)

MASSACHUSETTS
6th
Feb. 16, 1788

NEW YORK
11th
July 26, 1788

RHODE ISLAND
13th
May 29, 1790

CONNECTICUT
5th
Jan. 9, 1788

PENNSYLVANIA
2nd
Dec. 12, 1787

NEW JERSEY
3rd
Dec. 18, 1787

DELAWARE
1st
Dec. 8, 1787

VIRGINIA
10th
June 26, 1788

MARYLAND
7th
Apr. 26, 1788

SPANISH LOUISIANA

Kentucky District

NORTH CAROLINA
12th
Nov. 21, 1789

Tennessee District

SOUTH CAROLINA
8th
May 23, 1788

GEORGIA
4th
Jan. 2, 1788

Disputed with Spain

SPANISH FLORIDA

Majority for ratification

Majority against ratification

Divided

No returns (unsettled areas)

1st   Order in which the 13 states ratified

> **CHRONOLOGY**

1787
– Pro-Constitution essays called *The Federalist Papers* begin to be published.

1788
– U.S. Constitution is ratified.

protection that a stronger national government would afford against hostile Indians and Spanish Florida to the south.

Another three easy victories came in Connecticut, Maryland, and South Carolina. Again, merchants, lawyers, and urban artisans in general favored the new Constitution, as did large landowners and slaveholders. Antifederalists in these states tended to be rural, western, and noncommercial, men whose access to news was limited and whose participation in state government was tenuous.

Massachusetts was the first state to give the Federalists serious difficulty. The vote to select the ratification delegates decidedly favored the Antifederalists, whose strength lay in the western areas of the state, home to Shays's Rebellion. One rural delegate from Worcester County voiced widely shared suspicions: "These lawyers and men of learning and money men that talk so finely, and gloss over matters so smoothly, to make us poor illiterate people swallow down the pill, expect to get into Congress themselves; they expect to be the managers of the Constitution and get all the power and all the money into their own hands, and then they will swallow up all us little folks." Nevertheless, the Antifederalists' lead was slowly eroded by a vigorous newspaper campaign. In the end, the Federalists won in Massachusetts by a very slim margin and only with promises that amendments to the Constitution would be taken up in the first Congress.

By May 1788, eight states had ratified; only one more was needed. North Carolina and Rhode Island were hopeless for the Federalist cause, and New

CHAPTER LOCATOR | What kind of government did the Articles of Confederation create? | How did the states define citizenship and freedom?

228   CHAPTER 8
BUILDING A REPUBLIC

Hampshire seemed nearly as bleak. More worrisome was the failure to win over the largest and most economically critical states, Virginia and New York.

The Antifederalists

The **Antifederalists** were a composite group, united mainly in their desire to block the Constitution. Although much of their strength came from backcountry areas long suspicious of eastern elites, many Antifederalist leaders came from the same social background as Federalist leaders. The Antifederalists also drew strength in states that were already on sure economic footing, such as New York, which could afford to remain independent. Probably the biggest appeal of the Antifederalists' position lay in the long-nurtured fear that distant power might infringe on people's liberties.

But by the time eight states had ratified the Constitution, the Antifederalists faced a difficult task. First, they were no longer defending the status quo now that the momentum lay with the Federalists. Second, it was difficult to defend the confederation government with its admitted flaws. Even so, the Antifederalists remained genuinely fearful that the new government would be too distant from the people and could thus become corrupt or tyrannical. "The difficulty, if not impracticability, of exercising the equal and equitable powers of government by a single legislature over an extent of territory that reaches from the Mississippi to the western lakes, and from them to the Atlantic ocean, is an insuperable objection to the adoption of the new system," wrote Mercy Otis Warren, an Antifederalist woman writing under the name "A Columbia Patriot."

The new government was indeed distant. In the proposed House of Representatives, the only directly democratic element of the Constitution, one member represented some 30,000 people. How could that member really know or communicate with his whole constituency, Antifederalists worried. They also worried that representatives would always be elites and thus "ignorant of the sentiments of the middling and much more of the lower class of citizens, strangers to their ability, unacquainted with their wants, difficulties, and distress," as one Maryland man fretted.

The Federalists generally agreed that the elite would be favored for national elections. Indeed, Federalists wanted power to reside with intelligent, virtuous leaders like themselves. They did not envision a government constituted of every class of people. "Fools and knaves have voice enough in government already," quipped one Federalist, without being guaranteed representation in proportion to their total population. Alexander Hamilton claimed that mechanics and laborers preferred to have their social betters represent them. Antifederalists disagreed: "In reality, there will be no part of the people represented, but the rich. . . . It will literally be a government in the hands of the few to oppress and plunder the many."

Antifederalists fretted over many specific features of the Constitution, such as the prohibition on state-issued paper money, or the federal power to control the time and place of elections. The most widespread objection was the Constitution's glaring omission of any guarantees of individual liberties in a bill of rights like those contained in many state constitutions.

Antifederalists
▶ Opponents of the ratification of the Constitution. Antifederalists feared that a powerful and distant central government would be out of touch with the needs of citizens. They also complained that the Constitution failed to guarantee individual liberties in a bill of rights.

Why did the Articles of Confederation fail?

How did the Constitution change how the nation was governed?

What were the objections to ratification of the Constitution?

Conclusion: What was the "republican remedy"?

✓ LearningCurve
Check what you know.
bedfordstmartins.com
/roarkunderstanding

229

In the end, a small state—New Hampshire—provided the decisive ninth vote for ratification on June 21, 1788, following an intensive and successful lobbying effort by Federalists.

The Big Holdouts: Virginia and New York

Four states still remained outside the new Union, and a glance at a map demonstrated the necessity of pressing the Federalist case in the two largest, Virginia and New York (see Map 8.3). In Virginia, an influential Antifederalist group led by Patrick Henry and George Mason made the outcome uncertain. The Federalists finally but barely won ratification by proposing twenty specific amendments that the new government would promise to consider.

New York voters tilted toward the Antifederalists out of a sense that a state so large and powerful need not relinquish so much authority to the new federal government. But New York was also home to some of the most persuasive Federalists. Starting in October 1787, Alexander Hamilton collaborated with James Madison and New York lawyer John Jay on a series of eighty-five essays on the political philosophy of the new Constitution. Published in New York newspapers and later republished as *The Federalist Papers*, the essays set out the failures of the Articles of Confederation and offered an analysis of the complex nature of the Federalist position. In one of the most compelling essays, number 10, Madison challenged the Antifederalists' conviction that republican government had to be small-scale. Madison argued that a large and diverse population was itself a guarantee of liberty. In a national government, no single faction could ever be large enough to subvert the freedom of other groups. "Extend the sphere, and you take in a greater variety of parties and interests; you make it less probable that a majority of the whole will have a common motive to invade the rights of other citizens," Madison asserted. He called it "a republican remedy for the diseases most incident to republican government."

At New York's ratifying convention, Antifederalists predominated, but impassioned debate and lobbying—plus the dramatic news of Virginia's ratification—finally tipped the balance to the Federalists. Even so, the Antifederalists' approval of the document was accompanied by a list of twenty-four individual rights and thirty-three structural changes they hoped to see in the Constitution. New York's ratification ensured the legitimacy of the new government, yet it took another year and a half for Antifederalists in North Carolina to come around. Fiercely independent Rhode Island held out until May 1790, and even then it ratified by only a two-vote margin.

In less than twelve months, the U.S. Constitution was both written and ratified. (See appendix I, page A-3.) The Federalists had faced a formidable task, but by building momentum and ensuring consideration of a bill of rights, they did indeed carry the day.

> **QUICK REVIEW**

Why did Antifederalists oppose the Constitution?

CHAPTER LOCATOR | What kind of government did the Articles of Confederation create? | How did the states define citizenship and freedom?

230 CHAPTER 8
BUILDING A REPUBLIC

Conclusion: What was the "republican remedy"?

THUS ENDED ONE OF THE MOST intellectually tumultuous and creative periods in American history.

The period began in 1775 with a confederation government that could barely be ratified because of its requirement of unanimity, but there was no reaching unanimity on the western lands, an impost, and the proper way to respond to unfair taxation in a republican state. The new Constitution offered a different approach to these problems by loosening the grip of impossible unanimity and by embracing the ideas of a heterogeneous public life and a carefully balanced government that together would prevent any one part of the public from tyrannizing another. The genius of James Madison was to anticipate that diversity of opinion was not only an unavoidable reality but also a hidden strength of the new society beginning to take shape. This is what he meant in Federalist essay number 10 when he spoke of the "republican remedy" for the troubles most likely to befall a government in which the people are the source of authority.

Despite Madison's optimism, political differences remained keen and worrisome to many. The Federalists still hoped for a society in which leaders of exceptional wisdom would discern the best path for public policy. They looked backward to a society of hierarchy, rank, and benevolent rule by an aristocracy of talent, but they created a government with forward-looking checks and balances as a guard against corruption, which they figured would most likely emanate from the people. The Antifederalists also looked backward, but to an old order of small-scale direct democracy and local control, in which virtuous people kept a close eye on potentially corruptible rulers. The Antifederalists feared a national government led by distant, self-interested leaders who needed to be held in check. In the 1790s, these two conceptions of republicanism and of leadership would be tested in real life.

Why did the Articles of Confederation fail? | How did the Constitution change how the nation was governed? | What were the objections to ratification of the Constitution? | Conclusion: What was the "republican remedy"? | LearningCurve Check what you know. bedfordstmartins.com /roarkunderstanding

231

CHAPTER 8 STUDY GUIDE

STEP 1 GET STARTED ONLINE

✓ LearningCurve ▪ bedfordstmartins.com/roarkunderstanding

Now that you've read the chapter, make it stick by completing the LearningCurve activity.

STEP 2 EXPLAIN WHY IT MATTERS

Put your reading into practice. Identify each term below, and then explain why it matters in U.S. history.

TERM	WHO OR WHAT & WHEN	WHY IT MATTERS
Articles of Confederation (p. 206)		
republicanism (p. 210)		
gradual emancipation (p. 213)		
Newburgh Conspiracy (p. 216)		
Treaty of Fort Stanwix (p. 217)		
Northwest Ordinance (p. 219)		
Shays's Rebellion (p. 222)		
Virginia Plan (p. 224)		
New Jersey Plan (p. 224)		
three-fifths clause (p. 225)		
Federalists (p. 227)		
Antifederalists (p. 229)		

STEP 3 MOVE BEYOND THE BASICS

To demonstrate a more advanced understanding, fill in the chart below with the powers and responsibilities of the various branches of government under the Articles of Confederation and under the Constitution. What were the important differences between the two?

	Powers and responsibilities under Articles of Confederation	Powers and responsibilities under U.S. Constitution
Congress		
Executive branch		
Federal judiciary		
States		

STEP **4**

PUT IT ALL TOGETHER Now, take a step back and try to explain the big picture. Remember to use specific examples from the chapter in your answers.

THE ARTICLES OF CONFEDERATION

▶ How did the confederation government deal with the problem of western lands?

▶ What do the state constitutions drawn up during the confederation period tell us about the range of political opinion during the Revolutionary War and the years immediately following?

THE CREATION OF A NEW CONSTITUTION

▶ What forces and events combined to produce momentum for the creation of a new constitution?

▶ What political compromises were embodied in the Constitution?

THE FIGHT FOR RATIFICATION

▶ Where was support for the Constitution strongest? Where was it weakest? Why?

▶ Why did the Federalists ultimately prevail over the Antifederalists? What were the Federalists' most important weapons in the debate over the Constitution?

LOOKING BACKWARD, LOOKING AHEAD

▶ How did pre-revolutionary experiences with colonial legislatures and the British government shape the Articles of Confederation? The United States Constitution?

▶ What issues were left unresolved by the framers of the Constitution? Why?

> IN YOUR OWN WORDS

Imagine that you must give an oral report to the class answering the following question: **What were the most significant events that led to the formulation and ratification of the U.S. Constitution?** What would be the most important points to include and why?

9
FORMING THE NEW NATION

1789–1800

> **What were the developments that led to the establishment of political parties with distinctive agendas by the end of the 1790s?**
Chapter 9 examines the efforts to achieve political stability in the decade following the ratification of the Constitution. It explores Alexander Hamilton's plans to bring economic stability to the federal government and the external threats and internal arguments the new United States faced.

LearningCurve
bedfordstmartins.com/roarkunderstanding
After reading the chapter, use LearningCurve to retain what you've read.

> What were the sources of political stability in the 1790s?

> What were Hamilton's economic policies?

> What external threats did the United States face in the 1790s?

> How did partisan rivalries shape the politics of the late 1790s?

> Conclusion: Why did the new nation ultimately form political parties?

George Washington takes the oath of office. Federal Hall, Philadelphia, April 30, 1789. Courtesy, The Henry Francis du Pont Winterthur Museum.

> What were the sources of political stability in the 1790s?

AFTER THE STRUGGLES of the 1780s, the most urgent task in establishing the new government was to secure stability. Leaders sought ways to heal old divisions, and the first presidential election offered the means to do that in the person of George Washington, who enjoyed widespread veneration. People trusted him to exercise the untested and perhaps elastic powers of the presidency.

Congress had important work as well in initiating the new government. Congress quickly agreed on the Bill of Rights, which answered the concerns of many Antifederalists. Beyond politics, cultural change in the area of gender also enhanced political stability. The private virtue of women was mobilized to bolster the public virtue of male citizens and to enhance political stability. Republicanism was forcing a rethinking of women's relation to the state.

Washington Inaugurates the Government

George Washington was elected president in February 1789 by a unanimous vote of the electoral college. (John Adams got just half as many votes; he became vice president, but his pride was wounded.) Washington perfectly embodied the republican ideal of disinterested, public-spirited leadership. Indeed, he cultivated that image through astute ceremonies such as the dramatic surrender of his

CHAPTER LOCATOR | What were the sources of political stability in the 1790s?

236 CHAPTER 9
FORMING THE NEW NATION

sword to the Continental Congress at the end of the war, symbolizing the subservience of military power to the law.

Once in office, Washington calculated his moves, knowing that every step set a precedent and that any misstep could be dangerous for the fragile government. Congress debated a title for Washington, ranging from "His Highness" to "His Majesty, the President"; Washington favored "His High Mightiness." But in the end, republican simplicity prevailed. The final title was simply "President of the United States of America," and the established form of address became "Mr. President," a subdued yet dignified title reserved for property-owning white males.

Washington's genius in establishing the presidency lay in his capacity for implanting his own reputation for integrity into the office itself. In the political language of the day, he was "virtuous," meaning that he took pains to elevate the public good over private interest and projected honesty and honor over ambition. He remained aloof, resolute, and dignified, to the point of appearing wooden at times. He encouraged pomp and ceremony to create respect for the office, traveling with six horses to pull his coach, hosting formal balls, and surrounding himself with uniformed servants. He even held weekly "levees," as European monarchs did, hour-long audiences granted to distinguished visitors (including women), at which Washington appeared attired in black velvet, with a feathered hat and a polished sword. The president and his guests bowed, avoiding the egalitarian familiarity of a handshake. But he always managed, perhaps just barely, to avoid the extreme of royal splendor.

Washington chose talented and experienced men to preside over the newly created Departments of War, Treasury, and State.

> Washington's Cabinet	
Secretary of war	General Henry Knox
Secretary of the treasury	Alexander Hamilton
Secretary of state	Thomas Jefferson
Attorney general	Edmund Randolph
Chief justice of the Supreme Court	John Jay

Soon Washington began to hold regular meetings with these men, thereby establishing the precedent of a presidential cabinet. No one anticipated that two decades of party turbulence would emerge from the brilliant but explosive mix of Washington's first cabinet.

The Bill of Rights

An important piece of business for the First Congress, meeting in 1789, was the passage of the **Bill of Rights**. Seven states had ratified the Constitution on the condition that guarantees of individual liberties and limitations to federal power be swiftly incorporated. The Federalists of 1787 had thought an enumeration of rights unnecessary, but in 1789 Congressman James Madison of Virginia understood that healing the divisions of the 1780s was of prime importance: "It will be

> **CHRONOLOGY**

1789
– George Washington is inaugurated as the first president.
– First Congress meets.

1790
– Judith Sargent Murray publishes "On the Equality of the Sexes."

1791
– States ratify Bill of Rights.

Bill of Rights
▶ The first ten amendments to the Constitution, officially ratified by 1791. The First through Eighth Amendments dealt with individual liberties, and the Ninth and Tenth concerned the boundary between federal and state authority.

| What were Hamilton's economic policies? | What external threats did the United States face in the 1790s? | How did partisan rivalries shape the politics of the late 1790s? | Conclusion: Why did the new nation ultimately form political parties? | ✔ LearningCurve Check what you know. bedfordstmartins.com /roarkunderstanding |

237

a desirable thing to extinguish from the bosom of every member of the community, any apprehensions that there are those among his countrymen who wish to deprive them of the liberty for which they valiantly fought and honorably bled."

Drawing on existing state constitutions with bills of rights, Madison enumerated guarantees of freedom of speech, the press, and religion; the right to petition and assemble; and the right to be free from unwarranted searches and seizures. One amendment asserted the right to keep and bear arms in support of a "well-regulated militia," to which Madison added, "but no person religiously scrupulous of bearing arms, shall be compelled to render military service in person." That provision for what a later century would call "conscientious objector" status failed to gain acceptance in Congress.

In September 1789, Congress approved a set of twelve amendments and sent them to the states for approval; by 1791, ten were eventually ratified. The First through Eighth Amendments dealt with individual liberties, and the Ninth and Tenth concerned the boundary between federal and state authority.

Still, not everyone was entirely satisfied. State ratifying conventions had submitted some eighty proposed amendments. Congress never considered proposals to change structural features of the new government, and Madison had no intention of reopening debates about the length of the president's term or the power to levy excise taxes.

Significantly, no one complained about one striking omission in the Bill of Rights: the right to vote. Only much later was voting seen as a fundamental liberty requiring protection by constitutional amendment—indeed, by four amendments. The Constitution deliberately left the definition of eligible voters to the states because of the existing wide variation in local voting practices. Most of these practices were based on property qualifications, but some touched on religion and, in one unusual case (New Jersey), on sex and race (see chapter 8).

The Republican Wife and Mother

The exclusion of women from political activity did not mean they had no civic role or responsibility. A flood of periodical articles in the 1790s by both male and female writers reevaluated courtship, marriage, and motherhood in light of republican ideals. Tyrannical power in the ruler, whether king or husband, was declared a thing of the past. Affection, not duty, bound wives to their husbands and citizens to their government. In republican marriages, the writers claimed, women had the capacity to reform the morals and manners of men. One male author promised women that "the solidity and stability of the liberties of your country rest with you; since Liberty is never sure, 'till Virtue reigns triumphant. . . . While you thus keep our country virtuous, you maintain its independence."

Until the 1790s, public virtue was strictly a masculine quality. But another sort of virtue enlarged in importance: sexual chastity, a private asset prized as a feminine quality. Essayists of the 1790s explicitly advised young women to use sexual virtue to increase public virtue in men. "Love and courtship . . . invest a lady with more authority than in any other situation that falls to the lot of human beings," one male essayist proclaimed.

Republican ideals also cast motherhood in a new light. Throughout the 1790s, advocates for female education, still a controversial proposition, argued that education would produce better mothers, who in turn would produce better citizens,

a concept historians call republican motherhood. Benjamin Rush, a Pennsylvania physician and educator, called for female education because "our ladies should be qualified . . . in instructing their sons in the principles of liberty and government." A series of essays by Judith Sargent Murray of Massachusetts favored education that would remake women into self-confident, rational beings. Her first essay, published in 1790, was boldly titled "On the Equality of the Sexes." In a subsequent essay on education, Murray asserted that educated women would retain their "characteristic trait" of sweetness, thus reassuring readers that education would not undermine women's compliant nature.

Although women's obligations as wives and mothers were now infused with political meaning, traditional gender relations remained unaltered. The analogy between marriage and civil society worked precisely because of the self-subordination inherent in the term *virtue*. Men should put the public good first, before selfish desires, just as women must put their husbands and families first, before themselves. Women might gain literacy and knowledge, but only in the service of improved domestic duty. In Federalist America, wives and citizens alike should feel affection for and trust in their rulers; neither should ever rebel.

QUICK REVIEW

How did political leaders in the 1790s attempt to overcome the divisions of the 1780s?

What were Hamilton's economic policies?	What external threats did the United States face in the 1790s?	How did partisan rivalries shape the politics of the late 1790s?	Conclusion: Why did the new nation ultimately form political parties?	☑ LearningCurve Check what you know. bedfordstmartins.com /roarkunderstanding

What were Hamilton's economic policies?

Alexander Hamilton,
by John Trumbull

Hamilton was confident, handsome, audacious, brilliant, and very hardworking. Ever slender, in marked contrast to the more corpulent leaders of his day, he posed for this portrait in 1792, at the age of thirty-seven and at the height of his power.
CSFB Collection of Americana, NYC.

> CHRONOLOGY

1790
– Congress approves Hamilton's debt plan.
– National capital is moved to Philadelphia.

1791
– Bank of the United States is chartered.
– Congress passes whiskey tax.
– Hamilton issues *Report on Manufactures*.

1793
– Eli Whitney invents cotton gin.

1794
– Whiskey Rebellion.

COMPARED WITH THE severe financial instability of the 1780s, the 1790s brimmed with opportunity, as seen in improved trade, in transportation, and in banking. In 1790, the federal government moved from New York City to Philadelphia, a more central location with a substantial mercantile class. There, Alexander Hamilton, secretary of the treasury, embarked on multiple plans to solidify the government's economic base. But controversy ensued. His ambitious plans to fund the national debt, set up a national bank, promote manufacturing through trade laws, and raise revenue through a tax on whiskey mobilized severe opposition.

Agriculture, Transportation, and Banking

Dramatic increases in international grain prices, caused by underproduction in war-stricken Europe, motivated American farmers to boost agricultural production for the export trade. From the Connecticut River valley to the Chesapeake, farmers planted more wheat, generating new jobs for millers, coopers, dockworkers, and shipbuilders.

CHAPTER LOCATOR | What were the sources of political stability in the 1790s?

Cotton production also boomed, spurred by market demand from British textile manufacturers and a mechanical invention. Limited amounts of smooth-seed cotton had long been grown in the coastal areas of the South, but this variety of cotton did not thrive in the drier inland regions. Greenseed cotton grew well inland, but its rough seeds stuck to the cotton fibers and were labor-intensive to remove. In 1793, Yale graduate Eli Whitney devised a machine called a gin that easily separated out the seeds; cotton production soared.

A surge of road building further stimulated the economy. Before 1790, one road connected Maine to Georgia, but with the establishment of the U.S. Post Office in 1792, road mileage increased sixfold. Private companies also built toll roads, such as the Lancaster Turnpike west of Philadelphia, the Boston-to-Albany turnpike, and a third road from Virginia to Tennessee. By 1800, a dense network of dirt, gravel, and plank roadways connected towns in southern New England and the Middle Atlantic states, spurring the establishment of commercial stage companies. A trip from New York to Boston took four days; from New York to Philadelphia, less than two (**Map 9.1**). In 1790, Boston had only three stagecoach companies; by 1800, there were twenty-four.

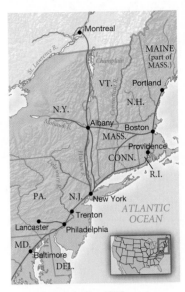

Major Roads in the 1790s

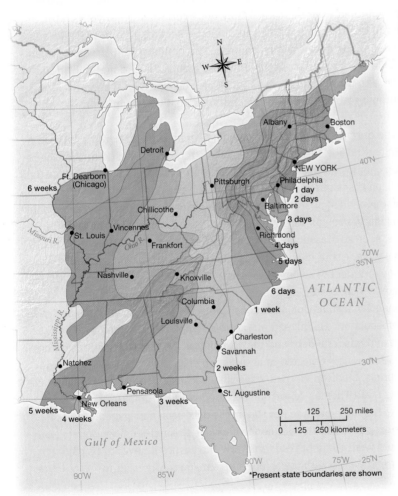

*Present state boundaries are shown

MAP 9.1 ■ Travel Times from New York City in 1800

Notice that travel out of New York extends over a much greater distance in the first week than in subsequent weeks. River corridors in the West and East speeded up travel — but only going downriver. Also notice that travel by sea (along the coast) was much faster than land travel.

> MAP ACTIVITY

READING THE MAP: Compare this map to the map "Major Roads in the 1790s" (above) and to Map 9.2 (page 249). What physical and cultural factors account for the slower travel times west of Pittsburgh?

CONNECTIONS: Why did Americans in the 1790s become so interested in traveling long distances? How did travel times affect the U.S. economy?

What were Hamilton's economic policies?

What external threats did the United States face in the 1790s?

How did partisan rivalries shape the politics of the late 1790s?

Conclusion: Why did the new nation ultimately form political parties?

✓ LearningCurve
Check what you know.
bedfordstmartins.com
/roarkunderstanding

241

A third development signaling economic resurgence was the growth of commercial banking. During the 1790s, the number of banks nationwide multiplied tenfold, from three to twenty-nine in 1800. Banks drew in money chiefly through the sale of stock. They then made loans in the form of banknotes, paper currency backed by the gold and silver from stock sales. By issuing two or three times as much money in banknotes as they held in hard money, they were creating new money for the economy.

The U.S. population expanded along with economic development, propelled by large average family size and better than adequate food and land resources. As measured by the first two federal censuses in 1790 and 1800, the population grew from 3.9 million to 5.3 million, an increase of 35 percent.

The Public Debt and Taxes

Report on Public Credit

▶ Hamilton's January 1790 report recommending that the national debt be funded — but not repaid immediately — at full value. Hamilton's goal was to make the new country creditworthy, not debt-free. Critics of his plan complained that it would benefit speculators.

The upturn in the economy, plus the new taxation powers of the government, suggested that the government might soon repay its wartime debt, amounting to more than $52 million owed to foreign and domestic creditors. But Hamilton had a different plan. He issued a ***Report on Public Credit*** in January 1790, recommending that the debt be funded — but not repaid immediately — at full value. This meant that old certificates of debt would be rolled over into new bonds, which would earn interest until they were retired several years later. There would still be a public debt, but it would be secure, giving its holders a direct financial stake in the new government. The bonds would circulate, injecting millions of dollars of new money into the economy. "A national debt if not excessive will be to us a national blessing; it will be a powerful cement of our union," Hamilton wrote to a financier. Hamilton's goal was to make the new country creditworthy, not debt-free.

Funding the debt in full was controversial because speculators had already bought up debt certificates cheaply, and Hamilton's report touched off further speculation. Hamilton compounded controversy with his proposal to add to the federal debt another $25 million that some state governments still owed to individuals. During the war, states had obtained supplies by issuing IOUs to farmers, merchants, and moneylenders. Some states, such as Virginia and New York, had paid off these debts entirely. Others, such as Massachusetts, had partially paid them off through heavy taxation of the people. About half the states had made little headway. Hamilton called for the federal government to assume these state debts and combine them with the federal debt, in effect consolidating federal power over the states.

Congressman James Madison strenuously objected to putting windfall profits in the pockets of speculators. He instead proposed a complex scheme to pay both the original holders of the federal debt and the speculators, each at fair fractions of the face value. He also strongly objected to assumption of all the states' debts. A large debt was dangerous, Madison warned, especially because it would lead to high taxation. Secretary of State Thomas Jefferson was also fearful of Hamilton's proposals: "No man is more ardently intent to see the public debt soon and sacredly paid off than I am. This exactly marks the difference between Colonel Hamilton's views and mine, that I would wish the debt paid tomorrow; he wishes it never to be paid, but always to be a thing where with to corrupt and manage the legislature."

CHAPTER LOCATOR | What were the sources of political stability in the 1790s?

CHAPTER 9
242 FORMING THE NEW NATION

The Return for SOUTH CAROLINA having been made since the foregoing Schedule was originally printed, the whole Enumeration is here given complete, except for the N. Western Territory, of which no Return has yet been published.

DISTICTS	Free white Males of 16 years and upwards, including heads of families.	Free white Males under sixteen years.	Free white Females, including heads of families.	All other free persons.	Slaves.	Total.
Vermont	22435	22328	40505	255	16	85539
N. Hampshire	36086	34851	70160	630	158	141885
Maine	24384	24748	46870	538	NONE	96540
Massachusetts	95453	87289	190582	5463	NONE	378787
Rhode Island	16019	15799	32652	3407	948	68825
Connecticut	60523	54403	117448	2808	2764	237946
New York	83700	78122	152320	4654	21324	340120
New Jersey	45251	41416	83287	2762	11423	184139
Pennsylvania	110788	106948	206363	6537	3737	434373
Delaware	11783	12143	22384	3899	8887	59094
Maryland	55915	51339	101395	8043	103036	319728
Virginia	110936	116135	215046	12866	292627	747610
Kentucky	15154	17057	28922	114	12430	73677
N. Carolina	69988	77506	140710	4975	100572	393751
S. Carolina	35576	37722	66880	1801	107094	249073
Georgia	13103	14044	25739	398	29264	82548
	807094	791850	1541263	59150	694280	3893635

Total number of Inhabitants of the United States exclusive of S. Western and N. Territory.	Free white Males of 21 years and upwards.	Free Males under 21 years of age.	Free white Females.	All other Persons.	Slaves.	Total
S. W. territory	6271	10277	15365	361	3417	35691
N. Ditto	—	—	—	—	—	—

This page summarizes the tally of the first federal census, data that determined representation in Congress and proportional taxation of the states. Notice the five classifications: free white males sixteen or older, the same under sixteen, free white females, "all other free persons," and slaves. Separating white males at sixteen provided a rough measure of military strength. U.S. Census Bureau.

> VISUAL ACTIVITY

READING THE IMAGE: Which northern states still had slaves? Which state had the largest population? Which had the largest white population?

CONNECTIONS: Why did the census separate males from females? Free from enslaved? Who might "all other free persons" include? Since women, children, and "all other free persons" counted for purposes of apportionment, could it be said that those groups were represented in the new government?

A solution to this impasse arrived when Jefferson invited Hamilton and Madison to dinner. Over good food and wine, Hamilton secured the reluctant Madison's promise to restrain his opposition. In return, Hamilton pledged to back efforts to locate the nation's new capital city in the South, along the Potomac River, an outcome that was sure to please Virginians. In early July 1790, Congress voted for the Potomac site, and in late July Congress passed the debt package, assumption and all.

The First Bank of the United States and the *Report on Manufactures*

The second and third major elements of Hamilton's economic plan were his proposal to create a national Bank of the United States and his program to encourage domestic manufacturing. Arguing that banks were the "nurseries of national wealth," Hamilton modeled his bank plan on European central banks that used their government's money to invigorate the economy. According to Hamilton's plan,

What were Hamilton's economic policies?	What external threats did the United States face in the 1790s?	How did partisan rivalries shape the politics of the late 1790s?	Conclusion: Why did the new nation ultimately form political parties?	LearningCurve Check what you know. bedfordstmartins.com /roarkunderstanding

the central bank was to be capitalized at $10 million, a sum larger than all the hard money in the entire nation. The federal government would hold 20 percent of the bank's stock, making the bank in effect the government's fiscal agent, holding its revenues derived from import duties, land sales, and various other taxes. The other 80 percent of the bank's capital would come from private investors, who could buy stock in the bank with either hard money (silver or gold) or the recently funded and thus sound federal securities. Because of its size and the privilege of being the only national bank, the central bank would help stabilize the economy by exerting prudent control over credit, interest rates, and the value of the currency.

Concerned that a few rich bankers might have undue influence over the economy, Madison tried but failed to stop the plan in Congress. Jefferson advised President Washington that the Constitution did not permit Congress to charter banks. Hamilton countered that Congress had explicit powers to regulate commerce and a broad mandate "to make all laws which shall be necessary and proper for carrying into execution the foregoing powers." Washington sided with Hamilton and signed the Bank of the United States into law in February 1791, giving it a twenty-year charter.

When the bank's privately held stock went on sale in Philadelphia, Boston, and New York City in July, it sold out in a few hours, touching off a lively period of speculative trading by hundreds of urban merchants and artisans. A discouraged Madison reported that in New York "the Coffee House is an eternal buzz with the gamblers," and wide swings in the stock's price pained Jefferson: "The spirit of gaming, once it has seized a subject, is incurable. The tailor who has made thousands in one day, tho' he has lost them the next, can never again be content with the slow and moderate earnings of his needle."

The third component of Hamilton's plan was issued in December 1791 in the *Report on Manufactures*, a proposal to encourage the production of American-made goods. Domestic manufacturing was in its infancy, and Hamilton aimed to mobilize the new powers of the federal government to grant subsidies to manufacturers and to impose moderate tariffs on those same products from overseas. Hamilton's plan targeted manufacturing of iron goods, arms and ammunition, coal, textiles, wood products, and glass. The *Report on Manufactures*, however, was never approved by Congress, and indeed never even voted on. Many confirmed agriculturalists in Congress feared that manufacturing was a curse rather than a blessing. Madison and Jefferson in particular were alarmed by stretching the "general welfare" clause of the Constitution to include public subsidies to private businesses.

Report on Manufactures
▶ A proposal by Treasury Secretary Alexander Hamilton in 1791 calling for the federal government to encourage domestic manufacturers with subsidies while imposing tariffs on foreign imports. Congress initially rejected the measure.

The Whiskey Rebellion

Hamilton's plan to restore public credit required new taxation to pay the interest on the large national debt. In deference to the merchant class, Hamilton did not propose a general increase in import duties, nor did he propose land taxes, which would have fallen hardest on the nation's wealthiest landowners. Instead, he convinced Congress in 1791 to pass a 25 percent excise tax on whiskey, to be paid by farmers bringing grain to the distillery and then passed on to whiskey consumers in higher prices. Even Madison approved, in the hope that the tax might promote "sobriety and thereby prevent disease and untimely deaths."

CHAPTER LOCATOR | What were the sources of political stability in the 1790s?

244 CHAPTER 9
FORMING THE NEW NATION

Not surprisingly, the new excise tax proved unpopular. In 1791, farmers in Kentucky and the western parts of Pennsylvania, Virginia, Maryland, and the Carolinas forcefully conveyed their resentment to Congress. One farmer complained that he had already paid half his grain to the local distillery for distilling his rye, and now the distiller was taking the new whiskey tax out of the farmer's remaining half. "If this is not an oppressive tax, I am at a loss to describe what is so," the farmer wrote. Congress responded with modest modifications to the tax in 1792, but even so, discontent — along with tax evasion — was rampant. In some places, crowds threatened to tar and feather tax collectors. Four counties in Pennsylvania established committees of correspondence and held rallies. Hamilton admitted to Congress that the revenue was far less than anticipated. But rather than abandon the law, he tightened up the prosecution of tax evaders.

In western Pennsylvania, Hamilton had one ally, a stubborn tax collector named John Neville who refused to quit even after a group of spirited farmers burned him in effigy. In May 1794, Neville filed charges against seventy-five farmers and distillers for tax evasion. His action touched off the **Whiskey Rebellion**. In July, a group of forty men ambushed him and a federal marshal in Allegheny County. Then a crowd of five hundred burned down Neville's house. At the end of July, seven thousand Pennsylvania farmers planned a march — or perhaps an attack, some thought — on Pittsburgh to protest the tax.

In response, President Washington nationalized the Pennsylvania militia and set out, with Hamilton at his side, at the head of thirteen thousand soldiers. A worried Philadelphia newspaper criticized the show of force: "Shall torrents of blood be spilled to support an odious excise system?" But in the end, no blood was spilled. By the time the army arrived in late September, the demonstrators had dispersed. No battles were fought, and no shots were exchanged. Twenty men were rounded up and charged with high treason, but only two were convicted, and Washington soon pardoned both.

Had the federal government overreacted? Thomas Jefferson thought so; he saw the event as a replay of Shays's Rebellion of 1786, when tax protesters had been met with military force (see chapter 8). The rebel farmers agreed; they felt entitled to protest oppressive taxation. Hamilton and Washington, however, thought that laws passed by a republican government must be obeyed. To them, the Whiskey Rebellion presented an opportunity for the new federal government to flex its muscles and stand up to civil disorder.

Whiskey Rebellion

▶ July 1794 uprising by farmers in western Pennsylvania in response to enforcement of an unpopular excise tax on whiskey. The federal government responded with a military presence that caused dissidents to disperse before blood was shed.

QUICK REVIEW <

Why were Hamilton's economic policies controversial?

| What were Hamilton's economic policies? | What external threats did the United States face in the 1790s? | How did partisan rivalries shape the politics of the late 1790s? | Conclusion: Why did the new nation ultimately form political parties? | ✔ LearningCurve Check what you know. bedfordstmartins.com /roarkunderstanding |

245

What external threats did the United States face in the 1790s?

WHILE THE WHISKEY REBELS challenged federal leadership from within the country, disorder threatened the United States from external sources as well. From 1789 onward, serious trouble brewed in four directions. To the southwest, Creek Indians pushed back against the westward-moving white southern population, giving George Washington an opportunity to test diplomacy. To the northwest, a powerful confederation of Indian tribes in the Ohio Country resisted white encroachment, resulting in a brutal war. At the same time, conflicts between the major European powers forced Americans to take sides and nearly pulled the country into another war. And to the south, a Caribbean slave rebellion raised fears that racial war might be imported to the United States. Despite these grave prospects, Washington won reelection to the presidency unanimously in the fall of 1792.

CHAPTER LOCATOR | What were the sources of political stability in the 1790s?

Creeks in the Southwest

An urgent task of the new government was to take charge of Indian affairs while avoiding the costs of warfare. Some twenty thousand Indians affiliated with the Creeks occupied lands extending from Georgia into what is now Mississippi, and border skirmishes with land-hungry Georgians were becoming a frequent occurrence. Washington and his secretary of war, Henry Knox, singled out one Creek chief, Alexander McGillivray, and sent a delegation to Georgia for preliminary treaty negotiations.

McGillivray had a mixed-race heritage that prepared him to be a major cultural broker. His French-Creek mother conferred a legitimate claim to Creek leadership, while his Scottish fur-trading father provided exposure to literacy and numeracy. Fluent in English and near fluent in Spanish, McGillivray spoke several Creek languages and had even studied Greek and Latin. In the 1770s, he worked for the British distributing gifts to various southern tribes; in the 1780s, he gained renown for brokering negotiations with the Spanish in Florida.

The chief reluctantly met with Knox's delegates and spurned the substantial concessions the American negotiators offered, chief among them a guarantee of the Creeks' extensive tribal lands. McGillivray sent the negotiators away, enjoying, as he wrote to a Spanish trader, the spectacle of the self-styled "masters of the new world" having "to bend and supplicate for peace at the feet of a people whom shortly before they despised."

A year later, Secretary Knox reopened diplomatic relations. To coax McGillivray to the treaty table, Knox invited him to New York City to meet with the president. McGillivray arrived in a triumphal procession of various lesser Creek chiefs and was accorded the honors of a head of state.

The negotiations stretched out for a month, resulting in the 1790 Treaty of New York that looked much like Knox's original plan.

> Treaty of New York

- Creek tribal lands were guaranteed. Federal troops were to provide boundary protection against land-seeking settlers.
- The Creeks were assured of annual payments in money and trade goods.
- The Creeks promised to accept the United States as its only trading partner, thus excluding Spain.

Actually, both sides had made promises they could not keep. McGillivray figured that the Creeks' interests were best served by maintaining creative tension between the American and Spanish authorities, and by 1792 he had signed an agreement with the Spanish governor of New Orleans, in which each side offered mutual pledges to protect against encroachments by Georgia settlers. By the time Alexander McGillivray died in 1793, his purported leadership of the Creeks was in serious question, and the Treaty of New York joined the list of treaties never implemented. Its promise of federal protection of Creek boundaries was unrealistic from the start, and its pledge of full respect for Creek sovereignty also was only a promise on paper.

1789
- French Revolution begins.
- Fort Washington is erected in western Ohio.

1790
- Indians in Ohio defeat General Josiah Harmar.
- Treaty of New York.

1791
- Ohio Indians defeat General Arthur St. Clair.
- Haitian Revolution begins.

1793
- War between Great Britain and France begins in Europe.
- Washington issues Neutrality Proclamation.

1794
- Battle of Fallen Timbers.

1795
- Treaty of Greenville.
- Jay Treaty.

| What were Hamilton's economic policies? | **What external threats did the United States face in the 1790s?** | How did partisan rivalries shape the politics of the late 1790s? | Conclusion: Why did the new nation ultimately form political parties? | ✓ LearningCurve Check what you know. bedfordstmartins.com /roarkunderstanding |

At the very start of the new government, in dealing with the Creeks, Washington and Knox tried to find a different way to approach Indian affairs, one rooted more in British than in American experience. But in the end, the demographic imperative of explosive white population growth and westward-moving, land-seeking settlers, together with the economic imperative of land speculation, meant that confrontation with the native population was nearly inevitable. As Washington wrote in 1796, "I believe scarcely any thing short of a Chinese Wall, or line of Troops will restrain Land Jobbers, and the encroachment of Settlers, upon Indian Territory."

Ohio Indians in the Northwest

Tribes of the Ohio Valley were even less willing to negotiate with the new federal government. Left vulnerable by the 1784 Treaty of Fort Stanwix (see chapter 8)—in which Iroquois tribes in New York had relinquished Ohio lands to the Americans—the Shawnee, Delaware, Miami, and other tribes in Ohio stood their ground. To confuse matters further, British troops still occupied half a dozen forts in the Northwest, protecting an ongoing fur trade between British traders and Indians and thereby sustaining Indians' claims to that land.

Under the terms of the Northwest Ordinance (see chapter 8), the federal government started to survey and map eastern Ohio, and settlers were eager to buy. So Washington sent units of the U.S. Army into Ohio's western half to subdue the various tribes. Fort Washington, built on the Ohio River in 1789 at the site of present-day Cincinnati, became the command post for three major invasions of Indian country (**Map 9.2**). The first occurred in the fall of 1790, when General Josiah Harmar marched with 1,400 men into Ohio's northwest region, burning Indian villages. His inexperienced troops were ambushed by Miami and Shawnee Indians led by their chiefs, Little Turtle and Blue Jacket. Harmar lost one-eighth of his soldiers and retreated.

Harmar's defeat spurred enhanced efforts to clear Ohio for permanent American settlement. General Arthur St. Clair, the military governor of the Northwest Territory, had pursued peaceful tactics in the 1780s, signing questionable treaties with Indians for land in eastern Ohio. In the wake of Harmar's bungled operation, St. Clair geared up for military action, and in the fall of 1791 he led two thousand men (accompanied by two hundred women camp followers) north from Fort Washington along Harmar's route. A surprise attack at the headwaters of the Wabash River left 55 percent of the Americans dead or wounded; only three of the women escaped alive. The Indians captured valuable weaponry and scalped and dismembered the dying on the field of battle. With more than nine hundred lives lost, this was the most stunning American loss in the history of the U.S. Indian wars.

Washington doubled the U.S. military presence in Ohio and appointed a new commander, General Anthony Wayne of Pennsylvania. About the Ohio natives, Wayne wrote, "I have always been of the opinion that we never should have a permanent peace with those Indians until they were made to experience our superiority." Throughout 1794, Wayne's army engaged in skirmishes with various tribes. Chief Little Turtle of the Miami tribe advised negotiation; in his view, Wayne's large army looked overpowering. But Blue Jacket of the Shawnees counseled continued warfare, and his view prevailed.

CHAPTER LOCATOR | What were the sources of political stability in the 1790s?

248 CHAPTER 9
FORMING THE NEW NATION

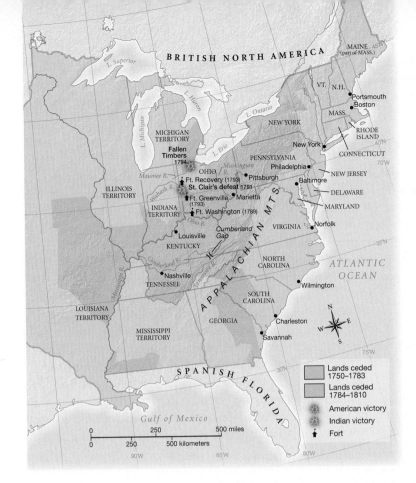

MAP 9.2 ■ Western Expansion and Indian Land Cessions to 1810

By the first decade of the nineteenth century, intense Indian wars had resulted in significant cessions of land to the U.S. government by treaty.

> MAP ACTIVITY

READING THE MAP: Locate the Appalachians. The Proclamation Line of 1763 that ran along these mountains forbade colonists to settle west of the line. How well was that purpose met?

CONNECTIONS: How much did the population of the United States grow between 1750 and 1790? How did this growth affect western settlement?

The decisive action came in August 1794 at the battle of Fallen Timbers, near the Maumee River. The confederated Indians—mainly Ottawas, Potawatomis, Shawnees, and Delawares numbering around eight hundred—ambushed the Americans but were underarmed, and Wayne's troops made effective use of their guns and bayonets. The Indians withdrew and sought refuge at nearby Fort Miami, still held by the British, but their former allies locked the gate and refused protection. The surviving Indians fled to the woods, their ranks decimated.

Fallen Timbers was a major defeat for the Indians. The Americans had destroyed cornfields and villages on the march north, and with winter approaching, the Indians' confidence was sapped. They reentered negotiations in a much less powerful bargaining position. In 1795, about a thousand Indians representing nearly a dozen tribes met with Wayne and other American emissaries to work out the **Treaty of Greenville**. The Americans offered treaty goods (calico shirts, axes, knives, blankets, kettles, mirrors, ribbons, thimbles, and abundant wine and liquor casks) worth $25,000 and promised additional shipments every year. The government's idea was to create a dependency on American goods to keep the Indians friendly. In exchange, the Indians ceded most of Ohio to the Americans; only the northwest part of the territory was reserved solely for the Indians.

The treaty brought temporary peace to the region, but it did not restore a peaceful life to the Indians. The annual allowance from the United States too often came in the form of liquor. "More of us have died since the Treaty of Greenville

Treaty of Greenville

▶ 1795 treaty between the United States and various Indian tribes in Ohio. The United States gave the tribes treaty goods valued at $25,000. In exchange, the Indians ceded most of Ohio to the Americans. The treaty brought only temporary peace to the region.

| What were Hamilton's economic policies? | **What external threats did the United States face in the 1790s?** | How did partisan rivalries shape the politics of the late 1790s? | Conclusion: Why did the new nation ultimately form political parties? | ✓ LearningCurve Check what you know. bedfordstmartins.com /roarkunderstanding |

249

than we lost by the years of war before, and it is all owing to the introduction of liquor among us," said Chief Little Turtle in 1800. "This liquor that they introduce into our country is more to be feared than the gun and tomahawk."

France and Britain

While Indian battles engaged the American military in the west, another war overseas was also closely watched. In 1789, monarchy came under attack in France, bringing on a revolution that inspired Americans in many states to celebrate the victory of the French people. Even fashions expressed symbolic solidarity: Some American women donned sashes and cockades made with ribbons of the French Revolution's red, white, and blue colors. Pro-French headgear for committed women included an elaborate turban, leading one horrified Federalist newspaper editor to chastise the "fiery frenchified dames" thronging Philadelphia's streets. In Charleston, South Carolina, a pro-French pageant in 1793 united two women as partners, one representing France and the other America. The women repudiated their husbands "on account of ill treatment" and pledged mutual "union and friendship." Most likely, this ceremony was not the country's first civil union but instead a richly metaphorical piece of street theater in which the spurned husbands represented the French and British monarchs. In addition to these symbolic actions, the growing exchange of political and intellectual ideas across the Atlantic helped plant the seeds of a woman's rights movement in America.

Sentiments against the French Revolution also ran deep. Vice President John Adams, who had lived in France in the 1780s, trembled to think of radicals in France or America. "Too many Frenchmen, after the example of too many Americans, pant for the equality of persons and property," Adams said. "The impracticability of this, God Almighty has decreed, and the advocates for liberty, who attempt it, will surely suffer for it."

French Dress Style: Woman with Cockade

In the early 1790s, some Americans showed enthusiasm for the French Revolution by wearing a tricolor cockade — a distinctive bow made from red, white, and blue ribbons. Bibliothèque Nationale de France.

CHAPTER LOCATOR | What were the sources of political stability in the 1790s?

250 CHAPTER 9 FORMING THE NEW NATION

Support for the French Revolution remained a matter of personal conviction until 1793, when Britain and France went to war and divided loyalties now framed critical foreign policy debates. Pro-French Americans remembered France's critical help during the American Revolution and wanted to offer aid now. But those shaken by the report of the guillotining of thousands of French people — including the king — as well as those with strong commercial ties to Britain sought ways to stay neutral.

In May 1793, President Washington issued the Neutrality Proclamation, which contained friendly assurances to both sides, in an effort to stay out of European wars. Yet American ships continued to trade between the French West Indies and France. In early 1794, the British expressed their displeasure by capturing more than three hundred of these vessels near the West Indies. Clearly, the president thought, something had to be done to assert American power.

Washington tapped John Jay, the chief justice of the Supreme Court and a man of strong pro-British sentiments, to negotiate commercial relations in the British West Indies and secure compensation for the seized American ships. Jay was also directed to address southerners' demands for reimbursement for the slaves evacuated by the British during the war as well as western settlers' demands to end the British occupation of frontier forts. Jay returned from his diplomatic mission with the **Jay Treaty**, a treaty that no one could love. First, the Jay Treaty failed to address the captured cargoes or the lost property in slaves. Second, it granted the British a lenient eighteen months to withdraw from the frontier forts, as well as continued rights in the fur trade. (This provision disheartened the Indians just then negotiating the Treaty of Greenville in Ohio. It was a significant factor in their decision to make peace.) Finally, the treaty called for repayment with interest of the debts that some American planters still owed to British firms dating from the Revolutionary War. In exchange for such generous terms, Jay secured limited trading rights in the West Indies and agreement that some issues — boundary disputes with Canada and the damage and loss claims of shipowners — would be decided later by arbitration commissions.

When newspapers published the terms of the treaty, powerful opposition quickly emerged. In Massachusetts, disrespectful anti-Jay graffiti appeared on walls, and effigies of Jay along with copies of the treaty were ceremoniously burned. Nevertheless, the treaty passed the Senate in 1795 by a vote of 20 to 10. The corresponding vote in the House, on funding the implementation of the treaty, passed by only 3 votes. The bitter votes in Congress divided along the same lines as the Hamilton-Jefferson split on economic policy.

The Haitian Revolution

In addition to the Indian troubles and the European war across the Atlantic, another bloody conflict to the south polarized and even terrorized many Americans in the 1790s. The French colony of Saint Domingue, in the western third of the large Caribbean island of Hispaniola, became engulfed in revolution starting in 1791. Bloody war raged for more than a decade, resulting in 1804 in the birth of the Republic of Haiti, the first and only independent black state to arise out of a successful slave revolution.

Jay Treaty

▶ 1795 treaty between the United States and Britain, negotiated by John Jay. It secured limited trading rights in the West Indies but failed to ensure timely removal of British forces from western forts and reimbursement for slaves removed by the British after the Revolution.

What were Hamilton's economic policies?

What external threats did the United States face in the 1790s?

How did partisan rivalries shape the politics of the late 1790s?

Conclusion: Why did the new nation ultimately form political parties?

✓ LearningCurve
Check what you know.
bedfordstmartins.com
/roarkunderstanding

251

Haitian Revolution

▶ The 1791–1804 conflict involving diverse Haitian participants and armies from three European countries. At its end, Haiti became a free, independent, black-run country. The Haitian Revolution fueled fears of slave insurrections in the United States.

Haitian Revolution, 1791–1804

The **Haitian Revolution** was a complex event involving many participants, including the diverse local population and, eventually, three European countries. Some 30,000 whites dominated the island in 1790, running sugar and coffee plantations with close to half a million blacks, two-thirds of them of African birth. The white French colonists were not the only plantation owners, however. About 28,000 free mixed-race people (*gens de couleur*) owned one-third of the island's plantations and nearly a quarter of the slave labor force. Despite their economic status, these mixed-race planters were barred from political power, but they aspired to it.

The French Revolution of 1789 was the immediate catalyst for rebellion in this already tense society. First, white colonists challenged the white royalist government in an effort to link Saint Domingue with the new revolutionary government in France. Next, the mixed-race planters rebelled in 1791, demanding equal civil rights with the whites. No sooner was this revolt viciously suppressed than another part of the island's population rose up; thousands of slaves armed with machetes and torches wreaked devastation. In 1793, the civil war escalated to include French, Spanish, and British troops fighting the inhabitants and also one another. Led by former slave Toussaint L'Ouverture, slaves and free blacks in alliance with Spain occupied the northern regions of the island, leaving a thousand plantations in ruins and tens of thousands of people dead. Thousands of white and mixed-race planters, along with some of their slaves, fled to Spanish Louisiana and southern cities in the United States.

White Americans followed the revolution in horror through newspapers and refugees' accounts. A few sympathized with the impulse for liberty, but many more feared that violent black insurrection might spread to the United States. Many black American slaves also followed the revolution, for the news of the success of a first-ever massive revolution by slaves traveled quickly in this oral culture.

The Haitian Revolution provoked naked fear of a race war in white southerners. Thomas Jefferson, agonizing over the contagion of liberty in 1797, wrote another Virginia slaveholder that "if something is not done, and soon done, we shall be the murderers of our own children . . . ; the revolutionary storm, now sweeping the globe, will be upon us, and happy if we make timely provision to give it an easy passage over our land. From the present state of things in Europe and America, the day which brings our combustion must be near at hand; and only a single spark is wanting to make that day to-morrow."

> **QUICK REVIEW**

Why did the United States feel vulnerable to international threats in the 1790s?

CHAPTER LOCATOR | What were the sources of political stability in the 1790s?

How did partisan rivalries shape the politics of the late 1790s?

Cartoon of the Lyon-Griswold Fight in Congress

Political tensions ran high in 1798. On the floor of Congress, Federalist Roger Griswold called Republican Matthew Lyon a coward. Lyon responded with some well-aimed spit, the first departure from the gentleman's code of honor. Griswold raised his cane to strike Lyon, whereupon Lyon grabbed fire tongs to defend himself. James Madison later commented that the two should have dueled, the honorable way to avenge insults. Library of Congress.

BY THE MID-1790s, polarization over the French Revolution, Haiti, the Jay Treaty, and Hamilton's economic plans had led to two distinct and consistent rival political groups: **Federalists** and **Republicans.** Federalist leaders supported Britain in foreign policy and commercial interests at home, while Republicans rooted for liberty in France and worried about monarchical Federalists at home. The labels did not yet describe full-fledged political parties; such division was still thought to be a sign of failure of the experiment in government. Washington's decision not to seek a third term led to serious partisan electioneering in the presidential and congressional elections of 1796. Federalist John Adams won the presidency, but party strife accelerated over failed diplomacy in France, bringing the country to the brink of war. Pro-war and antiwar antagonism created a major crisis over political free speech, militarism, and fears of sedition and treason.

The Election of 1796

Washington struggled to appear to be above party politics, and in his farewell address he stressed the need to maintain a "unity of government" reflecting a unified body politic. He also urged the country to "steer clear of permanent alliances with any portion of the foreign world." The leading contenders for his position, John Adams of Massachusetts and Thomas Jefferson of Virginia, in theory agreed with him, but around them raged a party contest split along pro-British versus pro-French lines.

Federalists

▶ Originally the term for the supporters of the ratification of the U.S. Constitution in 1787–1788. In the 1790s, it became the name for one of the two dominant political groups that emerged during that decade. Federalist leaders of the 1790s supported Britain in foreign policy and commercial interests at home. Prominent Federalists included George Washington, Alexander Hamilton, and John Adams.

Republicans

▶ One of the two dominant political groups that emerged in the 1790s. Republicans supported the revolutionaries in France and worried about monarchical Federalists at home. Prominent Republicans included Thomas Jefferson and James Madison.

What were Hamilton's economic policies?

What external threats did the United States face in the 1790s?

How did partisan rivalries shape the politics of the late 1790s?

Conclusion: Why did the new nation ultimately form political parties?

✓ LearningCurve
Check what you know.
bedfordstmartins.com
/roarkunderstanding

253

> CHRONOLOGY

1796
– John Adams is elected president.

1797
– XYZ affair.

1798
– Quasi-War with France erupts.
– Alien and Sedition Acts.
– Virginia and Kentucky Resolutions.

1800
– Thomas Jefferson is elected president.

John Adams

The artist Gilbert Stuart began painting this portrait in 1800 when Adams was sixty-five. A friend once described Adams's shortcoming as a politician: "He can't dance, drink, game, flatter, promise, dress, swear with gentlemen, and small talk and flirt with the ladies." National Gallery of Art, Washington, D.C.

The leading Federalists informally caucused and chose Adams as their candidate, with Thomas Pinckney of South Carolina to run with him. The Republicans settled on Aaron Burr of New York to pair with Jefferson. The Constitution did not anticipate parties and tickets. Instead, each electoral college voter could cast two votes for any two candidates, but on only one ballot. The top vote-getter became president, and the next-highest assumed the vice presidency. (This procedural flaw was corrected by the Twelfth Amendment, adopted in 1804.) With only one ballot, careful maneuvering was required to make sure that the chief rivals for the presidency did not land in the top two spots.

A failed effort by Alexander Hamilton to influence the outcome of the election landed the country in just such a position. Hamilton did not trust Adams; he preferred Pinckney, and he tried to influence southern electors to throw their support to the South Carolinian. But his plan backfired: Adams was elected president with 71 electoral votes; Jefferson came in second with 68 and thus became vice president. Pinckney got 59 votes, while Burr trailed with 30.

Adams's inaugural speech pledged neutrality in foreign affairs and respect for the French people, which made Republicans hopeful. To please Federalists, Adams retained three cabinet members from Washington's administration—the secretaries of state, treasury, and war. But the three were Hamilton loyalists, passing off Hamilton's judgments and advice as their own to the unwitting Adams. Vice President Jefferson extended a conciliatory hand to Adams, but the Hamiltonian cabinet ruined the honeymoon. Jefferson's advice was spurned, and he withdrew from active counsel of the president.

The XYZ Affair

From the start, Adams's presidency was in crisis. France retaliated for the British-friendly Jay Treaty by abandoning its 1778 alliance with the United States. French privateers—armed private vessels—started detaining American ships carrying British goods; by March 1797, more than three hundred American vessels had been seized. To avenge these insults, Federalists started murmuring openly about

CHAPTER LOCATOR | What were the sources of political stability in the 1790s?

254 CHAPTER 9 FORMING THE NEW NATION

war with France. Adams preferred negotiations and dispatched a three-man commission to France in the fall of 1797. But at the same time, he asked Congress to approve expenditures on increased naval defense.

When the three American commissioners arrived in Paris, French officials would not receive them. Finally, the French minister of foreign affairs, Talleyrand, sent three French agents—unnamed and later known to the American public as X, Y, and Z—to the American commissioners with the information that $250,000 might grease the wheels of diplomacy and that a $12 million loan to the French government would be the price of a peace treaty. Incensed, the commissioners brought news of the bribery attempt to the president.

Americans reacted to the **XYZ affair** with shock and anger. Even staunch pro-French Republicans began to reevaluate their allegiance. The Federalist-dominated Congress appropriated money for an army of ten thousand soldiers and repealed all prior treaties with France. In 1798, twenty naval warships launched the United States into its first undeclared war, called the Quasi-War by historians to underscore its uncertain legal status. The main scene of action was the Caribbean, where more than one hundred French ships were captured.

There was no home-front unity in this time of undeclared war; antagonism only intensified between Federalists and Republicans. Republican newspapers heaped abuse on Adams. One denounced him as "a person without patriotism, without philosophy, and a mock monarch." Pro-French mobs roamed the streets of Philadelphia, the capital, and Adams, fearing for his personal safety, stocked weapons in his presidential quarters. Federalists, too, went on the offensive. In Newburyport, Massachusetts, they lit a huge bonfire and burned issues of the state's Republican newspapers. Officers in a New York militia unit drank a menacing toast on July 4, 1798: "One and but one party in the United States." A Federalist editor ominously declared that "he who is not for us is against us."

The Alien and Sedition Acts

With tempers so dangerously high and fears that political dissent was akin to treason, Federalist leaders moved to muffle the opposition. In mid-1798, Congress passed the Sedition Act, which not only made conspiracy and revolt illegal but also criminalized any speech or words that defamed the president or Congress. One Federalist warned of the threat that existed "to overturn and ruin the government by publishing the most shameless falsehoods against the representatives of the people." In all, twenty-five men, almost all Republican newspaper editors, were charged with sedition; twelve were convicted.

Congress also passed two Alien Acts. The first extended the waiting period for an alien to achieve citizenship from five to fourteen years and required all aliens to register with the federal government. The second empowered the president in time of war to deport or imprison without trial any foreigner suspected of being a danger to the United States. The clear intent of these laws was to harass French immigrants already in the United States and to discourage others from coming.

Republicans strongly opposed the **Alien and Sedition Acts** on the grounds that they were in conflict with the Bill of Rights, but they did not have the votes to revoke the acts in Congress, nor could the federal judiciary, dominated by Federalist judges, be counted on to challenge the acts. Jefferson and Madison

XYZ affair
▶ A 1797 incident in which American negotiators in France were rebuffed for refusing to pay a substantial bribe. The incident led the United States into an undeclared war with France, known as the Quasi-War, which intensified antagonism between Federalists and Republicans.

Alien and Sedition Acts
▶ 1798 laws passed to suppress political dissent. The Sedition Act criminalized conspiracy and criticism of government leaders. The two Alien Acts extended the waiting period for citizenship and empowered the president to deport or imprison without trial any foreigner deemed a danger.

What were Hamilton's economic policies?

What external threats did the United States face in the 1790s?

How did partisan rivalries shape the politics of the late 1790s?

Conclusion: Why did the new nation ultimately form political parties?

☑ LearningCurve
Check what you know.
bedfordstmartins.com
/roarkunderstanding

255

Virginia and Kentucky Resolutions

▶ 1798 resolutions condemning the Alien and Sedition Acts submitted to the federal government by the Virginia and Kentucky state legislatures. The resolutions tested the idea that state legislatures could judge the constitutionality of federal laws and nullify them.

turned to the state legislatures, the only other competing political arena, to press their opposition. Each man anonymously drafted a set of resolutions condemning the acts and convinced the legislatures of Virginia and Kentucky to present them to the federal government in late fall 1798. The **Virginia and Kentucky Resolutions** tested the novel argument that state legislatures have the right to judge and even nullify the constitutionality of federal laws, bold claims that held the risk that one or both men could be accused of sedition. The resolutions in fact made little dent in the Alien and Sedition Acts, but the idea of a state's right to nullify federal law did not disappear. It would resurface several times in decades to come, most notably in a major tariff dispute in 1832 and in the sectional arguments that led to the Civil War.

Amid all the war hysteria and sedition fears in 1798, President Adams regained his balance. He was uncharacteristically restrained in pursuing opponents under the Sedition Act, and he finally refused to declare war on France, as extreme Federalists wished. No doubt he was beginning to realize how much he had been the dupe of Hamilton. He also shrewdly realized that France was not eager for war and that a peaceful settlement might be close at hand. In January 1799, a peace initiative from France arrived in the form of a letter assuring Adams that diplomatic channels were open again and that new peace commissioners would be welcomed in France.

Adams accepted this overture and appointed new negotiators. By late 1799, the Quasi-War with France had subsided, and in 1800 the negotiations resulted in a treaty declaring "a true and sincere friendship" between the United States and France. But Federalists were not pleased; Adams lost the support of a significant part of his own party and sealed his fate as the first one-term president of the United States.

The election of 1800 was openly organized along party lines. The self-designated national leaders of each group met to handpick their candidates for president and vice president. Adams's chief opponent was Thomas Jefferson. When the election was finally over, President Jefferson mounted the inaugural platform to announce, "We are all republicans, we are all federalists," an appealing rhetoric of harmony appropriate to an inaugural address. But his formulation perpetuated a denial of the validity of party politics, a denial that ran deep in the founding generation of political leaders.

> ## QUICK REVIEW

How did war between Britain and France intensify the political divisions in the United States?

CHAPTER LOCATOR | What were the sources of political stability in the 1790s?

256   CHAPTER 9 FORMING THE NEW NATION

Conclusion: Why did the new nation ultimately form political parties?

<

AMERICAN POLITICAL LEADERS began operating the new government in 1789 with great hopes of unifying the country and overcoming selfish factionalism. The enormous trust in President Washington was the central foundation for those hopes, and Washington did not disappoint, becoming a model Mr. President with a blend of integrity and authority. Stability was further aided by easy passage of the Bill of Rights (to appease Antifederalists) and by attention to cultivating a virtuous citizenry of upright men supported and rewarded by republican womanhood. Yet the hopes of the honeymoon period soon turned to worries and then fears as major political disagreements flared up.

At the core of the conflict was a group of talented men—Hamilton, Madison, Jefferson, and Adams—so recently allies but now opponents. They diverged over Hamilton's economic program, over relations with the British and the Jay Treaty, over the French and Haitian revolutions, and over preparedness for war abroad and free speech at home. Hamilton was perhaps the driving force in these conflicts, but the antagonism was not about mere personality. Parties were taking shape not around individuals, but around principles, such as ideas about what constituted enlightened leadership, how powerful the federal government should be, who was the best ally in Europe, and when oppositional political speech turned into treason.

In his inaugural address of 1801, Jefferson offered his conciliatory assurance that Americans were at the same time "all republicans" and "all federalists," suggesting that both groups shared two basic ideas—the value of republican government, in which power derived from the people, and the value of the unique federal system of shared governance structured by the Constitution. But by 1800, Federalist and Republican defined competing philosophies of government. To at least some of his listeners, Jefferson's assertion of harmony across budding party lines could only have seemed bizarre. For the next two decades, these two groups would battle each other, each fearing that the success of the other might bring about the demise of the country.

| What were Hamilton's economic policies? | What external threats did the United States face in the 1790s? | How did partisan rivalries shape the politics of the late 1790s? | **Conclusion: Why did the new nation ultimately form political parties?** | ✓ LearningCurve Check what you know. bedfordstmartins.com /roarkunderstanding |

257

CHAPTER 9 STUDY GUIDE

STEP 1

GET STARTED ONLINE

✓ LearningCurve ■ bedfordstmartins.com/roarkunderstanding

Now that you've read the chapter, make it stick by completing the LearningCurve activity.

STEP 2

EXPLAIN WHY IT MATTERS

Put your reading into practice. Identify each term below, and then explain why it matters in U.S. history.

TERM	WHO OR WHAT & WHEN	WHY IT MATTERS
Bill of Rights (p. 237)		
Report on Public Credit (p. 242)		
Report on Manufactures (p. 244)		
Whiskey Rebellion (p. 245)		
Treaty of Greenville (p. 249)		
Jay Treaty (p. 251)		
Haitian Revolution (p. 252)		
Federalists (p. 253)		
Republicans (p. 253)		
XYZ affair (p. 255)		
Alien and Sedition Acts (p. 255)		
Virginia and Kentucky Resolutions (p. 256)		

STEP 3

MOVE BEYOND THE BASICS

To demonstrate a more advanced understanding, assess the positions and policies of the Federalists and the Republicans. Is it accurate to describe them as political parties? Why or why not?

	Federalists	Republicans
States' rights		
Government influence on economy		
Social and political hierarchy		
Relations with Britain		
Relations with France		

PUT IT ALL TOGETHER Now, take a step back and try to explain the big picture. Remember to use specific examples from the chapter in your answers.

DOMESTIC AFFAIRS

▶ What important precedents did George Washington set? How did he use the presidency to bring political stability to the country?

▶ How did Hamilton imagine the future of the United States? How did his vision conflict with that of Jefferson?

NATIONAL SECURITY

▶ What were the most important threats to America's national security in the 1790s? How did the Washington and Adams administrations respond to those threats?

▶ How did the French Revolution contribute to the split between Federalists and Republicans in the United States?

FEDERALISTS AND REPUBLICANS

▶ What led to the factionalizing of American politics in the 1790s?

▶ How did the development of political factions affect the country domestically? In its external affairs?

LOOKING BACKWARD, LOOKING AHEAD

▶ How did the government Washington headed differ from the government created by the Articles of Confederation?

▶ What steps had been taken toward the creation of national political parties by 1800? What steps were still required before a true party system was in place?

> **IN YOUR OWN WORDS**

Imagine that you must give an oral report to the class answering the following question: What were the developments that led to the establishment of political parties with distinctive agendas by the end of the 1790s? What would be the most important points to include and why?

 Do it online at the Student Site ■ bedfordstmartins.com/roarkunderstanding

10
A MATURING REPUBLIC

1800–1824

> **What were the most important political, social, cultural, and diplomatic changes in the early decades of the nineteenth century?** Chapter 10 explores the changing political landscape of the nation from the election of Thomas Jefferson in 1800 to the election of John Quincy Adams in 1824. It examines the foreign and domestic challenges and opportunities that shaped American politics, as well as the shifting political culture that resulted in the expansion of voting rights for white men, the disfranchisement of most black men, and new educational opportunities for white women.

 LearningCurve

bedfordstmartins.com/roarkunderstanding
After reading the chapter, use LearningCurve to
retain what you've read.

> How did Jefferson attempt to undo the Federalist innovations of earlier administrations?

> What was the significance of the Louisiana Purchase for the United States?

> Why did Congress declare war on Great Britain in 1812?

> How did the civil status of American women and men differ in the early Republic?

> Why did partisan conflict increase during the administrations of Monroe and Adams?

> Conclusion: How did republican simplicity become complex?

The Artist in His Museum, a self-portrait by American painter, inventor, and museum founder Charles Willson Peale, 1822. The Granger Collection, New York.

> How did Jefferson attempt to undo the Federalist innovations of earlier administrations?

Thomas Jefferson, by John Trumbull This portrait of Jefferson was made in the late 1780s, when he was a young widower and lived in Paris as a diplomat with his daughters and slave Sally Hemings. In 1802, a scandal erupted when a journalist charged that Jefferson had fathered several children by Hemings. DNA evidence and historical evidence of Jefferson's whereabouts during the start of Hemings's pregnancies make a powerful case that he did father at least some of the children. Monticello/Thomas Jefferson Memorial Foundation, Inc.

CHRONOLOGY

1800
- Thomas Jefferson and Aaron Burr tie in electoral college.
- Gabriel's rebellion is reported.

1801
- House of Representatives elects Jefferson president.
- Barbary War with Tripoli begins.

1803
- *Marbury v. Madison.*

1805
- United States defeats Tripoli.

THE FIRST PRESIDENTIAL election of the new century was an all-out partisan battle. A panicky Federalist newspaper in Connecticut predicted that a victory by Thomas Jefferson would produce a bloody civil war and usher in an immoral reign of "murder, robbery, rape, adultery and incest." Apocalyptic fears gripped parts of the South, where a frightful slave uprising seemed a possible consequence of Jefferson's victory. But nothing nearly so dramatic occurred. Jefferson later called his election the "revolution of 1800," referring to his repudiation of Federalist practices and his cutbacks in military spending and taxes. While he cherished a republican simplicity in governance, he inevitably encountered events that required decisive and sometimes expensive government action, including military action overseas to protect American shipping.

Turbulent Times: Election and Rebellion

The election of 1800 was historic for procedural reasons: It was the first election to be decided by the House of Representatives. Probably by mistake, Republican

CHAPTER LOCATOR | How did Jefferson attempt to undo the Federalist innovations of earlier administrations? | What was the significance of the Louisiana Purchase for the United States?

262 CHAPTER 10 A MATURING REPUBLIC

voters in the electoral college gave Jefferson and his running mate, Senator Aaron Burr of New York, an equal number of votes, an outcome possible because of the single balloting to choose both president and vice president (**Map 10.1**). (To fix this problem, the Twelfth Amendment to the Constitution, adopted in 1804, provided for distinct ballots for the two offices.) The tie meant that the House had to choose between those two men, leaving the Federalist candidate, John Adams, out of the race. The vain and ambitious Burr declined to concede, so the sitting Federalist-dominated House of Representatives, in its waning days in early 1801, got to choose the president.

Some Federalists preferred Burr, believing that his character flaws made him susceptible to Federalist pressure. But the influential Alexander Hamilton, though no friend of Jefferson, recognized that the high-strung Burr would be more dangerous in the presidency. Jefferson was a "contemptible hypocrite" in Hamilton's opinion, but at least he was not corrupt. Thirty-six ballots and six days later, Jefferson got the votes he needed to win the presidency. This election demonstrated a remarkable feature of the new government: No matter how hard fought the campaign, the leadership of the nation could shift from one group to its rivals in a peaceful transfer of power.

As the country struggled over its white leadership crisis, a twenty-four-year-old blacksmith named Gabriel, the slave of Thomas Prossor, plotted rebellion in Virginia. Inspired by the Haitian Revolution (see chapter 9), Gabriel was said to be organizing a thousand slaves to march on the state capital of Richmond and take the governor, James Monroe, hostage. On the appointed day, however, a few nervous slaves went to the authorities with news of Gabriel's rebellion, and within days scores of implicated conspirators were jailed and brought to trial.

One of the jailed rebels compared himself to the most venerated icon of the early Republic: "I have nothing more to offer than what General Washington would have had to offer, had he been taken by the British and put to trial by them." Such talk worried white Virginians, and in the fall of 1800 twenty-seven black men were hanged for allegedly contemplating rebellion. Finally, Jefferson advised Governor Monroe to halt the hangings. "The world at large will forever condemn us if we indulge a principle of revenge," Jefferson wrote.

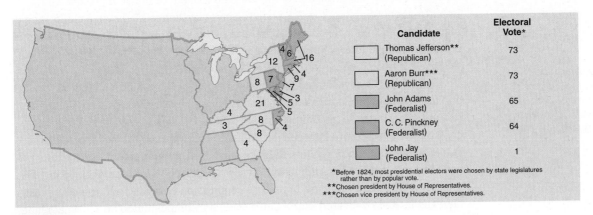

MAP 10.1 ■ The Election of 1800

| Why did Congress declare war on Great Britain in 1812? | How did the civil status of American women and men differ in the early Republic? | Why did partisan conflict increase during the administrations of Monroe and Adams? | Conclusion: How did republican simplicity become complex? | ✓ LearningCurve Check what you know. bedfordstmartins.com /roarkunderstanding |

263

The Jeffersonian Vision of Republican Simplicity

Once elected, Thomas Jefferson turned his attention to establishing his administration in clear contrast to the Federalists. For his inauguration, he dressed in everyday clothing to strike a tone of republican simplicity, and he walked to the Capitol for the modest swearing-in ceremony. As president, he scaled back Federalist building plans for Washington City and cut the government budget.

Martha Washington and Abigail Adams had received the wives of government officials at weekly teas, thereby cementing social relations in the governing class. But Jefferson, a longtime widower, disdained female gatherings and avoided the women of Washington City. He abandoned George Washington's practice of holding weekly formal receptions. He preferred small dinner parties with carefully chosen politicos, either all Republicans or all Federalists (and all male). At these intimate dinners, the president exercised influence and strengthened informal relationships that would help him govern.

Jefferson was no Antifederalist; he had supported the Constitution in 1788. But events of the 1790s had caused him to worry about the stretching of powers in the executive branch. Jefferson had watched with distrust as Hamiltonian policies refinanced the public debt, established a national bank, and secured commercial ties with Britain (see chapter 9). To him, these policies seemed to promote the interests of greedy speculators and profiteers at the expense of the rest of the country. In Jefferson's vision, the source of true liberty in America was the independent farmer, someone who owned and worked his land both for himself and for the market.

Jefferson set out to dismantle Federalist innovations. He reduced the size of the army by a third, preferring a militia-based defense, and he cut back the navy to six ships. With the consent of Congress, he abolished all federal taxes based on population or whiskey. Government revenue would now derive solely from customs duties and the sale of western land. This strategy benefited the South, where three-fifths of the slaves counted for representation but not for taxation now. By the end of his first term, Jefferson had deeply reduced Hamilton's cherished national debt.

A limited federal government, according to Jefferson, maintained a postal system, federal courts, and coastal lighthouses; it collected customs duties and conducted the census. The president had one private secretary, a young man named Meriwether Lewis, and Jefferson paid him out of his own pocket. The Department of State employed 8 people: Secretary James Madison, 6 clerks, and a messenger. The Treasury Department was by far the largest unit, with 73 revenue commissioners, auditors, and clerks, plus 2 watchmen. The entire payroll of the executive branch amounted to a mere 130 people in 1801.

However, 217 government workers lay beyond Jefferson's command, all judicial and military appointments made by John Adams as his last act in office. Jefferson refused to honor those "midnight judges" whose hires had not yet been fully processed. One disappointed job seeker, William Marbury, sued the new secretary of state, James Madison, for failure to make good on the appointment. This action gave rise to a landmark Supreme Court case, *Marbury v. Madison*, decided in 1803. The Court ruled that although Marbury's commission was valid and the new president should have delivered it, the Court could not compel him to do so. What made

Marbury v. Madison

▶ 1803 Supreme Court case that established the concept of judicial review in finding that parts of the Judiciary Act of 1789 were in conflict with the Constitution. The Supreme Court assumed legal authority to overrule acts of other branches of the government.

CHAPTER LOCATOR | How did Jefferson attempt to undo the Federalist innovations of earlier administrations? | What was the significance of the Louisiana Purchase for the United States?

the case significant was little noted at the time: The Court found that the grounds of Marbury's suit, resting in the Judiciary Act of 1789, were in conflict with the Constitution. For the first time, the Supreme Court disallowed a federal law on the grounds that it was unconstitutional.

Dangers Overseas: The Barbary Wars

Jefferson's desire to keep government and the military small met a severe test in the western Mediterranean Sea, where U.S. trading interests ran afoul of several states on the northern coast of Africa. For well over a century, Morocco, Algiers, Tunis, and Tripoli, called the Barbary States by Americans, controlled all Mediterranean shipping traffic by demanding large annual payments (called "tribute") for safe passage. Countries electing not to pay found their ships and crews at risk for seizure. After several years in which about a hundred American crew members were taken captive, the United States agreed to pay $50,000 a year in tribute.

In May 1801, when the monarch of Tripoli failed to secure a large increase in his tribute, he declared war on the United States. Jefferson considered such payments extortion, and he sent four warships to the Mediterranean to protect U.S. shipping. From 1801 to 1803, U.S. frigates engaged in skirmishes with Barbary privateers.

Then, in late 1803, the USS *Philadelphia* ran aground near Tripoli's harbor and was captured along with its 300-man crew. In early 1804, a U.S. naval ship commanded by Lieutenant Stephen Decatur sailed into the harbor after dark and set the *Philadelphia* on fire, rendering it useless to the Tripolitan monarch. Later that year, a small force of U.S. ships attacked the harbor and damaged or destroyed nineteen Tripolitan ships and bombarded the city, winning high praise

The Burning of the Frigate *Philadelphia* in Tripoli Harbor, 1804

After the capture of the warship *Philadelphia* in 1803, Commander Stephen Decatur engineered a daring nighttime raid to destroy the vessel. With his men concealed, Decatur sailed into the harbor using an Arabic-speaking pilot to fool harbor sentries. The Americans quickly boarded the *Philadelphia* and set it ablaze, forcing the Tripolitan guards to swim to shore. Decatur departed with only one injured man. The Mariners Museum, Newport News, Virginia.

Why did Congress declare war on Great Britain in 1812?

How did the civil status of American women and men differ in the early Republic?

Why did partisan conflict increase during the administrations of Monroe and Adams?

Conclusion: How did republican simplicity become complex?

✓ LearningCurve
Check what you know.
bedfordstmartins.com
/roarkunderstanding

and respect from European governments. Yet the sailors from the *Philadelphia* remained in captivity.

In 1805, William Eaton, an American officer stationed in Tunis, requested a thousand Marines to invade Tripoli, but Secretary of State James Madison rejected the plan. On his own, Eaton assembled a force of four hundred men (mostly Greek and Egyptian mercenaries plus eight Marines) and marched them over five hundred miles of desert for a surprise attack on Tripoli's second-largest city. Amazingly, he succeeded. The monarch of Tripoli yielded, released the prisoners taken from the *Philadelphia*, and negotiated a treaty in 1805 with the United States.

Periodic attacks by Algiers and Tunis continued to plague American ships during Jefferson's second term of office and into his successor's presidency. This Second Barbary War ended in 1815 when the hero of 1804, Stephen Decatur, now a captain, arrived on the northern coast of Africa with a fleet of twenty-seven ships. By show of force, he engineered three treaties that put an end to the tribute system and provided reparations for damages to U.S. ships. Decatur was widely hailed for restoring honor to the United States.

> ## QUICK REVIEW

How did Jefferson's views of the role of the federal government differ from those of his predecessors?

CHAPTER LOCATOR | How did Jefferson attempt to undo the Federalist innovations of earlier administrations? | What was the significance of the Louisiana Purchase for the United States?

CHAPTER 10

266   A MATURING REPUBLIC

What was the significance of the Louisiana Purchase for the United States?

Comanche Feats of Horsemanship, 1834

Pennsylvania artist George Catlin toured the Great Plains and captured Comanche equestrian warfare in training. "Every young man," Catlin wrote, learned "to drop his body upon the side of his horse at the instant he is passing, effectually screened from his enemies' weapons. . . . [H]e will hang whilst his horse is at fullest speed, carrying with him his bow and his shield, and also his long lance . . . which he will wield upon his enemy as he passes; rising and throwing his arrows over the horse's back, or with equal ease and equal success under the horse's neck." Smithsonian American Art Museum, Washington, DC/Art Resource, NY.

JEFFERSON SET ASIDE his cautious exercise of federal power to take advantage of an unexpected offer from France to buy the Louisiana Territory. The president sent four expeditions into the prairie and mountains to explore this huge acquisition of land. The powerful Osage of the Arkansas River valley responded to overtures for an alliance and were soon lavishly welcomed by Jefferson in Washington City, but the even more powerful Comanche of the southern Great Plains stood their ground against all invaders. Meanwhile, the expedition by Lewis and Clark, the longest and northernmost trek of the four launched by Jefferson, mapped U.S. terrain all the way to the Pacific Ocean, giving a boost to expansionist aspirations.

> CHRONOLOGY

1803
– Louisiana Purchase.

1804
– Jefferson meets with Osage Indians.

1804–1806
– Lewis and Clark expedition.

1807
– United States establishes trade with Comanche Indians.

Why did Congress declare war on Great Britain in 1812?

How did the civil status of American women and men differ in the early Republic?

Why did partisan conflict increase during the administrations of Monroe and Adams?

Conclusion: How did republican simplicity become complex?

☑ **LearningCurve**
Check what you know.
bedfordstmartins.com
/roarkunderstanding

The Louisiana Purchase

In 1763, at the end of the Seven Years' War, a large area west of the United States shifted from France to Spain, but Spain never effectively controlled it (see chapter 6). Centered on the Great Plains, it was home to Indian tribes, most notably the powerful and expansionist Comanche nation. New Orleans was Spain's principal stronghold, a city strategically sited on the Mississippi River near its outlet to the Gulf of Mexico. Spain profited modestly from trade taxes it imposed on the small flow of agricultural products shipped down the river from American farms in the western parts of Kentucky and Tennessee.

Spanish officials in New Orleans and St. Louis worried that their sparse population could not withstand an anticipated westward movement of Americans. At first, they hoped for a Spanish-Indian alliance to halt the expected demographic wave, but defending many hundreds of miles along the Mississippi River against Americans on the move was a daunting prospect. Thus, in 1800 Spain struck a secret deal to return this trans-Mississippi territory to France, in the hopes that a French Louisiana would provide a buffer zone between Spain's more valuable holdings in northern Mexico and the land-hungry Americans. The French emperor Napoleon accepted the transfer and agreed to Spain's condition that France could not sell Louisiana to anyone without Spain's permission.

From the U.S. perspective, Spain had proved a weak western neighbor, but France was another story. Jefferson was so alarmed by the rumored transfer that he instructed Robert R. Livingston, America's minister in France, to try to buy New Orleans. When Livingston hinted that the United States might seize it if buying was not an option, the French negotiator asked him to name his price for the entire Louisiana Territory from the Gulf of Mexico north to Canada. Livingston shrewdly stalled and within days accepted the bargain price of $15 million (**Map 10.2**).

On the verge of war with Britain, France needed both money and friendly neutrality from the United States, and it got both from the quick sale of the Louisiana Territory. In addition, the recent and costly loss of Haiti as a colony made a French presence in New Orleans less feasible as well. But in selling Louisiana to the United States, France had broken its agreement with Spain, which protested that the sale was illegal.

Moreover, there was no clarity on the western border of this land transfer. Spain claimed that the border was about one hundred miles west of the Mississippi River, while in Jefferson's eyes it was some eight hundred miles farther west, defined by the crest of the Rocky Mountains. When Livingston pressured the French negotiator to clarify his country's understanding of the boundary, the negotiator replied, "I can give you no direction. You have made a noble bargain for yourself, and I suppose you will make the most of it."

Jefferson gained congressional approval for the **Louisiana Purchase**, but without the votes of Federalist New England, which was anxious about the geographic balance of power under threat by such a large acquisition of land. In late 1803, the American army took formal control of the Louisiana Territory, and the United States nearly doubled in size — at least on paper.

Louisiana Purchase

▶ 1803 purchase of French territory west of the Mississippi River that stretched from the Gulf of Mexico to Canada. The Louisiana Purchase nearly doubled the size of the United States and opened the way for future American expansion west.

CHAPTER LOCATOR | How did Jefferson attempt to undo the Federalist innovations of earlier administrations? | **What was the significance of the Louisiana Purchase for the United States?**

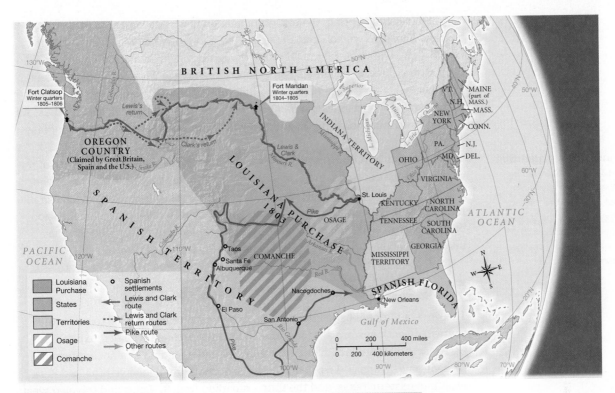

MAP 10.2 ■ Jefferson's Expeditions in the West, 1804–1806

The Louisiana Purchase of 1803 brought the United States a large territory without clear boundaries. Jefferson sent off four scientific expeditions to take stock of the land's possibilities and to assess the degree of potential antagonism from Indian and Spanish inhabitants.

> MAP ACTIVITY

READING THE MAP: How did the size of the newly acquired territory compare to the land area of the existing American states and territories? What natural features of the land might have suggested boundaries for the Louisiana Purchase? Did those natural features coincide with actual patterns of human habitation already in place?

CONNECTIONS: What political events in Europe created the opportunity for the Jefferson administration to purchase Louisiana? How did the acquisition of Louisiana affect Spain's hold on North America?

The Lewis and Clark Expedition

Jefferson quickly launched four government-financed expeditions up the river valleys of the new territory to establish relationships with Indian tribes and to determine Spanish influence and presence. The first set out in 1804 to explore the upper reaches of the Missouri River. Jefferson appointed twenty-eight-year-old Meriwether Lewis, his secretary, to head the expedition and instructed him to investigate Indian cultures, to collect plant and animal specimens, and to chart the geography of the West. Congress wanted the expedition to scout locations for military posts, negotiate fur trade agreements, and identify river routes to the West (see Map 10.2).

For his co-leader, Lewis chose Kentuckian William Clark, a veteran of the 1790s Indian wars. With a crew of forty-five, the explorers left St. Louis in the spring of 1804, working their way northwest up the Missouri River. They camped for the winter at a Mandan village in what is now central North Dakota.

Why did Congress declare war on Great Britain in 1812?	How did the civil status of American women and men differ in the early Republic?	Why did partisan conflict increase during the administrations of Monroe and Adams?	Conclusion: How did republican simplicity become complex?	☑ LearningCurve Check what you know. bedfordstmartins.com /roarkunderstanding

The following spring, the explorers headed west, accompanied by a sixteen-year-old Shoshoni woman named Sacajawea. Kidnapped by Mandans at about age ten, she had been sold to a French trapper as a slave/wife. Hers was not a unique story among Indian women; such women knew several languages, making them valuable translators and mediators. Further, Sacajawea and her new baby allowed the American expedition to appear peaceful to suspicious tribes. As Lewis wrote in his journal, "No woman ever accompanies a war party of Indians in this quarter."

The **Lewis and Clark expedition** reached the Pacific Ocean at the mouth of the Columbia River in November 1805. When the two leaders returned home the following year, they were greeted as national heroes. They had established favorable relations with dozens of Indian tribes; they had collected invaluable information on the peoples, soils, plants, animals, and geography of the West; and they had inspired a nation of restless explorers and solitary imitators.

Lewis and Clark expedition
▶ 1804–1806 expedition led by Meriwether Lewis and William Clark that explored the trans-Mississippi West for the U.S. government. The expedition's mission was scientific, political, and geographic.

Osage and Comanche Indians

The three additional expeditions set forth between 1804 and 1806 to probe the contested southwestern border of the Louisiana Purchase. The first exploring party ascended the Red River to the Ouachita River, ending at a hot springs in present-day Arkansas. Two years later, the second group followed the Red River west into eastern Texas, and the third embarked from St. Louis and traveled west, deep into the Rockies. This third group, led by Zebulon Pike, had gone too far, in the view of the Spaniards: Pike and his men were arrested, taken to northern Mexico, and soon released.

Of the scores of Indian tribes in this lower Great Plains region, two enjoyed reputations for territorial dominance. The Osage ruled the land between the Missouri and the lower Arkansas rivers, while the trading and raiding grounds of the Comanche stretched from the upper Arkansas River to the Rockies and south into Texas, a vast area called Comanchería. Both were formidable tribes that proved equal to the Spaniards. The Osage accomplished this through careful diplomacy and periodic shows of strength, the Comanche by expert horsemanship, a brisk trade in guns and captives, and a readiness to employ deadly force.

In 1804, Jefferson invited Osage tribal leaders to Washington City and greeted them with ceremonies and gifts. He positioned the Osage as equals of the Americans: "The great spirit has given you strength & has given us strength, not that we might hurt one another, but to do each other all the good in our power." Jefferson wanted a trade agreement that would introduce new agricultural tools to the Osage: hoes and ploughs for the men; spinning wheels and looms for the women. These gendered tools signified a departure from the native gender system in which women tended crops while men hunted game. With an agricultural civilization, men would give up the hunt and thus need far less land to sustain their communities. In exchange, the Osage asked for protection against Indian refugees displaced by American settlers east of the Mississippi. Jefferson's Osage alliance soon proved to be quite expensive, driven up by the costs of providing defense, brokering treaties, and giving gifts all around. In 1806, a second ceremonial visit to Washington and other eastern cities by a dozen Osage leaders cost the federal government $10,000.

CHAPTER LOCATOR | How did Jefferson attempt to undo the Federalist innovations of earlier administrations? | What was the significance of the Louisiana Purchase for the United States?

CHAPTER 10
270 A MATURING REPUBLIC

These promising peace initiatives were short-lived. By 1808, intertribal warfare was on the rise, and the governor of the Louisiana Territory declared that the U.S. government no longer had an obligation to protect the Osage. Jefferson's presidency was waning, and soon the practice of whittling away Indian lands through coercive treaties reasserted itself. Four treaties between 1808 and 1839 shrank the Osage lands, and by the 1860s they had been relocated to present-day Oklahoma.

By contrast, the Comanche resisted attempts to dominate them. European maps marking Spanish ownership of vast North American lands simply did not correspond to the reality on the ground, and for decades after the Louisiana Purchase of 1803, nothing much changed. In 1807, a newly appointed U.S. Indian agent invited Comanche leaders to Natchitoches in Louisiana, where he proclaimed an improbable solidarity with the Comanche: "It is now so long since our Ancestors came from beyond the great Water that we have no remembrance of it. We ourselves are Natives of the Same land that you are, in other words white Indians, we therefore Should feel & live together like brothers & Good Neighbours." Trade relations flourished, with American traders allowed to enter Comanchería to attend local market fairs, selling weapons, cloth, and household metal goods in exchange for horses, bison, and furs. No matter what the map of the United States looked like, on the ground Comanchería remained under the control of the Comanches and thus off-limits to settlement by white Americans until the late nineteenth century (see Map 10.2).

QUICK REVIEW <

What impact did the Louisiana Purchase have on U.S. relations with Spain and the Indian nations within the territory?

Why did Congress declare war on Great Britain in 1812?

How did the civil status of American women and men differ in the early Republic?

Why did partisan conflict increase during the administrations of Monroe and Adams?

Conclusion: How did republican simplicity become complex?

☑ LearningCurve
Check what you know.
bedfordstmartins.com
/roarkunderstanding

Why did Congress declare war on Great Britain in 1812?

This British engraving celebrates the British army's attack on Washington, D.C., in 1814. Disciplined troops control the street in front of the burning White House; the dome of the blazing Capitol is on the right. Anne S. K. Brown Military Collection, Brown University Library.

JEFFERSON EASILY RETAINED the presidency in the election of 1804, trouncing Federalist Charles Cotesworth Pinckney of South Carolina. A more difficult problem was the threat of war with both France and Britain, which led Jefferson to try a novel tactic, an embargo. His successor, James Madison, continued with a modified embargo, but his much narrower margin of victory over Pinckney in the election of 1808 indicated growing dissatisfaction with the Jefferson-Madison handling of foreign policy.

Madison broke with Jefferson on one very domestic matter: He allowed his gregarious wife, Dolley Madison, to participate in serious politics. Under James Madison's leadership, the country declared war in 1812 on Britain and on a confederacy of Indians in the old Northwest. The two-year war cost the young nation its White House and its Capitol, but victory was proclaimed at the end nonetheless.

Impressment and Embargo

In 1803, France and Britain went to war, and both repeatedly warned the United States not to ship arms to the other. Britain acted on these threats in 1806, stopping U.S. ships to inspect cargoes for military aid to France and seizing suspected deserters from the British navy, along with many Americans. Ultimately, 2,500 U.S. sailors were "impressed" (taken by force) by the British, who needed them for

CHAPTER LOCATOR | How did Jefferson attempt to undo the Federalist innovations of earlier administrations? | What was the significance of the Louisiana Purchase for the United States?

272 CHAPTER 10 A MATURING REPUBLIC

The *Chesapeake* Incident,
June 22, 1807

their war with France. In retaliation against the **impressment** of American sailors, Jefferson convinced Congress to pass a nonimportation law banning certain British-made goods.

Jefferson found one event particularly provoking. In June 1807, the American ship *Chesapeake*, harboring some British deserters, was ordered to stop by the British frigate *Leopard*. The *Chesapeake* refused, and the *Leopard* opened fire, killing three Americans — right at the mouth of Chesapeake Bay, well within U.S. territory. In response, Congress passed the **Embargo Act of 1807**, prohibiting U.S. ships from traveling to all foreign ports, a measure that brought a swift halt to all overseas trade carried in American vessels. Though a drastic measure, the embargo was meant to forestall war by forcing concessions from the British through economic pressure.

The Embargo Act of 1807 was a disaster. From 1790 to 1807, U.S. exports had increased fivefold, but the embargo brought commerce to a standstill. In New England, the heart of the shipping industry, unemployment rose. Grain plummeted in value, river traffic halted, tobacco rotted in the South, and cotton went unpicked. Protest petitions flooded Washington. The federal government suffered, too, for import duties were a significant source of revenue. The Federalist Party, in danger of fading away after its weak showing in the election of 1804, began to revive.

As the presidential election of 1808 approached, Republican caucuses — informal political groups that orchestrated the selection of candidates — chose Secretary of State James Madison as their nominee. The Federalist caucuses again chose Charles Cotesworth Pinckney. Madison won, but Pinckney secured 47 electoral votes, nearly half of Madison's total. Support for the Federalists remained centered in New England, and Republicans still held the balance of power nationwide.

impressment

▶ A British naval practice of seizing sailors on American ships under the claim that they were deserters from the British navy. Some 2,500 American men were taken by force into service, a grievance that helped propel the United States to declare war on Britain.

Embargo Act of 1807

▶ Act of Congress that prohibited U.S. ships from traveling to foreign ports and effectively banned overseas trade in an attempt to deter Britain from halting U.S. ships at sea. The embargo caused grave hardships for Americans engaged in overseas commerce.

Dolley Madison and Social Politics

Although women could not vote and supposedly left politics to men, the female relatives of Washington politicians took on several overtly political functions that greased the wheels of the affairs of state. They networked through dinners, balls, receptions, and the intricate custom of "calling," in which men and women paid brief visits at each other's homes. Webs of friendship and influence in turn facilitated female political lobbying. It was not uncommon for women in this social set to write letters of recommendation for men seeking government work.

When James Madison became president, Dolley Madison, called by some the "presidentress," struck a balance between queenliness and republican openness. She dressed the part in resplendent clothes, and she opened three elegant rooms in the executive mansion for a weekly open-house party called "Mrs. Madison's crush" or "squeeze." In contrast to George and Martha Washington's stiff, brief

Why did Congress declare war on Great Britain in 1812?	How did the civil status of American women and men differ in the early Republic?	Why did partisan conflict increase during the administrations of Monroe and Adams?	Conclusion: How did republican simplicity become complex?	✓ LearningCurve Check what you know. bedfordstmartins.com /roarkunderstanding

1803
– United States is warned not to ship war goods to Britain or France.

1807
– *Chesapeake* incident.
– Embargo Act.

1808
– James Madison is elected president.

1809
– Treaty of Fort Wayne.
– Non-Intercourse Act.

1811
– Battle of Tippecanoe.

1812
– United States declares war on Great Britain.

1813
– Tecumseh dies at battle of the Thames.

1814
– British attack Washington City.
– Treaty of Ghent.
– Hartford Convention.

1815
– Battle of New Orleans.

Dolley Madison, by Gilbert Stuart

The "presidentress" of the Madison administration sat for this official portrait in 1804. She wears a high-fashion empire-style dress, a style worn by many women at the coronation of the emperor Napoleon in Paris. The style featured a light fabric (muslin or chiffon) that dropped from a high waistline straight to the ground, with short sleeves and a daringly low neckline, as shown here. © White House Historical Association.

receptions, the Madisons' parties went on for hours, with scores or even hundreds of guests milling about, talking, and eating. Members of Congress, cabinet officers, distinguished guests, envoys from foreign countries, and their womenfolk attended with regularity. Mrs. Madison's weekly squeeze was an essential event for gaining political access, trading information, and establishing informal channels that would smooth the governing process.

In 1810–1811, the Madisons' house acquired its present name, the White House. The many guests simultaneously experienced both the splendor of the executive mansion and the atmosphere of republicanism that made it accessible to so many. Dolley Madison, ever an enormous political asset to her rather shy husband, understood well the symbolic function of the White House to enhance the power and legitimacy of the presidency.

Tecumseh and Tippecanoe

While the Madisons cemented alliances at home, difficulties with Britain and France overseas and with Indians in the old Northwest continued to increase. The Shawnee chief Tecumseh was, by all accounts, a charismatic leader. The Ohio Country, where Tecumseh was born in 1768, was home to some dozen Indian tribes. During the Revolutionary War, the region became a battleground, and Tecumseh lost his father and two brothers to American fighters. The Revolution's end in 1783 brought no peace to Indian country. The youthful Tecumseh fought at the battle of Fallen Timbers (see chapter 9), a major Indian defeat, and stood by as eight treaties ceded much of Ohio to the Americans between 1795 and 1805. Some resigned Indians looked for ways to accommodate, taking up farming, trade, and intermarriage with white settlers. Others spent their treaty payments on alcohol. Tecumseh's younger brother Tenskwatawa led an embittered life of idleness and

CHAPTER LOCATOR | How did Jefferson attempt to undo the Federalist innovations of earlier administrations? | What was the significance of the Louisiana Purchase for the United States?

Tecumseh

This 1848 engraving was adapted from an earlier drawing of Tecumseh made in a live sitting by a French fur trader in 1808. The engraver has given Tecumseh a British army officer's uniform, showing that he fought on the British side in the War of 1812. Notice the head covering and the medallion around Tecumseh's neck, marking his Indian identity. Library of Congress.

drink. But Tecumseh rejected accommodation and instead campaigned for a return to ancient ways. Donning traditional animal-skin clothing, he traveled around the Great Lakes region persuading tribes to join his pan-Indian confederacy. The territorial governor of Indiana, William Henry Harrison, both admired and feared Tecumseh, calling him "one of those uncommon geniuses which spring up occasionally to produce revolutions."

Even Tecumseh's dissolute brother was born anew. After a near-death experience in 1805, Tenskwatawa revived and recounted a startling vision of meeting the Master of Life. Renaming himself the Prophet, he urged his many Indian followers to regard whites as children of the Evil Spirit, destined to be destroyed.

In the years after 1805, Tecumseh actively solidified his confederacy, while the more northern tribes renewed their ties with supportive British agents in Canada, a potential source of food and weapons. If the United States went to war with Britain, there would clearly be serious repercussions on the frontier.

Shifting demographics put the Indians under pressure. The 1810 census counted some 230,000 Americans in Ohio, while another 40,000 inhabited the territories of Indiana, Illinois, and Michigan. The Indian population of the same area was much smaller, probably about 70,000.

Up to 1805, Indiana's territorial governor, William Henry Harrison, had negotiated a series of treaties in a divide-and-conquer strategy aimed at extracting Indian lands for paltry payments. But with the rise to power of Tecumseh and his brother Tenskwatawa, the Prophet, Harrison's strategy faltered. A fundamental part of Tecumseh's message was the assertion that all Indian lands were held in common by all the tribes. "No tribe has the right to sell [these lands], even to each other, much less to strangers . . . ," Tecumseh said. "Sell a country! Why not sell

Why did Congress declare war on Great Britain in 1812?

How did the civil status of American women and men differ in the early Republic?

Why did partisan conflict increase during the administrations of Monroe and Adams?

Conclusion: How did republican simplicity become complex?

☑ LearningCurve
Check what you know.
bedfordstmartins.com /roarkunderstanding

Battle of Tippecanoe, 1811

the air, the great sea, as well as the earth? Didn't the Great Spirit make them all for the use of his children?" In 1809, while Tecumseh was away on a recruiting trip, Harrison assembled the leaders of the Potawatomi, Miami, and Delaware tribes to negotiate the Treaty of Fort Wayne. After promising (falsely) that this was the last cession of land the United States would seek, Harrison secured three million acres at about two cents per acre.

When he returned, Tecumseh was furious with both Harrison and the tribal leaders. Leaving his brother in charge at Prophetstown on the Tippecanoe River, the Shawnee chief left to seek alliances with tribes in the South. In November 1811, Harrison decided to attack Prophetstown with a thousand men. The two-hour battle resulted in the deaths of sixty-two Americans and forty Indians before the Prophet's forces fled. The Americans won the **battle of Tippecanoe**, but Tecumseh was now more ready than ever to make war on the United States.

The War of 1812

The Indian conflicts in the old Northwest soon merged into the wider conflict with Britain, now known as the War of 1812. Between 1809 and 1812, Madison teetered between declaring either Britain or France America's primary enemy, as attacks by both countries on U.S. ships continued. In 1809, Congress replaced Jefferson's embargo with the Non-Intercourse Act, which prohibited trade only with Britain and France and their colonies, thus opening up other trade routes to alleviate the economic distress of American shippers, farmers, and planters. By 1811, the country was seriously divided and on the verge of war.

The new Congress seated in March 1811 contained several dozen young Republicans from the West and South who would come to be known as the **War Hawks**. Led by thirty-four-year-old Henry Clay from Kentucky and twenty-nine-year-old John C. Calhoun from South Carolina, they welcomed a war with Britain both to justify attacks on the Indians and to bring an end to impressment. Many were also expansionists, looking to occupy Florida and threaten Canada. Clay was elected Speaker of the House, and Calhoun won a seat on the Foreign Relations Committee. The War Hawks approved major defense expenditures, and the army soon quadrupled in size.

In June 1812, Congress declared war on Great Britain in a vote divided along sectional lines: New England and some Middle Atlantic states opposed the war, fearing its effect on commerce, while the South and West were strongly for it. Ironically, Britain had just announced that it would stop the search and seizure of American ships, but the war momentum would not be slowed. The Foreign Relations Committee issued an elaborate justification titled *Report on the Causes and Reasons for War*, written mainly by Calhoun and containing extravagant language about Britain's "lust for power," "unbounded tyranny," and "mad ambition."

battle of Tippecanoe
▶ An attack on Shawnee Indians at Prophetstown on the Tippecanoe River in 1811 by American forces headed by William Henry Harrison, Indiana's territorial governor. Tenskwatawa, the Prophet, fled with his followers. Tecumseh, his brother, deepened his resolve to make war on the United States.

War Hawks
▶ Young men newly elected to the Congress of 1811 who were eager for war against Britain in order to end impressments, fight Indians, and expand into neighboring British territory. Leaders included Henry Clay of Kentucky and John C. Calhoun of South Carolina.

CHAPTER LOCATOR | How did Jefferson attempt to undo the Federalist innovations of earlier administrations? | What was the significance of the Louisiana Purchase for the United States?

276 CHAPTER 10 A MATURING REPUBLIC

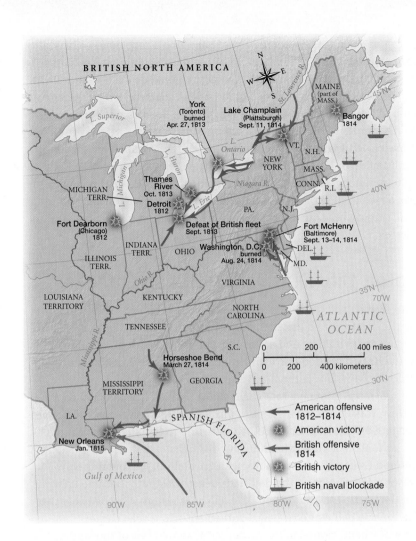

MAP 10.3 ■ **The War of 1812**

During the War of 1812, battles were fought along the Canadian border and in the Chesapeake region. The most important American victory came in New Orleans two weeks after a peace agreement had been signed in England.

These were fighting words in a war that was in large measure about insult and honor.

The War Hawks proposed an invasion of Canada, confidently predicting victory in four weeks. Instead, the war lasted two and a half years, and Canada never fell. The northern invasion turned out to be a series of blunders that revealed America's grave unpreparedness for war against the unexpectedly powerful British and Indian forces (**Map 10.3**). By the fall of 1812, the outlook was grim.

Worse, the New England states were slow to raise troops, and some New England merchants carried on illegal trade with Britain. The fall presidential election pitted Madison against DeWitt Clinton of New York, nominally a Republican but able to attract the Federalist vote. Clinton picked up all of New England's electoral votes, with the exception of Vermont's, and also took New York, New Jersey, and part of Maryland. Madison won in the electoral college, 128 to 89, but his margin of victory was considerably smaller than in 1808.

In late 1812 and early 1813, the tide began to turn in the Americans' favor. First came some victories at sea. Then the Americans attacked York (now Toronto) and burned it in April 1813. A few months later, Commodore Oliver Hazard Perry

Why did Congress declare war on Great Britain in 1812?

How did the civil status of American women and men differ in the early Republic?

Why did partisan conflict increase during the administrations of Monroe and Adams?

Conclusion: How did republican simplicity become complex?

✓ LearningCurve
Check what you know.
bedfordstmartins.com
/roarkunderstanding

277

defeated the British fleet at the western end of Lake Erie. Emboldened, General Harrison drove an army into Canada from Detroit and in October 1813 defeated the British and Indians at the battle of the Thames, where Tecumseh was killed.

Creek Indians in the South who had allied with Tecumseh's confederacy were also plunged into war. Some 10,000 living in the Mississippi Territory put up a spirited fight against U.S. forces for ten months. But the **Creek War** ended suddenly in March 1814 when a general named Andrew Jackson led 2,500 Tennessee militiamen in a bloody attack called the Battle of Horseshoe Bend. More than 550 Indians were killed, and several hundred more died trying to escape across a river. Later that year, General Jackson extracted from the defeated tribe a treaty relinquishing thousands of square miles of their land to the United States.

Washington City Burns: The British Offensive

In August 1814, British ships sailed into Chesapeake Bay, landing 5,000 troops and throwing the capital into a panic. The British troops burned the White House, the Capitol, a newspaper office, and a well-stocked arsenal. Instead of trying to hold the city, the British headed north and attacked Baltimore, but a fierce defense by the Maryland militia thwarted that effort.

In another powerful offensive that same month, British troops marched from Canada into New York State, but a series of mistakes cost them a naval skirmish at Plattsburgh on Lake Champlain, and they retreated to Canada. Five months later, another large British army landed in lower Louisiana and, in early January 1815, encountered General Andrew Jackson and his militia just outside New Orleans. Jackson's forces carried the day, and Jackson instantly became known as the hero of the **battle of New Orleans**. No one in the United States knew that negotiators in Europe had signed a peace agreement two weeks earlier.

The Treaty of Ghent, signed in December 1814, settled few of the surface issues that had led to war. Neither country could claim victory, and no land changed hands. Instead, the treaty reflected a mutual agreement to give up certain goals. The Americans dropped their plea for an end to impressments, which in any case subsided as soon as Britain and France ended their war in 1815. They also gave up any claim to Canada. The British agreed to stop all aid to the Indians. Nothing was said about shipping rights.

Antiwar Federalists in New England could not gloat over the war's ambiguous conclusion because of an ill-timed and seemingly unpatriotic move on their part. The region's leaders had convened a secret meeting in Hartford, Connecticut, in December 1814 to discuss a series of proposals aimed at reducing the South's power and breaking Virginia's lock on the presidency.

> **> Proposals Supported at the Hartford Convention**

- Abolition of the Constitution's three-fifths clause as a basis of representation.
- Requirement of a two-thirds vote instead of a simple majority for imposing embargoes, admitting states, or declaring war.
- Limit of one term for presidents.
- Prohibition of the election of successive presidents from the same state.

Creek War
▶ Part of the War of 1812 involving the Creek nation in the Mississippi Territory and Tennessee militiamen. General Andrew Jackson's forces defeated the Creeks at the Battle of Horseshoe Bend in 1814, forcing them to sign away much of their land.

battle of New Orleans
▶ The final battle in the War of 1812, fought and won by General Andrew Jackson and his militiamen against the much larger British army in New Orleans. The celebrated battle made no difference since the peace had already been negotiated.

CHAPTER LOCATOR | How did Jefferson attempt to undo the Federalist innovations of earlier administrations? | What was the significance of the Louisiana Purchase for the United States?

CHAPTER 10
278 A MATURING REPUBLIC

They even discussed secession from the Union but rejected that path. Coming just as peace was achieved, however, the **Hartford Convention** looked very unpatriotic. The Federalist Party never recovered, and within a few years it was reduced to a shadow of its former self, even in New England.

No one really won the War of 1812. The war did, however, give rise to a new spirit of nationalism. The paranoia over British tyranny evident in the 1812 declaration of war was laid to rest, replaced by pride in a more equal relationship with the old mother country. Indeed, in 1817 the two countries signed the Rush-Bagot disarmament treaty (named after its two negotiators), which limited each country to a total of four naval vessels, each with just a single cannon, to patrol the vast watery border between them. It was the most successful disarmament treaty for a century to come.

The biggest winners in the War of 1812 were the young men, once called War Hawks, who took up the banner of the Republican Party and carried it in new, expansive directions. These young politicians favored trade, western expansion, internal improvements, and the energetic development of new economic markets. The biggest losers of the war were the Indians. Tecumseh was dead, his brother the Prophet was discredited, the prospects of an Indian confederacy were dashed, the Creeks' large homeland was seized, and the British protectors were gone.

Hartford Convention

▶ A secret meeting of New England Federalist politicians held in late 1814 to discuss constitutional changes to reduce the South's political power and thus help block policies that injured northern commercial interests.

QUICK REVIEW ◁

Was the War of 1812 inevitable? Why or why not?

Why did Congress declare war on Great Britain in 1812?

How did the civil status of American women and men differ in the early Republic?

Why did partisan conflict increase during the administrations of Monroe and Adams?

Conclusion: How did republican simplicity become complex?

✓ LearningCurve
Check what you know.
bedfordstmartins.com
/roarkunderstanding

279

How did the civil status of American women and men differ in the early Republic?

Portrait of Emma Willard

Emma Willard, founder of the famed and rigorous Troy Female Seminary, was an exemplary role model to her students. Elizabeth Cady, a student in the 1830s and later an important figure in the woman's rights movement, recalled that Willard had a "profound self respect (a rare quality in a woman) which gave her a dignity truly regal." Her confidence shines through in this portrait. Emma Willard School.

DOLLEY MADISON'S PIONEERING role as "presidentress" showed that elite women could assume an active presence in civic affairs. But, as with the 1790s cultural compromise that endorsed female education to make women better wives and mothers (see chapter 9), Mrs. Madison and her female circle practiced politics to further their husbands' careers. There was little talk of the "rights of woman." Indeed, from 1800 to 1825, key institutions central to the shaping of women's lives — the legal system, marriage, and religion — proved fairly resistant to change. Nonetheless, the trend toward increased commitment to female education that began in the 1780s and 1790s continued in the first decades of the nineteenth century.

Women and the Law

In English common law, wives had no independent legal or political personhood. The legal doctrine of *feme covert* (covered woman) held that a wife's civic life was completely subsumed by her husband's. A wife was obligated to obey her

feme covert

▶ Legal doctrine grounded in British common law that held that a wife's civic life was subsumed by her husband's. Married women lacked independence to own property, make contracts, or keep wages earned. The doctrine shaped women's status in the early Republic.

CHAPTER LOCATOR | How did Jefferson attempt to undo the Federalist innovations of earlier administrations? | What was the significance of the Louisiana Purchase for the United States?

280 CHAPTER 10
A MATURING REPUBLIC

husband; her property was his, her domestic and sexual services were his, and even their children were legally his. Women had no right to keep their wages, to make contracts, or to sue or be sued. American state legislatures generally passed up the opportunity to rewrite the laws of domestic relations even though they redrafted other British laws in light of republican principles. Lawyers never paused to defend, much less to challenge, the assumption that unequal power relations lay at the heart of marriage.

The one aspect of family law that changed in the early Republic was divorce. Before the Revolution, only New England jurisdictions recognized a limited right to divorce; by 1820, every state except South Carolina did so. However, divorce was uncommon and in many states could be obtained only by petition to the state's legislature, a daunting obstacle for many ordinary people. A mutual wish to terminate a marriage was never sufficient grounds for a legal divorce. A New York judge affirmed that "it would be aiming a deadly blow at public morals to decree a dissolution of the marriage contract merely because the parties requested it. Divorces should never be allowed, except for the protection of the innocent party, and for the punishment of the guilty." States upheld the institution of marriage both to protect persons they thought of as naturally dependent (women and children) and to regulate the use and inheritance of property. (Unofficial self-divorce, desertion, and bigamy were remedies that ordinary people sometimes chose to get around the law, but all of these practices were socially unacceptable.) Legal enforcement of marriage as an unequal relationship played a major role in maintaining gender inequality in the nineteenth century.

Single adult women could own and convey property, make contracts, initiate lawsuits, and pay taxes. They could not vote (except in New Jersey before 1807), serve on juries, or practice law, so their civil status was limited. Single women's economic status was often limited as well, as much by custom as by law. Job prospects were few and low-paying. Unless they had inherited adequate property or could live with married siblings, single adult women in the early Republic very often were poor.

None of the legal institutions that structured white gender relations applied to black slaves. As property themselves, under the jurisdiction of slave owners, they could not freely consent to any contractual obligations, including marriage. The protective features of state-sponsored unions were thus denied to black men and women in slavery. But this also meant that slave unions did not establish unequal power relations between partners backed by the force of law, as did marriages among the free.

Women and Church Governance

In most Protestant denominations around 1800, white women made up the majority of congregants. Yet church leadership of most denominations rested in men's hands. There were some exceptions, however. In Baptist congregations in New England, women served along with men on church governance committees, deciding on the admission of new members, voting on hiring ministers, and even debating doctrinal points. Quakers, too, had a history of recognizing women's spiritual talents. Some were accorded the status of minister, capable of leading and speaking in Quaker meetings.

> CHRONOLOGY

1790–1820
– In an era of religious ferment, a small number of women openly engage in preaching.

1821
– Emma Willard founds Troy Female Seminary in New York.

1822
– Catharine Beecher founds Hartford Seminary in Connecticut.

Why did Congress declare war on Great Britain in 1812?

How did the civil status of American women and men differ in the early Republic?

Why did partisan conflict increase during the administrations of Monroe and Adams?

Conclusion: How did republican simplicity become complex?

☑ LearningCurve
Check what you know.
bedfordstmartins.com
/roarkunderstanding

281

In this early woodcut, Jemima Wilkinson, "the Publick Universal Friend," wears a clerical collar and body-obscuring robe, in keeping with the claim that the former Jemima was now a person without gender. With hair pulled back tight on the head and curled at the neck in a masculine style of the 1790s, was Wilkinson masculinized, or did the "Universal Friend" truly transcend gender? Rhode Island Historical Society.

Between 1790 and 1820, a small and highly unusual set of women openly engaged in preaching. Most were from Freewill Baptist groups centered in New England and upstate New York. Others came from small Methodist sects, and yet others rejected any formal religious affiliation. Probably fewer than a hundred such women existed, but several dozen traveled beyond their local communities, creating converts and controversy.

The best-known exhorting woman was Jemima Wilkinson, who called herself "the Publick Universal Friend." After a near-death experience from a high fever, Wilkinson proclaimed her body no longer female or male but the incarnation of the "Spirit of Light." She dressed in men's clothes, wore her hair in a masculine style, shunned gender-specific pronouns, and preached openly in Rhode Island and Philadelphia. In the early nineteenth century, Wilkinson established a town called New Jerusalem in western New York with some 250 followers.

The decades from 1790 to the 1820s marked a period of unusual confusion, ferment, and creativity in American religion. New denominations blossomed, new styles of religiosity gripped adherents, and an extensive periodical press devoted to religion popularized all manner of theological and institutional innovations. In such a climate, the age-old tradition of gender subordination came into question here and there among the most radically democratic of the churches. But the presumption of male authority over women was deeply entrenched in American culture. Even denominations that had allowed women to participate in church governance began to pull back, and most churches reinstated patterns of hierarchy along gender lines.

Female Education

First in the North and then in the South, states and localities began investing in public schools to foster an educated citizenry deemed essential in a republic. Young girls attended district schools along with boys, and by 1830, girls had made rapid gains, in many places approaching male literacy rates.

More advanced female education came from a growing number of private academies. Some dozen were established in the 1790s, and by 1830 that number had grown to nearly two hundred. Students came from elite families as well as those of middling families with intellectual aspirations, such as ministers' daughters.

CHAPTER LOCATOR | How did Jefferson attempt to undo the Federalist innovations of earlier administrations? | What was the significance of the Louisiana Purchase for the United States?

282 CHAPTER 10 A MATURING REPUBLIC

The three-year curriculum included both ornamental arts and solid academics. The former strengthened female gentility: drawing, needlework, music, and French conversation. The academic subjects included English grammar, literature, history, the natural sciences, geography, and elocution (the art of effective public speaking). The most ambitious female academies equaled the training offered at male colleges such as Harvard, Yale, Dartmouth, and Princeton, with classes in Latin, rhetoric, theology, moral philosophy, algebra, geometry, and even chemistry and physics.

Two of the best-known female academies were the Troy Female Seminary in New York, founded by Emma Willard in 1821, and the Hartford Seminary in Connecticut, founded by Catharine Beecher in 1822. Both prepared their female students to teach, on the grounds that women made better teachers than did men. Author Harriet Beecher Stowe, educated at her sister's school and then a teacher there, agreed: "If men have more knowledge they have less talent at communicating it. Nor have they the patience, the long-suffering, and gentleness necessary to superintend the formation of character."

The most immediate value of advanced female education lay in the self-cultivation and confidence it provided. Female graduation exercises showcased speeches and recitations performed in front of a mixed-sex audience of family, friends, and local notables. Academies also took care to promote a pleasing female modesty. Female pedantry or intellectual immodesty triggered the stereotype of the "bluestocking," a British term of hostility for a too-learned woman doomed to fail in the marriage market.

By the mid-1820s, the total annual enrollment at the female academies equaled enrollment at the nearly six dozen male colleges in the United States. Both groups accounted for only about 1 percent of their age cohorts in the country at large, indicating that advanced education was clearly limited to a privileged few. Most female graduates in time married and raised families, but first many of them became teachers at academies and district schools. A large number also became authors, contributing essays and poetry to newspapers, editing periodicals, and publishing novels. The new attention to the training of female minds laid the foundation for major changes in the gender system as girl students of the 1810s matured into adult women of the 1830s.

QUICK REVIEW <

In what ways did women influence society in the early Republic?

Why did Congress declare war on Great Britain in 1812?

How did the civil status of American women and men differ in the early Republic?

Why did partisan conflict increase during the administrations of Monroe and Adams?

Conclusion: How did republican simplicity become complex?

LearningCurve
Check what you know.
bedfordstmartins.com
/roarkunderstanding

> Why did partisan conflict increase during the administrations of Monroe and Adams?

"We Owe Allegiance to No Crown"

John A. Woodside, a Philadelphia sign painter, made his living creating advertisements for hotels, taverns, and city fire engines. He specialized in patriotic paintings and banners carried in parades. At some point in his long career from 1815 to 1850, he created this scene of a youthful sailor receiving a laurel wreath, the ancient Greek symbol of victory, by a breezy Miss Liberty (identified by the liberty cap on a stick). Picture Research Consultants & Archives.

> **VISUAL ACTIVITY**

READING THE IMAGE: What might the chain at the sailor's feet indicate? What do you think the slogan on the banner means? What do you see in the picture that would help date it? (Hint: Examine the flag. And for the truly curious, consider the history of styles for men's facial hair.)
CONNECTIONS: How and why does the painting reference the War of 1812? Regardless of the painting's date, what message do you think Woodside is trying to convey here?

VIRGINIANS CONTINUED THEIR hold on the presidency with the election of James Monroe in 1816 and again in 1820, when Monroe garnered all but one electoral vote. The collapse of the Federalist Party ushered in an apparent period of one-party rule, but politics remained highly partisan. At the state level, increasing political engagement sparked a drive for universal white male suffrage. At the national level, ill feelings were stirred by a sectional crisis in 1820 over the admission of Missouri to the Union, and foreign policy questions involving European claims to Latin America animated sharp disagreements as well. Four candidates vied for the presidency in 1824 in an election decided by the House of Representatives. One-party rule was far from harmonious.

CHAPTER LOCATOR | How did Jefferson attempt to undo the Federalist innovations of earlier administrations? | What was the significance of the Louisiana Purchase for the United States?

284 CHAPTER 10 A MATURING REPUBLIC

From Property to Democracy

Up to 1820, presidential elections occurred in the electoral college, at a remove from ordinary voters. The excitement generated by state elections, however, created an insistent pressure for greater democratization of presidential elections.

In the 1780s, twelve of the original thirteen states enacted property qualifications based on the theory that only male freeholders — landowners, as distinct from tenants or servants — had sufficient independence of mind to be entrusted with the vote. Of course, not everyone accepted that restricted idea of the people's role in government (see chapter 8). In the 1790s, Vermont became the first state to enfranchise all adult males, and four other states soon broadened suffrage considerably by allowing all male taxpayers to vote. As new states joined the Union, most opted for suffrage for all free white men, which added pressure for eastern states to consider broadening their suffrage laws. Between 1800 and 1830, greater democratization became a contentious issue.

Not everyone favored expanded suffrage; propertied elites tended to defend the status quo. But others managed to get legislatures to call new constitutional conventions in which questions of suffrage, balloting procedures, apportionment, and representation were debated. By 1820, half a dozen states passed suffrage reform, some choosing universal manhood suffrage while others tied the vote to tax status or militia service. In the remainder of the states, the defenders of landed property qualifications managed to delay expanded suffrage for two more decades. But it was increasingly hard to persuade the disfranchised that landowners alone had a stake in government. Proponents of the status quo began to argue instead that the "industry and good habits" necessary to achieve a propertied status in life were what gave landowners the right character to vote. Opponents fired back blistering attacks. One delegate to New York's constitutional convention said, "More integrity and more patriotism are generally found in the labouring class of the community than in the higher orders." Owning land was no more predictive of wisdom and good character than it was of a person's height or strength, said another observer.

Both sides of the debate generally agreed that character mattered, and many ideas for ensuring an electorate of proper wisdom came up for discussion. The exclusion of paupers and felons convicted of "infamous crimes" found favor in legislation in many states. Literacy tests and raising the voting age to a figure in the thirties were debated but ultimately discarded. In one exceptional moment, at the Virginia constitutional convention in 1829, a delegate wondered aloud why unmarried women over the age of twenty-one could not vote; he was quickly silenced with the argument that all women lacked the "free agency and intelligence" necessary for wise voting.

Free black men's enfranchisement was another story, generating much discussion at all the conventions. Under existing freehold qualifications, a small number of propertied black men could vote; universal or taxpayer suffrage would inevitably enfranchise many more. Many delegates at the various state conventions spoke against that extension, claiming that blacks as a race lacked prudence, independence, and knowledge. With the exception of New York, which retained the existing property qualification for black voters as it removed it for whites, the general pattern was one of expanded suffrage for whites and a total eclipse of suffrage for blacks.

> CHRONOLOGY

1816
- James Monroe is elected president.

1819
- Adams-Onís Treaty.

1820
- Missouri Compromise.

1823
- Monroe Doctrine is asserted.

1825
- John Quincy Adams is elected president by House of Representatives.

Why did Congress declare war on Great Britain in 1812?

How did the civil status of American women and men differ in the early Republic?

Why did partisan conflict increase during the administrations of Monroe and Adams?

Conclusion: How did republican simplicity become complex?

☑ LearningCurve
Check what you know.
bedfordstmartins.com
/roarkunderstanding

The Missouri Compromise

The politics of race produced the most divisive issue during Monroe's term. In February 1819, Missouri — so recently the territory of the powerful Osage Indians — applied for statehood. Since 1815, four other states (Indiana, Mississippi, Illinois, and Alabama) had joined the Union, following the blueprint laid out by the Northwest Ordinance of 1787. But Missouri posed a problem. Although much of its area was on the same latitude as the free state of Illinois, its territorial population included ten thousand slaves brought there by southern planters.

The problem led a New York congressman, James Tallmadge Jr., to propose two amendments to the statehood bill. The first stipulated that slaves born in Missouri after statehood would be free at age twenty-five, and the second declared that no new slaves could be imported into the state. Tallmadge's model was New York's gradual emancipation law of 1799 (see chapter 8). It did not strip slave owners of their current property, and it allowed them full use of the labor of newborn slaves well into their prime productive years. Still, southern congressmen objected because in the long run the amendments would make Missouri a free state, presumably no longer allied with southern economic and political interests. Just as southern economic power rested on slave labor, southern political power drew extra strength from the slave population because of the three-fifths rule. In 1820, the South owed seventeen of its seats in the House of Representatives to its slave population.

Tallmadge's amendments passed in the House by a close and sharply sectional vote of North against South. The ferocious debate led a Georgia representative to observe that the question had started "a fire which all the waters of the ocean could not extinguish. It can be extinguished only in blood." The Senate, with an even number of slave and free states, voted down the amendments, and Missouri statehood was postponed until the next congressional term.

In 1820, a compromise emerged. Maine, once part of Massachusetts, applied for statehood as a free state, balancing against Missouri as a slave state. The Senate further agreed that the southern boundary of Missouri — latitude 36°30' — extended west, would become the permanent line dividing slave from free states, guaranteeing the North a large area where slavery was banned (**Map 10.4**). The House also approved the **Missouri Compromise**, thanks to expert deal brokering by Kentucky's Henry Clay. The whole package passed because seventeen northern congressmen decided that minimizing sectional conflict was the best course and voted with the South.

President Monroe and former president Jefferson at first worried that the Missouri crisis would reinvigorate the Federalist Party as the party of the North. But even ex-Federalists agreed that the split between free and slave states was too dangerous a fault line to be permitted to become a shaper of national politics. When new parties did develop in the 1830s, they took pains to bridge geography, each party developing a presence in both the North and the South. Monroe and Jefferson also worried about the future of slavery. Both understood slavery to be deeply problematic, but, as Jefferson said, "We have the wolf by the ears, and we can neither hold him, nor safely let him go. Justice is in one scale, and self-preservation in the other."

Missouri Compromise

▶ 1820 congressional compromise engineered by Henry Clay that paired Missouri's entrance into the Union as a slave state with Maine's entrance as a free state. The compromise also established Missouri's southern border as the permanent line dividing slave from free states.

CHAPTER LOCATOR | How did Jefferson attempt to undo the Federalist innovations of earlier administrations? | What was the significance of the Louisiana Purchase for the United States?

286 CHAPTER 10 A MATURING REPUBLIC

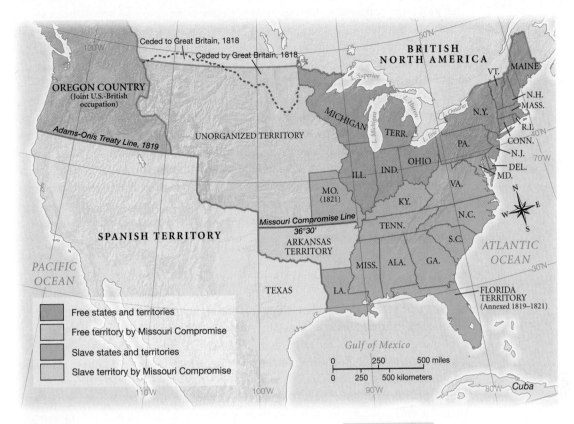

MAP 10.4 ■ The Missouri Compromise, 1820

After a difficult battle in Congress, Missouri entered the Union in 1821 as part of a package of compromises. Maine was admitted as a free state to balance slavery in Missouri, and a line drawn at latitude 36°30' put most of the rest of the Louisiana Territory off-limits to slavery in the future.

> **MAP ACTIVITY**

READING THE MAP: How many free and how many slave states were there before the Missouri Compromise? What did the admission of Missouri as a slave state threaten to do?

CONNECTIONS: Who precipitated the crisis over Missouri, what did he propose, and where did the idea come from? Who proposed the Missouri Compromise, and who benefited from it?

The Monroe Doctrine

New foreign policy challenges arose even as Congress struggled with the slavery issue. In 1816, U.S. troops led by General Andrew Jackson invaded Spanish Florida in search of Seminole Indians harboring escaped slaves. Once there, Jackson declared himself the commander of northern Florida, demonstrating his power in 1818 by executing two British men who he claimed were dangerous enemies. In asserting rule over the territory, and surely in executing the two British subjects on Spanish land, Jackson had gone too far. Privately, President Monroe was distressed and pondered court-martialing Jackson, prevented only by Jackson's immense popularity as the hero of the battle of New Orleans. Instead, John Quincy Adams, the secretary of state, negotiated with Spain the Adams-Onís Treaty, which delivered Florida to the United States in 1819. In exchange, the Americans agreed to abandon any claim to Texas or Cuba. Southerners viewed

Why did Congress declare war on Great Britain in 1812?

How did the civil status of American women and men differ in the early Republic?

Why did partisan conflict increase during the administrations of Monroe and Adams?

Conclusion: How did republican simplicity become complex?

✓ LearningCurve
Check what you know.
bedfordstmartins.com
/roarkunderstanding

287

this as a large concession, having eyed both places as potential acquisitions for future slave states.

Spain at that moment was preoccupied with its colonies in South America. One after another, Chile, Colombia, Peru, and finally Mexico declared themselves independent in the early 1820s. To discourage Spain and other European countries from reconquering these colonies, Monroe in 1823 formulated a declaration of principles on South America, known in later years as the Monroe Doctrine. The president warned that "the American Continents, by the free and independent condition which they have assumed and maintain, are henceforth not to be considered as subjects for future colonization by any European power." Any attempt to interfere in the Western Hemisphere would be regarded as "the manifestation of an unfriendly disposition towards the United States." In exchange for noninterference by Europeans, Monroe pledged that the United States would stay out of European struggles.

The Election of 1824

Monroe's nonpartisan administration was the last of its kind, a throwback to eighteenth-century ideals, as was Monroe, with his powdered wig and knee breeches. Monroe's cabinet contained men of sharply different philosophies, all calling themselves Republicans. Secretary of State John Quincy Adams represented the urban Northeast; as secretary of war, South Carolinian John C. Calhoun spoke for the planter aristocracy; and William H. Crawford of Georgia, secretary of the treasury, was a proponent of Jeffersonian states' rights and limited federal power. Even before the end of Monroe's first term, these men and others began to maneuver for the election of 1824.

Crucially helping them to maneuver were their wives, who accomplished some of the work of modern campaign managers by courting men — and women — of influence. Louisa Catherine Adams had a weekly party for guests numbering in the hundreds. The somber Adams lacked charm — "I am a man of reserved, cold, austere, and forbidding manners," he once wrote — but his abundantly charming (and hardworking) wife made up for that. She attended to the etiquette of social calls, sometimes making two dozen in a morning, and counted sixty-eight members of Congress as her regular guests.

John Quincy Adams (and Louisa Catherine) were ambitious for the presidency, but so were others. Candidate Henry Clay, Speaker of the House and negotiator of the Treaty of Ghent with Britain in 1814, promoted a new "American System," a package of protective tariffs to encourage manufacturing and federal expenditures for internal improvements such as roads and canals. Treasury Secretary William Crawford was a favorite of Republicans from Virginia and New York, even after he suffered an incapacitating stroke in mid-1824. John C. Calhoun was another serious contender, having served in Congress and in several cabinets. A southern planter, he attracted northern support for his backing of internal improvements and protective tariffs.

The final candidate was an outsider and a latecomer: General Andrew Jackson of Tennessee. Jackson had far less national political experience than the others, but he enjoyed great celebrity from his military career. When Jackson's supporters put his name forward for the presidency and voters in the West and South reacted with

CHAPTER LOCATOR | How did Jefferson attempt to undo the Federalist innovations of earlier administrations? | What was the significance of the Louisiana Purchase for the United States?

288 CHAPTER 10 A MATURING REPUBLIC

enthusiasm, Adams was dismayed, and Calhoun dropped out of the race and shifted his attention to winning the vice presidency.

Along with democratizing the vote, eighteen states (out of the full twenty-four) had put the power to choose members of the electoral college directly in the hands of voters, making the 1824 election the first one to have a popular vote tally for the presidency. Jackson proved by far to be the most popular candidate, winning 153,544 votes. Adams was second with 108,740, Clay won 47,136 votes, and the debilitated Crawford garnered 46,618.

In the electoral college, Jackson received 99 votes, Adams 84, Crawford 41, and Clay 37 (**Map 10.5**). Jackson lacked a majority, so the House of Representatives stepped in for the second time in U.S. history. Each congressional delegation had one vote; according to the Constitution's Twelfth Amendment, passed in 1804, only the top three candidates joined the runoff. Thus, Henry Clay was out of the race and in a position to bestow his support on another candidate.

Jackson's supporters later characterized the election of 1824 as the "corrupt bargain." Clay backed Adams, and Adams won by one vote in the House in February 1825. Clay's support made sense on several levels. Despite strong mutual dislike, he and Adams agreed on issues such as federal support to build roads and canals. Moreover, Clay was uneasy with Jackson's volatile temperament and unstated political views and with Crawford's diminished capacity. What made Clay's decision look "corrupt" was that immediately after the election Adams offered to appoint Clay secretary of state — and Clay accepted.

In fact, there probably was no concrete bargain; Adams's subsequent cabinet appointments demonstrated his lack of political astuteness. But Andrew Jackson felt that the election had been stolen from him, and he wrote bitterly that "the Judas of the West [Clay] has closed the contract and will receive the thirty pieces of silver."

MAP 10.5 ■ The Election of 1824

Candidate*	Electoral Vote	Popular Vote	Percent of Popular Vote
John Q. Adams	84	108,740	30.5
Andrew Jackson	99	153,544	43.1
Henry Clay	37	47,136	13.2
W. H. Crawford	41	46,618	13.1

*No distinct political parties

Note: Because no candidate garnered a majority in the electoral college, the election was decided in the House of Representatives. Although Clay was eliminated from the running, as Speaker of the House he influenced the final decision in favor of Adams.

Why did Congress declare war on Great Britain in 1812?

How did the civil status of American women and men differ in the early Republic?

Why did partisan conflict increase during the administrations of Monroe and Adams?

Conclusion: How did republican simplicity become complex?

☑ LearningCurve
Check what you know.
bedfordstmartins.com
/roarkunderstanding

The Adams Administration

John Quincy Adams, like his father, was a one-term president. His career had been built on diplomacy, not electoral politics, and despite his wife's deftness in the art of political influence, his own political horse sense was not well developed. With his cabinet choices, he welcomed his opposition into his inner circle. He asked Crawford to stay on in the Treasury. He retained an openly pro-Jackson postmaster general even though that position controlled thousands of nationwide patronage appointments. He even asked Jackson to become secretary of war. With Calhoun as vice president (elected without opposition by the electoral college) and Clay at the State Department, the whole argumentative crew would have been thrust into the executive branch. Crawford and Jackson had the good sense to decline the appointments.

Adams had lofty ideas for federal action during his presidency, and the plan he put before Congress was sweeping. Adams called for federally built roads, canals, and harbors. He proposed a national university in Washington as well as government-sponsored scientific research. He wanted to build observatories to advance astronomical knowledge and to promote precision in timekeeping, and he backed a decimal-based system of weights and measures. In all these endeavors, Adams believed he was continuing the legacy of Jefferson and Madison, using the powers of government to advance knowledge. But his opponents feared he was too Hamiltonian, using federal power inappropriately to advance commercial interests.

Whether he was more truly Federalist or Republican was a moot point. Lacking the give-and-take political skills required to gain congressional support, Adams was unable to implement much of his program. He scorned the idea of courting voters to gain support and using the patronage system to enhance his power. He often made appointments to placate enemies rather than to reward friends. A story of a toast offered to the president may well have been mythical, but it came to summarize Adams's precarious hold on leadership. A dignitary raised a glass and said, "May he strike confusion to his foes," to which another voice scornfully chimed in, "as he has already done to his friends."

> **QUICK REVIEW**

How did the collapse of the Federalist Party influence the administrations of James Monroe and John Quincy Adams?

CHAPTER LOCATOR | How did Jefferson attempt to undo the Federalist innovations of earlier administrations? | What was the significance of the Louisiana Purchase for the United States?

Conclusion: How did republican simplicity become complex?

T**HE JEFFERSONIAN REPUBLICANS** at first tried to undo much of what the Federalists had created in the 1790s, but their promise of a simpler government gave way to the complexities of domestic and foreign issues. The Louisiana Purchase and the Barbary Wars required a powerful government response, and the challenges posed by Britain on the seas finally drew America into declaring war on the onetime mother country. The War of 1812, joined by restive Indian nations allied with the British, was longer and more costly than anticipated, and it ended inconclusively.

The war elevated to national prominence General Andrew Jackson, whose popularity with voters in the 1824 election surprised traditional politicians and threw the one-party rule of Republicans into a tailspin. John Quincy Adams had barely assumed office in 1825 before the election campaign of 1828 was off and running. Reformed suffrage laws ensured that appeals to the mass of white male voters would be the hallmark of all nineteenth-century elections after 1824. In such a system, Adams and men like him were at a great disadvantage.

Ordinary American women, whether white or free black, had no place in government. All-male legislatures maintained women's *feme covert* status, keeping wives dependent on husbands. A few women found a pathway to greater personal autonomy through religion, while many others benefited from expanded female education in schools and academies. These substantial gains in education would blossom into a major transformation of gender in the 1830s and 1840s.

Two other developments would prove momentous in later decades. The bitter debate over slavery that surrounded the Missouri Compromise accentuated the serious divisions between northern and southern states — divisions that would only widen in the decades to come. And Jefferson's long embargo and Madison's wartime trade stoppage gave a big boost to American manufacturing by removing competition with British factories. When peace returned in 1815, the years of independent development burst forth into a period of sustained economic growth that continued nearly unabated into the mid-nineteenth century.

| Why did Congress declare war on Great Britain in 1812? | How did the civil status of American women and men differ in the early Republic? | Why did partisan conflict increase during the administrations of Monroe and Adams? | Conclusion: How did republican simplicity become complex? | ✓ LearningCurve Check what you know. bedfordstmartins.com /roarkunderstanding |

291

CHAPTER 10 STUDY GUIDE

STEP 1

GET STARTED ONLINE

✓ **LearningCurve** ▪ bedfordstmartins.com/roarkunderstanding

Now that you've read the chapter, make it stick by completing the LearningCurve activity.

STEP 2

EXPLAIN WHY IT MATTERS

Put your reading into practice. Identify each term below, and then explain why it matters in U.S. history.

TERM	WHO OR WHAT & WHEN	WHY IT MATTERS
Marbury v. Madison (p. 264)		
Louisiana Purchase (p. 268)		
Lewis and Clark expedition (p. 270)		
impressment (p. 273)		
Embargo Act of 1807 (p. 273)		
battle of Tippecanoe (p. 276)		
War Hawks (p. 276)		
Creek War (p. 278)		
battle of New Orleans (p. 278)		
Hartford Convention (p. 279)		
feme covert (p. 280)		
Missouri Compromise (p. 286)		

STEP 3

MOVE BEYOND THE BASICS

To demonstrate a more advanced understanding, assess the positions and policies of the early-nineteenth-century presidents. What core assumptions and beliefs informed each president's policies and positions? How did each successive president change the presidency?

Aspects and developments	Jefferson	Madison	Monroe	J. Q. Adams
Power of the presidency				
Expansion of the nation				
Domestic affairs				
Foreign affairs				
Difficulties				
Successes				

PUT IT ALL TOGETHER

Now, take a step back and try to explain the big picture. Remember to use specific examples from the chapter in your answers.

JEFFERSON AND REPUBLICANISM

▶ What steps did Jefferson take in the aftermath of the Louisiana Purchase to help facilitate western expansion of the United States?

▶ How did foreign policy issues shape the Jefferson presidency?

MADISON AND THE WAR OF 1812

▶ Where was support for the War of 1812 strongest? Where was it weakest? Why?

▶ How did the status of women change in the early decades of the nineteenth century? In what ways did some women exert political influence?

MONROE, ADAMS, AND PARTISANSHIP

▶ What forces led to the expansion of the voting rights in the early nineteenth century?

▶ In what ways did the election of 1824 mark a turning point in American politics?

LOOKING BACKWARD, LOOKING AHEAD

▶ How did the partisanship of the 1820s differ from the partisanship of the 1790s? What explains the changes you note?

▶ What problems were solved by the Missouri Compromise? What tensions and conflicts were left unresolved?

Candidate*	Electoral Vote	Popular Vote	Percent of Popular Vote
John Q. Adams	84	108,740	30.5
Andrew Jackson	99	153,544	43.1
Henry Clay	37	47,136	13.2
W. H. Crawford	41	46,618	13.1

*No distinct political parties

Note: Because no candidate garnered a majority in the electoral college, the election was decided in the House of Representatives. Although Clay was eliminated from the running as Speaker of the House he influenced the final decision in favor of Adams.

> ## IN YOUR OWN WORDS

Imagine that you must give an oral report to the class answering the following question: **What were the most important political, social, and cultural changes in the early decades of the nineteenth century?** What would be the most important points to include and why?

11
THE EXPANDING REPUBLIC

1815–1840

> **What were the most important causes and consequences of the market revolution from 1815 to 1840?** Chapter 11 explores the impact of the economic expansion known as the market revolution on American life. It also traces political developments and Indian policy under the presidency of Andrew Jackson as well as the contemporaneous appearance of reform movements.

LearningCurve
bedfordstmartins.com/roarkunderstanding
After reading the chapter, use LearningCurve to
retain what you've read.

The *Clermont*. Robert Fulton's steamboat travels up the Hudson River from New York City. The Granger Collection, New York.

> Why did the United States experience a market revolution after 1815?

> Why did Andrew Jackson defeat John Quincy Adams so dramatically in the 1828 election?

> What was Andrew Jackson's impact on the presidency?

> How did social and cultural life change in the 1830s?

> Why was Martin Van Buren a one-term president?

> Conclusion: The Age of Jackson or the era of reform?

Why did the United States experience a market revolution after 1815?

The Erie Canal at Lockport

The Erie Canal, completed in 1825, was impressive not only for its length of 350 miles but also for its elevation, requiring the construction of eighty-three locks. The biggest engineering challenge came at Lockport, twenty miles northeast of Buffalo, where the canal traversed a steep slate escarpment. Work crews — mostly immigrant Irishmen — used gunpowder and grueling physical labor to blast the deep artificial gorge shown here. Department of Rare Books and Special Collections, Rush Rhees Library, University of Rochester.

THE RETURN OF PEACE IN 1815 unleashed powerful forces that revolutionized the organization of the economy. Spectacular changes in transportation facilitated the movement of commodities, information, and people, while textile mills and other factories created many new jobs, especially for young unmarried women. Innovations in banking, legal practices, and tariff policies promoted swift economic growth.

This was not yet an industrial revolution, as was beginning in Britain, but rather a market revolution fueled by traditional sources — water, wood, beasts of burden, and human muscle. What was new was the accelerated pace of economic activity and the scale of the distribution of goods. The new nature and scale of production and consumption changed Americans' economic behavior, attitudes, and expectations.

CHAPTER LOCATOR | Why did the United States experience a market revolution after 1815? | Why did Andrew Jackson defeat John Quincy Adams so dramatically in the 1828 election?

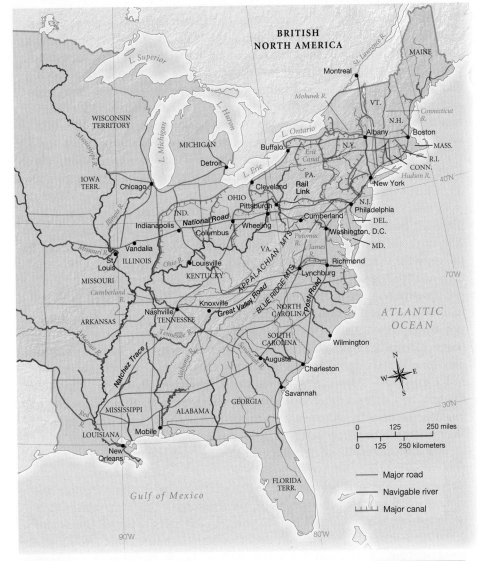

MAP 11.1 ■ Routes of Transportation in 1840

Transportation advances cut travel times significantly. On the Erie Canal, goods and people could move from New York City to Buffalo in four days, a two-week trip by road. Steamboats cut travel time from New York to New Orleans from four weeks by road to less than two weeks by river.

> MAP ACTIVITY

READING THE MAP: In what parts of the country were canals built most extensively? Were most of them within a single state's borders, or did they encourage interstate travel and shipping?
CONNECTIONS: What impact did the Erie Canal have on the development of New York City? How did improvements in transportation affect urbanization in other parts of the country?

Improvements in Transportation

Before 1815, transportation in the United States was slow and expensive; it cost as much to ship a crate over thirty miles of domestic roads as it did to send it across the Atlantic Ocean. A stagecoach trip from Boston to New York City took four days. But between 1815 and 1840, networks of roads, canals, steamboats, and finally railroads dramatically raised the speed and lowered the cost of travel (**Map 11.1**).

What was Andrew Jackson's impact on the presidency?	How did social and cultural life change in the 1830s?	Why was Martin Van Buren a one-term president?	Conclusion: The Age of Jackson or the era of reform?	✓ LearningCurve Check what you know. bedfordstmartins.com /roarkunderstanding

1807
– Robert Fulton sets off steamboat craze.

1816
– Second Bank of the United States is chartered.

1819
– Economic panic.

1825
– Erie Canal is completed in New York.

1829
– Baltimore and Ohio railroad is begun.

1834
– Female mill workers strike in Lowell, Massachusetts, and again in 1836.

Erie Canal
▶ Canal finished in 1825, covering 350 miles between Albany and Buffalo and linking the port of New York City with the entire Great Lakes region. The canal turned New York City into the country's premier commercial city.

Improved transportation moved goods into wider markets. It moved passengers, too, allowing young people as well as adults to take up new employment in cities or factory towns. Transportation also facilitated the flow of political information via the U.S. mail, with its bargain postal rates for newspapers, periodicals, and books. Enhanced public transport was expensive and produced uneven economic benefits, so presidents from Jefferson to Monroe were reluctant to fund it with federal dollars. Instead, private investors pooled resources and chartered transport companies, receiving significant subsidies and monopoly rights from state governments. Turnpike and roadway mileage increased dramatically after 1815, reducing shipping costs. Stagecoach companies proliferated, and travel time on main routes was cut in half.

Water travel was similarly transformed. In 1807, Robert Fulton's steam-propelled boat, the *Clermont*, churned up the Hudson River from New York City to Albany, touching off a steamboat craze on eastern rivers and the Great Lakes. By the early 1830s, more than seven hundred steamboats were in operation on the Ohio and Mississippi rivers.

Steamboats were not benign advances, however. The urgency to cut travel time led to overstoked furnaces, sudden boiler explosions, and terrible mass fatalities. By the mid-1830s, nearly three thousand Americans had been killed in steamboat accidents, leading to the first federal attempt to regulate safety on vessels used for interstate commerce. Environmental costs were also large: Steamboats had to load fuel—"wood up"—every twenty miles or so, resulting in mass deforestation. By the 1830s, the banks of many main rivers were denuded of trees, and forests miles back from the rivers fell to the ax. The smoke from wood-burning steamboats created America's first significant air pollution.

Canals were another major innovation of the transportation revolution. Canal boats powered by mules moved slowly—less than five miles per hour—but the low-friction water enabled one mule to pull a fifty-ton barge. Several states commenced major government-sponsored canal enterprises, the most impressive being the **Erie Canal**, finished in 1825, covering 350 miles between Albany and Buffalo and linking the port of New York City with the entire Great Lakes region. Wheat and flour moved east, household goods and tools moved west, and passengers went in both directions. By the 1830s, the cost of shipping by canal fell to less than one-tenth of the cost of overland transport, and New York City quickly blossomed into the premier commercial city in the United States.

In the 1830s, private railroad companies heavily subsidized by state legislatures began to give canals competition. The nation's first railroad, the Baltimore and Ohio, laid thirteen miles of track in 1829, and by 1840 three thousand more miles of track materialized nationwide. Rail lines in the 1830s were generally short, on the order of twenty to one hundred miles. They did not yet provide an efficient distribution system for goods, but passengers flocked to experience the marvelous speeds of fifteen to twenty miles per hour. Railroads and other advances in transportation served to unify the country culturally and economically.

CHAPTER LOCATOR | **Why did the United States experience a market revolution after 1815?** | Why did Andrew Jackson defeat John Quincy Adams so dramatically in the 1828 election?

This daguerreotype (the earliest form of photograph) shows a young woman tending a power loom in a textile mill. In the 1830s, women weavers generally tended two machines at a time. In the 1840s, some companies increased the workload to four. American Textile History Museum.

Factories, Workingwomen, and Wage Labor

Transportation advances accelerated manufacturing after 1815, creating an ever-expanding market for goods. The two leading industries, textiles and shoes, altered methods of production and labor relations. Textile production was greatly spurred by the development of water-driven machinery built near fast-coursing rivers. Shoe manufacturing, still using the power and skill of human hands, involved only a reorganization of production. Both industries pulled young women into wage-earning labor for the first time.

The earliest American textile factory was built in the 1790s by an English immigrant in Pawtucket, Rhode Island. By 1815, nearly 170 spinning mills stood along New England rivers. While British manufacturers hired entire families for mill work, American factory owners innovated by hiring young women, assumed to be cheap to hire because of their limited employment options and their short-term prospects, since most left to get married.

In 1821, a group of Boston entrepreneurs founded the town of Lowell on the Merrimack River, centralizing all aspects of cloth production: combing, shrinking, spinning, weaving, and dyeing. By 1836, the eight **Lowell mills** employed more than five thousand young women, who lived in carefully managed company-owned boardinghouses. A typical

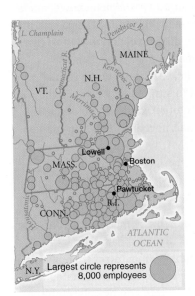

Cotton Textile Industry, ca. 1840

Largest circle represents 8,000 employees

Lowell mills

▶ Water-powered textile mills constructed along the Merrimack River in Lowell, Massachusetts, that pioneered the extensive use of female laborers. By 1836, the eight mills there employed more than five thousand young women, who lived in boardinghouses under close supervision.

| What was Andrew Jackson's impact on the presidency? | How did social and cultural life change in the 1830s? | Why was Martin Van Buren a one-term president? | Conclusion: The Age of Jackson or the era of reform? | ✓ **LearningCurve** Check what you know. bedfordstmartins.com /roarkunderstanding |

mill worker earned \$2 to \$3 for a seventy-hour week, more than a seamstress or domestic servant could earn but less than a young man's wages.

Despite the long hours, young women embraced factory work as a means to earn spending money and build savings before marriage; several banks in town held the nest eggs of thousands of workers. Also welcome was the unprecedented, though still limited, personal freedom of living in an all-female social space, away from parents and domestic tasks. In the evening, the women could engage in self-improvement activities, such as attending lectures. In 1837, 1,500 mill girls crowded Lowell's city hall to hear the sisters Angelina and Sarah Grimké speak about the evils of slavery.

In the mid-1830s, worldwide growth and competition in the cotton market impelled mill owners to speed up work and decrease wages. The workers protested, emboldened by their communal living arrangement and by their relative independence as temporary employees. In 1834 and again in 1836, hundreds of women at the Lowell mills went out on strike. Such strikes spread; in 1834, mill workers in Dover, New Hampshire, denounced their owners for trying to turn them into "slaves." Their assertiveness surprised many, but ultimately the ease of replacing them undermined their bargaining power, and owners in the 1840s began to shift to immigrant families as their primary labor source.

The shoe manufacturing industry centered in eastern New England reorganized production and hired women, including wives, as shoebinders. Male shoemakers still cut the leather and made the soles in shops, but female shoebinders working from home now stitched the upper parts of the shoes. Working from home meant that wives could contribute to family income—unusual for most wives in that period—and still perform their domestic chores.

In the economically turbulent 1830s, shoebinder wages fell. Unlike mill workers, female shoebinders worked in isolation, a serious hindrance to organized protest. In Lynn, Massachusetts, a major shoemaking center, women used female church networks to organize resistance, communicating via religious newspapers. The Lynn shoebinders who demanded higher wages in 1834 built on a collective sense of themselves as women. "Equal rights should be extended to all—to the weaker sex as well as the stronger," they proclaimed.

In the end, the Lynn shoebinders' protests failed to achieve wage increases. At-home workers all over New England continued to accept low wages, and even in Lynn many women shied away from organized protest, preferring to situate their work in the context of family duty (helping their husbands finish the shoes) instead of market relations.

Bankers and Lawyers

Entrepreneurs like the Lowell factory owners relied on innovations in the banking system to finance their ventures. Between 1814 and 1816, the number of state-chartered banks in the United States more than doubled, from fewer than 90 to 208. By 1830, there were 330, and by 1840 hundreds more. Banks stimulated the economy by making loans to merchants and manufacturers and by enlarging the money supply. Borrowers were issued loans in the form of banknotes—certificates

CHAPTER LOCATOR | Why did the United States experience a market revolution after 1815? | Why did Andrew Jackson defeat John Quincy Adams so dramatically in the 1828 election?

300 CHAPTER 11 THE EXPANDING REPUBLIC

unique to each bank—that were used as money for all transactions. Neither federal nor state governments issued paper money, so banknotes became the country's currency.

Bankers exercised great power over the economy, deciding who would get loans and what the discount rates would be. The most powerful bankers sat on the board of directors for the **second Bank of the United States**, headquartered in Philadelphia and featuring eighteen branches throughout the country. The twenty-year charter of the first Bank of the United States had expired in 1811, and the second Bank of the United States opened for business in 1816 under another twenty-year charter. The rechartering of this bank would become a major issue in the 1832 presidential campaign.

Lawyer-politicians too exercised economic power, by refashioning commercial law to enhance the prospects of private investment. In 1811, states started to rewrite their laws of incorporation (allowing the chartering of businesses by states), and the number of corporations expanded rapidly, from about twenty in 1800 to eighteen hundred by 1817. Incorporation protected individual investors from being held liable for corporate debts. State lawmakers also wrote laws of eminent domain, empowering states to buy land for roads and canals even from unwilling sellers. In such ways, entrepreneurial lawyers created the legal foundation for an economy that favored ambitious individuals interested in maximizing their own wealth.

Not everyone applauded these developments. Andrew Jackson, himself a skillful lawyer turned politician, spoke for a large and mistrustful segment of the population when he warned about the potential abuses of power "which the moneyed interest derives from a paper currency which they are able to control [and] from the multitude of corporations with exclusive privileges which they have succeeded in obtaining in the different states." Jacksonians believed that ending government-granted privileges was the way to maximize individual liberty and economic opportunity.

second Bank of the United States

▶ National bank with multiple branches chartered in 1816 for twenty years. Intended to help regulate the economy, the bank became a major issue in Andrew Jackson's reelection campaign in 1832, framed in political rhetoric about aristocracy versus democracy.

Booms and Busts

One aspect of the economy that the lawyer-politicians could not control was the threat of financial collapse. The boom years from 1815 to 1818 exhibited a volatility that resulted in the first sharp, large-scale economic downturn in U.S. history. Americans called this downturn a "panic," and the pattern was repeated in the 1830s. Some blamed the panic of 1819 on the second Bank of the United States for failing to control an economic bubble and then contracting the money supply, sending tremors throughout the economy. The crunch was made worse by a financial crisis in Europe in the spring of 1819. Overseas, prices for American cotton, tobacco, and wheat plummeted by more than 50 percent. Thus, when the banks began to call in their outstanding loans, American debtors involved in the commodities trade could not come up with the money. Business and personal bankruptcies skyrocketed. The intricate web of credit and debt relationships meant that almost everyone with even a toehold in the new commercial economy was affected by the panic. Thousands of Americans lost their savings and property, and unemployment estimates suggest that half a million people lost their jobs.

| What was Andrew Jackson's impact on the presidency? | How did social and cultural life change in the 1830s? | Why was Martin Van Buren a one-term president? | Conclusion: The Age of Jackson or the era of reform? | ✓ LearningCurve Check what you know. bedfordstmartins.com /roarkunderstanding |

301

Recovery took several years. Unemployment declined, but bitterness lingered, ready to be stirred up by politicians in the decades to come. The dangers of a system dependent on extensive credit were now clear. In one folksy formulation that circulated around 1820, a farmer compared credit to "a man pissing in his breeches on a cold day to keep his arse warm—very comfortable at first but I dare say . . . you know how it feels afterwards."

By the mid-1820s, the economy was back on track, driven by increases in productivity, consumer demand for goods, and international trade. Despite the panic of 1819, credit financing continued to fuel the system. A network of credit and debt relations grew dense by the 1830s in a system that encouraged speculation and risk taking. A pervasive optimism about continued growth supported the elaborate system, but a single business failure could produce many innocent victims. Well after the panic of 1819, an undercurrent of anxiety about rapid economic change continued to shape the political views of many Americans.

> QUICK REVIEW

What role did state governments and private businesses play in the market revolution?

CHAPTER LOCATOR | Why did the United States experience a market revolution after 1815?   Why did Andrew Jackson defeat John Quincy Adams so dramatically in the 1828 election?

CHAPTER 11
302   THE EXPANDING REPUBLIC

Jackson Forever!
The Hero of Two Wars and of Orleans!
The Man of the People!
HE WHO COULD NOT BARTER NOR BARGAIN FOR THE
PRESIDENCY!

Who, although "A Military Chieftain," valued the purity of Elections and of the Electors, MORE than the Office of PRESIDENT itself! Although the greatest in the gift of his countrymen, and the highest in point of dignity of any in the world,

BECAUSE
It should be derived from the
PEOPLE!

No Gag Laws! No Black Cockades! No Reign of Terror! No Standing Army or Navy Officers, when under the pay of Government, to browbeat, or

KNOCK DOWN

Old Revolutionary Characters, or our Representatives while in the discharge of their duty. To the Polls then, and vote for those who will support

OLD HICKORY
AND THE ELECTORAL LAW.

Campaign Poster for the 1828 Election

This poster praises Andrew Jackson as a war hero and a "man of the people" and reminds its readers that Jackson, who won the largest popular vote in 1824, did not stoop to "bargain for the presidency," as John Quincy Adams presumably had in his dealing with Henry Clay.
© Collection of the New-York Historical Society.

Why did Andrew Jackson defeat John Quincy Adams so dramatically in the 1828 election?

JUST AS THE MARKET REVOLUTION held out the promise, if not the reality, of economic opportunity for all who worked, the political transformation of the 1830s held out the promise of political opportunity for hundreds of thousands of new voters. During Andrew Jackson's presidency (1829–1837), the second American party system took shape, defined by Jackson's charismatic personality expressed in his efforts to dominate Congress. Not until 1836, however, would the parties have distinct names and consistent programs transcending the particular personalities running for office. Over those years, more men could and did vote, responding to new methods of arousing voter interest.

> ## > KEY FACTORS

- First presidential race in which the popular vote determined the outcome.
- Nearly half the free male population voted.
- First national election to be dominated by character issues.

Popular Politics and Partisan Identity

The election of 1828, pitting Andrew Jackson against John Quincy Adams, was the first presidential contest in which the popular vote determined the outcome. In twenty-two out of twenty-four states, voters—not state legislatures—designated

What was Andrew Jackson's impact on the presidency?

How did social and cultural life change in the 1830s?

Why was Martin Van Buren a one-term president?

Conclusion: The Age of Jackson or the era of reform?

LearningCurve
Check what you know.
bedfordstmartins.com
/roarkunderstanding

the number of electors committed to a particular candidate. More than a million voters participated, three times the number in 1824 and nearly half the free male population, reflecting the high stakes that voters perceived in the Adams-Jackson rematch. Throughout the 1830s, voter turnout continued to rise and reached 70 percent in some localities, partly because of the disappearance of property qualifications in all but three states and partly because of heightened political interest.

The 1828 election inaugurated new campaign styles. State-level candidates routinely gave speeches at rallies, picnics, and banquets. Adams and Jackson still declined such appearances as undignified, but Henry Clay of Kentucky, campaigning for Adams, earned the nickname "the Barbecue Orator." Campaign rhetoric became more informal and even blunt. The Jackson camp established many Hickory Clubs, trading on Jackson's popular nickname, "Old Hickory," from a common Tennessee tree suggesting resilience and toughness.

Partisan newspapers in ever-larger numbers defined issues and publicized political personalities as never before. Improved printing technology and rising literacy rates fueled a great expansion of newspapers of all kinds (**Table 11.1**). Party leaders dispensed subsidies and other favors to secure the support of papers, even in remote towns and villages. Political news stories traveled swiftly in the mail, gaining coverage by reprintings in sympathetic newspapers. Presidential campaigns were now coordinated in a national arena.

TABLE 11.1 ■ The Growth of Newspapers, 1820–1840

	1820	1830	1835	1840
U.S. population (in millions)	9.6	12.8	15.0	17.1
Number of newspapers published	500	800	1,200	1,400
Daily newspapers	42	65	—	138

Whigs

▶ Political party that evolved out of the National Republicans after 1834. With a Northeast power base, the Whigs supported federal action to promote commercial development and generally looked favorably on the reform movements associated with the Second Great Awakening.

Democrats

▶ Political party that evolved out of the Democratic Republicans after 1834. Strongest in the South and West, the Democrats embraced Andrew Jackson's vision of limited government, expanded political participation for white men, and the promotion of an ethic of individualism.

Politicians at first identified themselves as Jackson or Adams men, honoring the fiction of Republican Party unity. By 1832, however, the terminology had evolved to National Republicans, who favored federal action to promote commercial development, and Democratic Republicans, who promised to be responsive to the will of the majority. Between 1834 and 1836, National Republicans came to be called **Whigs**, while Jackson's party became simply the **Democrats**.

The Election of 1828 and the Character Issue

The campaign of 1828 was the first national election dominated by scandal and character questions. Claims about morality, honor, and discipline became central because voters used them to comprehend the kind of public official each man would make. Jackson and Adams presented two radically different styles of manhood.

John Quincy Adams was vilified by his opponents as an elitist, a bookish academic, and even a monarchist. They attacked his "corrupt bargain" of 1824—the alleged election deal between Adams and Henry Clay (see chapter 10). Adams's

CHAPTER LOCATOR | Why did the United States experience a market revolution after 1815?   Why did Andrew Jackson defeat John Quincy Adams so dramatically in the 1828 election?

304 CHAPTER 11
THE EXPANDING REPUBLIC

supporters countered by playing on Jackson's fatherless child-hood to portray him as the bastard son of a prostitute. Worse, the cloudy circumstances around his marriage to Rachel Donelson Robards in 1791 gave rise to the story that Jackson was a seducer and an adulterer, having married a woman whose divorce from her first husband was not entirely legal. Pro-Adams newspapers howled that Jackson was sinful and impulsive, while portraying Adams as pious, learned, and virtuous.

Editors in favor of Adams played up Jackson's violent temper, as evidenced by his participation in many duels, brawls, and canings. Jackson's supporters used the same stories to project Old Hickory as a tough frontier hero who knew how to command obedience. As for learning, Jackson's rough frontier education gave him a "natural sense," wrote a Boston editor, that "can never be acquired by reading books—it can only be acquired, in perfection, by reading men."

Jackson won a sweeping victory, with 56 percent of the popular vote and 178 electoral votes to Adams's 83 (**Map 11.2**). Old Hickory took most of the South and West and carried Pennsylvania and New York as well; Adams carried the remainder of the East. Jackson's vice president was John C. Calhoun, who had just served as vice president under Adams but had broken with Adams's policies.

After 1828, national politicians no longer deplored the existence of political parties. They were coming to see that parties mobilized and delivered voters, sharpened candidates' differences, and created party loyalty that surpassed loyalty to individual candidates and elections. Adams and Jackson clearly symbolized the competing ideas of the emerging parties: a moralistic, top-down party (the Whigs) ready to make major decisions to promote economic growth competing against a contentious, energetic party (the Democrats) ready to embrace liberty-loving individualism.

Candidate	Electoral Vote	Popular Vote	Percent of Popular Vote
Andrew Jackson (Democratic Republican)	178	647,286	56
John Q. Adams (National Republican)	83	508,064	44

MAP 11.2 ■ The Election of 1828

Jackson's Democratic Agenda

Jackson's supporters went wild at his March 1829 inauguration. Thousands cheered his ten-minute inaugural address, the shortest in history. An open reception at the White House turned into a near riot as well-wishers jammed the premises, used windows as doors, stood on furniture for a better view of the great man, and broke thousands of dollars' worth of china and glasses. During his presidency, Jackson continued to offer unprecedented hospitality to the public. The courteous Jackson, committed to his image as president of the "common man," held audiences with unannounced visitors throughout his two terms.

Past presidents had tried to lessen party conflict by including men of different factions in their cabinets, but Jackson would have only loyalists, a political tactic followed by most later presidents. For secretary of state, the key job, he tapped New Yorker Martin Van Buren, one of the shrewdest politicians of the day. Throughout the federal government, from postal clerks to ambassadors,

What was Andrew Jackson's impact on the presidency?

How did social and cultural life change in the 1830s?

Why was Martin Van Buren a one-term president?

Conclusion: The Age of Jackson or the era of reform?

✔ LearningCurve
Check what you know.
bedfordstmartins.com
/roarkunderstanding

Jackson replaced competent civil servants with party loyalists. Jackson's appointment practices were termed a "spoils system" by his opponents, after a Democratic politician coined the affirmative slogan "to the victor belong the spoils."

Jackson's agenda quickly emerged. Fearing that intervention in the economy inevitably favored some groups at the expense of others, Jackson favored a Jeffersonian limited federal government. He therefore opposed federal support of transportation and grants of monopolies and charters that benefited wealthy investors. Like Jefferson, he anticipated the rapid settlement of the country's interior, where land sales would spread economic democracy to settlers. Thus, establishing a federal policy to remove the Indians from this area had high priority. Jackson was freer than previous presidents with the use of the presidential veto power over Congress. In 1830, he vetoed a highway project in Maysville, Kentucky, Henry Clay's home state. The Maysville Road veto articulated Jackson's principled stand that citizens' tax dollars could be spent only on projects of a "general, not local" character.

> ## QUICK REVIEW

Why role did character play in the 1828 election?

CHAPTER LOCATOR | Why did the United States experience a market revolution after 1815? | Why did Andrew Jackson defeat John Quincy Adams so dramatically in the 1828 election?

What was Andrew Jackson's impact on the presidency?

Andrew Jackson as "the Great Father"

In 1828, a new process of commercial lithography brought political cartooning to new prominence. Out of some sixty satirical cartoons lampooning Jackson, only one featured his controversial Indian policy. This cropped cartoon lacks the cartoonist's caption, important for understanding the artist's intent. Still, the visual humor of Jackson cradling Indians packs an immediate punch.

William L. Clements Library.

> VISUAL ACTIVITY

READING THE IMAGE: Examine the body language conveyed in the various characters' poses. Are the Indians depicted as children or as powerless, miniature adults? What is going on in the picture on the wall?

CONNECTIONS: Does the cartoon suggest that Jackson offers protection to Indians? What does the picture on the wall contribute to our understanding of the artist's opinion of Jackson's Indian removal policy?

IN HIS TWO TERMS AS PRESIDENT, Andrew Jackson worked to implement his vision of a politics of opportunity for all white men. To open land for white settlement, he favored the relocation of all eastern Indian tribes. He dramatically confronted John C. Calhoun and South Carolina when that state tried to nullify the tariff of 1828. Disapproving of all government-granted privilege, Jackson challenged and defeated the Bank of the United States. In all this, he greatly enhanced the power of the presidency.

What was Andrew Jackson's impact on the presidency?

How did social and cultural life change in the 1830s?

Why was Martin Van Buren a one-term president?

Conclusion: The Age of Jackson or the era of reform?

☑ LearningCurve
Check what you know.
bedfordstmartins.com
/roarkunderstanding

307

> CHRONOLOGY

1828
- Tariff of Abominations.

1830
- Indian Removal Act.

1832
- Massacre of Sauk and Fox Indians.
- *Worcester v. Georgia.*
- Jackson vetoes charter renewal of Bank of the United States.

1833
- South Carolina nullifies federal tariffs.

1838
- Cherokee Trail of Tears.

Indian Removal Act of 1830
▶ Act that directed the mandatory relocation of eastern tribes to territory west of the Mississippi. Jackson insisted that his goal was to save the Indians. Indians resisted the controversial act, but in the end most were forced to comply.

Indian Policy and the Trail of Tears

Probably nothing defined Jackson's presidency more than his efforts to solve what he saw as the Indian problem. Thousands of Indians lived in the South and the old Northwest, and many remained in New England and New York. In his first message to Congress in 1829, Jackson declared that removing the Indians to territory west of the Mississippi was the only way to save them. White civilization destroyed Indian resources and thus doomed the Indians, he claimed: "That this fate surely awaits them if they remain within the limits of the states does not admit of a doubt. Humanity and national honor demand that every effort should be made to avert so great a calamity." Jackson never publicly wavered from this seemingly noble theme, returning to it in his next seven annual messages.

Prior administrations had experimented with different Indian policies. Starting in 1819, Congress funded missionary associations eager to "civilize" native peoples by converting them to Christianity and to whites' agricultural practices. The federal government had also pursued aggressive treaty making with many tribes, dealing with the Indians as foreign nations (see chapters 9 and 10). By contrast, Jackson saw Indians as subjects of the United States (neither foreigners nor citizens) who needed to be relocated to assure their survival. Congress agreed and passed the **Indian Removal Act of 1830**. About 100 million acres of eastern land would be vacated for eventual white settlement under this act authorizing ethnic expulsion (**Map 11.3**).

The Indian Removal Act generated widespread controversy. Newspapers, public lecturers, and local clubs debated the expulsion law, and public opinion, especially in the North, was heated. "One would think that the guilt of African slavery was enough for the nation to bear, without the additional crime of injustice to the aborigines," one writer declared in 1829. In an unprecedented move, thousands of northern white women signed anti-removal petitions. Between 1830 and 1832, women's petitions rolled into Washington, arguing that sovereign peoples on the road to Christianity were entitled to stay on their land. Jackson ignored the petitions.

For many northern tribes, diminished by years of war, removal was already under way. But not all went quietly. In 1832 in western Illinois, Black Hawk, a leader of the Sauk and Fox Indians who had fought in alliance with Tecumseh in the War of 1812 (see chapter 10), resisted removal. Volunteer militias attacked and chased the Indians into southern Wisconsin, where, after several skirmishes and a deadly battle (later called the Black Hawk War), Black Hawk was captured and some four hundred of his people were massacred.

The large southern tribes—the Creek, Chickasaw, Choctaw, Seminole, and Cherokee—proved even more resistant to removal. Georgia Cherokees had already taken several assimilationist steps. They had adopted written laws, including, in 1827, a constitution modeled on the U.S. Constitution. Two hundred of the wealthiest Cherokee men had intermarried with whites, adopting white styles of housing, dress, and cotton agriculture, including the ownership of slaves. They developed a written alphabet and published a newspaper and Christian prayer books in their language. These features helped make their cause attractive to the northern white women who petitioned the government on their behalf. Yet most of the seventeen thousand Cherokees maintained cultural continuity with past traditions.

CHAPTER LOCATOR | Why did the United States experience a market revolution after 1815? | Why did Andrew Jackson defeat John Quincy Adams so dramatically in the 1828 election?

308 CHAPTER 11
THE EXPANDING REPUBLIC

MAP 11.3 ■ Indian Removal and the Trail of Tears

The federal government under President Andrew Jackson pursued a vigorous policy of Indian removal in the 1830s, forcibly moving tribes west to land known as Indian Territory (present-day Oklahoma). In 1838, as many as a quarter of the Cherokee Indians died on the route known as the Trail of Tears.

> MAP ACTIVITY

READING THE MAP: From which states were most of the Native Americans removed? Through which states did the Trail of Tears go?
CONNECTIONS: Before Jackson's presidency, how did the federal government view Native Americans, and what policy initiatives were undertaken by the government and private groups? How did Jackson change the government's policy toward Native Americans?

In 1831, when Georgia announced its plans to seize all Cherokee property, the tribal leadership took their case to the U.S. Supreme Court. In *Worcester v. Georgia* (1832), the Court upheld the territorial sovereignty of the Cherokee people, recognizing their existence as "a distinct community, occupying its own territory, in which the laws of Georgia can have no force." An angry President Jackson ignored the Court and pressed the Cherokee tribe to move west: "If they now refuse to accept the liberal terms offered, they can only be liable for whatever evils and difficulties may arise. I feel conscious of having done my duty to my red children."

What was Andrew Jackson's impact on the presidency?	How did social and cultural life change in the 1830s?	Why was Martin Van Buren a one-term president?	Conclusion: The Age of Jackson or the era of reform?	✓ LearningCurve Check what you know. bedfordstmartins.com /roarkunderstanding

The Cherokee tribe remained in Georgia for two more years without significant violence. Then, in 1835, a small, unauthorized faction of the acculturated leaders signed a treaty selling all the tribal lands to the state, which rapidly resold the land to whites. Chief John Ross, backed by several thousand Cherokees, petitioned the U.S. Congress to ignore the bogus treaty, but to no avail. Most Cherokees refused to move, so in May 1838, the deadline for voluntary removal, federal troops arrived to remove them. Under armed guard, the Cherokees embarked on a 1,200-mile journey west that came to be called the **Trail of Tears.** Nearly a quarter of the Cherokees died en route from the hardship. Survivors joined the fifteen thousand Creek, twelve thousand Choctaw, five thousand Chickasaw, and several thousand Seminole Indians also forcibly relocated to Indian Territory (which became the state of Oklahoma in 1907).

In his farewell address to the nation in 1837, Jackson professed his belief in the humanitarian benefits of Indian removal: "This unhappy race . . . are now placed in a situation where we may well hope that they will share in the blessings of civilization and be saved from the degradation and destruction to which they were rapidly hastening while they remained in the states." Perhaps Jackson genuinely believed that removal was necessary, but for the forcibly removed tribes, the costs of relocation were high.

Trail of Tears

▶ Forced westward journey of Cherokees from their lands in Georgia to present-day Oklahoma in 1838. Despite favorable legal action, the Cherokees endured a grueling 1,200-mile march overseen by federal troops. Nearly a quarter of the Cherokees died en route.

The Tariff of Abominations and Nullification

Just as Indian removal in Georgia had pitted a state against a federal power, in the form of a Supreme Court ruling, a second explosive issue also pitted a state against federal regulation. This was the issue of federal tariff policy, strongly opposed by South Carolina.

Federal tariffs as high as 33 percent on imports such as textiles and iron goods had been passed in 1816 and again in 1824 in an effort to shelter new American manufacturers from foreign competition. Some southern congressmen opposed the steep tariffs, fearing they would reduce overseas shipping and thereby hurt cotton exports. In 1828, Congress passed a revised tariff that came to be known as the Tariff of Abominations. A bundle of conflicting duties, some as high as 50 percent, the legislation contained provisions that either pleased or angered every economic and sectional interest.

South Carolina in particular suffered from the Tariff of Abominations. Worldwide prices for cotton had declined in the late 1820s, and the falloff in shipping caused by the high tariffs further hurt the South. In 1828, a group of South Carolina politicians headed by John C. Calhoun advanced a doctrine called **nullification.** They argued that when Congress overstepped its powers, states had the right to nullify Congress's acts. As precedents, they pointed to the Virginia and Kentucky Resolutions of 1798, intended to invalidate the Alien and Sedition Acts (see chapter 9). Congress had erred in using tariff policy to benefit specific industries, they claimed; tariffs should be used only to raise revenue.

On assuming the presidency in 1829, Jackson ignored the South Carolina statement of nullification and shut out Calhoun, his new vice president, from influence or power. Tariff revisions in early 1832 brought little relief to the South. Calhoun resigned the vice presidency and became a senator to better serve his state. Finally, strained to their limit, South Carolina leaders took the radical step

nullification

▶ Theory asserting that states could nullify acts of Congress that exceeded congressional powers. South Carolina advanced the theory of nullification in 1828 in response to an unfavorable federal tariff. A show of force by Andrew Jackson, combined with tariff revisions, ended the crisis.

CHAPTER LOCATOR | Why did the United States experience a market revolution after 1815? | Why did Andrew Jackson defeat John Quincy Adams so dramatically in the 1828 election?

310 CHAPTER 11 THE EXPANDING REPUBLIC

of declaring federal tariffs null and void in their state as of February 1, 1833. The constitutional crisis was out in the open.

In response, Jackson sent armed ships to Charleston harbor and threatened to invade the state. He pushed through Congress the Force Bill, defining South Carolina's stance as treason and authorizing military action to collect federal tariffs. At the same time, Congress moved quickly to pass a revised tariff that was more acceptable to the South, reducing tariffs to their 1816 level. On March 1, 1833, Congress passed both the new tariff and the Force Bill. South Carolina withdrew its nullification of the old tariff—and then nullified the Force Bill. It was a symbolic gesture, since Jackson's show of muscle was no longer necessary.

Yet the question of federal power versus states' rights was far from settled. The implied threat behind nullification was secession, a position articulated in 1832 by some South Carolinians whose concerns went beyond tariff policy. In the 1830s, the political moratorium on discussions of slavery agreed on at the time of the Missouri Compromise (see chapter 10) was coming unglued, and new northern voices opposed to slavery gained increasing attention. If and when a northern-dominated federal government decided to end slavery, the South Carolinians thought, the South should nullify such laws or else remove itself from the Union.

The Bank War and Economic Boom

Along with the tariff and nullification, President Jackson fought another political battle, over the Bank of the United States. With twenty-nine branches, the bank handled the federal government's deposits, extended credit and loans, and issued banknotes—by 1830, the most stable currency in the country. Jackson, however, thought the bank concentrated undue economic power in the hands of a few.

National Republican (Whig) senators Daniel Webster and Henry Clay decided to force the issue. They convinced the bank to apply for charter renewal in 1832, well before the fall election, even though the existing charter ran until 1836. They fully expected that Congress's renewal would force Jackson to follow through on his rhetoric with a veto, that the unpopular veto would cause Jackson to lose the election, and that the bank would survive on an override vote by a new Congress swept into power on the anti-Jackson tide.

At first, the plan seemed to work. The bank applied for rechartering, Congress voted to renew, and Jackson, angry over being manipulated, issued his veto. But it was a brilliantly written veto, positioning Jackson as the champion of the democratic masses. "Many of our rich men have not been content with equal protection and equal benefits, but have besought us to make them richer by act of Congress," Jackson wrote.

Jackson's translation of the bank controversy into a language of class antagonism and egalitarian ideals resonated with many Americans. Jackson won the election easily, gaining 55 percent of the popular vote and 219 electoral votes to Clay's 49. Jackson's party still controlled Congress, so no override was possible. The second Bank of the United States would cease to exist after 1836.

Jackson wanted to destroy the bank sooner. Calling it a "monster," he ordered the sizable federal deposits to be removed from its vaults and redeposited into Democratic-inclined state banks. In retaliation, the Bank of the United States raised interest rates and called in loans. This action caused a brief decline in the

What was Andrew Jackson's impact on the presidency?

How did social and cultural life change in the 1830s?

Why was Martin Van Buren a one-term president?

Conclusion: The Age of Jackson or the era of reform?

LearningCurve
Check what you know.
bedfordstmartins.com
/roarkunderstanding

311

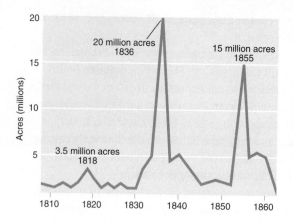

FIGURE 11.1 ■ Western Land Sales, 1810–1860

Land sales peaked in the 1810s, 1830s, and 1850s as Americans rushed to speculate in western land sold by the federal government. The surges in 1818 and 1836 demonstrate the volatile, speculative economy that suddenly collapsed in the panics of 1819 and 1837.

economy in 1833 and actually enhanced Jackson's claim that the bank was too powerful for the good of the country.

Unleashed and unregulated, the economy went into high gear in 1834. Just at this moment, an excess of silver from Mexican mines made its way into American banks, giving bankers license to print ever more banknotes. From 1834 to 1837, inflation soared; prices of basic goods rose more than 50 percent. States quickly chartered hundreds of new private banks, each issuing its own banknotes. Entrepreneurs borrowed and invested money, and the webs of credit and debt relationships that were the hallmark of the American economy grew denser yet. The market in western land sales also heated up. In 1834, about 4.5 million acres of the public domain had been sold, the highest annual volume since 1818. By 1836, the total reached an astonishing 20 million acres (**Figure 11.1**).

In one respect, the economy attained an admirable goal: The national debt disappeared, and from 1835 to 1837, for the only time in American history, the government had a monetary surplus. But much of that surplus consisted of questionable bank currencies — "bloated, diseased" currencies, in Jackson's vivid terminology. While the boom was on, however, few stopped to worry about the consequences if and when the bubble burst.

> ## QUICK REVIEW

What were the most significant policies of Andrew Jackson's presidency?

CHAPTER LOCATOR | Why did the United States experience a market revolution after 1815? | Why did Andrew Jackson defeat John Quincy Adams so dramatically in the 1828 election?

How did social and cultural life change in the 1830s?

Images of the Family at Home

Hundreds of itinerant amateur artists journeyed the back roads and small villages of antebellum America, earning a modest living painting individuals and families. This picture from the 1830s exhibits a common convention — the arrangement of family members by age and by sex, as if to emphasize the ideal of separate spheres. Museum of Fine Arts, Boston, Gift of Maxim Karolik for the M. and M. Karolik Collection of American Watercolors and Drawings, 1800–1875.

THE GROWING ECONOMY, booming by the mid-1830s, transformed social and cultural life. For many families, especially in the commercialized Northeast, standards of living rose, consumption patterns changed, and the nature and location of work were altered. All this had a direct impact on the duties of men and women and on the training of youths for the economy of the future.

Along with economic change came an unprecedented revival of evangelical religion known as the Second Great Awakening. Among the most serious adherents of evangelical Protestantism were men and women of the new merchant classes. Not content with individual perfection, many of these people sought to perfect society as well, by defining excessive alcohol consumption, nonmarital sex, and slavery as three major evils of modern life in need of correction. Three social movements championing temperance, moral reform, and abolition gained strength from evangelistic Christianity.

The Family and Separate Spheres

The centerpiece of new ideas about gender relations was the notion that husbands found their status and authority in the new world of work, leaving wives to tend the hearth and home. Sermons, advice books, periodicals, and novels reinforced the idea that men and women inhabited separate spheres and had separate duties. "To woman it belongs . . . to elevate the intellectual character of her household [and] to kindle the fires of mental activity in childhood," wrote Mrs. A. J. Graves in a popular book titled *Advice to American Women*. For men, by contrast, "the absorbing passion for gain, and the pressing demands of business, engross their whole attention."

| What was Andrew Jackson's impact on the presidency? | **How did social and cultural life change in the 1830s?** | Why was Martin Van Buren a one-term president? | Conclusion: The Age of Jackson or the era of reform? | ☑ LearningCurve Check what you know. bedfordstmartins.com /roarkunderstanding |

313

> CHRONOLOGY

1817
– American Colonization Society is founded.

1826
– American Temperance Society is founded.

1829
– David Walker publishes *An Appeal . . . to the Coloured Citizens of the World.*

1830–1831
– Charles Grandison Finney preaches in Rochester, New York.

1831
– William Lloyd Garrison starts *Liberator*.

1832
– New England Anti-Slavery Society is founded.

1833
– New York and Philadelphia antislavery societies are founded.
– New York Female Moral Reform Society is founded.

1836
– American Temperance Union is founded.

In particular, the home, now said to be the exclusive domain of women, was sentimentalized as the source of intimacy, love, and safety, a refuge from the cruel and competitive world of market relations.

Some new aspects of society gave substance to this formulation of separate spheres. Men's work was undergoing profound change after 1815 and increasingly brought cash to the household, especially in the manufacturing and urban Northeast. Farmers and tradesmen sold products in a market, and bankers, bookkeepers, shoemakers, and canal diggers earned regular salaries or wages. Furthermore, many men now worked away from the home, at an office or a store.

A woman's domestic role was more complicated than the cultural prescriptions indicated. Although the vast majority of married white women did not hold paying jobs, their homes required time-consuming labor. But the advice books treated housework as a loving familial duty, thus rendering it invisible in an economy that evaluated work by how much cash it generated. In reality, many wives contributed to family income by taking in boarders or sewing for pay. Wives in the poorest classes, including most free black wives, did not have the luxury of husbands earning adequate wages; for them, work as servants or laundresses helped augment family income.

Idealized notions about the feminine home and the masculine workplace gained acceptance in the 1830s because of the cultural ascendancy of the commercialized Northeast, with its domination of book and periodical publishing. Beyond white families of the middle and upper classes, however, these new gender ideals had limited applicability. Despite their apparent authority in printed material of the period, these gender ideals were never all-pervasive.

The Education and Training of Youths

The market economy required expanded opportunities for training youths of both sexes. By the 1830s, in both the North and the South, state-supported public school systems were the norm, designed to produce pupils of both sexes able, by age twelve to fourteen, to read, write, and participate in marketplace calculations. Literacy rates for white females climbed dramatically, rivaling the rates for white males for the first time. The fact that taxpayers paid for children's education created an incentive to seek an inexpensive teaching force. By the 1830s, school districts replaced male teachers with young females, for, as a Massachusetts report on education put it, "females can be educated cheaper, quicker, and better, and will teach cheaper after they are qualified."

Advanced education continued to expand in the 1830s, with an additional two dozen colleges for men and several more female seminaries offering education on a par with the male colleges. Still, only a very small percentage of young people attended institutions of higher learning. The vast majority of male youths left public school at age fourteen to apprentice in specific trades or to embark on business careers by seeking entry-level clerkships, abundant in the growing urban centers. Young women headed for mill towns or cities in unprecedented numbers, seeking work in the expanding service sector as seamstresses and domestic servants. Changes in patterns of youth employment meant that large numbers of youngsters escaped the watchful eyes of their parents, a cause of great concern for moralists of the era. Advice books published by the hundreds instructed youths in the virtues of hard work and delayed gratification.

CHAPTER LOCATOR | Why did the United States experience a market revolution after 1815? | Why did Andrew Jackson defeat John Quincy Adams so dramatically in the 1828 election?

314 CHAPTER 11 THE EXPANDING REPUBLIC

The Second Great Awakening

A newly invigorated version of Protestantism gained momentum in the 1820s and 1830s as the economy reshaped gender and age relations. The earliest manifestations of this fervent piety, which historians call the **Second Great Awakening**, appeared in 1801 in Kentucky, when a crowd of ten thousand people camped out on a hillside at Cane Ridge for a revival meeting that lasted several weeks. By the 1810s and 1820s, "camp meetings" had spread to the Atlantic seaboard states, accelerating and intensifying the emotional impact of the revival.

The gatherings attracted women and men hungry for a more immediate access to spiritual peace, one not requiring years of soul-searching. One eyewitness reported that "some of the people were singing, others praying, some crying for mercy. . . . At one time I saw at least five hundred swept down in a moment as if a battery of a thousand guns had been opened upon them, and then immediately followed shrieks and shouts that rent the very heavens."

From 1800 to 1820, church membership doubled in the United States, much of it among the evangelical groups. Methodists, Baptists, and Presbyterians formed the core of the new movement, which attracted women more than men; wives and mothers typically recruited husbands and sons to join them.

A central leader of the Second Great Awakening was a lawyer turned minister named Charles Grandison Finney. Finney lived in western New York, where the completion of the Erie Canal in 1825 fundamentally altered the social and economic landscape overnight. Growth and prosperity came with other, less admirable side effects, such as prostitution, drinking, and gaming. Finney saw New York canal towns as ripe for evangelical awakening. In Rochester, he sustained a six-month revival through the winter of 1830–31, generating thousands of converts.

Finney's message, directed primarily at the business classes, argued for a public-spirited outreach to the less-than-perfect to foster their salvation. Evangelicals promoted Sunday schools to bring piety to children; they battled to honor the Sabbath by ending mail delivery, stopping public transport, and closing shops on

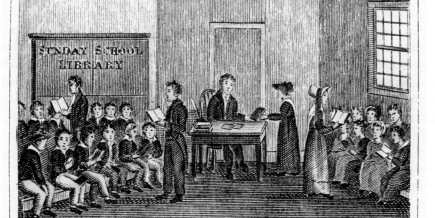

SUNDAY SCHOOL.

Sunday School

In the 1820s, free Sunday Schools for indigent children became a popular national movement, and by 1832 the American Sunday School Union formed to generate curriculum materials and provide volunteer teachers, both male and female, mainly from the newly awakened Protestant churches. Students, both white and free black, often worked six days a week, leaving only the Sabbath free for schooling. The Granger Collection, NYC.

What was Andrew Jackson's impact on the presidency?

How did social and cultural life change in the 1830s?

Why was Martin Van Buren a one-term president?

Conclusion: The Age of Jackson or the era of reform?

✔ LearningCurve
Check what you know.
bedfordstmartins.com
/roarkunderstanding

315

Sundays. Many women formed missionary societies that distributed millions of Bibles and religious tracts. Through such avenues, evangelical religion offered women expanded spheres of influence. Finney adopted the tactics of Jacksonian-era politicians—publicity, argumentation, rallies, and speeches—to sell his cause. His object, he said, was to get Americans to "vote in the Lord Jesus Christ as the governor of the Universe."

The Temperance Movement and the Campaign for Moral Reform

The evangelical fervor animated vigorous campaigns to eliminate alcohol abuse and eradicate sexual sin. Millions of Americans took the temperance pledge to abstain from strong drink, and thousands became involved in efforts to end prostitution.

Alcohol consumption had risen steadily in the decades up to 1830. All classes imbibed. A lively saloon culture fostered masculine camaraderie along with extensive alcohol consumption among laborers, while in elite homes the after-dinner whiskey or sherry was commonplace. Colleges before 1820 routinely served students a pint of ale with meals, and the military included rum in the daily ration.

Organized opposition to drinking first surfaced in the 1810s among health and religious reformers. In 1826, Lyman Beecher, a Connecticut minister of an "awakened" church, founded the **American Temperance Society**, which warned that drinking led to poverty, idleness, crime, and family violence. Temperance lecturers spread the word, and middle-class drinking began a steep decline. One powerful tool of persuasion was the temperance pledge, which many business owners began to require of employees.

In 1836, leaders of the temperance movement regrouped into a new society, the American Temperance Union, which demanded total abstinence from its adherents. The intensified war against alcohol moved beyond individual moral suasion into the realm of politics as reformers sought to deny taverns liquor licenses. By 1845, temperance advocates had put an impressive dent in alcohol consumption, which diminished to one-quarter of the per capita consumption of 1830.

More controversial than temperance was a social movement called "moral reform," which first aimed at public morals in general but quickly narrowed to a campaign to eradicate sexual sin. In 1833, a group of Finneyite women started the **New York Female Moral Reform Society**. Its members insisted that uncontrolled male sexual expression, manifested in seduction and prostitution, posed a serious threat to society in general and to women in particular. Within five years, more than four thousand auxiliary groups of women had sprung up, mostly in New England, New York, Pennsylvania, and Ohio.

In its analysis of the causes of licentiousness and its conviction that women had a duty to speak out about unspeakable things, the Moral Reform Society pushed the limits of what even the men in the evangelical movement could tolerate. Yet these women did not regard themselves as radicals. They were simply pursuing the logic of a gender system that defined home protection and morality as women's special sphere and a religious conviction that called for the eradication of sin.

American Temperance Society

▶ Organization founded in 1826 by Lyman Beecher that linked drinking with poverty, idleness, ill health, and violence. Temperance lecturers traveled the country gaining converts to the cause. The temperance movement had considerable success, contributing to a sharp drop in American alcohol consumption.

New York Female Moral Reform Society

▶ An organization of religious women inspired by the Second Great Awakening to eradicate sexual sin and male licentiousness. Formed in 1833, it spread to hundreds of auxiliaries and worked to curb male licentiousness, prostitution, and seduction.

CHAPTER LOCATOR | Why did the United States experience a market revolution after 1815? | Why did Andrew Jackson defeat John Quincy Adams so dramatically in the 1828 election?

Organizing against Slavery

More radical still was the movement in the 1830s to abolish the sin of slavery. Previously, the American Colonization Society, founded in 1817 by Maryland and Virginia planters, promoted gradual individual emancipation of slaves followed by colonization in Africa. By the early 1820s, several thousand ex-slaves had been transported to Liberia on the West African coast. But not surprisingly, newly freed men and women often were not eager to emigrate; their African roots were three or more generations in the past. Colonization was too gradual (and too expensive) to have much impact on American slavery.

Around 1830, northern challenges to slavery intensified, beginning in free black communities. In 1829, a Boston printer named David Walker published *An Appeal . . . to the Coloured Citizens of the World,* which condemned racism, invoked the egalitarian language of the Declaration of Independence, and hinted at racial violence if whites did not change their prejudiced ways. In 1830, at the inaugural National Negro Convention meeting in Philadelphia, forty blacks from nine states discussed the racism of American society and proposed emigration to Canada. In 1832 and 1833, a twenty-eight-year-old black woman named Maria Stewart delivered public lectures on slavery and racial prejudice to black audiences in Boston. Her lectures gained wider circulation when they were published in a national publication called the *Liberator.*

The *Liberator,* founded in 1831 in Boston, took antislavery agitation to new heights. Its founder and editor, William Lloyd Garrison, advocated immediate abolition: "On this subject, I do not wish to think, or speak, or write, with moderation. No! No! Tell a man whose house is on fire to give a moderate alarm; tell him to moderately rescue his wife from the hands of the ravisher; tell the mother to gradually extricate her babe from the fire into which it has fallen . . .—but urge me not to use moderation in a cause like the present." In 1832, Garrison's supporters started the New England Anti-Slavery Society.

Similar groups were organized in Philadelphia and New York in 1833. Soon a dozen antislavery newspapers and scores of antislavery lecturers were spreading

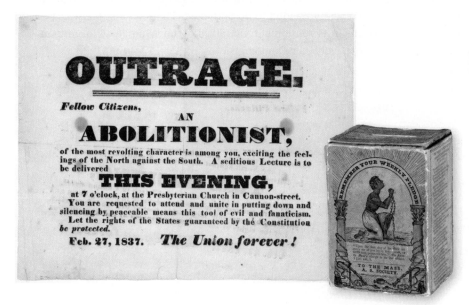

Controversy over Abolitionism

Mob violence erupted in northern cities with regularity when abolitionist speakers came to town. This 1837 poster from Poughkeepsie, New York, exemplifies the extremely inflammatory language that kindled riots. Antislavery societies raised money to support these lecture tours, one way being the weekly pledge. This contribution box is inscribed with biblical passages and the symbolic yet disturbing image of the slave in chains. Poster: Library of Congress; box: Boston Public Library/Rare Books Department—Courtesy of the Trustees.

What was Andrew Jackson's impact on the presidency?

How did social and cultural life change in the 1830s?

Why was Martin Van Buren a one-term president?

Conclusion: The Age of Jackson or the era of reform?

✓ LearningCurve
Check what you know.
bedfordstmartins.com /roarkunderstanding

317

the word and inspiring the formation of new local societies, which numbered 1,300 by 1837. Confined entirely to the North, their membership totaled a quarter of a million men and women.

Many white northerners, even those who opposed slavery, were not prepared to embrace the abolitionist call for emancipation. From 1834 to 1838, there were more than a hundred eruptions of serious mob violence against abolitionists and free blacks. In one incident, Illinois abolitionist editor Elijah Lovejoy was killed by a rioting crowd attempting to destroy his printing press. When Angelina and Sarah Grimké, sisters from South Carolina who opposed slavery, lectured in 1837, some authorities tried to intimidate them and deny them meeting space. The following year, rocks shattered windows when Angelina Grimké gave a speech at a female antislavery convention in Philadelphia. After the women vacated the building, a mob burned the building to the ground.

Despite these dangers, large numbers of northern women played a prominent role in abolition. They formed women's auxiliaries and held fairs to sell handmade crafts to support male lecturers in the field. They circulated antislavery petitions, presented to the U.S. Congress with tens of thousands of signatures. At first, women's petitions were framed as respectful memorials to Congress about the evils of slavery, but soon they demanded political action to end slavery in the District of Columbia, under Congress's jurisdiction.

By the late 1830s, the cause of abolition divided the nation as no other issue did. Even among abolitionists, significant divisions emerged. The Grimké sisters, radicalized by the public reaction to their speaking tour, began to write and speak about woman's rights. Angelina Grimké compared the silencing of women to the silencing of slaves: "The denial of our duty to act, is a bold denial of our right to act; and if we have no right to act, then may we well be termed 'the white slaves of the North'—for, like our brethren in bonds, we must seal our lips in silence and despair." The Grimkés were opposed by moderate abolitionists who were unwilling to mix the new and controversial issue of woman's rights with their first cause, the rights of blacks.

The many men and women active in reform movements in the 1830s found their initial inspiration in evangelical Protestantism's dual message: Salvation was open to all, and society needed to be perfected. Their activist mentality squared well with the interventionist tendencies of the Whig Party forming in opposition to Andrew Jackson's Democrats.

> **QUICK REVIEW**

How did evangelical Protestantism contribute to the reform movements of the 1830s?

CHAPTER LOCATOR | Why did the United States experience a market revolution after 1815? | Why did Andrew Jackson defeat John Quincy Adams so dramatically in the 1828 election?

318 CHAPTER 11
THE EXPANDING REPUBLIC

Why was Martin Van Buren a one-term president?

Panic of 1837 Cartoon A sad family with an unemployed father faces sudden hardship in this cartoon showing the consequences of the panic of 1837. The wife and children complain of hunger, the house is stripped nearly bare, and rent collectors loom in the doorway. Faint pictures on the wall show Andrew Jackson and Martin Van Buren presiding over the economic devastation of the family. Library of Congress.

BY THE MID-1830s, a vibrant and tumultuous political culture occupied center stage in American life. Andrew Jackson, too ill to stand for a third term, made way for Martin Van Buren, who faced tough opposition from an array of opposing Whigs and even from slave-owning Jacksonians. Van Buren was a skilled politician, but soon after his inauguration the country faced economic collapse. A shattering panic in 1837, followed by another in 1839, brought the country its worst economic depression yet.

| What was Andrew Jackson's impact on the presidency? | How did social and cultural life change in the 1830s? | **Why was Martin Van Buren a one-term president?** | Conclusion: The Age of Jackson or the era of reform? | ✓ **LearningCurve** Check what you know. bedfordstmartins.com /roarkunderstanding |

> CHRONOLOGY

1835
- Abolitionist literature is burned in Charleston, South Carolina.

1836
- Martin Van Buren is elected president.
- Congress institutes "gag rule" against antislavery petitions.

1837
- Economic panic.

1839
- Economic panic.

1840
- William Henry Harrison is elected president.

The Politics of Slavery

Sophisticated party organization was the specialty of Martin Van Buren, nick-named "the Little Magician" for his consummate political skills. First a senator and then a governor, the New Yorker became Jackson's secretary of state and then his running mate in 1832, replacing John C. Calhoun. His eight years in the volatile Jackson administration required the full measure of his political deftness as he sought repeatedly to save Jackson from both his enemies and his own obstinacy.

Jackson clearly favored Van Buren for the nomination in 1836, but starting in 1832, the major political parties had developed nominating conventions to choose their candidates. In 1835, Van Buren got the convention nod unanimously, to the dismay of his archrival, Calhoun, who then worked to discredit Van Buren among southern proslavery Democrats. Van Buren spent months assuring them that he was a "northern man with southern principles." This was a credible line, since his Dutch family hailed from the Hudson River counties where New York slavery had once flourished, and his own family had owned slaves as late as the 1810s, permitted under New York's gradual emancipation law.

Calhoun was able to stir up trouble for Van Buren because southerners were becoming increasingly alarmed by the rise of northern antislavery sentiment. When, in late 1835, abolitionists prepared to circulate in the South a million pamphlets condemning slavery, a mailbag of their literature was hijacked at the post office in Charleston, South Carolina, and ceremoniously burned along with effigies of leading abolitionists. President Jackson condemned the theft but issued approval for individual postmasters to exercise their own judgment about whether to allow incendiary materials to reach their destination. Abolitionists saw this as censorship of the mail.

The petitioning tactics of abolitionists escalated sectional tensions. When hundreds of antislavery petitions inundated Congress, proslavery congressmen responded by passing a "gag rule" in 1836. The gag rule prohibited entering the documents into the public record on the grounds that what the abolitionists prayed for was unconstitutional and, further, an assault on the rights of white southerners, as one South Carolina representative put it. Abolitionists like the Grimké sisters considered the gag rule to be an abridgment of free speech. They also argued that, tabled or not, the petitions were effective. "The South already turns pale at the number sent," Angelina Grimké said in a speech exhorting more petitions to be circulated.

Van Buren shrewdly seized on both mail censorship and the gag rule to express his prosouthern sympathies. Abolitionists were "fanatics," he repeatedly claimed, possibly under the influence of "foreign agents" (British abolitionists). He dismissed the issue of abolition in the District of Columbia as "inexpedient" and promised that if he was elected president, he would not allow any interference in southern "domestic institutions."

Elections and Panics

Although the elections of 1824, 1828, and 1832 clearly bore the stamp of Jackson's personality, by 1836 the party apparatus was sufficiently developed to give Van Buren, a backroom politician, a shot at the presidency. Local and state committees

CHAPTER LOCATOR | Why did the United States experience a market revolution after 1815? | Why did Andrew Jackson defeat John Quincy Adams so dramatically in the 1828 election?

existed throughout the country, and more than four hundred newspapers were Democratic partisans.

The Whigs had also built state-level organizations and newspaper loyalty. They had no top contender with nationwide support, so three regional candidates opposed Van Buren. Senator Daniel Webster of Massachusetts could deliver New England, home to reformers, merchants, and manufacturers; Senator Hugh Lawson White of Tennessee attracted proslavery voters still suspicious of the northern Magician; and the aging General William Henry Harrison, now residing in Ohio and remembered for his Indian war heroics in 1811, pulled in the western anti-Indian vote. Not one of the three candidates had the ability to win the presidency, but together they came close to denying Van Buren a majority vote. Van Burenites called the three-Whig strategy a deliberate plot to derail the election and move it to the House of Representatives.

In the end, Van Buren won with 170 electoral votes, while the other three received a total of 113. But Van Buren's victories came from narrow majorities, far below those Jackson had commanded. Although Van Buren had pulled together a national Democratic Party with wins in both the North and the South, he had done it at the cost of committing northern Democrats to the proslavery agenda. And running three candidates had maximized the Whigs' success by drawing Whigs into office at the state level.

When Van Buren took office in March 1837, the financial markets were already quaking; by April, the country was plunged into crisis. The causes of the **panic of 1837** were multiple and far-ranging.

panic of 1837
▶ Major economic crisis that led to several years of hard times in the United States from 1837 to 1841. Sudden bankruptcies, contraction of credit, and runs on banks worked hardships nationwide. The causes were multiple and global and not well understood.

> Causes of the Panic of 1837

- Bad harvests in Europe and a large trade imbalance between Britain and the United States caused the Bank of England to start calling in loans to American merchants.
- Failures in various crop markets and a 30 percent downturn in international cotton prices contributed to the growing disaster.
- Cotton merchants in the South could no longer meet their obligations to New York creditors, whose firms began to fail.
- Frightened citizens quickly tried to withdraw their money from the banks.
- Businesses rushed to liquefy their remaining assets to pay off debts.

The prices of stocks, bonds, and real estate fell 30 to 40 percent. The familiar events of the panic of 1819 unfolded again, with terrifying rapidity, and the credit market tumbled like a house of cards. Newspapers describing the economic free fall generally used the language of emotional states—excitement, anxiety, terror, panic. Such words focused on human reactions to the crisis rather than on the structural features of the economy that had interacted to amplify the downturn. The vocabulary for understanding the wider economy was still quite limited, making it hard to track the bigger picture of the workings of capitalism.

Instead, many observers looked to politics, religion, and character flaws to explain the crisis. Some Whig leaders were certain that Jackson's antibank and hard-money policies were responsible for the ruin. New Yorker Philip Hone, a wealthy Whig, called the Jackson administration "the most disastrous in the

What was Andrew Jackson's impact on the presidency?

How did social and cultural life change in the 1830s?

Why was Martin Van Buren a one-term president?

Conclusion: The Age of Jackson or the era of reform?

✓ LearningCurve
Check what you know.
bedfordstmartins.com
/roarkunderstanding

321

annals of the country" for its "wicked interference" in banking and monetary matters. Others framed the devastation as retribution for the frenzy of speculation that had gripped the nation. A religious periodical in Boston hoped that Americans would now moderate their greed: "We were getting to think that there was no end to the wealth, and could be no check to the progress of our country; that economy was not needed, that prudence was weakness." In this view, the panic was a wakeup call, a blessing in disguise. Others identified the competitive, profit-maximizing capitalist system as the cause and looked to Britain and France for new socialist ideas calling for the common ownership of the means of production. American socialists, though few in number, were vocal and imaginative, and in the early 1840s several thousand developed utopian alternative communities (as discussed in chapter 12).

The panic of 1837 subsided by 1838, but in 1839 another run on the banks and ripples of business failures deflated the economy, creating a second panic. President Van Buren called a special session of Congress to consider creating an independent treasury system to perform some of the functions of the defunct Bank of the United States. Such a system, funded by government deposits, would deal only in hard money and would exert a powerful moderating influence on inflation and the credit market. But Van Buren encountered strong resistance in Congress, even among Democrats. The treasury system finally won approval in 1840, but by then Van Buren's chances of winning a second term in office were virtually nil.

In 1840, the Whigs settled on William Henry Harrison to oppose Van Buren. The campaign drew on voter involvement as no other presidential campaign ever had. The Whigs borrowed tricks from the Democrats: Harrison was touted as a common man born in a log cabin (in reality, he was born on a Virginia plantation), and campaign parades featured toy log cabins held aloft. His Indian-fighting days, now thirty years behind him, were played up to give him a Jacksonian aura. Whigs staged festive rallies around the country, drumming up mass appeal with candlelight parades and song shows, and women participated in rallies as never before. Some 78 percent of eligible voters cast ballots—the highest percentage ever in American history.

Harrison took 53 percent of the popular vote and won a resounding 234 electoral college votes to Van Buren's 60. A Democratic editor lamented, "We have taught them how to conquer us!"

> ## QUICK REVIEW

What were the most significant issues of Martin Van Buren's presidency?

CHAPTER LOCATOR | Why did the United States experience a market revolution after 1815? | Why did Andrew Jackson defeat John Quincy Adams so dramatically in the 1828 election?

322   CHAPTER 11
THE EXPANDING REPUBLIC

ECONOMIC TRANSFORMATIONS LOOM large in explaining the fast-paced changes of the 1830s. Transportation advances put goods and people in circulation, augmenting urban growth and helping to create a national culture, and water-powered manufacturing began to change the face of wage labor. Trade and banking mushroomed, and western land once occupied by Indians was auctioned off in a landslide of sales. Two periods of economic downturn—including the panic of 1819 and the panics of 1837 and 1839—offered sobering lessons about speculative fever.

Andrew Jackson symbolized this age of opportunity for many. His fame as an aggressive general, an Indian fighter, a champion of the common man, and a defender of slavery attracted growing numbers of voters to the emergent Democratic Party, which championed personal liberty, free competition, and egalitarian opportunity for all white men.

Jackson's constituency was challenged by a small but vocal segment of the population troubled by serious moral problems that Jacksonians preferred to ignore. Inspired by the Second Great Awakening, reformers targeted personal vices (illicit sex and intemperance) and social problems (prostitution, poverty, and slavery) and joined forces with evangelicals and wealthy lawyers and merchants (in both the North and the South) who appreciated a national bank and protective tariffs. The Whig Party was the party of activist moralism and state-sponsored entrepreneurship. Whig voters were, of course, male, but thousands of reform-minded women broke new ground by signing political petitions on the issues of Indian removal and slavery. A few exceptional women, like Sarah and Angelina Grimké, captured the national limelight by offering powerful testimony against slavery and in the process pioneering new pathways for women to contribute a moral voice to politics.

National politics in the 1830s were more divisive than at any time since the 1790s. The new party system of Democrats and Whigs reached far deeper into the electorate than had the Federalists and Republicans. Stagecoaches and steamboats carried newspapers from the cities to the backwoods, politicizing voters and creating party loyalty. Politics acquired immediacy and excitement, causing nearly four out of five white men to cast ballots in 1840.

High rates of voter participation would continue into the 1840s and 1850s. Unprecedented urban growth, westward expansion, and early industrialism marked those decades, sustaining the Democrat-Whig split in the electorate. But critiques of slavery, concerns for free labor, and an emerging protest against women's second-class citizenship complicated the political scene of the 1840s, leading to third-party political movements. One of these third parties, called the Republican Party, would achieve dominance in 1860 with the election of an Illinois lawyer, Abraham Lincoln, to the presidency.

What was Andrew Jackson's impact on the presidency?

How did social and cultural life change in the 1830s?

Why was Martin Van Buren a one-term president?

Conclusion: The Age of Jackson or the era of reform?

LearningCurve
Check what you know.
bedfordstmartins.com/roarkunderstanding

CHAPTER 11 STUDY GUIDE

 STEP 1 GET STARTED ONLINE

 LearningCurve ▪ bedfordstmartins.com/roarkunderstanding

Now that you've read the chapter, make it stick by completing the LearningCurve activity.

STEP 2 EXPLAIN WHY IT MATTERS

Put your reading into practice. Identify each term below, and then explain why it matters in U.S. history.

TERM	WHO OR WHAT & WHEN	WHY IT MATTERS
Erie Canal (p. 298)		
Lowell mills (p. 299)		
second Bank of the United States (p. 301)		
Whigs (p. 304)		
Democrats (p. 304)		
Indian Removal Act of 1830 (p. 308)		
Trail of Tears (p. 310)		
nullification (p. 310)		
Second Great Awakening (p. 315)		
American Temperance Society (p. 316)		
New York Female Moral Reform Society (p. 316)		
panic of 1837 (p. 321)		

STEP 3 MOVE BEYOND THE BASICS

To demonstrate a more advanced understanding, consider change over time as it affected the American economy, politics, society, and culture. What was the relationship between each of the developments?

	1815	1830–1840
Transportation		
Industry and labor		
Economy		
Politics		
Social reform and cultural developments		

STEP 4 PUT IT ALL TOGETHER

Now, take a step back and try to explain the big picture. Remember to use specific examples from the chapter in your answers.

THE MARKET REVOLUTION

▶ Why were improvements in transportation so crucial to America's economic growth and development in the early nineteenth century?

▶ What changes in workers' lives and status accompanied industrialization?

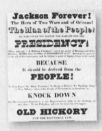

THE AGE OF JACKSON

▶ What does Andrew Jackson's rise to the presidency tell us about popular politics in the 1820s?

▶ How did Andrew Jackson change the presidency? How did he see and manipulate the relationship among the president, Congress, and the courts?

THE ERA OF REFORM

▶ How did the Second Great Awakening lead to a variety of social reform movements? What impact did these various reform movements have on politics and society in the 1830s?

▶ What role did women play in the reform movements of the early nineteenth century?

LOOKING BACKWARD, LOOKING AHEAD

▶ How did the second American party system differ from the first party system? How did it differ from the partisanship of the 1790s?

▶ How do the reform movements of the 1820s and 1830s shed light on the causes of the sectional tensions that would dominate the 1840s and 1850s?

> ## IN YOUR OWN WORDS

Imagine that you must give an oral report to the class answering the following question: What were the most important causes and consequences of the market revolution from 1815 to 1840? What would be the most important points to include and why?

 Do it online at the Student Site ▪ bedfordstmartins.com/roarkunderstanding

12

THE NEW WEST AND THE FREE NORTH

1840–1860

> **How was freedom defined in the North and West in the mid-nineteenth century?**

Chapter 12 focuses on how the concept of freedom helped shape economics, politics, and social reform. It explores the factors that propelled American economic growth, territorial expansion, political debate, and social reform. It also examines the growing tensions between the ideology of free labor and slavery.

LearningCurve

bedfordstmartins.com/roarkunderstanding
After reading the chapter, use LearningCurve to retain what you've read.

Westward the Star of Empire Takes Its Way. Artist Andrew Melrose depicted a mid-nineteenth-century landscape of agricultural and technological progress. Museum of the American West, Autry National Center, 92.147.1.

> What factors contributed to the United States' "industrial evolution"?

> How did the free-labor ideal account for economic inequality?

> What factors spurred westward expansion?

> Why did the United States go to war with Mexico?

> How did reform movements change after 1840?

> Conclusion: How was white freedom in the West and North defined?

> What factors contributed to the United States' "industrial evolution"?

Harvesting Grain with Cradles This late-nineteenth-century painting shows a grain harvest during the mid-nineteenth century at Bishop Hill, Illinois, a Swedish community where the artist, Olof Krans, and his parents settled in 1850. The men swing cradles, slowly cutting a swath through the grain; the women gather the cut grain into sheaves to be hauled away later for threshing. Although most Bishop Hill farmers had only a few family members and a hired hand or two, they could call upon the labor of the many men and women from the community at harvest time. Notice that all the work is done by hand; there is no machine in sight. Private Collection/Art Resource, NY.

DURING THE 1840S AND 1850S, Americans experienced a profound economic transformation. Since 1800, the total output of the U.S. economy had multiplied twelvefold. Four fundamental changes in American society fueled this remarkable economic growth.

> Changes That Led to Economic Growth

- Millions of Americans moved from farms to towns and cities.
- Factory workers (primarily in towns and cities) increased to about 20 percent of the labor force by 1860.
- A shift from water power to steam as a source of energy raised productivity, especially in factories and transportation. Railroads in particular harnessed steam power, speeding transport and cutting costs.
- Agricultural productivity nearly doubled between 1800 and 1860, spurring the nation's economic growth more than any other factor.

Historians often refer to this cascade of changes as an industrial revolution. However, these changes did not cause an abrupt discontinuity in America's economy or society, which remained overwhelmingly agricultural. Old methods of production continued alongside the new. The changes in the American economy during the 1840s and 1850s might better be termed "industrial evolution."

CHAPTER LOCATOR | **What factors contributed to the United States' "industrial evolution"?** | How did the free-labor ideal account for economic inequality?

CHAPTER 12
328 THE NEW WEST AND THE FREE NORTH

Agriculture and Land Policy

The foundation of the United States' economic growth lay in agriculture. As farmers pushed westward in a quest for cheap land, they encountered the Midwest's comparatively treeless prairie, where they could spend less time clearing land and more time with a plow and hoe. Rich prairie soils yielded bumper crops, enticing farmers to migrate to the Midwest by the tens of thousands between 1830 and 1860.

Laborsaving improvements in farm implements also boosted agricultural productivity. Inventors tinkered to craft stronger, more efficient plows. In 1837, John Deere made a strong, smooth steel plow that sliced through prairie soil so cleanly that farmers called it the "singing plow." Deere's company produced more than ten thousand plows a year by the late 1850s. Human and animal muscles provided the energy for plowing, but Deere's plows permitted farmers to break more ground and plant more crops.

Improvements in wheat harvesting also increased farmers' productivity. In 1850, most farmers harvested wheat by hand, cutting two or three acres a day. In the 1840s, Cyrus McCormick and others experimented with designs for **mechanical reapers**, and by the 1850s a McCormick reaper that cost between $100 and $150 allowed a farmer to harvest twelve acres a day. Improved reapers and plows allowed farmers to cultivate more land, doubling the corn and wheat harvests between 1840 and 1860.

Federal land policy made possible the leap in agricultural productivity. Up to 1860, the United States continued to be land-rich and labor-poor. Territorial acquisitions made the nation a great deal richer in land, adding more than a billion acres with the Louisiana Purchase (see chapter 10) and vast territories following the Mexican-American War. The federal government made most of this land available for purchase to attract settlers and to generate revenue. Millions of ordinary farmers bought federal land for just $1.25 an acre, or $50 for a forty-acre farm that could support a family. Millions of other farmers squatted on unclaimed federal land and carved out farms. By making land available on relatively easy terms, federal land policy boosted the increase in agricultural productivity that fueled the nation's impressive economic growth.

Manufacturing and Mechanization

Changes in manufacturing arose from the nation's land-rich, labor-poor economy. Western expansion and government land policies buoyed agriculture, keeping millions of people on the farm — 80 percent of the nation's 31 million people lived in rural areas in 1860 — and thereby limiting the supply of workers for manufacturing and elevating wages. Because of this relative shortage of workers, American manufacturers searched constantly for ways to save labor.

Mechanization allowed manufacturers to produce more with less labor. In general, factory workers produced twice as much (per unit of labor) as agricultural workers. The practice of manufacturing and then assembling interchangeable parts spread from gun making to other industries and became known as the **American system**. Using standardized parts produced by machine allowed manufacturers to employ unskilled workers, whose wages were much lower than those of highly trained craftsmen.

Manufacturing and agriculture meshed into a dynamic national economy. New England led the nation in manufacturing, shipping goods such as guns, clocks, plows, and axes west and south, while southern and western states sent

> **CHRONOLOGY**

1837
– Steel plow is patented.

1840s
– Practical mechanical reapers are created.

1844
– Samuel F. B. Morse demonstrates telegraph.

1850
– Railroads are granted six square miles of land for every mile of track.

1861
– California is connected to the nation by telegraph.

mechanical reapers
▶ Tools usually powered by horses or oxen that enabled farmers to harvest twelve acres of wheat a day, compared with the two or three acres a day possible with manual harvesting methods.

American system
▶ The practice of manufacturing and then assembling interchangeable parts. A system that spread quickly across American industries, the use of standardized parts allowed American manufacturers to employ unskilled workers at low wages.

What factors spurred westward expansion?

Why did the United States go to war with Mexico?

How did reform movements change after 1840?

Conclusion: How was white freedom in the West and North defined?

☑ LearningCurve
Check what you know.
bedfordstmartins.com /roarkunderstanding

329

commodities such as wheat, pork, whiskey, tobacco, and cotton north and east. Between 1840 and 1860, coal production in Pennsylvania, Ohio, and elsewhere multiplied eightfold, cutting prices in half and powering innumerable coal-fired steam engines. Nonetheless, by 1860 coal accounted for less than a fifth of the nation's energy consumption, and even in manufacturing, muscles provided thirty times more energy than steam did.

American manufacturers specialized in producing for the gigantic domestic market rather than for export. British goods dominated the international market and usually were cheaper and better than American-made products. U.S. manufacturers supported tariffs to minimize British competition, but their best protection from British competitors was to please their American customers, most of them farmers. The burgeoning national economy was accelerated by the growth of railroads, which linked farmers and factories in new ways.

Railroads: Breaking the Bonds of Nature

Railroads captured Americans' imagination because they seemed to break the bonds of nature. When canals and rivers froze in winter or became impassable during summer droughts, trains steamed ahead, averaging more than twenty miles an hour during the 1850s. Above all, railroads gave cities not blessed with canals or navigable rivers a way to compete for rural trade.

In 1850, trains steamed along 9,000 miles of track, almost two-thirds of it in New England and the Middle Atlantic states. By 1860, several railroads spanned the Mississippi River, connecting frontier farmers to the nation's 30,000 miles of track, approximately as much as in all of the rest of the world combined (**Map 12.1**).

In addition to speeding transportation, railroads propelled the growth of other industries, such as iron and communications. Iron production grew five times faster than the population during the decades up to 1860, in part to meet railroads' demand. Railroads also stimulated the fledgling telegraph industry. In 1844, Samuel F. B. Morse demonstrated the potential of his telegraph by transmitting an electronic message between Washington, D.C., and Baltimore. By 1861, more than fifty thousand miles of telegraph wire stretched across the continent to the Pacific Ocean, often alongside railroad tracks, accelerating communications of all sorts.

In contrast to the government ownership of railroads common in other industrial nations, private corporations built and owned almost all American railroads. But the railroads received massive government aid, especially federal land grants. Up to 1850, the federal government had granted a total of seven million acres of federal land to various turnpike, highway, and canal projects. In 1850, Congress approved a precedent-setting grant to railroads of six square miles of federal land for each mile of track laid. By 1860, Congress had granted railroads more than twenty million acres of federal land, thereby underwriting construction costs and promoting the expansion of the rail network, the settlement of federal land, and the integration of the domestic market.

The railroad boom of the 1850s signaled the growing industrial might of the American economy. Like other industries, railroads succeeded because they served both farms and cities. But transportation was not revolutionized overnight. Most Americans in 1860 were still far more familiar with horses than with locomotives.

The economy of the 1840s and 1850s linked an expanding, westward-moving population in farms and cities with muscles, animals, machines, steam, and

The Telegraph

Samuel F. B. Morse is credited with inventing the telegraph because of his patent in June 1840, but, as one contemporary observed, Morse's talent consisted of "combining and applying the discoveries of others in the invention of a particular instrument and process for telegraphic purposes." Morse sent the first message in 1844 on this telegraph using a code he devised that represented each letter and number with dots and dashes.
Division of Political History, Smithsonian Institution, Washington, D.C.

MAP 12.1 ■ Railroads in 1860

Railroads were a crucial component of the revolutions in transportation and communications that transformed nineteenth-century America. The railroad system reflected the differences in the economies of the North and South.

> MAP ACTIVITY

READING THE MAP: In which sections of the country was most of the railroad track laid by the middle of the nineteenth century? What cities served as the busiest railroad hubs?

CONNECTIONS: How did the expansion of railroad networks affect the American economy? Why was the U.S. government willing to grant more than twenty million acres of public land to the private corporations that ran the railroads?

railroads. Abraham Lincoln planted corn and split fence rails as a young man before he moved to Springfield, Illinois, and became a successful attorney who defended, among others, railroad corporations. His mobility — westward, from farm to city, from manual to mental labor, and upward — illustrated the direction of economic change and the opportunities that beckoned enterprising individuals.

QUICK REVIEW

Why did the United States become a leading industrial power in the nineteenth century?

What factors spurred westward expansion?	Why did the United States go to war with Mexico?	How did reform movements change after 1840?	Conclusion: How was white freedom in the West and North defined?	LearningCurve Check what you know. bedfordstmartins.com /roarkunderstanding

> How did the free-labor ideal account for economic inequality?

A German Immigrant in New York

This 1855 painting depicts a German immigrant in New York City asking directions from an African American man who is cutting firewood. Like many other German immigrants, the man shown here appears relatively well off. Compare his clothing with that of the sawyer and the white laborer on the right. The German appears to be speaking respectfully to the black sawyer, suggesting that he did not fully share assumptions of white supremacy common among native-born white working men. North Carolina Museum of Art, Raleigh, purchased with funds from the State of North Carolina (52.9.2).

> KEY FACTORS

1840s–1850s
- Free-labor ideal developed to describe the economic and social successes and shortcomings in the North and West.
- Almost 4.5 million immigrants arrived in the United States, three-fourths of them from Ireland and Germany.

THE NATION'S IMPRESSIVE economic performance did not reward all Americans equally. Native-born white men tended to do better than immigrants. With few exceptions, women were excluded from opportunities open to men. Tens of thousands of women worked as seamstresses, laundresses, domestic servants, factory hands, and teachers but had little opportunity to aspire to higher-paying jobs. In the North and West, slavery was slowly eliminated in the half century after the American Revolution, but most free African Americans were relegated to dead-end jobs as laborers and servants. Discrimination against immigrants, women, and free blacks did not trouble most white men. With certain notable exceptions, they considered it proper and just, the outcome of the free-labor system that rewarded hard work and, ideally, education.

CHAPTER LOCATOR | What factors contributed to the United States' "industrial evolution"? | **How did the free-labor ideal account for economic inequality?**

332 CHAPTER 12 THE NEW WEST AND THE FREE NORTH

The Free-Labor Ideal

During the 1840s and 1850s, leaders throughout the North and West emphasized a set of ideas that seemed to explain why the changes under way in their society benefited some people more than others. They referred again and again to the advantages of what they termed *free labor*. (The word *free* referred to laborers who were not slaves. It did not mean laborers who worked for nothing.) By the 1850s, free-labor ideas described a social and economic ideal that accounted for both the successes and the shortcomings of the economy and society taking shape in the North and West.

> ## > The Free-Labor Ideology
>
> - Hard work, self-reliance, and independence were highly valued.
> - Self-made men had a chance at success.
> - Free labor benefited farmers and artisans as well as wageworkers.
> - The free-labor ideal affirmed an egalitarian vision of human potential.
> - This ideology inspired calls for universal public education for young children throughout the North and West.

In rural areas, where the labor of children was more difficult to spare, schools typically enrolled no more than half the school-age children. Textbooks and teachers — most of whom were young women — drummed into students the valued traits of the free-labor system: self-reliance, discipline, and, above all else, hard work. "Remember that all the ignorance, degradation, and misery in the world is the result of indolence and vice," one textbook intoned. Both in and outside school, free-labor ideology emphasized labor as much as freedom.

Economic Inequality

The free-labor ideal made sense to many Americans, especially in the North and West, because it seemed to describe their own experiences. Abraham Lincoln frequently referred to his humble beginnings as a hired laborer and implicitly invited his listeners to consider how far he had come. In 1860, his assets of $17,000 easily placed him in the wealthiest 5 percent of the population. A few men became much richer. Most Americans, however, measured success in more modest terms. The average wealth of adult white men in the North in 1860 barely topped $2,000. Nearly half of American men had no wealth at all; about 60 percent owned no land. Because property possessed by married women was normally considered to belong to their husbands, women typically had less wealth than men. Free African Americans had still less; 90 percent of them were propertyless.

Free-labor spokesmen considered these economic inequalities a natural outgrowth of freedom — the inevitable result of some individuals being both luckier and more able and willing to work. These inequalities also demonstrate the gap between the promise and the performance of the free-labor ideal. Economic growth permitted many men to move from being landless squatters to landowning farmers and from being hired laborers to independent, self-employed producers. But many more Americans remained behind, landless and working for wages.

| What factors spurred westward expansion? | Why did the United States go to war with Mexico? | How did reform movements change after 1840? | Conclusion: How was white freedom in the West and North defined? | ✔ LearningCurve Check what you know. bedfordstmartins.com /roarkunderstanding |

333

Even those who realized their aspirations often had a precarious hold on their independence. Bad debts, market volatility, crop failure, sickness, or death could quickly eliminate a family's gains.

Seeking out new opportunities in pursuit of free-labor ideals created restless social and geographic mobility. While fortunate people such as Abraham Lincoln rose far beyond their social origins, others shared the misfortune of a merchant who, an observer noted, "has been on the sinking list all his life." In search of better prospects, roughly two-thirds of the rural population moved every decade, and population turnover in cities was even greater.

Immigrants and the Free-Labor Ladder

The risks and uncertainties of free labor did not deter millions of immigrants from entering the United States during the 1840s and 1850s. Almost 4.5 million immigrants arrived between 1840 and 1860, six times more than had come during the previous two decades (**Figure 12.1**). Nearly three-fourths of the immigrants who arrived in the United States between 1840 and 1860 came from either Germany or Ireland.

In America's labor-poor economy, Irish laborers could earn more in one day than they could in several weeks in Ireland. In America, one immigrant explained in 1853, there was "plenty of work and plenty of wages plenty to eat and no land lords thats enough what more does a man want." But many immigrants also craved respect and decent working conditions.

FIGURE 12.1 ■ Antebellum Immigration, 1840–1860

After increasing gradually for several decades, immigration shot up in the mid-1840s. Between 1848 and 1860, nearly 3.5 million immigrants entered the United States.

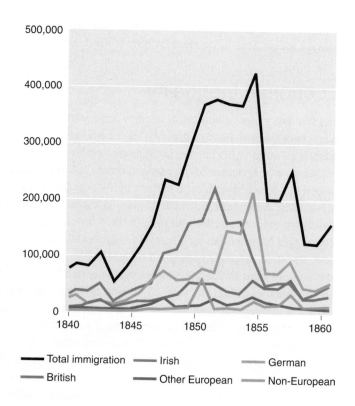

CHAPTER LOCATOR | What factors contributed to the United States' "industrial evolution"? | How did the free-labor ideal account for economic inequality?

334 CHAPTER 12
THE NEW WEST AND THE FREE NORTH

Amid the opportunities for some immigrants and native-born laborers, the free-labor system often did not live up to its promise. Many wage laborers could not realistically aspire to become independent, self-sufficient property holders, despite the claims of free-labor proponents.

> German and Irish Immigrants

Germans	Irish
1.4 million German immigrants entered the United States between 1840 and 1860.	Nearly 1.7 million Irish immigrants arrived between 1840 and 1860.
Majority were skilled tradesmen and their families.	Nearly all were poor and often weakened by hunger and disease.
Roughly one-quarter were farmers.	Potato blight caused a catastrophic famine in Ireland in 1845 and returned repeatedly in subsequent years.
Many were Protestants.	Almost all were Catholics.
Relatively few worked as wage laborers or domestic servants.	Roughly three-quarters worked as laborers or domestic servants.

QUICK REVIEW <

What values or assumptions underlay free-labor ideology?

What factors spurred westward expansion?

Why did the United States go to war with Mexico?

How did reform movements change after 1840?

Conclusion: How was white freedom in the West and North defined?

 LearningCurve
Check what you know.
bedfordstmartins.com
/roarkunderstanding

335

> What factors spurred westward expansion?

Pioneer Family on the Trail West

In 1860, W. G. Chamberlain photographed these unidentified travelers momentarily at rest by the upper Arkansas River in Colorado. We do not know their fates, but we can only hope that they fared better than the Sager family. In 1844, Henry and Naomi Sager and their children set out from Missouri to Oregon. Still far from Oregon, Henry Sager died of fever. Twenty-six days later, Naomi died, leaving seven children. The Sager children, under the care of other families in the wagon train, pressed on. After traveling two thousand miles, they arrived in Oregon, where Marcus and Narcissa Whitman, whose own daughter had drowned, adopted all seven of the Sager children.

Denver Public Library, Western History Division # F3226.

> **VISUAL ACTIVITY**

READING THE IMAGE: Based on this photograph, what were some of the difficulties faced by pioneers traveling west?

CONNECTIONS: How did wagon trains change the western United States?

BEGINNING IN THE 1840S, the nation's swelling population, booming economy, and boundless confidence propelled a new era of rapid westward migration. Under the banner of manifest destiny, American migrants encountered Native Americans who inhabited the plains, deserts, and rugged coasts of the West; the British, who claimed the Oregon Country; and Mexicans, whose flag flew over the vast expanse of the Southwest. Nevertheless, by 1850 the United States stretched to the Pacific, and the nation had more than doubled its size.

The human cost of aggressive expansionism was high. The young Mexican nation lost a war and half of its territory. Two centuries of Indian wars, which ended east of the Mississippi during the 1830s, continued for another half century in the West.

Manifest Destiny

Most Americans believed that the superiority of their institutions and white culture bestowed on them a God-given right to spread across the continent. They imagined the West as a howling wilderness, empty and undeveloped. If they recognized Indians and Mexicans at all, they dismissed them as primitives who would have to be redeemed, shoved aside, or exterminated. The West provided young men especially an arena in which to "show their manhood." Most Americans believed that the West needed the civilizing power of the hammer and the plow, the ballot box and the pulpit, which had transformed the East.

In 1845, a New York political journal edited by John L. O'Sullivan coined the term **manifest destiny** to justify white settlers taking the land they coveted. O'Sullivan called on Americans to resist any effort to thwart "the fulfillment of our manifest destiny to overspread the continent allotted by Providence for the free development of our yearly multiplying millions . . . [and] for the development of the great experiment of liberty and federative self-government entrusted to us." Almost overnight, the magic phrase *manifest destiny* swept the nation, providing an ideological shield for conquering the West.

As important as national pride and racial arrogance were to manifest destiny, economic gain made up its core. Land hunger drew hundreds of thousands of Americans westward. Some politicians, moreover, had become convinced that national prosperity depended on capturing the rich trade of the Far East. To trade with Asia, the United States needed the Pacific coast ports that stretched from San Diego to Puget Sound. The United States and Asia must "talk together, and trade together," Missouri senator Thomas Hart Benton declared. "Commerce is a great civilizer." In the 1840s, American economic expansion came wrapped in the rhetoric of uplift and civilization.

Oregon and the Overland Trail

American expansionists and the British competed for the Oregon Country — a vast region bounded on the west by the Pacific Ocean, on the east by the Rocky Mountains, on the south by the forty-second parallel, and on the north by Russian Alaska. In 1818, the United States and Great Britain decided on "joint occupation" that would leave Oregon "free and open" to settlement by both countries. By the 1820s, a handful of American fur traders and "mountain men" roamed the region.

In the late 1830s, settlers began to trickle along the **Oregon Trail**, following a path blazed by the mountain men (**Map 12.2**). The first wagon trains headed west in 1841, and by 1843 about 1,000 emigrants a year set out from Independence, Missouri. By 1869, when the first transcontinental railroad was completed, approximately 350,000 migrants had traveled west in wagon trains.

Emigrants encountered the Plains Indians, a quarter of a million Native Americans scattered over the area between the Mississippi River and the Rocky Mountains. Some were farmers who lived peaceful, sedentary lives, but a majority — the Sioux, Cheyenne, Shoshoni, and Arapaho of the central plains and the Kiowa, Wichita, and Comanche of the southern plains — were horse-mounted, nomadic, nonagricultural peoples whose warriors symbolized the "savage Indian" in the minds of whites.

Horses, which had been brought to North America by Spaniards in the sixteenth century, permitted the Plains tribes to become highly mobile hunters of buffalo. They came to depend on buffalo for nearly everything — food, clothing, shelter, and fuel. Competition for buffalo led to war between the tribes. Young men were introduced to warfare early, learning to ride ponies at breakneck speed while firing off arrows and, later, rifles with astounding accuracy. "A Comanche on his feet is out of his element," observed western artist George Catlin, "but the moment he lays his hands upon his horse, his *face* even becomes handsome, and he gracefully flies away like a different being."

> CHRONOLOGY

1836
– Battle of the Alamo.
– Texas declares independence from Mexico.

1841
– First wagon trains head west on Oregon Trail.

1845
– Term *manifest destiny* is coined.

1846
– Bear Flag Revolt.

1847
– Mormons settle in Utah.

1850
– Utah Territory is annexed.

1851
– Fort Laramie conference marks the beginning of Indian concentration.

1857
– Mormon War.

manifest destiny
▶ Term coined in 1845 by journalist John L. O'Sullivan to justify American expansion. O'Sullivan claimed that it was the nation's "manifest destiny" to transport its values and civilization westward. Manifest destiny framed the American conquest of the West as part of a divine plan.

Oregon Trail
▶ Route from Independence, Missouri, to Oregon traveled by American settlers starting in the late 1830s. Disease and accidents caused many more deaths along the trail than did Indian attacks, which migrants feared.

| What factors spurred westward expansion? | Why did the United States go to war with Mexico? | How did reform movements change after 1840? | Conclusion: How was white freedom in the West and North defined? | ☑ LearningCurve Check what you know. bedfordstmartins.com /roarkunderstanding |

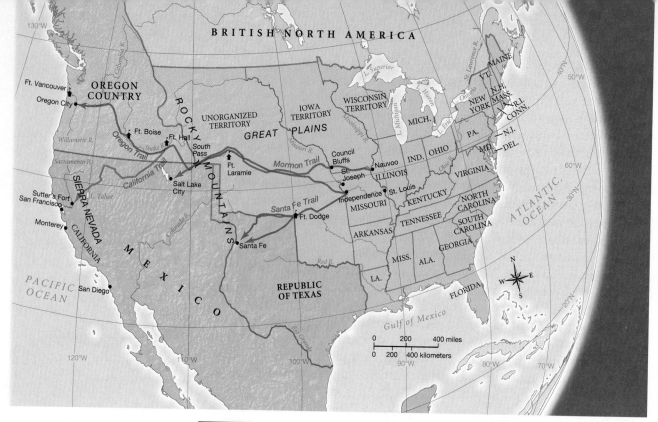

MAP 12.2 ■ Major Trails West

In the 1830s, wagon trains began snaking their way to the Southwest and the Pacific coast. Deep ruts, some of which can still be seen today, soon marked the most popular routes.

Plains Indians and Trails West in the 1840s and 1850s

The Plains Indians struck fear in the hearts of whites on the wagon trains. But Native Americans had far more to fear from whites. Indians killed fewer than four hundred emigrants on the Oregon Trail between 1840 and 1860, while whites brought alcohol and deadly epidemics. Moreover, white hunters slaughtered buffalo for the international hide market and sometimes just for sport.

The government constructed a chain of forts along the Oregon Trail (see Map 12.2) and adopted a new Indian policy: "concentration." In 1851, government negotiators at the Fort Laramie conference persuaded the Plains Indians to sign agreements that cleared a wide corridor for wagon trains by restricting Native Americans to specific areas that whites promised they would never violate. This policy of concentration became the seedbed for the subsequent policy of reservations. But whites would not keep out of Indian territory, and Indians would not easily give up their traditional ways of life. Struggle for control of the West meant warfare for decades to come.

Still, Indians threatened emigrants less than life on the trail did. Emigrants could count on at least six months of grueling travel. With nearly two thousand miles to go and traveling no more than fifteen miles a day, the pioneers endured parching heat, drought, treacherous rivers, disease, physical and emotional exhaustion, and, if the snows closed the mountain passes before they got through, freezing and starvation. It was said that a person could walk from Missouri to the Pacific stepping only on the graves of those who had died heading west.

Men usually found Oregon "one of the greatest countries in the world." From "the Cascade mountains to the Pacific, the whole country can be cultivated," exclaimed one eager settler. When women reached Oregon, they found that neighbors were scarce and things were in a "primitive state." Work seemed unending. "I am a very old woman," declared twenty-nine-year-old Sarah Everett. "My face is thin sunken and wrinkled, my hands bony withered and hard." Another settler observed, "A woman that can not endure almost as much as a horse has no business here." Yet despite the ordeal of the trail and the difficulties of starting from scratch, emigrants kept coming.

The Mormon Exodus

Not every wagon train heading west was bound for the Pacific Slope. One remarkable group of religious emigrants halted near the Great Salt Lake in what was then Mexican territory. After years of persecution in the East, the **Mormons** fled west to find religious freedom and communal security.

In the 1820s, an upstate New York farm boy named Joseph Smith Jr. said that he was visited by an angel who led him to golden tablets buried near his home. With the aid of magic stones, he translated the mysterious language on the tablets to produce *The Book of Mormon,* which he published in 1830. It told the story of an ancient Hebrew civilization in the New World and predicted the appearance of an American prophet who would reestablish Jesus Christ's undefiled kingdom in America. Converts, attracted to the promise of a pure faith in the midst of antebellum America's social turmoil and rampant materialism, flocked to the new Church of Jesus Christ of Latter-Day Saints (the Mormons).

Neighbors branded Mormons heretics and drove Smith and his followers from New York to Ohio, then to Missouri, and finally in 1839 to Nauvoo, Illinois, where they built a prosperous community. But after Smith sanctioned "plural marriage" (polygamy), non-Mormons arrested Smith and his brother. On June 27, 1844, a mob stormed the jail and shot both men dead.

The embattled church turned to an extraordinary new leader, Brigham Young, who in 1847 oversaw a great exodus to a new home beside the Great Salt Lake. Young described the region as a barren waste, "the paradise of the lizard, the cricket and the rattlesnake." Within ten years, however, the Mormons developed an irrigation system that made the desert bloom. Under Young's stern leadership, the Mormons built a thriving community.

In 1850, the Mormon kingdom was annexed to the United States as the Utah Territory. Shortly afterward, Brigham Young announced that many Mormons practiced polygamy. Although only one Mormon man in five had more than one wife (Young had twenty-three), Young's statement forced the U.S. government to establish its authority in Utah. In 1857, 2,500 U.S. troops invaded Salt Lake City in what was known as the Mormon War. The bloodless occupation illustrated that most Americans viewed the Mormons as a threat to American morality and institutions.

The Mexican Borderlands

In the Mexican Southwest, westward-moving Anglo-American pioneers confronted northern-moving Spanish-speaking frontiersmen. On this frontier as elsewhere, national cultures, interests, and aspirations collided. Mexico won its

Mormons
▶ Members of the Church of Jesus Christ of Latter-Day Saints, founded by Joseph Smith in 1830. Most Americans deemed the Mormons heretics. After Smith's death at the hands of an angry mob in 1844, Brigham Young led the Mormons to Utah in 1846.

| What factors spurred westward expansion? | Why did the United States go to war with Mexico? | How did reform movements change after 1840? | Conclusion: How was white freedom in the West and North defined? | ✔ LearningCurve Check what you know. bedfordstmartins.com /roarkunderstanding |

339

MAP 12.3 ■ Texas and Mexico in the 1830s

As Americans spilled into lightly populated and loosely governed northern Mexico, Texas and then other Mexican provinces became contested territory.

independence from Spain in 1821 (**Map 12.3**), but the young nation was plagued by civil wars, economic crises, quarrels with the Roman Catholic Church, and devastating raids by the Comanche, Apache, and Kiowa. Mexico found it increasingly difficult to defend its northern provinces, especially when faced with a neighbor convinced of its superiority and bent on territorial acquisition.

The American assault began quietly. In the 1820s, Anglo-American traders drifted into Santa Fe, a remote outpost in the northern province of New Mexico. The traders made the long trek southwest along the Santa Fe Trail (see Map 12.2) with wagons crammed with inexpensive American manufactured goods and returned home with Mexican silver, furs, and mules.

The Mexican province of Texas attracted a flood of Americans who had settlement, not long-distance trade, on their minds (see Map 12.3). Wanting to populate and develop its northern territory, the Mexican government granted the American Stephen F. Austin a huge tract of land along the Brazos River. In the 1820s, Austin offered land at only ten cents an acre, and thousands of Americans poured across the border. Most were Southerners who brought cotton and slaves with them.

By the 1830s, the settlers had established a thriving plantation economy in Texas. Americans numbered 35,000, while the *Tejano* (Spanish-speaking) population was fewer than 8,000. Few Anglo-American settlers were Roman Catholic,

CHAPTER LOCATOR | What factors contributed to the United States' "industrial evolution"? | How did the free-labor ideal account for economic inequality?

340 CHAPTER 12
THE NEW WEST AND THE FREE NORTH

spoke Spanish, or cared about assimilating into Mexican culture. The Mexican government in 1830 banned further immigration to Texas from the United States and outlawed the introduction of additional slaves. The Anglo-Americans made it clear that they wanted to be rid of the "despotism of the sword and the priesthood" and to govern themselves.

When the Texan settlers rebelled, General Antonio López de Santa Anna ordered the Mexican army northward. In February 1836, the army arrived at the outskirts of San Antonio. Commanded by Colonel William B. Travis from Alabama, the rebels included the Tennessee frontiersman Davy Crockett and the Louisiana adventurer James Bowie, as well as a handful of Tejanos. They took refuge in a former Franciscan mission known as the Alamo. Santa Anna sent wave after wave of his 2,000-man army crashing against the walls until the attackers finally broke through and killed all 187 rebels. A few weeks later, outside the small town of Goliad, Mexican forces captured and executed almost 400 Texans as "pirates and outlaws." In April 1836, at San Jacinto, General Sam Houston's army adopted the massacre of Goliad as a battle cry and crushed Santa Anna's troops in a surprise attack. The Texans had succeeded in establishing the **Lone Star Republic**, and the following year the United States recognized the independence of Texas from Mexico.

Earlier, in 1824, in an effort to increase Mexican migration to the province of California, the Mexican government granted *ranchos* — huge estates devoted to cattle raising — to new settlers. *Rancheros* ruled over near-feudal empires worked by Indians whose condition sometimes approached that of slaves. In 1834, *rancheros* persuaded the Mexican government to confiscate the Franciscan missions and make their lands available to new settlement, a development that accelerated the decline of the California Indians. Devastated by disease, the Indians, who had numbered approximately 300,000 when the Spanish arrived in 1769, had declined to half that number by 1846.

Despite the efforts of the Mexican government, California in 1840 had a population of only 7,000 Mexican settlers. Non-Mexican settlers numbered only 380, but among them were Americans who championed manifest destiny. They sought to convince American emigrants who were traveling the Oregon Trail to head southwest on the California Trail (see Map 12.2). As a New York newspaper put it in 1845, "Let the tide of emigration flow toward California and the American population will soon be sufficiently numerous to play the Texas game." Few Americans in California wanted a war, but many dreamed of living again under the U.S. flag.

In 1846, American settlers in the Sacramento Valley took matters into their own hands. Prodded by John C. Frémont, a former army captain and an explorer who had arrived with a party of sixty buckskin-clad frontiersmen spoiling for a fight, the Californians raised an independence movement known as the Bear Flag Revolt. By then, James K. Polk, a champion of aggressive expansion, sat in the White House.

Lone Star Republic
▶ Independent republic, also known as the Republic of Texas, that was established by a rebellion of Texans against Mexican rule. The victory at San Jacinto in April 1836 helped ensure the region's independence and recognition by the United States.

QUICK REVIEW ◁

Why did westward migration expand dramatically in the mid-nineteenth century?

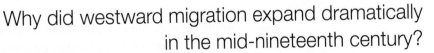

| What factors spurred westward expansion? | Why did the United States go to war with Mexico? | How did reform movements change after 1840? | Conclusion: How was white freedom in the West and North defined? | ☑ LearningCurve Check what you know. bedfordstmartins.com /roarkunderstanding |

Why did the United States go to war with Mexico?

Polk and Dallas Banner, 1844 In 1844, Democratic presidential nominee James K. Polk and vice presidential nominee George M. Dallas campaigned under this cotton banner. The extra star spilling over into the red and white stripes symbolizes Polk's vigorous support for annexing the huge slave republic of Texas, which had declared its independence from Mexico eight years earlier. Collection of Janice L. and David J. Frent.

ALTHOUGH EMIGRANTS ACTED as the advance guard of American empire, there was nothing automatic about the U.S. annexation of territory in the West. Acquiring territory required political action. In the 1840s, the politics of expansion became entangled with sectionalism and the slavery question. Texas, Oregon, and the Mexican borderlands also thrust the United States into dangerous diplomatic crises with Great Britain and Mexico.

Aggravation between Mexico and the United States escalated to open antagonism in 1845 when the United States annexed Texas. Absorbing territory still claimed by Mexico set the stage for war. But it was President James K. Polk's insistence on having Mexico's other northern provinces that made war certain. The war was not as easy as Polk anticipated, but it ended in American victory and the acquisition of a new American West. The discovery of gold in one of the nation's new territories, California, prompted a massive wave of emigration that nearly destroyed Native American and Californio society.

The Politics of Expansion

Texans had sought admission to the Union almost since winning their independence from Mexico in 1836. Almost constant border warfare between Mexico and the Republic of Texas in the decade following the revolution underscored the precarious nature of independence. But any suggestion of adding another slave state to the Union outraged most Northerners, who applauded westward expansion but imagined the expansion of liberty, not slavery.

John Tyler, who became president in April 1841 when William Henry Harrison died one month after taking office, understood that Texas was a dangerous issue. Adding to the danger, Great Britain began sniffing around Texas, apparently contemplating adding the young republic to its growing empire. In

CHAPTER LOCATOR | What factors contributed to the United States' "industrial evolution"? | How did the free-labor ideal account for economic inequality?

1844, Tyler, an ardent expansionist, decided to risk annexing the Lone Star Republic. However, howls of protest erupted across the North. Future Massachusetts senator Charles Sumner deplored the "insidious" plan to annex Texas and carve from it "great slaveholding states." The Senate soundly rejected the annexation treaty.

During the election of 1844, the Whig nominee for president, Henry Clay, in an effort to woo northern voters, came out against annexation of Texas. "Annexation and war with Mexico are identical," he declared. The Democratic nominee, Tennessean James K. Polk, vigorously backed annexation. To make annexation palatable to Northerners, the Democrats shrewdly yoked the annexation of Texas to the annexation of Oregon, thus tapping the desire for expansion in the free states of the North as well as in the slave states of the South.

When Clay finally recognized the popularity of expansion, he waffled, hinting that he might accept the annexation of Texas after all. His retreat succeeded only in alienating antislavery opinion in the North. In the November election, Polk won a narrow victory.

In his inaugural address on March 4, 1845, Polk underscored his faith in America's manifest destiny. "This heaven-favored land," he proclaimed, enjoyed the "most admirable and wisest system of well-regulated self-government . . . ever devised by human minds." He asked, "Who shall assign limits to the achievements of free minds and free hands under the protection of this glorious Union?"

The nation did not have to wait for Polk's inauguration to see results from his victory. One month after the election, President Tyler announced that the triumph of the Democratic Party provided a mandate for the annexation of Texas "promptly and immediately." In February 1845, after a fierce debate between antislavery and proslavery forces, Congress approved a joint resolution offering the Republic of Texas admission to the United States. Texas entered as the fifteenth slave state.

While Tyler delivered Texas, Polk had promised Oregon, too. But Polk was close to war with Mexico and could not afford a war with Britain over U.S. claims in Canada. He renewed an old offer to divide Oregon along the forty-ninth parallel. When Britain accepted the compromise, the nation gained an enormous territory peacefully. When the Senate approved the treaty in June 1846, the United States and Mexico were already at war.

The Mexican-American War, 1846–1848

From the day he entered the White House, Polk craved Mexico's remaining northern provinces: California and New Mexico, land that today makes up California, Nevada, Utah, most of New Mexico and Arizona, and parts of Wyoming and Colorado. Since the 1830s, Comanches, Kiowas, Apaches, and others had attacked Mexican ranches and towns, killing thousands, and the Polk administration invoked Mexico's inability to control its northern provinces to denigrate its claims to them. Polk hoped to buy the territory, but when the Mexicans refused to sell, he concluded that military force would be needed to realize the United States' manifest destiny.

Polk ordered General Zachary Taylor to march his 4,000-man army 150 miles south from its position on the Nueces River, the southern boundary of Texas according to the Mexicans, to the banks of the Rio Grande, the boundary claimed

1841
– Vice President John Tyler becomes president when William Henry Harrison dies.

1844
– James K. Polk is elected president.

1845
– Texas enters Union as slave state.

1846
– Congress declares war on Mexico.
– United States and Great Britain divide Oregon Country.

1848
– Treaty of Guadalupe Hidalgo.

1849
– California gold rush begins.

What factors spurred westward expansion? | **Why did the United States go to war with Mexico?** | How did reform movements change after 1840? | Conclusion: How was white freedom in the West and North defined? | ✓ LearningCurve Check what you know. bedfordstmartins.com /roarkunderstanding

343

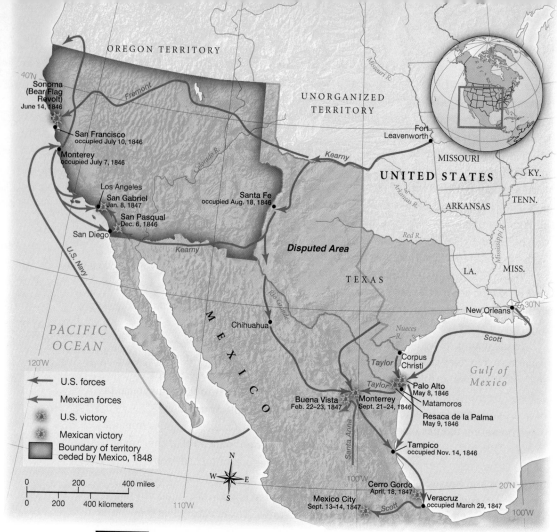

MAP 12.4 ■ The Mexican-American War, 1846–1848

American and Mexican soldiers skirmished across much of northern Mexico, but the major battles took place between the Rio Grande and Mexico City.

by Texans (**Map 12.4**). Viewing the American advance as aggression, Mexican cavalry on April 25, 1846, attacked a party of American soldiers, killing or wounding sixteen and capturing the rest.

On May 11, the president told Congress, "Mexico has passed the boundary of the United States, has invaded our territory, and shed American blood upon American soil." Thus "war exists, and, notwithstanding all our efforts to avoid it, exists by the act of Mexico herself." Congress passed a declaration of war and began raising an army. The U.S. Army was pitifully small, only 8,600 soldiers. Faced with the nation's first foreign war, against a Mexican army that numbered more than 30,000, Polk called for volunteers. Eventually, more than 112,000 white Americans (40 percent of whom were immigrants; blacks were banned) joined the army to fight in Mexico.

Despite the flood of volunteers, the war divided the nation. Northern Whigs in particular condemned the war. The Massachusetts legislature claimed that the war was being fought for the "triple object of extending slavery, of strengthening the slave power, and of obtaining control of the free states." On January 12, 1848,

This family had its portrait taken in 1847, in the middle of the war. Mexican civilians were vulnerable to atrocities committed by the invading army. Volunteers, who made up a large part of U.S. troops, received little training and resisted discipline. The "lawless Volunteers stop at no outrage," Brigadier General William Worth declared. "Innocent blood has been basely, cowardly, and barbarously shed in cold blood." Unknown photographer. Daguerreotype, ca. 1847, $2\frac{7}{8} \times \frac{3}{16}$ inches, Amon Carter Museum, Fort Worth, Texas, P1981.65.18.

a gangly freshman Whig representative from Illinois rose in the House of Representatives. Before Abraham Lincoln sat down, he had questioned Polk's intelligence, honesty, and sanity. The president ignored the upstart representative, but antislavery, antiwar Whigs kept up the attack throughout the conflict.

President Polk expected a short war in which U.S. armies would occupy Mexico's northern provinces and defeat the Mexican army in a decisive battle or two, after which Mexico would sue for peace and the United States would keep the territory its armies occupied. At first, Polk's strategy seemed to work. In May 1846, Zachary Taylor's troops drove south from the Rio Grande and routed the Mexican army, first at Palo Alto, then at Resaca de la Palma (see Map 12.4). "Old Rough and Ready," as Taylor was affectionately known among his adoring troops, became an instant war hero. Polk rewarded Taylor for his victories by making him commander of the Mexican campaign.

A second prong of the campaign centered on Colonel Stephen Watts Kearny, who led a 1,700-man army from Missouri into New Mexico. Without firing a shot, U.S. forces took Santa Fe in August 1846. Kearny then marched to San Diego, where he encountered a major Mexican rebellion against American rule. In January 1847, after several clashes and severe losses, U.S. forces occupied Los Angeles. California and New Mexico were in American hands.

By then, Taylor had driven deep into the interior of Mexico. In September 1846, he had taken the city of Monterrey. Taylor then pushed his 5,000 troops southwest, where the Mexican hero of the Alamo, General Antonio López de Santa Anna, was concentrating an army of 21,000. On February 23, 1847, Santa Anna's troops attacked Taylor at Buena Vista. The Americans won the day but suffered heavy casualties. The Mexicans suffered even greater losses (some 3,400 dead, wounded, and missing, compared with 650 Americans). During the night, Santa Anna withdrew his battered army.

The series of uninterrupted victories in northern Mexico fed the American troops' sense of invincibility. "No American force has ever thought of being defeated by any

| What factors spurred westward expansion? | **Why did the United States go to war with Mexico?** | How did reform movements change after 1840? | Conclusion: How was white freedom in the West and North defined? | ☑ LearningCurve Check what you know. bedfordstmartins.com /roarkunderstanding |

345

amount of Mexican troops," one soldier declared. The Americans worried about other hazards, however. "I can assure you that fighting is the least dangerous & arduous part of a soldier's life," one young man declared. Letters home told of torturous marches across arid wastes alive with tarantulas, scorpions, and rattlesnakes. Others recounted dysentery, malaria, smallpox, cholera, and yellow fever. Of the 13,000 American soldiers who died (some 50,000 Mexicans perished), fewer than 2,000 fell to Mexican bullets and shells. Disease killed most of the others. Medicine was so primitive that, as one Tennessee man observed, "nearly all who take sick die."

Victory in Mexico

Despite heavy losses on the battlefield, Mexico refused to trade land for peace. One American soldier captured the Mexican mood: "They cannot submit to be deprived of California after the loss of Texas, and nothing but the conquest of their Capital will force them to such a humiliation." Polk had arrived at the same conclusion. While Taylor occupied the north, General Winfield Scott would land an army on the Gulf coast of Mexico and march 250 miles inland to the capital. Polk's plan entailed enormous risk because Scott would have to cut himself off from supplies and lead his men deep into enemy country against a much larger army.

An amphibious landing on March 9, 1847, near Veracruz put some 10,000 American troops ashore. After furious shelling, Veracruz surrendered. In April 1847, Scott's forces moved westward, following the path blazed more than three centuries earlier by Hernán Cortés to "the halls of Montezuma" (see chapter 2).

After the defeat at Buena Vista, Santa Anna had returned to Mexico City, where he rallied his ragged troops and marched them east to set a trap for Scott in the mountain pass at Cerro Gordo. Knifing through Mexican lines, the Americans almost captured Santa Anna, who fled the field on foot. So complete was the victory that Scott gloated to Taylor, "Mexico no longer has an army." But Santa Anna, ever resilient, again rallied the Mexican army. Some 30,000 troops took up defensive positions on the outskirts of Mexico City and began melting down church bells to cast new cannons.

In August 1847, Scott began his assault on the Mexican capital. The fighting proved the most brutal of the war. Santa Anna backed his army into the city, fighting each step of the way. At the battle of Churubusco, the Mexicans took 4,000 casualties in a single day and the Americans more than 1,000. At the castle of Chapultepec, American troops scaled the walls and fought the Mexican defenders hand to hand. After Chapultepec, Mexico City officials persuaded Santa Anna to evacuate the city to save it from destruction, and on September 14, 1847, Scott rode in triumphantly.

On February 2, 1848, American and Mexican officials signed the **Treaty of Guadalupe Hidalgo** in Mexico City.

Treaty of Guadalupe Hidalgo

▶ February 1848 treaty that ended the Mexican-American War. Mexico gave up all claims to Texas north of the Rio Grande and ceded New Mexico and California to the United States. The United States agreed to pay Mexico $15 million and to assume American claims against Mexico.

> **> Terms of the Treaty of Guadalupe Hidalgo**

- Mexico agreed to give up all claims to Texas north of the Rio Grande and to cede the provinces of New Mexico and California to the United States.
- The United States agreed to pay Mexico $15 million and to assume $3.25 million in claims that American citizens had against Mexico.

CHAPTER LOCATOR | What factors contributed to the United States' "industrial evolution"? | How did the free-labor ideal account for economic inequality?

CHAPTER 12

346 THE NEW WEST AND THE FREE NORTH

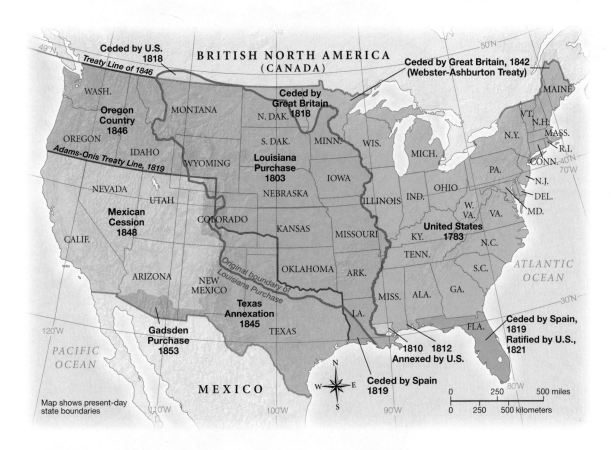

MAP 12.5 ■ Territorial Expansion by 1860

Less than a century after its founding, the United States spread from the Atlantic seaboard to the Pacific coast. War, purchase, and diplomacy had gained a continent.

> **MAP ACTIVITY**

READING THE MAP: List the countries from which the United States acquired land. Which nation lost the most land because of U.S. expansion?
CONNECTIONS: Who coined the term *manifest destiny*? When? What does it mean? What areas targeted for expansion were the subjects of debate during the presidential campaign of 1844?

The American triumph had enormous consequences. Less than three-quarters of a century after its founding, the United States had achieved its self-proclaimed manifest destiny to stretch from the Atlantic to the Pacific (**Map 12.5**). It would enter the industrial age with vast new natural resources and a two-ocean economy, while Mexico faced a sharply diminished economic future.

Golden California

Another consequence of the Mexican defeat was that California gold poured into American, not Mexican, pockets. In January 1848, James Marshall discovered gold in the American River in the foothills of the Sierra Nevada. His discovery set off the **California gold rush**, one of the wildest mining stampedes in the world's history. Between 1849 and 1852, more than 250,000 "forty-niners," as the would-be miners were known, descended on the Golden State. In less than two years, Marshall's discovery transformed California from foreign territory to statehood.

California gold rush

▶ Mining rush initiated by James Marshall's discovery of gold in the foothills of the Sierra Nevada in 1848. The hope of striking it rich drew more than 250,000 aspiring miners to California between 1849 and 1852, an influx that accelerated the push for statehood.

What factors spurred westward expansion?

Why did the United States go to war with Mexico?

How did reform movements change after 1840?

Conclusion: How was white freedom in the West and North defined?

☑ LearningCurve
Check what you know.
bedfordstmartins.com
/roarkunderstanding

This young man exhibits the spirit of individual effort that was the foundation of free-labor ideals. Posing with a pick and shovel to loosen gold-bearing deposits and a pan to wash away debris, the man appears determined to succeed as a miner by his own muscles and sweat. Hard work with these tools, the picture suggests, promised rewards and maybe riches. *Collection of Matthew Isenburg.*

Gold fever quickly spread around the world. A stream of men of various races and nationalities poured into California. Only a few struck it rich, and life in the goldfields was nasty, brutish, and often short. The prospectors faced cholera and scurvy, exorbitant prices for food (eggs cost a dollar apiece), deadly encounters with claim jumpers, and endless backbreaking labor.

Violent crime was an everyday occurrence, and establishing civic order was made more difficult by California's diversity. The Chinese attracted special scrutiny from Anglos. By 1851, 25,000 Chinese lived in California, and their religion, language, dress, queues (long pigtails), eating habits, and use of opium convinced many Anglos that they were not fit citizens of the Golden State. In 1850, the California legislature passed the Foreign Miners' Tax Law, which levied high taxes on non-Americans to drive them from the goldfields, except as hired laborers working on claims owned by Americans. The Chinese were segregated residentially and occupationally and, along with blacks and Indians, were denied public education and the right to testify in court.

Opponents demanded a halt to Chinese immigration, but Chinese leaders in San Francisco fought back. Admitting deep cultural differences, they insisted that "in the important matters we are good men. We honor our parents; we take care of our children; we are industrious and peaceable; we trade much; we are trusted

CHAPTER LOCATOR | What factors contributed to the United States' "industrial evolution"? | How did the free-labor ideal account for economic inequality?

CHAPTER 12
348 THE NEW WEST AND THE FREE NORTH

for small and large sums; we pay our debts; and are honest, and of course must tell the truth." Their protestations offered little protection, however, and racial violence grew.

Anglo-American prospectors asserted their dominance over other groups, especially Native Americans and the Californios, Spanish and Mexican settlers who had lived in California for decades. Despite the U.S. government's pledge to protect Mexican and Spanish land titles, Americans took the land of the *rancheros* and through discriminatory legislation pushed Hispanic professionals, merchants, and artisans into the ranks of unskilled labor. Mariano Vallejo, a leading Californio, said of the forty-niners, "The good ones were few and the wicked many."

For Indians, the gold rush was catastrophic. Numbering about 150,000 in 1848, the Indian population of California fell to 25,000 by 1854. Starvation, disease, and a declining birthrate took a heavy toll. Indians also fell victim to wholesale murder. The nineteenth-century historian Hubert Howe Bancroft described white behavior toward Indians during the gold rush as "one of the last human hunts of civilization, and the basest and most brutal of them all."

The forty-niners created dazzling wealth: In 1852, 81 million ounces of gold, nearly half of the world's production, came from California. However, most miners eventually took up farming, opened small businesses, or worked for wages for the corporations that took over the mining industry. Others Americans traded furs, hides, and lumber and engaged in whaling and the China trade in tea, silk, and porcelain. Still, as one Californian observed, the state was separated "by thousands of miles of plains, deserts, and almost impossible mountains" from the rest of the Union. Some dreamers imagined a railroad that would someday connect the Golden State with the thriving agriculture and industry of the East. Others imagined a country transformed not by transportation but by progressive individual and institutional reform.

Chinese Man

This daguerreotype of an unidentified Chinese man was made by Isaac Wallace Baker, a photographer who traveled through California's mining camps in his wagon studio. One of the earliest known portraits of an Asian in California, the portrait shows a proud man boldly displaying his queue (long braid). This was almost certainly an act of defiance, for Anglos ridiculed Chinese cultural traditions, and vigilantes chased down men who wore queues. Copyright the Dorothea Lange Collection, Oakland Museum of California, City of Oakland. Gift of Paul S. Taylor.

QUICK REVIEW <

What were the most significant consequences of the U.S. war with Mexico?

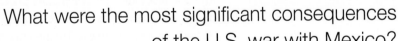

What factors spurred westward expansion?

Why did the United States go to war with Mexico?

How did reform movements change after 1840?

Conclusion: How was white freedom in the West and North defined?

✓ **LearningCurve** Check what you know. bedfordstmartins.com /roarkunderstanding

> How did reform movements change after 1840?

Abolitionist Meeting This rare daguerreotype portrays an abolitionist meeting in New York in 1850. Frederick Douglass, who had escaped from slavery in Maryland, is seated on the platform next to the woman at the table. One of the nation's most eloquent abolitionists, Douglass also supported equal rights for women. The man behind Douglass is Gerrit Smith, a wealthy and militant abolitionist whose funds supported many reform activities. Collection of the J. Paul Getty Museum, Malibu, CA.

WHILE MANIFEST DESTINY, the Mexican-American War, and the California gold rush transformed the nation's boundaries, many Americans sought personal and social reform. The emphasis on self-discipline and individual effort at the core of the free-labor ideal led Americans to believe that insufficient self-control caused the major social problems of the era. Evangelical Protestants struggled to control individuals' propensity to sin. Temperance advocates exhorted drinkers to control their taste for alcohol. Only about one-third of Americans belonged to a church in 1850, but the influence of evangelical religion reached far beyond church members.

The evangelical temperament — a conviction of righteousness coupled with energy, self-discipline, and faith that the world could be improved — animated

CHAPTER LOCATOR | What factors contributed to the United States' "industrial evolution"? | How did the free-labor ideal account for economic inequality?

350 CHAPTER 12
THE NEW WEST AND THE FREE NORTH

most reformers. However, a few activists pointed out that certain fundamental injustices lay beyond the reach of individual self-control. Transcendentalists and utopians believed that perfection required rejecting the competitive, individualistic values of mainstream society. Woman's rights activists and abolitionists sought to reverse the subordination of women and to eliminate the enslavement of blacks by changing laws, social institutions, attitudes, and customs. These reformers confronted the daunting challenge of repudiating widespread beliefs in male supremacy and white supremacy and somehow challenging the entrenched institutions that reinforced those views: the family and slavery.

The Pursuit of Perfection: Transcendentalists and Utopians

A group of New England writers who came to be known as transcendentalists believed that individuals should conform neither to the dictates of the materialistic world nor to the dogma of formal religion. Instead, people should look within themselves for truth and guidance. The leading transcendentalist, Ralph Waldo Emerson — an essayist, poet, and lecturer — proclaimed that the power of the solitary individual was nearly limitless. But the inward gaze and confident egoism of transcendentalism represented less an alternative to mainstream values than an extreme form of the rampant individualism of the age.

Unlike transcendentalists who sought to turn inward, a few reformers tried to change the world by organizing utopian communities as alternatives to prevailing social arrangements. Although these communities never attracted more than a few thousand people, the activities of their members demonstrated dissatisfaction with the larger society and efforts to realize their visions of perfection.

Some communities set out to become models of perfection whose success would point the way toward a better life for everyone. During the 1840s, more than two dozen communities organized themselves around the ideas of Charles Fourier. Members of Fourierist phalanxes, as these communities were called, believed that individualism and competition were evils that denied the basic truth that "men . . . are brothers and not competitors." Phalanxes aspired to replace competition with harmonious cooperation based on communal ownership of property. But Fourierist communities failed to realize their lofty goals, and few survived more than two or three years.

The **Oneida community** went beyond the Fourierist notion of communalism. John Humphrey Noyes, the charismatic leader of Oneida, believed that American society's commitment to private property made people greedy and selfish. Noyes claimed that the root of private property lay in marriage, in men's conviction that their wives were their exclusive property. Drawing from a substantial inheritance, Noyes organized the Oneida community in New York in 1848 to abolish marital property rights by permitting sexual intercourse between any consenting man and woman in the community. Noyes also required all members to relinquish their economic property to the community. Most of their neighbors considered Oneidans adulterers and blasphemers. Yet the practices that set Oneida apart from its mainstream neighbors strengthened the community, and it survived long after the Civil War.

> **CHRONOLOGY**

1840s
- Fourierist communities are founded.

1848
- Oneida community is organized.
- Seneca Falls convention.

1849
- Harriet Tubman escapes from slavery and becomes a leader of the underground railroad.

Oneida community

▶ Utopian community organized by John Humphrey Noyes in New York in 1848. Noyes's opposition to private property led him to denounce marriage as the root of the problem. The community embraced sexual and economic communalism, to the dismay of its mainstream neighbors.

What factors spurred westward expansion?

Why did the United States go to war with Mexico?

How did reform movements change after 1840?

Conclusion: How was white freedom in the West and North defined?

✓ LearningCurve
Check what you know.
bedfordstmartins.com
/roarkunderstanding

351

Woman's Rights Activists

Women participated in the many reform activities that grew out of evangelical churches. Women church members outnumbered men two to one and worked to put their religious ideas into practice by joining peace, temperance, antislavery, and other societies. Involvement in reform organizations gave a few women activists practical experience in such political arts as speaking in public, running a meeting, drafting resolutions, and circulating petitions.

In 1848, about three hundred reformers led by Elizabeth Cady Stanton and Lucretia Mott gathered at Seneca Falls, New York, for the first national woman's rights convention in the United States. As Stanton recalled, "The general discontent I felt with women's portion as wife, mother, housekeeper, physician, and spiritual guide, [and] the wearied anxious look of the majority of women impressed me with a strong feeling that some active measure should be taken to right the wrongs of society in general, and of women in particular." The **Seneca Falls Declaration of Sentiments** set an ambitious agenda to demand civil liberties for women and to right the wrongs of society. The declaration proclaimed that "the history of mankind is a history of repeated injuries and usurpations on the part of man toward woman, having in direct object the establishment of an absolute tyranny over her." In the style of the Declaration of Independence (see appendix I, page A-1), the Seneca Falls declaration demanded that women "have immediate admission to all the rights and privileges which belong to them as citizens of the United States," particularly the "inalienable right to the elective franchise."

Nearly two dozen other woman's rights conventions assembled before 1860, repeatedly calling for suffrage and an end to discrimination against women. But women had difficulty receiving a respectful hearing, much less achieving legislative action. Even so, the Seneca Falls declaration served as a pathbreaking

Seneca Falls Declaration of Sentiments

▶ Declaration issued in 1848 at the first national woman's rights convention in the United States, which was held in Seneca Falls, New York. The document adopted the style of the Declaration of Independence and demanded equal rights for women, including the franchise.

Bloomers and Woman's Emancipation

This 1851 British cartoon lampoons bloomers, the trouserlike garment worn beneath shortened skirts by two cigar-smoking American women. Bloomers were invented in the United States as an alternative to the uncomfortable, confining, and awkward dresses worn by the "respectable" women on the right. In the 1850s, Elizabeth Cady Stanton and other woman's rights activists wore bloomers and urged all American women to do likewise. Miriam and Ira D. Wallach Division of Art, Prints, and Photographs, The New York Public Library. Astor, Lenox, and Tilden Foundations.

BLOOMERISM—AN AMERICAN CUSTOM.

CHAPTER LOCATOR | What factors contributed to the United States' "industrial evolution"? | How did the free-labor ideal account for economic inequality?

352 CHAPTER 12 THE NEW WEST AND THE FREE NORTH

manifesto of dissent against male supremacy and of support for woman suffrage, and it inspired many women to challenge the barriers that limited their opportunities.

Stanton and other activists sought fair pay and expanded employment opportunities for women by appealing to free-labor ideology. Woman's rights advocate Paula Wright Davis urged Americans to stop discriminating against able and enterprising women: "Let [women] . . . open a Store, . . . learn any of the lighter mechanical Trades, . . . study for a Profession, . . . be called to the lecture-room, [and] . . . the Temperance rostrum . . . [and] let her be appointed [to serve in the Post Office]." Some women pioneered in these and many other occupations during the 1840s and 1850s. Woman's rights activists also succeeded in protecting married women's rights to their own wages and property in New York in 1860. But discrimination against women persisted, as most men believed that free-labor ideology required no compromise of male supremacy.

Abolitionists and the American Ideal

During the 1840s and 1850s, abolitionists continued to struggle to draw the nation's attention to the plight of slaves and the need for emancipation. Former slaves Frederick Douglass, Henry Bibb, and Sojourner Truth lectured to reform audiences throughout the North about the cruelties of slavery. Abolitionists published newspapers, held conventions, and petitioned Congress, but they never attracted a mass following among white Americans. Many white Northerners became convinced that slavery was wrong, but they still believed that blacks were inferior. Many other white Northerners shared the common view of white Southerners that slavery was necessary and even desirable. The westward extension of the nation during the 1840s offered abolitionists an opportunity to link their unpopular ideal to a goal that many white Northerners found much more attractive — limiting the geographic expansion of slavery, an issue that moved to the center of national politics during the 1850s (as discussed in chapter 14).

Black leaders rose to prominence in the abolitionist movement during the 1840s and 1850s. African Americans had actively opposed slavery for decades, but a new generation of leaders came to the forefront in these years. Frederick Douglass, Henry Highland Garnet, William Wells Brown, Martin R. Delany, and others became impatient with white abolitionists' appeals to the conscience of the white majority. To express their own uncompromising ideas, black abolitionists founded their own newspapers and held their own antislavery conventions, although they still cooperated with sympathetic whites.

The commitment of black abolitionists to battling slavery grew out of their own experiences with white supremacy. The 250,000 free African Americans in the North and West constituted less than 2 percent of the total population in 1860. They confronted the humiliations of racial discrimination in nearly every arena of daily life. Only Maine, Massachusetts, New Hampshire, and Vermont permitted black men to vote; New York imposed a special property-holding requirement on black — but not white — voters, effectively excluding most black men from the franchise. The pervasive racial discrimination both handicapped and energized black abolitionists. Some cooperated with the efforts of the **American Colonization Society** to send freed slaves and other black Americans to Liberia in West Africa. Others sought to move to Canada, Haiti, or elsewhere. Most black

American Colonization Society

▶ An organization dedicated to sending freed slaves and other black Americans to Liberia in West Africa. Although some African Americans cooperated with the movement, others campaigned against segregation and discrimination.

What factors spurred westward expansion?

Why did the United States go to war with Mexico?

How did reform movements change after 1840?

Conclusion: How was white freedom in the West and North defined?

✓ LearningCurve
Check what you know.
bedfordstmartins.com
/roarkunderstanding

353

American leaders refused to embrace emigration and worked against racial prejudice in their own communities, organizing campaigns against segregation, particularly in transportation and education. Their most notable success came in 1855 when Massachusetts integrated its public schools. Elsewhere, white supremacy continued unabated.

Outside the public spotlight, free African Americans in the North and West contributed to the antislavery cause by quietly aiding fugitive slaves. Harriet Tubman escaped from slavery in Maryland in 1849 and repeatedly risked her freedom and her life to return to the South to escort slaves to freedom. When the opportunity arose, free blacks in the North provided fugitive slaves with food, a safe place to rest, and a helping hand. An outgrowth of the antislavery sentiment and opposition to white supremacy that unified nearly all African Americans in the North, this **underground railroad** ran mainly through black neighborhoods, black churches, and black homes.

underground railroad
▶ Network consisting mainly of black homes, black churches, and black neighborhoods that helped slaves escape to the North by supplying shelter, food, and general assistance.

> ## QUICK REVIEW

Why were women especially prominent in many nineteenth-century reform efforts?

CHAPTER LOCATOR | What factors contributed to the United States' "industrial evolution"? | How did the free-labor ideal account for economic inequality?

CHAPTER 12
354 THE NEW WEST AND THE FREE NORTH

Conclusion: How was white freedom in the West and North defined?

DURING THE 1840S AND 1850S, a cluster of interrelated developments — population growth, steam power, railroads, and the growing mechanization of agriculture and manufacturing — meant greater economic productivity, a burst of output from farms and factories, and prosperity for many. Diplomacy with Great Britain and war with Mexico handed the United States 1.2 million square miles and more than 1,000 miles of Pacific coastline. One prize of manifest destiny, California, almost immediately rewarded its new owners with tons of gold. Most Americans believed that the new territory and vast riches were appropriate rewards for the nation's stunning economic progress and superior institutions.

To Northerners, industrial evolution confirmed the choice they had made to eliminate slavery and promote free labor as the key to independence, equality, and prosperity. Like Abraham Lincoln, millions of Americans could point to their personal experiences as evidence of the practical truth of the free-labor ideal. But millions of others knew that in the free-labor system, poverty and wealth continued to rub shoulders. Free-labor enthusiasts denied that the problems were inherent in the country's social and economic systems. Instead, they argued, most social ills — including poverty and dependency — sprang from individual deficiencies. Consequently, many reformers focused on personal self-control and discipline, on avoiding sin and alcohol. Other reformers focused on woman's rights and the abolition of slavery. They challenged widespread conceptions of male supremacy and black inferiority, but neither group managed to overcome the prevailing free-labor ideology based on individualism, racial prejudice, and notions of male superiority.

By midcentury, half of the nation had prohibited slavery, and half permitted it. The North and the South were animated by different economic interests, cultural values, and political aims. Each celebrated its regional identity and increasingly disparaged that of the other. Not even the victory over Mexico could bridge the deepening divide between North and South.

| What factors spurred westward expansion? | Why did the United States go to war with Mexico? | How did reform movements change after 1840? | **Conclusion: How was white freedom in the West and North defined?** | ✓ **LearningCurve** Check what you know. bedfordstmartins.com /roarkunderstanding |

355

CHAPTER 12 STUDY GUIDE

STEP 1 GET STARTED ONLINE

 LearningCurve ■ bedfordstmartins.com/roarkunderstanding

Now that you've read the chapter, make it stick by completing the LearningCurve activity.

STEP 2 EXPLAIN WHY IT MATTERS

Put your reading into practice. Identify each term below, and then explain why it matters in U.S. history.

TERM	WHO OR WHAT & WHEN	WHY IT MATTERS
mechanical reapers (p. 329)		
American system (p. 329)		
manifest destiny (p. 337)		
Oregon Trail (p. 337)		
Mormons (p. 339)		
Lone Star Republic (p. 341)		
Treaty of Guadalupe Hidalgo (p. 346)		
California gold rush (p. 347)		
Oneida community (p. 351)		
Seneca Falls Declaration of Sentiments (p. 352)		
American Colonization Society (p. 353)		
underground railroad (p. 354)		

STEP 3 MOVE BEYOND THE BASICS

To demonstrate a more advanced understanding, assess the key economic developments described in the chapter and their contributions to industrialization. How did agriculture and manufacturing benefit and complement each other?

	Key developments	Consequences/who benefited
Agricultural technology		
Federal land policy		
Mechanization and energy sources		
Railroads		

STEP 4 PUT IT ALL TOGETHER

Now, take a step back and try to explain the big picture. Remember to use specific examples from the chapter in your answers.

INDUSTRIAL DEVELOPMENT AND WESTWARD EXPANSION

▶ What were the social consequences of American industrial development in the first half of the nineteenth century?

▶ What role did American nationalism and economic opportunity play in promoting westward expansion?

THE MEXICAN-AMERICAN WAR

▶ Where was support for war with Mexico strongest? Where was there the least support? Why?

▶ How did victory in the Mexican-American War contribute to rising tensions over slavery?

REFORM

▶ What common concerns linked the reform movements of the 1840s and 1850s?

▶ What role did women play in reform movements in the decades before the Civil War?

LOOKING BACKWARD, LOOKING AHEAD

▶ How had America's economy and society changed between 1800 and 1860?

▶ How did American expansion and industrial development contribute to the sectional conflicts that culminated in the Civil War?

> IN YOUR OWN WORDS

Imagine that you must give an oral report to the class answering the following question: How was freedom defined in the North and West in the mid-nineteenth century? What would be the most important points to include and why?

 Do it online at the Student Site ■ bedforstmartins.com/roarkunderstanding

13

UNDERSTANDING THE SLAVE SOUTH

1820–1860

> **How did slavery shape the institutions and values of the antebellum South?** Chapter 13 explores the emergence and development of a distinctive slave society in the American South. It examines the causes and consequences of the divergence of North and South, the social world of the plantation, and the lives of nonslaveholding whites and free blacks. Finally, it assesses the impact of slavery on southern politics.

LearningCurve
bedfordstmartins.com/roarkunderstanding
After reading the chapter, use LearningCurve to retain what you've read.

Slave quarter. This early photograph depicts a slave family in Savannah, Georgia, ca. 1860. Collection of the New-York Historical Society.

> Why did the South become so distinctly different from the North?

> What was plantation life like for masters and mistresses?

> What was plantation life like for slaves?

> How did nonslaveholding southern whites work and live?

> What place did free blacks occupy in the South?

> How did slavery shape southern politics?

> Conclusion: How did slavery come to define the South?

Why did the South become so distinctly different from the North?

Steamboats and Cotton in New Orleans, circa 1858

Smokestacks of dozens of steamboats overlook hundreds of bales of cotton at the foot of Canal Street. This photograph by Jay Dearborn Edwards captures something of the magnitude of the cotton trade in the South's largest city and major port. Few Southerners doubted that cotton was king. Historic New Orleans Collection.

> CHRONOLOGY

1808
– External slave trade is outlawed.

1820s–1830s
– Southern legislatures enact slave codes.
– Southern intellectuals fashion a systematic defense of slavery.

1830
– Southern slaves number approximately two million.

1836
– Arkansas is admitted to Union as slave state.

1840
– Cotton accounts for more than 60 percent of nation's exports.

1845
– Texas and Florida are admitted to Union as slave states.

1860
– Southern slaves number nearly four million, one-third of South's population.

FROM THE EARLIEST SETTLEMENTS, inhabitants of the southern colonies had shared a great deal with northern colonists. Most whites in both sections were British and Protestant, spoke a common language, and celebrated their victorious revolution against British rule. The creation of the new nation under the Constitution in 1789 forged political ties that bound all Americans. The beginnings of a national economy fostered economic interdependence and communication across regional boundaries. White Americans everywhere praised the prosperous young nation, and they looked forward to its seemingly boundless future.

Despite these national similarities, Southerners and Northerners grew increasingly different. The French political observer Alexis de Tocqueville believed he knew why. "I could easily prove," he asserted in 1831, "that almost all the differences which may be noticed between the character of the Americans in the Southern and Northern states have originated in slavery." Slavery made the South different, and it was the differences between the North and South, not the similarities, that increasingly shaped antebellum American history.

CHAPTER LOCATOR | Why did the South become so distinctly different from the North? | What was plantation life like for masters and mistresses?

Cotton Kingdom, Slave Empire

In the first half of the nineteenth century, millions of Americans migrated west. In the South, hard-driving slaveholders seeking virgin acreage for new plantations, ambitious farmers looking for patches of cheap land for small farms, striving herders and drovers pushing their hogs and cattle toward fresh pastures — everyone felt the pull of western land.

But more than anything it was cotton that propelled Southerners westward. South of the **Mason-Dixon line**, climate and geography were ideally suited for the cultivation of cotton. By the 1830s, cotton fields stretched from the Atlantic seaboard to central Texas. Heavy migration led to statehood for Arkansas in 1836 and for

Mason-Dixon line

▶ A surveyors' mark that had established the boundary between Maryland and Pennsylvania in colonial times. By the 1830s, the boundary divided the free North and the slave South.

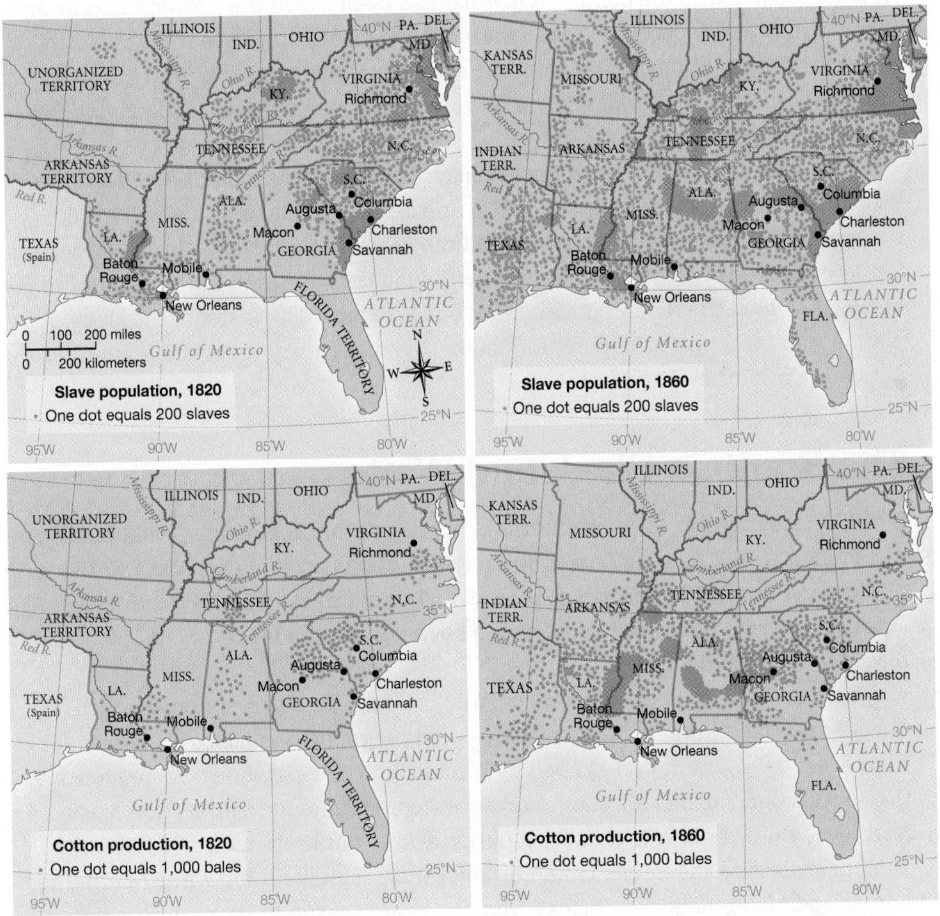

Slave population, 1820
One dot equals 200 slaves

Slave population, 1860
One dot equals 200 slaves

Cotton production, 1820
One dot equals 1,000 bales

Cotton production, 1860
One dot equals 1,000 bales

MAP 13.1 ■ Cotton Kingdom, Slave Empire: 1820 and 1860

As the production of cotton soared, the slave population increased dramatically. Slaves continued to toil in tobacco and rice fields, but in Alabama, Mississippi, and Texas, they increasingly worked on cotton plantations.

> MAP ACTIVITY

READING THE MAP: Where was slavery most prevalent in 1820? In 1860? How did the spread of slavery compare with the spread of cotton?

CONNECTIONS: How much of the world's cotton was produced in the American South in 1860? How did the number of slaves in the American South compare with that in the rest of the world? What does this suggest about the South's cotton kingdom?

| What was plantation life like for slaves? | How did nonslaveholding southern whites work and live? | What place did free blacks occupy in the South? | How did slavery shape southern politics? | Conclusion: How did slavery come to define the South? | ✔ **LearningCurve** Check what you know. bedfordstmartins.com /roarkunderstanding |

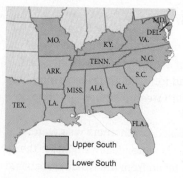

The Upper and Lower South

- ▢ Upper South
- ▢ Lower South

cotton kingdom

▶ Term for the South that reflected the dominance of cotton in the southern economy. Cotton was particularly important in the tier of states from South Carolina west to Texas. Cotton cultivation was the key factor in the growth of slavery.

Texas and Florida in 1845. Cotton production soared to nearly 5 million bales in 1860, when the South produced three-fourths of the world's supply. The South — especially that tier of states from South Carolina west to Texas called the Lower South — had become the **cotton kingdom** (**Map 13.1**, page 361).

The cotton kingdom was also a slave empire. The South's cotton boom rested on the backs of slaves. As cotton agriculture expanded westward, whites shipped more than a million enslaved men, women, and children from the Atlantic coast across the continent in what has been called the "Second Middle Passage," a massive deportation that dwarfed the transatlantic slave trade to North America. Victims of this brutal domestic slave trade marched hundreds of miles southwest to new plantations in the Lower South. Cotton, slaves, and plantations moved west together.

The slave population grew enormously. Southern slaves numbered fewer than 700,000 in 1790, about 2 million in 1830, and almost 4 million by 1860. By 1860, the South contained more slaves than all the other slave societies in the New World combined. The extraordinary growth was not the result of the importation of slaves, which the federal government outlawed in 1808. Instead, the slave population grew through natural reproduction; by midcentury, most U.S. slaves were native-born Southerners.

The South in Black and White

By 1860, one in every three Southerners was black (approximately 4 million blacks to 8 million whites). In the Lower South states of Mississippi and South Carolina, blacks constituted the majority (**Figure 13.1**). The contrast with the North was striking: In 1860, only one Northerner in seventy-six was black (about 250,000 blacks to 19 million whites).

The presence of large numbers of African Americans had profound consequences for the South. Southern culture — language, food, music, religion, and even accents — was in part shaped by blacks. But the most direct consequence of the South's biracialism was southern whites' commitment to white supremacy. Northern whites believed in racial superiority, too, but their dedication to white supremacy lacked the intensity and urgency increasingly felt by white Southerners who lived among millions of blacks who had every reason to strike back.

After 1820, attacks on slavery — from slaves and from northern abolitionists — caused white Southerners to make extraordinary efforts to strengthen slavery. State legislatures constructed **slave codes** (laws) that required the total submission of slaves. As the Louisiana code stated, a slave "owes his master . . . a respect without bounds, and an absolute obedience." The laws also underlined the authority of all whites, not just masters. Any white could "correct" slaves who did not stay "in their place."

Intellectuals joined legislators in the campaign to strengthen slavery. The South's academics, writers, and clergy employed every imaginable defense. They

slave codes

▶ Laws enacted in southern states in the 1820s and 1830s that required the total submission of slaves. Attacks by antislavery activists and by slaves convinced southern legislators that they had to do everything in their power to strengthen the institution of slavery.

CHAPTER LOCATOR | Why did the South become so distinctly different from the North? | What was plantation life like for masters and mistresses?

362 CHAPTER 13 UNDERSTANDING THE SLAVE SOUTH

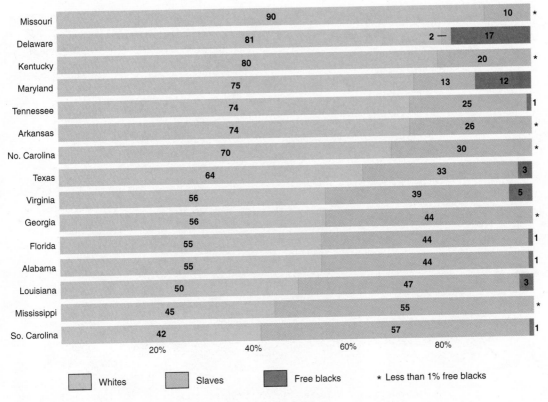

Missouri	90			10	*
Delaware	81		2 —	17	
Kentucky	80			20	*
Maryland	75		13	12	
Tennessee	74		25		1
Arkansas	74		26		*
No. Carolina	70		30		*
Texas	64		33		3
Virginia	56		39		5
Georgia	56		44		*
Florida	55		44		1
Alabama	55		44		1
Louisiana	50		47		3
Mississippi	45		55		*
So. Carolina	42		57		1

20% 40% 60% 80%

■ Whites   ■ Slaves   ■ Free blacks   * Less than 1% free blacks

FIGURE 13.1 ■ Black and White Populations in the South, 1860

Blacks represented a much larger fraction of the population in the South than in the North, but considerable variation existed from state to state. Only one Missourian in ten, for example, was black, while Mississippi and South Carolina had black majorities. States in the Upper South were "whiter" than states in the Lower South, despite the Upper South's greater number of free blacks.

argued that slaves were legal property, and wasn't the protection of property the bedrock of American liberty? History also endorsed slavery, they claimed. Weren't the great civilizations — such as those of the Hebrews, Greeks, and Romans — slave societies? They argued that the Bible, properly interpreted, also sanctioned slavery. Old Testament patriarchs owned slaves, they observed, and in the New Testament, Paul returned the runaway slave Onesimus to his master. Proslavery spokesmen claimed that the freeing of slaves would lead to the sexual mixing of the races, or **miscegenation**.

George Fitzhugh of Virginia defended slavery by attacking the North's free-labor economy and society. Gouging capitalists exploited wageworkers unmercifully, Fitzhugh declared, and he contrasted the North's vicious free-labor system with the humane relations that he said prevailed between masters and slaves because slaves were valuable capital that masters sought to protect. John C. Calhoun, an influential southern politician, declared that in the states where slavery had been abolished, "the condition of the African, instead of being improved, has become worse," while in the slave states, the Africans "have improved greatly in every respect."

But at the heart of the defense of slavery lay the claim of black inferiority. Black enslavement was both necessary and proper, slavery's defenders argued, because Africans were lesser beings. Rather than exploitative, slavery was a mass civilizing

miscegenation

▶ Interracial sex. Proslavery spokesmen played on the fears of whites when they suggested that giving blacks equal rights would lead to miscegenation. In reality, slavery led to considerable sexual abuse of black women by their white masters.

What was plantation life like for slaves?	How did nonslaveholding southern whites work and live?	What place did free blacks occupy in the South?	How did slavery shape southern politics?	Conclusion: How did slavery come to define the South?	☑ LearningCurve Check what you know. bedfordstmartins.com /roarkunderstanding

The Fruits of Amalgamation

In this lithograph from 1839, Edward W. Clay of Philadelphia attacked abolitionists by imagining the miscegenation (also known as "amalgamation") that would come from emancipation. He drew a beautiful white woman, her two biracial children, and her dark-skinned, ridiculously overdressed husband, resting his feet in his wife's lap. Courtesy, American Antiquarian Society.

effort that lifted lowly blacks from barbarism and savagery, taught them disciplined work, and converted them to soul-saving Christianity. According to Virginian Thomas R. Dew, most slaves were grateful. He declared that "the slaves of a good master are his warmest, most constant, and most devoted friends."

African slavery encouraged southern whites to unify around race rather than to divide by class. The grubbiest, most tobacco-stained white man could proudly proclaim his superiority to all blacks and his equality with the most refined southern planter. Georgia attorney Thomas R. R. Cobb observed that every white Southerner "feels that he belongs to an elevated class. It matters not that he is no slaveholder; he is not of the inferior race; he is a freeborn citizen." Consequently, the "poorest meets the richest as an equal; sits at his table with him; salutes him as a neighbor; meets him in every public assembly, and stands on the same social platform." In the South, Cobb boasted, "there is no war of classes." By providing every white Southerner membership in the ruling race, slavery helped whites bridge differences in wealth, education, and culture.

CHAPTER LOCATOR | Why did the South become so distinctly different from the North? | What was plantation life like for masters and mistresses?

364 CHAPTER 13 UNDERSTANDING THE SLAVE SOUTH

The Plantation Economy

As important as slavery was in unifying white Southerners, only about a quarter of the white population lived in slaveholding families. Most slaveholders owned fewer than five slaves. Only about 12 percent of slaveholders owned twenty or more, the number of slaves that historians consider necessary to distinguish a **planter** from a farmer. Despite their small numbers, planters dominated the southern economy. In 1860, 52 percent of the South's slaves lived and worked on **plantations**. Plantation slaves produced more than 75 percent of the South's export crops, the backbone of the region's economy.

The South's major cash crops — tobacco, sugar, rice, and cotton — grew on plantations (**Map 13.2**). Tobacco, the original plantation crop in North America, had

planter
▶ A substantial landowner who tilled his estate with twenty or more slaves. Planters dominated the social and political world of the South. Their values and ideology influenced the values of all southern whites.

plantation
▶ A large farm worked by twenty or more slaves. Although small farms were more numerous, plantations produced more than 75 percent of the South's export crops.

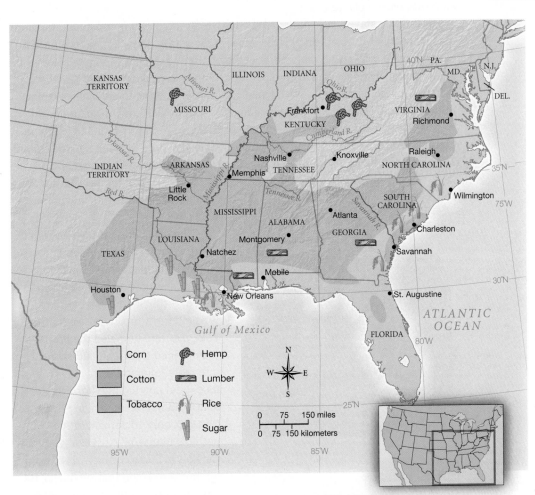

MAP 13.2 ■ The Agricultural Economy of the South, 1860

Cotton dominated the South's agricultural economy, but the region grew a variety of crops and was largely self-sufficient in foodstuffs.

> MAP ACTIVITY

READING THE MAP: In what type of geographic areas were rice and sugar grown? After cotton, what crop commanded the greatest agricultural area in the South? In which region of the South was this crop predominantly found?

CONNECTIONS: What role did the South play in the U.S. economy in 1860? How did the economy of the South differ from that of the North?

| What was plantation life like for slaves? | How did nonslaveholding southern whites work and live? | What place did free blacks occupy in the South? | How did slavery shape southern politics? | Conclusion: How did slavery come to define the South? | ✓ LearningCurve Check what you know. bedfordstmartins.com /roarkunderstanding |

shifted westward in the nineteenth century from the Chesapeake to Tennessee and Kentucky. Large-scale sugar production began in 1795, when Étienne de Boré built a modern sugar mill in what is today New Orleans, and sugar plantations were confined almost entirely to Louisiana. Commercial rice production began in the seventeenth century, and like sugar, rice was confined to a small geographic area, a narrow strip of coast stretching from the Carolinas into Georgia.

But by the nineteenth century, cotton reigned as king of the South's plantation crops. Cotton became commercially significant in the 1790s after the invention of a new cotton gin by Eli Whitney (see chapter 9). Cotton was relatively easy to grow and took little capital to get started — just enough for land, seed, and simple tools. Thus, small farmers as well as planters grew cotton. But planters, whose extensive fields were worked by gangs of slaves, produced three-quarters of the South's cotton, and cotton made planters rich.

Plantation slavery also enriched the nation. By 1840, cotton accounted for more than 60 percent of American exports. Most of the cotton was shipped to Great Britain, the world's largest manufacturer of cotton textiles. Much of the profit from the sale of cotton overseas returned to planters, but some went to northern middlemen who bought, sold, insured, warehoused, and shipped cotton to the mills in Great Britain. As one New York merchant observed, "Cotton has enriched all through whose hands it has passed." As middlemen invested their profits in the booming northern economy, industrial development received a burst of much-needed capital. Furthermore, southern plantations benefited northern industry by providing an important market for textiles, agricultural tools, and other manufactured goods.

The economies of the North and South steadily diverged. While the North developed a mixed economy — agriculture, commerce, and manufacturing — the South remained overwhelmingly agricultural. Year after year, planters funneled the profits they earned from land and slaves back into more land and more slaves. With its capital flowing into agriculture, the South did not develop many factories. By 1860, only 10 percent of the nation's industrial workers lived in the South. Some cotton mills sprang up, but the region that produced 100 percent of the nation's cotton manufactured less than 7 percent of its cotton textiles.

Without significant economic diversification, the South developed fewer cities than did the North and West. In 1860, it was the least urban region in the country. Whereas nearly

The Cotton Gin

Machines for separating cotton fibers from seeds that clung to the fiber — cotton gins (the word *gin* is short for *engine*) — had been around for centuries, but none cleaned cotton quickly and efficiently. In 1793, Eli Whitney, a young New Englander living on a Georgia plantation, built a simple little device that was crude but effective. Smithsonian Institution, National Museum of American History, Behring Center.

CHAPTER LOCATOR | Why did the South become so distinctly different from the North? | What was plantation life like for masters and mistresses?

366 CHAPTER 13 UNDERSTANDING THE SLAVE SOUTH

37 percent of New England's population lived in cities, less than 12 percent of Southerners were urban dwellers. Because the South had so few cities and industrial jobs, it attracted small numbers of European immigrants. Seeking economic opportunity, not competition with slaves (whose labor would keep wages low), immigrants steered northward. In 1860, 13 percent of all Americans were born abroad. But in nine of the fifteen slave states, only 2 percent or less of the population was foreign-born.

Northerners claimed that slavery was a backward labor system, and compared with Northerners, Southerners invested less of their capital in industry, transportation, and public education. But planters' pockets were never fuller than in the 1850s. Planters' decisions to reinvest in agriculture ensured the momentum of the plantation economy and the political and social relationships rooted in it.

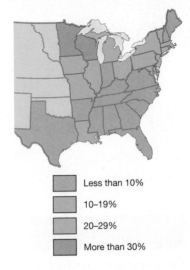

Less than 10%

10–19%

20–29%

More than 30%

Immigrants as a Percentage of State Populations, 1860

QUICK REVIEW <

Why did the nineteenth-century southern economy remain primarily agricultural?

| What was plantation life like for slaves? | How did nonslaveholding southern whites work and live? | What place did free blacks occupy in the South? | How did slavery shape southern politics? | Conclusion: How did slavery come to define the South? | ☑ LearningCurve Check what you know. bedfordstmartins.com /roarkunderstanding |

What was plantation life like for masters and mistresses?

Southern Man with Children and Their Mammy

Obviously prosperous and looking like a man accustomed to giving orders and being obeyed, this patriarch poses around 1848 with his young daughters and their nurse. The absent mother may be dead, and her death might account for the inclusion of the African American domestic servant in the family circle. Collection of the J. Paul Getty Museum, Malibu, CA.

NOWHERE WAS THE CONTRAST between northern and southern life more vivid than on the plantations of the South. A plantation typically included a "big house," where the plantation owner and his family lived, and a slave quarter. Near the big house were the kitchen, storehouse, smokehouse (for curing and preserving meat), and hen coop. More distant were the barns, toolsheds, artisans' workshops, and overseer's house. Large plantations sometimes had an infirmary and a chapel for slaves. Depending on the crop, there was also a tobacco shed, a rice mill, a sugar refinery, or a cotton gin house. Lavish or plain, plantations everywhere had an underlying similarity (**Figure 13.2**).

The plantation was the home of masters, mistresses, and slaves. A hierarchy of rigid roles and duties governed their relationships. Presiding was the master, who by law ruled his wife, children, and slaves as dependents under his dominion and protection.

Paternalism and Male Honor

Whereas smaller planters supervised the labor of their slaves themselves, larger planters hired overseers who went to the fields with the slaves, leaving the planters free to concentrate on marketing, finance, and the general affairs of the plantation. Planters also found time to escape to town to discuss cotton prices, to the courthouse and legislature to debate politics, and to the woods to hunt and fish.

Increasingly, planters characterized their mastery in terms of what they called "Christian guardianship" and what historians have called **paternalism**. The concept of paternalism denied that the form of slavery practiced in the South was brutal and exploitative. Instead, paternalism claimed that plantations benefited all. In exchange for the slaves' work and obedience, masters provided basic care and necessary guidance for a childlike, dependent people. In 1814, Thomas Jefferson captured the essence of the advancing ideal: "We should endeavor, with those whom fortune has thrown on our

paternalism

▶ The theory of slavery that emphasized reciprocal duties and obligations between masters and their slaves, with slaves providing labor and obedience and masters providing basic care and direction. Whites employed the concept of paternalism to deny that the slave system was brutal and exploitative.

CHAPTER LOCATOR | Why did the South become so distinctly different from the North? | **What was plantation life like for masters and mistresses?**

hands, to feed & clothe them well, protect them from ill usage, require such reasonable labor only as is performed voluntarily by freemen, and be led by no repugnancies to abdicate them, and our duties to them." A South Carolina rice planter insisted, "I manage them as my children."

Paternalism was part propaganda and part self-delusion. But it was also economically shrewd. Masters increasingly recognized slaves as valuable assets, particularly after the nation closed its external slave trade in 1808 and the cotton boom stimulated the demand for slaves. The expansion of the slave labor force could come only from natural reproduction. As one slave owner declared in 1849, "It behooves those who own them to make them last as long as possible."

One consequence of paternalism and economic self-interest was a small improvement in slaves' welfare. Diet improved, although nineteenth-century slaves still ate mainly fatty pork and cornmeal. Housing improved, although the cabins still had cracks large enough, slaves said, for cats to slip through. Clothing improved, although slaves seldom received much more than two crude outfits a year and perhaps a pair of cheap shoes. Workdays remained sunup to sundown, but most planters ceased the colonial practice of punishing slaves by branding and mutilation.

Paternalism should not be mistaken for "Ol' Massa's" kindness and goodwill. It encouraged better treatment because it made economic sense to provide at least minimal care for valuable slaves. Nor did paternalism require that planters put aside their whips. State laws gave masters nearly "uncontrolled authority over the body" of the slave, according to one North Carolina judge, and whipping remained planters' basic form of coercion.

Paternalism never won universal acceptance among planters, but by the nineteenth century it had become a kind of communal standard. With its notion that slavery imposed on masters a burden and a duty, paternalism provided slaveholders with a means of rationalizing their rule. But it also provided some slaves with leverage in controlling the conditions of their lives. Slaves learned to manipulate the slaveholder's need to see himself as a good master. To avoid a reputation as a cruel tyrant, planters sometimes negotiated with slaves, rather than just resorting to the whip. Masters sometimes granted slaves small garden plots in which they could work for themselves after working all day in the fields, or they gave slaves a few days off and a dance when they had gathered the last of the cotton.

Virginia statesman Edmund Randolph argued that slavery created in white southern men a "quick and acute sense of personal liberty" and a "disdain for every abridgment of personal independence." Indeed, prickly individualism and aggressive independence became crucial features of the southern concept of honor. Social standing, political advancement, and even self-esteem rested on an honorable reputation. Defending honor became a male passion. Andrew Jackson's mother reportedly told her son, "Never tell a lie, nor take what is not your own, nor sue anybody for slander or assault and battery. *Always settle them cases yourself.*"

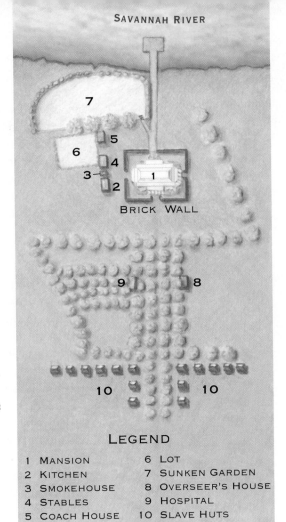

FIGURE 13.2 ■ A Southern Plantation

Slavery determined how masters laid out their plantations, where they situated their "big houses" and slave quarters, and what kinds of buildings they constructed. This model of the Hermitage, the mansion built in 1830 for Henry McAlpin, a Georgia rice planter, shows the overseer's house poised in a grove of oak trees halfway between the owner's mansion and the slave huts. The placement of the mansion at the end of an extended road leading up from the river underscored McAlpin's affluence and authority.

Adapted from *Back of the Big House: The Architecture of Plantation Slavery* by John Michael Vlach. Copyright © 1993 by the University of North Carolina Press. Reprinted with permission of the University of North Carolina Press. Original illustration property of the Historic American Buildings Survey, a division of the National Park Service.

| What was plantation life like for slaves? | How did nonslaveholding southern whites work and live? | What place did free blacks occupy in the South? | How did slavery shape southern politics? | Conclusion: How did slavery come to define the South? | ✓ LearningCurve Check what you know. bedfordstmartins.com /roarkunderstanding |

Plantation Masters
- Often characterized their roles in terms of paternalism.
- On larger plantations, hired overseers to supervise slaves in the field.
- Were increasingly interested in extending the lives of slave property.

Plantation Mistresses
- Were expected to conform to gender norms for white women.
- Lived within a system that both glorified and subordinated them.
- Lived privileged lives but also experienced disadvantages.

chivalry
▶ The South's romantic ideal of male-female relationships. Chivalry's underlying assumptions about the weakness of white women and the protective authority of men resembled the paternalistic defense of slavery.

Southerners also expected an honorable gentleman to be a proper patriarch. Nowhere in America was masculine power more accentuated. The master's absolute dominion sometimes led to miscegenation. Laws prohibited interracial sex, but as long as slavery gave white men extraordinary power, slave women were forced to submit to the sexual demands of the men who owned them.

In time, as the children of one elite family married the children of another, ties of blood and kinship, as well as ideology and economic interest, linked planters to one another. Aware of what they shared as slaveholders, planters worked together to defend their common interests. The values of the big house — slavery, honor, male domination — washed over the boundaries of plantations and flooded all of southern life.

The Southern Lady and Feminine Virtues

Like their northern counterparts, southern ladies were expected to possess the feminine virtues of piety, purity, chastity, and obedience within the context of marriage, motherhood, and domesticity. Countless toasts praised the southern lady as the perfect complement to her husband, the commanding patriarch. She was physically weak, "formed only for the less laborious occupations," and thus dependent on male protection. To gain this protection, she exhibited modesty and delicacy, possessed beauty and grace, and cultivated refinement and charm.

Chivalry — the South's romantic ideal of male-female relationships — glorified the lady while it subordinated her. Chivalry's underlying assumptions about the weakness of women and the protective authority of men resembled the paternalistic defense of slavery. Just as the slaveholder's mastery was written into law, so too were the paramount rights of husbands. Married women lost almost all their property rights to their husbands. Women throughout the nation found divorce difficult, but southern women found it almost impossible.

Daughters of planters confronted chivalry's demands at an early age. At their private boarding schools, they learned to be southern ladies, reading literature, learning languages, and studying the appropriate drawing-room arts. Elite women began courting young and married early. Kate Carney exaggerated only slightly when she despaired in her diary: "Today, I am seventeen, getting quite old, and am not married." Yet marriage meant turning their fates over to their husbands and making enormous efforts to live up to their region's lofty ideal.

Proslavery advocates claimed that slavery freed white women from drudgery. Surrounded "by her domestics," declared Thomas R. Dew, "she ceases to be a mere beast of burden" and "becomes the cheering and animating center of the family circle." In reality, however, having servants required the plantation mistress to work long hours. She managed the big house, directly supervising as many as a dozen slaves. But unlike her husband, the mistress had no overseer. All house servants answered directly to her. She assigned them tasks each morning, directed their work throughout the day, and punished them when she found fault.

Whereas masters used their status as slaveholders as a springboard into public affairs, mistresses' lives were circumscribed by the plantation. Masters left when they pleased, but mistresses needed chaperones to travel. When they could, they went to church, but women spent most days at home, where they often became lonely. In 1853, Mary Kendall wrote how much she enjoyed her sister's

CHAPTER LOCATOR | Why did the South become so distinctly different from the North? | What was plantation life like for masters and mistresses?

CHAPTER 13
370 UNDERSTANDING THE SLAVE SOUTH

The Price of Blood This 1868 painting by T. S. Noble depicts a transaction between a slave trader and a rich planter. The trader nervously pretends to study the contract, while the planter waits impatiently for the completion of the sale. The planter's mulatto son, who is being sold, looks away. The children of white men and slave women were property and could be sold by the father/master. Morris Museum of Art, Augusta, GA.

> VISUAL ACTIVITY

READING THE IMAGE: Who is absent from the painting, and what does this suggest about the tragedy of miscegenation?
CONNECTIONS: The white male planter represented the pinnacle of southern society. How did white women, black men, and black women fit into this strict hierarchy?

letter: "For about three weeks I did not have the pleasure of seeing one white female face, there being no white family except our own upon the plantation."

No feature of plantation life generated more anguish among mistresses than miscegenation. Mary Boykin Chesnut of Camden, South Carolina, confided in her diary: "Ours is a monstrous system, a wrong and iniquity. Like the patriarchs of old, our men live all in one house with their wives and their concubines; and the mulattos one sees in every family partly resemble the white children. Any lady is ready to tell you who is the father of all the mulatto children in everybody's household but her own. Those, she seems to think drop from the clouds."

But most planters' wives, including Chesnut, accepted slavery. After all, the privileged life of a mistress rested on slave labor as much as a master's did. Mistresses enjoyed the rewards of their class and race. But these rewards came at a price. Still, the heaviest burdens of slavery fell not on those who lived in the big house, but on those who toiled to support them.

QUICK REVIEW <

Why did the ideology of paternalism gain currency among planters in the nineteenth century?

| What was plantation life like for slaves? | How did nonslaveholding southern whites work and live? | What place did free blacks occupy in the South? | How did slavery shape southern politics? | Conclusion: How did slavery come to define the South? | ✔ **LearningCurve** Check what you know. bedfordstmartins.com /roarkunderstanding |

> What was plantation life like for slaves?

Slave Quarter, South Carolina

On large plantations, several score of African Americans lived in cabins that were often arranged along what slaves called "the street." The dwellings in this picture were better built than the typical rickety, one-room, dirt-floored slave cabin. During the daylight hours of the workweek, when most men and women labored in the fields, the quarter was mostly empty. At night and on Sundays, it was a busy place. Collection of the New-York Historical Society.

> ## KEY FACTORS

- An overwhelming majority of plantation slaves worked as field hands.
- Nine out of ten house slaves were women.
- Family and religion provided refuge for slaves.
- Slaves resisted by running away; outright rebellion was rare.

ON MOST PLANTATIONS, only a few hundred yards separated the big house and the slave quarter. But the distance was great enough to provide slaves with some privacy. Out of eyesight and earshot of the big house, slaves drew together and built lives of their own. They created families, worshipped God, and developed an African American community and culture. Individually and collectively, slaves found ways to resist their bondage.

Despite the rise of plantations, almost half of the South's slaves lived and worked elsewhere. Most labored on small farms, where they wielded a hoe alongside another slave or two and perhaps their master. But by 1860, almost half a million slaves (one in eight) did not work in agriculture at all. Some lived in towns and cities, where they worked as domestics, day laborers, bakers, barbers, tailors, and more. Other slaves, far from urban centers, toiled as fishermen, lumbermen, railroad workers, and deckhands on riverboats. Slaves could also be found in most of the South's factories. Nevertheless, a majority of slaves (52 percent) counted plantations as their workplaces and homes.

CHAPTER LOCATOR | Why did the South become so distinctly different from the North? | What was plantation life like for masters and mistresses?

372   CHAPTER 13
UNDERSTANDING THE SLAVE SOUTH

Work

Whites enslaved blacks for their labor, and all slaves who were capable of productive labor worked. Former slave Carrie Hudson recalled that children who were "knee high to a duck" were sent to the fields to carry water to thirsty workers or to protect ripening crops from hungry birds. Others helped in the slave nursery, caring for children even younger than themselves, or in the big house, where they swept floors or shooed flies in the dining room. When slave boys and girls reached the age of eleven or twelve, masters sent most of them to the fields. After a lifetime of labor, old women left the fields to care for the small children and spin yarn, and old men moved on to mind livestock and clean stables.

The overwhelming majority of plantation slaves worked as field hands. Planters sometimes assigned men and women to separate gangs, the women working at lighter tasks and the men doing the heavy work of clearing and breaking the land. But women also did heavy work. "I had to work hard," Nancy Boudry remembered, and "plow and go and split wood just like a man." The backbreaking labor and the monotonous routines caused one ex-slave to observe that the "history of one day is the history of every day."

A few slaves (about one in ten) became house servants. Nearly all of those (nine out of ten) were women. They cooked, cleaned, babysat, washed clothes, and did the dozens of other tasks the master and mistress required. House servants were constantly on call, with no time that was entirely their own. Since no servant could please constantly, most bore the brunt of white frustration and rage. Ex-slave Jacob Branch of Texas remembered, "My poor mama! Every washday old Missy give her a beating."

Even rarer than house servants were skilled artisans. In the cotton South, no more than one slave in twenty (almost all men) worked in a skilled trade. Most were blacksmiths and carpenters, but slaves also worked as masons, mechanics, millers, and shoemakers. Skilled slave fathers took pride in teaching their crafts to their sons. "My pappy was one of the black smiths and worked in the shop," John Mathews remembered. "I had to help my pappy in the shop when I was a child and I learnt how to beat out the iron and make wagon tires, and make plows."

Isaac Jefferson

In this 1845 daguerreotype, seventy-year-old Isaac Jefferson proudly poses in the apron he wore while practicing his crafts as a tinsmith and nail maker. Isaac, his wife, and their two children, all slaves of Thomas Jefferson, were deeded to Jefferson's daughter Mary when she married in 1797. Isaac worked at Jefferson's home, Monticello, until 1820, when he moved to Petersburg, Virginia. When work was slow on the home plantation, slave owners often would hire out their skilled artisans to neighbors who needed a carpenter, blacksmith, mason, or tinsmith. Special Collections Department, University of Virginia Library.

| What was plantation life like for slaves? | How did nonslaveholding southern whites work and live? | What place did free blacks occupy in the South? | How did slavery shape southern politics? | Conclusion: How did slavery come to define the South? | ✓ LearningCurve Check what you know. bedfordstmartins.com /roarkunderstanding |

Rarest of all slave occupations was that of slave driver. Probably no more than one male slave in a hundred worked in this capacity. These men were well named, for their primary task was driving other slaves to work harder in the fields. In some drivers' hands, the whip never rested. Ex-slave Jane Johnson of South Carolina called her driver the "meanest man, white or black, I ever see." But other drivers showed all the restraint they could. "Ole Gabe didn't like that whippin' business," West Turner of Virginia remembered. "When Marsa was there, he would lay it on 'cause he had to. But when old Marsa wasn't lookin', he never would beat them slaves."

Normally, slaves worked from what they called "can to can't," from "can see" in the morning to "can't see" at night. Even with a break at noon for a meal and rest, it made for a long day. For slaves, Lewis Young recalled, "work, work, work, 'twas all they do."

Family and Religion

From dawn to dusk, slaves worked for the master, but at night and all day Sunday and usually Saturday afternoon, slaves were left largely to themselves. Bone tired perhaps, they nonetheless used the time to develop and enjoy what mattered most to them.

Though severely battered, the black family survived slavery. Young men and women in the quarter fell in love, married, and set up housekeeping in cabins of their own. But no laws recognized slave marriage, and therefore no master was legally obligated to honor the bond. While plantation records show that some slave marriages were long-lasting, the massive deportation associated with the Second Middle Passage destroyed hundreds of thousands of slave families.

In 1858, a slave named Abream Scriven wrote to his wife, who lived on a neighboring plantation in South Carolina. "My dear wife," he began, "I take the pleasure of writing you . . . with much regret to inform you I am Sold to man by the name of Peterson, a Treader and Stays in New Orleans." Before he left for Louisiana, Scriven asked his wife to "give my love to my father and mother and tell them good Bye for me. And if we do not meet in this world I hope to meet in heaven. . . . My dear wife for you and my children my pen cannot express the griffe I feel to be parted from you all." He closed with words no master would have permitted in a slave's marriage vows: "I remain your truly husband until Death." The letter makes clear Scriven's love for his family; it also demonstrates slavery's massive assault on family life in the quarter.

Masters sometimes permitted slave families to work on their own, "overwork," as it was called. In the evenings and on Sundays, they tilled gardens, raised pigs and fowl, and chopped wood, selling the products in the market for a little pocket change. "Den each fam'ly have some chickens and sell dem and de eggs and maybe go huntin' and sell de hides and git some money," a former Alabama slave remembered. "Den us buy what am Sunday clothes with dat money, sech as hats and pants and shoes and dresses."

Religion also provided slaves with a refuge and a reason for living. In the nineteenth century, evangelical Baptists and Methodists had great success in converting slaves from their African beliefs. Planters promoted Christianity in the quarter because they believed that the slaves' salvation was part of the obligation of paternalism; they also hoped that religion would make slaves more obedient. South Carolina

CHAPTER LOCATOR | Why did the South become so distinctly different from the North? | What was plantation life like for masters and mistresses?

slaveholder Charles Colcock Jones, the leading missionary to the slaves, instructed them "to count their Masters 'worthy of all honour,' as those whom God has placed over them in this world." But slaves laughed up their sleeves at such messages. "That old white preacher just was telling us slaves to be good to our masters," one ex-slave said with a chuckle. "We ain't cared a bit about that stuff he was telling us 'cause we wanted to sing, pray, and serve God in our own way."

Meeting in their cabins or secretly in the woods, slaves created an African American Christianity that served their needs, not the masters'. Laws prohibited teaching slaves to read, but a few could read enough to struggle with the Bible. They interpreted the Christian message themselves. Rather than obedience, their faith emphasized justice. Slaves believed that God kept score and that the accounts of this world would be settled in the next. But the slaves' faith also spoke to their experiences in this world. In the Old Testament, they discovered Moses, who delivered his people from slavery, and in the New Testament, they found Jesus, who offered salvation to all. Jesus' message of equality provided a potent antidote to the planters' claim that blacks were an inferior people whom God condemned to slavery.

Christianity did not entirely drive out traditional African beliefs. Even slaves who were Christians sometimes continued to believe that conjurers, witches, and spirits possessed the power to injure and protect. Moreover, slaves' Christian music, preaching, and rituals reflected the influence of Africa, as did many of their secular activities, such as wood carving, quilt making, dancing, and storytelling. But by the mid-nineteenth century, black Christianity had assumed a central place in slaves' quest for freedom. In the words of one spiritual, "O my Lord delivered Daniel / O why not deliver me too?"

Resistance and Rebellion

Slaves did not suffer slavery passively. They were, as whites said, "troublesome property." Slaves understood that accommodation to what they could not change was the price of survival, but in a hundred ways they protested their bondage. Theoretically, the master was all-powerful and the slave powerless. But sustained by their families, religion, and community, slaves engaged in day-to-day resistance against their enslavers.

The spectrum of slave resistance ranged from mild to extreme. Telling a pointed story by the fireside in a slave cabin was probably the mildest form of protest. But when the weak got the better of the strong, as they did in tales of Br'er Rabbit and Br'er Fox (Br'er is a contraction of Brother), listeners could enjoy the thrill of a vicarious victory over their masters. Protest in the fields was riskier and included putting rocks in their cotton bags before having them weighed, feigning illness, and pretending to be so thickheaded that they could not understand the simplest instruction. Slaves broke so many hoes that owners outfitted the tools with oversized handles. Slaves so mistreated the work animals that masters switched from horses to mules, which could absorb more abuse. Although slaves worked hard in the master's fields, they also sabotaged his interests.

Running away was a common form of protest, but except along the borders with northern states and with Mexico, escape to freedom was almost impossible. Most runaways could hope only to escape for a few days. They sought temporary

| What was plantation life like for slaves? | How did nonslaveholding southern whites work and live? | What place did free blacks occupy in the South? | How did slavery shape southern politics? | Conclusion: How did slavery come to define the South? | ✔ LearningCurve Check what you know. bedfordstmartins.com /roarkunderstanding |

375

Horrid Massacre in Virginia

In August 1831, the slave Nat Turner led a bloody rebellion. Although the local militia quickly killed or captured all the rebels except Turner, rebelling slaves had slaughtered fifty-seven whites. When Turner was finally captured, he was tried, convicted, and executed. Although there was never another rebellion as deadly as Turner's, images of black violence continued to haunt white imaginations. Library of Congress.

respite from hard labor or avoided punishment, and their "lying out," as it was known, usually ended when the runaway, worn-out and ragged, gave up or was finally chased down by slave-hunting dogs.

Although resistance was common, outright rebellion — a violent assault on slavery by large numbers of slaves — was very rare. Conditions gave rebels almost no chance of success. By 1860, whites in the South outnumbered blacks two to one and were heavily armed. Moreover, communication between plantations was difficult, and the South provided little protective wilderness into which rebels could retreat and defend themselves.

Despite steady resistance and occasional rebellion, slaves did not have the power to end their bondage. Slavery thwarted their hopes and aspirations. It broke some and crippled others. But slavery's destructive power had to contend with the resiliency of the human spirit. Slaves fought back physically, culturally, and spiritually. Not only did they survive bondage, but they also created in the quarter a vibrant African American culture that buoyed them up during long hours in the fields and brought them joy and hope in the few hours they had to themselves.

> **QUICK REVIEW**

What types of resistance did slaves participate in, and why did slave resistance rarely take the form of rebellion?

CHAPTER LOCATOR | Why did the South become so distinctly different from the North? | What was plantation life like for masters and mistresses?

Gathering Corn in Virginia

In this romanticized agricultural scene, painter Felix O. C. Darley depicts members of a white farm family gathering its harvest by hand. In reality, growing corn was hard work. The artist, however, is less concerned with realism than with extolling rural family labor as virtuous and noble. Darley surrounds the southern yeomen with an aura of republican independence, dignity, and freedom. Warner Collection of Gulf States Paper Corporation.

MOST WHITES IN THE South did not own slaves, not even one. In 1860, more than six million of the South's eight million whites lived in slaveless households. Some nonslaveholding whites lived in cities and worked as artisans, mechanics, and traders. Others lived in the country and worked as storekeepers, parsons, and school-teachers. But most "plain folk" were small farmers. Perhaps three out of four were **yeomen**, small farmers who owned their own land. As in the North, farm ownership provided a family with an economic foundation, social respectability, and political standing. Unlike their northern counterparts, however, southern yeomen lived in a region whose economy and society were increasingly dominated by unfree labor.

In an important sense, the South had more than one white yeomanry. The huge southern landscape provided space enough for two yeoman societies, separated roughly along geographic lines. Yeomen throughout the South had much in common, but the life of a small farm family in the cotton belt (the flatlands that spread from South Carolina to Texas) differed from the life of a family in the upcountry (the area of hills and mountains). And some rural slaveless whites were not yeomen; they owned no land at all and were sometimes desperately poor.

yeomen

▶ Farmers who owned and worked their own small plots of land. Yeomen living within the plantation belt were more dependent on planters than were yeomen in the upcountry, where small farmers dominated.

| What was plantation life like for slaves? | **How did nonslaveholding southern whites work and live?** | What place did free blacks occupy in the South? | How did slavery shape southern politics? | Conclusion: How did slavery come to define the South? | ✓ **LearningCurve** Check what you know. bedfordstmartins.com /roarkunderstanding |

377

The Cotton Belt

plantation belt

▶ Flatlands that spread from South Carolina to east Texas and were dominated by large plantations.

upcountry

▶ The hills and mountains of the South whose higher elevation, colder climate, rugged terrain, and poor transportation made the region less hospitable than the flatlands to slavery and large plantations.

Upcountry of the South

Plantation-Belt Yeomen

Plantation-belt yeomen lived within the orbit of the planter class. Small farms outnumbered plantations in the **plantation belt**, but they were dwarfed in importance. Small farmers grew mainly food crops, particularly corn, and produced only a few 400-pound bales of cotton each year. Large planters measured their cotton crop in hundreds of bales. Small farmers' cotton tied them to planters. Unable to afford cotton gins or baling presses of their own, they relied on slave owners to gin and bale their cotton. With no link to merchants in the port cities, plantation-belt yeomen also turned to better-connected planters to ship and sell their cotton.

A network of relationships laced small farmers and planters together. Planters hired out surplus slaves to ambitious yeomen who wanted to expand cotton production. They sometimes chose overseers from among the sons of local farm families. Plantation mistresses occasionally nursed ailing neighbors. Family ties could span class lines, making planter and yeoman kin as well as neighbors. Yeomen helped police slaves by riding in slave patrols, which nightly scoured country roads to make certain that no slaves were moving about without permission. On Sundays, plantation dwellers and plain folk came together in church to worship.

Plantation-belt yeomen may have envied, and at times even resented, wealthy slaveholders, but small farmers learned to accommodate. Planters made accommodation easier by going out of their way to behave as good neighbors and avoid direct exploitation of slaveless whites in their community. As a consequence, rather than raging at the oppression of the planter regime, the typical plantation-belt yeoman sought entry into it. He dreamed of adding acreage to his farm, buying a few slaves of his own, and retiring from exhausting field work.

Upcountry Yeomen

By contrast, the hills and mountains of the South resisted the spread of slavery and plantations. In the western parts of Virginia, North Carolina, and South Carolina; in northern Georgia and Alabama; and in eastern Tennessee and Kentucky, the higher elevation, colder climate, rugged terrain, and poor transportation made it difficult for commercial agriculture to make headway. As a result, yeomen dominated, and planters and slaves were scarce.

All members of the **upcountry** farm family worked, their tasks depending on their sex and age. Husbands labored in the fields, and with their sons they cleared, plowed, planted, and cultivated primarily food crops — corn, wheat, beans, sweet potatoes, and perhaps some fruit. Women and their daughters labored in and about the cabin. One upcountry farmer remembered that his mother "worked in the house cooking, spinning, weaving [and doing] patchwork." Women also tended the vegetable garden, kept a cow and some chickens, preserved food, cleaned their homes, fed their families, and cared for their children. Male and female tasks were equally crucial to the farm's success, but as in other white southern households, the male patriarch ruled the domestic sphere.

The typical upcountry yeoman also grew a little cotton or tobacco, but food production was more important than cash crops. Not much currency changed hands in the upcountry. Barter was common. A yeoman might trade his small

CHAPTER LOCATOR | Why did the South become so distinctly different from the North? | What was plantation life like for masters and mistresses?

CHAPTER 13
378 UNDERSTANDING THE SLAVE SOUTH

cotton or tobacco crop to a country store owner for a little salt, bullets, needles, and nails, or swap extra sweet potatoes for a plow from a blacksmith or for leather from a tanner. Networks of exchange and mutual assistance tied individual homesteads to the larger community. Farm families joined together in logrolling, house and barn raising, and cornhusking.

Even the hills had some plantations and slaves, but the few upcountry folks who owned slaves usually had only two or three. As a result, slaveholders had much less social and economic power, and yeomen had more. But the upcountry did not oppose slavery. As long as plain folk there were free to lead their own lives, they defended slavery and white supremacy just as staunchly as other white Southerners.

Poor Whites

The majority of nonslaveholding white Southerners were hardworking, landholding small farmers, but Northerners held a different image of this group. They believed that slavery had condemned most whites to poverty and backwardness. One antislavery advocate charged that the South harbored three classes: "the slaves on whom devolves all the regular industry, the slaveholders who reap all the fruits, and an idle and lawless rabble who live dispersed over vast plains little removed from absolute barbarism." Critics called this third class a variety of derogatory names: hillbillies, crackers, rednecks, and poor white trash. According to critics, poor whites were not just whites who were poor. They were also supposedly ignorant, diseased, and degenerate.

Contrary to northern opinion, only about one in four nonslaveholding rural white men was landless and very poor. Some worked as tenants, renting land and struggling to make a go of it. Others survived by herding pigs and cattle. And still others worked for meager wages, ditching, mining, logging, and laying track for railroads.

Some poor white men earned reputations for mayhem and violence. One visitor claimed that a "bowie-knife was a universal, and a pistol a not at all unusual companion." Edward Isham, an illiterate roustabout, spent about as much time fighting as he did working. When he wasn't engaged in ear-biting, eye-gouging free-for-alls, he gambled, drank, stole, had run-ins with the law, and in 1860 murdered a respected slaveholder, for which he was hanged.

Unlike Isham, most poor white men worked hard and dreamed of becoming yeomen. The Lipscomb family illustrates the possibility of upward mobility. In 1845, Smith and Sally Lipscomb and their children abandoned their worn-out land in South Carolina for Benton County, Alabama. "Benton is a mountainous country but ther is a heep of good levil land to tend in it," Smith wrote back to his brother. Alabama, Smith said, "will be better for the rising generation if not for ourselves but I think it will be the best for us all that live any length of time."

Because they had no money to buy land, they squatted on seven unoccupied acres. With the help of neighbors, they built a 22-by-24-foot cabin, a detached kitchen, and two stables. In the first year, Smith and his sons produced several bales of cotton and enough food for the table. The women worked just as hard in the cabin, and Sally contributed to the family's income by selling homemade shirts

What was plantation life like for slaves?

How did nonslaveholding southern whites work and live?

What place did free blacks occupy in the South?

How did slavery shape southern politics?

Conclusion: How did slavery come to define the South?

✓ LearningCurve
Check what you know.
bedfordstmartins.com
/roarkunderstanding

and socks. In time, the Lipscombs bought land and joined the Baptist church, completing their transformation to respectable yeomen.

Many poor whites succeeded in climbing the economic ladder, but in the 1850s upward mobility slowed. The cotton boom of that decade caused planters to expand their operations, driving the price of land beyond the reach of poor families. Whether they gained their own land or not, however, poor whites shared common cultural traits with yeoman farmers.

The Culture of the Plain Folk

The lives of most plain folk revolved around farms, family, a handful of neighbors, the local church, and perhaps a country store. Work occupied most hours, but plain folk still found time for pleasure. "Dancing they are all fond of," a visitor to North Carolina discovered, "especially when they can get a fiddle, or bagpipe." But the most popular pastimes of men and boys were fishing and hunting. A traveler in Mississippi recalled that his host sent "two of his sons, little fellows that looked almost too small to shoulder a gun," for food. "One went off towards the river and the other struck into the forest, and in a few hours we were feasting on delicious venison, trout and turtle."

Plain folk did not have much "book learning." Private academies charged fees that yeomen could not afford, and public schools were scarce. Although most people managed to pick up the "three R's," approximately one southern white man in five was illiterate in 1860, and the rate for white women was even higher. "People here prefer talking to reading," a Virginian remarked. Telling stories, reciting ballads, and singing hymns were important activities in yeoman culture.

Plain folk spent more hours in revival tents than in classrooms. Preachers spoke day and night to save souls. Baptists and Methodists adopted revivalism most readily and by midcentury had become the South's largest religious groups. By emphasizing free choice and individual worth, the plain folk's religion was hopeful and affirming. Hymns and spirituals provided guides to right and wrong — praising humility and steadfastness, condemning drunkenness and profanity. Above all, hymns spoke of the eventual release from worldly sorrows and the assurance of eternal salvation.

> **QUICK REVIEW**

Why did the lives of plantation-belt yeomen and upcountry yeomen diverge?

CHAPTER LOCATOR | Why did the South become so distinctly different from the North? | What was plantation life like for masters and mistresses?

380 CHAPTER 13 UNDERSTANDING THE SLAVE SOUTH

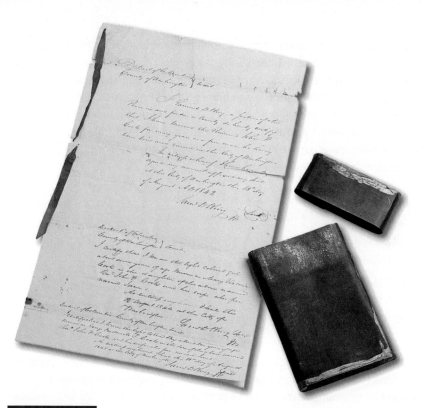

Freedom Paper This legal document attests to the free status of the Reverend John F. Cook of Washington, D.C., his daughter Mary, and his son George. Cook was a free black man who kept his "freedom paper" in this watertight tin, which he probably carried with him at all times. Moorland-Spingarn Research Center, Howard University, Washington, D.C.

What place did free blacks occupy in the South?

ALL WHITE SOUTHERNERS — slaveholders and slaveless alike — considered themselves superior to all blacks. But not every black Southerner was a slave. In 1860, some 260,000 (approximately 6 percent) of the region's 4.1 million African Americans were free. What is surprising is not that their numbers were small but that they existed at all. According to proslavery thinking, blacks were supposed to be slaves; only whites were supposed to be free. Blacks who were free stood out, and whites made them targets of oppression. But a few found success despite the restrictions placed on them by white Southerners.

Precarious Freedom

The population of **free blacks** swelled after the Revolutionary War, when the natural rights philosophy of the Declaration of Independence, the egalitarian message of evangelical Protestantism, and a depression in the tobacco economy led to a brief flurry of emancipation — the act of freeing a person from slavery. The soaring numbers of free blacks worried white Southerners, who, because of the cotton boom, wanted more slaves, not more blacks who were free.

free blacks

▶ African Americans who were not enslaved. Southern whites worried about the increasing numbers of free blacks. In the 1820s and 1830s, state legislatures stemmed the growth of the free black population and shrank the liberty of free blacks.

| What was plantation life like for slaves? | How did nonslaveholding southern whites work and live? | **What place did free blacks occupy in the South?** | How did slavery shape southern politics? | Conclusion: How did slavery come to define the South? | ✓ **LearningCurve** Check what you know. bedfordstmartins.com /roarkunderstanding |

1822

– Denmark Vesey is executed.

1820s–1830s

– Southern legislatures restrict free blacks.

1860

– Some 260,000 free blacks live in the South.

In the 1820s and 1830s, state legislatures stemmed the growth of the free black population and shrank the liberty of those blacks who had gained their freedom. New laws denied masters the right to free their slaves. Increasingly, whites subjected free blacks to the same laws as slaves. Free blacks could not testify under oath in a court of law or serve on juries. "Free negroes belong to a degraded caste of society," a South Carolina judge said in 1848. "They are in no respect on a perfect equality with the white man. . . . They ought, by law, to be compelled to demean themselves as inferiors."

> **Limits on Free Blacks**

- Subjected to special taxes.
- Prohibited from interstate travel.
- Denied the right to have schools.
- Denied the right to participate in politics.
- Required to carry "freedom papers" to prove they were not slaves.

Laws confined most free African Americans to poverty and dependence. Typically, free blacks were rural, uneducated, unskilled agricultural laborers and domestic servants who had to scramble to survive. Opportunities of any kind — for work, education, or community — were slim. Planters believed that free blacks set a bad example for slaves, subverting the racial subordination that was the essence of slavery.

Whites feared that free blacks might lead slaves in rebellion. In 1822, whites in Charleston accused Denmark Vesey, a free black carpenter, of conspiring with plantation slaves to slaughter Charleston's white inhabitants. The authorities rounded up scores of suspects, who, prodded by torture and the threat of death, implicated others in a "plot to riot in blood, outrage, and rapine." Although the city fathers never found any weapons and Vesey and most of the accused steadfastly denied the charges of conspiracy, officials hanged thirty-five black men, including Vesey, and banished another thirty-seven blacks from the state.

Achievement despite Restrictions

Despite increasingly harsh laws and stepped-up persecution, free African Americans made the most of the advantages their status offered. Unlike slaves, free blacks could legally marry and pass on their heritage of freedom to their children. Freedom also meant that they could choose occupations and own property. For most, however, these economic rights proved only theoretical, for a majority of the South's free blacks remained propertyless.

Still, some free blacks escaped the poverty and degradation whites thrust on them. Particularly in the South's cities, a free black elite emerged. Consisting of light-skinned African Americans, they worked at skilled trades, as tailors, carpenters, mechanics, and the like. They operated schools for their children and traveled in and out of their states, despite laws forbidding both activities. They worshipped with whites (in separate seating) and lived scattered about in white neighborhoods, not in ghettos. And some owned slaves. Of the 3,200 black slaveholders (barely 1 percent of the free black population), most owned only a few family members whom they could not legally free. Others owned slaves in large numbers and exploited them for labor.

One such free black slave owner was William Ellison of South Carolina. Born a slave in 1790, Ellison bought his freedom in 1816 and set up business as a cotton gin maker, a trade he had learned as a slave. By 1835, he was prosperous enough to purchase the home of a former governor of the state. By the time of his death in 1861, he had become a cotton planter, with sixty-three slaves and an 800-acre plantation.

Most free blacks neither became slaveholders nor sought to raise a slave rebellion, as whites accused Denmark Vesey of doing. Rather, most free blacks simply tried to preserve their freedom, which was under increasing attack. Unlike blacks in the North whose freedom was secure, free blacks in the South clung to a precarious freedom by seeking to impress whites with their reliability, economic contributions, and good behavior.

QUICK REVIEW

Why did many state legislatures pass laws restricting free blacks' rights in the 1820s and 1830s?

| What was plantation life like for slaves? | How did nonslaveholding southern whites work and live? | **What place did free blacks occupy in the South?** | How did slavery shape southern politics? | Conclusion: How did slavery come to define the South? | ☑ LearningCurve Check what you know. bedfordstmartins.com /roarkunderstanding |

> How did slavery shape southern politics?

Gen. James Chesnut, Jr., C.S.A.

BY THE MID-NINETEENTH CENTURY, all southern white men — planters and plain folk — and no southern black men, even those who were free, could vote. The nonslaveholding white majority wielded less political power than their numbers indicated. The slaveholding white minority wielded more. With a well-developed sense of class interest, slaveholders engaged in party politics, campaigns, and officeholding, and as a result they received significant benefits from state governments. Nonslaveholding whites were concerned mainly with preserving their liberties and keeping their taxes low. They asked government for little of an economic nature, and they received little.

Slaveholders sometimes worried about nonslaveholders' loyalty to slavery, but most whites accepted the planters' argument that the existing social order served all Southerners' interests. Slavery rewarded every white man — no matter how poor — with membership in the South's white ruling race. It also provided the means by which nonslaveholders might someday advance into the ranks of the planters. White men in the South argued furiously about many things, but they agreed that they should take land from Indians, promote agriculture, uphold white supremacy and masculine privilege, and defend slavery from its enemies.

> KEY FACTORS

- Suffrage was extended throughout the South to all adult white males by 1850.
- Slaveholding white men were most active in politics and were far more likely to hold political office than those without slaves.

CHAPTER LOCATOR | Why did the South become so distinctly different from the North? | What was plantation life like for masters and mistresses?

The Democratization of the Political Arena

In the first half of the nineteenth century, Southerners eliminated the wealth and property requirements that had once restricted political participation. Most southern states also removed the property requirements for holding state offices. To be sure, undemocratic features lingered. Plantation districts still wielded disproportionate power in several state legislatures. Nevertheless, southern politics took place within an increasingly democratic political structure, as it did elsewhere in the nation.

White male suffrage ushered in an era of vigorous electoral competition in the South. Eager voters rushed to the polls to exercise their new rights. Candidates crisscrossed their electoral districts, treating citizens to barbecues and bands, rum and races, as well as stirring oratory. In the South, it seemed, "everybody talked politics everywhere," even the "illiterate and shoeless."

As politics became aggressively democratic, it also grew fiercely partisan. From the 1830s to the 1850s, Whigs and Democrats battled for the electorate's favor. Both parties presented themselves as the plain white folk's best friend. All candidates declared their allegiance to republican equality and pledged themselves to defend the people's liberty. And each party sought to portray the other as a collection of rich, snobbish, selfish men who had antidemocratic designs up their silk sleeves.

Planter Power

Whether Whig or Democrat, southern officeholders were likely to be slave owners. By 1860, the percentage of slave owners in state legislatures ranged from 41 percent in Missouri to nearly 86 percent in North Carolina. Legislators not only tended to own slaves; they also often owned large numbers. The percentage of planters (individuals with twenty or more slaves) in southern legislatures in 1860 ranged from 5.3 percent in Missouri to 55.4 percent in South Carolina. Even in North Carolina, where only 3 percent of the state's white families belonged to the planter class, more than 36 percent of state legislators were planters. Almost everywhere nonslaveholders were in the majority, but plain folk did not throw the planters out of office.

Upper-class dominance of southern politics reflected the elite's success in persuading the yeoman majority that what was good for slaveholders was also good for plain folk. In reality, the South had, on the whole, done well by common white men. Most had farms of their own. They participated as equals in a democratic political system. They enjoyed an elevated social status, above all blacks and in theory equal to all other whites. They commanded patriarchal authority over their households. And as long as slavery existed, they could dream of joining the planter class. Slaveless white men found much to celebrate in the slave South.

Most slaveholders took pains to win the plain folk's trust and to nurture their respect. One nonslaveholder told his wealthy neighbor that he had a bright political future because he never thought himself "too good to sit down & talk to a poor man." Mary Boykin Chesnut complained about the fawning attention her husband, a U.S. senator from South Carolina, showed to poor men, including one who

| What was plantation life like for slaves? | How did nonslaveholding southern whites work and live? | What place did free blacks occupy in the South? | **How did slavery shape southern politics?** | Conclusion: How did slavery come to define the South? | ✔ LearningCurve Check what you know. bedfordstmartins.com /roarkunderstanding |

385

had "mud sticking up through his toes." Smart candidates found ways to convince wary plain folk of their democratic convictions and egalitarian sentiments, whether they were genuine or not. Walter L. Steele, who ran for a seat in the North Carolina legislature in 1846, detested campaigning for votes, but he learned, he said, to speak with a "candied tongue."

In addition to politics, slaveholders defended slavery in other ways. In the 1830s, Southerners decided that slavery was too important to debate. "So interwoven is [slavery] with our interest, our manners, our climate and our very being," one man declared in 1833, "that no change can ever possibly be effected without a civil commotion from which the heart of a patriot must turn with horror." Powerful whites dismissed slavery's critics from college faculties, drove them from pulpits, and hounded them from political life. Sometimes antislavery Southerners fell victim to vigilantes and mob violence. One could defend slavery; one could even delicately suggest mild reforms. But no Southerner could any longer safely call slavery evil or advocate its destruction.

In the South, therefore, the rise of the common man occurred alongside the continuing, even growing, power of the planter class. Rather than pitting slaveholders against nonslaveholders, elections remained an effective means of binding the region's whites together. Elections affirmed the sovereignty of white men, whether planter or plain folk, and the subordination of African Americans. Those twin themes played well among white women as well. Though unable to vote, white women supported equality for whites and slavery for blacks. In the antebellum South, the politics of slavery helped knit together all of white society.

> **QUICK REVIEW**

How did planters retain political power
in a democratic system?

CHAPTER LOCATOR | Why did the South become so distinctly different from the North? | What was plantation life like for masters and mistresses? |

386 CHAPTER 13
UNDERSTANDING THE SLAVE SOUTH

Conclusion: How did slavery come to define the South?

BY THE EARLY NINETEENTH CENTURY, northern states had either abolished slavery or put it on the road to extinction, while southern states were building the largest slave society in the New World. Regional differences increased over time, not merely because the South became more and more dominated by slavery, but also because developments in the North rapidly propelled it in a very different direction.

By 1860, one-third of the South's population was enslaved. Bondage saddled blacks with enormous physical and spiritual burdens: hard labor, harsh treatment, broken families, and, most important, the denial of freedom itself. Although degraded and exploited, they were not defeated. Out of African memories and New World realities, blacks created a life-affirming African American culture that sustained and strengthened them. Their families, religion, and community provided defenses against white racism and power. Defined as property, they refused to be reduced to things. Perceived as inferior beings, they rejected the notion that they were natural slaves.

The South was not merely a society with slaves; it had become a slave society. Slavery shaped the region's economy, culture, social structure, and politics. Whites south of the Mason-Dixon line believed that racial slavery was necessary and just. By making all blacks a pariah class, all whites gained a measure of equality and harmony.

Many features of southern life helped to confine class tensions among whites: the wide availability of land, rapid economic mobility, the democratic nature of political life, the patriarchal power among all white men, and, most of all, slavery and white supremacy. All stress along class lines did not disappear, however, and anxious slaveholders continued to worry that yeomen would defect from the pro-slavery consensus. But during the 1850s, white Southerners' nearly universal acceptance of slavery would increasingly unite them in political opposition to their northern neighbors.

| What was plantation life like for slaves? | How did nonslaveholding southern whites work and live? | What place did free blacks occupy in the South? | How did slavery shape southern politics? | Conclusion: How did slavery come to define the South? | ✓ LearningCurve Check what you know. bedfordstmartins.com /roarkunderstanding |

CHAPTER 13 STUDY GUIDE

STEP 1 **GET STARTED ONLINE**

 LearningCurve ■ bedfordstmartins.com/roarkunderstanding
Now that you've read the chapter, make it stick by completing the LearningCurve activity.

STEP 2 **EXPLAIN WHY IT MATTERS**

Put your reading into practice. Identify each term below, and then explain why it matters in U.S. history.

TERM	WHO OR WHAT & WHEN	WHY IT MATTERS
Mason-Dixon line (p. 361)		
cotton kingdom (p. 362)		
slave codes (p. 362)		
miscegenation (p. 363)		
planter (p. 365)		
plantation (p. 365)		
paternalism (p. 368)		
chivalry (p. 370)		
yeomen (p. 377)		
plantation belt (p. 378)		
upcountry (p. 378)		
free blacks (p. 381)		

STEP 3 **MOVE BEYOND THE BASICS**

To demonstrate a more advanced understanding, assess the key characteristics and trends in the North (see chapter 12) and the South in the nineteenth century. How did slavery shape white racial attitudes in both the North and the South?

Key characteristics and trends	North	South
Agriculture		
Urbanization/industrialization		
White racial attitudes		
Economic diversity/labor		
Population/immigration		

STEP 4 **PUT IT ALL TOGETHER** Now, take a step back and try to explain the big picture. Remember to use specific examples from the chapter in your answers.

REGIONAL DIVERGENCE

▶ How and why did the economies of the North and South steadily diverge over the course of the first half of the nineteenth century?

▶ How did the presence of large numbers of African Americans shape southern culture?

PLANTATION LIFE

▶ How did plantation owners see the relationship between master and slave? How did slavery shape other social relationships in the antebellum South?

▶ In what ways did slaves create communities for themselves and develop methods to resist their bondage?

SOUTHERN SOCIETY AND POLITICS

▶ How did southern yeomen see themselves and their place in southern society? How was slavery a part of that place?

▶ How did slavery shape southern politics?

LOOKING BACKWARD, LOOKING AHEAD

▶ How did southern slave society change from the eighteenth to nineteenth centuries?

▶ Why did many white Southerners come to believe that slavery had to be preserved at any cost? How might that have influenced national politics?

> **IN YOUR OWN WORDS**

Imagine that you must give an oral report to the class answering the following question: **How did slavery shape the institutions and values of the antebellum South?** What would be the most important points to include and why?

 Do it online at the Student Site ■ bedfordstmartins.com/roarkunderstanding

14

THE HOUSE DIVIDED

1846–1861

> **How did the issue of slavery drive the United States toward Civil War in the mid-nineteenth century?** Chapter 14 explores the politics of slavery in the years leading up to the Civil War. It examines how the recurring issue of the expansion of slavery into newly acquired territories deepened sectional divisions, undermined existing political parties, and helped create new ones. Finally, it looks at the events that ultimately led to secession and civil war.

**LearningCurve**

bedfordstmartins.com/roarkunderstanding
After reading the chapter, use LearningCurve to
retain what you've read.

> Why did the acquisition of land from Mexico contribute to sectional tensions?

> What factors helped unravel the balance between slave and free states?

> How did the party system change in the 1850s?

> Why did northern fear of the "Slave Power" intensify in the 1850s?

> Why did some southern states secede immediately after Lincoln's election?

> Conclusion: Why did political compromise fail?

Henry Clay offers his "California compromise" to the U.S. Senate, February 5, 1860. The Granger Collection, New York.

Why did the acquisition of land from Mexico contribute to sectional tensions?

Oak Home Farm, San Joaquin County, California

The discovery of gold in California initiated a stampede west, but not everyone wanted to be a prospector. In 1860, an unknown artist painted this idyllic view of the farm of W. I. Overhiser in California's fertile San Joaquin Valley. Thousands of miles away, farmers compared farmsteads like Overhiser's with their own. Many judged life more bountiful in the West and trekked across the country to try to strike it rich in western agriculture. University of California at Berkeley, Bancroft Library.

VICTORY IN THE MEXICAN-AMERICAN WAR brought vast new territories in the West into the United States. The gold rush of 1849 transformed the sleepy frontier of California into a booming economy (see chapter 12). The 1850s witnessed new "rushes," for gold in Colorado and silver in Nevada's Comstock Lode. The phenomenal economic growth of the West demanded the attention of the federal government, but it quickly became clear that Northerners and Southerners had very different visions of the West, particularly the place of slavery in its future. From 1846, when it first appeared that the war with Mexico might mean new territory for the United States, politicians battled over whether to ban slavery from former Mexican land or permit it to expand to the Pacific. In 1850, Congress patched together a plan that Americans hoped would last.

The Wilmot Proviso and the Expansion of Slavery

Most Americans agreed that the Constitution left the issue of slavery to the individual states to decide. Northern states had done away with slavery, while southern states had retained it. But what about slavery in the nation's territories? The Constitution states that "Congress shall have power to . . . make all needful rules

CHAPTER LOCATOR | Why did the acquisition of land from Mexico contribute to sectional tensions? | What factors helped unravel the balance between slave and free states?

392 CHAPTER 14 THE HOUSE DIVIDED

and regulations respecting the territory . . . belonging to the United States." The debate about slavery, then, turned toward Congress.

> ### > Slavery in the Territories: Contradictory Precedents

- 1787: Northwest Ordinance bans slavery north of the Ohio River.
- 1803: Congress allows slavery to remain in the newly acquired Louisiana Territory.
- 1820: The Missouri Compromise prohibits slavery in part of the Louisiana Territory but allows it in the rest.

The spark for the national debate appeared in August 1846 when a Democratic representative from Pennsylvania, David Wilmot, proposed that Congress bar slavery from all lands acquired in the war with Mexico. The Mexicans had abolished slavery in their country, and Wilmot declared, "God forbid that we should be the means of planting this institution upon it."

Regardless of party affiliation, Northerners lined up behind the **Wilmot Proviso**. Many supported free soil, by which they meant territory in which slavery would be prohibited, because they wanted to preserve the West for **free labor**, for hardworking, self-reliant free men, not for slaveholders and slaves. But support also came from those who were simply anti-South. New slave territories would eventually mean new slave states. Wilmot himself said his proposal would blunt "the power of slaveholders" in the national government.

Additional support for free soil came from Northerners who were hostile to blacks and wanted to reserve new land for whites. Wilmot himself blatantly encouraged racist support when he declared, "I would preserve for free white labor a fair country, a rich inheritance, where the sons of toil, of my own race and own color, can live without the disgrace which association with negro slavery brings upon free labor." It is no wonder that some called the Wilmot Proviso the "White Man's Proviso."

The thought that slavery might be excluded in the territories outraged white Southerners. Like Northerners, they regarded the West as a ladder for economic and

Mexican Cession, 1848

social opportunity. They also believed that the exclusion of slavery was a slap in the face to southern veterans of the Mexican-American War. "When the war-worn soldier returns home," one Alabaman asked, "is he to be told that he cannot carry his property to the country won by his blood?" In addition, southern leaders also sought to maintain political parity with the North to protect the South's interests, especially slavery. The need seemed especially urgent in the 1840s, when the North's population and wealth were booming. James Henry Hammond of South Carolina predicted that ten new states would be carved from the acquired Mexican land. If free soil won, the North would "ride over us roughshod" in Congress, he claimed. "Our only safety is in *equality* of power."

> ## CHRONOLOGY

1846
- Wilmot Proviso is introduced.

1847
- Wilmot Proviso is defeated in Senate.
- "Popular sovereignty" compromise is offered.

1848
- Free-Soil Party is founded.
- Zachary Taylor is elected president.

1849
- California gold rush.

1850
- Taylor dies; Vice President Millard Fillmore becomes president.
- Compromise of 1850 becomes law.

Wilmot Proviso
▶ Proposal put forward by Representative David Wilmot of Pennsylvania in August 1846 to ban slavery in territory acquired from the Mexican-American War. The Proviso enjoyed widespread support in the North, but Southerners saw it as an attack on their interests.

free labor
▶ Term referring to work conducted free from constraint and according to the laborer's own inclinations and will. The ideal of free labor lay at the heart of the North's argument that slavery should not be extended into the western territories.

How did the party system change in the 1850s? | Why did northern fear of the "Slave Power" intensify in the 1850s? | Why did some southern states secede immediately after Lincoln's election? | Conclusion: Why did political compromise fail? | ✓ LearningCurve Check what you know. bedfordstmartins.com /roarkunderstanding

393

Because Northerners had a majority in the House, they easily passed the Wilmot Proviso. In the Senate, however, where slave states outnumbered free states fifteen to fourteen, Southerners defeated it in 1847. Senator John C. Calhoun of South Carolina denied that Congress had the constitutional authority to exclude slavery from the nation's territories. He argued that because the territories were the "joint and common property" of all the states, Congress could not bar citizens of one state from migrating with their property (including slaves) to the territories. Whereas Wilmot demanded that Congress slam shut the door to slavery, Calhoun called on Congress to hold the door wide open.

In 1847, Senator Lewis Cass of Michigan offered a compromise through the doctrine of **popular sovereignty**, by which the people who settled the territories would decide for themselves slavery's fate. This solution, Cass argued, sat squarely in the American tradition of democracy and local self-government. Popular sovereignty's most attractive feature was its ambiguity about the precise moment when settlers could determine slavery's fate. Northern advocates believed that the decision on slavery could be made as soon as the first territorial legislature assembled. With free-soil majorities likely because of the North's greater population, they would shut the door to slavery immediately. Southern supporters believed that popular sovereignty guaranteed that slavery would be unrestricted throughout the entire territorial period. Only when settlers in a territory drew up a constitution and applied for statehood could they decide the issue of slavery. By then, slavery would have sunk deep roots. As long as the matter of timing remained vague, popular sovereignty gave hope to both sides.

When Congress ended its session in 1848, no plan had won a majority in both houses. Northerners who demanded no new slave territory anywhere, ever, and Southerners who demanded entry for their slave property into all territories, or else, staked out their extreme positions. Unresolved in Congress, the territorial question naturally became an issue in the presidential election of 1848.

popular sovereignty

▶ The idea that government is subject to the will of the people. Applied to the territories, popular sovereignty meant that the residents of a territory should determine, through their legislatures, whether to allow slavery.

General Taylor Cigar Case

This papier-mâché cigar case portrays General Zachary Taylor, Whig presidential candidate in 1848, in a colorful scene from the Mexican-American War. Shown here as a dashing, elegant officer, Taylor was in fact a short, thickset, and roughly dressed Indian fighter who had spent his career commanding small frontier garrisons. The inscription reminds voters that Taylor was a victor in the first four battles fought in the war and directs attention away from the fact that in politics, he was a rank amateur. Collection of Janice L. and David J. Frent.

CHAPTER LOCATOR | Why did the acquisition of land from Mexico contribute to sectional tensions? | What factors helped unravel the balance between slave and free states?

394   CHAPTER 14
THE HOUSE DIVIDED

The Election of 1848

When President James Polk chose not to seek reelection, the Democratic convention nominated Lewis Cass of Michigan, the man most closely associated with popular sovereignty. The Whigs nominated a Mexican-American War hero, General Zachary Taylor. The Whigs declined to adopt a party platform, betting that the combination of a military hero and total silence on the slavery issue would unite their divided party. Taylor, who owned more than one hundred slaves on plantations in Mississippi and Louisiana, was hailed by Georgia politician Robert Toombs as a "Southern man, a slaveholder, a cotton planter."

Antislavery Whigs balked. Senator Charles Sumner called for a major political realignment, "one grand Northern party of Freedom." In the summer of 1848, antislavery Whigs and anti-slavery Democrats founded the Free-Soil Party, nominating a Democrat, Martin Van Buren, for president and a Whig, Charles Francis Adams, for vice president. The platform boldly proclaimed, "Free soil, free speech, free labor, and free men."

The November election dashed the hopes of the Free-Soilers. They did not carry a single state. Taylor won the all-important electoral vote 163 to 127, carrying eight of the fifteen slave states and seven of the fifteen free states (**Map 14.1**). (Wisconsin had entered the Union earlier in 1848 as the fifteenth free state.) Northern voters were not yet ready for Sumner's "one grand Northern party of Freedom," but the struggle over slavery in the territories had shaken the major parties badly.

Candidate	Electoral Vote	Popular Vote	Percent of Popular Vote
Zachary Taylor (Whig)	163	1,360,099	47.4
Lewis Cass (Democrat)	127	1,220,544	42.5
Martin Van Buren (Free-Soil)	0	291,263	10.1

MAP 14.1 ■ The Election of 1848

Debate and Compromise

Believing that he could avoid further sectional strife if California and New Mexico skipped the territorial stage, new president Zachary Taylor encouraged the set-tlers to apply for admission to the Union as states. Predominantly antislavery, the settlers began writing free-state constitutions. "For the first time," Mississippian Jefferson Davis lamented, "we are about permanently to destroy the balance of power between the sections."

Congress convened in December 1849, beginning one of the most contentious and most significant sessions in its history. President Taylor urged Congress to admit California as a free state immediately and to admit New Mexico, which lagged behind a few months, as soon as it applied. Southerners exploded. A North Carolinian declared that Southerners who would "consent to be thus degraded and enslaved, ought to be whipped through their fields by their own negroes."

Into this rancorous scene stepped Senator Henry Clay of Kentucky, who offered a series of resolutions meant to answer and balance "all questions in con-troversy between the free and slave states, growing out of the subject of slavery." Admit California as a free state, he proposed, but organize the rest of the South-west without restrictions on slavery. Require Texas to abandon its claim to parts

How did the party system change in the 1850s? | Why did northern fear of the "Slave Power" intensify in the 1850s? | Why did some southern states secede immediately after Lincoln's election? | Conclusion: Why did political compromise fail? | ✔ LearningCurve Check what you know. bedfordstmartins.com /roarkunderstanding

395

of New Mexico, but compensate it by assuming its preannexation debt. Abolish the domestic slave trade in Washington, D.C., but confirm slavery itself in the nation's capital. Affirm Congress's lack of authority to interfere with the interstate slave trade, and enact a more effective fugitive slave law.

Both antislavery advocates and "fire-eaters" (as radical Southerners who urged secession from the Union were called) savaged Clay's plan. Senator Salmon P. Chase of Ohio ridiculed it as "sentiment for the North, substance for the South." Senator Henry S. Foote of Mississippi denounced it as more offensive to the South than the speeches of abolitionists William Lloyd Garrison, Wendell Phillips, and Frederick Douglass combined. The most ominous response came from John C. Calhoun, who argued that the fragile political unity of North and South depended on continued equal representation in the Senate, which Clay's plan for a free California destroyed. "As things now stand," he said in February 1850, the South "cannot with safety remain in the Union."

Massachusetts senator Daniel Webster then addressed the Senate. Like Clay, Webster defended compromise. He told Northerners that the South had legitimate complaints, but he told Southerners that secession from the Union would mean civil war. He argued that the Wilmot Proviso's ban on slavery in the territories was unnecessary because the harsh climate effectively prohibited the expansion of cotton and slaves into the new American Southwest. "I would not take pains uselessly to reaffirm an ordinance of nature, nor to reenact the will of God," Webster declared.

Free-soil forces recoiled from what they saw as Webster's desertion. Senator William H. Seward of New York responded that Webster's and Clay's compromise with slavery was "radically wrong and essentially vicious." He rejected Calhoun's argument that Congress lacked the constitutional authority to exclude slavery from the territories. In any case, Seward said, there was a "higher law than the

MAP 14.2 ■ The Compromise of 1850

The patched-together sectional agreement was both clumsy and unstable. Few Americans — in either the North or the South — supported all five parts of the Compromise.

CHAPTER LOCATOR | Why did the acquisition of land from Mexico contribute to sectional tensions?   What factors helped unravel the balance between slave and free states?

396   CHAPTER 14
THE HOUSE DIVIDED

Constitution" — the law of God — to ensure freedom in all the public domain. Claiming that God was a Free-Soiler did nothing to cool the superheated political atmosphere.

In May 1850, the Senate considered a bill that joined Clay's resolutions into a single comprehensive package. Clay bet that a majority of Congress wanted compromise and that the members would vote for the package. But the omnibus strategy backfired. Free-Soilers and proslavery Southerners voted down the comprehensive plan.

Fortunately for those who favored a settlement, Senator Stephen A. Douglas, a rising Democratic star from Illinois, broke the bill into its parts and skillfully ushered each through Congress. The agreement Douglas won in September 1850 was very much the one Clay had proposed in January. Millard Fillmore, who had become president when Zachary Taylor died in July, signed into law each bill, collectively known as the **Compromise of 1850** (**Map 14.2**). The nation breathed a sigh of relief, for the Compromise preserved the Union and peace for the moment.

Compromise of 1850
▶ Laws passed in 1850 meant to resolve the dispute over the spread of slavery in the territories. Key elements included the admission of California as a free state and the Fugitive Slave Act. The compromise soon unraveled.

> **Compromise of 1850**

- California entered the Union as a free state.
- New Mexico and Utah became territories where slavery would be decided by popular sovereignty.
- Texas accepted its boundary with New Mexico and received $10 million from the federal government.
- Congress ended the slave trade in the District of Columbia but enacted a more stringent fugitive slave law that stipulated that all citizens were expected to assist officials in apprehending runaway slaves.

QUICK REVIEW <

How might the Compromise of 1850 have eased sectional tensions?

How did the party system change in the 1850s?

Why did northern fear of the "Slave Power" intensify in the 1850s?

Why did some southern states secede immediately after Lincoln's election?

Conclusion: Why did political compromise fail?

✓ LearningCurve
Check what you know.
bedfordstmartins.com
/roarkunderstanding

What factors helped unravel the balance between slave and free states?

135,000 SETS, 270,000 VOLUMES SOLD.

UNCLE TOM'S CABIN

FOR SALE HERE.

AN EDITION FOR THE MILLION, COMPLETE IN 1 Vol., PRICE 37 1-2 CENTS.
" " IN GERMAN, IN 1 Vol., PRICE 50 CENTS.
" " IN 2 Vols,. CLOTH, 6 PLATES, PRICE $1.50.
SUPERB ILLUSTRATED EDITION, IN 1 Vol., WITH 153 ENGRAVINGS,
PRICES FROM $2.50 TO $5.00.

The Greatest Book of the Age.

Uncle Tom's Cabin Poster

After Congress passed the Fugitive Slave Act in 1850, Harriet Beecher Stowe's outraged sister-in-law told her, "Now Hattie, if I could use a pen as you can, I would write something that will make this whole nation feel what an accursed thing slavery is." This poster advertising the novel Stowe wrote calls it "The Greatest Book of the Age." The novel fueled the growing antislavery crusade. The Granger Collection, NY.

THE COMPROMISE OF 1850 began to come apart almost immediately. The implementation of the Fugitive Slave Act brought the horrors of slavery into the North. Moreover, millions of Northerners who never saw a runaway slave confronted slavery through Harriet Beecher Stowe's *Uncle Tom's Cabin*, a novel that vividly depicts the brutality of the South's "peculiar institution." Congress did its part to undo the Compromise as well. Four years after Congress stitched the sectional compromise together, it ripped the threads out. With the Kansas-Nebraska Act in 1854, it again posed the question of slavery in the territories, the deadliest of all sectional issues.

Uncle Tom's Cabin
▶ Enormously popular antislavery novel written by Harriet Beecher Stowe and published in 1852. It helped to solidify northern sentiment against slavery and to confirm white Southerners' sense that no sympathy remained for them in the free states.

The Fugitive Slave Act

The issue of runaway slaves was as old as the Constitution, which contained a provision for the return of any "person held to service or labor in one state" who escaped to another. In 1793, a federal law gave muscle to the provision by authorizing slave owners to enter other states to recapture their slave property. Proclaiming the 1793 law a license to kidnap free blacks, northern states in the 1830s began passing "personal liberty laws" that provided fugitives with some protection.

CHAPTER LOCATOR | Why did the acquisition of land from Mexico contribute to sectional tensions? | **What factors helped unravel the balance between slave and free states?**

398 CHAPTER 14 THE HOUSE DIVIDED

Some northern communities also formed vigilance committees to help runaways. Each year, a few hundred slaves escaped into free states and found friendly northern "conductors" who put them aboard the underground railroad, which was not a railroad at all but a series of secret "stations" (hideouts) on the way to Canada.

Furious about northern interference, Southerners in 1850 insisted on the stricter fugitive slave law that was part of the Compromise. According to the **Fugitive Slave Act**, to seize an alleged slave, a slaveholder simply had to appear before a commissioner and swear that the runaway was his. The commissioner earned $10 for every individual returned to slavery but only $5 for those set free. Most galling to Northerners, the law stipulated that all citizens were expected to assist officials in apprehending runaways.

In Boston in February 1851, an angry crowd overpowered federal marshals and snatched a runaway named Shadrach from a courtroom, put him on the underground railroad, and whisked him off to Canada. Three years later, when another Boston crowd rushed the courthouse in a failed attempt to rescue runaway Anthony Burns, a guard was shot dead. To white Southerners, it seemed that fanatics of the "higher law" creed had whipped Northerners into a frenzy of massive resistance.

Actually, the overwhelming majority of fugitives claimed by slaveholders were reenslaved peacefully. But brutal enforcement of the unpopular law had a radicalizing effect in the North, particularly in New England. To Southerners, it seemed that Northerners had betrayed the Compromise. "The continued existence of the United States as one nation," warned the *Southern Literary Messenger*, "depends upon the full and faithful execution of the Fugitive Slave Bill."

> **Fugitive Slave Act**
> ▶ A law included in the Compromise of 1850 to help attract southern support for the legislative package. Its strict provisions for capturing runaway slaves provoked outrage in the North and intensified antislavery sentiment in the region.

Uncle Tom's Cabin

The spectacle of shackled African Americans being herded south seared the conscience of every Northerner who witnessed such a scene. But even more Northerners were turned against slavery by a novel. Harriet Beecher Stowe, a white Northerner who had never set foot on a plantation, made the South's slaves into flesh-and-blood human beings almost more real than life.

A member of a famous clan of preachers, teachers, and reformers, Stowe despised the slave catchers and wrote to expose the sin of slavery. Published as a book in 1852, *Uncle Tom's Cabin, or Life among the Lowly* became a blockbuster hit, selling 300,000 copies in its first year and more than 2 million copies within ten years. Stowe's characters leaped from the page. Here was the gentle slave Uncle Tom, a Christian saint who forgave those who beat him to death; the courageous slave Eliza, who fled with her child across the frozen Ohio River; and the fiendish overseer Simon Legree, whose Louisiana plantation was a nightmare of torture and death.

Stowe aimed her most powerful blows at slavery's destructive impact on the family. Her character Eliza succeeds in keeping her son from being sold away, but other mothers are not so fortunate. When told that her infant has been sold, Lucy drowns herself. Driven half mad by the sale of a son and a daughter, Cassy decides "never again [to] let a child live to grow up!" She gives her third child an opiate and

| How did the party system change in the 1850s? | Why did northern fear of the "Slave Power" intensify in the 1850s? | Why did some southern states secede immediately after Lincoln's election? | Conclusion: Why did political compromise fail? | ☑ **LearningCurve** Check what you know. bedfordstmartins.com /roarkunderstanding |

399

1852
- *Uncle Tom's Cabin* is published.
- Franklin Pierce is elected president.

1853
- Gadsden Purchase.

1854
- Kansas-Nebraska Act.

watches as "he slept to death." Northerners shed tears and sang praises to *Uncle Tom's Cabin*.

What Northerners accepted as truth, Southerners denounced as slander. The Virginian George F. Holmes proclaimed Stowe a member of the "Woman's Rights" and "Higher Law" schools and dismissed the novel as a work of "intense fanaticism." Although it is impossible to measure precisely the impact of a novel on public opinion, *Uncle Tom's Cabin* clearly helped to crystallize northern sentiment against slavery and to confirm white Southerners' suspicion that they no longer received any sympathy in the free states.

Other writers — ex-slaves who knew life in slave cabins firsthand — also produced stinging indictments of slavery. Solomon Northup's compelling *Twelve Years a Slave* (1853) sold 27,000 copies in two years, and the powerful *Narrative of the Life of Frederick Douglass, as Told by Himself* (1845) eventually sold more than 30,000 copies. But no work touched the North's conscience as did the novel by a free white woman. A decade after its publication, when Stowe visited Abraham Lincoln at the White House, he reportedly said, "So you are the little woman who wrote the book that made this great war."

The Kansas-Nebraska Act

As the 1852 election approached, the Democrats and Whigs sought to close the sectional rifts that had opened within their parties. For their presidential nominee, the Democrats turned to Franklin Pierce of New Hampshire. Pierce's well-known sympathy with southern views on public issues caused his northern critics to include him among the "doughfaces," northern men malleable enough to champion southern causes. The Whigs chose another Mexican-American War hero, General Winfield Scott of Virginia. But the Whigs' northern and southern factions were hopelessly divided, and the Democrat Pierce carried twenty-seven states to Scott's four and won the electoral college vote 254 to 42 (see Map 14.4, page 404). The Free-Soil Party lost almost half of the voters who had turned to it in the tumultuous political atmosphere of 1848.

Eager to leave the sectional controversy behind, the new president turned swiftly to foreign expansion. Manifest destiny remained robust. Pierce's major objective was Cuba, but when antislavery Northerners blocked Cuba's acquisition to keep more slave territory from entering the Union, he turned to Mexico. In 1853, diplomat James Gadsden negotiated a $10 million purchase of some 30,000 square miles of land in present-day Arizona and New Mexico. The Gadsden Purchase furthered the dream of a transcontinental railroad to California and Pierce's desire for a southern route through Mexican territory. Talk of a railroad ignited rivalries in cities from New Orleans to Chicago as they maneuvered to become the eastern terminus. Inevitably in the 1850s, the contest for a transcontinental railroad became a sectional struggle over slavery.

Gadsden Purchase, 1853

CHAPTER LOCATOR | Why did the acquisition of land from Mexico contribute to sectional tensions? | What factors helped unravel the balance between slave and free states?

CHAPTER 14
400 THE HOUSE DIVIDED

Illinois's Democratic senator Stephen A. Douglas badly wanted the transcontinental railroad for Chicago. Any railroad that ran west from Chicago would pass through a region that Congress in 1830 had designated a "permanent" Indian reserve (see chapter 11). Douglas proposed giving this vast area between the Missouri River and the Rocky Mountains an Indian name, Nebraska, and then throwing the Indians out. Once the region achieved territorial status, whites could survey and sell the land, establish a civil government, and build a railroad.

Nebraska lay within the Louisiana Purchase and, according to the Missouri Compromise of 1820, was closed to slavery (see chapter 10). Douglas needed southern votes to pass his Nebraska legislation, but Southerners had no incentive to create another free territory or to help a northern city win the transcontinental railroad. Southerners, however, agreed to help if Congress organized Nebraska according to popular sovereignty. That meant giving slavery a chance in Nebraska Territory and reopening the dangerous issue of slavery expansion.

In January 1854, Douglas introduced his bill to organize Nebraska Territory, leaving to the settlers themselves the decision about slavery. At southern insistence, Douglas added an explicit repeal of the Missouri Compromise. Free-Soilers branded Douglas's plan "a gross violation of a sacred pledge" and an "atrocious plot" to transform free land into a "dreary region of despotism, inhabited by masters and slaves."

Free state or territory

Slave state or territory

Voters to decide on allowing slavery, Compromise of 1850

Voters to decide on allowing slavery, Kansas-Nebraska Act, 1854

MAP 14.3 ■ The Kansas-Nebraska Act, 1854

Americans hardly thought twice about dispossessing the Indians of land guaranteed them by treaty, but many worried about the outcome of repealing the Missouri Compromise and opening up the region to slavery.

> MAP ACTIVITY

READING THE MAP: How many slave states and how many free states does the map show? Estimate the percentage of new territory likely to be settled by slaveholders.

CONNECTIONS: Who would be more likely to support changes in government legislation to discontinue the Missouri Compromise — slaveholders or free-soil advocates? Why?

| How did the party system change in the 1850s? | Why did northern fear of the "Slave Power" intensify in the 1850s? | Why did some southern states secede immediately after Lincoln's election? | Conclusion: Why did political compromise fail? | ✓ LearningCurve Check what you know. bedfordstmartins.com /roarkunderstanding |

Kansas-Nebraska Act

▶ 1854 law that divided Indian territory into Kansas and Nebraska, repealed the Missouri Compromise, and left the new territories to decide the issue of slavery on the basis of popular sovereignty. The measure led to bloody fighting in Kansas.

Undaunted, Douglas skillfully shepherded the explosive bill through Congress in May 1854. Nine-tenths of the southern members (Whigs and Democrats) and half of the northern Democrats cast votes in favor of the bill. Like Douglas, most northern supporters believed that popular sovereignty would make Nebraska free territory. The **Kansas-Nebraska Act** divided the huge territory in two: Nebraska and Kansas (**Map 14.3**, page 401). With this act, the government pushed the Plains Indians farther west, making way for farmers and railroads.

> **QUICK REVIEW**

Why did the Compromise of 1850 fail to achieve sectional peace?

CHAPTER LOCATOR | Why did the acquisition of land from Mexico contribute to sectional tensions? | What factors helped unravel the balance between slave and free states?

402 CHAPTER 14
THE HOUSE DIVIDED

How did the party system change in the 1850s?

John and Jessie Frémont Poster

The election of 1856 marked the first time a candidate's wife appeared on campaign items. Jessie Benton Frémont helped plan her husband's campaign, coauthored his election biography, and drew northern women into political activity as never before. "What a shame that women can't vote!" declared abolitionist Lydia Maria Child. "We'd carry 'our Jessie' into the White House on our shoulders, wouldn't we." Museum of American Political Life.

SINCE THE EARLY 1830s, Whigs and Democrats had organized and channeled political conflict in the nation. This party system dampened sectionalism and strengthened the Union. To achieve national political power, the Whigs and Democrats had to retain their strength in both the North and the South. Strong northern and southern wings required that each party compromise and find positions acceptable to both sections.

The Kansas-Nebraska controversy shattered this stabilizing political system. In place of two national parties with bisectional strength, the mid-1850s witnessed the development of one party heavily dominated by one section and another party entirely limited to the other section. Rather than "national" parties, the country had what one critic disdainfully called "geographic" parties, a development that thwarted political compromise between the sections.

The Old Parties: Whigs and Democrats

As early as the Mexican-American War, members of the Whig Party had clashed over the future of slavery in annexed Mexican lands. By 1852, the Whig Party could please its proslavery southern wing or its antislavery northern wing, but not both. The Whigs' miserable showing in the election of 1852 made it clear that they were no longer a strong national party. By 1856, after more than two decades of contesting the Democrats, they were hardly a party at all (**Map 14.4**).

How did the party system change in the 1850s?	Why did northern fear of the "Slave Power" intensify in the 1850s?	Why did some southern states secede immediately after Lincoln's election?	Conclusion: Why did political compromise fail?	✔️ **LearningCurve** Check what you know. bedfordstmartins.com /roarkunderstanding

1848

Candidate	Electoral Vote	Popular Vote	Percent of Popular Vote
Zachary Taylor (Whig)	163	1,360,099	47.4
Lewis Cass (Democrat)	127	1,220,544	42.5
Martin Van Buren (Free-Soil)	0	291,263	10.1

1852

Candidate	Electoral Vote	Popular Vote	Percent of Popular Vote
Franklin Pierce (Democrat)	254	1,601,274	50.9
Winfield Scott (Whig)	42	1,386,580	44.1
John P. Hale (Free-Soil)	5	155,825	5.0

1856

Candidate	Electoral Vote	Popular Vote	Percent of Popular Vote
James Buchanan (Democrat)	174	1,838,169	45.3
John C. Frémont (Republican)	114	1,341,264	33.1
Millard Fillmore (American)	8	874,534	21.6

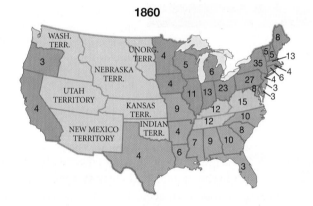

1860

Candidate	Electoral Vote	Popular Vote	Percent of Popular Vote
Abraham Lincoln (Republican)	180	1,866,452	39.9
John C. Breckinridge (Southern Democrat)	72	847,953	18.1
Stephen A. Douglas (Northern Democrat)	12	1,375,157	29.4
John Bell (Constitutional Union)	39	590,631	12.6

MAP 14.4 ■ Political Realignment, 1848–1860

In 1848, slavery and sectionalism began taking their toll on the country's party system. The Whig Party was an early casualty. By 1860, national parties — those that contended for votes in both the North and the South — had been replaced by regional parties.

> MAP ACTIVITY

READING THE MAP: Which states did the Democrats pick up in 1852 compared with 1848? Which of these states did the Democrats lose in 1856? Compare the general geographic location of the states won by the Republicans in 1856 with those won in 1860.

CONNECTIONS: In the 1860 election, which party benefited the most from the western and midwestern states added to the Union since 1848? Why do you think these states chose to back this party?

CHAPTER LOCATOR | Why did the acquisition of land from Mexico contribute to sectional tensions? | What factors helped unravel the balance between slave and free states?

The collapse of the Whig Party left the Democrats as the country's only national party. Popular sovereignty provided a doctrine that many Democrats could support. Even so, popular sovereignty very nearly undid the party. When Stephen Douglas applied the doctrine to the part of the Louisiana Purchase where slavery had been barred, he divided northern Democrats and destroyed the dominance of the Democratic Party in the free states. After 1854, the Democrats were a southern-dominated party. Still, gains in the South more than balanced Democratic losses in the North, and during the 1850s Democrats elected two presidents and won majorities in Congress in almost every election.

The breakup of the Whigs and the disaffection of many northern Democrats set millions of Americans politically adrift. As they searched for new political harbors, Americans found that the death of the old party system created a multitude of fresh political alternatives.

> CHRONOLOGY

1854
- American (Know-Nothing) Party emerges.
- Republican Party is founded.

1856
- James Buchanan is elected president.

The New Parties: Know-Nothings and Republicans

Dozens of new political organizations vied for voters' attention. Out of the confusion, two emerged as true contenders. One grew out of the slavery controversy, a coalition of indignant antislavery Northerners. The other arose from an entirely different split in American society, between native Protestants and Roman Catholic immigrants.

The wave of immigrants that arrived in America from 1845 to 1855 produced a nasty backlash among Protestant Americans, who feared that the Republic was about to drown in a sea of Roman Catholics from Ireland and Germany (see Figure 12.1, page 334). Nativists (individuals who were anti-immigrant) began to organize, first into secret fraternal societies and then in 1854 into a political party. Recruits swore never to vote for either foreign-born or Roman Catholic candidates and not to reveal any information about the organization. When questioned, they said, "I know nothing." Officially, they were the American Party, but most Americans called them Know-Nothings.

The Know-Nothings enjoyed dazzling success in 1854 and 1855. They captured state legislatures throughout the nation and claimed dozens of seats in Congress. Democrats and Whigs described the Know-Nothings' phenomenal record as a

Campaign Flag of the Know-Nothing Party

Convinced that the incendiary issue of slavery had blinded Americans to the greater dangers of uncontrolled immigration and foreign influence, the Know-Nothings nominated Millard Fillmore for president in 1856. Milwaukee County Historical Society.

| How did the party system change in the 1850s? | Why did northern fear of the "Slave Power" intensify in the 1850s? | Why did some southern states secede immediately after Lincoln's election? | Conclusion: Why did political compromise fail? | ✔ LearningCurve Check what you know. bedfordstmartins.com /roarkunderstanding |

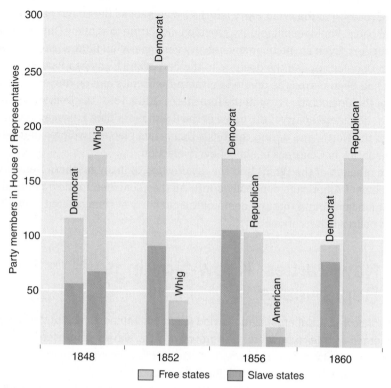

FIGURE 14.1 ■ Changing Political Landscape, 1848–1860

The polarization of American politics between free states and slave states occurred in little more than a decade.

"tornado," a "hurricane," and "a freak of political insanity." But by 1855, an observer might reasonably have concluded that the Know-Nothings had emerged as the successor to the Whigs.

The Know-Nothings were not the only new party making noise, however. One of the new antislavery organizations provoked by the Kansas-Nebraska Act called itself the **Republican Party**. The Republicans attempted to unite all those who opposed the extension of slavery into any territory of the United States (**Figure 14.1**).

The Republican creed tapped into the basic beliefs and values of Northerners. Slavery, Republicans believed, degraded the dignity of white labor by associating work with blacks and servility. As evidence, they pointed to the South, where, one Republican claimed, nonslaveholding whites "retire to the outskirts of civilization, where they live a semi-savage life, sinking deeper and more hopelessly into barbarism with every succeeding generation." Republicans warned that the insatiable slaveholders of the South, whom antislavery Northerners called the "Slave Power," were conspiring through their control of the Democratic Party to expand slavery, subvert liberty, and undermine the Constitution.

Only by restricting slavery to the South, Republicans believed, could free labor flourish elsewhere. In the North, one Republican declared in 1854, "every man holds his fortune in his own right arm; and his position in society, in life, is to be tested by his own individual character." Without slavery, western territories would provide vast economic opportunity for free men. Powerful images of liberty and opportunity attracted a wide range of Northerners to the Republican cause.

Republican Party

▶ Antislavery party formed in 1854 following passage of the Kansas-Nebraska Act. The Republicans attempted to unite all those who opposed the extension of slavery into any territory of the United States.

CHAPTER LOCATOR | Why did the acquisition of land from Mexico contribute to sectional tensions? | What factors helped unravel the balance between slave and free states?

406   CHAPTER 14
THE HOUSE DIVIDED

Women as well as men rushed to the new Republican Party. Indeed, three women helped found the party in Ripon, Wisconsin, in 1854. Although they could not vote and suffered from other legal handicaps, women nevertheless participated in partisan politics by writing campaign literature, marching in parades, giving speeches, and lobbying voters. Women's antislavery fervor attracted them to the Republican Party, and participation in party politics in turn nurtured the woman's rights movement. Susan B. Anthony, who attended Republican meetings throughout the 1850s, found that her political activity made her disfranchisement all the more galling. She and other women in the North worked on behalf of antislavery and woman suffrage and the right of married women to control their own property.

The Election of 1856

The election of 1856 revealed that the Republicans had become the Democrats' main challenger, and slavery in the territories, not nativism, was the election's principal issue. When the Know-Nothings insisted on a platform that endorsed the Kansas-Nebraska Act, most of the Northerners walked out, and the party came apart. The few Know-Nothings who remained nominated ex-president Millard Fillmore.

The Republican platform focused mostly on "making every territory free." When Republicans labeled slavery a "relic of barbarism," they signaled that they had written off the South. For president, they nominated the soldier and California adventurer John C. Frémont. Frémont lacked political credentials, but his wife, Jessie Frémont, the daughter of Senator Thomas Hart Benton of Missouri, knew the political map well. Though careful to maintain a proper public image, the vivacious young mother and antislavery zealot helped attract voters and draw women into politics.

The Democrats, successful in 1852 in bridging sectional differences by nominating a northern man with southern principles, chose another "doughface," James Buchanan of Pennsylvania. They portrayed the Republicans as extremists ("Black Republican Abolitionists") whose support for the Wilmot Proviso risked pushing the South out of the Union.

The Democratic strategy carried the day for Buchanan, who won 174 electoral votes against Frémont's 114 and Fillmore's 8 (see Map 14.4, page 404). But the big news was that the Republicans, despite being a brand-new party, carried all but five of the states north of the Mason-Dixon line. Sectionalism had fashioned a new party system, one that spelled danger for the Democrats and the Republic. Indeed, war had already broken out between proslavery and antislavery forces in distant Kansas Territory.

QUICK REVIEW <

Why did the Whig Party disintegrate in the 1850s?

How did the party system change in the 1850s?

Why did northern fear of the "Slave Power" intensify in the 1850s?

Why did some southern states secede immediately after Lincoln's election?

Conclusion: Why did political compromise fail?

☑ LearningCurve
Check what you know.
bedfordstmartins.com
/roarkunderstanding

407

Why did northern fear of the "Slave Power" intensify in the 1850s?

Armed Settlers Near Lawrence, Kansas

Armed with rifles, knives, swords, and pistols, these tough antislavery men gathered for a photograph near the free-soil town of Lawrence in 1856. Equally well-armed proslavery men attacked and briefly occupied Lawrence that same year. Kansas State Historical Society.

EVENTS IN KANSAS TERRITORY in the mid-1850s underscored the Republicans' contention that the slaveholding South presented a profound threat to "free soil, free labor, and free men." Kansas reeled with violence that Republicans argued was southern in origin. Republicans also pointed to the brutal beating by a Southerner of a respected northern senator on the floor of Congress. Even the Supreme Court, in the Republicans' view, reflected the South's drive toward minority rule and tyranny. Then, in 1858, the issues dividing North and South received an extraordinary hearing in a senatorial contest in Illinois, when the nation's foremost Democrat debated a resourceful Republican.

"Bleeding Kansas"

Three days after the House of Representatives approved the Kansas-Nebraska Act in 1854, Senator William H. Seward of New York boldly challenged the South. "Come on then, Gentlemen of the Slave States," he cried, "since there is no escaping your challenge, I accept it in behalf of the cause of freedom. We will engage in competition for the virgin soil of Kansas, and God give the victory to the side which is stronger in numbers as it is in right." Because of Stephen Douglas, popular sovereignty would determine whether Kansas became slave or free.

Emigrant aid societies sprang up to promote settlement from free states or slave states. Missourians, already bordered on the east by the free state of Illinois and on the north by the free state of Iowa, especially thought it important to secure Kansas for slavery. Thousands of rough frontiersmen, egged on by Missouri senator David Rice Atchison, invaded Kansas. "There are eleven hundred coming over from Platte County to vote," Atchison reported, "and if that ain't

CHAPTER LOCATOR | Why did the acquisition of land from Mexico contribute to sectional tensions? | What factors helped unravel the balance between slave and free states?

enough we can send five thousand — enough to kill every God-damned abolitionist in the Territory." Not surprisingly, proslavery candidates swept the territorial elections in November 1854. When Kansas's first territorial legislature met, it enacted a raft of proslavery laws. Ever-pliant President Pierce endorsed the work of the fraudulently elected legislature. Free-soil Kansans did not. They elected their own legislature, which promptly banned both slaves and free blacks from the territory. Organized into two rival governments and armed to the teeth, Kansans verged on civil war.

Fighting broke out on the morning of May 21, 1856, when several hundred proslavery men raided the town of Lawrence, the center of free-state settlement. The "Sack of Lawrence," as free-soil forces called it, inflamed northern opinion. Elsewhere in Kansas, news of events in Lawrence provoked John Brown, a free-soil settler, to announce that "it was better that a score of bad men should die than that one man who came here to make Kansas a Free State should be driven out" and to lead the posse that massacred five allegedly proslavery settlers along Pottawatomie Creek. After that, guerrilla war engulfed the territory.

Just as **"Bleeding Kansas"** gave the fledgling Republican Party fresh ammunition for its battle against the Slave Power, so too did an event that occurred in the nation's capital. In May 1856, Senator Charles Sumner of Massachusetts delivered a speech titled "The Crime against Kansas," which included a scalding personal attack on South Carolina senator Andrew P. Butler. Preston Brooks, a young South Carolina member of the House and a kinsman of Butler's, felt compelled to defend the honor of his aged relative. On May 22, Brooks entered the Senate, where he found Sumner working at his desk. He beat Sumner over the head with his cane until Sumner lay bleeding and unconscious on the floor. Brooks resigned his seat in the House, only to be promptly reelected. In the North, the southern hero became an arch-villain. Like "Bleeding Kansas," "Bleeding Sumner" provided the Republican Party with a potent symbol of the South's "twisted and violent civilization."

The *Dred Scott* Decision

Political debate over slavery in the territories became so heated in part because the Constitution lacked precision on the issue. In 1857, in the case of *Dred Scott v. Sandford*, the Supreme Court announced its understanding of the meaning of the Constitution regarding slavery in the territories. The Court's decision demonstrated that it enjoyed no special immunity from the sectional and partisan passions that were convulsing the land.

In 1833, an army doctor bought the slave Dred Scott in St. Louis, Missouri, and took him as his personal servant to Fort Armstrong, Illinois, and then to Fort Snelling in Wisconsin Territory. Back in St. Louis in 1846, Scott, with the help of white friends,

"Bleeding Kansas," 1850s

> CHRONOLOGY

1856
– "Bleeding Kansas."
– "Sack of Lawrence."
– Pottawatomie massacre.

1857
– *Dred Scott* decision.
– Congress rejects Lecompton constitution.
– Panic of 1857.

1858
– Lincoln-Douglas debates; Douglas wins Senate seat.

"Bleeding Kansas"
► Term for the bloody struggle between proslavery and antislavery factions in Kansas in the fall of 1854 following its organization as a territory. Corrupt election tactics led to a proslavery victory, but free-soil Kansans established a rival territorial government, and violence quickly ensued.

How did the party system change in the 1850s? | **Why did northern fear of the "Slave Power" intensify in the 1850s?** | Why did some southern states secede immediately after Lincoln's election? | Conclusion: Why did political compromise fail? | ✓ LearningCurve Check what you know. bedfordstmartins.com /roarkunderstanding

409

This portrait of Dred Scott was painted in 1857, the year of the Supreme Court's decision. African Americans in the North were particularly alarmed by the Court's ruling. Although the Court rejected his suit, he gained his freedom in May 1857 when a white man purchased and freed Scott and his family. Collection of the New-York Historical Society.

Dred Scott decision

▶ 1857 Supreme Court decision that ruled the Missouri Compromise unconstitutional. The Court ruled against the slave Dred Scott, who claimed that travels with his master into free states made him and his family free. The decision also denied the federal government the right to exclude slavery in the territories and declared that African Americans were not citizens.

sued to prove that he and his family were legally entitled to their freedom. Scott argued that living in Illinois, a free state, and Wisconsin, a free territory, had made his family free and that they remained free even after returning to Missouri, a slave state.

In 1857, Chief Justice Roger B. Taney, who hated Republicans and detested racial equality, wrote the Court's *Dred Scott* decision. The Court explicitly declared the Missouri Compromise unconstitutional, even though it had already been voided by the Kansas-Nebraska Act.

> ## > *Dred Scott* Decision

- Scott could not legally claim violation of his constitutional rights because he was not a citizen of the United States.
- The laws of Dred Scott's home state, Missouri, determined his status, and thus his travels in free areas did not make him free.
- Congress did not have the power to prohibit slavery in the territories.

The Taney Court's extreme proslavery decision outraged Republicans. By denying the federal government the right to exclude slavery in the territories, it cut the legs out from under the Republican Party. Moreover, as the *New York Tribune* lamented, the decision cleared the way for "all our Territories . . . to be ripened into Slave States." Particularly frightening to African Americans in the North was the Court's declaration that free blacks were not citizens and had no rights.

In a seven-to-two decision, the Court validated an extreme statement of the South's territorial rights. John C. Calhoun's claim that Congress had no authority to exclude slavery became the law of the land. White Southerners cheered, but the *Dred Scott* decision actually strengthened the young Republican Party. Indeed,

CHAPTER LOCATOR | Why did the acquisition of land from Mexico contribute to sectional tensions? | What factors helped unravel the balance between slave and free states?

410 CHAPTER 14
THE HOUSE DIVIDED

that "outrageous" decision, one Republican argued, was "the best thing that could have happened," for it provided powerful evidence of the Republicans' claim that a hostile Slave Power conspired against northern liberties.

Prairie Republican: Abraham Lincoln

By reigniting the sectional flames, the *Dred Scott* case provided Republican politicians with fresh challenges and fresh opportunities. Abraham Lincoln had long since put behind him his hardscrabble log-cabin beginnings in Kentucky and Indiana. Now living in Springfield, Illinois, he earned good money as a lawyer, but politics was his life. "His ambition was a little engine that knew no rest," observed his law partner William Herndon. Lincoln had served as a Whig in the Illinois state legislature and in the House of Representatives, but he had not held public office since 1849.

Convinced that slavery was a "monstrous injustice," a "great moral wrong," and an "unqualified evil to the negro, the white man, and the State," Lincoln condemned the Kansas-Nebraska Act of 1854 for giving slavery a new life and in 1856 joined the Republican Party. He accepted that the Constitution permitted slavery in those states where it existed, but he believed that Congress could contain its spread. Penned in, Lincoln believed, plantation slavery would wither, and in time Southerners would end slavery themselves.

Lincoln held what were, for his times, moderate racial views. Although he denounced slavery and defended black humanity, he also viewed black equality as impractical and unachievable. "Negroes have natural rights . . . as other men have," he said, "although they cannot enjoy them here." Insurmountable white prejudice made it impossible to extend full citizenship to blacks in America, he believed. In Lincoln's mind, social stability and black progress required that slavery end and that blacks leave the country.

Lincoln envisioned the western territories as "places for poor people to go to, and better their conditions." But slavery's expansion threatened free men's basic right to succeed. The Kansas-Nebraska Act and the *Dred Scott* decision persuaded him that slaveholders were engaged in a dangerous conspiracy to nationalize slavery. The next step, Lincoln warned, would be "another Supreme Court decision, declaring that the Constitution of the United States does not permit a State to exclude slavery from its limits." Unless the citizens of Illinois woke up, he warned, the Supreme Court would make "Illinois a slave State."

In Lincoln's view, the nation could not "endure, permanently half slave and half free." Either opponents of slavery would arrest its spread and place it on the "course of ultimate extinction," or its advocates would see that it became legal in "*all* the States, *old* as well as *new* — *North* as well as *South*." Lincoln's convictions that slavery was wrong and that Congress must stop its spread formed the core of the Republican ideology. In 1858, Republicans in Illinois chose him to challenge the nation's premier Democrat, who was seeking reelection to the U.S. Senate.

The Lincoln-Douglas Debates

When Stephen Douglas learned that the Republican Abraham Lincoln would be his opponent for the Senate, he observed: "He is the strong man of the party—full of wit, facts, dates—and the best stump speaker, with his droll ways and dry jokes, in the West. He is as honest as he is shrewd, and if I beat him my victory will be hardly won."

| How did the party system change in the 1850s? | **Why did northern fear of the "Slave Power" intensify in the 1850s?** | Why did some southern states secede immediately after Lincoln's election? | Conclusion: Why did political compromise fail? | ☑ LearningCurve Check what you know. bedfordstmartins.com /roarkunderstanding |

411

Not only did Douglas have to contend with a formidable foe, but the previous year the nation's economy had experienced a sharp downturn. Prices had plummeted, thousands of businesses had failed, and many were unemployed. As a Democrat, Douglas had to go before the voters as a member of the party whose policies stood accused of causing the panic of 1857.

Douglas's response to another crisis in 1857, however, helped shore up his standing in Illinois. Proslavery forces in Kansas met in the town of Lecompton, drafted a proslavery constitution, and applied for statehood. Everyone knew that free-soilers outnumbered proslavery settlers, but President Buchanan instructed Congress to admit Kansas as the sixteenth slave state. Senator Douglas broke with the Democratic administration and denounced the Lecompton constitution; Congress killed the Lecompton bill. (When Kansans reconsidered the Lecompton constitution in an honest election, they rejected it six to one. Kansas entered the Union in 1861 as a free state.) By denouncing the fraudulent proslavery constitution, Douglas declared his independence from the South and, he hoped, made himself acceptable at home.

A relative unknown and a decided underdog in the Illinois election, Lincoln challenged Douglas to debate him face-to-face. The two met in seven communities for what would become a legendary series of debates. Thousands stood straining to hear the two men debate the crucial issues of the age — slavery and freedom.

Lincoln badgered Douglas with the question of whether he favored the spread of slavery. He tried to force Douglas into the damaging admission that the Supreme Court had repudiated Douglas's own territorial solution, popular sovereignty. At Freeport, Illinois, Douglas admitted that settlers could not now pass legislation barring slavery, but he argued that they could ban slavery just as effectively by not passing protective laws, such as those found in slave states. Southerners condemned Douglas's "Freeport Doctrine" and charged him with trying to steal the victory they had gained with the *Dred Scott* decision. Lincoln chastised his opponent for his "don't care" attitude about slavery, for "blowing out the moral lights around us."

Douglas worked the racial issue. He called Lincoln an abolitionist and an egalitarian enamored of "our colored brethren." Put on the defensive, Lincoln reaffirmed his faith in white rule: "I will say, then, that I am not, nor ever have been, in favor of bringing about in any way the social and political equality of the white and black race." But unlike Douglas, Lincoln was no negrophobe. He tried to steer the debate back to what he considered the true issue: the morality and future of slavery. "Slavery is wrong," Lincoln repeated, because "a man has the right to the fruits of his own labor."

As Douglas predicted, the election was hard-fought and closely contested. Until the adoption of the Seventeenth Amendment in 1913, citizens voted for state legislators, who in turn selected U.S. senators. Since Democrats won a slight majority in the Illinois legislature, the members returned Douglas to the Senate. But the **Lincoln-Douglas debates** thrust Lincoln, the prairie Republican, into the national spotlight.

Lincoln-Douglas debates
▶ Series of debates on the issue of slavery and freedom between Democrat Stephen Douglas and Republican Abraham Lincoln, held as part of the 1858 U.S. senatorial race in Illinois. Douglas became senator, but the debates helped catapult Lincoln to national prominence.

> **QUICK REVIEW**

Why did the *Dred Scott* decision strengthen northern suspicions of a Slave Power conspiracy?

CHAPTER LOCATOR | Why did the acquisition of land from Mexico contribute to sectional tensions? | What factors helped unravel the balance between slave and free states?

412 CHAPTER 14
THE HOUSE DIVIDED

Why did some southern states secede immediately after Lincoln's election?

Abraham Lincoln

While in New York City to give a political address, Lincoln had this dignified photograph taken by Mathew Brady. "While I was there I was taken to one of the places where they get up such things," Lincoln explained, sounding more innocent than he was, "and I suppose they got my shadow, and can multiply copies indefinitely." Multiply they did. From the Lincoln Financial Foundation Collection, courtesy of the Indiana State Museum and Allen County Public Library.

FROM THE REPUBLICAN PERSPECTIVE, the Kansas-Nebraska Act, the Brooks-Sumner affair, the *Dred Scott* decision, and the Lecompton constitution amounted to irrefutable evidence of the South's aggressive promotion of slavery. White Southerners, of course, saw things differently. They were the ones who were under siege, they declared. They believed that Northerners were itching to use their numerical advantage to attack slavery, and not just in the territories. Republicans had made it clear that they were unwilling to accept the *Dred Scott* ruling as the last word on the issue of slavery expansion. And John Brown's attempt to incite a slave insurrection in Virginia in 1859 proved that Northerners would do anything to end slavery.

Talk of leaving the Union had been heard for years, but until the final crisis, Southerners had used secession as a ploy to gain concessions within the Union, not to destroy it. Then the 1850s delivered powerful blows to Southerners' confidence that they could remain in the Union and protect slavery. When the Republican Party won the White House in 1860, many Southerners concluded that they would have to leave.

> CHRONOLOGY

1859
– John Brown raids Harpers Ferry.

1860
– Abraham Lincoln is elected president.
– South Carolina secedes from Union.

1861
– Six other Lower South states secede.
– Confederate States of America is formed.

How did the party system change in the 1850s?

Why did northern fear of the "Slave Power" intensify in the 1850s?

Why did some southern states secede immediately after Lincoln's election?

Conclusion: Why did political compromise fail?

☑ LearningCurve
Check what you know.
bedfordstmartins.com
/roarkunderstanding

John Brown's Raid

John Brown, an ardent abolitionist and the man who instigated the massacre at Pottawatomie, Kansas, in 1856, took his war against slavery into the South. On October 16, 1859, he and twenty-one men, including five African Americans, invaded Harpers Ferry, Virginia. His band quickly seized the town's army and rifle works, but the invaders were immediately surrounded, first by local militia and then by Colonel Robert E. Lee, who commanded the U.S. troops in the area. When Brown refused to surrender, federal soldiers charged with bayonets. Seventeen men, two of whom were slaves, lost their lives. Although a few of Brown's raiders escaped, federal forces killed ten and captured seven, among them Brown.

For his attack on Harpers Ferry, John Brown stood trial for treason, murder, and incitement of slave insurrection. "To hang a fanatic is to make a martyr of him and fledge another brood of the same sort," cautioned one newspaper, but on December 2, 1859, Virginia executed Brown. In life, he was a ne'er-do-well, but, as the poet Stephen Vincent Benét observed, "he knew how to die." Brown told his wife that he was "determined to make the utmost possible out of a defeat." He told the court: "If it is deemed necessary that I should forfeit my life for the furtherance of the ends of justice, and mingle my blood further with the blood of . . . millions in this slave country whose rights are disregarded by wicked, cruel, and unjust enactments, I say, let it be done."

After Brown's execution, Americans across the land contemplated the meaning of his life and death. Some Northerners celebrated his "splendid martyrdom." Ralph Waldo Emerson likened Brown to Christ when he declared that Brown made "the gallows as glorious as the cross." Most Northerners did not advocate bloody rebellion, however. Like Lincoln, they concluded that Brown's noble anti-slavery ideals could not "excuse violence, bloodshed, and treason."

Still, when northern churches marked John Brown's hanging with tolling bells, hymns, and prayer vigils, white Southerners contemplated what they had in common with people who "regard John Brown as a martyr and a Christian hero, rather than a murderer and robber." Georgia senator Robert Toombs announced solemnly that Southerners must "never permit this Federal government to pass into the traitorous hands of the black Republican party."

Republican Victory in 1860

When the Democrats converged on Charleston, South Carolina, for their convention in April 1860, fire-eating Southerners denounced Stephen Douglas and demanded a platform that included federal protection of slavery in the territories. When the delegates approved a platform with popular sovereignty, representatives from the entire Lower South and Arkansas stomped out of the convention. The remaining Democrats adjourned to meet a few weeks later in Baltimore, where they nominated Douglas for president.

When bolting southern Democrats reconvened, they approved a platform with a federal slave code and nominated Vice President John C. Breckinridge of Kentucky. Southern moderates, however, refused to support Breckinridge. They formed the Constitutional Union Party to provide voters with a Unionist choice. Instead of adopting a platform and confronting the slavery question, the

John Brown Going to His Hanging, by Horace Pippin, 1942

The grandparents of Horace Pippin, a Pennsylvania artist, were slaves. His grandmother witnessed the hanging of John Brown, and this painting recalls the scene she so often described to him. Pippin used a muted palette to establish the bleak setting, but he also managed to convey its striking intensity. Historically accurate, the painting depicts Brown tied and sitting erect on his coffin, passing resolutely before the silent, staring white men. The black woman in the lower right corner presumably is Pippin's grandmother. Romare Bearden, another African American artist, recalled the central place of John Brown in black memory: "Lincoln and John Brown were as much a part of the actuality of the Afro-American experience, as were the domino games and the hoe cakes for Sunday morning breakfast. I vividly recall the yearly commemorations for John Brown." Pennsylvania Academy of Fine Arts, Philadelphia. John Lambert Fund.

> VISUAL ACTIVITY

READING THE IMAGE: What was the artist trying to convey about the tone of John Brown's execution? According to the painting, what were the feelings of those gathered to witness the event?

CONNECTIONS: How did Brown's trial and execution contribute to the growing split between North and South?

Constitutional Union Party merely approved a vague resolution pledging "to recognize no political principle other than *the Constitution . . . the Union . . . and the Enforcement of the Laws.*" For president, they nominated former senator John Bell of Tennessee.

The Republicans smelled victory, but they needed to carry nearly all the free states to win. To make their party more appealing, they expanded their platform

How did the party system change in the 1850s?

Why did northern fear of the "Slave Power" intensify in the 1850s?

Why did some southern states secede immediately after Lincoln's election?

Conclusion: Why did political compromise fail?

✓ LearningCurve
Check what you know.
bedfordstmartins.com
/roarkunderstanding

beyond antislavery. They hoped that free homesteads, a protective tariff, a transcontinental railroad, and a guarantee of immigrant political rights would provide an agenda broad enough to unify the North. While reasserting their commitment to stop the spread of slavery, they also denounced John Brown's raid as "among the gravest of crimes" and confirmed the security of slavery in the South.

The foremost Republican, William H. Seward, had made enemies with his radical "higher law" doctrine, which claimed that there was a higher moral law than the Constitution, and with his "irrepressible conflict" speech, in which he declared that North and South were fated to collide. Lincoln, however, since bursting onto the national scene in 1858, had demonstrated his clear purpose, good judgment, and solid Republican credentials. That, and his residence in Illinois, a crucial state, made him attractive to the party. On the third ballot, the delegates chose Lincoln. Defeated by Douglas in a state contest less than two years earlier, Lincoln now stood ready to take him on for the presidency.

The election of 1860 was like none other in American politics. It took place in the midst of the nation's severest crisis. Four major candidates crowded the presidential field. Rather than a four-cornered contest, however, the election broke into two contests, each with two candidates. In the North, Lincoln faced Douglas; in the South, Breckinridge confronted Bell. So outrageous did Southerners consider the Republican Party that they did not even permit Lincoln's name to appear on the ballot in ten of the fifteen slave states.

On November 6, 1860, Lincoln swept all of the eighteen free states except New Jersey, which split its electoral votes between him and Douglas. Although Lincoln received only 39 percent of the popular vote, he won easily in the electoral college with 180 votes, 28 more than he needed for victory (**Map 14.5**). Lincoln did not win because his opposition was splintered. Even if the votes of his three opponents had been combined, Lincoln still would have won. He won

Candidate	Electoral Vote	Popular Vote	Percent of Popular Vote
Abraham Lincoln (Republican)	180	1,866,452	39.9
John C. Breckinridge (Southern Democrat)	72	847,953	18.1
Stephen A. Douglas (Northern Democrat)	12	1,375,157	29.4
John Bell (Constitutional Union)	39	590,631	12.6

MAP 14.5 ■ The Election of 1860

CHAPTER LOCATOR | Why did the acquisition of land from Mexico contribute to sectional tensions? | What factors helped unravel the balance between slave and free states?

CHAPTER 14
416 THE HOUSE DIVIDED

because his votes were concentrated in the free states, which contained a majority of electoral votes. Ominously, however, Breckinridge, running on a southern-rights platform, won the entire Lower South, plus Delaware, Maryland, and North Carolina.

Secession Winter

Anxious Southerners immediately began debating what to do. Although Breckinridge had carried the South, a vote for "southern rights" was not necessarily a vote for secession. Besides, slightly more than half of the Southerners who had voted had cast ballots for Douglas and Bell, two stout defenders of the Union.

Southern Unionists tried to calm the fears that Lincoln's election triggered. Former congressman Alexander Stephens of Georgia asked what Lincoln had done to justify something as extreme as secession. Had he not promised to respect slavery where it existed? In Stephens's judgment, secession might lead to war, which would loosen the hinges of southern society and possibly even open the door to slave insurrection. "Revolutions are much easier started than controlled," he warned. "I consider slavery much more secure in the Union than out of it."

Secessionists emphasized the dangers of delay. "Mr. Lincoln and his party assert that this doctrine of equality applies to the negro," former Georgia governor Howell Cobb declared, "and necessarily there can exist no such thing as property in our equals." Lincoln's election without a single electoral vote from the South meant that Southerners were no longer able to defend themselves within the Union, Cobb argued. Why wait, he asked, for abolitionists to attack? As for war, there would be none. The Union was a voluntary compact, and Lincoln would not coerce patriotism. If Northerners did resist with force, secessionists argued, one southern woodsman could whip five of Lincoln's greasy mechanics.

For all their differences, southern whites agreed that they had to defend slavery. John Smith Preston of South Carolina spoke for the overwhelming majority when he declared, "The South cannot exist without slavery." They disagreed about whether the mere presence of a Republican in the White House made it necessary to exercise what they considered a legitimate right to secede.

South Carolina seceded from the Union on December 20, 1860. By February 1861, the six other Lower South states followed in South Carolina's footsteps. In general, slaveholders spearheaded secession, while nonslaveholders in the Piedmont and mountain counties, where slaves were relatively few, displayed the greatest attachment to the Union. In February, representatives from South Carolina, Georgia, Florida, Alabama, Mississippi, Louisiana, and Texas met in Montgomery, Alabama, where they created the **Confederate States of America**. Mississippi senator Jefferson Davis became president, and Alexander Stephens of Georgia, who had spoken so eloquently about the dangers of revolution, became vice president. In March 1861, Stephens declared that the Confederacy's "cornerstone" was "the great truth that the negro is not equal to the white man; that slavery, subordination to the superior race, is his natural and moral condition."

Lincoln's election had split the Union. Now secession split the South. Seven slave states seceded during the winter, but the eight slave states of the Upper South rejected secession, at least for the moment. The Upper South had a smaller

Confederate States of America
▶ Government formed by Lower South states on February 7, 1861, following their secession from the Union. Secessionists argued that the election of a Republican to the presidency imperiled slavery and that the South no longer had political protection within the Union.

| How did the party system change in the 1850s? | Why did northern fear of the "Slave Power" intensify in the 1850s? | **Why did some southern states secede immediately after Lincoln's election?** | Conclusion: Why did political compromise fail? | ✓ LearningCurve Check what you know. bedfordstmartins.com /roarkunderstanding |

417

Secession of the Lower South,
December 1860–February 1861

stake in slavery. Barely half as many white families in the Upper South held slaves (21 percent) as in the Lower South (37 percent). Slaves represented twice as large a percentage of the population in the Lower South (48 percent) as in the Upper South (23 percent). Consequently, whites in the Upper South had fewer fears that Republican ascendancy meant economic catastrophe, social chaos, and racial war. Lincoln would need to do more than just be elected to provoke them into secession.

The nation had to wait until March 4, 1861, when Lincoln took office, to see what he would do. He chose to stay in Springfield after his election and to say nothing. "Lame-duck" president James Buchanan sat in Washington and did nothing. Congress's efforts at cobbling together a peace-saving compromise came to nothing.

Lincoln began his inaugural address with reassurances to the South. He had "no lawful right" to interfere with slavery where it existed, he declared again, adding for emphasis that he had "no inclination to do so." Conciliatory about slavery, Lincoln proved inflexible about the Union. The Union, he declared, was "perpetual." Secession was "anarchy" and "legally void." The Constitution required him to execute the law "in all the States."

The decision for war or peace rested in the South's hands, Lincoln said. "You can have no conflict, without being yourselves the aggressors. You have no oath registered in Heaven to destroy the government, while I shall have the most solemn one to 'preserve, protect, and defend' it."

> **QUICK REVIEW**

Why were the states of the Lower and Upper South divided on the question of secession during the winter of 1860–1861?

CHAPTER LOCATOR | Why did the acquisition of land from Mexico contribute to sectional tensions? | What factors helped unravel the balance between slave and free states?

418   CHAPTER 14
THE HOUSE DIVIDED

A**S THEIR ECONOMIES,** societies, and cultures diverged in the nineteenth century, Northerners and Southerners expressed different concepts of the American promise and the place of slavery within it. Their differences crystallized into political form in 1846 when David Wilmot proposed banning slavery in any territory won in the Mexican-American War. "As if by magic," a Boston newspaper observed, "it brought to a head the great question that is about to divide the American people." Discovery of gold and other precious metals in the West added urgency to the controversy over slavery in the territories. Congress attempted to address the issue with the Compromise of 1850, but the Fugitive Slave Act and the publication of *Uncle Tom's Cabin* hardened northern sentiments against slavery and confirmed southern suspicions of northern ill will. The bloody violence that erupted in Kansas in 1856 and the incendiary *Dred Scott* decision in 1857 further eroded hope for a solution to this momentous question.

During the extended crisis of the Union that stretched from 1846 to 1861, the slavery question intertwined with national politics. The traditional Whig and Democratic parties struggled to hold together as new parties, most notably the Republican Party, emerged. Politicians fixed their attention on the expansion of slavery, but from the beginning Americans recognized that the controversy had less to do with slavery in the territories than with the future of slavery in the nation.

For more than seventy years, statesmen had found compromises that accepted slavery and preserved the Union. But as each section grew increasingly committed to its labor system, Americans discovered that accommodation had limits. In 1859, John Brown's militant antislavery pushed white Southerners to the edge. In 1860, Lincoln's election convinced whites in the Lower South that slavery and the society they had built on it were at risk in the Union, and they seceded. But it remained to be seen whether disunion would mean war.

| How did the party system change in the 1850s? | Why did northern fear of the "Slave Power" intensify in the 1850s? | Why did some southern states secede immediately after Lincoln's election? | Conclusion: Why did political compromise fail? | ✓ LearningCurve Check what you know. bedfordstmartins.com /roarkunderstanding |

CHAPTER 14 STUDY GUIDE

STEP 1

GET STARTED ONLINE

 LearningCurve ■ bedfordstmartins.com/roarkunderstanding

Now that you've read the chapter, make it stick by completing the LearningCurve activity.

STEP 2

EXPLAIN WHY IT MATTERS

Put your reading into practice. Identify each term below, and then explain why it matters in U.S. history.

TERM	WHO OR WHAT & WHEN	WHY IT MATTERS
Wilmot Proviso (p. 393)		
free labor (p. 393)		
popular sovereignty (p. 394)		
Compromise of 1850 (p. 397)		
Uncle Tom's Cabin (p. 398)		
Fugitive Slave Act (p. 399)		
Kansas-Nebraska Act (p. 402)		
Republican Party (p. 406)		
"Bleeding Kansas" (p. 409)		
Dred Scott decision (p. 410)		
Lincoln-Douglas debates (p. 412)		
Confederate States of America (p. 417)		

STEP 3

MOVE BEYOND THE BASICS

To demonstrate a more advanced understanding, use the table below to sketch the political landscape of the 1850s. How did slavery help transform the American political landscape?

Party	Who supported this party?	Position on slavery	Views on expansion	Perspectives on immigration
Democratic Party				
Whig Party				
Republican Party				
American (Know-Nothing) Party				

STEP 4 PUT IT ALL TOGETHER Now, take a step back and try to explain the big picture. Remember to use specific examples from the chapter in your answers.

EXPANSION AND SECTIONALISM

▶ Why was the Wilmot Proviso so controversial? What did the response to the Proviso reveal about the diverging visions of America in the North and in the South?

▶ Why was the expansion of slavery not only a moral issue for abolitionists but also an economic concern to both Northerners and Southerners?

POLITICAL INSTABILITY

▶ Why did the Compromise of 1850 ultimately fail?

▶ What were the consequences of the events of the 1840s and 1850s for America's political parties? How did the party system change under the pressure of the sectional divide?

THE ROAD TO SECESSION

▶ If most Northerners and Southerners wanted to avoid war, why did war come?

▶ Why did so many Southerners see the election of Abraham Lincoln as a threat to their way of life? Why did more than half of the southern electorate vote for pro-Union candidates?

LOOKING BACKWARD, LOOKING AHEAD

▶ Why, in the early nineteenth century, was compromise on the issue of slavery possible? Why did so many reject compromise in the 1840s and 1850s?

▶ What consequences might Southerners have imagined would follow from secession? What might have led them to underestimate Lincoln's determination to fight for the Union?

> IN YOUR OWN WORDS Imagine that you must give an oral report to the class answering the following question: **How did the issue of slavery drive the United States toward Civil War in the mid-nineteenth century?** What would be the most important points to include and why?

 Do it online at the Student Site ■ bedfordstmartins.com/roarkunderstanding

15

THE CRUCIBLE OF WAR

1861–1865

> **How did the Civil War change the nation, North and South?** Chapter 15 traces the course of the Civil War, exploring the connections between events on the battlefield and the political, social, and economic divisions on the home fronts. It explains how the war became a fight for black freedom and examines why the North ultimately won the war.

LearningCurve
bedfordstmartins.com/roarkunderstanding
After reading the chapter, use LearningCurve to
retain what you've read.

"Price Raid," October 1864. This 1865 illustration by Samuel J. Reader shows a regiment of Kansas militia captured by Confederate soldiers in Texas. Reader was one of the captives. Kansas State Historical Society.

> Why did both the Union and the Confederacy consider control of the border states crucial?

> Why did each side expect to win?

> How did each side fare in the early years of the war?

> How did the war for union become a fight for black freedom?

> What problems did the Confederacy face at home?

> How did the war affect the economy and politics of the North?

> How did the Union finally win the war?

> Conclusion: In what ways was the Civil War a "Second American Revolution"?

Why did both the Union and the Confederacy consider control of the border states crucial?

Fort Sumter Bombardment Located on an artificial island inside the entrance to Charleston harbor, Fort Sumter had walls eight to twelve feet thick. The fort was so undermanned that when Confederate shells began raining down on April 12, U.S. troops could answer back with only a few of the fort's forty-eight guns. Minnesota Historical Society.

ABRAHAM LINCOLN faced the worst crisis in the history of the nation: disunion. He revealed his strategy to save the Union in his inaugural address on March 4, 1861. He was firm yet conciliatory. First, he denied the right of secession and sought to stop its spread by avoiding any act that would push the skittish Upper South (North Carolina, Virginia, Maryland, Delaware, Kentucky, Tennessee, Missouri, and Arkansas) out of the Union. Second, he sought to reassure the seceding Lower South (South Carolina, Georgia, Florida, Alabama, Mississippi, Louisiana, and Texas) that the Republicans would not abolish slavery. Lincoln believed that Unionists there would assert themselves and overturn the secession decision.

His counterpart, Jefferson Davis, fully intended to establish the Confederate States of America as an independent republic. To achieve permanence, Davis had to sustain the secession fever that had carried the Lower South out of the Union. Even if the Lower South held firm, however, the Confederacy would remain weak without additional states. Davis watched for opportunities to add new stars to the Confederate flag.

CHAPTER LOCATOR | **Why did both the Union and the Confederacy consider control of the border states crucial?** | Why did each side expect to win? | How did each side fare in the early years of the war?

424 CHAPTER 15 THE CRUCIBLE OF WAR

Both men wanted to achieve their objectives peacefully. As Lincoln later observed, "Both parties deprecated war, but one of them would *make* war rather than let the nation survive, and the other would *accept* war rather than let it perish. And the war came."

Attack on Fort Sumter

Major Robert Anderson and some eighty U.S. soldiers occupied **Fort Sumter**, which was perched on a tiny island at the entrance to Charleston harbor in South Carolina. Lincoln decided to hold the fort, but Anderson and his men were running dangerously short of food. In early April 1861, Lincoln authorized a peaceful expedition to bring supplies, but not military reinforcements, to the fort. The president understood that he risked war, but his plan honored his inaugural promises to defend federal property and to avoid using military force unless first attacked. Masterfully, Lincoln had shifted the fateful decision of war or peace to Jefferson Davis.

On April 9, Davis and his cabinet met to consider the situation in Charleston harbor. Davis argued for military action, but his secretary of state, Robert Toombs of Georgia, replied: "Mr. President, at this time it is suicide, murder, and will lose us every friend at the North. You will wantonly strike a hornet's nest which extends from mountain to ocean, and legions now quiet will swarm out and sting us to death." But Davis ordered Confederate troops in Charleston to take the fort before the relief expedition arrived. Thirty-three hours of bombardment on April 12 and 13 reduced the fort to rubble. On April 14, Major Anderson offered his surrender and lowered the U.S. flag. The Confederates had Fort Sumter, but they also had war.

On April 15, when Lincoln called for 75,000 militiamen to serve for ninety days to put down the rebellion, several times that number rushed to defend the flag. Stephen A. Douglas, the recently defeated Democratic candidate for president, pledged his support and noted, "There can be no neutrals in this war, *only patriots — or traitors.*"

The Upper South Chooses Sides

The Upper South faced a horrendous choice: either to fight against the Lower South or to fight against the Union. Many who only months earlier had rejected secession now embraced the Confederacy. Thousands felt betrayed, believing that Lincoln had promised to achieve a peaceful reunion by waiting patiently for Unionists to retake power in the seceding states. It was a "politician's war," one man declared, but he conceded that "this is no time now to discuss the causes, but it is the duty of all who regard Southern institutions of value to side with the South, make common cause with the Confederate States and sink or swim with them."

Virginia, Arkansas, Tennessee, and North Carolina joined the Confederacy (**Map 15.1**). But in the border states of Delaware, Maryland, Kentucky, and Missouri, Unionism triumphed. Only in Delaware, where slaves accounted for less than 2 percent of the population, was the victory easy. In Maryland, Lincoln suspended the writ of habeas corpus, essentially setting aside constitutional

> **CHRONOLOGY**

1861
- Attack on Fort Sumter.
- Four Upper South states join Confederacy.

Fort Sumter

▶ Union fort on an island at the entrance to Charleston harbor in South Carolina. After Confederate leaders learned that President Lincoln intended to resupply Fort Sumter, Confederate forces attacked the fort on April 12, 1861, thus marking the start of the Civil War.

| How did the war for union become a fight for black freedom? | What problems did the Confederacy face at home? | How did the war affect the economy and politics of the North? | How did the Union finally win the war? | Conclusion: In what ways was the Civil War a "Second American Revolution"? | ✓ **LearningCurve** Check what you know. bedfordstmartins.com /roarkunderstanding |

MAP 15.1 ■ Secession, 1860–1861

After Lincoln's election, the fifteen slave states debated what to do. Seven states quickly left the Union, four left after the firing on Fort Sumter, and four remained loyal to the Union.

Seceded before fall of Fort Sumter

Seceded after fall of Fort Sumter

Slave state loyal to Union

Free state

Territory

1 Order of secession

guarantees that protect citizens from arbitrary arrest and detention, and he ordered U.S. troops into Baltimore. Maryland's legislature rejected secession.

The struggle turned violent in the West. In Missouri, Unionists won a narrow victory, but southern-sympathizing guerrilla bands roamed the state for the duration of the war, terrorizing civilians and soldiers alike. In Kentucky, Unionists also narrowly defeated secession, but the prosouthern minority claimed otherwise.

Lincoln understood that the border states — particularly Kentucky — contained indispensable resources, population, and wealth and also controlled major rivers and railroads. "I think to lose Kentucky is nearly the same as to lose the whole game," Lincoln said. "Kentucky gone, we can not hold Missouri, nor, as I think, Maryland. These all against us, . . . we would as well consent to separation at once."

In the end, only eleven of the fifteen slave states joined the Confederate States of America. Moreover, the four seceding Upper South states contained significant numbers of people who felt little affection for the Confederacy. Dissatisfaction was so rife in the western counties of Virginia that in 1863 citizens there voted to create the separate state of West Virginia, loyal to the Union. Still, the acquisition of four new states greatly strengthened the Confederacy's drive for national independence.

> **QUICK REVIEW**

Why did the attack on Fort Sumter force the Upper South to choose sides?

CHAPTER LOCATOR | Why did both the Union and the Confederacy consider control of the border states crucial? | **Why did each side expect to win?** | How did each side fare in the early years of the war?

426 CHAPTER 15
THE CRUCIBLE OF WAR

Why did each side expect to win?

Union Ordnance, Yorktown, Virginia

As the North successfully harnessed its enormous industrial capacity to meet the needs of the war, cannons, mortars, and shells poured out of its factories. A fraction of that abundance is seen here at Yorktown in 1862, ready for transportation to Union troops in the field. Library of Congress.

ONLY SLAVEHOLDERS had a direct economic stake in preserving slavery, but most whites in the Confederacy defended the institution, the way of life built on it, and the Confederate nation. The degraded and subjugated status of blacks elevated the status of the poorest whites. "It is enough that one simply belongs to the superior and ruling race, to secure consideration and respect." Moreover, Yankee "aggression" was no longer a mere threat; it was real and at the South's door.

For Northerners, the South's failure to accept the democratic election of a president and its firing on the nation's flag challenged the rule of law, the authority of the Constitution, and the ability of the people to govern themselves. As an Indiana soldier told his wife, a "good government is the best thing on earth. Property is nothing without it, because it is not protected; a family is nothing without it, because they cannot be educated."

Northerners and Southerners rallied behind their separate flags, fully convinced that they were in the right and that God was on their side. Yankees took heart from their superior power, but the rebels believed they had advantages that nullified every northern strength. Both sides mobilized swiftly in 1861, and each devised what it believed would be a winning military and diplomatic strategy.

How They Expected to Win

The balance sheet of northern and southern resources reveals enormous advantages for the Union (**Figure 15.1**). The twenty-three states remaining in the Union had a population of 22.3 million; the eleven Confederate states had a population of only 9.1 million, of whom 3.67 million (40 percent) were slaves. The North's economic advantages were even more overwhelming. Yet Southerners expected to win — for some good reasons — and they came very close to doing so.

| How did the war for union become a fight for black freedom? | What problems did the Confederacy face at home? | How did the war affect the economy and politics of the North? | How did the Union finally win the war? | Conclusion: In what ways was the Civil War a "Second American Revolution"? | ✓ **LearningCurve** Check what you know. bedfordstmartins.com /roarkunderstanding |

Confederate Expectations

- "King Cotton" could help create alliances based on Europe's (especially Britain's) reliance on cotton imports.
- Defensive war strategy meant the South could win simply by outlasting the Union.
- President Jefferson Davis was an experienced military commander.

Union Expectations

- Superior navy could blockade trade between the Confederacy and Europe.
- Superior numbers meant a larger army.
- Greater industrial capacity meant a stronger army.
- President Abraham Lincoln appointed well-qualified men to key positions in government.

Southerners knew they bucked the military odds, but hadn't the liberty-loving colonists in 1776 also done so? "Britain could not conquer three million," a Louisianan proclaimed, and "the world cannot conquer the South." How could anyone doubt the outcome of a contest between lean, hard, country-born rebel warriors defending family, property, and liberty, and soft, flabby, citified Yankee mechanics waging an unconstitutional war?

The South's confidence also rested on its belief that northern prosperity depended on the South's cotton. Without cotton, New England textile mills would stand idle. Without planters purchasing northern manufactured goods, northern factories would drown in their own unsold surpluses. And without the foreign exchange earned by the overseas sales of cotton, the financial structure of the entire Yankee nation would collapse.

Cotton would also make Europe a powerful ally of the Confederacy, Southerners reasoned. Of the 900 million pounds of cotton Britain imported annually, more than 700 million pounds came from the American South. If the supply was interrupted, sheer economic need would make Britain (and perhaps France) a Confederate ally. And because the British navy ruled the seas, the North would find Britain a formidable foe.

The Confederacy devised a military strategy to exploit its advantages and minimize its limitations. It recognized that a Union victory required the North to defeat and subjugate the South, but a Confederate victory required only that the

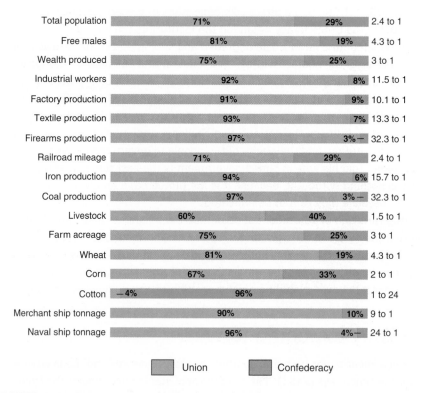

	Union	Confederacy	Ratio
Total population	71%	29%	2.4 to 1
Free males	81%	19%	4.3 to 1
Wealth produced	75%	25%	3 to 1
Industrial workers	92%	8%	11.5 to 1
Factory production	91%	9%	10.1 to 1
Textile production	93%	7%	13.3 to 1
Firearms production	97%	3%	32.3 to 1
Railroad mileage	71%	29%	2.4 to 1
Iron production	94%	6%	15.7 to 1
Coal production	97%	3%	32.3 to 1
Livestock	60%	40%	1.5 to 1
Farm acreage	75%	25%	3 to 1
Wheat	81%	19%	4.3 to 1
Corn	67%	33%	2 to 1
Cotton	4%	96%	1 to 24
Merchant ship tonnage	90%	10%	9 to 1
Naval ship tonnage	96%	4%	24 to 1

FIGURE 15.1 ■ Resources of the Union and Confederacy

The Union's enormous statistical advantages failed to convince Confederates that their cause was doomed.

CHAPTER LOCATOR | Why did both the Union and the Confederacy consider control of the border states crucial? | **Why did each side expect to win?** | How did each side fare in the early years of the war?

CHAPTER 15
428 THE CRUCIBLE OF WAR

South stay at home, blunt invasions, avoid battles that risked annihilating its army, and outlast the North's will to fight. When an opportunity presented itself, the South would strike the invaders. Like the American colonists, the South could win independence by not losing the war.

The Lincoln administration countered with a strategy designed to take advantage of its superior resources. Lincoln declared a naval blockade of the Confederacy to deny it the ability to sell cotton abroad, giving the South far fewer dollars to pay for war goods. Lincoln also ordered the Union army into Virginia, at the same time planning a march through the Mississippi valley that would cut the Confederacy in two.

Lincoln and Davis Mobilize

Mobilization required effective political leadership, and at first glance the South appeared to have the advantage. Jefferson Davis brought to the Confederate presidency a distinguished political career, including experience in the U.S. Senate. He was also a West Point graduate, a combat veteran and authentic hero of the Mexican-American War, and a former secretary of war. Dignified and ramrod straight, with "a jaw sawed in steel," Davis appeared to be everything a nation could want in a wartime leader.

By contrast, Abraham Lincoln brought to the White House one lackluster term in the House of Representatives and almost no administrative experience. His sole brush with anything military was as a captain in the militia in the Black Hawk War, a brief struggle in Illinois in 1832 in which whites expelled the last Indians from the state. The lanky, disheveled Illinois lawyer-politician looked anything but military or presidential in his bearing.

Davis, however, proved to be less than he appeared. Although he worked hard, he had no gift for military strategy yet intervened often in military affairs. He was an even less able political leader. Quarrelsome and proud, he had an acid tongue that made enemies the Confederacy could ill afford.

With Lincoln the North got far more than met the eye. He proved himself a master politician and a superb leader. When forming his cabinet, Lincoln appointed the ablest men, no matter that they were often his chief rivals and critics. He appointed Salmon P. Chase secretary of the treasury, knowing that Chase had presidential ambitions. As secretary of state, he chose his chief opponent for the Republican nomination in 1860, William H. Seward. Despite his civilian background, Lincoln displayed an innate understanding of military strategy. No one was more crucial in mapping the Union war plan.

Lincoln and Davis began gathering their armies. Confederates had to build almost everything from scratch, and Northerners had to channel their superior numbers and industrial resources to war. On the eve of the war, the federal army numbered only 16,000 men. One-third of the officers followed the example of the Virginian Robert E. Lee, resigning their commissions and heading south. The U.S. Navy was in better shape. Forty-two ships were in service, and a large merchant marine would in time provide more ships and sailors for the Union cause.

The Confederacy made prodigious efforts to supply its armies, but even when factories produced what soldiers needed, southern railroads often could not

| How did the war for union become a fight for black freedom? | What problems did the Confederacy face at home? | How did the war affect the economy and politics of the North? | How did the Union finally win the war? | Conclusion: In what ways was the Civil War a "Second American Revolution"? | ✓ LearningCurve Check what you know. bedfordstmartins.com /roarkunderstanding |

429

deliver the goods. And each year, more railroads were captured, destroyed, or left in disrepair. Food production proved less of a problem, but food sometimes rotted before it reached the soldiers. The one bright spot was the Confederacy's Ordnance Bureau, headed by Josiah Gorgas. In April 1864, Gorgas proudly observed: "Where three years ago we were not making a gun, a pistol nor a sabre, no shot nor shell . . . we now make all these in quantities to meet the demands of our large armies."

Recruiting and supplying huge armies required enormous new revenues. At first, the Union and the Confederacy sold war bonds, which essentially were loans from patriotic citizens. In addition, both sides turned to taxes. Eventually, both began printing paper money. Inflation soared, but the Confederacy suffered more because it financed a greater part of its wartime costs through the printing press. Prices in the Union rose by about 80 percent during the war, while inflation in the Confederacy topped 9,000 percent.

Within months of the bombardment of Fort Sumter, both sides found men to fight and ways to supply them. But the underlying strength of the northern economy gave the Union the decided advantage. With their military and industrial muscles beginning to ripple, Northerners became itchy for action that would smash the rebellion. Horace Greeley's *New York Tribune* began to chant: "Forward to Richmond! Forward to Richmond!"

> **QUICK REVIEW**

Why did the South believe it could win the war despite its numerical disadvantages?

CHAPTER LOCATOR | Why did both the Union and the Confederacy consider control of the border states crucial? | Why did each side expect to win? | How did each side fare in the early years of the war?

430 CHAPTER 15 THE CRUCIBLE OF WAR

How did each side fare in the early years of the war?

The Dead of Antietam In October 1862, photographer Mathew Brady opened an exhibition that presented the battle of Antietam as the soldiers saw it. A *New York Times* reporter observed: "Mr. Brady has done something to bring to us the terrible reality and earnestness of the war. If he has not brought bodies and laid them in our door-yards and along [our] streets, he had done something very like it." Library of Congress.

DURING THE FIRST YEAR and a half of the war, armies fought major campaigns in both the East and the West. While the eastern campaign was more dramatic, Lincoln had trouble finding a capable general, and the fighting ended in a stalemate. Battles in the West proved more decisive. Union general Ulysses S. Grant won important victories in Kentucky and Tennessee. As Yankee and rebel armies pounded each other on land, the navies fought on the seas and on the rivers of the South. In Europe, Confederate and U.S. diplomats competed for advantage in the corridors of power. All the while, casualty lists on both sides reached appalling lengths.

Stalemate in the Eastern Theater

In the summer of 1861, Lincoln ordered the 35,000 Union troops assembling outside Washington to attack the 20,000 Confederates defending Manassas, a railroad junction in Virginia about thirty miles southwest of Washington. On July 21, the army forded Bull Run, a branch of the Potomac River, and engaged the southern forces (**Map 15.2**). But fast-moving southern reinforcements blunted the Union attack and then counterattacked. What began as an orderly Union retreat turned into a panicky stampede.

By Civil War standards, the casualties (wounded and dead) at the **battle of Bull Run** (or **Manassas**, as Southerners called the battle) were light, about 2,000

battle of Bull Run (Manassas)

▶ First major battle of the Civil War, fought at a railroad junction in northern Virginia on July 21, 1861. The Union suffered a sobering defeat, while the Confederates felt affirmed in their superiority and the inevitability of Confederate nationhood.

How did the war for union become a fight for black freedom?

What problems did the Confederacy face at home?

How did the war affect the economy and politics of the North?

How did the Union finally win the war?

Conclusion: In what ways was the Civil War a "Second American Revolution"?

✓ **LearningCurve** Check what you know. bedfordstmartins.com /roarkunderstanding

431

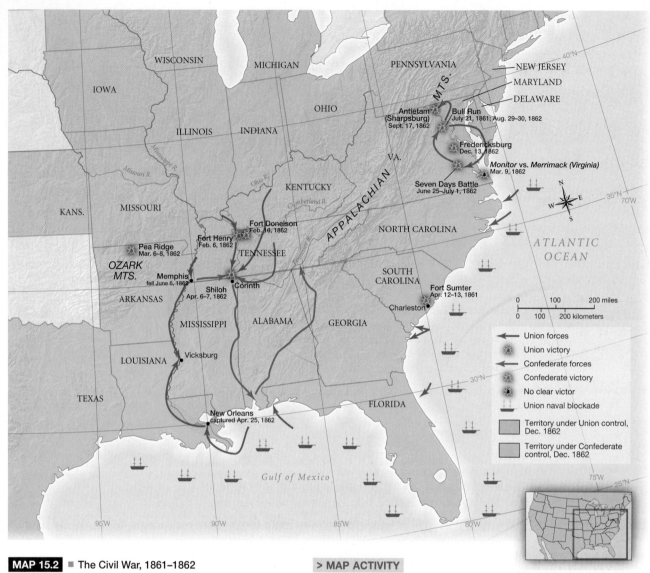

MAP 15.2 ■ The Civil War, 1861–1862

While most eyes were focused on the eastern theater, especially the ninety-mile stretch of land between Washington, D.C., and the Confederate capital of Richmond, Virginia, Union troops were winning strategic victories in the West.

> MAP ACTIVITY

READING THE MAP: In which states did the Confederacy and the Union each win the most battles during this period? Which side used or followed water routes most for troop movements and attacks?

CONNECTIONS: Which major cities in the South and West fell to Union troops in 1862? Which strategic area did those Confederate losses place in Union hands? How did this outcome affect the later movement of troops and supplies?

Confederates and 1,600 Federals. The significance of the battle lay in the lessons Northerners and Southerners drew from it. For Southerners, it confirmed the superiority of rebel fighting men and the inevitability of Confederate nationhood. While victory fed southern pride, defeat sobered Northerners. It was a major setback, admitted the *New York Tribune*, but "let us go to work, then, with a will." Within four days of the disaster, the president authorized the enlistment of 1 million men for three years.

CHAPTER LOCATOR | Why did both the Union and the Confederacy consider control of the border states crucial? | Why did each side expect to win? | **How did each side fare in the early years of the war?**

Lincoln also appointed the young George B. McClellan commander of the newly named Army of the Potomac. Having graduated from West Point second in his class, the thirty-four-year-old McClellan believed that he was a great soldier and that Lincoln was a dunce, the "original Gorilla." A superb administrator and organizer, McClellan energetically whipped his dispirited soldiers into shape, but for all his energy, McClellan lacked decisiveness. Lincoln wanted a general who would advance, take risks, and fight, but McClellan went into winter quarters. "If General McClellan does not want to use the army I would like to *borrow* it," Lincoln declared in frustration.

Finally, in May 1862, McClellan launched his long-awaited offensive. He transported his highly polished army, now 130,000 strong, to the mouth of the James River and began slowly moving up the Yorktown peninsula toward Richmond. When he was within six miles of the Confederate capital, General Joseph Johnston hit him like a hammer. In the assault, Johnston was wounded and was replaced by Robert E. Lee, who would become the South's most celebrated general. Lee named his command the Army of Northern Virginia.

The contrast between Lee and McClellan could hardly have been greater. McClellan brimmed with conceit; Lee was courteous and reserved. On the battlefield, McClellan grew timid and irresolute, and Lee became audaciously, even recklessly, aggressive. And Lee had at his side in the peninsula campaign military men of real talent: Thomas J. Jackson, nicknamed "Stonewall" for holding the line at Manassas, and James E. B. ("Jeb") Stuart, a dashing twenty-nine-year-old cavalry commander who rode circles around Yankee troops.

Lee's assault initiated the Seven Days Battle (June 25–July 1) and began McClellan's march back down the peninsula. By the time McClellan reached safety, 30,000 men from both sides had died or been wounded. Although Southerners suffered twice the casualties of Northerners, Lee had saved Richmond. Lincoln fired McClellan and replaced him with General John Pope.

In August, north of Richmond, at the second battle of Bull Run, Lee's smaller army battered Pope's forces and sent them scurrying back to Washington. Lincoln ordered Pope to Minnesota to pacify the Indians and restored McClellan to command.

Believing that he had the enemy on the run, Lee pushed his army across the Potomac and invaded Maryland. A victory on northern soil would dislodge Maryland from the Union, Lee reasoned, and might even cause Lincoln to sue for peace. On September 17, 1862, McClellan's forces engaged Lee's army at Antietam Creek (see Map 15.2). With "solid shot . . . cracking skulls like eggshells," according to one observer, the armies went after each other. At Miller's Cornfield, the firing was so intense that "every stalk of corn in the . . . field was cut as closely as could have been done with a knife." By nightfall, 6,000 men lay dead or dying on the battlefield, and 17,000 more had been wounded. The **battle of Antietam** would be the bloodiest day of the war and sent the battered Army of Northern Virginia limping back home. McClellan claimed to have saved the North, but Lincoln again removed him from command of the Army of the Potomac and appointed General Ambrose Burnside.

Though bloodied, Lee found an opportunity in December to punish the enemy at Fredericksburg, Virginia, where Burnside's 122,000 Union troops faced 78,500 Confederates dug in behind a stone wall on the heights above the

> CHRONOLOGY

1861
– First battle of Bull Run (Manassas).

1862
– Grant captures Fort Henry and Fort Donelson.
– Battle of Glorieta Pass.
– Battle of Pea Ridge.
– Battle of Shiloh.
– Virginia peninsula campaign.
– Battle of Antietam.
– Battle of Fredericksburg.

Peninsula Campaign, 1862

battle of Antietam
▶ Battle fought in Maryland on September 17, 1862, between the Union forces of George McClellan and Confederate troops of Robert E. Lee. The battle, a Union victory that left 6,000 dead and 17,000 wounded, was the bloodiest day of the war.

How did the war for union become a fight for black freedom? | What problems did the Confederacy face at home? | How did the war affect the economy and politics of the North? | How did the Union finally win the war? | Conclusion: In what ways was the Civil War a "Second American Revolution"? | ✓ **LearningCurve** Check what you know. bedfordstmartins.com /roarkunderstanding

433

Rappahannock River. Half a mile of open ground separated the armies. "A chicken could not live on that field when we open on it," a Confederate artillery officer predicted. Yet Burnside ordered a frontal assault. When the shooting ceased, the Federals counted nearly 13,000 casualties, the Confederates fewer than 5,000. The battle of Fredericksburg was one of the Union's worst defeats. As 1862 ended, the North seemed no nearer to ending the rebellion than it had been when the war began. Rather than checkmate, military struggle in the East had reached stalemate.

Union Victories in the Western Theater

While most eyes focused on events in the East, the decisive early encounters of the war were taking place between the Appalachian Mountains and the Ozarks (see Map 15.2). Confederates wanted Missouri and Kentucky, states they claimed but did not control. Federals wanted to split Arkansas, Louisiana, and Texas from the Confederacy by taking control of the Mississippi River and to occupy Tennessee, one of the Confederacy's main producers of food, mules, and iron — all vital resources.

Before Union forces could march on Tennessee, they needed to secure Missouri to the west. Union troops swept across Missouri to the border of Arkansas, where in March 1862 they encountered a 16,000-man Confederate army, which included three regiments of Indians from the so-called Five Civilized Tribes — the Choctaw, Chickasaw, Creek, Seminole, and Cherokee. The Union victory at the battle of Pea Ridge left Missouri free of Confederate troops, but guerrilla bands led by the notorious William Clarke Quantrill and "Bloody Bill" Anderson burned, tortured, scalped, and murdered Union civilians and soldiers until the final year of the war.

Battle of Glorieta Pass, 1862

Even farther west, Confederate armies sought to fulfill Jefferson Davis's vision of a slaveholding empire stretching all the way to the Pacific. Both sides recognized the immense value of the gold and silver mines of California, Nevada, and Colorado. And both sides bolstered their armies in the Southwest with Mexican Americans. A quick strike by Texas troops took Santa Fe, New Mexico, in the winter of 1861–62. Then in March 1862, a band of Colorado miners ambushed and crushed southern forces at Glorieta Pass, outside Santa Fe, effectively ending dreams of a Confederate empire beyond Texas.

The principal western battles took place in Tennessee, where General Ulysses S. Grant emerged as the key northern commander. Grant, a West Point graduate who had served in Mexico, was a thirty-nine-year-old dry-goods clerk in Galena, Illinois, when the war began. Gentle at home, he became pugnacious on the battlefield. "The art of war is simple," he said. "Find out where your enemy is, get at him as soon as you can and strike him as hard as you can, and keep moving on." Grant's philosophy of war as attrition would take a huge toll in

CHAPTER LOCATOR | Why did both the Union and the Confederacy consider control of the border states crucial? | Why did each side expect to win? | How did each side fare in the early years of the war?

434 CHAPTER 15 THE CRUCIBLE OF WAR

human life, but it played to the North's superiority in manpower. Later, to critics who wanted the president to sack Grant because of his drinking, Lincoln would say, "*I can't spare this man. He fights.*"

In February 1862, operating in tandem with U.S. Navy gunboats, Grant captured Fort Henry on the Tennessee River and Fort Donelson on the Cumberland (see Map 15.2). Defeat forced the Confederates to withdraw from all of Kentucky and most of Tennessee, but Grant followed.

On April 6, General Albert Sidney Johnston's army surprised Grant at Shiloh Church in Tennessee. Union troops were badly mauled the first day, but Grant remained cool and brought up reinforcements throughout the night. The next morning, the Union army counterattacked, driving the Confederates before it. The **battle of Shiloh** was terribly costly to both sides; there were 20,000 casualties, among them General Johnston. Grant later said that after Shiloh he "gave up all idea of saving the Union except by complete conquest."

Although no one knew it at the time, Shiloh ruined the Confederacy's bid to control the theater of operations in the West. The Yankees quickly captured the strategic town of Corinth, Mississippi; the river city of Memphis; and the South's largest city, New Orleans. By the end of 1862, the far West and most—but not all—of the Mississippi valley lay in Union hands. At the same time, the outcome of the struggle in another theater of war was also becoming clearer.

battle of Shiloh

▶ Battle at Shiloh Church, Tennessee, on April 6–7, 1862, between Albert Sidney Johnston's Confederate forces and Ulysses S. Grant's Union army. The Union army ultimately prevailed, though at great cost to both sides. Shiloh ruined the Confederacy's bid to control the war in the West.

> Major Battles of the Civil War, 1861–1862	
April 12–13, 1861	Attack on Fort Sumter
July 21, 1861	First battle of Bull Run (Manassas)
February 6, 1862	Battle of Fort Henry
February 16, 1862	Battle of Fort Donelson
March 6–8, 1862	Battle of Pea Ridge
March 9, 1862	Battle of the *Merrimack* (the *Virginia*) and the *Monitor*
March 26, 1862	Battle of Glorieta Pass
April 6–7, 1862	Battle of Shiloh
May–July 1862	McClellan's peninsula campaign
June 6, 1862	Fall of Memphis
June 25–July 1, 1862	Seven Days Battle
August 29–30, 1862	Second battle of Bull Run (Manassas)
September 17, 1862	Battle of Antietam
December 13, 1862	Battle of Fredericksburg

| How did the war for union become a fight for black freedom? | What problems did the Confederacy face at home? | How did the war affect the economy and politics of the North? | How did the Union finally win the war? | Conclusion: In what ways was the Civil War a "Second American Revolution"? | ✓ LearningCurve Check what you know. bedfordstmartins.com /roarkunderstanding |

435

The Atlantic Theater

When the war began, the U.S. Navy's blockade fleet consisted of about three dozen ships to patrol more than 3,500 miles of southern coastline, and rebel merchant ships were able to slip in and out of southern ports nearly at will. Taking on cargoes in the Caribbean, sleek Confederate blockade runners brought in vital supplies — guns and medicine. But with the U.S. Navy commissioning a new blockader almost weekly, the naval fleet eventually numbered 150 ships on duty, and the Union navy dramatically improved its score.

Unable to build a conventional navy equal to the expanding U.S. fleet, the Confederates experimented with a radical new maritime design: the ironclad warship. At Norfolk, Virginia, the wooden hull of the *Merrimack* was layered with two-inch-thick armor plate. Rechristened *Virginia*, the ship steamed out in March 1862 and sank two wooden federal ships (see Map 15.2). When the *Virginia* returned to finish off the federal blockaders the next morning, it was challenged by the *Monitor*, a Union ironclad of even more radical design, topped with a revolving turret holding two eleven-inch guns. On March 9, the two ships hurled shells at each other for two hours, but the battle ended in a draw.

The Confederacy never found a way to break the **Union blockade** despite exploring many naval innovations, including a new underwater vessel — the submarine. By 1865, the blockaders were intercepting about half of the southern ships attempting to break through. The Union navy, a southern naval officer observed, "shut the Confederacy out from the world, deprived it of supplies, weakened its military and naval strength." The Confederacy was sealed off, with devastating results.

International Diplomacy

What the Confederates could not achieve on the seas, they sought to achieve through international diplomacy. They based their hope for European intervention on King Cotton. In theory, cotton-starved European nations would have no choice but to break the Union blockade and recognize the Confederacy. Southern hopes were not unreasonable, for at the height of the "cotton famine" in 1862, when 2 million British workers were unemployed, Britain tilted toward recognition. Along with several other European nations, Britain granted the Confederacy "belligerent" status, which enabled it to buy goods and build ships in European ports. But no country challenged the Union blockade or recognized the Confederate States of America as a nation, a bold act that probably would have drawn that country into war.

King Cotton diplomacy failed for several reasons. A bumper cotton crop in 1860 meant that the warehouses of British textile manufacturers bulged with surplus cotton throughout 1861. In 1862, when a cotton shortage did occur, European manufacturers found new sources in India, Egypt, and elsewhere. In addition, the development of a brisk trade between the Union and Britain — British war materiel for American grain and flour — helped offset the decline in textiles and encouraged Britain to remain neutral (**Figure 15.2**).

CHAPTER LOCATOR | Why did both the Union and the Confederacy consider control of the border states crucial? | Why did each side expect to win? | How did each side fare in the early years of the war?

CHAPTER 15
THE CRUCIBLE OF WAR

436

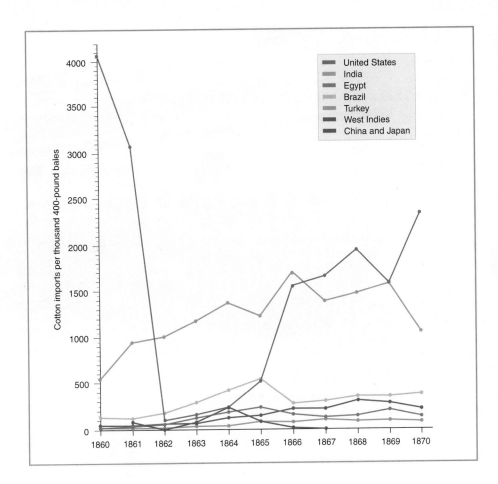

FIGURE 15.2 ■ European Cotton Imports, 1860–1870

In 1860, the South enjoyed a near monopoly in supplying cotton to Europe's textile mills, but the Civil War almost entirely halted its exports. Figures for Europe's importation of cotton for 1861 to 1865 reveal one of the reasons the Confederacy's King Cotton diplomacy failed: Europeans found other sources of cotton. Which countries were most important in filling the void? When the war ended in 1865, cotton production resumed in the South, and exports to Europe again soared. Did the South regain its near monopoly? How would you characterize the United States' competitive position five years after the war?

Europe's temptation to intervene disappeared for good in 1862. Union military successes in the West made Britain and France think twice about linking their fates to the struggling Confederacy. Moreover, in September 1862, Lincoln announced a new policy that made an alliance with the Confederacy an alliance with slavery — a commitment the French and British, who had outlawed slavery in their empires and looked forward to its eradication worldwide, were not willing to make. After 1862, the South's cause was linked irrevocably with slavery and reaction, and the Union's cause was linked with freedom and democracy. The Union, not the Confederacy, had won the diplomatic stakes.

QUICK REVIEW <

Why did the Confederacy's bid for international support fail?

| How did the war for union become a fight for black freedom? | What problems did the Confederacy face at home? | How did the war affect the economy and politics of the North? | How did the Union finally win the war? | Conclusion: In what ways was the Civil War a "Second American Revolution"? | LearningCurve Check what you know. bedfordstmartins.com /roarkunderstanding |

How did the war for union become a fight for black freedom?

Company E, Fourth U.S. Colored Infantry, Fort Lincoln, Virginia

The Lincoln administration was slow to accept black soldiers into the Union army, in part because of lingering doubts about their ability to fight. But Colonel Thomas W. Higginson, the white commander of the Union's First South Carolina Infantry, which was made up of former slaves, celebrated his men's courage: "No officer in this regiment now doubts that the key to the successful prosecution of this war lies in the unlimited employment of black troops. . . . Instead of leaving their homes and families to fight they are fighting for their homes and families." Before the war was over, ex-slaves and free blacks filled 145 Union regiments. Library of Congress.

FOR A YEAR AND A HALF, Lincoln insisted that the North fought strictly to save the Union and not to abolish slavery. Nevertheless, the war for union became a war for African American freedom. Each month the conflict dragged on, it became clearer that the Confederate war machine depended heavily on slavery. Rebel armies used slaves to build fortifications, haul materiel, tend horses, and perform camp chores. On the southern home front, slaves labored in ironworks and shipyards, and they grew the food that fed both soldiers and civilians. Slavery undergirded the Confederacy as certainly as it had the Old South. Union military commanders and politicians alike gradually realized that to defeat the Confederacy, the North would have to destroy slavery. Lincoln's Emancipation Proclamation began the work, and soon African Americans flooded into the Union army, where they fought against the Confederacy and for black freedom.

From Slaves to Contraband

Lincoln detested human bondage, but as president he felt compelled to act prudently in the interests of the Union. He doubted his right under the Constitution

CHAPTER LOCATOR

| Why did both the Union and the Confederacy consider control of the border states crucial? | Why did each side expect to win? | How did each side fare in the early years of the war? |

438 CHAPTER 15 THE CRUCIBLE OF WAR

to tamper with the "domestic institutions" of any state, even states in rebellion. An astute politician, Lincoln worked within the tight limits of public opinion. The issue of black freedom was particularly explosive in the loyal border states, where slaveholders threatened to jump into the arms of the Confederacy at even the hint of emancipation.

Black freedom also raised alarms in the free states. The Democratic Party gave notice that adding emancipation to the goal of union would make the war strictly a Republican affair. Moreover, many white Northerners were not about to risk their lives to satisfy what they considered abolitionist "fanaticism." "We Won't Fight to Free the Nigger," one popular banner read. They feared that emancipation would propel "two or three million semi-savages" northward, where they would crowd into white neighborhoods, compete for white jobs, and mix with white "sons and daughters."

Yet proponents of emancipation pressed Lincoln as relentlessly as did the anti-emancipation forces. Abolitionists argued that by seceding, Southerners had forfeited their right to the protection of the Constitution and that Lincoln could — as the price of their treason — legally confiscate their property in slaves. When Lincoln refused, abolitionists scalded him. Frederick Douglass labeled him "the miserable tool of traitors and rebels."

The Republican-dominated Congress declined to leave slavery policy entirely in President Lincoln's hands. In August 1861, Congress approved the Confiscation Act, which allowed the seizure of any slave employed directly by the Confederate military. It also fulfilled the free-soil dream of prohibiting slavery in the territories and abolished slavery in Washington, D.C. Democrats and border-state representatives voted against even these mild measures.

Slaves, not politicians, became the most insistent force for emancipation. By escaping their masters by the tens of thousands and running away to Union lines, they forced slavery on the North's wartime agenda. Runaways made Northerners answer a crucial question: Were the runaways now free, or were they still slaves who, according to the fugitive slave law, had to be returned to their masters? At first, Yankee military officers sent the fugitives back. But Union armies needed laborers, and at Fort Monroe, Virginia, General Benjamin F. Butler called them **contraband of war**, meaning "confiscated property," and put them to work. Congress made Butler's practice national policy in March 1862 when it forbade returning fugitive slaves to their masters. Slaves were still not legally free, but there was a tilt toward emancipation.

Lincoln's policy of noninterference with slavery gradually crumbled. To calm Northerners' racial fears, Lincoln offered colonization, the deportation of African Americans from the United States to Haiti, Panama, or elsewhere. Congress voted a small amount of money to underwrite colonization, but practical limitations and stiff black opposition sank the scheme.

While Lincoln was developing his own antislavery initiatives, he snuffed out actions that he believed would jeopardize northern unity. He was particularly alert to Union commanders who tried to dictate slavery policy from the field. In August 1861, when John C. Frémont, former Republican presidential nominee and now commander of federal troops in Missouri, freed the slaves belonging to Missouri rebels, Lincoln forced the general to revoke his edict. The following May, when General David Hunter freed the slaves in Georgia, South Carolina, and

> CHRONOLOGY

1861
– First Confiscation Act.

1862
– Second Confiscation Act.
– Militia Act.

1863
– Emancipation Proclamation is issued.

contraband of war
▶ General Benjamin F. Butler's term for runaway slaves, who were considered confiscated property of war, not fugitives, and put to work in the Union army. This policy proved to be a step on the road to emancipation.

| How did the war for union become a fight for black freedom? | What problems did the Confederacy face at home? | How did the war affect the economy and politics of the North? | How did the Union finally win the war? | Conclusion: In what ways was the Civil War a "Second American Revolution"? | ✓ LearningCurve Check what you know. bedfordstmartins.com /roarkunderstanding |

Florida, Lincoln countermanded his order. Events moved so rapidly, however, that Lincoln found it impossible to control federal policy on slavery.

From Contraband to Free People

On August 22, 1862, Lincoln replied to an angry abolitionist who demanded that he attack slavery. "My paramount objective in this struggle *is* to save the Union," Lincoln said, "and is *not* either to save or destroy slavery. If I could save the Union without freeing *any* slave I would do it, and if I could save it by freeing *all* the slaves I would do it; and if I could save it by freeing some and leaving others alone I would also do that." At first glance, Lincoln seemed to restate his old position that union was the North's sole objective. Instead, Lincoln announced that slavery was no longer untouchable and that he would emancipate every slave if doing so would preserve the Union.

By the summer of 1862, events were tumbling rapidly toward emancipation. On July 17, Congress adopted the second Confiscation Act. The first had confiscated slaves employed by the Confederate military; the second declared all slaves of rebel masters "forever free of their servitude." In theory, this breathtaking measure freed most Confederate slaves, for slaveholders formed the backbone of the rebellion. Congress had traveled far since the war began.

Lincoln had, too. By the summer of 1862, the president had come to believe that emancipation was "a military necessity, absolutely essential to the preservation of the Union." In September, he announced his preliminary **Emancipation Proclamation**, which promised to free *all* the slaves in the seceding states on January 1, 1863. The limitations of the proclamation — it exempted the loyal border states and the Union-occupied areas of the Confederacy — caused some to ridicule the act. The *Times* (London) observed cynically, "Where he has no power Mr. Lincoln will set the negroes free, where he retains power he will consider them as slaves." But Lincoln had no power to free slaves in loyal states, and invading Union armies would liberate slaves in the Confederacy as they advanced.

By presenting emancipation as a "military necessity," Lincoln hoped to disarm his conservative critics. Emancipation would deprive the Confederacy of valuable slave laborers, shorten the war, and thus save lives. Democrats, however, fumed

Emancipation Proclamation

▶ President Lincoln's proclamation issued on January 1, 1863, declaring all slaves in Confederate-controlled territory free. The proclamation made the Civil War a war to free slaves; however, its limitations — exemptions for loyal border states and Union-occupied areas of the Confederacy — made some ridicule the act.

CHAPTER LOCATOR | Why did both the Union and the Confederacy consider control of the border states crucial? | Why did each side expect to win? | How did each side fare in the early years of the war?

440 CHAPTER 15
THE CRUCIBLE OF WAR

that the "shrieking and howling abolitionist faction" had captured the White House and made it "a nigger war." Democrats gained thirty-four congressional seats in the November 1862 elections. House Democrats quickly proposed a resolution branding emancipation "a high crime against the Constitution." The Republicans, who maintained narrow majorities in both houses of Congress, barely beat it back.

As promised, on New Year's Day 1863, Lincoln issued the final Emancipation Proclamation. In addition to freeing the slaves in the rebel states, the Emancipation Proclamation also committed the federal government to the fullest use of African Americans to defeat the Confederate enemy.

The War of Black Liberation

Even before Lincoln proclaimed emancipation a Union war aim, African Americans in the North had volunteered to fight. But the War Department, doubtful of blacks' abilities and fearful of white reaction to serving side by side with them, refused to make black men soldiers. Instead, the army employed black men as manual laborers; black women sometimes found employment as laundresses and cooks. The navy, however, accepted blacks from the outset, including runaway slaves.

As Union casualty lists lengthened, Northerners gradually and reluctantly turned to African Americans to fill the army's blue uniforms. With the Militia Act of July 1862, Congress authorized enrolling blacks in "any military or naval service for which they may be found competent." After the Emancipation Proclamation, whites — like it or not — were fighting and dying for black freedom, and few insisted that blacks remain out of harm's way behind the lines. Indeed, whites insisted that blacks share the danger, especially after March 1863, when Congress resorted to the draft to fill the Union army.

The military was far from color-blind. The Union army established segregated black regiments, paid black soldiers $10 per month rather than the $13 it paid whites, refused blacks the opportunity to become commissioned officers, punished blacks as if they were slaves, and assigned blacks to labor battalions rather than to combat units. Still, when the war ended, 179,000 African American men had served in the Union army.

In time, whites allowed blacks to put down their shovels and to shoulder rifles. At the battles of Port Hudson and Milliken's Bend on the Mississippi River and at Fort Wagner in Charleston harbor, black courage under fire finally dispelled notions that African Americans could not fight. More than 38,000 black soldiers died in the Civil War, a mortality rate that was higher than that of white troops. Blacks played a crucial role in the triumph of the Union and the destruction of slavery in the South.

QUICK REVIEW <

Why did the Union change policy in 1863 to allow black men to serve in the army?

| How did the war for union become a fight for black freedom? | What problems did the Confederacy face at home? | How did the war affect the economy and politics of the North? | How did the Union finally win the war? | Conclusion: In what ways was the Civil War a "Second American Revolution"? | ✓ LearningCurve Check what you know. bedfordstmartins.com /roarkunderstanding |

441

What problems did the Confederacy face at home?

Confederate Soldiers and Their Slaves

Soldiers of the Seventh Tennessee Cavalry pose with their slaves. Many slaveholders took "body servants" with them to war. These slaves cooked, washed, and cleaned for the white soldiers. In 1861, James H. Langhorne reported to his sister: "Peter . . . is charmed with being with me & 'being a soldier.' I gave him my old uniform overcoat & he says he is going to have his picture taken . . . to send to the servants." Do you think Peter was "puttin' on ol' massa" or just glad to be free of plantation labor? Daguerreotype courtesy of Tom Farish. Photographed by Michael Latil.

> VISUAL ACTIVITY

READING THE IMAGE: What can we glean from this image about a Confederate soldier's life in the military?

CONNECTIONS: This daguerreotype likely was not taken for any purpose other than to capture the camaraderie of four southern cavalrymen, yet the inclusion of the two slaves speaks volumes. What are the possible ramifications of slaveholders bringing "body servants" to war?

BY SECEDING, Southerners brought on themselves a firestorm of unimaginable fury. Monstrous losses on the battlefield nearly bled the Confederacy to death. Southerners on the home front also suffered, even at the hands of their own government. Efforts by the Davis administration in Richmond to centralize power in order to fight the war convinced some men and women that the Confederacy had betrayed them. They charged Richmond with tyranny when it impressed goods and slaves and drafted men into the army. War also meant severe economic deprivation. Shortages and inflation hurt everyone, some more than others. By 1863, unequal suffering meant that planters and yeomen who had stood together began to drift apart. Most disturbing of all, slaves became open participants in the destruction of slavery and the Confederacy.

Revolution from Above

As a Confederate general observed, Southerners were engaged in a total war "in which the whole population and the whole production . . . are to be put on a war

CHAPTER LOCATOR | Why did both the Union and the Confederacy consider control of the border states crucial? | Why did each side expect to win? | How did each side fare in the early years of the war?

442   CHAPTER 15   THE CRUCIBLE OF WAR

footing, where every institution is to be made auxiliary to war." Jefferson Davis faced the task of building an army and a navy from almost nothing, supplying them from factories that were scarce and anemic, and paying for it all from a treasury that did not exist. Finding eager soldiers proved easiest. Hundreds of officers defected from the U.S. Army, and hundreds of thousands of eager young rebels volunteered to follow them.

The Confederacy's economy and finances proved tougher problems. Because of the Union blockade, the government had no choice but to build an industrial sector itself. Government-owned clothing and shoe factories, mines, arsenals, and powder works sprang up. The government also harnessed private companies, such as the huge Tredegar Iron Works in Richmond, to the war effort. Paying for the war became the most difficult task. A flood of paper money caused debilitating inflation. By Christmas 1864, a Confederate soldier's monthly pay no longer bought a pair of socks. The Confederacy manufactured much more than most people imagined possible, but it never produced all that the South needed.

Richmond's war-making effort brought unprecedented government intrusion into the private lives of Confederate citizens. In April 1862, the Confederate Congress passed the first conscription (draft) law in American history. All able-bodied white males between the ages of eighteen and thirty-five (later seventeen and fifty) were liable to serve in the rebel army. The government adopted a policy of impressment, which allowed officials to confiscate food, horses, wagons, and whatever else they wanted from private citizens and to pay for them at below-market rates. After March 1863, the Confederacy legally impressed slaves, employing them as military laborers.

Richmond's centralizing efforts ran head-on into the South's traditional values of states' rights and unfettered individualism. Southerners lashed out at what Georgia governor Joseph E. Brown denounced as the "dangerous usurpation by Congress of the reserved right of the States." Richmond and the states struggled for control of money, supplies, and soldiers, with damaging consequences for the war effort.

Hardship Below

Hardships on the home front fell most heavily on the poor. The draft stripped yeoman farms of men, leaving the women and children to grow what they ate. Government agents took 10 percent of harvests as a "tax-in-kind" on agriculture. Like inflation, shortages afflicted the entire population, but the rich lost luxuries while the poor lost necessities. In the spring of 1863, bread riots broke out in a dozen cities and villages across the South. In Richmond, a mob of nearly a thousand hungry women broke into shops and took what they needed.

"Men cannot be expected to fight for the Government that permits their wives & children to starve," one Southerner observed. Although a few wealthy individuals shared their bounty and the Confederate and state governments made efforts at social welfare, every attempt fell short. When the war ended, one-third of the soldiers had already gone home. A Mississippi deserter explained, "We are poor men and are willing to defend our country but our families [come] first."

Yeomen perceived a profound inequality of sacrifice. They called it "a rich man's war and a poor man's fight." The draft law permitted a man who had

> CHRONOLOGY

1862
– Confederate Congress authorizes draft.

1863
– Bread riots break out in the South.

How did the war for union become a fight for black freedom?

What problems did the Confederacy face at home?

How did the war affect the economy and politics of the North?

How did the Union finally win the war?

Conclusion: In what ways was the Civil War a "Second American Revolution"?

✓ LearningCurve
Check what you know.
bedfordstmartins.com /roarkunderstanding

443

money to hire a substitute to take his place. Moreover, the "twenty-Negro law" exempted one white man on every plantation with twenty or more slaves. The government intended this law to provide protection for white women and to see that slaves tended the crops, but yeomen perceived it as rich men evading military service. A Mississippian complained that stay-at-home planters sent their slaves into the fields to grow cotton while in plain view "poor soldiers' wives are plowing with their own hands to make a subsistence for themselves and children — while their husbands are suffering, bleeding and dying for their country." In fact, most slaveholders went off to war, but the extreme suffering of common folk and the relative immunity of planters increased class friction.

The Richmond government hoped that the crucible of war would mold a region into a nation. Officials actively promoted Confederate nationalism to "excite in our citizens an ardent and enduring attachment to our Government and its institutions." Clergymen assured their congregations that God had blessed slavery and the new nation. Jefferson Davis claimed that the Confederacy was part of a divine plan and asked citizens to observe national days of fasting and prayer. But these efforts failed to win over thousands of die-hard Unionists, and animosity between yeomen and planters increased. The war also threatened to rip the southern social fabric along its racial seam.

The Disintegration of Slavery

The legal destruction of slavery was the product of presidential proclamation, congressional legislation, and eventually constitutional amendment, but the practical destruction of slavery was the product of war, what Lincoln called war's "friction and abrasion." Slaves took advantage of the upheaval to reach for freedom. Some half a million of the South's 4 million slaves ran away to Union military lines. More than 100,000 runaways took up arms as federal soldiers and sailors and attacked slavery directly. Other men and women stayed in the slave quarter, where they staked their claim to more freedom.

War disrupted slavery in a dozen ways. Almost immediately, it called the master away, leaving the mistress to assume responsibility for the plantation. But mistresses could not maintain traditional standards of slave discipline in wartime, and the balance of power shifted. Slaves got to the fields late, worked indifferently, and quit early. Some slaveholders responded violently; most saw no alternative but to strike bargains — offering gifts or part of the crop — to keep slaves at home and at work. Slaveholders had believed that they "knew" their slaves, but they learned that they did not. When the war began, a North Carolina woman praised her slaves as "diligent and respectful." When it ended, she said, "As to the idea of a *faithful servant, it is all a fiction.*"

> **QUICK REVIEW**

How did wartime hardship in the South contribute to class friction?

CHAPTER LOCATOR

Why did both the Union and the Confederacy consider control of the border states crucial?

Why did each side expect to win?

How did each side fare in the early years of the war?

444   CHAPTER 15
THE CRUCIBLE OF WAR

| U.S. Sanitary Commission, Brandy Station, Virginia, 1863 |

The burden of caring for millions of Union soldiers was more than the government could shoulder. Private initiative in the form of the U.S. Sanitary Commission brought additional medical attention to the Union wounded and boosted the comfort and morale of soldiers in the camps. National Archives.

How did the war affect the economy and politics of the North?

ALTHOUGH LITTLE FIGHTING took place on northern soil, almost every family had a son, husband, father, or brother in uniform. Moreover, total war blurred the distinction between home front and battlefield. As in the South, men marched off to fight, but preserving the country was also women's work. For civilians as well as soldiers, for women as well as men, war was transforming.

The need to build and fuel the Union war machine strengthened the federal government and boosted the economy. The Union sent nearly 2 million men into the military yet managed to increase production in almost every area. But because the rewards and burdens of patriotism were distributed unevenly, the North experienced sharp, even violent, divisions. Workers confronted employers, whites confronted blacks, and Democrats confronted Republicans. Still, Northerners on the home front remained fervently attached to the Union.

The Government and the Economy

When the war began, the United States had no national banking system, no national currency, and no federal income tax. But the secession of eleven slave states cut the Democrats' strength in Congress in half and destroyed their capacity to resist Republican economic programs. Before the war ended, the Republicans had turned their economic vision into law.

> CHRONOLOGY

1863
- National Banking Act.
- Congress authorizes draft.
- New York City draft riots.

| How did the war for union become a fight for black freedom? | What problems did the Confederacy face at home? | **How did the war affect the economy and politics of the North?** | How did the Union finally win the war? | Conclusion: In what ways was the Civil War a "Second American Revolution"? | ✓ **LearningCurve** Check what you know. bedfordstmartins.com /roarkunderstanding |

445

- The Legal Tender Act (February 1862) creates a national currency.
- The National Banking Act (February 1863) establishes a system of national banks.
- Congress also enacts a series of sweeping tax laws, including the first income tax.

The Republicans' wartime legislation also aimed at integrating the West into the Union. In May 1862, Congress approved the Homestead Act, which offered 160 acres of public land to settlers who would live and labor on it. The Homestead Act bolstered western loyalty and in time resulted in more than a million new farms. The Pacific Railroad Act in July 1862 provided massive federal assistance for building a transcontinental railroad that ran from Omaha to San Francisco when completed in 1869. To achieve this goal, Congress also offered subsidies for the Pony Express mail service and a transcontinental telegraph.

In addition, Congress created the Department of Agriculture and passed the Land-Grant College Act (also known as the Morrill Act after its sponsor, Representative Justin Morrill of Vermont), which set aside public land to support universities that emphasized "agriculture and mechanical arts." The Lincoln administration immeasurably strengthened the North's effort to win the war, but its ideas also permanently changed the nation.

Women and Work at Home and at War

More than a million farm men were called to the military, and farm women added men's chores to their own. "I met more women driving teams on the road and saw more at work in the fields than men," a visitor to Iowa reported in the fall of 1862. Rising production testified to their success in plowing, planting, and harvesting. Rapid mechanization assisted farm women in their new roles. Cyrus McCormick sold 165,000 of his reapers during the war years. The combination of high prices for farm products and increased production ensured that war and prosperity joined hands in the rural North.

In cities, women stepped into jobs vacated by men, particularly in manufacturing, and also into essentially new occupations such as government secretaries and clerks. The number of women working for wages rose 40 percent during the war. As more and more women entered the workforce, employers cut wages. In 1864, New York seamstresses working fourteen-hour days earned only $1.54 a week. Urban workers resorted increasingly to strikes to wrench decent salaries from their employers, but their protests rarely succeeded.

Most middle-class white women stayed home and contributed to the war effort in traditional ways. They sewed, wrapped bandages, and sold homemade goods at local fairs to raise money to aid the soldiers. Other women expressed their patriotism in an untraditional way. Defying prejudices about female delicacy, thousands of women on both sides volunteered to nurse the wounded. Many northern female volunteers worked through the U.S. Sanitary Commission, a huge civilian organization that bought and distributed clothing, food, and medicine, recruited doctors and nurses, and buried the dead.

Some volunteers went on to become paid military nurses. Dorothea Dix, well known for her efforts to reform insane asylums, was named superintendent of female nurses in April 1861. By 1863, some 3,000 nurses served under her. Most

CHAPTER LOCATOR | Why did both the Union and the Confederacy consider control of the border states crucial? | Why did each side expect to win? | How did each side fare in the early years of the war?

CHAPTER 15
446 THE CRUCIBLE OF WAR

nurses worked in hospitals behind the battle lines, but some, like Clara Barton, who later founded the American Red Cross, worked in battlefield units. Women who served in the war went on to lead the postwar movement to establish training schools for female nurses.

Politics and Dissent

At first, the bustle of economic and military mobilization seemed to silence politics, but bipartisan unity did not last. Within a year, Democrats were labeling the Republican administration a "reign of terror" and denouncing as unconstitutional Republican policies expanding federal power, subsidizing private business, and emancipating the slaves. In turn, Republicans were calling Democrats the party of "Dixie, Davis, and the Devil."

When the Republican-dominated Congress enacted the draft law in March 1863, Democrats had another grievance. The law required that all men between the ages of twenty and forty-five enroll and make themselves available for a lottery that would decide who went to war. It also allowed a draftee to hire a substitute or simply to pay a $300 fee and get out of his military obligation. As in the South, common folk could be heard chanting, "A rich man's war and a poor man's fight."

Linking the draft and emancipation, Democrats argued that Republicans employed an unconstitutional means (the draft) to achieve an unconstitutional end (emancipation). In the summer of 1863, antidraft, antiblack mobs went on rampages in northern cities. In July in New York City, Democratic Irish workingmen — crowded into filthy tenements, gouged by inflation, enraged by the draft, and dead set against fighting to free blacks — erupted in four days of rioting. The **New York City draft riots** killed at least 105 people, most of them black.

Lincoln called Democratic opposition to the war "the fire in the rear" and believed that it was even more threatening to national survival than were Confederate armies. The antiwar wing of the Democratic Party, the Peace Democrats — whom some called "Copperheads," after the poisonous snake — found their chief spokesman in Ohio congressman Clement Vallandigham. Vallandigham demanded: "Stop fighting. Make an armistice. . . . Withdraw your army from the seceding States."

In September 1862, in an effort to stifle opposition to the war, Lincoln placed under military arrest any person who discouraged enlistments, resisted the draft, or engaged in "disloyal" practices. Before the war ended, his administration imprisoned nearly 14,000 individuals, most in the border states. The administration's heavy-handed tactics suppressed free speech, but the campaign fell short of a reign of terror, for the majority of the prisoners were not northern Democratic opponents but Confederates, blockade runners, and citizens of foreign countries, and most of those arrested gained quick release. Still, the administration's net captured Vallandigham, who was arrested, convicted of treason, and banished.

New York City draft riots

▶ Four days of rioting in New York City in July 1863 triggered by efforts to enforce the military draft. Democratic Irish workingmen — suffering economic hardship, infuriated by the draft, and opposed to emancipation — killed at least 105 people, most of them black.

QUICK REVIEW

Why was the U.S. Congress able to pass such a bold legislative agenda during the war?

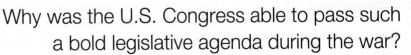

How did the war for union become a fight for black freedom?

What problems did the Confederacy face at home?

How did the war affect the economy and politics of the North?

How did the Union finally win the war?

Conclusion: In what ways was the Civil War a "Second American Revolution"?

☑ LearningCurve
Check what you know.
bedfordstmartins.com
/roarkunderstanding

Ruins of Richmond

As the Confederate government evacuated Richmond during the evening of April 2, 1865, demolition squads set fire to everything that had military or industrial value. Huge explosions devastated the arsenal, the ruins of which are shown here. As one witness observed, "The old war-scarred city seemed to prefer annihilation to conquest." Library of Congress.

siege of Vicksburg

▶ Six-week siege by General Ulysses S. Grant intended to starve out Vicksburg, Mississippi. On July 4, 1863, the 30,000 Confederate troops holding the city surrendered. The victory gave the Union control of the Mississippi River and, together with Gettysburg, marked a major turning point of the war.

IN THE EARLY MONTHS of 1863, the Union's prospects looked bleak, and the Confederate cause stood at high tide. Then, in July 1863, the tide began to turn. The military man most responsible for this shift was Ulysses S. Grant. Elevated to supreme command in 1864, Grant knit together a powerful war machine that integrated a sophisticated command structure, modern technology, and complex logistics and supply systems. Grant's plan was simple: Killing more of the enemy than he killed of you equaled "the complete over-throw of the rebellion."

The North ground out the victory battle by bloody battle. Still, Southerners were not deterred. The fighting escalated in the last two years of the war. As national elections approached in the fall of 1864, Lincoln expected a war-weary North to reject him. Instead, northern voters declared their willingness to continue the war in the defense of the ideals of union and freedom. Lincoln lived to see victory, but only days after Lee surrendered, the president died from an assassin's bullet.

Vicksburg and Gettysburg

Vicksburg, Mississippi, situated on the eastern bank of the Mississippi River, stood between Union forces and complete control of the river. In May 1863, Union forces under Grant laid siege to the city in an effort to starve out the enemy. As the **siege of Vicksburg** dragged on, civilians ate mules and rats to survive. After six weeks, on July 4, 1863, nearly 30,000 rebels marched out of Vicksburg, stacked their arms, and surrendered unconditionally. A Yankee captain wrote home to his

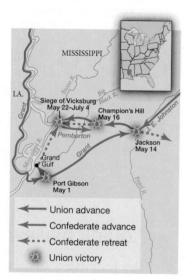

Vicksburg Campaign, 1863

CHAPTER LOCATOR

| Why did both the Union and the Confederacy consider control of the border states crucial? | Why did each side expect to win? | How did each side fare in the early years of the war? |

wife: "The backbone of the Rebellion is this day broken. The Confederacy is divided. . . . Vicksburg is ours. The Mississippi River is opened, and Gen. Grant is to be our next President."

On the same Fourth of July, word arrived that Union forces had crushed General Lee at Gettysburg, Pennsylvania (**Map 15.3**). Emboldened by his victory at Chancellorsville in May, Lee and his 75,000-man army had invaded Pennsylvania. On June 28, Union forces under General George G. Meade intercepted the

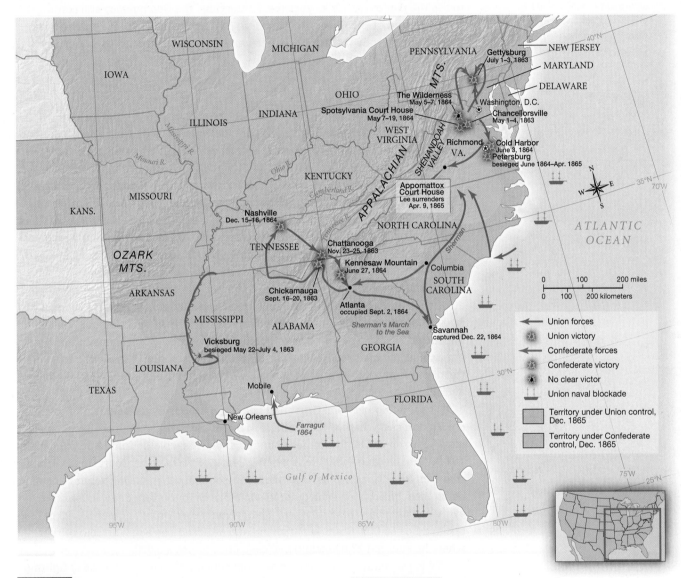

MAP 15.3 ■ The Civil War, 1863–1865

Ulysses S. Grant's victory at Vicksburg divided the Confederacy at the Mississippi River. William Tecumseh Sherman's march from Chattanooga to Savannah divided it again. In northern Virginia, Robert E. Lee fought fiercely, but Grant's larger, better-supplied armies prevailed.

> MAP ACTIVITY

READING THE MAP: Describe the difference between Union and Confederate naval capacity. Were the battles shown on the map fought primarily in Union-controlled or in Confederate-controlled territory? (Look at the land areas on the map.)

CONNECTIONS: Did former slaves serve in the Civil War? If so, on which side(s), and what did they do?

| How did the war for union become a fight for black freedom? | What problems did the Confederacy face at home? | How did the war affect the economy and politics of the North? | **How did the Union finally win the war?** | Conclusion: In what ways was the Civil War a "Second American Revolution"? | LearningCurve Check what you know. bedfordstmartins.com /roarkunderstanding |

battle of Gettysburg

▶ Battle fought at Gettysburg, Pennsylvania (July 1–3, 1863), between Union forces under General George G. Meade and Confederate forces under General Robert E. Lee. The Union emerged victorious, and Lee lost more than one-third of his men. Together with Vicksburg, Gettysburg marked a major turning point of the war.

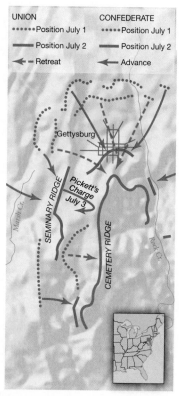

Battle of Gettysburg, July 1–3, 1863

Confederates at the small town of Gettysburg, where Union soldiers occupied the high ground. In three days of furious fighting, the Confederates failed to dislodge the Federals. The **battle of Gettysburg** cost Lee more than one-third of his army — 28,000 casualties. "It's all my fault," he lamented. On the night of July 4, 1863, he marched his battered army back to Virginia.

The twin disasters at Vicksburg and Gettysburg proved to be the turning point of the war. The Confederacy could not replace the nearly 60,000 soldiers who were captured, wounded, or killed. It is hindsight, however, that permits us to see the pair of battles as decisive. At the time, the Confederacy still controlled the heartland of the South, and Lee still had a vicious sting. War-weariness threatened to erode the North's will to win before Union armies could destroy the Confederacy's ability to go on.

Grant Takes Command

In September 1863, Union general William Rosecrans placed his army in a dangerous situation in Chattanooga, Tennessee, where he had retreated after defeat at the battle of Chickamauga (see Map 15.3). Rebels surrounded the disorganized bluecoats and threatened to starve them into submission. Grant, now commander of Union forces between the Mississippi River and the Appalachians, arrived in nearby Chattanooga in October. Within weeks, he opened an effective supply line, broke the siege, and routed the Confederate army. The victory at Chattanooga on November 25 opened the door to Georgia. In March 1864, Lincoln asked Grant to come east to become the general in chief of all Union armies.

In Washington, General Grant implemented his grand strategy for a war of attrition. He ordered a series of simultaneous assaults from Virginia all the way to Louisiana. Two actions proved particularly significant. In one, General William Tecumseh Sherman, whom Grant appointed his successor to command the western armies, plunged southeast toward Atlanta. In the other, Grant, who took control of the Army of the Potomac, went head-to-head with Lee in Virginia in May and June of 1864.

The fighting between Grant and Lee was particularly savage. At the battle of the Wilderness, where a dense tangle of forest often made it impossible to see more than ten paces, the armies pounded away at each other until approximately 18,000 Yankees and 11,000 rebels had fallen. At Spotsylvania Court House, frenzied men fought hand to hand for eighteen hours in the rain. One veteran remembered men "piled upon each other in some places four layers deep, exhibiting every ghastly phase of mutilation." Spotsylvania cost Grant another 18,000 casualties and Lee 10,000. Grant kept moving and attacked Lee again at Cold Harbor, where he suffered 13,000 additional casualties to Lee's 5,000.

Twice as many Union soldiers as rebel soldiers died in four weeks of fighting in Virginia, but because Lee had only half as many troops as Grant, his losses were equivalent to Grant's. Grant knew that the South could not replace the losses. Moreover, the campaign carried Grant to the outskirts of Petersburg, just south of Richmond, where he abandoned the costly tactic of the frontal assault and began a siege that immobilized both armies and dragged on for nine months.

Simultaneously, Sherman invaded Georgia. Skillful maneuvering, constant skirmishing, and one pitched battle, at Kennesaw Mountain, brought Sherman to

CHAPTER LOCATOR | Why did both the Union and the Confederacy consider control of the border states crucial? | Why did each side expect to win? | How did each side fare in the early years of the war?

450 CHAPTER 15
THE CRUCIBLE OF WAR

Atlanta, which fell on September 2. Intending to "make Georgia howl," Sherman marched out of Atlanta on November 15 with 62,000 battle-hardened veterans, heading for Savannah, 285 miles away on the Atlantic coast. One veteran remembered, "[We] destroyed all we could not eat, stole their niggers, burned their cotton & gins, spilled their sorghum, burned & twisted their R. Roads and raised Hell generally." **Sherman's March to the Sea** aimed at destroying the will of white Southerners to continue the war. A few weeks earlier, General Philip H. Sheridan had carried out his own scorched-earth campaign in the Shenandoah Valley. When Sherman's troops entered an undefended Savannah in mid-December, the general telegraphed Lincoln that he had "a Christmas gift" for him. A month earlier, Union voters had bestowed on the president an even greater gift.

> Major Battles of the Civil War, 1863–1865

May 1–4, 1863	Battle of Chancellorsville
July 1–3, 1863	Battle of Gettysburg
July 4, 1863	Fall of Vicksburg
September 16–20, 1863	Battle of Chickamauga
November 23–25, 1863	Battle of Chattanooga
May 5–7, 1864	Battle of the Wilderness
May 7–19, 1864	Battle of Spotsylvania Court House
June 3, 1864	Battle of Cold Harbor
June 27, 1864	Battle of Kennesaw Mountain
September 2, 1864	Fall of Atlanta
November–December 1864	Sheridan sacks Shenandoah Valley Sherman's March to the Sea
December 15–16, 1864	Battle of Nashville
December 22, 1864	Fall of Savannah
April 2–3, 1865	Fall of Petersburg and Richmond
April 9, 1865	Lee surrenders at Appomattox Court House

The Election of 1864

In the summer of 1864, with Sherman temporarily checked outside Atlanta and Grant bogged down in the siege of Petersburg, the Democratic Party smelled victory in the fall elections. Lincoln himself concluded, "It seems exceedingly probable that this administration will not be re-elected."

The Democrats were badly divided, however. "Peace" Democrats insisted on an armistice, while "war" Democrats supported the conflict but opposed Republican

> CHRONOLOGY

1863
- Vicksburg falls to Union forces.
- Lee is defeated at battle of Gettysburg.

1864
- Grant is appointed Union general in chief.
- Wilderness campaign.
- Atlanta falls to Union forces.
- Lincoln is reelected.

1865
- Richmond falls to Union forces.
- Lee surrenders at Appomattox Court House.
- Lincoln is assassinated.
- Andrew Johnson becomes president.

Sherman's March to the Sea

▶ Military campaign from September through December 1864 in which Union forces under General William Tecumseh Sherman marched from Atlanta, Georgia, to the coast at Savannah. Carving a path of destruction as it progressed, Sherman's army aimed at destroying white Southerners' will to continue the war.

How did the war for union become a fight for black freedom?

What problems did the Confederacy face at home?

How did the war affect the economy and politics of the North?

How did the Union finally win the war?

Conclusion: In what ways was the Civil War a "Second American Revolution"?

✓ LearningCurve
Check what you know.
bedfordstmartins.com /roarkunderstanding

451

means of fighting it. The party tried to paper over the chasm by nominating a war candidate, General George McClellan, but adopting a peace platform that demanded that "immediate efforts be made for a cessation of hostilities." Republicans denounced the peace plank as a cut-and-run plan that "virtually proposed to surrender the country to the rebels in arms against us."

The capture of Atlanta in September turned the political tide in favor of the Republicans. Lincoln received 55 percent of the popular vote, but his electoral margin was a whopping 212 to McClellan's 21. Lincoln's party won a resounding victory, one that gave him a mandate to continue the war until slavery and the Confederacy were dead.

The Confederacy Collapses

As 1865 dawned, military disaster littered the Confederate landscape. With the destruction of John B. Hood's army at Nashville in December 1864, the interior of the Confederacy lay in Yankee hands (see Map 15.3). Sherman's troops, resting momentarily in Savannah, eyed South Carolina hungrily. Farther north, Grant had Lee's army pinned down in Petersburg, a few miles from Richmond.

Some Confederates turned their backs on the rebellion. News from the battlefield made it difficult not to conclude that the Yankees had beaten them. Soldiers' wives begged their husbands to return home to keep their families from starving, and the stream of deserters grew dramatically. Still, white Southerners had demonstrated a remarkable endurance for their cause. Half of the 900,000 Confederate soldiers had been killed or wounded, and ragged, hungry women and children had sacrificed throughout one of the bloodiest wars then known to history.

The end came with a rush. On February 1, 1865, Sherman's troops stormed out of Savannah into South Carolina, the "cradle of the Confederacy." In Virginia, Lee abandoned Petersburg on April 2, and Richmond fell on April 3. Grant pursued Lee until he surrendered on April 9, 1865, at Appomattox Court House, Virginia. Grant offered generous peace terms. He allowed Lee's men to return home and to keep their horses to help "put in a crop to carry themselves and their families through the next winter." With Lee gone, the remaining Confederate armies lost hope and gave up within two weeks. After four years, the war was over.

No one was more relieved than Lincoln, but his celebration was restrained. He told his cabinet that his postwar burdens would weigh almost as heavily as those of wartime. Seeking a distraction, Lincoln attended Ford's Theatre on the evening of Good Friday, April 14, 1865. John Wilkes Booth, an actor with southern sympathies, slipped into the president's box and shot Lincoln, who died the next morning. Vice President Andrew Johnson became president. The man who had led the nation through the war would not lead it during the postwar search for a just peace.

> **QUICK REVIEW**

Why were the siege of Vicksburg and the battle of Gettysburg crucial to the outcome of the war?

CHAPTER LOCATOR | Why did both the Union and the Confederacy consider control of the border states crucial? | Why did each side expect to win? | How did each side fare in the early years of the war?

452   CHAPTER 15
THE CRUCIBLE OF WAR

Conclusion: In what ways was the Civil War a "Second American Revolution"?

A TRANSFORMED NATION EMERGED from the crucible of war. Antebellum America was decentralized politically and loosely integrated economically. To bend the resources of the country to a Union victory, Congress enacted legislation that reshaped the nation's political and economic character. It created a transcontinental railroad and miles of telegraph lines to bind the West to the rest of the nation. The massive changes brought about by the war — the creation of a national government, a national economy, and a national spirit — led one historian to call the American Civil War the "Second American Revolution."

The Civil War also had a profound effect on individual lives. Millions of men put on blue or gray uniforms and fought and suffered for what they passionately believed was right. The war disrupted families, leaving women at home with additional responsibilities and giving others wartime work in factories, offices, and hospitals. It offered blacks new and more effective ways to resist slavery and agitate for equality.

The war devastated the South. Three-fourths of southern white men of military age served in the Confederate army, and half of them were wounded or killed or died of disease. The war destroyed two-fifths of the South's livestock, wrecked half of the farm machinery, and blackened dozens of cities and towns. The struggle also cost the North a heavy price: 360,000 lives. But rather than devastating the land, the war set the countryside and cities humming with business activity. The radical shift in power from South to North signaled a new direction in American development: the long decline of agriculture and the rise of industrial capitalism.

Most revolutionary of all, the war ended slavery. Ironically, the South's war to preserve slavery destroyed it. Nearly 200,000 black men dedicated their wartime service to its eradication. Because slavery was both a labor and a racial system, the institution was entangled in almost every aspect of southern life. Slavery's uprooting inevitably meant fundamental change. But the full meaning of abolition remained unclear in 1865, and the status of ex-slaves would be the principal task of reconstruction.

How did the war for union become a fight for black freedom?

What problems did the Confederacy face at home?

How did the war affect the economy and politics of the North?

How did the Union finally win the war?

Conclusion: In what ways was the Civil War a "Second American Revolution"?

LearningCurve Check what you know. bedfordstmartins.com /roarkunderstanding

453

CHAPTER 15 STUDY GUIDE

STEP 1 **GET STARTED ONLINE**

✓ LearningCurve ▪ bedfordstmartins.com/roarkunderstanding
Now that you've read the chapter, make it stick by completing the LearningCurve activity.

STEP 2 **EXPLAIN WHY IT MATTERS**

Put your reading into practice. Identify each term below, and then explain why it matters in U.S. history.

TERM	WHO OR WHAT & WHEN	WHY IT MATTERS
Fort Sumter (p. 425)		
battle of Bull Run (Manassas) (p. 431)		
battle of Antietam (p. 433)		
battle of Shiloh (p. 435)		
Union blockade (p. 436)		
King Cotton diplomacy (p. 436)		
contraband of war (p. 439)		
Emancipation Proclamation (p. 440)		
New York City draft riots (p. 447)		
siege of Vicksburg (p. 448)		
battle of Gettysburg (p. 450)		
Sherman's March to the Sea (p. 451)		

STEP 3 **MOVE BEYOND THE BASICS**

To demonstrate a more advanced understanding, assess the strengths and weaknesses of the North and South at the outset of the Civil War. Why did the war take much longer than most people imagined at the outset?

Category	South	North
Population		
Industry		
Financial resources		
Leadership		
War strategy		

PUT IT ALL TOGETHER Now, take a step back and try to explain the big picture. Remember to use specific examples from the chapter in your answers.

THE EARLY YEARS OF THE WAR

▶ Why did the North, with all its advantages, fail to achieve a rapid victory over the South?

▶ Why did the South fail to attract international support for its cause?

THE HOME FRONT

▶ Why did Lincoln decide to issue the Emancipation Proclamation? How did Northerners respond to this decision?

▶ Why did conditions in the South deteriorate as the war went on? How did problems on the home front undermine the South's war effort?

UNION VICTORY

▶ What was Grant's strategy? How did it turn the tide of the war?

▶ Is it possible to identify a point at which Union victory became inevitable? Explain your reasoning.

LOOKING BACKWARD, LOOKING AHEAD

▶ Argue for or against the following statement: "The root cause of the Civil War was the failure of the architects of the Constitution to resolve the issue of slavery once and for all."

▶ What changes that occurred during the Civil War might have forecast what a northern victory would mean for the nation?

> **IN YOUR OWN WORDS**

Imagine that you must give an oral report to the class answering the following question: **How did the Civil War change the nation, North and South? What would be the most important points** to include and why?

16

RECONSTRUCTING A NATION

1863–1877

> What were the achievements and failures of reconstruction? Chapter 16 explores the era of reconstruction, in which the nation struggled to define the defeated South's status and the meaning of freedom for ex-slaves. Following the Civil War, the nation entered one of its most confused and violent periods as victorious Northerners, defeated white Southerners, and newly freed African Americans battled to shape the postwar South.

LearningCurve
bedfordstmartins.com/roarkunderstanding
After reading the chapter, use LearningCurve to
retain what you've read.

Voting day, June 5, 1867. Black freedmen line up to vote in Washington, D.C. The Granger Collection, New York.

> Why did Congress object to Lincoln's wartime plan for reconstruction?

> How did the North respond to the passage of black codes in the southern states?

> How radical was congressional reconstruction?

> What brought the elements of the South's Republican coalition together?

> Why did reconstruction collapse?

> Conclusion: Was reconstruction "a revolution but half accomplished"?

Why did Congress object to Lincoln's wartime plan for reconstruction?

Military Auction of Condemned Property, Beaufort, South Carolina, 1865

During the war, thousands of acres of land in the South came into federal hands as abandoned property or as a result of seizures because of nonpayment of taxes. The government authorized the sale of some of this land at public auction. This rare photograph shows expectant blacks (and a few whites) gathered in Beaufort, South Carolina, for a sale.

The Huntington Library, San Marino, California.

RECONSTRUCTION DID NOT WAIT for the end of war. As the odds of a northern victory increased, thinking about reunification quickened. Immediately, a question arose: Who had authority to devise a plan for reconstructing the Union? President Abraham Lincoln firmly believed that reconstruction was a matter of executive responsibility. Congress just as firmly asserted its jurisdiction. Fueling the argument were significant differences about the terms of reconstruction. In their eagerness to formulate a plan for political reunification, neither Lincoln nor Congress gave much attention to the South's land and labor problem or to the aspirations of freedmen. But as the war rapidly eroded slavery and traditional plantation agriculture, Yankee military commanders in the Union-occupied areas of the Confederacy had no choice but to oversee the emergence of a new labor system.

"To Bind Up the Nation's Wounds"

As early as 1863, Lincoln began contemplating how "to bind up the nation's wounds" and achieve "a lasting peace." While deep compassion for the enemy guided his thinking about peace, his plan for reconstruction aimed primarily at shortening the war and ending slavery.

Lincoln's Proclamation of Amnesty and Reconstruction in December 1863 set out his terms. Lincoln's plan did not require ex-rebels to extend social or political rights to ex-slaves, nor did it anticipate a program of long-term federal assistance to freedmen. Clearly, the president looked forward to the rapid, forgiving restoration of the broken Union.

Lincoln's easy terms enraged abolitionists such as Wendell Phillips of Boston, who charged that the president "makes the negro's freedom a mere sham." He "is

> CHRONOLOGY

1863
– Proclamation of Amnesty and Reconstruction.

1864
– Lincoln refuses to sign Wade-Davis bill.

1865
– Freedmen's Bureau is established.

CHAPTER LOCATOR | **Why did Congress object to Lincoln's wartime plan for reconstruction?** | How did the North respond to the passage of black codes in the southern states?

458 CHAPTER 16 RECONSTRUCTING A NATION

- Lincoln offered a full pardon, restoring property (except slaves) and political rights, to most rebels willing to renounce secession and to accept emancipation.
- High-ranking Confederate military and political officers and a few other groups were to be excluded from this offer.
- When 10 percent of a state's voting population had taken an oath of allegiance, the state could organize a new government and be readmitted into the Union.

willing that the negro should be free but seeks nothing else for him." Phillips and other northern radicals called instead for a thorough overhaul of southern society. Their ideas proved to be too drastic for most Republicans during the war years, but Congress agreed that Lincoln's plan was inadequate.

In July 1864, Congressman Henry Winter Davis of Maryland and Senator Benjamin Wade of Ohio jointly sponsored their own less forgiving reconstruction bill. When Lincoln refused to sign the bill and let it die, Wade and Davis charged the president with usurpation of power.

> ## Wade-Davis Bill

- The bill demanded that at least half of the voters in a conquered rebel state take the oath of allegiance before reconstruction could begin.
- It banned almost all ex-Confederates from participating in the drafting of new state constitutions.
- It guaranteed the equality of freedmen before the law.

Undeterred, Lincoln continued to nurture the formation of loyal state governments under his own plan. Four states — Louisiana, Arkansas, Tennessee, and Virginia — fulfilled the president's requirements, but Congress refused to seat representatives from the "Lincoln states." In his last public address in April 1865, Lincoln defended his plan but for the first time publicly expressed his endorsement of suffrage for southern blacks, at least "the very intelligent, and . . . those who serve our cause as soldiers." The announcement demonstrated that Lincoln's thinking about reconstruction was still evolving. Four days later, he was dead.

Land and Labor

Of all the problems raised by the North's victory in the war, none proved more critical than the South's transition from slavery to free labor. As federal armies invaded and occupied the Confederacy, hundreds of thousands of slaves became free workers. In addition, Union armies controlled vast territories in the South where legal title to land had become unclear. The Confiscation Acts passed during the war punished "traitors" by taking away their property. The question of what to do with federally occupied land and how to organize labor on it engaged ex-slaves, ex-slaveholders, Union military commanders, and federal government officials long before the war ended.

In the Mississippi valley, occupying federal troops announced a new labor code. It required landholders to give up whipping, to sign contracts with ex-slaves, and to

| How radical was congressional reconstruction? | What brought the elements of the South's Republican coalition together? | Why did reconstruction collapse? | Conclusion: Was reconstruction "a revolution but half accomplished"? | ✓ LearningCurve Check what you know. bedfordstmartins.com /roarkunderstanding |

pay wages. The code required black laborers to enter into contracts, work diligently, and remain subordinate and obedient. Military leaders clearly had no intention of promoting a social or economic revolution. The effort resulted in a hybrid system that one contemporary called "compulsory free labor," something that satisfied no one.

Planters complained because the new system fell short of slavery. Blacks could not be "transformed by proclamation," a Louisiana sugar planter declared. Without the right to whip, he argued, the new labor system did not have a chance. Either Union soldiers must "compel the negroes to work," or the planters themselves must "be authorized and sustained in using force."

African Americans found the new regime too reminiscent of slavery to be called free labor. Its chief deficiency, they believed, was the failure to provide them with land of their own. Freedmen believed they had a moral right to land because they and their ancestors had worked it without compensation for more than two centuries. "What's the use of being free if you don't own land enough to be buried in?" one man asked. Several wartime developments led freedmen to believe that the federal government planned to undergird black freedom with landownership.

In January 1865, General William Tecumseh Sherman set aside part of the coast south of Charleston for black settlement. By June 1865, some 40,000 freedmen sat on 400,000 acres of "Sherman land." In addition, in March 1865, Congress passed a bill establishing the Bureau of Refugees, Freedmen, and Abandoned Lands. The **Freedmen's Bureau**, as it was called, distributed food and clothing to destitute Southerners and eased the transition of blacks from slaves to free persons. Congress also authorized the agency to divide abandoned and confiscated land into 40-acre plots, to rent them to freedmen, and eventually to sell them "with such title as the United States can convey." By June 1865, the Bureau had situated nearly 10,000 black families on half a million acres abandoned by fleeing planters. Other ex-slaves eagerly anticipated farms of their own.

Despite the flurry of activity, wartime reconstruction failed to produce agreement about whether the president or Congress had the authority to devise policy or what proper policy should be.

Freedmen's Bureau
▶ Government organization created in March 1865 to distribute food and clothing to destitute Southerners and to ease the transition of slaves to free persons. Early efforts by the Freedmen's Bureau to distribute land to the newly freed blacks were later overturned by President Andrew Johnson.

The African American Quest for Autonomy

Ex-slaves never had any doubt about what they wanted from freedom. They had only to contemplate what they had been denied as slaves. Slaves had to remain on their plantations; freedom allowed blacks to see what was on the other side of the hill. Slaves had to be at work in the fields by dawn; freedom permitted blacks to sleep through a sunrise. Freedmen also tested the etiquette of racial subordination. "Lizzie's maid passed me today when I was coming from church *without speaking to me*," huffed one plantation mistress.

To whites, emancipation looked like pure anarchy. Blacks, they said, had reverted to their natural condition: lazy, irresponsible, and wild. Actually, former slaves were experimenting with freedom, but they could not long afford to roam the countryside, neglect work, and casually provoke whites. Soon, most were back at work in whites' kitchens and fields.

But they continued to dream of land and economic independence. "The way we can best take care of ourselves is to have land," one former slave declared in

CHAPTER LOCATOR | Why did Congress object to Lincoln's wartime plan for reconstruction? | How did the North respond to the passage of black codes in the southern states?

CHAPTER 16
460 RECONSTRUCTING A NATION

Harry Stephens and Family, 1866 Dressed in their Sunday best, this Virginia family sits proudly for a photograph. Many black families were not as fortunate as the Stephens family and spent years seeking missing family members. The Metropolitan Museum of Art, Gilman Collection, Purchase, The Horace W. Goldsmith Foundation Gift, 2005 (2005.100.277)/Art Resource, NY.

1865, "and turn it and till it by our own labor." Freedmen also wanted to learn to read and write. "I wishes the Childern all in School," one black veteran asserted. "It is beter for them then to be their Sureing a mistes [mistress]."

The restoration of broken families was another persistent black aspiration. Thousands of freedmen took to the roads in 1865 to look for kin who had been sold away or to free those who were being held illegally as slaves. A black soldier from Missouri wrote his daughters that he was coming for them. "I will have you if it cost me my life," he declared. "Your Miss Kitty said that I tried to steal you," he told them. "But I'll let her know that god never intended for a man to steal his own flesh and blood." And he swore that "if she meets me with ten thousand soldiers, she [will] meet her enemy."

Independent worship was another continuing aspiration. African Americans greeted freedom with a mass exodus from white churches, where they had been required to worship when slaves. Some joined the newly established southern branches of all-black northern churches, such as the African Methodist Episcopal Church. Others formed black versions of the major southern denominations, Baptists and Methodists.

QUICK REVIEW

To what extent did Lincoln's wartime plan for reconstruction reflect the concerns of newly freed slaves?

How radical was congressional reconstruction?

What brought the elements of the South's Republican coalition together?

Why did reconstruction collapse?

Conclusion: Was reconstruction "a revolution but half accomplished"?

✔️ **LearningCurve** Check what you know. bedfordstmartins.com /roarkunderstanding

461

How did the North respond to the passage of black codes in the southern states?

The Black Codes

Titled "Selling a Freeman to Pay His Fine at Monticello, Florida," this 1867 drawing from a northern magazine equates black codes with the institution of slavery. The ascension of Andrew Johnson to the presidency emboldened many southern states to pass laws severely restricting blacks' freedom. Granger Collection.

ABRAHAM LINCOLN DIED on April 15, 1865, just hours after John Wilkes Booth shot him at a Washington, D.C., theater. Chief Justice Salmon P. Chase immediately administered the oath of office to Vice President Andrew Johnson of Tennessee. Congress had adjourned in March and would not reconvene until December. Throughout the summer and fall, Johnson drew up and executed a plan of reconstruction without congressional advice.

Congress returned to the capital in December to find that, as far as the president and former Confederates were concerned, reconstruction was completed. Most Republicans, however, thought Johnson's plan made far too few demands of ex-rebels. They claimed that Johnson's leniency had acted as midwife to the rebirth of the Old South, that he had achieved political reunification at the cost of black freedom. Republicans in Congress then proceeded to dismantle Johnson's program and substitute a program of their own.

Johnson's Program of Reconciliation

Born in 1808 in Raleigh, North Carolina, Andrew Johnson was the son of illiterate parents. Self-educated and ambitious, Johnson moved to Tennessee, where he built a career in politics championing the South's common white people and assailing its "illegitimate, swaggering, bastard, scrub aristocracy." The only senator from a Confederate state to remain loyal to the Union, Johnson held the planter class responsible for secession.

A Democrat all his life, Johnson occupied the White House only because the Republican Party in 1864 had needed a vice presidential candidate who would

CHAPTER LOCATOR | Why did Congress object to Lincoln's wartime plan for reconstruction? | **How did the North respond to the passage of black codes in the southern states?**

appeal to loyal, Union-supporting Democrats. Johnson vigorously defended states' rights (but not secession) and opposed Republican efforts to expand the power of the federal government. A steadfast supporter of slavery, Johnson had owned slaves until 1862, when Tennessee rebels, angry at his Unionism, confiscated them. When he grudgingly accepted emancipation, it was more because he hated planters than because he sympathized with slaves. "Damn the negroes," he said. "I am fighting those traitorous aristocrats, their masters." The new president harbored unshakable racist convictions. Africans, Johnson said, were "inferior to the white man in point of intellect — better calculated in physical structure to undergo drudgery and hardship."

Like Lincoln, Johnson stressed the rapid restoration of civil government in the South. Like Lincoln, he promised to pardon most, but not all, ex-rebels. Johnson recognized the state governments created by Lincoln but set out his own requirements for restoring the other rebel states to the Union.

> CHRONOLOGY

1865
- Lincoln is assassinated; Andrew Johnson becomes president.
- Black codes are enacted.
- Thirteenth Amendment becomes part of Constitution.

1866
- Civil Rights Act.

> **Johnson's Plan to Restore Confederate States to the Union**

- Citizens of a state had to renounce the right of secession.
- They had to deny that the debts of the Confederacy were legal and binding.
- They had to ratify the Thirteenth Amendment abolishing slavery, which became part of the Constitution in December 1865.

Johnson also returned all confiscated and abandoned land to pardoned ex-Confederates, even if it was in the hands of freedmen. Reformers were shocked by Johnson's quick and easy plan of reconstruction. Instead of punishing treason and making planters pay as he had promised, Johnson canceled the promising beginnings made by General Sherman and the Freedmen's Bureau to settle blacks on land of their own. As one freedman observed, "Things was hurt by Mr. Lincoln getting killed."

White Southern Resistance and Black Codes

In the summer of 1865, delegates across the South gathered to draw up the new state constitutions required by Johnson's plan of reconstruction. They refused to accept even the president's mild requirements. Refusing to renounce secession, the South Carolina and Georgia conventions merely "repudiated" their secession ordinances, preserving in principle their right to secede. South Carolina and Mississippi refused to disown their Confederate war debts. Mississippi rejected the Thirteenth Amendment. Despite this defiance, Johnson did nothing. White Southerners began to think that by standing up for themselves they could shape the terms of reconstruction.

New state governments across the South adopted a series of laws known as **black codes**, which made a travesty of black freedom. The codes sought to keep ex-slaves subordinate to whites by subjecting them to every sort of discrimination. Several states made it illegal for blacks to own a gun. Mississippi made insulting gestures and language by blacks a criminal offense. The codes barred blacks from jury duty. Not a single southern state granted any black the right to vote.

black codes

▶ Laws passed by state governments in the South in 1865 that sought to keep ex-slaves subordinate to whites. At the core of the black codes lay the desire to force freedmen back to the plantations.

How radical was congressional reconstruction?

What brought the elements of the South's Republican coalition together?

Why did reconstruction collapse?

Conclusion: Was reconstruction "a revolution but half accomplished"?

✓ LearningCurve
Check what you know.
bedfordstmartins.com /roarkunderstanding

463

At the core of the black codes, however, lay the matter of labor. Legislators sought to hustle freedmen back to the plantations. Whites were almost universally opposed to black landownership, and South Carolina attempted to limit blacks to either farmwork or domestic service by requiring them to pay annual taxes of $10 to $100 to work in any other occupation. Mississippi declared that blacks who did not possess written evidence of employment could be declared vagrants and be subject to involuntary plantation labor. Under so-called apprenticeship laws, courts bound thousands of black children — orphans and others whose parents were deemed unable to support them — to work for planter "guardians."

Johnson, a staunch defender of states' rights and white supremacy, refused to intervene. He also recognized that his do-nothing response offered him political advantage. A conservative Tennessee Democrat at the head of a northern Republican Party, he had begun to look southward for political allies. By pardoning powerful whites, by accepting governments even when they failed to satisfy his minimal demands, and by acquiescing in the black codes, Johnson won useful southern friends.

In the fall elections of 1865, white Southerners dramatically expressed their mood. To represent them in Congress, they chose former Confederates. Of the eighty senators and representatives they sent to Washington, fifteen had served in the Confederate army, ten of them as generals. Another sixteen had served in civil and judicial posts in the Confederacy. Nine others had served in the Confederate Congress. One — Alexander Stephens — had been vice president of the Confederacy. As one Georgian remarked, "It looked as though Richmond had moved to Washington."

Expansion of Federal Authority and Black Rights

Southerners had blundered monumentally. They had assumed that what Andrew Johnson was willing to accept, Republicans would accept as well. But southern intransigence compelled even moderates to conclude that ex-rebels were a "generation of vipers," still untrustworthy and dangerous. The black codes became a symbol of southern intentions to "restore all of slavery but its name." "We tell the white men of Mississippi," the *Chicago Tribune* roared, "that the men of the North will convert the State of Mississippi into a frog pond before they will allow such laws to disgrace one foot of the soil in which the bones of our soldiers sleep and over which the flag of freedom waves."

The moderate majority of the Republican Party wanted only assurance that slavery and treason were dead. They did not champion black equality, the confiscation of plantations, or black voting, as did the radical minority within the party. But southern obstinacy had succeeded in forging unity (at least temporarily) among Republican factions. In December 1865, Republicans refused to seat the southern representatives elected in the fall elections. Rather than accept Johnson's claim that the "work of restoration" was done, Congress challenged his executive power.

CHAPTER LOCATOR | Why did Congress object to Lincoln's wartime plan for reconstruction? | How did the North respond to the passage of black codes in the southern states?

464 CHAPTER 16 RECONSTRUCTING A NATION

Republican senator Lyman Trumbull of Illinois declared that the president's policy meant that an ex-slave would "be tyrannized over, abused, and virtually reenslaved without some legislation by the nation for his protection." Early in 1866, the moderates produced two bills that strengthened the federal shield. The first, the Freedmen's Bureau bill, prolonged the life of the agency established by the previous Congress. Arguing that the Constitution never contemplated a "system for the support of indigent persons," President Andrew Johnson vetoed the bill. Congress failed by a narrow margin to override the president's veto.

The moderates designed their second measure, what would become the **Civil Rights Act of 1866**, to nullify the black codes by affirming African Americans' rights to "full and equal benefit of all laws and proceedings for the security of person and property as is enjoyed by white citizens." The act required the end of racial discrimination in state laws and represented an extraordinary expansion of black rights and federal authority. The president argued that the civil rights bill amounted to "unconstitutional invasion of states' rights" and vetoed it.

In April 1866, an incensed Republican Party again pushed the civil rights bill through Congress and overrode the presidential veto. In July, it passed another Freedmen's Bureau bill and overrode Johnson's veto. For the first time in American history, Congress had overridden presidential vetoes of major legislation. As a worried South Carolinian observed, Johnson had succeeded in uniting the Republicans and probably touched off "a fight this fall such as has never been seen."

Civil Rights Act of 1866

▶ Legislation passed by Congress in 1866 that nullified the black codes and affirmed that black Americans should have equal benefit of the law. President Andrew Johnson vetoed this expansion of black rights and federal authority, but Congress later overrode his veto.

QUICK REVIEW ◁

When the southern states passed the black codes, how did the U.S. Congress respond?

| How radical was congressional reconstruction? | What brought the elements of the South's Republican coalition together? | Why did reconstruction collapse? | Conclusion: Was reconstruction "a revolution but half accomplished"? | ✓ LearningCurve Check what you know. bedfordstmartins.com /roarkunderstanding |

> How radical was congressional reconstruction?

State Convention at Richmond, Virginia

Between 1867 and 1869, every southern state except Tennessee held a convention to draft a new constitution. In Virginia, where blacks were more than 40 percent of the population, they made up about 20 percent of the convention. Richmond History Center.

BY THE SUMMER OF 1866, President Andrew Johnson and Congress had dropped their gloves and stood toe-to-toe in a bare-knuckle contest unprecedented in American history. Johnson made it clear that he would not budge on either constitutional issues or policy. Moderate Republicans responded by amending the Constitution. But the obstinacy of Johnson and white Southerners pushed Republican moderates ever closer to the radicals and to acceptance of additional federal intervention in the South. Congress also voted to impeach the president. In time, Congress debated whether to make voting rights color-blind, while women sought to make voting rights sex-blind as well.

The Fourteenth Amendment and Escalating Violence

Fourteenth Amendment

▶ Constitutional amendment passed in 1866 that made all native-born or naturalized persons U.S. citizens and prohibited states from abridging the rights of national citizens. The amendment aimed to provide a guarantee of equality before the law for black citizens.

In June 1866, Congress passed the **Fourteenth Amendment** to the Constitution, and two years later the states ratified it. The most important provisions of this complex amendment made all native-born or naturalized persons American citizens and prohibited states from abridging the "privileges and immunities" of citizens, depriving them of "life, liberty, or property without due process of law," and denying them "equal protection of the laws." By making blacks national citizens, the amendment provided a national guarantee of equality before the law. In essence, it protected blacks against violation by southern state governments.

CHAPTER LOCATOR | Why did Congress object to Lincoln's wartime plan for reconstruction? | How did the North respond to the passage of black codes in the southern states?

466 CHAPTER 16
RECONSTRUCTING A NATION

The Fourteenth Amendment also dealt with voting rights. It gave Congress the right to reduce the congressional representation of any state that withheld suffrage from some of its adult male population. In other words, white Southerners could either allow black men to vote or see their representation in Washington slashed.

The Fourteenth Amendment's suffrage provisions ignored the small band of women who had emerged from the war demanding "the ballot for the two disenfranchised classes, negroes and women." Founding the American Equal Rights Association in 1866, Susan B. Anthony and Elizabeth Cady Stanton lobbied for "a government by the people, and the whole people; for the people and the whole people." They felt betrayed when their old antislavery allies refused to work for their goals. "It was the Negro's hour," Frederick Douglass explained. Senator Charles Sumner suggested that woman suffrage could be "the great question of the future."

The Fourteenth Amendment provided for punishment of any state that excluded voters on the basis of race, but not on the basis of sex. The amendment also introduced the word *male* into the Constitution when it referred to a citizen's right to vote. Stanton predicted that "if that word 'male' be inserted, it will take us a century at least to get it out."

Tennessee approved the Fourteenth Amendment in July, and Congress promptly welcomed the state's representatives and senators back. Had President Johnson counseled other southern states to ratify this relatively mild amendment, they might have listened. Instead, Johnson advised Southerners to reject the Fourteenth Amendment and to rely on him to trounce the Republicans in the fall congressional elections.

Johnson had decided to make the Fourteenth Amendment the overriding issue of the 1866 elections and to gather its white opponents into a new conservative party, the National Union Party. The president's strategy suffered a setback when whites in several southern cities went on rampages against blacks. Mobs killed thirty-four blacks in New Orleans and forty-six blacks in Memphis. The slaughter shocked Northerners and renewed skepticism about Johnson's claim that southern whites could be trusted. "Who doubts that the Freedmen's Bureau ought to be abolished forthwith," a New Yorker observed sarcastically, "and the blacks remitted to the paternal care of their old masters, who 'understand the nigger, you know, a great deal better than the Yankees can.'"

The 1866 elections resulted in an overwhelming Republican victory. Johnson had bet that Northerners would not support federal protection of black rights and that a racist backlash would blast the Republican Party. But the war was still fresh in northern minds, and as one Republican explained, southern whites "with all their intelligence were traitors, the blacks with all their ignorance were loyal."

Radical Reconstruction and Military Rule

When Johnson continued to urge Southerners to reject the Fourteenth Amendment, every southern state except Tennessee voted it down. "The last one of the sinful ten," thundered Representative James A. Garfield of Ohio, "has flung back into our teeth the magnanimous offer of a generous nation." After the South rejected the moderates' program, the radicals seized the initiative.

Each act of defiance by southern whites had boosted the standing of the radicals within the Republican Party. Radicals such as Massachusetts senator Charles

1866
- Congress approves Fourteenth Amendment.
- American Equal Rights Association is founded.

1767
- Military Reconstruction Act.
- Tenure of Office Act.

1868
- Impeachment trial of President Johnson.

1869
- Congress approves Fifteenth Amendment.

| How radical was congressional reconstruction? | What brought the elements of the South's Republican coalition together? | Why did reconstruction collapse? | Conclusion: Was reconstruction "a revolution but half accomplished"? | ✓ LearningCurve Check what you know. bedfordstmartins.com /roarkunderstanding |

467

Sumner and Pennsylvania representative Thaddeus Stevens united in demanding civil and political equality. Southern states were "like clay in the hands of the potter," Stevens declared in January 1867, and he called on Congress to begin reconstruction all over again.

In March 1867, Congress passed the **Military Reconstruction Act** and overturned the Johnson state governments and initiated military rule of the South.

Military Reconstruction Act

▶ Congressional act of March 1867 that initiated military rule of the South. Congressional reconstruction divided the ten unreconstructed Confederate states into five military districts, each under the direction of a Union general. It also established the procedure by which unreconstructed states could reenter the Union.

> **> Military Reconstruction Act**

- The ten unreconstructed Confederate states were divided into five military districts.
- Congress placed a Union general in charge of each district and instructed him to "suppress insurrection, disorder, and violence" and to begin political reform.
- After the military had completed voter registration, which would include black men, voters in each state would elect delegates to conventions that would draw up new state constitutions.
- Each constitution would guarantee black suffrage.
- When the voters of each state had approved the constitution and the state legislature had ratified the Fourteenth Amendment, the state could submit its work to Congress.
- If Congress approved the constitution, the state's senators and representatives could be seated, and political reunification would be accomplished.

Reconstruction Military Districts, 1867

Radicals proclaimed the provision for black suffrage "a prodigious triumph," for it extended far beyond the limited suffrage provisions of the Fourteenth Amendment. When combined with the disfranchisement of thousands of ex-rebels, it promised to cripple any neo-Confederate resurgence and guarantee Republican state governments in the South.

Despite its bold suffrage provision, the Military Reconstruction Act of 1867 disappointed those who also advocated the confiscation of southern plantations and their redistribution to ex-slaves. Thaddeus Stevens agreed with the freedman who said, "Give us our own land and we take care of ourselves, but without land, the old masters can hire us or starve us, as they please." But most Republicans believed they had provided blacks with what they needed: equal legal rights and the ballot. If blacks were to get land, they would have to gain it themselves.

Declaring that he would rather sever his right arm than sign such a formula for "anarchy and chaos," Andrew Johnson vetoed the Military Reconstruction Act, but Congress overrode his veto. With the passage of the Reconstruction Acts of 1867, congressional reconstruction was virtually completed. Congress left whites owning most of the South's land but, in a departure that justified the term "radical reconstruction," had given black men the ballot.

Impeaching a President

Despite his defeats, Andrew Johnson had no intention of yielding control of reconstruction. In a dozen ways, he sabotaged Congress's will and encouraged southern whites to resist. He issued a flood of pardons, waged war against the

CHAPTER LOCATOR | Why did Congress object to Lincoln's wartime plan for reconstruction? | How did the North respond to the passage of black codes in the southern states?

CHAPTER 16
468 RECONSTRUCTING A NATION

Freedmen's Bureau, and replaced Union generals eager to enforce Congress's Reconstruction Acts with conservative officers eager to defeat them. Johnson claimed that he was merely defending the "violated Constitution." At bottom, however, the president subverted congressional reconstruction to protect southern whites from what he considered the horrors of "Negro domination."

Radicals argued that Johnson's abuse of constitutional powers and his failure to fulfill constitutional obligations to enforce the law were impeachable offenses. According to the Constitution, the House of Representatives can impeach and the Senate can try any federal official for "treason, bribery, or other high crimes and misdemeanors." But moderates interpreted the Constitution to mean violation of criminal statutes. As long as Johnson refrained from breaking the law, impeachment (the process of formal charges of wrongdoing against the president or other federal official) remained stalled.

Then in August 1867, Johnson suspended Secretary of War Edwin M. Stanton from office. As required by the Tenure of Office Act, a law passed in March 1867 that demanded the approval of the Senate for the removal of any government official who had been appointed with Senate approval, the president requested the Senate to consent to Stanton's dismissal. When the Senate balked, Johnson removed Stanton anyway. "Is the President crazy, or only drunk?" asked a dumbfounded Republican moderate. "I'm afraid his doings will make us all favor impeachment."

News of Johnson's open defiance of the law convinced every Republican in the House to vote for a resolution impeaching the president. Supreme Court chief justice Salmon Chase presided over the Senate trial, which lasted from March until May 1868. When the vote came, thirty-five senators voted guilty and nineteen not guilty. The impeachment forces fell one vote short of the two-thirds needed to convict.

After his trial, Johnson called a truce, and for the remaining ten months of his term, congressional reconstruction proceeded unhindered by presidential interference. Without interference from Johnson, Congress revisited the suffrage issue.

The Fifteenth Amendment and Women's Demands

In February 1869, Republicans passed the **Fifteenth Amendment** to the Constitution, which prohibited states from depriving any citizen of the right to vote because of "race, color, or previous condition of servitude." The Reconstruction Acts of 1867 already required black suffrage in the South; the Fifteenth Amendment extended black voting nationwide.

Some Republicans, however, found the final wording of the Fifteenth Amendment "lame and halting." Rather than absolutely guaranteeing the right to vote, the amendment merely prohibited exclusion on grounds of race. The distinction would prove to be significant. In time, white Southerners would devise tests of literacy and property and other apparently nonracial measures that would effectively disfranchise blacks yet not violate the Fifteenth Amendment. But an amendment that fully guaranteed the right to vote courted defeat outside the South. Rising antiforeign sentiment — against the Chinese in California and

Fifteenth Amendment
▶ Constitutional amendment passed in February 1869 prohibiting states from depriving any citizen of the right to vote because of "race, color, or previous condition of servitude." It extended black suffrage nationwide. Woman suffrage advocates were disappointed that the amendment failed to extend voting rights to women.

| How radical was congressional reconstruction? | What brought the elements of the South's Republican coalition together? | Why did reconstruction collapse? | Conclusion: Was reconstruction "a revolution but half accomplished"? | ✓ LearningCurve Check what you know. bedfordstmartins.com /roarkunderstanding |

469

European immigrants in the Northeast — caused states to resist giving up total
control of suffrage requirements. In March 1870, after three-fourths of the states
had ratified it, the Fifteenth Amendment became part of the Constitution.

Woman suffrage advocates, however, were sorely disappointed with the Fifteenth Amendment's failure to extend voting rights to women. Elizabeth Cady
Stanton and Susan B. Anthony condemned the Republicans' "negro first" strategy
and pointed out that women remained "the only class of citizens wholly unrepre-
sented in the government." The Fifteenth Amendment severed the early feminist
movement from its abolitionist roots. Over the next several decades, feminists
established an independent suffrage crusade that drew millions of women into
political life.

Republicans took enough satisfaction in the Fifteenth Amendment to
promptly scratch the "Negro question" from the agenda of national politics. Even
Wendell Phillips, a steadfast crusader for equality, concluded that the black man
now held "sufficient shield in his own hands. . . . Whatever he suffers will be
largely now, and in future, his own fault." Northerners had no idea of the violent
struggles that lay ahead.

> QUICK REVIEW

Why did Congress impeach President
Andrew Johnson?

CHAPTER LOCATOR | Why did Congress object
to Lincoln's wartime plan
for reconstruction? | How did the North
respond to the passage
of black codes in the
southern states?

470 CHAPTER 16
RECONSTRUCTING A NATION

What brought the elements of the South's Republican coalition together?

NORTHERNERS BELIEVED they had discharged their responsibilities with the Reconstruction Acts and the amendments to the Constitution, but Southerners knew that the battle had just begun. Black suffrage established the foundation for the rise of the Republican Party in the South. Gathering together outsiders and outcasts, southern Republicans won elections, wrote new state constitutions, and formed new state governments.

Challenging the established class for political control was dangerous business. Equally dangerous were the confrontations that took place on southern farms and plantations, where blacks sought to give fuller meaning to their newly won legal and political equality. Freedom remained contested territory, and Southerners fought pitched battles with one another to determine the contours of their new world.

Freedmen, Yankees, and Yeomen

African Americans made up the majority of southern Republicans. After gaining voting rights in 1867, nearly all eligible black men registered to vote as Republicans. "It is the hardest thing in the world to keep a negro away from the polls," observed an Alabama white man. Southern blacks did not all have identical political priorities, but they united in their desire for education and equal treatment before the law.

> CHRONOLOGY

1866
– Ku Klux Klan is founded.

1867
– Southern African Americans gain voting rights under the Military Reconstruction Act.
– Southern states hold elections for delegates to state conventions.

1875
– One-half of South Carolina's and Mississippi's children, the majority black, attend school.
– Sharecropping is the dominant labor system for rural southern blacks.

| How radical was congressional reconstruction? | **What brought the elements of the South's Republican coalition together?** | Why did reconstruction collapse? | Conclusion: Was reconstruction "a revolution but half accomplished"? | ✓ LearningCurve Check what you know. bedfordstmartins.com /roarkunderstanding |

carpetbaggers

► Southerners' pejorative term for northern migrants who sought opportunity in the South after the Civil War. Northern migrants formed an important part of the southern Republican Party.

scalawags

► A derogatory term that Southerners applied to southern white Republicans, who were seen as traitors to the South. Most were yeoman farmers.

Ku Klux Klan

► A social club of Confederate veterans that quickly developed into a paramilitary organization supporting Democrats. With too few Union troops in the South to control the region, the Klan went on a rampage of violence to defeat Republicans and restore white supremacy.

Northern whites who made the South their home after the war were a second element of the South's Republican Party. Conservative white Southerners called them **carpetbaggers**, opportunists who stuffed all their belongings in a single carpet-sided suitcase and headed south to "fatten on our misfortunes." But most Northerners who moved south were young men who looked upon the South as they did the West — as a promising place to make a living. Northerners in the southern Republican Party supported programs that encouraged vigorous economic development along the lines of the northern free-labor model.

Southern whites made up the third element of the South's Republican Party. Approximately one out of four white Southerners voted Republican. The other three condemned the one who did as a traitor to his region and his race and called him a **scalawag**, a term for runty horses and low-down, good-for-nothing rascals. Yeoman farmers accounted for the majority of southern white Republicans. Some were Unionists who emerged from the war with bitter memories of Confederate persecution. Others were small farmers who wanted to end state governments' favoritism toward plantation owners. Yeomen supported initiatives for public schools and for expanding economic opportunity in the South.

The South's Republican Party, then, was made up of freedmen, Yankees, and yeomen — an improbable coalition. The mix of races, regions, and classes inevitably meant friction as each group maneuvered to define the party. But Reconstruction represents an extraordinary moment in American politics: Blacks and whites joined together in the Republican Party to pursue political change. Formally, of course, only men participated in politics — casting ballots and holding offices — but white and black women also played a part in the political struggle by joining in parades and rallies, attending stump speeches, and even campaigning.

Most whites in the South condemned southern Republicans as illegitimate and felt justified in doing whatever they could to stamp them out. Violence against blacks — the "white terror" — took brutal institutional form in 1866 with the formation in Tennessee of the **Ku Klux Klan**, a social club of Confederate veterans that quickly developed into a paramilitary organization supporting Democrats. The Klan went on a rampage of violence to defeat Republicans and restore white supremacy. Rapid demobilization of the Union army after the war left only twenty thousand troops to patrol the entire South. Without effective military protection, southern Republicans had to take care of themselves.

Republican Rule

In the fall of 1867, southern states held elections for delegates to state constitutional conventions, as required by the Reconstruction Acts. About 40 percent of the white electorate stayed home because they had been disfranchised or because they had decided to boycott politics. Republicans won three-fourths of the seats. About 15 percent of the Republican delegates to the conventions were Northerners who had moved south, 25 percent were African Americans, and 60 percent were white Southerners. As a British visitor observed, the delegate elections reflected "the mighty revolution that had taken place in America."

The reconstruction constitutions introduced two broad categories of changes in the South: those that reduced aristocratic privilege and increased democratic equality and those that expanded the state's responsibility for the general welfare. In the first

CHAPTER LOCATOR | Why did Congress object to Lincoln's wartime plan for reconstruction? | How did the North respond to the passage of black codes in the southern states?

472 CHAPTER 16 RECONSTRUCTING A NATION

category, the constitutions adopted universal male suffrage, abolished property qualifications for holding office, and made more offices elective and fewer appointed. In the second category, they enacted prison reform; made the state responsible for caring for orphans, the insane, and the deaf and mute; and exempted debtors' homes from seizure.

To Democrats, however, these progressive constitutions looked like wild revolution. Democrats were blind to the fact that no constitution confiscated and redistributed land, as virtually every former slave wished, or disfranchised ex-rebels wholesale, as most southern Unionists advocated. And they were convinced that the new constitutions initiated "Negro domination." In fact, although 80 percent of Republican voters were black men, only 6 percent of Southerners in Congress during reconstruction were black (**Figure 16.1**). The sixteen black men in Congress included exceptional men, such as Representative James T. Rapier of Alabama. No state legislature experienced "Negro rule," despite black majorities in the populations of some states.

Southern voters ratified the new constitutions and swept Republicans into power. When the former Confederate states ratified the Fourteenth Amendment, Congress readmitted them. Southern Republicans then turned to a staggering array of problems. Wartime destruction littered the landscape. Making matters worse, racial harassment and reactionary violence dogged Southerners who sought reform. In this desperate context, Republicans struggled to rebuild and reform the region.

Activity focused on three areas — education, civil rights, and economic development. Every state inaugurated a system of public education. Before the Civil War, whites had deliberately kept slaves illiterate, and planter-dominated governments rarely spent tax money to educate the children of yeomen. By 1875, half of Mississippi's and South Carolina's eligible children were attending school. Although schools were underfunded, literacy rates rose sharply. Public schools were racially segregated, but education remained for many blacks a tangible, deeply satisfying benefit of freedom and Republican rule.

State legislatures also attacked racial discrimination and defended civil rights. Republicans especially resisted efforts to segregate blacks from whites in public transportation. Mississippi levied fines and jail terms for owners of railroads and steamboats that pushed blacks into "smoking cars" or to lower decks. But passing color-blind laws was far easier than enforcing them. A Mississippian complained: "Education amounts to nothing, good behavior counts for nothing, even money cannot buy for a colored man or woman decent treatment and the comforts that white people claim and can obtain." Despite the laws, segregation — later called Jim Crow — developed at white insistence and became a feature of southern life long before the end of the Reconstruction era.

Republican governments also launched ambitious programs of economic development. They envisioned a South of diversified agriculture, roaring factories, and booming towns. State legislatures chartered scores of banks and industrial companies, appropriated funds to fix ruined levees and drain swamps, and went on a railroad-building binge. These efforts fell far short of solving the South's economic troubles, however. Republican spending to stimulate economic growth also meant rising taxes and enormous debt that siphoned funds from schools and other programs.

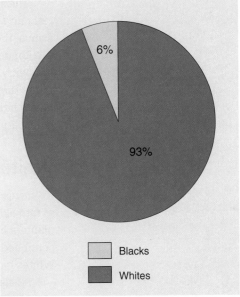

FIGURE 16.1 ■ Southern Congressional Delegations, 1865–1877

The statistics contradict the myth of black domination of congressional representation during reconstruction.

How radical was congressional reconstruction?

What brought the elements of the South's Republican coalition together?

Why did reconstruction collapse?

Conclusion: Was reconstruction "a revolution but half accomplished"?

☑ LearningCurve Check what you know. bedfordstmartins.com /roarkunderstanding

The southern Republicans' record, then, was mixed. To their credit, the biracial party adopted an ambitious agenda to change the South. But money was scarce, the Democrats continued their harassment, and factionalism threatened the Republican Party from within. Moreover, corruption infected Republican governments. Nonetheless, the Republican Party made headway in its efforts to purge the South of aristocratic privilege and racist oppression. Republican governments had less success in overthrowing the long-established white oppression of black farm laborers in the rural South.

White Landlords, Black Sharecroppers

Ex-slaves who wished to escape slave labor and ex-masters who wanted to reinstitute old ways clashed repeatedly. Except for having to pay subsistence wages, planters had not been required to offer many concessions to emancipation. They continued to believe that African Americans would not work without coercion. Whites moved quickly to restore as much of slavery as they could get away with.

Ex-slaves resisted every effort to turn back the clock. They believed that land of their own would anchor their economic independence and end planters' interference in their personal lives. They could then, for example, make their own decisions about whether women and children would labor in the fields. Indeed, within months after the war, perhaps one-third of black women abandoned field labor to work on chores in their own cabins just as poor white women did. Black women also negotiated about work ex-mistresses wanted done in the big house. Hundreds of thousands of black children enrolled in school. But without their own land, ex-slaves had little choice but to work on plantations.

Although forced to return to the planters' fields, they resisted efforts to restore slavelike conditions. Instead of working for wages, a South Carolinian observed, "the negroes all seem disposed to rent land," which increased their independence from whites. Out of this tug-of-war between white landlords and black laborers emerged a new system of southern agriculture.

Sharecropping was a compromise that offered something to both ex-masters and ex-slaves but satisfied neither. Under the new system, planters divided their cotton plantations into small farms that freedmen rented, paying with a share of each year's crop, usually half. Sharecropping gave blacks more freedom than the system of wages and labor gangs and released them from day-to-day supervision by whites. Black families abandoned the old slave quarters and built separate cabins for themselves on the patches of land they rented (**Map 16.1**). Still, most black families remained dependent on white landlords, who had the power to evict them at the end of each growing season. For planters, sharecropping offered a way to resume agricultural production, but it did not allow them to restore the old slave plantation.

Sharecropping introduced the country merchant into the agricultural equation. Landlords supplied sharecroppers with land, mules, seeds, and tools, but blacks also needed credit to obtain essential food and clothing before they harvested their crop. Under an arrangement called a crop lien, a merchant would advance goods to a sharecropper in exchange for a *lien*, or legal claim, on the farmer's future crop. Some merchants charged exorbitant rates of interest, as much as 60 percent, on the goods they sold. At the end of the growing season, after the landlord had taken half of the farmer's crop for rent, the merchant took most of the rest. Sometimes,

sharecropping

▶ Labor system that emerged in the South during reconstruction. Under this system, planters divided their plantations into small farms that freedmen rented, paying with a share of each year's crop. Sharecropping gave blacks some freedom, but they remained dependent on white landlords and country merchants.

CHAPTER LOCATOR | Why did Congress object to Lincoln's wartime plan for reconstruction? | How did the North respond to the passage of black codes in the southern states?

474 CHAPTER 16
RECONSTRUCTING A NATION

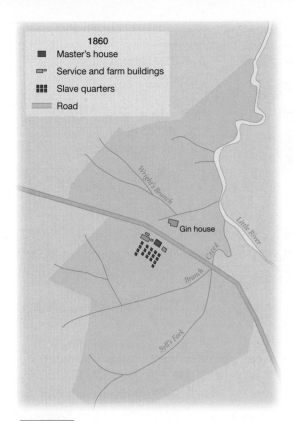

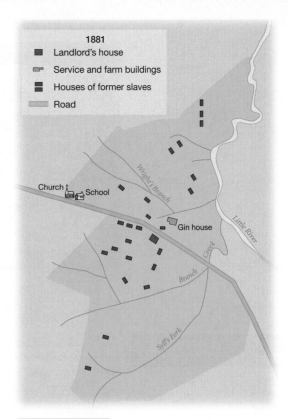

MAP 16.1 ■ A Southern Plantation in 1860 and 1881

These maps of the Barrow plantation in Georgia illustrate some of the ways in which ex-slaves expressed their freedom. Freedmen and freedwomen deserted the clustered living quarters behind the master's house, scattered over the plantation, built family cabins, and farmed rented land. The former Barrow slaves also worked together to build a school and a church.

> **MAP ACTIVITY**

READING THE MAP: Compare the number and size of the slave quarters in 1860 with the homes of the former slaves in 1881. How do they differ? Which buildings were prominently located along the road in 1860, and which could be found along the road in 1881?

CONNECTIONS: How might the former master feel about the new configuration of buildings on the plantation in 1881? In what ways did the new system of sharecropping replicate the old system of plantation agriculture? In what ways was it different?

the farmer did not earn enough to repay the debt to the merchant, and he would have to borrow more from the merchant and begin the cycle again.

An experiment at first, sharecropping soon dominated the cotton South. Lien merchants forced tenants to plant cotton, which was easy to sell, instead of food crops. The result was excessive production of cotton and falling cotton prices, developments that cost thousands of small white farmers their land and pushed them into the great army of sharecroppers. The new sharecropping system of agriculture took shape just as the political power of Republicans in the South began to buckle under Democratic pressure.

QUICK REVIEW

How did politics and economic concerns shape reconstruction in the South?

| How radical was congressional reconstruction? | **What brought the elements of the South's Republican coalition together?** | Why did reconstruction collapse? | Conclusion: Was reconstruction "a revolution but half accomplished"? |  LearningCurve Check what you know. bedfordstmartins.com /roarkunderstanding |

Why did reconstruction collapse?

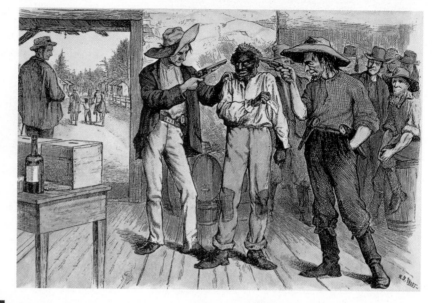

"Of Course He Wants to Vote the Democratic Ticket"

This Republican cartoon from the October 21, 1876, issue of *Harper's Weekly* comments sarcastically on the possibility of honest elections in the South. The caption reads, "You're free as air, ain't you? Say you are or I'll blow yer black head off."
Granger Collection.

BY 1870, after a decade of war and reconstruction, Northerners wanted to put "the southern problem" behind them. Practical business-minded men came to dominate the Republican Party, replacing the band of reformers and idealists who had been prominent in the 1860s. Civil war hero Ulysses S. Grant succeeded Andrew Johnson as president in 1869 and quickly became an issue himself, proving that brilliance on the battlefield does not necessarily translate into competence in the White House. As northern commitment to defend black freedom eroded, southern commitment to white supremacy intensified. Without northern protection, southern Republicans were no match for the Democrats' economic coercion, political fraud, and bloody violence. One by one, Republican state governments fell in the South. The election of 1876 both confirmed and completed the collapse of reconstruction.

Candidate	Electoral Vote	Popular Vote	Percent of Popular Vote
Ulysses S. Grant (Republican)	214	3,012,833	52.7
Horatio Seymour (Democrat)	80	2,703,249	47.3
Nonvoting states (Reconstruction)			

MAP 16.2 ■ The Election of 1868

Grant's Troubled Presidency

In 1868, the Republican Party's presidential nomination went to Ulysses S. Grant, the North's favorite general. His Democratic opponent, Horatio Seymour of New York, ran on a platform that blasted reconstruction as "a flagrant usurpation of power . . . unconstitutional, revolutionary, and void." The

CHAPTER LOCATOR | Why did Congress object to Lincoln's wartime plan for reconstruction? | How did the North respond to the passage of black codes in the southern states?

Republicans answered by "waving the bloody shirt" — that is, they reminded voters that the Democrats were "the party of rebellion." Grant gained a narrow 309,000-vote margin in the popular vote and a substantial victory (214 votes to 80) in the electoral college (**Map 16.2**).

Grant was not as good a president as he was a general. The talents he had demonstrated on the battlefield — decisiveness, clarity, and resolution — were less obvious in the White House. Grant sought both justice for blacks and sectional reconciliation. But he surrounded himself with fumbling kinfolk and old friends from his army days and made a string of dubious appointments that led to a series of damaging scandals. Charges of corruption tainted his vice president, Schuyler Colfax, and brought down two of his cabinet officers. Though never personally implicated in any scandal, Grant was aggravatingly naive and blind to the rot that filled his administration.

In 1872, anti-Grant Republicans bolted and launched the Liberal Party. To clean up the graft and corruption, Liberals proposed ending the spoils system,

> CHRONOLOGY

1868
- Ulysses S. Grant is elected president.

1871
- Ku Klux Klan Act.

1872
- Liberal Party is formed.
- President Grant is reelected.

1873
- Economic depression sets in.
- *Slaughterhouse* cases.
- Colfax massacre.

1874
- Democrats win majority in House of Representatives.

1877
- In the disputed presidential election of 1876, Rutherford Hayes is declared the winner.

Grant and Scandal

This anti-Grant cartoon by Thomas Nast, the nation's most celebrated political cartoonist, shows the president falling headfirst into the barrel of fraud and corruption that tainted his administration. During Grant's eight years in the White House, many members of his administration failed him. Sometimes duped, sometimes merely loyal, Grant stubbornly defended wrongdoers, even to the point of perjuring himself to keep an aide out of jail. Library of Congress.

> VISUAL ACTIVITY

READING THE IMAGE: How does Thomas Nast portray President Grant's role in corruption? According to this cartoon, what caused the problems?
CONNECTIONS: How responsible was President Grant for the corruption that plagued his administration?

| How radical was congressional reconstruction? | What brought the elements of the South's Republican coalition together? | **Why did reconstruction collapse?** | Conclusion: Was reconstruction "a revolution but half accomplished"? | LearningCurve Check what you know. bedfordstmartins.com /roarkunderstanding |

by which victorious parties rewarded loyal workers with public office, and replacing it with a nonpartisan civil service commission that would oversee competitive examinations for appointment to office. Liberals also demanded that the federal government remove its troops from the South and restore "home rule" (southern white control). Democrats liked the Liberals' southern policy and endorsed the Liberal presidential candidate, Horace Greeley, the longtime editor of the *New York Tribune*. The nation, however, still felt enormous affection for the man who had saved the Union and reelected Grant with 56 percent of the popular vote.

Northern Resolve Withers

Although Grant genuinely wanted to see blacks' civil and political rights protected, he understood that most Northerners had grown weary of reconstruction and were increasingly willing to let southern whites manage their own affairs. Citizens wanted to shift their attention to other issues, especially after the nation slipped into a devastating economic depression in 1873. More than eighteen thousand businesses collapsed, leaving more than a million workers on the streets. Northern businessmen wanted to invest in the South but believed that recurrent federal intrusion was itself a major cause of instability in the region. Republican leaders began to question the wisdom of their party's alliance with the South's lower classes — its small farmers and sharecroppers. One member of Grant's administration proposed allying with the "thinking and influential native southerners . . . the intelligent, well-to-do, and controlling class."

Congress, too, wanted to leave reconstruction behind, but southern Republicans made that difficult. When the South's Republicans begged for federal protection from increasing Klan violence, Congress enacted three laws in 1870 and 1871 that were intended to break the back of white terrorism. The severest of the three, the Ku Klux Klan Act (1871), made interference with voting rights a felony. Federal marshals arrested thousands of Klansmen and came close to destroying the Klan, but they did not end all terrorism against blacks. Congress also passed the Civil Rights Act of 1875, which boldly outlawed racial discrimination in transportation, public accommodations, and juries. But federal authorities never enforced the law aggressively, and segregated facilities remained the rule throughout the South.

By the early 1870s, the Republican Party had lost its leading champions of African American rights to death or defeat at the polls. Other Republicans concluded that the quest for black equality was mistaken or hopelessly naive. In May 1872, Congress restored the right of office holding to all but three hundred ex-rebels. Many Republicans had come to believe that traditional white leaders offered the best hope for honesty, order, and prosperity in the South.

Underlying the North's abandonment of reconstruction was unyielding racial prejudice. Northerners had learned to accept black freedom during the war, but deep-seated prejudice prevented many from accepting black equality. Even the actions they took on behalf of blacks often served partisan political advantage. Northerners generally supported Indiana senator Thomas A. Hendricks's harsh declaration that "this is a white man's Government, made by the white man for the white man."

CHAPTER LOCATOR | Why did Congress object to Lincoln's wartime plan for reconstruction? | How did the North respond to the passage of black codes in the southern states?

CHAPTER 16
478   RECONSTRUCTING A NATION

The U.S. Supreme Court also did its part to undermine reconstruction. The Court issued a series of decisions that significantly weakened the federal government's ability to protect black Southerners. In the *Slaughterhouse* cases (1873), the Court distinguished between national and state citizenship and ruled that the Fourteenth Amendment protected only those rights that stemmed from the federal government, such as voting in federal elections and interstate travel. Since the Court decided that most rights derived from the states, it sharply curtailed the federal government's authority to defend black citizens. Even more devastating, the *United States v. Cruikshank* ruling (1876) said that the reconstruction amendments gave Congress the power to legislate against discrimination only by states, not by individuals. The "suppression of ordinary crime," such as assault, remained a state responsibility. The Supreme Court did not declare reconstruction unconstitutional but eroded its legal foundation.

The mood of the North found political expression in the election of 1874, when for the first time in eighteen years the Democrats gained control of the House of Representatives. As one Republican observed, the people had grown tired of the "negro question, with all its complications, and the reconstruction of Southern States, with all its interminable embroilments." Reconstruction had come apart. Rather than defend reconstruction from its southern enemies, Northerners steadily backed away from the challenge. By the early 1870s, southern Republicans faced the forces of reaction largely on their own.

White Supremacy Triumphs

Reconstruction was a massive humiliation to most white Southerners. Republican rule meant intolerable insults: Black militiamen patrolled town streets, black laborers negotiated contracts with former masters, black maids stood up to former mistresses, black voters cast ballots, and black legislators such as James T. Rapier enacted laws. Republican governments in the South attracted more hatred than did any other political regimes in American history. The northern retreat from reconstruction permitted southern Democrats to set things right.

Taking the name **Redeemers**, Democrats in the South promised to replace "bayonet rule" (a few federal troops continued to be stationed in the South) with "home rule." They promised that honest, thrifty Democrats would supplant corrupt tax-and-spend Republicans. Above all, Redeemers swore to save southern civilization from a descent into "African barbarism." As one man put it, "We must render this either a white man's government, or convert the land into a Negro man's cemetery."

Southern Democrats adopted a multipronged strategy to overthrow Republican governments. First, they sought to polarize the parties around color. They went about gathering all the South's white voters into the Democratic Party, leaving the Republicans to depend on blacks, who made up a minority of the population in almost every southern state. To dislodge whites from the Republican Party, Democrats fanned the flames of racial prejudice. A South Carolina Democrat crowed that his party appealed to the "proud Caucasian race, whose sovereignty on earth God has proclaimed." Local newspapers published the names of whites who kept company with blacks, and neighbors ostracized offenders.

Redeemers
▶ Name taken by southern Democrats who harnessed white rage in order to overthrow Republican rule and black political power and thus, they believed, save southern civilization.

How radical was congressional reconstruction?

What brought the elements of the South's Republican coalition together?

Why did reconstruction collapse?

Conclusion: Was reconstruction "a revolution but half accomplished"?

✔ LearningCurve
Check what you know.
bedfordstmartins.com
/roarkunderstanding

479

This silk ribbon from the 1868 presidential campaign between Republican Ulysses S. Grant and his Democratic opponent, New York governor Horatio Seymour, openly declares the Democrats' goal of white supremacy. During the campaign, Democratic vice presidential nominee Francis P. Blair Jr. promised that a Seymour victory would restore "white people" to power by declaring the reconstruction governments in the South "null and void." Collection of Janice L. and David J. Frent.

Democrats also exploited the severe economic plight of small white farmers by blaming it on Republican financial policy. Government spending soared during reconstruction, and small farmers saw their tax burden skyrocket. "This is tax time," a South Carolinian reported. "We are nearly all on our head about them. They are so high & so little money to pay with" that farmers "[are] selling every egg and chicken they can get." In 1871, Mississippi reported that one-seventh of the state's land — 3.3 million acres — had been forfeited for nonpayment of taxes. The small farmers' economic distress had a racial dimension. Because few freedmen succeeded in acquiring land, they rarely paid taxes. In Georgia in 1874, blacks made up 45 percent of the population but paid only 2 percent of the taxes. From the perspective of a small white farmer, Republican rule meant that he was paying more taxes and paying them to aid blacks.

If racial pride, social isolation, and financial hardship proved insufficient to drive yeomen from the Republican Party, Democrats turned to terrorism. "Night riders" targeted white Republicans as well as blacks for murder and assassination. Whether white or black, a "dead Radical is very harmless," South Carolina Democratic leader Martin Gary told his followers.

But the primary victims of white violence were black Republicans. Violence escalated to an unprecedented ferocity on Easter Sunday in 1873 in tiny Colfax, Louisiana. The black majority in the area had made Colfax a Republican stronghold until 1872, when Democrats turned to intimidation and fraud to win the local election. Republicans refused to accept the result and eventually occupied the courthouse in the middle of the town. After three weeks, 165 white men attacked. They overran the Republicans' defenses and set the courthouse on fire. When the blacks tried to surrender, the whites murdered them. At least 81 black men were slaughtered that day. Although the federal government indicted the attackers, the Supreme Court ruled that it did not have the right to prosecute. And since local whites would not prosecute neighbors who killed blacks, the defendants in the Colfax massacre went free.

Even before adopting the all-out white supremacist tactics of the 1870s, Democrats had taken control of the governments of Virginia, Tennessee, and North Carolina. The new campaign brought fresh gains. The Redeemers retook Georgia in 1871, Texas in 1873, and Arkansas and Alabama in 1874. As Mississippi's election approached in 1876, Governor Adelbert Ames appealed to Washington for federal troops to control the violence, only to hear from the attorney general that the "whole public are tired of these annual autumnal outbreaks in the South." Abandoned, Mississippi Republicans succumbed to the Democratic onslaught in the fall elections. By 1876, only three Republican state governments survived in the South (**Map 16.3**).

CHAPTER LOCATOR | Why did Congress object to Lincoln's wartime plan for reconstruction? | How did the North respond to the passage of black codes in the southern states?

CHAPTER 16
480 RECONSTRUCTING A NATION

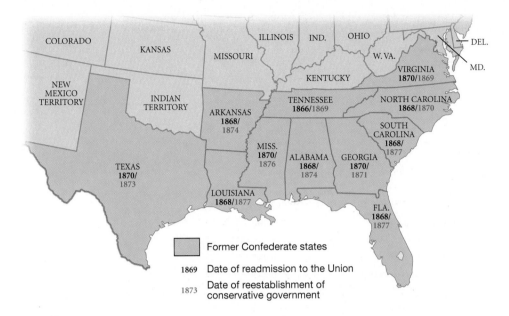

Former Confederate states	
1869	Date of readmission to the Union
1873	Date of reestablishment of conservative government

MAP 16.3 ■ The Reconstruction of the South

Myth has it that Republican rule of the former Confederacy was not only harsh but long. In most states, however, conservative southern whites stormed back into power in months or just a few years. By the election of 1876, Republican governments could be found in only three states, and they soon fell.

> MAP ACTIVITY

READING THE MAP: List in chronological order the readmission of the former Confederate states to the Union. Which states reestablished conservative governments most quickly?

CONNECTIONS: What did the former Confederate states need to do in order to be readmitted to the Union? How did reestablished conservative governments react to reconstruction?

An Election and a Compromise

The year 1876 witnessed one of the most tumultuous elections in American history. The election took place in November, but not until March 2 of the following year did the nation know who would be inaugurated president on March 4. The Democrats nominated New York's governor, Samuel J. Tilden, who immediately targeted the corruption of the Grant administration and the "despotism" of Republican reconstruction. The Republicans put forward Rutherford B. Hayes, governor of Ohio. Privately, Hayes considered "bayonet rule" a mistake but concluded that waving the bloody shirt remained the Republicans' best political strategy.

On election day, Tilden tallied 4,288,590 votes to Hayes's 4,036,000. But in the all-important electoral college, Tilden fell one vote short of the majority required for victory. The electoral votes of three states — South Carolina, Louisiana, and Florida, the only remaining Republican governments in the South — remained in doubt because both Republicans and Democrats in those states claimed victory. To win, Tilden needed only one of the nineteen contested votes. Hayes had to have all of them.

Congress had to decide who had actually won the elections in the three southern states and thus who would be president. The Constitution provided no guidance for this situation. Moreover, Democrats controlled the House, and Republicans controlled the Senate. Congress created a special electoral

| How radical was congressional reconstruction? | What brought the elements of the South's Republican coalition together? | **Why did reconstruction collapse?** | Conclusion: Was reconstruction "a revolution but half accomplished"? | ☑ LearningCurve Check what you know. bedfordstmartins.com /roarkunderstanding |

481

MAP 16.4 ■ The Election of 1876

Candidate	Electoral Vote	Popular Vote	Percent of Popular Vote
Rutherford B. Hayes (Republican)	185*	4,036,298	47.9**
Samuel J. Tilden (Democrat)	184	4,288,590	51.0

*19 electoral votes were disputed.

**Percentages do not total 100 because some popular votes went to other parties.

commission to arbitrate the disputed returns. All of the commissioners voted their party affiliation, giving every state to the Republican Hayes and putting him over the top in electoral votes (**Map 16.4**).

Some outraged Democrats vowed to resist Hayes's victory. Rumors flew of an impending coup and renewed civil war. But the impasse was broken when negotiations behind the scenes resulted in an informal understanding known as the **Compromise of 1877**. In exchange for a Democratic promise not to block Hayes's inauguration and to deal fairly with the freedmen, Hayes vowed to refrain from using the army to uphold the remaining Republican regimes in the South and to provide the South with substantial federal subsidies for railroads.

Stubborn Tilden supporters bemoaned the "stolen election" and damned "His Fraudulency," Rutherford B. Hayes. Old-guard radicals such as William Lloyd Garrison denounced Hayes's bargain as a "policy of compromise, of credulity, of weakness, of subserviency, of surrender." But the nation as a whole celebrated, for the country had weathered a grave crisis. The last three Republican state governments in the South fell quickly once Hayes abandoned them and withdrew the U.S. Army. Reconstruction came to an end.

Compromise of 1877

▶ Informal agreement in which Democrats agreed not to block Rutherford Hayes's inauguration and to deal fairly with freedmen; in return, Hayes vowed not to use the army to uphold the remaining Republican regimes in the South and to provide the South with substantial federal subsidies for railroads. The compromise brought the Reconstruction era to an end.

> **QUICK REVIEW**

How did the Supreme Court undermine reconstruction?

CHAPTER LOCATOR | Why did Congress object to Lincoln's wartime plan for reconstruction? | How did the North respond to the passage of black codes in the southern states?

CHAPTER 16
482 RECONSTRUCTING A NATION

Conclusion: Was reconstruction "a revolution but half accomplished"?

IN 1865, when General Carl Schurz visited the South, he discovered "a revolution but half accomplished." White Southerners resisted the passage from slavery to free labor, from white racial despotism to equal justice, and from white political monopoly to biracial democracy. The old elite wanted to get "things back as near to slavery as possible," Schurz reported, while African Americans such as James T. Rapier and some whites were eager to exploit the revolutionary implications of defeat and emancipation.

Although the northern-dominated Republican Congress refused to provide for blacks' economic welfare, it employed constitutional amendments to require ex-Confederates to accept legal equality and share political power with black men. Conservative southern whites fought ferociously to recover their power and privilege. When Democrats regained control of politics, whites used both state power and private violence to wipe out many of the gains of Reconstruction, leading one observer to conclude that the North had won the war but the South had won the peace.

The Redeemer counterrevolution, however, did not mean a return to slavery. Northern victory in the Civil War ensured that ex-slaves no longer faced the auction block and could send their children to school, worship in their own churches, and work independently on their own rented farms. Sharecropping, with all its hardships, provided more autonomy and economic welfare than bondage had. It was limited freedom, to be sure, but it was not slavery.

The Civil War and emancipation set in motion the most profound upheaval in the nation's history. War destroyed the largest slave society in the New World and gave birth to a modern nation-state. Washington, D.C., increased its role in national affairs, and the victorious North set the nation's compass toward the expansion of industrial capitalism and the final conquest of the West.

Despite massive changes, however, the Civil War remained only a "half accomplished" revolution. By not fulfilling the promises the nation seemed to hold out to black Americans at war's end, Reconstruction represents a tragedy of enormous proportions. The failure to protect blacks and guarantee their rights had enduring consequences. It was the failure of the first reconstruction that made the modern civil rights movement necessary.

| How radical was congressional reconstruction? | What brought the elements of the South's Republican coalition together? | Why did reconstruction collapse? | Conclusion: Was reconstruction "a revolution but half accomplished"? | ✓ LearningCurve Check what you know. bedfordstmartins.com /roarkunderstanding |

483

CHAPTER 16 STUDY GUIDE

STEP 1

GET STARTED ONLINE

LearningCurve ■ bedfordstmartins.com/roarkunderstanding

Now that you've read the chapter, make it stick by completing the LearningCurve activity.

STEP 2

EXPLAIN WHY IT MATTERS

Put your reading into practice. Identify each term below, and then explain why it matters in U.S. history.

TERM	WHO OR WHAT & WHEN	WHY IT MATTERS
Freedmen's Bureau (p. 460)		
black codes (p. 463)		
Civil Rights Act of 1866 (p. 465)		
Fourteenth Amendment (p. 466)		
Military Reconstruction Act (p. 468)		
Fifteenth Amendment (p. 469)		
carpetbaggers (p. 472)		
scalawags (p. 472)		
Ku Klux Klan (p. 472)		
sharecropping (p. 474)		
Redeemers (p. 479)		
Compromise of 1877 (p. 482)		

STEP 3

MOVE BEYOND THE BASICS

To demonstrate a more advanced understanding, indicate below how each phase of reconstruction addressed the key issues involved.

Phase of reconstruction	Requirements for readmission	Role/rights of freedmen	Achievements	Failures
Wartime reconstruction (Lincoln)				
Presidential reconstruction (Johnson)				
Congressional reconstruction				

STEP 4 **PUT IT ALL TOGETHER**   Now, take a step back and try to explain the big picture. Remember to use specific examples from the chapter in your answers.

PRESIDENTIAL AND CONGRESSIONAL RECONSTRUCTION

▸ What role did the black codes play in shaping the course of reconstruction?

▸ What steps did Congress take between 1865 and 1869 to assist ex-slaves in their lives as freedmen? How effective were these actions?

SOUTHERN RECONSTRUCTION IN ACTION

▸ How did white Southerners respond during reconstruction? Consider both Democrats and Republicans in your response.

▸ How did southern African Americans attempt to shape their own lives during reconstruction?

THE END OF RECONSTRUCTION

▸ How and why did the decline of northern support for reconstruction help southern Democrats "redeem" the South?

▸ Why did white supremacy become the foundation of southern politics in the 1870s?

LOOKING BACKWARD, LOOKING AHEAD

▸ How did long-held racial views among whites, in both the South and the North, shape reconstruction?

▸ What were the lasting accomplishments of reconstruction? What were its most important failures?

> **IN YOUR OWN WORDS**   Imagine that you must give an oral report to the class answering the following question: What were the achievements and failures of reconstruction? What would be the most important points to include and why?

 Do it online at the Student Site ▪ **bedfordstmartins.com/roarkunderstanding**

17

CONTESTING THE WEST

1865–1900

> **What was most significant about American expansion after the Civil War?** Chapter 17 explores the westward expansion of the United States in the late nineteenth century. It examines the impact of expansion on Native Americans, the role mining played in the creation of the American West, the cultural diversity of the West, and American settlement and exploitation of western lands.

LearningCurve
bedfordstmartins.com/roarkunderstanding
After reading the chapter, use LearningCurve to
retain what you've read.

Cliffs of the Upper Colorado. When artist Thomas Moran arrived in Wyoming Territory in 1871, these towering buttes were his first sight. Smithsonian American Art Museum, Washington, D.C./Art Resource, NY.

> What did U.S. expansion mean for Native Americans?

> In what ways did different Indian groups defy and resist colonial rule?

> How did mining shape American expansion?

> How did the fight for land and resources in the West unfold?

> Conclusion: How did the West set the tone for the Gilded Age?

What did U.S. expansion mean for Native Americans?

Crazy Horse at the Little Big Horn

This pictograph by Amos Bad Heart Bull, an Oglala Sioux from the Pine Ridge Reservation, pictures Crazy Horse at the center of the Battle of the Little Big Horn. Although the artist was only seven years old in 1876, he based his pictures on the recollections of his uncle and other Oglala elders. The Granger Collection, New York.

WHILE THE EUROPEAN POWERS expanded their authority and wealth through imperialism and colonialism in far-flung empires abroad, the United States focused its attention on the West. From the U.S. Army attack on the remainder of the Comanche empire to the conquest of the Black Hills, whites pushed Indians aside as they moved west. As posited by historian Frederick Jackson Turner in 1893, American exceptionalism derived from the ways in which the history of the United States differed from that of European nations, and he cited America's western frontier as a cause. In what has become known as Turner's "frontier thesis," the availability of land provided a "safety valve," releasing social tensions and providing opportunities for social mobility for Americans. Yet expansion in the trans-Mississippi West involved the conquest, displacement, and rule over native peoples — a process best understood in the global context of imperialism and colonialism.

The U.S. government, through trickery and conquest, pushed the Indians off their lands (**Map 17.1**) and onto designated Indian territories or reservations. The

CHAPTER LOCATOR | What did U.S. expansion mean for Native Americans?

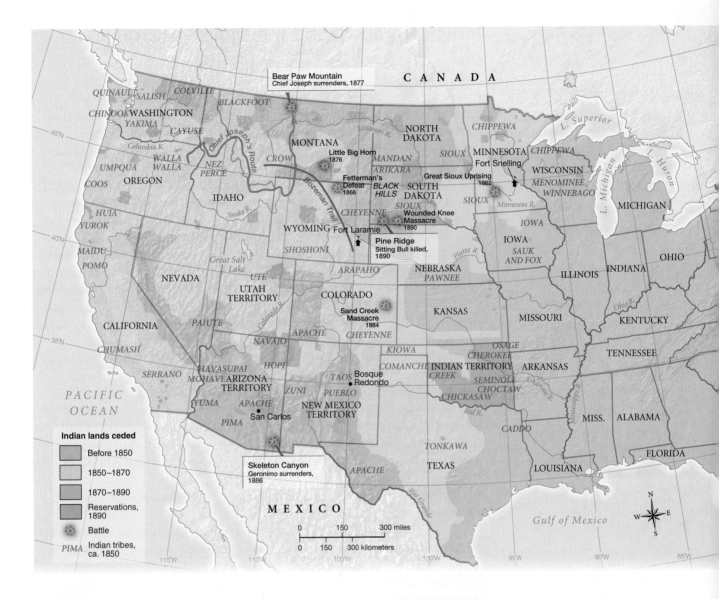

MAP 17.1 ■ The Loss of Indian Lands, 1850–1890

By 1890, western Indians were isolated on small, scattered reservations. Native Americans had struggled to retain their land in major battles, from the Santee Uprising in Minnesota in 1862 to the massacre at Wounded Knee, South Dakota, in 1890.

> MAP ACTIVITY

READING THE MAP: Where was the largest reservation located in 1890? Which states on this map show no reservations in 1890? Compare this map to Map 17.3 on page 509.
CONNECTIONS: Why did the federal government force Native Americans onto reservations? What developments prompted these changes?

Indian wars that followed the Civil War depleted the Native American population and handed the lion's share of Indian land over to white settlers. The decimation of the bison herds pushed the Plains Indians onto reservations, where they lived as wards of the state. Through the lens of colonialism, we can see how the United States, with its commitment to an imperialist, expansionist ideology, colonized the West.

| In what ways did different Indian groups defy and resist colonial rule? | How did mining shape American expansion? | How did the fight for land and resources in the West unfold? | Conclusion: How did the West set the tone for the Gilded Age? | ✓ **LearningCurve** Check what you know. bedfordstmartins.com /roarkunderstanding |

> CHRONOLOGY

1851
– First Treaty of Fort Laramie.

1862
– Great Sioux Uprising (Santee Uprising).

1864
– Sand Creek massacre.

1867
– Treaty of Medicine Lodge.

1868
– Second Treaty of Fort Laramie.

1870
– Hunters begin to decimate bison herds.

1874
– Gold is discovered in Black Hills.

1876
– Battle of the Little Big Horn.

1881
– Sitting Bull surrenders.

1893
– Frederick Jackson Turner presents "frontier thesis."

reservations
▶ Land given by the federal government to American Indians beginning in the 1860s in an attempt to reduce tensions between Indians and western settlers. On reservations, Indians subsisted on meager government rations and faced a life of poverty and starvation.

Indian Removal and the Reservation System

Manifest destiny — the belief that the United States had a "God-given" right to aggressively spread the values of white civilization and expand the nation from ocean to ocean — dictated U.S. policy toward Indians and other nations with claims in North America. In the name of manifest destiny, Americans forced the removal of the Five Civilized Tribes of the South (the Cherokee, Chocktaw, Chickasaw, Creek, and Seminole peoples) to Oklahoma in the 1830s; colonized Texas and won its independence from Mexico in 1836; conquered California, Arizona, New Mexico, and parts of Utah and Colorado in the Mexican-American War of 1846–1848; and invaded Oregon in the mid-1840s.

By midcentury, hordes of settlers crossed the Great Plains on their way to the goldfields of California or the rich farmland of Washington and Oregon. In their path stood a solid wall of Indian land, much of it in **reservations** granted by the U.S. government in its policy of Indian removal. In 1851, some ten thousand Plains Indians came together at Fort Laramie in Wyoming to negotiate a treaty that ceded a wide swath of their land to allow passage of wagon trains headed west. In return, the government promised that the remaining Indian land would remain inviolate.

The Indians who "touched the pen" to the 1851 Treaty of Fort Laramie hoped to preserve their land and culture in the face of the white onslaught. Settlers and miners cut down trees, polluted streams, and killed off the bison. Whites brought alcohol, guns, and something even more deadly — disease. Between 1780 and 1870, the population of the Plains tribes declined by half. "If I could see this thing, if I knew where it came from, I would go there and fight it," a Cheyenne warrior lamented. Disease also shifted the power from Woodland agrarian tribes to the Lakota (Western) Sioux, who fled the contagion by pursuing an equestrian nomadic existence that displaced weaker tribes in the western plains.

Poverty and starvation stalked the reservations. Confined by armed force, the Indians eked out an existence on stingy government rations. Styled as stepping-stones on the road to "civilization," Indian reservations closely resembled colonial societies where native populations, ruled by outside bureaucrats, saw their culture assaulted, their religious practices outlawed, their children sent away to school, and their way of life attacked in the name of progress and civilization.

To Americans raised on theories of racial superiority, the Indians constituted, in the words of one Colorado militia major, "an obstacle to civilization . . . [and] should be exterminated." This attitude pervaded the military. In November 1864 at the Sand Creek massacre in Colorado Territory, Colonel John M. Chivington and his Colorado militia descended on a village of Cheyenne, mostly women and children. Their leader, Black Kettle, raised a white flag and an American flag to signal surrender, but the charging cavalry ignored his signal and butchered 270 Indians. Chivington watched as his men scalped and mutilated their victims and later justified the killing of Indian children with the terse remark, "Nits make lice." The city of Denver treated Chivington and his men as heroes, but a congressional inquiry eventually castigated the soldiers for their "fiendish malignity" and condemned the "savage cruelty" of the massacre.

CHAPTER LOCATOR | What did U.S. expansion mean for Native Americans?

The Decimation of the Great Bison Herds

After the Civil War, the accelerating pace of industrial expansion brought about the near extinction of the American bison (buffalo). The development of larger, more accurate rifles combined with the growth of the nation's transcontinental rail system, which cut the range in two and divided the herds, hastened the bison's decline. For the Sioux and other nomadic tribes of the plains, the buffalo constituted a way of life — a source of food, fuel, and shelter and a central part of their religion and rituals. To the railroads, the buffalo were a nuisance, at best a cheap source of meat for their workers and a target for sport. "It will not be long before all the buffaloes are extinct near and between the railroads," Ohio senator John Sherman predicted in 1868.

The decimation of the great bison herds contributed to the army's conquest of the Plains Indians. General Philip Sheridan acknowledged as much when he applauded white hide hunters for "destroying the Indians' commissary." With their food supply gone, Indians had to choose between starvation and the reservation. "A cold wind blew across the prairie when the last buffalo fell," the great Sioux leader Sitting Bull lamented, "a death wind for my people."

On the southern plains in 1867, more than five thousand warring Comanches, Kiowas, and Southern Arapahos gathered at Medicine Lodge Creek in Kansas to negotiate the Treaty of Medicine Lodge. They sought to preserve limited land and hunting by moving the tribe to a reservation. Three years later, hide hunters poured into the region, and within a decade they had nearly exterminated the southern bison herds. Luther Standing Bear recounted the sight and stench: "I saw the bodies of hundreds of dead buffalo lying about, just wasting, and the odor was terrible. . . . They were letting our food lie on the plains to rot." With the buffalo gone, the Indians faced starvation and became dependent on the stingy allotments provided on the reservations.

Indian Wars and the Collapse of Comanchería

The Indian wars in the West marked the last resistance of a Native American population devastated by disease and demoralized by the reservation policy pursued by the federal government. The Dakota Sioux in Minnesota went to war in 1862. For years, under the leadership of Chief Little Crow, the Dakota — also known as the Santee — had pursued a policy of accommodation, ceding land in return for the promise of annuities. But with his people on the

"Slaughtered for the Hide"

In 1874, *Harper's Weekly* featured this illustration of a buffalo-hide hunter skinning a carcass on the southwestern plains. City father Colonel Richard Dodge wrote of the carnage, "The air was foul with sickening stench, and the vast plain which only a short twelve months before teemed with animal life, was a dead, solitary putrid desert." Library of Congress.

> VISUAL ACTIVITY

READING THE IMAGE: What virtues and stereotypes of the West does this magazine cover extol?
CONNECTIONS: How does the magazine's subtitle, "Journal of Civilization," fit the picture?

| In what ways did different Indian groups defy and resist colonial rule? | How did mining shape American expansion? | How did the fight for land and resources in the West unfold? | Conclusion: How did the West set the tone for the Gilded Age? | ✓ LearningCurve Check what you know. bedfordstmartins.com /roarkunderstanding |

491

verge of starvation (the local Indian agent told the hungry Dakota, "Go and eat grass"), Little Crow led his angry warriors in a desperate campaign against the intruders, killing more than 1,000 settlers. American troops quelled the Great Sioux Uprising (also called the Santee Uprising) and marched 1,700 Sioux to Fort Snelling, where 400 Indians were put on trial for murder and 38 died in the largest mass execution in American history.

Farther west, the great Indian empire of Comanchería had stretched from the Canadian plains to Mexico in the eighteenth century. By 1865, it numbered fewer than five thousand Comanche, ranging from west Texas north to Oklahoma. Through decades of dealings with the Spanish and the French, the Comanche had built a complex empire based on trade in horses, hides, guns, and captives. Expert riders, the Comanche waged war in the saddle, giving the U.S. Cavalry reason to hate and fear them.

After the Civil War, President Ulysses S. Grant faced the prospect of protracted Indian war on the Great Plains. Reluctant to spend more money and sacrifice more lives in battle, Grant adopted a "peace policy" designed to segregate and control the Indians while opening up land to white settlers. This policy won the support of both friends of the Indians and those who coveted the Indians' land. The army herded the Indians onto reservations (see Map 17.1), where the U.S. Bureau of Indian Affairs hired agents who, in the words of Paiute Sarah Winnemucca, did "nothing but fill their pockets." In 1871, Grant's peace policy in the West gave way to all-out warfare as the U.S. Army dispatched three thousand soldiers to wipe out the remains of Comanchería. Raiding parties of Comanche virtually obliterated white settlements in west Texas. To defeat the Indians, the army adopted the tactics of burning and destroying everything in their path using the tactics that General William Tecumseh Sherman had used in his march through Georgia during the Civil War. At the decisive battle of Palo Duro Canyon in 1874, only three Comanche warriors died in battle, but U.S. soldiers took the Indians' camp, burning more than two hundred tepees, hundreds of robes and blankets, and thousands of pounds of winter supplies and shooting more than a thousand horses. Coupled with the decimation of the bison, the army's scorched-earth policy led to the final collapse of the Comanche people. The surviving Indians of Comanchería, now numbering fewer than 1,500, reluctantly retreated to the reservation at Fort Sill.

The Fight for the Black Hills

On the northern plains, the fever for gold fueled the conflict between Indians and Euro-Americans. In 1866, the Cheyenne united with the Sioux in Wyoming to protect their hunting grounds in the Powder River valley, which were threatened by the construction of the Bozeman Trail connecting Fort Laramie with the goldfields in Montana. Captain William Fetterman, who had boasted that with eighty men he could ride through the Sioux nation, was killed along with all of his troops in an Indian attack. The Sioux's impressive victories led to the second Treaty of Fort Laramie in 1868, in which the United States agreed to abandon the Bozeman Trail and guaranteed the Indians control of the Black Hills, land sacred to the Lakota Sioux.

The government's fork-tongued promises induced some of the tribes to accept the treaty. The great Sioux chief Red Cloud led many of his people onto the reser-

Comanchería

▶ Indian empire based on trade in horses, hides, guns, and captives that stretched from the Canadian plains to Mexico in the eighteenth century. By 1865, fewer than five thousand Comanches lived in the empire, which ranged from west Texas north to Oklahoma.

Black Hills

▶ Mountains in western South Dakota and northeast Wyoming that are sacred to the Lakota Sioux. In the 1868 Treaty of Fort Laramie, the United States guaranteed Indians control of the Black Hills but broke its promise after gold was discovered there in 1874.

CHAPTER LOCATOR | What did U.S. expansion mean for Native Americans?

vation. Red Cloud soon regretted his decision. "Think of it!" he told a visitor to the Pine Ridge Reservation. "I, who used to own . . . country so extensive that I could not ride through it in a week . . . must tell Washington when I am hungry. I must beg for that which I own." Several Sioux chiefs, among them Crazy Horse and Sitting Bull, refused to sign the treaty. Crazy Horse said that he wanted no part of the "piecemeal penning" of his people.

In 1874, the discovery of gold in the Black Hills of the Dakotas led the government to break its promise to Red Cloud. Miners began pouring into the region, and the Northern Pacific Railroad made plans to lay track. Lieutenant Colonel George Armstrong Custer trumpeted news of the gold strike. At first, the government offered to purchase the Black Hills. But the Lakota Sioux refused to sell. The army responded by issuing an ultimatum ordering all Lakota Sioux and Northern Cheyenne bands onto the Pine Ridge Reservation and threatening to hunt down those who refused.

In the summer of 1876, the army launched a three-pronged attack led by Custer, General George Crook, and Colonel John Gibbon. Crazy Horse stopped Crook at the Battle of the Rosebud. Custer, leading the second prong of the army's offensive, divided his troops and ordered an attack. On June 25, he spotted signs of the Indians' camp. Crying "Hurrah Boys, we've got them," he led 265 men of the Seventh Cavalry into the largest gathering of Indians ever assembled on the Great Plains (more than 8,000) camped along the banks of the Greasy Grass River (whites called it the Little Big Horn). Indian warriors led by Sitting Bull and Crazy Horse set upon Custer and his men and quickly annihilated them. "It took us about as long as a hungry man to eat his dinner," the Cheyenne chief Two Moons recalled.

"Custer's Last Stand," as the **Battle of the Little Big Horn** was styled in myth, turned out to be the last stand for the Sioux. The nomadic bands that had massed at the Little Big Horn scattered, and the army hunted them down. "Wherever we went," wrote the Oglala holy man Black Elk, "the soldiers came to kill us." In 1877, Crazy Horse was captured and killed. Four years later, in 1881, Sitting Bull surrendered. The government took the Black Hills and confined the Lakota to the reservation. The Sioux never accepted the loss of the Black Hills. In 1923, they filed suit, demanding the return of the land illegally taken from them. After a protracted court battle lasting nearly sixty years, the U.S. Supreme Court ruled in 1980 that the government had illegally violated the Treaty of Fort Laramie and upheld an award of $122.5 million in compensation to the tribes. The Sioux refused the settlement and continue to press for the return of the Black Hills.

Battle of the Little Big Horn

▶ 1876 battle begun when American cavalry under George Armstrong Custer attacked an encampment of Indians who refused to remove to a reservation. Indian warriors led by Crazy Horse and Sitting Bull annihilated the American soldiers, but their victory was short-lived.

QUICK REVIEW <

How did the slaughter of the bison contribute to the Plains Indians' removal to reservations?

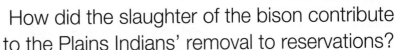

| In what ways did different Indian groups defy and resist colonial rule? | How did mining shape American expansion? | How did the fight for land and resources in the West unfold? | Conclusion: How did the West set the tone for the Gilded Age? | 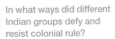 LearningCurve Check what you know. bedfordstmartins.com /roarkunderstanding |

In what ways did different Indian groups defy and resist colonial rule?

Ghost Dancers Arapaho women at the Darlington Agency in Indian Territory (Oklahoma) participate in the Ghost Dance. Different tribes performed variations of the dance, but generally dancers formed a circle and danced until they reached the trancelike state shown here. Whites feared the dancers and demanded that the army dispatch troops to subdue them. The result was the killing of Sitting Bull and the massacre at Wounded Knee. National Anthropological Archives, Smithsonian Institution, Washington, D.C. (#81-9626).

> CHRONOLOGY

1877
– Chief Joseph surrenders.

1879
– Carlisle Indian School opens.

1886
– Geronimo surrenders.

1887
– Dawes Allotment Act.

1889
– Rise of Ghost Dance.

1890
– Sitting Bull is killed.
– Massacre at Wounded Knee, South Dakota.

IMPERIALISTIC ATTITUDES of whites toward Indians continued to evolve in the late nineteenth century. To "civilize" the Indians, the U.S. government sought to force assimilation on their children. Reservations became increasingly unpopular among whites who coveted Indian land. A new policy of allotment gained favor. It promised to put Indians on parcels of land, forcing them into farming, and then to redistribute the rest of the land to settlers. In the face of this ongoing assault on their way of life, Indians actively resisted, contested, and adapted to colonial rule.

Indian Schools and the War on Indian Culture

Indian schools constituted the cultural battleground of the Indian wars in the West, their avowed purpose being "to destroy the Indian . . . and save the man." In 1877,

CHAPTER LOCATOR | What did U.S. expansion mean for Native Americans?

Congress appropriated funds for Indian education, reasoning that it was less expensive to educate Indians than to kill them. Virginia's Hampton Institute, created in 1868 to school newly freed slaves, accepted its first Indian students in 1878. Although many Indian schools operated on the reservations, authorities much preferred boarding facilities that isolated students from the "contamination" of tribal values.

Many Native American parents resisted sending their children away. When all else failed, the military kidnapped the children and sent them off to school. An agent at the Mescalero Apache Agency in Arizona Territory reported in 1886 that "it became necessary to visit the camps unexpectedly with a detachment of police, and seize such children as were proper and take them away to school, willing or unwilling." The parents put up a struggle. "Some hurried their children off to the mountains or hid them away in camp, and the police had to chase and capture them like so many wild rabbits," the agent observed. "This unusual proceeding created quite an outcry. The men were sullen and muttering, the women loud in their lamentations and the children almost out of their wits with fright."

Once at school, the children were stripped and scrubbed, their clothing and belongings confiscated, and their hair hacked off and doused with kerosene to kill lice. Issued stiff new uniforms, shoes, and what one boy recalled as the "torture" of woolen long underwear, the children often lost not only their possessions but also their names: Hehakaavita (Yellow Elk) became Thomas Goodwood; Polingaysi Qoyawayma became Elizabeth White.

The **Carlisle Indian School** in Pennsylvania, founded in 1879, became the model for later institutions. To encourage assimilation, Carlisle pioneered the "outing system" — sending students to live with white families during summer vacations. The policy reflected the school's slogan: "To civilize the Indian, get him into civilization. To keep him civilized, let him stay."

Carlisle Indian School

▶ Institution established in Pennsylvania in 1879 to educate and assimilate American Indians. It pioneered the "outing system" in which Indian students were sent to live with white families in order to accelerate acculturation.

In what ways did different Indian groups defy and resist colonial rule?

How did mining shape American expansion?

How did the fight for land and resources in the West unfold?

Conclusion: How did the West set the tone for the Gilded Age?

✔ LearningCurve
Check what you know.
bedfordstmartins.com/roarkunderstanding

Merrill Gates, a member of the Board of Indian Commissioners, summed up the goal of Indian education: "To get the Indian out of the blanket and into trousers, — *and trousers with a pocket in them, and with a pocket that aches to be filled with dollars!*" Gates's faith in the "civilizing" power of the dollar reflected the unabashed materialism of the age.

The Dawes Act and Indian Land Allotment

In the 1880s, the practice of rounding up Indians and herding them onto reservations lost momentum in favor of allotment — a new policy designed to encourage assimilation through farming and the ownership of private property. Americans vowing to avenge Custer urged the government to get tough with the Indians. Reservations, they argued, took up too much good land that white settlers could put to better use. At the same time, people sympathetic to the Indians were appalled at the desperate poverty on the reservations and feared for the Indians' survival. Helen Hunt Jackson, in her classic work *A Century of Dishonor* (1881), convinced many readers that the Indians had been treated unfairly. "Our Indian policy," the *New York Times* concluded, "is usually spoliation behind the mask of benevolence."

The Indian Rights Association, a group of mainly white easterners formed in 1882, campaigned for the dismantling of the reservations, now viewed as obstacles to progress. To "cease to treat the Indian as a red man and treat him as a man" meant putting an end to tribal communalism and fostering individualism. "Selfishness," declared Senator Henry Dawes of Massachusetts, "is at the bottom of civilization." Dawes called for "allotment in severalty" — the institution of private property.

In 1887, Congress passed the **Dawes Allotment Act**, dividing up reservations and allotting parcels of land to individual Indians as private property.

Dawes Allotment Act

▶ 1887 law that divided up reservations and allotted parcels of land to individual Indians as private property. In the end, the U.S. government sold almost two-thirds of "surplus" Indian land to white settlers. The Dawes Act dealt a crippling blow to traditional tribal culture.

> **Provisions of the Dawes Allotment Act**

- Indian heads of household received an allotment of 160 acres from reservation lands.
- Single persons over eighteen and orphans under eighteen received 80 acres.
- Indians who took allotments earned U.S. citizenship.
- The government reserved the right to sell "surplus" reservation lands to white settlers.

The Dawes Act effectively reduced Indian land from 138 million acres to a scant 48 million. The legislation, in the words of one critic, worked "to despoil the Indians of their lands and to make them vagabonds on the face of the earth." By 1890, the United States controlled 97.5 percent of the territory formerly occupied by Native Americans.

Indian Resistance and Survival

Faced with the extinction of their entire way of life, different groups of Indians responded in different ways. In the 1870s, Comanche and Kiowa raiding parties

CHAPTER LOCATOR | What did U.S. expansion mean for Native Americans?

496 CHAPTER 17 CONTESTING THE WEST

frustrated the U.S. Army by brazenly using the reservations as a seasonal supply base during the winter months. When spring came, they resumed their nomadic hunting way of life.

Some tribes, including the Crow and Shoshoni, chose to fight alongside the army against their old enemies, the Sioux. The Crow chief Plenty Coups explained why he allied with the United States: "Not because we loved the white man . . . or because we hated the Sioux . . . but because we plainly saw that this course was the only one which might save our beautiful country for us." The Crow and Shoshoni got to stay in their homelands and avoided the fate of other tribes shipped to reservations far away.

Indians who refused to stay on reservations risked being hunted down. The Nez Percé war is perhaps the most harrowing example of the army's policy. In 1863, the government dictated a treaty drastically reducing Nez Percé land. Most of the chiefs refused to sign the treaty and did not move to the reservation. When the army cracked down in 1877, some eight hundred Nez Percé people, many of them women and children, fled across the mountains of Idaho, Wyoming, and Montana, heading for the safety of Canada. At the end of their 1,300-mile trek, 50 miles from freedom, they stopped to rest in the snow. The army caught up with them and attacked. Yellow Wolf recalled their plight: "Children crying with cold. No fire. There could be no light. Everywhere the crying, the death wail." After a five-day siege, the Nez Percé leader, Chief Joseph, surrendered. His speech, reported by a white soldier, would become famous. "I am tired of fighting," he said as he surrendered his rifle. "Our chiefs are killed. It is cold and we have no blankets. The little children are freezing to death. . . . I am tired. My heart is sick and sad. From where the sun now stands, I will fight no more forever."

In the Southwest, the Apaches resorted to armed resistance. They roamed the Sonoran Desert of southern Arizona and northern Mexico, perfecting a hit-and-run guerrilla warfare that terrorized white settlers and bedeviled the army in the 1870s and 1880s. General George Crook combined a policy of dogged pursuit with judicious diplomacy. Crook relied on Indian scouts to track the raiding parties, recruiting nearly two hundred Apaches, Navajos, and Paiutes. By 1882, Crook had succeeded in persuading most of the Apaches to settle on the San Carlos Reservation in Arizona Territory. A desolate piece of desert inhabited by scorpions and rattlesnakes, San Carlos, in the words of one Apache, was "the worst place in all the great territory stolen from the Apaches."

Geronimo, a respected shaman (medicine man) of the Chiricahua Apache, refused to stay at San Carlos and repeatedly led raiding parties in the early 1880s. His warriors attacked ranches to obtain ammunition and horses. Among

Chief Joseph

Chief Joseph came to symbolize the heroic resistance of the Nez Percé. General Nelson Miles promised the Nez Percé that they could return to their homeland if they surrendered. But he betrayed them, as he would betray the Apache people seven years later. The Nez Percé were shipped off to Indian Territory (Oklahoma). National Anthropological Archives, Smithsonian Institution, Washington, D.C. (#2906).

In what ways did different Indian groups defy and resist colonial rule?

How did mining shape American expansion?

How did the fight for land and resources in the West unfold?

Conclusion: How did the West set the tone for the Gilded Age?

✓ LearningCurve Check what you know. bedfordstmartins.com /roarkunderstanding

Geronimo's band was Lozen, a woman who rode with the warriors, armed with a rifle and a cartridge belt. The sister of a great chief described her as being as "strong as a man, braver than most, and cunning in strategy." In the spring of 1885, Geronimo and his followers, including Lozen, went on a ten-month offensive, moving from the Apache sanctuary in the Sierra Madre to raid and burn ranches and towns on both sides of the Mexican border. General Crook caught up with Geronimo in the fall and persuaded him to return to San Carlos, only to have him slip away on the way back to the reservation. Chagrined, Crook resigned his post. General Nelson Miles, Crook's replacement, adopted a policy of hunt and destroy.

Geronimo's band of thirty-three Apaches, including women and children, eluded Miles's troops for more than five months. The pursuit left Miles's cavalry ragged. Over time, Lieutenant Leonard Wood had discarded his horse and was reduced to wearing nothing "but a pair of canton flannel drawers, and an old blouse, a pair of moccasins and a hat without a crown." Eventually, Miles's scouts cornered Geronimo in 1886 at Skeleton Canyon, where he agreed to march north and negotiate a settlement. "We have not slept for six months," he admitted, "and we are worn out." After General Miles induced them to surrender, the government rounded up nearly five hundred Apaches and sent them as prisoners to the South, even though fewer than three dozen Apaches had been considered "hostile." By 1889, more than a quarter of them had died, some as a result of illnesses contracted in the damp lowland climate of Florida and Alabama and some by suicide. Their plight roused public opinion, and in 1892 they were moved to Fort Sill in Oklahoma and later to New Mexico.

Geronimo lived to become something of a celebrity. He appeared at the St. Louis Exposition in 1904, and he rode in President Theodore Roosevelt's inaugural parade in 1905. In a newspaper interview, he confessed, "I want to go to my old home before I die. . . . Want to go back to the mountains again. I asked the Great White Father to allow me to go back, but he said no." None of the Apaches were permitted to return to Arizona; when Geronimo died in 1909, he was buried in Oklahoma.

On the plains, many tribes turned to a nonviolent form of resistance — a compelling new religion called the **Ghost Dance**. The Paiute shaman Wovoka, drawing on a cult that had developed in the 1870s, combined elements of Christianity and traditional Indian religion to found the Ghost Dance religion in 1889. Wovoka claimed that he had received a vision in which the Great Spirit spoke through him to all Indians, prophesying that if they would unite in the Ghost Dance ritual, whites would be destroyed in an apocalypse and the buffalo would return. His religion, born of despair and with a message of hope, spread like wildfire over the plains. The Ghost Dance was performed in Idaho, Montana, Utah, Wyoming, Colorado, Nebraska, Kansas, the Dakotas, and Indian Territory by tribes as diverse as the Sioux, Arapaho, Cheyenne, Pawnee, and Shoshoni. Dancers often went into hypnotic trances, dancing until they dropped from exhaustion.

The Ghost Dance was nonviolent, but it frightened whites, especially when the Sioux taught that wearing a white ghost shirt made Indians immune to soldiers' bullets. Soon whites began to fear an uprising. "Indians are dancing in the snow and are wild and crazy," wrote the Bureau of Indian Affairs agent at the Pine Ridge Reservation in South Dakota. Frantic, he pleaded for reinforcements.

Ghost Dance

▶ Religion founded in 1889 by Paiute shaman Wovoka. It combined elements of Christianity and traditional Indian religion and served as a nonviolent form of resistance for Indians in the late nineteenth century. The Ghost Dance frightened whites and was violently suppressed.

"We are at the mercy of these dancers. We need protection, and we need it now."
President Benjamin Harrison dispatched several thousand federal troops to Sioux
country to handle any outbreak.

In December 1890, when Sitting Bull attempted to join the Ghost Dance, he
was killed by Indian police as they tried to arrest him at his cabin on the Standing
Rock Reservation. His people, fleeing the scene, joined with a larger group of
Miniconjou Sioux, who were apprehended by the Seventh Cavalry, Custer's old
regiment, near Wounded Knee Creek, South Dakota. As the Indians laid down
their arms, a soldier attempted to take a rifle from a deaf Miniconjou man, and the
gun went off. The soldiers opened fire. In the ensuing melee, more than two hundred Indian men, women, and children were mowed down in minutes by the
army's brutally efficient Hotchkiss rapid-fire guns. Settler Jules Sandoz surveyed
the scene the day after the massacre at **Wounded Knee**. "Here in ten minutes an
entire community was as the buffalo that bleached on the plains," he wrote.
"There was something loose in the world that hated joy and happiness as it hated
brightness and color, reducing everything to drab agony and gray."

It had taken Euro-Americans 250 years to wrest control of the eastern half of
the United States from the Indians. It took them less than 40 years to take the
western half. The subjugation of the American Indians marked the first chapter in
a national mission of empire that would anticipate overseas imperialistic adventures in Asia, Latin America, the Caribbean, and the Pacific islands.

Wounded Knee
▶ 1890 massacre of Sioux
Indians by the Seventh Cavalry
at Wounded Knee Creek, South
Dakota. Sent to suppress the
Ghost Dance, the soldiers
opened fire on the Sioux as they
attempted to surrender. More
than two hundred Sioux men,
women, and children were killed.

QUICK REVIEW

How and why did U.S. Indian policy
change between 1870 and 1890?

In what ways did
different Indian groups
defy and resist colonial
rule?

How did mining shape
American expansion?

How did the fight for
land and resources in the
West unfold?

Conclusion: How did
the West set the tone for
the Gilded Age?

☑ LearningCurve
Check what you know.
bedfordstmartins.com
/roarkunderstanding

How did mining shape American expansion?

"Mining on the Comstock" This illustration, made at Gold Hill, Nevada, in 1876, shows a sectional view of a mine, highlighting the square-set timber method. Note also the tunnels, incline, cooling-off room, blower, and air shaft, along with a collection of miner's tools. Mines like this one honeycombed the hills of Gold City and neighboring Virginia City on the Comstock Lode in Nevada. University of California at Berkeley, Bancroft Library.

Comstock Lode

▶ Silver ore deposit discovered in 1859 in Nevada. Discovery of the Comstock Lode touched off a mining rush that brought a diverse population into the region and led to the establishment of a number of boomtowns, including Virginia City, Nevada.

MINING STOOD AT THE CENTER of the United States' quest for empire in the West. The California gold rush of 1849 touched off the frenzy. The four decades following witnessed equally frenetic rushes for gold and other metals, most notably on the **Comstock Lode** in Nevada and later in New Mexico, Colorado, the Dakotas, Montana, Idaho, Arizona, and Utah (**Map 17.2**). At first glance, the mining West may seem much different from the East, but by the 1870s the term *urban industrialism* described Virginia City, Nevada, as accurately as it did Pittsburgh or Cleveland. A close look at life on the Comstock Lode indicates some of the patterns and paradoxes of western mining. The diversity of peoples drawn to the West by the promise of mining riches and land made the region the most cosmopolitan in the nation, as well as the most contested.

Life on the Comstock Lode

By 1859, refugees from California's played-out goldfields flocked to the Washoe basin in Nevada. While searching for gold, Washoe miners stumbled on the richest vein of silver ore on the continent — the legendary Comstock Lode, named for prospector Henry Comstock.

CHAPTER LOCATOR | What did U.S. expansion mean for Native Americans?

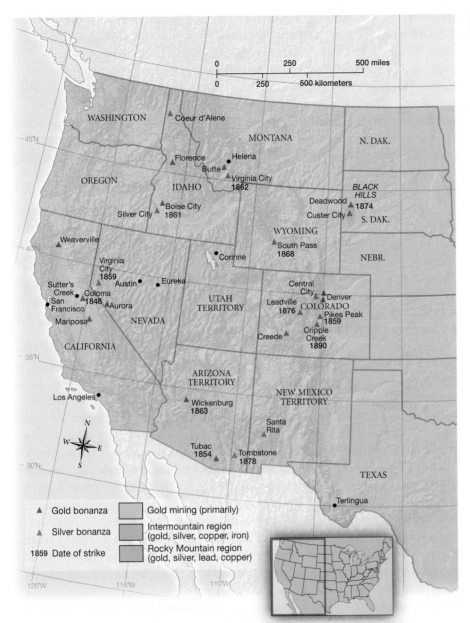

MAP 17.2 ■ Western Mining, 1848–1890

Rich deposits of gold, silver, copper, lead, and iron larded the mountains of the West. Miners from all over the world flocked to the mines. Few struck it rich, but many stayed on as paid workers in the increasingly mechanized corporate mines.

▲ Gold bonanza

▲ Silver bonanza

1859 Date of strike

Gold mining (primarily)

Intermountain region (gold, silver, copper, iron)

Rocky Mountain region (gold, silver, lead, copper)

To exploit even potentially valuable silver claims required capital and expensive technology well beyond the means of the prospector. An active San Francisco stock market sprang up to finance operations on the Comstock. Shrewd businessmen soon recognized that the easiest way to get rich was to sell their claims or to form mining companies and sell shares of stock. The most unscrupulous mined the wallets of gullible investors by selling shares in bogus mines. Speculation, misrepresentation, and outright thievery ran rampant. In twenty years, more than $300 million poured from the earth in Nevada alone, most of it going to speculators in San Francisco.

The promise of gold and silver drew thousands to the mines of the West. As Mark Twain observed in Virginia City's *Territorial Enterprise*, "All the peoples of

In what ways did different Indian groups defy and resist colonial rule?

How did mining shape American expansion?

How did the fight for land and resources in the West unfold?

Conclusion: How did the West set the tone for the Gilded Age?

✓ LearningCurve
Check what you know.
bedfordstmartins.com
/roarkunderstanding

501

the earth had representative adventures in the Silverland." Irish, Chinese, Germans, English, Scots, Welsh, Canadians, Mexicans, Italians, Scandinavians, French, Swiss, Chileans, and other South and Central Americans came to share in the bonanza. With them came a sprinkling of Russians, Poles, Greeks, Japanese, Spaniards, Hungarians, Portuguese, Turks, Pacific Islanders, and Moroccans, as well as other North Americans, African Americans, and American Indians. This polyglot population, typical of mining boomtowns, made Virginia City in the 1870s more cosmopolitan than New York or Boston. In the part of Utah Territory that eventually became Nevada, as many as 30 percent of the people came from outside the United States, compared with 25 percent in New York and 21 percent in Massachusetts.

Irish immigrants formed the largest ethnic group in the mining district. In Virginia City, fully one-third of the population claimed at least one parent from Ireland. Irish women constituted the largest group of women on the Comstock. As servants, boardinghouse owners, and washerwomen, they made up a significant part of the workforce. By contrast, the Chinese community, numbering 642 in 1870, remained overwhelmingly male. Virulent anti-Chinese sentiment barred the men from work in the mines, but despite the violent anti-Asian rhetoric, the mining community came to depend on Chinese labor.

The discovery of precious metals on the Comstock spelled disaster for the Indians. No sooner had the miners struck pay dirt than they demanded that army troops "hunt Indians" and establish forts to protect transportation to and from the diggings. This sudden and dramatic intrusion left Nevada's native tribes — the Northern Paiute and Bannock Shoshoni — exiles in their own land. At first they resisted, but over time they adapted and preserved their culture and identity despite the havoc wreaked by western mining and settlement.

In 1873, Comstock miners uncovered a new vein of ore, a veritable cavern of gold and silver. This "Big Bonanza" speeded the transition from small-scale industry to corporate oligopoly, creating a radically new social and economic environment. The Comstock became a laboratory for new mining technology. Huge stamping mills pulverized rock with pistonlike hammers driven by steam engines. Enormous Cornish pumps sucked water from the mine shafts, and huge ventilators circulated air in the underground chambers. No backwoods mining camp, Virginia City was an industrial center with more than 1,200 stamping mills working on average a ton of ore every day. Almost 400 men worked in milling, nearly 300 labored in manufacturing industries, and roughly 3,000 toiled in the mines. The Gould and Curry mine covered sixty acres. Most of the miners who came to the Comstock ended up as laborers for the big companies.

New technology eliminated some of the dangers of mining but often created new ones. In the hard-rock mines of the West, accidents in the 1870s disabled one out of every thirty miners and killed one in eighty. Ross Moudy, who worked as a miner in Cripple Creek, Colorado, recalled how a stockholder visiting the mine nearly fell to his death. The terrified visitor told the miner next to him that "instead of being paid $3 a day, they ought to have all the gold they could take out." On the Comstock Lode, because of the difficulty of obtaining skilled labor, the richness of the ore, and the need for a stable workforce, labor unions formed early and held considerable bargaining power. Comstock miners commanded $4 a day, the highest wage in the mining West.

CHAPTER LOCATOR | What did U.S. expansion mean for Native Americans?

The mining towns of the "Wild West" are often portrayed as lawless outposts, filled with saloons and rough gambling dens and populated almost exclusively by men. The truth is more complex, as Virginia City's development attests. An established urban community built to serve an industrial giant, Virginia City in its first decade boasted churches, schools, theaters, an opera house, and hundreds of families. By 1870, women composed 30 percent of the population, and 75 percent of the women listed their occupation in the census as housekeeper. Mary McNair Mathews, a widow from Buffalo, New York, who lived on the Comstock in the 1870s, worked as a teacher, nurse, seamstress, laundress, and lodging-house operator. She later published a book on her adventures.

By 1875, Virginia City boasted a population of 25,000 people, making it one of the largest cities between St. Louis and San Francisco. The city, dubbed the "Queen of the Comstock," hosted American presidents as well as legions of lesser dignitaries. Virginia City represented, in the words of a recent chronicler, "the distilled essence of America's newly established course — urban, industrial, acquisitive, and materialistic, on the move, 'a living polyglot' of cultures that collided and converged."

The Diverse Peoples of the West

The West of the late nineteenth century was a polyglot place, as much so as the big cities of the East. The sheer number of peoples who mingled in the West produced a complex blend of racism and prejudice. One historian has noted, not entirely facetiously, that there were at least eight oppressed "races" in the West — Indians, Latinos, Chinese, Japanese, blacks, Mormons, strikers, and radicals.

African Americans who ventured out to the territories faced hostile settlers determined to keep the West "for whites only." In response, they formed all-black communities such as Nicodemas, Kansas. That settlement, founded by thirty black Kentuckians in 1877, grew to a community of seven hundred by 1880. Isolated and often separated by great distances, small black settlements grew up throughout the West, in Nevada, Utah, and the Pacific Northwest, as well as in Kansas. Black soldiers who served in the West during the Indian wars often stayed on as settlers. Called buffalo soldiers because Native Americans thought their hair resembled that of the bison, these black troops numbered up to 25,000. In the face of discrimination, poor treatment, and harsh conditions, the buffalo soldiers served with distinction and boasted the lowest desertion rate in the army.

Hispanic peoples had lived in Texas and the Southwest since Juan de Oñate led pioneer settlers up the Rio Grande in 1598. Hispanics had occupied the Pacific coast since San Diego was founded in 1769. Overnight, they were reduced to a "minority" after the United States annexed Texas in 1845 and took land stretching to California after the Mexican-American War ended in 1848. At first, the Hispanic owners of large *ranchos* in California, New Mexico, and Texas greeted conquest as an economic opportunity. But racial prejudice soon ended their optimism. Californios (Mexican residents of California), who had been granted American citizenship by the Treaty of Guadalupe Hidalgo (1848), faced discrimination by Anglos who sought to keep them out of California's mines and commerce. Whites illegally squatted on *rancho* land while protracted litigation over Spanish and Mexican land grants forced the Californios into court. Although the U.S. Supreme Court eventually

In what ways did different Indian groups defy and resist colonial rule?

How did mining shape American expansion?

How did the fight for land and resources in the West unfold?

Conclusion: How did the West set the tone for the Gilded Age?

✔ LearningCurve
Check what you know.
bedfordstmartins.com
/roarkunderstanding

503

validated most of their claims, it took so long — seventeen years on average — that many Californios sold their property to pay taxes and legal bills.

Swindles, trickery, and intimidation dispossessed scores of Californios. Many ended up segregated in urban barrios (neighborhoods) in their own homeland. Their percentage of California's population declined from 82 percent in 1850 to 19 percent in 1880 as Anglos migrated to the state. In New Mexico and Texas, Mexicans remained a majority of the population but became increasingly impoverished as Anglos dominated business and took the best jobs. Skirmishes between Hispanics and whites in northern New Mexico over the fencing of the open range lasted for decades. Groups of Hispanics with names such as *Las Manos Negras* (the Black Hands) cut fences and burned barns. In Texas, violence along the Rio Grande pitted Tejanos (Mexican residents of Texas) against the Texas Rangers, who saw their role as "keeping Mexicans in their place."

Like the Mexicans, the Mormons faced prejudice and hostility. The followers of Joseph Smith, the founder and prophet of the Church of Jesus Christ of Latter-Day Saints, fled west to Utah Territory in 1844 to avoid religious persecution. They believed they had a divine right to the land, and their messianic militancy made others distrust them. The Mormon practice of polygamy (church leader Brigham Young had twenty-seven wives) also came under attack. To counter the criticism of polygamy, the Utah territorial legislature gave women the right to vote in 1870, the first universal woman suffrage act in the nation. (Wyoming had granted suffrage to white women in 1869.) Although women's rights advocates argued that the newly enfranchised women would "do away with the horrible institution of polygamy," it remained in force. Not until 1890 did the church hierarchy yield to pressure and renounce polygamy. The fierce controversy over polygamy postponed statehood for Utah until 1896.

Of all the newcomers, the Chinese suffered the most brutal treatment at the hands of employers and other laborers. Drawn by the promise of gold, more than 20,000 Chinese had joined the rush to California by 1852. Miners determined to keep "California for Americans" succeeded in passing prohibitive foreign license laws to keep the Chinese out of the mines. But Chinese immigration continued. In the 1860s, when white workers moved on to find riches in the bonanza mines of Nevada, Chinese laborers took jobs abandoned by the whites. Railroad magnate Charles Crocker hired Chinese gangs to work on the Central Pacific, reasoning that "the race that built the Great Wall" could lay tracks across the treacherous Sierra Nevada. Some 12,000 Chinese, representing 90 percent of Crocker's workforce, completed America's first transcontinental railroad in 1869.

By 1870, more than 63,000 Chinese immigrants lived in America, 77 percent of them in California. A 1790 federal statute that limited naturalization to "white persons" was modified after the Civil War to extend naturalization to blacks ("persons of African descent"). But the Chinese and other Asians continued to be denied access to citizenship. As perpetual aliens, they constituted a reserve army of transnational laborers that many saw as a threat to American labor.

In 1876, the Workingmen's Party formed to fight for Chinese exclusion. Racial and cultural animosities stood at the heart of anti-Chinese agitation. Denis Kearney, the fiery San Francisco leader of the movement, made clear this racist bent when he urged legislation to "expel every one of the moon-eyed lepers." Nor

CHAPTER LOCATOR | What did U.S. expansion mean for Native Americans?

504 CHAPTER 17 CONTESTING THE WEST

Chinese Workers

Chinese section hands, wearing their distinctive conical hats, are shown here working on a railroad. Charles Crocker was the first to hire Chinese laborers to work on the Central Pacific railroad in the 1860s, reasoning that the race that built the Great Wall could build tracks through the Sierra Nevada. California Historical Society, FN-25345.

was California alone in its anti-immigrant nativism. As the country confronted growing ethnic and racial diversity with the rising tide of global immigration in the decades following the Civil War, many questioned the principle of racial equality at the same time they argued against the assimilation of "nonwhite" groups. In this climate, Congress passed the **Chinese Exclusion Act** in 1882, effectively barring Chinese immigration and setting a precedent for further immigration restrictions.

The Chinese Exclusion Act led to a sharp drop in the Chinese population — from 105,465 in 1880 to 89,863 in 1900 — because Chinese immigrants, overwhelmingly male, did not have families to sustain their population. Eventually, Japanese immigrants, including women as well as men, replaced the Chinese, particularly in agriculture. As "nonwhite" immigrants, they could not become naturalized citizens, but their children born in the United States claimed the rights of citizenship. Japanese parents, seeking to own land, purchased it in their children's names. Although anti-Asian prejudice remained strong in California and elsewhere in the West, Asian immigrants formed an important part of the economic fabric of the western United States.

Chinese Exclusion Act

▶ 1882 law that effectively barred Chinese immigration and set a precedent for further immigration restrictions. The Chinese population in America dropped sharply as a result of the passage of the act, which was fueled by racial and cultural animosities.

QUICK REVIEW <

What role did mining play in shaping the society and economy of the American West?

In what ways did different Indian groups defy and resist colonial rule?	**How did mining shape American expansion?**	How did the fight for land and resources in the West unfold?	Conclusion: How did the West set the tone for the Gilded Age?	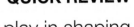 LearningCurve Check what you know. bedfordstmartins.com /roarkunderstanding

505

How did the fight for land and resources in the West unfold?

Railroad Locomotive In the years following the Civil War, the locomotive replaced the covered wagon, enabling settlers to travel from Chicago or St. Louis to the West Coast in two days. The first transcontinental railroad, completed in 1869, soon led to the creation of competing systems, so that by the 1880s travelers going west could choose from four railroad lines. Library of Congress.

Homestead Act of 1862
▶ An act that promised 160 acres in the trans-Mississippi West free to any citizen or prospective citizen who settled on the land for five years. The act spurred American settlement of the West. Altogether, nearly one-tenth of the United States was granted to settlers.

first transcontinental railroad
▶ Railroad completed in 1869 that was the first to span the North American continent. Built in large part by Chinese laborers, this railroad and others opened access to new areas, fueled land speculation, and actively recruited settlers.

IN THE THREE DECADES following 1870, more land was settled than in all the previous history of the country. Americans by the hundreds of thousands packed up and moved west, goaded if not by the hope of striking gold, then by the promise of owning land to farm or ranch. The agrarian West shared with the mining West a persistent restlessness, an equally pervasive addiction to speculation, and a penchant for exploiting natural resources and labor.

Two factors stimulated the land rush in the trans-Mississippi West. The **Homestead Act of 1862** promised 160 acres free to any citizen or prospective citizen, male or female, who settled on the land for five years. Even more important, transcontinental railroads opened up new areas and actively recruited settlers. After the completion of the **first transcontinental railroad** in 1869, homesteaders abandoned the covered wagon, and by the 1880s they could choose from four competing rail lines and make the trip west in a matter of days.

CHAPTER LOCATOR | What did U.S. expansion mean for Native Americans?

Although the country was rich in land and resources, not all who wanted to own land achieved their goal. During the transition from the family farm to large commercial farming, small farms and ranches gave way to vast spreads worked by migrant labor or paid farmworkers and cowhands. Just as industry corporatized and consolidated in the East, the period from 1870 to 1900 witnessed corporate consolidation in mining, ranching, and agriculture.

Moving West: Homesteaders and Speculators

A Missouri homesteader remembered packing as her family pulled up stakes and headed west to Oklahoma in 1890. "We were going to God's Country," she wrote. "You had to work hard on that rocky country in Missouri. I was glad to be leaving it. . . . We were going to a new land and get rich."

Settlers who headed west in search of "God's Country" faced hardship, loneliness, and deprivation. To carve a farm from the raw prairie of Iowa, the plains of Nebraska, or the forests of the Pacific Northwest took more than fortitude and backbreaking toil. It took luck. Blizzards, tornadoes, grasshoppers, hailstorms, drought, prairie fires, accidental death, and disease were only a few of the catastrophes that could befall even the best farmer. Homesteaders on free land still needed as much as $1,000 for a house, a team of farm animals, a well, fencing, and seed. Poor farmers called "sodbusters" did without even these basics, living in houses made from sod (blocks of grass-covered earth) or dugouts carved into hillsides and using muscle instead of machinery.

"Father made a dugout and covered it with willows and grass," one Kansas girl recounted. When it rained, the dugout flooded, and "we carried the water out in buckets, then waded around in the mud until it dried." Rain wasn't the only problem. "Sometimes the bull snakes would get in the roof and now and then one would lose his hold and fall down on the bed. . . . Mother would grab the hoe . . . and after the fight was over Mr. Bull Snake was dragged outside."

For women on the frontier, obtaining simple daily necessities such as water and fuel meant backbreaking labor. Out on the plains, where water was scarce, women often had to trudge to the nearest creek or spring. "A yoke was made to place across [Mother's] shoulders, so as to carry at each end a bucket of water," one daughter recollected, "and then water was brought a half mile from spring to house." Gathering fuel was another heavy chore. Without ready sources of coal or firewood, the most prevalent fuel was "chips" — chunks of dried cattle and buffalo dung, found in abundance on the plains.

Despite the hardships, some homesteaders succeeded in building comfortable lives. The dugout made way for the sod hut — a more substantial dwelling; the log cabin yielded to a white clapboard home with a porch and a rocking chair. For others, the promise of the West failed to materialize. Already by the 1870s, much of the best land had been taken. Too often, homesteaders found that only the least desirable tracts were left — poor land, far from markets, transportation, and society. "There is plenty of land for sale in California," one migrant complained in 1870, but "the majority of the available lands are held by speculators, at prices far beyond the reach of a poor man." The railroads, flush from land grants provided by the state and federal governments, owned huge swaths of

> CHRONOLOGY

1862
– Homestead Act.

1869
– First transcontinental railroad is completed.

1879
– Exodusters move to Kansas.

1886–1887
– Severe blizzards decimate cattle.

1889
– Two million acres in Oklahoma are opened for settlement.

1893
– Last land rush in Oklahoma Territory.

Midwestern Settlement before 1862

In what ways did different Indian groups defy and resist colonial rule?

How did mining shape American expansion?

How did the fight for land and resources in the West unfold?

Conclusion: How did the West set the tone for the Gilded Age?

✓ LearningCurve
Check what you know.
bedfordstmartins.com
/roarkunderstanding

507

land in the West and actively recruited buyers. Altogether, the land grants totaled approximately 180 million acres — an area almost one-tenth the size of the United States (**Map 17.3**). Of the 2.5 million farms established between 1860 and 1900, homesteading accounted for only one in five; the vast majority of farmland sold for a profit.

As land grew scarce on the prairie in the 1870s, farmers began to push farther west, moving into western Kansas, Nebraska, and eastern Colorado — the region called the Great American Desert by settlers who had passed over it on their way to California and Oregon. Many agricultural experts warned that the semiarid land (where less than twenty inches of rain fell annually) would not support a farm on the 160 acres allotted to homesteaders. But their words of caution were drowned out by the extravagant claims of western promoters, many employed by the railroads to sell off their land grants. "Rain follows the plow" became the slogan of western boosters, who insisted that cultivation would alter the climate of the region and bring more rainfall. Instead, drought followed the plow. Droughts were a cyclical fact of life on the Great Plains. Plowed up, the dry topsoil blew away in the wind. A period of relatively good rainfall in the early 1880s encouraged farming; then a protracted drought in the late 1880s and early 1890s sent starving farmers reeling back from the plains. Thousands left, some in wagons carrying the slogan "In God we trusted, in Kansas we busted."

Fever for fertile land set off a series of spectacular land runs in Oklahoma. When two million acres of land in former Indian Territory opened for settlement in 1889, thousands of homesteaders massed on the border. At the opening pistol shot, "with a shout and a yell the swift riders shot out, then followed the light buggies or wagons," a reporter wrote. "Above all, a great cloud of dust hover[ed] like smoke over a battlefield." By nightfall, Oklahoma boasted two tent cities with more than ten thousand residents. In the last frenzied land rush on Oklahoma's Cherokee strip in 1893, several settlers were killed in the stampede, and nervous men guarded their claims with rifles. As public land grew scarce, the hunger for land grew fiercer for both farmers and ranchers.

Ranchers and Cowboys

Cattle ranchers followed the railroads onto the plains, establishing a cattle kingdom from Texas to Wyoming between 1865 and 1885. Cowboys drove huge herds, as many as three thousand head of cattle that grazed on public lands as they followed cattle tracks like the Chisholm Trail from Texas to railheads in Kansas.

Barbed wire, invented in 1874, revolutionized the cattle business and sounded the death knell for the open range. As the largest ranches in Texas began to fence, nasty fights broke out between big ranchers and "fence cutters," who resented the end of the open range. One old-timer observed, "Those persons, Mexicans and Americans, without land but who had cattle were put out of business by fencing." Fencing forced small-time ranchers who owned land but could not afford to buy barbed wire or sink wells to sell out for the best price they could get. The displaced ranchers, many of them Mexicans,

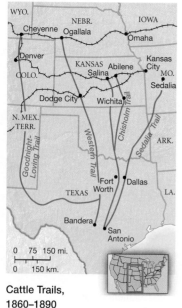

Cattle Trails, 1860–1890

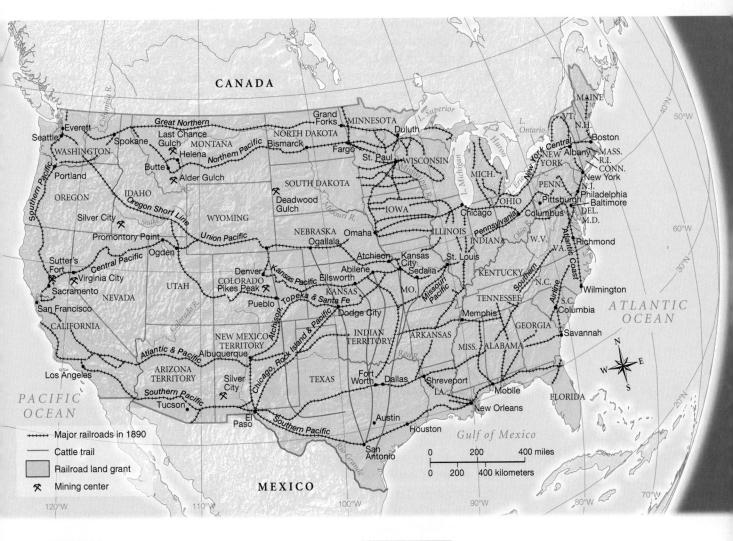

MAP 17.3 ■ Federal Land Grants to Railroads and the Development of the West, 1850–1900

Railroads received land grants totaling more than 180 million acres, an area as large as Texas. Built well ahead of demand, the western railroads courted settlers, often onto land not fit for farming.

> MAP ACTIVITY

READING THE MAP: Which mining cities and towns were located directly on a railroad line? Which towns were located at the junction of more than one line or railroad branch?

CONNECTIONS: In what ways did the growth of the railroads affect the population of the West? What western goods and products did the railroads help bring east and to ports for shipping around the world?

ended up as wageworkers on the huge spreads owned by Anglos or by European syndicates.

On the range, the cowboy gave way to the cattle king and, like the miner, became a wage laborer. Many cowboys were African Americans (as many as five thousand in Texas alone). Writers of western literature chose to ignore the presence of black cowboys like Deadwood Dick (Nat Love), who was portrayed as a white man in the dime novels of the era.

In what ways did different Indian groups defy and resist colonial rule?

How did mining shape American expansion?

How did the fight for land and resources in the West unfold?

Conclusion: How did the West set the tone for the Gilded Age?

✓ LearningCurve
Check what you know.
bedfordstmartins.com
/roarkunderstanding

By 1886, cattle overcrowded the range. Severe blizzards during the winter of 1886–87 decimated the herds. "A whole generation of cowmen," wrote one chronicler, "went dead broke." Fencing worsened the situation. During blizzards, cattle stayed alive by keeping on the move. But when they ran up against barbed wire fences, they froze to death. In the aftermath of the "Great Die Up," new labor-intensive forms of cattle ranching replaced the open-range model.

Tenants, Sharecroppers, and Migrants

In the post–Civil War period, as agriculture became a big business tied by the railroads to national and global markets, an increasing number of laborers worked land that they would never own. In the southern United States, farmers labored under particularly heavy burdens. The Civil War wiped out much of the region's capital, which had been invested in slaves, and crippled the plantation economy. Newly freed slaves rarely obtained land of their own and often ended up as farm laborers. "The colored folks stayed with the old boss man and farmed and worked on the plantations," a black Alabama sharecropper observed bitterly. "They were still slaves, but they were free slaves." Some freed people did manage to pull together enough resources to go west. In 1879, more than fifteen thousand black Exodusters, as the black settlers were known, moved from Mississippi and Louisiana to take up land in Kansas.

California's Mexican cowboys, or *vaqueros*, commanded decent wages throughout the Southwest. But by 1880, as the coming of the railroads ended the long cattle drives and as large feedlots began to replace the open range, the value of their skills declined. Many vaqueros ended up as migrant laborers, often on land their families had once owned. Similarly, in Texas, Tejanos (Mexican residents of Texas) found themselves displaced. After the heyday of cattle ranching ended in the late 1880s, cotton production rose in the southeastern regions of the state. Ranchers turned their pastures into sharecroppers' plots and hired displaced cowboys, most of them Mexicans, as seasonal laborers for as little as seventy-five cents a day, thereby creating a growing army of agricultural wageworkers.

Land monopoly and large-scale farming fostered tenancy and migratory labor on the West Coast. By the 1870s, less than 1 percent of California's population owned half the state's available agricultural land. The rigid economics of large-scale commercial agriculture and the seasonal nature of the crops spawned a ragged army of migratory agricultural laborers. Derisively labeled "blanket men" or "bindle stiffs," these transients worked the fields in the growing season and wintered in the flophouses of San Francisco. After passage of the Chinese Exclusion Act of 1882, Mexicans, Filipinos, and Japanese immigrants filled the demand for migratory workers.

Commercial Farming and Industrial Cowboys

In the late nineteenth century, the population of the United States remained overwhelmingly rural. The 1870 census showed that nearly 80 percent of the nation's people lived on farms and in villages of fewer than 8,000 inhabitants. By 1900, the figure had dropped to 66 percent (**Figure 17.1**). At the same time, the number of farms rose. Rapid growth in the West increased the number of the nation's farms from 2 million in 1860 to more than 5.7 million in 1900.

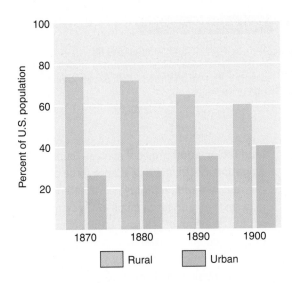

FIGURE 17.1 ■ Changes in Rural and Urban Populations, 1870–1900

Between 1870 and 1900, the number of urban dwellers increased; however, even as the number of rural inhabitants fell, the number of farms increased. Mechanization made it possible to farm with fewer hands, fueling the exodus from farm to city throughout the second half of the nineteenth century.

New technology and farming techniques revolutionized American farm life. Mechanized farm machinery halved the time and labor cost of production and made it possible to cultivate vast tracts of land. Meanwhile, urbanization provided farmers with expanding markets for their produce, and railroads carried crops to markets thousands of miles away. Even before the start of the twentieth century, American agriculture had entered the era of what would come to be called agribusiness — farming as a big business — with the advent of huge commercial farms.

As farming moved onto the prairies and plains, mechanization took command. Steel plows, reapers, mowers, harrows, seed drills, combines, and threshers replaced human muscle. Horse-drawn implements gave way to steam-powered machinery. By 1880, a single combine could do the work of twenty men, vastly increasing the acreage a farmer could cultivate. Mechanization spurred the growth of bonanza wheat farms, some more than 100,000 acres, in California and the Red River Valley of North Dakota and Minnesota. This agricultural revolution meant that Americans raised more than four times the corn, five times the hay, and seven times the wheat and oats they had before the Civil War.

Like cotton farmers in the South, western grain and livestock farmers increasingly depended on foreign markets for their livelihood. A fall in global market prices meant that a farmer's entire harvest went to pay off debts. In the depression that followed the panic of 1893, many heavily mortgaged farmers lost their land to creditors. As a Texas cotton farmer complained, "By the time the World Gets their Liveing out of the Farmer as we have to Feed the World, we the Farmer has nothing Left but a Bear Hard Liveing." Commercial farming, along with mining, represented another way in which the West developed its own brand of industrialism. The far West's industrial economy sprang initially from California gold and the vast territory that came under American control following the Mexican-American War. In the ensuing rush on land and resources, environmental factors interacted with economic and social forces to produce enterprises as vast in scale and scope as anything found in the East.

Two Alsatian immigrants, Henry Miller and Charles Lux, pioneered the West's mix of agriculture and industrialism. Beginning as meat wholesalers, Miller and Lux quickly expanded their business to encompass cattle, land, and

In what ways did different Indian groups defy and resist colonial rule?

How did mining shape American expansion?

How did the fight for land and resources in the West unfold?

Conclusion: How did the West set the tone for the Gilded Age?

Mechanical planters came into use in the 1860s. The Farmers Friend Manufacturing Company of Dayton, Ohio, advertised its lever and treadle corn planter in the early 1880s. Ohio History Society.

land reclamation projects such as dams and irrigation systems. With a labor force of migrant workers, a highly coordinated corporate system, and large sums of investment capital, the firm of Miller & Lux became one of America's industrial behemoths. Eventually, these "industrial cowboys" grazed a herd of 100,000 cattle on 1.25 million acres of company land in California, Oregon, and Nevada and employed more than 1,200 migrant laborers on their corporate ranches. Miller & Lux dealt with the labor problem by offering free meals to migratory workers, thus keeping wages low while winning goodwill among an army of unemployed who competed for the work. When the company's Chinese cooks rebelled at washing the dishes resulting from the free meals, the migrant laborers were forced to eat after the ranch hands and use their dirty plates. By the 1890s, more than eight hundred migrants a year followed what came to be known as the "Dirty Plate Route" on Miller & Lux ranches throughout California.

Since the days of Thomas Jefferson, agrarian life had been linked with the highest ideals of a democratic society. Now agrarianism itself had been transformed. The farmer was no longer a self-sufficient yeoman but often a businessman or a wage laborer tied to a global market. And even as farm production soared, industrialization outstripped it. More and more farmers left the fields for urban factories or found work in the "factories in the fields" of the new industrialized agribusiness. Now that the future seemed to lie not with the small farmer but with industrial enterprises, was democracy itself at risk? This question would ignite a farmers' revolt in the 1880s and dominate political debate in the 1890s.

> QUICK REVIEW

Why did many homesteaders find it difficult to acquire good land in the West?

CHAPTER LOCATOR | What did U.S. expansion mean for Native Americans?

CHAPTER 17
512   CONTESTING THE WEST

IN 1871, AUTHOR MARK TWAIN published *Roughing It*, a chronicle of his days spent in mining towns in California and Nevada. There he found corrupt politics, vulgar display, and mania for speculation, the same cupidity he later skewered in *The Gilded Age* (1873), his biting satire of greed and corruption in the nation's capital. Far from being an antidote to the tawdry values of the East — an innocent idyll out of place and time — the American West, with its get-rich-quick ethos and its addiction to gambling and speculation, helped set the tone for the Gilded Age.

Twain's view countered that of Frederick Jackson Turner and perhaps better suited a West that witnessed the reckless overbuilding of railroads; the consolidation of business in mining and ranching; the rise of commercial farming; corruption and a penchant for government handouts; racial animosity, whether in the form of Indian wars or Chinese exclusion; the exploitation of labor and natural resources, which led to the decimation of the great bison herds, the pollution of rivers with mining wastes, and the overgrazing of the plains; and the beginnings of an imperial policy that would provide a template for U.S. adventures abroad. Turner, intent on promoting what was unique about the frontier, failed to note that the same issues that came to dominate debate east of the Mississippi — the growing power of big business, the exploitation of land and labor, corruption in politics, and ethnic and racial tensions exacerbated by colonial expansion and unparalleled immigration — took center stage in the West at the end of the nineteenth century.

| In what ways did different Indian groups defy and resist colonial rule? | How did mining shape American expansion? | How did the fight for land and resources in the West unfold? | **Conclusion: How did the West set the tone for the Gilded Age?** | ✓ LearningCurve Check what you know. bedfordstmartins.com /roarkunderstanding |

513

CHAPTER 17 STUDY GUIDE

STEP 1 GET STARTED ONLINE

 LearningCurve ■ bedfordstmartins.com/roarkunderstanding
Now that you've read the chapter, make it stick by completing the LearningCurve activity.

STEP 2 EXPLAIN WHY IT MATTERS

Put your reading into practice. Identify each term below, and then explain why it matters in U.S. history.

TERM	WHO OR WHAT & WHEN	WHY IT MATTERS
reservations (p. 490)		
Comanchería (p. 492)		
Black Hills (p. 492)		
Battle of the Little Big Horn (p. 493)		
Carlisle Indian School (p. 495)		
Dawes Allotment Act (p. 496)		
Ghost Dance (p. 498)		
Wounded Knee (p. 499)		
Comstock Lode (p. 500)		
Chinese Exclusion Act (p. 505)		
Homestead Act of 1862 (p. 506)		
first transcontinental railroad (p. 506)		

STEP 3 MOVE BEYOND THE BASICS

To demonstrate a more advanced understanding, describe the policies and goals of the federal government with respect to the West in the late nineteenth century.

	Federal policies and legislation	Goals
Indian peoples		
Diverse peoples of the West		
Land and natural resources		
Transportation		

STEP 4

PUT IT ALL TOGETHER

Now, take a step back and try to explain the big picture. Remember to use specific examples from the chapter in your answers.

NATIVE AMERICANS

▶ How did American Indians respond to the flood of westward migration after the Civil War?

▶ How did American Indians respond to changes in federal Indian policy between 1865 and 1900?

NATURAL RESOURCES AND TRANSPORTATION IN THE WEST

▶ Why was mining so important in the economy and society of the West and of the nation?

▶ What role did the railroad play in the development of the West?

THE WEST AND ETHNIC DIVERSITY

▶ What was the impetus for and impact of the Chinese Exclusion Act?

▶ How did racial and ethnic prejudice affect relations among westerners?

LOOKING BACKWARD, LOOKING AHEAD

▶ How did western expansion before the Civil War differ from western expansion after the Civil War?

  ▶ What new political and economic issues and tensions did American expansion raise?

  ▶ How did American lives and livelihoods change as a result of migration to the West?

> **IN YOUR OWN WORDS**

Imagine that you must give an oral report to the class answering the following question: What was most significant about American expansion after the Civil War? What would be the most important points to include and why?

18

DEFINING THE GILDED AGE IN BUSINESS AND POLITICS

1865–1900

> **What were the most important business and political developments of the Gilded Age?**

Chapter 18 explores the years between 1865 and 1895, the era commonly known as the Gilded Age. It examines the acceleration of industrialization and the growing interplay of business and politics. This chapter also examines the role of race and gender in social and political life and explores the impact of economic changes on the politics and culture of the late nineteenth century.

 **LearningCurve**
bedfordstmartins.com/roarkunderstanding
After reading the chapter, use LearningCurve to retain what you've read.

The Lost Bet, 1893. Artist Joseph Klir painted this scene of a Chicago parade after a local Republican agreed to pull his Democratic friend if Grover Cleveland won the 1892 presidential election. Library of Congress.

> How did the railroads stimulate big business?

> Why did the ideas of social Darwinism appeal to many Americans in the late nineteenth century?

> What factors influenced political life in the late nineteenth century?

> What issues shaped party politics in the late nineteenth century?

> What role did economic issues play in party realignment?

> Conclusion: Why did business dominate the Gilded Age?

How did the railroads stimulate big business?

"What a Funny Little Government"

The power wielded by John D. Rockefeller and his Standard Oil Company is satirized here by cartoonist Horace Taylor. Rockefeller is pictured holding the White House and the Treasury Department in the palm of his hand, while in the background the U.S. Capitol has been converted into an oil refinery. Collection of the New-York Historical Society.

> VISUAL ACTIVITY

READING THE IMAGE: According to Horace Taylor, what kind of relationship did John D. Rockefeller have with the federal government? What did the public think of it?

CONNECTIONS: How much influence did industrialists such as Rockefeller exert over the national government in the late nineteenth century?

Gilded Age

▶ A period of enormous economic growth and ostentatious displays of wealth during the last quarter of the nineteenth century. Industrialization dramatically changed in U.S. society and created a newly dominant group of rich entrepreneurs and an impoverished working class.

IN THE YEARS following the Civil War, the American economy underwent a transformation. Where once wealth had been measured in tangible assets — property, livestock, buildings — the economy now ran on money and the new devices of business — paper currency, securities, and anonymous corporate entities. Wall Street, the heart of the country's financial system, increasingly affected Main Street. The scale and scope of American industry expanded dramatically. Old industries like iron transformed into modern industries typified by the behemoth U.S. Steel. Discovery and invention stimulated new industries, from oil refining to electric light and power. The reckless expansion of the railroad in the decades after the Civil War played the key role in the transformation of the American economy.

Jay Gould, Andrew Carnegie, John D. Rockefeller, and other business leaders pioneered new strategies to seize markets and consolidate power. Always with an eye to making the most of their opportunities, these tycoons set the tone in the get-rich-quick era of freewheeling capitalism that came to be called the **Gilded Age**.

CHAPTER LOCATOR | **How did the railroads stimulate big business?** | Why did the ideas of social Darwinism appeal to many Americans in the late nineteenth century?

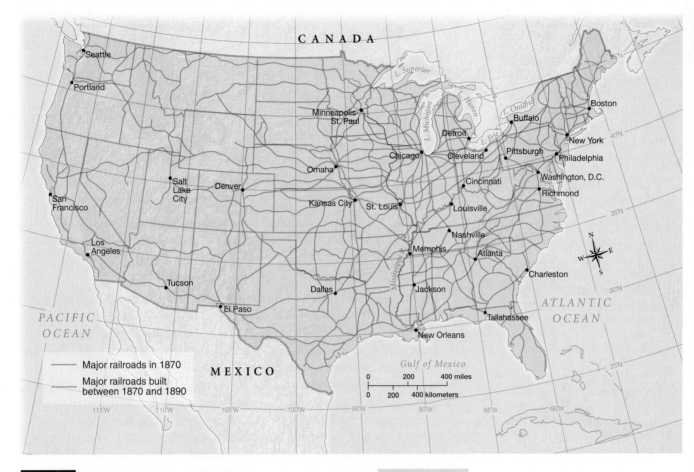

MAP 18.1 ■ Railroad Expansion, 1870–1890

Railroad mileage nearly quadrupled between 1870 and 1890, with the greatest growth occurring in the trans-Mississippi West. New transcontinental lines were completed in the 1880s. Fueled by speculation and built ahead of demand, the western railroads made fortunes for individual speculators. But they rarely paid for themselves and speeded the decline of Native Americans.

> **MAP ACTIVITY**

READING THE MAP: Where were most of the railroad lines located in 1870? By 1890, how many railroads reached the West Coast? What was the end point of the only western route? **CONNECTIONS:** Why were so many rails laid between 1870 and 1890? How did the railroads affect the nation's economy?

Railroads: America's First Big Business

The military conquest of America's inland empire and the dispossession of Native Americans (see chapter 17) were fed by an elaborate new railroad system built on speculation and government giveaways. Between 1870 and 1880, overbuilding doubled the amount of track in the country; in the following decade, the nation's railroad mileage nearly doubled again. By 1900, the nation boasted more than 193,000 miles of railroad track — more than in all of Europe and Russia combined (**Map 18.1** and **Figure 18.1**). Privately owned but publicly financed by enormous land grants from the federal government and the states, the railroads epitomized the insidious nexus of business and politics in the Gilded Age.

| What factors influenced political life in the late nineteenth century? | What issues shaped party politics in the late nineteenth century? | What role did economic issues play in party realignment? | Conclusion: Why did business dominate the Gilded Age? | ✔ LearningCurve Check what you know. bedfordstmartins.com /roarkunderstanding |

FIGURE 18.1 ■ Railroad Track Mileage, 1890

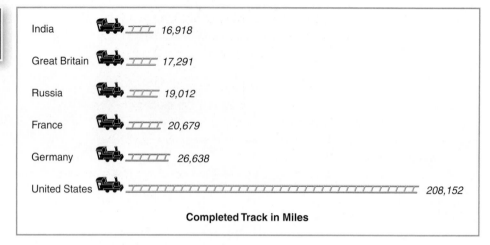

By 1850, the railway network in Great Britain was already well established, and most of the main lines in Germany had been built. France was slower to invest in railroads, but during the period 1850 to 1860, the government invested heavily in laying track, and the French soon caught up with, and then bypassed, their European neighbors. Russia's railway development experienced its greatest growth in the late nineteenth century. This growth was driven by the country's need to access its newly developing industrial regions and the vast natural resources of its far-flung territories in Asia. Like Russia, most of India's railroad growth occurred late in the century. This development was financed by the British, who were eager to tap the economic potential of their profitable overseas colony. By 1890, the United States had laid more railroad track than Britain, Germany, France, Russia, and India combined. Most of this growth occurred in the period 1870 to 1890, when railroad mileage in the United States nearly quadrupled. The vast area of the United States and its western territories accounted for some of the disparity between railroad mileage here and in Europe. England, France, and Germany combined contained less land than the states east of the Mississippi River.

To understand how the railroads came to dominate American life, there is no better place to start than with the career of Jay Gould, the era's most notorious speculator. Jason "Jay" Gould bought his first railroad before he turned twenty-five. It was only sixty-two miles long, in bad repair, and on the brink of failure, but within two years he sold it at a profit of $130,000.

The secretive Gould operated in the stock market like a shark, looking for vulnerable railroads, buying enough stock to take control, and threatening to undercut his competitors until they bought him out at a high profit. The railroads that fell into his hands fared badly and often went bankrupt. Gould's genius lay not in providing transportation, but in cleverly buying and selling railroad stock on Wall Street. Millionaires like Gould adopted the strategy of expansion and consolidation, which in turn encouraged overbuilding of the railroads and stimulated a national market.

The New York Stock Exchange expanded as the volume of stock increased sixfold between 1869 and 1901. As the scale and complexity of the financial system increased, the line between investment and speculation blurred, causing many Americans to question if speculators manipulating paper profits fueled the boom and bust cycles that led to panic and depression, putting hardworking Americans out of jobs.

The dramatic growth of the railroads created the country's first big business. Before the Civil War, even the largest textile mill in New England employed no more than 800 workers. By contrast, the Pennsylvania Railroad by the 1870s boasted a payroll of more than 55,000 workers. Capitalized at more than $400 million, the Pennsylvania Railroad constituted the largest private enterprise in the world.

The big business of railroads bestowed enormous riches on a handful of tycoons. Both Gould and his competitor "Commodore" Cornelius Vanderbilt amassed fortunes estimated at $100 million. Such staggering wealth eclipsed that of upper-class Americans from previous generations and left a legacy of lavish spending for an elite crop of ultra-rich heirs.

The Republican Party, firmly entrenched in Washington, worked closely with business interests, subsidizing the transcontinental railroad system with

CHAPTER LOCATOR | How did the railroads stimulate big business? | Why did the ideas of social Darwinism appeal to many Americans in the late nineteenth century?

land grants of a staggering 100 million acres of public land and $64 million in tax incentives and direct aid. States and local communities joined the railroad boom, knowing that only those towns and villages along the tracks would grow and flourish.

A revolution in communication accompanied and supported the growth of the railroads. The telegraph, developed by Samuel F. B. Morse, marched across the continent alongside the railroad. By transmitting coded messages along electrical wire, the telegraph formed the "nervous system" of the new industrial order. Telegraph service quickly replaced Pony Express mail carriers in the West and transformed business by providing instantaneous communication. Again, Jay Gould took the lead. In 1879, through stock manipulation, he seized control of Western Union, the company that monopolized the telegraph industry.

The railroads soon fell on hard times. Already by the 1870s, lack of planning led to overbuilding. Across the nation, railroads competed fiercely for business. A manufacturer in an area served by competing railroads could get substantially reduced shipping rates in return for promises of steady business. Because railroad owners lost money through this kind of competition, they tried to set up agreements, or "pools," to divide up territory and set rates. But these informal gentlemen's agreements invariably failed because men like Jay Gould, intent on undercutting all competitors, refused to play by the rules.

The public's alarm at the control wielded by the new railroad magnates and the tactics they employed provided a barometer of attitudes toward big business itself. When Gould died in 1892, he was, as he himself admitted, "the most hated man in America."

Andrew Carnegie, Steel, and Vertical Integration

If Jay Gould was the man Americans loved to hate, Andrew Carnegie became one of America's heroes. Unlike Gould, Carnegie turned his back on speculation and worked to build something enduring — Carnegie Steel, the biggest steel business in the world during the Gilded Age.

The growth of the steel industry proceeded directly from railroad building. The first railroads ran on iron rails, which cracked and broke with alarming frequency. Steel, both stronger and more flexible than iron, remained too expensive for use in rails until Englishman Henry Bessemer developed a way to make steel more cheaply. Andrew Carnegie, among the first to champion the new "King Steel," came to dominate the emerging industry.

Carnegie, a Scottish immigrant, landed in New York in 1848 at the age of twelve. He rose from a job cleaning bobbins in a textile factory to become one of the richest men in America. Before he died, he gave away more than $300 million, most notably to public libraries. His generosity, combined with his own rise from poverty, burnished his public image.

While Carnegie was a teenager, his skill as a telegraph operator caught the attention of Tom Scott, superintendent of the Pennsylvania Railroad. Scott hired Carnegie, soon promoted him, and lent him the money for his first foray into

> CHRONOLOGY

1869
– First transcontinental railroad is completed.

1870
– John D. Rockefeller incorporates Standard Oil Company.

1872
– Andrew Carnegie builds world's largest steel plant.

1876
– Alexander Graham Bell demonstrates the telephone.

1882
– John D. Rockefeller develops the trust.

What factors influenced political life in the late nineteenth century?

What issues shaped party politics in the late nineteenth century?

What role did economic issues play in party realignment?

Conclusion: Why did business dominate the Gilded Age?

☑ LearningCurve
Check what you know.
bedfordstmartins.com
/roarkunderstanding

521

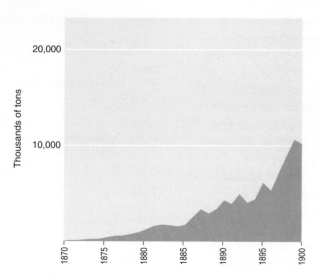

FIGURE 18.2 ■ Iron and Steel Production, 1870–1900

Iron and steel production in the United States grew from nearly none in 1870 to 10 million tons a year by 1900. The secrets to the great increase in steel production were the use of the Bessemer process and vertical integration, pioneered by Andrew Carnegie. By 1900, Carnegie's mills alone produced more steel than did all of Great Britain. With corporate consolidation after 1900, the rate of growth in steel proved even more spectacular.

Wall Street investment. As a result of this crony capitalism, Carnegie became a millionaire before his thirtieth birthday. At that point, Carnegie turned away from speculation. "My preference was always manufacturing," he wrote. "I wished to make something tangible." By applying the lessons of cost accounting and efficiency that he had learned with the Pennsylvania Railroad, Carnegie turned steel into the nation's first manufacturing big business (**Figure 18.2**).

In 1872, Andrew Carnegie built the world's largest, most up-to-date steel mill in Braddock, Pennsylvania. At that time, steelmakers produced about 70 tons a week. Within two decades, Carnegie's blast furnaces poured out an incredible 10,000 tons a week. His formula for success was simple: "Cut the prices, scoop the market, run the mills full; watch the costs and profits will take care of themselves." Carnegie pioneered a system of business organization called vertical integration, in which all aspects of the business were under Carnegie's control — from the mining of iron ore, to its transport on the Great Lakes, to the production of steel. As one observer noted, "There was never a price, profit, or royalty paid to any outsider."

The great productivity Carnegie encouraged came at a high price. He deliberately pitted his managers against one another, firing the losers and rewarding the winners with a share in the company. Workers achieved the output Carnegie demanded by enduring low wages, dangerous working conditions, and twelve-hour days six days a week. One worker, observing the contradiction between Carnegie's generous endowment of public libraries and his labor policy, observed, "After working twelve hours, how can a man go to a library?"

By 1900, Andrew Carnegie had become the best-known manufacturer in the nation, and the age of iron had yielded to an age of steel. Steel from Carnegie's mills supported the elevated trains in New York and Chicago, formed the skeleton of the Washington Monument, supported the first steel bridge to span the Mississippi, and girded America's first skyscrapers. As a captain of industry, Carnegie's only rival was the titan of the oil industry, John D. Rockefeller.

John D. Rockefeller, Standard Oil, and the Trust

In the days before the automobile and gasoline, crude oil was refined into lubricating oil for machinery and kerosene for lamps, the major source of lighting in the nineteenth century. The amount of capital needed to buy or build an oil refinery in the 1860s and 1870s remained relatively low — roughly what it cost to lay one mile of railroad track. As a result, the new petroleum industry experienced riotous competition. Ultimately, John D. Rockefeller and his Standard Oil Company succeeded in controlling nine-tenths of the oil-refining business.

Rockefeller grew up the son of a shrewd Yankee who peddled quack cures for cancer. Under his father's rough tutelage, Rockefeller learned how to drive a hard bargain. In 1865, at the age of twenty-five, he controlled the largest oil refinery in Cleveland. Like a growing number of business owners, Rockefeller abandoned partnership or single proprietorship to embrace the corporation as the business structure best suited to maximize profit and minimize personal liability. In 1870, he incorporated his oil business, founding the Standard Oil Company.

As the largest refiner in Cleveland, Rockefeller demanded illegal rebates from the railroads in exchange for his steady business. The secret rebates enabled Rockefeller to drive out his competitors through predatory pricing. The railroads needed Rockefeller's business so badly that they gave him a share of the rates that his competitors paid. A Pennsylvania Railroad official later confessed that Rockefeller extracted such huge rebates that the railroad, which could not risk losing his business, sometimes ended up paying him to transport Standard's oil. Rebates enabled Rockefeller to undercut his competitors and pressure competing refiners to sell out or face ruin.

To gain legal standing for Standard Oil's secret deals, Rockefeller in 1882 pioneered a new form of corporate structure — the **trust**. The trust differed markedly from Carnegie's vertical approach in steel. Rockefeller used horizontal integration to control not the entire process, but just one aspect of oil production — refining. Several trustees held stock in various refinery companies "in trust" for Standard's stockholders. This elaborate stock swap allowed the trustees to coordinate policy among the refineries by gobbling up all the small, competing refineries. Buyers often did not know they were actually selling out to Standard. By the end of the century, Rockefeller enjoyed a virtual monopoly of the oil-refining business. The Standard Oil trust, valued at more than $70 million, paved the way for trusts in sugar, whiskey, matches, and many other products.

trust
▶ A system in which corporations give shares of their stock to trustees who hold the stocks "in trust" for their stockholders, thereby coordinating the industry to ensure profits to the participating corporations and to curb competition.

When the federal government responded to public pressure to outlaw the trust in 1890, Standard Oil changed tactics and reorganized as a holding company. Instead of stockholders in competing companies acting through trustees to set prices and determine territories, the holding company simply brought competing companies under one central administration. Now one business, not an assortment of individual refineries, Standard Oil controlled competition without violating antitrust laws that forbade competing companies from forming "combinations in restraint of trade." By the 1890s, Standard Oil ruled more than 90 percent of the oil business, employed 100,000 people, and was the biggest, richest, most feared, and most admired business organization in the world.

John D. Rockefeller enjoyed enormous success in business, but he was not well liked by the public. Editor and journalist Ida M. Tarbell's "History of the Standard Oil Company," which ran for three years (1902–1905) in serial form in *McClure's Magazine*, largely shaped the public's harsh view of Rockefeller. Her history chronicled the illegal methods Rockefeller had used to take over the oil industry. By the time Tarbell finished her story, Rockefeller slept with a loaded revolver by his bed. Standard Oil and the man who created it had become the symbol of heartless monopoly.

| What factors influenced political life in the late nineteenth century? | What issues shaped party politics in the late nineteenth century? | What role did economic issues play in party realignment? | Conclusion: Why did business dominate the Gilded Age? | ☑ LearningCurve Check what you know. bedfordstmartins.com /roarkunderstanding |

523

TABLE 18.1 ■ Notable American
Inventions, 1865–1899

1865	Railroad sleeping car
1867	Typewriter
1868	Railroad refrigerator car
1870	Stock ticker
1874	Barbed wire
1876	Telephone
1877	Phonograph
1879	Electric lightbulb
1882	Electric fan
1885	Adding machine
1886	Coca-Cola
1888	Kodak camera
1890	Electric chair
1891	Zipper
1895	Safety razor
1896	Electric stove
1899	Tape recorder

New Inventions: The Telephone and the Telegraph

The second half of the nineteenth century was an age of invention (**Table 18.1**). Men like Thomas Alva Edison and Alexander Graham Bell became folk heroes. But no matter how dramatic the inventors or the inventions, the new electric and telephone industries pioneered by Edison and Bell soon eclipsed their inventors and fell under the control of bankers and industrialists.

Alexander Graham Bell came to America from Scotland at the age of twenty-four with a passion to find a way to teach the deaf to speak (his wife and mother were deaf). Instead, he developed a way to transmit voice over wire — the telephone. Bell's invention astounded the world when he demonstrated it at the Philadelphia Centennial Exposition in 1876. In 1880, Bell's company, American Bell, pioneered "long lines" (long-distance telephone service), creating American Telephone and Telegraph (AT&T) as a subsidiary. In 1900, AT&T developed a complicated structure that enabled Americans to communicate not only locally but also across the country. And unlike a telegraph message, the telephone connected

AN UNRESTRAINED DEMON.

The Dangers of Electricity

This 1889 cartoon graphically portrays the dangers of electricity. Innocent pedestrians are electrocuted by the wires as a policeman runs for help. The skull in the wires attached to the electric lightbulb warns that this new technology can be deadly. And the carnage portrayed illustrates the point. Granger Collection.

CHAPTER LOCATOR | How did the railroads stimulate big business? | Why did the ideas of social Darwinism appeal to many Americans in the late nineteenth century?

CHAPTER 18
524 DEFINING THE GILDED AGE IN BUSINESS AND POLITICS

both parties immediately and privately. Bell's invention proved a boon to business, contributing to speed and efficiency. The number of telephones soared, reaching 310,000 in 1895 and more than 1.5 million in 1900.

Even more than Alexander Graham Bell, inventor Thomas Alva Edison embodied the old-fashioned virtues of Yankee ingenuity and rugged individualism that Americans most admired. A self-educated dynamo, he worked twenty hours a day in his laboratory in Menlo Park, New Jersey, vowing to turn out "a minor invention every ten days and a big thing every six months or so." He almost made good on his promise. At the height of his career, he averaged a patent every eleven days and invented such "big things" as the phonograph, the motion picture camera, and the filament for the incandescent lightbulb.

Edison, in competition with George W. Westinghouse, pioneered the use of electricity as an energy source. By the late nineteenth century, electricity had become a part of American urban life. It powered trolley cars and lighted factories, homes, and office buildings. Indeed, electricity became so prevalent in urban life that it symbolized the city, whose bright lights contrasted with rural America, left largely in the dark.

The day of the inventor quietly yielded to the heyday of the corporation. In 1892, the electric industry consolidated. Reflecting a nationwide trend in business, Edison General Electric dropped the name of its inventor, becoming simply General Electric (GE). For years, an embittered Edison refused to set foot inside a GE building. GE, a prime example of the trend toward business consolidation, soon dominated the market.

QUICK REVIEW

What tactics and strategies did American business owners employ during the Gilded Age?

| What factors influenced political life in the late nineteenth century? | What issues shaped party politics in the late nineteenth century? | What role did economic issues play in party realignment? | Conclusion: Why did business dominate the Gilded Age? | ✓ LearningCurve Check what you know. bedfordstmartins.com /roarkunderstanding |

> Why did the ideas of social Darwinism appeal to many Americans in the late nineteenth century?

Homestead Steelworks

The Homestead steelworks, outside Pittsburgh, is pictured shortly after J. P. Morgan created U.S. Steel, the precursor of today's USX. Try to count the smokestacks in the picture. Air pollution on this scale posed a threat to the health of citizens and made for a dismal landscape. Workers complained that trees would not grow in Homestead. Hagley Museum & Library.

finance capitalism
▶ Investment sponsored by banks and bankers that typified the American business scene at the end of the nineteenth century. After the panic of 1893, bankers stepped in and reorganized major industries to stabilize them, leaving power concentrated in the hands of a few influential capitalists.

EVEN AS ROCKEFELLER and Carnegie built their empires, the era of the "robber barons," as they were dubbed by their detractors, was drawing to a close. Increasingly, businesses replaced partnerships and sole proprietorships with the anonymous corporate structure that would come to dominate the twentieth century. At the same time, mergers led to the creation of huge new corporations.

Banks and financiers played a key role in this consolidation, so much so that the decades at the turn of the twentieth century can be characterized as a period of **finance capitalism** — investment sponsored by banks and bankers. When the depression that followed the panic of 1893 bankrupted many businesses, bankers stepped in to bring order and to reorganize major industries. During these years, a new social philosophy later known as social Darwinism helped to justify consolidation and to inhibit state or federal regulation of business. A conservative Supreme Court further frustrated attempts to control business by consistently declaring unconstitutional legislation designed to regulate railroads or to outlaw trusts and monopolies.

CHAPTER LOCATOR | How did the railroads stimulate big business?

Why did the ideas of social Darwinism appeal to many Americans in the late nineteenth century?

J. P. Morgan and Finance Capitalism

John Pierpont Morgan, the preeminent finance capitalist of the late nineteenth century, loathed competition and sought whenever possible to eliminate it by substituting consolidation and central control. Morgan's passion for order made him the architect of business mergers. At the turn of the twentieth century, he dominated American banking, exerting an influence so powerful that his critics charged he controlled a vast "money trust" even more insidious than Rockefeller's Standard Oil.

Morgan acted as a power broker in the reorganization of the railroads and the creation of industrial giants such as General Electric and U.S. Steel. When the railroads collapsed, Morgan quickly took over and eliminated competition by creating what he called "a community of interest." By the time he finished "Morganizing" the railroads, a handful of directors controlled two-thirds of the nation's track.

In 1898, Morgan moved into the steel industry, directly challenging Andrew Carnegie. The pugnacious Carnegie cabled his partners in the summer of 1900: "Action essential: crisis has arrived . . . have no fear as to the result; victory certain." The press trumpeted news of the impending fight between the feisty Scot and the haughty Wall Street banker. But for all his belligerence, the sixty-six-year-old Carnegie yearned to retire to Scotland. Morgan, who disdained haggling, agreed to pay Carnegie's asking price, $480 million (the equivalent of about $10 billion in today's currency). According to legend, when Carnegie later teased Morgan, saying that he should have asked $100 million more, Morgan replied, "You would have got it if you had."

Morgan's acquisition of Carnegie Steel signaled the passing of the old entrepreneurial order personified by Andrew Carnegie and the arrival of a new, anonymous corporate world. Morgan quickly moved to pull together Carnegie's chief competitors to form a huge new corporation, United States Steel, known today as USX. Created in 1901 and capitalized at $1.4 billion, U.S. Steel was the largest corporation in the world.

Even more than Carnegie or Rockefeller, Morgan left his stamp on the twentieth century and formed the model for corporate consolidation that economists and social scientists justified with a new social theory later known as social Darwinism.

Social Darwinism, Laissez-Faire, and the Supreme Court

John D. Rockefeller Jr., the son of the founder of Standard Oil, once remarked to his Baptist Bible class that the Standard Oil Company, like the American Beauty rose, resulted from "pruning the early buds that grew up around it." The elimination of competition, he declared, was "merely the working out of a law of nature

> CHRONOLOGY

1883
– William Graham Sumner articulates his philosophy of social Darwinism in *What Social Classes Owe to Each Other*.

1889
– Andrew Carnegie publishes "The Gospel of Wealth."

1901
– U.S. Steel is incorporated and capitalized at $1.4 billion.

What factors influenced political life in the late nineteenth century?

What issues shaped party politics in the late nineteenth century?

What role did economic issues play in party realignment?

Conclusion: Why did business dominate the Gilded Age?

✓ LearningCurve
Check what you know.
bedfordstmartins.com
/roarkunderstanding

527

and a law of God." The comparison of the business world to the natural world resembled the theory of evolution formulated by the British naturalist Charles Darwin. In his monumental work *On the Origin of Species* (1859), Darwin theorized that in the struggle for survival, adaptation to the environment triggered among species a natural selection process that led to evolution. Herbert Spencer in Britain and William Graham Sumner in the United States developed the theory of **social Darwinism**. The social Darwinists insisted that societal progress came about as a result of relentless competition in which the strong survived and the weak died out.

social Darwinism
▶ A social theory popularized in the late nineteenth century by Herbert Spencer and William Graham Sumner. Proponents believed that only relentless competition could produce social progress and that wealth was a sign of "fitness" and poverty a sign of "unfitness" for survival.

In social terms, the idea of the "survival of the fittest," coined by Herbert Spencer, had profound significance, as Sumner, a professor of political economy at Yale University, made clear in his book *What Social Classes Owe to Each Other* (1883). "The drunkard in the gutter is just where he ought to be, according to the fitness and tendency of things," Sumner insisted. Conversely, "millionaires are the product of natural selection," and although "they get high wages and live in luxury," Sumner claimed, "the bargain is a good one for society."

Social Darwinists equated wealth and power with "fitness" and believed that any efforts by the rich to aid the poor would only tamper with the laws of nature and slow down evolution. Social Darwinism acted to curb social reform while at the same time glorifying great wealth. In an age when Rockefeller and Carnegie amassed hundreds of millions of dollars (billions in today's currency) and the average worker earned $500 a year, social Darwinism justified economic inequality.

Andrew Carnegie softened some of the harshness of social Darwinism in his essay "The Gospel of Wealth," published in 1889. The millionaire, Carnegie wrote, acted as a "mere trustee and agent for his poorer brethren, bringing to their service his superior wisdom, experience, and ability to administer, doing for them better than they could or would do for themselves." Carnegie preached philanthropy and urged the rich to "live unostentatious lives" and "administer surplus wealth for the good of the people." His **gospel of wealth** earned much praise but won few converts. Most millionaires followed the lead of J. P. Morgan, who contributed to charity but hoarded private treasures in his marble library.

gospel of wealth
▶ The idea that the financially successful should use their wisdom, experience, and wealth to help the poor. Andrew Carnegie promoted this view in an 1889 essay in which he maintained that the wealthy should serve as stewards for society as a whole.

With its emphasis on the free play of competition and the survival of the fittest, social Darwinism encouraged the economic theory of laissez-faire (French for "let it alone"). Business argued that government should not meddle in economic affairs, except to protect private property (or support high tariffs and government subsidies). A conservative Supreme Court agreed. During the 1880s and 1890s, the Court increasingly reinterpreted the Constitution, judging corporations to be "persons" in order to protect business from taxation, regulation, labor organization, and antitrust legislation.

Only in the arena of politics did Americans tackle the social issues raised by corporate capitalism.

> **QUICK REVIEW**

How did social Darwinism shape American society and business in the late nineteenth century?

CHAPTER LOCATOR | How did the railroads stimulate big business? | Why did the ideas of social Darwinism appeal to many Americans in the late nineteenth century?

528   CHAPTER 18
DEFINING THE GILDED AGE IN BUSINESS AND POLITICS

What factors influenced political life in the late nineteenth century?

"Woman's Holy War"

This political cartoon styles the temperance campaign as "Woman's Holy War" and shows a woman knight in armor (demurely seated sidesaddle on her charger), wielding a battle-ax and trampling on barrels of liquor. The image of temperance women as ax-wielding Amazons proved a popular satiric image. The cartoon appeared in 1874, the year the Woman's Christian Temperance Union was founded. Picture Research Consultants & Archives.

FOR MANY AMERICANS, politics provided a source of identity, a means of livelihood, and a ready form of entertainment. No wonder voter turnout averaged a hefty 77 percent (compared with roughly 60 percent in the 2008 presidential election). A variety of factors contributed to the complicated interplay of politics and culture. Patronage provided an economic incentive for voter participation, but ethnicity, religion, sectional loyalty, race, and gender all influenced the political life of the period.

Political Participation and Party Loyalty

Political parties in power doled out federal, state, and local government jobs to their loyal supporters. With hundreds of thousands of jobs to be filled, the choice of party affiliation could mean the difference between a paycheck and an empty pocket. Money greased the wheels of this system of patronage, dubbed the **spoils system** from the adage "to the victor go the spoils." With their livelihoods tied to their party identity, government employees had a powerful incentive to vote in great numbers.

spoils system
► System in which politicians doled out government positions to their loyal supporters. This patronage system led to widespread corruption during the Gilded Age.

| What factors influenced political life in the late nineteenth century? | What issues shaped party politics in the late nineteenth century? | What role did economic issues play in party realignment? | Conclusion: Why did business dominate the Gilded Age? | ☑ LearningCurve Check what you know. bedfordstmartins.com /roarkunderstanding |

529

> CHRONOLOGY

1869
– National Woman Suffrage Association is founded.

1874
– Woman's Christian Temperance Union (WCTU) is founded.

1890
– General Federation of Women's Clubs (GFWC) is founded.

1892
– Ida B. Wells launches antilynching campaign.

Political affiliation provided a sense of group identity for many voters proud of their loyalty to the Democrats or the Republicans. Democrats, who traced the party's roots back to Thomas Jefferson, called theirs "the party of the fathers." The Republican Party, founded in the 1850s, still claimed strong loyalties in the North as a result of its alignment with the Union during the Civil War. Republicans proved particularly adept at evoking Civil War loyalty, using a tactic called "waving the bloody shirt."

Religion and ethnicity also played a significant role in politics. In the North, Protestants from the old-line denominations, particularly Presbyterians and Methodists, flocked to the Republican Party, which championed a series of moral reforms, including local laws requiring businesses to close on Sunday in observance of the Sabbath. In the cities, the Democratic Party courted immigrants and working-class Catholic and Jewish voters and charged, rightly, that Republican moral crusades often masked attacks on immigrant culture.

Sectionalism and the New South

After the end of Reconstruction, most white voters in the former Confederate states remained loyal Democrats, creating the so-called solid South that lasted for the next seventy years. Labeling the Republican Party the agent of "Negro rule," Democrats urged white southerners to "vote the way you shot." Yet the South proved far from solid for the Democrats on the state and local levels, leading to shifting political alliances and to third-party movements that challenged Democratic attempts to define politics along race lines and maintain the Democrats as the white man's party.

The South's economy, devastated by the war, foundered at the same time the North experienced an unprecedented industrial boom. Soon an influential group of southerners called for a New South modeled on the industrial North. Henry Grady, the ebullient young editor of the *Atlanta Constitution,* used his paper's influence to exhort the South to use its natural advantages — cheap labor and abundant natural resources — to go head-to-head in competition with northern industry. And even as southern Democrats took back control of state governments, they embraced northern promoters who promised prosperity and profits.

The railroads came first, opening up the region for industrial development. Southern railroad mileage grew fourfold from 1865 to 1890. The number of cotton spindles also soared as textile mill owners abandoned New England in search of the cheap labor and proximity to raw materials promised in the South. By 1900, the South had become the nation's leading producer of cloth, and more than 100,000 southerners, many of them women and children, worked in the region's textile mills.

The New South prided itself most on its iron and steel industry, which grew up in the area surrounding Birmingham, Alabama. During this period, the smokestack replaced the white-pillared plantation as the symbol of the New South. Andrew Carnegie toured the region in 1889 and observed, "The South is Pennsylvania's most formidable industrial enemy." But southern industry remained controlled by northern investors, who had no intention of letting the South beat the North at its own game. Elaborate mechanisms rigged the price of southern steel, inflating it, as one northern insider confessed, "for the purpose of

CHAPTER LOCATOR | How did the railroads stimulate big business? | Why did the ideas of social Darwinism appeal to many Americans in the late nineteenth century?

530   CHAPTER 18
DEFINING THE GILDED AGE IN BUSINESS AND POLITICS

protecting the Pittsburgh mills and in turn the Pittsburgh steel users." Similarly, in the lumber and mining industries, investors in the North and abroad, not southerners, reaped the lion's share of the profits.

In only one industry did the South truly dominate — tobacco. Capitalizing on the invention of a machine for rolling cigarettes, the American Tobacco Company, founded by the Duke family of North Carolina, eventually dominated the industry. As cigarettes replaced chewing tobacco in popularity at the turn of the twentieth century, a booming market developed for Duke's "ready mades." Soon the company sold 400,000 cigarettes a day.

In practical terms, the industrialized New South proved an illusion. Much of the South remained agricultural, caught in the grip of the insidious crop lien system (see chapter 16). White southern farmers, desperate to get out of debt, sometimes joined with African Americans to pursue their goals politically. Between 1865 and 1900, voters in every southern state experimented with political alliances that crossed the color line and threatened the status quo.

Gender, Race, and Politics

Gender — society's notion of what constitutes acceptable masculine or feminine behavior — influenced politics throughout the nineteenth century. From the early days of the Republic, citizenship had been defined in male terms. Citizenship and its prerogatives (voting and officeholding) served as a badge of manliness and rested on its corollary, patriarchy — the power and authority men exerted over their wives and families. With the advent of universal (white) male suffrage in the early nineteenth century, gender eclipsed class as the defining feature of citizenship; men's dominance over women provided the common thread that knit all white men together politically. The concept of separate spheres dictated political participation for men only. Once the public sphere of political participation became equated with manhood, women found themselves increasingly restricted to the private sphere of the home.

Women were not alone in their limited access to the public sphere. Blacks continued to face discrimination well after Reconstruction, especially in the New South. Segregation, commonly practiced through **Jim Crow** laws (as discussed in chapter 21), prevented ex-slaves from riding in the same train cars as whites, from eating in the same restaurants, or from using the same toilet facilities.

Jim Crow

▶ System of racial segregation in the South lasting from after the Civil War into the twentieth century. Jim Crow laws segregated African Americans in public facilities such as trains and streetcars, curtailed their voting rights, and denied other basic civil rights.

Amid the turmoil of the post-Reconstruction South, some groups struck cross-racial alliances. In Virginia, the "Readjusters," a coalition of blacks and whites determined to "readjust" (lower) the state debt and spend more money on public education, captured state offices from 1879 to 1883. Groups like the Readjusters believed that universal political rights could be extended to black males while maintaining racial segregation in the private sphere. Democrats fought back by arguing that black voting would lead to racial mixing, and many whites returned to the Democratic fold to protect "white womanhood."

The notion that black men threatened white southern womanhood reached its most vicious form in the practice of lynching — the killing and mutilation of black men by white mobs. By 1892, the practice had become so prevalent that a courageous black editor, Ida B. Wells, launched an antilynching movement. That year, a white mob lynched a friend of Wells's whose grocery store competed too successfully

What factors influenced political life in the late nineteenth century? | What issues shaped party politics in the late nineteenth century? | What role did economic issues play in party realignment? | Conclusion: Why did business dominate the Gilded Age? | ✓ LearningCurve Check what you know. bedfordstmartins.com /roarkunderstanding

531

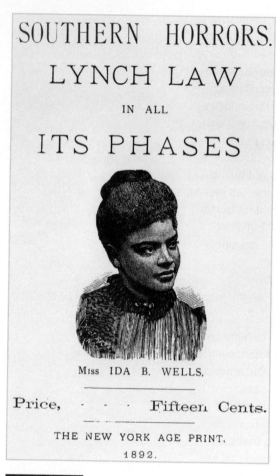

Ida B. Wells

Ida B. Wells began her antilynching campaign in 1892 after a friend's murder led her to examine lynching in the South. She spread her message in lectures and pamphlets like this one, distributed for fifteen cents. Wells brought the horror of lynching to a national and international audience and became a founding member of the National Association for the Advancement of Colored People (NAACP). Manuscript, Archives, and Rare Books Division, Schomburg Center for Research in Black Culture, The New York Public Library, Astor, Lenox, and Tilden Foundations.

with a white-owned store. Wells shrewdly concluded that lynching served "as an excuse to get rid of Negroes who were acquiring wealth and property and thus keep the race terrorized." She began to collect data on lynching and discovered that in the decade between 1882 and 1892 lynching rose in the South by an overwhelming 200 percent, with at least 241 black people killed. The vast increase in lynching testified to the retreat of the federal government following Reconstruction and to white southerners' determination to maintain supremacy through terrorism and intimidation.

Wells articulated lynching as a problem of gender as well as race. She insisted that the myth of black attacks on white southern women masked the reality that mob violence had more to do with economics and the shifting social structure of the South than with rape. She demonstrated in a sophisticated way how the southern patriarchal system, having lost its control over blacks with the end of slavery, used its control over white women to circumscribe the liberty of black men.

Wells's outspoken stance immediately resulted in reprisal. While she was traveling in the North, vandals ransacked her office in Tennessee and destroyed her printing equipment. Yet the warning that she would be killed on sight if she ever returned to Memphis only stiffened her resolve. As she wrote in her autobiography, *Crusade for Justice* (1928), "Having lost my paper, had a price put on my life and been made an exile . . . , I felt that I owed it to myself and to my race to tell the whole truth now that I was where I could do so freely."

Lynching did not end during Wells's lifetime, but her forceful voice brought the issue to national and international prominence. At her funeral in 1931, black leader W. E. B. Du Bois eulogized Wells as the woman who "began the awakening of the conscience of the nation." Wells's determined campaign against lynching provided just one example of women's political activism during the Gilded Age. The suffrage and temperance movements, along with the growing popularity of women's clubs, dramatized how women refused to be relegated to a separate sphere that kept them out of politics.

Women's Activism

In 1869, Elizabeth Cady Stanton and Susan B. Anthony formed the National Woman Suffrage Association, the first independent woman's rights organization in the United States, to fight for the vote for women. But women found ways to act politically long before they voted and cleverly used their moral authority as wives and mothers to move from the domestic sphere into the realm of politics.

The extraordinary activity of women's clubs in the period following the Civil War provides just one example. Women's clubs proliferated beginning in the 1860s. Newspaper reporter Jane Cunningham Croly (pen name Jennie June)

CHAPTER LOCATOR | How did the railroads stimulate big business? | Why did the ideas of social Darwinism appeal to many Americans in the late nineteenth century?

CHAPTER 18

532   DEFINING THE GILDED AGE IN BUSINESS AND POLITICS

founded the Sorosis Club in New York City in 1868, after the New York Press Club denied entry to women journalists wishing to attend a banquet honoring the British author Charles Dickens. In 1890, Croly brought state and local clubs together under the umbrella of the General Federation of Women's Clubs (GFWC). Not wishing to alienate southern women, the GFWC barred black women's clubs from joining, despite vehement objections. Women's clubs soon abandoned literary pursuits to devote themselves to "civic usefulness," endorsing an end to child labor, supporting the eight-hour workday, and helping pass pure food and drug legislation.

The temperance movement (the movement to end drunkenness) attracted by far the largest number of organized women in the late nineteenth century. By the late 1860s and the 1870s, the liquor business was flourishing, with about one saloon for every fifty males over the age of fifteen. During the winter of 1873–74, temperance women adopted a radical new tactic. Armed with Bibles and singing hymns, they marched on taverns and saloons and refused to leave until the proprietors signed a pledge to quit selling liquor. Known as the Woman's Crusade, the movement spread like a prairie fire through small towns in Ohio, Indiana, Michigan, and Illinois and soon moved east into New York, New England, and Pennsylvania. Before it was over, more than 100,000 women had marched in more than 450 cities and towns.

The women's tactics may have been new, but the temperance movement dated back to the 1820s. Originally, the movement was led by Protestant men who organized clubs to pledge voluntary abstinence from liquor. By the 1850s, temperance advocates won significant victories when states, starting with Maine, passed laws to prohibit the sale of liquor. The Woman's Crusade dramatically brought the issue of temperance back into the national spotlight and led to the formation of a new organization, the **Woman's Christian Temperance Union (WCTU)** in 1874. Composed entirely of women, the WCTU advocated total abstinence from alcohol.

Temperance provided women with a respectable outlet for their increasing resentment of women's inferior status and their growing recognition of women's capabilities. In its first five years, the WCTU relied on education and moral suasion, but when Frances Willard became president in 1879, she politicized the organization (as discussed in chapter 20). When the women of the WCTU joined with the Prohibition Party (formed in 1869 by a group of evangelical clergymen), one wag observed, "Politics is a man's game, an' women, childhern, and prohyibitionists do well to keep out iv it." By sharing power with women, the Prohibitionist men violated the old political rules and risked attacks on their honor and manhood.

Even though women found ways to affect the political process, especially in third parties, it remained true that politics, particularly presidential politics, remained an exclusively male prerogative.

Woman's Christian Temperance Union (WCTU)

▶ All-women organization founded in 1874 to advocate for total abstinence from alcohol. The WCTU provided important political training for women, which many used in the suffrage movement.

QUICK REVIEW <

How did race and gender influence politics?

| What factors influenced political life in the late nineteenth century? | What issues shaped party politics in the late nineteenth century? | What role did economic issues play in party realignment? | Conclusion: Why did business dominate the Gilded Age? |  LearningCurve Check what you know. bedfordstmartins.com /roarkunderstanding |

What issues shaped party politics in the late nineteenth century?

Civil Service Exam In this 1890s photograph, prospective police officers in Chicago take the written civil service exam. Civil service meant that politicians and party bosses could no longer use jobs in the government to reward the party faithful. Chicago Historical Society.

THE PRESIDENTS OF THE GILDED AGE, from Rutherford B. Hayes (1877–1881) to William McKinley (1897–1901), are largely forgotten men, primarily because so little was expected of them. The dominant creed of laissez-faire, coupled with the dictates of social Darwinism, warned the president and the government to leave business alone. Still, presidents in the Gilded Age grappled with corruption and party strife, and they struggled toward the creation of new political ethics designed to replace patronage with a civil service system that promised to award jobs on the basis of merit, not party loyalty.

Corruption and Party Strife

The political corruption and party factionalism that characterized the administration of Ulysses S. Grant (1869–1877) (see chapter 16) continued to trouble the nation in the 1880s. The spoils system remained the driving force in party politics at all levels of government. Pro-business Republicans generally held a firm grip on the White House, while Democrats had better luck in Congress. Both parties relied on patronage to cement party loyalty.

A small but determined group of reformers championed a new ethics that would preclude politicians from getting rich from public office. The selection of

U.S. senators particularly concerned them. Under the Constitution, senators were selected by state legislatures, not directly elected by the voters. Powerful business interests often contrived to control state legislatures and through them U.S. senators. As journalist Henry Demarest Lloyd quipped, Standard Oil "had done everything to the Pennsylvania legislature except to refine it." In this climate, a constitutional amendment calling for the direct election of senators faced stiff opposition from entrenched interests.

Republican president Rutherford B. Hayes, whose disputed election in 1876 signaled the end of Reconstruction in the South (see chapter 16), tried to steer a middle course between spoilsmen and reformers. Hayes proved a hardworking, well-informed executive who wanted peace, prosperity, and an end to party strife. Yet the Republican Party remained divided into factions led by strong party bosses who boasted that they could make or break any president.

> CHRONOLOGY

1880
– James A. Garfield is elected president.

1881
– Garfield is assassinated; Vice President Chester A. Arthur becomes president.

1883
– Pendleton Civil Service Act.

1884
– Grover Cleveland is elected president.

> Republican Factions in 1880	
Stalwarts	Supporters of the patronage system, led by master spoilsman Senator Roscoe Conkling of New York.
Half Breeds	Less openly corrupt than the Stalwarts, led by Conkling's archrival, Senator James G. Blaine of Maine.
Mugwumps	Reform-minded Republicans from Massachusetts and New York who deplored the spoils system and advocated civil service reform.

President Hayes's middle course pleased no one, and he soon managed to alienate all factions of his party. Few were surprised when he announced that he would not seek reelection in 1880. To avoid choosing among its factions, the Republican Party in 1880 nominated a dark-horse candidate, Representative James A. Garfield of Ohio. To foster party unity, they picked Stalwart Chester A. Arthur as the vice presidential candidate. The Democrats made an attempt to overcome sectionalism by selecting former Union general Winfield Scott Hancock. Hancock garnered only lukewarm support, receiving just 155 electoral votes to Garfield's 214, although the popular vote was less lopsided.

Garfield's Assassination and Civil Service Reform

Garfield, like Hayes, faced the difficult task of remaining independent while pacifying the party bosses and placating the reformers. On July 2, 1881, less than four months after taking office, Garfield was shot and died two months later. His assailant, Charles Guiteau, though clearly insane, turned out to be a disappointed office seeker, motivated by political partisanship. He told the police officer who arrested him, "I did it; I will go to jail for it: Arthur is president, and I am a Stalwart."

The press almost universally condemned Republican factionalism for creating the political climate that produced Guiteau. Attacks on the spoils system increased, and both parties claimed credit for passage of the Pendleton Civil

What factors influenced political life in the late nineteenth century?

What issues shaped party politics in the late nineteenth century?

What role did economic issues play in party realignment?

Conclusion: Why did business dominate the Gilded Age?

☑ LearningCurve
Check what you know.
bedfordstmartins.com
/roarkunderstanding

535

Service Act of 1883, which established a permanent Civil Service Commission consisting of three members appointed by the president. Some fourteen thousand jobs came under a merit system that required examinations for office and made it impossible to remove jobholders for political reasons. The new law also prohibited federal jobholders from contributing to political campaigns, thus drying up the major source of the party bosses' revenue. Businesses soon stepped in as the nation's chief political contributors. Ironically, **civil service reform** gave business an even greater influence in political life.

civil service reform

▶ Effort in the 1880s to end the spoils system and reduce government corruption. The Pendleton Civil Service Act of 1883 created the Civil Service Commission to award government jobs under a merit system that required examinations for office and made it impossible to remove jobholders for political reasons.

Reform and Scandal: The Campaign of 1884

James G. Blaine assumed leadership of the Republican Party and at long last captured the presidential nomination in 1884. A magnetic Irish American, Blaine inspired such devotion that his supporters called themselves Blainiacs. But Mugwump reformers bolted the party and embraced the Democrats' presidential nominee, Governor Grover Cleveland of New York. The burly, beer-drinking Cleveland distinguished himself from a generation of politicians by the simple

Campaign Pins, 1884

These gilt campaign pins from the election of 1884 show Republican candidate James G. Blaine, on the right, thumbing his nose at Democratic candidate Grover Cleveland. The gilt pins are a symbol for Gilded Age politics, an era characterized by corruption and party strife. Collection of Janice L. and David J. Frent.

CHAPTER LOCATOR | How did the railroads stimulate big business? | Why did the ideas of social Darwinism appeal to many Americans in the late nineteenth century?

536 CHAPTER 18
DEFINING THE GILDED AGE IN BUSINESS AND POLITICS

motto "A public office is a public trust." First as mayor of Buffalo and later as governor of New York, he built a reputation for honesty, economy, and administrative efficiency. The Democrats, who had not won the presidency since 1856, had high hopes for his candidacy, especially after the Mugwumps threw their support to Cleveland, announcing, "The paramount issue this year is moral rather than political."

The Mugwumps soon regretted their words. In July, Cleveland's hometown paper, the *Buffalo Telegraph*, dropped the bombshell that the candidate had fathered an illegitimate child in an affair with a local widow. Cleveland, a bachelor, stoically accepted responsibility for the child. Crushed by the scandal, the Mugwumps lost much of their enthusiasm. At public rallies, Blaine's partisans taunted Cleveland, chanting, "Ma, Ma, where's my Pa?"

Blaine set a new campaign style by launching a whirlwind national tour. On a last-minute stop in New York City, the exhausted candidate committed a misstep that may have cost him the election. He overlooked a remark by a supporter, a local clergyman who cast a slur on Catholic voters by styling the Democrats as the party of "Rum, Romanism, and Rebellion." Linking drinking (rum) and Catholicism (Romanism) offended Irish Catholic voters, whom Blaine had counted on to desert the Democratic Party and support him because of his Irish background.

With less than a week to go until the election, Blaine had no chance to recover from the negative publicity. He lost New York State by fewer than 1,200 votes and with it the election. In the final tally, Cleveland defeated Blaine by a scant 23,005 votes nationwide but won with 219 electoral votes to Blaine's 182 (**Map 18.2**), ending twenty-four years of Republican control of the presidency. Cleveland's followers had the last word. To the chorus of "Ma, Ma, where's my Pa?" they retorted, "Going to the White House, ha, ha, ha."

Candidate	Electoral Vote	Popular Vote	Percent of Popular Vote
Grover Cleveland (Democrat)	219	4,874,986	48.5*
James G. Blaine (Republican)	182	4,851,981	48.3

*Percentages do not total 100 because some popular votes went to other parties.

MAP 18.2 ■ The Election of 1884

QUICK REVIEW <

How did the question of civil service reform contribute to divisions within the Republican Party?

What factors influenced political life in the late nineteenth century?

What issues shaped party politics in the late nineteenth century?

What role did economic issues play in party realignment?

Conclusion: Why did business dominate the Gilded Age?

✓ LearningCurve
Check what you know.
bedfordstmartins.com
/roarkunderstanding

537

What role did economic issues play in party realignment?

FOUR YEARS LATER, in the election of 1888, fickle voters turned Cleveland out, electing Republican Benjamin Harrison, the grandson of President William Henry Harrison. Then, in the only instance in American history when a president once defeated at the polls returned to office, the voters brought Cleveland back in the election of 1892. What factors account for such a surprising turnaround? The 1880s witnessed a remarkable political realignment as a set of economic concerns replaced appeals to Civil War sectional loyalties. The tariff, federal regulation of the railroads and trusts, and the campaign for free silver restructured American politics. Then a Wall Street panic in 1893 set off a major depression that further fed political unrest.

The Tariff and the Politics of Protection

The tariff became a potent political issue in the 1880s. The concept of a protective tariff to raise the price of imported goods and stimulate American industry dated

CHAPTER LOCATOR | How did the railroads stimulate big business? | Why did the ideas of social Darwinism appeal to many Americans in the late nineteenth century?

back to the founding days of the Republic. Republicans turned the tariff to political ends in 1861 by enacting a measure that both raised revenues for the Civil War and rewarded their industrial supporters, who wanted protection from foreign competition. After the war, the pro-business Republicans continued to raise the tariff. Manufactured goods such as steel and textiles, and some agricultural products, including sugar and wool, benefited from protection. Most farm products, notably wheat and cotton, did not. By the 1880s, the tariff produced more than $2.1 billion in revenue. Not only did the high tariff pay off the nation's Civil War debt and fund pensions for Union soldiers, but it also created a huge surplus that sat idly in the Treasury's vaults while the government argued about how (or even whether) to spend it.

To many Americans, particularly southern and midwestern farmers who sold their crops in a world market but had to buy goods priced artificially high because of the protective tariff, the answer was simple: Reduce the tariff. But the Republican Party seized on the tariff question to forge a new national coalition. "Fold up the bloody shirt and lay it away," James G. Blaine advised a colleague in 1880. "It's of no use to us. You want to shift the main issue to protection." By encouraging an alliance among industrialists, labor, and western producers of raw materials — groups seen to benefit from the tariff — Blaine hoped to solidify the North, Midwest, and West against the solidly Democratic South. Although the tactic failed for Blaine in the presidential election of 1884, it worked for the Republicans four years later.

Cleveland, who had straddled the tariff issue in the election of 1884, startled the nation in 1887 by calling for tariff reform. The president attacked the tariff as a tax levied on American consumers by powerful industries. And he pointed out that high tariffs impeded the expansion of American markets abroad at a time when American industries needed to expand. The Republicans countered by arguing that "tariff tinkering" would only unsettle prosperous industries, drive down wages, and shrink the farmers' home market. Republican Benjamin Harrison, who supported the high tariff, ousted Cleveland from the White House in 1888, carrying all the western and northern states except Connecticut and New Jersey.

Back in power, the Republicans brazenly passed the highest tariff in the nation's history in 1890. The new tariff, sponsored by Republican representative William McKinley of Ohio, stirred up a hornet's nest of protest across the United States. The American people had elected Harrison to preserve protection but not to enact a higher tariff. Democrats condemned the McKinley tariff and labeled the Republican Congress that passed it the "Billion Dollar Congress" for its carnival of spending, which depleted the nation's surplus by enacting a series of pork barrel programs shamelessly designed to bring federal money to congressmen's constituencies. In the congressional election of 1890, angry voters swept the hapless Republicans, including tariff sponsor McKinley, out of office. Two years later, Harrison himself was defeated, and Grover Cleveland returned to the White House. Such were the changes in the political winds whipped up by the tariff issue.

Controversy over the tariff masked deeper divisions in American society. Conflict between workers and farmers on the one side and bankers and corporate giants on the other erupted throughout the 1880s and came to a head in the 1890s. Both sides in the tariff debate spoke to concern over class conflict when they insisted that their respective plans, whether McKinley's high tariff or Cleveland's tariff reform, would bring prosperity and harmony. For their part, many working

> CHRONOLOGY

1873
– Wall Street panic leads to major economic depression.

1887
– Interstate Commerce Act.

1890
– McKinley tariff.
– Sherman Antitrust Act.

1893
– Wall Street panic touches off national depression.

1895
– J. P. Morgan bails out U.S. Treasury.

What factors influenced political life in the late nineteenth century?

What issues shaped party politics in the late nineteenth century?

What role did economic issues play in party realignment?

Conclusion: Why did business dominate the Gilded Age?

☑ LearningCurve
Check what you know.
bedfordstmartins.com
/roarkunderstanding

539

people shared the sentiment voiced by one labor leader that the tariff was "only a scheme devised by the old parties to throw dust in the eyes of laboring men."

Railroads, Trusts, and the Federal Government

American voters may have divided on the tariff, but increasingly they agreed on the need for federal regulation of the railroads and federal legislation to curb the power of the "trusts" (a term loosely applied to all large business combinations). As early as the 1870s, angry farmers in the Midwest who suffered from the unfair shipping practices of the railroads organized to fight for railroad regulation. The Patrons of Husbandry, or the Grange, founded in 1867 as a social and educational organization for farmers, soon became an independent political movement. By electing Grangers to state office, farmers made it possible for several midwestern states to pass laws in the 1870s and 1880s regulating the railroads. At first, the Supreme Court ruled in favor of state regulation (*Munn v. Illinois*, 1877). But in 1886, the Court reversed itself, ruling that because railroads crossed state boundaries, they fell outside state jurisdiction (*Wabash v. Illinois*). With more than three-fourths of railroads crossing state lines, the Supreme Court's decision effectively quashed the states' attempts at railroad regulation.

Anger at the *Wabash* decision finally led to the first federal law regulating the railroads, the Interstate Commerce Act, passed in 1887 during Cleveland's first administration. The act established the nation's first federal regulatory agency, the **Interstate Commerce Commission (ICC)**, to oversee the railroad industry. In its early years, the ICC was never strong enough to pose a serious threat to the railroads. For example, it could not end rebates to big shippers. In its early decades, the ICC proved more important as a precedent than effective as a watchdog.

Concern over the growing power of the trusts led Congress to pass the **Sherman Antitrust Act** in 1890. The act outlawed pools and trusts, ruling that businesses could no longer enter into agreements to restrict competition. It did nothing to restrict huge holding companies such as Standard Oil, however, and proved to be a weak sword against the trusts. In the following decade, the government successfully struck down only six trusts but used the law four times against labor by outlawing unions as a "conspiracy in restraint of trade." In 1895, the conservative Supreme Court dealt the antitrust law a crippling blow in *United States v. E. C. Knight Company*. In its decision, the Court ruled that "manufacture" did not constitute "trade." This semantic quibble drastically narrowed the law, in this case allowing the American Sugar Refining Company, which had bought out a number of other sugar companies (including E. C. Knight) and controlled 98 percent of the production of sugar, to continue its virtual monopoly.

Both the ICC and the Sherman Antitrust Act testified to the nation's concern about corporate abuses of power and to a growing willingness to use federal measures to intervene on behalf of the public interest. As corporate capitalism became more and more powerful, public pressure toward government intervention grew. Yet not until the twentieth century would more active presidents sharpen and use these weapons effectively against the large corporations.

Interstate Commerce Commission (ICC)

▶ Federal regulatory agency designed to oversee the railroad industry. Congress created it through the 1887 Interstate Commerce Act after the Supreme Court decision in *Wabash v. Illinois* (1886) effectively denied states the right to regulate railroads. The ICC proved weak and did not immediately pose a threat to the industry.

Sherman Antitrust Act

▶ 1890 act that outlawed pools and trusts, ruling that businesses could no longer enter into agreements to restrict competition. Government inaction, combined with the Supreme Court's narrow reading of the act in the *United States v. E. C. Knight Company* decision, undermined the law's effectiveness.

CHAPTER LOCATOR | How did the railroads stimulate big business? | Why did the ideas of social Darwinism appeal to many Americans in the late nineteenth century?

540 CHAPTER 18 DEFINING THE GILDED AGE IN BUSINESS AND POLITICS

The Fight for Free Silver

While the tariff and regulation of the trusts gained many backers, the silver issue stirred passions like no other issue of the day. On one side stood those who believed that gold constituted the only honest money. Many who supported the gold standard were eastern creditors who did not wish to be paid in devalued dollars. On the opposite side stood a coalition of western silver barons and poor farmers from the West and South who called for **free silver**. Farmers from the West and South hoped to increase the money supply with silver dollars and create inflation, which would give them some debt relief by enabling them to

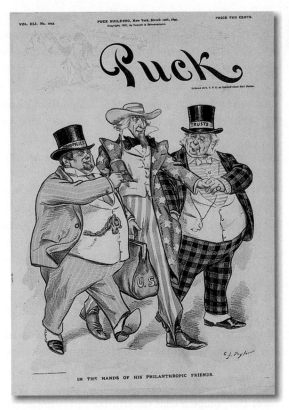

IN THE HANDS OF HIS PHILANTHROPIC FRIENDS.

pay off their creditors with cheaper dollars. The mining interests, who had seen the silver bonanza in the West drive down the price of the precious metal, wanted the government to buy silver and mint silver dollars.

During the depression following the panic of 1873, critics of hard money organized the Greenback Labor Party, an alliance of farmers and urban wage laborers. The Greenbackers favored issuing paper currency not tied to the gold supply, citing the precedent of the greenbacks issued during the Civil War. The government had the right to define what constituted legal tender, the Greenbackers reasoned: "Paper is equally money, when . . . issued according to law." They proposed that the nation's currency be based on its wealth — land, labor, and capital — and not simply on its reserves of gold. The Greenback Labor Party captured more than a million votes and elected fourteen members to Congress in 1878. Although conservatives considered the Greenbackers dangerous cranks, their views eventually prevailed in the 1930s, when the country abandoned the gold standard.

After the Greenback Labor Party collapsed, proponents of free silver came to dominate the monetary debate in the 1890s. Advocates of free silver pointed out that until 1873 the country had enjoyed a system of bimetallism — the minting of both silver and gold into coins. In that year, at the behest of those who favored gold, the Republican Congress had voted to stop buying and minting silver, an act silver supporters denounced as the "crime of '73." By sharply contracting the money supply at a time when the nation's economy was burgeoning, the Republicans had enriched bankers and investors at the expense of cotton and wheat farmers and industrial wageworkers. In 1878 and again in 1890, with the Sherman Silver Purchase Act, Congress took steps to ease the tight money policy

free silver

▶ Term used in the late nineteenth century by those who advocated minting silver dollars in addition to supporting the gold standard and the paper currency backed by gold. Poor farmers from the West and South hoped this would result in inflation, effectively providing them with debt relief. Western silver barons wanted the government to buy silver and mint silver dollars, thereby raising the price of silver.

What factors influenced political life in the late nineteenth century? | What issues shaped party politics in the late nineteenth century? | **What role did economic issues play in party realignment?** | Conclusion: Why did business dominate the Gilded Age? | ☑ LearningCurve Check what you know. bedfordstmartins.com /roarkunderstanding

541

and appease advocates of silver by passing legislation requiring the government to buy silver and issue silver certificates. Though good for the mining interests, the laws did little to promote the inflation desired by farmers. Soon monetary reformers began to call for "the free and unlimited coinage of silver," a plan whereby nearly all the silver mined in the West would be minted into coins, with sixteen ounces of silver equal in value to one ounce of gold.

By the 1890s, the silver issue crossed party lines. The Democrats hoped to use it to achieve a union between western and southern voters. Unfortunately for them, Democratic president Grover Cleveland supported the gold standard as vehemently as any Republican. After a panic on Wall Street in the spring of 1893, Cleveland called a special session of Congress and bullied the legislature into repealing the Silver Purchase Act because he believed it threatened economic confidence. Repeal proved disastrous for Cleveland. It did nothing to bring prosperity and dangerously divided the country. Angry farmers warned Cleveland not to travel west of the Mississippi River if he valued his life.

Panic and Depression

President Cleveland had scarcely begun his second term in 1893 when the country plunged into the worst depression it had yet seen. In the face of economic disaster, Cleveland clung to the economic orthodoxy of the gold standard. In the winter of 1894–95, the president walked the floor of the White House, sleepless over the prospect that the United States might go bankrupt. Individuals and investors, rushing to trade in their banknotes for gold, strained the country's monetary system. The Treasury's gold reserves dipped so low that unless they could be buttressed, the unthinkable might happen: The U.S. Treasury might not be able to meet its obligations.

At this juncture, J. P. Morgan stepped in. A group of bankers would purchase $65 million in U.S. government bonds, paying in gold. Cleveland knew that such a scheme would unleash a thunder of protest, yet to save the gold standard, the president had no choice. But if President Cleveland's action managed to salvage the gold standard, it did not save the country from hardship. In the winter of 1894–95, people faced unemployment, cold, and hunger. Cleveland, a firm believer in limited government, insisted that nothing could be done to help: "I do not believe that the power and duty of the General Government ought to be extended to the relief of individual suffering which is in no manner properly related to the public service or benefit." Nor did it occur to Cleveland that his great faith in the gold standard prolonged the depression, favored creditors over debtors, and caused immense hardship for millions of Americans.

> **QUICK REVIEW**

What role did the gold standard play in the economic crisis of the 1890s?

CHAPTER LOCATOR | How did the railroads stimulate big business? | Why did the ideas of social Darwinism appeal to many Americans in the late nineteenth century?

542   CHAPTER 18
DEFINING THE GILDED AGE IN BUSINESS AND POLITICS

Conclusion: Why did business dominate the Gilded Age?

THE GOLD DEAL BETWEEN J. P. Morgan and Grover Cleveland underscored a dangerous reality: The federal government was so weak that its solvency depended on a private banker. This lopsided power relationship signaled the dominance of business in the era Mark Twain satirically but accurately characterized as the Gilded Age. Birthed by the railroads, the new economy spawned greed, corruption, and vulgarity on a grand scale. Speculators like Jay Gould not only built but also wrecked railroads to turn paper profits; the get-rich-quick ethic of the gold miner infused the whole continent; and business boasted openly of buying politicians, who in turn lined their pockets at the public's expense.

Nevertheless, the Gilded Age was not without its share of solid achievements. Where dusty roads and cattle trails once sprawled across the continent, steel rails now bound the country together, creating a national market that enabled America to make the leap into the industrial age. Factories and refineries poured out American steel and oil at unprecedented rates. Businessmen like Carnegie, Rockefeller, and Morgan developed new strategies to consolidate American industry. New inventions, including the telephone and electric light and power, changed Americans' everyday lives. By the end of the nineteenth century, the country had achieved industrial maturity. It boasted the largest, most innovative, most productive economy in the world. No other era in the nation's history witnessed such a transformation.

Yet the changes that came with these developments worried many Americans and gave rise to the era's political turmoil. Race and gender profoundly influenced American politics, leading to new political alliances. The fearless activist Ida B. Wells fought racism in its most brutal form — lynching. Women's organizations championed causes, notably suffrage and temperance, and challenged prevailing views of woman's proper sphere. Reformers fought corruption by instituting civil service. And new issues — the tariff, the regulation of the trusts, and currency reform — restructured the nation's politics.

The Gilded Age witnessed a nation transformed. Fueled by expanding industry, cities grew exponentially, bulging at the seams with new inhabitants from around the globe and bristling with new bridges, subways, and skyscrapers. The frenzied growth of urban America brought wealth and opportunity, but also the exploitation of labor, racism toward newcomers, and social upheaval that lent a new urgency to calls for social reform.

What factors influenced political life in the late nineteenth century?

What issues shaped party politics in the late nineteenth century?

What role did economic issues play in party realignment?

Conclusion: Why did business dominate the Gilded Age?

☑ LearningCurve
Check what you know.
bedfordstmartins.com
/roarkunderstanding

543

CHAPTER 18 STUDY GUIDE

STEP 1

GET STARTED ONLINE

 LearningCurve ▪ bedfordstmartins.com/roarkunderstanding
Now that you've read the chapter, make it stick by completing the LearningCurve activity.

STEP 2

EXPLAIN WHY IT MATTERS

Put your reading into practice. Identify each term below, and then explain why it matters in U.S. history.

TERM	WHO OR WHAT & WHEN	WHY IT MATTERS
Gilded Age (p. 518)		
trust (p. 523)		
finance capitalism (p. 526)		
social Darwinism (p. 528)		
gospel of wealth (p. 528)		
spoils system (p. 529)		
Jim Crow (p. 531)		
Woman's Christian Temperance Union (WCTU) (p. 533)		
civil service reform (p. 536)		
Interstate Commerce Commission (ICC) (p. 540)		
Sherman Antitrust Act (p. 540)		
free silver (p. 541)		

STEP 3

MOVE BEYOND THE BASICS

To demonstrate a more advanced understanding, describe the positions that various political parties held on the key economic issues of the Gilded Age and assess the impact of regional differences on these issues.

Key economic issues	Democrats	Republicans	Third parties	Regional differences
Tariffs				
Railroads				
Trusts				
Free silver				

STEP 4

PUT IT ALL TOGETHER

Now, take a step back and try to explain the big picture. Remember to use specific examples from the chapter in your answers.

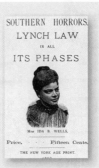

THE RISE OF BIG BUSINESS

▶ What role did railroads and new technologies play in the rise of American big business?

▶ How did the business pioneers of the late nineteenth century organize and grow their businesses?

LATE-NINETEENTH-CENTURY POLITICS

▶ How did ideas about gender and race shape late-nineteenth-century politics?

▶ How did new social philosophical theories justify business and political practices in the late nineteenth century?

ECONOMIC ISSUES AND POLITICAL CONFLICT

▶ How did each Gilded Age president react to economic issues? How did Supreme Court decisions affect economic issues?

▶ What made free silver such a powerful and emotional issue in the late nineteenth century?

LOOKING BACKWARD, LOOKING AHEAD

▶ How did the role of business in politics in the late nineteenth century differ from its role in the first half of the century?

▶ How did the rise of big business affect the economic and political landscape of early-twentieth-century America? In what ways did Americans try to deal with the excesses of big business?

> **IN YOUR OWN WORDS**

Imagine that you must give an oral report to the class answering the following question: **What were the most important business and political developments of the Gilded Age?** What would be the most important points to include and why?

> **Do it online at the Student Site ▪ bedfordstmartins.com/roarkunderstanding**

19

THE GROWTH OF AMERICA'S CITIES

1870–1900

> **What were the most important outcomes of the expansion of American cities in the late nineteenth century?** Chapter 19 explores urban growth and its consequences. It focuses on the nature of industrial labor and tensions between workers and employers and assesses the impact of urbanization on daily life. Finally, the chapter examines efforts by city government and private citizens to respond to the demands of rapid population growth.

LearningCurve
bedfordstmartins.com/roarkunderstanding
After reading the chapter, use LearningCurve to
retain what you've read.

PRICE 25¢

NEW YORK
ILLUSTRATED

> Why did American cities experience explosive growth in the late nineteenth century?

> What kinds of work did people do in industrial America?

> Why did the fortunes of the Knights of Labor rise in the late 1870s and decline in the 1890s?

> How did urban industrialism shape home life and the world of leisure?

> How did municipal governments respond to the challenges of urban expansion?

> Conclusion: Who built the cities?

Brooklyn Bridge. Completed in 1883, the Brooklyn Bridge realized builder John Roebling's dream of creating "a great work of art" as well as a superbly engineered bridge. Picture Research Consultants & Archives.

> Why did American cities experience explosive growth in the late nineteenth century?

Russian Immigrant Family

A Russian immigrant family is shown leaving Ellis Island in 1900. The white slips of paper pinned to their coats indicate that they have been processed. The family is well dressed, but the scarcity of their possessions testifies to their struggles. The woman carries her belongings in a white cloth sack, and the man holds a suitcase and bedding. Keystone-Mast Collection, UCR/California Museum of Photography, University of California, Riverside.

"WE CANNOT ALL LIVE IN CITIES, yet nearly all seem determined to do so," New York editor Horace Greeley complained. The last three decades of the nineteenth century witnessed an urban explosion. Cities and towns grew more than twice as rapidly as the total population. By 1900, the United States boasted three cities with more than a million inhabitants—New York, Chicago, and Philadelphia.

Patterns of **global migration** contributed to the rise of the city. In the port cities of the East Coast, more than fourteen million people arrived, many from southern and eastern Europe, and huddled together in dense urban ghettos. The word *slum* entered the American vocabulary along with a growing concern over the rising tide of newcomers. In the city, the widening gap between rich and poor became more visible. The gap was made more visible by changes in the city landscape brought about by advances in transportation and technology.

global migration

▶ Movement of populations across large distances such as oceans and continents. In the late nineteenth century, large-scale immigration from southern and eastern Europe into the United States contributed to the growth of cities and changes in American demographics.

The Urban Explosion: A Global Migration

The United States grew up in the country and moved to the city, or so it seemed by the end of the nineteenth century. Between 1870 and 1900, eleven million people moved into cities. Burgeoning industrial centers such as Pittsburgh, Chicago, New York, and Cleveland acted as giant magnets, attracting workers from the countryside. But rural Americans were by no means the only ones migrating to cities.

CHAPTER LOCATOR | Why did American cities experience explosive growth in the late nineteenth century? | What kinds of work did people do in industrial America?

548 CHAPTER 19 THE GROWTH OF AMERICA'S CITIES

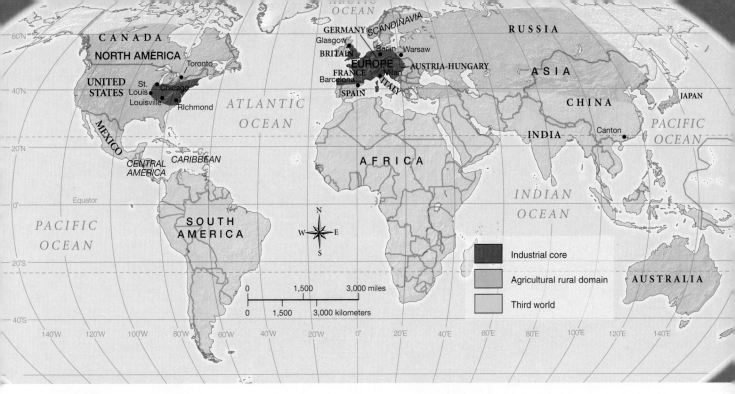

MAP 19.1 ■ Economic Regions of the World, 1890s

The global nature of the world economy at the turn of the twentieth century is indicated by three interconnected geographic regions. At the center stands the industrial core — western Europe and the northeastern United States. The second region — the agricultural periphery — supplied immigrant laborers to the industries in the core. Beyond these two regions lay a vast area tied economically to the industrial core by colonialism.

> MAP ACTIVITY

READING THE MAP: What types of economic regions were contained in the United States in this period? Which continents held most of the industrial core? Which held most of the agricultural rural domain? Which held the greatest portion of the third world?

CONNECTIONS: Which of these three regions provided the bulk of immigrant workers to the United States? What major changes prompted the global migration at the end of the nineteenth century?

Worldwide in scope, the movement from rural areas to urban industrial centers attracted millions of immigrants to American shores.

By the 1870s, the world could be conceptualized as three interconnected geographic regions (**Map 19.1**). At the center stood an industrial core that encompassed the eastern United States and western Europe. Surrounding this industrial core lay a vast agricultural domain from the Canadian wheat fields to the hinterlands of northern China. Capitalist development in the late nineteenth century shattered traditional patterns of economic activity in this rural periphery. As old patterns broke down, these rural areas exported, along with other raw materials, new recruits for the industrial labor force.

Beyond this second circle lay an even larger third world. Colonial ties between this part of the world and the industrial core strengthened in the late nineteenth century, but most of the people living there stayed put. They worked on plantations and railroads, and in mines and ports, as part of a huge export network managed by foreign powers that staked out spheres of influence and colonies in this vast region.

| Why did the fortunes of the Knights of Labor rise in the late 1870s and decline in the 1890s? | How did urban industrialism shape home life and the world of leisure? | How did municipal governments respond to the challenges of urban expansion? | Conclusion: Who built the cities? | ✓ LearningCurve Check what you know. bedfordstmartins.com /roarkunderstanding |

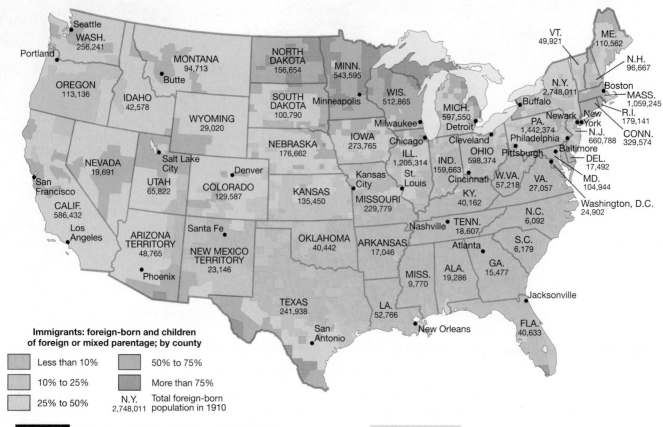

Immigrants: foreign-born and children of foreign or mixed parentage; by county

- Less than 10%
- 10% to 25%
- 25% to 50%
- 50% to 75%
- More than 75%

N.Y. 2,748,011 — Total foreign-born population in 1910

MAP 19.2 ■ The Impact of Immigration, to 1910

Immigration flowed in all directions — south from Canada, north from Mexico and Latin America, east from Asia, and west from Europe.

> MAP ACTIVITY

READING THE MAP: Which states had high percentages of immigrants? Which cities attracted the most immigrants? Which cities attracted the fewest?

CONNECTIONS: Why did most immigrants gravitate toward the cities? Why do you think the South drew such a low percentage of immigrants?

In the 1870s, railroad expansion and low steamship fares gave the world's peoples a newfound mobility, enabling industrialists to draw on a global population for cheap labor. When Andrew Carnegie opened his first steel mill in 1872, his superintendent hired workers he called "buckwheats" — young American boys just off the farm. By the 1890s, however, Carnegie's workforce was liberally sprinkled with other rural boys, Hungarians and Slavs who had migrated to the United States, willing to work for low wages.

Altogether, more than 25 million immigrants came to the United States between 1850 and 1920. They came from all directions: east from Asia, south from Canada, north from Latin America, and west from Europe (**Map 19.2**). Part of a worldwide migration, immigrants traveled to South America and Australia as well as to the United States. Yet more than 70 percent of all European immigrants chose North America as their destination.

The largest number of immigrants to the United States came from the British Isles and from German-speaking lands (**Figure 19.1**). The vast majority of immigrants were white; Asians accounted for fewer than one million immigrants, and other people

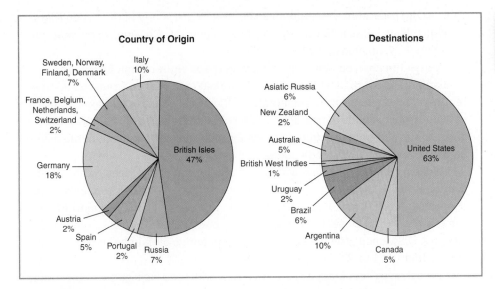

Country of Origin

- Sweden, Norway, Finland, Denmark 7%
- Italy 10%
- France, Belgium, Netherlands, Switzerland 2%
- Germany 18%
- Austria 2%
- Spain 5%
- Portugal 2%
- Russia 7%
- British Isles 47%

Destinations

- Asiatic Russia 6%
- New Zealand 2%
- Australia 5%
- British West Indies 1%
- Uruguay 2%
- Brazil 6%
- Argentina 10%
- Canada 5%
- United States 63%

> GLOBAL COMPARISON

FIGURE 19.1 ■ European Emigration, 1870–1890

European emigration between 1870 and 1890 shows that people from Germany, Austria, and the British Isles formed the largest group of out-migrants. After 1890, the origin of European emigrants tilted south and east, with Italians and eastern Europeans growing in number. The United States took in nearly two-thirds of the European emigrants. What factors account for the popularity of the United States?

of color numbered even fewer. Yet ingrained racial prejudices increasingly influenced the country's perception of immigration patterns. One of the classic formulations of the history of European immigration divided immigrants into two distinct waves that have been called the "old" and the "new" immigration. According to this theory, before 1880 the majority of immigrants came from northern and western Europe, with Germans, Irish, English, and Scandinavians making up approximately 85 percent of the newcomers. After 1880, the pattern shifted, with more and more ships carrying passengers from southern and eastern Europe. Italians, Hungarians, eastern European Jews, Turks, Armenians, Poles, Russians, and other Slavic peoples accounted for more than 80 percent of all immigrants by 1896. Implicit in the distinction was an invidious comparison between "old" pioneer settlers and "new" unskilled laborers. Yet this sweeping generalization spoke more to perception than to reality. In fact, many of the earlier immigrants from Ireland, Germany, and Scandinavia came not as settlers or farmers, but as wageworkers, and they were met with much the same disdain as the Italians and Slavs who followed them.

Steamship companies courted immigrants—a highly profitable, self-loading cargo. By the 1880s, the price of a ticket from Liverpool had dropped to less than $25. Would-be immigrants eager for information about the United States relied on letters from friends and relatives, advertisements, and word of mouth—sources that were not always dependable or truthful. Even photographs proved deceptive: Workers dressed in their Sunday best looked more prosperous than they actually were to relatives in the old country, where only the very wealthy wore white collars or silk dresses. No wonder people left for the United States believing, as one Italian immigrant observed, "that if they were ever fortunate enough to reach America, they would fall into a pile of manure and get up brushing the diamonds out of their hair."

Most of the newcomers stayed in the nation's cities. By 1900, almost two-thirds of the country's immigrant population resided in cities. Many of the immigrants were too poor to move on. (The average laborer immigrating to the United States carried only about $21.50.) Although the foreign-born rarely outnumbered the native-born population, taken together immigrants and their American-born

| Why did the fortunes of the Knights of Labor rise in the late 1870s and decline in the 1890s? | How did urban industrialism shape home life and the world of leisure? | How did municipal governments respond to the challenges of urban expansion? | Conclusion: Who built the cities? | ✔ LearningCurve Check what you know. bedfordstmartins.com /roarkunderstanding |

551

> CHRONOLOGY

1880s
- Immigration from southern and eastern Europe rises.

1890
- Jacob Riis publishes *How the Other Half Lives.*

1890s
- African American migration from the South begins.

1892
- Ellis Island opens.

1896
- President Grover Cleveland vetoes immigrant literacy test.

children did constitute a majority in some areas, particularly in the nation's largest cities: Philadelphia, 55 percent; Boston, 66 percent; Chicago, 75 percent; and New York City, an amazing 80 percent in 1900.

Not all the newcomers came to stay. Perhaps eight million European immigrants—most of them young men—worked for a year or a season and then returned to their homelands. Immigration officers called these immigrants, many of them Italians, "birds of passage" because they followed a regular pattern of migration to and from the United States. By 1900, almost 75 percent of the new immigrants were young, single men.

Women generally had less access to funds for travel and faced tighter family control. Because the traditional sexual division of labor relied on women's unpaid domestic labor and care of the very young and the very old, women most often came to the United States as wives, mothers, or daughters, not as single wage laborers. Only among the Irish did women immigrants outnumber men by a small margin from 1871 to 1891.

Jews from eastern Europe most often came with their families and came to stay. Beginning in the 1880s, a wave of violent pogroms, or persecutions, in Russia and Poland prompted the departure of more than a million Jews in the next two decades. Most of the Jewish immigrants settled in the port cities of the East, creating distinct ethnic enclaves, like Hester Street in the heart of New York City's Lower East Side, which rang with the calls of pushcart peddlers and vendors hawking their wares, from pickles to feather beds.

Racism and the Cry for Immigration Restriction

Ethnic diversity and racism played a role in dividing skilled workers (those with a craft or specialized ability) from the globe-hopping proletariat of unskilled workers (those who supplied muscle or tended machines). Skilled workers, frequently members of older immigrant groups, criticized the newcomers. One Irish worker complained, "There should be a law . . . to keep all the Italians from comin' in and takin' the bread out of the mouths of honest people."

The Irish worker's resentment brings into focus the impact of racism on America's immigrant laborers. Throughout the nineteenth century and into the twentieth, members of the educated elite as well as the uneducated viewed ethnic and even religious differences as racial characteristics, referring to the Polish or the Jewish "race." Americans judged "new" immigrants of southern and eastern European "races" as inferior. Each wave of newcomers was deemed somehow inferior to the established residents. The Irish who criticized the Italians so harshly had themselves been stigmatized as a lesser "race" a generation earlier.

Immigrants not only brought their own religious and racial prejudices to the United States but also absorbed the popular prejudices of American culture. Social Darwinism, with its strongly racist overtones, decreed that whites stood at the top of the evolutionary ladder. But who was "white"? Skin color supposedly served as a marker for the "new" immigrants—"swarthy" Italians; dark-haired, olive-skinned Jews. But even blond, blue-eyed Poles were not considered white. The social construction of "race" is nowhere more apparent than in the testimony of an Irish dockworker who boasted that he hired only "white

CHAPTER LOCATOR | Why did American cities experience explosive growth in the late nineteenth century? | What kinds of work did people do in industrial America?

CHAPTER 19
552 THE GROWTH OF AMERICA'S CITIES

men," a category that he insisted excluded "Poles and Italians." For the new immigrants, Americanization and assimilation would prove inextricably part of becoming "white."

For African Americans, the cities of the North promised not just economic opportunity but also an escape from institutionalized segregation and persecution. Throughout the South, Jim Crow laws—restrictions that segregated blacks—became common in the decades following Reconstruction. Intimidation and lynching terrorized blacks. "To die from the bite of frost is far more glorious than at the hands of a mob," proclaimed the *Defender*, Chicago's largest African American newspaper. In the 1890s, many blacks moved north, settling for the most part in the growing cities. Racism relegated them to poor jobs and substandard living conditions, but by 1900 New York, Philadelphia, and Chicago had the largest black communities in the nation. Although the most significant African American migration out of the South would occur during and after World War I, the great exodus was already under way.

On the West Coast, Asian immigrants became scapegoats of the changing economy. Hard times in the 1870s made them a target for disgruntled workers. Prohibited from owning land, the Chinese migrated to the cities. In 1870, San Francisco housed a Chinese population estimated at 12,022, and it continued to grow until passage of the Chinese Exclusion Act in 1882 (see chapter 17). For the first time in the nation's history, U.S. law excluded an immigrant group on the basis of race.

Huang Zunxian came to San Francisco in 1882 as Chinese consul general. Disillusioned with the anti-Chinese violence he saw all around him, he wrote a series of angry poems that took Americans to task for their hypocrisy. One of them read:

> They have sealed the gates tightly,
> Door after door with guards beating alarms.
>
>   . . . .
>
> Anyone with a yellow-colored face
> Is beaten even if guiltless.
>
>   . . . .
>
> The American eagle strides the heavens soaring,
> With half of the globe clutched in his claw.
> Although the Chinese arrived later,
> Couldn't you leave them a little space?

Despite the Chinese Exclusion Act, some Chinese managed to come to America using a loophole that allowed relatives to join their families. Meanwhile, the number of Japanese immigrants rapidly grew, leading to the creation in 1910 of an immigration station at Angel Island in San Francisco Bay through which many Asians entered the United States.

On the East Coast, the volume of immigration from Europe in the last two decades of the century proved unprecedented. In 1888 alone, more than half a million Europeans landed in America, 75 percent of them in New York City. The Statue of Liberty, a gift from the people of France erected in 1886, stood sentinel in the harbor.

| Why did the fortunes of the Knights of Labor rise in the late 1870s and decline in the 1890s? | How did urban industrialism shape home life and the world of leisure? | How did municipal governments respond to the challenges of urban expansion? | Conclusion: Who built the cities? | ✔ LearningCurve Check what you know. bedfordstmartins.com /roarkunderstanding |

553

Ellis Island

▶ Immigration facility opened in 1892 in New York harbor that processed new immigrants coming into New York City. In the late nineteenth century, some 75 percent of European immigrants to America came through New York.

When the federal government took over immigration in 1890, it built a facility on **Ellis Island** in New York harbor, which opened in 1892. After fire gutted the wooden building, a new brick edifice replaced it in 1900. Its overcrowded halls became the gateway to the United States for millions. To many Americans, the "new" immigrants seemed impossible to assimilate. "These people are not Americans," editorialized the popular journal *Public Opinion;* "they are the very scum and offal of Europe." Terence V. Powderly, head of the broadly inclusive Knights of Labor, complained that the newcomers "herded together like animals and lived like beasts." Blue-blooded Yankees led by Senator Henry Cabot Lodge of Massachusetts formed an unlikely alliance with leaders of organized labor—who feared that immigrants would drive down wages—to press for immigration restrictions. In 1896, Congress approved a literacy test for immigrants, but President Grover Cleveland promptly vetoed it. "It is said," the president reminded Congress, "that the quality of recent immigration is undesirable. The time is quite within recent memory when the same thing was said of immigrants, who, with their descendants, are now numbered among our best citizens."

The Social Geography of the City

During the Gilded Age, the social geography of the city changed enormously. Cleveland, Ohio, provides a good example. In the 1870s, Cleveland was a small city in both population and area. Oil magnate John D. Rockefeller could, and often did, walk from his large brick house on Euclid Avenue to his office downtown. On his way, he passed the small homes of his clerks and other middle-class families. Behind these homes ran miles of alleys crowded with the dwellings of Cleveland's working class. Farther out, on the shores of Lake Erie, close to the factories and foundries, clustered the shanties of the city's poorest laborers.

Within two decades, the Cleveland that Rockefeller knew no longer existed. The coming of mass transit transformed the walking city. In its place emerged a central business district surrounded by concentric rings of residences organized by ethnicity and income. First the horsecar in the 1870s and then the electric streetcar in the 1880s made it possible for those who could afford the five-cent fare to work downtown and flee after work to the "cool green rim" of the city. Social segregation—the separation of rich and poor, and of recent immigrants and old-stock Americans—became one of the major social changes engendered by the rise of the industrial metropolis.

Race and ethnicity affected the way cities evolved. Newcomers to the nation's cities faced hostility and not surprisingly sought out their kin and country folk as they struggled to survive. Distinct ethnic neighborhoods often formed around a synagogue or church. African Americans typically experienced the greatest residential segregation, but every large city had its ethnic enclaves—Little Italy, Chinatown, Bohemia Flats, Germantown—where English was rarely spoken.

Poverty, crowding, dirt, and disease constituted the daily reality of New York City's immigrant poor—a plight documented by photojournalist Jacob Riis in his best-selling book *How the Other Half Lives* (1890). By taking his camera into the hovels of the poor, Riis opened the nation's eyes to conditions in the city's slums.

While Riis's audience shivered at his revelations about the "other half," many middle-class Americans worried equally about the excesses of the wealthy. They

CHAPTER LOCATOR | Why did American cities experience explosive growth in the late nineteenth century? | What kinds of work did people do in industrial America?

554 CHAPTER 19
THE GROWTH OF AMERICA'S CITIES

feared the class antagonism fueled by the growing chasm between rich and poor and shared Riis's view that "the real danger to society comes not only from the tenements, but from the ill-spent wealth which reared them."

The excesses of the Gilded Age's newly minted millionaires were nowhere more visible than in the lifestyle of the Vanderbilts. Alva Vanderbilt launched herself into New York society in 1883 with a costume party so opulent that her sister-in-law Alice Vanderbilt appeared as that miraculous new invention, the electric light, resplendent in a white satin evening dress studded with diamonds.

Such ostentatious displays of wealth became especially alarming when they were coupled with disdain for the well-being of ordinary people. When a reporter in 1882 asked William Vanderbilt whether he considered the public good when running his railroads, he shot back, "The public be damned." The fear that America had become a plutocracy—a society ruled by the rich—gained credence from the fact that the wealthiest 1 percent of the population owned more than half the real and personal property in the country. As the new century dawned, reformers would form a progressive movement to address the problems of urban industrialism and the substandard living and working conditions it produced.

QUICK REVIEW

What global trends were reflected in the growth of America's cities in the late nineteenth century?

Why did the fortunes of the Knights of Labor rise in the late 1870s and decline in the 1890s?

How did urban industrialism shape home life and the world of leisure?

How did municipal governments respond to the challenges of urban expansion?

Conclusion: Who built the cities?

LearningCurve
Check what you know.
bedfordstmartins.com
/roarkunderstanding

> What kinds of work did people do in industrial America?

Clerical Worker A stenographer takes dictation in an 1890s office. Notice that the apron, that symbol of feminine domesticity, accompanied women into the workplace. In the 1880s, with the invention of the typewriter, many women put their literacy skills to use in the nation's offices. Brown Brothers.

THE NUMBER OF INDUSTRIAL WAGEWORKERS in the United States exploded in the second half of the nineteenth century, more than tripling from 5.3 million in 1860 to 17.4 million in 1900. These workers toiled in a variety of settings. Many skilled workers and artisans still earned a living in small workshops. But with the rise of corporate capitalism, large factories, mills, and mines increasingly dotted the landscape. Sweatshops and the contracting out of pieces of assembly work, including finishing garments by hand, provided work experiences different from those of factory operatives and industrial workers. Pick-and-shovel labor constituted the lowest-paid labor, while managers, as well as women "typewriters" and salesclerks, formed a new white-collar segment of America's workforce. Children also worked in growing numbers in mills and mines across the country.

America's Diverse Workers

Common laborers formed the backbone of the American labor force. They built the railroads and subways, tunneled under New York's East River to anchor the Brooklyn Bridge, and helped lay the foundation of industrial America. These "human machines" generally came from the most recent immigrant groups. Initially, the Irish wielded the picks and shovels that built American cities, but by the turn of the century, as the Irish bettered their lot, Slavs and Italians took up their tools.

CHAPTER LOCATOR | Why did American cities experience explosive growth in the late nineteenth century? | **What kinds of work did people do in industrial America?**

CHAPTER 19
556 THE GROWTH OF AMERICA'S CITIES

At the opposite end of labor's hierarchy stood skilled craftsmen like iron puddler James J. Davis, a Welsh immigrant who worked in the Pennsylvania mills. Using brains along with brawn, puddlers earned good wages—Davis drew up to $7 a day, when there was work. But most industry and manufacturing work in the nineteenth century remained seasonal; few workers could count on year-round pay. In addition, two major depressions twenty years apart—one beginning in 1873, the other in 1893—brought unemployment and hardship. With no social safety net, even the best worker could not guarantee security for his family. "The fear of ending in the poor-house is one of the terrors that dog a man through life," Davis confessed.

Employers attempted to replace people with machines, breaking down skilled work into ever-smaller tasks that could be performed by unskilled factory operatives. New England's textile mills provide a classic example. Mary, a weaver at the mills in Fall River, Massachusetts, went to work in the 1880s at the age of twelve. Mechanization of the looms had reduced the job of the weaver to watching for breaks in the thread. "At first the noise is fierce, and you have to breathe the cotton all the time, but you get used to it," Mary told a reporter from *Independent* magazine. "When the bobbin flies out and a girl gets hurt, you can't hear her shout—not if she just screams, you can't. She's got to wait, 'till you see her. . . . Lots of us is deaf."

During the 1880s, the number of foreign-born mill workers almost doubled. At Fall River, Mary and her Scots-Irish family resented the new immigrants. "The Polaks learn weavin' quick," she remarked, using a common derogatory term to identify a rival group. "They just as soon live on nothin' and work like that. But it won't do 'em much good for all they'll make out of it." Employers encouraged racial and ethnic antagonism because it inhibited labor organization.

Mechanization transformed the garment industry as well. The introduction of the foot-pedaled sewing machine in the 1850s and the use of mechanical cloth-cutting knives drove out independent tailors, who were replaced by pieceworkers. Sadie Frowne, a sixteen-year-old Polish Jew, worked in a Brooklyn **sweatshop** in the 1890s. Frowne sewed for eleven hours a day in a 20-by-14-foot room containing fourteen machines. "The machines go like mad all day, because the faster you work the more money you get," she recalled. She earned about $4.50 a week and, by rigid economy, tried to save $2 from her weekly pay. Young and single, Frowne typified the woman wage earner in the late nineteenth century. In 1890, the average workingwoman was twenty-two and had been working since the age of fifteen, laboring twelve hours a day six days a week and earning less than $6 a week.

The Family Economy: Women and Children

In 1900, the typical male worker in manufacturing earned $500 a year, about $12,000 in today's dollars. Many working-class families, whether native-born or immigrant, lived in or near poverty, their economic survival dependent on the contributions of all family members, regardless of sex or age. "Father," asked one young immigrant girl, "does everybody in America live like this? Go to work early, come home late, eat and go to Sleep? And the next day again work, eat, and sleep?" Most workers did. The **family economy** meant that everyone contributed to maintain even the most meager household.

sweatshops

▶ Small rooms used for clothing piecework beginning in the later nineteenth century. As mechanization transformed the garment industry with the introduction of foot-pedaled sewing machines and mechanical cloth-cutting knives, independent tailors were replaced with sweatshop workers hired by contractors to sew pieces into clothing.

family economy

▶ Economic contributions of multiple members of a household that were necessary to the survival of the family. From the late nineteenth century into the twentieth, many working-class families depended on the wages of all family members, regardless of sex or age.

| Why did the fortunes of the Knights of Labor rise in the late 1870s and decline in the 1890s? | How did urban industrialism shape home life and the world of leisure? | How did municipal governments respond to the challenges of urban expansion? | Conclusion: Who built the cities? | ☑ **LearningCurve** Check what you know. bedfordstmartins.com /roarkunderstanding |

557

The faces and hands of the two bootblacks shown here with a third boy on a New York City street in 1896 testify to their grimy trade. Boys as young as six worked on city streets as bootblacks and newsboys. For these child workers, education was a luxury they could not afford. Alice Austin photo, Staten Island Historical Society.

In the cities, boys as young as six years old plied their trades as bootblacks and newsboys. Often working under an adult contractor, these children earned as little as fifty cents a day. Many of them were homeless—orphaned or cast off by their families. "We wuz six, and we ain't got no father," a child of twelve told reporter Jacob Riis. "Some of us had to go."

Child labor increased each decade after 1870. The percentage of children under fifteen engaged in paid labor did not drop until after World War I. The 1900 census estimated that 1,750,178 children ages ten to fifteen were employed, an increase of more than a million over thirty years. Children in this age range consti-tuted more than 18 percent of the industrial labor force.

The number of women working for wages in nonagricultural occupations more than doubled between 1870 and 1900 (**Figure 19.2**). Yet white married women, even among the working class, rarely worked for wages outside the home. In 1890, only 3 percent were employed. Black women, married and unmar-ried, worked out of the home for wages in much greater numbers. The 1890 cen-sus showed that 25 percent of married African American women were employed, often as domestics in the houses of white families.

White-Collar Workers: Managers, "Typewriters," and Salesclerks

In the late nineteenth century, a managerial revolution created a new class of white-collar workers who worked in offices and stores. As skilled workers saw their crafts replaced by mechanization, some moved into management positions.

CHAPTER LOCATOR | Why did American cities experience explosive growth in the late nineteenth century? | What kinds of work did people do in industrial America?

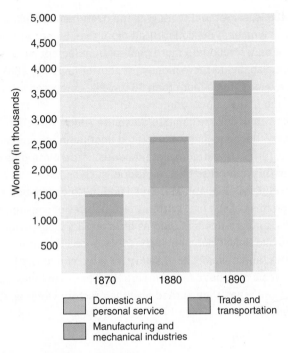

FIGURE 19.2 ■ Women and Work, 1870–1890

In 1870, close to 1.5 million women worked in nonagricultural occupations. By 1890, that number had more than doubled to 3.7 million. More and more women sought work in manufacturing and mechanical industries, although domestic service still constituted the largest employment arena for women.

"The middle class is becoming a salaried class," a writer for the *Independent* magazine observed, "and is rapidly losing the economic and moral independence of former days." As large business organizations consolidated, corporate development separated management from ownership, and the job of directing the firm became the province of salaried executives and managers, the majority of whom were white men drawn from the 8 percent of Americans who held high school diplomas.

The new white-collar workforce also included women **"typewriters"** and salesclerks. In the decades after the Civil War, as businesses became larger and more far-flung, the need for more elaborate and exact records, as well as the greater volume of correspondence, led to the hiring of more office workers. The adding machine, the cash register, and the typewriter came into general use in the 1880s. Employers seeking literate workers soon turned to nimble-fingered women. Educated men had many other career choices, but for middle-class white women, secretarial work constituted one of the very few areas where they could put their literacy to use for wages.

Sylvie Thygeson was typical of the young women who went to work as secretaries. Thygeson grew up in an Illinois prairie town and went to work as a country schoolteacher after graduating from high school in 1884. Realizing that teaching school did not pay a living wage, she mastered typing and stenography and found work as a secretary to help support her family. According to her account, she made "a fabulous sum of money" (possibly $25 a month). Nevertheless, she gave up her job after a few years when she met and married her husband.

"typewriters"

▶ Women who were hired by businesses in the decades after the Civil War to keep records and conduct correspondence, often using equipment such as typewriters. Secretarial work constituted one of the very few areas where middle-class women could use their literacy for wages.

Why did the fortunes of the Knights of Labor rise in the late 1870s and decline in the 1890s? | How did urban industrialism shape home life and the world of leisure? | How did municipal governments respond to the challenges of urban expansion? | Conclusion: Who built the cities? | ✔ LearningCurve Check what you know. bedfordstmartins.com /roarkunderstanding

559

But by the 1890s, secretarial work was the overwhelming choice of native-born, single white women, who constituted more than 90 percent of the female clerical force. Not only considered more genteel than factory work or domestic labor, office work also meant more money for shorter hours. In 1883, Boston's clerical workers on average made more than $6 a week, compared with less than $5 for women working in manufacturing.

As a new consumer culture came to dominate American urban life in the late nineteenth century, department stores offered another employment opportunity for women in the cities. Boasting ornate facades, large plate-glass display windows, and marble and brass fixtures, stores such as Macy's in New York, Wanamaker's in Philadelphia, and Marshall Field in Chicago stood as monuments to the material promise of the era. Within these palaces of consumption, cash girls, stock clerks, and wrappers earned as little as $3 a week, while at the top of the scale, buyers like Belle Cushman of the fancy goods department at Macy's earned $25 a week, an unusually high salary for a woman in the 1870s. Salesclerks counted themselves a cut above factory workers. Their work was neither dirty nor dangerous, and even when they earned less than factory workers, they felt a sense of superiority.

> **QUICK REVIEW**

How did business expansion and consolidation change workers' occupations in the late nineteenth century?

CHAPTER LOCATOR | Why did American cities experience explosive growth in the late nineteenth century? | What kinds of work did people do in industrial America?

CHAPTER 19
560   THE GROWTH OF AMERICA'S CITIES

Why did the fortunes of the Knights of Labor rise in the late 1870s and decline in the 1890s?

Destruction from the Great Railroad Strike of 1877

Pictures of the devastation caused in Pittsburgh during the Great Railroad Strike shocked many Americans. When militiamen fired on striking workers, killing more than twenty strikers, the mob retaliated by destroying a two-mile area along the track, reducing it to a smoldering rubble. Property damage totaled $2 million. In the aftermath, the curious came out to view the destruction. Carnegie Library of Pittsburgh.

BY THE LATE NINETEENTH CENTURY, industrial workers were losing ground in the workplace. In the fierce competition to reduce prices and cut costs, industrialists invested heavily in new machinery that replaced skilled workers with unskilled labor. The erosion of skills and the redefinition of labor as mere "machine tending" left the worker with a growing sense of individual helplessness that spurred collective action. The 1870s and 1880s witnessed the emergence of two labor unions—the Knights of Labor and the American Federation of Labor. In 1877, in the midst of a depression, labor flexed its muscle in the Great Railroad Strike. But unionism would suffer a major setback after the mysterious Haymarket bombing in 1886.

The Great Railroad Strike of 1877

Economic depression following the panic of 1873 threw as many as three million people out of work. Those who were lucky enough to keep their jobs watched as pay cuts eroded wages until they could no longer feed their families. In the summer of 1877, the Baltimore and Ohio (B&O) Railroad announced a 10 percent wage cut at the same time it declared a 10 percent dividend to its stockholders. Angry

| Why did the fortunes of the Knights of Labor rise in the late 1870s and decline in the 1890s? | How did urban industrialism shape home life and the world of leisure? | How did municipal governments respond to the challenges of urban expansion? | Conclusion: Who built the cities? | ✓ LearningCurve Check what you know. bedfordstmartins.com /roarkunderstanding |

Strike activity

MAP 19.3 ■ The Great Railroad Strike of 1877

Starting in West Virginia and Pennsylvania, the strike spread as far north as Albany, New York, and as far west as San Francisco, bringing rail traffic to a standstill. Called the Great Uprising, the strike heralded the beginning of a new era of working-class protest and trade union organization.

Great Railroad Strike

▶ Nationwide strike that began in 1877 with West Virginia railroad brakemen who protested against sharp wage reductions. The strike quickly spread to include roughly 600,000 workers. When it grew violent, President Rutherford B. Hayes used federal troops to break the strike. Despite the strike's failure, union membership surged.

> CHRONOLOGY

1869
– Knights of Labor is founded.

1873
– Panic on Wall Street touches off a depression.

1877
– Great Railroad Strike.

1886
– American Federation of Labor (AFL) is founded.
– Haymarket bombing.

brakemen in West Virginia, whose wages had already fallen from $70 to $30 a month, walked out on strike. One B&O worker described the hardship that drove him to take such desperate action: "We eat our hard bread and tainted meat two days old on the sooty cars up the road, and when we come home, find our wives complaining that they cannot even buy hominy and molasses for food."

The West Virginia brakemen's strike touched off the **Great Railroad Strike** of 1877, a nationwide uprising that spread rapidly to Pittsburgh and Chicago, St. Louis and San Francisco (**Map 19.3**). Within a few days, nearly 100,000 railroad workers had walked off the job. An estimated 500,000 sympathetic laborers soon joined the train workers. In Reading, Pennsylvania, militiamen refused to fire on the strikers, saying, "We may be militiamen, but we are workmen first." Rail traffic ground to a halt; the nation lay paralyzed.

Violence erupted as the strike spread. In Pittsburgh, militia brought in from Philadelphia fired on the crowds, killing twenty people. Angry workers retaliated by reducing an area two miles long beside the tracks to rubble. Before the day ended, the militia had shot twenty more workers, and the railroad had sustained more than $2 million in property damage.

Within eight days, the governors of nine states, acting at the prompting of the railroad owners and managers, defined the strike as an "insurrection" and called for federal troops. President Rutherford B. Hayes, after hesitating briefly, called out the army. By the time the troops arrived, the violence had run its course. Federal troops did not shoot a single striker in 1877. But they struck a blow against labor by acting as strikebreakers—opening rail traffic, protecting nonstriking

CHAPTER LOCATOR

Why did American cities experience explosive growth in the late nineteenth century?

What kinds of work did people do in industrial America?

562
CHAPTER 19
THE GROWTH OF AMERICA'S CITIES

"scab" train crews, and maintaining peace along the line. In three weeks, the strike was over.

Middle-class Americans initially sympathized with the conditions that led to the strike. But they quickly condemned the strikers for the violence and property damage that occurred. The *New York Times* editorialized about the "dangerous classes," and the *Independent* magazine offered the following advice on how to deal with "rioters": "If the club of a policeman, knocking out the brains of the rioter, will answer then well and good; but if it does not promptly meet the exigency, then bullets and bayonets . . . constitutes [*sic*] the one remedy and one duty of the hour."

"The strikes have been put down by force," President Hayes noted in his diary on August 5. "But now for the real remedy. Can't something be done by education of the strikers, by judicious control of the capitalists, by wise general policy to end or diminish the evil? The railroad strikers, as a rule, are good men, sober, intelligent, and industrious." While Hayes acknowledged the workers' grievances, most businessmen condemned the idea of labor unions as agents of class warfare. For their part, workers quickly recognized that they held little power individually and flocked to join unions. As labor leader Samuel Gompers noted, the nation's first national strike dramatized the frustration and unity of the workers and served as an alarm bell to labor "that sounded a ringing message of hope to us all."

The Knights of Labor and the American Federation of Labor

The **Knights of Labor**, the first mass organization of America's working class, proved the chief beneficiary of labor's newfound consciousness. The Noble and Holy Order of the Knights of Labor had been founded in 1869 as a secret society of workers who envisioned a "universal brotherhood" of all workers, from common laborers to master craftsmen. Secrecy and ritual served to bind Knights together at the same time that it discouraged company spies and protected members from reprisals.

Although the Knights played no active role in the 1877 railroad strike, membership swelled as a result of the growing interest in labor organizing that followed the strike. In 1878, the Knights abandoned secrecy and launched an ambitious campaign to organize workers. The Knights attempted to bridge the boundaries of ethnicity, gender, ideology, race, and occupation. Leonora Barry served as general investigator for women's work from 1886 to 1890, helping the Knights recruit teachers, waitresses, housewives, and domestics along with factory and sweatshop workers. Women composed perhaps 20 percent of the membership. The Knights also recruited more than 95,000 black workers. That the Knights of Labor often fell short of its goals to unify the working class proved less surprising than the scope of its efforts. Under the direction of Grand Master Workman Terence V. Powderly, the Knights became the dominant force in labor during the 1880s.

The Knights of Labor was not without rivals. Many skilled workers belonged to craft unions organized by trade. Among the largest and richest of these unions stood the Amalgamated Association of Iron and Steel Workers, founded in 1876 and counting twenty thousand skilled workers as members. Trade unionists spurned the broad reform goals of the Knights and focused on workplace issues. Samuel Gompers founded the Organized Trades and Labor Unions in 1881 and reorganized it in 1886 into the **American Federation of Labor (AFL)**, which

Knights of Labor

▶ The first mass organization of America's working class. Founded in 1869, the Knights of Labor attempted to bridge the boundaries of ethnicity, gender, ideology, race, and occupation to build a "universal brotherhood" of all workers.

American Federation of Labor (AFL)

▶ Organization created by Samuel Gompers in 1886 that coordinated the activities of craft unions throughout the United States. The AFL worked to achieve immediate benefits for skilled workers. Its narrow goals for unionism became popular after the Haymarket bombing.

| Why did the fortunes of the Knights of Labor rise in the late 1870s and decline in the 1890s? | How did urban industrialism shape home life and the world of leisure? | How did municipal governments respond to the challenges of urban expansion? | Conclusion: Who built the cities? | ☑ LearningCurve Check what you know. bedfordstmartins.com /roarkunderstanding |

563

- Public ownership of railroads
- An income tax
- Equal pay for women workers
- Abolition of child labor
- One union of all workers (except gamblers, stockbrokers, lawyers, bankers, and liquor dealers) without class distinctions

coordinated the activities of craft unions throughout the United States. His plan was simple: Organize skilled workers such as machinists and locomotive engineers — those with the most bargaining power — and use strikes to gain immediate objectives such as higher pay and better working conditions. At first, Gompers drew few converts. The AFL had only 138,000 members in 1886, compared with 730,000 for the Knights of Labor. But events soon brought down the Knights, and Gompers's brand of unionism came to prevail.

Haymarket and the Specter of Labor Radicalism

While the AFL and the Knights of Labor competed for members, more radical labor groups, including socialists and anarchists, believed that reform was futile and called instead for social revolution. Both the socialists and the anarchists, sensitive to criticism that they preferred revolution in theory to improvements here and now, rallied around the popular issue of the eight-hour workday.

Since the 1840s, labor had sought to end the twelve-hour workday, which was standard in industry and manufacturing. By the mid-1880s, it seemed clear to many workers that labor shared too little in the new prosperity of the decade, and pressure mounted for the eight-hour workday. Labor championed the popular issue and launched major rallies in cities across the nation. Supporters of the movement set May 1, 1886, as the date for a nationwide general strike in support of the eight-hour workday.

All factions of the labor movement came together in Chicago on May Day. A group of labor radicals led by anarchist Albert Parsons, a *Mayflower* descendant, and August Spies, a German socialist, spearheaded the eight-hour movement in Chicago. Chicago's Knights of Labor rallied to the cause even though Terence Powderly and the union's national leadership, worried about the increasing activism of the rank and file, refused to endorse the movement for shorter hours. Samuel Gompers was on hand, too, to lead the city's trade unionists, although he privately urged the AFL assemblies not to participate in the general strike.

The cautious labor leaders stood in sharp contrast to the dispossessed workers out on strike across town at Chicago's huge McCormick reaper works. There strikers watched helplessly as the company brought in strikebreakers to take their jobs and marched the "scabs" to work under the protection of the Chicago police and security guards supplied by the Pinkerton Detective Agency. Cyrus McCormick Jr., son of the inventor of the mechanical reaper, viewed labor organization as a threat to his power as well as to his profits; he was determined to smash the union.

Haymarket bombing

▶ May 4, 1886, conflict in which both workers and policemen were killed or wounded during a labor demonstration in Chicago. The violence began when someone threw a bomb into the ranks of police at the gathering. The incident created a backlash against labor activism.

CHAPTER LOCATOR | Why did American cities experience explosive growth in the late nineteenth century? | What kinds of work did people do in industrial America?

564   CHAPTER 19
THE GROWTH OF AMERICA'S CITIES

During the May Day rally, 45,000 workers paraded peacefully down Michigan Avenue in support of the eight-hour day. Trouble came two days later, when strikers attacked strikebreakers outside the McCormick works and police opened fire, killing or wounding six men. Angry radicals urged workers to "arm yourselves and appear in full force" at a rally in Haymarket Square.

On the evening of May 4, the turnout at Haymarket was disappointing. No more than two or three thousand gathered in the drizzle to hear Spies, Parsons, and the other speakers. Mayor Carter Harrison, known as a friend of labor, mingled conspicuously in the crowd, pronounced the meeting peaceable, and went home to bed. Sometime later, police captain John "Blackjack" Bonfield marched his men into the crowd, by now fewer than three hundred people, and demanded that it disperse. Suddenly, someone threw a bomb into the police ranks. After a moment of stunned silence, the police drew their revolvers. "Fire and kill all you can," shouted a police lieutenant. When the melee ended, seven policemen and an unknown number of others lay dead. An additional sixty policemen and thirty or forty civilians suffered injuries.

News of the "Haymarket riot" provoked a nationwide convulsion of fear, followed by blind rage directed at anarchists, labor unions, strikers, immigrants, and the working class in general. Eight men, including Parsons and Spies, went on trial in Chicago. "Convict these men," thundered the state's attorney, Julius S. Grinnell, "make examples of them, hang them, and you save our institutions." Although the state could not link any of the defendants to the **Haymarket bombing**, the jury nevertheless found them all guilty. Four men were hanged, one committed suicide, and three received prison sentences.

The bomb blast at Haymarket had lasting repercussions. To commemorate the death of the Haymarket martyrs, labor made May 1 an annual international celebration of the worker. But the Haymarket bomb, in the eyes of one observer, proved "a godsend to all enemies of the labor movement." It effectively scotched the eight-hour movement and dealt a blow to the Knights of Labor. With the labor movement everywhere under attack, many skilled workers turned to the American Federation of Labor. Gompers's narrow economic strategy made sense at the time and enabled one segment of the workforce—the skilled—to organize effectively and achieve tangible gains.

"The Chicago Riot"

Inflammatory pamphlets published in the wake of the Haymarket bombing aimed to scare the public. In this charged atmosphere, the anarchist speakers at the rally were tried and convicted for the bombing even though witnesses testified that none of them had thrown the bomb. Even today, the identity of the bomb thrower remains uncertain. Chicago Historical Society.

> **VISUAL ACTIVITY**

READING THE IMAGE: What does the cover suggest about the views of the author of the pamphlet?
CONNECTIONS: In what ways does this pamphlet reflect the public climate following the Haymarket bombing?

QUICK REVIEW <

What were the long-term effects of the Great Railroad Strike of 1877 and the Haymarket bombing of 1886?

Why did the fortunes of the Knights of Labor rise in the late 1870s and decline in the 1890s?	How did urban industrialism shape home life and the world of leisure?	How did municipal governments respond to the challenges of urban expansion?	Conclusion: Who built the cities?	 LearningCurve Check what you know. bedfordstmartins.com /roarkunderstanding

How did urban industrialism shape home life and the world of leisure?

Beach Scene at Coney Island

Coney Island became a symbol of commercialized leisure and mechanical excitement at the turn of the twentieth century. This fanciful rendering of Coney Island captures men and women frolicking in the waves. Notice the modest woolen bathing outfits. Men box and play ball, a woman flies on a parachute, a uniformed policeman wades into the fray, while the Ferris wheel dominates onshore. Sunday crowds reportedly reached 100,000. Library of Congress.

THE GROWTH OF URBAN INDUSTRIALISM not only dramatically altered the workplace but also transformed home and family life, and it gave rise to new forms of commercialized leisure. Industrialization redefined the very concepts of work and home. Increasingly, men went out to work for wages, while most white married women stayed home, either working in the home without pay—cleaning, cooking, and rearing children—or supervising paid domestic servants who did the housework.

cult of domesticity

▶ Nineteenth-century belief that women's place was in the home, where they should create havens for their families. This sentimentalized ideal led to an increase in the hiring of domestic servants, thus freeing white middle-class women to spend time in pursuits outside the home.

Domesticity and "Domestics"

The separation of the workplace and the home that marked the shift to industrial society led to a new ideology, one that sentimentalized the home and women's role in it. The cultural ideal dictating that a woman's place was in the home, where she would create a haven for her family, began to develop in the early nineteenth century. It has been called the **cult of domesticity**, a phrase used to prescribe an ideal of middle-class, white womanhood that dominated the period from 1820 to the end of the nineteenth century.

CHAPTER LOCATOR | Why did American cities experience explosive growth in the late nineteenth century? | What kinds of work did people do in industrial America?

566 CHAPTER 19 THE GROWTH OF AMERICA'S CITIES

The cult of domesticity and the elaboration of the middle-class home led to a major change in patterns of hiring household help. The live-in servant, or domestic, became a fixture in the North, replacing the hired girl of the previous century. In American cities by 1870, 15 to 30 percent of all households included live-in domestic servants, more than 90 percent of them women. Earlier in the mid-nineteenth century, native-born women increasingly took up other work and left domestic service to immigrants. In the East, the maid was so often Irish that "Bridget" became a generic term for female domestics. The South continued to rely on poorly paid black female "help."

Servants by all accounts resented the long hours and lack of privacy. "She is liable to be rung up at all hours," one study of domestics reported. "Her very meals are not secure from interruption, and even her sleep is not sacred." Domestic service became the occupation of last resort, a "hard and lonely life" in the words of one female servant.

For women of the white middle class, domestics were a boon, freeing them from household drudgery and giving them more time to spend with their children, to pursue club work, or to work for reforms. Thus, while domestic service supported the cult of domesticity, it created for those women who could afford it opportunities that expanded their horizons outside the home. They became involved in women's clubs as well as the temperance and suffrage movements.

Cheap Amusements

Growing class divisions manifested themselves in patterns of leisure as well as in work and home life. The poor and working class took their leisure, when they had any, not in the crowded tenements that housed their families, but increasingly in the cities' new dance halls, music houses, ballparks, and amusement arcades, which by the 1890s formed a familiar part of the urban landscape.

Young workingwomen no longer met prospective husbands only through their families. Fleeing crowded tenements, the young sought each other's company in dance halls and other commercial retreats. Young workingwomen counted on being "treated" by men, a transaction that often implied sexual payback. Their behavior sometimes blurred the line between respectability and promiscuity. The dance halls became a favorite target of reformers who feared they lured teenage girls into prostitution.

For men, baseball became a national pastime in the 1870s—then, as now, one force in urban life capable of uniting a city across class lines. Cincinnati mounted the first entirely paid team, the Red Stockings, in 1869. Soon professional teams proliferated in cities across the nation, and Mark Twain hailed baseball as "the very symbol, the outward and visible expression, of the drive and push and rush and struggle of the raging, tearing, booming nineteenth century."

Why did the fortunes of the Knights of Labor rise in the late 1870s and decline in the 1890s? | **How did urban industrialism shape home life and the world of leisure?** | How did municipal governments respond to the challenges of urban expansion? | Conclusion: Who built the cities? | ✔ LearningCurve Check what you know. bedfordstmartins.com /roarkunderstanding

567

The increasing commercialization of entertainment in the late-nineteenth-century city was best seen at Coney Island. A two-mile stretch of sand nine miles from Manhattan by trolley or steamship, Coney Island in the 1890s was transformed into the site of some of the largest and most elaborate amusement parks in the country. Promoter George Tilyou built Steeplechase Park in 1897, advertising "10 hours of fun for 10 cents." With its mechanical thrills and fun-house laughs, the amusement park encouraged behavior that one schoolteacher aptly described as "everyone with the brakes off." By 1900, as many as a million New Yorkers flocked to Coney Island on any given weekend, making the amusement park the unofficial capital of a new mass culture.

> ## QUICK REVIEW

How and why did recreation and leisure change in the last decades of the nineteenth century?

CHAPTER LOCATOR | Why did American cities experience explosive growth in the late nineteenth century? | What kinds of work did people do in industrial America?

568 CHAPTER 19
THE GROWTH OF AMERICA'S CITIES

How did municipal governments respond to the challenges of urban expansion?

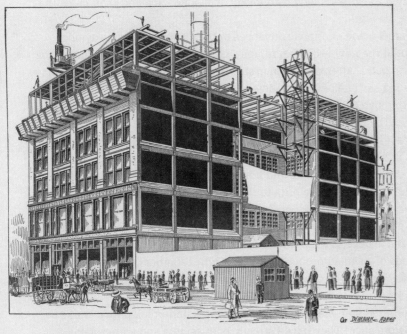

VIEW OF CONSTRUCTION OF "THE FAIR" BUILDING, CHICAGO.
Illustrating Paper by W. L. B. Jenney, Architect, published in this number.

Chicago Skyscraper Going Up

With the advent of structural steel, skyscrapers like this one in progress in Chicago in 1891 became prominent features of the American urban landscape. This architect's rendering of the Fair Building, a department store designed by William Le Baron Jenney, shows a modern skyscraper whose foundations supported the structural steel skeleton so that the walls could simply "hang" on the outside of the building, because they no longer had to support the structure. Newberry Library (*Inland Architect*, Nov. 1891).

PRIVATE ENTERPRISE, not planners, built the cities of the United States. With a few notable exceptions, cities simply mushroomed, formed by the dictates of profit and the exigencies of local politics. With the rise of the city came the need for public facilities, transportation, and services that would tax the imaginations of America's architects and engineers and set the scene for the rough-and-tumble of big-city government, politics, and bossism.

Building Cities of Stone and Steel

Skyscrapers and mighty bridges dominated the imagination and the urban landscape. Less imposing but no less significant were the paved streets, the parks and public libraries, and the subways and sewers. In the late nineteenth century,

| Why did the fortunes of the Knights of Labor rise in the late 1870s and decline in the 1890s? | How did urban industrialism shape home life and the world of leisure? | **How did municipal governments respond to the challenges of urban expansion?** | Conclusion: Who built the cities? | ✓ LearningCurve Check what you know. bedfordstmartins.com /roarkunderstanding |

569

1871
- Boss Tweed's rule in New York City ends.
- Chicago's Great Fire.

1883
- Brooklyn Bridge opens.

1893
- World's Columbian Exposition.
- Panic on Wall Street touches off a major economic depression.

1895
- Boston Public Library opens in Copley Square.

1897
- Nation's first subway system opens in Boston.

Americans rushed to embrace new technology of all kinds, making their cities the most modern in the world.

Structural steel made enormous advances in building possible. No symbol better represented the new urban landscape than the Brooklyn Bridge, which took fourteen years to build. After the massive steel and stone structure opened in May 1883, it was hailed as "one of the wonders of the world." A decade after the completion of the Brooklyn Bridge, engineers used the new technology of structural steel to construct the Williamsburg Bridge. More prosaic and utilitarian than its neighbor, the new bridge was never as acclaimed, but it was longer by four feet and completed in half the time. It became the model for future building as the age of steel supplanted the age of stone and iron.

Chicago, not New York, gave birth to the modern skyscraper. Rising from the ashes of the Great Fire of 1871, which destroyed three square miles and left eighteen thousand people homeless, Chicago offered a generation of skilled architects and engineers the chance to experiment. Commercial architecture became an art form at the hands of a skilled group of architects who together constituted the "Chicago school." Employing the dictum "Form follows function," they built startlingly modern structures.

Across the United States, municipal governments undertook public works on a scale never before seen. They paved streets, built sewers and water mains, replaced gas lamps with electric lights, ran trolley tracks on the old horsecar lines, and dug underground to build subways, tearing down the unsightly elevated tracks that had clogged city streets. Boston completed the nation's first subway system in 1897, and New York and Philadelphia soon followed.

Cities became more beautiful with the creation of urban public parks to complement the new buildings that quickly filled city lots. Much of the credit for America's greatest parks goes to one man—landscape architect Frederick Law Olmsted. New York City's Central Park, completed in 1873, became the first landscaped public park in the United States. Olmsted and his partner, Calvert Vaux, directed the planting of more than five million trees, shrubs, and vines to transform the eight hundred acres between 59th Street and 110th Street into an oasis for urban dwellers. "We want a place," he wrote, where people "may stroll for an hour, seeing, hearing, and feeling nothing of the bustle and jar of the streets."

American cities did not overlook the mind in their efforts at improvement. They created a comprehensive free public school system that educated everyone from the children of the middle class to the sons and daughters of immigrant workers. Yet the exploding urban population strained the system and led to crowded and inadequate facilities. In 1899, more than 544,000 pupils attended school in New York City's five boroughs. Municipalities across the United States provided free secondary school education for all who wished to attend, even though only 8 percent of Americans completed high school.

To educate those who couldn't go to school, American cities created the most extensive free public library system in the world. In 1895, the Boston Public Library opened its bronze doors in its new Copley Square location under the inscription "Free to All." Designed in the style of a Renaissance palazzo, with more than 700,000 books on the shelves ready to be checked out, the library earned the description "a palace of the people."

CHAPTER LOCATOR | Why did American cities experience explosive growth in the late nineteenth century? | What kinds of work did people do in industrial America?

CHAPTER 19
570 THE GROWTH OF AMERICA'S CITIES

Despite the Boston Public Library's motto "Free to All," the poor did not share equally in the advantages of city life. The parks, the libraries, and even the subways and sewers benefited some city dwellers more than others. Few library cards were held by Boston's laborers, who worked six days a week and found the library closed on Sunday. And in the 1890s, there was nothing central about New York's Central Park. It was a four-mile walk from the tenements of Hester Street to the park's entrance at 59th Street and Fifth Avenue. Then, as now, the comfortable majority, not the indigent minority, reaped a disproportionate share of the benefits in the nation's big cities.

Any story of the American city, it seems, must be a tale of two cities—or, given the cities' great diversity, a tale of many cities within each metropolis. At the turn of the twentieth century, a central paradox emerged: The enduring monuments of America's cities—the bridges, skyscrapers, parks, and libraries—stood as the undeniable achievements of the same system of municipal government that reformers dismissed as boss-ridden, criminal, and corrupt.

City Government and the "Bosses"

The physical growth of the cities required the expansion of public services and the creation of entirely new facilities: streets, subways, elevated trains, bridges, docks, sewers, and public utilities. There was work to be done and money to be made. The rise of the professional politician—the colorful big-city boss—resulted from urban growth, and **bossism** became a national phenomenon. Though corrupt and often criminal, the boss saw to the building of the city and provided needed social services for the new residents in return for their political support. Yet not even the big-city boss could be said to rule the unruly city. The governing of America's cities resembled more a tug-of-war than boss rule.

The most notorious of all the city bosses was William Marcy "Boss" Tweed of New York City. At midcentury, Boss Tweed's Democratic Party "machine" held sway. A machine was really no more than a political party organized at the grassroots level. Its purpose was to win elections and reward its followers, often with jobs on the city's payroll. New York's citywide Democratic machine, Tammany Hall, commanded an army of party functionaries. They formed a shadow government more powerful than the city's elected officials.

As chairman of the Tammany general committee, Tweed kept the Democratic Party together and ran the city through the use of bribery and graft. "As long as I count the votes," he shamelessly boasted, "what are you going to do about it?" The excesses of the Tweed ring soon led to a clamor for reform and cries of "Throw the rascals out." Tweed's rule ended in 1871. Eventually, he was tried and convicted, and later died in jail. New York was not the only city to experience bossism and corruption. The British visitor James Bryce concluded in 1888, "There is no denying that the government of cities is the one conspicuous failure of the United States." More than 80 percent of the nation's thirty largest cities experienced some form of boss rule in the decades around the turn of the twentieth century. However, infighting among powerful ward bosses often meant that no single boss enjoyed exclusive power in the big cities.

bossism

▶ Pattern of urban political organization that arose in the late nineteenth century in which an often corrupt "boss" maintains an inordinate level of power through command of a political machine that distributes services to its constituents.

| Why did the fortunes of the Knights of Labor rise in the late 1870s and decline in the 1890s? | How did urban industrialism shape home life and the world of leisure? | **How did municipal governments respond to the challenges of urban expansion?** | Conclusion: Who built the cities? | ✓ LearningCurve Check what you know. bedfordstmartins.com /roarkunderstanding |

571

Urban reformers and proponents of good government (derisively called "goo goos" by their rivals) challenged machine rule and sometimes succeeded in electing reform mayors. But the reformers rarely managed to stay in office for long. Their detractors called them "mornin' glories," observing that they "looked lovely in the mornin' and withered up in a short time." The bosses enjoyed continued success largely because the urban political machine helped the cities' immigrants and poor, who remained the bosses' staunchest allies. "What tells in holding your district," a Tammany ward boss observed, "is to go right down among the poor and help them in the different ways they need help. It's philanthropy, but it's politics, too—mighty good politics."

The big-city boss, through the skillful orchestration of rewards, exerted powerful leverage and lined up support for his party from a broad range of constituents, from the urban poor to wealthy industrialists. In 1902, when journalist Lincoln Steffens began "The Shame of the Cities," a series of articles exposing city corruption, he found that business leaders who fastidiously refused to mingle socially with the bosses nevertheless struck deals with them. "He is a self-righteous fraud, this big businessman," Steffens concluded. "I found him buying boodlers [bribers] in St. Louis, defending grafters in Minneapolis, originating corruption in Pittsburgh, sharing with bosses in Philadelphia, deploring reform in Chicago, and beating good government with corruption funds in New York."

For all the color and flamboyance of the big-city boss, he was simply one of many actors in the drama of municipal government. Old-stock aristocrats, new professionals, saloon keepers, pushcart peddlers, and politicians all fought for their interests in the hurly-burly of city government. They didn't much like each other, and they sometimes fought savagely. But they learned to live with one another. Compromise and accommodation—not boss rule—best characterized big-city government by the turn of the twentieth century, although the cities' reputation for corruption left an indelible mark on the consciousness of the American public.

White City or City of Sin?

Americans have always been of two minds about the city. They like to boast of its skyscrapers and bridges, its culture and sophistication, and they pride themselves on its bigness and bustle. At the same time, they fear it as the city of sin, the home of immigrant slums, the center of vice and crime. Nowhere did the divided view of the American city take form more graphically than in Chicago in 1893. In that year, Chicago hosted the **World's Columbian Exposition**, the grandest world's fair in the nation's history. The fairground, only five miles down the shore of Lake Michigan from downtown Chicago, offered a lesson in what Americans on the eve of the twentieth century imagined a city might be. Christened the "White City," the fairground seemed light-years away from Chicago, with its stockyards, slums, and bustling terminals. Frederick Law Olmsted and architect Daniel Burnham supervised the transformation of a swampy wasteland into a pristine paradise of lagoons, fountains, wooded islands, gardens, and imposing white buildings.

World's Columbian Exposition

▶ World's fair held in Chicago in 1893 that attracted millions of visitors. The elaborately designed pavilions of the "White City" included exhibits of technological innovation and of cultural exoticism. The white buildings embodied an urban ideal that contrasted with the realities of Chicago life.

CHAPTER LOCATOR | Why did American cities experience explosive growth in the late nineteenth century? | What kinds of work did people do in industrial America?

This painting by H. D. Nichols captures the monumental architecture of the White City built for the World's Columbian Exposition in 1893. Monumental, harmonious, and pristine, the White City was designed by Daniel Burnham and Frederick Law Olmsted to awe and overwhelm fairgoers. And so it did, drawing millions of visitors from America and abroad. Chicago Historical Society.

"Sell the cookstove if necessary and come," novelist Hamlin Garland wrote to his parents on the farm. And come they did, in spite of the panic and depression that broke out only weeks after the fair opened in May 1893. In six months, fairgoers purchased more than 27 million tickets, turning a profit of nearly half a million dollars for promoters. Visitors from home and abroad strolled the elaborate grounds and visited the exhibits—everything from a model of the Brooklyn Bridge carved in soap to the latest goods and inventions. Half carnival, half culture, the great fair offered something for everyone. On the Midway Plaisance, crowds thrilled to the massive wheel built by G. W. G. Ferris and watched agog as Little Egypt danced the hootchy-kootchy.

In October, the fair closed its doors in the midst of the worst depression the country had yet seen. During the winter of 1894, Chicago's unemployed and homeless took over the grounds, vandalized the buildings, and frightened the city's comfortable citizens out of their wits. When reporters asked Daniel Burnham, its chief architect, what should be done with the moldering remains of the White City, he responded, "It should be torched." And it was. In July 1894, in a clash between federal troops and striking railway workers, incendiaries set fires that leveled the fairgrounds.

| Why did the fortunes of the Knights of Labor rise in the late 1870s and decline in the 1890s? | How did urban industrialism shape home life and the world of leisure? | **How did municipal governments respond to the challenges of urban expansion?** | Conclusion: Who built the cities? | ✓ LearningCurve Check what you know. bedfordstmartins.com /roarkunderstanding |

573

In the end, the White City remained what it had always been, a dream-scape. Buildings that looked like marble were actually constructed of staff, a plaster substance that began to crumble even before fire destroyed the fairgrounds. Perhaps it was not so strange, after all, that the legacy of the White City could be found on Coney Island, where two new amusement parks, Luna and Dreamland, sought to combine, albeit in a more tawdry form, the beauty of the White City and the thrill of the Midway Plaisance. More enduring than the White City itself was what it represented: the emergent industrial might of the United States, at home and abroad, with its inventions, manufactured goods, and growing consumer culture.

> QUICK REVIEW

How did city life change in the late nineteenth century?

CHAPTER LOCATOR | Why did American cities experience explosive growth in the late nineteenth century? | What kinds of work did people do in industrial America?

AS MUCH AS THE GREAT INDUSTRIALISTS and financiers, as much as engineers and landscape architects, it was common workers, most of them immigrants, who built the nation's cities. The unprecedented growth of urban, industrial America resulted from the labor of millions of men, women, and children who toiled in workshops and factories, in sweatshops and mines, on railroads and construction sites across America.

America's cities in the late nineteenth century teemed with life. Townhouses and tenements jostled for space with skyscrapers and great department stores, while parks, ball fields, amusement arcades, and public libraries provided the city masses with recreation and entertainment. Municipal governments, straining to build the new cities, experienced the rough-and-tumble of machine politics as bosses and their constituents looked to profit from city growth.

For America's workers, urban industrialism along with the rise of big business and corporate consolidation drastically changed the workplace. Industrialists replaced skilled workers with new machines that could be operated by cheaper unskilled labor. And during hard times, employers did not hesitate to cut workers' already meager wages. As the Great Railroad Strike of 1877 demonstrated, when labor united, it could bring the nation to attention. Organization held out the best hope for the workers; first the Knights of Labor and later the American Federation of Labor won converts among the nation's working class.

The rise of urban industrialism challenged the American promise, which for decades had been dominated by Jeffersonian agrarian ideals. Could such a promise exist in the changing world of cities, tenements, immigrants, and huge corporations? In the great depression that came in the 1890s, mounting anger and frustration would lead farmers and workers to join forces and create a grassroots movement to fight for change under the banner of a new People's Party.

| Why did the fortunes of the Knights of Labor rise in the late 1870s and decline in the 1890s? | How did urban industrialism shape home life and the world of leisure? | How did municipal governments respond to the challenges of urban expansion? | Conclusion: Who built the cities? | ✓ LearningCurve Check what you know. bedfordstmartins.com /roarkunderstanding |

575

CHAPTER 19 STUDY GUIDE

STEP 1

GET STARTED ONLINE

LearningCurve ▪ bedfordstmartins.com/roarkunderstanding
Now that you've read the chapter, make it stick by completing the LearningCurve activity.

STEP 2

EXPLAIN WHY IT MATTERS

Put your reading into practice. Identify each term below, and then explain why it matters in U.S. history.

TERM	WHO OR WHAT & WHEN	WHY IT MATTERS
global migration (p. 548)		
Ellis Island, (p. 554)		
sweatshops (p. 557)		
family economy (p. 557)		
"typewriters" (p. 559)		
Great Railroad Strike (p. 562)		
Knights of Labor (p. 563)		
American Federation of Labor (AFL) (p. 563)		
Haymarket bombing (p. 565)		
cult of domesticity (p. 566)		
bossism (p. 571)		
World's Columbian Exposition (p. 572)		

STEP 3

MOVE BEYOND THE BASICS

To demonstrate a more advanced understanding, describe the key characteristics of American cities at the turn of the twentieth century and the impact that these characteristics had on city life.

Characteristic	The American city, ca. 1900	Impact on city life
Population		
Diversity		
Social structure		
Work and labor relations		
Politics		
Domestic life		
Leisure		

Now, take a step back and try to explain the big picture. Remember to use specific examples from the chapter in your answers.

URBANIZATION

▶ What factors led immigrants to American cities in the late nineteenth century? How did their arrival change the cities in which they settled?

▶ How and why did the social geography of the American city change in the late nineteenth century?

INDUSTRY AND LABOR

▶ What new social divisions accompanied business expansion and industrialization?

▶ What kinds of organizations did workers form in the late nineteenth century, and why did they start them? How successful were they?

CITY LIFE

▶ How did urban industrialism transform home and family life?

▶ What led to the rise of the big-city boss? Whose interests did late-nineteenth-century city governments serve?

LOOKING BACKWARD, LOOKING AHEAD

▶ How did early-twentieth-century American cities differ from their early-nineteenth-century counterparts?

▶ How did the rise of urban industrialism change Americans' sense of themselves as a people?

> ## IN YOUR OWN WORDS

Imagine that you must give an oral report to the class answering the following question: What were the most important outcomes of the expansion of American cities in the late nineteenth century? What would be the most important points to include and why?

 Do it online at the Student Site ■ **bedfordstmartins.com/roarkunderstanding**

20
DISSENT, DEPRESSION, AND WAR

1890–1900

> Why was the decade of the 1890s such a turbulent time in U.S. history? Chapter 20 explores the political and economic conflicts of the 1890s through the lenses of diverse groups of Americans. It also examines the major shift in U.S. foreign policy in the last decade of the nineteenth century.

LearningCurve
bedfordstmartins.com/roarkunderstanding
After reading the chapter, use LearningCurve to retain what you've read.

The Unemployed — Scene at a Country Railway Station. The Graphic, Chicago, September 9, 1893.
Chicago History Museum.

> Why did American farmers organize alliances in the late nineteenth century?

> What led to the labor wars of the 1890s?

> How were women involved in late-nineteenth-century politics?

> How did economic problems affect American politics in the 1890s?

> Why did the United States largely abandon its isolationist foreign policy in the 1890s?

> Conclusion: What was the connection between domestic strife and foreign policy?

> Why did American farmers organize alliances in the late nineteenth century?

Nebraska Farm Family

A Nebraska farm family poses in front of their sod hut in Custer County, Nebraska, in 1889. The house is formed of blocks of sod cut from the prairie. This photo testifies to the hard, lonely life of farmers on the Great Plains. Nebraska State Historical Society.

HARD TIMES in the 1880s and 1890s created a groundswell of agrarian revolt. A bitter farmer wrote from Minnesota: "I settled on this Land in good Faith Built House and Barn. Broken up Part of the Land. Spent years of hard Labor in grubbing fencing and Improving." About to lose his farm to foreclosure, he lamented, "Are they going to drive us out like trespassers . . . and give us away to the Corporations?"

Farm prices fell decade after decade, even as American farmers' share of the world market grew (**Figure 20.1**). In parts of Kansas, corn sold for as little as ten cents a bushel, and angry farmers burned their crops for fuel rather than take them to market. At the same time, consumer prices soared (**Figure 20.2**). In Kansas alone, almost half the farms had fallen into the hands of the banks by 1894 through foreclosure. Farmers soon banded together into Farmers' Alliances, which gave birth to a broad political movement.

The Farmers' Alliance

At the heart of the farmers' problems stood a banking system dominated by eastern commercial banks committed to the gold standard, a railroad rate system both capricious and unfair, and rampant speculation that drove up the price of land. In the West, farmers rankled under a system that allowed railroads to charge them

> CHRONOLOGY

1876
– First Farmers' Alliance forms in Lampasas County, Texas.

1892
– Farmers' Alliance forms the People's Party and launches the Populist movement.

CHAPTER LOCATOR | Why did American farmers organize alliances in the late nineteenth century? | What led to the labor wars of the 1890s?

580 CHAPTER 20
DISSENT, DEPRESSION, AND WAR

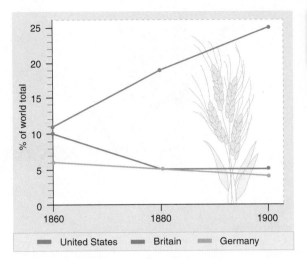

FIGURE 20.1 ■ **Share of World Wheat Market, 1860–1900**

Although many countries produced wheat for home markets, Britain, Germany, and the United States were among the largest wheat exporters. Exporting wheat worldwide became viable after the completion of the transcontinental railroad in 1869. The resulting growth of the railroads, coupled with the development of improved mechanical reapers throughout the second half of the century, led to the mechanization of U.S. agriculture, allowing wheat farmers to harvest ever-larger crops.

exorbitant freight rates while granting rebates to large shippers (see chapter 18). In the South, lack of currency and credit drove farmers to the stopgap credit system of the crop lien. Determined to do something, farmers banded together to fight for change.

Farm protest was not new. In the 1870s, farmers had supported the Grange and the Greenback Labor Party. As the farmers' situation grew more desperate, they organized, forming regional alliances. The first **Farmers' Alliance** came together in 1876 in Lampasas County, Texas, to fight "landsharks and horse thieves." In frontier farmhouses in Texas, in log cabins in the backwoods of Arkansas, and in the rural parishes of Louisiana, separate groups of farmers formed similar alliances for self-help.

As the movement grew in the 1880s, farmers' groups consolidated into two regional alliances: the Northwestern Farmers' Alliance, active in Kansas, Nebraska, and other midwestern Granger states; and the more radical Southern Farmers' Alliance. Traveling lecturers preached the Alliance message. Worn-out men and careworn women did not need to be convinced that something was wrong. By 1890, the Southern Farmers' Alliance alone counted more than three million members.

Radical in its inclusiveness, the Southern Alliance reached out to African Americans, women, and industrial workers. Through cooperation with the Colored Farmers' Alliance, an African American group founded in Texas in the 1880s, blacks and whites attempted to make common cause. As Georgia's Tom Watson, a Southern Alliance stalwart, pointed out, "The colored tenant is in the same boat as the white tenant, . . . and . . . the accident of color can make no difference in the interests of farmers, croppers, and laborers." Women rallied to the Alliance banner. "I am going to work for prohibition, the Alliance, and for Jesus as long as I live," swore one woman.

At the heart of the Alliance movement stood a series of farmers' cooperatives. By "bulking" their cotton — that is, selling it together — farmers could negotiate a better price. And by setting up trade stores and exchanges, they sought to escape the grasp of the merchant/creditor. Through the cooperatives, the Farmers'

Farmers' Alliance

▶ Movement to form local organizations to advance farmers' collective interests that gained popularity in the 1880s. Over time, farmers' groups consolidated into two regional alliances: the Northwestern Farmers' Alliance and the Southern Farmers' Alliance. In 1892, the Farmers' Alliance gave birth to the People's Party and launched the Populist movement.

| How were women involved in late-nineteenth-century politics? | How did economic problems affect American politics in the 1890s? | Why did the United States largely abandon its isolationist foreign policy in the 1890s? | Conclusion: What was the connection between domestic strife and foreign policy? | ✓ LearningCurve Check what you know. bedfordstmartins.com /roarkunderstanding |

FIGURE 20.2 ■ Consumer Prices and Farm Income, 1865–1910

Around 1870, consumer prices and farm income were about equal. During the 1880s and 1890s, however, farmers suffered great hardships as prices for their crops steadily declined and the cost of consumer goods continued to rise.

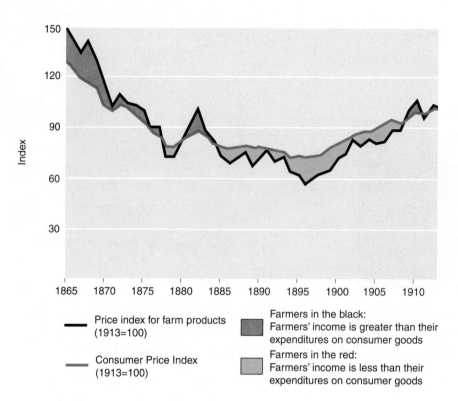

Price index for farm products (1913=100)

Consumer Price Index (1913=100)

Farmers in the black: Farmers' income is greater than their expenditures on consumer goods

Farmers in the red: Farmers' income is less than their expenditures on consumer goods

Alliance promised to change the way farmers lived. "We are going to get out of debt and be free and independent people once more," exulted one Georgia farmer. But the Alliance faced insurmountable difficulties in running successful cooperatives. Opposition by merchants, bankers, wholesalers, and manufacturers made it impossible for the cooperatives to get credit. As the cooperative movement died, the Farmers' Alliance moved into politics.

The Populist Movement

In the earliest days of the Alliance movement, a leader of the Southern Farmers' Alliance insisted, "The Alliance is a strictly white man's nonpolitical, secret business association." But by 1892, it was none of those things. Advocates of a third party carried the day at a convention of laborers, farmers, and common folk in 1892 in St. Louis, where the Farmers' Alliance gave birth to the **People's Party** and launched the Populist movement. The same spirit of religious revival that animated the Farmers' Alliance infused the People's Party. Convinced that the money and banking systems worked to the advantage of the wealthy few, they demanded economic democracy. To help farmers get the credit they needed at reasonable rates, southern farmers hit on the ingenious idea of a subtreasury — a plan that would allow farmers to store their nonperishable crops until prices rose and to receive commodity credit from the federal government to obtain needed supplies.

People's Party (Populist Party)

▶ Political party formed in 1892 by the Farmers' Alliance to advance the goals of the Populist movement. Populists sought economic democracy, promoting land, electoral, banking, and monetary reform. Republican victory in the presidential election of 1896 effectively destroyed the People's Party.

CHAPTER LOCATOR | Why did American farmers organize alliances in the late nineteenth century? | What led to the labor wars of the 1890s?

582 CHAPTER 20
DISSENT, DEPRESSION, AND WAR

The sweeping array of Populist reforms enacted in the Populist platform changed the agenda of politics for decades to come. More than just a response to hard times, Populism presented an alternative vision of American economic democracy.

> The Populist Platform

- Championed land reform, including a plan to reclaim excessive land granted to railroads or sold to foreign investors.
- Proposed government ownership of the railroads and telegraph system to put an end to discriminatory rates.
- Supported free silver to ease the nation's tight money supply.
- Called for electoral reforms, such as the direct election of senators and the secret ballot, and the right to initiate legislation, to recall elected officials, and to submit issues to the people by means of a referendum.
- Supported the eight-hour workday.

QUICK REVIEW

Why did the Farmers' Alliance decide to form a political party?

How were women involved in late-nineteenth-century politics?

How did economic problems affect American politics in the 1890s?

Why did the United States largely abandon its isolationist foreign policy in the 1890s?

Conclusion: What was the connection between domestic strife and foreign policy?

☑ LearningCurve
Check what you know.
bedfordstmartins.com
/roarkunderstanding

> What led to the labor wars of the 1890s?

National Guard Occupying Pullman, Illinois

After President Grover Cleveland called out troops to put down the Pullman strike in 1894, the National Guard occupied the town of Pullman. The intervention enabled owner George M. Pullman to bring in strikebreakers and defeat the unions. Chicago Historical Society.

WHILE FARMERS UNITED to fight for change, industrial laborers fought their own battles in a series of bloody strikes historians have called the "labor wars." Industrial workers took a stand in the 1890s. At issue was the right of workers to organize and to speak through unions, to bargain collectively, and to fight for better working conditions, higher wages, shorter hours, and greater worker control in the face of increased mechanization. Three major conflicts — the lockout of steelworkers in Homestead, Pennsylvania, in 1892; the miners' strike in Cripple Creek, Colorado, in 1894; and the Pullman boycott that same year — raised fundamental questions about the rights of labor and the sanctity of private property.

The Homestead Lockout

In 1892, steelworkers in Pennsylvania squared off against Andrew Carnegie in a decisive struggle over the right to organize in the Homestead steel mills. When the Amalgamated Iron and Steel Workers, one of the largest and richest craft unions in the American Federation of Labor (AFL), attempted to renew its contract at Carnegie's Homestead mill, Carnegie resolved to crush the union. The union's leaders were told that since "the vast majority of our employees are Non union, the Firm has decided that the minority must give place to the majority."

CHAPTER LOCATOR | Why did American farmers organize alliances in the late nineteenth century? | **What led to the labor wars of the 1890s?**

CHAPTER 20
584 DISSENT, DEPRESSION, AND WAR

While it was true that only 800 skilled workers belonged to the elite Amalgamated, the union had long enjoyed the support of the plant's 3,000 non-union workers. Slavs, who did much of the unskilled work, made common cause with the Welsh, Scottish, and Irish skilled workers who belonged to the union.

Carnegie preferred not to be directly involved in the union busting, so that spring he sailed to Scotland and left Henry Clay Frick, the toughest antilabor man in the industry, in charge. By summer, a strike looked inevitable. Frick prepared by erecting a fifteen-foot fence around the Homestead plant and topping it with barbed wire. Workers aptly dubbed it "Fort Frick." Frick then hired 316 mercenaries from the Pinkerton National Detective Agency at the rate of $5 per day, more than double the wage of the average Homestead worker.

On June 28, the **Homestead lockout** began when Frick locked the doors of the mills and prepared to bring in strikebreakers. Hugh O'Donnell, the young Irishman who led the union, vowed to prevent "scabs" from entering the plant. On July 6 at 4 a.m., a lookout spotted two barges moving up the Monongahela River in the fog. Frick was attempting to smuggle his Pinkertons into Homestead.

Workers sounded the alarm, and within minutes a crowd of more than a thousand, hastily armed with rifles, hoes, and fence posts, rushed to the riverbank. When the Pinkertons attempted to come ashore, gunfire broke out, and more than a dozen Pinkertons and some thirty strikers fell, killed or wounded. The Pinkertons retreated to the barges. For twelve hours, the workers, joined by their family members, threw everything they had at the barges, from fireworks to dynamite. Finally, the Pinkertons hoisted a white flag and arranged with O'Donnell to surrender. With three workers dead and scores wounded, the crowd, numbering perhaps ten thousand, was in no mood for conciliation. As the hated "Pinks" came up the hill, they were forced to run a gantlet of screaming, cursing men, women, and children. When a young guard dropped to his knees, weeping for mercy, a woman used her umbrella to poke out his eye. One Pinkerton had been killed in the siege on the barges. In the grim rout that followed their surrender, not one avoided injury. In the aftermath of the battle, the workers took control of the plant and elected a council to run the community. At first, public opinion favored their cause. A congressman castigated Carnegie for "skulking in his castle in Scotland." Populists, meeting in St. Louis, condemned the use of "hireling armies."

The action of the Homestead workers struck at the heart of the capitalist system, pitting the workers' right to their jobs against the rights of private property. The workers' insistence that "we are not destroying the property of the company — merely protecting our rights" did not prove as compelling to the courts and the state as the property rights of the owners. Four days after the confrontation, Pennsylvania's governor, who sympathized with the workers, nonetheless yielded to pressure from Frick and ordered eight thousand National Guard troops into Homestead to protect Carnegie's property. The workers, thinking they had nothing to fear from the militia, welcomed the troops with a brass band. But the troops' occupation not only protected Carnegie's property but also enabled Frick to reopen the mills and bring in strikebreakers. "We have been deceived," one worker complained bitterly. "We have stood idly by and let the town be occupied by soldiers who come here, not as our protectors, but as the protectors of non-union men. . . . If we undertake to resist the seizure of our jobs, we will be shot down like dogs."

> CHRONOLOGY

1892
- Homestead lockout.

1893
- Stock market crash touches off economic depression.

1894
- Miners' strike in Cripple Creek, Colorado.
- Pullman boycott is crushed.

Homestead lockout

▶ 1892 lockout of workers at the Homestead, Pennsylvania, steel mill after Andrew Carnegie refused to renew the union contract and workers prepared to strike. Union supporters attacked the Pinkerton National Detective Agency guards hired to protect the mill, but the National Guard soon broke the strike.

| How were women involved in late-nineteenth-century politics? | How did economic problems affect American politics in the 1890s? | Why did the United States largely abandon its isolationist foreign policy in the 1890s? | Conclusion: What was the connection between domestic strife and foreign policy? | ✓ LearningCurve Check what you know. bedfordstmartins.com /roarkunderstanding |

The nation's attention was riveted on labor strife at the Homestead steel mill in the summer of 1892. *Frank Leslie's Illustrated Weekly* ran a cover story on the violence that Pinkerton agents faced from an armed crowd of men, women, and children who were enraged that Henry Clay Frick had hired the Pinkertons to bring in strikebreakers. Beaten and overwhelmed by the strikers, the Pinkertons surrendered. The New-York Historical Society Library.

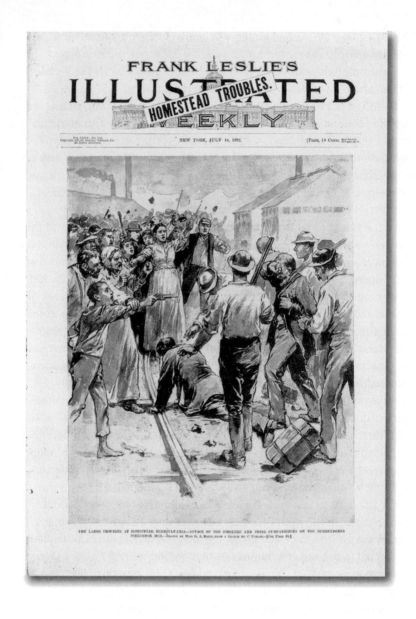

Then, in a misguided effort to ignite a general uprising, Alexander Berkman, a Russian immigrant and anarchist, attempted to assassinate Frick. Berkman bungled his attempt. Shot twice and stabbed with a dagger, Frick survived and showed considerable courage, allowing a doctor to remove the bullets but refusing to leave his desk until the day's work was completed. "I do not think that I shall die," Frick remarked coolly, "but whether I do or not, the Company will pursue the same policy and it will win."

After the assassination attempt, public opinion turned against the workers. Berkman was quickly tried and sentenced to prison. Although the Amalgamated and the AFL denounced his action, the incident linked anarchism and unionism. O'Donnell later wrote, "The bullet from Berkman's pistol, failing in its foul intent, went straight through the heart of the Homestead strike." The Homestead mill reopened in November, and the men returned to work, except for the union leaders, now blacklisted in every steel mill in the country. With the owners firmly in charge, the company slashed wages, reinstated the twelve-hour workday, and eliminated five hundred jobs.

The workers at Homestead had been taught a lesson. They would never again, in the words of the National Guard commander, "believe the works are their's [*sic*] quite as much as Carnegie's." Another forty-five years would pass before steelworkers, unskilled as well as skilled, successfully unionized. In the meantime, Carnegie's production tripled, even in the midst of a depression. "Ashamed to tell you profits these days," Carnegie wrote a friend in 1899. And no wonder: Carnegie's profits had grown from $4 million in 1892 to $40 million in 1900.

The Cripple Creek Miners' Strike of 1894

Less than a year after the Homestead lockout, a panic on Wall Street in the spring of 1893 touched off a bitter economic depression. In the West, silver mines fell on hard times, leading to the **Cripple Creek miners' strike of 1894**. When mine owners moved to lengthen the workday from eight to ten hours, the newly formed Western Federation of Miners (WFM) vowed to hold the line in Cripple Creek, Colorado. In February 1894, the WFM threatened to strike all mines working more than eight-hour shifts. The mine owners divided: Some quickly settled with the WFM; others continued to demand ten-hour shifts, provoking a strike.

The striking miners received help from many quarters. Working miners paid $15 a month to a strike fund, and miners in neighboring districts sent substantial contributions. The miners enjoyed the support and assistance of local businesses and grocers, who provided credit to the strikers. With these advantages, the Cripple Creek strikers could afford to hold out for their demands.

Even more significant, Governor Davis H. Waite, a Populist elected in 1892, had strong ties to the miners and refused to use the power of the state against the strikers. Governor Waite asked the strikers to lay down their arms and demanded that the mine owners disperse their hired deputies. The miners agreed to arbitration and selected Waite as their sole arbitrator. By May, the recalcitrant mine owners capitulated, and the union won an eight-hour day.

Governor Waite's intervention demonstrated the pivotal power of the state in the nation's labor wars. Having a Populist in power made a difference. A decade later, in 1904, with Waite out of office, mine owners relied on state troops to take back control of the mines, defeating the WFM and blacklisting all of its members. In retrospect, the Cripple Creek miners' strike of 1894 proved the exception to the rule of state intervention on the side of private property.

Cripple Creek miners' strike of 1894
▶ Strike led by the Western Federation of Miners in response to an attempt to lengthen their workday to ten hours. With the support of local businessmen and the Populist governor of Colorado, the miners successfully maintained an eight-hour day.

Eugene V. Debs and the Pullman Strike

The economic depression that began in 1893 swelled the ranks of the unemployed to three million. "A fearful crisis is upon us," wrote a labor publication. Nowhere were workers more demoralized than in the model town of Pullman, on the outskirts of Chicago.

In the wake of the Great Railroad Strike of 1877, George M. Pullman, the builder of Pullman railroad cars, moved his plant and workers nine miles south

How were women involved in late-nineteenth-century politics?

How did economic problems affect American politics in the 1890s?

Why did the United States largely abandon its isolationist foreign policy in the 1890s?

Conclusion: What was the connection between domestic strife and foreign policy?

☑ LearningCurve
Check what you know.
bedfordstmartins.com
/roarkunderstanding

A Pullman Craftsworker

Pullman Palace cars were known for their luxurious details. Here, a painter working in the 1890s applies elaborate decoration to the exterior of a Pullman car. The Pullman workers' strike in 1894 stemmed in part from the company's efforts to undermine the status of craftsworkers by reducing them to low-paid piecework. The fight to control the workplace contributed to the labor wars of the 1890s. Chicago Historical Society.

of Chicago and built a model town. The town of Pullman boasted parks, fountains, playgrounds, an auditorium, a library, a hotel, shops, and markets, along with 1,800 units of housing. Noticeably absent was a saloon.

The housing in Pullman was clearly superior to that in neighboring areas, but workers paid a high price to live there. Pullman's rents ran 10 to 20 percent higher than housing costs in nearby communities. In addition, George Pullman refused to "sell an acre under any circumstances." As long as he controlled the town absolutely, he held the powerful whip of eviction over his employees and could quickly get rid of "troublemakers." Although observers at first praised the beauty and orderliness of the town, critics by the 1890s compared Pullman's model town to a "gilded cage" for workers.

The depression brought hard times to Pullman. Workers saw their wages slashed five times between May and December 1893, with cuts totaling at least 28 percent. At the same time, Pullman refused to lower the rents in his model town, insisting that "the renting of the dwellings and the employment of workmen at Pullman are in no way tied together." When workers went to the bank to cash their paychecks, they found that the rent had been taken out. One worker discovered only forty-seven cents in his pay envelope for two weeks' work. When the bank teller asked him whether he wanted to apply it to his back rent, he retorted, "If Mr. Pullman needs that forty-seven cents worse than I do, let him have it." At the same time, Pullman continued to pay his stockholders an 8 percent dividend, and the company accumulated a $25 million surplus.

At the heart of the labor problems at Pullman lay not only economic inequity but also the company's attempt to control the work process, substituting piecework for day wages and undermining skilled craftsworkers. During the spring of 1894, Pullman's desperate workers, seeking help, flocked to the ranks of the American Railway Union (ARU), led by the charismatic Eugene V. Debs. The ARU,

CHAPTER LOCATOR | Why did American farmers organize alliances in the late nineteenth century? | **What led to the labor wars of the 1890s?**

588 CHAPTER 20 DISSENT, DEPRESSION, AND WAR

unlike the skilled craft unions of the AFL, pledged to organize all railway workers — from engineers to engine wipers.

George Pullman responded to union organization at his plant by firing three of the union's leaders the day after they protested wage cuts. Angry men and women walked off the job in disgust. What began as a spontaneous protest in May 1894 quickly blossomed into a strike that involved more than 90 percent of Pullman's 3,300 workers. Pullman countered by shutting down the plant. In June, the Pullman strikers appealed to the ARU to come to their aid. Debs pleaded with the workers to find another solution. But when George Pullman refused arbitration, the ARU membership voted to boycott all Pullman cars. Beginning on June 29, switchmen across the United States refused to handle any train that carried Pullman cars.

The conflict escalated quickly. The General Managers Association (GMA), an organization of managers from twenty-four different railroads, acted in concert to quash the **Pullman boycott**. They recruited strikebreakers and fired all the pro-testing switchmen. Their tactics set off a chain reaction. Entire train crews walked off the job in a show of solidarity with the Pullman workers. By July 2, rail lines from New York to California lay paralyzed. Even the GMA was forced to con-cede that the railroads had been "fought to a standstill."

The boycott remained surprisingly peaceful. In contrast to the Great Railroad Strike of 1877, no major riots broke out, and no serious property damage occurred. Debs fired off telegrams to all parts of the country advising his followers to avoid violence and respect law and order. But the nation's newspapers, fed press releases by the GMA, distorted the issues and misrepresented the strike. Across the country, papers ran headlines like "Wild Riot in Chicago" and "Mob Is in Control."

In Washington, Attorney General Richard B. Olney, a lawyer with strong ties to the railroads, determined to put down the strike. In his way stood the gover-nor of Illinois, John Peter Altgeld, who, observing that the boycott remained peaceful, refused to call out troops. To get around Altgeld, Olney convinced President Grover Cleveland that federal troops had to intervene to protect the mails. To further cripple the boycott, two conservative Chicago judges issued an injunction so sweeping that it prohibited Debs from speaking in public. By issuing the injunction, the court made the boycott a crime punishable by a jail sentence for contempt of court, a civil process that did not require a jury trial. Even the conservative *Chicago Tribune* judged the injunction "a menace to liberty . . . a weapon ever ready for the capitalist." Furious, Debs risked jail by refusing to honor it.

Olney's strategy worked. President Grover Cleveland called out the army. On July 5, nearly 8,000 troops marched into Chicago. Violence immediately erupted. In one day, troops killed 25 workers and wounded more than 60. In the face of bullets and bayonets, the strikers held firm. "Troops cannot move trains," Debs reminded his followers, a fact that was borne out as the railroads remained paralyzed despite the military intervention. But if the army could not put down the boycott, the injunc-tion did. Debs was arrested and imprisoned for contempt of court. With its leader in jail, its headquarters raided and ransacked, and its members demoralized, the ARU collapsed along with the boycott. Pullman reopened his factory, hiring new workers to replace many of the strikers and leaving 1,600 without jobs.

Pullman boycott

▶ Nationwide railroad workers' boycott of trains carrying Pullman cars in 1894 after Pullman workers, suffering radically reduced wages, joined the American Railway Union (ARU) and union leaders were fired in response. The boycott ended after the U.S. Army fired on strikers and ARU leader Eugene Debs was jailed.

How were women involved in late-nineteenth-century politics?

How did economic problems affect American politics in the 1890s?

Why did the United States largely abandon its isolationist foreign policy in the 1890s?

Conclusion: What was the connection between domestic strife and foreign policy?

☑ **LearningCurve**
Check what you know.
bedfordstmartins.com
/roarkunderstanding

In the aftermath of the strike, a special commission investigated the events at Pullman, taking testimony from 107 witnesses, from the lowliest workers to George M. Pullman himself. Stubborn and self-righteous, Pullman spoke for the business orthodoxy of his era, steadfastly affirming the right of business to safeguard its interests through confederacies such as the GMA and at the same time denying labor's right to organize. "If we were to receive these men as representatives of the union," he stated, "they could probably force us to pay any wages which they saw fit."

From his jail cell, Eugene Debs reviewed the events of the Pullman strike. With the courts and the government ready to side with industrialists in defense of private property, strikes seemed futile, and unions remained helpless. Workers would have to take control of the state itself. Debs went into jail a trade unionist and came out six months later a socialist. At first, he turned to the Populist Party, but after its demise he formed the Socialist Party in 1900 and ran for president five times.

> ## QUICK REVIEW

Why were the labor conflicts of the 1890s so often marked by violence?

CHAPTER LOCATOR | Why did American farmers organize alliances in the late nineteenth century? | What led to the labor wars of the 1890s?

590 CHAPTER 20 DISSENT, DEPRESSION, AND WAR

Woman's Christian Temperance Union Postcard

The Woman's Christian Temperance Union distributed postcards like this to attack the liquor trade. This card is typical in its portrayal of saloon backers as traitors to the nation. Notice the man trampling on the American flag as he casts his ballot — a sly allusion to the need for woman suffrage. Collection of Joyce M. Tice.

How were women involved in late-nineteenth-century politics?

"DO EVERYTHING," Frances Willard urged her followers in 1881. The new president of the Woman's Christian Temperance Union (WCTU) meant what she said. The WCTU followed a trajectory that was common for women in the late nineteenth century. As women organized to deal with issues that touched their homes and families, they moved into politics, lending new urgency to the cause of woman suffrage. Urban industrialism dislocated women's lives no less than men's. Like men, women sought political change and organized to promote issues central to their lives, campaigning for temperance and woman suffrage.

Frances Willard and the Woman's Christian Temperance Union

A visionary leader, Frances Willard spoke for a group left almost entirely out of the U.S. electoral process. In 1890, only one state, Wyoming, allowed women to vote in national elections. But lack of the franchise did not mean that women were apolitical. The Woman's Christian Temperance Union demonstrated the breadth of women's political activity in the late nineteenth century.

Women supported the temperance movement because they felt particularly vulnerable to the effects of drunkenness. Dependent on men's wages, women and children suffered when money went for drink. The drunken, abusive husband

How were women involved in late-nineteenth-century politics?	How did economic problems affect American politics in the 1890s?	Why did the United States largely abandon its isolationist foreign policy in the 1890s?	Conclusion: What was the connection between domestic strife and foreign policy?	✓ LearningCurve Check what you know. bedfordstmartins.com /roarkunderstanding

591

1879
- Frances Willard becomes president of the Woman's Christian Temperance Union.

1884
- Frances Willard calls for woman suffrage.

1890
- National American Woman Suffrage Association is formed.
- Wyoming is the only state allowing women to vote in national elections.

epitomized the evils of a nation in which women remained second-class citizens. The WCTU, composed entirely of women, viewed all women's interests as essentially the same and therefore did not hesitate to use the singular *woman* to emphasize gender solidarity. Although mostly white and middle-class, WCTU members resolved to speak for their entire sex.

When Frances Willard became the WCTU's president in 1879, she radically changed the direction of the organization. Social action replaced prayer as women's answer to the threat of drunkenness. Viewing alcoholism as a disease rather than a sin and poverty as a cause rather than a result of drink, the WCTU became involved in labor issues, joining with the Knights of Labor to press for better working conditions for women workers. Describing workers in a textile mill, a WCTU member wrote in the organization's *Union Signal* magazine, "It is dreadful to see these girls, stripped almost to the skin . . . and running like racehorses from the beginning to the end of the day." She concluded, "The hard slavish work is drawing the girls into the saloon."

Willard capitalized on the cult of domesticity as a shrewd political tactic. Using "home protection" as her watchword, she argued as early as 1884 that women needed the vote to protect home and family. By the 1890s, the WCTU's grassroots network of local unions included 200,000 dues-paying members and had spread to all but the most isolated rural areas of the country.

Willard worked to create a broad reform coalition in the 1890s, embracing the Knights of Labor, the People's Party, and the Prohibition Party. Until her death in 1898, she led, if not a woman's rights movement, then the first organized mass movement of women united around a women's issue. By 1900, thanks largely to the WCTU, women could claim a generation of experience in political action — speaking, lobbying, organizing, drafting legislation, and running private charitable institutions. As Willard observed, "All this work has tended more toward the liberation of women than it has toward the extinction of the saloon."

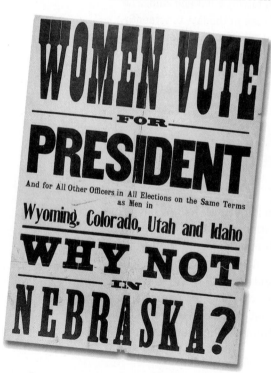

Campaigning for Woman Suffrage

In 1896, women voted in only four states — Wyoming, Colorado, Idaho, and Utah. The West led the way in the campaign for woman suffrage, with Wyoming Territory granting women the vote as early as 1869. The poster calls on Nebraska to join the suffrage column. Nebraska State Historical Society.

CHAPTER LOCATOR | Why did American farmers organize alliances in the late nineteenth century? | What led to the labor wars of the 1890s?

592 CHAPTER 20
DISSENT, DEPRESSION, AND WAR

Elizabeth Cady Stanton, Susan B. Anthony, and the Movement for Woman Suffrage

Unlike the WCTU, the organized movement for woman suffrage remained small and relatively weak in the late nineteenth century. In 1869, Elizabeth Cady Stanton and her ally, Susan B. Anthony, launched the National Woman Suffrage Association demanding the vote for women (see chapter 18). A more conservative group, the American Woman Suffrage Association (AWSA), formed the same year. Composed of men as well as women, the AWSA believed that women should vote in local but not national elections.

By 1890, the split had healed, and the newly united **National American Woman Suffrage Association (NAWSA)** launched campaigns on the state level to gain the vote for women. Twenty years had made a great change. Woman suffrage, though not yet generally supported, was no longer considered a crackpot idea, thanks in part to the WCTU's support of the "home protection" ballot. The NAWSA honored Elizabeth Cady Stanton by electing her its first president, but Susan B. Anthony, who took the helm in 1892, emerged as the leading figure in the new united organization.

Stanton and Anthony, both in their seventies, were coming to the end of their public careers. Since the days of the Seneca Falls woman's rights convention, they had worked for reforms for their sex, including property rights, custody rights, and the right to education and gainful employment. But the prize of woman suffrage still eluded them. Women suffered a bitter defeat in a California referendum on woman suffrage in 1896. Never losing faith, Susan B. Anthony remarked in her last public appearance, in 1906, "Failure is impossible."

National American Woman Suffrage Association (NAWSA)

▶ Organization formed in 1890 that united the National Woman Suffrage Association and the American Woman Suffrage Association. The NAWSA pursued state-level campaigns to gain the vote for women. With successes in Idaho, Colorado, and Utah, woman suffrage had become more accepted by the 1890s.

> ## Nineteenth-Century Woman Suffrage Victories

- 1869: Wyoming
- 1893: Colorado
- 1896: Idaho, Utah

QUICK REVIEW <

How did women's temperance activism contribute to the cause of woman suffrage?

How were women involved in late-nineteenth-century politics?	How did economic problems affect American politics in the 1890s?	Why did the United States largely abandon its isolationist foreign policy in the 1890s?	Conclusion: What was the connection between domestic strife and foreign policy?	✓ LearningCurve Check what you know. bedfordstmartins.com /roarkunderstanding

How did economic problems affect American politics in the 1890s?

Coxey's Army A contingent of Coxey's army stops to rest on its way to Washington, D.C. A "petition in boots," Coxey's followers were well dressed. Music was an important component of the march, including the anthem "Marching with Coxey." Band members are pictured on the right with their instruments. Despite their peaceful pose, the marchers stirred the fears of many Americans, who predicted an uprising of the unemployed. Ohio Historical Society.

THE DEPRESSION that began in the spring of 1893 and lasted for more than four years put nearly half of the labor force out of work, a higher percentage than during the Great Depression of the 1930s. The human cost of the depression was staggering. "I Take my pen in hand to let you know that we are Starving to death," a Kansas farm woman wrote to the governor in 1894. "Last cent gone," wrote a young widow in her diary. "Children went to work without their breakfasts." Following the harsh dictates of social Darwinism and laissez-faire, the majority of America's elected officials believed that it was inappropriate for the government to intervene. But the scope of the depression made it impossible for churches and local agencies to supply sufficient relief, and increasingly Americans called on the federal government to take action. Armies of the unemployed marched on Washington to demand relief, and the Populist Party experienced a surge of support as the election of 1896 approached.

CHAPTER LOCATOR | Why did American farmers organize alliances in the late nineteenth century? | What led to the labor wars of the 1890s?

Coxey's Army

Masses of unemployed Americans marched to Washington, D.C., in the spring of 1894 to call attention to their plight and to urge Congress to enact a public works program to end unemployment. Jacob S. Coxey of Massilon, Ohio, led the most publicized contingent. Convinced that men could be put to work building badly needed roads for the nation, Coxey proposed a scheme to finance public works through non-interest-bearing bonds. "What I am after," he maintained, "is to try to put this country in a condition so that no man who wants work shall be obliged to remain idle." His plan won support from the AFL and the Populists. Starting out from Ohio with one hundred men, **Coxey's army**, as it was dubbed, swelled as it marched east through the spring snows of the Alleghenies. In Pennsylvania, Coxey recruited several hundred from the ranks of those left unemployed by the Homestead lockout.

On May 1, Coxey's army arrived in Washington. When Coxey defiantly marched his men onto the Capitol grounds, police set upon the demonstrators with nightsticks, cracking skulls and arresting Coxey and his lieutenants. Coxey went to jail for twenty days and was fined $5 for "walking on the grass." But other armies of the unemployed, totaling possibly as many as five thousand people, were still on their way. The more daring contingents commandeered entire trains, stirring fears of revolution. Journalists who covered the march did little to quiet the nation's fears. They delighted in military terminology, describing themselves as "war correspondents." To boost newspaper sales, they gave to the episode a tone of urgency and heightened the sense of a nation imperiled.

By August, the leaderless, tattered armies dissolved. Although the "On to Washington" movement proved ineffective in forcing federal relief legislation, Coxey's army dramatized the plight of the unemployed and acted, in the words of one participant, as a "living, moving object lesson." Like the Populists, Coxey's army called into question the underlying values of the new industrial order and demonstrated how ordinary citizens turned to means outside the regular party system to influence politics in the 1890s.

The People's Party and the Election of 1896

Even before the depression of 1893, the Populists had railed against the status quo. "We meet in the midst of a nation brought to the verge of moral, political, and material ruin," Ignatius Donnelly had declared in his keynote address at the creation of the People's Party in St. Louis in 1892. "The fruits of the toil of millions are boldly stolen to build up colossal fortunes for a few. . . . From the same prolific womb of governmental injustice we breed the two great classes — tramps and millionaires."

The fiery rhetoric frightened many who saw in the People's Party a call not to reform but to revolution. Throughout the country, the press denounced the

> **CHRONOLOGY**

1894
- Coxey's army marches to Washington, D.C.

1896
- Democrats and Populists support William Jennings Bryan for president.
- William McKinley is elected president.

Coxey's army

▶ Unemployed men who marched to Washington, D.C., in 1894 to urge Congress to enact a public works program to end unemployment. Jacob S. Coxey of Ohio led the most publicized contingent. The movement failed to force federal relief legislation.

How were women involved in late-nineteenth-century politics?	**How did economic problems affect American politics in the 1890s?**	Why did the United States largely abandon its isolationist foreign policy in the 1890s?	Conclusion: What was the connection between domestic strife and foreign policy?	✓ LearningCurve Check what you know. bedfordstmartins.com /roarkunderstanding

595

Candidate	Electoral Vote	Popular Vote	Percent of Popular Vote
Grover Cleveland (Democrat)	277	5,555,426	46.1
Benjamin Harrison (Republican)	145	5,182,690	43.0
James B. Weaver (People's)	22	1,029,846	8.5

MAP 20.1 ■ The Election of 1892

Populists as "cranks, lunatics, and idiots." When one self-righteous editor dismissed them as "calamity howlers," Populist governor Lorenzo Lewelling of Kansas shot back, "If that is so I want to continue to howl until those conditions are improved."

The People's Party captured more than a million votes in the presidential election of 1892, a respectable showing for a new party (**Map 20.1**). But increasingly, sectional and racial animosities threatened its unity. Realizing that race prejudice obscured the common economic interests of black and white farmers, Populist Tom Watson of Georgia openly courted African Americans, appearing on platforms with black speakers and promising "to wipe out the color line." When angry Georgia whites threatened to lynch a black Populist preacher, Watson rallied two thousand gun-toting Populists to the man's defense. Although many Populists remained racist in their attitudes toward African Americans, the spectacle of white Georgians riding through the night to protect a black man from lynching was symbolic of the enormous changes the Populist Party promised in the South.

As the presidential election of 1896 approached, the depression intensified cries for reform not only from the Populists but also throughout the electorate. Depression worsened the tight money problem caused by the deflationary pressures of the gold standard. Once again, proponents of free silver stirred rebellion in the ranks of both the Democratic and the Republican parties. When the Republicans nominated Ohio governor William McKinley on a platform pledging the preservation of the gold standard, western advocates of free silver representing miners and farmers walked out of the convention. Open rebellion also split the Democratic Party as vast segments in the West and South repudiated President Grover Cleveland because of his support for gold. In South Carolina, Benjamin Tillman won his race for Congress by promising, "Send me to Washington and I'll stick my pitchfork into [Cleveland's] old ribs!"

The spirit of revolt animated the Democratic National Convention in Chicago in the summer of 1896. William Jennings Bryan of Nebraska, the thirty-six-year-old "boy orator from the Platte," whipped the convention into a frenzy with his passionate call for free silver with a ringing exhortation: "Do not crucify mankind upon a cross of gold." Pandemonium broke loose as delegates stampeded to nominate Bryan, the youngest candidate ever to run for the presidency.

The juggernaut of free silver rolled out of Chicago and on to St. Louis, where the People's Party met a week after the Democrats adjourned. Many western Populists urged the party to ally with the Democrats and endorse Bryan. A major obstacle in the path of fusion, however, was Bryan's running mate, Arthur M. Sewall. A Maine railway director and bank president, Sewall, who had been placed on the ticket to appease conservative Democrats, embodied everything the Populists detested. Moreover, die-hard southern Populists wanted no part of fusion. Southern Democrats had resorted to fraud and violence to steal elections from the Populists in southern states, and support for a Democratic ticket proved hard to swallow.

Populists struggled to work out a compromise. To show that they remained true to their principles, delegates first voted to support all the planks of the 1892

CHAPTER LOCATOR | Why did American farmers organize alliances in the late nineteenth century? | What led to the labor wars of the 1890s?

596 CHAPTER 20 DISSENT, DEPRESSION, AND WAR

platform, added to it a call for public works projects for the unemployed, and only narrowly defeated a plank for woman suffrage. To deal with the problem of fusion, the convention selected the vice presidential candidate first. The nomination of Tom Watson undercut opposition to Bryan's candidacy. And although Bryan quickly sent a telegram to protest that he would not drop Sewall as his running mate, mysteriously his message never reached the convention floor. Fusion triumphed. Bryan won nomination by a lopsided vote. The Populists did not know it, but their cheers for Bryan signaled the death knell for the People's Party.

Few contests in the nation's history have been as fiercely fought as the presidential election of 1896. On one side stood Republican William McKinley, backed by the wealthy industrialist and party boss Mark Hanna. Hanna played on the business community's fears of Populism to raise a Republican war chest more than double the amount of any previous campaign. On the other side, William Jennings Bryan, with few assets beyond his silver tongue, struggled to make up in energy and eloquence what his party lacked in campaign funds. He crisscrossed the country in a whirlwind tour, by his own reckoning visiting twenty-seven states and speaking to more than five million Americans.

On election day, four out of five voters went to the polls in an unprecedented turnout. The silver states of the Rocky Mountains lined up solidly for Bryan. The Northeast went for McKinley. The Midwest tipped the balance. In the end, the election hinged on between 100 and 1,000 votes in several key states, including Wisconsin, Iowa, and Minnesota. Although McKinley won twenty-three states to Bryan's twenty-two, the electoral vote showed a lopsided 271 to 176 in McKinley's favor (**Map 20.2**).

The biggest losers in 1896 turned out to be the Populists. On the national level, they polled fewer than 300,000 votes, a million less than in 1894. In the clamor to support Bryan, Populists in the South, determined to beat McKinley at any cost, swallowed their differences and drifted back to the Democratic Party.

But if Populism proved unsuccessful at the polls, it nevertheless set the domestic political agenda for the United States in the next decades, highlighting issues such as railroad regulation, banking and currency reform, electoral reforms, and an enlarged role for the federal government in the economy. Meanwhile, as the decade ended, the bugle call to arms turned America's attention to foreign affairs. The struggle for social justice gave way to a war for empire as the United States asserted its power on the world stage.

Candidate	Electoral Vote	Popular Vote	Percent of Popular Vote
William McKinley (Republican)	271	7,104,779	51.1
William J. Bryan (Democrat-People's)	176	6,502,925	47.7

MAP 20.2 ■ The Election of 1896

QUICK REVIEW

Why was the People's Party unable to translate national support into victory in the 1896 election?

How were women involved in late-nineteenth-century politics?	**How did economic problems affect American politics in the 1890s?**	Why did the United States largely abandon its isolationist foreign policy in the 1890s?	Conclusion: What was the connection between domestic strife and foreign policy?	✓ LearningCurve Check what you know. bedfordstmartins.com /roarkunderstanding

Why did the United States largely abandon its isolationist foreign policy in the 1890s?

The Open Door

The trade advantage that the United States gained through the Open Door policy is portrayed in this political cartoon. Uncle Sam stands prominently in the "open door," while representatives of the other great powers seek admittance to the "Flowery Kingdom" of China. In fact, the Open Door policy promised equal access for all powers to the China trade, not U.S. preeminence as the cartoon implies. Culver Pictures.

> VISUAL ACTIVITY

READING THE IMAGE: How does the cartoon portray the role of the United States in international diplomacy?
CONNECTIONS: In what ways does this image misrepresent the reality of American and European involvement in China and of the Open Door policy?

THROUGHOUT MUCH OF THE SECOND HALF of the nineteenth century, U.S. interest in foreign policy took a backseat to territorial expansion in the American West. The United States fought the Indian wars while European nations carved out empires in Asia, Africa, Latin America, and the Pacific.

At the turn of the twentieth century, the United States pursued a foreign policy consisting of two currents — isolationism and expansionism. Although the determination to remain detached from European politics had been a hallmark of U.S. foreign policy since the nation's founding, Americans simultaneously believed in manifest destiny — the "obvious" right to expand the nation from ocean to ocean. With its own inland empire secured, the United States looked outward. Determined to protect its sphere of influence in the Western Hemisphere and to expand its trading in Asia, the nation moved away from isolationism and toward a more active role on the world stage that led to intervention in China's Boxer uprising and war with Spain.

Markets and Missionaries

The depression of the 1890s provided a powerful impetus to American commercial expansion. As markets weakened at home, American businesses looked abroad for profits. As the depression deepened, one diplomat warned that Americans "must turn [their] eyes abroad, or they will soon look inward upon discontent."

CHAPTER LOCATOR | Why did American farmers organize alliances in the late nineteenth century? | What led to the labor wars of the 1890s?

Exports constituted a small but significant percentage of the profits of American business in the 1890s (**Figure 20.3**). And where American interests led, businessmen expected the government's power and influence to follow to protect their investments. Companies like Standard Oil actively sought to use the U.S. government as their agent, often putting foreign service employees on the payroll. "Our ambassadors and ministers and consuls," wrote John D. Rockefeller appreciatively, "have aided to push our way into new markets and to the utmost corners of the world."

America's foreign policy often appeared little more than a sidelight to business development. In Hawai'i (first called the Sandwich Islands), American sugar interests fomented a rebellion in 1893, toppling the increasingly independent Queen Lili'uokalani. They pushed Congress to annex the islands to avoid the high McKinley tariff on sugar. When President Cleveland learned that Hawai'ians opposed annexation, he withdrew the proposal from Congress. But expansionists still coveted the islands and looked for an opportunity to push through annexation.

Business interests alone did not account for the new expansionism that seized the nation during the 1890s. As Alfred Thayer Mahan, leader of a growing group of American expansionists, confessed, "Even when material interests are the original exciting cause, it is the sentiment to which they give rise, the moral tone which emotion takes that constitutes the greater force." Much of that moral tone was set by American missionaries intent on spreading the gospel of Christianity to the "heathen." No area on the globe constituted a greater challenge than China.

> CHRONOLOGY

1894
- President Grover Cleveland nixes attempt to annex Hawai'i.

1895
- Cleveland enforces Monroe Doctrine in border dispute between British Guiana and Venezuela.

1898
- U.S. battleship *Maine* explodes in Havana harbor.
- Congress declares war on Spain.
- U.S. Navy destroys Spanish fleet in Manila Bay, the Philippines.
- U.S. troops defeat Spanish forces in Cuba.
- Treaty of Paris ends war with Spain.
- United States annexes Hawai'i.

1899–1900
- Secretary of State John Hay enunciates Open Door policy in China.
- Boxer uprising in China.

1901
- European powers impose Boxer Protocol on Chinese government.

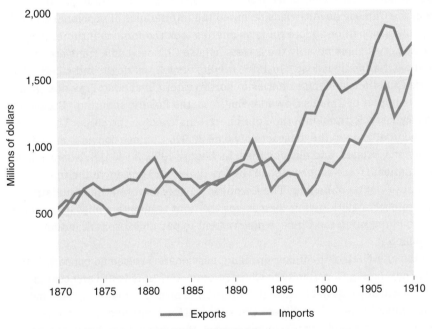

FIGURE 20.3 ■ **Expansion in U.S. Trade, 1870–1910**

Between 1870 and 1910, American exports more than tripled. Imports generally rose, but they were held in check by the high protective tariffs championed by Republican presidents from Ulysses S. Grant to William Howard Taft. A decline in imports is particularly noticeable after the passage of the prohibitive McKinley tariff in 1890.

| How were women involved in late-nineteenth-century politics? | How did economic problems affect American politics in the 1890s? | **Why did the United States largely abandon its isolationist foreign policy in the 1890s?** | Conclusion: What was the connection between domestic strife and foreign policy? | ✓ LearningCurve Check what you know. bedfordstmartins.com /roarkunderstanding |

An 1858 agreement, the Tianjin treaty admitted foreign missionaries to China. Although Christians converted only 100,000 in a population of 400 million, the Chinese nevertheless resented the interference of missionaries in village life. Opposition to foreign missionaries took the form of antiforeign secret societies, most notably the Boxers, whose Chinese name translated to "Righteous Harmonious Fist." In 1899, the Boxers hunted down and killed Chinese Christians and missionaries in northwestern Shandong Province. With the tacit support of China's Dowager Empress, the Boxers, shouting "Uphold the Ch'ing Dynasty, Exterminate the Foreigners," marched on the cities. Their rampage eventually led to the massacre of some 30,000 Chinese converts and 250 foreign nuns, priests, and missionaries. In August 1900, 2,500 U.S. troops joined an international force sent to rescue the foreigners and put down the uprising in the Chinese capital of Beijing. The European powers imposed the humiliating Boxer Protocol in 1901, giving themselves the right to maintain military forces in Beijing and requiring the Chinese government to pay an exorbitant indemnity of $333 million.

In the aftermath of the **Boxer uprising**, missionaries voiced no concern at the paradox of bringing Christianity to China at gunpoint. "It is worth any cost in money, worth any cost in bloodshed," argued one bishop, "if we can make millions of Chinese true and intelligent Christians." Merchants and missionaries alike shared such moralistic reasoning. Indeed, they worked hand in hand; trade and Christianity marched into Asia together. "Missionaries," admitted the American clergyman Charles Denby, "are the pioneers of trade and commerce. . . . The missionary, inspired by holy zeal, goes everywhere and by degrees foreign commerce and trade follow."

Boxer uprising

▶ 1899–1900 uprising in China led by the Boxers, an antiforeign society, in which 30,000 Chinese converts and 250 foreign Christians were killed. An international force rescued foreigners in Beijing, and European powers imposed the humiliating Boxer Protocol on China in 1901.

CHAPTER LOCATOR | Why did American farmers organize alliances in the late nineteenth century? | What led to the labor wars of the 1890s?

600 CHAPTER 20 DISSENT, DEPRESSION, AND WAR

The Monroe Doctrine and the Open Door Policy

The emergence of the United States as a world power pitted the nation against other colonial powers, particularly Germany and Japan, that posed a threat to the twin pillars of America's expansionist foreign policy. The first, the Monroe Doctrine, came to be interpreted as establishing the Western Hemisphere as an American "sphere of influence" and warned European powers to stay away or risk war. The second, the Open Door, dealt with maintaining market access to China.

American diplomacy actively worked to buttress the Monroe Doctrine, with its assertion of American hegemony (domination) in the Western Hemisphere. In the 1880s, Republican secretary of state James G. Blaine promoted hemispheric peace and trade through Pan-American cooperation but at the same time used American troops to intervene in Latin American border disputes. In 1895, President Cleveland risked war with Great Britain to enforce the Monroe Doctrine when a conflict developed between Venezuela and British Guiana. After American saber rattling, the British backed down and accepted U.S. mediation in the area despite their territorial claims in Guiana.

In Central America, American business triumphed in a bloodless takeover that saw French and British interests routed. The United Fruit Company of Boston virtually dominated the Central American nations of Costa Rica and Guatemala, while an importer from New Orleans turned Honduras into a "banana republic" (a country run by U.S. business interests). Thus, by 1895, the United States, through business as well as diplomacy, had successfully achieved hegemony in Latin America and the Caribbean, forcing even the British to concur that "the infinite resources [of the United States] combined with its isolated position render it master of the situation and practically invulnerable as against any or all other powers."

At the same time that American foreign policy warned European powers to stay out of the Western Hemisphere, the United States competed for trade in the Eastern Hemisphere. As American interests in China grew, the United States became more aggressive in defending its presence in Asia and the Pacific. In 1889, it risked war with Germany to guarantee U.S. naval access to Pago Pago in the Samoan Islands, a port for refueling on the way to Asia. Germany, seeking dominance over the islands, sent warships to the region. But before fighting broke out, a typhoon destroyed the German and American ships. The potential combatants later divided the islands amicably in the 1899 Treaty of Berlin.

In the 1890s, China, weakened by years of internal warfare, was partitioned into spheres of influence by Britain, Japan, Germany, France, and Russia. Concerned about the integrity of China and no less about American trade, Secretary of State John Hay in 1899–1900 wrote a series of notes calling for an "open door" policy that would ensure trade access to all and maintain Chinese sovereignty. The notes were greeted by the major powers with polite evasion. Nevertheless, Hay skillfully managed to maneuver them into doing his bidding, and in 1900 he boldly announced the Open Door as international policy. The United States, by insisting on the Open Door policy, managed to secure access to Chinese markets, expanding its economic power while avoiding the problems of maintaining a far-flung colonial empire on the Asian mainland. But as the Spanish-American War soon demonstrated, Americans found it hard to resist the temptations of overseas empire.

Monroe Doctrine

▶ President James Monroe's 1823 declaration that the Western Hemisphere was closed to further colonization or interference by European powers. In exchange, Monroe pledged that the United States would not become involved in European struggles. The United States strengthened the doctrine during the late nineteenth century.

Open Door policy

▶ Policy successfully insisted upon by Secretary of State John Hay in 1899–1900 recommending that the major powers of the United States, Britain, Japan, Germany, France, and Russia should all have access to trade with China and that Chinese sovereignty should be maintained.

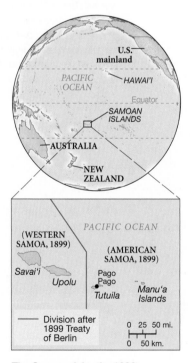

The Samoan Islands, 1889

How were women involved in late-nineteenth-century politics?

How did economic problems affect American politics in the 1890s?

Why did the United States largely abandon its isolationist foreign policy in the 1890s?

Conclusion: What was the connection between domestic strife and foreign policy?

☑ LearningCurve
Check what you know.
bedfordstmartins.com
/roarkunderstanding

"A Splendid Little War"

Spanish-American War

▶ 1898 war between Spain and the United States that began as an effort to free Cuba from Spain's colonial rule. This popular war left the United States an imperial power in control of Cuba and with colonies in Puerto Rico, Guam, and the Philippines.

The **Spanish-American War** began as a humanitarian effort to free Cuba from Spain's colonial grasp and ended with the United States itself acquiring territory overseas and fighting a dirty guerrilla war with Filipino nationalists who, like the Cubans, sought independence. Behind the contradiction stood the twin pillars of American foreign policy: The Monroe Doctrine made Spain's presence in Cuba unacceptable, and U.S. determination to keep open the door to Asia made the Philippines attractive. Precedent for the nation's imperial adventures also came from the recent Indian wars in the American West, which provided a template for the subjugation of native peoples in the name of civilization.

Looking back on the Spanish-American War of 1898, Secretary of State John Hay judged it "a splendid little war; begun with the highest motives, carried on with magnificent intelligence and spirit, favored by that fortune which loves the brave." At the close of a decade marred by bitter depression, social unrest, and political upheaval, the war offered Americans a chance to wave the flag and march in unison. War fever proved as infectious as the tune of a John Philip Sousa march. Few argued the merits of the conflict until it was over and the time came to divide the spoils.

Yellow Journalism

Most cartoonists followed the lead of William Randolph Hearst and Joseph Pulitzer in promoting war with Spain. Cartoonist Grant Hamilton drew this cartoon for *Judge* magazine in 1898. It shows a brutish Spain (the "Devil's Deputy") with bloody hands trampling on a sailor from the *Maine*. Cuba is prostrate, and a pile of skulls represents civilians "starved to death by Spain." Collection of the New-York Historical Society.

CHAPTER LOCATOR | Why did American farmers organize alliances in the late nineteenth century? | What led to the labor wars of the 1890s?

CHAPTER 20
602 DISSENT, DEPRESSION, AND WAR

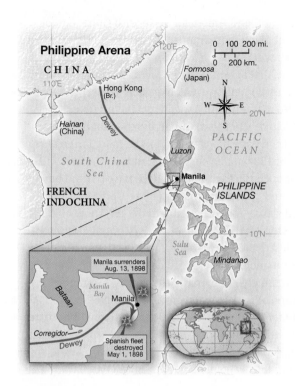

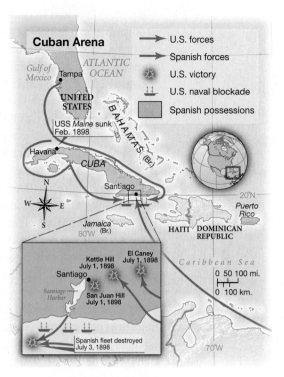

MAP 20.3 ■ The Spanish-American War, 1898

The Spanish-American War was fought in two theaters, the Philippine Islands and Cuba. Five days after President William McKinley called for a declaration of war, Admiral George Dewey captured Manila. The war lasted only eight months. Troops landed in Cuba in mid-June and by mid-July had destroyed the Spanish fleet.

> MAP ACTIVITY

READING THE MAP: Which countries held imperial control over countries and territories immediately surrounding the Philippine Islands and Cuba?
CONNECTIONS: What role did American newspapers play in the start of the war? How did the results of the war serve American aims in both Asia and the Western Hemisphere?

The war began with moral outrage over the treatment of Cuban revolutionaries, who had launched a fight for independence against the Spanish colonial regime in 1895. In an attempt to isolate the guerrillas, the Spanish general Valeriano Weyler herded Cubans into crowded and unsanitary concentration camps, where thousands died of hunger, disease, and exposure. Starvation soon spread to the cities. By 1898, fully a quarter of the island's population had perished in the Cuban revolution.

As the Cuban rebellion dragged on, pressure for American intervention mounted. American newspapers fueled public outrage at Spain. A fierce circulation war raged in New York City between William Randolph Hearst's *Journal* and Joseph Pulitzer's *World*. Their competition provoked what came to be called **yellow journalism**, named for the colored ink used in a popular comic strip. The Cuban war provided a wealth of dramatic copy. Newspapers fed the American people a daily diet of "Butcher" Weyler and Spanish atrocities. Hearst sent artist Frederic Remington to document the horror, and when Remington wired home, "There is no trouble here. There will be no war," Hearst shot back, "You furnish the pictures and I'll furnish the war."

American interests in Cuba were, in the words of the U.S. minister to Spain, more than "merely theoretical or sentimental." American business had more than

yellow journalism

▶ Term first given to sensationalistic newspaper reporting and cartoon images rendered in yellow. A circulation war between two New York City papers provoked the tactics of yellow journalism that fueled popular support for the Spanish-American War in 1898.

How were women involved in late-nineteenth-century politics?

How did economic problems affect American politics in the 1890s?

Why did the United States largely abandon its isolationist foreign policy in the 1890s?

Conclusion: What was the connection between domestic strife and foreign policy?

☑ **LearningCurve**
Check what you know.
bedfordstmartins.com /roarkunderstanding

$50 million invested in Cuban sugar, and American trade with Cuba, a brisk $100 million a year before the rebellion, had dropped to near zero. Nevertheless, the business community balked, wary of a war with Spain. When industrialist Mark Hanna, the Republican kingmaker and senator from Ohio, urged restraint, a hotheaded Theodore Roosevelt exploded, "We will have this war for the freedom of Cuba, Senator Hanna, in spite of the timidity of commercial interests."

To expansionists like Roosevelt, more than Cuban independence was at stake. As assistant secretary of the navy, Roosevelt took the helm in the absence of his boss and in the summer of 1897 audaciously ordered the U.S. fleet to Manila in the Philippines. In the event of conflict with Spain, Roosevelt put the navy in a position to capture the islands and gain a stepping-stone to China.

President McKinley moved slowly toward intervention. In a show of American force, he dispatched the battleship *Maine* to Cuba. On the night of February 15, 1898, a mysterious explosion destroyed the *Maine*, killing 267 crew members. The source of the explosion remained unclear, but inflammatory stories in the press enraged Americans. Rallying to the cry "Remember the *Maine*," Congress declared war on Spain. In a surge of patriotism, more than a million men rushed to enlist. War brought with it a unity of purpose and national harmony that ended a decade of political dissent and strife. "In April, everywhere over this good fair land, flags were flying," wrote Kansas editor William Allen White. "At the stations, crowds gathered to hurrah for the soldiers, and to throw hats into the air, and to unfurl flags."

Five days after McKinley signed the war resolution, a U.S. Navy squadron destroyed the Spanish fleet in Manila Bay (**Map 20.3**). The stunning victory caught most Americans by surprise. Few had ever heard of the Philippines. Even McKinley confessed that he could not locate the archipelago on the map. Nevertheless, he dispatched U.S. troops to secure the islands.

The war in Cuba ended almost as quickly as it began. The first troops landed on June 22, and after a handful of battles the Spanish forces surrendered on July 17. The war lasted just long enough to elevate Theodore Roosevelt to the status of bona fide war hero. Roosevelt resigned his navy post and formed the Rough Riders, a regiment composed of a sprinkling of Ivy League polo players and a number of western cowboys Roosevelt befriended during his stint as a cattle rancher in the Dakotas. The Rough Riders' charge up Kettle Hill and Roosevelt's role in the decisive battle of San Juan Hill made front-page news. Overnight, Roosevelt became the most famous man in America. By the time he sailed home from Cuba, a coalition of independent Republicans was already plotting his political future.

The Debate over American Imperialism

After a few brief campaigns in Cuba and Puerto Rico brought the Spanish-American War to an end, the American people woke up in possession of an empire that stretched halfway around the globe. As part of the spoils of war, the United States acquired Cuba, Puerto Rico, Guam, and the Philippines. And Republicans quickly moved to annex Hawai'i in July 1898.

Contemptuous of the Cubans, whom General William Shafter declared "no more fit for self-government than gun-powder is for hell," the U.S. government directed a Cuban constitution and refused to give up military control of the

CHAPTER LOCATOR | Why did American farmers organize alliances in the late nineteenth century? | What led to the labor wars of the 1890s?

604   CHAPTER 20   DISSENT, DEPRESSION, AND WAR

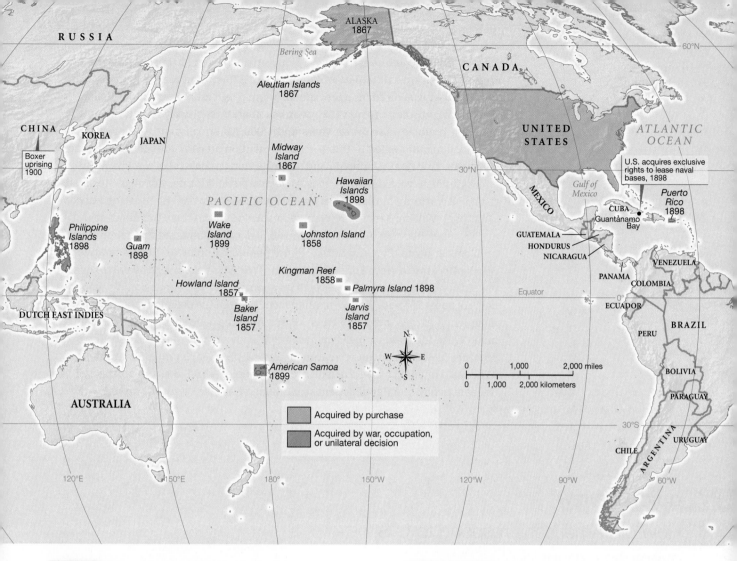

MAP 20.4 ■ U.S. Overseas Expansion through 1900

The United States extended its interests abroad with a series of territorial acquisitions. Although Cuba was granted independence, the Platt Amendment kept the new nation firmly under U.S. control. In the wake of the Spanish-American War, the United States woke up to find that it held an empire extending halfway around the globe.

> **MAP ACTIVITY**

READING THE MAP: Does the map indicate that more territory was acquired by purchase or by war, occupation, or unilateral decision? How many purchases of land outside the continental United States did the government make?

CONNECTIONS: What foreign policy developments occurred in the 1890s? How did American political leaders react to them? Where was U.S. expansion headed and why?

island until the Cubans accepted the so-called Platt Amendment — a series of provisions that granted the United States the right to intervene to protect Cuba's "independence," as well as the power to oversee Cuban debt so that European creditors would not find an excuse for intervention. For good measure, the United States gave itself a ninety-nine-year lease on a naval base at Guantánamo. In return, McKinley promised to implement an extensive sanitation program to clean up the island, making it more attractive to American investors.

In the formal Treaty of Paris (1898), Spain ceded the Philippines to the United States, along with the former Spanish colonies of Puerto Rico and Guam (**Map 20.4**).

| How were women involved in late-nineteenth-century politics? | How did economic problems affect American politics in the 1890s? | **Why did the United States largely abandon its isolationist foreign policy in the 1890s?** | Conclusion: What was the connection between domestic strife and foreign policy? | ✓ LearningCurve Check what you know. bedfordstmartins.com /roarkunderstanding |

Empire did not come cheap. When Spain initially balked at these terms, the United States agreed to pay an indemnity of $20 million for the islands. Nor was the cost measured in money alone. Filipino revolutionaries under Emilio Aguinaldo, who had greeted U.S. troops as liberators, bitterly fought the new masters. It would take seven years and 4,000 American dead — almost ten times the number killed in Cuba — not to mention an estimated 20,000 Filipino casualties, to defeat Aguinaldo and secure American control of the Philippines.

At home, a vocal minority, mostly Democrats and former Populists, resisted the country's foray into overseas empire, judging it unwise, immoral, and unconstitutional. William Jennings Bryan, who enlisted in the army but never saw action, concluded that American expansionism only distracted the nation from problems at home. Pointing to the central paradox of the war, Representative Bourke Cockran of New York admonished, "We who have been the destroyers of oppression are asked now to become its agents." But the expansionists won the day. As Senator Knute Nelson of Minnesota assured his colleagues, "We come as ministering angels, not as despots." Fresh from the conquest of Native Americans in the West, the nation largely embraced the heady mixture of racism and missionary zeal that fueled American adventurism abroad. The *Washington Post* trumpeted, "The taste of empire is in the mouth of the people," thrilled at the prospect of "an imperial policy, the Republic renascent, taking her place with the armed nations."

> **QUICK REVIEW**

How did Americans respond to U.S. overseas expansion?

CHAPTER LOCATOR | Why did American farmers organize alliances in the late nineteenth century? | What led to the labor wars of the 1890s?

Conclusion: What was the connection between domestic strife and foreign policy?

A DECADE OF DOMESTIC STRIFE ended amid the blare of martial music and the waving of flags. The Spanish-American War drowned out the calls for social reform that had fueled the Populist politics of the 1890s. During that decade, angry farmers facing hard times looked to the Farmers' Alliance to fight for their vision of economic democracy, workers staged bloody battles across the country to assert their rights, and women like Frances Willard preached temperance and suffrage. Together, they formed a new People's Party to fight for change.

The bitter depression that began in 1893 led to increased labor strife. The Pullman boycott brutally dramatized the power of property and the conservatism of the laissez-faire state. But workers' willingness to confront capitalism on the streets of Chicago, Homestead, Cripple Creek, and a host of other sites across America eloquently testified to labor's growing determination, unity, and strength.

As the depression deepened, the sight of Coxey's army of unemployed marching on Washington to demand federal intervention in the economy signaled a growing shift in the public mind against the standpat politics of laissez-faire. The call for the government to take action to better the lives of workers, farmers, and the dispossessed manifested itself in the fiercely fought presidential campaign of William Jennings Bryan in 1896. With the outbreak of the Spanish-American War in 1898, the decade ended on a harmonious note with patriotic Americans rallying around the flag. But even though Americans basked in patriotism and contemplated empire, old grievances had not been laid to rest. The People's Party had been beaten, but the Populist spirit lived on in the demands for greater government involvement in the economy, expanded opportunities for direct democracy, and a more equitable balance of profits and power between the people and the big corporations. A new generation of progressive reformers took up the unfinished reform agenda in the first decades of the twentieth century.

How were women involved in late-nineteenth-century politics?

How did economic problems affect American politics in the 1890s?

Why did the United States largely abandon its isolationist foreign policy in the 1890s?

Conclusion: What was the connection between domestic strife and foreign policy?

LearningCurve
Check what you know.
bedfordstmartins.com
/roarkunderstanding

607

CHAPTER 20 STUDY GUIDE

STEP 1

GET STARTED ONLINE

✓ **LearningCurve** ▪ bedfordstmartins.com/roarkunderstanding
Now that you've read the chapter, make it stick by completing the LearningCurve activity.

STEP 2

EXPLAIN WHY IT MATTERS

Put your reading into practice. Identify each term below, and then explain why it matters in U.S. history.

TERM	WHO OR WHAT & WHEN	WHY IT MATTERS
Farmers' Alliance (p. 581)		
People's Party (Populist Party) (p. 582)		
Homestead lockout (p. 585)		
Cripple Creek miners' strike of 1894 (p. 587)		
Pullman boycott (p. 589)		
National American Woman Suffrage Association (NAWSA) (p. 593)		
Coxey's army (p. 595)		
Boxer uprising (p. 600)		
Monroe Doctrine (p. 601)		
Open Door policy (p. 601)		
Spanish-American War (p. 602)		
yellow journalism (p. 603)		

STEP 3

MOVE BEYOND THE BASICS

To demonstrate a more advanced understanding, describe the issues, goals, actions, and successes and failures of activists, reformers, and foreign-policy makers in the 1890s.

Group	Issues and goals	Actions	Successes and failures
Farmers			
Laborers			
Women			
Foreign-policy makers			

PUT IT ALL TOGETHER

Now, take a step back and try to explain the big picture. Remember to use specific examples from the chapter in your answers.

ECONOMICS

► What key issues fueled farm protest in the late nineteenth century? How did the Farmers' Alliance attempt to address these issues?

► What strategies and tactics did unions employ in the late nineteenth century? How did companies fight back?

POLITICS

► How did reform movements provide a vehicle for women's involvement in public political life?

► How did the depression of the mid-1890s shape the politics of the decade?

EMPIRE

► How did U.S. foreign policy reflect the tension between American tendencies toward isolationism and expansionism?

► How did the Spanish-American War change the place of the United States in global politics?

LOOKING BACKWARD, LOOKING AHEAD

► What were the United States' most important strengths and weaknesses in 1900? How had the nation's place in the world changed since 1800?

► Defend or refute the following statement: "With its victory in the Spanish-American War in 1898, the United States became an imperial power."

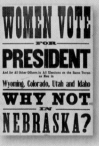

> ## IN YOUR OWN WORDS

Imagine that you must give an oral report to the class answering the following question: Why was the decade of the 1890s such a turbulent time in U.S. history? What would be the most important points to include and why?

 Do it online at the Student Site ■ bedfordstmartins.com/roarkunderstanding

21

PROGRESSIVISM FROM THE GRASS ROOTS UP

1890–1916

> **What were the most significant changes in the United States as a result of the Progressive Era?** Chapter 21 examines the efforts of progressive reformers to combat the ills of industrial America. It explores the initiatives of reformers at the grassroots level and examines their core values and beliefs. The chapter then considers the impact that the progressive agenda had on local, state, and national politics. Finally, it looks at the limits of progressive reform.

LearningCurve
bedfordstmartins.com/roarkunderstanding
After reading the chapter, use LearningCurve to
retain what you've read.

> How did grassroots progressives attack the problems of industrial America?

> What were the key tenets of progressive theory?

> How did Theodore Roosevelt advance the progressive agenda?

> How did progressivism evolve during Woodrow Wilson's first term?

> What were the limits of progressive reform?

> Conclusion: How did the liberal state transform during the Progressive Era?

Progressive social work. An Infant Welfare Society nurse instructs an immigrant mother on clean home care in 1910. Chicago History Museum.

How did grassroots progressives attack the problems of industrial America?

Jane Addams Jane Addams was twenty-nine years old when she founded Hull House in 1889. Her insistence that settlement house work benefited educated women as well as her immigrant neighbors marked the distance from philanthropy to progressive reform. *Twenty Years at Hull-House*, her autobiography published in 1910, is shown in the inset. Photo: Jane Addams Memorial Collection (JAMC neg. 14), Special Collections, University of Illinois at Chicago, photographer: Max Platz; book: Newberry Library.

AS THE GAP BETWEEN RICH and poor widened in the 1890s, a group of reformers demonstrated a willingness to use the government to counterbalance the power of private interests and in doing so redefined liberalism in the twentieth century. Faith in activism united an otherwise diverse group of progressive reformers. A sense of Christian mission inspired some. Others, fearing social upheaval, sought to remove some of the worst evils of urban industrialism — tenements, child labor, and harsh working conditions.

Much of progressive reform began at the grassroots level and percolated upward into local, state, and eventually national politics as reformers attacked the social problems fostered by urban industrialism. Although **progressivism** flourished in many different settings across the country, urban problems inspired the progressives' greatest efforts. In their zeal to "civilize the city," reformers founded settlement houses, professed a new Christian social gospel, and campaigned against vice and crime in the name of "social purity." Allying with the working class, women progressives sought to better the lot of sweatshop garment workers

progressivism
▶ A reform movement that often advocated government activism to mitigate the problems created by urban industrialism. Progressivism reached its peak in 1912 with the creation of the Progressive Party. The term *progressivism* has come to mean any general effort advocating for social welfare programs.

CHAPTER LOCATOR | **How did grassroots progressives attack the problems of industrial America?** | What were the key tenets of progressive theory?

and to end child labor. These local reform efforts often ended up being debated in state legislatures and in the U.S. Congress.

Civilizing the City

Progressives attacked the problems of the city on many fronts. The settlement house movement, which began in England, came to the United States in 1886 with the opening of the University Settlement House in New York City. Other **settlement houses** soon followed. In the summer of 1889, reformer Jane Addams leased two floors of a dilapidated mansion on Chicago's West Side. For Addams, personal action marked the first step in her search for solutions to the social problems created by urban industrialism. She wanted to help her immigrant neighbors, and she wanted to offer meaningful work to educated women like herself. Addams's emphasis on the reciprocal relationship between the social classes made Hull House different from other philanthropic enterprises. She wished to do things with, not just for, Chicago's poor.

In the next decade, Hull House expanded from two rented floors in the old brick mansion to some thirteen buildings housing a remarkable variety of activities. Addams provided public baths, opened a restaurant for working women too tired to cook after their long shifts, and sponsored a nursery and kindergarten. Hull House offered classes, lectures, art exhibits, musical instruction, and college extension courses. It boasted a gymnasium, a theater, a manual training workshop, a labor museum, and the first public playground in Chicago.

In 1893, the needs of poor urban neighborhoods that had motivated Jane Addams led Lillian Wald, a nurse, to recruit several other nurses to move to New York City's Lower East Side "to live in the neighborhood as nurses, identify ourselves with it socially, and . . . contribute to it our citizenship." Wald's Henry Street settlement pioneered public health nursing.

Women, particularly college-educated women like Addams and Wald, formed the backbone of the settlement house movement and stood in the vanguard of the progressive movement. Settlement houses gave college-educated women eager to use their knowledge a place to put their talents to work in the service of society and to champion progressive reform. Settlements grew in number from six in 1891 to more than four hundred in 1911. In the process, settlement house women created a new profession — social work.

> **CHRONOLOGY**

1889
- Jane Addams opens Hull House in Chicago.

1893
- Lillian Wald opens Henry Street settlement house in New York.

1903
- Women's Trade Union League (WTUL) is founded.

1908
- *Muller v. Oregon.*

1909
- Garment workers' strike.

1911
- Triangle fire.

settlement houses
▶ Settlements established in poor neighborhoods beginning in the 1880s. Reformers like Jane Addams and Lillian Wald believed that only by living among the poor could they help bridge the growing class divide. College-educated women formed the backbone of the settlement house movement.

> Progressives and Urban Reform	
Settlement house movement	Effort by reformers to bridge the social divide by living and working among the poor.
Social gospel	Call for churches and their members to play an active role in social reform. Advocates questioned social Darwinism and the gospel of wealth.
Social purity movement	Campaign to attack vice, particularly prostitution. The movement brought together ministers who wished to stamp out sin, doctors concerned about the spread of sexually transmitted diseases, and women reformers. Advanced progressives linked prostitution to poverty and championed higher wages for women.

How did Theodore Roosevelt advance the progressive agenda?	How did progressivism evolve during Woodrow Wilson's first term?	What were the limits of progressive reform?	Conclusion: How did the liberal state transform during the Progressive Era?	✔ LearningCurve Check what you know. bedfordstmartins.com /roarkunderstanding

For their part, churches confronted urban social problems by enunciating a new social gospel, one that saw its mission as not simply to reform individuals but to reform society. Charles M. Sheldon's popular book *In His Steps* (1898) called on men and women to Christianize capitalism by asking the question "What would Jesus do?" Ministers also played an active role in the social purity movement, the campaign to attack vice.

Attacks on alcohol went hand in hand with the push for social purity. The Anti-Saloon League, formed in 1895 under the leadership of Protestant clergy, added to the efforts of the Woman's Christian Temperance Union in campaigning to end the sale of liquor. Reformers pointed to links between drinking and a variety of other problems, including prostitution, wife and child abuse, unemployment, and industrial accidents. The powerful liquor lobby fought back, spending liberally in election campaigns, fueling the charge that liquor corrupted the political process.

An element of nativism (dislike of foreigners) ran through the movement for prohibition, as it did in a number of progressive reforms. The Irish, the Italians, and the Germans were among the groups stigmatized by temperance reformers for their drinking. Progressives campaigned to enforce the Sunday closing of taverns, stores, and other commercial establishments and pushed for state legislation to outlaw the sale of liquor. By 1912, seven states were "dry."

> ### > Core Progressive Attitudes

- A willingness to take action
- The belief that environment, not heredity alone, determined human behavior
- Optimism that reform could be achieved through government action without radically altering America's economy or institutions

---

Progressives and the Working Class

Day-to-day contact with their neighbors made settlement house workers particularly sympathetic to labor. When Mary Kenney O'Sullivan complained that her bookbinders' union met in a dirty, noisy saloon, Jane Addams invited them to meet at Hull House. And during the Pullman strike in 1894, Hull House residents organized strike relief. "Hull-House has been so unionized," grumbled one Chicago businessman, "that it has lost its usefulness and become a detriment and harm to the community." But to the working class, the support of middle-class reformers marked a significant gain.

Attempts to forge a cross-class alliance became institutionalized in 1903 with the creation of the Women's Trade Union League (WTUL). The WTUL brought together women workers and middle-class "allies." Its goal was to organize workingwomen into unions under the auspices of the American Federation of Labor (AFL). Although the alliance between workingwomen, primarily immigrants and daughters of immigrants, and their middle-class allies was not without tension, the WTUL helped workingwomen achieve significant gains.

The WTUL's most notable success came in 1909 in the "uprising of the twenty thousand," when hundreds of women employees of the Triangle Shirtwaist Company in New York City went on strike to protest low wages, dangerous working conditions,

CHAPTER LOCATOR | How did grassroots progressives attack the problems of industrial America? | What were the key tenets of progressive theory?

614 CHAPTER 21 PROGRESSIVISM FROM THE GRASS ROOTS UP

and management's refusal to recognize their union, the International Ladies' Garment Workers Union. In support, an estimated twenty thousand garment workers, most of them teenage girls and many of them Jewish and Italian immigrants, stayed out on strike through the winter, picketing in the bitter cold. By the time the strike ended in February 1910, the workers had won important demands in many shops. The solidarity shown by the women workers proved to be the strike's greatest achievement. As Clara Lemlich, one of the strike's leaders, exclaimed, "They used to say that you couldn't even organize women. They wouldn't come to union meetings. They were 'temporary' workers. Well we showed them!"

But for all its success, the uprising of the twenty thousand failed fundamentally to change conditions for women workers, as the tragic Triangle fire dramatized in 1911. A little over a year after the shirtwaist makers' strike ended, fire alarms sounded at the Triangle Shirtwaist factory. The ramshackle building, full of lint and combustible cloth, burned to rubble in half an hour. A WTUL member described the scene below on the street: "Two young girls whom I knew to be working in the vicinity came rushing toward me, tears were running from their eyes and they were white and shaking as they caught me by the arm. 'Oh,' shrieked one of them, 'they are jumping. Jumping from ten stories up! They are going through the air like bundles of clothes.'"

The terrified Triangle workers had little choice but to jump. Flames blocked one exit, and the other door had been locked to prevent workers from pilfering. The flimsy, rusted fire escape collapsed under the weight of fleeing workers, killing dozens. Trapped, 54 workers on the top floors jumped to their deaths. Of 500 workers, 146 died and scores of others were injured. The owners of the Triangle firm went to trial for negligence, but they avoided conviction when authorities determined that a careless smoker had started the fire. The Triangle Shirtwaist Company reopened in another firetrap within a matter of weeks.

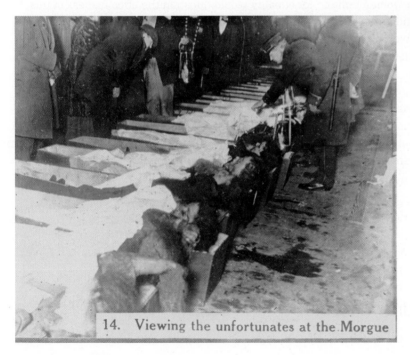

14. Viewing the unfortunates at the Morgue

Triangle Fire Morgue

After the Triangle fire on March 26, 1911, New York City set up a makeshift morgue at the end of Manhattan's Charities Pier. There, the remains of more than a hundred young women and two dozen young men were laid out in coffins for their friends and relatives to identify. Small personal items often provided the only clues to the victims' identity. Hadwin Collection, Kheel Center, Cornell University, Ithaca, NY.

| How did Theodore Roosevelt advance the progressive agenda? | How did progressivism evolve during Woodrow Wilson's first term? | What were the limits of progressive reform? | Conclusion: How did the liberal state transform during the Progressive Era? | ✓ **LearningCurve** Check what you know. bedfordstmartins.com /roarkunderstanding |

615

Outrage and a sense of futility overwhelmed Rose Schneiderman, a leading WTUL organizer, who made a bitter speech at the memorial service for the dead Triangle workers. "I would be a traitor to those poor burned bodies if I came here to talk good fellowship," she told her audience. "We have tried you good people of the public and we have found you wanting. . . . I know from my experience it is up to the working people to save themselves . . . by a strong working class movement." The Triangle fire severely tested the bonds of the cross-class alliance. Schneiderman and other WTUL leaders determined that organizing and striking were no longer enough, particularly when the AFL paid so little attention to women workers. Increasingly, the WTUL turned its efforts to lobbying for protective legislation — laws that would limit hours and regulate women's working conditions.

The National Consumers League (NCL) also fostered cross-class alliance and advocated for protective legislation. When Florence Kelley took over the leadership of the NCL in 1899, she urged middle-class women to boycott stores and exert pressure for decent wages and working conditions for women employees. Frustrated by the reluctance of the private sector to reform, the NCL promoted protective legislation to better working conditions for women.

Advocates of protective legislation had won a major victory in 1908 when the U.S. Supreme Court, in *Muller v. Oregon*, reversed its previous rulings and upheld an Oregon law that limited to ten the number of hours women could work in a day. A mass of sociological evidence put together by Florence Kelley of the NCL and Josephine Goldmark of the WTUL convinced the Court that long hours endangered women and therefore the entire human race. The Court's ruling set a precedent, but one that separated the well-being of women workers from that of men by arguing that women's reproductive role justified special treatment. Later generations of women fighting for equality would question the effectiveness of this strategy and argue that it ultimately closed good jobs to women. The WTUL, however, greeted protective legislation as a first step in the attempt to ensure the safety of all workers.

Reform also fueled the fight for woman suffrage. For women like Jane Addams, involvement in social reform inevitably led to support for woman suffrage. These new suffragists emphasized the reforms that could be accomplished if women had the vote. Addams insisted that in an urban, industrial society, a good housekeeper could not be sure the food she fed her family, or the water and milk they drank, were pure unless she became involved in politics and wielded the ballot — and not just the broom — to protect her family.

> **QUICK REVIEW**

What types of people were drawn to the progressive movement, and why?

CHAPTER OVERVIEW | How did grassroots progressives attack the problems of industrial America? | What were the key tenets of progressive theory?

CHAPTER 21
616 PROGRESSIVISM FROM THE GRASS ROOTS UP

What were the key tenets of progressive theory?

Tom Johnson

The reform mayor of Cleveland from 1901 to 1909, Tom Johnson is shown here campaigning in Cleveland's Wade Park in 1908. To get a three-cent streetcar fare and win the support of the working classes, Johnson instituted municipal ownership of the transit system. The Western Reserve Historical Society, Cleveland, Ohio.

PROGRESSIVISM EMPHASIZED action and experimentation. Dismissing the view that humans should leave progress to the dictates of natural selection, a new group of reform Darwinists argued that evolution could be advanced more rapidly if men and women used their intellects to improve society. In their zeal for action, progressives often showed an unchecked admiration for speed and efficiency that promoted scientific management and a new cult to improve productivity. These varied strands of progressive theory found practical application in state and local politics, where reformers challenged traditional laissez-faire government.

Reform Darwinism and Social Engineering

The active, interventionist approach of the progressives directly challenged social Darwinism, with its insistence on survival of the fittest. A new group of sociologists argued that progress could be advanced more rapidly if people used their intellects to alter their environment. The best statement of this **reform Darwinism** came from sociologist Lester Frank Ward, who, in his book

reform Darwinism

▶ Sociological theory developed in the 1880s that argued humans could speed up evolution by altering their environment. A challenge to the laissez-faire approach of social Darwinism, reform Darwinism insisted that the liberal state should play an active role in solving social problems.

How did Theodore Roosevelt advance the progressive agenda?

How did progressivism evolve during Woodrow Wilson's first term?

What were the limits of progressive reform?

Conclusion: How did the liberal state transform during the Progressive Era?

✓ **LearningCurve**
Check what you know.
bedfordstmartins.com
/roarkunderstanding

1883
– Lester Frank Ward champions reform Darwinism in *Dynamic Sociology*.

1910
– Progressive Hiram Johnson is elected governor of California.

1911
– Frederick Winslow Taylor pioneers "systematized shop management."

1914
– Journalist Walter Lippmann calls for scientific techniques to control social change.

Dynamic Sociology (1883), insisted that the "blind natural forces in society must give way to human foresight." This theory condemned the laissez-faire approach, insisting that the liberal state should play a more active role in solving social problems.

Efficiency and *expertise* became progressives' watchwords. In *Drift and Mastery* (1914), journalist and critic Walter Lippmann called for skilled "*technocrats*" to use scientific techniques to control social change. Unlike the Populists, who advocated a greater voice for the masses, progressives, for all their interest in social justice, insisted that experts be put in charge. At its extreme, the application of expertise and social engineering took the form of scientific management. In 1911, Frederick Winslow Taylor pioneered "systematized shop management." Obsessed with making humans and machines produce more and faster, he meticulously timed workers with a stopwatch and attempted to break down their work into its simplest components, one repetitious action after another. He won many converts among corporate managers, but workers hated the monotony of systematized shop management and argued that it led to speedup — pushing workers to produce more in less time and for less pay. Nevertheless, many progressives applauded the increased productivity and efficiency of Taylor's system.

Progressive Government: City and State

Progressivism burst forth at every level of government in 1900, but nowhere more forcefully than in Cleveland with the election of Democrat Thomas Loftin Johnson as mayor. A self-made millionaire by age forty, Johnson moved to Cleveland in 1899, where he began his career in politics. During his mayoral campaign, he pledged to reduce the streetcar fare from five cents to three cents. His election touched off a seven-year war between Johnson and the streetcar moguls. To get his three-cent fare, Johnson had Cleveland buy the streetcar system, a tactic of municipal ownership progressives called "gas and water socialism." Reelected four times, Johnson fought for fair taxation and championed greater democracy through the use of the initiative and referendum to let voters introduce legislation, and the recall to get rid of elected officials and judges. These devices allowed voters to have a direct say in legislative and judicial matters. Under Johnson's administration, Cleveland became, in the words of journalist Lincoln Steffens, the "best governed city in America."

In Wisconsin, Republican Robert M. La Follette converted to the progressive cause early in the twentieth century. La Follette capitalized on the grassroots movement for reform to launch his long political career as governor (1901–1905) and U.S. senator (1906–1925). La Follette brought scientists and professors into his administration and used the university, just down the street from the statehouse in Madison, as a resource. As governor, La Follette lowered railroad rates, raised railroad taxes, improved education, preached conservation, established factory regulation and workers' compensation, instituted the first direct primary in the country, and inaugurated the first state income tax. Under his leadership, Wisconsin earned the title "laboratory of democracy." A fiery orator, "Fighting Bob" La Follette united his supporters around issues that transcended party

CHAPTER OVERVIEW | How did grassroots progressives attack the problems of industrial America? | **What were the key tenets of progressive theory?**

CHAPTER 21
618 PROGRESSIVISM FROM THE GRASS ROOTS UP

loyalties. Democrats and Republicans like Tom Johnson and Robert La Follette crossed party lines to work for reform.

West of the Rockies, progressivism arrived somewhat later and found a champion in Republican Hiram Johnson of California, who served as governor from 1911 to 1917 and later as a U.S. senator. Since the 1870s, the Southern Pacific Railroad had dominated California politics. Johnson ran for governor in 1910 on the promise to "kick the Southern Pacific out of politics." With the support of the reform wing of the Republican Party and the promise "to return the government to the people," he won handily. As governor, he introduced the direct primary; supported the initiative, referendum, and recall; strengthened the state's railroad commission; supported conservation; and signed an employer's liability law.

QUICK REVIEW <

How did progressives justify their demand for a more activist government?

| How did Theodore Roosevelt advance the progressive agenda? | How did progressivism evolve during Woodrow Wilson's first term? | What were the limits of progressive reform? | Conclusion: How did the liberal state transform during the Progressive Era? | ✓ LearningCurve Check what you know. bedfordstmartins.com /roarkunderstanding |

619

How did Theodore Roosevelt advance the progressive agenda?

Theodore Roosevelt Aptly described by a contemporary observer as "a steam engine in trousers," Theodore Roosevelt, at forty-two, was the youngest president ever to occupy the White House. He brought to the office energy, intellect, and activism in equal measure. Roosevelt boasted that he used the presidency as a "bully pulpit"—a forum from which he advocated reforms ranging from trust-busting to conservation. Library of Congress.

O N SEPTEMBER 6, 1901, President William McKinley was shot by Leon Czolgosz, an anarchist, while attending the Pan-American Exposition in Buffalo, New York. Eight days later, McKinley died, and Theodore Roosevelt became president. Roosevelt immediately reassured the shocked nation that he intended "to continue absolutely unbroken" the policies of McKinley. But Roosevelt was quite different from McKinley. An activist and a moralist, imbued with the progressive spirit, Roosevelt would turn the White House into a "bully pulpit," advocating conservation and antitrust reforms and championing the nation's emergence as a world power. In the process, Roosevelt would work to shift the nation's center of power from Wall Street to Washington.

After serving nearly two full terms as president, Roosevelt left office at the height of his powers. Any man would have found it difficult to follow in his footsteps, but his handpicked successor, William Howard Taft, proved hopelessly ill suited to the task. Taft's presidency was marked by a progressive stalemate, a bitter break with Roosevelt, and a schism in the Republican Party.

CHAPTER OVERVIEW | How did grassroots progressives attack the problems of industrial America? | What were the key tenets of progressive theory?

The Square Deal

At age forty-two, Theodore Roosevelt became the youngest man ever to move into the White House. A patrician by birth and an activist by temperament, Roosevelt brought to the job enormous talent and energy.

Roosevelt recognized that the path to power did not lie in the good government leagues formed by his well-bred friends. "If it is the muckers that govern," he wrote, "then I want to see if I cannot hold my own with them." Roosevelt's rise in politics was swift and sure. He went from the New York assembly at the age of twenty-three to the presidency in less than twenty years, with time out as a cowboy in the Dakotas, police commissioner of New York City, assistant secretary of the navy, and a colonel of the Rough Riders. Elected governor of New York in 1898, he alienated the state's Republican boss, who finagled to get him "kicked upstairs" as a candidate for the vice presidency in 1900. The party bosses reasoned that Roosevelt could do little harm as vice president. But one bullet proved the error of their logic.

Once president, Roosevelt would harness his explosive energy to strengthen the power of the federal government, putting business on notice that it could no longer count on a laissez-faire government to give it free rein. In Roosevelt's eyes, self-interested capitalists like John D. Rockefeller, whose Standard Oil trust monopolized the refinery business, constituted "the most dangerous members of the criminal class — the criminals of great wealth." The "absolutely vital question" facing the country, Roosevelt wrote to a friend in 1901, was "whether or not the government has the power to control the trusts." The Sherman Antitrust Act of 1890 had been badly weakened by a conservative Supreme Court and by attorneys general more willing to use it against labor unions than against monopolies. To determine whether the law had any teeth left, Roosevelt, in one of his first acts as president, ordered his attorney general to begin a secret antitrust investigation of the Northern Securities Company, a behemoth that monopolized railroad traffic in the Northwest.

Just five months after Roosevelt took office, Wall Street rocked with the news that the government had filed an antitrust suit against Northern Securities. As one newspaper editor sarcastically observed, "Wall Street is paralyzed at the thought that a President of the United States would sink so low as to try to enforce the law." Roosevelt's thunderbolt put Wall Street on notice that the new president expected to be treated as an equal and was willing to use government as a weapon to curb business excesses. Perhaps sensing the new mood, the Supreme Court, in a significant turnaround, upheld the Sherman Act and called for the dissolution of Northern Securities in 1904.

"Hurrah for Teddy the Trustbuster," cheered the papers. Roosevelt went on to use the Sherman Act against forty-three trusts, including such giants as American Tobacco, Du Pont, and Standard Oil. Always the moralist, he insisted on a "rule of reason." He would punish "bad" trusts (those that broke the law) and leave "good" ones alone. In practice, he preferred regulation to antitrust suits. In 1903, he pressured Congress to pass the Elkins Act, outlawing railroad rebates. And he created the new cabinet-level Department of Commerce and Labor, with the subsidiary Bureau of Corporations to act as a corporate watchdog.

> CHRONOLOGY

1901
- William McKinley is assassinated; Theodore Roosevelt becomes president.

1902
- Antitrust lawsuit is filed against Northern Securities Company.
- Roosevelt mediates anthracite coal strike.

1903
- Panama Canal construction begins.

1904
- Roosevelt Corollary to Monroe Doctrine.

1906
- Pure Food and Drug Act and Meat Inspection Act.
- Hepburn Act.

1907
- Panic on Wall Street.
- "Gentlemen's Agreement" with Japan.

1908
- William Howard Taft is elected president.

How did Theodore Roosevelt advance the progressive agenda?

How did progressivism evolve during Woodrow Wilson's first term?

What were the limits of progressive reform?

Conclusion: How did the liberal state transform during the Progressive Era?

✓ LearningCurve
Check what you know.
bedfordstmartins.com
/roarkunderstanding

621

In his handling of the anthracite coal strike in 1902, Roosevelt again demonstrated his willingness to assert the authority of the presidency, this time to mediate between labor and management. In May, 147,000 coal miners in Pennsylvania went on strike. The United Mine Workers (UMW) demanded a reduction in the workday from twelve to ten hours, an equitable system of weighing each miner's output, and a 10 percent wage increase, along with recognition of the union. When asked about the appalling conditions in the mines that led to the strike, George Baer, the mine operators' spokesman, scoffed, "The miners don't suffer, why they can't even speak English."

The strike dragged on through the summer and into the fall. Hoarding and profiteering drove the price of coal from $2.50 to $6.00 a ton. As winter approached, coal shortages touched off near riots in the nation's big cities. At this juncture, Roosevelt stepped in. Instead of sending in troops, he determined to mediate. His unprecedented intervention served notice that government counted itself an independent force in business and labor disputes. At the same time, it gave unionism a boost by granting the UMW a place at the table.

At the meeting, Baer and the mine owners refused to talk with the union representative — a move that angered the attorney general and insulted the president. Beside himself with rage over the "woodenheaded obstinacy and stupidity" of management, Roosevelt threatened to seize the mines and run them with federal troops. This quickly brought management to the table. In the end, the miners won a reduction in hours and a wage increase, but the owners succeeded in preventing formal recognition of the UMW.

Taken together, Roosevelt's actions in the Northern Securities case and the anthracite coal strike marked a dramatic departure from the presidential passivity of the Gilded Age. Roosevelt's actions demonstrated conclusively that government intended to act as a countervailing force to the power of the big corporations. Pleased with his role in the anthracite strike, Roosevelt announced that all he had tried to do was give labor and capital a "square deal."

The phrase "Square Deal" became Roosevelt's campaign slogan in the 1904 election. Roosevelt easily defeated the Democrats, who abandoned their former candidate, William Jennings Bryan, to support Judge Alton B. Parker, a "safe" choice they hoped would lure business votes away from Roosevelt. In the months before the election, the president prudently toned down his criticism of big business. Roosevelt swept into office with the largest popular majority — 57.9 percent — any candidate had polled up to that time.

Roosevelt the Reformer

"Tomorrow I shall come into my office in my own right," Roosevelt is said to have remarked on the eve of his election. "Then watch out for me!" Roosevelt's stunning victory gave him a mandate for reform. He would need all the popularity and political savvy he could muster, however, to guide his reform measures through Congress. The Senate remained controlled by a staunchly conservative Republican "old guard," with many senators on the payrolls of the corporations Roosevelt sought to curb. Roosevelt's pet project remained railroad regulation. The Elkins Act prohibiting rebates had not worked. Roosevelt determined that the only solution lay in giving the Interstate Commerce Commission (ICC) real power to set rates and prevent discriminatory practices. But the right to determine the price of goods or services was an age-old prerogative of private enterprise, and one that business had no intention of yielding to government.

The Hepburn Act of 1906 marked the crowning legislative achievement of Roosevelt's presidency. It gave the ICC the power to set rates subject to court review. Committed progressives like Robert La Follette judged the law a defeat for reform. Die-hard conservatives branded it a "piece of populism." Both sides exaggerated. The law left the courts too much power and failed to provide adequate means for the ICC to determine rates, but its passage proved a landmark in federal control of private industry. For the first time, a government commission had the power to investigate private business records and to set rates.

Always an apt reader of the public temper, Roosevelt witnessed a growing appetite for reform. Revelations of corporate and political wrongdoing as well as social injustice filled the papers and boosted the sales of popular magazines. Roosevelt counted many of the new investigative journalists among his friends. But he warned them against going too far, citing the allegorical character in *Pilgrim's Progress* who was too busy raking muck to notice higher things. Roosevelt's criticism gave the American vocabulary a new word, *muckraker*, which journalists soon appropriated as a title of honor.

Muckraking, as Roosevelt well knew, provided enormous help in securing progressive legislation. In the spring of 1906, publicity generated by the muckrakers about poisons in patent medicines goaded the Senate, with Roosevelt's backing, into passing a pure food and drug bill. Opponents in the House of Representatives hoped to keep the legislation locked up in committee. There it would have died, were it not for the publication of Upton Sinclair's novel *The Jungle* (1906), with its sensational account of filthy conditions in meatpacking plants. A massive public outcry led to the passage of the Pure Food and Drug Act and the Meat Inspection Act in 1906.

In the waning years of his administration, Roosevelt allied with the more progressive elements of the Republican Party. In speech after speech, he attacked "malefactors of great wealth." Styling himself a "radical," he claimed credit for leading the "ultra conservative" party of McKinley to a position of "progressive conservatism and conservative radicalism."

When an economic panic developed in the fall of 1907, business interests quickly blamed the president. Once again, J. P. Morgan stepped in to avert disaster, this time switching funds from one bank to another to prop up weak institutions. For his services, he claimed the Tennessee Coal and Iron Company, an independent steel business that U.S. Steel had long coveted. Morgan dispatched his lieutenants to Washington, where they told Roosevelt that the sale of the company would aid the economy "but little benefit" U.S. Steel. Willing to take the word of a gentleman, Roosevelt tacitly agreed not to institute antitrust proceedings against U.S. Steel over the acquisition. Roosevelt's promise would give rise to the charge that he acted as a tool of the Morgan interests.

THE JUNGLE
BY
UPTON SINCLAIR
DOUBLEDAY, PAGE & C?
NEW YORK

The Jungle

Novelist Upton Sinclair, a lifelong socialist, wrote *The Jungle* to expose the evils of capitalism. But readers were more horrified by his descriptions of the unsanitary conditions in the meatpacking industry, where the novel's hapless hero sees rats, filth, and diseased animals processed into meat products. The public outcry surrounding *The Jungle* contributed to the enactment of pure food and drug legislation and a federal meat inspection law.
Picture Research Consultants, Inc.

muckraking

▶ Early-twentieth-century style of journalism that exposed the corruption of big business and government. Theodore Roosevelt coined the term after a character in *Pilgrim's Progress* who was too busy raking muck to notice higher things.

| How did Theodore Roosevelt advance the progressive agenda? | How did progressivism evolve during Woodrow Wilson's first term? | What were the limits of progressive reform? | Conclusion: How did the liberal state transform during the Progressive Era? | ✓ LearningCurve Check what you know. bedfordstmartins.com /roarkunderstanding |

The charge of collusion between business and government underscored the extent to which corporate leaders like Morgan found federal regulation preferable to unbridled competition or harsher state measures. During the Progressive Era, enlightened business leaders cooperated with government in the hope of avoiding antitrust prosecution. Convinced that regulation and not trust-busting offered the best way to deal with big business, Roosevelt never acknowledged that his regulatory policies fostered an alliance between business and government that today is called corporate liberalism.

Roosevelt and Conservation

In the area of conservation, Roosevelt proved indisputably ahead of his time. When he took office, some 43 million acres of forestland remained as government reserves. He more than quadrupled that number to 194 million acres. To conserve natural resources, he fought western cattle barons, lumber kings, mining interests, and powerful leaders in Congress, including Speaker of the House Joseph Cannon, who vowed to spend "not one cent for scenery."

As the first president to have lived and worked in the West, Roosevelt came to the White House convinced of the need for better management of the nation's rivers and forests as well as the preservation of wildlife and wilderness. During his presidency, he placed the nation's conservation policy in the hands of scientifically trained experts like his chief forester, Gifford Pinchot. Pinchot preached conservation — the efficient use of natural resources. Willing to permit grazing, lumbering, and the development of hydroelectric power, conservationists fought private interests only when they felt business acted irresponsibly or threatened to monopolize water and electric power. Preservationists like John Muir, founder of the Sierra Club, believed that the wilderness needed to be protected. Roosevelt — a fervent Darwinian naturalist and an (overly) enthusiastic game hunter, a conservationist who built big dams, and a preservationist who saved the redwoods — aimed to have it both ways.

In 1907, Congress attempted to put the brakes on Roosevelt's conservation program by passing a law limiting his power to create forest reserves in six western states. In the days leading up to the law's enactment, Roosevelt feverishly created twenty-one new reserves and enlarged eleven more, saving 16 million acres from development. Once again, Roosevelt had outwitted his adversaries. "Opponents of the forest service turned handsprings in their wrath," he wrote, "but the threats . . . were really only a tribute to the efficiency of our action." Worried that private utilities were gobbling up waterpower sites and creating a monopoly of hydroelectric power, he connived with Pinchot to withdraw 2,565 power sites from private use by designating them "ranger stations." Firm in his commitment to wild America, Roosevelt proved willing to stretch the law when it served his ends. His legacy is more than 234 million acres of American wilderness saved for posterity (**Map 21.1**).

The Big Stick

Roosevelt's activism extended to his foreign policy. A fierce proponent of America's interests abroad, he relied on executive power to pursue a vigorous for-

CHAPTER OVERVIEW | How did grassroots progressives attack the problems of industrial America? | What were the key tenets of progressive theory?

624   CHAPTER 21
PROGRESSIVISM FROM THE GRASS ROOTS UP

eign policy, sometimes stretching the powers of the presidency beyond legal limits. In his relations with the European powers, he relied on military strength and diplomacy, a combination he aptly described with the aphorism "Speak softly but carry a big stick."

A strong supporter of the Monroe Doctrine, Roosevelt jealously guarded the U.S. sphere of influence in the Western Hemisphere. His proprietary attitude toward the Caribbean became evident in the case of the Panama Canal. Roosevelt had long been a supporter of a canal linking the Caribbean and the Pacific. By enabling ships to move quickly from the Atlantic to the Pacific, a canal would trim 8,000 miles from a coast-to-coast voyage and effectively double the U.S. Navy's power. Having decided on a route across the Panamanian isthmus (a narrow strip

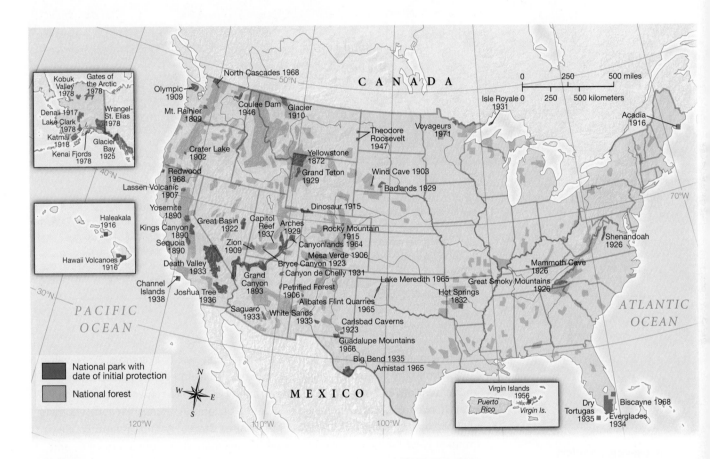

MAP 21.1 ■ National Parks and Forests

The national park system in the West began with Yellowstone in 1872. Grand Canyon, Yosemite, Kings Canyon, and Sequoia followed in the 1890s. During his presidency, Theodore Roosevelt added six parks—Crater Lake, Wind Cave, Petrified Forest, Lassen Volcanic, Mesa Verde, and Zion. Even more significant were the 234 million acres of wilderness he saved for posterity.

> MAP ACTIVITY

READING THE MAP: Collectively, do national parks or national forests encompass more land? According to the map, how many national parks were created before 1910? How many were created after 1910?

CONNECTIONS: How do conservation and preservation differ? Why did Roosevelt believe that saving land in the West was important? What principles guided the national land use policy of the Roosevelt administration?

How did Theodore Roosevelt advance the progressive agenda? | How did progressivism evolve during Woodrow Wilson's first term? | What were the limits of progressive reform? | Conclusion: How did the liberal state transform during the Progressive Era? | ✔ LearningCurve Check what you know. bedfordstmartins.com /roarkunderstanding

625

THE WORLD'S CONSTABLE.

"The World's Constable"

In this political cartoon from 1905, President Theodore Roosevelt, dressed as a constable, wields the club of "The New Diplomacy" in one hand, with "Arbitration" tucked under his arm. The Roosevelt Corollary to the Monroe Doctrine made the United States the Western Hemisphere's policeman, a role Roosevelt relished. The Granger Collection, NYC.

> **VISUAL ACTIVITY**

READING THE IMAGE: How does this political cartoon visually represent Roosevelt's foreign policy? Does it appear to be supportive or critical of his policies? How does it treat the other peoples of the world?

CONNECTIONS: What aspects of Roosevelt's foreign policy ideas and actions are depicted in the cartoon?

Roosevelt Corollary

▶ Theodore Roosevelt's 1904 follow-up to the Monroe Doctrine in which he declared that the United States had the right to intervene in Latin America to stop "brutal wrongdoing" and protect American interests. The corollary warned European powers to keep out of the Western Hemisphere.

of land connecting North and South America), then part of Colombia, Roosevelt in 1902 offered the Colombian government a one-time sum of $10 million and an annual rent of $250,000. When the government in Bogotá refused to accept the offer, Roosevelt became incensed at what he called the "homicidal corruptionists" in Colombia for trying to "blackmail" the United States. At the prompting of a group of New York investors, the Panamanians staged an uprising in 1903, and with unseemly haste the U.S. government recognized the new government within twenty-four hours. The Panamanians promptly accepted the $10 million, and the building got under way. The canal would take eleven years and $375 million to complete; it opened in 1914 (**Map 21.2**).

In the wake of the Panama affair, a confrontation with Germany over Venezuela, and yet another default on a European debt, this time in the Dominican Republic, Roosevelt grew concerned that financial instability in Latin America would lead European powers to interfere. In 1904, he announced the **Roosevelt Corollary** to the Monroe Doctrine.

CHAPTER OVERVIEW | How did grassroots progressives attack the problems of industrial America? | What were the key tenets of progressive theory?

- The United States had a right to act as "an international police power" in the Western Hemisphere.
- The United States would not intervene in Latin America as long as nations there conducted their affairs with "decency," but it would step in to stop "brutal wrongdoing."
- The Roosevelt Corollary served notice to European powers to stay out of the Western Hemisphere.

In Asia, Roosevelt inherited the Open Door policy initiated by Secretary of State John Hay in 1899, designed to ensure U.S. commercial entry into China. As European powers raced to secure Chinese trade and territory, Roosevelt was tempted to use force to gain economic or possibly territorial concessions. Realizing that Americans would not support an aggressive Asian policy, the president sensibly held back.

MAP 21.2 ■ The Panama Canal, 1914

The Panama Canal, completed in 1914, bisects the isthmus in a series of massive locks and dams. As Theodore Roosevelt had planned, the canal greatly strengthened the U.S. Navy by allowing ships to move from the Atlantic to the Pacific in a matter of days.

> MAP ACTIVITY

READING THE MAP: How long was the trip from New York to San Francisco before the Panama Canal was built? After it was built?

CONNECTIONS: How did Roosevelt's desire for a canal lead to independence for Panama? How did the canal benefit the U.S. Navy?

| How did Theodore Roosevelt advance the progressive agenda? | How did progressivism evolve during Woodrow Wilson's first term? | What were the limits of progressive reform? | Conclusion: How did the liberal state transform during the Progressive Era? | ✓ LearningCurve Check what you know. bedfordstmartins.com /roarkunderstanding |

The Roosevelt Corollary in Action

In his relations with Europe, Roosevelt sought to establish the United States as a rising force in world affairs. When tensions flared between France and Germany in Morocco in 1905, Roosevelt mediated at a conference in Algeciras, Spain, where he worked to maintain a balance of power that helped neutralize German ambitions. His skillful mediation gained him a reputation as an astute player on the world stage and demonstrated the nation's new presence in world affairs.

Roosevelt earned the Nobel Peace Prize in 1906 for his role in negotiating an end to the Russo-Japanese War, which had broken out when the Japanese invaded Chinese Manchuria, threatening Russia's sphere of influence in the area. Once again, Roosevelt sought to maintain a balance of power, in this case working to curb Japanese expansionism. Roosevelt admired the Japanese, judging them "the most dashing fighters in the world," but he did not want Japan to become too strong in Asia.

When good relations with Japan were jeopardized by discriminatory legislation in California calling for segregated public schools for Asians, Roosevelt smoothed over the incident and negotiated the "Gentlemen's Agreement" in 1907, which allowed the Japanese to save face by voluntarily restricting immigration to the United States. To demonstrate America's naval power and to counter Japan's growing bellicosity, Roosevelt dispatched the Great White Fleet, sixteen of the navy's most up-to-date battleships, on a "goodwill mission" around the world. U.S. relations with Japan improved, and in the 1908 Root-Takahira agreement the two nations pledged to maintain the Open Door and support the status quo in the Pacific. Roosevelt's show of American force constituted a classic example of his dictum "Speak softly but carry a big stick."

The Troubled Presidency of William Howard Taft

On the eve of his election in 1904, Roosevelt promised that he would not seek another term. So he retired from the presidency in 1909 at age fifty and removed himself from the political scene by going on safari in Africa. He turned the White House over to his handpicked successor, William Howard Taft, a lawyer who had served as governor-general of the Philippines. In the presidential election of 1908, Taft soundly defeated the perennial Democratic candidate, William Jennings Bryan.

A genial man with a talent for law, Taft had no experience in elective office, no feel for politics, and no nerve for controversy. His ambitious wife coveted the office and urged him to seek it. He would have been better off listening to his mother, who warned, "Roosevelt is a good fighter and enjoys it, but the malice of politics would make you miserable."

Once in office, Taft proved a perfect tool in the hands of Republicans who yearned for a return to the days of a less active executive. A lawyer by training and instinct, Taft believed that it was up to the courts, not the president, to arbitrate social issues. Roosevelt had carried presidential power to a new level, often flouting the separation of powers and showing thinly veiled contempt for Congress and the courts. Taft found it difficult to condone Roosevelt's actions. Wary of the progressive insurgents in Congress, Taft relied increasingly on

CHAPTER OVERVIEW | How did grassroots progressives attack the problems of industrial America? | What were the key tenets of progressive theory?

628 CHAPTER 21
PROGRESSIVISM FROM THE GRASS ROOTS UP

William Howard Taft

When President Theodore Roosevelt tapped William Howard Taft as his successor in 1908, Taft had never held an elected office. Taft had little aptitude for politics, and his actions angered progressives, leading Roosevelt to challenge him for the presidency in 1912. Library of Congress.

conservatives in the Republican Party. As a progressive senator lamented, "Taft is a ponderous and amiable man completely surrounded by men who know exactly what they want."

Taft's troubles began on the eve of his inaugural, when he called a special session of Congress to deal with the tariff. Roosevelt had been too politically astute to tackle the troublesome tariff issue, even though he knew that rates needed to be lowered. Taft blundered into the fray. The Payne-Aldrich bill that emerged was amended in the Senate so that it actually raised the tariff, benefiting big business and the trusts at the expense of consumers. As if paralyzed, Taft neither fought for changes nor vetoed the measure. On a tour of the Midwest in 1909, he was greeted with jeers when he claimed, "I think the Payne bill is the best bill that the Republican Party ever passed." In the eyes of a growing number of Americans, Taft's praise of the tariff made him either a fool or a liar.

Taft's legalism soon got him into hot water in the area of conservation. He undid Roosevelt's work to preserve hydroelectric power sites when he learned that they had been improperly designated as ranger stations. And when Gifford Pinchot publicly denounced Taft's secretary of the interior as a tool of western land-grabbers, Taft fired Pinchot, touching off a storm of controversy that damaged Taft and alienated Roosevelt.

When Roosevelt returned to the United States in June 1910, he received a hero's welcome and attracted a stream of visitors and reporters seeking his advice and opinions. Hurt, Taft kept his distance. By late summer, Roosevelt had taken sides with the progressive insurgents in his party. "Taft is utterly hopeless as a leader," Roosevelt confided to his son as he set out on a speaking tour of the West. Reading the mood of the country, Roosevelt began to sound more and more like a candidate.

How did Theodore Roosevelt advance the progressive agenda?

How did progressivism evolve during Woodrow Wilson's first term?

What were the limits of progressive reform?

Conclusion: How did the liberal state transform during the Progressive Era?

✓ LearningCurve
Check what you know.
bedfordstmartins.com
/roarkunderstanding

Taft's "Dollar Diplomacy"

U.S. intervention

With the Republican Party divided, the Democrats swept the congressional elections of 1910. Branding the Payne-Aldrich tariff "the mother of trusts," they captured a majority in the House of Representatives and won several key governorships. The revitalized Democratic Party could look to new leaders, among them the progressive governor of New Jersey, Woodrow Wilson.

The new Democratic majority in the House, working with progressive Republicans in the Senate, achieved a number of key reforms, including legislation to regulate mine and railroad safety, to create the Children's Bureau in the Department of Labor, and to establish an eight-hour day for federal workers. Two significant constitutional amendments — the Sixteenth Amendment, which provided for a modest graduated income tax, and the Seventeenth Amendment, which called for the direct election of senators (formerly chosen by state legislatures) — went to the states, where they would win ratification in 1913. While Congress rode the high tide of progressive reform, Taft sat on the sidelines.

In foreign policy, Taft continued Roosevelt's policy of extending U.S. influence abroad, but here, too, Taft had a difficult time following Roosevelt. Taft's "dollar diplomacy" championed commercial goals rather than the strategic aims Roosevelt had pursued. Taft naively assumed he could substitute "dollars for bullets." In the Caribbean, he provoked anti-American feeling by dispatching U.S. Marines to Nicaragua and the Dominican Republic in 1912 pursuant to the Roosevelt Corollary. In Asia, he openly avowed his intent to promote "active intervention to secure for . . . our capitalists opportunity for profitable investment." Lacking Roosevelt's understanding of power politics, Taft failed to recognize that an aggressive commercial policy could not exist without the willingness to use military might to back it up.

Taft faced the limits of dollar diplomacy when revolution broke out in Mexico in 1911. Under pressure to protect American investments, he mobilized troops along the border. In the end, however, with no popular support for a war with Mexico, he had to fall back on diplomatic pressure to salvage American interests.

Taft's greatest dream was to encourage world peace through the use of a world court and arbitration. He unsuccessfully sponsored a series of arbitration treaties that Roosevelt, who prized national honor more than international law, vehemently opposed as weak and cowardly. By 1910, Roosevelt had become a vocal critic of Taft's foreign policy.

The final breach between Taft and Roosevelt came in 1911, when Taft's attorney general filed an antitrust suit against U.S. Steel. In its brief against the corporation, the government cited Roosevelt's agreement with the Morgan interests in the 1907 acquisition of Tennessee Coal and Iron. The incident greatly embarrassed Roosevelt. Thoroughly enraged, he lambasted Taft's "archaic" antitrust policy and hinted that he might be persuaded to run for president again.

> **QUICK REVIEW**

What advances in the progressive agenda were
made at the federal level between 1901 and 1913?

CHAPTER OVERVIEW | How did grassroots progressives attack the problems of industrial America? | What were the key tenets of progressive theory?

CHAPTER 21
630 PROGRESSIVISM FROM THE GRASS ROOTS UP

1912 Election Cartoon

In this 1912 political cartoon, an elephant—the mascot of the Republican Party (the Grand Old Party, or GOP)—and a donkey—representing the Democratic Party—react in alarm as a bull moose charges into the fray. The bull moose, with its spectacles and gleaming teeth, caricatures Theodore Roosevelt, the new Progressive Party's presidential candidate. Granger Collection.

How did progressivism evolve during Woodrow Wilson's first term?

DISILLUSIONMENT WITH TAFT resulted in a split in the Republican Party and the creation of a new Progressive Party that rallied around Theodore Roosevelt. In the election of 1912, four candidates styled themselves "progressives," but it was Democrat Woodrow Wilson who, with a minority of the popular vote, won the presidency.

Born in Virginia and raised in Georgia, Woodrow Wilson became the first southerner elected president since 1844 and only the second Democrat to occupy the White House since Reconstruction. A believer in states' rights, Wilson nevertheless promised legislation to break the hold of the trusts. This lean, ascetic scholar was, as one biographer conceded, a man whose "political convictions were never as fixed as his ambition." Building on the base built by Roosevelt in strengthening presidential power, Wilson exerted leadership to achieve banking reform and worked through his party in Congress to accomplish the Democratic agenda. Before he was finished, Wilson presided over progressivism at high tide and lent his support to many of the Progressive Party's social reforms.

> **CHRONOLOGY**

1912
– Roosevelt runs for president on Progressive Party ticket.
– Woodrow Wilson is elected president.

1913
– Federal Reserve Act.

1914
– Federal Trade Commission (FTC) is created.
– Clayton Antitrust Act.

How did Theodore Roosevelt advance the progressive agenda?

How did progressivism evolve during Woodrow Wilson's first term?

What were the limits of progressive reform?

Conclusion: How did the liberal state transform during the Progressive Era?

✓ LearningCurve
Check what you know.
bedfordstmartins.com
/roarkunderstanding

Progressive Insurgency and the Election of 1912

Convinced that Taft was inept, in February 1912 Roosevelt announced his candidacy for the Republican nomination. Taft, with uncharacteristic strength, refused to step aside. Roosevelt took advantage of newly passed primary election laws and ran in thirteen states, winning 278 delegates to Taft's 48. But at the Chicago convention, Taft's bosses refused to seat the Roosevelt delegates. Fistfights broke out on the convention floor as Taft won nomination on the first ballot. Crying robbery, Roosevelt's supporters bolted the party.

Seven weeks later, in the same Chicago auditorium, the hastily organized Progressive Party met to nominate Roosevelt. Full of reforming zeal, the delegates chose Roosevelt and Hiram Johnson to head the new party and approved the most ambitious platform since that of the Populists.

> Progressive Party Platform

- Woman suffrage
- Presidential primaries
- Conservation of natural resources
- An end to child labor
- Workers' compensation
- A minimum wage that would include women workers
- Social security
- A federal income tax

Roosevelt arrived in Chicago to accept the nomination and announced that he felt "as fit as a bull moose," giving the new party a nickname and a mascot. But for all the excitement and the cheering, the new Progressive Party was doomed, and the candidate knew it. The people may have supported the party, but the politicians, even progressives such as La Follette, stayed within the Republican fold. "I am under no illusion about it," Roosevelt confessed to a friend. "It is a forlorn hope." But he had gone too far to turn back. The Democrats, delighted at the split in the Republican ranks, nominated Woodrow Wilson, the governor of New Jersey. After only eighteen months in office, the former professor of political science and president of Princeton University found himself running for president of the United States.

Voters in 1912 could choose among four candidates who claimed to be progressives. Taft, Roosevelt, and Wilson each embraced the label, and even the Socialist candidate, Eugene V. Debs, styled himself a progressive. That the term *progressive* could stretch to cover these diverse candidates underscored major disagreements in progressive thinking about the relationship between business and government. Taft, in spite of his trust-busting, was generally viewed as the candidate of the old guard. The real contest for the presidency was between Roosevelt and Wilson and the two political philosophies summed up in their respective campaign slogans: "**The New Nationalism**" and "**The New Freedom**."

The New Nationalism
▶ Theodore Roosevelt's 1912 campaign slogan, which reflected his commitment to federal planning and regulation. Roosevelt wanted to use the federal government to act as a "steward for the people" to regulate giant corporations.

The New Freedom
▶ Woodrow Wilson's 1912 campaign slogan, which reflected his belief in limited government and states' rights. Wilson promised to use antitrust legislation to eliminate big corporations and to improve opportunities for small businesses and farmers.

The New Nationalism expressed Roosevelt's belief in federal planning and regulation. He accepted the inevitability of big business but demanded that government act as "a steward of the people" to regulate the giant corporations. Wilson, schooled in the Democratic principles of limited government and states' rights, set a markedly different course with his New Freedom. Wilson promised to use antitrust legislation to get rid of big corporations and to give small businesses and farmers better opportunities in the marketplace.

The energy and enthusiasm of the Bull Moosers made the race seem closer than it was. In the end, the Republican vote split, while the Democrats remained united. No candidate claimed a majority in the race. Wilson captured a bare 42 percent of the popular vote. Roosevelt and his Bull Moose Party won 27 percent, an unprecedented tally for a new party. Taft came in third with 23 percent. The Socialist Party, led by Debs, captured 6 percent (**Map 21.3**). The Republican Party moved in a conservative direction, while the Progressive Party essentially collapsed after Roosevelt's defeat. It had always been, in the words of one astute observer, "a house divided against itself and already mortgaged."

Candidate	Electoral Vote	Popular Vote	Percent of Popular Vote
Woodrow Wilson (Democrat)	435	6,293,454	41.9
Theodore Roosevelt (Progressive)	88	4,119,538	27.4
William H. Taft (Republican)	8	3,484,980	23.2
Eugene V. Debs (Socialist)	0	900,672	6.1

MAP 21.3 ■ The Election of 1912

Wilson's Reforms: Tariff, Banking, and the Trusts

With the Democrats thoroughly in control of Congress, Wilson immediately called for tariff reform. "The object of the tariff," Wilson told Congress, "must be effective competition." The Democratic House of Representatives hastily passed the Underwood tariff, which lowered rates by 15 percent. To compensate for lost revenue, the House approved a moderate federal income tax made possible by the ratification of the Sixteenth Amendment a month earlier. In the Senate, lobbyists for industries quietly went to work to get the tariff raised, but Wilson rallied public opinion by attacking the "industrious and insidious lobby." In the harsh glare of publicity, the Senate passed the Underwood tariff.

Wilson next turned his attention to banking. During the panic of 1907, the government once again had to turn to J. P. Morgan to avoid economic catastrophe. But by the time Wilson came to office, Morgan's legendary power had come under close scrutiny. In 1913, a Senate committee investigated the "money trust," calling J. P. Morgan himself to testify. The committee uncovered an alarming concentration of banking power. J. P. Morgan and Company and its affiliates held 341 directorships in 112 corporations, controlling assets of more than $22 billion (more than $1 trillion in today's dollars). The sensational findings led to reform.

The Federal Reserve Act of 1913 marked the most significant piece of domestic legislation of Wilson's presidency.

How did Theodore Roosevelt advance the progressive agenda?

How did progressivism evolve during Woodrow Wilson's first term?

What were the limits of progressive reform?

Conclusion: How did the liberal state transform during the Progressive Era?

✓ LearningCurve
Check what you know.
bedfordstmartins.com
/roarkunderstanding

633

- Established a national banking system composed of twelve regional banks, privately controlled but regulated and supervised by the Federal Reserve Board, which was appointed by the president.
- Gave the United States its first efficient banking and currency system.
- Provided for a greater degree of government control over banking.
- Made currency more elastic and credit adequate for the needs of business and agriculture.

Wilson, flush with success, tackled the trust issue next. When Congress reconvened in January 1914, he supported the introduction and passage of the Clayton Antitrust Act to outlaw "unfair competition" — practices such as price discrimination and interlocking directorates (directors from one corporation sitting on the board of another). In the midst of the successful fight for the Clayton Act, Wilson changed course and threw his support behind the creation of the Federal Trade Commission (FTC), precisely the kind of federal regulatory agency that Roosevelt had advocated in his New Nationalism. The FTC, created in 1914, had not only wide investigatory powers but also the authority to prosecute corporations for "unfair trade practices" and to enforce its judgments by issuing "cease and desist" orders. Despite his campaign promises, Wilson's antitrust program worked to regulate rather than to break up big business.

Wilson, Reluctant Progressive

By the fall of 1914, Wilson declared that the progressive movement had fulfilled its mission and that the country needed "a time of healing." Progressives watched in dismay as Wilson repeatedly obstructed or obstinately refused to endorse further reforms. He failed to support labor's demand for an end to court injunctions against labor unions. He twice threatened to veto legislation providing farm credits for nonperishable crops. He refused to support child labor legislation or woman suffrage. Wilson used the rhetoric of the New Freedom to justify his actions, claiming that his administration would condone "special privileges to none." But, in fact, his stance often reflected the interests of his small-business constituency.

In the face of Wilson's obstinacy, reform might have ended in 1913 had not politics intruded. In the congressional elections of 1914, the Republican Party, no longer split by Roosevelt's Bull Moose faction, won substantial gains. Democratic strategists recognized that Wilson needed to pick up support in the Midwest and the West by capturing votes from former Bull Moose progressives. Wilson responded belatedly by lending his support to reform in the months leading up to the election of 1916. In a sharp about-face, he cultivated union labor, farmers, and social reformers. To please labor, he appointed progressive Louis Brandeis to the Supreme Court. To woo farmers, he threw his support behind legislation to obtain rural credits. And he won praise from labor by supporting workers' compensation

CHAPTER OVERVIEW | How did grassroots progressives attack the problems of industrial America? | What were the key tenets of progressive theory?

CHAPTER 21

634 PROGRESSIVISM FROM THE GRASS ROOTS UP

and the Keating-Owen child labor law (1916), which outlawed the regular employment of children younger than sixteen. When a railroad strike threatened in the months before the election, Wilson ordered Congress to establish an eight-hour day on the railroads. He had moved a long way from his New Freedom of 1912, and as Wilson noted, the Democrats had "come very near to carrying out the platform of the Progressive Party." Wilson's shift toward reform, along with his claim that he had kept the United States out of the war in Europe (as discussed in chapter 22), helped him win reelection in 1916.

QUICK REVIEW <

How did party politics change between 1912 and 1916, and what impact did this change have on progressivism?

How did Theodore Roosevelt advance the progressive agenda?

How did progressivism evolve during Woodrow Wilson's first term?

What were the limits of progressive reform?

Conclusion: How did the liberal state transform during the Progressive Era?

✓ LearningCurve
Check what you know.
bedfordstmartins.com
/roarkunderstanding

635

What were the limits of progressive reform?

DINNER GIVEN AT THE WHITE HOUSE BY PRESIDENT ROOSEVELT TO BOOKER T. WASHINGTON, OCTOBER 17th, 1901.

Booker T. Washington and Theodore Roosevelt Dine at the White House

Theodore Roosevelt invited Booker T. Washington to the White House in 1901, stirring up a hornet's nest of controversy that continued into the election of 1904. This Republican campaign piece shows Roosevelt and a light-skinned Washington sitting under a portrait of Abraham Lincoln. Democrats' campaign buttons pictured Washington with darker skin and implied that Roosevelt had "painted the White House black" and favored "race mingling." Collection of Janice L. and David J. Frent.

WHILE PROGRESSIVISM CALLED for a more active role for the liberal state, at heart it was a movement that sought reforms designed to preserve American institutions and stem the tide of more radical change. Its basic conservatism can be seen by comparing it with the more radical movements of socialism, radical labor, and birth control — and by looking at the groups progressive reform left behind, including women, Asians, and African Americans.

Radical Alternatives

The year 1900 marked the birth of the Social Democratic Party in America, later called simply the **Socialist Party**. Like the progressives, the socialists were middle-class and native-born. They had broken with the older, more militant Socialist Labor Party precisely because of its dogmatic approach and immigrant constituency. The new group of socialists proved eager to appeal to a broad mass of disaffected Americans.

Socialist Party
▶ Political party formed in 1900 that advocated cooperation over competition and promoted the breakdown of capitalism. Its members, who were largely middle-class and native-born, saw both the Republican and the Democratic parties as hopelessly beholden to capitalism.

CHAPTER OVERVIEW | How did grassroots progressives attack the problems of industrial America? | What were the key tenets of progressive theory?

The Socialist Party chose as its presidential standard-bearer Eugene V. Debs, whose experience in the Pullman strike of 1894 (see chapter 20) convinced him that "there is no hope for the toiling masses of my countrymen, except by the pathways mapped out by Socialism." Debs would run for president five times, in every election (except 1916) from 1900 to 1920. The socialism Debs advocated preached cooperation over competition and urged men and women to liberate themselves from "the barbarism of private ownership and wage slavery." In the 1912 election, Debs indicted both old parties as "Tweedledee and Tweedledum," each dedicated to the preservation of capitalism and the continuation of the wage system. Styling the Socialist Party the "revolutionary party of the working class," he urged voters to rally to his standard. Debs's best showing came in 1912, when his 6 percent of the popular vote totaled more than 900,000 votes.

Farther to the left and more radical than the socialists stood the **Industrial Workers of the World (IWW)**, nicknamed the Wobblies. In 1905, Debs, along with Western Federation of Miners leader William Dudley "Big Bill" Haywood, created the IWW, "one big union" dedicated to organizing the most destitute segment of the workforce, the unskilled workers disdained by Samuel Gompers's AFL: western miners, migrant farmworkers, lumbermen, and immigrant textile workers. Haywood, a craggy-faced miner with one eye (he had lost the other in a childhood accident), was a charismatic leader and a proletarian intellectual. Seeing workers on the lowest rung of the social ladder as the victims of violent repression, the IWW advocated direct action, sabotage, and the general strike — tactics designed to trigger a workers' uprising and overthrow the capitalist state. The IWW never had more than 10,000 members at any one time, although possibly as many as 100,000 workers belonged to the union at one time or another in the early twentieth century. Nevertheless, the IWW's influence on the country extended far beyond its numbers (as discussed in chapter 22).

In contrast to political radicals like Debs and Haywood, Margaret Sanger promoted the **birth control movement** as a means of social change. Sanger, a nurse who had worked among the poor on New York's Lower East Side, coined the term *birth control* in 1915 and launched a movement with broad social implications. Sanger and her followers saw birth control not only as a sexual and medical reform but also as a means to alter social and political power relationships and to alleviate human misery. By having fewer babies, the working class could constrict the size of the workforce and make possible higher wages and at the same time refuse to provide "cannon fodder" for the world's armies.

The desire for family limitation was widespread, and in this sense birth control was nothing new. The birthrate in the United States had been falling consistently throughout the nineteenth century. The average number of children per family dropped from 7.0 in 1800 to 3.6 by 1900. But the open advocacy of contraception, the use of artificial means to prevent pregnancy, struck many people as both new and shocking. And it was illegal. Anthony Comstock, New York City's commissioner of vice, promoted laws in the 1870s making it a felony not only to sell contraceptive devices like condoms and cervical caps but also to publish information on how to prevent pregnancy.

When Margaret Sanger used her militant feminist paper, the *Woman Rebel,* to promote birth control, the Post Office confiscated Sanger's publication and

Industrial Workers of the World (IWW)
▶ Umbrella union and radical political group founded in 1905 that was dedicated to organizing unskilled workers to oppose capitalism. Nicknamed the Wobblies, the IWW advocated direct action by workers, including sabotage and general strikes, in hopes of triggering a widespread workers' uprising.

birth control movement
▶ Movement launched in 1915 by Margaret Sanger in New York City's Lower East Side. Birth control advocates hoped that contraception would alter social and political power relationships: By having fewer babies, the working class could constrict the size of the workforce, thus making possible higher wages, and at the same time refuse to provide soldiers for the world's armies.

How did Theodore Roosevelt advance the progressive agenda?

How did progressivism evolve during Woodrow Wilson's first term?

What were the limits of progressive reform?

Conclusion: How did the liberal state transform during the Progressive Era?

☑ LearningCurve
Check what you know.
bedfordstmartins.com
/roarkunderstanding

637

> CHRONOLOGY

1896
– *Plessy v. Ferguson*.

1900
– Socialist Party is founded.

1905
– Industrial Workers of the World (IWW) is founded.

1906
– Atlanta race riot.

1907
– National Association for the Advancement of Colored People (NAACP) is formed.

1913
– Suffragists march in Washington, D.C.

1916
– Margaret Sanger opens first U.S. birth control clinic.

brought charges of obscenity against her. Facing arrest, she fled to Europe, only to return in 1916 as something of a national celebrity. In her absence, birth control had become linked with free speech and had been taken up as a liberal cause. Under public pressure, the government dropped the charges against Sanger, who undertook a nationwide tour to publicize the birth control cause.

Sanger then took direct action, opening the nation's first birth control clinic in the Brownsville section of Brooklyn in October 1916. Located in the heart of a Jewish and Italian immigrant neighborhood, the clinic attracted 464 clients. On the tenth day, police shut down the clinic and threw Sanger in jail. By then, she had become a national figure, and the cause she championed had gained legitimacy, if not legality. Sanger soon reopened her clinic. After World War I, the birth control movement would become much less radical as Sanger turned to medical doctors for support and mouthed popular racist genetic theories. But in its infancy, birth control was part of a radical vision for reforming the world that made common cause with the socialists and the IWW in challenging the limits of progressive reform.

Progressivism for White Men Only

The day before President Woodrow Wilson's inauguration in March 1913, the largest mass march to that date in the nation's history took place as more than five thousand demonstrators took to the streets in Washington to demand the vote for women. A rowdy crowd on hand to celebrate the Democrats' triumph attacked the marchers. Men spat at the suffragists and threw lighted cigarettes and matches at their clothing. "If my wife were where you are," a burly cop told one suffragist, "I'd break her head." But for all the marching, Wilson pointedly ignored woman suffrage in his inaugural address the next day.

The march served as a reminder that the political gains of progressivism were not spread equally throughout the population. As the twentieth century dawned, women still could not vote in most states, although they had won major victories in the West. Increasingly, however, woman suffrage had become an international movement.

Alice Paul, a Quaker social worker who had visited England and participated in suffrage activism there, returned to the United States in 1910 in time to plan the mass march on the eve of Wilson's inauguration and to lobby for a federal amendment to give women the vote. Paul's dramatic tactics alienated many in the National American Woman Suffrage Association. In 1916, Paul founded the militant National Woman's Party, which became the radical voice of the suffrage movement.

Women weren't the only group left out in progressive reform. Progressivism, as it was practiced in the West and South, was tainted with racism by seeking to limit the rights of Asians and African Americans. Anti-Asian bigotry in the West led to a

Woman Suffrage Parade

Women marched in a suffrage parade in Washington, D.C., in 1913. The women had to fend off angry crowds who attacked them and tried to break up the parade. Inez Milholland led the march on horseback, replicating the "white knight" on this program. Attacked by the mob, Milholland spurred her horse into the crowd shouting, "You men ought to be ashamed of yourselves." The Granger Collection, New York.

CHAPTER OVERVIEW | How did grassroots progressives attack the problems of industrial America? | What were the key tenets of progressive theory?

638   CHAPTER 21
PROGRESSIVISM FROM THE GRASS ROOTS UP

renewal of the Chinese Exclusion Act in 1902. At first, California governor Hiram Johnson stood against the strong anti-Asian prejudice of his state. But in 1913, he caved in to popular pressure and signed the Alien Land Law, which barred Japanese immigrants from purchasing land in California.

South of the Mason-Dixon line, the progressives' racism targeted African Americans. Progressives preached the disfranchisement of black voters as a "reform." During the bitter electoral fights that had pitted Populists against Democrats in the 1890s, the party of white supremacy held its power by votes purchased or coerced from African Americans. Southern progressives proposed to reform the electoral system by eliminating black voters. Beginning in 1890 with Mississippi, southern states curtailed the African American vote through devices such as poll taxes (fees required for voting) and literacy tests.

The Progressive Era also witnessed the rise of Jim Crow laws to segregate public facilities. The new railroads precipitated segregation in the South where it had rarely existed before, at least on paper. Soon, separate railcars, separate waiting rooms, separate bathrooms, and separate dining facilities for blacks sprang up across the South. In courtrooms in Mississippi, blacks were required to swear on a separate Bible.

In the face of this growing repression, Booker T. Washington, the preeminent black leader of the day, urged caution and restraint. A former slave, Washington opened the Tuskegee Institute in Alabama in 1881 to teach vocational skills to African Americans. He emphasized education and economic progress for his race and urged African Americans to put aside issues of political and social equality. In an 1895 speech in Atlanta that came to be known as the Atlanta Compromise, he stated, "In all things that are purely social we can be as separate as the fingers, yet one as the hand in all things essential to mutual progress." Washington's accommodationist policy appealed to whites and elevated "the wizard of Tuskegee" to the role of national spokesman for African Americans.

The year after Washington proclaimed the Atlanta Compromise, the Supreme Court upheld the legality of racial segregation, affirming in *Plessy v. Ferguson* (1896) the constitutionality of the doctrine of "separate but equal." Blacks could be segregated in separate schools, restrooms, and other facilities as long as the facilities were "equal" to those provided for whites. Of course, facilities for blacks rarely proved equal.

Woodrow Wilson brought to the White House southern attitudes toward race and racial segregation. He instituted segregation in the federal workforce, especially the Post Office, and approved segregated drinking fountains and restrooms in the nation's capital. When critics attacked the policy, Wilson insisted that segregation was "in the interest of the Negro."

In 1906, a major race riot in Atlanta called into question Booker T. Washington's strategy of uplift and accommodation. For three days in September, the streets of Atlanta ran red with blood as angry white mobs chased and cornered any blacks they happened upon. An estimated 250 African Americans died in the riots — members of Atlanta's black middle class along with the poor and derelict. Professor William Crogman of Clark College noted the central irony of the riot: "Here we have worked and prayed and tried to make good men and women of our colored population," he observed, "and at our very doorstep the whites kill these

Plessy v. Ferguson
▶ 1896 Supreme Court ruling that upheld the legality of racial segregation. According to the ruling, blacks could be segregated in separate schools, restrooms, and other facilities as long as the facilities were "equal" to those provided for whites.

How did Theodore Roosevelt advance the progressive agenda?

How did progressivism evolve during Woodrow Wilson's first term?

What were the limits of progressive reform?

Conclusion: How did the liberal state transform during the Progressive Era?

☑ LearningCurve
Check what you know.
bedfordstmartins.com
/roarkunderstanding

639

good men." The riot caused many African Americans to question Washington's strategy of gradualism and accommodation.

Foremost among Washington's critics stood W. E. B. Du Bois, a Harvard graduate who urged African Americans to fight for civil rights and racial justice. In *The Souls of Black Folk* (1903), Du Bois attacked the "Tuskegee Machine," comparing Washington to a political boss who used his influence to silence his critics and reward his followers. Du Bois founded the Niagara movement in 1905, calling for universal male suffrage, civil rights, and leadership composed of a black intellectual elite. The Atlanta riot only bolstered his resolve. In 1909, the Niagara movement helped found the National Association for the Advancement of Colored People (NAACP), a coalition of blacks and whites that sought legal and political rights for African Americans through the courts. In the decades that followed, the NAACP came to represent the future for African Americans, while Booker T. Washington, who died in 1915, represented the past.

> **QUICK REVIEW**

How did race, class, and gender shape the limits of progressive reform?

CHAPTER OVERVIEW | How did grassroots progressives attack the problems of industrial America? | What were the key tenets of progressive theory?

CHAPTER 21

640　PROGRESSIVISM FROM THE GRASS ROOTS UP

Conclusion: How did the liberal state transform during the Progressive Era?

PROGRESSIVISM'S GOAL WAS TO REFORM the existing system — by government intervention if necessary — but without uprooting any of the traditional American political, economic, or social institutions. As Theodore Roosevelt, the bellwether of the movement, insisted, "The only true conservative is the man who resolutely sets his face toward the future." Roosevelt was such a man, and progressivism was such a movement. But although progressivism was never radical, progressives' willingness to use the power of government to regulate business and achieve a measure of social justice redefined liberalism in the twentieth century, tying it to the expanded power of the state.

Progressivism contained many paradoxes. A diverse coalition of individuals and interests, the progressive movement began at the grass roots but left as its legacy a stronger presidency and unprecedented federal involvement in the economy and social welfare. A movement that believed in social justice, progressivism often promoted social control. And while progressives called for greater democracy, they fostered elitism with their worship of experts and efficiency, and they often failed to champion equality for women and minorities.

Whatever its inconsistencies and limitations, progressivism took action to deal with the problems posed by urban industrialism. Progressivism saw grass-roots activists address social problems on the local and state levels and search for national solutions. By increasing the power of the presidency and expanding the power of the state, progressives worked to bring about greater social justice and to achieve a better balance between government and business. Jane Addams and Theodore Roosevelt could lay equal claim to the movement that redefined liberalism and launched the liberal state of the twentieth century. War on a global scale would provide progressivism with yet another challenge even before it had completed its ambitious agenda.

| How did Theodore Roosevelt advance the progressive agenda? | How did progressivism evolve during Woodrow Wilson's first term? | What were the limits of progressive reform? | Conclusion: How did the liberal state transform during the Progressive Era? | ✓ LearningCurve Check what you know. bedfordstmartins.com /roarkunderstanding |

641

CHAPTER 21 STUDY GUIDE

STEP 1 GET STARTED ONLINE

 LearningCurve ■ bedfordstmartins.com/roarkunderstanding

Now that you've read the chapter, make it stick by completing the LearningCurve activity.

STEP 2 EXPLAIN WHY IT MATTERS

Put your reading into practice. Identify each term below, and then explain why it matters in U.S. history.

TERM	WHO OR WHAT & WHEN	WHY IT MATTERS
progressivism (p. 612)		
settlement houses (p. 613)		
social gospel (p. 614)		
reform Darwinism (p. 617)		
muckraking (p. 623)		
Roosevelt Corollary (p. 626)		
The New Nationalism (p. 632)		
The New Freedom (p. 632)		
Socialist Party (p. 636)		
Industrial Workers of the World (IWW) (p. 637)		
birth control movement (p. 637)		
Plessy v. Ferguson (p. 639)		

STEP 3 MOVE BEYOND THE BASICS

To demonstrate a more advanced understanding, describe the actions and successes of the progressives at the local, state, and national levels between 1890 and 1916. Then, consider the limitations of the progressive movement

Decade	Key actions	Resulting reforms	Limitations/setbacks
1890s			
1900s			
1910s			

PUT IT ALL TOGETHER

Now, take a step back and try to explain the big picture. Remember to use specific examples from the chapter in your answers.

PROGRESSIVES AND PROGRESSIVISM

▶ How did progressivism differ from earlier reform movements?

▶ Why was grassroots activism so important to the progressive movement?

THEODORE ROOSEVELT AND PROGRESSIVISM

▶ What progressive ideals were embodied in Roosevelt's Square Deal?

▶ What were the limits of progressive reform during Roosevelt's presidency?

WOODROW WILSON AND PROGRESSIVISM

▶ How did Wilson's progressivism differ from Roosevelt's?

▶ How did Wilson's progressive agenda change during his presidency?

LOOKING BACKWARD, LOOKING AHEAD

▶ To what extent, in both the short term and the long term, did progressivism reflect the agendas of African Americans, working-class Americans, and women?

▶ What progressive ideas and policies continue to influence American social and political life today?

> ## IN YOUR OWN WORDS

Imagine that you must give an oral report to the class answering the following question: **What were the most significant changes in the United States as a result of the Progressive Era?** What would be the most important points to include and why?

 Do it online at the Student Site ▪ **bedfordstmartins.com/roarkunderstanding**

22

THE UNITED STATES AND WORLD WAR I

1914–1920

> **What were the most important outcomes of World War I for the United States?** Chapter 22 explores the nature and impact of U.S. involvement in World War I. It examines Woodrow Wilson's role in taking the country to war and in shaping the peace that followed. The chapter also considers the contribution of American armed forces to the Allied victory, the impact of the war on the home front, and the domestic tensions during and immediately following the war.

LearningCurve

bedfordstmartins.com/roarkunderstanding
After reading the chapter, use LearningCurve to retain what you've read.

> What was Woodrow Wilson's foreign policy agenda?

> What role did the United States play in World War I?

> What impact did the war have on the home front?

> What part did Woodrow Wilson play at the Paris peace conference?

> Why was America's transition from war to peace so turbulent?

> Conclusion: What was the domestic cost of foreign victory?

Writing home. A Salvation Army worker writes a letter for a wounded American soldier, 1918.
National Archives.

What was Woodrow Wilson's foreign policy agenda?

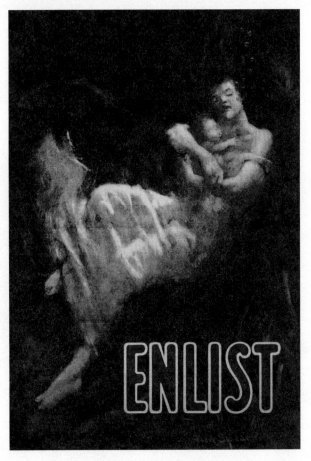

"Enlist"

This poster depicting a young mother and her baby beneath the cold waters of the Atlantic Ocean brought home the terrible cost of Germany's sinking of the British passenger liner *Lusitania* in 1915. Burned into American memory, the *Lusitania* remained a compelling reason to enlist in the armed forces after the United States entered the war in 1917.
Library of Congress.

SHORTLY AFTER WINNING election to the presidency in 1912, Woodrow Wilson confided to a friend: "It would be an irony of fate if my administration had to deal with foreign affairs." Indeed, Wilson had focused his life and career on domestic concerns, and in his campaign for the presidency hardly mentioned the world abroad.

Wilson, however, could not avoid the world and the rising tide of militarism, nationalism, and violence that beat against American shores. Economic interests compelled the nation outward. Moreover, Wilson was drawn abroad by his own progressive political principles. He believed that the United States had a moral duty to champion national self-determination, peaceful free trade, and political democracy. "We have no selfish ends to serve," he proclaimed. "We desire no conquest, no dominion. . . . We are but one of the champions of the rights of mankind." Yet as president, Wilson was as ready as any American president to apply military solutions to problems of foreign policy. This readiness led Wilson and the United States into military conflict in Mexico and then in Europe.

CHAPTER LOCATOR | **What was Woodrow Wilson's foreign policy agenda?** | What role did the United States play in World War I?

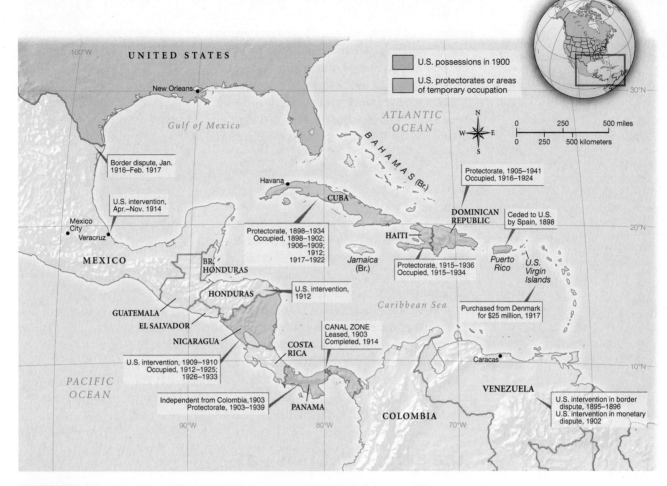

MAP 22.1 ■ U.S. Involvement in Latin America and the Caribbean, 1895–1941

Victory against Spain in 1898 made Puerto Rico an American possession and Cuba a protectorate. The United States later gained control of the Panama Canal Zone. The nation protected its expanding economic interests with military force by propping up friendly, though not necessarily democratic, governments.

Taming the Americas

When he took office, Wilson sought to distinguish his foreign policy from that of his Republican predecessors. To Wilson, Theodore Roosevelt's "big stick" and William Howard Taft's "dollar diplomacy" appeared crude flexing of military and economic muscle. To signal a new direction, Wilson appointed William Jennings Bryan, a pacifist, as secretary of state.

But Wilson and Bryan, like Roosevelt and Taft, also believed that the Monroe Doctrine gave the United States special rights and responsibilities in the Western Hemisphere. Wilson thus authorized U.S. military intervention in Nicaragua, Haiti, and the Dominican Republic, paving the way for U.S. banks and corporations to take financial control. All the while, Wilson believed that U.S. actions were promoting order and democracy. "I am going to teach the South American Republics to elect good men!" he declared (**Map 22.1**).

Wilson's most serious involvement in Latin America came in Mexico. When General Victoriano Huerta seized power by violent means, most European nations

| What impact did the war have on the home front? | What part did Woodrow Wilson play at the Paris peace conference? | Why was America's transition from war to peace so turbulent? | Conclusion: What was the domestic cost of foreign victory? | ✔ LearningCurve Check what you know. bedfordstmartins.com /roarkunderstanding |

1914

– U.S. Marines occupy Veracruz, Mexico.
– Archduke Franz Ferdinand is assassinated.
– Austria-Hungary declares war on Serbia.
– Germany attacks Russia and France.
– Great Britain declares war on Germany.

1915

– German U-boat sinks the *Lusitania*.

1916

– Pancho Villa attacks Americans in Mexico and New Mexico.
– Wilson is reelected.

1917

– Zimmermann telegram is intercepted.
– United States declares war on Germany.

promptly recognized Mexico's new government, but Wilson refused, declaring that he would not support a "government of butchers." In April 1914, Wilson sent 800 Marines to seize the port of Veracruz to prevent the unloading of a large shipment of arms for Huerta. Huerta fled to Spain, and the United States welcomed a more compliant government.

But a rebellion erupted among desperately poor farmers who believed that the new government, aided by U.S. business interests, had betrayed the revolution's promise to help the common people. In January 1916, the rebel army, commanded by Francisco "Pancho" Villa, seized a train carrying gold to Texas from an American-owned mine in Mexico and killed the 17 American engineers aboard. In March, Villa's men crossed the border for a predawn raid on Columbus, New Mexico, where they killed 18 Americans. Wilson promptly dispatched 12,000 troops, led by Major General John J. Pershing. But Villa avoided capture, and in January 1917 Wilson recalled Pershing so that he might prepare the army for the possibility of fighting in the Great War.

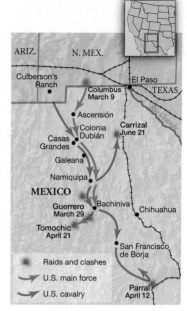

U.S. Intervention In Mexico, 1916–1917

The European Crisis

Before 1914, Europe had enjoyed decades of peace, but just beneath the surface lay the potentially destructive forces of nationalism and imperialism. The consolidation of the German and Italian states into unified nations and the similar ambition of Russia to create a Pan-Slavic union initiated new rivalries throughout Europe. As the conviction spread that colonial possessions were a mark of national greatness, competition expanded onto the world stage. Most ominously, Germany's efforts under Kaiser Wilhelm II to challenge Great Britain's world supremacy by creating industrial muscle at home, an empire abroad, and a mighty navy threatened the balance of power and thus the peace.

European nations sought to avoid an explosion by developing a complex web of military and diplomatic alliances. By 1914, Germany, Austria-Hungary, and Italy (the **Triple Alliance**) stood opposed to Great Britain, France, and Russia (the **Triple Entente**, also known as "the Allies"). But in their effort to prevent war through a balance of power, Europeans had actually magnified the possibility of large-scale conflict (**Map 22.2**). Treaties, some of them secret, obligated members of the alliances to come to the aid of another member if attacked.

The fatal sequence began on June 28, 1914, in the city of Sarajevo, when a Bosnian Serb terrorist assassinated Archduke Franz Ferdinand, heir to the Austro-Hungarian throne. On July 18, Austria-Hungary declared war on Serbia. The elaborate alliance system meant that the war could not remain local. Russia announced that it would back the Serbs. Compelled by treaty to support Austria-Hungary, Germany on August 3 attacked Russia and France. In response, on

CHAPTER LOCATOR | What was Woodrow Wilson's foreign policy agenda? | What role did the United States play in World War I?

CHAPTER 22
648 THE UNITED STATES AND WORLD WAR I

MAP 22.2 ■ European Alliances after the Outbreak of World War I

With Germany and Austria-Hungary wedged between their Entente rivals and all parties fully armed, Europe was poised for war when Archduke Franz Ferdinand of Austria-Hungary was assassinated in Sarajevo in June 1914.

August 4, Great Britain, upholding its pact with France, declared war on Germany. Within weeks, Europe was engulfed in war. The conflict became a world war when Japan, seeing an opportunity to rid itself of European competition in China, joined the cause against Germany.

The Ordeal of American Neutrality

Woodrow Wilson promptly announced that because the war engaged no vital American interest and involved no significant principle, the United States would remain neutral. Neutrality entitled the United States to trade safely with all nations at war, he declared. Unfettered trade, Wilson believed, was not only a right under international law but also a necessity because in 1913 the U.S. economy had slipped into a recession that wartime disruption of European trade could drastically worsen.

What impact did the war have on the home front?

What part did Woodrow Wilson play at the Paris peace conference?

Why was America's transition from war to peace so turbulent?

Conclusion: What was the domestic cost of foreign victory?

☑ **LearningCurve**
Check what you know.
bedfordstmartins.com
/roarkunderstanding

Sinking of the *Lusitania*, 1915

Lusitania

▶ British passenger liner torpedoed by a German U-boat on May 7, 1915. The attack killed 1,198 passengers, including 128 Americans. The incident challenged American neutrality during World War I and moved the United States on a path toward entering the war.

Although Wilson proclaimed neutrality, his sympathies, like those of many Americans, lay with Great Britain and France. Americans gratefully remembered crucial French assistance in the American Revolution and shared with the British a language, a culture, and a commitment to liberty. Germany, by contrast, was a monarchy with strong militaristic traditions. Still, Wilson insisted on neutrality, in part because he feared the conflict's effects on the United States as a nation of immigrants. As he told the German ambassador, "We definitely have to be neutral, since otherwise our mixed populations would wage war on each other."

Britain's powerful fleet controlled the seas and quickly set up an economic blockade of Germany. The United States vigorously protested, but Britain refused to give up its naval advantage. The blockade actually had little economic impact on the United States. Between 1914 and the spring of 1917, while trade with Germany evaporated, war-related exports to Britain — food, clothing, steel, and munitions — escalated by some 400 percent. Although the British blockade violated American neutrality, the Wilson administration gradually acquiesced, thus beginning the fateful process of alienation from Germany.

Germany retaliated with a submarine blockade of British ports. German *Unterseebooten*, or U-boats, threatened notions of "civilized" warfare. Unlike surface warships that could harmlessly stop freighters and prevent them from entering a war zone, submarines relied on sinking their quarry. And once they sank a ship, the tiny U-boats could not pick up survivors. Nevertheless, in February 1915, Germany announced that it intended to sink on sight enemy ships en route to the British Isles. On May 7, 1915, a German U-boat torpedoed the British passenger liner *Lusitania*, killing 1,198 passengers, 128 of them U.S. citizens.

American newspapers featured drawings of drowning women and children, and some demanded war. Calmer voices pointed out that Germany had warned prospective passengers and that the *Lusitania* carried millions of rounds of ammunition and so was a legitimate target. Secretary of State Bryan resisted the hysteria and declared that a ship carrying war materiel "should not rely on passengers to protect her from attack — it would be like putting women and children in front of an army." He counseled Wilson to warn American citizens that they traveled on ships of belligerent countries at their own risk.

Wilson sought a middle course that would retain his commitment to peace and neutrality without condoning German attacks on passenger ships. On May 10, 1915, he announced that any further destruction of ships would be regarded as "deliberately unfriendly" and might lead the United States to break diplomatic relations with Germany. Wilson essentially demanded that Germany abandon unrestricted submarine warfare. Bryan resigned, predicting that the president had placed the United States on a collision course with Germany. Wilson replaced Bryan with Robert Lansing, who believed that Germany's antidemocratic character and goal of "world dominance" meant that it "must not be permitted to win this war."

After Germany apologized for the civilian deaths on the *Lusitania*, tensions subsided. And in 1916, Germany went further, promising no more submarine attacks without warning and without provisions for the safety of civilians. Wilson's supporters celebrated the success of his middle-of-the-road strategy.

Wilson's diplomacy proved helpful in his bid for reelection in 1916. In the contest against Republican Charles Evans Hughes, the Democratic Party ran Wilson under the slogan "He kept us out of war." The Democrats' case for Wilson's neutrality

CHAPTER LOCATOR | What was Woodrow Wilson's foreign policy agenda? | What role did the United States play in World War I?

650 CHAPTER 22 THE UNITED STATES AND WORLD WAR I

appealed to enough of those in favor of peace to eke out a majority. Wilson won, but only by the razor-thin margins of 600,000 popular and 23 electoral votes.

The United States Enters the War

Step-by-step, the United States backed away from "absolute neutrality." The consequence of protesting the German blockade of Great Britain but accepting the British blockade of Germany was that by 1916 the United States was supplying the Allies with 40 percent of their war materiel. When France and Britain ran short of money to pay for U.S. goods and asked for loans, Wilson argued that "loans by American bankers to any foreign government which is at war are inconsistent with the true spirit of neutrality." But rather than jeopardize America's wartime prosperity, Wilson allowed billions of dollars in loans that kept American goods flowing to Britain and France.

In January 1917, Germany decided that it could no longer afford to allow neutral shipping to reach Great Britain and announced that its navy would resume unrestricted submarine warfare and sink without warning any ship, enemy or neutral, found in the waters off Great Britain. Germany understood that the decision would probably bring the United States into the war but gambled that the submarines would strangle the British economy and allow German armies to win a military victory in France before American troops arrived in Europe.

Resisting demands for war, Wilson continued to hope for a negotiated peace and only broke off diplomatic relations with Germany. Then on February 25, 1917, British authorities informed Wilson of a secret telegram sent by the German foreign secretary, Arthur Zimmermann, to the German minister in Mexico. It promised that in the event of war between Germany and the United States, Germany would see that Mexico regained its "lost provinces" of Texas, New Mexico, and Arizona if Mexico would declare war against the United States. Wilson angrily responded to the Zimmermann telegram by asking Congress to approve a policy of "armed neutrality" that would allow merchant ships to fight back against any attackers.

In March, German submarines sank five American vessels off Britain, killing 66 Americans. On April 2, the president asked Congress to issue a declaration of war. He accused Germany of "warfare against all mankind" and declared that America fought to "vindicate the principles of peace and justice." He promised a world made "safe for democracy." On April 6, 1917, Congress voted to declare war.

Wilson feared what war would do at home. He said despairingly, "Once lead this people into war, and they'll forget there ever was such a thing as tolerance. To fight you must be brutal and ruthless, and the spirit of ruthless brutality will infect Congress, the courts, the policeman on the beat, the man in the street."

QUICK REVIEW <

Why did President Wilson fail to maintain U.S. neutrality during World War I?

What impact did the war have on the home front?

What part did Woodrow Wilson play at the Paris peace conference?

Why was America's transition from war to peace so turbulent?

Conclusion: What was the domestic cost of foreign victory?

LearningCurve
Check what you know.
bedfordstmartins.com
/roarkunderstanding

> What role did the United States play in World War I?

Life in the Trenches

One U.S. soldier in a rat-infested trench watches for danger, while others sit or lie in exhausted sleep. This trench is dry for the moment, but with the rains came mud so deep that wounded men drowned in it. Barbed wire, machine-gun nests, and mortars backed by heavy artillery protected the trenches. Trenches with millions of combatants stretched from French ports on the English Channel all the way to Switzerland. Such holes were miserable, but a decent shave with a Gillette safety razor and a friendly game of checkers offered temporary relief to doughboys (as the American soldiers were called). Inevitably, however, the whistles would blow, sending the young men rushing toward enemy lines. Photo: Imperial War Museum; shaving kit and checkers set: Collection of Colonel Stuart S. Corning Jr./ Picture Research Consultants, Inc.

> VISUAL ACTIVITY

READING THE IMAGE: What do these images suggest about the reality of life for American soldiers during World War I?

CONNECTIONS: How do you suppose the photograph of the trench compares with the doughboys' expectations of military service in France?

AMERICAN SOLDIERS SAILED FOR FRANCE filled with a sense of democratic mission. Some of them maintained their idealism to the end. American soldiers, many of whom had been drafted, joined the fighting just after the Russians had withdrawn from the war, leaving France as the main battleground. Although black soldiers faced discrimination, many eventually won respect under the French command. The majority of American soldiers, however, found little that was gallant in rats, lice, and poison gas and — despite the progressives' hopes — little to elevate the human soul in a landscape of utter destruction and death.

The Call to Arms

When America entered the war, Britain and France were nearly exhausted after almost three years of conflict. Millions of soldiers had perished; food and morale

CHAPTER LOCATOR | What was Woodrow Wilson's foreign policy agenda?

What role did the United States play in World War I?

CHAPTER 22

652 THE UNITED STATES AND WORLD WAR I

were dangerously low. Another Allied power, Russia, was in turmoil. In March 1917, a revolution had forced Czar Nicholas II to abdicate, and eight months later, in a separate peace with Germany, the **Bolshevik** revolutionary government withdrew Russia from the war. Peace with Russia allowed Germany to withdraw hundreds of thousands of its soldiers from the eastern front and to deploy them against the Allies on the western front in France.

On May 18, 1917, Wilson signed a sweeping Selective Service Act, authorizing a draft of all young men into the armed forces. Conscription transformed a tiny volunteer armed force of 80,000 men into a vast army and navy. Draft boards eventually inducted 2.8 million men into the armed services, in addition to the 2 million who volunteered.

Among the 4.8 million men under arms, 370,000 were black Americans. Although African Americans remained understandably skeptical about President Wilson's war for democracy, most followed W. E. B. Du Bois's advice to "close ranks" and to temporarily "forget our special grievances" until the nation had won the war. During training, black recruits suffered the same prejudices that they encountered in civilian life. Rigidly segregated, they faced abuse and miserable conditions, and they usually shouldered shovels rather than rifles.

Training camps sought to transform raw white recruits into fighting men. Progressives in the government were also determined that the camps turn out soldiers with the highest moral and civic values. YMCA workers and veterans of the settlement house and playground movements led recruits in games, singing, and college extension courses. The army asked soldiers to stop thinking about sex, explaining that a "man who is thinking below the belt is not efficient." Wilson's choice to command the army on the battlefields of France, Major General John "Black Jack" Pershing, was as morally upright as he was militarily uncompromising. Described by one observer as "lean, clean, keen," he gave progressives perfect confidence.

The War in France

At the front, the **American Expeditionary Force (AEF)** discovered a desperate situation. The war had degenerated into a stalemate of armies dug into hundreds of miles of trenches that stretched across France. Huddling in the mud among the corpses and rats, soldiers were separated from the enemy by only a few hundred yards of "no-man's-land." When ordered "over the top," troops raced desperately toward the enemy's trenches, only to be entangled in barbed wire, enveloped in poison gas, and mowed down by machine guns. The three-day battle of the Somme in 1916 cost the French and British forces 600,000 dead and wounded and the Germans 500,000. The deadliest battle of the war allowed the Allies to advance their trenches only a few meaningless miles.

Still, U.S. troops saw almost no combat in 1917. The major exception was the 92nd Division of black troops. When Pershing received an urgent call for troops from the French, he sent the 92nd to the front to be integrated with the French army because he did not want to lose command over the white troops he valued more. In the 191 days they spent in battle — longer than any other American outfit — the 369th Regiment of the 92nd Division won more medals than any other American combat unit. Black soldiers recognized the irony of having to serve with the French to gain respect.

> **CHRONOLOGY**

1917
– Selective Service Act.

1918
– Russia arranges separate peace with Germany.

1918
– U.S. Marines see first major combat.
– Armistice ending World War I is signed.

Bolshevik
▶ Russian revolutionary. Bolsheviks forced Czar Nicholas II to abdicate and seized power in Russia in 1917. In a separate peace with Germany, the Bolshevik government withdrew Russia from World War I.

American Expeditionary Force (AEF)
▶ U.S. armed forces under the command of General John Pershing who fought under a separate American command in Europe during World War I. They helped defeat Germany when they entered the conflict in full force in 1918.

What impact did the war have on the home front? | What part did Woodrow Wilson play at the Paris peace conference? | Why was America's transition from war to peace so turbulent? | Conclusion: What was the domestic cost of foreign victory?

✓ LearningCurve
Check what you know.
bedfordstmartins.com
/roarkunderstanding

653

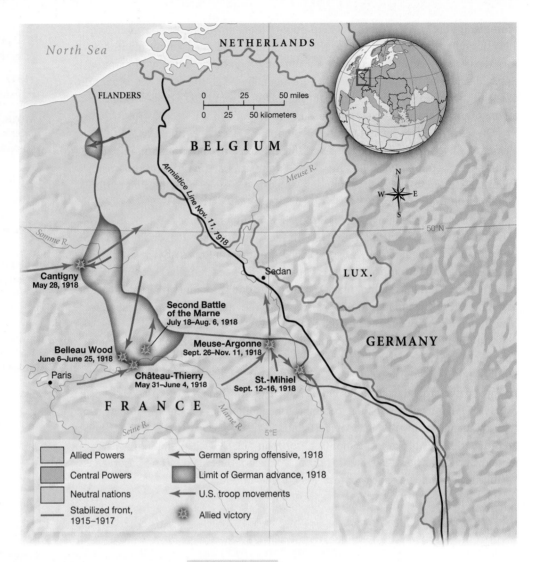

MAP 22.3 ■ The American Expeditionary Force, 1918

In the last year of the war, the AEF joined the French army on the western front to respond to the final German offensive and pursue the retreating enemy until surrender.

> MAP ACTIVITY

READING THE MAP: Across which rivers did the Germans advance in 1918? Where did the armistice line of November 11, 1918, lie in relation to the stabilized front of 1915–1917? Through which countries did the armistice line run?

CONNECTIONS: What events paved the way for the AEF to join the combat effort in 1918? What characteristic(s) differentiated American troops from other Allied forces and helped them achieve victory?

White troops continued to train and sightsee until March 1918, when a million German soldiers punched a hole in the Allied lines. Pershing finally committed the AEF to combat. In May and June, at Cantigny and then at Château-Thierry, the eager but green Americans checked the German advance with a series of assaults (**Map 22.3**). Then they headed toward the forest stronghold of Belleau Wood, moving against streams of retreating Allied soldiers who cried defeat: "La guerre est finie!" (The war is over!). A French officer commanded the Americans to retreat

CHAPTER LOCATOR | What was Woodrow Wilson's foreign policy agenda? | What role did the United States play in World War I?

CHAPTER 22
654 THE UNITED STATES AND WORLD WAR I

with them, but the American commander replied sharply, "Retreat, hell. We just got here." After charging through a wheat field against withering machine-gun fire, the Marines plunged into hand-to-hand combat. Victory came hard, but a German report praised the enemy's spirit, noting that "the Americans' nerves are not yet worn out." Indeed, it was German morale that was on the verge of cracking.

In the summer of 1918, the Allies launched a massive counteroffensive that would end the war. A quarter of a million U.S. troops joined in the rout of German forces along the Marne River. In September, more than a million Americans took part in the assault that threw the Germans back from positions along the Meuse River. In November, a revolt against the German government sent Kaiser Wilhelm II fleeing to Holland. On November 11, 1918, a delegation from the newly established German republic met with the French high command to sign an armistice that brought the fighting to an end.

The adventure of the AEF was brief, bloody, and victorious. When Germany had resumed unrestricted U-boat warfare in 1917, it had been gambling that it could defeat Britain and France before the Americans could raise and train an army and ship it to France. The German military had miscalculated badly. By the end, 112,000 AEF soldiers perished from wounds and disease, while another 230,000 Americans suffered injuries but survived. European nations, however, suffered much greater losses: 2.2 million Germans, 1.9 million Russians, 1.4 million French, and 900,000 Britons had been killed. Where they had fought, the landscape was as blasted and barren as the moon.

QUICK REVIEW

How did the American Expeditionary Force
contribute to the defeat of Germany?

What impact did the war have on the home front?

What part did Woodrow Wilson play at the Paris peace conference?

Why was America's transition from war to peace so turbulent?

Conclusion: What was the domestic cost of foreign victory?

LearningCurve
Check what you know.
bedfordstmartins.com
/roarkunderstanding

What impact did the war have on the home front?

Picketing the White House for the Vote

Mrs. William L. Colt pickets the White House to demand women's right to vote. Because of such direct pressure and in recognition of women's service to the defense industry at home and as nurses and Red Cross workers in France, Woodrow Wilson finally pledged support for the suffrage amendment. © Bettmann/Corbis.

MANY PROGRESSIVES HOPED that the war would improve the quality of American life as well as free Europe from tyranny and militarism. Mobilization helped propel the crusades for woman suffrage and prohibition to success. Progressives enthusiastically channeled industrial and agricultural production into the vast war effort. Labor shortages caused by workers entering the military provided new opportunities for women in the booming wartime economy. With labor at a premium, unionized workers gained higher pay and shorter hours. To instill loyalty in Americans whose ancestry was rooted in the belligerent nations, President Wilson launched a campaign to foster patriotism. But fanning patriotism led to suppressing dissent. When the government launched a harsh assault on civil liberties, mobs gained license to attack those whom they considered disloyal. As Wilson feared, democracy took a beating at home when the nation undertook its crusade for democracy abroad.

The Progressive Stake in the War

Progressives embraced the idea that the war could be an agent of national improvement. The Wilson administration, realizing that the federal government would have to assert greater control to mobilize the nation's human and physical resources, created new agencies to manage the war effort. Bernard Baruch

CHAPTER LOCATOR | What was Woodrow Wilson's foreign policy agenda? | What role did the United States play in World War I?

headed the War Industries Board, charged with stimulating and directing industrial production. Baruch brought industrial management and labor together into a team that produced everything from boots to bullets and made U.S. troops the best-equipped soldiers in the world.

Herbert Hoover headed the Food Administration. He led remarkably successful "Hooverizing" campaigns for "meatless" Mondays and "wheatless" Wednesdays and other ways of conserving resources. With farmers guaranteed high prices, the American heartland not only supplied the needs of U.S. citizens and armed forces but also became the breadbasket of America's allies. As the war went on, wartime agencies multiplied.

> Wartime Agencies

Railroad Administration	Directed railroad traffic
Fuel Administration	Coordinated the coal industry and other fuel suppliers
Shipping Board	Organized the merchant marine
National War Labor Policies Board	Resolved labor disputes

Industrial leaders found that wartime agencies enforced efficiency, which helped corporate profits triple. Some working people also had cause to celebrate. Mobilization meant high prices for farmers and plentiful jobs at high wages in the new war industries (**Figure 22.1**). Because increased industrial production required

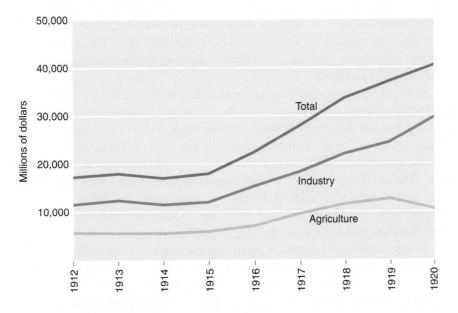

Agriculture: cash receipts.
Industry: includes mining, electric power, manufacturing, construction, and communications.

FIGURE 22.1 ■ Industrial Wages, 1912–1920

With help from unions and progressive reformers, wageworkers gradually improved their economic condition. The entry of millions of young men into the armed forces during World War I caused labor shortages and led to a rapid surge in industrial wages.

> CHRONOLOGY

1916
– Republican and Progressive parties endorse woman suffrage.

1917
– Committee on Public Information is created.
– Espionage Act and Trading with the Enemy Act.

1918
– President Wilson endorses woman suffrage.
– Sedition Act.
– Republicans win a majority in both houses of Congress.

1920
– Prohibition begins.
– American women get the vote.

| What impact did the war have on the home front? | What part did Woodrow Wilson play at the Paris peace conference? | Why was America's transition from war to peace so turbulent? | Conclusion: What was the domestic cost of foreign victory? | ☑ LearningCurve Check what you know. bedfordstmartins.com /roarkunderstanding |

657

peaceful labor relations, the National War Labor Policies Board enacted the eight-hour day, a living minimum wage, and collective bargaining rights in some industries. The American Federation of Labor (AFL) saw its membership soar from 2.7 million to more than 5 million.

The war also provided a huge boost to the crusade to ban alcohol. By 1917, prohibitionists had convinced nineteen states to go dry. Liquor's opponents now argued that banning alcohol would make the cause of democracy powerful and pure. At the same time, shutting down the distilleries would save millions of bushels of grain that could feed the United States and its allies. "Shall the many have food or the few drink?" the drys asked. In December 1917, Congress passed the **Eighteenth Amendment**, which banned the manufacture, transportation, and sale of alcohol. After swift ratification by the states, the prohibition amendment went into effect on January 1, 1920.

Eighteenth Amendment (prohibition)

▶ Constitutional amendment banning the manufacture, transportation, and sale of alcohol. Congress passed the amendment in December 1917, and it was ratified in January 1920. World War I provided a huge boost to the crusade to ban alcohol.

Women, War, and the Battle for Suffrage

Women had made real strides during the Progressive Era, and war presented new opportunities. More than 25,000 women served in France. About half were nurses. The others drove ambulances; ran canteens for the Salvation Army, Red Cross, and YMCA; worked with French civilians in devastated areas; and acted as telephone operators and war correspondents. Like men who joined the war effort, they believed that they were taking part in a great national venture. "I am more than willing to live as a soldier and know of the hardships I would have to undergo," one canteen worker declared when applying to go overseas, "but I want to help my country. . . . I want . . . to do the *real* work." And like men, women struggled against disillusionment in France. One woman explained: "Over in America, we thought we knew something about the war . . . but when you get here the difference is [like the one between] studying the laws of electricity and being struck by lightning."

At home, long-standing barriers against hiring women fell when millions of workingmen became soldiers and few new immigrant workers crossed the Atlantic. Tens of thousands of women found work in defense plants as welders, metalworkers, and heavy machine operators and with the railroads. A black woman, a domestic before the war, celebrated her job as a laborer in a railroad yard: "We . . . do not have to work as hard as at housework which requires us to be on duty from six o'clock in the morning until nine or ten at night, with might[y] little time off and at very poor wages." Other women found white-collar work. Between 1910 and 1920, the number of women clerks doubled. Before the war ended, more than a million women had found work in war industries.

The most dramatic advance for women came in the political arena. Adopting a state-by-state approach before the war, suffragists had achieved some success (**Map 22.4**). More commonly, voting rights for women met strong hostility and defeat. After 1910, suffrage leaders added a federal campaign to amend the Constitution to the traditional state-by-state strategy for suffrage.

The radical wing of the suffragists, led by Alice Paul, picketed the White House, where the marchers unfurled banners that proclaimed "America Is Not a Democracy. Twenty Million Women Are Denied the Right to Vote." They

CHAPTER LOCATOR | What was Woodrow Wilson's foreign policy agenda? | What role did the United States play in World War I?

CHAPTER 22
658 THE UNITED STATES AND WORLD WAR I

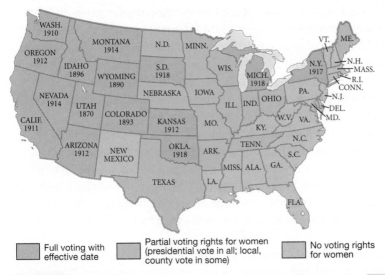

Full voting with effective date

Partial voting rights for women (presidential vote in all; local, county vote in some)

No voting rights for women

MAP 22.4 ■ Women's Voting Rights before the Nineteenth Amendment

The long campaign for women's voting rights reversed the pioneer epic that moved from east to west. From its first successes in the new democratic West, suffrage rolled eastward toward the entrenched, male-dominated public life of the Northeast and South.

> MAP ACTIVITY

READING THE MAP: What was the first state to grant woman suffrage? How many states extended full voting rights to women before 1914? How many extended these rights during World War I (1914–1918)?
CONNECTIONS: Suffragists redirected their focus during the war. What strategies did they use then?

chained themselves to fences and went to jail, where many engaged in hunger strikes. But membership in the mainstream organization, the National American Woman Suffrage Association, led by Carrie Chapman Catt, soared to some two million. Seeing the handwriting on the wall, the Republican and Progressive parties endorsed woman suffrage in 1916.

In 1918, Wilson gave his support to suffrage, calling the amendment "vital to the winning of the war." He conceded that it would be wrong not to reward the wartime "partnership of suffering and sacrifice" with a "partnership of privilege and right." By linking their cause to the wartime emphasis on national unity, the advocates of woman suffrage finally triumphed. In 1919, Congress passed the **Nineteenth Amendment (woman suffrage)**, granting women the vote, and by August 1920 the required two-thirds of the states had ratified it.

Rally around the Flag — or Else

When Congress committed the nation to war, only a handful of peace advocates resisted the tide of patriotism. A group of professional women, led by settlement house leader Jane Addams and economics professor Emily Greene Balch, denounced what Addams described as "the pathetic belief in the regenerative results of war." After America entered the conflict, advocates for peace were labeled cowards and traitors.

Nineteenth Amendment (woman suffrage)

▶ Constitutional amendment granting women the vote. Congress passed the amendment in 1919, and it was ratified in August 1920. Like proponents of prohibition, the advocates of woman suffrage triumphed by linking their cause to the war.

What impact did the war have on the home front? | What part did Woodrow Wilson play at the Paris peace conference? | Why was America's transition from war to peace so turbulent? | Conclusion: What was the domestic cost of foreign victory?

✓ LearningCurve
Check what you know.
bedfordstmartins.com
/roarkunderstanding

To suppress criticism of the war, Wilson stirred up patriotic fervor. In 1917, the president created the Committee on Public Information under the direction of George Creel. Creel sent "Four-Minute Men," a squad of 75,000 volunteers, around the country to give brief pep talks that celebrated successes on the battlefields and in the factories. Posters, pamphlets, and cartoons depicted brave American soldiers and sailors defending freedom and democracy against the evil "Huns," the derogatory nickname applied to German soldiers.

America rallied around Creel's campaign. The film industry cranked out pro-war melodramas and taught audiences to hiss at the German kaiser. Colleges and universities generated war propaganda in the guise of scholarship. When Professor James McKeen Cattell of Columbia University urged that America seek peace with Germany short of victory, university president Nicholas Murray Butler fired him on the grounds that "what had been folly is now treason."

A firestorm of anti-German passion erupted. Across the nation, "100% American" campaigns enlisted ordinary people to sniff out disloyalty. German, the most widely taught foreign language in 1914, practically disappeared from the nation's schools. Targeting German-born Americans, the *Saturday Evening Post* declared that it was time to rid the country of "the scum of the melting pot." Anti-German action reached its extreme with the lynching of Robert Prager, a German-born baker with socialist leanings. Persuaded by the defense lawyer who praised what he called a "patriotic murder," the jury at the trial of the killers took only twenty-five minutes to acquit.

D. W. Griffith's *Hearts of the World*

Hollywood joined the government's efforts to stir up rage against the Germans. In a 1918 film made by D. W. Griffith for the British and French governments, a hulking German is about to whip a defenseless farm woman. Library of Congress.

CHAPTER LOCATOR | What was Woodrow Wilson's foreign policy agenda? | What role did the United States play in World War I?

CHAPTER 22
660 THE UNITED STATES AND WORLD WAR I

As hysteria increased, the campaign reached absurd levels. Menus across the nation changed German toast to French toast and sauerkraut to liberty cabbage. In Milwaukee, vigilantes mounted a machine gun outside the Pabst Theater to prevent the staging of Schiller's *Wilhelm Tell*, a powerful protest against tyranny. The fiancée of one of the war's leading critics, caught dancing on the dunes of Cape Cod, was held on suspicion of signaling to German submarines.

The Wilson administration's zeal in suppressing dissent contrasted sharply with its war aims of defending democracy. In the name of self-defense, the Espionage Act (June 1917), the Trading with the Enemy Act (October 1917), and the Sedition Act (May 1918) gave the government sweeping powers to punish any opinion or activity it considered "disloyal, profane, scurrilous, or abusive." When Postmaster General Albert Burleson blocked mailing privileges for dissenting publications, dozens of journals were forced to close down. Of the 1,500 individuals eventually charged with sedition, all but a dozen had merely spoken words the government found objectionable. One of them was Eugene V. Debs, the leader of the Socialist Party, who was convicted under the Espionage Act for speeches condemning the war as a capitalist plot and sent to the Atlanta penitentiary.

The president hoped that national commitment to the war would silence partisan politics, but his Republican rivals used the war as a weapon against the Democrats. The trick was to oppose Wilson's conduct of the war but not the war itself. Republicans outshouted Wilson on the nation's need to mobilize for war but then complained that Wilson's War Industries Board was a tyrannical agency that crushed free enterprise. As the war progressed, Republicans gathered power against the Democrats, who had narrowly reelected Wilson in 1916.

In 1918, Republicans gained a narrow majority in both the House and the Senate. The end of Democratic control of Congress not only halted further domestic reform but also meant that the United States would advance toward military victory in Europe with political power divided between a Democratic president and a Republican Congress likely to challenge Wilson's plans for international cooperation.

QUICK REVIEW <

How did progressive ideals fare during wartime?

What impact did the war have on the home front?

What part did Woodrow Wilson play at the Paris peace conference?

Why was America's transition from war to peace so turbulent?

Conclusion: What was the domestic cost of foreign victory?

LearningCurve
Check what you know.
bedfordstmartins.com
/roarkunderstanding

The three leaders in charge of putting the world back together after the Great War — from left to right, British prime minister David Lloyd George, French premier Georges Clemenceau, and U.S. president Woodrow Wilson — stride toward the peace conference at the Versailles palace. Clemenceau is caught offering animated instruction to Wilson, whom he considered naively idealistic. Gamma Liaison/Getty Images.

What part did Woodrow Wilson play at the Paris peace conference?

Fourteen Points

▶ Woodrow Wilson's plan, proposed in 1918, to create a new democratic world order with lasting peace. Wilson's plan affirmed basic liberal ideals, supported the right to self-determination, and called for the creation of a League of Nations. Wilson compromised on his plan at the 1919 Paris peace conference, and the U.S. Senate refused to ratify the resulting treaty.

League of Nations

▶ International organization proposed in Woodrow Wilson's Fourteen Points designed to secure political independence and territorial integrity for all states and thus ensure enduring peace. The U.S. Senate refused to ratify the Treaty of Versailles, and the United States never became a member.

WILSON DECIDED TO REAFFIRM his noble war ideals by announcing his peace aims before the end of hostilities. He hoped the victorious Allies would adopt his plan for international democracy, but he was sorely disappointed. America's allies understood that Wilson's principles jeopardized their own postwar plans for the acquisition of enemy territory, new colonial empires, and reparations. Wilson also faced strong opposition at home from those who feared that his enthusiasm for international cooperation would undermine American sovereignty.

Wilson's Fourteen Points

On January 8, 1918, President Wilson revealed to Congress his **Fourteen Points**, his blueprint for a new democratic world order. The first five points affirmed basic liberal ideals: an end to secret treaties; freedom of the seas; removal of economic barriers to free trade; reduction of weapons of war; and recognition of the rights of colonized peoples. The next eight points supported the right to self-determination of European peoples who had been dominated by Germany or its allies. Wilson's fourteenth point called for a "general association of nations" — a **League of Nations**—to provide "mutual guarantees of political independence and territorial integrity to great and small states alike." A League of Nations reflected Wilson's

CHAPTER LOCATOR | What was Woodrow Wilson's foreign policy agenda? | What role did the United States play in World War I?

662 CHAPTER 22 THE UNITED STATES AND WORLD WAR I

lifelong dream of a "parliament of man." Only such an organization of "peace-loving nations," he believed, could justify the war and secure a lasting peace.

The Paris Peace Conference

From January 18 to June 28, 1919, the eyes of the world focused on Paris. Wilson, inspired by his mission, decided to head the U.S. delegation. He said he owed it to the American soldiers. "It is now my duty," he announced, "to play my full part in making good what they gave their life's blood to obtain." A dubious British diplomat retorted that Wilson was drawn to Paris "as a debutante is entranced by the prospect of her first ball." The decision to leave the country at a time when his political opponents challenged his leadership was risky enough, but his stubborn refusal to include prominent Republicans in the delegation proved foolhardy and eventually cost him his dream of a new world order.

> Allied Leaders at the Paris Peace Conference	
United States	Woodrow Wilson
Great Britain	David Lloyd George
France	Georges Clemenceau
Italy	Vittorio Orlando

After four terrible years of war, the common people of Europe almost worshipped Wilson, believing that he would create a safer, more decent world. When the peace conference convened at Louis XIV's magnificent palace at Versailles, however, Wilson encountered a different reception. To the Allied leaders, Wilson appeared a naive and impractical moralist. His desire to gather former enemies within a new international democratic order showed how little he understood hard European realities. Georges Clemenceau, premier of France, claimed that Wilson "believed you could do everything by formulas" and "empty theory." Disparaging the Fourteen Points, he added, "God himself was content with ten commandments."

The Allies wanted to fasten blame for the war on Germany, totally disarm it, and make it pay so dearly that it would never threaten its neighbors again. The French demanded retribution in the form of territory containing Germany's richest mineral resources. The British made it clear that they were not about to give up the powerful weapon of naval blockade for the vague principle of freedom of the seas.

The Allies forced Wilson to make drastic compromises. In return for France's moderating its territorial claims, he agreed to support Article 231 of the peace treaty, assigning war guilt to Germany. Though saved from permanently losing Rhineland territory to the French, Germany was outraged at being singled out as the instigator of the war and being saddled with more than $33 billion in damages. Many Germans felt that their nation had been betrayed. After agreeing to an armistice in the belief that peace terms would be based in Wilson's generous Fourteen Points, they faced hardship and humiliation instead.

Wilson had better success in establishing the principle of self-determination. But from the beginning, Secretary of State Robert Lansing knew that the president's concept of self-determination was "simply loaded with dynamite." Lansing

> CHRONOLOGY

1918
– Wilson gives Fourteen Points speech.

1919
– Paris peace conference begins.
– Treaty of Versailles is signed.

1920
– Senate votes against ratification of Treaty of Versailles.

What impact did the war have on the home front? | **What part did Woodrow Wilson play at the Paris peace conference?** | Why was America's transition from war to peace so turbulent? | Conclusion: What was the domestic cost of foreign victory? | ✔ LearningCurve Check what you know. bedfordstmartins.com /roarkunderstanding

wondered, "What unit has he in mind? Does he mean a race, a territorial area, or a community?" Even Wilson was vague about what self-determination actually meant. "When I gave utterance to those words," he admitted, "I said them without the knowledge that nationalities existed, which are coming to us day after day." Lansing suspected that the notion "will raise hopes which can never be realized. It will, I fear, cost thousands of lives. In the end it is bound to be discredited, to be called the dream of an idealist who failed to realize the danger until it was too late."

Yet partly on the basis of self-determination, the conference redrew the map of Europe and parts of the rest of the world. Portions of Austria-Hungary were ceded to Italy, Poland, and Romania, and the remainder was reassembled into Austria, Hungary, Czechoslovakia, and Yugoslavia — independent republics whose boundaries were drawn with attention to concentrations of major ethnic groups. More arbitrarily, the Ottoman empire was carved up into small mandates (including Palestine) run by local leaders but under the control of France and Great Britain. The conference reserved the mandate system for those regions it deemed insufficiently "civilized" to have full independence. Thus, the reconstructed nations — each beset with ethnic and nationalist rivalries — faced the challenge of making a new democratic government work (**Map 22.5**). Many of today's bitterest disputes — in the Balkans and Iraq, between Greece and Turkey, between Arabs and Jews — have roots in the decisions made in Paris in 1919.

MAP 22.5 ■ Europe after World War I

The post–World War I settlement redrew boundaries to create new nations based on ethnic groupings. Within defeated Germany and Russia, this outcome left bitter peoples who resolved to recover the territory taken from them.

CHAPTER LOCATOR | What was Woodrow Wilson's foreign policy agenda? | What role did the United States play in World War I?

CHAPTER 22
664 THE UNITED STATES AND WORLD WAR I

Wilson hoped that self-determination would also dictate the fate of Germany's colonies in Asia and Africa. But the Allied nations, which had taken over the colonies during the war, allowed the League of Nations only a mandate to administer them. Technically, the mandate system rejected imperialism, but in reality it allowed the Allies to maintain control. Thus, while denying Germany its colonies, the Allies retained and added to their own empires.

The cause of democratic equality suffered another setback when the peace conference rejected Japan's call for a statement of racial equality in the treaty. Wilson's belief in the superiority of whites, as well as his apprehension about how white Americans would respond to such a declaration, led him to oppose the clause. To soothe hurt feelings, Wilson agreed to grant Japan a mandate over the Shantung Peninsula in northern China, which had formerly been controlled by Germany. The gesture mollified Japan's moderate leaders, but the military faction preparing to take over the country used bitterness toward racist Western colonialism to build support for expanding Japanese power throughout Asia.

Closest to Wilson's heart was finding a new way to manage international relations. In Wilson's view, war had discredited the old strategy of balance of power. Instead, he proposed a League of Nations that would provide collective security. The league would establish rules of international conduct and resolve conflicts between nations through rational and peaceful means. When the Allies agreed to the league, Wilson was overjoyed. He believed that the league would rectify the errors his colleagues had forced on him in Paris.

To some Europeans and Americans, the **Versailles treaty** came as a bitter disappointment. Wilson's admirers were shocked that the president dealt in compromise like any other politician. But without Wilson's presence, the treaty that was signed on June 28, 1919, surely would have been more vindictive. Wilson returned home in July 1919 consoled that, despite his frustrations, he had gained what he most wanted — a League of Nations. In Wilson's judgment, "We have completed in the least time possible the greatest work that four men have ever done."

The Fight for the Treaty

The tumultuous reception Wilson received when he arrived home persuaded him, probably correctly, that the American people supported the treaty. When the president submitted the treaty to the Senate in July 1919, he warned that failure to ratify it would "break the heart of the world." By then, however, criticism of the treaty was mounting, especially from Americans convinced that their countries of ethnic origin — Ireland, Italy, and Germany — had not been given fair treatment. Others worried that the president's concessions at Versailles had jeopardized the treaty's capacity to provide a workable plan for rebuilding Europe and to guarantee world peace.

In the Senate, Republican "irreconcilables" condemned the treaty for entangling the United States in world affairs. A larger group of Republicans did not object to American participation in world politics but feared that membership in the League of Nations would jeopardize the nation's ability to act independently. No Republican, in any case, was eager to hand Wilson and the Democrats a foreign policy victory with the 1920 presidential election little more than a year away.

At the center of Republican opposition was Wilson's archenemy, Senator Henry Cabot Lodge of Massachusetts. Lodge was no isolationist, but he thought

Versailles treaty

▶ Treaty signed on June 28, 1919, that ended World War I. The agreement redrew the map of the world and assigned Germany sole responsibility for the war and saddled it with a debt of $33 billion in war damages. Many Germans felt betrayed by the treaty.

What impact did the war have on the home front? | **What part did Woodrow Wilson play at the Paris peace conference?** | Why was America's transition from war to peace so turbulent? | Conclusion: What was the domestic cost of foreign victory? | ✔ LearningCurve Check what you know. bedfordstmartins.com /roarkunderstanding

665

"Refusing to Give the Lady a Seat"

When stiff opposition to American membership in the League of Nations developed in the United States, friends of the league mounted a counterattack. This cartoon skewers the three leading Republican opponents of the league — Senators William Borah of Idaho, Henry Cabot Lodge of Massachusetts, and Hiram Johnson of California — who stubbornly refuse to budge an inch for the angel of peace. Picture Research Consultants & Archives.

that much of the Fourteen Points was a "general bleat about virtue being better than vice." Lodge expected the United States' economic and military power to propel the nation into a major role in world affairs. But he insisted that membership in the League of Nations, which would require collective action to maintain peace, threatened the nation's independence in foreign relations.

With Lodge as its chairman, the Senate Foreign Relations Committee produced several amendments, or "reservations," that sought to limit the consequences of American membership in the league. For example, several reservations required approval of both the House and the Senate before the United States could participate in league-sponsored economic sanctions or military action.

It gradually became clear that ratification of the treaty depended on acceptance of the Lodge reservations. Democratic senators, who overwhelmingly supported the treaty, urged Wilson to accept Lodge's terms, arguing that they left the essentials of the treaty intact. Wilson, however, insisted that the reservations cut "the very heart out of the treaty."

Wilson decided to take his case directly to the people. On September 3, 1919, still exhausted from the peace conference, he set out by train on the most ambitious speaking tour ever undertaken by a president. On September 25 in Pueblo, Colorado, Wilson collapsed and had to return to Washington. There, he suffered a massive stroke that partially paralyzed him. From his bedroom, Wilson sent messages instructing Democrats in the Senate to hold firm against any and all reservations. Wilson commanded enough loyalty to ensure a vote against the Lodge reservations. But when the treaty without reservations came before the Senate in March 1920, the combined opposition of the Republican irreconcilables and reservationists left Wilson six votes short of the two-thirds majority needed for passage.

The nations of Europe organized the League of Nations at Geneva, Switzerland. Although Woodrow Wilson received the Nobel Peace Prize in 1920 for his central role in creating the league, the United States never became a member. Whether American membership could have prevented the world war that would begin in Europe in 1939 is highly unlikely, but the United States' failure to join certainly weakened the league from the start. In refusing to accept relatively minor compromises with Senate moderates, Wilson lost his treaty and American membership in the league.

> **QUICK REVIEW**

Why did the Senate fail to ratify the Versailles treaty?

CHAPTER LOCATOR | What was Woodrow Wilson's foreign policy agenda? | What role did the United States play in World War I?

CHAPTER 22
666 THE UNITED STATES AND WORLD WAR I

Wearing their Sunday best and carrying the rest of what they owned in two suitcases, this southern family waits to board a northern-bound train in 1912. In Chicago, the League on Urban Conditions among Negroes, which became the Urban League, sought to ease the transition of southern blacks to life in the North. Photographs and Prints Division, Schomburg Center for Research in Black Culture, New York Public Library, Astor, Lenox, and Tilden Foundations.

Why was America's transition from war to peace so turbulent?

THE DEFEAT OF WILSON'S plan for international democracy proved the crowning blow to progressives who had hoped that the war could boost reform at home. When the war ended, Americans wanted to demobilize swiftly. In the process, servicemen, defense workers, and farmers lost their war-related jobs. The volatile combination — of unemployed veterans returning home, a stalled economy, and leftover wartime patriotism looking for a new cause — threatened to explode. Wartime anti-German passion was quickly succeeded by the Red scare, an anti-radical campaign broad enough to ensnare unionists, socialists, dissenters, and African Americans and Mexicans who had committed no offense but to seek to escape rural poverty as they moved north.

Economic Hardship and Labor Upheaval

Americans demanded that the nation return to a peacetime economy. The government abruptly abandoned its wartime economic controls and canceled war contracts. In a matter of months, 3 million soldiers mustered out of the military and flooded the job market just as war production ceased.

What impact did the war have on the home front?

What part did Woodrow Wilson play at the Paris peace conference?

Why was America's transition from war to peace so turbulent?

Conclusion: What was the domestic cost of foreign victory?

☑ LearningCurve
Check what you know.
bedfordstmartins.com
/roarkunderstanding

1915–1920
- Great migration of half a million blacks out of the South.

1918
- Global influenza epidemic starts.

1919
- Wave of labor strikes.
- Red scare.
- U.S. Supreme Court limits free speech in *Schenck v. United States*.

1920
- American Civil Liberties Union is founded.
- Palmer raids.
- Warren G. Harding is elected president.

Unemployment soared. At the same time, consumers went on a postwar spending spree that drove inflation skyward. In 1919 alone, prices rose 75 percent over prewar levels.

Most of the gains workers had made during the war evaporated. Business turned against the eight-hour day and attacked labor unions. With inflation eating up their paychecks, workers fought back. The year 1919 witnessed nearly 3,600 strikes involving 4 million workers. The most spectacular strike occurred in February 1919 in Seattle, where shipyard workers had been put out of work by demobilization. When a coalition of the radical Industrial Workers of the World (IWW, known as Wobblies) and the moderate American Federation of Labor called a general strike, the largest work stoppage in American history shut down the city. Newspapers claimed that the walkout was "a Bolshevik effort to start a revolution." The suppression of the Seattle general strike by city officials cost the AFL many of its wartime gains and contributed to the destruction of the IWW soon afterward.

A strike by Boston policemen in the fall of 1919 underscored postwar hostility toward labor militancy. Although the police were paid less than pick-and-shovel laborers, they won little sympathy. Once the officers stopped walking their beats, looters sacked the city. Massachusetts governor Calvin Coolidge called in the National Guard to restore order. The public welcomed Coolidge's anti-union assurance that "there is no right to strike against the public safety by anybody, anywhere, any time."

Labor strife climaxed in the grim steel strike of 1919. Faced with the industry's plan to revert to seven-day weeks, twelve-hour days, and weekly wages of about $20, Samuel Gompers, head of the AFL, called for a strike. In September, 350,000 workers in fifteen states walked out. The steel industry hired 30,000 strikebreakers and convinced the public that the strikers were radicals bent on subverting democracy and capitalism. In January 1920, after 18 striking workers were killed, the strike collapsed. That devastating defeat initiated a sharp decline in the fortunes of the labor movement, a trend that would continue for almost twenty years.

The Red Scare

Suppression of labor strikes was one response to the widespread fear of internal subversion that swept the nation in 1919. The **Red scare** ("Red" referred to the color of the Bolshevik flag) had homegrown causes: the postwar recession, labor unrest, terrorist acts, and the difficulties of reintegrating millions of returning veterans. But unsettling events abroad also added to Americans' anxieties.

Two epidemics swept the globe in 1918. One was Spanish influenza, which brought on a lethal accumulation of fluid in the lungs. A nurse near the front lines in France observed that victims "run a high temperature, so high that we can't believe it's true. . . . It is accompanied by vomiting and dysentery. When they die, as about half of them do, they turn a ghastly dark gray and are taken out at once and cremated." Before the flu virus had run its course, 40 million people had died worldwide, including some 700,000 Americans.

The other epidemic was Russian bolshevism, which seemed to most Americans equally contagious and deadly. Bolshevism became even more menacing in March 1919, when the new Soviet leaders created the Comintern, a worldwide association of Communists sworn to revolution in capitalist countries. A Communist revolution in the United States was extremely unlikely, but edgy Americans, faced with a flurry of

Red scare

▶ The widespread fear of internal subversion and Communist revolution that swept the United States in 1919 and resulted in suppression of dissent. Labor unrest, postwar recession, the difficult peacetime readjustment, and the Soviet establishment of the Comintern all contributed to the scare.

CHAPTER LOCATOR | What was Woodrow Wilson's foreign policy agenda? | What role did the United States play in World War I?

CHAPTER 22
668 THE UNITED STATES AND WORLD WAR I

terrorist acts, believed otherwise. Dozens of prominent individuals had received bombs through the mail. On September 16, 1920, a wagon filled with dynamite and iron exploded on Wall Street, killing 38 and maiming 143 others.

Even before the Wall Street bombing, the government had initiated a hunt for domestic revolutionaries. Led by Attorney General A. Mitchell Palmer, the campaign targeted men and women who harbored ideas that Palmer believed could lead to violence, even though the individuals may not have done anything illegal. In January 1920, Palmer ordered a series of raids that netted 6,000 alleged subversives. Finding no revolutionary conspiracies, Palmer nevertheless ordered 500 noncitizen suspects deported.

His action came in the wake of a campaign against the most notorious radical alien, Russian-born Emma Goldman. Before the war, Goldman's passionate support of labor strikes, women's rights, and birth control had made her a symbol of radicalism. In 1919, after a stay in prison for denouncing military conscription, she was ordered deported by J. Edgar Hoover, the director of the Justice Department's Radical Division.

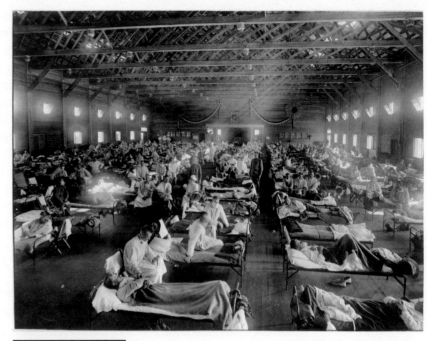

Emergency Hospital

Despite its name, the Spanish flu was first observed in 1918 in Kansas. Army camps, with their close troop quarters, proved perfect incubators. This emergency hospital at Camp Funston, Kansas, is filled with some of the flu's early victims. Crowded troopships quickly spread the virus to Europe. Civilians were not immune. In October 1918 in Philadelphia, more than 4,500 people died in a single week. National Museum of Health & Medicine, Armed Forces Institute of Pathology.

The effort to rid the country of alien radicals was matched by efforts to crush troublesome citizens. Law enforcement officials and vigilante groups joined hands against so-called Reds. In November 1919 in the rugged lumber town of Centralia, Washington, a menacing crowd gathered in front of the IWW hall. Nervous Wobblies inside opened fire, killing three people. Three IWW members were arrested and later convicted of murder, but another, ex-soldier Wesley Everett, was carried off by the mob, which castrated him, hung him from a bridge, and then riddled his body with bullets. His death was officially ruled a suicide.

Public institutions joined the attack on civil liberties. Local libraries removed dissenting books. Schools fired unorthodox teachers. Police shut down radical newspapers. State legislatures refused to seat elected representatives who professed socialist ideas. And in 1919, Congress removed its lone socialist representative, Victor Berger, on the pretext that he was a threat to national safety.

That same year, the Supreme Court provided a formula for restricting free speech. In upholding the conviction of socialist Charles Schenck for publishing a pamphlet urging resistance to the draft during wartime (*Schenck v. United States*), the Court established a "clear and present danger" test. Utterances such as Schenck's during a time of national peril, Justice Oliver Wendell Holmes wrote, were equivalent to shouting "Fire!" in a crowded theater.

Schenck v. United States

▶ 1919 Supreme Court decision that established a "clear and present danger" test for restricting free speech. The Court upheld the conviction of socialist Charles Schenck for urging resistance to the draft during wartime.

What impact did the war have on the home front?

What part did Woodrow Wilson play at the Paris peace conference?

Why was America's transition from war to peace so turbulent?

Conclusion: What was the domestic cost of foreign victory?

☑ LearningCurve
Check what you know.
bedfordstmartins.com
/roarkunderstanding

In 1920, the assault on civil liberties provoked the creation of the American Civil Liberties Union (ACLU), which was dedicated to defending an individual's constitutional rights. One of the ACLU's founders, Roger Baldwin, declared, "So long as we have enough people in this country willing to fight for their rights, we'll be called a democracy." The ACLU championed the targets of Attorney General Palmer's campaign — politically radical immigrants, trade unionists, socialists and Communists, and antiwar activists who still languished in jail.

The Red scare eventually collapsed because of its excesses. In particular, the antiradical campaign lost credibility after Palmer warned that radicals were planning to celebrate the Bolshevik Revolution with a nationwide wave of violence on May 1, 1920. Officials called out state militias, mobilized bomb squads, and even placed machine-gun nests at major city intersections. When May 1 came and went without a single disturbance, the public mood turned from fear to scorn.

The Great Migrations of African Americans and Mexicans

Before the Red scare lost steam, the government raised alarms about the loyalty of African Americans. A Justice Department investigation concluded that Reds were fomenting racial unrest among blacks. Although the report was wrong about Bolshevik influence, it was correct in noticing a new stirring among African Americans.

In 1900, nine of every ten blacks still lived in the South, where poverty, disfranchisement, segregation, and violence dominated their lives. Whites remained committed to keeping blacks down. "If we own a good farm or horse, or cow, or bird-dog, or yoke of oxen," a black sharecropper in Mississippi observed in 1913, "we are harassed until we are bound to sell, give away, or run away, before we can have any peace in our lives."

The First World War provided African Americans with the opportunity to escape the South's cotton fields and kitchens. When war channeled almost 5 million American workers into military service and almost ended European immigration, northern industrialists turned to black labor. Black men found work in northern steel mills, shipyards, munitions plants, railroad yards, automobile factories, and mines. From 1915 to 1920, half a million blacks (approximately 10 percent of the South's black population) boarded trains bound for Philadelphia, Detroit, Cleveland, Chicago, St. Louis, and other industrial cities.

Thousands of migrants wrote home to tell family and friends about their experiences in the North. One man announced proudly that he had recently been promoted to "first assistant to the head carpenter." He added, "I should have been here twenty years ago. I just begin to feel like a man. . . . My children are going to the same school with the whites and I don't have to [h]umble to no one. I have registered — will vote the next election and there ain't any 'yes sir' — it's all yes and no and Sam and Bill."

But the North was not the promised land. Black men stood on the lowest rungs of the labor ladder. Jobs of any kind proved scarce for black women, and most worked as domestic servants as they did in the South. The existing black middle class sometimes shunned the less educated, less sophisticated rural southerners crowding into northern cities. Many whites, fearful of losing jobs and status, lashed out against the new migrants. Savage race riots ripped through two

Mexican Women Arriving in El Paso, 1911

These Mexican women, carrying bundles and wearing traditional shawls, try to get their bearings upon arriving in El Paso, Texas — the Ellis Island for Mexican immigrants. They were part of the first modern wave of Mexican immigration to the United States. Women like them found work in the fields, canneries, and restaurants of the Southwest, as well as at home taking in sewing, laundry, and boarders. Courtesy of the Rio Grande Historical Collections, New Mexico State University, Las Cruces, NM.

dozen northern cities. In 1918, the nation witnessed ninety-six lynchings of blacks, some of them decorated war veterans still in uniform.

Still, most black migrants stayed in the North and encouraged friends and family to follow. By 1940, more than one million blacks had left the South, profoundly changing their own lives and the course of the nation's history. Black enclaves such as Harlem in New York and the South Side of Chicago, "cities within cities," emerged in the North. These assertive communities provided a foundation for black protest and political organization in the years ahead.

At nearly the same time, another migration was under way in the American Southwest. Between 1910 and 1920, the Mexican-born population in the United States soared from 222,000 to 478,000. Mexican immigration resulted from developments on both sides of the border. When Mexicans revolted against dictator Porfirio Díaz in 1910, initiating a ten-year civil war, migrants flooded northward. In the United States, the Chinese Exclusion Act of 1882 and later the disruption of World War I cut off the supply of cheap foreign labor and caused western employers in the expanding rail, mining, construction, and agricultural industries to look south to Mexico for workers.

Like immigrants from Europe and black migrants from the South, Mexicans in the American Southwest dreamed of a better life. And like the others, they found both opportunity and disappointment. Wages were better than in Mexico, but life in the fields, mines, and factories was hard, and living conditions — in boxcars, labor camps, or urban barrios — were dismal. Signs warning "No Mexicans Allowed" increased rather than declined. Mexicans were considered excellent prospects for manual labor but not for citizenship. Among Mexican Americans, some of whom had lived in the Southwest for more than a century, *los recién llegados* (the recent arrivals) encountered mixed reactions. One Mexican American expressed this ambivalence: "We are all Mexicans anyway because the gueros [Anglos] treat us all alike." But he also called for immigration quotas because the recent arrivals drove down wages and incited white prejudice that affected all Mexican Americans.

Despite friction, large-scale immigration into the Southwest meant a resurgence of the Mexican cultural presence, which became the basis for

| What impact did the war have on the home front? | What part did Woodrow Wilson play at the Paris peace conference? | **Why was America's transition from war to peace so turbulent?** | Conclusion: What was the domestic cost of foreign victory? | ☑ LearningCurve Check what you know. bedfordstmartins.com /roarkunderstanding |

671

Candidate	Electoral Vote	Popular Vote	Percent of Popular Vote
Warren G. Harding (Republican)	404	16,143,407	60.5
James M. Cox (Democrat)	127	9,130,328	34.2
Eugene V. Debs (Socialist)	0	919,799	3.4

MAP 22.6 ■ The Election of 1920

greater solidarity and political action for the ethnic Mexican population. In 1929 in Texas, Mexican Americans formed the League of United Latin American Citizens.

Postwar Politics and the Election of 1920

A thousand miles away in Washington, D.C., President Woodrow Wilson, bedridden and paralyzed, ignored the mountain of domestic troubles — labor strikes, the Red scare, race riots, immigration backlash — and insisted that the 1920 election would be a "solemn referendum" on the League of Nations. Dutifully, the Democratic nominees for president, James M. Cox of Ohio, and for vice president, Franklin Delano Roosevelt of New York, campaigned on Wilson's international ideals. The Republican Party chose the handsome, gregarious Warren Gamaliel Harding, a senator from Ohio.

Harding found the winning formula when he declared that "America's present need is not heroics, but healing; not nostrums [questionable remedies] but normalcy." But what was "normalcy"? Harding explained: "By 'normalcy' I don't mean the old order but a regular steady order of things. I mean normal procedure, the natural way, without excess." Eager to put wartime crusades and postwar strife behind them, voters responded by giving Harding the largest presidential victory ever: 60.5 percent of the popular vote and 404 out of 531 electoral votes (**Map 22.6**). Harding's election lifted the national pall, signaling a new, more easy-going era.

> **QUICK REVIEW**

How did the Red scare contribute to the erosion of civil liberties after the war?

CHAPTER LOCATOR | What was Woodrow Wilson's foreign policy agenda? | What role did the United States play in World War I?

672 CHAPTER 22 THE UNITED STATES AND WORLD WAR I

AMERICA'S EXPERIENCE IN WORLD WAR I was exceptional. For much of the world, the Great War produced great destruction — blackened fields, ruined factories, and millions of casualties. But in the United States, war and prosperity marched hand in hand. America emerged from the war with the strongest economy in the world and a position of international preeminence.

Still, the nation paid a heavy price both at home and abroad. American soldiers and sailors encountered unprecedented horrors — submarines, poison gas, machine guns — and more than 100,000 died. But rather than redeeming the sacrifice of these men as Woodrow Wilson promised, the peace that followed the armistice tarnished it.

At home, rather than permanently improving working conditions, advancing public health, and spreading educational opportunity, as progressives had hoped, the war threatened to undermine the achievements of the previous two decades. Moreover, rather than promoting democracy, the war bred fear, intolerance, and repression that led to a crackdown on dissent and a demand for conformity. Reformers could count only woman suffrage as a permanent victory.

Woodrow Wilson had promised more than anyone could deliver. Progressive hopes of extending democracy and liberal reform nationally and internationally were dashed. In 1920, a bruised and disillusioned society stumbled into a new decade. The era coming to an end had called on Americans to crusade and sacrifice. The new era promised peace, prosperity, and a good time.

| What impact did the war have on the home front? | What part did Woodrow Wilson play at the Paris peace conference? | Why was America's transition from war to peace so turbulent? | Conclusion: What was the domestic cost of foreign victory? | ☑ LearningCurve Check what you know. bedfordstmartins.com /roarkunderstanding |

673

CHAPTER 22 STUDY GUIDE

STEP 1

GET STARTED ONLINE

✓ LearningCurve ▪ bedfordstmartins.com/roarkunderstanding
Now that you've read the chapter, make it stick by completing the LearningCurve activity.

STEP 2

EXPLAIN WHY IT MATTERS

Put your reading into practice. Identify each term below, and then explain why it matters in U.S. history.

TERM	WHO OR WHAT & WHEN	WHY IT MATTERS
Triple Alliance (p. 648)		
Triple Entente (p. 648)		
Lusitania (p. 650)		
Bolshevik (p. 653)		
American Expeditionary Force (AEF) (p. 653)		
Eighteenth Amendment (prohibition) (p. 658)		
Nineteenth Amendment (woman suffrage) (p. 659)		
Fourteen Points (p. 662)		
League of Nations (p. 662)		
Versailles treaty (p. 665)		
Red scare (p. 668)		
Schenck v. United States (p. 669)		

STEP 3

MOVE BEYOND THE BASICS

To demonstrate a more advanced understanding, describe U.S. entry into World War I and list the government initiatives in three areas: wartime agencies, legislation, and propaganda. How did these various initiatives help the war effort?

	Description or list	Reasons for	Effects of
U.S. entry into World War I			
Wartime agencies			
Legislation			
Propaganda			

PUT IT ALL TOGETHER

Now, take a step back and try to explain the big picture. Remember to use specific examples from the chapter in your answers.

THE PATH TO WAR

▶ Describe Woodrow Wilson's foreign policy during his first term in office. How did Wilson see the relationship between the United States and the rest of the world?

▶ Is it fair to describe the American people as "isolationist" prior to America's entry into World War I? Why or why not?

THE HOME FRONT

▶ How did the war affect the progressive agenda? How did progressives use the war to achieve their goals?

▶ To what extent did U.S. participation in World War I involve the domestic efforts of the American people?

A TROUBLED PEACE

▶ What vision did Wilson have of the postwar world? Why did the Senate refuse to endorse his vision, as embodied in the Treaty of Versailles?

▶ What led to the Red scare, and why did it eventually subside?

LOOKING BACKWARD, LOOKING AHEAD

▶ Why did a majority of Americans initially oppose the country's entry into World War I? What events and experiences in the country's past helped shape prewar public opinion?

▶ How did World War I change the place of the United States in the world? What role in world affairs was America poised to take as it entered the 1920s?

> IN YOUR OWN WORDS

Imagine that you must give an oral report to the class answering the following question: What were the most important outcomes of World War I for the United States? What would be the most important points to include and why?

 Do it online at the Student Site ▪ bedfordstmartins.com/roarkunderstanding

23

FROM NEW ERA TO GREAT DEPRESSION

1920–1932

> **What were the high points and the low points of the 1920s?** Chapter 23 examines the central role of business in the 1920s, the cultural change and conflicts of the decade, and the events that led to the collapse of the American economy by the end of the decade. The chapter also explores the policies of the Republican administrations of the era and the failure of the federal government to respond effectively to the economic catastrophe.

LearningCurve

bedfordstmartins.com/roarkunderstanding
After reading the chapter, use LearningCurve to
retain what you've read.

> How did big business shape the "New Era" of the 1920s?

> In what ways did the Roaring Twenties challenge traditional values?

> Why did the relationship between urban and rural America deteriorate in the 1920s?

> How did President Hoover respond to the economic crash of 1929?

> What was life like in the early years of the depression?

> Conclusion: Why did the hope of the 1920s turn to despair?

"Sheik with Sheba." Cover of *Judge* magazine, by A. John Held Jr. The Granger Collection, New York.

How did big business shape the "New Era" of the 1920s?

Henry and Edsel Ford

In this 1924 photograph, Henry Ford looks fondly at his first car while his son, Edsel, stands next to the ten millionth Model T. Henry Ford Museum and Greenfield Village.

ONCE WOODROW WILSON LEFT the White House, energy flowed away from government activism and civic reform and toward private economic endeavor. The rise of a freewheeling economy and a heightened sense of individualism caused Secretary of Commerce Herbert Hoover to declare that America had entered a "New Era," one of many labels used to describe the complex 1920s. Some terms focus on the decade's high-spirited energy and cultural change: Roaring Twenties, Jazz Age, Flaming Youth. Others echo the rising importance of money — Dollar Decade, Golden Twenties — or reflect the sinister side of gangster profiteering — Lawless Decade. Still others emphasize the lonely confusion of the Lost Generation and the stress and anxiety of the Aspirin Age.

America in the twenties was many things, but President Calvin Coolidge got at an essential truth when he declared: "The business of America is business." Politicians and diplomats proclaimed business the heart of American civilization as they promoted its products at home and abroad. Average men and women bought into the idea that business and its wonderful goods were what made America great, as they snatched up the flood of new consumer items American factories sent forth. Nothing caught Americans' fancy more powerfully than the automobile.

CHAPTER LOCATOR | How did big business shape the "New Era" of the 1920s? | In what ways did the Roaring Twenties challenge traditional values?

CHAPTER 23
678 FROM NEW ERA TO GREAT DEPRESSION

A Business Government

Republicans controlled the White House from 1921 to 1933. The first of the three Republican presidents was Warren Gamaliel Harding, the Ohio senator who in his 1920 campaign called for a "return to normalcy," by which he meant the end of public crusades and a return to private pursuits. Harding appointed a few men of real stature to his cabinet. Herbert Hoover, the former head of the wartime Food Administration, became secretary of commerce. But wealth and friendship also counted: Andrew Mellon, one of the richest men in America, became secretary of the treasury, and Harding handed out jobs to his friends, members of his old "Ohio gang." This curious combination of merit and cronyism made for a disjointed administration.

When Harding was elected in 1920 (see chapter 22, Map 22.6), the unemployment rate hit 20 percent, the highest ever up to that point. The bankruptcy rate of farmers increased tenfold. Harding pushed measures to regain national prosperity — high tariffs to protect American businesses, price supports for agriculture, and the dismantling of wartime government control over industry in favor of unregulated private business. "Never before, here or anywhere else," the U.S. Chamber of Commerce said proudly, "has a government been so completely fused with business."

Harding's policies to boost American enterprise made him very popular, but ultimately his small-town congeniality and trusting ways did him in. Some of his friends in the Ohio gang were up to their necks in lawbreaking. Three of Harding's appointees would go to jail. Interior Secretary Albert Fall was convicted of accepting bribes of more than $400,000 for leasing oil reserves on public land in Teapot Dome, Wyoming, and **Teapot Dome** became a synonym for political corruption.

On August 2, 1923, when Harding died from a heart attack, Vice President Calvin Coolidge became president. Coolidge, who once said that "the man who builds a factory builds a temple, the man who works there worships there," continued and extended Harding's policies of promoting business and limiting government. Secretary of the Treasury Andrew Mellon reduced the government's control over the economy and cut taxes for corporations and wealthy individuals. New rules for the Federal Trade Commission severely restricted its power to regulate business. Secretary of Commerce Herbert Hoover hedged government authority by encouraging trade associations that ideally would keep business honest and efficient through voluntary cooperation.

Coolidge found an ally in the Supreme Court. The Court ruled against closed shops — businesses where only union members could be employed — while confirming the right of owners to form exclusive trade associations. In 1923, the Court declared unconstitutional the District of Columbia's minimum-wage law for women, asserting that the law interfered with the freedom of employer and employee to make labor contracts. The Court and the president attacked government intrusion in the free market, even when the prohibition of government regulation threatened the welfare of workers.

The election of 1924 confirmed the defeat of the progressive principle that the state should take a leading role in ensuring the general welfare. To oppose Coolidge, the Democrats nominated John W. Davis, a corporate lawyer whose conservative views differed little from Republican principles. Only the Progressive Party and its presidential nominee, Senator Robert La Follette of Wisconsin, offered

> CHRONOLOGY

1920
- Warren G. Harding is elected president.

1922
- Teapot Dome scandal.
- Five-Power Naval Treaty.

1923
- Harding dies; Vice President Calvin Coolidge becomes president.

1924
- Dawes Plan.
- Coolidge is elected president.

1928
- Kellogg-Briand pact.

1929
- Publication of *Middletown*.

Teapot Dome
▶ Nickname for the scandal in which Interior Secretary Albert Fall accepted $400,000 in bribes for leasing oil reserves on public land in Teapot Dome, Wyoming. It was part of a larger pattern of corruption that marred Warren G. Harding's presidency.

| Why did the relationship between urban and rural America deteriorate in the 1920s? | How did President Hoover respond to the economic crash of 1929? | What was life like in the early years of the depression? | Conclusion: Why did the hope of the 1920s turn to despair? | ☑ LearningCurve Check what you know. bedfordstmartins.com /roarkunderstanding |

a genuine alternative. When La Follette championed labor unions, regulation of business, and protection of civil liberties, Republicans coined the slogan "Coolidge or Chaos." Voters chose Coolidge in a landslide. Coolidge was right when he declared, "This is a business country, and it wants a business government." What was true of the government's relationship to business at home was also true abroad.

Promoting Prosperity and Peace Abroad

After orchestrating the Senate's successful effort to block U.S. membership in the League of Nations, Henry Cabot Lodge boasted, "We have torn Wilsonism up by the roots." But repudiation of Wilsonian internationalism and rejection of collective security through the League of Nations did not mean that the United States retreated into isolationism. The United States emerged from World War I with its economy intact and enjoyed a decade of stunning growth. New York replaced London as the center of world finance, and the United States became the world's chief creditor. Economic involvement in the world and the continuing chaos in Europe made withdrawal impossible.

One of the Republicans' most ambitious foreign policy initiatives was the Washington Disarmament Conference, which convened in 1921 to establish a global balance of naval power. Secretary of State Charles Evans Hughes shaped the **Five-Power Naval Treaty of 1922** committing Britain, France, Japan, Italy, and the United States to a proportional reduction of naval forces. The treaty led to the scrapping of more than two million tons of warships, by far the world's greatest success in disarmament. By fostering international peace, President Harding also helped make the world a safer place for American trade.

A second major effort on behalf of world peace came in 1928, when Secretary of State Frank Kellogg joined French foreign minister Aristide Briand to produce the Kellogg-Briand pact. Nearly fifty nations signed the solemn pledge to renounce war and settle international disputes peacefully.

But Republican administrations preferred private-sector diplomacy to state action. With the blessing of the White House, a team of American financiers led by Charles Dawes swung into action when Germany suspended its war reparation payments in 1923. Impoverished, Germany was staggering under the massive bill of $33 billion presented by the victorious Allies in the Versailles treaty. When Germany failed to meet its annual payment, France occupied Germany's industrial Ruhr Valley, creating the worst international crisis since the war. In 1924, the Dawes Plan halved Germany's annual reparation payments, initiated fresh American loans to Germany, and caused the French to retreat from the Ruhr. Although the United States failed to join the League of Nations, it continued to exercise significant economic and diplomatic influence abroad. These Republican successes overseas helped fuel prosperity at home.

Automobiles, Mass Production, and Assembly-Line Progress

The automobile industry emerged as the largest single manufacturing industry in the nation. The pioneer of the mass production of automobiles was Henry Ford.

Five-Power Naval Treaty of 1922

▶ Treaty that committed Britain, France, Japan, Italy, and the United States to a proportional reduction of naval forces, producing the world's greatest success in disarmament up to that time. Republicans orchestrated its development at the 1921 Washington Disarmament Conference.

CHAPTER LOCATOR | How did big business shape the "New Era" of the 1920s? | In what ways did the Roaring Twenties challenge traditional values?

680 CHAPTER 23 FROM NEW ERA TO GREAT DEPRESSION

When the 1920s began, he had already produced six million automobiles; by 1927, the figure reached fifteen million. In 1920, a Ford car cost $845; in 1928, the price was less than $300, within range of most of the country's skilled workingmen. Ford shrewdly located his company in Detroit, knowing that key materials for his automobiles were manufactured in nearby states (**Map 23.1**). Keystone of the American economy, the automobile industry not only employed hundreds of thousands of workers directly but also brought whole industries into being — filling stations, garages, fast-food restaurants, and "guest cottages" (motels). The need for tires, glass, steel, highways, oil, and refined gasoline for automobiles provided millions of related jobs. By 1929, one American in four found employment directly or indirectly in the automobile industry. "Give us our daily bread" was no longer addressed to the Almighty, one commentator quipped, but to Detroit.

Detroit and the Automobile Industry in the 1920s

Automobiles changed where people lived, what work they did, how they spent their leisure, even how they thought. Hundreds of small towns decayed because the automobile enabled rural people to bypass them in favor of more distant cities and towns. In cities, streetcars began to disappear as workers moved to the suburbs and commuted to work along crowded highways. Nothing shaped modern America more than the automobile, and efficient mass production made the automobile revolution possible.

Mass production by the assembly-line technique became standard in almost every factory, from automobiles to meatpacking to cigarettes. To improve efficiency, corporations reduced assembly-line work to the simplest, most repetitive tasks. Changes on

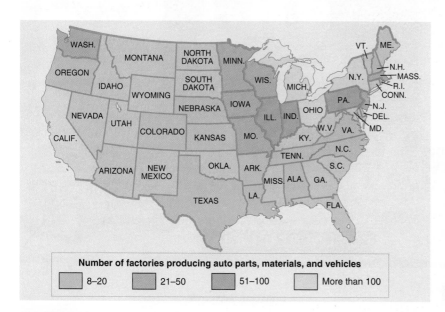

Number of factories producing auto parts, materials, and vehicles

| 8–20 | 21–50 | 51–100 | More than 100 |

MAP 23.1 ■ Auto Manufacturing

By the mid-1920s, the massive coal and steel industries of the Midwest had made that region the center of the new automobile industry. A major road-building program by the federal government carried the thousands of new cars produced each day to every corner of the country.

> MAP ACTIVITY

READING THE MAP: How many states had factories involved with the manufacture of automobiles? In what regions was auto manufacturing concentrated?

CONNECTIONS: On what related industries did auto manufacturing depend? How did the integration of the automobile into everyday life affect American society?

Why did the relationship between urban and rural America deteriorate in the 1920s?

How did President Hoover respond to the economic crash of 1929?

What was life like in the early years of the depression?

Conclusion: Why did the hope of the 1920s turn to despair?

✓ LearningCurve
Check what you know.
bedfordstmartins.com
/roarkunderstanding

the assembly line and in management, along with technological advances, significantly boosted overall efficiency. Between 1922 and 1929, productivity in manufacturing increased 32 percent. Average wages, however, increased only 8 percent.

Industries also developed programs for workers that came to be called **welfare capitalism**. Some businesses improved safety and sanitation inside factories. They also instituted paid vacations and pension plans. Welfare capitalism encouraged loyalty to the company and discouraged traditional labor unions. One labor organizer in the steel industry bemoaned the success of welfare capitalism. "So many workmen here had been lulled to sleep by the company union, the welfare plans, the social organizations fostered by the employer," he declared, "that they had come to look upon the employer as their protector, and had believed vigorous trade union organization unnecessary for their welfare."

welfare capitalism

▸ Industrial programs for workers that became popular in the 1920s. Some businesses improved safety and sanitation inside factories. They also instituted paid vacations and pension plans. This encouraged loyalty to companies and discouraged independent labor unions.

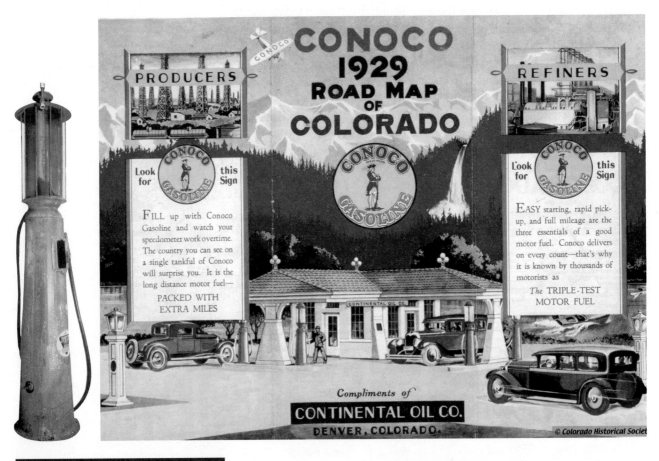

Colorado Filling Station and Gas Pump

By 1929, when Conoco (Continental Oil Company) produced this lavish map featuring Colorado's spectacular mountains, nearly every oil company was supplying road maps as part of its campaign to boost tourism. This appealing drive-through station is a far cry from the first retail outlets for gas — blacksmith shops and hardware stores, the same places individuals bought kerosene for their lamps. Because motorists did not trust what they could not see, companies in the 1910s introduced glass-cylinder, gravity-flow gas pumps. Courtesy, Colorado Historical Society.

> **VISUAL ACTIVITY**

READING THE IMAGE: What do this road map and accompanying image of a gravity-flow gasoline pump tell us about American consumer culture on the eve of the Great Depression?

CONNECTIONS: Does the road map accurately reflect the economic direction of the U.S. economy in 1929?

CHAPTER LOCATOR | How did big business shape the "New Era" of the 1920s? | In what ways did the Roaring Twenties challenge traditional values?

CHAPTER 23
682 FROM NEW ERA TO GREAT DEPRESSION

Consumer Culture

Mass production fueled corporate profits and national economic prosperity. During the 1920s, per capita income increased by a third, the cost of living stayed the same, and unemployment remained low. But the rewards of the economic boom were not evenly distributed. Americans who labored with their hands inched ahead, while white-collar workers enjoyed significantly more spending money and more leisure time to spend it. Mass production of a broad range of new products — automobiles, radios, refrigerators, electric irons, washing machines — produced a consumer goods revolution.

In this new era of abundance, more people than ever conceived of the American dream in terms of the things they could acquire. *Middletown* (1929), a study of the inhabitants of Muncie, Indiana, revealed that Muncie had become, above all, "a culture in which everything hinges on money." Moreover, faced with technological and organizational change beyond their comprehension, many citizens had lost confidence in their ability to play an effective role in civic affairs. More and more they became passive consumers, deferring to the supposed expertise of leaders in politics and economics.

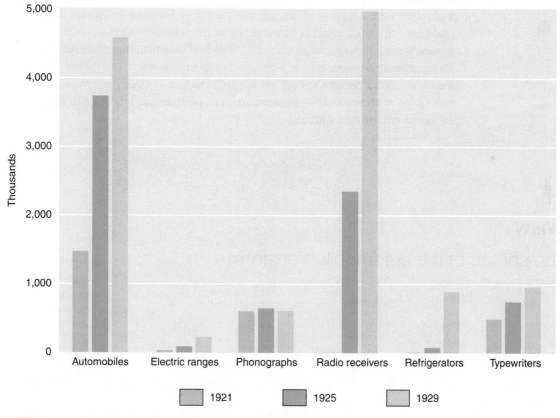

FIGURE 23.1 ■ Production of Consumer Goods, 1920–1929

Transportation, communications, and entertainment changed the lives of consumers in the 1920s. Laborsaving devices for the home were popular, but the vastly greater sales of automobiles and radios showed that consumerism was powerful in moving people's attention beyond their homes.

Why did the relationship between urban and rural America deteriorate in the 1920s?

How did President Hoover respond to the economic crash of 1929?

What was life like in the early years of the depression?

Conclusion: Why did the hope of the 1920s turn to despair?

LearningCurve
Check what you know.
bedfordstmartins.com
/roarkunderstanding

The rapidly expanding business of advertising stimulated the desire for new products and attacked the traditional values of thrift and saving. Advertising linked material goods to the fulfillment of every spiritual and emotional need. Americans increasingly defined and measured their social status, and indeed their personal worth, on the yardstick of material possessions. Happiness itself rode on owning a car and choosing the right cigarettes and toothpaste.

By the 1920s, the United States had achieved the physical capacity to satisfy Americans' material wants (**Figure 23.1**, page 683). The economic problem shifted from production to consumption: Who would buy the goods flying off American assembly lines? One solution was to expand America's markets in foreign countries, and government and business joined in that effort. Another solution to the problem of consumption was to expand the market at home.

Henry Ford realized early on that "mass production requires mass consumption." He understood that automobile workers not only produced cars but would also buy them if they made enough money. "One's own employees ought to be one's own best customers," Ford said. In 1914, he raised wages in his factories to $5 a day, more than twice the going rate. High wages made for workers who were more loyal and more exploitable, and high wages returned as profits when workers bought Fords.

Many people's incomes, however, were too puny to satisfy the growing desire for consumer goods. The solution was installment buying — a little money down, a payment each month — which allowed people to purchase expensive items they could not otherwise afford or to purchase items before saving the necessary money. As one newspaper announced, "The first responsibility of an American to his country is no longer that of a citizen, but of a consumer." During the 1920s, America's motto became spend, not save. Old values — "Use it up, wear it out, make it do or do without" — seemed about as pertinent as a horse and buggy. American culture had shifted.

> **QUICK REVIEW**

How did the spread of the automobile transform the United States?

In what ways did the Roaring Twenties challenge traditional values?

"The Girls' Rebellion"

The August 1924 cover of *Redbook*, a popular women's magazine, portrays the kind of postadolescent girl who was making respectable families frantic. Flappers scandalized their middle-class parents by flouting the old moral code. This young woman sports the "badges of flapperhood," including what one critic called an "intoxication of rouge." Fictionalized, emotion-packed stories such as this brought the new woman into every woman's home. Picture Research Consultants & Archives.

A NEW ETHIC OF PERSONAL FREEDOM excited many Americans to seek pleasure without guilt in a whirl of activity that earned the decade the name "Roaring Twenties." Prohibition made lawbreakers of millions of otherwise decent folk. Flappers and "new women" challenged traditional gender boundaries. Other Americans enjoyed the Roaring Twenties through the words and images of vastly expanded mass communication, especially radio and movies. In America's big cities, particularly New York, a burst of creativity produced the "New Negro," who confounded and disturbed white Americans. The "Lost Generation" of writers, profoundly disillusioned with mainstream America's cultural direction, fled the country.

Prohibition

Republicans generally sought to curb the powers of government, but the twenties witnessed a great exception to this rule when the federal government implemented one of the last reforms of the Progressive Era: the Eighteenth Amendment, which banned the manufacture and sale of alcohol and took effect in January 1920 (see chapter 22). Drying up the rivers of liquor that Americans consumed, supporters of **prohibition** claimed, would eliminate crime, boost production, and lift the nation's morality. Instead, prohibition initiated a fourteen-year orgy of lawbreaking unparalleled in the nation's history.

prohibition
▶ The ban on the manufacture and sale of alcohol that went into effect in January 1920 with the Eighteenth Amendment. Prohibition proved almost impossible to enforce. By the end of the 1920s, most Americans wished it to end, and it was finally repealed in 1933.

Why did the relationship between urban and rural America deteriorate in the 1920s?

How did President Hoover respond to the economic crash of 1929?

What was life like in the early years of the depression?

Conclusion: Why did the hope of the 1920s turn to despair?

☑ **LearningCurve**
Check what you know.
bedfordstmartins.com
/roarkunderstanding

> CHRONOLOGY

1920
- Prohibition begins.
- Women get the vote.

1921
- Sheppard-Towner Act.

1923
- Equal Rights Amendment is defeated in Congress.

1927
- Charles Lindbergh flies nonstop across the Atlantic.

1929
- St. Valentine's Day murders.

The Treasury Department agents charged with enforcing prohibition faced a staggering task. Although they smashed more than 172,000 illegal stills in 1925 alone, loopholes in the law almost guaranteed failure. Sacramental wine was permitted, allowing fake clergy to party with bogus congregations. Farmers were allowed to ferment their own "fruit juices." Doctors and dentists could prescribe liquor for medicinal purposes.

In 1929, a Treasury agent in Indiana reported intense local resistance to enforcement of prohibition. "Conditions in most important cities very bad," he declared. "Lax and corrupt public officials great handicap . . . prevalence of drinking among minor boys and the . . . middle or better classes of adults." The "speakeasy," an illegal nightclub, became a common feature of the urban landscape. Speakeasies' dance floors led to the sexual integration of the formerly all-male drinking culture, changing American social life forever. Detroit, probably America's wettest city, was home to more than 20,000 illegal drinking establishments, making the alcohol business the city's second-largest industry, behind automobile manufacturing.

Eventually, serious criminals took over the liquor trade. During the first four years of prohibition, Chicago witnessed more than two hundred gang-related killings as rival mobs struggled for control of the lucrative liquor trade. The most notorious event came on St. Valentine's Day 1929, when Alphonse "Big Al" Capone's Italian-dominated mob machine-gunned seven members of a rival Irish

Confiscated Liquor

Revenue agents, some holding rifles, proudly display the bootleg liquor they have confiscated during a raid in Washington, D.C., in 1922. The carefully staged scene and the photographer on the roof indicate that the agents were eager to publicize their success. Successes like this were common during prohibition, but the criminalization of liquor could not permanently defeat "Satan in a bottle." The Granger Collection, NYC.

CHAPTER LOCATOR | How did big business shape the "New Era" of the 1920s? | In what ways did the Roaring Twenties challenge traditional values?

gang. Federal authorities finally sent Capone to prison for income tax evasion. "I violate the Prohibition law — sure," he told a reporter. "Who doesn't? The only difference is, I take more chances than the man who drinks a cocktail before dinner."

Americans overwhelmingly favored the repeal of the Eighteenth Amendment. In 1931, a panel of distinguished experts reported that prohibition, which supporters had defended as "a great social and economic experiment," had failed. The social and political costs of prohibition outweighed the benefits. Prohibition fueled criminal activity, corrupted the police, demoralized the judiciary, and caused ordinary citizens to disrespect the law. In 1933, the nation ended prohibition, making the Eighteenth Amendment the only constitutional amendment to be repealed.

The New Woman

Of all the changes in American life in the 1920s, none sparked more heated debate than the alternatives offered to the traditional roles of women. Increasing numbers of women worked and went to college, defying older gender norms. Even mainstream magazines such as the *Saturday Evening Post* began publishing stories about young, college-educated women who drank gin cocktails, smoked cigarettes, and wore skimpy dresses and dangly necklaces. Before the Great War, the **new woman** dwelt in New York City's bohemian Greenwich Village, but afterward the mass media brought her into middle-class America's living rooms.

When the Nineteenth Amendment, ratified in 1920, granted women the vote, feminists felt liberated and expected women to reshape the political landscape. A Kansas woman declared, "I went to bed last night a slave[;] I awoke this morning a *free woman*." Women began pressuring Congress to pass laws that especially concerned women, including measures to protect women in factories and grant federal aid to schools. Black women lobbied particularly for federal courts to assume jurisdiction over the crime of lynching. But women's only significant national legislative success came in 1921 when Congress enacted the Sheppard-Towner Act, which extended federal assistance to states seeking to reduce high infant mortality rates.

A number of factors helped thwart women's political influence. Male domination of both political parties, the rarity of female candidates, and lack of experience in voting, especially among recent immigrants, kept many women away from the polls. In the South, poll taxes, literacy tests, and outright terrorism continued to decimate the vote of African Americans, men and women alike.

Most important, rather than forming a solid voting bloc, feminists divided. Some argued for women's right to special protection; others demanded equal protection. The radical National Woman's Party fought for an Equal Rights Amendment that stated flatly: "Men and women shall have equal rights throughout the United States." The more moderate League of Women Voters feared that the amendment's wording threatened state laws that provided women special protection, such as preventing them from working on certain machines. Put before Congress in 1923, the Equal Rights Amendment went down to defeat, and radical women were forced to work for the causes of birth control, legal equality for minorities, and the end of child labor through other means.

new woman

▶ Alternative image of womanhood that came into the American mainstream in the 1920s. The mass media frequently portrayed young, college-educated women who drank, smoked, and wore skimpy dresses. New women also challenged American convictions about separate spheres for women and men and the sexual double standard.

Why did the relationship between urban and rural America deteriorate in the 1920s?

How did President Hoover respond to the economic crash of 1929?

What was life like in the early years of the depression?

Conclusion: Why did the hope of the 1920s turn to despair?

☑ LearningCurve
Check what you know.
bedfordstmartins.com
/roarkunderstanding

687

Economically, more women worked for pay — approximately one in four by 1930 — but they clustered in "women's jobs." The proportion of women working as secretaries, stenographers, and typists skyrocketed. Women almost monopolized the occupations of librarian, nurse, elementary school teacher, and telephone operator. Women also represented 40 percent of salesclerks by 1930. More female white-collar workers meant that fewer women were interested in protective legislation for women; new women wanted salaries and opportunities equal to men's.

Increased earnings gave working women more buying power in the new consumer culture. A stereotype soon emerged of the flapper, so called because of the short-lived fad of wearing unbuckled galoshes. The flapper had short "bobbed" hair, and she wore lipstick and rouge. She spent freely on the latest styles — dresses with short skirts, drop waists, bare arms, and no petticoats — and she danced all night to wild jazz.

The new woman both reflected and propelled the modern birth control movement. Margaret Sanger, the crusading pioneer for contraception during the Progressive Era (see chapter 21), restated her principal conviction in 1920: "No woman can call herself free until she can choose consciously whether she will or will not be a mother." By shifting strategy in the twenties, Sanger courted the conservative American Medical Association; linked birth control with the eugenics movement, which advocated limiting reproduction among "undesirable" groups; and thus made contraception a respectable subject for discussion.

Flapper style and values spread from coast to coast through films, novels, magazines, and advertisements. New women challenged American convictions about separate spheres for women and men, the double standard of sexual conduct, and Victorian ideas of proper female appearance and behavior. Although only a minority of American women became flappers, all women, even those who remained at home, felt the great changes of the era.

The New Negro

The 1920s witnessed the emergence not only of the "new woman" but also of the "New Negro." African Americans who challenged the caste system that confined dark-skinned Americans to the lowest levels of society confronted whites who insisted that race relations would not change.

The prominent African American intellectual W. E. B. Du Bois and the National Association for the Advancement of Colored People (NAACP) aggressively pursued the passage of a federal antilynching law to counter mob violence against blacks in the South. At the same time, the Jamaican-born visionary Marcus Garvey urged African Americans to rediscover the heritage of Africa, take pride in their own achievements, and maintain racial purity by avoiding miscegenation. In 1917, Garvey launched the Universal Negro Improvement Association (UNIA) to help African Americans gain economic and political independence entirely outside white society. In 1919, the UNIA created its own shipping company, the Black Star Line, to support the "Back to Africa" movement among black Americans. In 1927, the federal government pinned charges of illegal practices on Garvey and deported him to Jamaica. Nevertheless, the issues Garvey raised about racial pride, black identity, and the search for equality persisted, and his legacy remains at the center of black nationalist thought.

CHAPTER LOCATOR | How did big business shape the "New Era" of the 1920s? | In what ways did the Roaring Twenties challenge traditional values?

CHAPTER 23
688 FROM NEW ERA TO GREAT DEPRESSION

Still, most African Americans maintained hope in the American promise. In New York City, hope and talent came together. New York City's black population jumped 115 percent (from 152,000 to 327,000) in the 1920s, and in Harlem in uptown Manhattan an extraordinary mix of black artists, sculptors, novelists, musicians, and poets set out to create a distinctive African American culture that drew on their identities as Americans and Africans. As scholar Alain Locke put it in 1925, they introduced to the world the **New Negro**, who rose from the ashes of slavery and segregation to proclaim African Americans' creative genius.

The emergence of the New Negro came to be known as the Harlem Renaissance. Building on the independence and pride displayed by black soldiers during the war, black artists sought to defeat the fresh onslaught of racial discrimination and violence with poems, paintings, and plays. "We younger Negro artists . . . intend to express our individual dark-skinned selves without fear or shame," poet Langston Hughes said of the Harlem Renaissance. "If white people are pleased, we are glad. If they are not, it doesn't matter. We know we are beautiful. And ugly, too."

The Harlem Renaissance produced dazzling talent. Despite such vibrancy, Harlem for most whites remained a separate black ghetto known only for its lively nightlife. Fashionable whites crowded into Harlem's segregated nightclubs, the most famous of which was the Cotton Club, where they believed they could hear

New Negro

▶ Term referring to African Americans who, through the arts, challenged American racial hierarchy. The New Negro emerged in New York City in the 1920s in what became known as the Harlem Renaissance, which produced dazzling literary, musical, and artistic talent.

Duke Ellington at the Cotton Club

Duke Ellington, at the piano, presides over the floor show at the Cotton Club in Harlem, where black performers played for white audiences. During the years from 1927 to 1931, when his orchestra was the house band at the Cotton Club, Ellington recorded more than one hundred of his compositions, establishing him as America's greatest composer and bandleader. The Frank Driggs Collection.

| Why did the relationship between urban and rural America deteriorate in the 1920s? | How did President Hoover respond to the economic crash of 1929? | What was life like in the early years of the depression? | Conclusion: Why did the hope of the 1920s turn to despair? | ✓ LearningCurve Check what you know. bedfordstmartins.com /roarkunderstanding |

"real" jazz, a relatively new musical form, in its "natural" surroundings. The vigor of the Harlem Renaissance left a powerful legacy for black Americans, but the creative burst did little in the short run to dissolve the prejudice of white society.

> Leaders of the Harlem Renaissance	
James Weldon Johnson	writer, civil rights leader
Langston Hughes, Claude McKay, Countee Cullen	poets
Zora Neale Hurston	novelist
Aaron Douglas	artist

Entertainment for the Masses

In the 1920s, popular culture, like consumer goods, was mass-produced and mass-consumed. The proliferation of movies, radios, music, and sports meant that Americans found plenty to do, and in doing the same things, they helped create a national culture.

Nothing offered escapist delights like the movies. Hollywood, California, discovered the successful formula of combining opulence, sex, and adventure. Admission was cheap, and by 1929 the movies were drawing more than 80 million people in a single week, as many as lived in the entire country. Rudolph Valentino, described as "catnip to women," and Clara Bow, the "It Girl" (everyone knew what *it* was), became household names. Most loved of all was the comic Charlie Chaplin, whose famous character, the wistful Little Tramp, showed an endearing inability to cope with the rules and complexities of modern life.

Americans also found heroes in sports. Baseball solidified its place as the national pastime in the 1920s. It remained essentially a game played by and for the working class. In George Herman "Babe" Ruth, baseball had the most cherished free spirit of the time. The rowdy escapades of the "Sultan of Swat" demonstrated that sports offered a way to break out of the ordinariness of everyday life. By "his sheer exuberance," one sportswriter declared, Ruth "has lightened the cares of the world."

The public also fell in love with a young boxer from the grim mining districts of Colorado. As a teenager, Jack Dempsey had made his living hanging around saloons betting he could beat anyone in the house. When he took the heavy-weight crown just after World War I, he was revered as the people's champ, a stand-in for the average American who felt increasingly confined by bureaucracy and machine-made culture.

Football, essentially a college sport, held greater sway with the upper classes. But in keeping with the times, football moved toward a more commercial spectacle. Harold "Red" Grange, "the Galloping Ghost," led the way by going from stardom at the University of Illinois to the Chicago Bears in the new professional football league.

The decade's hero worship reached its zenith in the celebration of Charles Lindbergh, a young pilot who set out on May 20, 1927, to become the first person to fly nonstop across the Atlantic. Newspapers tagged Lindbergh "the Lone Eagle" — the perfect hero for an age that celebrated individual accomplishment. "Charles Lindbergh," one journalist proclaimed, "is the stuff out of which have

CHAPTER LOCATOR | How did big business shape the "New Era" of the 1920s? | In what ways did the Roaring Twenties challenge traditional values?

CHAPTER 23
690   FROM NEW ERA TO GREAT DEPRESSION

been made the pioneers that opened up the wilderness. His are the qualities which we, as a people, must nourish." Lindbergh realized, however, that technical and organizational complexity was fast reducing chances for solitary achievement. Consequently, he titled his book about the flight *We* (1927) to include the machine that had made it all possible.

Another machine — the radio — became crucial to mass culture in the 1920s. The nation's first licensed radio station, KDKA in Pittsburgh, began broadcasting in 1920, and soon American airwaves buzzed with news, sermons, soap operas, sports, comedy, and music. Because they could now reach prospective customers in their own homes, advertisers bankrolled radio's rapid growth. Between 1922 and 1929, the number of radio stations in the United States increased from 30 to 606. In just seven years, homes with radios jumped from 60,000 to a staggering 10.25 million.

The Lost Generation

Some writers and artists felt alienated from America's mass-culture society, which they found shallow, anti-intellectual, and materialistic. They believed that business culture blighted American life. Silly movie stars disgusted them. Young, white, and mostly college educated, these expatriates, as they came to be called, felt embittered by the war and renounced the progressives who had promoted it as a crusade. For them, Europe — not Hollywood or Harlem — seemed the place to seek their renaissance.

The American-born writer Gertrude Stein, long established in Paris, remarked famously as the young exiles gathered around her, "They are the lost generation." Most of the expatriates, however, believed to the contrary that they had finally found themselves. The Lost Generation helped launch the most creative period in American art and literature in the twentieth century. The novelist whose spare, clean style best exemplified the expatriate efforts to make art mirror basic reality was Ernest Hemingway. Admirers found the terse language and hard lessons of his novel *The Sun Also Rises* (1926) to be perfect expressions of a world stripped of illusions.

Many writers who remained in America were exiles in spirit. Before the war, intellectuals had eagerly joined progressive reform movements. Afterward, they were more likely critics of American cultural vulgarity. Novelist Sinclair Lewis in *Main Street* (1920) and *Babbitt* (1922) satirized his native Midwest as a cultural wasteland. Humorists such as James Thurber created outlandish characters to poke fun at American stupidity and inhibitions. And southern writers, led by William Faulkner, explored the South's grim class and race heritage. Worries about alienation surfaced as well. F. Scott Fitzgerald spoke sadly in *This Side of Paradise* (1920) of a disillusioned generation "grown up to find all Gods dead, all wars fought, all faiths in man shaken."

QUICK REVIEW <

How did the new freedoms of the 1920s challenge older conceptions of gender and race?

Why did the relationship between urban and rural America deteriorate in the 1920s?

How did President Hoover respond to the economic crash of 1929?

What was life like in the early years of the depression?

Conclusion: Why did the hope of the 1920s turn to despair?

LearningCurve Check what you know. bedfordstmartins.com /roarkunderstanding

Why did the relationship between urban and rural America deteriorate in the 1920s?

WKKK Badge

Half a million women were members of the Women of the Ku Klux Klan (WKKK). Klanswomen fit perfectly within the KKK because the organization proclaimed itself the defender of the traditional virtues of pure womanhood and decent homes. This badge from Harrisburg, Pennsylvania, advertises the local WKKK's support for a "home for orphan and dependent children." Collection of Janice L. and David J. Frent.

LARGE AREAS OF THE COUNTRY did not share in the wealth of the 1920s. By the end of the decade, 40 percent of the nation's farmers were landless, and 90 percent of rural homes lacked indoor plumbing, gas, or electricity. Rural America's traditional distrust of urban America turned to despair in the 1920s when the census reported that the majority of the population had shifted to the city (**Map 23.2**). Urban domination over the nation's political and cultural life and sharply rising economic disparity drove rural Americans in often ugly, reactionary directions.

Cities seemed to stand for everything rural areas stood against. Rural America imagined itself as solidly Anglo-Saxon (despite the presence of millions of African Americans in the South and Mexican Americans, Native Americans, and Asian Americans in the West), and the cities seemed to be filled with undesirable immigrants. Rural America was the home of old-time Protestant religion, and the cities teemed with Catholics, Jews, liberal Protestants, and atheists. Rural America championed old-fashioned moral standards — abstinence and self-denial — while the cities spawned every imaginable vice. In the 1920s, frustrated rural people sought to recapture their country by helping to push through prohibition, dam the flow of immigrants, revive the Ku Klux Klan, defend the Bible as literal truth, and defeat an urban Roman Catholic for president.

CHAPTER LOCATOR | How did big business shape the "New Era" of the 1920s? | In what ways did the Roaring Twenties challenge traditional values?

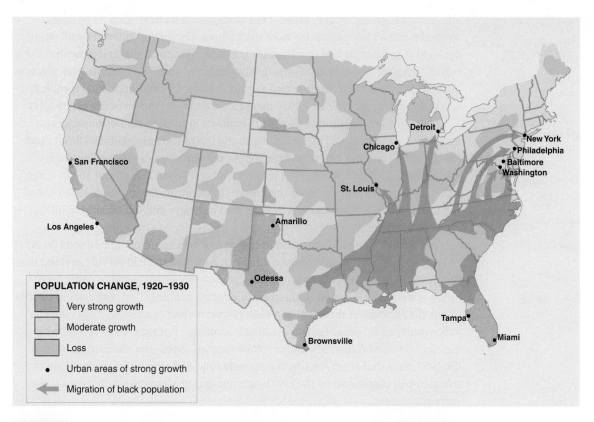

POPULATION CHANGE, 1920–1930

- Very strong growth
- Moderate growth
- Loss
- • Urban areas of strong growth
- ← Migration of black population

MAP 23.2 ■ The Shift from Rural to Urban Population, 1920–1930

The movement of whites and Hispanics toward urban and agricultural opportunity made Florida, the West, and the Southwest the regions of fastest population growth. By contrast, large numbers of blacks left the rural South to find a better life in the North. Almost all migrating blacks went from the countryside to cities in distant parts of the nation, while white and Hispanic migrants tended to move shorter distances toward familiar places.

> MAP ACTIVITY

READING THE MAP: Which states had the strongest growth? To which cities did southern blacks predominantly migrate?

CONNECTIONS: What conditions in the countryside made the migration to urban areas appealing to many rural Americans? In what social and cultural ways did rural America view itself as different from urban America?

Rejecting the Undesirables

Before the war, when about a million immigrants arrived each year, some Americans warned that unassimilable foreigners were smothering the nation. War against Germany and its allies expanded nativist and antiradical sentiment. After the war, large-scale immigration resumed (another 800,000 immigrants arrived in 1921) at a moment when industrialists no longer needed new factory laborers. Returning veterans, as well as African American and Mexican migration, had relieved labor shortages. Moreover, union leaders feared that millions of poor immigrants would undercut their efforts to organize American workers. Rural America's God-fearing Protestants were particularly alarmed that most of the immigrants were Catholic or Jewish. In 1921, Congress responded by severely restricting immigration.

In 1924, Congress very nearly slammed the door shut. The **Johnson-Reed Act** limited the number of immigrants to no more than 161,000 a year and established quotas for each European nation. The act revealed the fear and bigotry that fueled

Johnson-Reed Act

▶ 1924 law that severely restricted immigration to the United States to no more than 161,000 a year, with quotas for each European nation. The racist restrictions were designed to staunch the flow of immigrants from southern and eastern Europe and from Asia.

| Why did the relationship between urban and rural America deteriorate in the 1920s? | How did President Hoover respond to the economic crash of 1929? | What was life like in the early years of the depression? | Conclusion: Why did the hope of the 1920s turn to despair? | ✓ LearningCurve Check what you know. bedfordstmartins.com /roarkunderstanding |

> CHRONOLOGY

1921
- Congress restricts immigration.

1924
- Johnson-Reed Act.
- Indian Citizenship Act.

1925
- Scopes trial.

1927
- Nicola Sacco and Bartolomeo Vanzetti are executed.

1928
- Herbert Hoover is elected president.

anti-immigration legislation. While it cut immigration by more than 80 percent, it squeezed some nationalities far more than others. Backers of Johnson-Reed, who declared that America had become the "garbage can and the dumping ground of the world," manipulated quotas to ensure entry only to "good" immigrants from western Europe. The law effectively reversed the trend toward immigration from southern and eastern Europe, which by 1914 had amounted to 75 percent of the yearly total.

The 1924 law reaffirmed the 1880s legislation barring Chinese immigrants and added Japanese and other Asians to the list of the excluded. But it left open immigration from the Western Hemisphere because farmers in the Southwest demanded continued access to cheap agricultural labor. During the 1920s, some half a million Mexicans crossed the border. In addition, Congress in 1924 passed the Indian Citizenship Act, which extended suffrage and citizenship to all American Indians.

Antiforeign hysteria climaxed in the trial of two anarchist immigrants from Italy, Nicola Sacco and Bartolomeo Vanzetti. Arrested in 1920 for robbery and murder in South Braintree, Massachusetts, the men were sentenced to death by a judge who openly referred to them as "anarchist bastards." In response to doubts about the fairness of the verdict, a blue-ribbon review committee found the trial judge guilty of a "grave breach of official decorum" but refused to recommend a motion for retrial. When Massachusetts executed Sacco and Vanzetti on August 23, 1927, fifty thousand American mourners followed the caskets, convinced that the men had died because they were immigrants and radicals, not because they were murderers.

The Rebirth of the Ku Klux Klan

Ku Klux Klan

▶ Secret society that first thwarted black freedom after the Civil War but was reborn in 1915 to fight against perceived threats posed by blacks, immigrants, radicals, feminists, Catholics, and Jews. The new Klan spread well beyond the South in the 1920s.

The nation's sour antiforeign mood struck a responsive chord in members of the secret society called the **Ku Klux Klan**. The Klan first appeared in the South during Reconstruction to thwart black freedom and expired with the reestablishment of white supremacy (see chapter 16). In 1915, the Klan was reborn at Stone Mountain, Georgia, but when the new Klan extended its targets beyond black Americans, it quickly spread beyond the South. Under a banner proclaiming "100 percent Americanism," the Klan promised to defend family, morality, and traditional American values against the threats posed by blacks, immigrants, radicals, feminists, Catholics, and Jews.

Building on the frustrations of rural America, the Klan in the 1920s spread throughout the nation, almost controlling Indiana and influencing politics in Illinois, California, Oregon, Texas, Louisiana, Oklahoma, and Kansas. In 1926, Klan imperial wizard Hiram Wesley Evans described the assault of modernity: "One by one all our traditional moral standards went by the boards or were so disregarded that they ceased to be binding," he explained. "The sacredness of our Sabbath, of our homes, of chastity, and finally even of our right to teach our own children in schools [represented] fundamental facts and truth torn away from us."

Eventually, social changes, along with lawless excess, crippled the Klan. Immigration restrictions eased the worry about invading foreigners, and sensational wrongdoing by Klan leaders cost it the support of traditional moralists. Grand Dragon David Stephenson of Indiana, for example, went to jail for the kidnapping and rape of a woman who subsequently committed suicide. Yet the

CHAPTER LOCATOR | How did big business shape the "New Era" of the 1920s?

In what ways did the Roaring Twenties challenge traditional values?

694   CHAPTER 23
FROM NEW ERA TO GREAT DEPRESSION

social grievances, economic problems, and religious anxieties of the countryside and small towns remained alive, ready to be ignited.

The Scopes Trial

In 1925 in a Tennessee courtroom, old-time religion and the new spirit of science went head-to-head. The confrontation occurred after several southern states passed legislation against the teaching of Charles Darwin's theory of evolution in the public schools. Scientists and civil liberties organizations clamored for a challenge to the law, and John Scopes, a young biology teacher in Dayton, Tennessee, offered to test his state's ban on teaching evolution. When Scopes came to trial, Clarence Darrow, a brilliant defense lawyer from Chicago, volunteered to defend him. Darrow, an avowed agnostic, took on the prosecution's William Jennings Bryan, three-time Democratic nominee for president, fervent fundamentalist, and symbol of rural America.

The **Scopes trial** quickly degenerated into a media circus. The first trial to be covered live on radio, it attracted a nationwide audience. When, under relentless questioning by Darrow, Bryan declared on the witness stand that he did indeed believe that the world had been created in six days and that Jonah had lived in the belly of a whale, his humiliation in the eyes of most urban observers was complete. Nevertheless, the Tennessee court upheld the law and punished Scopes with a $100 fine. Although fundamentalism won the battle, it lost the war. Baltimore journalist H. L. Mencken had the last word in a merciless obituary for Bryan, who died just a week after the trial ended. Portraying the "monkey trial" as a battle between the country and the city, Mencken flayed Bryan as a "charlatan, a mountebank, a zany without shame or dignity," motivated solely by "hatred of the city men who had laughed at him for so long."

As Mencken's acid prose indicated, Bryan's humiliation was not purely a victory of reason and science. It also revealed the disdain urban people felt for country people and the values they clung to. The Ku Klux Klan revival and the Scopes trial dramatized and inflamed divisions between city and country, intellectuals and the uneducated, the privileged and the poor, the scoffers and the faithful.

Scopes trial
▶ 1925 trial of John Scopes, a biology teacher in Dayton, Tennessee, for violating his state's ban on teaching evolution. The trial created a nationwide media frenzy and came to be seen as a showdown between urban and rural values.

Al Smith and the Election of 1928

The presidential election of 1928 brought many of the developments of the 1920s — prohibition, immigration, religion, and the clash of rural and urban values — into sharp focus. Republicans emphasized the economic success of their party's pro-business government and turned to Herbert Hoover, the energetic secretary of commerce and leading public symbol of 1920s prosperity. But because both parties generally agreed that the American economy was basically sound, the campaign turned on social issues that divided Americans.

The Democrats nominated four-time governor of New York Alfred E. Smith. Smith seemed to represent all that rural Americans feared and resented. A child of immigrants, Smith got his start in politics with the help of New York's Tammany Hall political machine, to many the epitome of big-city corruption. He denounced immigration quotas, signed New York State's anti-Klan bill, and opposed prohibition,

| Why did the relationship between urban and rural America deteriorate in the 1920s? | How did President Hoover respond to the economic crash of 1929? | What was life like in the early years of the depression? | Conclusion: Why did the hope of the 1920s turn to despair? | ✔ LearningCurve Check what you know. bedfordstmartins.com /roarkunderstanding |

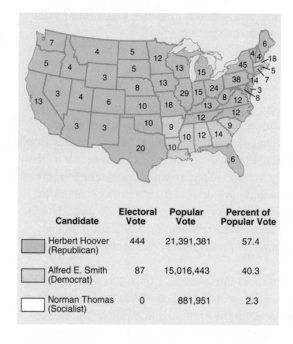

Candidate	Electoral Vote	Popular Vote	Percent of Popular Vote
Herbert Hoover (Republican)	444	21,391,381	57.4
Alfred E. Smith (Democrat)	87	15,016,443	40.3
Norman Thomas (Socialist)	0	881,951	2.3

MAP 23.3 ■ The Election of 1928

believing that it was a nativist attack on immigrant customs. Prohibition forces dubbed him "Alcohol Al," but Smith's greatest vulnerability in the heartland was his religion. He was the first Catholic to run for president. A Methodist bishop in Virginia denounced Roman Catholicism as "the Mother of ignorance, superstition, intolerance and sin" and begged Protestants not to vote for a candidate who represented "the kind of dirty people that you find today on the sidewalks of New York."

Hoover, who neatly combined the images of morality, efficiency, service, and prosperity, won the election by a landslide (**Map 23.3**). He received nearly 58 percent of the vote and gained 444 electoral votes to Smith's 87. The only bright spot for Democrats was the nation's cities, which voted Democratic, indicating the rising strength of ethnic minorities, including Smith's fellow Catholics.

> **QUICK REVIEW**

How did some Americans resist cultural change?

CHAPTER LOCATOR | How did big business shape the "New Era" of the 1920s? | In what ways did the Roaring Twenties challenge traditional values?

CHAPTER 23
696 FROM NEW ERA TO GREAT DEPRESSION

How did President Hoover respond to the economic crash of 1929?

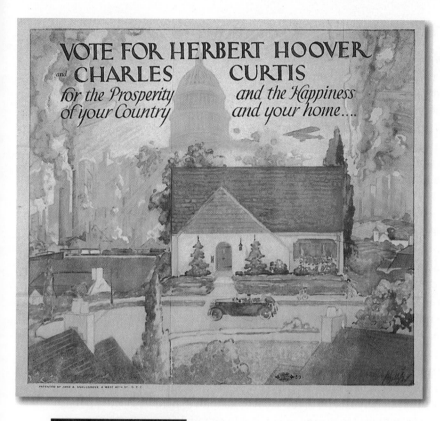

Hoover Campaign Poster

This poster effectively illustrates Herbert Hoover's 1928 campaign message: Republican administrations in the 1920s had produced middle-class prosperity, complete with a house in the suburbs and the latest automobile. To remind voters that Hoover as secretary of commerce had promoted industry that made the suburban dream possible, the poster portrays smoking chimneys at a discreet distance. Collection of Janice L. and David J. Frent.

AT HIS INAUGURATION IN 1929, Herbert Hoover told the American people, "Given a chance to go forward with the policies of the last eight years, we shall soon with the help of God be in sight of the day when poverty will be banished from this nation." Those words came back to haunt Hoover when eight months later the prosperity he touted collapsed in the stock market crash of 1929. The nation ended nearly three decades of barely interrupted economic growth. Like much of the world, the United States fell into the most serious economic depression of all time. Hoover's limited response to economic catastrophe proved inadequate.

| Why did the relationship between urban and rural America deteriorate in the 1920s? | **How did President Hoover respond to the economic crash of 1929?** | What was life like in the early years of the depression? | Conclusion: Why did the hope of the 1920s turn to despair? | ☑ LearningCurve Check what you know. bedfordstmartins.com /roarkunderstanding |

697

> CHRONOLOGY

1929
- Stock market collapses.

1930
- Congress authorizes $420 million for public works projects.
- Hawley-Smoot tariff.

1932
- Reconstruction Finance Corporation is established.

Herbert Hoover: The Great Engineer

When Herbert Hoover became president in 1929, he seemed the perfect choice to lead a prosperous business nation. His rise from poor Iowa orphan to one of the world's most celebrated mining engineers personified America's rags-to-riches ideal. His success in managing efforts to feed civilian victims of the fighting during World War I won him acclaim as "the Great Humanitarian" and led Woodrow Wilson to name him head of the Food Administration once the United States entered the war. Hoover's reputation soared even higher as secretary of commerce in the Harding and Coolidge administrations.

Hoover belonged to the progressive wing of his party. "The time when the employer could ride roughshod over his labor[ers] is disappearing with the doctrine of 'laissez-faire' on which it is founded," he declared in 1909. He urged a limited business-government partnership that would manage the sweeping changes Americans were experiencing. Hoover brought a reform agenda to the White House: "We want to see a nation built of home owners and farm owners. We want to see their savings protected. We want to see them in steady jobs. We want to see more and more of them insured against death and accident, unemployment and old age. We want them all secure."

But Hoover also had ideological and political liabilities. Principles that appeared strengths in the prosperous 1920s — individual self-reliance, industrial self-management, and a limited federal government — became straitjackets when economic catastrophe struck. Moreover, Hoover had never held an elected public office, had a poor political touch, and was too thin-skinned to be an effective politician. Prophetically, he confided to a friend his fear that "if some unprecedented calamity should come upon the nation . . . I would be sacrificed to the unreasoning disappointment of a people who expected too much." The distorted national economy set the stage for the calamity Hoover so feared.

The Distorted Economy

In the spring of 1929, the United States enjoyed a fragile prosperity. Although America had become the world's leading economy, it had done little to help rebuild Europe's shattered economy after World War I. Instead, the Republican administrations demanded that Allied nations repay their war loans, creating a tangled web of debts and reparations that sapped Europe's economic vitality. Moreover, to boost American business, the United States enacted tariffs that prevented other nations from selling their goods to Americans. Fewer sales meant that foreign nations had less money to buy American goods. American banks propped up the nation's export trade by extending credit to foreign customers, deepening their debt.

America's domestic economy was also in trouble. Wealth was unevenly distributed. Farmers continued to suffer from low prices and chronic indebtedness; the average income of farm families was only $240 per year. The wages of industrial workers, though rising during the decade, failed to keep up with productivity and corporate profits. Overall, nearly two-thirds of all American families lived on less than the $2,000 per year that economists estimated would "supply only basic necessities." In sharp contrast, the wealthiest 1 percent of the population

CHAPTER LOCATOR | How did big business shape the "New Era" of the 1920s? | In what ways did the Roaring Twenties challenge traditional values?

received 15 percent of the nation's income — the amount received by the poorest 42 percent. The Coolidge administration worsened the deepening inequality by cutting taxes on the wealthy.

By 1929, the inequality of wealth produced a serious problem in consumption. The rich spent lavishly, but they could absorb only a tiny fraction of the nation's output. For a time, the new device of installment buying — buying on credit — kept consumer demand up. By the end of the decade, four out of five cars and two out of three radios were bought on credit.

Signs of economic trouble began to appear at mid-decade. New construction slowed down. Automobile sales faltered. Companies began cutting back production and laying off workers. Between 1921 and 1928, as investment and loan opportunities faded, five thousand banks failed, wiping out the life savings of hundreds of thousands.

The Crash of 1929

Even as the economy faltered, Americans remained upbeat. Hoping for even bigger slices of the economic pie, Americans speculated wildly in the stock market on Wall Street. Between 1924 and 1929, the values of stocks listed on the New York

Stock Market Crash

Edward Laning, a mural painter who lost his personal fortune in the stock market crash, gained a measure of revenge in this melodramatic version of the panic on the Stock Exchange floor. Stock Exchange president Richard Whitney stands illuminated and unperturbed in the center as prices and brokers collapse around him. A few years later, however, Whitney went to prison for stealing from other people's accounts to cover his own losses. Collection of John. P. Axelrod/ Picture Research Consultants & Archives.

Why did the relationship between urban and rural America deteriorate in the 1920s?

How did President Hoover respond to the economic crash of 1929?

What was life like in the early years of the depression?

Conclusion: Why did the hope of the 1920s turn to despair?

✓ LearningCurve
Check what you know.
bedfordstmartins.com
/roarkunderstanding

Stock Exchange increased by more than 400 percent. Buying stocks on margin — that is, putting up only part of the money at the time of purchase — accelerated. Many people got rich this way, but those who bought on credit could finance their loans only if their stocks increased in value.

Finally, in the autumn of 1929, the market hesitated. Investors nervously began to sell their overvalued stocks. The dip quickly became a panic on October 24, the day that came to be known as Black Thursday. More panic selling came on Black Tuesday, October 29, the day the market suffered a greater fall than ever before. In the next six months, the stock market lost six-sevenths of its total value.

It was once thought that the crash alone caused the Great Depression. It did not. In 1929, the national and international economies were already riddled with severe problems. But the dramatic losses in the stock market crash and the fear of risking what was left acted as a great brake on economic activity. The collapse on Wall Street shattered the New Era's confidence that America would enjoy perpetually expanding prosperity.

Hoover and the Limits of Individualism

When the bubble broke, Americans expressed relief that Herbert Hoover resided in the White House. Not surprisingly for a man who had been such an active secretary of commerce, Hoover acted quickly to arrest the decline. In November 1929, to keep the stock market collapse from ravaging the entire economy, Hoover called a White House conference of business and labor leaders. He urged them to join in a voluntary plan for recovery: Businesses would maintain production and keep their workers on the job; labor would accept existing wages, hours, and conditions. Within a few months, however, the bargain fell apart. As demand for their products declined, industrialists cut production, sliced wages, and laid off workers. Poorly paid or unemployed workers could not buy much, and their decreased spending led to further cuts in production and further loss of jobs. Thus began the terrible spiral of economic decline.

> Hoover's Attempts to Deal with the Depression	
1929	• Agricultural Marketing Act allowed the federal government to buy surplus agricultural products to raise prices.
1930	• Hawley-Smoot tariff established the highest tariff rates in U.S. history. • Congress authorized $420 million for public works projects to give the unemployed jobs.
1932	• Reconstruction Finance Corporation was established to lend federal money to banks and corporations.

Reconstruction Finance Corporation (RFC)

▶ Federal agency established by Herbert Hoover in 1932 to help American industry by lending government funds to endangered banks and corporations, which Hoover hoped would benefit people at the bottom through trickle-down economics. In practice, this strategy provided little help to the poor.

But with each year of Hoover's term, the economy weakened. Tariffs did not end the suffering of farmers because foreign nations retaliated with increased tariffs of their own that crippled American farmers' ability to sell abroad. With the establishment of the **Reconstruction Finance Corporation (RFC)**, Hoover employed the theory of trickle-down economics: Pump money into the economy at the top, and in the long run the people at the bottom would benefit. Or as one wag put it, "Feed the sparrows by feeding the horses." In the end, very little of what critics of the RFC called a "millionaires' dole" trickled down to the poor.

Meanwhile, hundreds of thousands of workers lost their jobs each month. By 1932, an astounding one-quarter of the American workforce — nearly thirteen million people — were unemployed. There was no direct federal assistance, and state services and private charities were swamped. The depression that began in 1929 devastated much of the world, but no other industrialized nation provided such feeble support to the jobless. Cries grew louder for the federal government to give hurting people relief.

Hoover's response revealed the limits of his conception of the government's proper role in fighting the economic disaster. He compared direct federal aid to the needy to the "dole" in Britain, which he thought destroyed the moral fiber of the chronically unemployed. The poor, he said, could rely on their neighbors to protect them "from hunger and cold." In 1931, he allowed the Red Cross to distribute government-owned agricultural surpluses to the hungry. In 1932, he relaxed his principles further to offer small federal loans, not gifts, to the states to help them in their relief efforts. But Hoover's circumscribed notions of legitimate government action proved vastly inadequate to address the problems of restarting the economy and ending human suffering.

QUICK REVIEW <

Why did the American economy collapse in 1929?

| Why did the relationship between urban and rural America deteriorate in the 1920s? | How did President Hoover respond to the economic crash of 1929? | What was life like in the early years of the depression? | Conclusion: Why did the hope of the 1920s turn to despair? | ✓ LearningCurve Check what you know. bedfordstmartins.com /roarkunderstanding |

701

> What was life like in the early years of the depression?

An Unemployed Youth

Joblessness was frightening and humiliating. Brought up to believe that if you worked hard, you got ahead, the unemployed had difficulty seeing failure to find work as anything other than personal failure. We can only imagine this young man's story. Utterly alone, sitting on a bench that might be his bed, his head in his hands, he looks emotionally battered and perhaps defeated. Library of Congress.

IN 1930, SUFFERING on a massive scale set in. Men and women hollow-eyed with hunger grew increasingly bewildered and angry in the face of cruel contradictions. They saw agricultural surpluses pile up in the countryside and knew that their children were going to bed hungry. They saw factories standing idle, yet they knew that they and millions of others were willing to work. The gap between the American people and leaders who failed to resolve these contradictions widened as the depression deepened. By 1932, America's economic problems had created a dangerous social and political crisis.

The Human Toll

Statistics only hint at the human tragedy of the Great Depression. When Herbert Hoover took office in 1929, the American economy stood at its peak. When he left in 1933, it had reached its twentieth-century low (**Figure 23.2**). In 1929, national income was $88 billion. By 1933, it had declined to $40 billion. In 1929, unemployment was 3.1 percent, or 1.5 million workers. By 1933, unemployment stood at

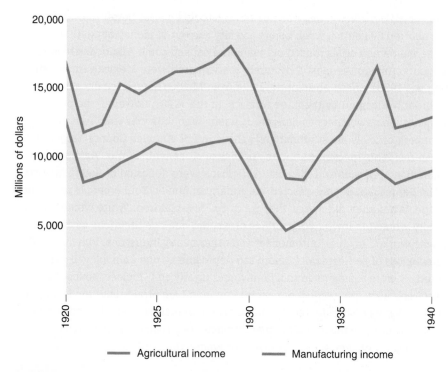

> CHRONOLOGY

1931
- Scottsboro Boys are arrested.
- Harlan County, Kentucky, coal strike.

1932
- River Rouge factory demonstration.
- National Farmers' Holiday Association is formed.

FIGURE 23.2 ■ Manufacturing and Agricultural Income, 1920–1940

After economic collapse, recovery in the 1930s began under New Deal auspices. The sharp declines in 1937–1938, when federal spending was reduced, indicated that New Deal stimuli were still needed to restore manufacturing and agricultural income.

25 percent, almost 13 million workers. By 1932, more than 9,000 banks had shut their doors, wiping out millions of savings accounts.

Jobless, homeless victims wandered in search of work, and the tramp, or hobo, became one of the most visible figures of the decade. Riding the rails or hitchhiking, a million vagabonds moved southward and westward looking for seasonal agricultural work. Other unemployed men and women, sick or less hopeful, huddled in doorways, overcome, one man remembered, by "helpless despair and submission." Scavengers haunted alleys behind restaurants in search of food. "I don't want to steal," a Pennsylvania man wrote to the governor in 1931, "but I won't let my wife and boy cry for something to eat. . . . How long is this going to keep up? I cannot stand it any longer."

Rural poverty was most acute. Tenant farmers and sharecroppers, mainly in the South, came to symbolize how poverty crushed the human spirit. Eight and a half million people, three million of them black, crowded into cabins without plumbing, electricity, or running water. They subsisted — just barely — on salt pork, cornmeal, molasses, beans, peas, and whatever they could hunt or fish. When economist John Maynard Keynes was asked whether anything like this degradation had existed before, he replied, "Yes, it was called the Dark Ages and it lasted four hundred years."

There was no federal assistance to meet this human catastrophe, only a patchwork of strapped charities and destitute state and local agencies. For a family of four without any income, the best the city of Philadelphia could do was

Why did the relationship between urban and rural America deteriorate in the 1920s?

How did President Hoover respond to the economic crash of 1929?

What was life like in the early years of the depression?

Conclusion: Why did the hope of the 1920s turn to despair?

✓ LearningCurve
Check what you know.
bedfordstmartins.com
/roarkunderstanding

703

provide $5.50 per week. That was not enough to live on but better than Detroit, which allotted 60 cents a week before the city ran out of money altogether.

The deepening crisis roused old fears and caused some Americans to look for scapegoats. Among the most thoroughly scapegoated were Mexican Americans. During the 1920s, cheap agricultural labor from Mexico flowed legally across the U.S. border, welcomed by the large farmers. In the 1930s, however, the public denounced the newcomers as dangerous aliens who took jobs from Americans. Government officials, most prominently those in Los Angeles County, targeted Mexican residents for deportation regardless of citizenship status. As many as half a million Mexicans and Mexican Americans were deported or fled to Mexico.

The depression deeply affected the American family. Young people postponed marriage. When they did marry, they produced few children. White women, who generally worked in low-paying service areas, did not lose their jobs as often as men who worked in steel, automobile, and other heavy industries. Idle husbands suffered a loss of self-esteem. "Before the depression," one unemployed man reported, "I wore the pants in this family, and rightly so." Jobless, he lost "self-respect" and also "the respect of my children, and I am afraid that I am losing my wife." Employers discriminated against married women workers, but necessity continued to drive women into the marketplace. As a result, by 1940 some 25 percent more women were employed for wages than in 1930.

Denial and Escape

President Hoover assured the American nation that economic recovery was on its way, but the president's optimism was contradicted by makeshift shantytowns, called "Hoovervilles," that sprang up on the edges of America's cities. Bitter jokes circulated about the increasingly unpopular president. One told of Hoover asking for a nickel to telephone a friend. Flipping him a dime, an aide said, "Here, call them both."

While Hoover practiced denial, other Americans sought refuge from reality at the movies. Throughout the depression, between 60 million and 75 million people (nearly two-thirds of the nation) scraped together enough change to fill the movie palaces every week. Box office hits such as *Forty-second Street* and *Gold Diggers of 1933* capitalized on the hope that prosperity lay just around the corner. But a few filmmakers grappled with realities rather than escape them. *The Public Enemy* (1931) taught hard lessons about gangsters' ill-gotten gains. Indeed, under the new production code of 1930, designed to protect public morals, all movies had to find some way to show that crime did not pay.

Despite Hollywood's efforts to keep Americans on the right side of the law, crime increased. In the countryside, the plight of people who had lost their farms to bank foreclosures led to the romantic idea that bank robbers were only getting back what banks had stolen from the poor. Woody Guthrie, the populist folksinger from Oklahoma, captured the public's tolerance for outlaws in his tribute to a murderous bank robber with a choirboy face, "The Ballad of Pretty Boy Floyd":

> Yes, as through this world I've wandered
> I've seen lots of funny men;
> Some will rob you with a six-gun,
> And some with a fountain pen.

CHAPTER LOCATOR | How did big business shape the "New Era" of the 1920s? | In what ways did the Roaring Twenties challenge traditional values?

704   CHAPTER 23
FROM NEW ERA TO GREAT DEPRESSION

And as through your life you travel,
Yes, as through your life you roam,
You won't never see an outlaw
Drive a family from their home.

Working-Class Militancy

The nation's working class bore the brunt of the economic collapse. By 1931, William Green, head of the American Federation of Labor, had turned militant. "I warn the people who are exploiting the workers," he shouted, "that they can drive them only so far before they will turn on them and destroy them. They are taking no account of the history of nations in which governments have been overturned. Revolutions grow out of the depths of hunger."

The American people were slow to anger, but on March 7, 1932, several thousand unemployed autoworkers massed at the gates of Henry Ford's River Rouge factory in Dearborn, Michigan, to demand work. Pelted with rocks, Ford's private security forces responded with gunfire, killing four demonstrators. Forty thousand outraged citizens turned out for the unemployed men's funerals.

Farmers mounted uprisings of their own. When Congress refused to guarantee farm prices, several thousand farmers created the National Farmers' Holiday Association in 1932, so named because its members planned to take a "holiday" from shipping crops to market. Farm militants also resorted to what they called "penny sales." When banks foreclosed and put farms up for auction, neighbors warned others not to bid, bought the foreclosed property for a few pennies, and returned it to the bankrupt owners. Militancy won farmers little in the way of long-term solutions, but one individual observed that "the biggest and finest crop of revolutions you ever saw is sprouting all over the country right now."

Even those who had proved their patriotism by serving in World War I rose up in protest against the government. In 1932, tens of thousands of unemployed veterans traveled to Washington, D.C., to petition Congress for the immediate payment of the pension (known as a "bonus") that Congress had promised them in 1924. Hoover feared that the veterans would spark a riot and ordered the U.S. Army to evict the **Bonus Marchers** from their camp on the outskirts of the city. Tanks destroyed the squatters' encampments while five hundred soldiers wielding bayonets and tear gas sent the protesters fleeing. The spectacle of the army driving peaceful, petitioning veterans from the nation's capital further undermined public support for the beleaguered Hoover.

The Great Depression — the massive failure of capitalism — catapulted the Communist Party to its greatest size and influence in American history. Some 100,000 Americans — workers, intellectuals, college students — joined the Communist Party in the belief that only an overthrow of the capitalist system could save the victims of the depression. In 1931, the party, through its National Miners Union, moved into Harlan County, Kentucky, to support a strike by brutalized coal miners. Mine owners unleashed thugs against the strikers and eventually beat the miners down. But the Communist Party gained a reputation as the most dedicated and fearless champion of the union cause.

The left also led the fight against racism. While both major parties refused to challenge segregation in the South, the Socialist Party, led by Norman Thomas,

Harlan County Coal Strike, 1931

Bonus Marchers

▶ World War I veterans who marched on Washington, D.C., in 1932 to lobby for immediate payment of the pension ("bonus") promised them in 1924. President Herbert Hoover believed the bonuses would bankrupt the government and sent the U.S. Army to evict the veterans from the city.

Why did the relationship between urban and rural America deteriorate in the 1920s?

How did President Hoover respond to the economic crash of 1929?

What was life like in the early years of the depression?

Conclusion: Why did the hope of the 1920s turn to despair?

✓ LearningCurve
Check what you know.
bedfordstmartins.com
/roarkunderstanding

705

"Scottsboro Boys" Nine black youths, ranging in age from thirteen to twenty-one, were convicted of the rape of two white women and sentenced to death by an all-white jury in March 1931. None was executed, and eventually the state dropped the charges against the youngest four and granted paroles to the others. The last "Scottsboro Boy" left jail in 1950. © Bettmann/Corbis.

Scottsboro Boys

▶ Nine African American youths who were arrested for the alleged rape of two white women in Scottsboro, Alabama, in 1931. After an all-white jury sentenced the young men to death, the Communist Party took action that saved them from the electric chair.

attacked the system of sharecropping that left many African Americans in near servitude. The Communist Party also took action. When nine young black men in Scottsboro, Alabama (the **Scottsboro Boys**), were arrested on trumped-up rape charges in 1931, a team of lawyers sent by the party saved the defendants from the electric chair.

Radicals on the left often sparked action, but protests by moderate workers and farmers occurred on a far greater scale. Breadlines, soup kitchens, foreclosures, unemployment, government violence, and cold despair drove patriotic men and women to question American capitalism. "I am as conservative as any man could be," a Wisconsin farmer explained, "but any economic system that has in its power to set me and my wife in the streets, at my age — what can I see but red?"

> QUICK REVIEW

How did the depression reshape American politics?

CHAPTER LOCATOR | How did big business shape the "New Era" of the 1920s? | In what ways did the Roaring Twenties challenge traditional values?

Conclusion: Why did the hope of the 1920s turn to despair?

<

IN THE AFTERMATH of World War I, America turned its back on progressive crusades and embraced conservative Republican politics, the growing influence of corporate leaders, and business values. Changes in the nation's economy — Henry Ford's automobile revolution, mass production, advertising — propelled fundamental change throughout society. Living standards rose, economic opportunity increased, and Americans threw themselves into private pleasures — gobbling up the latest household goods and fashions, attending baseball and football games and boxing matches, gathering around the radio, and going to the movies. As big cities came to dominate American life, the culture of youth and flappers became the leading edge of what one observer called a "revolution in manners and morals." At home in Harlem and abroad in Paris, American literature, art, and music flourished.

For many Americans, however, none of the glamour and vitality had much meaning. The vast majority struggled to earn a decent living. Blue-collar America did not participate fully in white-collar prosperity. Country folk, deeply suspicious and profoundly discontented, championed prohibition, revived the Klan, attacked immigration, and defended old-time Protestant religion.

The crash of 1929 and the depression that followed starkly revealed the economy's crises of international trade and consumption. Hard times swept high living off the front pages of the nation's newspapers. Different images emerged: hoboes hopping freight trains, strikers confronting police, malnourished sharecroppers staring blankly into the distance, empty apartment buildings alongside cardboard shantytowns, and mountains of food rotting in the sun while guards with shotguns chased away the hungry.

The depression hurt everyone, but the poor were hurt most. As farmers and workers sank into aching hardship, businessmen rallied around Herbert Hoover to proclaim that private enterprise would get the country moving again. But things fell apart, and Hoover faced increasingly radical opposition. Membership in the Socialist and Communist parties surged, and more and more Americans contemplated desperate measures. By 1932, the depression had nearly brought the nation to its knees. America faced its greatest crisis since the Civil War, and citizens demanded new leaders who would save them from the "Hoover Depression."

Why did the relationship between urban and rural America deteriorate in the 1920s? | How did President Hoover respond to the economic crash of 1929? | What was life like in the early years of the depression? | Conclusion: Why did the hope of the 1920s turn to despair? | LearningCurve Check what you know. bedfordstmartins.com /roarkunderstanding

707

CHAPTER 23 STUDY GUIDE

STEP 1 **GET STARTED ONLINE**

✓ **LearningCurve** ■ bedfordstmartins.com/roarkunderstanding
Now that you've read the chapter, make it stick by completing the LearningCurve activity.

STEP 2 **EXPLAIN WHY IT MATTERS**

Put your reading into practice. Identify each term below, and then explain why it matters in U.S. history.

TERM	WHO OR WHAT & WHEN	WHY IT MATTERS
Teapot Dome (p. 679)		
Five-Power Naval Treaty of 1922 (p. 680)		
welfare capitalism (p. 682)		
prohibition (p. 685)		
new woman (p. 687)		
New Negro (p. 689)		
Johnson-Reed Act (p. 693)		
Ku Klux Klan (p. 694)		
Scopes trial (p. 695)		
Reconstruction Finance Corporation (RFC) (p. 700)		
Bonus Marchers (p. 705)		
Scottsboro Boys (p. 706)		

STEP 3 **MOVE BEYOND THE BASICS**

To demonstrate a more advanced understanding, describe the social, cultural, and economic trends that marked the 1920s as a "New Era" and the changes that occurred as the nation entered the Great Depression.

	Characteristics/developments in the 1920s	Changes from 1929 to 1932
Business and manufacturing/ urban life		
Agriculture/rural life		
Society: consumerism, religion, mass culture		
Population: gender, race relations, immigrants		
Government and politics		
The economy		

STEP 4

PUT IT ALL TOGETHER

Now, take a step back and try to explain the big picture. Remember to use specific examples from the chapter in your answers.

POSTWAR DEVELOPMENTS

▶ What place did big business hold in the politics and culture of the 1920s?

▶ How did the economic changes of the 1920s contribute to challenges to social, cultural, and ethical norms?

RESISTANCE TO CHANGE

▶ What explains the rising anti-immigrant mood of America in the 1920s?

▶ What cultural divisions between rural and urban America were highlighted by the election of 1928?

THE CRASH AND THE GREAT DEPRESSION

▶ What underlying weaknesses in the American and world economies led to the Great Depression?

▶ How did Herbert Hoover respond to the economic crisis that engulfed his presidency? Why were his efforts unsuccessful?

▶ What was the "human toll" of the Great Depression?

LOOKING BACKWARD, LOOKING AHEAD

▶ Were the 1920s truly a New Era? Why or why not?

　▶ How were American life and culture challenged by the economic collapse of 1929? How did economic disaster make political change possible?

> **IN YOUR OWN WORDS**

Imagine that you must give an oral report to the class answering the following question: What were the high points and the low points of the 1920s? What would be the most important points to include and why?

24

FORGING THE NEW DEAL

1932–1939

> **Why was the New Deal so important in U.S. history?** Chapter 24 traces the efforts of President Franklin D. Roosevelt to respond to the Great Depression through an effort known as the New Deal. The chapter explores the principles and political factors that shaped the New Deal and examines the successes and failures of the New Deal during the 1930s.

LearningCurve
bedfordstmartins.com/roarkunderstanding
After reading the chapter, use LearningCurve to retain what you've read.

> How did Franklin D. Roosevelt win the 1932 election?

> What were the goals and achievements of the first New Deal?

> Who opposed the New Deal and why?

> How did the second phase of the New Deal differ from the first?

> What major political trends changed during the late 1930s?

> Conclusion: What were the achievements and limitations of the New Deal?

"Work Pays America!" Poster from the New Deal's Works Progress Administration. Library of Congress.

> How did Franklin D. Roosevelt win the 1932 election?

UNLIKE THE MILLIONS of impoverished Americans, Franklin Delano Roosevelt came from a wealthy and privileged background that contributed to his optimism, self-confidence, and vitality. He drew on these personal qualities in his political career to bridge the economic, social, and cultural chasm that separated him from the struggles of ordinary people. During the twelve years he served as president (1933–1945), many elites came to hate him as a traitor to his class, while millions more Americans in his New Deal coalition, especially the hardworking poor and dispossessed, revered him because he cared about them and their problems.

The Making of a Politician

Born in 1882, Franklin Delano Roosevelt grew up on his father's leafy estate at Hyde Park on the Hudson River, north of New York City. Roosevelt prepared for a career in politics, hoping to follow in the political footsteps of his fifth cousin, Theodore Roosevelt. Unlike cousin Teddy, Franklin Roosevelt sought his political

CHAPTER LOCATOR | How did Franklin D. Roosevelt win the 1932 election? | What were the goals and achievements of the first New Deal?

712   CHAPTER 24
FORGING THE NEW DEAL

fortune in the Democratic Party. In 1920, he catapulted to the second spot on the national Democratic ticket as the vice presidential running mate of presidential nominee James M. Cox. Although Cox lost the election (see chapter 22), Roosevelt's energetic campaigning convinced Democratic leaders that he had a bright future.

In the summer of 1921, at the age of thirty-nine, Roosevelt caught polio, which paralyzed both his legs. For the rest of his life, he wore heavy steel braces, and he could walk a few steps only by leaning on another person. Tireless physical therapy helped him regain his vitality and intense desire for high political office, although he carefully avoided being photographed in the wheelchair he used routinely.

After his polio attack, Roosevelt frequented a polio therapy facility at Warm Springs, Georgia. There, he got to know southern Democrats, which helped make him a rare political creature: a New Yorker from the Democratic Party's urban and immigrant wing who got along with whites from the party's entrenched southern wing.

By 1928, Roosevelt had recovered sufficiently to campaign for governor of New York, and he squeaked out a victory. As governor of the nation's most populous state, Roosevelt showcased his activist policies, which became a dress rehearsal for his presidency.

As the Great Depression spread hard times throughout the nation, Governor Roosevelt believed that government should intervene to protect citizens from economic hardships rather than wait for the law of supply and demand to improve the economy. According to the laissez-faire views of many conservatives — especially Republicans, but also numerous Democrats — the depression simply represented market forces separating strong survivors from weak losers. Unlike Roosevelt, conservatives believed that government help for the needy sapped individual initiative and impeded the self-correcting forces of the market by rewarding people for losing the economic struggle to survive. Roosevelt lacked a full-fledged counterargument to these conservative claims, but he sympathized with the plight of poor people. "To these unfortunate citizens," he proclaimed, "aid must be extended by governments, not as a matter of charity but as a matter of social duty. . . . [No one should go] unfed, unclothed, or unsheltered."

To his supporters, Roosevelt seemed to be a leader determined to attack the economic crisis without deviating from democracy — unlike the fascist parties gaining strength in Europe — or from capitalism — unlike the Communists in power in the Soviet Union. Roosevelt's ideas about how to revive the economy were vague, but his many supporters appreciated his energy and activism. His conviction that government should do something to help Americans climb out of the economic abyss propelled him into the front ranks of the national Democratic Party.

The Election of 1932

Democrats knew that Herbert Hoover's unpopularity gave them a historic opportunity to recapture the White House in 1932. Since Abraham Lincoln's election, Republicans had occupied the White House three-fourths of the time, a trend Democrats hoped to reverse. Democrats, however, had to overcome warring factions that divided the party by region, religion, culture, and commitment to the status quo.

> KEY FACTORS

The 1932 Election
- The election was held in the midst of the Great Depression.
- Franklin Roosevelt believed that government should intervene to protect citizens from economic hardship.
- President Herbert Hoover was highly unpopular.
- Democrats had to overcome divisiveness within the party.
- Roosevelt promised a "new deal" during the campaign but provided few details.

Who opposed the New Deal and why?

How did the second phase of the New Deal differ from the first?

What major political trends changed during the late 1930s?

Conclusion: What were the achievements and limitations of the New Deal?

✓ LearningCurve
Check what you know.
bedfordstmartins.com
/roarkunderstanding

713

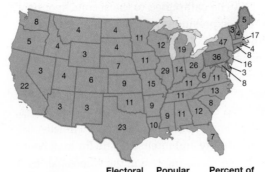

Candidate	Electoral Vote	Popular Vote	Percent of Popular Vote
Franklin D. Roosevelt (Democrat)	472	22,821,857	57.4
Herbert C. Hoover (Republican)	59	15,761,841	39.7
Norman Thomas (Socialist)	0	881,951	2.2
William Z. Foster (Communist)	0	102,991	0.3

MAP 24.1 ■ The Election of 1932

The southern, native-born, white, rural, Protestant, conservative wing of the Democratic Party found little common ground with the northern, immigrant, urban, disproportionately Catholic, liberal wing. Eastern-establishment Democratic dignitaries shared few goals with angry farmers and factory workers. Still, this unruly coalition managed to agree on Franklin Roosevelt as its presidential candidate.

In his acceptance speech, Roosevelt vowed to help "the forgotten man at the bottom of the pyramid" with "bold, persistent experimentation." Highlighting his differences with Hoover and the Republicans, he pledged "a new deal for the American people." Few details about what Roosevelt meant by "a new deal" emerged in the presidential campaign. He declared that "the people of America want more than anything else . . . two things: work . . . and a reasonable measure of security." Voters decided that whatever Roosevelt's new deal might be, it was better than reelecting Hoover.

Roosevelt won the 1932 presidential election in a historic landslide. He received 57 percent of the nation's votes, the first time a Democrat had won a majority of the popular vote since 1852 (**Map 24.1**). He amassed 472 electoral votes to Hoover's 59, carrying state after state that had voted Republican for

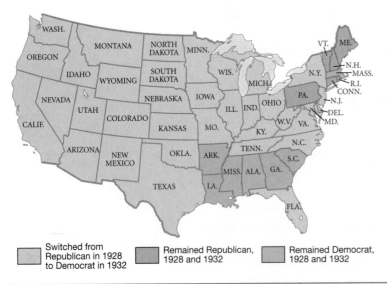

Switched from Republican in 1928 to Democrat in 1932

Remained Republican, 1928 and 1932

Remained Democrat, 1928 and 1932

MAP 24.2 ■ Electoral Shift, 1928–1932

The Democratic victory in 1932 signaled the rise of a New Deal coalition within which women and minorities, many of them new voters, made the Democrats the majority party for the first time in the twentieth century.

> **MAP ACTIVITY**

READING THE MAP: How many states voted Democratic in 1928? How many states voted Republican in 1932? How many states shifted from Republican to Democratic between 1928 and 1932?

CONNECTIONS: What factions within the Democratic Party opposed Franklin Roosevelt's candidacy in 1932, and why did they do so? To what do you attribute his landslide victory?

CHAPTER LOCATOR | How did Franklin D. Roosevelt win the 1932 election? | What were the goals and achievements of the first New Deal?

714 CHAPTER 24 FORGING THE NEW DEAL

years (**Map 24.2**). Roosevelt's coattails swept Democrats into control of Congress by large margins. The popular mandate for change was loud and clear.

Roosevelt's victory represented the emergence of what came to be known as the **New Deal coalition**. Attracting support from farmers, factory workers, immigrants, city folk, African Americans, women, and progressive intellectuals, Roosevelt launched a realignment of the nation's political loyalties. The New Deal coalition dominated American politics throughout Roosevelt's presidency and remained powerful long after his death in 1945. United less by ideology or support for specific policies, voters in the New Deal coalition instead expressed faith in Roosevelt's promise of a government that would somehow change things for the better. Nobody, including Roosevelt, knew exactly what the New Deal would change or whether the changes would revive the nation's ailing economy and improve Americans' lives. But Roosevelt and many others knew that the future of American capitalism and democracy was at stake.

New Deal coalition
▶ Political coalition that supported Franklin D. Roosevelt's New Deal and the Democratic Party, including farmers, factory workers, immigrants, city dwellers, women, African Americans, and progressive intellectuals. The coalition dominated American politics during and long after Roosevelt's presidency.

QUICK REVIEW ◀

Why did Franklin D. Roosevelt win the 1932 presidential election by such a large margin?

| Who opposed the New Deal and why? | How did the second phase of the New Deal differ from the first? | What major political trends changed during the late 1930s? | Conclusion: What were the achievements and limitations of the New Deal? | ✓ **LearningCurve** Check what you know. bedfordstmartins.com /roarkunderstanding |

> What were the goals and achievements of the first New Deal?

Eleanor Roosevelt Serving Unemployed Women

A tireless ambassador of the New Deal, Eleanor Roosevelt used her status as First Lady to highlight New Dealers' sympathy for the plight of the poor, unemployed, and neglected working people. Said one North Carolina woman, "One of my great pleasures was meeting Mrs. Roosevelt . . . she was so free of prejudice . . . she was always willing to take a stand."
© Bettmann/Corbis.

> CHRONOLOGY

1933
- Franklin D. Roosevelt becomes president.
- Roosevelt's "Hundred Days" launches the New Deal.
- Roosevelt declares a four-day "bank holiday."
- Federal Emergency Relief Administration (FERA) is created.

1934
- Securities and Exchange Commission (SEC) is created.

AT NOON ON MARCH 4, 1933, Americans gathered around their radios to hear the inaugural address of the newly elected president. Roosevelt began by asserting his "firm belief that the only thing we have to fear is fear itself — nameless, unreasoning, unjustified terror which paralyzes needed efforts to convert retreat into advance." He promised "direct, vigorous action," and the first months of his administration, termed "the Hundred Days," fulfilled that promise in a whirlwind of government initiatives that launched the New Deal.

Roosevelt and his advisers had three interrelated objectives: relief, recovery, and reform. The New Deal never fully achieved these goals. But by aiming for them, Roosevelt's experimental programs enormously expanded government's role in the nation's economy and society.

CHAPTER LOCATOR | How did Franklin D. Roosevelt win the 1932 election? | **What were the goals and achievements of the first New Deal?**

Relief	Provide help to the millions of poor and unemployed Americans victimized by the depression.
Recovery	Foster economic recovery of farms and businesses, thereby creating jobs and reducing the need for relief.
Reform	Reshape government and the economy to protect citizens against future economic downturns.

The New Dealers

To design and implement the New Deal, Roosevelt needed ideas and people. He convened a "Brains Trust" of economists and other leaders to offer suggestions and advice about the problems facing the nation. No New Dealers were more important than the president and his wife, Eleanor. The gregarious president radiated charm and good cheer, giving the New Deal's bureaucratic regulations a benevolent human face. Eleanor Roosevelt became the New Deal's unofficial ambassador. She served, she said, as "the eyes and ears of the New Deal," traveling throughout the nation meeting Americans of all colors and creeds.

As Roosevelt's programs swung into action, the millions of beneficiaries of the New Deal became grassroots New Dealers who expressed their appreciation by voting Democratic on election day. In this way, the New Deal created a durable political coalition of Democrats that reelected Roosevelt in 1936, 1940, and 1944.

Four guiding ideas shaped New Deal policies. First, Roosevelt and his advisers sought capitalist solutions to the economic crisis. They had no desire to eliminate private property or impose socialist programs, such as public ownership of productive resources. Instead, they hoped to save the capitalist economy by remedying its flaws.

Second, Roosevelt's Brains Trust persuaded him that the greatest flaw of America's capitalist economy was **underconsumption**, the root cause of the current economic paralysis. Underconsumption, New Dealers argued, resulted from the gigantic productive success of capitalism. Factories and farms produced more than they could sell to consumers, causing factories to lay off workers and farmers to lose money on bumper crops. Workers without wages and farmers without profits shrank consumption and choked the economy. Somehow, the balance between consumption and production needed to be restored.

Third, New Dealers believed that the immense size and economic power of American corporations needed to be counterbalanced by government and by organization among workers and small producers. Unlike progressive trust-busters, New Dealers did not seek to splinter big businesses. Roosevelt and his advisers hoped to counterbalance big economic institutions with government programs focused on protecting individuals and the public interest.

Fourth, New Dealers felt that government must somehow moderate the imbalance of wealth created by American capitalism. Wealth concentrated in a few hands reduced consumption by most Americans and thereby contributed to the current economic gridlock. Government needed to find a way to permit ordinary working people to share more fully in the fruits of the economy.

underconsumption
▶ A situation in which factories and farms produce more than consumers buy, causing factories to lay off workers and farmers to lose money. New Dealers believed that underconsumption was the root cause of the country's economic paralysis. Workers without wages and farmers without profits shrank consumption and choked the economy. The only way to increase consumption, New Dealers believed, was to provide jobs that put wages in consumers' pockets.

Who opposed the New Deal and why?

How did the second phase of the New Deal differ from the first?

What major political trends changed during the late 1930s?

Conclusion: What were the achievements and limitations of the New Deal?

☑ LearningCurve
Check what you know.
bedfordstmartins.com
/roarkunderstanding

717

Banking and Finance Reform

Roosevelt wasted no time making good on his inaugural pledge for "action now." As he took the oath of office on March 4, the nation's banking system was on the brink of collapse. Roosevelt immediately declared a four-day "bank holiday" in order to devise a plan to shore up banks and restore depositors' confidence. Working round the clock, New Dealers drafted the Emergency Banking Act, which propped up the private banking system with federal funds and subjected banks to federal regulation and oversight. To secure the confidence of depositors, Congress passed the Glass-Steagall Banking Act, setting up the **Federal Deposit Insurance Corporation**, which guaranteed bank customers that the federal government would reimburse them for deposits if their banks failed. In addition, the act required the separation of commercial banks (which accept deposits and make loans to individuals and small businesses) and investment banks (which make speculative investments with their funds), in an effort to insulate the finances of Main Street America from the risky speculations of Wall Street wheeler-dealers.

On Sunday night, March 12, while the banks were still closed, Roosevelt broadcast the first of a series of **fireside chats**. Speaking in a friendly, informal manner, he explained the new banking legislation that, he said, made it "safer to keep your money in a reopened bank than under the mattress." With such plain talk, Roosevelt translated complex matters into common sense. This and subsequent fireside chats forged a direct connection — via radio — between Roosevelt and millions of Americans, a connection felt by a man from Paris, Texas, who wrote to Roosevelt, "You are the one & only President that ever helped a Working Class of People. . . . Please help us some way I Pray to God for relief."

The banking legislation and fireside chat worked. Within a few days, most of the nation's major banks reopened, and they remained solvent as reassured depositors switched funds from their mattresses to their bank accounts (**Figure 24.1**).

In his inaugural address, Roosevelt criticized financiers for their greed and incompetence. To prevent the fraud, corruption, and insider trading that had tainted Wall Street and contributed to the crash of 1929, New Dealers created the Securities and Exchange Commission (SEC) in 1934 to oversee financial markets by licensing investment dealers, monitoring all stock transactions, and requiring corporate officers to make full disclosures about their companies. The SEC helped clean up and regulate Wall Street, which slowly recovered.

Federal Deposit Insurance Corporation

▶ Regulatory body established by the Glass-Steagall Banking Act that guaranteed the federal government would reimburse bank depositors if their banks failed. This key feature of the New Deal restored depositors' confidence in the banking system during the Great Depression.

fireside chats

▶ Series of informal radio addresses Franklin Roosevelt made to the nation in which he explained New Deal initiatives. The chats helped bolster Roosevelt's popularity and secured popular support for his reforms.

Relief and Conservation Programs

Patching the nation's financial structure provided little relief for the hungry and unemployed. A poor man from Nebraska asked Eleanor Roosevelt "if the folk who was borned here in America . . . are this Forgotten Man, the President had in mind, [and] if we are this Forgotten Man then we are still Forgotten." Since its founding, the federal government had never assumed responsibility for needy people, except in moments of natural disaster or emergencies such as the Civil War. Instead, churches, private charities, county and municipal governments, and occasionally states assumed the burden of poor relief, usually with meager payments. The depression necessitated unprecedented federal relief efforts, according to New Dealers.

CHAPTER LOCATOR | How did Franklin D. Roosevelt win the 1932 election? | **What were the goals and achievements of the first New Deal?**

CHAPTER 24
718   FORGING THE NEW DEAL

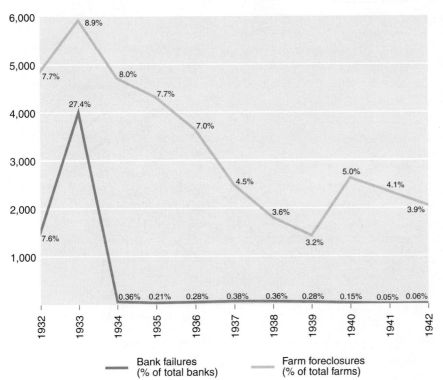

FIGURE 24.1 ■ Bank Failures and Farm Foreclosures, 1932–1942

New Deal legislation to stabilize the economy had its most immediate and striking effect in preventing banks, along with their depositors, from going under and farmers from losing their land.

Bank failures (% of total banks)   Farm foreclosures (% of total farms)

The Federal Emergency Relief Administration (FERA), established in May 1933, supported four million to five million households with $20 or $30 a month. The FERA also created jobs for the unemployed on thousands of public works projects, organized into the Civil Works Administration (CWA), which put paychecks worth more than $800 million into the hands of previously jobless workers. Earning wages between 40 and 60 cents an hour, laborers renovated schools, dug sewers, and rebuilt roads and bridges.

The most popular work relief program was the **Civilian Conservation Corps (CCC)**, established in March 1933. It offered unemployed young men a chance to earn wages while working to conserve natural resources, a long-standing interest of Roosevelt. Women were excluded from working in the CCC until Eleanor Roosevelt demanded that a token number of young women be hired. By the end of the program in 1942, three million CCC workers had left a legacy of vast new recreation areas, along with roads that made those areas accessible to millions of Americans. Just as important, the CCC, CWA, and other work relief efforts replaced the stigma of welfare with the dignity of jobs. As one woman said about her husband's work relief job, "We aren't on relief anymore. My husband is working for the Government."

The New Deal's most ambitious and controversial natural resources development project was the Tennessee Valley Authority (TVA), created in May 1933 to build dams along the Tennessee River to supply impoverished rural communities with cheap electricity (**Map 24.3**). The TVA set out to demonstrate that a partnership between the federal government and local residents could overcome the barriers of state governments and private enterprises to make efficient use of

Civilian Conservation Corps (CCC)

▶ Federal relief program established in March 1933 that provided assistance in the form of jobs to millions of unemployed young men and a token number of women. CCC workers worked on conservation projects throughout the nation.

Who opposed the New Deal and why?

How did the second phase of the New Deal differ from the first?

What major political trends changed during the late 1930s?

Conclusion: What were the achievements and limitations of the New Deal?

✔️ LearningCurve
Check what you know.
bedfordstmartins.com/roarkunderstanding

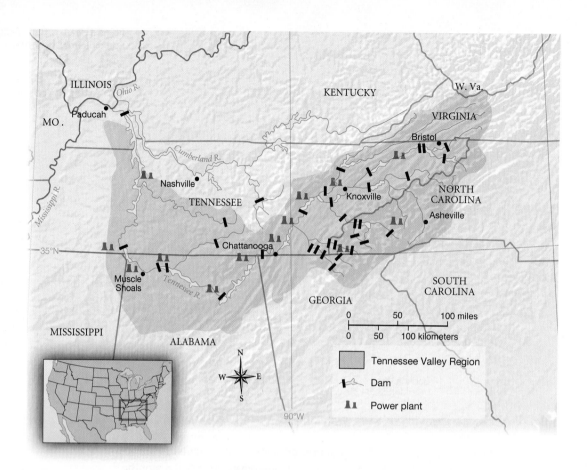

MAP 24.3 ■ The Tennessee Valley Authority

The New Deal created the Tennessee Valley Authority to modernize a vast impoverished region with hydroelectric power dams and, at the same time, to reclaim eroded land and preserve old folkways.

> MAP ACTIVITY

READING THE MAP: How many states were affected by the TVA? How many miles of rivers (approximately) were affected?
CONNECTIONS: What kinds of benefits—economic as well as social and cultural—did TVA programs bring to the region? How might the lives of a poor farming family in Alabama or Tennessee have changed after the mid-1930s owing to these programs?

abundant natural resources and break the ancient cycle of poverty. The TVA improved the lives of millions in the region with electric power, flood protection, soil reclamation, and jobs.

New sources of hydroelectric power helped the New Deal bring the wonders of electricity to country folk, fulfilling an old progressive dream. When Roosevelt became president, 90 percent of rural Americans lacked electricity. Private electric companies refused to build transmission lines into the sparsely settled country-side when they had a profitable market in more accessible and densely populated urban areas. Beginning in 1935, the Rural Electrification Administration (REA) made low-cost loans available to local cooperatives for power plants and transmission lines to serve rural communities. Within ten years, the REA delivered electricity to nine out of ten farms, giving rural Americans access for the first time to modern conveniences that urban people had enjoyed for decades.

CHAPTER LOCATOR | How did Franklin D. Roosevelt win the 1932 election? | What were the goals and achievements of the first New Deal?

Agricultural Initiatives

Farmers had been mired in a depression since the end of World War I. New Dealers diagnosed the farmers' plight as a classic case of overproduction and underconsumption. Following age-old practices, farmers tried to compensate for low crop prices by growing more crops. Of course, producing more crops pushed prices lower still. Farm families' income sank to $167 a year, barely one-tenth of the national average in 1932.

New Dealers sought to cut agricultural production, thereby raising crop prices and farmers' income. With more money in their pockets, farm families — who made up one-third of all Americans — would then buy more goods and lift consumption in the entire economy. To reduce production, the **Agricultural Adjustment Act (AAA)**, passed in May 1933, authorized the "domestic allotment plan," which paid farmers *not* to grow crops. Individual farmers who agreed not to plant crops on a portion of their fields (their "allotment") would receive a government payment compensating them for the crops they did not plant. While millions of Americans went to bed hungry, farmers slaughtered livestock and destroyed crops to qualify for their allotment payments.

With the formation of the Commodity Credit Corporation, the federal government allowed farmers to hold their harvested crops off the market and wait for a higher price. New Dealers also sponsored the Farm Credit Act (FCA) to provide long-term credit on mortgaged farm property, allowing debt-ridden farmers to avoid foreclosures that were driving thousands off their land (see Figure 24.1).

Crop allotments, commodity loans, and mortgage credit made farmers major beneficiaries of the New Deal. Crop prices rose impressively, farm income jumped 50 percent by 1936, and FCA loans financed 40 percent of farm mortgage debt by the end of the decade. These gains were distributed fairly equally among farmers in the corn, hog, and wheat region of the Midwest. In the South's cotton belt, however, landlords controlled the distribution of New Deal agricultural benefits and shamelessly rewarded themselves while denying benefits to many sharecroppers and tenant farmers — blacks and whites — by taking the land they worked out of production and assigning it to the allotment program. As the president of the Oklahoma Tenant Farmers' Union explained, large farmers who got "Triple-A" payments often used the money to buy tractors and then "forced their tenants and [share]croppers off the land," causing these "Americans to be starved and dispossessed of their homes in our land of plenty."

Agricultural Adjustment Act (AAA)

▶ New Deal legislation passed in May 1933 aimed at cutting agricultural production and raising crop prices and, consequently, farmers' income. Through the "domestic allotment plan," the AAA paid farmers to not grow crops.

Industrial Recovery

Unlike farmers, industrialists cut production with the onset of the depression. Between 1929 and 1933, industrial production fell more than 40 percent in an effort to balance low demand with low supply and thereby maintain prices. But falling industrial production meant that millions of working people lost their jobs. Unlike farmers, most working people needed jobs to eat. Mass unemployment also reduced consumer demand for industrial products, contributing to a downward spiral in both production and jobs, with no end in sight. Industries responded by reducing wages for employees who still had jobs, further reducing demand—a

Who opposed the New Deal and why?

How did the second phase of the New Deal differ from the first?

What major political trends changed during the late 1930s?

Conclusion: What were the achievements and limitations of the New Deal?

✓ LearningCurve
Check what you know.
bedfordstmartins.com
/roarkunderstanding

721

trend made worse by competition among industrial producers. New Dealers struggled to find a way to break this cycle of unemployment and underconsumption — a way consistent with corporate profits and capitalism.

The New Deal's National Industrial Recovery Act opted for a government-sponsored form of industrial self-government through the **National Recovery Administration (NRA)**, established in June 1933. The NRA encouraged industrialists to agree on rules, known as codes, to define fair working conditions, to set prices, and to minimize competition. The idea behind NRA codes was to stabilize existing industries and maintain their workforces. Industry after industry wrote elaborate codes addressing detailed features of production, pricing, and competition. In exchange for the relaxation of federal antitrust regulations that prohibited such business agreements, the participating businesses promised to recognize the right of working people to organize and engage in collective bargaining. To encourage consumers to patronize businesses with NRA codes, posters with the NRA's Blue Eagle appeared in shop windows throughout the nation.

New Dealers hoped that NRA codes would yield businesses with a social conscience, ensuring fair treatment of workers and consumers as well as promotion of the general economic welfare. Instead, NRA codes tended to strengthen conventional business practices. Large corporations wrote codes that served primarily their own interests rather than the needs of workers or the welfare of the national economy.

Many business leaders criticized NRA codes as heavy-handed government regulation of private enterprise. In reality, compliance with NRA codes was voluntary, and government enforcement efforts were weak to nonexistent. The NRA did little to reduce unemployment, raise consumption, or relieve the depression. In effect, it represented a peace offering to business leaders by Roosevelt and his advisers, conveying the message that the New Deal did not intend to wage war against profits or private enterprise. The peace offering failed, however. Most corporate leaders became entrenched opponents of Roosevelt and the New Deal.

National Recovery Administration (NRA)

▶ Federal agency established in June 1933 to promote industrial recovery. The NRA encouraged industrialists to voluntarily adopt codes that defined fair working conditions, set prices, and minimized competition. In practice, large corporations developed codes that served primarily their own interests rather than those of workers or the economy.

> ## QUICK REVIEW

How did the New Dealers try to steer the nation toward recovery from the Great Depression?

CHAPTER LOCATOR | How did Franklin D. Roosevelt win the 1932 election? | What were the goals and achievements of the first New Deal?

722   CHAPTER 24
FORGING THE NEW DEAL

Evicted Sharecroppers

The New Deal's Agricultural Adjustment Administration maintained farm prices by reducing acreage in production, often resulting in the eviction of tenant farmers when the land they worked was left idle. These African American sharecroppers protested AAA policies that caused cotton farmers to evict them from their homes. They were among the many rural laborers whose lives were made worse by New Deal agricultural policies. © Bettmann/Corbis.

THE FIRST NEW DEAL INITIATIVES engendered fierce criticism and political opposition. From the right, Republicans and business people charged that New Deal programs were too radical, undermining private property, economic stability, and democracy. Critics on the left faulted the New Deal for its failure to allay the human suffering caused by the depression and for its timidity in attacking corporate power and greed.

Resistance to Business Reform

New Deal programs rescued capitalism, but business leaders lambasted Roosevelt, even though their economic prospects improved more than those of most other Americans during the depression. Republicans and business leaders

| Who opposed the New Deal and why? | How did the second phase of the New Deal differ from the first? | What major political trends changed during the late 1930s? | Conclusion: What were the achievements and limitations of the New Deal? | ✓ LearningCurve Check what you know. bedfordstmartins.com /roarkunderstanding |

1934
- Upton Sinclair loses California governorship bid.
- American Liberty League is founded.
- Dr. Francis Townsend devises Old Age Revolving Pension scheme.

1935
- Father Charles Coughlin founds National Union for Social Justice.

denounced New Deal efforts to regulate or reform what they considered their private enterprises.

By 1935, two major business organizations, the National Association of Manufacturers and the Chamber of Commerce, had become openly anti–New Deal. Their critiques were amplified by the American Liberty League, founded in 1934, which blamed the New Deal for betraying basic constitutional guarantees of freedom and individualism. To them, the Agricultural Adjustment Act was a "trend toward fascist control of agriculture," relief programs marked "the end of democracy," and the National Recovery Administration was a plunge into the "quicksand of visionary experimentation."

Economists who favored rational planning in the public interest and labor leaders who sought to influence wages and working conditions by organizing unions attacked the New Deal from the left. In their view, the National Recovery Administration stifled enterprise by permitting monopolistic practices. They pointed out that industrial trade associations twisted NRA codes to suit their aims, thwarted competition, and engaged in price gouging. Labor leaders especially resented the NRA's willingness to allow businesses to form company-controlled unions while blocking workers from organizing genuine grassroots unions to bargain for themselves.

The Supreme Court stepped into this cross fire of criticisms in May 1935 and declared that the NRA unconstitutionally conferred powers reserved to Congress on an administrative agency. The NRA codes soon lost the little authority they had. The failure of the NRA demonstrated the depth of many Americans' resistance to economic planning and the stubborn refusal of business leaders to yield to government regulations or reforms.

Casualties in the Countryside

The Agricultural Adjustment Act weathered critical battering by champions of the old order better than the National Recovery Administration. Allotment checks for keeping land fallow and crop prices high created loyalty among farmers with enough acreage to participate. As a white farmer in North Carolina declared, "I stand for the New Deal and Roosevelt . . . , the AAA . . . and crop control."

Protests stirred, however, among those who did not qualify for allotments. The Southern Farm Tenants Union argued passionately that the AAA enriched large farmers while it impoverished small farmers who rented rather than owned their land. Like the NRA, the AAA tended to help most those who least needed help. Roosevelt's political dependence on southern Democrats caused him to avoid confronting economic and racial inequities in the South.

Displaced tenants often joined the army of migrant workers who straggled across rural America during the 1930s, some to flee Great Plains dust storms. Many migrants came from Mexico to work Texas cotton, Michigan beans, Idaho sugar beets, and California crops of all kinds. But since the number of people willing to take agricultural jobs usually exceeded the number of jobs available, wages fell, and native-born white migrants fought to reserve even these low-wage jobs for themselves. Hundreds of thousands of "Okies" streamed out of the Dust Bowl of Oklahoma, Kansas, Texas, and Colorado, where chronic drought and harmful agricultural practices blasted crops and hopes. Parched, poor, and

CHAPTER LOCATOR | How did Franklin D. Roosevelt win the 1932 election? | What were the goals and achievements of the first New Deal?

CHAPTER 24
724 FORGING THE NEW DEAL

windblown, Okies — like the Joad family immortalized in John Steinbeck's novel *The Grapes of Wrath* (1939) — migrated to the lush fields and orchards of California, congregating in labor camps and hoping to find work and a future. But migrant laborers seldom found steady or secure work. As one Okie said, "When they need us they call us migrants, and when we've picked their crop, we're bums and we got to get out."

Politics on the Fringes

Politically, the New Deal's staunchest opponents were in the Republican Party — organized, well-heeled, mainstream, and determined to challenge Roosevelt at every turn. But the New Deal also faced challenges from the political fringes, fueled by the hardship of the depression and the hope for a cure-all.

Socialists and Communists accused the New Deal of being the handmaiden of business elites and of rescuing capitalism from its self-inflicted crisis. Socialist author Upton Sinclair ran for governor of California in 1934 on a plan that the state take ownership of idle factories and unused land and then give them to cooperatives of working people, a first step toward putting the needs of people above profits. Sinclair lost the election, ending the most serious socialist electoral challenge to the New Deal.

Some intellectuals and artists sought to advance the cause of more radical change by joining left-wing organizations, including the American Communist Party. At its high point in the 1930s, the party had only about thirty thousand members, the large majority of them immigrants, especially Scandinavians in the upper Midwest and eastern European Jews in major cities. Individual Communists worked to organize labor unions, protect the civil rights of black people, and help the destitute, but the party preached the overthrow of "bourgeois democracy" and the destruction of capitalism in favor of Soviet-style communism. Such talk attracted few followers among the nation's millions of poor and unemployed. They wanted jobs and economic security within American capitalism and democracy, not violent revolution to establish a dictatorship of the Communist Party.

More powerful radical challenges to the New Deal sprouted from homegrown roots. Many Americans felt overlooked by New Deal programs that concentrated on finance, agriculture, and industry but did little to produce jobs or aid the poor. The merciless reality of the depression also continued to erode the security of people who still had jobs but worried constantly that they, too, might be pushed into the legions of the unemployed and penniless.

A Catholic priest in Detroit named Charles Coughlin spoke to and for many worried Americans in his weekly radio broadcasts, which reached a nationwide audience of 40 million. Father Coughlin expressed outrage at the suffering and inequities that he blamed on Communists, bankers, and "predatory capitalists" who, he claimed, appealing to widespread anti-Semitic sentiments, were mostly Jews. Coughlin became frustrated by Roosevelt's refusal to grant him influence, turned against the New Deal, and in 1935 founded the National Union for Social Justice, or Union Party, to challenge Roosevelt in the 1936 presidential election.

Dr. Francis Townsend, of Long Beach, California, also criticized the timidity of the New Deal. Angry that many of his retired patients lived in misery, Townsend

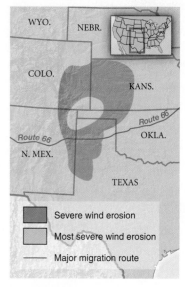

Severe wind erosion

Most severe wind erosion

Major migration route

The Dust Bowl

Who opposed the New Deal and why?

How did the second phase of the New Deal differ from the first?

What major political trends changed during the late 1930s?

Conclusion: What were the achievements and limitations of the New Deal?

LearningCurve
Check what you know.
bedfordstmartins.com
/roarkunderstanding

Huey Long

Huey Long's ability to adapt his stump-speech style to the radio made him the one rival politician who gave Roosevelt considerable concern in the mid-1930s. Corbis.

proposed in 1934 the creation of the Old Age Revolving Pension, which would pay every American over age sixty a pension of $200 a month. To receive the pension, senior citizens had to agree to spend the entire amount within thirty days, thereby stimulating the economy.

Townsend organized pension clubs and petitioned the federal government to enact his scheme. When the major political parties ignored his impractical plan, Townsend merged his forces with Coughlin's Union Party in time for the 1936 election.

A more formidable challenge to the New Deal came from the powerful southern wing of the Democratic Party. Huey Long, son of a backcountry Louisiana farmer, was elected governor of the state in 1928 with his slogan "Every man a king, but no one wears a crown." Unlike nearly all other southern white politicians who harped on white supremacy, Long championed the poor over the rich, country people over city folk, and the humble over elites. As governor, "the Kingfish" — as he liked to call himself — delivered on his promises to provide jobs and build roads, schools, and hospitals, but he also behaved ruthlessly to achieve his goals. Long delighted his supporters, who elected him to the U.S. Senate in

CHAPTER LOCATOR | How did Franklin D. Roosevelt win the 1932 election? | What were the goals and achievements of the first New Deal?

CHAPTER 24
726 FORGING THE NEW DEAL

1932, where he introduced a sweeping "soak the rich" tax bill that would outlaw personal incomes of more than $1 million and inheritances of more than $5 million. When the Senate rejected his proposal, Long decided to run for president, mobilizing more than five million Americans behind his "Share Our Wealth" plan. Like Townsend's scheme, Long's program promised far more than it could deliver. The Share Our Wealth campaign died when Long was assassinated in 1935, but his constituency and the wide appeal of a more equitable distribution of wealth persisted.

The challenges to the New Deal from both right and left stirred Democrats to solidify their winning coalition. In the midterm congressional elections of 1934 — normally a time when a president loses support — voters gave New Dealers a landslide victory. Democrats increased their majority in the House of Representatives and gained a two-thirds majority in the Senate.

QUICK REVIEW

Why did groups at both ends of the political spectrum criticize the New Deal?

Who opposed the New Deal and why?	How did the second phase of the New Deal differ from the first?	What major political trends changed during the late 1930s?	Conclusion: What were the achievements and limitations of the New Deal?	✓ LearningCurve Check what you know. bedfordstmartins.com /roarkunderstanding

How did the second phase of the New Deal differ from the first?

City Activities Mural

During the 1930s, artists — many of them employed by New Deal agencies — painted thousands of murals depicting the variety of American life. These murals often appeared in public buildings. The mural shown here, by Missouri-born artist Thomas Hart Benton, illustrates the seductive pleasures and the spirit to be found in American cities. © AXA Financial, Inc. Thomas Hart Benton, *City Activities with Subway,* from *America Today,* 1930. Distemper and egg tempera on gessoed linen with oil glaze 92 x 134½". Collection of AXA Financial, Inc., through its subsidiary, The Equitable Life Assurance Society of the U.S.

> **VISUAL ACTIVITY**

READING THE IMAGE: What features of urban experience does Benton emphasize in this mural? What ideas and attitudes, if any, link the people shown here?

CONNECTIONS: To what extent does the mural highlight activities distinct to U.S. cities, compared with urban life in Europe, Africa, or Asia?

THE POPULAR MANDATE for the New Deal revealed by the congressional elections persuaded Roosevelt to press ahead with bold new efforts to achieve relief, recovery, and reform. Despite the initiatives of the Hundred Days, the depression still strangled the economy. In 1935, Roosevelt capitalized on his congressional majorities to enact major new programs that signaled the emergence of an American welfare state.

Taken together, these New Deal efforts stretched a safety net under the lives of ordinary Americans, including such landmark initiatives as Social Security, which provided modest pensions for the elderly, and the Wagner Act, which encouraged the organization of labor unions. Although many citizens remained unprotected, New Deal programs helped millions with jobs, relief, and government support. Knitting together the safety net was the idea that, when individual Americans

CHAPTER LOCATOR | How did Franklin D. Roosevelt win the 1932 election? | What were the goals and achievements of the first New Deal?

suffered because of forces beyond their control, the federal government had the responsibility to support and protect them. The safety net of welfare programs tied the political loyalty of working people to the New Deal and the Democratic Party.

Relief for the Unemployed

First and foremost, Americans still needed jobs. Since the private economy left eight million people jobless by 1935, Roosevelt and his advisers launched a massive work relief program. With a congressional appropriation of nearly $5 billion — more than all government revenues in 1934 — the New Deal created the **Works Progress Administration (WPA)** in 1935 to give unemployed Americans government-funded jobs on public works projects. The WPA put millions of jobless citizens to work on roads, bridges, parks, public buildings, and more.

By 1936, WPA funds provided jobs for 7 percent of the nation's labor force. In effect, the WPA made the federal government the employer of last resort, creating useful jobs when the capitalist economy failed to do so. In hiring, WPA officials tended to discriminate in favor of white men and against women and racial minorities. Still, WPA jobs put thirteen million men and women to work and gave them paychecks worth $10 billion.

About three out of four WPA jobs involved construction and renovation of the nation's physical infrastructure. In addition, the WPA gave jobs to thousands of artists, musicians, actors, journalists, poets, and novelists. The WPA also organized sewing rooms for jobless women, giving them work and wages. These sewing rooms produced more than 100 million pieces of clothing that were donated to the needy. Throughout the nation, WPA projects displayed tangible evidence of the New Deal's commitment to public welfare.

Empowering Labor

During the Great Depression, factory workers who managed to keep their jobs worried constantly about being laid off while their wages and working hours were cut. When workers tried to organize labor unions to protect themselves, municipal and state governments usually sided with employers. Since the Gilded Age, state and federal governments had been far more effective at busting unions than at busting trusts. The New Deal dramatically reversed the federal government's stance toward unions. With legislation and political support, the New Deal encouraged an unprecedented wave of union organizing among the nation's working people. When the head of the United Mine Workers, John L. Lewis, told coal miners that "the President wants you to join a union," he exaggerated only a little. New Dealers believed that unions would counterbalance the organized might of big corporations by defending working people, maintaining wages, and replacing the bloody violence that often accompanied strikes with economic peace and commercial stability.

Violent battles on the nation's streets and docks showed the determination of militant labor leaders to organize unions that would protect jobs as well as wages. In 1934, striking workers in Toledo, Minneapolis, San Francisco, and elsewhere were beaten and shot by police and the National Guard. In Congress, labor leaders lobbied for the National Labor Relations Act, a bill sponsored by Senator Robert Wagner of New York that authorized the federal government to intervene in labor

Works Progress Administration (WPA)

▶ Federal New Deal program established in 1935 that provided government-funded public works jobs to millions of unemployed Americans during the Great Depression, in areas ranging from construction to the arts.

> CHRONOLOGY

1934
– Indian Reorganization Act.

1935
– Works Progress Administration (WPA) is created.
– Wagner Act.
– Committee for Industrial Organization (CIO) is founded.
– Social Security Act.

1937
– Sit-down strike at General Motors plant in Flint, Michigan.

Who opposed the New Deal and why?

How did the second phase of the New Deal differ from the first?

What major political trends changed during the late 1930s?

Conclusion: What were the achievements and limitations of the New Deal?

✓ LearningCurve
Check what you know.
bedfordstmartins.com
/roarkunderstanding

729

Wagner Act

▶ 1935 law that guaranteed industrial workers the right to organize into unions; also known as the National Labor Relations Act. Following passage of the act, union membership skyrocketed to 30 percent of the workforce, the highest in American history.

disputes and supervise the organization of labor unions. The **Wagner Act**, as it came to be called, guaranteed industrial workers the right to organize unions, putting the might of federal law behind the appeals of labor leaders. If the majority of workers at a company voted for a union, the union became the sole bargaining agent for the entire workplace, and the employer was required to negotiate with the elected union leaders. Roosevelt signed the Wagner Act in July 1935, for the first time providing federal support for labor organization — the most important New Deal reform of the industrial order.

The achievements that flowed from the Wagner Act and renewed labor militancy were impressive. When Roosevelt became president in 1933, union membership — composed almost entirely of skilled workers in trade unions affiliated with the American Federation of Labor (AFL) — stood at three million. With the support of the Wagner Act, union membership expanded to fourteen million by 1945. By then, 30 percent of the workforce was unionized, the highest in American history.

Most of the new union members were factory workers and unskilled laborers, many of them immigrants, women, and African Americans. For decades, established AFL unions had no desire to organize factory and unskilled workers. In 1935, under the aggressive leadership of the mine workers' John L. Lewis and the head of the Amalgamated Clothing Workers, Sidney Hillman, a coalition of unskilled workers formed the **Committee for Industrial Organization (CIO)**, later the Congress of Industrial Organizations). The CIO, helped by the Wagner Act, mobilized organizing drives in major industries, including the bitterly anti-union automobile and steel industries.

Committee for Industrial Organization (CIO)

▶ Coalition of mostly unskilled workers (later called Congress of Industrial Organizations) formed in 1935 that mobilized massive union organizing drives in major industries. By 1941, through the CIO-affiliated United Auto Workers, organizers had overcome violent resistance to unionize the entire automobile industry.

The bloody struggle by the CIO-affiliated United Auto Workers (UAW) to organize workers at General Motors climaxed in January 1937. Striking workers occupied the main assembly plant in Flint, Michigan, in a sit-down strike that slashed the plant's production of 15,000 cars a week to a mere 150. Stymied, General Motors eventually surrendered and agreed to make the UAW the sole bargaining agent for all the company's workers and to refrain from interfering with union activity. The UAW expanded its campaign until, after much violence, the entire industry was unionized by 1941.

The CIO hoped to ride organizing success in auto plants to victory in the steel mills. But after unionizing the giant U.S. Steel, the CIO ran up against determined opposition from smaller steel firms. Following a police attack that killed ten strikers at Republic Steel outside Chicago in May 1937, the battered steelworkers halted their organizing campaign. In steel and other major industries, such as the stridently anti-union southern textile mills, organizing efforts stalled until after 1941, when military mobilization created labor shortages that gave workers greater bargaining power.

Social Security and Tax Reform

Social Security

▶ New Deal program created in August 1935 that was designed to provide a modest income for elderly people. The act also created unemployment insurance with modest benefits. Social Security provoked sharp opposition from conservatives and the wealthy.

The single most important feature of the New Deal's emerging welfare state was **Social Security**. An ambitious, far-reaching, and permanent reform, Social Security was designed to provide a modest income to relieve the poverty of elderly people. Only about 15 percent of older Americans had private pension plans, and during the depression corporations and banks often failed to pay the meager pensions they had promised. Corporations routinely fired or demoted employees to avoid or reduce pension payments. Prompted by the popular but impractical panaceas of

CHAPTER LOCATOR | How did Franklin D. Roosevelt win the 1932 election? | What were the goals and achievements of the first New Deal?

CHAPTER 24

730 FORGING THE NEW DEAL

Dr. Townsend, Father Coughlin, and Huey Long, Roosevelt told Congress that "it is our plain duty to provide for that security upon which welfare depends . . . and undertake the great task of furthering the security of the citizen and his family through social insurance."

The political struggle for Social Security highlighted class differences among Americans. Support for the measure came from a coalition of advocacy groups for the elderly and the poor, traditional progressives, leftists, social workers, and labor unions. Arrayed against them were economic conservatives, including the American Liberty League, the National Association of Manufacturers, the Chamber of Commerce, and the American Medical Association. Enact the Social Security system, these conservatives and other Republicans warned, and the government will ruin private property, destroy initiative, and reduce proud individuals to spineless loafers. Despite this opposition, the large New Deal majority in Congress passed the Social Security Act in August 1935.

> ### > Key Provisions of Social Security

- Used tax contributions from workers and their employers to fund pensions for the elderly.
- Stipulated that, upon reaching retirement age, workers would earn benefits based on their contributions and years of work.
- Placed no means test on eligibility for benefits.
- Created unemployment insurance that provided modest benefits for workers who lost their jobs.

Not all workers benefited from the Social Security Act. It excluded domestic and agricultural workers, thereby making ineligible about half of all African Americans and more than half of all employed women — about five million people in all.

Although the first Social Security check (for $41.30) was not issued until 1940, the system gave millions of working people the assurance that when they became too old to work, they would receive a modest income from the federal government. This safety net protected many ordinary working people from fears of a penniless and insecure old age.

Fervent opposition to Social Security struck New Dealers as evidence that the rich had learned little from the depression. Roosevelt had long felt contempt for the moneyed elite who ignored the suffering of the poor. He looked for a way to redistribute wealth that would weaken conservative opposition, advance the cause of social equity, and defuse political challenges from Huey Long and Father Coughlin. Roosevelt charged in 1935 that large fortunes put "great and undesirable concentration of control in [the hands of] relatively few individuals." He urged a graduated tax on corporations, an inheritance tax, and an increase in maximum personal income taxes. Congress endorsed Roosevelt's basic principle by taxing those with higher incomes at a somewhat higher rate.

Neglected Americans and the New Deal

The patchwork of New Deal reforms erected a two-tier welfare state. In the top tier, organized workers in major industries were the greatest beneficiaries of New Deal

Who opposed the New Deal and why?

How did the second phase of the New Deal differ from the first?

What major political trends changed during the late 1930s?

Conclusion: What were the achievements and limitations of the New Deal?

☑ LearningCurve
Check what you know.
bedfordstmartins.com
/roarkunderstanding

731

Mary McLeod Bethune

At the urging of Eleanor Roosevelt, Mary McLeod Bethune, a southern educational and civil rights leader, became director of the National Youth Administration's Division of Negro Affairs. The first black woman to head a federal agency, Bethune used her position to promote social change. Here, Bethune protests the discriminatory hiring practices of the Peoples Drug Store chain in the nation's capital. Moorland-Spingarn Research Center, Howard University.

initiatives. In the bottom tier, millions of neglected Americans — women, children, and old folks, along with the unorganized, unskilled, uneducated, and unemployed — often fell through the New Deal safety net. Many working people remained more or less untouched by New Deal benefits. The average unemployment rate for the 1930s stayed high — 17 percent. Workers in industries that resisted unions received little help from the Wagner Act or the WPA. Tens of thousands of women in southern textile mills, for example, commonly received wages of less than ten cents an hour and were fired if they protested. Domestic workers, almost all of them women, and agricultural workers — many of them African, Hispanic, or Asian Americans — were neither unionized nor eligible for Social Security.

The New Deal neglected few citizens more than African Americans. About half of black Americans in cities were jobless, more than double the unemployment rate among whites. In the rural South, where the vast majority of African Americans lived, conditions were worse, given the New Deal agricultural policies such as the AAA that favored landowners, who often pushed blacks off the land they farmed. Disfranchisement by intimidation and legal subterfuge prevented southern blacks from protesting their plight at the ballot box. Protesters risked vicious retaliation from local whites. Bitter critics charged that the New Deal's NRA stood for "Negro Run Around" or "Negroes Ruined Again."

Roosevelt responded to such criticisms with great caution, since New Deal reforms required the political support of powerful conservative, segregationist, southern white Democrats who would be alienated by programs that aided blacks. A white Georgia relief worker expressed the common view that "any Nigger who gets over $8 a week is a spoiled Nigger, that's all." Stymied by the political clout of entrenched white racism, New Dealers still attracted support from black voters. Roosevelt's overtures to African Americans prompted northern black voters in the 1934 congressional elections to shift from the Republican to the Democratic Party, helping elect New Deal Democrats.

Eleanor Roosevelt sponsored the appointment of Mary McLeod Bethune — the energetic cofounder of the National Council of Negro Women — as head of the Division of Negro Affairs in the National Youth Administration. The highest-ranking black official in Roosevelt's administration, Bethune used her position to guide a small number of black professionals and civil rights activists to posts within New Deal agencies. Ultimately, about one in four African Americans got access to New Deal relief programs.

Despite these gains, by 1940 African Americans still suffered severe handicaps. Most of the thirteen million black workers toiled at low-paying menial jobs, unprotected by the New Deal safety net. Segregated and unequal schools were the norm, and only 1 percent of black students earned college degrees. In southern

CHAPTER LOCATOR | How did Franklin D. Roosevelt win the 1932 election? | What were the goals and achievements of the first New Deal?

CHAPTER 24
732   FORGING THE NEW DEAL

states, vigilante violence against blacks went unpunished. For these problems of black Americans, the New Deal offered few remedies.

Hispanic Americans fared no better. About a million Mexican Americans lived in the United States in the 1930s, most of them first- or second-generation immigrants who worked crops throughout the West. During the depression, field workers saw their low wages plunge lower still to about a dime an hour. To preserve scarce jobs for U.S. citizens, the federal government choked off immigration from Mexico, while state and local officials deported tens of thousands of Mexican Americans, many with their American-born children. New Deal programs throughout the West often discriminated against Hispanics and other people of color. A New Deal study concluded that "the Mexican is . . . segregated from the rest of the community as effectively as the Negro . . . [by] poverty and low wages."

Asian Americans had similar experiences. Asian immigrants were still excluded from U.S. citizenship and in many states were not permitted to own land. By 1930, more than half of Japanese Americans had been born in the United States, but they were still liable to discrimination. One young Asian American expressed the frustration felt by many others: "I am a fruit-stand worker. I would much rather it were doctor or lawyer . . . but my aspirations [were] frustrated long ago by circumstances. . . . I am only what I am, a professional carrot washer."

Native Americans also suffered neglect from New Deal agencies. As a group, they remained the poorest of the poor. Since the Dawes Act of 1887 (see chapter 17), the federal government had encouraged Native Americans to assimilate — to abandon their Indian identities and adopt the cultural norms of the majority society. Under the leadership of the New Deal's commissioner of Indian affairs, John Collier, the New Deal's Indian Reorganization Act (IRA) of 1934 largely reversed that policy. Collier claimed that "the most interesting and important fact about Indians" was that they "do not expect much, often they expect nothing at all; yet they are able to be happy." Given such views, the IRA provided little economic aid to Native Americans, but it did restore their right to own land communally and to have greater control over their own affairs. The IRA brought little immediate benefit to Native Americans, but it provided an important foundation for Indians' economic, cultural, and political resurgence a generation later.

Voicing common experiences among Americans neglected by the New Deal, singer and songwriter Woody Guthrie traveled the nation for eight years during the 1930s and heard other rambling men tell him "the story of their life": "how the home went to pieces, how . . . the crops got to where they wouldn't bring nothing, work in factories would kill a dog . . . and — always, always [you] have to fight and argue and cuss and swear . . . to try to get a nickel more out of the rich bosses."

QUICK REVIEW <

What features of a welfare state did the New Deal create and why?

Who opposed the New Deal and why?

How did the second phase of the New Deal differ from the first?

What major political trends changed during the late 1930s?

Conclusion: What were the achievements and limitations of the New Deal?

What major political trends changed during the late 1930s?

When bountiful harvests produced surplus crops that would depress prices if they were sent to market, the New Deal arranged to distribute some of them to needy Americans. Here, farmworkers in east-central Arizona near the New Mexico border line up to receive a ration of potatoes authorized by the New Deal agent checking the box of index cards. Library of Congress.

TO ACCELERATE the sputtering economic recovery, Roosevelt shifted the emphasis of the New Deal in the mid-1930s. Instead of seeking cooperation from conservative business leaders, he decided to rely on the growing New Deal coalition to enact reforms over the strident opposition of the Supreme Court, Republicans, and corporate interests.

Added to New Deal strength in farm states and big cities were some new allies on the left. Throughout Roosevelt's first term, socialists and Communists denounced the slow pace of change and accused the New Deal of failing to serve the interests of the workers who produced the nation's wealth. But by 1936, when Roosevelt won reelection in a landslide, many radicals switched from opposing the New Deal to supporting its relief programs and encouragement of labor unions. By 1937, Roosevelt believed the economy was improving and reduced government spending, triggering a sharp recession that undermined economic recovery and prolonged the depression.

CHAPTER LOCATOR | How did Franklin D. Roosevelt win the 1932 election? | What were the goals and achievements of the first New Deal?

The Election of 1936

Roosevelt believed that the presidential election of 1936 would test his leadership and progressive ideals. The depression still had a stranglehold on the economy. Conservative leaders believed that the New Deal's failure to lift the nation out of the depression indicated that Americans were ready for a change. Left-wing critics insisted that the New Deal had missed the opportunity to displace capitalism with a socialist economy and that voters would embrace candidates who recommended more radical remedies.

Republicans turned to Kansas governor Alfred (Alf) Landon as their presidential nominee, a moderate who stressed mainstream Republican proposals to achieve a balanced federal budget and less government bureaucracy. Roosevelt assailed his "old enemies . . . business and financial monopoly, speculation, reckless banking, [and] class antagonism" and proclaimed, "Never before in all our history have these forces been so united against one candidate. . . . They are unanimous in their hate for me — and I welcome their hatred."

Roosevelt triumphed spectacularly. He won 60.8 percent of the popular vote, making it the widest margin of victory in a presidential election to date. Third parties — including the Socialist and Communist parties — fell pitifully short of the support they expected and never again mounted a significant challenge to the New Deal. Congressional results were equally lopsided, with Democrats outnumbering Republicans more than three to one in both houses. In his inaugural address, Roosevelt announced, "I see one third of a nation ill-housed, ill-clad, [and] ill-nourished," and he promised to devote his second term to alleviating their hardship.

Court Packing

In the afterglow of his reelection triumph, Roosevelt pondered how to remove the remaining obstacles to New Deal reforms. He decided to target the Supreme Court. Conservative justices appointed by Republican presidents had invalidated eleven New Deal measures as unconstitutional interferences with free enterprise. Now, the justices were about to consider Social Security, the Wagner Act, the Securities and Exchange Commission, and other New Deal innovations.

To ensure that the Supreme Court did not dismantle the New Deal, Roosevelt proposed a **court-packing plan** that added one new justice for each existing judge who had served for ten years and was over the age of seventy. In effect, the proposed law would give Roosevelt the power to pack the Court with up to six New Dealers who could outvote the elderly, conservative, Republican justices.

But the president had not reckoned with Americans' deeply rooted deference to the independent authority of the Supreme Court. More than two-thirds of Americans believed that the Court should be free from political interference. Even New Deal supporters were disturbed by the court-packing scheme. The suggestion that individuals over age seventy had diminished mental capacity offended many elderly members of Congress, which defeated Roosevelt's plan in 1937.

Supreme Court justices still got the message. The four most conservative of the elderly justices retired. Roosevelt eventually named eight justices to the Court — more than any other president — ultimately giving New Deal laws safe passage through the Court.

> CHRONOLOGY

1936
- Franklin Roosevelt is reelected by a landslide.

1937
- Roosevelt's court-packing legislation is defeated.
- Economic recession.

1938
- Second Agricultural Adjustment Act.
- Fair Labor Standards Act.
- Congress rejects antilynching bill.

court-packing plan

▶ Law proposed by Franklin Roosevelt to add one new Supreme Court justice for each existing judge who had served for ten years and who was over the age of seventy. Roosevelt wanted to pack the Court with up to six New Dealers who could protect New Deal legislation, but the Senate defeated the bill in 1937.

Who opposed the New Deal and why?

How did the second phase of the New Deal differ from the first?

What major political trends changed during the late 1930s?

Conclusion: What were the achievements and limitations of the New Deal?

✓ LearningCurve
Check what you know.
bedfordstmartins.com
/roarkunderstanding

Reaction and Recession

Emboldened by their defeat of the court-packing plan, Republicans and southern Democrats rallied around their common conservatism to obstruct additional reforms. Former president Herbert Hoover proclaimed that the New Deal was the "repudiation of Democracy" and that "the Republican Party alone [was] the guardian of . . . the charter of freedom." Democrats' arguments over whether the New Deal needed to be expanded — and if so, how — undermined the consensus among reformers and sparked antagonism between Congress and the White House. The ominous rise of belligerent regimes in Germany, Italy, and Japan also slowed reform.

Roosevelt himself favored slowing the pace of the New Deal. He believed that existing New Deal measures had steadily boosted the economy and largely eliminated the depression crisis. In fact, the gross national product in 1937 briefly equaled the 1929 level before dropping lower for the rest of the decade. Unemployment declined to 14 percent in 1937 but quickly spiked upward and stayed higher until 1940. Roosevelt's unwarranted optimism about the economic recovery persuaded him that additional deficit spending by the federal government was no longer necessary.

Roosevelt's optimism failed to consider the stubborn realities of unemployment and poverty, and the reduction in deficit spending reversed the improving economy. Even at the high-water mark of recovery in the summer of 1937, seven million people lacked jobs. In the next few months, national income and production slipped so steeply that almost two-thirds of the economic gains since 1933 were lost by June 1938.

This economic reversal hurt the New Deal politically. Conservatives argued that this recession proved that New Deal measures produced only an illusion of progress. The way to weather the recession was to tax and spend less as well as to wait for the natural laws of supply and demand to restore prosperity. Many New Dealers insisted instead that the continuing depression demanded that Roosevelt revive federal spending and redouble efforts to stimulate the economy. In 1938, Congress heeded such pleas and enacted a massive new program of federal spending.

The recession scare of 1937–1938 taught the president the lesson that economic growth had to be carefully nurtured. The English economist John Maynard Keynes argued that only government intervention could pump enough money into the economy to restore prosperity, a concept that became known as Keynesian economics. Roosevelt never had the inclination or time to master Keynesian thought. But in a commonsense way, he understood that escape from the depression required a plan for large-scale spending to alleviate distress and stimulate economic growth (**Figure 24.2**).

The Last of the New Deal Reforms

From the moment he was sworn in, Roosevelt sought to expand the powers of the presidency. He believed that the president needed more authority to meet emergencies such as the depression and to administer the sprawling federal bureaucracy. Combined with a Democratic majority in Congress, a now-friendly Supreme Court, and the revival of deficit spending, the newly empowered White House seemed to be in a good position to move ahead with a revitalized New Deal.

Resistance to further reform was also on the rise, however. Conservatives argued that the New Deal had pressed government centralization too far. Even

CHAPTER LOCATOR | How did Franklin D. Roosevelt win the 1932 election? | What were the goals and achievements of the first New Deal?

736 CHAPTER 24 FORGING THE NEW DEAL

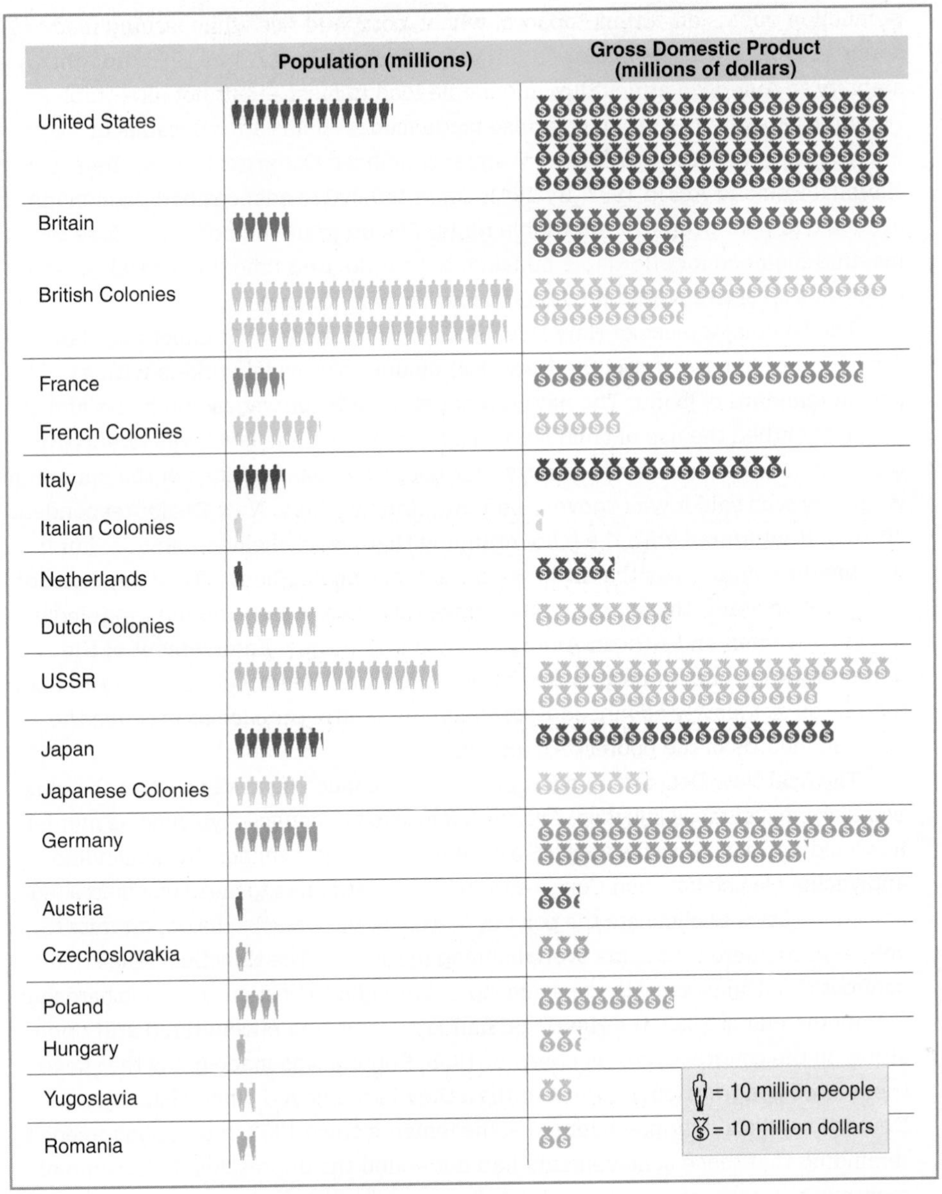

	Population (millions)	Gross Domestic Product (millions of dollars)
United States		
Britain		
British Colonies		
France		
French Colonies		
Italy		
Italian Colonies		
Netherlands		
Dutch Colonies		
USSR		
Japan		
Japanese Colonies		
Germany		
Austria		
Czechoslovakia		
Poland		
Hungary		
Yugoslavia		
Romania		

= 10 million people
= 10 million dollars

> GLOBAL COMPARISON

FIGURE 24.2 ■ National Populations and Economies, ca. 1938

Throughout the Great Depression, the United States remained more productive than any other nation in the world. Despite the lingering effects of the depression, by 1938 the United States produced more than twice as much as Germany and the Soviet Union, nearly three times as much as France and Japan, and more than five times as much as Italy. From the viewpoint of Germany, if the European nations listed here could be brought under German control, its economy would be greater than that of the United States and would become the mightiest in the world. Economically, how important were colonies to the major powers? In general, what do these data suggest about the relationship between population and gross domestic product?

the New Deal's friends became weary of one emergency program after another while economic woes continued to shadow New Deal achievements. By the midpoint of Roosevelt's second term, restive members of Congress balked at new initiatives. But enough support remained for one last burst of reform.

Agriculture still had strong claims on New Deal attention in the face of drought, declining crop prices, and impoverished sharecroppers and tenants. In 1937, the Agriculture Department created the Farm Security Administration (FSA) to provide housing and loans to help tenant farmers become independent. A black tenant farmer in North Carolina who received an FSA loan told a New Deal interviewer, "I wake up in the night sometimes and think I must be half-dead and gone to heaven." For those who owned farms, the New Deal offered renewed prosperity with a second Agricultural Adjustment Act (AAA) in 1938 that placed

| Who opposed the New Deal and why? | How did the second phase of the New Deal differ from the first? | **What major political trends changed during the late 1930s?** | Conclusion: What were the achievements and limitations of the New Deal? | ✓ LearningCurve Check what you know. bedfordstmartins.com /roarkunderstanding |

production quotas on cotton, tobacco, wheat, corn, and rice while issuing food stamps to allow poor people to obtain surplus food. The AAA of 1938 brought stability to American agriculture and ample food to most — but not all — tables.

Advocates for the urban poor also made modest gains after decades of neglect. New York senator Robert Wagner convinced Congress to pass the National Housing Act in 1937. By 1941, some 160,000 residences had been made available to poor people at affordable rents. The program did not come close to meeting the need for affordable housing, but for the first time the federal government took an active role in providing decent urban housing.

The last major piece of New Deal labor legislation, the Fair Labor Standards Act of June 1938, reiterated the New Deal pledge to provide workers with a decent standard of living. The new law set standards for wages and hours and at long last curbed the use of child labor. The minimum-wage level was twenty-five cents an hour for a maximum of forty-four hours a week. To critics of the minimum wage law who said it was "government interference," one New Dealer responded: "It was. It interfered with the fellow running that pecan shelling plant . . . [and] told him he couldn't pay that little widow seven cents an hour." To attract enough conservative votes, the act exempted domestic help and farm laborers — relegating most women and African Americans to lower wages. Enforcement of the minimum-wage standards was weak and haphazard. Nevertheless, the Fair Labor Standards Act slowly advanced Roosevelt's inaugural promise to improve the living standards of the poorest Americans.

The final New Deal reform effort failed to make much headway against the hidebound system of racial injustice. Although Roosevelt denounced lynching as murder, he would not jeopardize his vital base of southern political support by demanding antilynching legislation, and Congress voted down attempts to make lynching a federal crime. Laws to eliminate the poll tax — used to deny blacks the opportunity to vote — encountered the same overwhelming resistance. The New Deal refused to confront racial injustice with the same vigor it brought to bear on economic hardship.

By the end of 1938, the New Deal had lost steam and encountered stiff opposition. In the congressional elections of 1938, Republicans made gains that gave them more congressional influence than they had enjoyed since 1932. New Dealers could claim unprecedented achievements since 1933, but nobody needed reminding that those achievements had not ended the depression. In his annual message to Congress in January 1939, Roosevelt signaled a halt to New Deal reforms by speaking about preserving the progress already achieved rather than extending it. Roosevelt pointed to the ominous threats posed by fascist aggressors in Germany and Japan, and he proposed defense expenditures that surpassed New Deal appropriations for relief and economic recovery.

> **QUICK REVIEW**

Why did political support for
New Deal reforms decline?

CHAPTER LOCATOR | How did Franklin D. Roosevelt win the 1932 election? | What were the goals and achievements of the first New Deal?

738   CHAPTER 24
FORGING THE NEW DEAL

THE NEW DEAL demonstrated that a growing majority of Americans agreed with Roosevelt that the federal government should help those in need. Through programs that sought relief, recovery, and reform, the New Deal vastly expanded the size and influence of the federal government and changed the way many Americans viewed Washington. New Dealers achieved significant victories, such as Social Security, labor's right to organize, and guarantees that farm prices would be maintained through controls on production and marketing. New Deal measures marked the emergence of a welfare state, but its limits left millions of needy Americans with little aid.

Full-scale relief, recovery, and reform eluded the New Deal. Even though millions of Americans benefited from New Deal initiatives, both relief and recovery were limited and temporary. In 1940, the depression still plagued the economy. Perhaps the most impressive achievement of the New Deal was what did not happen. Although authoritarian governments and anticapitalist policies were common outside the United States during the 1930s, they were shunned by the New Deal. The greatest economic crisis the nation had ever faced did not cause Americans to abandon democracy, as happened in Germany, where Adolf Hitler seized dictatorial power. Nor did the nation turn to radical alternatives such as socialism or communism.

Republicans and other conservatives claimed that the New Deal amounted to a form of socialism that threatened democracy and capitalism. But rather than attack capitalism, Franklin Roosevelt sought to save it. And he succeeded. That success also marked the limits of the New Deal's achievements. Franklin Roosevelt believed that a shift of authority toward the federal government would allow capitalist enterprises to be balanced by the nation's democratic tradition. The New Deal stopped far short of challenging capitalism either by undermining private property or by imposing strict national planning.

New Dealers repeatedly described their programs as a kind of warfare against the depression of the 1930s. In the next decade, the Roosevelt administration had to turn from the economic crisis at home to participate in a worldwide conflagration to defeat the enemies of democracy abroad.

Nonetheless, many New Deal reforms continued for decades to structure the basic institutions of banking, the stock market, union organizations, agricultural markets, Social Security, minimum-wage standards, and more. Opponents of these measures and of the basic New Deal notion of an activist government remained powerful, especially in the Republican Party. They claimed that government was the problem, not the solution — a slogan that Republicans championed during and after the 1980s and that led, with the cooperation of some Democrats, to the dismantling of a number of New Deal programs, including the regulation of banking.

| Who opposed the New Deal and why? | How did the second phase of the New Deal differ from the first? | What major political trends changed during the late 1930s? | Conclusion: What were the achievements and limitations of the New Deal? | ✓ LearningCurve Check what you know. bedfordstmartins.com /roarkunderstanding |

739

CHAPTER 24 STUDY GUIDE

STEP 1
GET STARTED ONLINE

✓ LearningCurve ▪ bedfordstmartins.com/roarkunderstanding

Now that you've read the chapter, make it stick by completing the LearningCurve activity.

STEP 2
EXPLAIN WHY IT MATTERS

Put your reading into practice. Identify each term below, and then explain why it matters in U.S. history.

TERM	WHO OR WHAT & WHEN	WHY IT MATTERS
New Deal coalition (p. 715)		
underconsumption (p. 717)		
Federal Deposit Insurance Corporation (p. 718)		
fireside chats (p. 718)		
Civilian Conservation Corps (CCC) (p. 719)		
Agricultural Adjustment Act (AAA) (p. 721)		
National Recovery Administration (NRA) (p. 722)		
Works Progress Administration (WPA) (p. 729)		
Wagner Act (p. 730)		
Committee for Industrial Organization (CIO) (p. 730)		
Social Security (p. 730)		
court-packing plan (p. 735)		

STEP 3
MOVE BEYOND THE BASICS

To demonstrate a more advanced understanding, describe the following New Deal programs and legislation and assess how successful or unsuccessful each was in achieving relief, recovery, or reform.

Program/legislation	Description	How successful/unsuccessful?
Agricultural Adjustment Act		
Civilian Conservation Corps		
Emergency Banking Act		
Indian Reorganization Act		
National Recovery Administration		
Public Works Administration		
Social Security		
Tennessee Valley Authority		
Wagner Act		
Works Progress Administration		

STEP 4 PUT IT ALL TOGETHER

Now, take a step back and try to explain the big picture. Remember to use specific examples from the chapter in your answers.

FRANKLIN D. ROOSEVELT

▶ Why was Franklin Roosevelt so popular? Why did he win the elections of 1932 and 1936?

▶ How was Eleanor Roosevelt a part of her husband's political career?

THE NEW DEAL

▶ What were the greatest achievements of the New Deal, both generally and specifically?

▶ What were the differences between the first phase of the New Deal and the second?

THE OPPOSITION

▶ Who initially opposed the New Deal and why?

▶ Why did general support for the New Deal decline?

LOOKING BACKWARD, LOOKING AHEAD

▶ What was distinctive about the New Deal compared with previous government reforms in the twentieth century?

▶ What was the long-term significance of the New Deal?

> IN YOUR OWN WORDS

Imagine that you must give an oral report to the class answering the following question: Why was the New Deal so important in U.S. history? What would be the most important points to include and why?

25

THE UNITED STATES AND THE SECOND WORLD WAR

1939–1945

> **How did the Second World War change the United States, both domestically and internationally?** Chapter 25 examines the involvement of the United States in World War II. It first examines isolationism and neutrality in the years before the nation's declaration of war in 1941 and then explains the most important wartime events, including the impact of the war on the American home front.

**LearningCurve**

bedfordstmartins.com/roarkunderstanding
After reading the chapter, use LearningCurve to retain what you've read.

> How did the United States respond to international developments in the 1930s?

> How did the outbreak of war affect U.S. foreign policy?

> How did the United States mobilize for war?

> How did the Allies turn the tide in Europe and the Pacific?

> How did the war change life on the American home front?

> How did the Allies finally win the war?

> Conclusion: Why did the United States emerge as a superpower at the end of the war?

USS *Yorktown*. A Grumann F6F-3 "Hellcat" sits on the flight deck during Pacific operations, 1943. Photo by PhotoQuest/Getty Images.

> How did the United States respond to international developments in the 1930s?

WALT DISNEY *Goes South American*
IN HIS GAYEST MUSICAL TECHNICOLOR FEATURE

SALUDOS AMIGOS *(HELLO FRIENDS)*

Introducing JOE CARIOCA THE BRAZILIAN JITTERBIRD

DISTRIBUTED BY RKO RADIO PICTURES INC.

Promoting the Good Neighbor Policy

To encourage continuing friendly relations with Latin America during World War II, the Roosevelt administration urged Walt Disney to make the 1942 film *Saludos Amigos* — starring Donald Duck, Goofy, and "the Brazilian Jitterbird," Joe Carioca — largely for distribution south of the border. The good neighbor policy helped prevent Latin American nations from developing meaningful military alliances with the Axis powers during World War II. © Disney Enterprises, Inc.

THE FIRST WORLD WAR left a dangerous and ultimately deadly legacy. The victors — especially Britain, France, and the United States — sought to avoid future wars at almost any cost. The defeated nation, Germany, aspired to reassert its power and avenge its losses by means of renewed warfare. Italy and Japan felt humiliated by the Versailles peace settlement and saw war as a legitimate way to increase their global power. Japan invaded the northern Chinese province of Manchuria in 1931 with ambitions to expand throughout Asia. Italy, led by the fascist Benito Mussolini since 1922, hungered for an empire in Africa. In Germany, National Socialist Adolf Hitler rose to power in 1933 in a quest to dominate Europe and the world. These aggressive, militaristic, antidemocratic regimes seemed a smaller threat to most people in the United States during the 1930s than did the economic crisis at home. Shielded from external threats by the Atlantic and Pacific

CHAPTER LOCATOR | How did the United States respond to international developments in the 1930s? | How did the outbreak of war affect U.S. foreign policy?

oceans, Americans hoped to avoid entanglement in foreign woes and to concentrate on climbing out of the nation's economic abyss.

Roosevelt and Reluctant Isolation

Like most Americans during the 1930s, Franklin Roosevelt believed that the nation's highest priority was to attack the domestic causes and consequences of the Great Depression. But unlike most Americans, Roosevelt had long advocated an active role for the United States in international affairs.

The depression forced Roosevelt to retreat from his previous internationalism. He came to believe that energetic involvement in foreign affairs diverted resources and political support from domestic recovery. Once in office, Roosevelt sought to combine domestic economic recovery with a low-profile foreign policy that encouraged free trade and disarmament.

Roosevelt's pursuit of international amity was constrained by economic circumstances and American popular opinion. After an opinion poll demonstrated popular support for recognizing the Soviet Union, Roosevelt established formal diplomatic relations in 1933. But when the League of Nations condemned Japanese and German aggression, Roosevelt did not support the league's attempts to keep the peace because he feared jeopardizing isolationists' support for New Deal measures in Congress. America watched from the sidelines when Japan withdrew from the league and ignored the limitations on its navy imposed after World War I. The United States also looked the other way when Hitler rearmed Germany and recalled its representative to the league in 1933. Roosevelt worried that German and Japanese actions threatened world peace, but he reassured Americans that the nation would not "use its armed forces for the settlement of any [international] dispute anywhere."

The Good Neighbor Policy

In 1933, Roosevelt announced that the United States would pursue "the policy of the good neighbor" in international relations, which meant that no nation had the right to intervene in the internal or external affairs of another. The **good neighbor policy** did not indicate a U.S. retreat from empire in Latin America. Instead, it declared that, unlike in past decades, the United States would not depend on military force to exercise its influence in the region. Roosevelt refrained from sending troops to defend the interests of American corporations in Latin America. While Roosevelt's hands-off policy honored the principle of national self-determination, it also permitted the rise of dictators in Nicaragua, Cuba, and elsewhere, who exploited and terrorized their nations with private support from U.S. businesses.

Military nonintervention also did not prevent the United States from exerting its economic influence in Latin America. In 1934, Congress gave the president the power to reduce tariffs on goods imported into the United States from nations that agreed to lower their own tariffs on U.S. exports. By 1940, twenty-two nations had agreed to reciprocal tariff reductions, helping to double U.S. exports to Latin America and contributing to the New Deal's goal of boosting the domestic economy through free trade.

> CHRONOLOGY

1935–1937
– Neutrality acts.

1936
– Nazi Germany occupies the Rhineland.
– Italian armies conquer Ethiopia.
– Spanish civil war begins.

1937
– Japanese troops capture Nanjing.

good neighbor policy
▶ Foreign policy announced by Franklin Roosevelt in 1933 that promised the United States would not interfere in the internal or external affairs of another country, thereby ending U.S. military interventions in Latin America.

| How did the United States mobilize for war? | How did the Allies turn the tide in Europe and the Pacific? | How did the war change life on the American home front? | How did the Allies finally win the war? | Conclusion: Why did the United States emerge as a superpower at the end of the war? | ✔ LearningCurve Check what you know. bedfordstmartins.com /roarkunderstanding |

745

The Price of Noninvolvement

In Europe, fascist governments in Italy and Germany threatened military aggression. Britain and France made only verbal protests. Emboldened, Hitler plotted to avenge defeat in World War I by recapturing territories with German inhabitants, all the while accusing Jews of polluting the purity of the Aryan master race. The virulent anti-Semitism of Hitler and his Nazi Party unified non-Jewish Germans and attracted sympathizers among many other Europeans, even in France and Britain.

In Japan, a stridently militaristic government planned to follow the invasion of Manchuria in 1931 with conquests extending throughout Southeast Asia. The Manchurian invasion bogged down in a long and vicious war when Chinese Nationalists rallied around their leader, Jiang Jieshi (Chiang Kai-shek), to fight against the Japanese. Preparations for new Japanese conquests continued, however. In 1936, Japan openly violated naval limitation treaties and began to build a battle-ready fleet to seek naval superiority in the Pacific.

In the United States, the hostilities in Asia and Europe reinforced isolationist sentiments. Popular disillusionment with the failure of Woodrow Wilson's idealistic goals caused many Americans to question the nation's participation in World War I. In 1933, Gerald Nye, a Republican from North Dakota, chaired a Senate committee that concluded that greedy "merchants of death" — American weapons makers, bankers, and financiers — had dragged the nation into the war to line their own pockets. International tensions and the Nye committee report prompted Congress to pass a series of **neutrality acts** between 1935 and 1937 designed to avoid entanglement in foreign wars. The neutrality acts prohibited making loans and selling arms to nations at war.

By 1937, the growing conflicts overseas caused some Americans to call for a total embargo on all trade with warring countries. The Neutrality Act of 1937 attempted to reconcile the nation's desire for both peace and foreign trade with a "cash-and-carry" policy that required warring nations to pay cash for nonmilitary goods and to transport them in their own ships. This policy benefited the nation's economy, but it also helped foreign aggressors by supplying them with goods and thereby undermining peace.

The desire for peace in France, Britain, and the United States led Germany, Italy, and Japan to launch offensives on the assumption that the Western democracies lacked the will to oppose them. In March 1936, Nazi troops marched into the industry-rich Rhineland on Germany's western border, in blatant violation of the Treaty of Versailles. One month later, Italian armies completed their conquest of Ethiopia, projecting fascist power into Africa. In December 1937, Japanese invaders captured

neutrality acts

▶ Legislation passed in 1935 and 1937 that sought to avoid entanglement in foreign wars while protecting trade. The 1937 act prohibited selling arms to nations at war and required nations to pay cash for nonmilitary goods and to transport them in their own ships.

Spanish Civil War, 1936–1939

CHAPTER LOCATOR | How did the United States respond to international developments in the 1930s? | How did the outbreak of war affect U.S. foreign policy?

CHAPTER 25
746 THE UNITED STATES AND THE SECOND WORLD WAR

Nanjing (Nanking) and celebrated their triumph in the "Rape of Nanking," a deadly rampage that killed 200,000 Chinese civilians.

In Spain, a bitter civil war broke out in July 1936 when the Nationalists — fascist rebels led by General Francisco Franco — attacked the democratically elected Republican government. Both Germany and Italy reinforced Franco, while the Soviet Union provided much less aid to the Republican Loyalists. The Spanish civil war did not prompt European democracies or the U.S. government to help the Loyalists, despite sympathy for their cause. Abandoned by the Western nations, the Republican Loyalists were defeated in 1939, and Franco built a fascist bulwark in Spain.

Hostilities in Europe, Africa, and Asia alarmed Roosevelt and some Americans. The president sought to persuade most Americans to moderate their isolationism and find a way to support the victims of fascist aggression. Critics accused the president of seeking to replace "Americanism" with "internationalism." The popularity of isolationist sentiment convinced Roosevelt that he needed to maneuver carefully if the United States were to help prevent fascist aggressors from conquering Europe and Asia, leaving the United States an isolated island of democracy.

QUICK REVIEW

Why did isolationism during the 1930s concern Roosevelt?

| How did the United States mobilize for war? | How did the Allies turn the tide in Europe and the Pacific? | How did the war change life on the American home front? | How did the Allies finally win the war? | Conclusion: Why did the United States emerge as a superpower at the end of the war? | ✓ LearningCurve Check what you know. bedfordstmartins.com /roarkunderstanding |

How did the outbreak of war affect U.S. foreign policy?

Nazi Invasion of Poland

Adolf Hitler relished the early success of the German army's *blitzkrieg* against Poland in 1939. This photo shows Hitler reviewing a victory parade of his soldiers in Warsaw. After the conquest, Germans systematically murdered hundreds of thousands of Polish civilians and confined even more to slave labor camps. Photo by Hugo Jaeger/Timepix/Time Life Pictures/Getty Images.

BETWEEN 1939 AND 1941, fascist victories overseas eventually eroded American isolationism. At first, U.S. intervention was limited to providing material support to the enemies of Germany and Japan, principally Britain, China, and the Soviet Union. But Japan's surprise attack on Pearl Harbor eliminated that restraint, and the nation began to mobilize for an all-out assault on foreign foes.

Nazi Aggression and War in Europe

Under the spell of isolationism, Americans passively watched Hitler's relentless campaign to dominate Europe (**Map 25.1**). In 1938, Hitler incorporated Austria into Germany and turned his attention to the Sudetenland, which had been granted to Czechoslovakia by the World War I peace settlement. Hoping to avoid war, British prime minister Neville Chamberlain offered Hitler terms of **appeasement** that would give the Sudetenland to Germany if Hitler agreed to leave the rest of Czechoslovakia alone. Hitler accepted the terms but didn't keep his promise. By 1939, Hitler had annexed Czechoslovakia and demanded that Poland return the

appeasement
▶ British strategy aimed at avoiding a war with Germany in the late 1930s by not objecting to Hitler's policy of territorial expansion.

CHAPTER LOCATOR | How did the United States respond to international developments in the 1930s? | **How did the outbreak of war affect U.S. foreign policy?**

CHAPTER 25
748 THE UNITED STATES AND THE SECOND WORLD WAR

German territory it had gained after World War I. Recognizing that appeasement of Hitler had failed, Britain and France assured Poland that they would go to war with Germany if Hitler attacked. In turn, Hitler negotiated with Soviet premier Joseph Stalin, offering him concessions to prevent the Soviet Union from joining Britain and France in opposing a German attack on Poland. Despite the enduring hatred between fascist Germany and the Communist Soviet Union, the two powers signed the Nazi-Soviet treaty of nonaggression in August 1939, exposing Poland to an onslaught by both the German and Soviet armies.

At dawn on September 1, 1939, Hitler unleashed his *blitzkrieg* (literally, "lightning war") on Poland. "Act brutally!" Hitler exhorted his generals. "Send [every] man, woman, and child of Polish descent and language to their deaths, pitilessly and remorselessly." The attack triggered Soviet attacks on eastern Poland and declarations of war from France and Britain two days later, igniting a conflagration that raced around the globe. In September 1939, Germany seemed invincible, causing many people to fear that all of Europe would soon share Poland's fate.

After the Nazis overran Poland, Hitler soon launched a westward blitzkrieg. In the first six months of 1940, German forces smashed through Denmark, Norway, the Netherlands, Belgium, and France. The speed of the German attack trapped more than 300,000 British and French soldiers, who retreated to the port of Dunkirk, where an improvised armada of British vessels ferried them to safety across the English Channel. By mid-June 1940, France had surrendered the largest army in the world, signed an armistice that gave Germany control of nearly two-thirds of the countryside, and installed a collaborationist government at Vichy. With an empire that stretched across Europe from Poland to France, Hitler seemed poised to attack Britain.

The new British prime minister, Winston Churchill, vowed that Britain, unlike France, would never surrender to Hitler. "We shall fight on the seas and oceans [and] . . . in the air," he proclaimed, "whatever the cost may be, we shall fight on the beaches, . . . and in the fields and in the streets." Churchill's defiance stiffened British resolve against Hitler's attack, which began in mid-June 1940 when wave after wave of German bombers targeted British military installations and cities, killing tens of thousands of civilians. The outgunned Royal Air Force fought as doggedly as Churchill had predicted and finally won the Battle of Britain by November, clearing German bombers from British skies and handing Hitler his first defeat. Churchill praised the valiant British pilots, declaring that "never . . . was so much owed by so many to so few." Battered and exhausted by German attacks, Britain needed American help to continue to fight, as Churchill repeatedly wrote to Roosevelt in private.

From Neutrality to the Arsenal of Democracy

Most Americans condemned German aggression and favored Britain and France, but isolationism remained powerful. Roosevelt feared that if Congress did not repeal the arms embargo mandated by the Neutrality Act of 1937, France and Britain would soon succumb to the Nazi onslaught. Congress agreed in November 1939 to allow belligerent nations to buy arms, as well as nonmilitary supplies, on a cash-and-carry basis.

In practice, the revised neutrality law permitted Britain and France to purchase American war materiel and carry it across the Atlantic in their own ships,

> CHRONOLOGY

1938
- Hitler annexes Austria.

1939
- German troops occupy Czechoslovakia.
- Nazi-Soviet nonaggression pact.
- Germany's attack on Poland begins World War II.

1940
- Germany invades Denmark, Norway, France, Belgium, Luxembourg, and the Netherlands.
- British and French troops evacuate from Dunkirk.
- Battle of Britain.
- Tripartite Pact.

1941
- Lend-Lease Act.
- Germany invades Soviet Union.
- Japanese attack Pearl Harbor.
- United States enters World War II.

| How did the United States mobilize for war? | How did the Allies turn the tide in Europe and the Pacific? | How did the war change life on the American home front? | How did the Allies finally win the war? | Conclusion: Why did the United States emerge as a superpower at the end of the war? | ✔ LearningCurve Check what you know. bedfordstmartins.com /roarkunderstanding |

749

thereby shielding American vessels from attack by German submarines lurking in the Atlantic. Roosevelt searched for a way to aid Britain short of entering a formal alliance or declaring war against Germany. Churchill pleaded for American destroyers, aircraft, and munitions, but he had no money to buy them under the

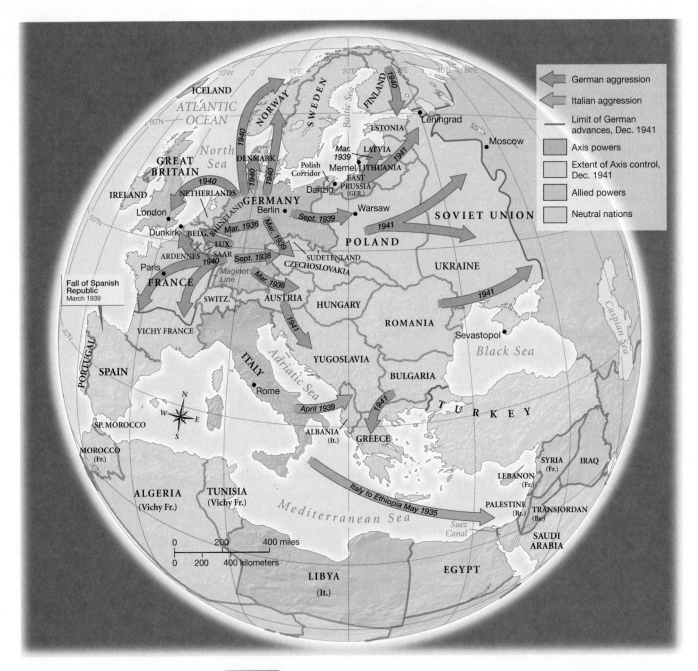

MAP 25.1 ■ Axis Aggression through 1941

Through a series of surprise military strikes before 1942, Mussolini sought to re-create the Roman empire in the Mediterranean while Hitler aimed to annex Austria and reclaim German territories occupied by France after World War I. When the German dictator began his campaign to rule "inferior" peoples by attacking Poland, World War II broke out.

CHAPTER LOCATOR | How did the United States respond to international developments in the 1930s? | How did the outbreak of war affect U.S. foreign policy?

CHAPTER 25
750 THE UNITED STATES AND THE SECOND WORLD WAR

prevailing cash-and-carry neutrality law. By late summer in 1940, Roosevelt concocted a scheme to deliver fifty old destroyers to Britain in exchange for American access to British bases in the Western Hemisphere, the first steps toward building a firm Anglo-American alliance against Hitler.

While German Luftwaffe (air force) pilots bombed Britain, Roosevelt decided to run for an unprecedented third term as president in 1940. But the presidential election, which Roosevelt won handily, provided no clear mandate for American involvement in the European war. The Republican candidate, Wendell Willkie, a former Democrat who generally favored New Deal measures and Roosevelt's foreign policy, attacked Roosevelt as a warmonger. Willkie's accusations caused the president to promise voters, "Your boys are not going to be sent into any foreign wars," a pledge counterbalanced by his repeated warnings about the threats to America posed by Nazi aggression.

Once reelected, Roosevelt maneuvered to support Britain in every way short of war. In a fireside chat shortly after Christmas 1940, he proclaimed that it was incumbent on the United States to become "the great arsenal of democracy" and send "every ounce and every ton of munitions and supplies that we can possibly spare to help the defenders who are in the front lines." In January 1941, Roosevelt proposed the **Lend-Lease Act.**

> **Lend-Lease Act**

- Allowed the British to obtain arms from the United States without paying cash but with the promise to reimburse the United States when the war ended.
- Supported the defense of democracy and human rights throughout the world, according to Roosevelt.
- Provided Britain with more than $50 billion of support during the war.

Lend-Lease Act

▶ Legislation in 1941 that enabled Britain to obtain arms from the United States without cash but with the promise to reimburse the United States when the war ended. The act reflected Roosevelt's desire to assist the British in any way possible, short of war.

Stymied in his plans for an invasion of England, Hitler turned his massive army eastward and on June 22, 1941, sprang a surprise attack on the Soviet Union, his ally in the 1939 Nazi-Soviet nonaggression pact. Neither Roosevelt nor Churchill had any love for Joseph Stalin or communism, but they both welcomed the Soviet Union to the anti-Nazi cause. Both Western leaders understood that Hitler's attack on Russia would provide relief for the hard-pressed British. Roosevelt quickly persuaded Congress to extend Lend-Lease to the Soviet Union, beginning the shipment of millions of tons of trucks, jeeps, and other equipment that, in all, supplied about 10 percent of Russian war materiel.

As Hitler's Wehrmacht (armed forces) raced across the Russian plains and Nazi U-boats tried to choke off supplies to Britain and the Soviet Union, Roosevelt met with Churchill aboard a ship near Newfoundland to cement the Anglo-American alliance. In August 1941, the two leaders issued the Atlantic Charter, pledging the two nations to freedom of the seas and free trade as well as the right of national self-determination.

Japan Attacks America

Although the likelihood of war with Germany preoccupied Roosevelt, Hitler exercised a measure of restraint in directly provoking America. Japanese ambitions in

| How did the United States mobilize for war? | How did the Allies turn the tide in Europe and the Pacific? | How did the war change life on the American home front? | How did the Allies finally win the war? | Conclusion: Why did the United States emerge as a superpower at the end of the war? | ✔ **LearningCurve** Check what you know. bedfordstmartins.com /roarkunderstanding |

751

Asia clashed more openly with American interests and commitments, especially in China and the Philippines. And unlike Hitler, the Japanese high command planned to attack the United States in order to pursue Japan's aspirations to rule an Asian empire it termed the Greater East Asia Co-Prosperity Sphere. Appealing to widespread Asian bitterness toward white colonial powers such as the British

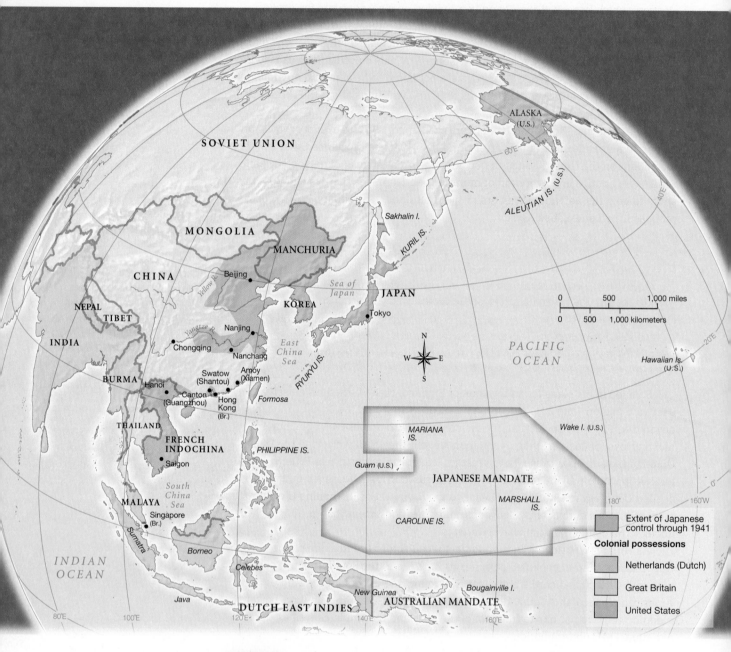

MAP 25.2 ■ Japanese Aggression through 1941

Beginning with the invasion of Manchuria in 1931, Japan sought to extend its imperialist control over most of East Asia. Japanese aggression was driven by the need for raw materials for the country's expanding industries and by the military government's devotion to martial honor.

CHAPTER LOCATOR

How did the United States respond to international developments in the 1930s?

How did the outbreak of war affect U.S. foreign policy?

CHAPTER 25

752 THE UNITED STATES AND THE SECOND WORLD WAR

in India and Burma, the French in Indochina (now Vietnam), and the Dutch in the East Indies (now Indonesia), the Japanese campaigned to preserve "Asia for the Asians." Japan's invasion of China — which had lasted for ten years by 1941 — proved that its true goal was Asia for the Japanese (**Map 25.2**). Japan coveted the raw materials available from China and Southeast Asia, and it ignored American demands to stop its campaign of aggression.

In 1940, Japan signaled a new phase of its imperial designs by entering a defensive alliance with Germany and Italy — the Tripartite Pact. To thwart Japanese plans to invade the Dutch East Indies, in July 1941 Roosevelt announced a trade embargo that denied Japan access to oil, scrap iron, and other goods essential for its war machines. Roosevelt hoped the embargo would strengthen factions within Japan that opposed the militarists.

Instead, the American embargo played into the hands of Japanese militarists headed by General Hideki Tojo, who seized control of the government in October 1941 and persuaded other leaders, including Emperor Hirohito, that swift destruction of American naval bases in the Pacific would leave Japan free to follow its destiny. On December 7, 1941, 183 aircraft lifted off six Japanese carriers and

Pearl Harbor Attack

This Japanese postcard celebrates the successful surprise attack on Pearl Harbor on December 7, 1941, highlighting the airborne supremacy of the Japanese, the weak defenses of the United States, and the smoking destruction caused by Japanese carrier-based aircraft. Brothers Wesley and Edward Heidt from Los Angeles were one of thirty-four pairs of brothers killed when Japanese warplanes sank the battleship *Arizona* at Pearl Harbor. www.museumofworldwarii.com.

| How did the United States mobilize for war? | How did the Allies turn the tide in Europe and the Pacific? | How did the war change life on the American home front? | How did the Allies finally win the war? | Conclusion: Why did the United States emerge as a superpower at the end of the war? | ☑ LearningCurve Check what you know. bedfordstmartins.com /roarkunderstanding |

753

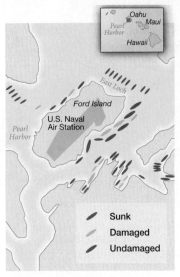

Bombing of Pearl Harbor,
December 7, 1941

Sunk

Damaged

Undamaged

attacked the U.S. Pacific Fleet at Pearl Harbor on the Hawai'ian island of Oahu. The devastating surprise attack sank all of the fleet's battleships, killed more than 2,400 Americans, and almost crippled U.S. war-making capacity in the Pacific. Luckily for the United States, Japanese pilots failed to destroy oil storage facilities at Pearl Harbor and any of the nation's aircraft carriers, which happened to be at sea during the attack.

The Japanese scored a stunning tactical victory at Pearl Harbor, but in the long run the attack proved a colossal blunder. The victory made many Japanese commanders overconfident about their military prowess. Worse for the Japanese, Americans instantly united in their desire to fight and avenge the attack. Roosevelt vowed that "this form of treachery shall never endanger us again." On December 8, Congress endorsed the president's call for a declaration of war. Both Hitler and Mussolini declared war against America on December 11, bringing the United States into all-out war with the Axis powers (Germany, Italy, and Japan) in both Europe and Asia.

> **QUICK REVIEW**

How did Roosevelt attempt to balance American isolationism with the military aggression of Germany and Japan in the late 1930s and early 1940s?

CHAPTER LOCATOR | How did the United States respond to international developments in the 1930s? | How did the outbreak of war affect U.S. foreign policy?

CHAPTER 25
754 THE UNITED STATES AND THE SECOND WORLD WAR

How did the United States mobilize for war?

African American Machine Gunners These African American soldiers prepare their machine gun for action on the side of a road near Pisa, Italy, in September 1944. They and other black soldiers who served in combat in segregated units repeatedly earned praise from their commanders for gallantry and courage under fire. © Bettmann/Corbis.

THE TIME HAD COME, Roosevelt announced, for the prescriptions of "Dr. New Deal" to be replaced by the stronger medicines of "Dr. Win-the-War." Military and civilian leaders rushed to secure the nation against possible attacks, causing Americans of Japanese descent to be stigmatized and sent to internment camps. Roosevelt and his advisers lost no time enlisting millions of Americans in the armed forces to bring the isolationist-era military to fighting strength for a two-front war. The war emergency also required economic mobilization unparalleled in the nation's history. As Dr. Win-the-War, Roosevelt set aside the New Deal goal of reform and plunged headlong into transforming the American economy into the world's greatest military machine, thereby achieving full employment and economic recovery, goals that had eluded the New Deal.

Home-Front Security

Shortly after declaring war against the United States, Hitler dispatched German submarines to hunt American ships along the Atlantic coast, where American pilots tried to destroy them. The U-boats had devastating success for about eight months, sinking hundreds of U.S. ships and threatening to disrupt the Lend-Lease

| How did the United States mobilize for war? | How did the Allies turn the tide in Europe and the Pacific? | How did the war change life on the American home front? | How did the Allies finally win the war? | Conclusion: Why did the United States emerge as a superpower at the end of the war? | ☑ LearningCurve Check what you know. bedfordstmartins.com /roarkunderstanding |

755

> CHRONOLOGY

1940
– Congress passes the Selective Service Act.

1942
– Internment of Japanese Americans.

lifeline to Britain and the Soviet Union. But by mid-1942, the U.S. Navy had chased German submarines into the mid-Atlantic.

Within the continental United States, Americans remained sheltered from the chaos and destruction the war was bringing to hundreds of millions in Europe and Asia. Nevertheless, the government worried constantly about espionage and internal subversion. The campaign for patriotic vigilance focused on German and Japanese foes, but Americans of Japanese descent became targets of official and popular persecution because of Pearl Harbor and long-standing racial prejudice against people of Asian descent.

About 320,000 people of Japanese descent lived in U.S. territory in 1941, two-thirds of them in Hawai'i, where they largely escaped such wartime persecution because they were essential and valued members of society. On the mainland, however, Japanese Americans were a tiny minority — even along the West Coast, where most of them worked on farms and in small businesses. Although an official military survey concluded that Japanese Americans posed no danger, popular hostility fueled a campaign to round up all mainland Japanese Americans — two-thirds of them U.S. citizens. "A Jap's a Jap. . . . It makes no difference whether he is an American citizen or not," one official declared.

On February 19, 1942, Roosevelt issued Executive Order 9066, which authorized sending all Americans of Japanese descent to ten makeshift **internment camps** located in remote areas of the West (**Map 25.3**). Japanese Americans lost homes and businesses worth about $400 million and lived out the war penned in by barbed wire and armed guards. Although several thousand Japanese Americans served with distinction in the U.S. armed forces and no case of subversion by a Japanese American was ever uncovered, the Supreme Court, in its 1944 *Korematsu* decision, upheld Executive Order 9066's blatant violation of constitutional rights as justified by "military necessity."

Building a Citizen Army

In 1940, Roosevelt encouraged Congress to pass the **Selective Service Act** to register men of military age who would be subject to a draft if the need arose. When

internment camps

▶ Makeshift prison camps, to which Americans of Japanese descent were sent as a result of Roosevelt's Executive Order 9066, issued in February 1942. In 1944, the Supreme Court upheld this blatant violation of constitutional rights as a "military necessity."

Selective Service Act

▶ Law enacted in 1940 requiring all men who would be eligible for a military draft to register in preparation for the possibility of a future conflict. The act also prohibited discrimination based on "race or color."

MAP 25.3 ▪ Western Relocation Authority Centers

Responding to prejudice and fear of sabotage, President Roosevelt authorized the roundup and relocation of all Americans of Japanese descent in 1942. Taken from their homes in the cities and fertile farmland of the far West, more than 120,000 Japanese Americans were confined in desolate camps scattered as far east as the Mississippi River.

▲ WRA relocation camp

▮ More than 1,000 Japanese Americans sent to relocation centers

CHAPTER LOCATOR | How did the United States respond to international developments in the 1930s? | How did the outbreak of war affect U.S. foreign policy?

CHAPTER 25
756 THE UNITED STATES AND THE SECOND WORLD WAR

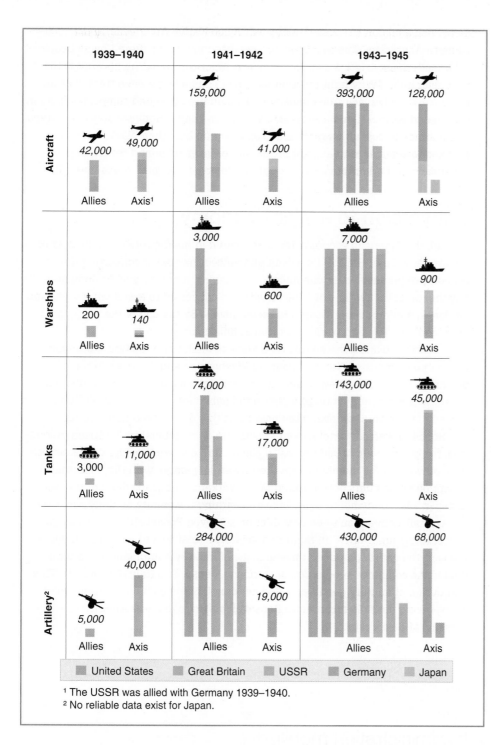

FIGURE 25.1 ■ Weapons Production by the Axis and Allied Powers during World War II

This chart demonstrates the massive contribution of the United States to Allied weapons production during World War II. In the air and on the sea, U.S. weapons predominated, after 1940 accounting for more aircraft and many more warships than those of Britain and the Soviet Union combined. Together, the three Allied powers produced about three times as many aircraft and five to eight times as many warships as the two Axis powers. On the ground, the Soviet Union led the other Allies in the production of tanks and artillery, an outgrowth of the colossal battles on the eastern front. What do these data suggest about the significance of America's entry into the war in December 1941? What do they suggest about the kind of warfare emphasized by each of the belligerents? What does the chronology of weapons production suggest about the course of the war?

war came, more than 16 million men and women served in uniform during the war, two-thirds of them draftees, mostly young men. Women were barred from combat duty, but they worked at nearly every noncombatant task, eroding traditional barriers to women's military service.

The Selective Service Act prohibited discrimination "on account of race or color," and almost a million African American men and women donned uniforms,

| How did the United States mobilize for war? | How did the Allies turn the tide in Europe and the Pacific? | How did the war change life on the American home front? | How did the Allies finally win the war? | Conclusion: Why did the United States emerge as a superpower at the end of the war? | ✓ LearningCurve Check what you know. bedfordstmartins.com /roarkunderstanding |

as did half a million Mexican Americans, 25,000 Native Americans, and 13,000 Chinese Americans. The racial insults and discrimination suffered by all people of color made some soldiers ask, as a Mexican American GI did on his way to the European front, "Why fight for America when you have not been treated as an American?" Only black Americans were trained in segregated camps, confined in segregated barracks, and assigned to segregated units. Homosexuals also served in the armed forces, although in much smaller numbers than black Americans. Allowed to serve as long as their sexual preferences remained covert, gay Americans, like other minorities, sought to demonstrate their worth under fire.

Conversion to a War Economy

In 1940, the American economy remained mired in the depression. Shortly after the attack on Pearl Harbor, Roosevelt announced the goal of converting the economy to produce "overwhelming . . . , crushing superiority of equipment in any theater of the world war." Factories were converted to assembling tanks and airplanes, and production soared to record levels. By the end of the war, jobs exceeded workers, and plants operated at full capacity.

To organize and oversee this tidal wave of military production, Roosevelt called upon business leaders to come to Washington and, for the token payment of a dollar a year, head new government agencies such as the War Production Board, which set production priorities and pushed for maximum output. Contracts flowed to large corporations, often on a basis that guaranteed their profits.

Booming wartime employment swelled union membership. To speed production, the government asked unions to pledge not to strike. Despite the relentless pace of work, union members kept their no-strike pledge, with the important exception of members of the United Mine Workers, who walked out of the coal mines in 1943, demanding a pay hike and earning the enmity of many Americans.

Overall, conversion to war production achieved Roosevelt's ambitious goal of "crushing superiority" in military goods. At a total cost of $304 billion during the war, the nation produced an avalanche of military equipment, more than double the combined production of Germany, Japan, and Italy (**Figure 25.1**). This outpouring of military goods supplied not only U.S. forces but also America's allies, giving tangible meaning to Roosevelt's pledge to make America the "arsenal of democracy."

> QUICK REVIEW

How did the Roosevelt administration mobilize the human and industrial resources necessary to fight a two-front war?

CHAPTER LOCATOR | How did the United States respond to international developments in the 1930s? | How did the outbreak of war affect U.S. foreign policy?

CHAPTER 25
758　THE UNITED STATES AND THE SECOND WORLD WAR

Marine Pinned Down on Saipan More than 100,000 American GIs assaulted the Japanese garrison on Saipan in the Mariana Islands in June 1944. The battle lasted nearly a month and inflicted 14,000 casualties on American troops. The intensity of the fighting is visible on the face of the Marine shown here. Marine Corps Photo, National Archives.

THE UNITED STATES CONFRONTED a daunting military challenge in December 1941. The attack on Pearl Harbor destroyed much of its Pacific Fleet. In the Atlantic, Hitler's U-boats sank American ships, while German armies occupied most of western Europe and relentlessly advanced eastward into the Soviet Union. Roosevelt and his military advisers believed that defeating Germany took top priority. To achieve that victory required preventing Hitler from defeating America's allies, Britain and the Soviet Union. If they fell, Hitler would command all the resources of Europe in a probable assault on the United States. To fight back effectively against Germany and Japan, the United States had to coordinate military and political strategy with its allies and muster all its human and economic assets. Victory over the Japanese fleet at the Battle of Midway, the successful elimination of Germany's menace to Allied shipping in the prolonged battle of the Atlantic, and the Allied assault on North Africa and then Italy established Allied naval superiority in the Atlantic and Pacific and began to challenge German domination of southern Europe.

Turning the Tide in the Pacific

In the Pacific theater, the Japanese assaulted American airfields in the Philippines and captured U.S. outposts on Guam and Wake Island. After capturing Singapore and Burma, Japan sought to complete its domination of the southern Pacific with an attack in January 1942 on the American stronghold in the Philippines (see Map 25.5, page 772). American defenders surrendered to the Japanese in May. By the summer of 1942, the Japanese had conquered the Dutch East Indies and were poised to strike Australia and New Zealand.

| How did the United States mobilize for war? | **How did the Allies turn the tide in Europe and the Pacific?** | How did the war change life on the American home front? | How did the Allies finally win the war? | Conclusion: Why did the United States emerge as a superpower at the end of the war? | ☑ LearningCurve Check what you know. bedfordstmartins.com /roarkunderstanding |

1942
- Japan captures the Philippines.
- Battles of Coral Sea and Midway.
- U.S. forces invade North Africa.

1943
- Allied leaders demand the unconditional surrender of the Axis powers.
- U.S. and British forces invade Sicily.

Battle of Midway

▶ June 3–6, 1942, naval battle in the Central Pacific in which American forces surprised and defeated the Japanese who had been massing an invasion force aimed at Midway Island. The battle put the Japanese at a disadvantage for the rest of the war.

In the spring of 1942, U.S. forces launched a major two-pronged counteroffensive that military officials hoped would reverse Japanese advances. Forces led by General Douglas MacArthur, commander of the U.S. armed forces in the Pacific theater, moved north from Australia and eventually attacked the Japanese in the Philippines. Far more decisively, Admiral Chester W. Nimitz sailed his battle fleet west from Hawai'i to retake Japanese-held islands in the southern and mid-Pacific. On May 7–8, 1942, in the Coral Sea just north of Australia, the American fleet and carrier-based warplanes defeated a Japanese armada that was sailing around the coast of New Guinea.

Nimitz then learned from an intelligence intercept that the Japanese were massing an invasion force aimed at Midway Island, an outpost guarding the Hawai'ian Islands. Nimitz maneuvered his carriers and cruisers to surprise the Japanese at the **Battle of Midway**. In a furious battle that raged on June 3–6, American ships and planes delivered a devastating blow to the Japanese navy. The Battle of Midway reversed the balance of naval power in the Pacific and put the Japanese at a disadvantage for the rest of the war. But the Japanese still occupied and defended the many places they had conquered.

The Campaign in Europe

After Pearl Harbor, Hitler's eastern-front armies marched ever deeper into the Soviet Union while his western-front forces prepared to invade Britain. As in World War I, the Germans attempted to starve the British into submission by destroying their seaborne lifeline. In 1941 and 1942, they sank Allied ships faster than new ones could be built.

Until mid-1943, the outcome of the war in the Atlantic remained in doubt. Then, newly invented radar detectors and production of sufficient destroyer escorts for merchant vessels allowed the Allies to prey upon the lurking U-boats. After U-boat crews suffered a 75 percent casualty rate, Hitler withdrew German submarines from the North Atlantic in late May 1943, allowing thousands of American supply ships to cross the Atlantic unimpeded. Winning the battle of the Atlantic allowed the United States to continue to supply its British and Soviet allies for the duration of the war and to reduce the imminent threat of a German invasion of Britain.

The most important strategic questions confronting the United States and its allies were when and where to open a second front against the Nazis. Stalin demanded that America and Britain mount an immediate and massive assault across the English Channel into western France to force Hitler to divert his armies from the eastern front and relieve the pressure on the Soviet Union. Churchill and Roosevelt instead delayed opening a second front, allowing the Germans and the Soviets to slug it out. Churchill and Roosevelt decided to strike first in North Africa to help secure Allied control of the Mediterranean.

In October and November 1942, British forces at El-Alamein in Egypt halted German general Erwin Rommel's drive to capture the Suez Canal, Britain's lifeline to the oil of the Middle East and to British colonies in India and South Asia (see Map 25.4, page 769). In November, an American army under General Dwight D. Eisenhower landed far to the west, in French Morocco. Propelled by American tank units commanded by General George Patton, the Allied armies defeated the Germans in North Africa in May 1943. The North African campaign pushed the Germans out of Africa, made the Mediterranean safe for Allied shipping, and opened the door for an Allied invasion of Italy.

CHAPTER LOCATOR | How did the United States respond to international developments in the 1930s? | How did the outbreak of war affect U.S. foreign policy?

760 CHAPTER 25 THE UNITED STATES AND THE SECOND WORLD WAR

Relief Column, Tunisia, North Africa This eyewitness painting depicts a column of American soldiers moving toward the front lines to relieve exhausted and wounded comrades in Tunisia in 1943. The artist, Peter Sanfilippo, a twenty-three-year-old private from Brooklyn, New York, wrote that the "arrival of a relief column of fresh soldiers . . . reassures a battered man's faith in his fellow comrades. The unnerved and wounded are resurrected in spirit to thrive, and thus persevere into a new day." Peter Sanfilippo/Veterans History Project, Library of Congress.

In January 1943, while the North African campaign was still under way, Roosevelt and Churchill met in Casablanca and announced that they would accept nothing less than the "unconditional surrender" of the Axis powers, ruling out peace negotiations. They concluded that they should capitalize on their success in North Africa and strike against Italy, consigning the Soviet Union to continue to bear the brunt of the Nazi war machine.

In July 1943, American and British forces landed in Sicily. Soon afterward, Mussolini was deposed in Italy, ending the reign of Italian fascism. Quickly, the Allies invaded the mainland, and the Italian government surrendered unconditionally. The Germans responded by rushing reinforcements to Italy, turning the Allies' Italian campaign into a series of battles to liberate Italy from German occupation.

German troops dug into strong fortifications and fought to defend every inch of Italy's rugged terrain. Allied forces continued to battle against stubborn German defenses for the remainder of the war, making the Italian campaign the war's deadliest for American infantrymen. One soldier wrote that his buddies "died like butchered swine."

QUICK REVIEW

How did the United States seek to counter the Japanese in the Pacific and the Germans in Europe?

| How did the United States mobilize for war? | **How did the Allies turn the tide in Europe and the Pacific?** | How did the war change life on the American home front? | How did the Allies finally win the war? | Conclusion: Why did the United States emerge as a superpower at the end of the war? | ☑ LearningCurve Check what you know. bedfordstmartins.com /roarkunderstanding |

How did the war change life on the American home front?

This poster encourages women and children to contribute to the war effort by collecting scrap metal for recycling into weaponry. The poster highlights the middle-class prosperity of the war years, a sharp contrast to the hard times of the 1930s. Chicago Historical Society.

WE'RE SCRAPPERS TOO

THE WAR EFFORT MOBILIZED Americans as never before. Factories churned out ever more bombs, bullets, tanks, ships, and airplanes, which workers rushed to assemble, leaving their farms and small towns and congregating in cities. Women took jobs with wrenches and welding torches, boosting the nation's workforce and fraying traditional notions that a woman's place was in the home rather than on the assembly line. Despite rationing and shortages, unprecedented government expenditures for war production brought prosperity to many Americans after years of depression-era poverty. Although Americans in uniform risked their lives on battlefields in Europe and Asia, Americans on the U.S. mainland enjoyed complete immunity from foreign attack — in sharp contrast to their Soviet and

CHAPTER LOCATOR | How did the United States respond to international developments in the 1930s? | How did the outbreak of war affect U.S. foreign policy?

British allies. The wartime ideology that contrasted Allied support for human rights with Axis tyranny provided justification for the many sacrifices Americans were required to make in support of the military effort. It also established a standard of basic human equality that became a potent weapon in the campaign for equal rights at home and in condemning the atrocities of the Holocaust perpetrated by the Nazis.

Women and Families, Guns and Butter

Millions of American women gladly took their places on assembly lines in defense industries. At the start of the war, about a quarter of adult women worked outside the home, but few women worked in factories, except for textile mills and sewing industries. But wartime mobilization of the economy and the siphoning of millions of men into the armed forces left factories begging for women workers.

Government advertisements urged women to take industrial jobs by assuring them that their household chores had prepared them for work on the "Victory Line." Millions of women responded. Advertisers often referred to a woman who worked in a war industry as "Rosie the Riveter," a popular wartime term. By the end of the war, women working outside the home numbered 50 percent more than in 1939. Contributing to the war effort also paid off in wages. A Kentucky woman remembered her job at a munitions plant, where she earned "the fabulous sum of $32 a week. To us it was an absolute miracle."

The majority of married women remained at home, occupied with domestic chores and child care. But they, too, supported the war effort, planting Victory Gardens, saving tin cans and newspapers for recycling into war materiel, and buying war bonds. Many families scrimped to cope with the 30 percent inflation during the war, but men and women in manufacturing industries enjoyed wages that grew twice as fast as inflation.

The war influenced how all families spent their earnings. Buying a new washing machine or car was out of the question, since factories that formerly built them now made military goods. Many other consumer goods — such as tires, gasoline, shoes, and meat — were rationed at home to meet military needs overseas. But most Americans readily found things to buy, including movie tickets, cosmetics, and music recordings.

The wartime prosperity and abundance enjoyed by most Americans contrasted with the experiences of their hard-pressed allies. Personal consumption fell by 22 percent in Britain, and food output plummeted to just one-third of pre-war levels in the Soviet Union, creating widespread hunger and even starvation.

The Double V Campaign

Fighting against Nazi Germany and its ideology of Aryan racial supremacy, Americans were confronted with the extensive racial prejudice in their own country. The *Pittsburgh Courier*, a leading black newspaper, asserted that the wartime emergency called for a **Double V campaign** seeking "victory over our enemies at home and victory over our enemies on the battlefields abroad."

In 1941, black organizations demanded that the federal government require companies receiving defense contracts to integrate their workforces. A. Philip

> CHRONOLOGY

1942
– Congress of Racial Equality is founded.

1943
– 242 race riots erupt in 47 American cities.

1944
– GI Bill of Rights.
– Roosevelt is reelected to fourth term.

Double V campaign
▶ World War II campaign in America to attack racism at home and abroad. The campaign pushed the federal government to require defense contractors to integrate their workforces. In response, Franklin Roosevelt authorized a committee to investigate and prevent racial discrimination in employment.

| How did the United States mobilize for war? | How did the Allies turn the tide in Europe and the Pacific? | **How did the war change life on the American home front?** | How did the Allies finally win the war? | Conclusion: Why did the United States emerge as a superpower at the end of the war? | ☑ LearningCurve Check what you know. bedfordstmartins.com /roarkunderstanding |

763

Randolph, head of the Brotherhood of Sleeping Car Porters, promised that 100,000 African American marchers would descend on Washington if the president did not eliminate discrimination in defense industries. Roosevelt decided to risk offending his white allies in the South and in unions, and he issued Executive Order 8802 in mid-1941. It authorized the Committee on Fair Employment Practices to investigate and prevent racial discrimination in employment.

Progress came slowly, however. In 1940, nine out of ten black Americans lived below the federal poverty line, and those who worked earned an average of just 39 percent of whites' wages. In search of better jobs and living conditions, 5.5 million black Americans migrated from the South to centers of industrial production in the North and West, making a majority of African Americans city dwellers for the first time in U.S. history. Severe labor shortages and government fair employment standards opened assembly-line jobs in defense plants to African Americans, causing black unemployment to drop by 80 percent during the war. But more jobs did not mean equal pay for blacks. The average income of black families rose during the war, but by the end of the conflict it still stood at only half of what white families earned.

Blacks' migration to defense jobs intensified racial antagonisms, which boiled over in the hot summer of 1943, when 242 race riots erupted in 47 cities. The worst mayhem occurred in Detroit, where a long-simmering conflict between whites and blacks over racially segregated housing ignited into a race war. In two days of violence, twenty-five blacks and nine whites were killed, and scores more were injured.

Racial violence created the impetus for the Double V campaign, officially supported by the National Association for the Advancement of Colored People (NAACP), which asserted black Americans' demands for the rights and privileges enjoyed by all other Americans — demands reinforced by the Allies' wartime ideology of freedom and democracy. While the NAACP focused on court challenges to segregation, a new organization founded in 1942, the Congress of Racial Equality, organized picketing and sit-ins against racially segregated restaurants and theaters. Still, the Double V campaign achieved only limited success against racial discrimination during the war.

Wartime Politics and the 1944 Election

Americans rallied around the war effort in unprecedented unity. In June 1944, Congress recognized the sacrifices made by millions of veterans, unanimously passing the landmark **GI Bill of Rights**, which put the financial resources of the federal government behind the abstract goals of freedom and democracy for which veterans were fighting.

GI Bill of Rights

▶ Legislation passed in 1944 authorizing the government to provide World War II veterans with funds for education, housing, and health care, as well as loans to start businesses and buy homes.

> **GI Bill of Rights**

- Gave military veterans government funds for education, housing, and health care.
- Provided loans to help veterans start businesses and buy homes.
- Empowered millions of GIs to better themselves and their families after the war.

CHAPTER LOCATOR | How did the United States respond to international developments in the 1930s? | How did the outbreak of war affect U.S. foreign policy?

CHAPTER 25

764 THE UNITED STATES AND THE SECOND WORLD WAR

After twelve turbulent years in the White House, Roosevelt was exhausted and gravely ill with heart disease, but he was determined to remain president until the war ended. His poor health made the selection of a vice presidential candidate unusually important. Convinced that many Americans had soured on liberal reform, Roosevelt chose Senator Harry S. Truman of Missouri as his running mate. A reliable party man from a southern border state, Truman satisfied urban Democratic leaders while not worrying white southerners who were nervous about challenges to racial segregation.

The Republicans, confident of a strong conservative upsurge in the nation, nominated as their presidential candidate the governor of New York, Thomas E. Dewey, who had made his reputation as a tough crime fighter. In the 1944 presidential campaign, Roosevelt's failing health alarmed many observers, but his frailty was outweighed by Americans' unwillingness to change presidents in the midst of the war and by Dewey's failure to persuade most voters that the New Deal was a creeping socialist menace. Voters gave Roosevelt a 53.5 percent majority, his narrowest presidential victory, ensuring his continued leadership as Dr. Win-the-War.

Reaction to the Holocaust

Since the 1930s, the Nazis had persecuted Jews in Germany and every German-occupied territory, causing many Jews to seek asylum beyond Hitler's reach. Thousands of Jews sought to immigrate to the United States, but 82 percent of

Mass Execution of Jewish Women and Children

On October 14, 1942, Jewish women and children from the village of Mizocz in present-day Ukraine were herded into a ravine, forced to undress and lie facedown, and then shot at point-blank range by German police. This rare photograph, taken by one of the authorities at the scene, shows Germans killing the women who survived the initial gunfire. United States Holocaust Memorial Museum.

| How did the United States mobilize for war? | How did the Allies turn the tide in Europe and the Pacific? | **How did the war change life on the American home front?** | How did the Allies finally win the war? | Conclusion: Why did the United States emerge as a superpower at the end of the war? | ✔ **LearningCurve** Check what you know. bedfordstmartins.com /roarkunderstanding |

765

The Holocaust, 1933–1945

Holocaust

▶ German effort during World War II to murder Europe's Jews, along with other groups the Nazis deemed "undesirable." Despite reports of the ongoing genocide, the Allies did almost nothing to interfere. In all, some 11 million people were killed in the Holocaust, most of them Jews.

Americans opposed admitting them, and they were turned away. In 1942, numerous reports reached the United States that Hitler was sending Jews, Gypsies, religious and political dissenters, homosexuals, and others to concentration camps, where old people, children, and others deemed too weak to work were systematically slaughtered and cremated, while the able-bodied were put to work at slave labor until they died of starvation and abuse. Other camps were devoted almost exclusively to murdering and cremating Jews. Despite reports of the brutal slave labor and killing camps, U.S. officials refused to grant asylum to Jewish refugees. Most Americans, including top officials, believed that reports were exaggerated.

Desperate to stem the killing, the World Jewish Congress appealed to the Allies to bomb the death camps and the railroad tracks leading to them in order to hamper the killing and block further shipments of victims. Intent on achieving military victory as soon as possible, the Allies repeatedly turned down such bombing requests, arguing that the air forces could not spare resources from their military missions.

The nightmare of the **Holocaust** was all too real. When Russian troops arrived at Auschwitz in Poland in January 1945, they found emaciated prisoners, skeletal corpses, gas chambers, pits filled with human ashes, and loot the Nazis had stripped from the dead, including hair, gold fillings, and false teeth. At last, the truth about the Holocaust began to be known beyond the Germans who had perpetrated and tolerated these atrocities and the men, women, and children who had succumbed to the genocide. By then, it was too late for the 11 million civilian victims — mostly Jews — of the Nazis' crimes against humanity.

> **QUICK REVIEW**

How did the war influence American society?

CHAPTER LOCATOR | How did the United States respond to international developments in the 1930s? | How did the outbreak of war affect U.S. foreign policy?

CHAPTER 25
766   THE UNITED STATES AND THE SECOND WORLD WAR

The Allied War Effort

The Russian poster shown here illustrates the combined efforts of the Allies, declaring, "We won't let the evil enemy escape the noose. He will not evade it." Museum of World War II, Natick, MA, www.museumofworldwarii.com.

> VISUAL ACTIVITY

READING THE IMAGE: What does the depiction of Hitler on this Russian poster suggest about his leadership and character?
CONNECTIONS: What does the poster suggest about the importance of the alliance among the major Allied powers?

BY FEBRUARY 1943, Soviet defenders had finally defeated the massive German offensive against Stalingrad, turning the tide of the war in Europe. After gargantuan sacrifices in fighting that had lasted for eighteen months, the Red Army forced Hitler's Wehrmacht to turn back toward the west. In the Pacific, the Allies had halted the expansion of the Japanese empire but now had the deadly task of dislodging Japanese defenders from the outposts they still occupied. Allied military planners devised a strategy to annihilate Axis resistance by taking advantage of America's industrial superiority. A secret plan to develop a superbomb harnessing atomic power came to fruition too late to use against Germany. But when the atomic bomb devastated the cities of Hiroshima and Nagasaki, Japan finally surrendered, averting the planned assault on the

| How did the United States mobilize for war? | How did the Allies turn the tide in Europe and the Pacific? | How did the war change life on the American home front? | **How did the Allies finally win the war?** | Conclusion: Why did the United States emerge as a superpower at the end of the war? | ☑ LearningCurve Check what you know. bedfordstmartins.com /roarkunderstanding |

767

1944
– D Day.

1945
– Yalta Conference.
– Roosevelt dies; Vice President Harry Truman becomes president.
– Germany surrenders.
– United States joins United Nations.
– United States drops atomic bombs on Hiroshima and Nagasaki.
– Japan surrenders, ending World War II.

Japanese homeland by hundreds of thousands of American soldiers and sailors and their allies.

From Bombing Raids to Berlin

While the Allied campaigns in North Africa and Italy were under way, British and American pilots flew bombing missions from England to German-occupied territories and to Germany itself as an airborne substitute for the delayed second front on the ground. During night raids, British bombers targeted general areas, hoping to hit civilians, create terror, and undermine morale. Beginning in August 1942, American pilots flew heavily armored B-17s from English airfields in daytime raids on industrial targets vital for the German war machine.

German air defenses took a fearsome toll on Allied pilots and aircraft. In 1943, two-thirds of American airmen did not survive to complete their twenty-five-mission tours of duty. In all, 85,000 American airmen were killed in the skies over Europe. Many others were shot down and held as prisoners of war. In February 1944, the arrival of America's durable and deadly P-51 Mustang fighter gave Allied bombers superior protection. The Mustangs slowly began to sweep the Luftwaffe from the skies, allowing bombers to penetrate deep into Germany and pound civilian and military targets around the clock.

In November 1943, Churchill, Roosevelt, and Stalin met in Teheran to discuss wartime strategy and the second front.

> Allied Agreement at Teheran

- Roosevelt conceded to Stalin that the Soviet Union would exercise de facto control of the eastern European countries that the Red Army occupied as it rolled back the German Wehrmacht.
- Stalin agreed to enter the war against Japan once Germany finally surrendered.
- Roosevelt and Churchill promised that they would launch a massive second-front assault in northern France, code-named Overlord, scheduled for May 1944.

General Dwight Eisenhower was assigned overall command of the Allied forces preparing to invade northern France, and mountains of military supplies were stockpiled in England. The huge deployment of Hitler's armies in the east, which were trying to halt the Red Army's westward offensive, left too few German troops to stop the millions of Allied soldiers waiting to attack France. More decisive, years of Allied air raids had decimated the German Luftwaffe, which could send aloft only 300 fighter planes against 12,000 Allied aircraft.

After frustrating delays caused by stormy weather, Eisenhower launched the largest amphibious assault in world history on **D Day**, June 6, 1944 (**Map 25.4**). Allied soldiers finally succeeded in securing the beachhead. An officer told his men, "The only people on this beach are the dead and those that are going to die — now let's get the hell out of here." And they did, finally surmounting the

D Day

▶ June 6, 1944, the date of the Allied invasion of northern France. D Day was the largest amphibious assault in world history. The invasion opened a second front against the Germans and moved the Allies closer to victory in Europe.

CHAPTER LOCATOR | How did the United States respond to international developments in the 1930s? | How did the outbreak of war affect U.S. foreign policy?

CHAPTER 25
768 THE UNITED STATES AND THE SECOND WORLD WAR

Legend:

- Axis powers, including annexed territory
- Extent of Axis control, early Nov. 1942
- Allied powers
- Neutral nations
- ← Allied forces
- ✳ Major battle (Allied victory)

ICELAND

ATLANTIC OCEAN

NORWAY

SWEDEN

FINLAND

• Murmansk
• Archangel

DENMARK

North Sea

Leningrad
Besieged
Sept. 1942–Jan. 1943

Sept. 1944

• Moscow

GREAT BRITAIN

IRELAND

• London

NETH.

Berlin
Captured
May 2, 1945

• Danzig

Warsaw

July 1944

SOVIET UNION

50N

Normandy
D Day
June 6, 1944

BELG.

LUX.

GERMANY

Apr. 1945

Mar. 1944

Aug. 1943

Stalingrad
Aug. 21, 1942–
Jan. 31, 1943

POLAND

UKRAINE

Battle of
the Bulge
Dec. 16, 1944–
Jan. 31, 1945

Paris
Liberated
Aug. 25, 1944

FRANCE

SWITZ.

AUSTRIA

SLOVAKIA

HUNGARY

Aug. 1944

40N

VICHY
FRANCE

Aug. 1944

CROATIA

SERBIA

ROMANIA

Black Sea

PORTUGAL

SPAIN

Corsica

N
W   E
S

Adriatic Sea

ITALY

MONTENEGRO

BULGARIA

TURKEY

Casablanca

SP. MOROCCO

Nov. 1942

Sardinia

Rome
Liberated
June 4, 1944

ALBANIA
(It.)

GREECE

30N

MOROCCO

Tunis
Occupied
May 12, 1943

Jul 1943

Sicily

Rhodes
(It.)

Cyprus
(Br.)

LEBANON
(Fr.)

SYRIA

IRAQ

FRENCH
NORTH AFRICA
(Vichy France)
Joined Allies Nov. 1942

TUNISIA

Crete (Gr.)

PALESTINE
(Br.)

TRANSJORDAN

Kasserine Pass
Feb. 14–26, 1943

Mediterranean Sea

Suez
Canal

SAUDI
ARABIA

ALGERIA

0   200   400 miles
0   200   400 kilometers

LIBYA
(It.)

El-Alamein
Oct. 23–Nov. 5, 1942

Alexandria

Nov. 1942

EGYPT

10W   0   10E   20E   30E   40E   50E

MAP 25.4 ■ The European Theater of World War II, 1942–1945

The Russian reversal of the German offensive at Stalingrad and Leningrad, combined with Allied landings in North Africa and Normandy, trapped Germany in a closing vise of Allied armies on all sides.

> MAP ACTIVITY

READING THE MAP: By November 1942, which nations or parts of nations in the European theater were under Axis control? Which had been absorbed by the Axis powers before the war? Which nations remained neutral? Which ones were affiliated with the Allies?

CONNECTIONS: What were the three fronts in the European theater? When did the Allies initiate actions on each front, and why did Churchill, Stalin, and Roosevelt disagree on the timing of the opening of these fronts?

How did the United States mobilize for war?	How did the Allies turn the tide in Europe and the Pacific?	How did the war change life on the American home front?	**How did the Allies finally win the war?**	Conclusion: Why did the United States emerge as a superpower at the end of the war?	✓ **LearningCurve** Check what you know. bedfordstmartins.com /roarkunderstanding

cliffs that loomed over the beach and destroying the German defenses. One GI who made the landing recalled the soldiers "were exhausted and we were exultant. We had survived D Day!"

Within a week, a flood of soldiers, tanks, and other military equipment propelled Allied forces toward Germany. On August 25, the Allies liberated Paris from four years of Nazi occupation. As the giant pincers of the Allied and Soviet armies closed on Germany in December 1944, Hitler ordered a counterattack to capture the Allies' essential supply port at Antwerp, Belgium. In the Battle of the Bulge (December 16, 1944, to January 31, 1945), as the Allies termed it, German forces drove fifty-five miles into Allied lines before being stopped at Bastogne. More than 70,000 Allied soldiers were killed, including more Americans than in any other battle of the war. The battle fatally depleted Hitler's reserves.

In February 1945, while Allied armies relentlessly pushed German forces backward, Churchill, Stalin, and Roosevelt met secretly at the Yalta Conference (named for the Russian resort town where it was held) to discuss their plans for the postwar world.

> **> Results of the Yalta Conference**

- Stalin promised to permit votes of self-determination in the eastern European countries occupied by the Red Army.
- The Allies pledged to support Jiang Jieshi (Chiang Kai-shek) as the leader of China.
- The Soviet Union obtained a role in the postwar governments of Korea and Manchuria in exchange for entering the war against Japan after the defeat of Germany.

The "Big Three" also agreed on the creation of a new international peace-keeping organization, the United Nations (UN). All nations would have a place in the UN General Assembly, but the Security Council would wield decisive power, and its permanent representatives from the Allied powers — China, France, Great Britain, the Soviet Union, and the United States — would possess a veto over UN actions. The Senate ratified the United Nations Charter in July 1945 by a vote of 89 to 2, reflecting the triumph of internationalism during the nation's mobilization for war.

While Allied armies sped toward Berlin, Allied warplanes dropped more bombs after D Day than in all the previous European bombing raids combined. By April 11, Allied armies reached the banks of the Elbe River and paused while the Soviets smashed into Berlin. The Red Army captured Berlin on May 2. Hitler had committed suicide on April 30, and the provisional German government surrendered unconditionally on May 7. The war in Europe was finally over, with the sacrifice of 135,576 American soldiers, nearly 250,000 British troops, and 9 million Russian combatants.

CHAPTER LOCATOR | How did the United States respond to international developments in the 1930s? | How did the outbreak of war affect U.S. foreign policy?

CHAPTER 25
770 THE UNITED STATES AND THE SECOND WORLD WAR

Roosevelt did not live to witness the end of the war. On April 12, he suffered a fatal stroke. Americans grieved for the man who had led them through years of depression and world war, and they worried about his untested successor, Vice President Harry Truman.

The Defeat of Japan

After the punishing defeats in the Coral Sea and at Midway, Japan had to fend off Allied naval and air attacks. In 1943, British and American forces, along with Indian and Chinese allies, launched an offensive against Japanese outposts in southern Asia, pushing through Burma and into China, where Jiang's armies continued to resist conquest. In the Pacific, Americans and their allies attacked Japanese strongholds by sea, air, and land, moving island by island toward the Japanese homeland (**Map 25.5**).

The island-hopping campaign began in August 1942, when American Marines landed on Guadalcanal in the southern Pacific. For the next six months, a savage battle raged for control of the strategic area. Finally, during the night of February 8, 1943, Japanese forces withdrew. The terrible losses on both sides indicated to the Marines how costly it would be to defeat Japan. After the battle, Joseph Steinbacher, a twenty-one-year-old from Alabama, sailed from San Francisco to New Guinea, where, he recalled, "all the cannon fodder waited to be assigned" to replace the killed and wounded.

In mid-1943, Allied forces launched offensives in New Guinea and the Solomon Islands that gradually secured the South Pacific. In the Central Pacific, amphibious forces conquered the Gilbert and Marshall islands, which served as forward bases for air assaults on the Japanese home islands. As the Allies attacked island after island, Japanese soldiers were ordered to refuse to surrender no matter how hopeless their plight.

While the island-hopping campaign kept pressure on Japanese forces, the Allies invaded the Philippines in the fall of 1944. In the four-day Battle of Leyte Gulf, one of the greatest naval battles in world history, the American fleet crushed the Japanese armada, clearing the way for Allied victory in the Philippines. While the Philippine campaign was under way, American forces captured two crucial islands — Iwo Jima and Okinawa — from which they planned to launch an attack on the Japanese homeland. To defend Okinawa, Japanese leaders ordered thousands of suicide pilots, known as *kamikaze*, to crash their bomb-laden planes into Allied ships. But instead of destroying the American fleet, they demolished the last vestige of the Japanese air force. By June 1945, the Japanese were nearly defenseless on the sea and in the air. Still, their leaders prepared to fight to the death for their homeland.

Joseph Steinbacher and other GIs who had suffered "horrendous" casualties in the Philippines were now told by their commanding officer: "Men, in a few short months we are going to invade [Japan]. . . . We will be going in on the first wave and are expecting ninety percent casualties the first day. . . . For the few of

How did the United States mobilize for war?

How did the Allies turn the tide in Europe and the Pacific?

How did the war change life on the American home front?

How did the Allies finally win the war?

Conclusion: Why did the United States emerge as a superpower at the end of the war?

✓ LearningCurve
Check what you know.
bedfordstmartins.com /roarkunderstanding

771

MAP 25.5 ■ The Pacific Theater of World War II, 1941–1945

To drive the Japanese from their far-flung empire, the Allies launched two combined naval and military offensives — one to recapture the Philippines and then attack Japanese forces in China, the other to hop from island to island in the Central Pacific toward the Japanese mainland.

> MAP ACTIVITY

READING THE MAP: What was the extent of Japanese control up until August 1942? Which nations in the Pacific theater sided with the Allies? Which nations remained neutral?

CONNECTIONS: Describe the economic and military motivations behind Japanese domination of the region. How and when did Japan achieve this dominance? Judging from this map, what strategic and geographic concerns might have prompted Truman and his advisers to consider using the atomic bomb against Japan?

CHAPTER LOCATOR

How did the United States respond to international developments in the 1930s?

How did the outbreak of war affect U.S. foreign policy?

CHAPTER 25
772 THE UNITED STATES AND THE SECOND WORLD WAR

us left alive the war will be over." Steinbacher later recalled his mental attitude at that moment: "I know that I am now a walking dead man and will not have a snowball's chance in hell of making it through the last great battle to conquer the home islands of Japan."

Atomic Warfare

In mid-July 1945, as Allied forces prepared for the final assault on Japan, American scientists tested a secret weapon at an isolated desert site near Los Alamos, New Mexico. In 1942, Roosevelt had authorized the top-secret **Manhattan Project** to find a way to convert nuclear energy into a superbomb before the Germans added such a weapon to their arsenal. More than 100,000 Americans, led by scientists, engineers, and military officers at Los Alamos, worked frantically to win the race for an atomic bomb. Germany surrendered two and a half months before the test on July 16, 1945, when scientists first witnessed an atomic explosion that sent a mushroom cloud of debris eight miles into the atmosphere. After watching the successful test of the bomb, J. Robert Oppenheimer, the head scientist at Los Alamos, remarked soberly, "Lots of boys not grown up yet will owe their life to it."

Manhattan Project
▶ Top-secret project authorized by Franklin Roosevelt in 1942 to develop an atomic bomb ahead of the Germans. The thousands of Americans who worked on the project at Los Alamos, New Mexico, succeeded in producing a successful atomic bomb by July 1945.

Hiroshima

This photo shows part of Hiroshima shortly after the atomic bomb dropped from the B-29 bomber named the *Enola Gay*, leveling the densely populated city. Deadly radiation from the bomb maimed and killed Japanese civilians for years afterward. National Archives.

How did the United States mobilize for war? | How did the Allies turn the tide in Europe and the Pacific? | How did the war change life on the American home front? | **How did the Allies finally win the war?** | Conclusion: Why did the United States emerge as a superpower at the end of the war?

✓ **LearningCurve**
Check what you know.
bedfordstmartins.com
/roarkunderstanding

President Truman saw no reason not to use the atomic bomb against Japan if doing so would save American lives. Despite numerous defeats, Japan still had more than 6 million reserves at home for a last-ditch defense against the anticipated Allied assault, which U.S. military advisers estimated would kill at least 250,000 Americans. But first Truman issued an ultimatum: Japan must surrender unconditionally or face utter ruin. When the Japanese failed to respond by the deadline, Truman ordered that an atomic bomb be dropped on a Japanese city. The bomb that Colonel Paul Tibbets and his crew released over Hiroshima on August 6 leveled the city and incinerated about 100,000 people. Three days later, after the Japanese government still refused to surrender, the second atomic bomb killed nearly as many civilians at Nagasaki.

With American assurance that the emperor could retain his throne after the Allies took over, Japan surrendered on August 14. On a troop ship departing from Europe for what would have been the final assault on Japan, an American soldier spoke for millions of others when he heard the wonderful news that the killing was over: "We are going to grow to adulthood after all."

While all Americans welcomed peace, Robert Oppenheimer and others worried about the consequences of unleashing atomic power. Almost every American, including Oppenheimer, believed that the atomic bomb had brought peace in 1945, but nobody knew what it would bring in the future.

> **QUICK REVIEW**

Why did Truman elect to use the atomic bomb against Japan?

CHAPTER LOCATOR | How did the United States respond to international developments in the 1930s? | How did the outbreak of war affect U.S. foreign policy?

CHAPTER 25
774   THE UNITED STATES AND THE SECOND WORLD WAR

Conclusion: Why did the United States emerge as a superpower at the end of the war?

AT A COST OF 405,399 American lives, the nation united with its allies to crush the Axis aggressors into unconditional surrender. Almost all Americans believed they had won a "good war" against totalitarian evil. The Allies saved Asia and Europe from enslavement and finally halted the Nazis' genocidal campaign against Jews and many others whom the Nazis considered inferior. To secure human rights and protect the world against future wars, the Roosevelt administration took the lead in creating the United Nations.

Wartime production lifted the nation out of the Great Depression. The gross national product soared to four times what it had been when Roosevelt became president in 1933. Jobs in defense industries eliminated chronic unemployment, provided wages for millions of women workers and African American migrants from southern farms, and boosted Americans' prosperity. Ahead stretched the challenge of maintaining that prosperity while reintegrating millions of uniformed men and women, with help from the benefits of the GI Bill.

By the end of the war, the United States had emerged as a global superpower. Wartime mobilization made the American economy the strongest in the world, buttressed by the military clout of the nation's nuclear monopoly. Although the war left much of the world a rubble-strewn wasteland, the American mainland had enjoyed immunity from attack. The Japanese occupation of China had left 50 million people without homes and millions more dead, maimed, and orphaned. The German offensive against the Soviet Union had killed more than 20 million Russian soldiers and civilians. Germany and Japan lay in ruins, their economies and societies as shattered as their military forces. But in the gruesome balance sheet of war, the Axis powers had inflicted far more grief, misery, and destruction on the global victims of their aggression than they had suffered in return.

As the dominant Western nation in the postwar world, the United States asserted its leadership in the reconstruction of Europe while occupying Japan and overseeing its economic and political recovery. America soon confronted new challenges in the tense aftermath of the war, as the Soviets seized political control of eastern Europe, a Communist revolution swept China, and national liberation movements emerged in the colonial empires of Britain and France. The forces unleashed by World War II would shape the United States and the rest of the world for decades to come. Before the ashes of World War II had cooled, America's wartime alliance with the Soviet Union fractured, igniting a Cold War between the superpowers. To resist global communism, the United States became, in effect, the policeman of the free world, repudiating the pre–World War II legacy of isolationism.

| How did the United States mobilize for war? | How did the Allies turn the tide in Europe and the Pacific? | How did the war change life on the American home front? | How did the Allies finally win the war? | Conclusion: Why did the United States emerge as a superpower at the end of the war? | ✓ LearningCurve Check what you know. bedfordstmartins.com /roarkunderstanding |

775

CHAPTER 25 STUDY GUIDE

 STEP 1 **GET STARTED ONLINE**

☑ **LearningCurve** ▪ bedfordstmartins.com/roarkunderstanding

Now that you've read the chapter, make it stick by completing the LearningCurve activity.

STEP 2 **EXPLAIN WHY IT MATTERS**

Put your reading into practice. Identify each term below, and then explain why it matters in U.S. history.

TERM	WHO OR WHAT & WHEN	WHY IT MATTERS
good neighbor policy (p. 745)		
neutrality acts (p. 746)		
appeasement (p. 748)		
Lend-Lease Act (p. 751)		
internment camps (p. 756)		
Selective Service Act (p. 756)		
Battle of Midway (p. 760)		
Double V campaign (p. 763)		
GI Bill of Rights (p. 764)		
Holocaust (p. 766)		
D Day (p. 768)		
Manhattan Project (p. 773)		

 STEP 3 **MOVE BEYOND THE BASICS**

To demonstrate a more advanced understanding, describe important developments in the United States and their impact during World War II. What impact did these developments have on women and racial minorities, on the New Deal and the political balance of power, and on the size and nature of the federal government?

	Developments	Impact
Economic activity		
Employment		
Government		
Politics and the New Deal		
Race relations		
Women's roles		

THE ONSET OF WORLD WAR II

▶ Why were the American people, as a whole, reluctant to become involved in World War II?

▶ How did Roosevelt use the economic power of the United States to aid Britain and the Soviet Union?

THE HOME FRONT

▶ How did the conversion to a war economy end the Great Depression? Who benefited most? What groups still struggled?

▶ What were the most important social consequences of America's involvement in World War II?

VICTORY

▶ How did the Allies achieve victory? What tensions among the Allies emerged in the final years of the war?

▶ What led to the decision to drop atomic bombs on Japan? In your opinion, was it a purely military decision, or were nonmilitary considerations important as well?

LOOKING BACKWARD, LOOKING AHEAD

▶ How did America's experience of World War I shape public opinion in 1939 and 1940 about U.S. involvement in World War II?

▶ How did World War II help set the stage for the social, economic, and political developments of the 1950s?

> **IN YOUR OWN WORDS**

Imagine that you must give an oral report to the class answering the following question: **How did the Second World War change the United States, both domestically and internationally?** What would be the most important points to include and why?

26

COLD WAR POLITICS IN THE TRUMAN YEARS

1945–1953

> **What was the impact of the Cold War on the United States?** Chapter 26 examines American politics and foreign policy in the years immediately following World War II. It explores the origins and impact of the Cold War, President Harry Truman's domestic and foreign policy agendas, and the effect of the Korean War on U.S. domestic politics.

LearningCurve

bedfordstmartins.com/roarkunderstanding
After reading the chapter, use LearningCurve to
retain what you've read.

IS THIS TOMORROW

MERICA UNDER COMMUNISM!

Cold War comic book. Four million copies of this 1947 comic book painted a terrifying picture of what would happen to Americans if the Soviets took over the country. Collection of Charles H. Christensen.

> What factors contributed to the Cold War?

> Why did Truman have limited success in implementing his domestic agenda?

> How did U.S. Cold War policy lead to the Korean War?

> Conclusion: What were the costs and consequences of the Cold War?

> What factors contributed to the Cold War?

Joseph Stalin: From Ally to Enemy

These two portrayals indicate how quickly the World War II alliance disintegrated into the Cold War. The photograph on the left, from a 1944 issue of the popular magazine *Look*, shows Stalin with two adoring schoolchildren. Only four years later, in 1948, *Look* published Stalin's life story, framing his photo with communism's emblem, the hammer and sickle. The Michael Barson Collection/Past Perfect.

WITH JAPAN'S SURRENDER in August 1945, Americans besieged the government for the return of their loved ones. Americans wanted to dismantle the large military establishment and expected the Allies to cooperate in the management of international peace. Postwar realities quickly dashed these hopes. The wartime alliance forged by the United States, Great Britain, and the Soviet Union crumbled, giving birth to a Cold War. The United States began to develop the means for containing the spread of Soviet power around the globe, including an enormous aid program for Europe, known as the Marshall Plan.

The Cold War Begins

"The guys who came out of World War II were idealistic," reported Harold Russell, a young paratrooper who had lost both hands in a training accident. "We felt the day had come when the wars were all over." But these hopes were quickly dashed. Once the Allies had overcome a common enemy, the prewar mistrust and antagonism between the Soviet Union and the West resurfaced over their very different visions of the postwar world.

The Western Allies' delay in opening a second front in Western Europe aroused Soviet suspicions during the war. The Soviet Union made supreme wartime sacrifices,

CHAPTER LOCATOR | **What factors contributed to the Cold War?**

losing more than twenty million citizens and vast portions of its agricultural and industrial capacity. Soviet leader Joseph Stalin wanted to make Germany pay for Soviet economic reconstruction and to expand Soviet influence in the world. Above all, he wanted friendly governments on the Soviet Union's borders in Eastern Europe. A ruthless dictator, Stalin also wanted to maintain his own power.

In contrast to the Soviet devastation, the United States emerged from the war as the most powerful nation on the planet, with a vastly expanded economy and a monopoly on atomic weapons. That sheer power, along with U.S. economic interests and a belief in the superiority of American institutions and intentions, all affected how American leaders approached the Soviet Union.

American officials believed that a healthy economy depended on opportunities abroad. American companies needed access to raw materials, markets for their goods, and security for their investments overseas. These needs could be met best in countries with similar economic and political systems. As President Harry S. Truman put it in 1947, "The American system can survive in America only if it becomes a world system." Yet leaders and citizens alike regarded their foreign policy not as a self-interested campaign for economic advantage, but as the means to preserve national security and bring freedom, democracy, and capitalism to the rest of the world. Laura Briggs, a woman from Idaho, spoke for many Americans who believed "it was our destiny to prove that we were the children of God and that our way was right for the world."

Recent history also shaped postwar foreign policy. Americans believed that World War II might have been avoided had Britain and France resisted rather than appeased Hitler's initial aggression. Navy Secretary James V. Forrestal argued against trying to "buy [the Soviets'] understanding and sympathy. We tried that once with Hitler." The man with ultimate responsibility for U.S. policy was a keen student of history but came to the White House with little international experience. Harry S. Truman anticipated Soviet-American cooperation, as long as the Soviet Union conformed to U.S. plans for the postwar world. Proud of his ability to make quick decisions, Truman determined to take a firm hand if the Soviets tried to expand, confident that America's nuclear monopoly gave him the upper hand.

The **Cold War** first emerged over clashing Soviet and American interests in Eastern Europe. Stalin insisted that wartime agreements gave him a free hand in the countries defeated or liberated by the Red Army, just as the United States was unilaterally reconstructing governments in Italy and Japan. The Soviet dictator used harsh methods to install Communist governments in neighboring Poland and Bulgaria. Elsewhere, Stalin initially tolerated non-Communist governments in Hungary and Czechoslovakia. In early 1946, he responded to pressure from the West and removed troops from Iran on the Soviet Union's southwest border, allowing U.S. access to the rich oil fields there.

Stalin saw hypocrisy when U.S. officials demanded democratic elections in Eastern Europe while supporting dictatorships friendly to U.S. interests in Latin America. The United States clung to its sphere of influence while opposing Soviet efforts to create its own. But the Western Allies were unwilling to match tough words with military force against the largest army in the world. They protested strongly but failed to prevent the Soviet Union from establishing satellite countries throughout Eastern Europe.

> CHRONOLOGY

1945
- Franklin Roosevelt dies; Vice President Harry Truman becomes president.

1946
- George F. Kennan drafts containment policy.
- United States grants independence to the Philippines.

1947
- National Security Act.
- Truman announces Truman Doctrine.
- U.S. aid to Greece and Turkey.

1948
- Marshall Plan is approved.
- United States recognizes Israel.

1948–1949
- Berlin crisis and airlift.

1949
- Communists take over China.
- North Atlantic Treaty Organization (NATO) is formed.
- Soviet Union explodes atomic bomb.
- Truman approves development of hydrogen bomb.

1951
- U.S. occupation of Japan ends.

Cold War

▶ Term given to the tense and hostile relationship between the United States and the Soviet Union from 1947 to 1989. The term *cold* was apt because the hostility stopped short of direct armed conflict.

| Why did Truman have limited success in implementing his domestic agenda? | How did U.S. Cold War policy lead to the Korean War? | Conclusion: What were the costs and consequences of the Cold War? | ✓ **LearningCurve** Check what you know. bedfordstmartins.com /roarkunderstanding |

In 1946, the wartime Allies contended over Germany's future. Both sides wanted to demilitarize Germany, but U.S. policymakers sought rapid industrial revival there to foster European economic recovery and thus America's own long-term prosperity. By contrast, the Soviet Union wanted Germany weak both militarily and economically, and Stalin demanded heavy reparations from Germany to help rebuild the devastated Soviet economy. Unable to settle their differences, the Allies divided Germany. The Soviet Union installed a puppet Communist government in the eastern section, and Britain, France, and the United States began to unify their occupation zones, eventually establishing the Federal Republic of Germany — West Germany — in 1949 (**Map 26.1**).

MAP 26.1 ■ The Division of Europe after World War II

The "iron curtain," a term coined by Winston Churchill to refer to the Soviet grip on Eastern and central Europe, divided the continent for nearly fifty years. Communist governments controlled the countries along the Soviet Union's western border, except for Finland, which remained neutral.

> **MAP ACTIVITY**

READING THE MAP: Is the division of Europe between NATO, Communist, and neutral countries about equal? Why would the location of Berlin pose a problem for the Western allies?

CONNECTIONS: When was NATO founded, and what was its purpose? How did the postwar division of Europe compare with the wartime alliances?

The war of words escalated early in 1946. Boasting of the superiority of the Soviet system, Stalin told a Moscow audience in February that capitalism inevitably produced war. One month later, Truman accompanied Winston Churchill to Westminster College in Fulton, Missouri, where the former prime minister denounced Soviet interference in Eastern and central Europe. "From Stettin in the Baltic to Trieste in the Adriatic, an **iron curtain** has descended across the Continent," Churchill said. Stalin saw Churchill's proposal for joint British-American action to combat Soviet aggression as "a call to war against the USSR (the Soviet Union)."

In February 1946, George F. Kennan, a career diplomat and expert on Russia, wrote a comprehensive rationale for what came to be called the policy of **containment**. Downplaying the influence of Communist ideology in Soviet policy, he instead stressed Soviet insecurity and Stalin's need to maintain authority at home, which, he believed, prompted Stalin to exaggerate threats from abroad and expand Soviet power. Kennan believed that the Soviet Union would retreat from its expansionist efforts if the United States would respond with "unalterable counterforce." This approach, he predicted, would eventually end in "either the breakup or the gradual mellowing of Soviet power." Not all public figures agreed. In September 1946, Secretary of Commerce Henry A. Wallace urged greater understanding of the Soviets' national security concerns, insisting that "we have no more business in the political affairs of Eastern Europe than Russia has in the political affairs of Latin America." State Department officials were furious at Wallace for challenging the administration's hard line against the Soviet Union, and Truman fired Wallace.

The Truman Doctrine and the Marshall Plan

In 1947, the United States began to implement the doctrine of containment that would guide foreign policy for the next four decades. It was not an easy transition; Americans approved of taking a hard line against the Soviet Union but wanted to keep their soldiers and tax dollars at home. In addition to selling containment to the public, Truman had to gain the support of a Republican-controlled Congress.

Crises in two Mediterranean countries triggered the implementation of containment. In February 1947, Britain informed the United States that its crippled economy could no longer sustain military assistance to Greece, where the autocratic government faced a leftist uprising, and to Turkey, which was trying to resist Soviet pressures. Truman promptly sought congressional authority to send the two countries military and economic aid. Meeting with congressional leaders, Undersecretary of State Dean Acheson predicted that if Greece and Turkey fell, communism would soon consume three-fourths of the world. After a stunned silence, Michigan senator Arthur Vandenberg, the Republican foreign policy leader, warned that to get approval, Truman would have to "scare hell out of the country."

Truman did just that. He warned that if Greece fell to the rebels, "confusion and disorder might well spread throughout the entire Middle East" and then create instability in Europe. According to what came to be called the **Truman Doctrine**, the United States must not only resist Soviet military power but also "support free peoples who are resisting attempted subjugation by armed

iron curtain
▶ Metaphor coined by Winston Churchill in 1946 to demarcate the line dividing Soviet-controlled countries in Eastern Europe from democratic nations in Western Europe following World War II.

containment
▶ The post–World War II foreign policy strategy that committed the United States to resisting the influence and expansion of the Soviet Union and communism. The strategy of containment shaped American foreign policy throughout the Cold War.

Truman Doctrine
▶ President Harry S. Truman's commitment to "support free peoples who are resisting attempted subjugation by armed minorities or outside pressures." First applied to Greece and Turkey in 1947, the Truman Doctrine became the justification for U.S. intervention in many countries during the Cold War.

Why did Truman have limited success in implementing his domestic agenda?

How did U.S. Cold War policy lead to the Korean War?

Conclusion: What were the costs and consequences of the Cold War?

✓ **LearningCurve**
Check what you know.
bedfordstmartins.com
/roarkunderstanding

minorities or by outside pressures." The president failed to convince some liberal members of Congress who wanted the United States to work through the United Nations and opposed propping up the authoritarian Greek government. But the administration won the day, setting a precedent for forty years of Cold War interventions that would aid any kind of government if the only alternative appeared to be communism. A much larger assistance program for Europe followed aid to Greece and Turkey. In May 1947, Acheson described a war-ravaged Western Europe, with "factories destroyed, fields impoverished, transportation systems wrecked, populations scattered and on the borderline of starvation." American citizens were sending generous amounts of private aid, but Europe needed large-scale assistance to keep desperate citizens from turning to socialism or communism.

In March 1948, Congress approved such assistance, which came to be called the **Marshall Plan**, after Secretary of State George C. Marshall, who proposed it. Over the next five years, the United States spent $13 billion ($117 billion in 2010 dollars) to restore the economies of sixteen Western European nations. Marshall invited all European nations and the Soviet Union to cooperate in a request for aid, but the Soviets objected to the American terms of free trade and financial disclosure. They ordered their Eastern European satellites to reject the offer.

Marshall Plan

▶ Aid program begun in 1948 to help European economies recover from World War II. Between 1948 and 1953, the United States provided $13 billion to seventeen Western European nations in a project that helped its own economy as well.

Marshall Plan Bread for Greek Children

Greece was one of sixteen European nations that participated in the European Recovery Program, more commonly known as the Marshall Plan. In this photograph taken in 1949, Greek children receive loaves of bread made from the first shipment of Marshall Plan flour from the United States. © Bettmann/Corbis.

CHAPTER LOCATOR | What factors contributed to the Cold War?

Humanitarian impulses as well as the goal of keeping Western Europe free of communism drove the adoption of this enormous aid program. But the Marshall Plan also helped boost the U.S. economy because the participating European nations spent most of the dollars to buy American products and Europe's economic recovery created new markets and opportunities for American investment. And by insisting that the recipient nations work together, the Marshall Plan marked the first step toward the European Union.

In February 1948, the Soviets staged a brutal coup and installed a Communist regime in Czechoslovakia, the last democracy left in Eastern Europe. Next, Stalin threatened Western access to Berlin. That former capital of Germany lay within Soviet-controlled East Germany, but all four Allies jointly occupied it. As the Western Allies moved to organize West Germany as a separate nation, the Soviets retaliated by blocking roads and rail lines between West Germany and the Western-held sections of Berlin, cutting off food, fuel, and other essentials to two million inhabitants. "We stay in Berlin, period," Truman vowed. To avoid a confrontation with Soviet troops, for nearly a year U.S. and British pilots airlifted 2.3 million tons of goods to sustain the West Berliners. Stalin hesitated to shoot down these cargo planes, and in 1949 he lifted the blockade. The city was then divided into East Berlin, under Soviet control, and West Berlin, which became part of West Germany.

Berlin Divided, 1948

Building a National Security State

In September 1949, the Soviet Union detonated its own atomic bomb. Truman then approved the development of a hydrogen bomb — equivalent to five hundred atomic bombs — rejecting the counterarguments of several scientists who had worked on the atomic bomb and of George Kennan, who warned of an endless arms race. The "superbomb" was ready by 1954, but the U.S. advantage was brief. In November 1955, the Soviets exploded their own hydrogen bomb.

> **The Six-Pronged Containment Program**

- Development of atomic weapons
- Stronger traditional military forces
- Military alliances with other nations
- Military and economic aid to friendly nations
- An espionage network and secret means to subvert Communist expansion
- A propaganda offensive to win support for the United States around the world

From the 1950s through the 1980s, deterrence formed the basis of American nuclear strategy. To deter a Soviet attack, the United States strove to maintain a nuclear force more powerful than that of the Soviets. Because the Russians pursued a similar policy, the superpowers became locked in an ever-escalating nuclear weapons race. Albert Einstein, whose mathematical discoveries had laid the foundations for nuclear weapons, commented grimly that the war that came after World War III would "be fought with sticks and stones."

Why did Truman have limited success in implementing his domestic agenda?

How did U.S. Cold War policy lead to the Korean War?

Conclusion: What were the costs and consequences of the Cold War?

✓ LearningCurve
Check what you know.
bedfordstmartins.com
/roarkunderstanding

785

Implementing the second component of containment, the United States beefed up its conventional military power to deter Soviet threats that might not warrant nuclear retaliation. The National Security Act of 1947 united the military branches under a single secretary of defense and created the National Security Council (NSC) to advise the president. During the Berlin crisis in 1948, Congress hiked military appropriations and enacted a peacetime draft. In addition, Congress granted permanent status to the women's military branches, though it limited their numbers and rank. With 1.5 million men and women in uniform in 1950, the military strength of the United States had quadrupled since the 1930s, and defense expenditures claimed one-third of the federal budget.

Collective security, the third prong of containment strategy, marked a sharp reversal of the nation's traditional foreign policy. In 1949, the United States joined Canada and Western European nations in its first peacetime military alliance, the **North Atlantic Treaty Organization (NATO)**, designed to counter a Soviet threat to Western Europe (see Map 26.1). For the first time in its history, the United States pledged to go to war if one of its allies was attacked.

The fourth element of defense strategy involved foreign assistance programs to strengthen friendly countries, such as aid to Greece and Turkey and the Marshall Plan. In addition, in 1949 Congress approved $1 billion of

North Atlantic Treaty Organization (NATO)

▶ Military alliance formed in 1949 among the United States, Canada, and Western European nations to counter any possible Soviet threat. It represented an unprecedented commitment by the United States to go to war if one of its allies was attacked.

Cold War Spying

"Intelligence," the gathering of information about the enemy, took on new importance with the Cold War and the creation of the Central Intelligence Agency (CIA) in 1947. While much intelligence work took place in Washington, where analysts combed through Communist newspapers, official reports, and speeches, secret agents gathered information behind the iron curtain with bugs and devices such as these cameras hidden in cigarette packs. Jack Naylor Collection/Picture Research Consultants & Archives.

CHAPTER LOCATOR | What factors contributed to the Cold War?

military aid to its NATO allies, and the government began economic assistance to nations in other parts of the world.

The fifth ingredient of containment improved the government's espionage. The National Security Act of 1947 created the **Central Intelligence Agency (CIA)** to gather information and to perform any activities "related to intelligence affecting the national security" that the NSC might authorize. Such functions included propaganda, sabotage, economic warfare, and support for "anti-communist elements in threatened countries of the free world." In 1948, secret CIA operations helped defeat Italy's Communist Party. Subsequently, CIA agents would intervene even more actively, helping to topple legitimate foreign governments and violating the rights of U.S. citizens.

Finally, the U.S. government sought, through cultural exchanges and propaganda, to win "hearts and minds" throughout the world. Truman expanded the Voice of America, created during World War II to broadcast U.S. propaganda abroad. In addition, the State Department sent books, exhibits, jazz musicians, and other performers to foreign countries as "cultural ambassadors."

By 1950, the United States had abandoned age-old tenets of foreign policy. Isolationism and neutrality had given way to a peacetime military alliance and efforts to control events far beyond U.S. borders. Short of war, the United States could not stop the descent of the iron curtain, but it aggressively and successfully promoted economic recovery and a military shield for the rest of Europe.

Central Intelligence Agency (CIA)

▶ Agency created by the National Security Act of 1947 to expand the government's espionage capacities and ability to thwart communism through covert activities, including propaganda, sabotage, economic warfare, and support for anti-Communist forces around the world.

Superpower Rivalry around the Globe

Efforts to implement containment moved beyond Europe. In Africa, Asia, and the Middle East, World War II accelerated a tide of national liberation movements against war-weakened imperial powers. By 1960, forty countries had won their independence. These nations, along with Latin America, came to be referred to collectively as the third world.

Like Woodrow Wilson during World War I, Roosevelt and Truman promoted the ideal of self-determination. The United States granted independence to the Philippines in 1946 and applauded the British withdrawal from India. U.S. policymakers encouraged democracy and capitalism in emerging nations and sought to preserve opportunities for American trade, while U.S. corporations coveted the vast oil reserves in the Middle East. Yet leaders of many liberation movements, impressed with Russia's rapid economic growth, adopted socialist or Communist ideas. Although few of these movements had formal ties with the Soviet Union, American leaders saw them as a threatening extension of Soviet power. Seeking to hold communism at bay by fostering economic development and political stability, in 1949 the Truman administration began a small program of aid to developing nations. Meanwhile, civil war raged in China, where the Communists, led by Mao Zedong (Mao Tse-tung), fought the official Nationalist government under Jiang Jieshi (Chiang Kai-shek). While the Communists gained popular support for their land reforms and valiant stand against the Japanese, Jiang's corrupt, incompetent government alienated much of the population. Failing to promote a settlement between Jiang and Mao, the United States provided $3 billion in aid to the Nationalists. Yet, recognizing the ineptness of Jiang's government, Truman refused to divert further resources from Europe to China.

Why did Truman have limited success in implementing his domestic agenda?

How did U.S. Cold War policy lead to the Korean War?

Conclusion: What were the costs and consequences of the Cold War?

✓ LearningCurve
Check what you know.
bedfordstmartins.com
/roarkunderstanding

787

In October 1949, Mao established the People's Republic of China (PRC), and the Nationalists fled to the island of Taiwan. Fearing a U.S.-supported invasion to recapture China for the Nationalists, Mao signed a mutual defense treaty with the Soviet Union. The United States refused to recognize the PRC, blocked its admission to the United Nations, and supported the Nationalist government in Taiwan. Only a massive U.S. military commitment could have stopped the Chinese Communists, yet some Republicans charged that Truman and "pro-Communists in the State Department" had "lost" China. With China in turmoil, U.S. policy shifted to helping Japan rapidly reindustrialize. In a short time, the Japanese economy was flourishing, and the official military occupation ended when the two nations signed a peace treaty and a mutual security pact in September 1951. Like West Germany, Japan now sat squarely within the American orbit, ready to serve as an economic hub in a vital area.

The one place where Cold War considerations did not control American policy was Palestine. In 1943, then-senator Harry Truman spoke passionately about Nazi Germany's annihilation of the Jews, asserting, "This is not a Jewish problem, it is an American problem — and we must . . . face it squarely and honorably." As president, he made good on his words. Jews had been migrating to Palestine, their biblical homeland, since the nineteenth century, resulting in tension and hostilities with the Palestinian Arabs. After World War II, as hundreds of thousands of European Jews sought refuge and a national homeland in Palestine, fighting and terrorism escalated on both sides.

Truman's foreign policy experts sought American-Arab friendship to contain Soviet influence in the Middle East and to secure access to Arabian oil. Uncharacteristically defying his advisers, the president responded instead to pleas from Jewish organizations, his moral commitment to Holocaust survivors, and his interest in the American Jewish vote for the 1948 election. When Jews in Palestine declared the state of Israel in May 1948, Truman quickly recognized the new country and made its defense the cornerstone of U.S. policy in the Middle East.

Israel, 1948

> **QUICK REVIEW**

Why did relations between the United States and the Soviet Union deteriorate after World War II?

CHAPTER LOCATOR | What factors contributed to the Cold War?

Truman's Whistle-Stop Campaign

Harry Truman rallies a crowd from his campaign train in Bridgeport, Pennsylvania, in October 1948. As he campaigned across the country, supporters often shouted, "Give 'em hell, Harry." Truman's support for civil rights cost him four southern states but helped him win votes from liberals and blacks. Truman Library.

> VISUAL ACTIVITY

READING THE IMAGE: This photo was taken one month before the election. Why might his opponent's campaign have dismissed the importance of these large crowds in support of Truman?
CONNECTIONS: President Truman was under attack by the Republicans and could not enact the Fair Deal. Almost everyone thought he would lose the election. Why do you think the American people responded so well to his campaign? In what ways have presidential campaigns changed since Harry Truman's time?

Why did Truman have limited success in implementing his domestic agenda?

REFERRING TO THE CIVIL WAR GENERAL who coined the phrase "War is hell," Truman said in December 1945, "Sherman was wrong. I'm telling you I find peace is hell." Challenged by crises abroad, Truman also faced shortages, strikes, inflation, and other problems as the economy shifted to peacetime production. At the same time, he tried to expand New Deal reform with his own Fair Deal agenda of initiatives in civil rights, housing, education, and health care — efforts hindered by the wave of anti-Communist hysteria sweeping the country.

Reconverting to a Peacetime Economy

Despite scarcities and deprivations, World War II had brought most Americans a higher standard of living than ever before. Economic experts as well as ordinary citizens worried about sustaining that standard and providing jobs for millions of returning soldiers. To that end, Truman asked Congress to enact a twenty-one-point program of social and economic reforms. He wanted the government to continue regulating the economy while it adjusted to peacetime production, and he sought government programs to provide basic essentials such as housing and

Why did Truman have limited success in implementing his domestic agenda?

How did U.S. Cold War policy lead to the Korean War?

Conclusion: What were the costs and consequences of the Cold War?

✓ LearningCurve
Check what you know.
bedfordstmartins.com
/roarkunderstanding

789

> CHRONOLOGY

1946
– Postwar labor unrest.
– President's Committee on Civil Rights is created.
– Employment Act.
– Republicans gain control of Congress.

1947
– *Mendez v. Westminster.*

1948
– Truman orders desegregation of military.
– American GI Forum is founded.
– Truman is elected president.

1950
– Senator Joseph McCarthy claims U.S. government harbors Communists.

health care to those in need. "Not even President Roosevelt ever asked for as much at one sitting," exploded Republican leader Joseph W. Martin Jr.

Congress approved one of Truman's key proposals — full-employment legislation — only after watering it down. The Employment Act of 1946 called on the federal government "to promote maximum employment, production, and purchasing power," thereby formalizing government's responsibility for maintaining a healthy economy. But it authorized no new powers to translate that obligation into effective action.

Inflation, not unemployment, turned out to be the biggest problem. Consumers had $30 billion in wartime savings to spend, but shortages of meat, automobiles, housing, and other items persisted. Until industry could make more goods available, consumer demand would continue to drive up prices. With a basket of groceries on her arm to dramatize rising costs, Democratic congresswoman Helen Gahagan Douglas of California urged Congress to maintain price and rent controls. Those efforts, however, fell to pressures from business groups and others determined to trim government powers.

Labor relations were another thorn in Truman's side. Organized labor emerged from the war with its 14.5 million members making up 35 percent of the civilian workforce. Yet union members feared the erosion of wartime gains and turned to the weapon they had surrendered during the war. Five million workers went out on strike in 1946, affecting nearly every major industry. Shortly before voting to strike, a former Marine and his coworkers calculated that an executive had spent more on a party than they would earn in a whole year at the steel mill. "That sort of stuff made us realize, hell we had to bite the bullet. . . . The bosses sure didn't give a damn for us." Although most Americans approved of unions in principle, they became fed up with strikes, blamed unions for shortages and rising prices, and called for government restrictions on organized labor. When the

FIGURE 26.1 ■ Women Workers in Selected Industries, 1940–1950
Women demolished the idea that some jobs were "men's work" during World War II, but they failed to maintain their gains in the manufacturing sector after the war.

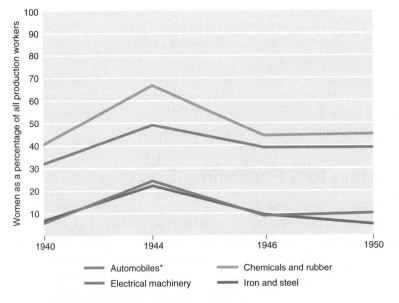

*During World War II, this industry did not produce cars, but rather military transportation such as jeeps, tanks, aircraft, etc.

CHAPTER LOCATOR | What factors contributed to the Cold War?

strikes subsided, workers had won wage increases of about 20 percent, but the loss of overtime pay along with rising prices left their purchasing power only slightly higher than in 1942.

Women workers fared even worse. Polls indicated that many women wanted to keep their wartime jobs, but most who remained in the workforce had to settle for relatively low-paying jobs in light industry or the service sector (**Figure 26.1**). Displaced from her shipyard work, Marie Schreiber took a cashier's job, lamenting, "You were back to women's wages, you know . . . practically in half." With the backing of women's organizations and union women, Congresswoman Douglas sponsored bills to require equal pay for equal work, to provide child care for employed mothers, and to create a government commission to study women's status. But at a time when women were viewed primarily as wives and mothers and opposition to further expansion of federal powers was strong, these initiatives went nowhere.

By 1947, the economy had stabilized, avoiding the postwar depression that so many had feared. Wartime profits enabled businesses to expand. Consumers could now spend their wartime savings on houses, cars, and appliances that had lain beyond their reach during the depression and war. Defense spending and foreign aid that enabled war-stricken countries to purchase American products also stimulated the economy. A soaring birthrate further sustained consumer demand. Although prosperity was far from universal, the United States entered into a remarkable economic boom that lasted through the 1960s (as discussed in chapter 27).

Another economic boost came from the only large welfare measure passed after the New Deal. The Servicemen's Readjustment Act (GI Bill), enacted in 1944, offered 16 million veterans job training and education; unemployment compensation until they found jobs; and low-interest loans to purchase homes, farms, and small businesses. By 1948, some 1.3 million veterans had bought houses with government loans. Helping 2.2 million ex-soldiers attend college, the subsidies sparked a boom in higher education. A drugstore clerk before his military service, Don Condren was able to get an engineering degree and buy his first house. "I think the GI Bill gave the whole country an upward boost economically," he said.

Yet the impact of the GI Bill was uneven. As wives and daughters of veterans, women benefited indirectly from the GI subsidies, but few women qualified for the employment and educational preferences available to some 15 million men. Moreover, GI programs were administered at the state and local levels, which resulted in routine discrimination especially in the South. Southern universities remained segregated, and historically black colleges could not accommodate all

Women's Role in Peacetime

Like many manufacturers during World War II, Proctor Electric Company was forced to convert to war production, so it switched from making appliances to producing bomb fuses, cartridges, and airplane wing flaps. After the war, the company hoped to profit from pent-up consumer demand. During the reconversion period, ads tempted consumers with products soon to come, as in this 1946 ad. What message about women's employment during and after the war is conveyed here? Picture Research Consultants & Archives.

Why did Truman have limited success in implementing his domestic agenda?

How did U.S. Cold War policy lead to the Korean War?

Conclusion: What were the costs and consequences of the Cold War?

LearningCurve
Check what you know.
bedfordstmartins.com
/roarkunderstanding

who wanted to attend. Black veterans were shuttled into menial labor. One decorated veteran reported that "my color bars me from most decent jobs, and if, instead of accepting menial work, I collect my $20 a week readjustment allowance, I am classified as a 'lazy nigger.'" Thousands of black veterans did benefit, but the GI Bill did not help all ex-soldiers equally.

Blacks and Mexican Americans Push for Their Civil Rights

"I spent four years in the army to free a bunch of Frenchmen and Dutchmen," an African American corporal declared, "and I'm hanged if I'm going to let the Alabama version of the Germans kick me around when I get home." Black veterans along with civilians resolved not to return to the racial injustices of prewar America. The migration of two million African Americans to northern and western cities meant that they could now vote and participate in ongoing struggles to end discrimination in housing and education. Pursuing civil rights through the courts and Congress, the National Association for the Advancement of Colored People (NAACP) counted half a million members.

In the postwar years, individual African Americans broke through the color barrier, achieving several "firsts." Jackie Robinson integrated major league baseball, playing for the Brooklyn Dodgers, and won the Rookie of the Year Award in 1947. In 1950, Ralph J. Bunche received the Nobel Peace Prize for his United Nations work, and Gwendolyn Brooks won the Pulitzer Prize for poetry. Still, little had changed for most African Americans, especially in the South, where violence greeted their attempts to assert their rights. Armed white men prevented Medgar Evers (who would become a key civil rights leader in the 1960s) and four other veterans from voting in Mississippi. A mob lynched Isaac Nixon for voting in Georgia, and an all-white jury acquitted the men accused of his murder. Segregation and economic discrimination were widespread in the North as well.

In waging the Cold War, the superpowers vied for the allegiance of newly independent nations with nonwhite populations, and Soviet propaganda repeatedly highlighted racial injustice in the United States. Secretary of State Dean Acheson noted that systematic segregation and discrimination endangered "our moral leadership of the free and democratic nations of the world."

"My very stomach turned over when I learned that Negro soldiers just back from overseas were being dumped out of army trucks in Mississippi and beaten," wrote Truman. Risking support from southern white voters, Truman spoke more boldly on civil rights than any previous president had. In 1946, he created the President's Committee on Civil Rights, and in February 1948 he asked Congress to enact the committee's recommendations. The first president to address the NAACP, Truman asserted that all Americans should have equal rights to housing, education, employment, and the ballot.

As with much of his domestic program, Truman failed to act aggressively on his bold words. Congress rejected his proposals for national civil rights legislation, although some northern and western states did pass laws against discrimination in employment and public accommodations. Running for reelection in 1948 and hoping to appeal to northern black and liberal voters, Truman issued an executive

Segregation The segregation visible on this bus was a feature of life in the South from the late nineteenth century until the 1960s. African Americans could not use white hospitals, cemeteries, schools, libraries, swimming pools, restrooms, or drinking fountains. They were relegated to balconies in movie theaters and kept apart from whites in all public meetings. Stan Wayman/Time Life Pictures/ Getty Images.

order to desegregate the armed services, but it lay unimplemented until the Korean War, when the cost of segregation to military efficiency became apparent. Although actual accomplishments fell far short of Truman's proposals, desegregation of the military and the administration's support of civil rights cases in the Supreme Court contributed to far-reaching changes.

Discussion of race and civil rights usually focused on African Americans, but Mexican Americans fought similar injustices. In 1929, they had formed the League of United Latin American Citizens (LULAC) to combat discrimination and segregation in the Southwest. Like black soldiers, Mexican American veterans believed, as one insisted, that "we had earned our credentials as American citizens." Problems with getting their veterans' benefits spurred the formation of a new organization in 1948 in Corpus Christi, Texas — the American GI Forum. Dr. Héctor Peréz García, president of the local LULAC and a Bronze Star combat surgeon, led the GI Forum, which became a national force for battling discrimination and electing sympathetic officials.

"Education is our freedom," read the GI Forum's motto, yet Mexican American children were routinely segregated in public schools. In 1945, with the help of LULAC, parents filed a class action suit in southern California, challenging school districts that barred their children from white schools. In the resulting decision, *Mendez v. Westminster* (1947), a federal court for the first time struck down school segregation. NAACP lawyer Thurgood Marshall filed a supporting brief in

---

| Why did **Truman** have limited success in implementing his domestic agenda? | How did U.S. Cold War policy lead to the Korean War? | Conclusion: What were the costs and consequences of the Cold War? | ✔ LearningCurve Check what you know. bedfordstmartins.com /roarkunderstanding |

the case, which foreshadowed the landmark *Brown* decision of 1954 (as discussed in chapter 27). Efforts to gain equal education, challenges to job discrimination in employment, and campaigns for political representation all demonstrated a growing mobilization of Mexican Americans in the Southwest.

The Fair Deal Flounders

In the 1946 congressional elections, Republicans won control of Congress for the first time in fourteen years, capitalizing on public frustrations with strikes and shortages and accusing the administration of "confusion, corruption, and communism." Many Republicans had campaigned against the New Deal in 1946, and in the Eightieth Congress they weakened some reform programs and enacted tax cuts favoring higher-income groups.

Organized labor took the most severe blow when Congress passed the **Taft-Hartley Act** over Truman's veto in 1947. Called a "slave labor" law by unions, the measure amended the Wagner Act (see chapter 24). It reduced the power of organized labor and made it more difficult to organize workers. States could now pass "right-to-work" laws, which banned the practice of requiring all workers to join a union once a majority had voted for it. Many states, especially in the South and West, rushed to enact such laws, encouraging industries to relocate there. Taft-Hartley maintained the New Deal principle of government protection for collective bargaining, but it put the government more squarely between labor and management.

In the 1948 election, Truman faced not only a resurgent Republican Party headed by New York governor Thomas E. Dewey but also two revolts within his own party. On the left, Henry A. Wallace, whose foreign policy views had cost him his cabinet seat, led the new Progressive Party. On the right, South Carolina governor J. Strom Thurmond headed the States' Rights Party — the Dixiecrats — formed by southern Democrats who walked out of the 1948 Democratic Party convention when it passed a liberal civil rights plank.

Truman launched a vigorous campaign, yet his prospects were so bleak that on election night the *Chicago Daily Tribune* printed its next day's issue with the headline "Dewey Defeats Truman." But even though the Dixiecrats won four southern states, Truman took 303 electoral votes to Dewey's 189, and his party regained control of Congress (**Map 26.2**). His unexpected victory attested to the broad support for his foreign policy and the enduring popularity of New Deal reform.

While most New Deal programs survived Republican attacks, Truman failed to enact his Fair Deal agenda. Congress made modest improvements in Social Security and raised the minimum wage, but it passed only one significant reform measure. The **Housing Act of 1949** authorized 810,000 units of government-constructed housing over the next six years and represented a landmark commitment by the government to address the housing needs of the poor. Yet it fell far short of

Taft-Hartley Act

▶ Law passed by the Republican-controlled Congress in 1947 that amended the Wagner Act and placed restrictions on organized labor that made it more difficult for unions to organize workers.

Housing Act of 1949

▶ Law authorizing the construction of 810,000 units of government housing. This landmark effort marked the first significant commitment of the federal government to meet the housing needs of the poor.

Candidate	Electoral Vote	Popular Vote	Percent of Popular Vote
Harry S. Truman (Democrat)	303	24,105,695	49.5
Thomas E. Dewey (Republican)	189	21,969,170	45.1
J. Strom Thurmond (States' Rights)	39	1,169,021	2.4
Henry A. Wallace (Progressive)	0	1,156,103	2.4

MAP 26.2 ■ The Election of 1948

actual need, and slum clearance frequently displaced the poor without providing alternatives.

With southern Democrats posing a primary obstacle, Congress rejected Truman's proposals for civil rights, a powerful medical lobby blocked plans for a universal health care program, and conflicts over race and religion thwarted federal aid to education. Truman's efforts to revise immigration policy were mixed. The McCarran-Walter Act of 1952 ended the outright ban on immigration and citizenship for Japanese and other Asians, but it authorized the government to bar suspected Communists and homosexuals and maintained the discriminatory quota system established in the 1920s. By late 1950, the Korean War embroiled the president in controversy and depleted his power as a legislative leader (see pages 798–99). Truman's failure to make good on his domestic proposals set the United States apart from most European nations, which by the 1950s had in place comprehensive health, housing, and employment security programs to underwrite the material well-being of their populations.

The Domestic Chill: McCarthyism

Truman's domestic program also suffered from a wave of anticommunism that weakened liberals. "Red-baiting" (attempting to link individuals or ideas with communism) and official retaliation against leftist critics of the government had flourished during the Red scare at the end of World War I (see chapter 22). A second Red scare followed World War II, born of partisan politics, the collapse of the Soviet-American alliance, foreign policy setbacks, and disclosures of Soviet espionage.

Republicans who had attacked the New Deal as a plot of radicals now jumped on events such as the Soviet takeover of Eastern Europe and the Communist triumph in China to accuse Democrats of fostering internal subversion. Wisconsin senator Joseph R. McCarthy avowed that "the Communists within our borders have been more responsible for the success of Communism abroad than Soviet Russia." McCarthy's charges — such as the allegation that retired general George C. Marshall belonged to a Communist conspiracy — were reckless and often ludicrous, but the press covered him avidly, and *McCarthyism* became a term synonymous with the anti-Communist crusade.

Revelations of Soviet espionage lent credibility to fears of internal communism. A number of ex-Communists, including Whittaker Chambers and Elizabeth Bentley, testified that they and others had provided secret documents to the Soviets. Most alarming of all, in 1950 a British physicist working on the atomic bomb project confessed that he was a spy and implicated several Americans, including Ethel and Julius Rosenberg. The Rosenbergs pleaded not guilty but were convicted of conspiracy to commit espionage and electrocuted in 1953.

Records opened in the 1990s showed that the Soviet Union did receive secret documents from Americans that probably hastened its development of nuclear weapons by a year or two. Yet the vast majority of individuals hunted down in the Red scare had done nothing more than at one time joining the Communist Party, associating with Communists, or supporting radical causes. And most of those activities had taken place long before the Cold War had made the Soviet Union an enemy. The hunt for subversives was conducted by both Congress and the

Why did Truman have limited success in implementing his domestic agenda?

How did U.S. Cold War policy lead to the Korean War?

Conclusion: What were the costs and consequences of the Cold War?

✓ LearningCurve
Check what you know.
bedfordstmartins.com
/roarkunderstanding

795

executive branch. Stung by charges of communism in the 1946 midterm elections, Truman issued Executive Order 9835 in March 1947, establishing loyalty review boards to investigate every federal employee. "A nightmare from which there [was] no awakening" was how State Department employee Esther Brunauer described it when both she and her husband, a chemist in the navy, lost their jobs because he had joined a Communist youth organization in the 1920s and associated with suspected radicals. Government investigators allowed anonymous informers to make charges and placed the burden of proof on the accused. More than two thousand civil service employees lost their jobs, and another ten thousand resigned as Truman's loyalty program continued into the mid-1950s. Years later, Truman admitted that it had been a mistake.

Congressional committees, such as the **House Un-American Activities Committee (HUAC)**, also investigated individuals' political associations. When those under scrutiny refused to name names, investigators charged that silence was tantamount to confession, and these "unfriendly witnesses" lost their jobs and suffered public ostracism. In 1947, HUAC investigated radical activity in Hollywood. Some actors and directors cooperated, but ten refused, citing their First Amendment rights. The "Hollywood Ten" served jail sentences for contempt of Congress and then found themselves blacklisted in the movie industry.

The domestic Cold War spread beyond the nation's capital. State and local governments investigated citizens, demanded loyalty oaths, fired employees suspected of disloyalty, banned books from public libraries, and more. Because the Communist Party had helped organize unions and championed racial justice, labor and civil rights activists fell prey to McCarthyism as well. African American activist Jack O'Dell remembered that segregationists pinned the tag of Communist on "anybody who supported the right of blacks to have civil rights."

McCarthyism caused untold harm to thousands of innocent individuals. Anti-Communist crusaders humiliated and discredited law-abiding citizens, hounded them from their jobs, and in some cases even sent them to prison. The anti-Communist crusade violated fundamental constitutional rights of freedom of speech and stifled the expression of dissenting ideas or unpopular causes.

House Un-American Activities Committee (HUAC)

▶ Congressional committee especially prominent during the early years of the Cold War that investigated Americans who might be disloyal to the government or might have associated with Communists or other radicals. It was one of the key institutions that promoted the second Red scare.

> **QUICK REVIEW**

What impact did the Cold War have on Truman's domestic agenda?

CHAPTER LOCATOR | What factors contributed to the Cold War?

How did U.S. Cold War policy lead to the Korean War?

POWs in Korea

These demoralized American soldiers reflect the grim situation for U.S. forces during the early months of the Korean War. Their North Korean captors forced them to march through Seoul in July 1950 carrying a banner proclaiming the righteousness of the Communist cause and attacking U.S. intervention. Wide World Photos, Inc.

THE COLD WAR ERUPTED into a shooting war in June 1950 when troops from Communist North Korea invaded South Korea. For the first time, Americans went into battle to implement containment. Confirming the global reach of the Truman Doctrine, U.S. involvement in Korea also marked the militarization of American foreign policy. The United States, in concert with the United Nations, ultimately held the line in Korea, but at a great cost in lives, dollars, and domestic unity.

Korea and the Military Implementation of Containment

The **Korean War** grew out of the artificial division of Korea after World War II. Having expelled the Japanese, the United States and the Soviet Union created two occupation zones separated by the thirty-eighth parallel (**Map 26.3**). With Moscow and Washington unable to agree on unification, the United Nations sponsored elections in South Korea in July 1948. The American-favored candidate, Syngman Rhee, was elected president, and the United States withdrew most of its troops. In the fall of 1948, the Soviets established the People's Republic of North Korea under Kim Il-sung and also withdrew. Although unsure whether Rhee's repressive government could sustain popular support, U.S. officials appreciated his anticommunism and provided economic and military aid to South Korea.

Korean War

▶ Conflict between North Korean forces, supported by China and the Soviet Union, and South Korean and U.S.-led UN forces over control of South Korea. Lasting from 1950 to 1953, the war represented the first time that the United States went to war to implement containment.

Why did Truman have limited success in implementing his domestic agenda?

How did U.S. Cold War policy lead to the Korean War?

Conclusion: What were the costs and consequences of the Cold War?

✓ **LearningCurve**
Check what you know.
bedfordstmartins.com
/roarkunderstanding

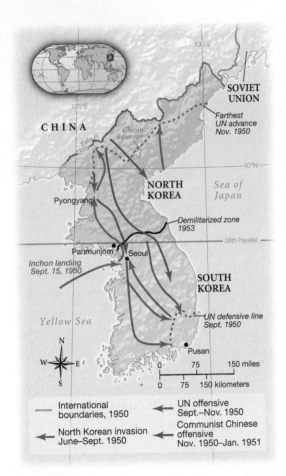

MAP 26.3 ■ The Korean War, 1950–1953

Although each side had plunged deep into enemy territory, the war ended in 1953 with the dividing line between North and South Korea nearly where it had been before the fighting began.

> MAP ACTIVITY

READING THE MAP: How far south did the North Korean forces progress at the height of their invasion? How far north did the UN forces get? What countries border Korea?

CONNECTIONS: What dangers did the forays of MacArthur's forces to within forty miles of the Korean-Chinese border pose? Why did Truman forbid MacArthur to approach that border? What political considerations on the home front influenced Truman's policy and military strategy regarding Korea?

Skirmishes between North and South Korean troops at the thirty-eighth parallel began in 1948. Then, in June 1950, 90,000 North Koreans swept into South Korea. Truman's advisers assumed that the Soviet Union or China had instigated the attack (an assumption later proved incorrect), and he quickly decided to intervene, viewing Korea as "the Greece of the Far East." With the Soviet Union absent from the Security Council, the United States obtained UN sponsorship of a collective effort to repel the attack. Authorized to appoint a commander for the UN force, Truman named World War II hero General Douglas MacArthur.

Sixteen nations sent troops to Korea, but the United States furnished most of the personnel and weapons, deploying almost 1.8 million troops and dictating strategy. By dispatching troops without asking Congress for a declaration of war, Truman violated the spirit if not the letter of the Constitution and contributed to the expansion of executive power that would characterize the Cold War. The first American soldiers rushed to Korea unprepared and ill equipped, and U.S. forces suffered severe defeats early in the war. The North Koreans took the capital of Seoul and drove deep into South Korea, forcing UN troops to retreat to Pusan. Then, in September 1950, General MacArthur launched a bold counteroffensive at Inchon, 180 miles behind North Korean lines. By October, UN and South Korean forces had retaken Seoul and pushed the North Koreans back to the thirty-eighth parallel. Now Truman had to decide whether to invade North Korea and seek to unify the country.

From Containment to Rollback to Containment

"Troops could not be expected . . . to march up to a surveyor's line and stop," remarked Secretary of State Dean Acheson, reflecting support for transforming the military objective from containment to elimination of the enemy and unification of Korea. Thus, for the only time during the Cold War, the United States tried to roll back communism by force. With UN approval, on September 27, 1950, Truman authorized MacArthur to cross the thirty-eighth parallel. Concerned about possible intervention by China, the president directed him to keep UN troops away from the Korean-Chinese border. Disregarding the order, MacArthur sent them to within forty miles of China, whereupon 300,000 Chinese soldiers crossed into Korea. With Chinese help, the North Koreans recaptured Seoul.

After three months of grueling battle, UN forces fought their way back to the thirty-eighth parallel. At that point, Truman decided to seek a negotiated settlement. MacArthur was furious when the goal of the war reverted to containment, which to him represented defeat. Taking his case to the public, he challenged

CHAPTER LOCATOR | What factors contributed to the Cold War?

both the president's authority to conduct foreign policy and the principle of civilian control of the military. Fed up with MacArthur's insubordination, Truman fired him in April 1951. Many Americans sided with MacArthur, reflecting their frustration with containment. Why should Americans die simply to preserve the status quo? Why not destroy the enemy once and for all? Those siding with MacArthur assumed that the United States was all-powerful and blamed the stalemate in Korea on the government's ineptitude or willingness to shelter subversives.

When Congress investigated MacArthur's dismissal, all of the top military leaders supported the president. According to the chairman of the Joint Chiefs of Staff, MacArthur wanted to wage "the wrong war, at the wrong place, at the wrong time, with the wrong enemy." Yet Truman never recovered from the political fallout. Nor was he able to end the war. Negotiations began in July 1951, but peace talks dragged on for two more years while twelve thousand more U.S. soldiers died.

Korea, Communism, and the 1952 Election

Popular discontent with President Truman's war boosted Republicans in the 1952 election. Their presidential nominee, General Dwight D. Eisenhower, was a popular hero. As supreme commander in Europe, he won widespread acclaim for leading the Allied armies to victory over Germany in World War II. In 1950, Truman appointed Eisenhower the first supreme commander of NATO forces.

Although Eisenhower believed that professional soldiers should stay out of politics, he found compelling reasons to run in 1952. He largely agreed with Truman's foreign policy, but he deplored the Democrats' propensity to solve domestic problems with costly new federal programs. He also disliked the foreign policy views of the leading Republican presidential contender, Senator Robert A. Taft, who attacked containment and sought to cut defense spending. Eisenhower defeated Taft for the nomination, but the old guard prevailed on the party platform. It excoriated containment as "negative, futile, and immoral" and charged the Truman administration with shielding "traitors to the Nation in high places." By choosing thirty-nine-year-old Senator Richard M. Nixon for his running mate, Eisenhower helped to appease the right wing of the party.

Richard Milhous Nixon grew up in southern California, worked his way through college and law school, served in the navy, and briefly practiced law before winning election to Congress in 1946. Nixon quickly made a name for himself as a member of HUAC (see page 796) and a key anti-Communist, moving to the Senate in 1950.

With his public approval ratings plummeting, Truman decided not to run for reelection. The Democrats nominated Adlai E. Stevenson, the popular governor of Illinois, who was acceptable to both liberals and southerners. Stevenson could not escape the domestic fallout from the Korean War, however; nor could he match Eisenhower's widespread appeal. Shortly before the election, Eisenhower announced dramatically, "I shall go to Korea," and voters registered their confidence in his ability to end the war. Cutting sharply into traditional Democratic territory, Eisenhower won several southern states and garnered 55 percent of the popular vote overall. His coattails carried a narrow Republican majority to Congress.

> CHRONOLOGY

1950
– Korean War begins.

1951
– Truman fires General Douglas MacArthur.

1952
– Dwight D. Eisenhower is elected president.

1953
– Korean War ends.

Why did Truman have limited success in implementing his domestic agenda?

How did U.S. Cold War policy lead to the Korean War?

Conclusion: What were the costs and consequences of the Cold War?

✓ LearningCurve
Check what you know.
bedfordstmartins.com
/roarkunderstanding

An Armistice and the War's Costs

Eisenhower made good on his pledge to end the Korean War. In July 1953, the two sides reached an armistice that left Korea divided, again roughly at the thirty-eighth parallel, with North and South separated by a two-and-a-half-mile-wide demilitarized zone (see Map 26.3). The war fulfilled the objective of containment, since the United States had backed up its promise to help nations that were resisting communism. Both Truman and Eisenhower managed to contain what amounted to a world war — involving twenty nations altogether — within a single country and to avoid the use of nuclear weapons.

> ### > The Human Toll of the Korean War
>
> - 36,000 Americans were killed, and 100,000 were wounded.
> - South Korea lost more than 1 million people to war-related causes.
> - More than 1.8 million North Koreans and Chinese were killed or wounded.

The Korean War had an enormous effect on defense policy and spending. In April 1950, just before the war began, the National Security Council completed a top-secret report, known as **NSC 68**, on the United States' military strength, warning that national survival required a massive military buildup. The Korean War brought about nearly all of the military expansion called for in NSC 68, vastly increasing U.S. capacity to act as a global power. Military spending shot up from $14 billion in 1950 to $50 billion in 1953 and remained above $40 billion thereafter. By 1952, defense spending claimed nearly 70 percent of the federal budget, and the size of the armed forces had tripled.

To General Matthew Ridgway, MacArthur's successor as commander of the UN forces, Korea taught the lesson that U.S. forces should never again fight a land war in Asia. Eisenhower concurred. Nevertheless, the Korean War induced the Truman administration to expand its role in Asia by increasing aid to the French, who were fighting to hang on to their colonial empire in Indochina. As U.S. Marines retreated from a battle against Chinese soldiers in 1950, they sang, prophetically, "We're Harry's police force on call, / So put back your pack on, / The next step is Saigon."

NSC 68

▶ Top-secret government report of April 1950 warning that national survival required a massive military buildup. The Korean War brought nearly all of the expansion that the report called for, and by 1952 defense spending claimed nearly 70 percent of the federal budget.

> QUICK REVIEW

How did the Korean War shape American foreign policy in the 1950s?

Conclusion: What were the costs and consequences of the Cold War?

H**OPING FOR CONTINUED** U.S.-Soviet cooperation rather than unilateral American intervention to resolve foreign crises, some liberal members of Congress had initially opposed the implementation of containment. By 1948, however, most had gotten behind Truman's decision to fight communism throughout the world, a decision that marked the most momentous foreign policy initiative in the nation's history.

More than any development in the postwar world, the Cold War defined American politics and society for decades to come. It transformed the federal government, shifting its priorities from domestic to external affairs, greatly expanding its budget, and substantially increasing the power of the president. Military spending helped transform the nation itself, as defense contracts promoted economic and population booms in the West and Southwest. The nuclear arms race put the people of the world at risk, consumed resources that might have been used to improve living standards, and skewed the economy toward dependence on military projects.

In sharp contrast to foreign policy, the domestic policies of the postwar years reflected continuity with the past. Some liberals in Congress avidly supported Truman's proposals for new programs in education, health, and civil rights, but a majority of members of Congress did not. Consequently, the poor and minorities suffered even while many other Americans enjoyed a higher standard of living in an economy boosted by Cold War spending and the reconstruction of Western Europe and Japan.

Another cost of the early Cold War years was the anti-Communist hysteria that swept the nation, narrowing the range of ideas acceptable for political discussion. Partisan politics and Truman's warnings about the Communist menace fueled McCarthyism, along with popular frustrations over the failure of containment to produce clear-cut victories. The Korean War, which ended in stalemate rather than the defeat of communism, exacerbated feelings of frustration. It would be a major challenge of the Eisenhower administration to restore national unity and confidence.

Why did Truman have limited success in implementing his domestic agenda?

How did U.S. Cold War policy lead to the Korean War?

Conclusion: What were the costs and consequences of the Cold War?

☑ **LearningCurve**
Check what you know.
bedfordstmartins.com
/roarkunderstanding

801

CHAPTER 26 STUDY GUIDE

STEP 1

GET STARTED ONLINE

LearningCurve ▪ bedfordstmartins.com/roarkunderstanding

Now that you've read the chapter, make it stick by completing the LearningCurve activity.

STEP 2

EXPLAIN WHY IT MATTERS

Put your reading into practice. Identify each term below, and then explain why it matters in U.S. history.

TERM	WHO OR WHAT & WHEN	WHY IT MATTERS
Cold War (p. 781)		
iron curtain (p. 783)		
containment (p. 783)		
Truman Doctrine (p. 783)		
Marshall Plan (p. 784)		
North Atlantic Treaty Organization (NATO) (p. 786)		
Central Intelligence Agency (CIA) (p. 787)		
Taft-Hartley Act (p. 794)		
Housing Act of 1949 (p. 794)		
House Un-American Activities Committee (HUAC) (p. 796)		
Korean War (p. 797)		
NSC 68 (p. 800)		

STEP 3

MOVE BEYOND THE BASICS

To demonstrate a more advanced understanding, describe the U.S. and Soviet actions and policies between 1945 and 1953 in Germany; Eastern Europe; Turkey, Greece, and the Middle East; China; and Korea.

The Cold War, 1945–1953	U.S. actions and policies	Soviet actions and policies
Germany		
Eastern Europe		
Turkey, Greece, and the Middle East		
Middle East		
China		
Korea		

THE UNITED STATES AND THE POSTWAR WORLD

► What interests did American and Soviet policymakers think were at stake in Eastern Europe? How did events in the region contribute to the growing Cold War?

► What was the policy of containment? What assumptions about Soviet power and intentions were at the heart of the policy?

TRUMAN AND THE FAIR DEAL

► How did Truman propose to expand the New Deal? In what areas did he succeed, and in what areas did he fail?

► What explains the rise of McCarthyism? Why did so many Americans believe that the country faced a grave internal threat to its security?

THE KOREAN WAR

► How did the policy of containment lead to American involvement in Korea?

► What impact did the Korean War have on American domestic politics?

LOOKING BACKWARD, LOOKING AHEAD

► How did American and Soviet experiences between 1918 and 1945 lay the groundwork for the Cold War?

► How did the Cold War set the stage for American life in the 1950s?

> **IN YOUR OWN WORDS**

Imagine that you must give an oral report to the class answering the following question: What was the impact of the Cold War on the United States? What would be the most important points to include and why?

 Do it online at the Student Site ■ bedfordstmartins.com/roarkunderstanding

27

THE POLITICS AND CULTURE OF ABUNDANCE

1952–1960

> **What were the successes and limitations of America's "culture of abundance" in the 1950s?** Chapter 27 examines the politics and culture of the 1950s. It explores President Dwight D. Eisenhower's domestic and foreign policies, the causes and consequences of the prosperity of the era, and the challenges to the status quo, in particular the challenge to racial segregation and discrimination.

LearningCurve
bedfordstmartins.com/roarkunderstanding
After reading the chapter, use LearningCurve to
retain what you've read.

A 1950s family poses proudly with their new sedan. Bettmann/Corbis BE042857.

> What was Eisenhower's "middle way" on domestic issues?

> How did Eisenhower's foreign policy differ from Truman's?

> What fueled the prosperity of the 1950s?

> How did prosperity affect American society and culture?

> How did African Americans fight for civil rights in the 1950s?

> Conclusion: What unmet challenges did peace and prosperity mask?

> What was Eisenhower's "middle way" on domestic issues?

MODERATION WAS THE GUIDING PRINCIPLE of Dwight D. Eisenhower's domestic agenda and leadership style. In 1953, he pledged a "middle way between untrammeled freedom of the individual and the demands for the welfare of the whole Nation," promising that his administration would "avoid government by bureaucracy as carefully as it avoids neglect of the helpless." Eisenhower generally resisted expanding the federal government's power, he acted reluctantly when the Supreme Court ordered schools to desegregate, and his administration terminated the federal trusteeship of dozens of Indian tribes. As a moderate Republican, however, Eisenhower supported the continuation of New Deal programs, and in some cases, such as the creation of a national highway system, he expanded federal action. Nicknamed "Ike," the confident war hero remained popular, but he was not able to lift the Republican Party to national dominance.

Modern Republicanism

In contrast to the old guard conservatives in his party who criticized containment and wanted to repeal much of the New Deal, Dwight D. Eisenhower preached "modern Republicanism." This meant resisting additional federal intervention in economic and social life but not turning the clock back to the 1920s. Democratic control of Congress after the elections of 1954 further contributed to Eisenhower's moderate approach.

CHAPTER LOCATOR | **What was Eisenhower's "middle way" on domestic issues?** | How did Eisenhower's foreign policy differ from Truman's?

806 CHAPTER 27
THE POLITICS AND CULTURE OF ABUNDANCE

The new president attempted to distance himself from the anti-Communist fervor that had plagued the Truman administration, even as he intensified Truman's loyalty program, allowing federal executives to dismiss thousands of employees on grounds of loyalty, security, or "suitability." Reflecting his inclination to avoid controversial issues, Eisenhower refused to denounce Senator Joseph McCarthy publicly. In 1954, McCarthy began to destroy himself when he hurled reckless charges of communism against military personnel during televised hearings. When the army's lawyer demanded of McCarthy, "Have you left no sense of decency?" those in the hearing room applauded. In 1954, the Senate voted to condemn him, marking the end of his influence but not the end of pursuing radicals.

Eisenhower sometimes echoed the conservative Republicans' conviction that government was best left to the states and economic decisions to private business. Yet he signed laws bringing ten million more workers under Social Security, increasing the minimum wage, and creating a new Department of Health, Education, and Welfare. And when the spread of polio neared epidemic proportions, Eisenhower obtained funds from Congress to distribute a vaccine, even though conservatives wanted to leave that responsibility to the states.

Eisenhower's greatest domestic initiative was the **Interstate Highway and Defense System Act of 1956** (**Map 27.1**). Promoted as essential to national defense and an impetus to economic growth, the act authorized construction of a national highway system, with the federal government paying most of the costs through increased fuel and vehicle taxes. The new highways accelerated the mobility of people and goods, and they benefited the trucking, construction, and automobile industries, which had lobbied hard for the law. Eventually, the monumental highway project exacted such unforeseen costs as air pollution, increased energy

> **CHRONOLOGY**

1952
– Dwight D. Eisenhower is elected president.

1954
– Senate condemns Senator Joseph McCarthy.

1956
– Interstate Highway and Defense System Act becomes law.
– Eisenhower is reelected.

Interstate Highway and Defense System Act of 1956
▶ Law authorizing the construction of a national highway system. Promoted as essential to national defense and an impetus to economic growth, the national highway system accelerated the movement of people and goods and changed the nature of American communities.

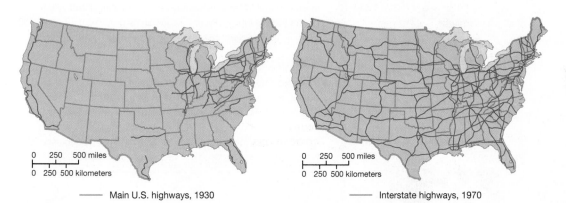

0 250 500 miles
0 250 500 kilometers
—— Main U.S. highways, 1930

0 250 500 miles
0 250 500 kilometers
—— Interstate highways, 1970

MAP 27.1 ■ The Interstate Highway System, 1930 and 1970

Built with federal funds authorized in the Interstate Highway and Defense System Act of 1956, superhighways soon crisscrossed the nation. Trucking, construction, gasoline, and travel were among the industries that prospered, but railroads suffered from the subsidized competition.

> **MAP ACTIVITY**

READING THE MAP: What regions of the United States had main highways in 1930? What regions did not? How had the situation changed by 1970?
CONNECTIONS: What impact did the growth of the interstate highway system have on migration patterns in the United States? What benefits did the new interstate highways bring to Americans and at what costs?

What fueled the prosperity of the 1950s?

How did prosperity affect American society and culture?

How did African Americans fight for civil rights in the 1950s?

Conclusion: What unmet challenges did peace and prosperity mask?

✓ LearningCurve
Check what you know.
bedfordstmartins.com
/roarkunderstanding

consumption, declining railroads and mass transportation, and the decay of central cities.

In other areas, Eisenhower restrained federal activity in favor of state governments and private enterprise. His large tax cuts directed most benefits to business and the wealthy, and he resisted federal aid to primary and secondary education as well as strong White House leadership on behalf of civil rights. Eisenhower opposed national health insurance, preferring the growing practice of private insurance provided by employers. Although Democrats sought to keep nuclear power in government hands, Eisenhower signed legislation authorizing the private manufacture and sale of nuclear energy.

Termination and Relocation of Native Americans

Eisenhower's efforts to limit the federal government were consistent with a new direction in Indian policy, which reversed the New Deal emphasis on strengthening tribal governments and preserving Indian culture (see chapter 24). After World War II, when some 25,000 Indians had left their homes for military service and another 40,000 for work in defense industries, policymakers began to favor assimilating Native Americans and ending their special relationship with the government.

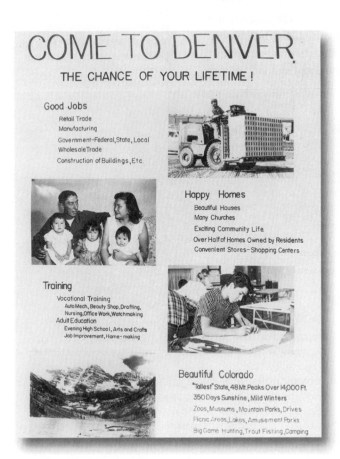

Indian Relocation

As part of its new emphasis on assimilation in the late 1940s and the 1950s, the Bureau of Indian Affairs distributed this leaflet to entice Native Americans to move from their reservations to cities. Thousands of Indians relocated in the years after World War II. The percentage of Indians living in urban areas grew from 13.4 in 1950 to 44 in 1970. National Archives.

> VISUAL ACTIVITY

READING THE IMAGE: Which of the features shown in this leaflet do you think would have been the most appealing to Native Americans living on reservations? Which might have evoked little interest?

CONNECTIONS: In what ways did the government's plan to assimilate Native Americans succeed? In what ways did it fail?

CHAPTER LOCATOR | What was Eisenhower's "middle way" on domestic issues? | How did Eisenhower's foreign policy differ from Truman's?

CHAPTER 27
808 THE POLITICS AND CULTURE OF ABUNDANCE

To some officials, the communal practices of Indians resembled socialism and stifled individual initiative. Eisenhower's commissioner of Indian affairs, Glenn Emmons, did not believe that tribal lands could produce income sufficient to eliminate poverty, but he also revealed the ethnocentrism of policymakers when he insisted that Indians wanted to "work and live like Americans." Moreover, Indians still held rights to water, land, minerals, and other resources that were increasingly attractive to state governments and private entrepreneurs.

By 1960, the government had implemented a three-part program of compensation, termination, and relocation. In 1946, Congress established the Indian Claims Commission to hear outstanding claims by Native Americans for land taken by the government. By the time it closed in 1978, the commission had settled 285 cases, with compensation exceeding $800 million. Yet the awards were based on land values at the time the land was taken and did not include interest.

The second policy, termination, also originated in the Truman administration, when Commissioner Dillon S. Myer asserted that his Bureau of Indian Affairs should do "nothing for Indians which Indians can do for themselves." Beginning in 1953, Eisenhower signed bills transferring jurisdiction over tribal land to state and local governments and ending the trusteeship relationship between Indians and the federal government. The loss of federal hospitals, schools, and other special arrangements devastated Indian tribes. As had happened after passage of the Dawes Act in 1887 (see chapter 17), some corporate interests and individuals took advantage of the opportunity to purchase Indian land cheaply. The government abandoned termination in the 1960s after some 13,000 Indians and more than one million acres of their land had been affected.

The Indian Relocation Program, the third piece of Native American policy, began in 1948 and involved more than 100,000 Native Americans by 1973. The government encouraged Indians to move to cities, where relocation centers were supposed to help with housing, job training, and medical care. Even though Indians were moved far from their reservations, about one-third returned.

Most who stayed in cities faced racism, unemployment, poor housing, and the loss of their traditional culture. "I wish we had never left home," said one woman whose husband was out of work and drinking heavily. "It's dirty and noisy, and people all around, crowded. . . . It seems like I never see the sky or trees." Reflecting long-standing disagreements among Indians themselves, some who overcame these obstacles applauded the program. But most urban Indians remained poor, and even many who had welcomed relocation worried that "we would lose our identity as Indian people, lose our culture and our [way] of living." Within two decades, a national pan-Indian movement — a by-product of this urbanization — emerged to resist assimilation and to demand much more for Indians (as discussed in chapter 28).

Major Indian Relocations, 1950–1970

The 1956 Election and the Second Term

Eisenhower easily defeated Adlai Stevenson in 1956, doubling his victory margin of 1952. Yet Democrats kept control of Congress, and in the midterm elections two years later, they all but wiped out the Republican Party, gaining a 64–34 majority

| What fueled the prosperity of the 1950s? | How did prosperity affect American society and culture? | How did African Americans fight for civil rights in the 1950s? | Conclusion: What unmet challenges did peace and prosperity mask? | ✓ LearningCurve Check what you know. bedfordstmartins.com /roarkunderstanding |

809

in the Senate and a 282–135 advantage in the House. Although Ike captured voters' hearts, a majority of Americans remained wedded to the programs and policies of the Democrats.

Eisenhower faced more serious leadership challenges in his second term. When the economy plunged into a recession in late 1957, he fought with Congress over the budget and vetoed bills to expand housing, urban development, and public works projects. The president and Congress did agree on the first, though largely symbolic, civil rights law in a century and on a larger federal role in education, largely in the interest of national security (as discussed on pages 815–16 and 828).

In the end, the first Republican administration after the New Deal left the functions of the federal government intact, though it tipped policy benefits somewhat toward corporate interests. Even with two recessions, unparalleled prosperity graced the Eisenhower years, and inflation was kept low. Eisenhower celebrated what he called the "wide diffusion of wealth and incomes" across the United States, yet amid the remarkable abundance were some forty million impoverished Americans. Rural deprivation was particularly pronounced, as was poverty among the elderly, African Americans, and other minorities.

> **QUICK REVIEW**

How did Eisenhower's domestic policies reflect his moderate political vision?

CHAPTER LOCATOR | What was Eisenhower's "middle way" on domestic issues? | How did Eisenhower's foreign policy differ from Truman's?

CHAPTER 27
810 THE POLITICS AND CULTURE OF ABUNDANCE

How did Eisenhower's foreign policy differ from Truman's?

The Nuclear Arms Race

Soviet Premier Nikita Khrushchev speaks at his arrival at Andrews Air Force Base in September 1959 for talks with President Eisenhower that both hoped would defuse the nuclear threat. Behind the two leaders are the Soviet ambassador, Mikhail Menshikov, and the U.S. Secretary of State, Christian Herter. At the close of their summit Eisenhower and Khrushchev issued a statement declaring that "the question of general disarmament is the most important one facing the world today." © Bettmann/Corbis.

AT HIS INAUGURATION IN 1953, Eisenhower warned that "forces of good and evil are massed and armed and opposed as rarely before in history." Like Truman, he saw communism as a threat to the nation's security and economic interests, and he wanted to keep the United States the most powerful country in the world. Eisenhower's foreign policy differed from Truman's, however, in three areas: its rhetoric, its means, and — after Stalin's death in 1953 — its movement toward accommodation with the Soviet Union.

Although some Republicans, such as Secretary of State John Foster Dulles, deplored containment as "negative, futile, and immoral," the Eisenhower administration practiced containment in Vietnam and intervened in Latin America and the Middle East. Eisenhower also pursued an ever-escalating arms race with the Soviet Union but sought to ease tensions between the superpowers toward the end of his presidency.

What fueled the prosperity of the 1950s?

How did prosperity affect American society and culture?

How did African Americans fight for civil rights in the 1950s?

Conclusion: What unmet challenges did peace and prosperity mask?

☑ **LearningCurve** Check what you know. bedfordstmartins.com /roarkunderstanding

> CHRONOLOGY

1953
– CIA organizes coup against Iranian government.

1954
– CIA organizes coup against Guatemalan government.
– Geneva accords reached.

1955
– Eisenhower and Khrushchev meet in Geneva.

1957
– Soviets launch *Sputnik.*

1958
– National Aeronautics and Space Administration (NASA) is established.
– National Defense Education Act is passed.

1960
– Soviets shoot down U.S. U-2 spy plane.

mutually assured destruction (MAD)
▶ Term for the standoff between the United States and Soviet Union based on the assumption that a nuclear first strike by either nation would result in massive retaliation and mutual destruction for each. Despite this possibility, both countries pursued an ever-escalating arms race.

domino theory
▶ Theory of containment articulated by President Dwight Eisenhower in the context of Vietnam. He warned that the fall of a non-Communist government to communism would trigger the spread of communism to neighboring countries.

The "New Look" in Foreign Policy

To meet his goals of balancing the budget and cutting taxes, Eisenhower was determined to control military expenditures. Moreover, he feared that massive defense spending would threaten the nation's economic strength. Reflecting American confidence in technology and opposition to a large peacetime army, Eisenhower's "New Look" in defense strategy concentrated U.S. military strength in nuclear weapons and missiles to deliver them. Instead of maintaining large ground forces of its own, the United States would arm friendly nations and back them up with an ominous nuclear arsenal, providing, according to one defense official, "more bang for the buck." Dulles believed that America's willingness to "go to the brink" of war with its intimidating nuclear weapons — a strategy called brinksmanship — would block any Soviet efforts to expand.

Nuclear weapons could not stop a Soviet nuclear attack, but in response to one, they could inflict enormous destruction. This certainty of "massive retaliation" was meant to deter the Soviets from launching an attack. Because the Soviet Union could respond similarly to an American first strike, this nuclear standoff became known as **mutually assured destruction,** or **MAD**. Leaders of both nations pursued an ever-escalating arms race.

Nuclear weapons could not roll back the iron curtain. When a revolt against the Soviet-controlled government began in Hungary in 1956, Dulles's liberation rhetoric proved to be empty. A radio plea from Hungarian freedom fighters cried, "SOS! They just brought us a rumor that the American troops will be here within one or two hours." But help did not come. Eisenhower was unwilling to risk U.S. soldiers and possible nuclear war, and Soviet troops soon suppressed the insurrection, killing or wounding thousands of Hungarians.

Applying Containment to Vietnam

A major challenge to the containment policy came in Southeast Asia. During World War II, Ho Chi Minh, a Vietnamese nationalist, had founded a coalition called the Vietminh to fight both the occupying Japanese forces and the French colonial rulers. In 1945, the Vietminh declared Vietnam's independence from France, and when France fought back, the area plunged into war. Because Ho declared himself a Communist, the Truman administration quietly began to provide aid to the French (see chapter 29, Map 29.2). American principles of national self-determination took a backseat to the battle against communism.

Eisenhower viewed communism in Vietnam much as Truman had regarded it in Greece and Turkey. In what became known as the **domino theory**, Eisenhower explained, "You have a row of dominoes, you knock over the first one, and what will happen to the last one is the certainty that it will go over very quickly." A Communist victory in Southeast Asia, he warned, could trigger the fall of Japan, Taiwan, and the Philippines. By 1954, the United States was paying 75 percent of the cost of France's war, but Eisenhower resisted a larger role. When the French asked for American troops and planes to avert almost certain defeat at Dien Bien Phu, Eisenhower, remembering the Korean War (see chapter 26), said no.

CHAPTER LOCATOR | What was Eisenhower's "middle way" on domestic issues? | How did Eisenhower's foreign policy differ from Truman's?

CHAPTER 27
812   THE POLITICS AND CULTURE OF ABUNDANCE

Dien Bien Phu fell in May 1954, and two months later in Geneva a truce was signed. The Geneva accords recognized Vietnam's independence and temporarily partitioned it at the seventeenth parallel, separating the Vietminh in the north from the puppet government established by the French in the south. Within two years, the Vietnamese people were to vote in elections for a unified government. Some officials warned against U.S. involvement in Vietnam, envisioning "nothing but grief in store for us if we remained in that area." Eisenhower and Dulles nonetheless moved to prop up the dominoes with a new alliance and put the CIA to work infiltrating and destabilizing North Vietnam. Fearing a Communist victory in the elections mandated by the Geneva accords, they supported South Vietnamese prime minister Ngo Dinh Diem's refusal to hold the vote.

Between 1955 and 1961, the United States provided $800 million to the South Vietnamese army (ARVN). Yet the ARVN proved grossly unprepared for the guerrilla warfare that began in the late 1950s. With help from Ho Chi Minh's government in Hanoi, Vietminh rebels in the south stepped up their guerrilla attacks on the Diem government. The insurgents gained support from the largely Buddhist peasants, who were outraged by the repressive regime of the Catholic, Westernized Diem. Unwilling to abandon containment, Eisenhower left his successor with a deteriorating situation and a firm commitment to defend South Vietnam against communism.

Geneva Accords, 1954

Interventions in Latin America and the Middle East

While supporting friendly governments in Asia, the Eisenhower administration sought to topple unfriendly ones in Latin America and the Middle East. U.S. officials saw internal civil wars in terms of the Cold War conflict between the superpowers and often viewed nationalist uprisings as Communist threats to democracy. They also acted against governments that threatened U.S. economic interests. The Eisenhower administration took this course of action out of sight of Congress and the public, making the CIA an important arm of foreign policy.

Guatemala's government, under the popularly elected reformist president Jacobo Arbenz, was not Soviet controlled, but it accepted support from the local Communist Party (see chapter 29, Map 29.1). In 1953, Arbenz moved to help landless, poverty-stricken peasants by nationalizing uncultivated land owned by the United Fruit Company, a U.S. corporation whose annual profits were twice the size of Guatemala's budget. United Fruit refused Arbenz's offer to compensate the company at the value of the land it had declared for tax purposes. Then, in response to the nationalization program, the CIA supported an opposition army that overthrew the elected government and installed a military dictatorship in 1954. United Fruit kept its land, and Guatemala succumbed to destructive civil wars that lasted through the 1990s.

In 1959, when Cubans' desire for political and economic autonomy erupted into a revolution led by Fidel Castro, a CIA agent promised "to take care of Castro just like we took care of Arbenz." American companies controlled major Cuban resources, and decisions made in Washington directly influenced the lives of the Cuban people. The 1959 **Cuban revolution** drove out the U.S.-supported dictator Fulgencio Batista and led the CIA to warn Eisenhower

Cuban revolution
▶ Uprising led by Fidel Castro that drove out U.S.-supported dictator Fulgencio Batista and eventually allied Cuba with the Soviet Union.

| What fueled the prosperity of the 1950s? | How did prosperity affect American society and culture? | How did African Americans fight for civil rights in the 1950s? | Conclusion: What unmet challenges did peace and prosperity mask? | ✔ LearningCurve Check what you know. bedfordstmartins.com /roarkunderstanding |

813

that "Communists and other extreme radicals appear to have penetrated the Castro movement." When the United States denied Castro's requests for loans, he turned to the Soviet Union. And when U.S. companies refused Castro's offer to purchase their Cuban holdings at their assessed value, he began to nationalize their property. Many anti-Castro Cubans fled to the United States and reported his atrocities. Before leaving office, Eisenhower broke off diplomatic relations with Cuba and authorized the CIA to train Cuban exiles for an invasion.

In the Middle East, the CIA intervened in Iran to oust an elected government, support an unpopular dictatorship, and maintain Western access to Iranian oil (see chapter 30, Map 30.2). In 1951, the Iranian parliament, led by Prime Minister Mohammed Mossadegh, nationalized the country's oil fields and refineries, which had been held primarily by a British company. Britain strongly objected to the takeover and eventually sought help from the United States.

Advisers convinced Eisenhower that Mossadegh, whom *Time* magazine had called "the Iranian George Washington," left Iran vulnerable to communism, and the president wanted to keep oil-rich areas "under the control of people who are friendly." With his authorization, CIA agents instigated a coup. In August 1953, Iranian army officers captured Mossadegh and reestablished the authority of the shah, Mohammad Reza Pahlavi, known for favoring Western interests and the Iranian wealthy classes. U.S. companies received a 40 percent share of Iran's oil concessions. But resentment over the intervention would poison U.S.-Iranian relations into the twenty-first century.

Elsewhere in the Middle East, Eisenhower continued Truman's support of Israel but also pursued friendships with Arab nations to secure access to oil and build a bulwark against communism. U.S. officials demanded that smaller nations take the American side in the Cold War, even when those nations preferred neutrality. In 1955, as part of this effort to win Arab allies, Secretary of State Dulles began talks with Egypt about American support to build the Aswan Dam on the Nile River. The following year, Egypt's leader, Gamal Abdel Nasser, sought arms from Communist Czechoslovakia, formed a military alliance with other Arab nations, and recognized the People's Republic of China. In retaliation, Dulles called off the deal for the dam.

In July 1956, Nasser responded by seizing the Suez Canal, then owned by Britain and France but scheduled to revert to Egypt within seven years. In response to the seizure, Israel, whose forces had been skirmishing with Egyptian troops along their common border since 1948, attacked Egypt, with help from Britain and France. Eisenhower opposed the intervention, recognizing that the Egyptians had claimed their own territory and that Nasser "embodie[d] the emotional demands of the people . . . for independence." Calling on the United Nations to arrange a truce, he pressured Britain and France to pull back, forcing Israel to retreat.

Despite staying out of the Suez crisis, Eisenhower made it clear in a January 1957 speech that the United States would actively combat communism in the Middle East. In March, Congress approved aid to any Middle Eastern nation "requesting assistance against armed aggression from any country controlled by international communism." The president invoked this **Eisenhower Doctrine** to send aid to Jordan in 1957 and troops to Lebanon in 1958 to counter anti-Western pressures on those governments.

Eisenhower Doctrine

▶ President Dwight Eisenhower's 1957 declaration that the United States would actively combat communism in the Middle East. Congress approved the policy, and Eisenhower sent aid to Jordan in 1957 and troops to Lebanon in 1958.

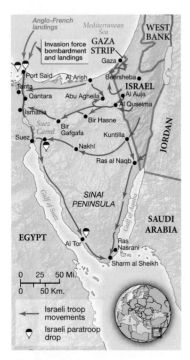

The Suez Crisis, 1956

CHAPTER LOCATOR | What was Eisenhower's "middle way" on domestic issues? | How did Eisenhower's foreign policy differ from Truman's?

814   CHAPTER 27
THE POLITICS AND CULTURE OF ABUNDANCE

The Nuclear Arms Race

While Eisenhower moved against perceived Communist inroads abroad, he also sought to reduce superpower tensions. After Stalin's death in 1953, Nikita Khrushchev emerged as a more moderate leader. Like Eisenhower, who remarked privately that the arms race would lead "at worst to atomic warfare, at best to robbing every people and nation on earth of the fruits of their own toil," Khrushchev wanted to reduce defense spending and the threat of nuclear devastation. Eisenhower and Khrushchev met in Geneva in 1955 at the first summit conference since the end of World War II. Although the meeting produced no new agreements, it symbolized what Eisenhower called "a new spirit of conciliation and cooperation."

In August 1957, the Soviets test-fired their first intercontinental ballistic missile (ICBM) and two months later beat the United States into space by launching *Sputnik*, the first man-made satellite to circle the earth. The United States launched a successful satellite of its own in January 1958, but *Sputnik* raised fears that the Soviets led not only in missile development and space exploration but also in science and education. In response, Eisenhower established the National

The Age of Nuclear Anxiety As schools routinely held "duck-and-cover" drills to prepare for possible Soviet attacks, children directly experienced the anxiety and insecurity of the 1950s nuclear arms race. The federal government distributed this pamphlet about how to protect oneself from an atomic attack. How effective do you think the strategy pictured here would be in a nuclear attack? Photo: Archive Photos/Getty Images; Pamphlet: Lynn Historical Society.

| What fueled the prosperity of the 1950s? | How did prosperity affect American society and culture? | How did African Americans fight for civil rights in the 1950s? | Conclusion: What unmet challenges did peace and prosperity mask? | ✔ LearningCurve Check what you know. bedfordstmartins.com /roarkunderstanding |

Aeronautics and Space Administration (NASA) and signed the National Defense Education Act, providing support for students in math, foreign languages, and science and technology.

Eisenhower assured the public that the United States possessed nuclear superiority. In fact, during his presidency the stockpile of nuclear weapons more than quadrupled. Yet these weapons could not guarantee security because both superpowers possessed sufficient nuclear capacity to devastate each other. Most Americans did not follow Civil Defense Administration recommendations to construct home bomb shelters, but they did realize how precarious nuclear weapons had made their lives.

In the midst of the arms race, the superpowers continued to talk, and by 1960 the two sides were close to a ban on nuclear testing. But just before a planned summit in Paris, a Soviet missile shot down an American U-2 spy plane over Soviet territory. The State Department first denied that U.S. planes had been violating Soviet airspace, but the Soviets produced the pilot and the photos taken on his flight. Eisenhower and Khrushchev met briefly in Paris, but the U-2 incident dashed all prospects for a nuclear arms agreement.

As Eisenhower left office, he warned about the growing influence of the **military-industrial complex**. Eisenhower had struggled against persistent pressures from defense contractors who, in tandem with the military, sought more dollars for newer, more powerful weapons systems. In his farewell address, he warned that the "conjunction of an immense military establishment and a large arms industry . . . exercised a total influence . . . in every city, every state house, every office of the federal government." The Cold War had created a warfare state.

military-industrial complex
▶ A term President Eisenhower used to refer to the military establishment and defense contractors who, he warned, exercised undue influence in city, state, and federal government.

> **QUICK REVIEW**

Where and how did Eisenhower practice containment?

CHAPTER LOCATOR | What was Eisenhower's "middle way" on domestic issues? | How did Eisenhower's foreign policy differ from Truman's?

CHAPTER 27
816 THE POLITICS AND CULTURE OF ABUNDANCE

Hotpoint Air Conditioner Ad, 1955

In 1902, Willis Haviland Carrier, a twenty-six-year-old American engineer, designed the first system to control temperature and humidity and installed it in a Brooklyn printing plant. Room air conditioners began to appear in the 1930s and spread rapidly in the 1950s, making possible the industrial and population explosion in the Sun Belt. While this ad promised consumers clean as well as cool air inside the house, it failed to note that air conditioning consumed large amounts of energy and contributed to outdoor air pollution. Hotpoint/General Electric Company.

STIMULATED BY COLD WAR spending and by technological advances, economic productivity increased enormously in the 1950s. A multitude of new items came on the market, and consumption became the order of the day. Millions of Americans enjoyed new homes in the suburbs, and higher education enrollments skyrocketed. Although every section of the nation enjoyed the new abundance, the Southwest and the South — the Sun Belt — especially boomed in production, commerce, and population.

Work itself was changing. Fewer people labored on farms, service-sector employment overtook manufacturing jobs, women's employment grew, and union membership soared. Not all Americans benefited from these changes; forty million lived in poverty. Most Americans, however, enjoyed a higher standard of living, prompting economist John Kenneth Galbraith to call the United States "the affluent society."

Technology Transforms Agriculture and Industry

Between 1940 and 1960, agricultural output mushroomed even while the number of farmworkers declined by almost one-third. Farmers achieved unprecedented

| What fueled the prosperity of the 1950s? | How did prosperity affect American society and culture? | How did African Americans fight for civil rights in the 1950s? | Conclusion: What unmet challenges did peace and prosperity mask? | ✓ LearningCurve Check what you know. bedfordstmartins.com /roarkunderstanding |

817

> CHRONOLOGY

1954
- Operation Wetback is launched.
- *Hernandez v. Texas.*

1960
- One-quarter of Americans live in suburbs.
- Women hold nearly one-third of all jobs.

productivity through greater crop specialization, intensive use of fertilizers, and, above all, mechanization. A single mechanical cotton picker replaced fifty people and cut the cost of harvesting a bale of cotton from $40 to $5.

The decline of family farms and the growth of large commercial farming, or agribusiness, were both causes and consequences of mechanization. Benefiting handsomely from federal price supports begun in the New Deal, larger farmers could afford technological improvements, while smaller producers lacked capital to purchase the machinery necessary to compete. Consequently, average farm size more than doubled between 1940 and 1964, and the number of farms fell by more than 40 percent.

Many small farmers who hung on constituted a core of rural poverty. Southern landowners replaced sharecroppers and tenants with machines. Hundreds of thousands of African Americans moved to cities, where racial discrimination and a lack of jobs mired many in urban poverty. A Mississippi mother reported that most of her relatives headed for Chicago when they realized that "it was going to be machines now that harvest the crops." Worrying that "it might be worse up there" for her children, she agonized, "I'm afraid to leave and I'm afraid to stay."

New technologies also transformed industrial production. Between 1945 and 1960, the number of labor-hours needed to manufacture a car fell by 50 percent. Technology revolutionized industries such as electronics, chemicals, and air transportation. It also promoted the growth of television, plastics, computers, and other newer industries. American businesses enjoyed access to cheap oil, ample markets abroad, and little foreign competition. Even with Eisenhower's conservative fiscal policies, government spending reached $80 billion annually and created new jobs.

Labor unions enjoyed their greatest success during the 1950s, and real earnings for production workers shot up 40 percent. As one worker put it, "We saw continual improvement in wages, fringe benefits like holidays, vacation, medical plans . . . all sorts of things that provided more security for people." In most industrial nations, government programs underwrote their citizens' security, but the United States developed a mixed system in which company-funded programs won by unions provided for retirement, health care, and the like. This system, often called a private welfare state, resulted in wide disparities among workers, disadvantaging those not unionized and those with irregular employment.

Technology Transforms Agriculture

The years from 1945 to 1970 saw a second agricultural revolution in the United States. In 1954, tractors outnumbered mules and horses on farms for the first time. In 1940, one farmer could feed 10.7 people. By 1970, that ratio was 1 to 75.8. This advertisement shows how one person could plant several rows of corn by barely lifting a finger. International Harvester Company.

While the number of organized workers continued to grow, union membership peaked at 27.1 percent of the labor force in 1957. Technological advances eliminated jobs in heavy industry. "You are going to have trouble collecting union dues from all of these machines," commented a Ford manager to union leader Walter Reuther. Moreover, the economy as a whole was shifting from production to service as more workers distributed goods, performed services, provided education, and carried out government work. Unions made some headway in these fields, especially among government employees, but most service industries resisted unionization.

The growing clerical and service occupations swelled the demand for female workers. By the end of the 1950s, women held nearly one-third of all jobs. The vast majority of them worked in offices, light manufacturing, domestic service, teaching, and nursing; because these occupations were occupied

CHAPTER LOCATOR | What was Eisenhower's "middle way" on domestic issues? | How did Eisenhower's foreign policy differ from Truman's?

CHAPTER 27
818 THE POLITICS AND CULTURE OF ABUNDANCE

primarily by women, wages were relatively low. In 1960, the average female full-time worker earned just 60 percent of the average male worker's wages. At the bottom of the employment ladder, black women took home only 42 percent of what white men earned.

Burgeoning Suburbs and Declining Cities

Although suburbs had existed since the nineteenth century, nothing symbolized the affluent society more than their tremendous expansion in the 1950s. Eleven million new homes went up in the suburbs, and by 1960 one in four Americans lived there. In 1949, families could purchase mass-produced houses in Levittown, a new 17,000-home development on Long Island, New York, for just under $8,000 each ($75,000 in 2012 dollars). Developments similar to Levittown, as well as more luxurious ones, quickly went up throughout the country. The government subsidized home ownership by guaranteeing low-interest mortgages and by making interest on mortgages tax deductible. Government-funded interstate highways running through urban areas also encouraged suburban development.

The growing suburbs helped polarize society, especially along racial lines. Each Levittown homeowner signed a contract pledging not to rent or sell to a non-Caucasian. The Supreme Court declared such covenants unenforceable in 1948, but suburban America remained dramatically segregated. Although some African Americans joined the suburban migration, most moved to cities in search of economic opportunity, doubling their numbers in most cities during the 1950s. These migrants, however, came to cities that were already in decline, losing not only population but also commerce and industry to the suburbs or to southern and western states.

The Rise of the Sun Belt

No regions experienced the postwar economic and population booms more intensely than the South and Southwest (**Map 27.2**). California overtook New York as the most populous state. Sports franchises followed fans: In 1958, the Brooklyn Dodgers moved to Los Angeles, joined by the Minneapolis Lakers three years later.

A pleasant natural environment attracted new residents, but no magnet proved stronger than economic opportunity. As railroads had fueled western growth in the nineteenth century, so the automobile and airplane spurred the post–World War II surge. Air-conditioning facilitated industrial development and by 1960 cooled nearly eight million homes in the **Sun Belt**, which stretched from Florida to California.

So important was the defense industry to the South and Southwest that the area was later referred to as the "Gun Belt." The aerospace industry boomed in such cities as Los Angeles and Dallas–Fort Worth, and military bases helped underwrite prosperity in cities such as San Diego and San Antonio. Although defense dollars benefited other regions, the Sun Belt captured the lion's share of Cold War spending. By the 1960s, nearly one of every three California workers held a defense-related job.

The surging populations and industries soon threatened the environment. Providing sufficient water and power to cities and to agribusiness meant building

Sun Belt
▶ Name applied to the Southwest and the South, an area that grew rapidly after World War II as a center of defense industries and non-unionized labor.

| What fueled the prosperity of the 1950s? | How did prosperity affect American society and culture? | How did African Americans fight for civil rights in the 1950s? | Conclusion: What unmet challenges did peace and prosperity mask? | ☑ LearningCurve Check what you know. bedfordstmartins.com /roarkunderstanding |

819

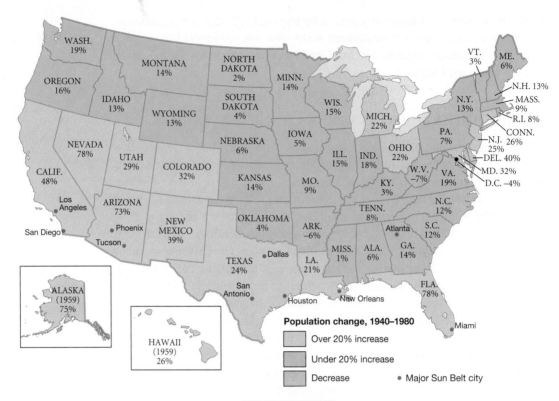

Population change, 1940–1980

- [ ] Over 20% increase
- [ ] Under 20% increase
- [ ] Decrease   ● Major Sun Belt city

MAP 27.2 ■ The Rise of the Sun Belt, 1940–1980

The growth of defense industries, a non-unionized labor force, and the spread of air-conditioning all helped spur economic development and population growth in the Southwest and the South. This made the Sun Belt the fastest-growing region of the country between 1940 and 1980.

> MAP ACTIVITY

READING THE MAP: Which states experienced population growth of more than 20 percent? Which states experienced the largest population growth?
CONNECTIONS: What stimulated the population boom in the Southwest? What role did the Cold War play in this expansion? What developments made the Southwest diverse in the composition of its population?

dams and reservoirs on free-flowing rivers. Native Americans lost fishing sites on the Columbia River, and dams on the Upper Missouri displaced nine hundred Indian families. Sprawling suburban settlement without efficient public transportation contributed to blankets of smog over Los Angeles and other cities.

The high-technology basis of economic development drew well-educated, highly skilled workers to the West, but economic promise also attracted the poor. "We see opportunity all around us here. . . . We smell freedom here, and maybe soon we can taste it," commented a black mother in California. Between 1945 and 1960, more than one-third of the African Americans who left the South moved west.

The Mexican American population also grew, especially in California and Texas. To supply California's vast agribusiness industry, the government continued the *bracero* program begun in 1942, under which Mexicans were permitted to enter the United States to work for a limited period. Until the program ended in 1964, more than 100,000 Mexicans entered the United States each year to labor in the fields — and many of them stayed, legally or illegally. But permanent Mexican immigration was not as welcome as Mexicans' low-wage labor. In 1954, the government launched a series of raids called "Operation Wetback," sending more than a million Mexicans back across the border.

At the same time, Mexican American citizens gained a victory in their ongoing struggle for civil rights in *Hernandez v. Texas*. In this 1954 case, the Supreme Court ruled unanimously that Mexican Americans constituted a distinct group and that their systematic exclusion from juries violated the Fourteenth Amendment guarantee of equal protection.

Free of the discrimination faced by minorities, white Americans enjoyed the fullest prosperity in the West. In April 1950, when California developers opened Lakewood, a large housing development in Los Angeles County, thirty thousand people lined up to buy houses at prices averaging $85,000 in 2012 dollars. Many of the new homeowners were veterans, blue-collar and lower-level white-collar workers whose defense-based jobs at aerospace corporations enabled them to fulfill the American dream of the 1950s. A huge shopping mall, Lakewood Center, offered myriad products of the consumer culture, and the workers' children lived at commuting distance from community colleges and six state universities.

Hernandez v. Texas
▶ 1954 Supreme Court decision that found that the systematic exclusion of Mexican Americans from juries violated the constitutional guarantee of equal protection.

The Democratization of Higher Education

California's university system exemplified a spectacular transformation of higher education. Between 1940 and 1960, college enrollments in the United States more than doubled, and more than 40 percent of young Americans attended college by the mid-1960s. The federal government subsidized the education of more than two million veterans, and the Cold War sent millions of federal dollars to universities for defense-related research. State governments vastly expanded the number of public colleges and universities, while municipalities began to build two-year community colleges.

All Americans did not benefit equally from the democratization of higher education. Although their college enrollments surged from 37,000 in 1941 to 90,000 in 1961, African Americans constituted only about 5 percent of all college students. For a time, the educational gap between white men and women grew, even though women's enrollments increased. In 1940, women had earned 40 percent of undergraduate degrees, but as veterans flocked to college campuses, women's proportion fell to 25 percent, rising to just 33 percent by 1960. Women were more likely than men to drop out of college after marriage, taking jobs to keep their husbands in school. Reflecting gender norms of the 1950s, most college women agreed that "it is natural for a woman to be satisfied with her husband's success and not crave personal achievement."

QUICK REVIEW ◁

How did technology contribute to changes in the economy, suburbanization, and the growth of the Sun Belt?

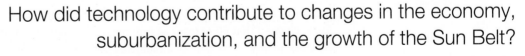

| **What fueled the prosperity of the 1950s?** | How did prosperity affect American society and culture? | How did African Americans fight for civil rights in the 1950s? | Conclusion: What unmet challenges did peace and prosperity mask? | ✓ LearningCurve Check what you know. bedfordstmartins.com /roarkunderstanding |

> How did prosperity affect American society and culture?

PROSPERITY IN THE 1950s intensified the transformation of the nation into a consumer society, changing the way Americans lived and converting the traditional work ethic into an ethic of consumption. The new medium of television both reflected and stimulated a consumer culture. People married at earlier ages, the birthrate soared, and dominant values celebrated family life and traditional gender roles. Undercurrents of rebellion, especially among young people, and women's increasing employment defied some of the dominant norms but did not greatly disrupt the complacency of the 1950s.

Consumption Rules the Day

Consumer items flooded American society in the 1950s. Although the purchase and display of consumer goods was not new (see chapter 23), by midcentury consumption had become a reigning value, vital for economic prosperity and essential to individuals' identity and status. In place of the traditional emphasis on work and savings, the consumer culture encouraged satisfaction and happiness through the acquisition of new products.

The consumer culture rested on a firm material base. Between 1950 and 1960, both the gross national product (the value of all goods and services produced) and median family income grew by 25 percent in constant dollars (**Figure 27.1**). Economists claimed that 60 percent of Americans enjoyed middle-class incomes in 1960. By then, nearly 90 percent of all families owned a television set, nearly all had a refrigerator, and most owned at least one car. The number of shopping centers quadrupled between 1957 and 1963.

CHAPTER LOCATOR | What was Eisenhower's "middle way" on domestic issues? | How did Eisenhower's foreign policy differ from Truman's?

CHAPTER 27
822 THE POLITICS AND CULTURE OF ABUNDANCE

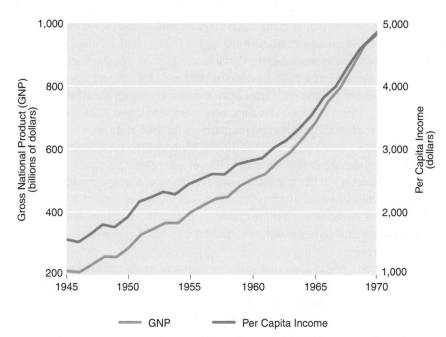

FIGURE 27.1 ■ The Postwar Economic Boom: GNP and Per Capita Income, 1945–1970

American dominance of the worldwide market, innovative technologies that led to new industries such as computers and plastics, population growth, and increases in worker productivity all contributed to the enormous economic growth of the United States after World War II.

Several forces spurred this unparalleled abundance. A population surge — from 152 million to 180 million during the 1950s — expanded demand for products and boosted industries ranging from housing to baby goods. Consumer borrowing also fueled the economic boom, as people made purchases on installment plans and began to use credit cards. Americans now enjoyed their possessions while they paid for them instead of saving their money for future purchases.

Although the sheer need to support themselves and their families explained most women's employment, a desire to secure some of the new abundance sent growing numbers of women to work. As one woman remarked, "My Joe can't put five kids through college . . . and the washer had to be replaced, and Ann was ashamed to bring friends home because the living room furniture was such a mess, so I went to work." The standards for family happiness imposed by the consumer culture increasingly required a second income.

The Revival of Domesticity and Religion

Despite married women's growing employment, a dominant ideology celebrated traditional family life and conventional gender roles. Both popular culture and public figures defined the ideal family as a male breadwinner, a full-time homemaker, and three or four children. Writer and feminist Betty Friedan gave a name to the idealization of women's domestic roles in her 1963 book *The Feminine Mystique*. Friedan criticized scholars, advertisers, and public officials for assuming that biological differences dictated different roles for men and women. According to this feminine mystique that they promulgated, women should find fulfillment in devotion to their homes, families, and serving others. Not many women directly challenged these ideas, but writer Edith Stern maintained that "many arguments about the joys of housewifery have been advanced, largely by those who have never had to work at it."

> CHRONOLOGY

1945–1960
– Baby boom.

1953
– *Playboy* begins publication.

1960
– Nearly 90 percent of American homes have a television set.

1963
– Betty Friedan publishes *The Feminine Mystique*.

What fueled the prosperity of the 1950s? | **How did prosperity affect American society and culture?** | How did African Americans fight for civil rights in the 1950s? | Conclusion: What unmet challenges did peace and prosperity mask? | ✓ LearningCurve Check what you know. bedfordstmartins.com /roarkunderstanding

823

Although the glorification of domesticity clashed with women's increasing employment, many Americans' lives did embody the family ideal. Postwar prosperity enabled people to marry earlier and to have more children. The American birthrate soared between 1945 and 1960, peaking in 1957 with 4.3 million births and producing the **baby boom** generation (**Figure 27.2**). Experts encouraged mothers to devote even more attention to child rearing, while they also urged fathers to cultivate family "togetherness" by spending more time with their children.

Interest in religion also surged in the 1950s. From 1940 to 1960, membership in churches and synagogues rose from 50 to 63 percent of all Americans. Polls reported that 95 percent of the population believed in God. Evangelism took on new life, most notably in the nationwide crusades of Baptist minister Billy Graham. Congress linked religion more closely to the state by adding "under God" to the pledge of allegiance and by requiring that "In God We Trust" be printed on all currency.

Religion helped to calm anxieties in the nuclear age, while ministers such as Graham made the Cold War a holy war, labeling communism "a great sinister anti-Christian movement masterminded by Satan." Some critics questioned the depth of the religious revival, attributing the growth in church membership to a desire for conformity and a need for social outlets. One commentator noted that 53 percent of Americans could not name any book of the New Testament.

Television Transforms Culture and Politics

Just as family life and religion offered a respite from Cold War anxieties, so too did the new medium of television. By 1960, nearly 90 percent of American

baby boom

▶ The surge in the American birthrate between 1945 and 1960, which peaked in 1957 with 4.3 million births. The baby boom both reflected and promoted Americans' postwar prosperity.

> GLOBAL COMPARISON

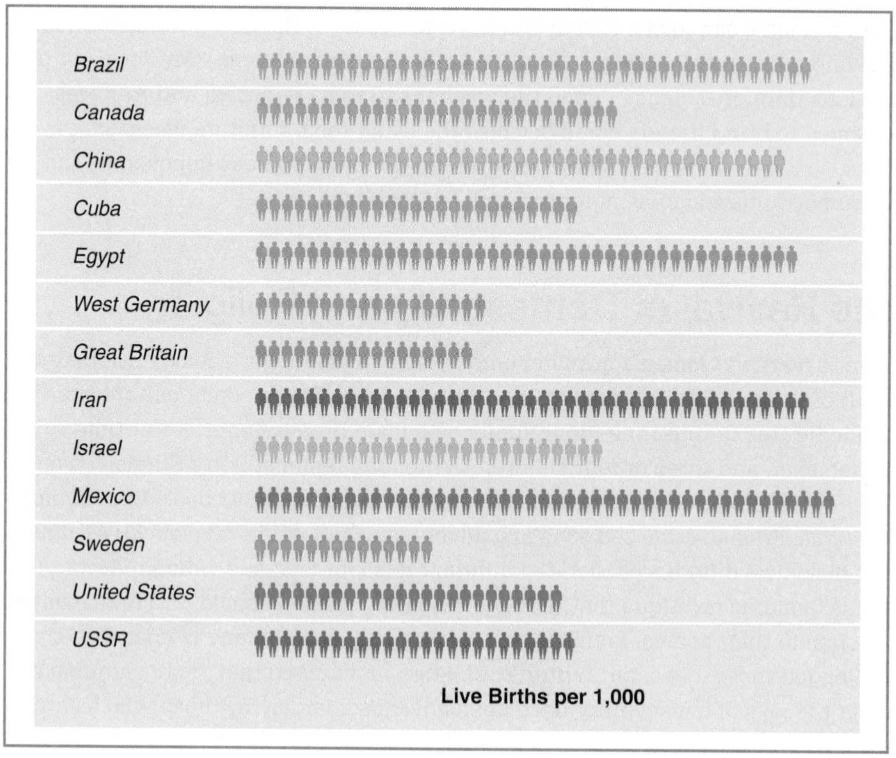

FIGURE 27.2 ■ The Baby Boom in International Perspective

The United States was not alone in welcoming bumper crops of babies in the 1950s. High fertility continued in nonindustrialized countries, while in Europe, as in the United States, birthrates rebounded from low levels during the Great Depression and World War II. Which countries had birthrates comparable to those of the United States? What might explain why countries such as Brazil, China, Iran, and Mexico had birthrates so much higher than those in the United States? What might explain why birthrates in Europe were lower than those in the United States?

Brazil	
Canada	
China	
Cuba	
Egypt	
West Germany	
Great Britain	
Iran	
Israel	
Mexico	
Sweden	
United States	
USSR	

Live Births per 1,000

CHAPTER LOCATOR | What was Eisenhower's "middle way" on domestic issues? | How did Eisenhower's foreign policy differ from Truman's?

CHAPTER 27
824 THE POLITICS AND CULTURE OF ABUNDANCE

homes boasted a television set, and the average viewer spent more than five hours each day in front of the screen. Audiences were especially attracted to situation comedies, which projected the family ideal and the feminine mystique into millions of homes.

Television also began to affect politics. Eisenhower's 1952 presidential campaign used TV ads for the first time, although he was not happy that "an old soldier should come to this." By 1960, television played a key role in election campaigns. Reflecting on his narrow victory, president-elect John F. Kennedy remarked, "We wouldn't have had a prayer without that gadget."

Television transformed politics in other ways. Money played a much larger role in elections because candidates needed to pay for expensive TV spots. The ability to appeal directly to voters in their living rooms put a premium on personal attractiveness and encouraged candidates to build their own campaign organizations, relying less on political parties. The declining strength of parties and the growing power of money in elections were not new trends, but TV helped accelerate them.

Unlike government-financed television in Europe, private enterprise paid for American TV. What NBC called a "selling machine in every living room" became the major vehicle for fostering consumption, and advertisers did not hesitate to interfere with shows that might jeopardize the sale of their products. In 1961, Newton Minow, chairman of the Federal Communications Commission, called television a "vast wasteland." While acknowledging some of TV's achievements, particularly documentaries and drama, Minow depicted it as "a procession of game shows, . . . formula comedies about totally unbelievable families, blood and thunder, mayhem, violence, sadism, murder . . . and cartoons." But viewers kept tuning in. In little more than a decade, television came to dominate Americans' leisure time, influence their consumption patterns, and shape their perceptions of the nation's leadership.

Countercurrents

Pockets of dissent underlay the complacency of the 1950s. Some intellectuals took exception to the materialism and conformity of the era. In *The Lonely Crowd* (1950), sociologist David Riesman lamented a shift from the "inner-directed" to the "other-directed" individual, as Americans replaced independent thinking with an eagerness to adapt to external standards of behavior and belief. Sharing that distaste for the importance of "belonging," William H. Whyte Jr., in his popular book *The Organization Man* (1956), blamed the modern corporation for making employees tailor themselves to the group. Vance Packard's 1959 best seller, *The Status Seekers*, decried "the vigorous merchandising of goods as status-symbols."

Implicit in much of the critique of consumer culture was concern about the loss of traditional masculinity. Consumption was associated with women and their presumed greater susceptibility to manipulation. Men, required to conform to get ahead, moved farther away from the masculine ideals of individualism and aggressiveness. Moreover, the increase in married women's employment compromised the male ideal of breadwinner. Into this gender confusion came *Playboy*, which began publication in 1953 and quickly gained a circulation of one million.

| What fueled the prosperity of the 1950s? | **How did prosperity affect American society and culture?** | How did African Americans fight for civil rights in the 1950s? | Conclusion: What unmet challenges did peace and prosperity mask? | ☑ LearningCurve Check what you know. bedfordstmartins.com /roarkunderstanding |

825

The new magazine idealized masculine independence in the form of bachelorhood and assaulted the middle-class norms of domesticity and respectability. By associating the sophisticated bachelor with good wine, music, furnishings, and the like, the magazine made consumption more masculine while promoting sexual freedom, at least for men.

In fact, two books published by Alfred Kinsey and other researchers at Indiana University — *Sexual Behavior in the Human Male* (1948) and *Sexual Behavior in the Human Female* (1953) — disclosed that Americans' sexual behavior often departed from the postwar family ideal. Large numbers of men and women reported that they had engaged in premarital sex and adultery; one-third of the men and one-seventh of the women reported homosexual experiences. Although Kinsey's sampling procedures later cast doubt on his ability to generalize across the population, the books became best sellers.

Less direct challenges to mainstream standards appeared in the everyday behavior of young Americans. "Roll over Beethoven and tell Tchaikovsky the news!" belted out Chuck Berry in his 1956 hit record celebrating **rock and roll**, a new form of music that combined country music with black rhythm and blues. White teenagers lionized Elvis Presley, who shocked their parents with his tight pants, hip-rolling gestures, and sensuous rock-and-roll music. "Before there was Elvis . . . I started going crazy for 'race music,'" recalled a white man of his teenage years. His recollection underscored African Americans' contributions to rock and roll, as well as the rebellion expressed by white youths' attraction to black music.

rock and roll

▶ A music genre created from country music and black rhythm and blues that emerged in the 1950s and captivated American youth.

The most blatant revolt against conventionality came from the self-proclaimed Beat generation, a small group of primarily male literary figures based in New York City and San Francisco. Rejecting nearly everything in mainstream culture — patriotism, consumerism, technology, conventional family life, discipline — writers such as Allen Ginsberg and Jack Kerouac celebrated spontaneity and absolute personal freedom, including drug consumption and freewheeling sex. The Beats' lifestyles shocked "square" Americans, but they would provide a model for a new movement of youthful dissidents in the 1960s.

Bold new styles in the visual arts also showed the 1950s to be more than a decade of bland conventionality. In New York City, "action painting" or "abstract expressionism" flowered, rejecting the idea that painting should represent recognizable forms. Jackson Pollock and other abstract expressionists poured, dripped, and threw paint on canvases or substituted sticks and other implements for brushes. The new form of painting so captivated and redirected the Western art world that New York replaced Paris as its center.

> QUICK REVIEW

Why did American consumption expand so dramatically in the 1950s, and what aspects of society and culture did it influence?

CHAPTER LOCATOR | What was Eisenhower's "middle way" on domestic issues? | How did Eisenhower's foreign policy differ from Truman's?

826 CHAPTER 27 THE POLITICS AND CULTURE OF ABUNDANCE

How did
African
Americans
fight for civil
rights in the
1950s?

Montgomery Civil Rights Leaders

During the Montgomery bus boycott, local white officials sought to intimidate African Americans with arrests and lawsuits. Here Rosa Parks, one of ninety-two defendants, enters the Montgomery County courthouse. Parks later said of her actions: "People always say that I didn't give up my seat because I was tired, but that isn't true. I was not tired physically. . . . I was not old. . . . I was forty-two. No, the only tired I was, was tired of giving in." Wide World Photos.

BUILDING ON THE CIVIL RIGHTS initiatives begun during World War II, African Americans posed the most dramatic challenge to the status quo of the 1950s as they sought to overcome discrimination and segregation. Although black protest was as old as American racism, in the 1950s grassroots movements arose that attracted national attention and the support of white liberals. Pressed by civil rights groups, the Supreme Court delivered significant institutional reforms, but the most important changes occurred among blacks themselves. Ordinary African Americans in substantial numbers sought their own liberation, building a movement that would transform race relations in the United States.

African Americans Challenge the Supreme Court and the President

Several factors spurred black protest in the 1950s. Between 1940 and 1960, more than three million African Americans moved from the South into areas where they had a political voice. Black leaders made sure that foreign policy officials realized

> CHRONOLOGY

1954
– *Brown v. Board of Education.*

1955–1956
– Montgomery, Alabama, bus boycott.

1957
– Southern Christian Leadership Conference (SCLC) is founded.
– Civil Rights Act of 1957.

What fueled the prosperity of the 1950s?

How did prosperity affect American society and culture?

How did African Americans fight for civil rights in the 1950s?

Conclusion: What unmet challenges did peace and prosperity mask?

✓ **LearningCurve**
Check what you know.
bedfordstmartins.com
/roarkunderstanding

827

how racist practices at home tarnished the U.S. image abroad and handicapped the United States in its competition with the Soviet Union. The very system of segregation meant that African Americans controlled certain organizational resources, such as churches, colleges, and newspapers, where leadership skills could be honed and networks developed.

The legal strategy of the major civil rights organization, the National Association for the Advancement of Colored People (NAACP), reached its crowning achievement with the Supreme Court decision in *Brown v. Board of Education* in 1954, which consolidated five separate suits. Oliver Brown, a World War II veteran in Topeka, Kansas, filed suit because his daughter had to pass by a white school near their home to attend a black school more than a mile away. In Virginia, sixteen-year-old Barbara Johns initiated a student strike over wretched conditions in her black high school, leading to another of the suits joined in *Brown*. The NAACP's lead lawyer, future Supreme Court justice Thurgood Marshall, urged the Court to overturn the "separate but equal" precedent established in *Plessy v. Ferguson* in 1896 (see chapter 21). A unanimous Court, headed by Chief Justice Earl Warren, declared, "Separate educational facilities are inherently unequal" and thus violated the Fourteenth Amendment.

Ultimate responsibility for enforcement of the decision lay with President Eisenhower, but he refused to endorse *Brown*. He also kept silent in 1955 when whites murdered Emmett Till, a fourteen-year-old black boy who had allegedly whistled at a white woman in Mississippi. Reflecting his own prejudice, his preference for limited federal intervention in the states, and a leadership style that favored consensus and gradual progress, Eisenhower kept his distance from civil rights issues. Such inaction fortified southern resistance.

In September 1957, Arkansas governor Orval Faubus sent National Guard troops to block the enrollment of nine black students in Little Rock's Central High School. Later, he allowed them to enter but withdrew the National Guard, leaving the students to face an angry white mob. "During those years when we desperately needed approval from our peers," Melba Patillo Beals remembered, "we were victims of the most harsh rejection imaginable." As television cameras transmitted the ugly scene, Eisenhower was forced to send regular army troops to Little Rock, the first federal military intervention in the South since Reconstruction. Paratroopers escorted the "Little Rock Nine" into the school, but resistance to integration continued across the South.

School segregation outside the South was not usually sanctioned by law, but northern school districts separated black and white students by manipulating neighborhood boundaries and with other devices. Even before *Brown*, black parents in dozens of northern cities challenged the assignment of their children to inferior "colored" schools. While their protests reaped some successes, the structure of residential segregation, often supported by official action, made school segregation a reality for African Americans in both the North and the South.

Eisenhower ordered the integration of public facilities in Washington, D.C., and on military bases, and he supported the first federal civil rights legislation since Reconstruction. Yet the Civil Rights Acts of 1957 and 1960 were little more than symbolic. Baseball star Jackie Robinson spoke for many African Americans when he wired Eisenhower in 1957: "We disagree that half a loaf is better than

Brown v. Board of Education

▶ 1954 Supreme Court ruling that overturned the "separate but equal" precedent established in *Plessy v. Ferguson* in 1896. The Court declared that separate educational facilities were inherently unequal and thus violated the Fourteenth Amendment.

CHAPTER LOCATOR | What was Eisenhower's "middle way" on domestic issues? | How did Eisenhower's foreign policy differ from Truman's?

CHAPTER 27
828 THE POLITICS AND CULTURE OF ABUNDANCE

none. Have waited this long for a bill with meaning — can wait a little longer." Eisenhower appointed the first black professional to his White House staff, but E. Frederick Morrow confided in his diary, "I feel ridiculous . . . trying to defend the administration's record on civil rights."

Montgomery and Mass Protest

What set the civil rights movement of the 1950s and 1960s apart from earlier acts of black protest was its widespread presence in the South, the large number of people involved, their willingness to confront white institutions directly, and the use of nonviolent protest and civil disobedience to bring about change. The Congress of Racial Equality and other groups had experimented with these tactics in the 1940s, organizing to integrate movie theaters, restaurants, and swimming pools in northern cities. In the South, the first sustained protest to claim national attention began in Montgomery, Alabama, on December 1, 1955.

School Integration in Little Rock, Arkansas

Nine African American teenagers — including Elizabeth Eckford, shown here — endured nearly three weeks of threats and hateful taunts as they sought to integrate Central High School. Even after President Eisenhower intervened to enable the "Little Rock Nine" to attend school, they were called names, tripped, spat on, and otherwise harassed by some white students. Francis Miller/TimePix/Getty.

What fueled the prosperity of the 1950s?

How did prosperity affect American society and culture?

How did African Americans fight for civil rights in the 1950s?

Conclusion: What unmet challenges did peace and prosperity mask?

☑ LearningCurve
Check what you know.
bedfordstmartins.com
/roarkunderstanding

829

That day, police arrested Rosa Parks for violating a local segregation ordinance. Riding a crowded bus home from work, she refused to give up her seat so that a white man could sit down. The bus driver called the police, who promptly arrested her. Parks had long been active in the local NAACP, headed by E. D. Nixon. They had already talked about challenging bus segregation. So had the Women's Political Council (WPC), led by Jo Ann Robinson, an English professor at Alabama State, who had once been humiliated by a bus driver when she accidentally sat in the white section.

When word came that Parks would fight her arrest, WPC leaders mobilized teachers and students to distribute fliers urging blacks to boycott the buses. E. D. Nixon called a mass meeting at a black church, where those assembled founded the Montgomery Improvement Association (MIA). The MIA arranged volunteer car pools and marshaled more than 90 percent of the black community to sustain the yearlong **Montgomery bus boycott**.

Elected to head the MIA was twenty-six-year-old Martin Luther King Jr., a young Baptist pastor with a doctorate in theology from Boston University. King addressed mass meetings at churches throughout the bus boycott, inspiring blacks' courage and commitment by linking racial justice to Christianity. He promised, "If you will protest courageously and yet with dignity and Christian love . . . historians will have to pause and say, 'There lived a great people — a black people — who injected a new meaning and dignity into the veins of civilization.'"

Montgomery blacks summoned their courage and determination in abundance. An older woman insisted, "I'm not walking for myself, I'm walking for my children and my grandchildren." Boycotters walked miles or carpooled to get to work, contributed their meager financial resources, and stood up to intimidation and police harassment. Authorities arrested several leaders, and whites firebombed King's house. Yet the movement persisted until November 1956, when the Supreme Court declared unconstitutional Alabama's laws requiring bus segregation. King's face on the cover of *Time* magazine in February 1957 marked his rapid rise to national and international fame. In January, black clergy from across the South had chosen King to head the Southern Christian Leadership Conference (SCLC), newly established to coordinate local protests against segregation and disfranchisement. The prominence of King and other ministers obscured the substantial numbers and critical importance of black women in the movement. King's fame and the media's focus on the South also hid the national scope of racial injustice and the struggles for racial equality in the North that both encouraged and benefited from the black freedom struggle in the South.

Montgomery bus boycott

▶ Yearlong boycott of Montgomery's segregated bus system in 1955–1956 by the city's African American population. The boycott brought Martin Luther King Jr. to national prominence and ended in victory when the Supreme Court declared segregated transportation unconstitutional.

> **QUICK REVIEW**

What were the goals and strategies of civil rights activists in the 1950s?

CHAPTER LOCATOR | What was Eisenhower's "middle way" on domestic issues? | How did Eisenhower's foreign policy differ from Truman's?

Conclusion: What unmet challenges did peace and prosperity mask?

AT AN AMERICAN EXHIBIT in Moscow in 1959, the consumer goods that Nixon proudly displayed to Khrushchev and the Cold War competition that crackled through their dialogue reflected two dominant themes of the 1950s: American prosperity and the success of both the United States and the Soviet Union in keeping their antagonism within the bounds of peace. The tremendous economic growth of the 1950s, which raised the standard of living for most Americans, resulted in part from Cold War defense spending.

Prosperity changed the very landscape of the United States. Suburban housing developments sprang up, interstate highways cut up cities and connected the country, farms declined in number but grew in size, and population and industry moved south and west. Daily habits and even values shifted as the economy became more service oriented and as the appearance of a host of new products intensified the growth of a consumer culture.

The prosperity, however, masked a number of developments and problems that Americans would soon face head-on: rising resistance to racial injustice, a 20 percent poverty rate, married women's movement into the labor force, and the emergence of a youth rebellion. Although defense spending and housing, highway, and education subsidies helped to sustain the economic boom, in general President Eisenhower tried to curb domestic programs and let private enterprise have its way. His administration maintained the welfare state inherited from the New Deal but resisted the expansion of federal programs.

In global affairs, Eisenhower exercised restraint on large issues, recognizing the limits of U.S. power. In the name of deterrence, he promoted the development of more destructive atomic weapons, but he withstood pressures for even larger defense budgets. Still, Eisenhower shared Harry Truman's assumption that the United States must fight communism everywhere, and when movements in Iran, Guatemala, Cuba, and Vietnam seemed too radical, too friendly to communism, or too inimical to American economic interests, he tried to undermine them, often with secret operations. Eisenhower presided over eight years of peace and prosperity, but his foreign policy inspired anti-Americanism and forged commitments and interventions that future generations would deem unwise. As Eisenhower's successors took on the struggle against communism and grappled with the domestic challenges of race, poverty, and urban decay that he had avoided, the tranquility and consensus of the 1950s would give way to the turbulence and conflict of the 1960s.

What fueled the prosperity of the 1950s?

How did prosperity affect American society and culture?

How did African Americans fight for civil rights in the 1950s?

Conclusion: What unmet challenges did peace and prosperity mask?

☑ LearningCurve
Check what you know.
bedfordstmartins.com
/roarkunderstanding

831

CHAPTER 27 STUDY GUIDE

STEP 1

GET STARTED ONLINE

LearningCurve ■ bedfordstmartins.com/roarkunderstanding

Now that you've read the chapter, make it stick by completing the LearningCurve activity.

STEP 2

EXPLAIN WHY IT MATTERS

Put your reading into practice. Identify each term below, and then explain why it matters in U.S. history.

TERM	WHO OR WHAT & WHEN	WHY IT MATTERS
Interstate Highway and Defense System Act of 1956 (p. 807)		
mutually assured destruction (MAD) (p. 812)		
domino theory (p. 812)		
Cuban revolution (p. 813)		
Eisenhower Doctrine (p. 814)		
military-industrial complex (p. 816)		
Sun Belt (p. 819)		
Hernandez v. Texas (p. 821)		
baby boom (p. 824)		
rock and roll (p. 826)		
Brown v. Board of Education (p. 828)		
Montgomery bus boycott (p. 830)		

STEP 3

MOVE BEYOND THE BASICS

To demonstrate a more advanced understanding, describe the social, political, and cultural aspects of life in the 1950s as it affected a range of Americans: the suburban middle class, the counterculture, and African Americans and other minorities.

	Developments	Impact on suburban middle class	Impact on African Americans and other minorities	Impact on the counterculture
Economic growth and consumerism				
Suburban growth/ domesticity				
Culture/values				
The Cold War				

PUT IT ALL TOGETHER

Now, take a step back and try to explain the big picture. Remember to use specific examples from the chapter in your answers.

THE COLD WAR

▶ What was the "New Look" in U.S. foreign policy under President Eisenhower?

▶ How did the United States use military intervention or CIA covert activities as a tool of foreign policy in the 1950s?

CULTURAL CURRENTS

▶ How did prosperity shape living patterns in the 1950s?

▶ What developments challenged the dominant norms regarding consumer culture in the 1950s?

CIVIL RIGHTS

▶ Why was *Brown v. Board of Education* such a pivotal case in the history of the civil rights movement?

▶ Why did the Montgomery bus boycott succeed?

LOOKING BACKWARD, LOOKING AHEAD

▶ Compare and contrast the culture and society of the 1920s with that of the 1950s.

▶ What tensions in 1950s America suggest defining aspects of the 1960s?

> ## IN YOUR OWN WORDS

Imagine that you must give an oral report to the class answering the following question: What were the successes and limitations of America's "culture of abundance" in the 1950s? What would be the most important points to include and why?

28
REFORM, REBELLION, AND REACTION
1960–1974

> How did protest movements change policies and society in the 1960s and 1970s? Chapter 28 examines the efforts to reform and transform American society in the 1960s and early 1970s. It explores the domestic agenda of Lyndon B. Johnson's administration, the role of the Supreme Court, and the evolution of the black freedom movement. The chapter also examines other movements inspired by the struggle for black civil rights, the backlash against reform, and the transformation of the liberal agenda under President Richard M. Nixon.

LearningCurve
bedfordstmartins.com/roarkunderstanding
After reading the chapter, use LearningCurve to
retain what you've read.

Birmingham, Alabama. Police officers attack civil rights demonstrators with fire hoses at Kelley Ingram Park in 1963. © Bob Adelman.

> What liberal reforms were advanced during the Kennedy and Johnson administrations?

> How did the civil rights movement evolve in the 1960s?

> What other rights movements emerged in the 1960s?

> What were the goals of the new wave of feminism?

> How did liberalism fare under President Nixon?

> Conclusion: What were the achievements and limitations of liberalism?

> What liberal reforms were advanced during the Kennedy and Johnson administrations?

A Tribute to Johnson for Medicare

George Niedermeyer, who lived in Hollywood, Florida, and received a Social Security pension, painted pieces of wood and glued them together to create this thank-you to President Lyndon Johnson for establishing Medicare. LBJ Library, photo by Henry Groskinsky.

AT THE DEMOCRATIC National Convention in 1960, John F. Kennedy announced "a New Frontier" that would confront "unsolved problems of peace and war, unconquered pockets of ignorance and prejudice, unanswered questions of poverty and surplus." Four years later, Lyndon B. Johnson invoked the ideal of a "Great Society, [which] rests on abundance and liberty for all [and] demands an end to poverty and racial injustice." Acting under the liberal faith that government should use its power to solve social and economic problems, end injustice, and promote the welfare of all citizens, the Democratic administrations of the 1960s won legislation on civil rights, poverty, education, medical care, housing, consumer safeguards, and environmental protection. These measures, along with pathbreaking Supreme Court decisions, responded to demands for rights from African Americans and other groups and addressed problems arising from rapid economic growth.

The Unrealized Promise of Kennedy's New Frontier

John F. Kennedy grew up in privilege, the child of an Irish Catholic businessman who became a New Deal official. Helped by a distinguished World War II navy

CHAPTER LOCATOR | What liberal reforms were advanced during the Kennedy and Johnson administrations? | How did the civil rights movement evolve in the 1960s?

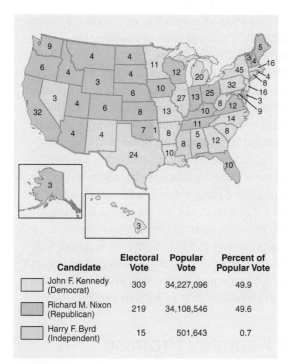

Candidate	Electoral Vote	Popular Vote	Percent of Popular Vote
John F. Kennedy (Democrat)	303	34,227,096	49.9
Richard M. Nixon (Republican)	219	34,108,546	49.6
Harry F. Byrd (Independent)	15	501,643	0.7

MAP 28.1 ■ The Election of 1960

record, Kennedy won election to the House of Representatives in 1946 and the Senate in 1952. With a powerful political machine, his family's fortune, and a dynamic personal appeal, Kennedy won the Democratic presidential nomination in 1960. He stunned many Democrats by choosing as his running mate Lyndon B. Johnson of Texas, whom liberals disparaged as a typical southern conservative.

In the general election, Kennedy narrowly defeated his Republican opponent, Vice President Richard M. Nixon, by a 118,550-vote margin (**Map 28.1**). African American voters contributed to his victory, and Kennedy also benefited from the nation's first televised presidential debates, at which he appeared cool and confident beside a nervous and pale Nixon.

The Kennedy administration projected energy, idealism, and glamour, although Kennedy was in most ways a cautious, pragmatic politician. At his inauguration, he called on Americans to serve the common good. "Ask not what your country can do for you," he implored, "ask what you can do for your country." Although Kennedy's idealism inspired many, he failed to persuade Congress to expand the welfare state with federal education and health care programs. Moreover, he resisted leadership on behalf of racial justice until civil rights activists gave him no choice.

Moved by the desperate conditions he observed while campaigning in Appalachia, Kennedy pushed poverty onto the national agenda. In 1962, he read Michael Harrington's *The Other America*, which described the poverty that left more than one in five Americans "maimed in body and spirit, existing at levels beneath those necessary for human decency." By 1962, Kennedy had won support for a $2 billion urban renewal program, providing incentives to businesses to locate in economically depressed areas and job training for the unemployed. In the summer of 1963, he asked aides to plan a full-scale attack on poverty.

Kennedy had promised to make economic growth a key objective, and he called for an enormous tax cut in 1963, which he promised would increase demand and create jobs. Passed in February 1964, the law contributed to an economic boom, as unemployment fell and the gross national product shot up. Some liberal critics of the tax cut, however, noted that it favored the well-off and argued instead for increased spending on social programs.

> CHRONOLOGY

1960
– John F. Kennedy is elected president.

1963
– In *Abington School District v. Schempp*, Supreme Court rules against requiring Bible reading and prayer in schools.
– Supreme Court rules that congressional districts must reflect "one person, one vote" in *Baker v. Carr*.
– President Kennedy is assassinated; Lyndon B. Johnson becomes president.

1964
– Civil Rights Act is passed.

1964–1966
– Congress passes most of Johnson's Great Society domestic programs.

1966
– *Miranda v. Arizona* ruling requires police officers to inform suspects of their rights.

1967
– Supreme Court strikes down state laws against interracial marriage in *Loving v. Virginia*.

What other rights movements emerged in the 1960s?

What were the goals of the new wave of feminism?

How did liberalism fare under President Nixon?

Conclusion: What were the achievements and limitations of liberalism?

✔ LearningCurve
Check what you know.
bedfordstmartins.com/roarkunderstanding

Kennedy's domestic efforts were in their infancy when an assassin's bullets struck him down on November 22, 1963. Within minutes of the shooting—which occurred as Kennedy's motorcade passed through Dallas, Texas—radio and television broadcast the unfolding horror to the nation. Stunned Americans struggled to understand what had happened. Soon after the assassination, police arrested Lee Harvey Oswald and concluded that he had fired the shots from a nearby building. Two days later, while officers were transferring Oswald from one jail to another, a local nightclub operator killed him. Suspicions arose that Oswald was murdered to cover up a conspiracy by ultraconservatives who hated Kennedy or by Communists who supported Castro's Cuba (as discussed in chapter 29). To get at the truth, President Johnson appointed a commission headed by Chief Justice Earl Warren, which concluded that both Oswald and his assassin had acted alone.

Kennedy's domestic record had been unremarkable in his first two years, but his attention to taxes, civil rights, and poverty in 1963 suggested an important shift. Whether Kennedy could have persuaded Congress to enact them remained in question. Journalist James Reston commented, "What was killed was not only the president but the promise. . . . We saw him only as a rising sun."

Civil Rights Act of 1964
▶ Law that responded to demands of the civil rights movement by making discrimination in employment, education, and public accommodations illegal. It was the strongest such measure since Reconstruction and included a ban on sex discrimination in employment.

Johnson Fulfills the Kennedy Promise

Lyndon B. Johnson assumed the presidency with a wealth of political experience. A self-made man from the Texas Hill Country, he had won election in 1937 to the House of Representatives and in 1948 to the Senate, where he served skillfully as Senate majority leader. His modest upbringing, his admiration for Franklin Roosevelt, and his ambition to outdo the New Deal president all spurred his commitment to reform. Equally compelling were external pressures generated by the black freedom struggle and the host of movements it helped inspire.

Lacking Kennedy's sophistication, Johnson excelled behind the scenes, where he could entice, maneuver, or threaten legislators to support his objectives. The famous "Johnson treatment" became legendary. In his ability to achieve his legislative goals, Johnson had few peers in American history.

Johnson entreated Congress to act so that "John Fitzgerald Kennedy did not live or die in vain." He signed Kennedy's tax cut bill in February 1964. More remarkable was passage of the **Civil Rights Act of 1964**, which made discrimination in employment, education, and public accommodations illegal. The strongest such measure since reconstruction, the law required every ounce of

The "Johnson Treatment"

Abe Fortas, a distinguished lawyer who had argued a major criminal rights case, *Gideon v. Wainwright* (1963), before the Supreme Court, was a close friend of and adviser to President Johnson. This photograph of the president and Fortas taken in July 1965 illustrates how Johnson used his body as well as his voice to bend people to his will. Yoichi R. Okamoto/LBJ Library Collection.

CHAPTER LOCATOR | What liberal reforms were advanced during the Kennedy and Johnson administrations? | How did the civil rights movement evolve in the 1960s?

CHAPTER 28
838 REFORM, REBELLION, AND REACTION

Johnson's political skill to pry sufficient votes from Republicans to balance the "nays" of southern Democrats. Senate Republican leader Everett Dirksen's aide reported that Johnson "never left him alone for thirty minutes."

Antipoverty legislation followed fast on the heels of the Civil Rights Act. Johnson announced "an unconditional war on poverty" in his January 1964 State of the Union message, and in August Congress passed the Economic Opportunity Act. The law authorized ten new programs, allocating $800 million—about 1 percent of the federal budget—for the first year.

> **> Programs of the Economic Opportunity Act**

- Head Start for preschoolers
- Work-study grants for college students
- Job Corps for unemployed young people
- Volunteers in Service to America (VISTA) to work with the disadvantaged
- Legal services for the poor
- Community Action Program requiring participation by the poor in antipoverty projects

The most novel and controversial part of the law, the Community Action Program (CAP), required "maximum feasible participation" of the poor themselves in antipoverty projects. Poor people began to organize to take control of their neighborhoods and to make welfare agencies, school boards, police departments, and housing authorities more accountable to the people they served. Even though Johnson backed off from pushing genuine representation for the poor, CAP gave people usually excluded from government an opportunity to act on their own behalf and develop leadership skills.

Policymaking for a Great Society

As the 1964 election approached, Johnson projected stability and security in the midst of a booming economy. Few voters wanted to risk the dramatic change promised by his Republican opponent, Arizona senator Barry M. Goldwater, who attacked the welfare state and entertained the use of nuclear weapons in Vietnam. Johnson achieved a record-breaking 61 percent of the popular vote, and Democrats won resounding majorities in the House (295–140) and Senate (68–32). Still, Goldwater's considerable grassroots support marked a growing movement on the right (as discussed in chapter 30).

"I want to see a whole bunch of coonskins on the wall," Johnson told his aides, using a hunting analogy to stress his ambitious legislative goals for what he called the "Great Society." The large Democratic majorities in Congress, his own political skills, and pressure from the black freedom struggle enabled Johnson to obtain legislation on discrimination, poverty, education, medical care, housing, consumer and environmental protection, and more. Reporters called the legislation of the Eighty-ninth Congress (1965–1966) "a political miracle."

| What other rights movements emerged in the 1960s? | What were the goals of the new wave of feminism? | How did liberalism fare under President Nixon? | Conclusion: What were the achievements and limitations of liberalism? | ✓ LearningCurve Check what you know. bedfordstmartins.com /roarkunderstanding |

War on Poverty

▶ President Lyndon Johnson's efforts, organized through the Office of Economic Opportunity, to ameliorate poverty, primarily through education and training as well as by including the poor in decision making.

Medicare and Medicaid

▶ Social programs enacted as part of Lyndon Johnson's Great Society. Medicare provided the elderly with universal compulsory medical insurance financed primarily by Social Security taxes. Medicaid authorized federal grants to supplement state-paid medical care for poor people of all ages.

Voting Rights Act of 1965

▶ Law passed during Lyndon Johnson's administration that empowered the federal government to intervene to ensure minorities access to the voting booth. As a result of the act, black voting and officeholding in the South shot up, initiating a major transformation in southern politics.

Immigration and Nationality Act of 1965

▶ Legislation passed during Lyndon Johnson's administration abolishing discriminatory immigration quotas based on national origins. Although it did limit the number of immigrants, including those from Latin America for the first time, it facilitated a surge in immigration later in the century.

The Economic Opportunity Act of 1964 was the opening shot in the **War on Poverty**. Congress doubled the program's funding in 1965, enacted new economic development measures for depressed regions, and authorized more than $1 billion to improve the nation's slums. Direct aid included a new food stamp program, giving poor people greater choice in obtaining food, and rent supplements that provided alternatives to public housing. Moreover, a movement of welfare mothers, the National Welfare Rights Organization, assisted by antipoverty lawyers, pushed administrators of Aid to Families with Dependent Children (AFDC) to ease restrictions on welfare recipients. The number of families receiving assistance jumped from less than one million in 1960 to three million by 1972, benefiting 90 percent of those eligible.

Central to Johnson's War on Poverty were efforts to equip the poor with the skills necessary to find jobs. His Elementary and Secondary Education Act of 1965 marked a turning point by involving the federal government in K–12 education. The measure sent federal dollars to local school districts with high poverty populations and provided equipment and supplies to private and parochial schools serving the poor. That same year, Congress passed the Higher Education Act, vastly expanding federal assistance to colleges and universities for buildings, programs, scholarships, and loans.

The federal government's responsibility for health care marked an even greater watershed. Faced with a powerful medical lobby that opposed national health insurance as "socialized medicine," Johnson focused on the elderly, who constituted a large portion of the nation's poor. Congress responded with the **Medicare** program, providing the elderly with universal medical insurance financed largely through Social Security taxes. A separate program, **Medicaid**, authorized federal grants to supplement state-paid medical care for poor people. By the twenty-first century, these two programs covered 87 million Americans, nearly 30 percent of the population.

Whereas programs such as Medicare fulfilled New Deal and Fair Deal promises, the Great Society's civil rights legislation represented a break with tradition. Racial minorities were neglected or discriminated against in many New Deal programs, and Truman's civil rights proposals bore few results. By contrast, the Civil Rights Act of 1964 made discrimination in employment, education, and public accommodations illegal. The **Voting Rights Act of 1965** banned literacy tests and authorized federal intervention to ensure access to the voting booth.

Another form of bias fell with the **Immigration and Nationality Act of 1965**, which abolished quotas based on national origins that discriminated against non–western European immigrants. The law maintained caps on the total number of immigrants and for the first time limited those from the Western Hemisphere; preference was now given to immediate relatives of U.S. citizens and to those with desirable skills. The measure's unanticipated consequences triggered a surge of immigration near the end of the century (as discussed in chapter 31).

Great Society benefits reached well beyond victims of discrimination and the poor. Medicare covered the elderly, regardless of income. A groundswell of consumer activism won legislation making cars safer and raising standards for the food, drug, and cosmetics industries. Johnson insisted that the Great Society meet "not just the needs of the body but the desire for beauty and hunger for

CHAPTER LOCATOR | What liberal reforms were advanced during the Kennedy and Johnson administrations? | How did the civil rights movement evolve in the 1960s?

840 CHAPTER 28 REFORM, REBELLION, AND REACTION

community." In 1965, he sent Congress the first presidential message on the environment, obtaining measures to control water and air pollution and to preserve the natural beauty of the American landscape. In addition, the National Arts and Humanities Act of 1965 funded artists, musicians, writers, and scholars and brought their work to public audiences.

The flood of reform legislation dwindled after 1966, when Democratic majorities in Congress diminished and a backlash against government programs arose. The Vietnam War dealt the largest blow to Johnson's ambitions, diverting his attention, spawning an antiwar movement that crippled his leadership, and devouring tax dollars that might have been used for reform (as discussed in chapter 29).

In 1968, Johnson pried out of Congress one more civil rights law, which banned discrimination in housing and jury service. He also signed the National Housing Act of 1968, which authorized an enormous increase in low-income housing—1.7 million units over three years—and put construction and ownership in private hands.

Assessing the Great Society

The reduction in poverty in the 1960s was considerable. The number of poor Americans fell from more than 20 percent of the population in 1959 to around 13 percent in 1968. Those who in Johnson's words "live on the outskirts of hope" saw new opportunities. To Rosemary Bray, what turned her family of longtime welfare recipients into taxpaying workers "was the promise of the civil rights movement and the war on poverty." A Mexican American who learned to be a sheet metal worker through a jobs program reported, "[My children] will finish high school and maybe go to college. . . . I see my family and I know the chains are broken."

Certain groups, especially the aged, fared better than others. Many male-headed families rose out of poverty, but impoverishment among female-headed families actually increased. Whites escaped poverty faster than racial and ethnic minorities. Great Society programs contributed to a burgeoning black middle class, yet one out of three African Americans remained poverty-stricken (**Figure 28.1**).

Conservative critics charged that Great Society programs discouraged initiative by giving the poor "handouts." Liberal critics claimed that focusing on training and education wrongly blamed the poor themselves rather than an economic system that could not provide enough adequately paying jobs. In contrast to the New Deal, the Great Society avoided structural reform of the economy and spurned public works projects as a means of providing jobs for the disadvantaged.

Some critics insisted that ending poverty required raising taxes in order to create jobs, overhaul welfare systems, and rebuild slums. Great Society programs did invest more heavily in the public sector, but they were funded from economic growth rather than from new taxes on the rich or middle class. There was no significant redistribution of income, despite large increases in subsidies for food stamps, housing, medical care, and AFDC. Economic prosperity allowed spending for the poor to rise and improved the lives of millions, but that spending never approached the amounts necessary to claim victory in the War on Poverty.

| What other rights movements emerged in the 1960s? | What were the goals of the new wave of feminism? | How did liberalism fare under President Nixon? | Conclusion: What were the achievements and limitations of liberalism? | ✓ LearningCurve Check what you know. bedfordstmartins.com /roarkunderstanding |

841

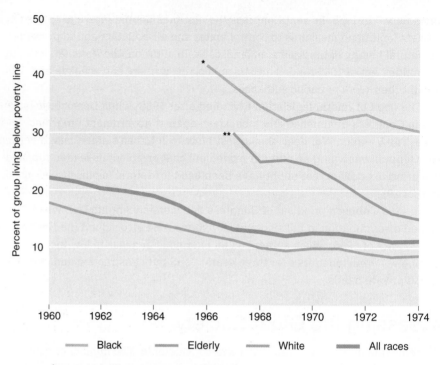

*Statistics on blacks for years 1960–1965 not available.
**Statistics on the elderly for years 1960–1966 not available.

FIGURE 28.1 ■ **Poverty in the United States, 1960–1974**

The short-term effects of economic growth and the Great Society's attack on poverty are seen here. Which groups experienced the sharpest decline in poverty, and what might account for the differences?

The Judicial Revolution

A key element of liberalism's ascendancy emerged in the Supreme Court under Chief Justice Earl Warren (1953–1969). In contrast to the federal courts of the Progressive Era and New Deal, which blocked reform, the **Warren Court** often moved ahead of Congress and public opinion. Expanding the Constitution's promise of equality and individual rights, the Court's decisions supported an activist government to prevent injustice and provided new protections to disadvantaged groups and accused criminals.

Following the pathbreaking *Brown v. Board of Education* school desegregation decision of 1954 (see chapter 27), the Court struck down southern states' stratagems to avoid integration and defended civil rights activists' rights to freedom of assembly and speech. In addition, a unanimous Court in *Loving v. Virginia* (1967) invalidated state laws banning interracial marriage, calling that institution one of the "basic civil rights of man." Chief Justice Warren considered *Baker v. Carr* (1963) his most important decision. The case grew out of a complaint that inequitably drawn Tennessee electoral districts gave sparsely populated rural districts far more representatives than densely populated urban areas. Using the Fourteenth Amendment guarantee of "equal protection of the laws," *Baker* established the principle of "one person, one vote" for state legislatures and the House of

Warren Court

▶ The Supreme Court under Chief Justice Earl Warren (1953–1969), which expanded the Constitution's promise of equality and civil rights. The Court issued landmark decisions in the areas of civil rights, criminal rights, reproductive freedom, and separation of church and state.

CHAPTER LOCATOR │ What liberal reforms were advanced during the Kennedy and Johnson administrations? │ How did the civil rights movement evolve in the 1960s?

842 CHAPTER 28
REFORM, REBELLION, AND REACTION

Representatives. As states redrew electoral districts, legislatures became more responsive to metropolitan interests.

The Warren Court also reformed the criminal justice system, overturning a series of convictions on the grounds that the accused had been deprived of "life, liberty, or property, without due process of law," guaranteed in the Fourteenth Amendment. In decisions that dramatically altered law enforcement practices, the Court declared that states, as well as the federal government, were subject to the Bill of Rights. *Gideon v. Wainwright* (1963) ruled that when an accused criminal could not afford to hire a lawyer, the state had to provide one. *Miranda v. Arizona* (1966) required police officers to inform suspects of their rights upon arrest. The Court also overturned convictions based on evidence obtained by unlawful arrest, by electronic surveillance, or without a search warrant. Critics accused the justices of "handcuffing the police" and letting criminals go free; liberals argued that these rulings promoted equal treatment in the criminal justice system.

The Court's decisions on religion provoked even greater outrage. *Abington School District v. Schempp* (1963) ruled that requiring Bible reading and prayer in the schools violated the First Amendment principle of separation of church and state. Later judgments banned official prayer in public schools even if students were not required to participate. The Court's supporters declared that the religion cases protected the rights of non-Christians and atheists. They noted that the Court left students free to pray on their own, but the decisions infuriated many Christians. Billboards demanding "Impeach Earl Warren" spoke for critics of the Court, who joined a larger backlash mounting against Great Society liberalism.

QUICK REVIEW <

How did the Kennedy and Johnson administrations exemplify a liberal vision of the federal government?

What other rights movements emerged in the 1960s?

What were the goals of the new wave of feminism?

How did liberalism fare under President Nixon?

Conclusion: What were the achievements and limitations of liberalism?

☑ LearningCurve
Check what you know.
bedfordstmartins.com
/roarkunderstanding

> How did the civil rights movement evolve in the 1960s?

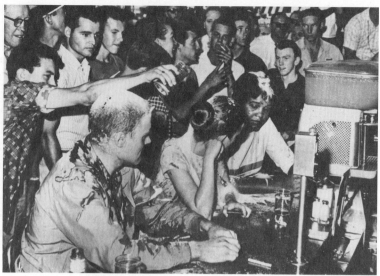

Lunch Counter Sit-in

John Salter Jr., a professor at Tougaloo College, and students Joan Trumpauer and Anne Moody take part in a 1963 sit-in at the Woolworth's lunch counter in Jackson, Mississippi. Shortly before this photograph was taken, whites had thrown two students to the floor, and police had arrested one student. Salter was spattered with mustard and ketchup. In 1968, Moody published *Coming of Age in Mississippi*, a popular book about her experiences in the black freedom struggle. State Historical Society of Wisconsin.

> **VISUAL ACTIVITY**

READING THE IMAGE: What does the photograph tell you about black civil rights activity of the early 1960s?

CONNECTIONS: How would you describe the changes in race relations between African Americans and whites in the United States in the first half of the 1960s?

AS MUCH AS SUPREME COURT DECISIONS, the black freedom struggle distinguished the liberalism of the 1960s from that of the New Deal. Before the Great Society reforms—and, in fact, contributing to them—African Americans had mobilized a movement that struck down legal separation and discrimination in the South and secured their voting rights. Whereas the first Reconstruction reflected the power of northern Republicans in the aftermath of the Civil War, the second Reconstruction depended heavily on the courage and determination of black people themselves to stand up to racist violence.

Civil rights activism that focused on the South and on legal rights won widespread acceptance. But when African Americans stepped up protest against racial injustice in the rest of the country and challenged the economic deprivation that equal rights left untouched, a strong backlash developed as the movement itself lost cohesion.

The Flowering of the Black Freedom Struggle

The Montgomery bus boycott of 1955–1956 gave racial issues national visibility and produced a leader in Martin Luther King Jr. In the 1960s, protest expanded dramatically, as blacks directly confronted the people and institutions that

CHAPTER LOCATOR | What liberal reforms were advanced during the Kennedy and Johnson administrations? | How did the civil rights movement evolve in the 1960s?

844 CHAPTER 28 REFORM, REBELLION, AND REACTION

segregated and discriminated against them: retail establishments, public parks and libraries, buses and depots, voting registrars, and police forces.

Massive direct action in the South began in February 1960, when four African American college students in Greensboro, North Carolina, requested service at the whites-only Woolworth's lunch counter. Within days, hundreds of young people joined them, and others launched sit-ins in thirty-one southern cities. From Southern Christian Leadership Conference headquarters, civil rights activist Ella Baker telephoned her young contacts at black colleges: "What are you going to do? It's time to move."

In April 1960, Baker helped student activists form a new organization, the Student Nonviolent Coordinating Committee (SNCC). Embracing civil disobedience and Martin Luther King Jr.'s principles of nonviolence, activists would confront their oppressors and stand up for their rights, but they would not respond if attacked. In the words of SNCC leader James Lawson, "Nonviolence nurtures the atmosphere in which reconciliation and justice become actual possibilities." SNCC, however, rejected the top-down leadership of King and the established civil rights organizations, adopting a structure that fostered decision making and leadership development at the grassroots level.

The activists' optimism and commitment to nonviolence soon underwent severe tests. Although some cities quietly met student demands, more typically activists encountered violence. Hostile whites poured food over demonstrators, burned them with cigarettes, called them "niggers," and pelted them with rocks. Local police attacked protesters with dogs, clubs, fire hoses, and tear gas, and they arrested thousands of demonstrators.

Another wave of protest occurred in May 1961, when the Congress of Racial Equality (CORE) organized Freedom Rides to integrate interstate transportation in the South. When a group of six whites and seven blacks reached Alabama, whites bombed their bus and beat them with baseball bats so fiercely that an observer "couldn't see their faces through the blood." CORE rebuffed President Kennedy's pleas to call off the rides. But after a huge mob attacked the riders in Montgomery, Alabama, Attorney General Robert Kennedy dispatched federal marshals to restore order. Freedom Riders arriving in Jackson, Mississippi, were promptly arrested, and several hundred spent weeks in jail. All told, more than four hundred blacks and whites participated in the Freedom Rides.

In the summer of 1962, SNCC and other groups began the Voter Education Project. They, too, met violence. Whites bombed black churches, threw tenant farmers out of their homes, and beat and jailed activists. In June 1963, a white man gunned down Mississippi NAACP leader Medgar Evers in front of his house. Similar violence met King's 1963 campaign in Birmingham, Alabama, to integrate public facilities and open jobs to blacks. The police attacked demonstrators with dogs, cattle prods, and fire hoses—brutalities that television broadcast around the world.

The largest demonstration drew 250,000 blacks and whites to the nation's capital in August 1963 in the March on Washington for Jobs and Freedom, inspired by the strategy of A. Philip Randolph in 1941 (see chapter 25). Speaking from the Lincoln Memorial, King put his indelible stamp on the day. "I have a dream," he repeated again and again, imagining the day "when all of God's children . . . will be able to join hands and sing . . . 'Free at last, free at last; thank God Almighty, we are free at last.'"

> CHRONOLOGY

1960
- Student Nonviolent Coordinating Committee (SNCC) is founded.

1961
- Freedom Rides.

1963
- March on Washington.

1964
- Civil Rights Act.
- Mississippi Freedom Summer Project.

1965
- Voting Rights Act.

1965–1968
- Riots in major cities.

1966
- Black Panther Party for Self-Defense is founded.

1968
- Martin Luther King Jr. is assassinated.

Civil Rights Freedom Rides, May 1961

| What other rights movements emerged in the 1960s? | What were the goals of the new wave of feminism? | How did liberalism fare under President Nixon? | Conclusion: What were the achievements and limitations of liberalism? | ✓ LearningCurve Check what you know. bedfordstmartins.com /roarkunderstanding |

The Children's Crusade

Children and teenagers played a key role in the civil rights campaign in Birmingham, Alabama, in May 1963. As shown here, police stopped the children and led them into jail. After more than a thousand young people filled the jails, police used water hoses and dogs against the next stream of demonstrators, bringing national attention to the protesters and some concessions from Birmingham's leaders. AP Photo/Bill Hudson.

The euphoria of the March on Washington faded as activists returned to face continued violence in the South. In 1964, the Mississippi Freedom Summer Project mobilized more than a thousand northern black and white college students to conduct voter registration drives. Resistance was fierce, and by the end of the summer only twelve hundred new voters had been allowed to register. Southern whites had killed several activists, beaten eighty, arrested more than a thousand, and burned thirty-five black churches. Hidden resistance came from the federal government itself, as the FBI spied on King and other leaders and expanded its activities to "expose, disrupt, misdirect, discredit, or otherwise neutralize" black protest.

Still, the movement persisted. In March 1965, Alabama state troopers used such violent force to turn back a voting rights march from Selma to the state capitol in Montgomery that the incident earned the name "Bloody Sunday" and com-

CHAPTER LOCATOR | What liberal reforms were advanced during the Kennedy and Johnson administrations? | How did the civil rights movement evolve in the 1960s?

pelled President Johnson to call up the Alabama National Guard to protect the marchers. Battered and hospitalized on Bloody Sunday, John Lewis, chairman of SNCC (and later a congressman from Georgia), called the Voting Rights Act, which passed that October, "every bit as momentous as the Emancipation Proclamation." Referring to the Selma march, he said, "We all felt we'd had a part in it."

The Response in Washington

Civil rights leaders would have to wear sneakers, Lyndon Johnson said, if they were going to keep up with him. But both Kennedy and Johnson, reluctant to alienate southern voters and their congressional representatives, tended to move only when events gave them little choice. In June 1963, Kennedy finally made good on his promise to seek strong antidiscrimination legislation. Pointing to the injustice suffered by blacks, Kennedy asked white Americans, "Who among us would then be content with the counsels of patience and delay?" Johnson took up Kennedy's commitment with passion, as scenes of violence against peaceful demonstrators appalled television viewers across the nation. The resulting public support, the "Johnson treatment," and the president's appeal to memories of the martyred Kennedy all produced the most important civil rights law since reconstruction.

The Civil Rights Act of 1964 guaranteed access for all Americans to public accommodations, public education, employment, and voting, and it extended constitutional protections to Indians on reservations. Title VII of the measure, banning discrimination in employment, not only attacked racial discrimination but also outlawed discrimination against women. Because Title VII applied to every aspect of employment, including wages, hiring, and promotion, it represented a giant step toward equal employment opportunity for white women as well as for racial minorities.

Responding to black voter registration drives in the South, Johnson demanded legislation to remove "every remaining obstacle to the right and the opportunity to vote." In August 1965, he signed the Voting Rights Act, empowering the federal government to intervene directly to enable African Americans to register and vote, thereby launching a major transformation in southern politics. Black voting rates shot up dramatically (**Map 28.2**). In turn, the number of African Americans holding political office in the South increased from a handful in 1964 to more than a thousand by 1972. Such gains translated into tangible benefits as black officials upgraded public facilities, police protection, and other basic services for their constituents.

Johnson also declared the need to realize "not just equality as a right and theory, but equality as fact and result." To this end, he issued an executive order in 1965 to require employers holding government contracts (affecting about one-third of the labor force) to take affirmative action to ensure equal opportunity. Extended to cover women in 1967, the affirmative action program required employers to counter the effects of centuries of oppression by acting forcefully to align their labor force with the available pool of qualified candidates. Most corporations came to see affirmative action as a good employment practice.

In 1968, Johnson maneuvered one final bill through Congress. While those in other regions often applauded the gains made by the black freedom struggle in the South, they were just as likely to resist claims for racial justice in their own locations.

| What other rights movements emerged in the 1960s? | What were the goals of the new wave of feminism? | How did liberalism fare under President Nixon? | Conclusion: What were the achievements and limitations of liberalism? | ☑ LearningCurve Check what you know. bedfordstmartins.com /roarkunderstanding |

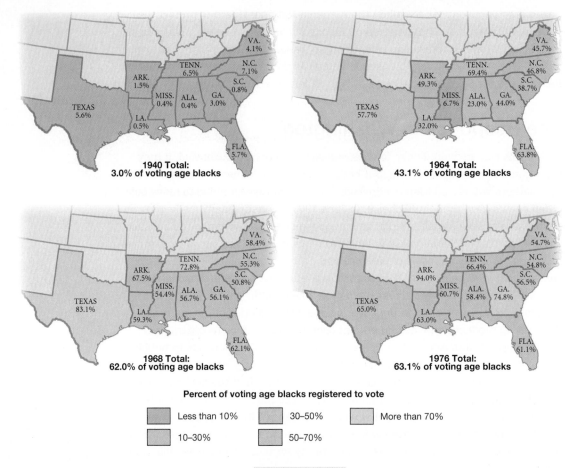

Percent of voting age blacks registered to vote

Less than 10%	30–50%	More than 70%
10–30%	50–70%	

MAP 28.2 ■ The Rise of the African American Vote, 1940–1976

Voting rates of southern blacks increased gradually in the 1940s and 1950s but shot up dramatically in the deep South after the Voting Rights Act of 1965 provided for federal agents to enforce African Americans' right to vote.

> **MAP ACTIVITY**

READING THE MAP: When did the biggest change in African American voter registration occur in the South? In 1968, which states had the highest and which had the lowest voter registration rates?

CONNECTIONS: What role did African American voters play in the 1960 election? What were the targets of two major voting drives in the 1960s?

In 1963, California voters rejected a law passed by the legislature banning discrimination in housing. And when Martin Luther King Jr. launched a campaign against de facto segregation in Chicago in 1966, thousands of whites jeered and threw stones at demonstrators. Johnson's efforts to get a federal open-housing law succeeded only in the wake of King's assassination in 1968. The Civil Rights Act of 1968 banned racial discrimination in housing and jury selection, and it authorized federal intervention when states failed to protect civil rights workers from violence.

Black Power and Urban Rebellions

By 1966, black protest engulfed the entire nation, demanding not just legal equality but also economic justice and abandoning passive resistance as a basic principle.

CHAPTER LOCATOR | What liberal reforms were advanced during the Kennedy and Johnson administrations? | How did the civil rights movement evolve in the 1960s?

848   CHAPTER 28
REFORM, REBELLION, AND REACTION

These developments were not completely new. African Americans had waged campaigns for decent jobs, housing, and education outside the South since the 1930s. Some African Americans had always armed themselves in self-defense, and many activists doubted that their passive suffering would change the hearts of racists. Still, the black freedom struggle began to appear more threatening to the white majority.

The new emphases resulted from a combination of heightened activism and unrealized promise. Legal equality could not quickly improve the material conditions of blacks, and black rage at oppressive conditions erupted in waves of urban uprisings from 1965 to 1968 (**Map 28.3**). In a situation where virtually all-white police forces patrolled black neighborhoods, incidents between police and local blacks typically sparked rioting and resulted in looting, destruction of property, injuries, and deaths. The worst riots occurred in Watts (Los Angeles) in August 1965, Newark and Detroit in July 1967, and the nation's capital in April 1968, but violence visited hundreds of cities.

In the North, Malcolm X posed a powerful challenge to the ethos of nonviolence. Calling for black pride and autonomy, separation from the "corrupt [white]

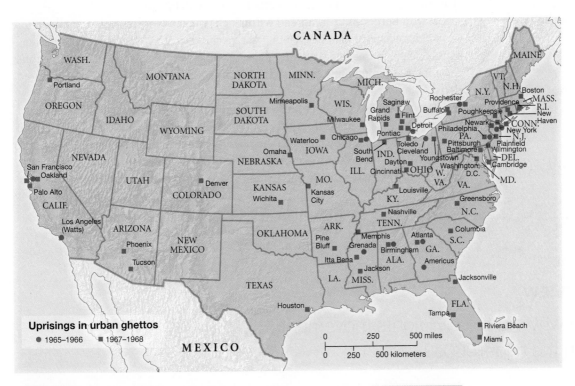

MAP 28.3 ■ Urban Uprisings, 1965–1968

When a white police officer in the Watts district of Los Angeles struck a twenty-one-year-old African American, whom he had just pulled over for driving drunk, one onlooker shouted, "We've got no rights at all — it's just like Selma." The altercation sparked a five-day uprising, during which young blacks set fires, looted, and attacked police and firefighters. When the riot ended, 34 people were dead, more than 3,000 were arrested, and scores of businesses had been wiped out. Similar but smaller-scale violence erupted in dozens of cities across the nation during the next three summers.

> MAP ACTIVITY

READING THE MAP: In what regions and cities of the United States were the 1960s uprisings concentrated? What years saw the greatest unrest?

CONNECTIONS: What were some of the causes of racial unrest in America's cities during this period? Whom did whites generally hold responsible for the violence and why?

| What other rights movements emerged in the 1960s? | What were the goals of the new wave of feminism? | How did liberalism fare under President Nixon? | Conclusion: What were the achievements and limitations of liberalism? | ✓ LearningCurve Check what you know. bedfordstmartins.com /roarkunderstanding |

society," and self-defense against white violence, Malcolm X attracted a large following, especially in urban ghettos. At a June 1966 rally in Greenwood, Mississippi, SNCC chairman Stokely Carmichael gave the ideas espoused by Malcolm X a new name when he shouted, "We want black power." Carmichael rejected integration and assimilation because that implied white superiority. African Americans were encouraged to develop independent businesses and control their own schools, communities, and political organizations. The phrase "Black is beautiful" emphasized pride in African American culture and connections to dark-skinned people around the world, who were claiming their independence from colonial domination. Black power quickly became the rallying cry in SNCC and CORE as well as other organizations such as the Black Panther Party for Self-Defense, organized in 1966 to combat police brutality.

black power movement

▶ Movement of the 1960s and 1970s that emphasized black racial pride and autonomy. Black power advocates encouraged African Americans to assert community control, and some within the movement also rejected the ethos of nonviolence.

The press paid inordinate attention to the **black power movement**, and civil rights activism encountered a severe white backlash. Although the urban riots of the mid-1960s erupted spontaneously, triggered by specific incidents of alleged police mistreatment, horrified whites blamed black power militants. By 1966, 85 percent of the white population—up from 34 percent two years earlier—thought that African Americans were pressing for too much too quickly.

Martin Luther King Jr. agreed with black power advocates about the need for "a radical reconstruction of society," yet he clung to nonviolence and integration as the means to this end. In 1968, the thirty-nine-year-old leader went to Memphis to support striking municipal sanitation workers. There, on April 4, he was murdered by an escaped white convict.

Although black power organizations captured the headlines, they failed to gain the massive support from African Americans that King and other leaders had attracted. Nor could they alleviate the poverty and racism entrenched in the entire country. Yet black power's emphasis on racial pride and its critique of American institutions resonated loudly and helped shape the protest activities of other groups.

> **QUICK REVIEW**

How and why did the civil rights movement change in the mid-1960s?

CHAPTER LOCATOR | What liberal reforms were advanced during the Kennedy and Johnson administrations? | How did the civil rights movement evolve in the 1960s?

850 CHAPTER 28 REFORM, REBELLION, AND REACTION

What other rights movements emerged in the 1960s?

THE CIVIL RIGHTS MOVEMENT'S undeniable moral claims helped make protest more respectable, while its successes encouraged other groups with grievances. Native Americans, Latinos, college students, women, gay men and lesbians, and others drew on the black freedom struggle for inspiration and models of activism. Many of these groups engaged in direct-action protests, expressed their own cultural nationalism, and challenged dominant institutions and values. Their grievances gained attention in the political arena, and they expanded justice and opportunity for many of their constituents.

| What other rights movements emerged in the 1960s? | What were the goals of the new wave of feminism? | How did liberalism fare under President Nixon? | Conclusion: What were the achievements and limitations of liberalism? | ✔ **LearningCurve** Check what you know. bedfordstmartins.com /roarkunderstanding |

1960
- Students for a Democratic Society (SDS) is established.

1962
- United Farm Workers (UFW) is founded.

1968
- American Indian Movement (AIM) is founded.

1969
- Stonewall riots.

1972
- "Trail of Broken Treaties" caravan to Washington, D.C.

American Indian Movement (AIM)

▶ Organization established in 1968 to address the problems Indians faced in American cities, including poverty and police harassment. AIM organized Indians to end relocation and termination policies and to win greater control over their cultures and communities.

Native American Protest

The cry "red power" reflected the influence of black radicalism on young Native Americans, whose activism took on fresh militancy and goals in the 1960s. The termination and relocation programs of the 1950s, contrary to their intent, stirred a sense of Indian identity across tribal lines and a determination to preserve traditional culture. Native Americans demonstrated and occupied land and public buildings, claiming rights to natural resources and territory they had owned collectively before European settlement.

In 1969, Native American militants captured world attention when several dozen seized Alcatraz Island, an abandoned federal prison in San Francisco Bay, claiming their right of "first discovery" of this land. For nineteen months, they used the occupation to publicize injustices against Indians, promote pan-Indian cooperation, and celebrate traditional cultures. One of the organizers, Dr. LaNada Boyer, the first Native American to attend the University of California, Berkeley, said of Alcatraz, "We were able to reestablish our identity as Indian people, as a culture, as political entities."

In Minneapolis in 1968, two Chippewa Indians, Dennis Banks and George Mitchell, founded the **American Indian Movement (AIM)** to attack problems in cities, where about 300,000 Indians lived. AIM sought to protect Indians from police harassment, secure antipoverty funds, and establish "survival schools" to teach Indian history and values. The movement's appeal quickly spread and filled many Indians with a new sense of purpose. Lakota activist and author Mary Crow Dog wrote that AIM's visit to her South Dakota reservation "loosened a sort of earthquake inside me." AIM leaders helped organize the "Trail of Broken Treaties" caravan to the nation's capital in 1972, when activists occupied the Bureau of Indian Affairs to express their outrage at the bureau's policies and interference in Indians' lives. In 1973, a much longer siege occurred on the Lakota Sioux reservation in South Dakota. Conflicts there between AIM militants and older tribal leaders led AIM to take over for seventy-two days the village of Wounded Knee, where U.S. troops had massacred more than two hundred Sioux Indians in 1890 (see chapter 17).

Although these dramatic occupations failed to achieve their specific goals, Indians won the end of relocation and termination policies, greater tribal sovereignty and control over community services, protection of Indian religious practices, and a measure of respect and pride. A number of laws and court decisions restored rights to ancestral lands and compensated tribes for land seized in violation of treaties.

Latino Struggles for Justice

The fastest-growing minority group in the 1960s was Latino, or Hispanic American, an extraordinarily varied population encompassing people of Mexican, Puerto Rican, Caribbean, and other Latin American origins. (The term *Latino* stresses their common bonds as a minority group in the United States. The older, less political term *Hispanic* also includes people with origins in Spain.) People of

CHAPTER LOCATOR | What liberal reforms were advanced during the Kennedy and Johnson administrations? | How did the civil rights movement evolve in the 1960s?

Puerto Rican and Caribbean descent populated East Coast cities, but more than half of the nation's Latino population—including some six million Mexican Americans—lived in the Southwest. In addition, thousands illegally crossed the border between Mexico and the United States yearly in search of economic opportunity.

Political organization of Mexican Americans dated back to the League of United Latin American Citizens (LULAC), founded in 1929, which fought segregation and discrimination through litigation (see chapter 26). In the 1960s, however, young Mexican Americans increasingly rejected traditional politics in favor of direct action. One symbol of this generational challenge was young activists' adoption of the term *Chicano* (from *mejicano*, the Spanish word for "Mexican").

The **Chicano movement** drew national attention to California, where Cesar Chavez and Dolores Huerta organized a movement to improve the wretched conditions of migrant agricultural workers. As the child of migrant farmworkers, Chavez lived in soggy tents, changed schools frequently, and encountered indifference and discrimination. One teacher, he recalled, "hung a sign on me that said, 'I am a clown, I speak Spanish.'" After serving in World War II, Chavez began to organize voter registration drives among Mexican Americans.

In contrast to Chavez, Dolores Huerta grew up in an integrated urban neighborhood and avoided the farmworkers' grinding poverty but witnessed subtle forms of discrimination. Once, a high school teacher challenged her authorship

Chicano movement

▶ Mobilization of Mexican Americans in the 1960s and 1970s to fight for civil rights, economic justice, and political power and to combat police brutality. Most notably, the movement worked to improve the lives of migrant farmworkers and to end discrimination in employment and education.

Cesar Chavez and Dolores Huerta

Under posters showing Senator Robert Kennedy and Mahatma Gandhi, Chavez and Huerta confer in 1968 during the United Farm Workers' struggle with grape growers for better wages and working conditions. Chavez, like Martin Luther King Jr., had studied the ideas of Gandhi, who used civil disobedience and nonviolence to gain independence for India. People across the country, including Robert Kennedy, supported the UFW's grape boycott. Arthur Schatz/TimePix/Getty Images.

What other rights movements emerged in the 1960s?

What were the goals of the new wave of feminism?

How did liberalism fare under President Nixon?

Conclusion: What were the achievements and limitations of liberalism?

☑ LearningCurve
Check what you know.
bedfordstmartins.com
/roarkunderstanding

of an essay because it was so well written. Believing that collective action was the key to progress, she and Chavez founded the United Farm Workers (UFW) in 1962. To gain leverage for striking workers, the UFW mounted a nationwide boycott of California grapes, winning support from millions of Americans and gaining a wage increase for the workers in 1970. Although the UFW struggled and lost membership during the 1970s, it helped politicize Mexican Americans and improve farmworkers' lives.

Other Chicanos pressed the Equal Employment Opportunity Commission (EEOC) to act against job discrimination against Mexican Americans. After LULAC, the American GI Forum (see chapter 26), and other groups picketed government offices, President Johnson responded in 1967 by appointing Vicente T. Ximenes as the first Mexican American EEOC commissioner and created a special committee on Mexican American issues.

Claiming "brown power," Chicanos organized to end discrimination in education, gain political power, and combat police brutality. In Denver, Rodolfo "Corky" Gonzales set up "freedom schools" where Chicano children learned Spanish and Mexican American history. The nationalist strains of Chicano protest were evident in La Raza Unida (the United Race), a political party founded in 1970 based on cultural pride and brotherhood. Along with blacks and Native Americans, Chicanos continued to be disproportionately impoverished, but they gradually won more political offices, more effective enforcement of antidiscrimination legislation, and greater respect for their culture.

Student Rebellion, the New Left, and the Counterculture

Although materially and legally more secure than their African American, Indian, and Latino counterparts, white youths also expressed dissent, participating in the black freedom struggle, student protests, the antiwar movement, and the new feminist movement. Challenging establishment institutions, young activists were part of a larger international phenomenon of student movements around the globe.

The central organization of white student protest was Students for a Democratic Society (SDS), formed in 1960. In 1962, the organizers wrote in their statement of purpose, "We are people of this generation, bred in at least modest comfort, housed now in universities, looking uncomfortably at the world we inherit." The idealistic students criticized the complacency of their elders, the remoteness of decision makers, and the powerlessness and alienation generated by a bureaucratic society. SDS aimed to mobilize a "New Left" around the goals of civil rights, peace, and universal economic security. Other forms of student activism soon followed.

The first large-scale white student protest arose at the University of California, Berkeley, in 1964, when university officials banned students from setting up tables to recruit support for various causes. Led by whites returning from civil rights work in the South, the "free speech" movement occupied the administration building, and more than seven hundred students were arrested before the California Board of Regents overturned the new restrictions.

CHAPTER LOCATOR | What liberal reforms were advanced during the Kennedy and Johnson administrations? | How did the civil rights movement evolve in the 1960s?

CHAPTER 28
854 REFORM, REBELLION, AND REACTION

Hundreds of student rallies and building occupations followed on campuses across the country, especially after 1965, when opposition to the Vietnam War mounted and students protested against universities' ties with the military (as discussed in chapter 29). Students also changed the collegiate environment. Women at the University of Chicago, for example, charged in 1969 that all universities "discriminate against women, impede their full intellectual development, deny them places on the faculty, exploit talented women and mistreat women students." At Howard University, African American students called for a "Black Awareness Research Institute," demanding that academic departments "place more emphasis on how these disciplines may be used to effect the liberation of black people."

> **Accomplishments of the Student Movement**

- Curricular reforms, such as the introduction of black studies, Latino studies, and women's studies programs
- Increased financial aid for minority and poor students
- Independence from paternalistic rules
- A larger voice in campus decision making

Student protest sometimes blended into a cultural revolution against nearly every conventional standard of behavior. Drawing on the ideas of the Beats of the 1950s (see chapter 27), the "hippies," as they were called, rejected mainstream values such as materialism, order, and sexual control. Seeking personal rather than political change, they advocated "Do your own thing" and drew attention with their long hair, wildly colorful clothing, and use of drugs. Across the country, thousands of radicals established communes in cities or on farms.

Rock and folk music defined both the counterculture and the political left. Music during the 1960s often carried insurgent political and social messages that reflected radical youth culture. "Eve of Destruction," a top hit of 1965, reminded young men at a time when the voting age was twenty-one, "You're old enough to kill but not for votin'." The 1969 Woodstock Music Festival, attended by 400,000 young people, epitomized the centrality of music to the youth rebellion. Hippies faded away in the 1970s, but many elements of the counterculture—rock music, jeans, and long hair, as well as new social attitudes—filtered into the mainstream. More tolerant approaches to sexual behaviors spawned what came to be called the "sexual revolution," with help from the birth control pill, which became available in the 1960s. Self-fulfillment became a dominant concern of many Americans, and questioning of authority became more widespread.

Gay Men and Lesbians Organize

More permissive sexual norms did not stretch easily to include tolerance of homosexuality. Gay men and lesbians escaped discrimination and ridicule only by concealing their very identities. Those who couldn't or wouldn't found themselves

| What other rights movements emerged in the 1960s? | What were the goals of the new wave of feminism? | How did liberalism fare under President Nixon? | Conclusion: What were the achievements and limitations of liberalism? | ✓ LearningCurve Check what you know. bedfordstmartins.com /roarkunderstanding |

fired from jobs, arrested for their sexual activities, deprived of their children, or accused of being "perverted." Nevertheless, some gays and lesbians began to organize.

Some of the first gay activism challenged the government's aggressive efforts to keep homosexuals out of the civil service. In October 1965, picketers outside the White House held signs calling discrimination against homosexuals "as immoral as discrimination against Negroes and Jews." Not until ten years later, however, did the Civil Service Commission formally end its anti-gay policy.

A turning point in gay activism came in 1969 when police raided a gay bar, the Stonewall Inn, in New York City's Greenwich Village, and gay men and lesbians fought back. "Suddenly, they were not submissive anymore," a police officer remarked. Energized by the defiance shown at the Stonewall riots, gay men and lesbians organized a host of new groups, such as the Gay Liberation Front and the National Gay and Lesbian Task Force.

In 1972, Ann Arbor, Michigan, passed the first antidiscrimination ordinance, and two years later Elaine Noble's election to the Massachusetts legislature marked the first time an openly gay candidate won state office. In 1973, gay activists persuaded the American Psychiatric Association to withdraw its designation of homosexuality as a mental disease. It would take decades for these initial gains to improve conditions for most homosexuals, but by the mid-1970s gay men and lesbians had a movement through which they could claim equal rights and express pride in their identities.

> **QUICK REVIEW**

How did the black freedom struggle influence other reform movements of the 1960s and 1970s?

CHAPTER LOCATOR | What liberal reforms were advanced during the Kennedy and Johnson administrations? | How did the civil rights movement evolve in the 1960s?

856 CHAPTER 28
REFORM, REBELLION, AND REACTION

Cover of the First Issue of *Ms.* Magazine

In 1972, Gloria Steinem and other journalists and writers published the premier issue of the first mass-circulation magazine for and controlled by women. *Ms.: The New Magazine for Women* ignored the recipes and fashion tips of typical women's magazines. It featured literature by women writers and articles on a broad range of feminist issues. Courtesy, Lang Communications.

BECOMING VISIBLE by the late 1960s, a multifaceted women's movement reached its high tide in the 1970s and persisted into the twenty-first century. By that time, despite a powerful countermovement, women had experienced tremendous transformations in their legal status, public opportunities, and personal and sexual relationships, while popular expectations about appropriate gender roles had shifted dramatically.

A Multifaceted Movement Emerges

Beginning in the 1940s, large demographic changes laid the preconditions for a resurgence of feminism. As more and more women took jobs, the importance of their paid work to the economy and their families challenged traditional views of women and awakened many women workers, especially labor union women, to the inferior conditions of their employment. The democratization of higher education brought more women to college campuses, where their aspirations exceeded the confines of domesticity and of routine, subordinate jobs.

Policy initiatives in the early 1960s reflected both these larger transformations and the efforts of women's rights activists. In 1961, Assistant Secretary of Labor Esther Peterson persuaded President Kennedy to create the President's Commission on the Status of Women. Its 1963 report documented widespread discrimination against women and recommended remedies. One of the commission's concerns was

What other rights movements emerged in the 1960s?	**What were the goals of the new wave of feminism?**	How did liberalism fare under President Nixon?	Conclusion: What were the achievements and limitations of liberalism?	✔ LearningCurve Check what you know. bedfordstmartins.com /roarkunderstanding

addressed even before it issued its report, when Congress passed the Equal Pay Act of 1963, making it illegal to pay women less than men for the same work.

Like other movements, the rise of feminism owed much to the black freedom struggle. Women gained protection from employment discrimination through Title VII of the Civil Rights Act of 1964 and the extension of affirmative action to women by piggybacking onto civil rights measures. They soon grew impatient when the government failed to take these new policies seriously. Determined to speed the process of change, writer and feminist Betty Friedan, civil rights activist Pauli Murray, several union women, and others founded the **National Organization for Women (NOW)** in 1966.

Simultaneously, a more radical feminism grew among civil rights and New Left activists. Frustrated with the unwillingness of male activists to take sexism seriously, many women walked out of New Left organizations and created an independent women's liberation movement throughout the nation.

Women's liberation began to gain public attention, especially when dozens of women picketed the Miss America beauty pageant in 1968, protesting against being forced "to compete for male approval [and] enslaved by ludicrous 'beauty' standards." Women began to speak publicly about personal experiences that had always been shrouded in secrecy, such as rape and abortion. Throughout the country, women joined consciousness-raising groups, where they discovered that what they had considered "personal" problems reflected an entrenched system of discrimination against and devaluation of women.

Radical feminists, who called their movement "women's liberation," differed from feminists in NOW and other more mainstream groups in several ways. NOW focused on equal treatment for women in the public sphere; women's liberation emphasized ending women's subordination in family and other personal relationships. Groups such as NOW wanted to integrate women into existing institutions; radical groups insisted that women's liberation required a total transformation of economic, political, and social institutions. Differences between these two strands of feminism blurred in the 1970s, as NOW and other mainstream groups embraced many of the issues raised by radicals.

Although NOW elected a black president, Aileen Hernandez, in 1970, the new feminism's leadership and constituency were predominantly white and middle-class. Women of color criticized white feminists for their inadequate attention to the disproportionate poverty experienced by minority women and to the additional layers of discrimination based on race or ethnicity. To black women, who were much more frequently compelled to work in the lowest-paying jobs for their families' survival, employment did not necessarily look like liberation.

In addition to struggling with vast differences among women, feminism also contended with the refusal of the mass media to take women's grievances seriously. When the House of Representatives passed an Equal Rights Amendment to the U.S. Constitution in 1970, the *New York Times* criticized it in an editorial titled "The Henpecked House." After Gloria Steinem founded *Ms: The New Magazine for Women* in 1972, feminists had their own mass-circulation periodical controlled by women and featuring articles on a broad range of feminist issues. *Ms.* reported on a multifaceted movement that included numerous organizations, reflecting the diverse experiences, backgrounds, and goals of American women. New women's organizations represented ethnic and racial minorities, labor union

National Organization for Women (NOW)

▶ Women's civil rights organization formed in 1966. Initially, NOW focused on eliminating gender discrimination in public institutions and the workplace, but by the 1970s it also embraced many of the issues raised by more radical feminists.

CHAPTER LOCATOR | What liberal reforms were advanced during the Kennedy and Johnson administrations? | How did the civil rights movement evolve in the 1960s?

858 CHAPTER 28 REFORM, REBELLION, AND REACTION

women, religious women, welfare mothers, lesbians, and more. Other new groups focused on single issues such as health, education, abortion rights, and violence against women. Common threads underlay the great diversity of organizations, issues, and activities. Feminism represented the belief that women were barred from, unequally treated in, or poorly served by the male-dominated public arena, encompassing politics, medicine, law, education, culture, and religion. Many feminists also sought equality in the private sphere, challenging traditional norms that identified women primarily as wives and mothers or sex objects, subservient to men.

Feminist Gains Spark a Countermovement

Although more an effect than a cause of women's rising employment, feminism lifted female aspirations and helped lower barriers to posts monopolized by men. Between 1970 and 2000, women's share of law degrees shot up from 5 percent to nearly 50 percent, and their proportion of medical degrees from less than 10 percent to more than 35 percent. Women gained political offices very slowly; yet by 2010, they constituted about 17 percent of Congress and more than 20 percent of all state executives and legislators. Despite some inroads into male-dominated occupations, women still concentrated in low-paying, traditionally female jobs. Employed women continued to bear primary responsibility for their homes and families, thereby working a "double day."

By the mid-1970s, feminism faced a powerful countermovement, organized around opposition to an Equal Rights Amendment (ERA) to the Constitution that would outlaw differential treatment of men and women under all state and federal laws. After Congress passed the ERA in 1972, Phyllis Schlafly, a conservative activist in the Republican Party, mobilized thousands of antifeminist women. These women, marching on state capitols, persuaded enough male legislators to block ratification so that when the time limit ran out in 1982, only thirty-five states had done so, three short of the necessary three-fourths majority. Powerful opposition likewise arose to feminists' quest for abortion rights. "Without the full capacity to limit her own reproduction," abortion rights activist Lucinda Cisler insisted, "a woman's other 'freedoms' are tantalizing mockeries that cannot be exercised." In 1973, the Supreme Court ruled in the landmark *Roe v. Wade* decision that the Constitution protects the right to abortion, which states cannot prohibit in the early stages of pregnancy. This decision galvanized many Americans who equated abortion with murder. Like ERA opponents, with whom they often overlapped, right-to-life activists believed that abortion disparaged motherhood and that feminism threatened their traditional roles. Beginning in 1977, abortion foes pressured Congress to restrict the right to abortion by prohibiting coverage under Medicaid and other government-financed health programs, and the Supreme Court allowed states to impose additional obstacles.

Despite resistance, feminists won other lasting gains. Title IX of the Education Amendments Act of 1972 banned sex discrimination in all aspects of education, such as admissions, athletics, and hiring. Congress also outlawed sex discrimination in credit in 1974, opened U.S. military academies to women in 1976, and prohibited discrimination against pregnant workers in 1978. Moreover, the Supreme Court struck down laws that treated men and women differently in Social Security, welfare and military benefits, and workers' compensation.

> CHRONOLOGY

1963
- President's Commission on the Status of Women issues report.
- Equal Pay Act makes it illegal to pay women less than men for the same work.

1966
- National Organization for Women (NOW) is founded.

1972
- Title IX bans sex discrimination in education.

1973
- Supreme Court rules in favor of abortion rights for women in *Roe v. Wade*.

Roe v. Wade

▶ 1973 Supreme Court ruling that the Constitution protects the right to abortion, which states cannot prohibit in the early stages of pregnancy. The decision galvanized social conservatives and made abortion a controversial policy issue for decades to come.

What other rights movements emerged in the 1960s?

What were the goals of the new wave of feminism?

How did liberalism fare under President Nixon?

Conclusion: What were the achievements and limitations of liberalism?

✓ LearningCurve
Check what you know.
bedfordstmartins.com/roarkunderstanding

859

At the state and local levels, women saw reforms in areas that radical feminists had first introduced. They won laws forcing police departments and the legal system to treat rape victims more justly and humanely. Activists also pushed domestic violence onto the public agenda, obtaining government financing for shelters for battered women as well as laws ensuring both greater protection for victims of domestic violence and more effective prosecution of abusers.

> QUICK REVIEW

What were the key goals of feminist reformers, and why did a countermovement arise to resist them?

CHAPTER LOCATOR | What liberal reforms were advanced during the Kennedy and Johnson administrations? | How did the civil rights movement evolve in the 1960s?

860 CHAPTER 28 REFORM, REBELLION, AND REACTION

How did liberalism fare under President Nixon?

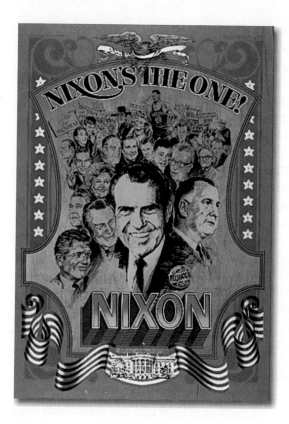

Poster for Nixon's 1968 Campaign

Seeking the presidency in 1968 — a turbulent year for protests, riots, and assassinations — Richard Nixon tried to appeal to a broad spectrum of voters, reflected in this campaign poster. While his slogan "Champion of the Forgotten America" spoke to white Americans alienated by the Great Society's programs for minorities and the poor, the appearance on the poster of the black Republican senator Edward Brooke and basketball player Wilt Chamberlain of the Los Angeles Lakers gave a nod to African Americans. Collection of Janice L. and David J. Frent.

OPPOSITION TO CIVIL RIGHTS MEASURES, Great Society reforms, and protest groups — along with frustrations over the war in Vietnam (as discussed in chapter 29) — delivered the White House to Republican Richard M. Nixon in 1968. Nixon attacked the Great Society for "pouring billions of dollars into programs that have failed" and promised to represent the "forgotten Americans, the non-shouters, the non-demonstrators." Yet his administration either promoted or accepted important elements of the liberal reform agenda, such as greater federal assistance to the poor and environmental reforms.

Extending the Welfare State and Regulating the Economy

A number of factors shaped the liberal policies of the Nixon administration. Democrats continued to control Congress, the Republican Party contained significant numbers of liberals and moderates, and Nixon saw political advantages in accepting some liberal programs. Serious economic problems also compelled new approaches, and although Nixon's real passion lay in foreign policy, he was eager to establish a domestic legacy.

| What other rights movements emerged in the 1960s? | What were the goals of the new wave of feminism? | **How did liberalism fare under President Nixon?** | Conclusion: What were the achievements and limitations of liberalism? | ✓ **LearningCurve** Check what you know. bedfordstmartins.com /roarkunderstanding |

> CHRONOLOGY

1968
– Richard M. Nixon is elected president.

1970
– Environmental Protection Agency is established.
– Clean Air Act.

Under Nixon, government assistance programs such as Social Security, housing, and food stamps grew, and Congress enacted a new billion-dollar program that provided Pell grants for low-income students to attend college. Noting the disparity between what Nixon said and what he did, his speechwriter, the arch-conservative Pat Buchanan, grumbled, "Vigorously did we inveigh against the Great Society, enthusiastically did we fund it."

Nixon also acted contrary to his antigovernment rhetoric when economic crises and energy shortages induced him to increase the federal government's power in the marketplace. By 1970, both inflation and unemployment had surpassed 6 percent, an unprecedented combination dubbed "stagflation." Domestic troubles were compounded by the decline of American dominance in the international economy. In 1971, for the first time in decades, the United States imported more than it exported. Because the amount of dollars in foreign hands exceeded U.S. gold reserves, the nation could no longer back up its currency with gold.

In 1971, Nixon abandoned the convertibility of dollars into gold and devalued the dollar to increase exports. To protect domestic manufacturers, he imposed a 10 percent surcharge on most imports, and he froze wages and prices, thus enabling the government to stimulate the economy without fueling inflation. In the short run, these policies worked, and Nixon was resoundingly reelected in 1972. Yet by 1974, unemployment had crept back up and inflation soared.

Skyrocketing energy prices intensified stagflation. Throughout the post–World War II economic boom, abundant domestic oil deposits and access to cheap Middle Eastern oil had encouraged the building of large cars and skyscrapers with no concern for fuel efficiency. By the 1970s, the United States was consuming one-third of the world's fuel resources.

In the fall of 1973, the United States faced its first energy crisis. Arab nations, furious at the administration's support of Israel during the Yom Kippur War (as discussed in chapter 29), cut off oil shipments to the United States. Long lines formed at gas stations, where prices had nearly doubled, and many homes were cold. In response, Nixon authorized temporary emergency measures allocating petroleum and establishing a national 55-mile-per-hour speed limit to save gasoline. The energy crisis eased, but the nation had yet to come to grips with its seemingly unquenchable demand for fuel and dependence on foreign oil.

Responding to Environmental Concerns

The oil crisis dovetailed with a rising environmental movement, which was pushing the government to conserve energy and protect nature and human beings from the hazards of rapid economic growth. Like the conservation movement born in the Progressive Era (see chapter 21), the new environmentalists sought to preserve natural areas for recreational and aesthetic purposes and to conserve natural resources for future use. Especially in the West, the post–World War II explosion of economic growth and mushrooming population, with the resulting demands for electricity and water, made such efforts seem even more critical.

The new environmentalists, however, went beyond conservationism to attack the ravaging effects of industrial development and technological advances on human life and health. Biologist Rachel Carson drew national attention in 1962 with her best seller *Silent Spring*, which described the harmful effects of toxic

CHAPTER LOCATOR | What liberal reforms were advanced during the Kennedy and Johnson administrations? | How did the civil rights movement evolve in the 1960s?

862 CHAPTER 28 REFORM, REBELLION, AND REACTION

Democratic senator Gaylord Nelson of Wisconsin suggested the idea of Earth Day "to shake up the political establishment and force this issue [environmentalism] onto the national agenda." As a result, on April 22, 1970, some twenty million people participated in grassroots demonstrations all over the country. This banner displayed on the Mall in Washington, D.C., focused on clean air. Other activists dramatized oil spills, toxic dumps, pesticides, polluted rivers and lakes, the loss of wilderness, and the extinction of wildlife. Dennis Brack/Black Star/Stockphoto.com.

chemicals such as the pesticide DDT. The Sierra Club and other older conservation organizations expanded their agendas, and a host of new groups arose. Millions of Americans expressed environmental concerns on the first observation of Earth Day in April 1970.

Responding to these concerns, Nixon called "clean air, clean water, open spaces . . . the birthright of every American" and urged Congress to "end the plunder of America's natural heritage." In 1970, he created the **Environmental Protection Agency (EPA)** to enforce environmental laws, conduct research, and reduce environmental and human health risks from pollutants. He also signed the Occupational Safety and Health Act, protecting workers against job-related accidents and disease, and the Clean Air Act of 1970, restricting factory and automobile emissions of carbon dioxide and other pollutants. Environmentalists claimed that Nixon failed to do enough, pointing particularly to his veto of the Clean Water Act of 1972, which Congress overrode. Yet his environmental initiatives surpassed those of previous administrations.

Environmental Protection Agency (EPA)

▶ Federal agency created by President Nixon in 1970 to enforce environmental laws, conduct environmental research, and reduce environmental and human health risks from pollutants.

Expanding Social Justice

Nixon's 1968 campaign had appealed to southern Democrats and white workers by exploiting hostility to black protest and new civil rights policies, but his administration had to answer to the courts and to Congress. In 1968, fourteen years

| What other rights movements emerged in the 1960s? | What were the goals of the new wave of feminism? | **How did liberalism fare under President Nixon?** | Conclusion: What were the achievements and limitations of liberalism? | ✓ LearningCurve Check what you know. bedfordstmartins.com /roarkunderstanding |

after the *Brown* decision, school desegregation had barely touched the South. Like Eisenhower, Nixon was reluctant to use federal power to compel integration, but the Supreme Court overruled the administration's efforts to delay court-ordered desegregation. By the time Nixon left office, fewer than one in ten southern black children attended totally segregated schools.

Nixon also began to implement affirmative action among federal contractors and unions, and his administration awarded more government contracts and loans to minority businesses. Congress took the initiative in other areas. In 1970, it extended the Voting Rights Act of 1965, and in 1972 it strengthened the Civil Rights Act of 1964 by enlarging the powers of the Equal Employment Opportunity Commission. In 1971, Congress also responded to the massive youth movement with the Twenty-sixth Amendment to the Constitution, which reduced the voting age to eighteen.

Several measures of the Nixon administration also specifically attacked sex discrimination, as the president confronted a growing feminist movement that included Republican feminists. Nixon vetoed a comprehensive child care bill and publicly opposed abortion, but he signed the pathbreaking Title IX, guaranteeing equality in all aspects of education, and allowed his Labor Department to push affirmative action.

President Nixon gave more public support for justice to Native Americans than to any other protest group. While not bowing to radical demands, the administration dealt cautiously with extreme protests. Nixon signed measures recognizing claims of Alaskan and New Mexican Indians and set in motion legislation restoring tribal lands and granting Indians more control over their schools and other service institutions.

> **QUICK REVIEW**

Why and how did Republican president Richard Nixon expand the liberal reforms of previous administrations?

CHAPTER LOCATOR | What liberal reforms were advanced during the Kennedy and Johnson administrations? | How did the civil rights movement evolve in the 1960s?

CHAPTER 28
864   REFORM, REBELLION, AND REACTION

SENATE MAJORITY LEADER Mike Mansfield was not alone in concluding that Lyndon Johnson "has done more than FDR ever did, or ever thought of doing." Building on initiatives from John F. Kennedy's New Frontier, the Great Society expanded the New Deal's focus on economic security, refashioning liberalism to embrace individual rights and to extend material well-being to groups left out of or discriminated against in New Deal programs. Yet opposition to Johnson's leadership grew so strong that by 1968 his liberal vision lay in ruins. "How," he asked, "was it possible that all these people could be so ungrateful to me after I have given them so much?"

African Americans could have responded by pointing out how slowly the government acted when efforts to win black rights met with violence. In addition, failed attempts to use Johnson's antipoverty programs to help poor blacks in the South reflected, in part, some of the more general shortcomings of the War on Poverty. Hastily planned and inadequately funded, antipoverty programs focused more on remediating individual shortcomings than on reforms that would ensure adequately paying jobs for all. Because Johnson launched an all-out war in Vietnam and refused to ask for sacrifices from prosperous Americans, the Great Society never commanded the resources necessary for victory over poverty.

Furthermore, black aspirations exceeded white Americans' commitment to genuine equality. When the civil rights movement attacked racial barriers long entrenched throughout the nation and sought equality in fact as well as in law, it faced a powerful backlash. By the end of the 1960s, the revolution in the legal status of African Americans was complete, but the black freedom struggle had lost momentum, and African Americans remained, with Native Americans and Chicanos, at the bottom of the economic ladder.

Johnson's critics overlooked the Great Society's more successful and lasting elements. Medicare and Medicaid continue to provide access to health care for the elderly and the poor. Federal aid for education and housing became permanent elements of national policy. Moreover, Richard Nixon's otherwise conservative administration implemented school desegregation in the South and affirmative action, initiated environmental reforms, and secured new rights for Native Americans and women. Women benefited from the decline of discrimination, and significant numbers of African Americans and other minority groups began to enter the middle class.

Yet the perceived shortcomings of government programs contributed to social turmoil and fueled the resurgence of conservative politics. Young radicals launched direct confrontations with the government and universities that, together with racial conflict, escalated into political discord and social disorder. The Vietnam War polarized American society as much as did domestic change; it devoured resources that might have been used for social reform and undermined faith in presidential leadership.

| What other rights movements emerged in the 1960s? | What were the goals of the new wave of feminism? | How did liberalism fare under President Nixon? | **Conclusion: What were the achievements and limitations of liberalism?** | ☑ LearningCurve Check what you know. bedfordstmartins.com /roarkunderstanding |

CHAPTER 28 STUDY GUIDE

STEP 1

GET STARTED ONLINE

LearningCurve ▪ bedfordstmartins.com/roarkunderstanding

Now that you've read the chapter, make it stick by completing the LearningCurve activity.

STEP 2

EXPLAIN WHY IT MATTERS

Put your reading into practice. Identify each term below, and then explain why it matters in U.S. history.

TERM	WHO OR WHAT & WHEN	WHY IT MATTERS
Civil Rights Act of 1964 (p. 838)		
War on Poverty (p. 840)		
Medicare and Medicaid (p. 840)		
Voting Rights Act of 1965 (p. 840)		
Immigration and Nationality Act of 1965 (p. 840)		
Warren Court (p. 842)		
black power movement (p. 850)		
American Indian Movement (AIM) (p. 852)		
Chicano movement (p. 853)		
National Organization for Women (NOW) (p. 858)		
Roe v. Wade (p. 859)		
Environmental Protection Agency (EPA) (p. 863)		

STEP 3

MOVE BEYOND THE BASICS

To demonstrate a more advanced understanding, describe the goals, strategies and tactics, and achievements of the major rights movements of the 1960s. Make sure to include a description of any divisions within the movements.

Rights movement	Goals	Strategies and tactics	Achievements
African Americans			
Latinos			
Native Americans			
Students			
Feminists			
Gays and lesbians			
Environmentalists			

STEP 4 PUT IT ALL TOGETHER

Now, take a step back and try to explain the big picture. Remember to use specific examples from the chapter in your answers.

LYNDON JOHNSON AND THE GREAT SOCIETY

▶ What were the most important domestic achievements of the Johnson administration? What were its most important failures?

▶ What assumptions about the relationship between government and society underlay Johnson's Great Society programs?

PROTEST AND REBELLION

▶ What role did students play in the civil rights struggles of the 1960s? How did the civil rights movement change toward the end of the decade?

▶ What were the key achievements of 1960s feminism? What goals did it fail to fulfill?

LIBERAL REFORM IN THE NIXON ADMINISTRATION

▶ What liberal initiatives did the Nixon administration embrace, and what explains these actions?

▶ Should Richard Nixon be considered an environmentalist? Why or why not?

LOOKING BACKWARD, LOOKING AHEAD

▶ How did the African American civil rights movement of the 1960s differ from the movement of the 1950s?

▶ What kinds of opposition emerged in the late 1960s to liberal reforms and radical protest? How might that trend influence politics in the decades after the 1960s?

> IN YOUR OWN WORDS

Imagine that you must give an oral report to the class answering the following question: **How did protest movements change policies and society in the 1960s and 1970s?** What would be the most important points to include and why?

 Do it online at the Student Site ▪ bedfordstmartins.com/roarkunderstanding

29

VIETNAM AND THE END OF THE COLD WAR CONSENSUS

1961–1975

> **Why was the United States unable to achieve its objectives in Vietnam?** Chapter 29 explores U.S. foreign policy from 1961 to 1975, placing the Vietnam War in the larger context of American politics and relations with the Soviet Union, China, and developing nations. It examines the escalation of U.S. involvement in Vietnam under Presidents John F. Kennedy and Lyndon B. Johnson, the polarizing effect of the war on American society and politics, and the gradual American withdrawal from Vietnam under President Richard M. Nixon.

LearningCurve
bedfordstmartins.com/roarkunderstanding
After reading the chapter, use LearningCurve to
retain what you've read.

> How did U.S. foreign policy change under Kennedy?

> Why did Johnson escalate American involvement in Vietnam?

> How did the war in Vietnam polarize the nation?

> How did U.S. foreign policy change under Nixon?

> Conclusion: Was Vietnam an unwinnable war?

Marines patrol near the DMZ. U.S. Marines patrol near the demilitarized zone in Vietnam during Operation Prairie, 1966. Larry Burrows.

How did U.S. foreign policy change under Kennedy?

Preparing for the Worst during the Cuban Missile Crisis

Waiting out the tense days after President Kennedy issued the ultimatum to the Soviet Union to halt shipments of missile materials to Cuba, many Americans tried to prepare for the worst possible outcome. Owners of Chalet Suzanne, a hotel in Lake Wales, Florida, canned several thousand cases of well water, labeled "NASK" for Nuclear Attack Survival Kit. Photo by David Woods.

JOHN F. KENNEDY MOVED quickly to pursue containment more aggressively and with more flexible means than the Eisenhower administration had. Kennedy declared that the United States would "pay any price, bear any burden, meet any hardship, support any friend, oppose any foe to assure the survival and the success of liberty."

> **> Key Elements of Kennedy's Foreign Policy**

- Expansion of the United States' ability to fight conventional battles and engage in guerrilla warfare
- Acceleration of the nation's space exploration program
- Increased attention to the third world
- Escalation of the nuclear arms race
- Commitment of U.S. arms and personnel to South Vietnam

Meeting the "Hour of Maximum Danger"

Underlying Kennedy's foreign policy was an assumption that the United States had "gone soft—physically, mentally, spiritually soft," as he put it in 1960. Calling the Eisenhower era "years of drift and impotency," Kennedy warned in his inaugural address that the nation faced a grave peril: "Each day the crises multiply. . . . Each day we draw nearer the hour of maximum danger."

Although the president exaggerated the threat to national security, several developments in 1961 heightened the sense of crisis and provided a rationalization for his military buildup. Shortly before Kennedy's inauguration, Soviet leader Nikita Khrushchev publicly encouraged "wars of national liberation," thereby aligning the Soviet Union with independence movements in the third world that were often anti-Western. His statement reflected in part the Soviet competition with China for the allegiance of emerging nations, but U.S. officials saw it as a threat to the status quo of containment.

MAP 29.1 ■ U.S. Involvement in Latin America and the Caribbean, 1954–1994

During the Cold War, the United States frequently intervened in Central American and Caribbean countries to suppress Communist or leftist movements.

> **MAP ACTIVITY**

READING THE MAP: How many and which Latin American countries did the United States invade directly? What was the extent of indirect U.S. involvement in other upheavals in the region?

CONNECTIONS: What role, if any, did geographic proximity play in U.S. policy toward the region? What was the significance of the Cuban missile crisis for U.S. foreign policy?

| Why did Johnson escalate American involvement in Vietnam? | How did the war in Vietnam polarize the nation? | How did U.S. foreign policy change under Nixon? | Conclusion: Was Vietnam an unwinnable war? | ✔ LearningCurve Check what you know. bedfordstmartins.com /roarkunderstanding |

1961
- Bay of Pigs invasion.
- Berlin Wall is erected.
- Kennedy increases military aid to South Vietnam.
- Peace Corps is created.

1962
- Cuban missile crisis.

1963
- President Kennedy is assassinated; Lyndon B. Johnson becomes president.

1969
- American astronauts land on the moon.

Bay of Pigs

▶ Failed U.S.-sponsored invasion of Cuba in 1961 by anti-Castro forces who planned to overthrow Fidel Castro's government. The disaster humiliated Kennedy and the United States. It alienated Latin Americans who saw the invasion as another example of Yankee imperialism.

Apollo program

▶ Project initiated by John F. Kennedy in 1961 to surpass the Soviet Union in space exploration and send a man to the moon.

Berlin Wall

▶ Structure erected by East Germany in 1961 to stop the massive exodus of East Germans into West Berlin, which was an embarrassment to the Communists.

Peace Corps

▶ Program launched by President Kennedy in 1961 through which young American volunteers helped with education, health, and other projects in developing countries around the world. More than 60,000 volunteers had served by the mid-1970s.

Cuba, just ninety miles off the Florida coast, posed the first crisis for Kennedy. The revolution led by Fidel Castro had moved Cuba into the Soviet orbit, and Eisenhower's Central Intelligence Agency (CIA) had been planning an invasion of the island by Cuban exiles living in Florida. Kennedy ordered the invasion to proceed even though his military advisers gave it only a fair chance of success.

On April 17, 1961, about 1,400 anti-Castro exiles trained and armed by the CIA landed at the **Bay of Pigs** on the south shore of Cuba (**Map 29.1**). Contrary to U.S. expectations, no popular uprising materialized to support the anti-Castro brigade. Kennedy refused to provide direct military support, and the invaders quickly fell to Castro's forces. The disaster humiliated Kennedy and the United States, posing a stark contrast to the president's inaugural promise of a new, more effective foreign policy. And it alienated Latin Americans who saw it as another example of Yankee imperialism.

Days before the Bay of Pigs invasion, the Soviet Union delivered a psychological blow when a Soviet astronaut became the first human to orbit the earth. Kennedy then called for a huge new commitment to the space program, with the goal of sending a man to the moon by 1970. Congress authorized the **Apollo program** and boosted appropriations for space exploration. John H. Glenn orbited the earth in 1962, and the United States beat the Soviets to the moon, landing two astronauts there in 1969.

Kennedy determined to show American toughness to Khrushchev, but when the two met in June 1961 in Vienna, Austria, Khrushchev took the offensive. The stunned Kennedy reported privately, "He just beat [the] hell out of me. . . . If he thinks I'm inexperienced and have no guts . . . we won't get anywhere with him." Khrushchev demanded an agreement recognizing the existence of two Germanys, and he threatened America's occupation rights in and access to West Berlin.

Khrushchev was concerned about the massive exodus of East Germans into West Berlin, a major embarrassment for the Communists. To stop this flow, in August 1961 East Germany erected a wall between East and West Berlin. With the **Berlin Wall** stemming the tide of escapees and Kennedy declaring West Berlin "the great testing place of Western courage and will," Khrushchev backed off from his threats.

Kennedy used the Berlin crisis to add $3.2 billion to the defense budget. He increased draft calls, and he also mobilized the reserves and National Guard, adding 300,000 troops to the military. This buildup of conventional forces provided for a "flexible response," offering "a wider choice than humiliation or all-out nuclear action."

New Approaches to the Third World

Complementing Kennedy's hard-line policy toward the Soviet Union were fresh approaches to the nationalist movements that had multiplied since the end of World War II. In 1960 alone, seventeen African nations gained their independence. Kennedy publicly supported third world aspirations, believing that the United States could win the hearts and minds of people in developing nations by helping to fulfill hopes for autonomy and democracy.

Kennedy launched his most dramatic third world initiative in 1961 with an idea borrowed from Senator Hubert H. Humphrey: the **Peace Corps**. The program recruited young people to work in developing countries, attracting many who had been moved by Kennedy's appeal for idealism and sacrifice in his inaugural

CHAPTER LOCATOR | How did U.S. foreign policy change under Kennedy?

address. Peace Corps volunteers worked directly with local people, opening schools, providing basic health care, and assisting with agriculture and small economic enterprises. By the mid-1970s, more than 60,000 volunteers had served in Latin America, Africa, and Asia. Peace Corps projects were generally welcomed, but they did not address the receiving countries' larger economic and political structures.

Kennedy also used direct military means to bring political stability to the third world. He rapidly expanded the elite special forces corps established under Eisenhower to aid groups fighting against Communist-leaning movements. These counterinsurgency forces, including the army's Green Berets and the navy's SEALs, were trained to wage guerrilla warfare and equipped with the latest technology. They would get their first test in Vietnam.

The Arms Race and the Nuclear Brink

The final piece of Kennedy's foreign policy was to strengthen American nuclear dominance. He increased the number of nuclear weapons based in Europe from 2,500 to 7,200 and multiplied fivefold the supply of intercontinental ballistic missiles (ICBMs). Concerned that this buildup would enable the United States to launch a first strike and wipe out Soviet missile sites before they could respond, the Soviet Union stepped up its own ICBM program. Thus began the most intense arms race in history.

The superpowers came perilously close to using their weapons during the **Cuban missile crisis** in 1962. Khrushchev decided to install nuclear missiles in Cuba to protect Castro's regime from further U.S. attempts at intervention and to balance the U.S. missiles aimed at the Soviet Union from Europe. On October 22, after the CIA showed Kennedy aerial photographs of missile launching sites under construction in Cuba, Kennedy announced that the military was on full alert and that the navy would turn back any Soviet vessel suspected of carrying offensive missiles to Cuba. He warned that any attack launched from Cuba would trigger a full nuclear assault against the Soviet Union.

With the superpowers on the brink of nuclear war, both Kennedy and Khrushchev also exercised caution. Kennedy refused advice from the military to bomb the missile sites. On October 24, Russian ships carrying nuclear warheads toward Cuba suddenly turned back. When one ship crossed the blockade line, Kennedy ordered the navy to follow the ship rather than attempt to stop it.

While Americans experienced the Cold War's most dangerous days, Kennedy and Khrushchev negotiated an agreement. The Soviets removed the missiles and pledged not to introduce new offensive weapons into Cuba. The United States promised not to invade the island. Secretly, Kennedy also agreed to remove U.S. missiles from Turkey. The Cuban crisis contributed to Khrushchev's fall from power two years later, while Kennedy emerged triumphant. The image of an inexperienced president fumbling the Bay of Pigs invasion gave way to that of a strong leader.

Having proved his toughness, Kennedy worked to ease superpower hostilities. In a major speech in June 1963, Kennedy called for a reexamination of Cold War assumptions, asking Americans "not to see conflict as inevitable." Acknowledging the superpowers' differences, Kennedy stressed what they had in common: "We all breathe the same air. We all cherish our children's future and we are all mortal."

Cuban missile crisis

▶ 1962 nuclear standoff between the Soviet Union and the United States when the Soviets attempted to deploy nuclear missiles in Cuba. In a negotiated settlement, the Soviet Union agreed to remove its missiles from Cuba, and the United States agreed to remove its missiles from Turkey.

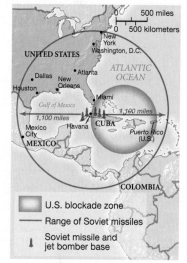

Cuban Missile Crisis, 1962

Why did Johnson escalate American involvement in Vietnam?

How did the war in Vietnam polarize the nation?

How did U.S. foreign policy change under Nixon?

Conclusion: Was Vietnam an unwinnable war?

✓ LearningCurve
Check what you know.
bedfordstmartins.com
/roarkunderstanding

In August 1963, the United States, the Soviet Union, and Great Britain signed a limited nuclear test ban treaty, reducing the threat of radioactive fallout from nuclear testing and raising hopes for further superpower accord.

A Growing War in Vietnam

In 1963, Kennedy criticized the idea of "a Pax Americana enforced on the world by American weapons of war," but he had already increased the flow of those weapons into South Vietnam. Kennedy's strong anticommunism and attachment to a vigorous foreign policy prepared him to expand the commitment that he had inherited from Eisenhower.

By the time Kennedy took office, more than $1 billion in aid and seven hundred U.S. military advisers had failed to stabilize South Vietnam. Two major obstacles stood in the way. First, the South Vietnamese insurgents—whom Americans called Vietcong—were an indigenous force whose initiative came from within. Because the Saigon government refused to hold elections, the rebels saw no choice but to take up arms. Increasingly, Ho Chi Minh's Communist government in North Vietnam supplied them with weapons and soldiers.

Second, the South Vietnamese government refused to satisfy insurgents' demands, but the Army of the Republic of Vietnam (ARVN) could not defeat them militarily. Ngo Dinh Diem, South Vietnam's premier from 1954 to 1963, chose self-serving military leaders for their personal loyalty rather than for their effectiveness. Many South Vietnamese, the majority of whom were Buddhists, saw the Catholic Diem as a corrupt and brutal tool of the West. The growing intervention by North Vietnam made matters worse. In 1960, the Hanoi government established the National Liberation Front, composed of South Vietnamese rebels but directed by the northern army. In addition, Hanoi constructed a network of infiltration routes, called the Ho Chi Minh Trail, in neighboring Laos and Cambodia, through which it sent people and supplies to help liberate the

MAP 29.2 ■ The Vietnam War, 1964–1975

The United States sent 2.6 million soldiers to Vietnam and spent more than $150 billion on the longest war in American history, but it was unable to prevent the unification of Vietnam under a Communist government.

> MAP ACTIVITY

READING THE MAP: What accords divided Vietnam into two nations? When were these accords signed, and where was the line of division drawn? Through what countries did the Ho Chi Minh Trail go?

CONNECTIONS: What was the Gulf of Tonkin incident, and how did the United States respond? What was the Tet Offensive, and how did it affect the war?

CHAPTER LOCATOR | How did U.S. foreign policy change under Kennedy?

South (**Map 29.2**). Violence escalated between 1960 and 1963, bringing the Saigon government close to collapse.

In response, Kennedy gradually escalated the U.S. commitment. By the spring of 1963, military aid had doubled, and 9,000 Americans served in Vietnam as military advisers, occasionally participating in actual combat. The South Vietnamese government promised reform but never made good on its promises.

American officials assumed that technology and sheer power could win in Vietnam. Yet advanced weapons were ill suited to the guerrilla warfare practiced by the enemy, whose surprise attacks were designed to weaken support for the South Vietnamese government. Moreover, U.S. weapons and strategy harmed the very people they were intended to save. Thousands of peasants were uprooted or fell victim to bombs—containing the highly flammable substance napalm—dropped by the South Vietnamese air force to quell the Vietcong. In 1962, U.S. planes began to spray herbicides such as **Agent Orange** to destroy the Vietcong's jungle hideouts and food supply.

With tacit permission from Washington, South Vietnamese military leaders executed a coup against Diem and his brother, who headed the secret police, in November 1963. Kennedy expressed shock at the murders but indicated no change in policy. In a speech to be given on the day he was assassinated, Kennedy referred specifically to Southeast Asia and warned, "We dare not weary of the task." At his death, 16,700 Americans were stationed in Vietnam, and 100 had died there.

Agent Orange

▶ Herbicide used extensively during the Vietnam War to destroy the Vietcong's jungle hideouts and food supply. Its use was later linked to a wide range of illnesses that veterans and the Vietnamese suffered after the war, including birth defects, cancer, and skin disorders.

QUICK REVIEW <

Why did Kennedy believe that engagement in Vietnam was crucial to his foreign policy?

| Why did Johnson escalate American involvement in Vietnam? | How did the war in Vietnam polarize the nation? | How did U.S. foreign policy change under Nixon? | Conclusion: Was Vietnam an unwinnable war? | ☑ **LearningCurve** Check what you know. bedfordstmartins.com /roarkunderstanding |

Why did Johnson escalate American involvement in Vietnam?

U.S. Military Helicopter

The particular conditions in Vietnam — the guerrilla tactics of the enemy, the conduct of fighting all over South Vietnam, and the mountains and dense jungles with limited landing areas — put a premium on helicopters' mobility and maneuverability. In addition to transporting troops and artillery, performing reconnaissance, picking up downed pilots, and evacuating the dead and wounded, helicopters mounted with machine guns and grenade launchers also served as attack vehicles. © Bettmann/Corbis.

LYNDON B. JOHNSON SHARED the Cold War assumptions that had shaped Kennedy's foreign policy. Retaining Kennedy's key advisers — Secretary of State Dean Rusk, Secretary of Defense Robert McNamara, and National Security Adviser McGeorge Bundy — Johnson continued the massive buildup of nuclear weapons as well as conventional and counterinsurgency forces. In 1965, he made the fateful decisions to order U.S. troops into combat in Vietnam and to initiate sustained bombing of the North. That same year, Johnson sent U.S. Marines to the Dominican Republic to crush a leftist rebellion.

An All-Out Commitment in Vietnam

The president who wanted to make his mark on domestic policy was compelled to deal with the commitments his predecessors had made in Vietnam. Some advisers, politicians, and international leaders questioned the wisdom of greater intervention there, viewing the situation as a civil war rather than Communist aggression. Most U.S. allies did not consider Vietnam crucial to containing communism and were not prepared to share the military burden. Senate majority leader Mike Mansfield wondered whether Vietnam could be won with a "limited expenditure

CHAPTER LOCATOR | How did U.S. foreign policy change under Kennedy?

of American lives and resources somewhere commensurate with our national interests." Disregarding the opportunity for disengagement that these critics saw in 1964, Johnson expressed his own doubt privately: "I don't think it's worth fighting for and I don't think we can get out."

Like Kennedy, Johnson remembered how Harry Truman had suffered politically when the Communists took over China. Along with most of his advisers, Johnson believed that American credibility was on the line, and he believed that conceding defeat in Vietnam would undermine his ability to achieve his Great Society.

Johnson understood the ineffectiveness of his South Vietnamese allies and agonized over sending young men into combat. Yet he continued to dispatch more military advisers, weapons, and economic aid and, in August 1964, seized an opportunity to increase the pressure on North Vietnam. While spying in the Gulf of Tonkin, off the coast of North Vietnam, two U.S. destroyers reported that North Vietnamese gunboats had fired on them (see Map 29.2). Johnson quickly ordered air strikes on North Vietnamese torpedo bases and oil storage facilities. Concealing the uncertainty about whether the second attack had even occurred, he won from Congress the **Gulf of Tonkin Resolution**, authorizing him to take "all necessary measures to repel any armed attacks against the forces of the United States and to prevent further aggression."

Soon after winning the election of 1964, Johnson widened the war. He rejected peace overtures from North Vietnam, which insisted on American withdrawal and a coalition government in South Vietnam as steps toward unification of the country. In February 1965, Johnson authorized Operation Rolling Thunder, a strategy of gradually intensified bombing of North Vietnam. Less than a month later, Johnson ordered the first U.S. combat troops to South Vietnam, and in July he shifted U.S. troops from defensive to offensive operations, dispatching 50,000 more soldiers (**Figure 29.1**). Although the administration downplayed the import of these decisions, they marked a critical turning point. Now it was genuinely America's war.

> CHRONOLOGY

1964
– Gulf of Tonkin Resolution.

1965
– Operation Rolling Thunder begins.
– First combat troops are sent to Vietnam.
– U.S. troops invade the Dominican Republic.

Gulf of Tonkin Resolution
▶ Resolution passed by Congress in 1964 in the wake of a naval confrontation in the Gulf of Tonkin. It gave the president virtually unlimited authority in conducting the Vietnam War. The Senate terminated the resolution following outrage over the U.S. invasion of Cambodia in 1970.

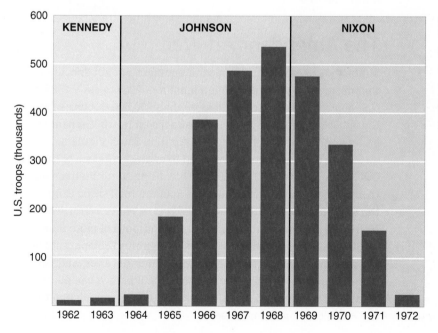

FIGURE 29.1 ■ U.S. Troops in Vietnam, 1962–1972

The steepest increases in the American military presence in Vietnam came with Johnson's escalation of the war in 1965 and 1966. Although Nixon reduced troop levels significantly in 1971 and 1972, the United States continued massive bombing attacks.

| Why did Johnson escalate American involvement in Vietnam? | How did the war in Vietnam polarize the nation? | How did U.S. foreign policy change under Nixon? | Conclusion: Was Vietnam an unwinnable war? | ✓ LearningCurve Check what you know. bedfordstmartins.com /roarkunderstanding |

Preventing Another Castro in Latin America

Closer to home, Johnson faced persistent problems in Latin America. Thirteen times during the 1960s, military coups toppled Latin American governments, and local insurgencies grew apace. The administration's response varied from case to case but centered on the determination to prevent any more Castro-type revolutions.

In 1964, riots erupted in the Panama Canal Zone, instigated by Panamanians who viewed the United States as a colonial power, since it had seized the land and made it a U.S. territory early in the century (see chapter 21). Johnson sent troops to quell the disturbance, but he also initiated negotiations that eventually returned the canal to Panamanian authority in 2000.

Elsewhere, Johnson's Latin American policy generated new cries of "Yankee imperialism." In 1961, voters in the Dominican Republic ousted a longtime dictator and elected a constitutional government headed by reformist Juan Bosch, who was overthrown by a military coup two years later. In 1965, when Bosch supporters launched an uprising against the military government, Johnson sent more than 20,000 soldiers to suppress what he perceived to be a leftist revolt and to take control of the island.

This first outright show of Yankee force in Latin America in four decades damaged the administration. Although Johnson had justified intervention as necessary to prevent "another Cuba," no Communists were found among the rebels, and U.S. intervention kept the reform-oriented Boschists from returning to power. Moreover, the president had not consulted the Dominicans or the Organization of American States, to which the United States had promised it would respect national sovereignty in Latin America.

U.S. Troops in the Dominican Republic

These U.S. paratroopers were among the 20,000 troops sent to the Dominican Republic in April and May 1965. The invasion restored peace but kept the popularly elected government of Juan Bosch from regaining office. Dominicans greeted the U.S. troops with anti-American slogans throughout the capital, Santo Domingo. Bosch himself said, "This was a democratic revolution smashed by the leading democracy in the world." © Bettmann/Corbis.

The Americanized War

Military success in the Dominican Republic no doubt encouraged the president to press on in Vietnam. From 1965 to early 1968, the U.S. military presence grew to more than 500,000 troops as the United States gradually escalated attacks on North Vietnam and on its ally, the National Liberation Front, in South Vietnam.

Even with restrictions imposed to contain criticism of the war, U.S. pilots dropped 643,000 tons of bombs on North Vietnam and more than twice that amount in the South, a total surpassing all the explosives the United States dropped in World War II. The North Vietnamese withstood monthly death tolls of more than 2,000. They applied ingenuity and sheer effort to compensate for the destruction of transportation lines, industrial sites, and power plants. In South Vietnam, the massive U.S. bombing campaign destroyed villages and fields, alienating the very population that the Americans had come to save.

CHAPTER LOCATOR | How did U.S. foreign policy change under Kennedy?

On the ground, General William Westmoreland's strategy of attrition was designed to seek out and kill the Vietcong and North Vietnamese regular army. With no fixed battlefront, helicopters carried troops to conduct offensives all over South Vietnam, and officials calculated progress not in territory seized but in "body counts" and "kill ratios"—the number of enemies killed relative to the cost in American and ARVN lives. According to Lieutenant Frederick Downs, "To win a battle, we had to kill them. For them to win, all they had to do was survive." The Americans "never owned anything except the ground they stood on."

Those Who Served

Teenagers fought the Vietnam War. In contrast to World War II, in which the average soldier was twenty-six years old, the average age for all soldiers in Vietnam was nineteen. Until the Twenty-sixth Amendment to the Constitution dropped the voting age from twenty-one to eighteen in 1971, most soldiers could not even vote for the officials who sent them to war. Men of all classes had fought in World War II,

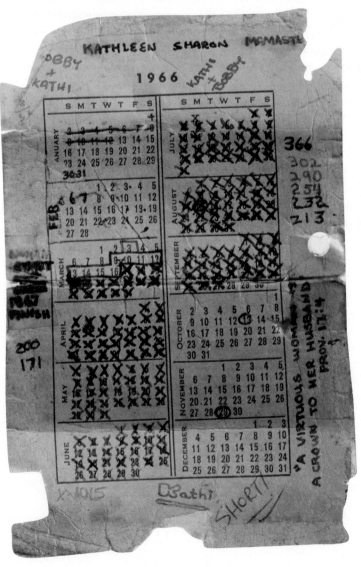

Counting the Days in Vietnam

Unlike previous wars, most soldiers served tours of duty in Vietnam lasting just one year. The soldier who carried this calendar expressed an obsession with time "in country" that many of his comrades shared. Soldiers considered themselves "short" when they had fewer than 100 days left. Bobby McMaster was thinking either of his wife or of the woman he would marry when, and if, he returned home. What might his inscription of the Bible verse on the right side of the calendar suggest about his feelings about the woman he left behind? © Bettmann/Corbis.

| Why did Johnson escalate American involvement in Vietnam? | How did the war in Vietnam polarize the nation? | How did U.S. foreign policy change under Nixon? | Conclusion: Was Vietnam an unwinnable war? | ✓ LearningCurve Check what you know. bedfordstmartins.com /roarkunderstanding |

but in Vietnam the poor and working class constituted about 80 percent of the troops. More privileged youths avoided the draft by using college deferments or family connections to get into the National Guard. Sent from Plainville, Kansas, to Vietnam in 1965, Mike Clodfelter could not recall "a single middle-class son of the town's businessmen, lawyers, doctors, or ranchers from my high school graduating class who experienced the Armageddon of our generation."

Much more than World War II, Vietnam was a men's war. Because the United States did not undergo full mobilization for Vietnam, officials did not seek women's sacrifices for the war effort. Still, between 7,500 and 10,000 women served in Vietnam, the vast majority of them nurses. Early in the war, African Americans constituted 31 percent of combat troops, often choosing the military over the meager opportunities in the civilian economy. Special forces ranger Arthur E. Woodley Jr. recalled, "The only way I could possibly make it out of the ghetto was to be the best soldier I possibly could." Death rates among black soldiers were disproportionately high until 1966, when the military adjusted personnel assignments to achieve a better racial balance.

The young troops faced extremely difficult conditions. Platoons fought in thick jungles filled with leeches, in rain and oppressive heat, always vulnerable to sniper bullets and land mines. Soldiers in previous wars had served "for the duration," but in Vietnam a soldier served a one-year tour of duty. A commander called it "the worst personnel policy in history," because men had less incentive to fight near the end of their tours, wanting merely to stay alive and whole.

American soldiers inflicted great losses on the enemy, yet the war remained a stalemate. The South Vietnamese government was an enormous obstacle to victory, as graft and corruption continued to flourish. In the intensified fighting and with the inability to distinguish friend from foe, ARVN and American troops killed and wounded thousands of South Vietnamese civilians and destroyed their villages. By 1968, nearly 30 percent of the population had become refugees. The failure to stabilize South Vietnam even as the U.S. military presence expanded enormously created grave challenges for the administration at home.

> **QUICK REVIEW**

Why did massive amounts of airpower and ground troops fail to bring U.S. victory in Vietnam?

CHAPTER LOCATOR | How did U.S. foreign policy change under Kennedy?

CHAPTER 29
880 VIETNAM AND THE END OF THE COLD WAR CONSENSUS

How did the war in Vietnam polarize the nation?

Mothers against the War

Founded in 1961 to work for nuclear disarmament, Women Strike for Peace (WSP) began to protest the Vietnam War in 1963. Identifying themselves as "concerned housewives" and mothers, members mobilized around the slogan "Not Our Sons, Not Your Sons, Not Their Sons." In February 1967, WSP held the first antiwar protest at the Pentagon. More than 2,000 women, some shown here, banged their shoes on Pentagon doors, which were locked as they approached. © Bettmann/Corbis.

SOON PRESIDENT JOHNSON was fighting a war on two fronts, as domestic opposition to the war swelled after 1965. In March 1968, torn between his domestic critics and the military's clamor for more troops, Johnson announced a halt to the bombing, a new effort at negotiations, and his decision not to pursue reelection. Throughout 1968, demonstrations, violence, and assassinations convulsed the increasingly polarized nation. Vietnam took center stage in the election, and voters narrowly favored the Republican candidate, former vice president Richard Nixon, who promised to achieve "peace with honor."

The Widening War at Home

Johnson's authorization of Operation Rolling Thunder expanded the previously quiet doubts and criticism into a mass movement against the war. In April 1965, Students for a Democratic Society (SDS) recruited 20,000 people for the first major antiwar protest in Washington, D.C. Thousands of students protested against Reserve Officers Training Corps (ROTC) programs, CIA and defense industry recruiters, and military research projects on their campuses. Environmentalists attacked the use of chemical weapons, such as the deadly Agent Orange.

Why did Johnson escalate American involvement in Vietnam?

How did the war in Vietnam polarize the nation?

How did U.S. foreign policy change under Nixon?

Conclusion: Was Vietnam an unwinnable war?

✓ **LearningCurve**
Check what you know.
bedfordstmartins.com
/roarkunderstanding

881

> CHRONOLOGY

1968
- Demonstrations against Vietnam War increase.
- Tet Offensive.
- Johnson decides not to seek a second term.
- Violence erupts near the Democratic convention in Chicago.
- Richard Nixon is elected president.

Antiwar sentiment entered society's mainstream. By 1968, media critics included the *New York Times*, the *Wall Street Journal*, *Life* magazine, and popular TV anchorman Walter Cronkite. Clergy, business people, scientists, and physicians formed their own groups to pressure Johnson to stop the bombing and start negotiations. Prominent Democratic senators urged Johnson to substitute negotiation for force.

Although the peace movement never claimed a majority of the population, it focused media attention on the war and severely limited the administration's options. The twenty-year-old consensus around Cold War foreign policy had shattered.

Many refused to serve. The World Boxing Association stripped Muhammad Ali of his heavyweight title when he refused to fight in what he called a "white man's war." More than 170,000 men gained conscientious objector status and performed nonmilitary duties at home or in Vietnam. About 60,000 fled the country to escape the draft, and more than 200,000 were accused of failing to register or of committing other draft offenses.

Opponents of the war held diverse views. Those who saw the conflict in moral terms wanted total withdrawal, claiming that their country had no right to interfere in a civil war and stressing the suffering of the Vietnamese people. A larger segment of antiwar sentiment reflected practical considerations—the belief that the war could not be won at a bearable cost. Those activists wanted Johnson to stop bombing North Vietnam and seek negotiations. Working-class people were no more antiwar than other groups, but they recognized the class dimensions of the war and the antiwar movement. A firefighter whose son had died in Vietnam said bitterly, "It's people like us who give up our sons for the country."

The antiwar movement outraged millions of Americans who supported the war. Some members of the generation who had fought against Hitler could not understand younger men's refusal to support their government. They expressed their anger at war protesters with bumper stickers that read "America: Love It or Leave It."

By 1967, the administration realized that "discontent with the war is now wide and deep." President Johnson used various means to silence critics. He equated opposition to the war with communism and assistance to the enemy. His administration deceived the public by making optimistic statements and concealing officials' doubts about the possibility of success in Vietnam. Johnson ordered the CIA to spy on peace advocates, and without the president's specific authorization, the FBI infiltrated the peace movement, disrupted its work, and spread false information about activists.

The Tet Offensive and Johnson's Move toward Peace

The year 1968 was marked by violent confrontations around the world. Protests against governments erupted from Mexico City to Paris to Tokyo, usually led by students in collaboration with workers. American society became increasingly polarized. On one side, the so-called hawks charged that the United States was fighting with one hand tied behind its back and called for intensification of the war. The doves wanted de-escalation or withdrawal. As U.S. troop strength neared half a million and military deaths approached 20,000 by the end of 1967,

CHAPTER LOCATOR | How did U.S. foreign policy change under Kennedy?

882   CHAPTER 29   VIETNAM AND THE END OF THE COLD WAR CONSENSUS most people were torn between weariness with the war and a desire to fulfill the United States' commitment. As one woman said, "I want to get out but I don't want to give up."

Grave doubts penetrated the administration itself. Secretary of Defense Robert McNamara, a principal architect of U.S. involvement, now believed that the North Vietnamese "won't quit no matter how much bombing we do." He feared for the image of the United States, "the world's greatest superpower, killing or seriously injuring 1,000 noncombatants a week, while trying to pound a tiny, backward nation into submission on an issue whose merits are hotly disputed." McNamara left the administration in early 1968 but did not publicly oppose the war.

A critical turning point came with the **Tet Offensive**. On January 30, 1968, the North Vietnamese and Vietcong launched a campaign of attacks on key cities, every major American base, and the U.S. Embassy in Saigon during Tet, the Vietnamese New Year holiday. Although the enemy lost ten times as many soldiers as ARVN and U.S. forces, Tet was psychologically devastating to the United States because it exposed the credibility gap between official statements and the war's reality. Newsman Walter Cronkite wondered, "What the hell is going on? I thought we were winning the war." The attacks created a million more South Vietnamese refugees as well as widespread destruction. Public approval of Johnson's handling of the war dropped to 26 percent.

In the aftermath of Tet, Johnson conferred with advisers in the Defense Department and an unofficial group of foreign policy experts who had been key architects of Cold War policies since the 1940s. Dean Acheson, Truman's secretary of state, summarized their conclusion: "We can no longer do the job we set out to do in the time we have left and we must begin to take steps to disengage."

On March 31, 1968, Johnson announced that the United States would sharply curtail its bombing of North Vietnam and that he was prepared to begin peace talks. He added the stunning declaration that he would not run for reelection. Thus, military strategy shifted from "Americanization" to "Vietnamization" of the war. But this was not a shift in policy. The goal remained a non-Communist South Vietnam; the United States would simply rely more heavily on the South Vietnamese to achieve it.

Negotiations began in Paris in May 1968. The United States would not agree to recognize the National Liberation Front, to a coalition government, or to American withdrawal. The North Vietnamese would agree to nothing less. Although the talks continued, so did the fighting.

Meanwhile, violence escalated at home. Protests struck two hundred college campuses in the spring of 1968. In the bloodiest action, students occupied buildings at Columbia University in New York City, condemning the university's war-related research and its treatment of African Americans. When negotiations failed, university officials called in the city police, who cleared the buildings, injuring scores of demonstrators and arresting hundreds. An ensuing student strike prematurely ended the academic year.

The Tumultuous Election of 1968

Disorder and violence also entered the election process. In June, two months after the murder of Martin Luther King Jr. and the riots that followed, Senator Robert F. Kennedy,

Tet Offensive

▶ Major campaign of attacks launched throughout South Vietnam in early 1968 by the North Vietnamese and Vietcong. A major turning point in the war, it exposed the credibility gap between official statements and the war's reality, and it shook Americans' confidence in the government.

| Why did Johnson escalate American involvement in Vietnam? | How did the war in Vietnam polarize the nation? | How did U.S. foreign policy change under Nixon? | Conclusion: Was Vietnam an unwinnable war? | ✓ LearningCurve Check what you know. bedfordstmartins.com /roarkunderstanding |

883

Protest in Chicago The worst violence surrounding the 1968 Democratic National Convention in Chicago came near the Hilton Hotel, where most of the delegates stayed. When some 3,000 protesters marching toward the convention site came up against a line of police, the police attacked not only the demonstrators but also reporters, hotel guests, and bystanders, driving a crowd through the plate-glass window of the hotel and injuring hundreds. AP Photo/Michael Boyer.

an antiwar candidate campaigning for the Democratic Party's presidential nomination, was killed by a Palestinian Arab refugee because of his support for Israel.

In August, protesters battled the police in Chicago, site of the Democratic National Convention. Several thousand demonstrators came to the city, some to support peace candidate Senator Eugene McCarthy, others to cause disruption. On August 25, when demonstrators jeered at orders to disperse, police attacked them with tear gas and clubs. Street battles continued for three days, culminating in a police riot on the night of August 28. Taunted by the crowd, the police sprayed Mace and clubbed not only those who had come to provoke violence but also reporters, peaceful demonstrators, and convention delegates.

The bloodshed in Chicago had little effect on the convention's outcome. Vice President Hubert H. Humphrey trounced McCarthy by nearly three to one for the Democratic nomination.

In contrast to the turmoil in Chicago, the Republican convention met peacefully and nominated former vice president Richard Nixon. In a bid for southern support, Nixon chose Maryland governor Spiro T. Agnew for his running mate. A strong third candidate entered the race when the American Independent Party nominated staunch segregationist George C. Wallace. The former Alabama governor appealed to Americans' dissatisfaction with the reforms and rebellions of the 1960s and their outrage at the assaults on traditional values. Nixon guardedly played on resentments that fueled the Wallace campaign, calling for "law and order" and attacking liberal Supreme Court decisions, busing for school desegregation, and protesters.

Nixon and Humphrey differed little on the central issue of Vietnam. Nixon promised "an honorable end" to the war but did not indicate how to achieve it. Humphrey had reservations about U.S. policy in Vietnam, yet as vice president he was tied to Johnson's policies. With nearly 13 percent of the total popular vote, Wallace produced the strongest third-party finish since 1924. Nixon edged out Humphrey by just half a million popular votes but won 301 electoral college votes to Humphrey's 191 and Wallace's 46. The Democrats maintained control of Congress.

The 1968 election revealed deep cracks in the coalition that had maintained Democratic dominance in Washington for the previous thirty years. Johnson's liberal policies on race shattered a century of Democratic Party rule in the South, which delivered all its electoral votes to Wallace and Nixon. Elsewhere, large numbers of blue-collar workers broke with labor's traditional alliance with the Democrats to vote for Wallace or Nixon, as did other groups that associated the Democrats with racial turmoil, poverty programs, changing sexual mores, and failure to turn the tide in Vietnam. These resentments would soon be mobilized into a resurging right in American politics (as discussed in chapter 30).

QUICK REVIEW

How did the Vietnam War shape
the election of 1968?

Why did Johnson escalate American involvement in Vietnam?

How did the war in Vietnam polarize the nation?

How did U.S. foreign policy change under Nixon?

Conclusion: Was Vietnam an unwinnable war?

LearningCurve
Check what you know.
bedfordstmartins.com
/roarkunderstanding

885

How did U.S. foreign policy change under Nixon?

Nixon in China

"This was the week that changed the world," proclaimed President Nixon in February 1972, emphasizing the stunning turnaround in relations with America's former enemy, the People's Republic of China. Nixon's trip was planned to dramatize the event on television and, aside from criticism from some conservatives, won overwhelming support from Americans. Here, Nixon and his wife, Pat, visit the Great Wall of China. Nixon Presidential Materials Project, National Archives and Record Administration.

détente

▶ Term (from the French for "loosening") given to the easing of conflict between the United States and the Soviet Union during the Nixon administration by focusing on issues of common concern, such as arms control and trade.

Helsinki accords

▶ 1975 agreement signed by U.S., Canadian, Soviet, and European leaders, recognizing the post–World War II borders in Europe and pledging the signatories to respect human rights and fundamental freedoms.

RICHARD M. NIXON TOOK office hoping to make his mark on history by applying his broad understanding of international relations to a changing world. Diverging from Republican orthodoxy, he made dramatic overtures to the Soviet Union and China. Yet anticommunism remained central to U.S. policy. Nixon backed repressive regimes around the world and aggressively pursued the war in Vietnam, despite mounting opposition to his policies. He expanded the conflict into Cambodia and Laos and ferociously bombed North Vietnam. Yet in the end, he was forced to settle for peace without victory.

Moving toward Détente with the Soviet Union and China

Nixon perceived that the "rigid and bipolar world of the 1940s and 1950s" was changing, and America's European allies were seeking to ease East-West tensions. Moreover, Nixon and his national security adviser Henry A. Kissinger believed they could exploit the increasing conflict between the Soviet Union and

CHAPTER LOCATOR | How did U.S. foreign policy change under Kennedy?

China. In addition, these two nations might be used to help the United States extricate itself from Vietnam.

In February 1972, following two years of secret negotiations, Nixon became the nation's first president to set foot on Chinese soil. Although his visit was largely symbolic, cultural and scientific exchanges followed, and American manufacturers began to find markets in China—small steps in the process of globalization that would take giant strides in the 1990s.

As Nixon and Kissinger had hoped, the warming of U.S.-Chinese relations furthered their strategy of **détente**, their term for easing conflict with the Soviet Union. Détente (from the French for "loosening") did not mean abandoning containment; instead, it focused on issues of common concern, such as arms control and trade. Containment would be achieved not just by military threat but also by ensuring that the Soviets and Chinese had stakes in a stable international order. Nixon's goal was "a stronger healthy United States, Europe, Soviet Union, China, Japan, each balancing the other."

Arms control, trade, and stability in Europe were three areas where the United States and the Soviet Union had common interests. In May 1972, Nixon visited Moscow, signing agreements on trade and cooperation in science and space. Most significantly, Soviet and U.S. leaders concluded arms limitation treaties that had grown out of the Strategic Arms Limitation Talks begun in 1969, agreeing to limit antiballistic missiles (ABMs) to two each. Giving up pursuit of a defense against nuclear weapons was a crucial move, because it denied both nations an ABM defense so secure against a nuclear attack that they would risk a first strike.

Although détente made little progress after 1974, U.S., Canadian, Soviet, and European leaders signed a historic agreement in 1975 in Helsinki, Finland, that formally recognized the post–World War II boundaries in Europe. The **Helsinki accords** were controversial because they acknowledged Soviet domination over Eastern Europe. Yet they also committed the signing countries to recognize "the universal significance of human rights and fundamental freedoms." Dissidents in the Soviet Union and its Eastern European satellites used this official promise of rights to challenge the Soviet dictatorship and help force its overthrow fifteen years later.

Shoring Up U.S. Interests around the World

Despite the thawing in U.S. relations with the Soviet Union and China, in Vietnam and elsewhere Nixon and Kissinger continued to view left-wing movements as threats to U.S. interests and actively resisted social revolutions that might lead to communism. The Nixon administration helped overthrow Salvador Allende, a self-proclaimed Marxist who was elected president of Chile in 1970. Since 1964, the CIA and U.S. corporations concerned about nationalization of their Chilean properties had assisted Allende's opponents. After Allende became president, Nixon ordered the CIA director to destabilize his government, and in 1973 the CIA helped the Chilean military engineer a coup, killing Allende and establishing a brutal dictatorship under General Augusto Pinochet.

In other parts of the world, too, the Nixon administration backed repressive regimes. In southern Africa, it eased pressures on white minority governments that tyrannized blacks. In the Middle East, the United States sent massive arms

> **CHRONOLOGY**

1970
- Nixon orders invasion of Cambodia.
- Students are killed at Kent State and Jackson State.

1971
- Portions of *Pentagon Papers* are published.

1972
- Nixon visits China.
- Nixon signs arms limitation treaties with Soviets.

1973
- Paris Peace Accords.
- CIA-backed military coup in Chile.
- Arab oil embargo following Yom Kippur War.

1975
- North Vietnam takes over South Vietnam, ending the war.
- Helsinki accords.

Chile

Why did Johnson escalate American involvement in Vietnam?

How did the war in Vietnam polarize the nation?

How did U.S. foreign policy change under Nixon?

Conclusion: Was Vietnam an unwinnable war?

☑ LearningCurve
Check what you know.
bedfordstmartins.com
/roarkunderstanding

887

Israeli Territorial Gains in the Six-Day War, 1967

- Israel before 1967
- Land gained by Israel in Six-Day War
- Land returned to Egypt, 1973–1981

Six-Day War

▶ 1967 conflict between Israel and the Arab nations of Egypt, Syria, and Jordan. Israel attacked Egypt after Egypt had massed troops on its border and cut off the sea passage to Israel's southern port. Israel won a stunning victory, seizing territory that amounted to twice its original size.

shipments to support the shah of Iran's harsh regime because Iran had enormous petroleum reserves and seemed a stable anti-Communist ally. Like his predecessors, Nixon pursued a delicate balance between defending Israel's security and seeking the goodwill of Arab nations strategically and economically important to the United States. Conflict between Israel and the Arab nations had escalated into the **Six-Day War** in 1967, when Israel attacked Egypt after Egypt had massed troops on the Israeli border and cut off sea passage to Israel's southern port. Although Syria and Jordan joined the war on Egypt's side, Israel won a stunning victory, seizing the Sinai Peninsula and Gaza Strip from Egypt, the Golan Heights from Syria, and the West Bank, where hundreds of thousands of Palestinians lived, from Jordan.

That decisive victory did not quell Middle Eastern turmoil. In October 1973, on the Jewish holiday of Yom Kippur, Egypt and Syria surprised Israel with a full-scale attack. When the Nixon administration sided with Israel, Arab nations retaliated with an oil embargo that created severe shortages in the United States. After Israel repulsed the attack, tensions remained high. The Arab countries refused to recognize Israel's right to exist, Israel began to settle its citizens in the West Bank and other territories occupied during the Six-Day War, and no solution could be found for the Palestinian refugees who had been displaced by the creation of Israel in 1948. The simmering conflict contributed to anti-American sentiment among Arabs who viewed the United States as Israel's supporter.

Vietnam Becomes Nixon's War

"I'm going to stop that war. Fast," Nixon asserted. He gradually withdrew ground troops, but he was no more willing than his predecessors to be the president who let South Vietnam fall to the Communists. That goal was tied to the larger objective of maintaining American credibility. Regardless of the wisdom of the initial intervention, Kissinger asserted, "The commitment of 500,000 Americans has settled the importance of Vietnam. For what is involved now is confidence in American promises."

From 1969 to 1972, Nixon and Kissinger pursued a three-pronged approach. First, they tried to strengthen the South Vietnamese military and government. ARVN forces grew to more than a million, and the South Vietnamese air force became the fourth largest in the world. The United States also promoted land reform, village elections, and the building of schools, hospitals, and transportation facilities. Second, Nixon gradually reduced the U.S. presence in Vietnam, a move that somewhat disarmed the antiwar movement at home. American forces decreased from 543,000 in 1968 to 140,000 by the end of 1971, although casualties remained high. Third, the United States replaced U.S. ground forces with intensive bombing. In the spring of 1969, Nixon began a ferocious air war in Cambodia, hiding it from Congress and the public for more than a year. Seeking to knock out North Vietnamese sanctuaries in Cambodia, the United States dropped more than 100,000 tons of bombs but succeeded only in sending the enemy to other hiding places. Echoing Johnson, Kissinger believed that a "fourth-rate power like North Vietnam" had to have a "breaking point," but the massive bombing failed to find it.

To support a new, pro-Western Cambodian government installed through a military coup and "to show the enemy that we were still serious about our commitment in Vietnam," Nixon ordered a joint U.S.-ARVN invasion of Cambodia in April 1970. That order made Vietnam "Nixon's war" and provoked outrage at home. Nixon made a belligerent speech emphasizing the importance of U.S. credibility: "If when the chips are down, the world's most powerful nation acts like a pitiful helpless giant, the forces of totalitarianism and anarchy will threaten free nations" everywhere.

In response, more than 100,000 people protested in Washington, D.C., and students boycotted classes on hundreds of campuses. At a rally on May 4 at Kent State University in Ohio, National Guard troops opened fire after students threw rocks at them, killing four and wounding ten others. "They're starting to treat their own children like they treat us," commented a black woman in Harlem. In a confrontation at Jackson State College in Mississippi on May 14, police shot into a dormitory, killing two black students.

Congressional reaction to the invasion of Cambodia revealed increasing concern about abuses of presidential power. In the name of national security, presidents since Franklin Roosevelt had conducted foreign policy without the consent or sometimes even the knowledge of Congress—for example, Eisenhower in Iran and Johnson in the Dominican Republic. But in their determination to win the war in Vietnam, Johnson and Nixon had taken extreme measures to deceive the public and silence their critics. The bombing and invasion of Cambodia infuriated enough legislators that the Senate voted to terminate the Gulf of Tonkin Resolution, which had given the president virtually a blank check in Vietnam, and to cut off funds for the Cambodian operation. The House refused to go along, but by the end of June 1970 Nixon had pulled all U.S. troops out of Cambodia.

In 1971, Vietnam veterans became a visible part of the peace movement, the first men in U.S. history to protest a war in which they had fought. They held a public investigation of "war crimes" in Vietnam, rallied in front of the Capitol, and cast away their war medals. In May 1971, veterans numbered among the 40,000 protesters who engaged in civil disobedience in an effort to shut down Washington.

U.S. Invasion of Cambodia, 1970

Pro-War Demonstrators

Supporters as well as opponents of the war in Vietnam took to the streets, as these New Yorkers did in support of the U.S. invasion of Cambodia in May 1970. Construction workers — called "hard hats" — and other union members marched with American flags and posters championing President Nixon's policies and blasting New York mayor John Lindsay for his antiwar position. Paul Fusco/Magnum Photos, Inc.

> VISUAL ACTIVITY

READING THE IMAGE: What do the hard hats in the photograph symbolize in terms of identity and politics?

CONNECTIONS: How were these union members related to the unraveling of the Democratic Party coalition?

| Why did Johnson escalate American involvement in Vietnam? | How did the war in Vietnam polarize the nation? | **How did U.S. foreign policy change under Nixon?** | Conclusion: Was Vietnam an unwinnable war? | ✓ LearningCurve Check what you know. bedfordstmartins.com /roarkunderstanding |

889

Officials made more than 12,000 arrests, which courts later ruled violations of protesters' rights.

After the spring of 1971, there were fewer massive antiwar demonstrations, but protest continued. Public attention focused on the court-martial of Lieutenant William Calley, which began in November 1970. During the trial, Americans learned that in March 1968 Calley's company had killed every inhabitant of the hamlet of My Lai, even though it had encountered no enemy forces and the four hundred villagers were nearly all old men, women, and children. The military covered up the atrocity for more than a year before a journalist exposed it. Eventually, twelve officers and enlisted men were charged with murder or assault, but only Calley was convicted.

Administration policy suffered another blow in June 1971 when the *New York Times* published portions of the **Pentagon Papers**, a secret internal study of the war begun in 1967. Nixon sent government lawyers to court to stop further publication, in part out of fear that other information would be leaked. The Supreme Court, however, ruled that suppression of the publication violated the First Amendment. Subsequent circulation of the *Pentagon Papers*, which revealed pessimism among officials even as they made rosy promises, heightened disillusionment with the war by casting doubts on the government's credibility. More than 60 percent of Americans polled in 1971 considered it a mistake to have sent American troops to Vietnam; 58 percent believed the war to be immoral.

Military morale sank in the last years of the war. Having been exposed to the antiwar movement at home, many of the remaining soldiers had less faith in the war than their predecessors had had. Racial tensions among soldiers mounted, many soldiers sought escape in illegal drugs, and enlisted men committed hundreds of "fraggings," attacks on officers. In a 1971 report, "The Collapse of the Armed Forces," a retired Marine Corps colonel described the lack of discipline: "Our army that now remains in Vietnam [is] near mutinous."

The Peace Accords

Nixon and Kissinger continued to believe that intensive firepower could bring the North Vietnamese to their knees. In March 1972, responding to a North Vietnamese offensive, the United States resumed sustained bombing of the North, mined Haiphong and other harbors for the first time, and announced a naval blockade. With peace talks stalled, in December Nixon ordered the most devastating bombing yet. Though costly to both sides, it brought renewed negotiations. On January 27, 1973, representatives of the United States, North Vietnam, South Vietnam, and the Vietcong (now called the Provisional Revolutionary Government) signed a formal peace accord in Paris. The agreement required removal of all U.S. troops and military advisers from South Vietnam but allowed North Vietnamese forces to remain. Both sides agreed to return prisoners of war. Nixon called the agreement "peace with honor," but in fact it allowed only a face-saving withdrawal.

Fighting resumed immediately among the Vietnamese. Nixon's efforts to support the South Vietnamese government, and indeed his ability to govern at all, were increasingly eroded by what came to be known as the Watergate scandal, which forced him to resign in 1974 (as discussed in chapter 30). In 1975, North Vietnam launched a new offensive, seizing Saigon on April 30. The Americans

Pentagon Papers

▶ Secret government documents published in 1971 containing an internal study of the Vietnam War. The documents further disillusioned the public by revealing that officials harbored pessimism about the war even as they made rosy public pronouncements about its progress.

hastily evacuated, along with 150,000 of their South Vietnamese allies. Confusion, humiliation, and tragedy marked the rushed departure. The United States lacked sufficient transportation capabilities and time to evacuate all those who had supported the South Vietnamese government and were desperate to leave. A journalist reported that his departing helicopter "took some ground fire from South Vietnamese soldiers who probably felt that the Americans had betrayed them."

During the four years it took Nixon to end the war, he had expanded the conflict into Cambodia and Laos and launched massive bombing campaigns. Although increasing numbers of legislators criticized the war, Congress never denied the funds to fight it. Only after the peace accords did the legislative branch try to reassert its constitutional authority in the making of war. The War Powers Act of 1973 required the president to secure congressional approval for any substantial, long-term deployment of troops abroad. The new law, however, did little to dispel the distrust of and disillusionment with the government that resulted from Americans' realization that their leaders had not told the truth about Vietnam.

The Legacy of Defeat

Antigovernment sentiment was just one of the war's legacies. It left bitter divisions among Americans, diverted money from domestic programs, and sounded the death knell for Johnson's Great Society. The war created federal budget deficits and triggered inflation that contributed to ongoing economic crises throughout the 1970s (as discussed in chapter 30).

Four presidents had declared that the survival of South Vietnam was essential for U.S. containment policy, but their predictions that a Communist victory in South Vietnam would set the dominoes cascading did not materialize. Although Vietnam, Laos, and Cambodia all fell within the Communist camp in the spring of 1975, the rest of Southeast Asia did not. When China and Vietnam reverted to their historically hostile relationship, the myth of a monolithic Communist power overrunning Asia evaporated.

The long pursuit of victory in Vietnam complicated the United States' relations with other nations, as even its staunchest ally, Britain, doubted the wisdom of the war. The use of terrifying American power against a small Asian country compromised efforts to win the hearts and minds of people in developing nations.

The cruelest legacy of Vietnam fell on those who had served. "The general public just wanted to ignore us," remembered Frederick Downs, while opponents of the war "wanted to argue with us until we felt guilty about what we had done over there." Many veterans believed in the war's purposes and felt betrayed by the government for not letting them win it. Other veterans blamed the government for sacrificing the nation's youth in an immoral, unnecessary war, expressing their sense of the war's futility by referring to their dead comrades as having been "wasted." Some veterans belonging to minority groups had more reason to doubt the nobility of their purpose. A Native American soldier assigned to resettle Vietnamese civilians found it to be "just like when they moved us to the rez [reservation]. We shouldn't have done that."

Evacuating South Vietnam

As Communist troops rolled south toward Saigon in the spring of 1975, desperate South Vietnamese attempted to flee along with the departing Americans. These South Vietnamese, carrying little or nothing, attempt to scale the wall of the U.S. Embassy to reach evacuation helicopters. Thousands of Vietnamese who wanted to be evacuated were left behind. Even though space for evacuees was desperately limited, South Vietnamese president Nguyen Van Thieu fled to Taiwan on a U.S. plane, taking with him fifteen tons of baggage. AP Images.

| Why did Johnson escalate American involvement in Vietnam? | How did the war in Vietnam polarize the nation? | How did U.S. foreign policy change under Nixon? | Conclusion: Was Vietnam an unwinnable war? | ✔ LearningCurve Check what you know. bedfordstmartins.com /roarkunderstanding |

891

TABLE 29.1 ■ Vietnam War Casualties

United States	
Battle deaths	47,434
Other deaths	10,786
Wounded	153,303
South Vietnam	
Killed in action	110,357
Military wounded	499,026
Civilians killed	415,000
Civilians wounded	913,000
Communist Regulars and Guerrillas	
Killed in action	66,000

Source: U.S. Department of Defense.

Because the Vietnam War was a civil war involving guerrilla tactics, combat was especially brutal (**Table 29.1**). The terrors of conventional warfare were multiplied, and so were the motivations to commit atrocities. The 1968 massacre at My Lai was only the most widely publicized war crime. To demonstrate the immorality of the war, peace advocates stressed the atrocities, contributing to a distorted image of the Vietnam veteran as dehumanized and violent.

Most veterans came home to public neglect. Government benefits were less generous to Vietnam veterans than they had been to those of the previous two wars. While two-thirds of Vietnam veterans said that they would serve again, and while most veterans readjusted well to civilian life, some suffered long after the war ended. The Veterans Administration estimated that nearly one-sixth of the veterans suffered from post-traumatic stress disorder, experiencing recurring nightmares, feelings of guilt and shame, violence, substance abuse, and suicidal tendencies. Thirty years after performing army intelligence work in Saigon, Doris Allen "still hit the floor sometimes when [she heard] loud bangs." Some who had served in Vietnam began to report birth defects, cancer, severe skin disorders, and other ailments. Veterans claimed a link between those illnesses and Agent Orange, which had exposed many to the deadly poison dioxin in Vietnam. In 1991, Congress began to provide assistance to veterans with diseases linked to the poison.

By then, the climate had changed. The war began to enter the realm of popular culture, with novels, TV shows, and hit movies depicting a broad range of military experience—from soldiers reduced to brutality, to men and women serving with courage and integrity. The incorporation of the Vietnam War into the collective experience was symbolized most dramatically in the Vietnam Veterans Memorial unveiled in Washington, D.C., in November 1982. Designed by Yale architecture student Maya Lin, the black, V-shaped wall inscribed with the names of 58,200 men and women lost in the war became one of the most popular sites in the nation's capital. In an article describing the memorial's dedication, a Vietnam combat veteran spoke to and for his former comrades: "Welcome home. The war is over."

> QUICK REVIEW

What strategies did Nixon implement to bring American involvement in Vietnam to a close?

CHAPTER LOCATOR | How did U.S. foreign policy change under Kennedy?

CHAPTER 29
892 VIETNAM AND THE END OF THE COLD WAR CONSENSUS

THE UNITED STATES SPENT $111 billion (more than $600 billion in 2013 dollars) and sent 2.6 million men and women to Vietnam. Of those, 58,200 never returned, and 150,000 suffered serious injury. The war shattered consensus at home, increased presidential power at the expense of congressional authority and public accountability, weakened the economy, and contributed to the downfall of two presidents.

Even as Nixon and Kissinger took steps to ease Cold War tensions with the major Communist powers—the Soviet Union and China—they also acted vigorously throughout the third world to install or prop up anti-Communist governments. They embraced their predecessors' commitment to South Vietnam as a necessary Cold War engagement: To do otherwise would threaten American credibility and make the United States appear weak. Defeat in Vietnam did not make the United States the "pitiful helpless giant" predicted by Nixon, but it did mark a relative decline of U.S. power and the impossibility of containment on a global scale.

One of the constraints on U.S. power was the tenacity of revolutionary movements determined to achieve national independence. Overestimating the effectiveness of American technological superiority, U.S. officials badly underestimated the sacrifices that the enemy was willing to make and failed to realize how easily the United States could be perceived as a colonial intruder. A second constraint on Eisenhower, Kennedy, Johnson, and Nixon was their resolve to avoid a major confrontation with the Soviet Union or China. For Johnson, who conducted the largest escalation of the war, caution was critical so as not to provoke direct intervention by the Communist superpowers. After China exploded its first atomic bomb in 1964, the potential heightened for the Vietnam conflict to escalate into worldwide disaster.

Third, in Vietnam the United States sought to prop up an extremely weak ally engaged in a civil war. The South Vietnamese government failed to win the support of its people, and the intense devastation the war brought to civilians only made things worse. Short of taking over the South Vietnamese government and military, the United States could do little to strengthen South Vietnam's ability to resist communism.

Finally, domestic opposition to the war, which by 1968 had spread to mainstream America, constrained the options of Johnson and Nixon. As the war dragged on, with increasing American casualties and growing evidence of the damage being inflicted on innocent Vietnamese, more and more civilians wearied of the conflict. Even some who had fought in the war joined the peace movement, sending their military ribbons and bitter letters of protest to the White House. In 1973, Nixon and Kissinger bowed to the resoluteness of the enemy and the limitations of U.S. power. As the war wound down, passions surrounding it contributed to a rising conservative movement that would substantially alter the post–World War II political order.

Why did Johnson escalate American involvement in Vietnam? | How did the war in Vietnam polarize the nation? | How did U.S. foreign policy change under Nixon? | **Conclusion: Was Vietnam an unwinnable war?** | ✔ **LearningCurve** Check what you know. bedfordstmartins.com /roarkunderstanding

893

CHAPTER 29 STUDY GUIDE

STEP 1

GET STARTED ONLINE

✓ LearningCurve ■ bedfordstmartins.com/roarkunderstanding

Now that you've read the chapter, make it stick by completing the LearningCurve activity.

STEP 2

EXPLAIN WHY IT MATTERS

Put your reading into practice. Identify each term below, and then explain why it matters in U.S. history.

TERM	WHO OR WHAT & WHEN	WHY IT MATTERS
Bay of Pigs (p. 872)		
Apollo program (p. 872)		
Berlin Wall (p. 872)		
Peace Corps (p. 872)		
Cuban missile crisis (p. 873)		
Agent Orange (p. 875)		
Gulf of Tonkin Resolution (p. 877)		
Tet Offensive (p. 883)		
détente (p. 886)		
Helsinki accords (p. 886)		
Six-Day War (p. 888)		
Pentagon Papers (p. 890)		

STEP 3

MOVE BEYOND THE BASICS

To demonstrate a more advanced understanding, describe the key American policy decisions regarding Vietnam between 1961 and 1974 and explain the rationale and impact of each decision. How was U.S. involvement in Vietnam shaped by policymakers' larger vision of global politics?

	Policy decision	Rationale	Impact
Kennedy administration			
Johnson administration			
Nixon administration			

PUT IT ALL TOGETHER

Now, take a step back and try to explain the big picture. Remember to use specific examples from the chapter in your answers.

KENNEDY'S FOREIGN POLICY

▶ How did Kennedy's view of America's place in the world affect his foreign policy decisions in 1961 and 1962?

▶ How were Kennedy's decisions with respect to Vietnam shaped by the Cold War?

JOHNSON AND VIETNAM

▶ Why did Lyndon Johnson disregard some of his advisers who urged him to disengage from Vietnam?

▶ How did the divisions over Vietnam contribute to Nixon's election in 1968?

NIXON'S FOREIGN POLICY

▶ What impact did Nixon's strategies in Vietnam have on the United States?

▶ How did Nixon's approach to foreign policy differ from that of his predecessors?

LOOKING BACKWARD, LOOKING AHEAD

▶ How did American foreign policy in the 1950s set the stage for the escalation of U.S. involvement in Vietnam in the 1960s?

▶ How did American foreign policy change between 1961 and 1975? What impact did the Vietnam conflict have on these changes?

> ## IN YOUR OWN WORDS

Imagine that you must give an oral report to the class answering the following question: **Why was the United States unable to achieve its objectives in Vietnam?** What would be the most important points to include and why?

30

THE CONSERVATIVE TURN

1969–1989

> **What were the effects of America's move to the political right on American society and on U.S. foreign policy?** Chapter 30 explores the rise of conservatism as a major force in late-twentieth-century American politics. It examines the emergence of new strands of conservatism in the 1960s, the evolution of conservatism in the post-Watergate years, and its full expression in the politics and policies of Ronald Reagan.

LearningCurve

bedfordstmartins.com/roarkunderstanding
After reading the chapter, use LearningCurve to
retain what you've read.

> How did the Nixon presidency reflect the rise of postwar conservatism?

> Why did the "outsider" presidency of Jimmy Carter fail to gain broad support?

> What conservative goals were realized in the Reagan administration?

> What strategies did liberals use to fight the conservative turn?

> How did Ronald Reagan's foreign policy affect the Cold War?

> Conclusion: What was the long-term impact of the conservative turn?

Inauguration of Ronald Reagan, 1981. Chief Justice Warren Burger administers the oath of office to President Ronald Reagan. Dirck Halstead/Getty Images.

How did the Nixon presidency reflect the rise of postwar conservatism?

School Busing Controversy over busing as a means to integrate public schools erupted in Boston when the 1974–1975 school year started. Opposition was especially high in white ethnic neighborhoods such as South Boston. Residents there resented liberal judges from the suburbs assigning them the burden of integration. Clashes between blacks and whites in Boston, such as this one in February 1975 outside Boston's Hyde Park High School, prompted authorities to dispatch police to protect black students. AP/Wide World.

RICHARD NIXON ACQUIESCED IN CONTINUING most Great Society programs and even approved pathbreaking environmental, minority, and women's rights measures. Yet his public rhetoric and some of his actions signaled the country's rightward move. Whereas Kennedy had appealed to Americans to contribute to the common good, Nixon invited Americans to "ask—not just what will government do for me, but what can I do for myself?" His words invoked individualism and reliance on private enterprise rather than on government, preferences that would grow stronger in the nation during the 1970s and beyond, as a new strand of conservatism joined the older movement that focused on anticommunism, a strong national defense, and a limited federal role in domestic affairs. New conservatives wanted to restore what they considered traditional moral values.

Just two years after Nixon won reelection by a huge margin, his abuse of power and efforts to cover up crimes committed by subordinates, revealed in the so-called Watergate scandal, forced the first presidential resignation in history. His successor, Gerald Ford, faced the aftermath of Watergate and severe economic problems, which returned the White House to the Democrats in 1976.

Emergence of a Grassroots Movement

Hidden beneath Lyndon Johnson's landslide victory over Arizona senator Barry Goldwater in 1964 lay a rising conservative movement. Defining his purpose as

CHAPTER LOCATOR | **How did the Nixon presidency reflect the rise of postwar conservatism?** | Why did the "outsider" presidency of Jimmy Carter fail to gain broad support?

"enlarging freedom at home and safeguarding it from the forces of tyranny abroad," Goldwater argued that government intrusions into economic life hindered prosperity, stifled personal responsibility, and interfered with individuals' rights to determine their own values. Conservatives assailed big government in domestic affairs but demanded a strong military to eradicate "Godless communism."

The grassroots movement supporting Goldwater's nomination was especially vigorous in the South and West, and it included middle-class suburban women and men, members of the rabidly anti-Communist John Birch Society, and college students in the new Young Americans for Freedom. A number of Sun Belt characteristics made this movement strong in places such as Orange County, California; Dallas, Texas; and Scottsdale, Arizona. Such predominantly white areas contained relatively homogeneous, skilled, and economically comfortable populations, as well as military bases and defense production facilities. The West harbored a long-standing tradition of Protestant morality, individualism, and opposition to interference by a remote federal government. That tradition continued with the emergence of the New Right, even though it was hardly consistent with the Sun Belt's economic dependence on defense spending and on huge federal projects providing water and power for the burgeoning region.

The South, which also benefited from military bases and the space program, shared the West's antipathy toward the federal government. Hostility to racial change, however, was much more central to the South's conservatism. After signing the Civil Rights Act of 1964, President Lyndon Johnson remarked privately, "I think we just delivered the South to the Republican Party." Indeed, Barry Goldwater carried five southern states in 1964.

Grassroots movements proliferated around what conservatives believed marked the "moral decline" of their nation. For example, in 1962 Mel and Norma Gabler got the Texas board of education to drop books that they believed undermined "the Christian-Judeo morals, values, and standards as given to us by God through . . . the Bible." Sex education roused the ire of Eleanor Howe in Anaheim, California, who felt that "nothing [in the sex education curriculum] depicted my values. . . . It wasn't so much the information. It was the shift in values." The Supreme Court's liberal decisions on school prayer, obscenity, and abortion also galvanized conservatives to restore "traditional values."

In the 1970s, grassroots protests against taxes grew alongside concerns about morality. As Americans struggled with inflation and unemployment, many found themselves

The Tax Revolt

Neighbors gather in Los Angeles to rally for Proposition 13, an initiative launched by conservative Howard Jarvis in 1978. Many homeowners rallied to Jarvis's antitax movement because rising land values had increased their property taxes sharply. After Californians passed Proposition 13, some thirty-seven states cut property taxes, and twenty-eight reduced income taxes. The tax issue helped the Republican Party end decades of Democratic dominance. Tony Korody/Getty Images.

What conservative goals were realized in the Reagan administration?

What strategies did liberals use to fight the conservative turn?

How did Ronald Reagan's foreign policy affect the Cold War?

Conclusion: What was the long-term impact of the conservative turn?

LearningCurve
Check what you know.
bedfordstmartins.com /roarkunderstanding

Percent of black students statewide
attending schools more than 50% white

▨	60% or more	▨	30–40%
▨	50–60%	▨	20–30%
▨	40–50%	▨	20% or less

Integration of Public Schools, 1968

paying higher taxes, especially higher property taxes as the value of their homes increased. In 1978, Californians revolted in a popular referendum, reducing property taxes by more than one-half and limiting the state legislature's ability to raise taxes. What a newspaper called a "primal scream by the People against Big Government" spread to other states.

Nixon Courts the Right

In his 1968 campaign, Richard Nixon exploited hostility to black protest and new civil rights policies, wooing white southerners and a considerable number of northern voters away from the Democratic Party. As president, he used this "southern strategy" to make further inroads into traditional Democratic strongholds in the 1972 election.

Nixon reluctantly enforced court orders to achieve high degrees of integration in southern schools, but he resisted efforts to deal with segregation outside the South. In northern and western cities, where segregation resulted from discrimination in housing and in the drawing of school district boundaries, half of all African American children attended nearly all-black schools. After courts began to order the transfer of students between schools in white and black neighborhoods to achieve desegregation, busing became a hot-button issue. "We've had all we can take of judicial interference with local schools," conservative spokeswoman Phyllis Schlafly railed in 1972.

Children had been riding buses to school for decades, but busing for racial integration provoked fury. Violence erupted in Boston in 1974 when a district judge found that school officials had maintained what amounted to a dual system based on race and ordered busing "if necessary to achieve a unitary school system." The whites most affected by busing came from working-class families left in cities abandoned by the more affluent and whose children often rode buses to predominantly black, overcrowded schools with deficient facilities. Clarence McDonough denounced the liberal officials who bused his "kid half way around Boston so that a bunch of politicians can end up their careers with a clear conscience." African Americans themselves were conflicted about sending their children on long rides to schools where white teachers might not welcome or respect them.

Whites eventually became more accepting of integration, especially after the creation of schools with specialized programs and other new mechanisms for desegregation offered greater choice. Nonetheless, integration propelled white flight to the suburbs. Nixon failed to persuade Congress to end court-ordered busing, but after he had appointed four new justices, the Supreme Court imposed strict limits on the use of that tool to achieve racial balance.

Nixon's judicial appointments also reflected the southern strategy. He criticized the Supreme Court under Chief Justice Earl Warren for being "unprecedentedly politically active . . . using their interpretation of the law to remake American society according to their own social, political, and ideological precepts." When Warren resigned in 1969, Nixon replaced him with Warren E. Burger, a federal appeals court judge who was a strict constructionist, inclined to interpret the Constitution narrowly and to limit government intervention on behalf of individual rights. The Burger Court restricted somewhat the protections of individual rights established by its predecessor, but it upheld many of the liberal programs of the 1960s. For

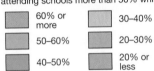

> CHRONOLOGY

1968
– Richard Nixon is elected president.

1969
– Warren E. Burger is appointed chief justice of Supreme Court.

1971
– Nixon vetoes child care bill.

1972
– Nixon campaign aides are arrested at Watergate.
– Nixon is reelected president.

1974
– Nixon resigns; Gerald Ford becomes president.
– Ford pardons Nixon.

1976
– Jimmy Carter is elected president.

1978
– *Regents of University of California v. Bakke.*

CHAPTER LOCATOR | **How did the Nixon presidency reflect the rise of postwar conservatism?** | Why did the "outsider" presidency of Jimmy Carter fail to gain broad support?

example, *Regents of the University of California v. Bakke* (1978) limited the range of affirmative action but allowed universities to attack the results of past discrimination if they avoided strict quotas and racial classifications.

Nixon's southern strategy and other repercussions of the civil rights revolution of the 1960s ended the Democratic hold on the "solid South." Beginning in 1964, a number of conservative southern Democrats changed their party affiliation, and by 2005 Republicans held the majority of southern seats in Congress and governorships in seven southern states.

In addition to exploiting racial fears, Nixon appealed to anxieties about women's changing roles and new demands. In 1971, he vetoed a bill providing federal funds for day care centers with a message that combined the old and new conservatism. Parents should purchase child care services "in the private, open market," he insisted, not rely on government. He appealed to social conservatives by warning about the measure's "family-weakening implications." In response to the movement to liberalize abortion laws, Nixon sided with "defenders of the right to life of the unborn," anticipating the Republican Party's eventual embrace of the issue.

The Election of 1972

Nixon's ability to attract Democrats and appeal to concerns about Vietnam, race, law and order, and traditional morality heightened his prospects for reelection in 1972. Although the war in Vietnam continued, antiwar protests diminished with the decrease in American ground forces and casualties. Nixon's economic initiatives had temporarily checked inflation and unemployment (see chapter 28), and his attacks on busing and antiwar protesters had won increasing support from the right.

A large field of contenders vied for the Democratic nomination, including New York congresswoman Shirley Chisholm, the first African American to make a serious bid for the presidency. South Dakota senator George S. McGovern came to the Democratic convention as the clear leader and was easily nominated, but he struggled against Nixon from the outset. Republicans portrayed McGovern as a left-wing extremist, and his support for busing, a generous welfare program, and immediate withdrawal from Vietnam alienated conservative Democrats.

Nixon achieved a landslide victory, winning 60.7 percent of the popular vote and every state except Massachusetts. Although the Democrats maintained control of Congress, Nixon won majorities among traditional Democrats — southerners, Catholics, urbanites, and blue-collar workers. The president, however, had little time to savor his triumph, as revelations began to emerge about crimes committed to ensure the victory.

Watergate

During the early-morning hours of June 17, 1972, five men working for Nixon's reelection crept into Democratic Party headquarters in the Watergate complex in Washington, D.C. Intending to repair a bugging device installed in an earlier break-in, they were discovered and arrested. Nixon and his aides then tried to cover up the intruders' connection to administration officials, setting in motion the scandal reporters dubbed **Watergate**.

Nixon was not the first president to lie to the public or to misuse power. Every president since Franklin D. Roosevelt had enlarged the powers of his office

Watergate
▶ Term referring to the 1972 break-in at Democratic Party headquarters in the Watergate complex in Washington, D.C., by men working for President Nixon's reelection, along with Nixon's efforts to cover it up. The Watergate scandal led to President Nixon's resignation.

What conservative goals were realized in the Reagan administration?

What strategies did liberals use to fight the conservative turn?

How did Ronald Reagan's foreign policy affect the Cold War?

Conclusion: What was the long-term impact of the conservative turn?

☑ **LearningCurve**
Check what you know.
bedfordstmartins.com
/roarkunderstanding

in the name of national security. This expansion of executive powers, often called the "imperial presidency," weakened the traditional checks and balances on the executive branch and opened the door to abuses. No president, however, had dared go as far as Nixon, who saw opposition to his policies as a personal attack and was willing to violate the Constitution to stop it.

Upon learning of the Watergate arrests, Nixon plotted to conceal links between the burglars and the White House, while publicly denying any connection. In April 1973, after investigations by a grand jury and the Senate suggested that White House aides had been involved in the cover-up effort, Nixon accepted official responsibility for Watergate but denied any knowledge of the break-in or cover-up. He also announced the resignations of three White House aides and the attorney general. In May, he authorized the appointment of an independent special prosecutor, Archibald Cox, to conduct an investigation.

Meanwhile, speaking before a Senate investigating committee, headed by Democrat Samuel J. Ervin of North Carolina, White House counsel John Dean described projects to harass "enemies" through tax audits and other illegal means and implicated the president in efforts to cover up the Watergate break-in. Another White House aide struck the decisive blow when he disclosed that all conversations in the Oval Office were taped. Both Cox and Ervin immediately asked for the tapes related to Watergate. When Nixon refused, citing executive privilege and separation of powers, Cox and Ervin won a unanimous decision from the Supreme Court ordering him to release the tapes.

Additional disclosures exposed Nixon's misuse of federal funds and tax evasion. In August 1973, Vice President Spiro Agnew resigned after an investigation revealed that he had taken bribes while governor of Maryland. Nixon's choice of House minority leader Gerald Ford of Michigan to succeed Agnew won widespread approval, but Agnew's resignation further tarnished the administration, and Nixon's popular support plummeted.

In February 1974, the House of Representatives voted to begin an impeachment investigation. In April, Nixon began to release edited transcripts of the tapes. The transcripts revealed Nixon's orders to aides in March 1973: "I don't give a shit what happens. I want you all to stonewall it, let them plead the Fifth Amendment, cover up or anything else, if it'll save it—save the plan." House Republican leader Hugh Scott of Pennsylvania called the documents a "deplorable, shabby, disgusting, and immoral performance by all."

In July 1974, the House Judiciary Committee voted to impeach the president on three counts: obstruction of justice, abuse of power, and contempt of Congress. Seven or eight Republicans on the committee sided with the majority, and it seemed certain that the House would follow suit. Georgia state legislator and civil rights activist Julian Bond commented, "The prisons of Georgia are full of people who stole $5 or $10, and this man tried to steal the Constitution."

To avoid impeachment, Nixon announced his resignation to a national television audience on August 8, 1974. Acknowledging some incorrect judgments, he insisted that he had always tried to do what was best for the nation. The next morning, Nixon ended a rambling, emotional farewell to his staff with some advice: "Always give your best, never get discouraged, never get petty; always remember, others may hate you, but those who hate you don't win unless you hate them, and then you destroy yourself."

CHAPTER LOCATOR | How did the Nixon presidency reflect the rise of postwar conservatism? | Why did the "outsider" presidency of Jimmy Carter fail to gain broad support?

CHAPTER 30
902　THE CONSERVATIVE TURN

The first U.S. president to resign, Richard Nixon refused to admit guilt, even though tapes of his conversations indicated that he had obstructed justice, abused his power, and lied. In the decades after his resignation, he gradually rehabilitated his reputation and became an elder statesman. Here, he and his wife, Pat, are escorted by his successor, Gerald Ford, and his wife, Betty, as they leave the White House. © Bettmann/Corbis.

The Ford Presidency and the 1976 Election

Upon taking office, Gerald R. Ford announced, "Our long national nightmare is over." But he shocked many Americans one month later by granting Nixon a pardon "for all offenses against the United States which he . . . has committed or may have committed or taken part in" during his presidency. Prompted by Ford's concern for Nixon's health and by his hope to get the country beyond Watergate, this sweeping pardon saved Nixon from nearly certain indictment and trial, and it provoked a tremendous outcry from Congress and the public. Democrats made impressive gains in the November congressional elections, while Ford's action gave Nixon a new political life. Without having to admit that he had violated the law, Nixon rebuilt his image over the next two decades into that of an elder statesman. Thirty of his associates ultimately pleaded guilty to or were convicted of crimes related to Watergate.

Congress's efforts to guard against the types of abuses revealed in the Watergate investigations had only limited effects. The Federal Election Campaign Act of 1974 established public financing of presidential campaigns and imposed some restrictions on contributions to curtail the selling of political favors. Yet politicians found other ways of raising money—for example, through political action committees (PACs), to which individuals could contribute more than they could to candidates. Moreover, the Supreme Court struck down limitations on campaign spending as violations of freedom of speech. Ever-larger campaign donations flowed to candidates from interest groups, corporations, labor unions, and wealthy individuals.

Congressional investigating committees discovered a host of illegal FBI and CIA activities stretching back to the 1950s, including harassment of political dissenters and plots to assassinate Fidel Castro and other foreign leaders. In response to these revelations, President Ford established new controls on covert operations, and Congress created permanent committees to oversee the

What conservative goals were realized in the Reagan administration?   What strategies did liberals use to fight the conservative turn?   How did Ronald Reagan's foreign policy affect the Cold War?   Conclusion: What was the long-term impact of the conservative turn?

✓ LearningCurve Check what you know. bedfordstmartins.com /roarkunderstanding

intelligence agencies. Yet these measures did little to diminish the public's cynicism about their government.

Disillusionment grew as the Ford administration struggled with serious economic problems: a low growth rate, high unemployment, a foreign trade deficit, and soaring energy prices. Ford carried these burdens into the election campaign of 1976, while contending with a major challenge from the Republican right. Blasting Nixon's and Ford's foreign policy of détente for causing the "loss of U.S. military supremacy," California governor Ronald Reagan came close to capturing the nomination.

The Democrats nominated James Earl "Jimmy" Carter Jr., former governor of Georgia. A graduate of the U.S. Naval Academy, Carter spent seven years as a nuclear engineer in the navy before returning to Plains, Georgia, to run the family peanut farming business. Carter stressed his faith as a "born-again Christian" and his distance from the government in Washington. Although he selected liberal senator Walter F. Mondale of Minnesota as his running mate, Carter's nomination nonetheless marked a rightward turn in the party.

Carter had considerable appeal as a candidate who carried his own bags, lived modestly, and taught a Bible class at his Baptist church. He also benefited from Ford's failure to solve the country's economic problems, which helped him win the traditional Democratic coalition of blacks, organized labor, and ethnic groups and even recapture some of the white southerners who had voted for Nixon in 1972. Still, on election day, Carter received just 50 percent of the popular vote to Ford's 48 percent, while Democrats retained substantial margins in Congress.

> **QUICK REVIEW**

How did Nixon's policies reflect the increasing influence
of conservatives on the Republican Party?

CHAPTER LOCATOR | How did the Nixon presidency reflect the rise of postwar conservatism? | Why did the "outsider" presidency of Jimmy Carter fail to gain broad support?

CHAPTER 30
904 THE CONSERVATIVE TURN

Jimmy Carter Honors Martin Luther King Jr.

On January 14, 1979, the day before the anniversary of King's birthday, President Carter and his wife, Rosalyn, worshipped at Ebenezer Baptist Church in Atlanta, Georgia, where both King and his father had been pastors. Carter had been pushing to establish King's birthday as a national holiday, but Congress did not enact such a law until 1983. Jimmy Carter Presidential Library.

JIMMY CARTER PROMISED a government that was "competent" as well as "decent, open, fair, and compassionate." He also warned Americans "that even our great Nation has its recognized limits, and that we can neither answer all questions nor solve all problems." Carter's humility and personal integrity helped revive trust in the presidency, but he faltered in the face of domestic and foreign crises.

Energy shortages and stagflation worsened, exposing Carter's deficiencies in working with Congress and in rallying public opinion. He achieved notable advances in environmental and energy policies, and he oversaw foreign policy successes concerning the Panama Canal, China, and the Middle East. Yet near the end of his term, Soviet-American relations deteriorated, new crises emerged in the Middle East, and the economy plummeted.

Retreat from Liberalism

Jimmy Carter vowed "to help the poor and aged, to improve education, and to provide jobs," but at the same time "not to waste money." When these goals conflicted, reform took second place to budget balancing. Carter's approach pleased Americans unhappy about their tax dollars being used to benefit the

What conservative goals were realized in the Reagan administration?

What strategies did liberals use to fight the conservative turn?

How did Ronald Reagan's foreign policy affect the Cold War?

Conclusion: What was the long-term impact of the conservative turn?

✔ **LearningCurve**
Check what you know.
bedfordstmartins.com
/roarkunderstanding

> CHRONOLOGY

1977
– United States signs Panama Canal treaty.

1978
– Congress deregulates airlines.

1979
– Camp David accords.
– Carter establishes formal diplomatic relations with China.
– Soviet Union invades Afghanistan.
– Hostage crisis in Iran begins.

1980
– Congress deregulates banking, trucking, and railroad industries.
– Congress passes Superfund legislation.

disadvantaged while stagflation eroded their own standard of living. But his fiscal stringency frustrated liberal Democrats pushing for major welfare reform and a national health insurance program. Carter himself said, "In many cases I feel more at home with the conservative Democratic and Republican members of Congress than I do with the others."

Although Carter did fulfill liberals' desire to make government more inclusive by appointing unprecedented numbers of women and minorities to cabinet, judicial, and diplomatic posts, a number of factors thwarted Carter's policy goals. His outsider status helped him win the election but left him without strong ties to party leaders in Congress. Democrats complained that Carter flooded them with comprehensive proposals without consultation or a strategy to get them enacted. Even if he had possessed Lyndon Johnson's political skills, Carter might not have done much better. The economic problems he inherited—unemployment, inflation, and sluggish economic growth—confounded economic doctrine. Usually, rising prices accompanied a humming economy with a strong demand for labor. Now, however, stagflation burdened the economy with both steep inflation and high unemployment.

Carter first targeted unemployment, signing bills that pumped $14 billion into the economy through public works and public service jobs programs and cutting taxes by $34 billion. Unemployment receded, but then inflation surged. Working people, wrote one journalist, "winced and ached" as their paychecks bought less and less, "hollowing their hopes and dreams, their plans for a house or their children's college education." To curb inflation, Carter curtailed federal spending, and the Federal Reserve Board tightened the money supply. Not only did these measures fail to halt inflation, which surpassed 13 percent in 1980, but they also contributed to rising unemployment, reversing the gains made in Carter's first two years.

Carter's commitment to holding down the federal budget frustrated Democrats pushing for comprehensive welfare reform, national health insurance, and a substantial jobs program that would make government the employer of last resort. His refusal to propose a comprehensive national health insurance plan, long a key Democratic Party objective, led to a bitter split with Massachusetts senator Ted Kennedy, who fought Carter for the 1980 presidential nomination. Carter's agreement to legislation to ensure solvency in the Social Security system resulted in higher payroll taxes on lower- and middle-income Americans.

By contrast, corporations and wealthy individuals gained from new legislation, such as a sharp cut in the capital gains tax. When the Chrysler Corporation approached bankruptcy, Congress provided $1.5 billion in loan guarantees to bail out the auto giant. Congress also acted on Carter's proposals to deregulate airlines in 1978 and the banking, trucking, and railroad industries in 1980, beginning a policy turn toward implementing conservatives' attachment to a free market and unfettered private enterprise.

Energy and Environmental Reform

Complicating the government's battle with stagflation was the nation's enormous energy consumption and dependence on foreign nations to fill one-third of its energy demands. Consequently, Carter proposed a comprehensive program to

CHAPTER LOCATOR | How did the Nixon presidency reflect the rise of postwar conservatism? | **Why did the "outsider" presidency of Jimmy Carter fail to gain broad support?**

906 CHAPTER 30
THE CONSERVATIVE TURN

The Fuel Shortage

This billboard appeared in 1980, while Iran held Americans hostage in Teheran (see pages 911–12). Gasoline shortages and rising gas prices vexed motorists all over the country. The shortages and high prices were sparked by the Iranian revolution, which brought to power Ayatollah Ruholla Khomeini, pictured on the billboard. The ad appeals to drivers to observe the fuel-saving 55-mile-per-hour national speed limit imposed in 1974 during the first oil crisis. John W. Hartman Center/Duke University Special Collections Library.

> VISUAL ACTIVITY

READING THE IMAGE: What assumptions does the billboard make about Americans' reactions to the Iran hostage crisis? What reasons does the ad give for drivers to respect the speed limit? What reasons are not mentioned?

CONNECTIONS: What impact did the hostage and oil crises have on American politics?

conserve energy, and he elevated its importance by establishing the Department of Energy. Beset with competing demands among energy producers and consumers, Congress picked Carter's program apart. The **National Energy Act of 1978** penalized manufacturers of gas-guzzling automobiles and provided other incentives for conservation and development of alternative fuels, such as wind and solar power, but the act fell far short of a long-term, comprehensive program.

In 1979, a new upheaval in the Middle East, the Iranian revolution, created the most severe energy crisis yet. In midsummer, shortages caused 60 percent of gasoline stations to close down, resulting in long lines and high prices. In response, Congress reduced controls on the oil and gas industry to stimulate American production and imposed a windfall profits tax on producers to redistribute some of the profits they would reap from deregulation.

European nations were just as dependent on foreign oil as was the United States, but they more successfully controlled consumption. They levied high taxes on gasoline, causing people to rely more on public transportation and manufacturers to produce more energy-efficient cars. In the automobile-dependent United States, however, with inadequate public transit, a sprawling population, and an aversion to taxes, politicians dismissed that approach. By the end of the century, the United States, with 6 percent of the world's population, would consume more than 25 percent of global oil production (**Map 30.1** and **Figure 30.1**).

A vigorous environmental movement opposed nuclear energy as an alternative fuel, warning of radiation leakage, potential accidents, and the hazards of radioactive wastes. In 1976, hundreds of members of the Clamshell Alliance

National Energy Act of 1978

▶ Legislation that penalized manufacturers of gas-guzzling automobiles and provided additional incentives for energy conservation and development of alternative fuels, such as wind and solar power. However, the act fell short of the long-term, comprehensive program that President Carter advocated.

What conservative goals were realized in the Reagan administration?

What strategies did liberals use to fight the conservative turn?

How did Ronald Reagan's foreign policy affect the Cold War?

Conclusion: What was the long-term impact of the conservative turn?

✔ LearningCurve
Check what you know.
bedfordstmartins.com
/roarkunderstanding

went to jail for attempting to block construction of a nuclear power plant in Seabrook, New Hampshire; other groups sprang up across the country to demand an environment safe from nuclear radiation and waste. The perils of nuclear energy claimed international attention in March 1979, when a meltdown of the reactor core was narrowly averted at the nuclear facility near Harrisburg, Pennsylvania. Popular opposition and the great expense of building nuclear power plants stalled further development of the industry, which provided 10 percent of the nation's electricity in the 1970s. A disaster at Love Canal in Niagara Falls, New York, advanced other environmental goals by underscoring the human costs of unregulated development. Residents suffering high rates of serious illness discovered that their homes sat amid highly

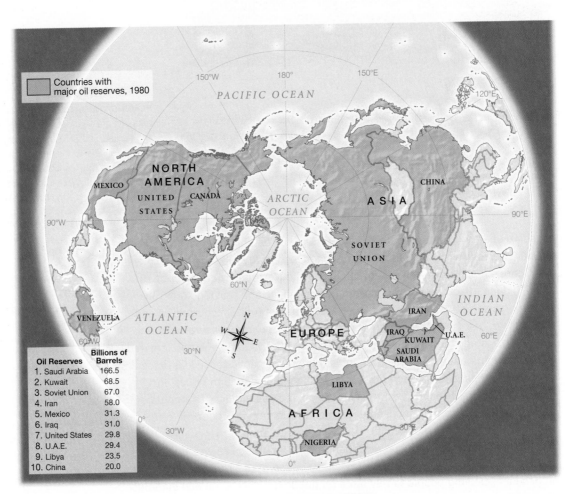

Oil Reserves	Billions of Barrels
1. Saudi Arabia	166.5
2. Kuwait	68.5
3. Soviet Union	67.0
4. Iran	58.0
5. Mexico	31.3
6. Iraq	31.0
7. United States	29.8
8. U.A.E.	29.4
9. Libya	23.5
10. China	20.0

MAP 30.1 ■ Worldwide Oil Reserves, 1980

Data produced by geologists and engineers enable experts to estimate the size of "proved oil reserves," quantities that are recoverable with existing technology and prices. In 1980, total worldwide reserves were estimated at 645 billion barrels. Recovery of reserves depends on many factors, including the location of the oil. Large portions of U.S. reserves, for example, lie under the Gulf of Mexico, where it is expensive to drill and where hurricanes can disrupt operations.

> MAP ACTIVITY

READING THE MAP: Where did the United States rank in 1980 in the possession of oil reserves? About what portion of the total oil reserves were located in the Middle East?

CONNECTIONS: When during the 1970s did the United States experience oil shortages? What caused these shortages?

CHAPTER LOCATOR | How did the Nixon presidency reflect the rise of postwar conservatism? | Why did the "outsider" presidency of Jimmy Carter fail to gain broad support?

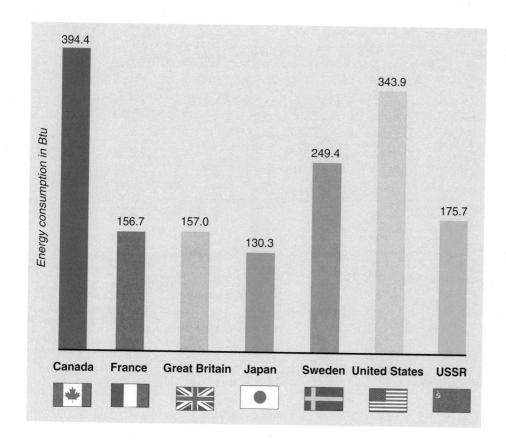

> GLOBAL
COMPARISON

FIGURE 30.1 ■ Energy Consumption per Capita, 1980

Relative to most other industrialized nations, the United States consumed energy voraciously, with a per capita rate of consumption in 1980 that was more than twice as high as that of Britain, France, and Japan and nearly twice as high as that of the Soviet Union. A number of factors influence a nation's energy consumption (shown here in British thermal units, or Btu), including standard of living, climate, size of landmass and dispersal of population, availability and price of energy, and government policies such as support for public transportation. What country had a per capita rate of consumption even higher than that of the United States?

toxic waste products from a nearby chemical company. Finally responding to the residents' claims in 1978, the state of New York agreed to help families relocate, and the Carter administration sponsored legislation in 1980 that created the so-called Superfund, $1.6 billion for cleanup of hazardous wastes left by the chemical industry around the country.

Carter also signed bills to improve clean air and water programs; to expand the Arctic National Wildlife Refuge preserve in Alaska; and to control strip-mining, which left destructive scars on the land. During the 1979 gasoline crisis, Carter attempted to balance the development of domestic fuel sources with environmental concerns, winning legislation to conserve energy and to provide incentives for the development of solar energy and environmentally friendly alternative fuels.

Promoting Human Rights Abroad

"We're ashamed of what our government is as we deal with other nations around the world," Jimmy Carter charged, promising to reverse U.S. support of dictators, secret diplomacy, interference in the internal affairs of other countries, and excessive reliance on military solutions. Human rights formed the cornerstone of his approach. The Carter administration applied economic pressure on governments that denied their citizens basic rights, refusing aid or trading privileges to nations such as Chile and El Salvador, as well as to the white minority governments of Rhodesia and South Africa. Yet in other instances, Carter sacrificed human rights

| What conservative goals were realized in the Reagan administration? | What strategies did liberals use to fight the conservative turn? | How did Ronald Reagan's foreign policy affect the Cold War? | Conclusion: What was the long-term impact of the conservative turn? | ✓ LearningCurve Check what you know. bedfordstmartins.com /roarkunderstanding |

909

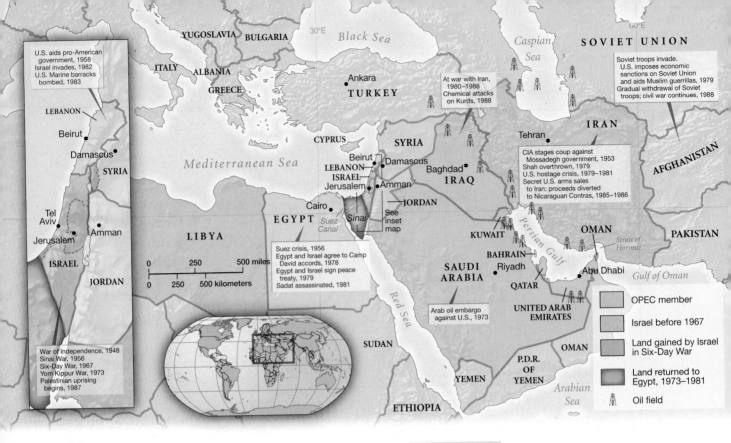

MAP 30.2 ■ The Middle East, 1948–1989

Determination to preserve access to the rich oil reserves of the Middle East and commitment to the security of Israel were the fundamental — and often conflicting — principles of U.S. foreign policy in that region.

Map labels and annotations:

U.S. aids pro-American government, 1958
Israel invades, 1982
U.S. Marine barracks bombed, 1983

At war with Iran, 1980–1988
Chemical attacks on Kurds, 1988

Soviet troops invade. U.S. imposes economic sanctions on Soviet Union and aids Muslim guerrillas, 1979
Gradual withdrawal of Soviet troops; civil war continues, 1988

CIA stages coup against Mossadegh government, 1953
Shah overthrown, 1979
U.S. hostage crisis, 1979–1981
Secret U.S. arms sales to Iran; proceeds diverted to Nicaraguan Contras, 1985–1986

Suez crisis, 1956
Egypt and Israel agree to Camp David accords, 1978
Egypt and Israel sign peace treaty, 1979
Sadat assassinated, 1981

War of Independence, 1948
Sinai War, 1956
Six-Day War, 1967
Yom Kippur War, 1973
Palestinian uprising begins, 1987

Arab oil embargo against U.S., 1973

Legend:
OPEC member
Israel before 1967
Land gained by Israel in Six-Day War
Land returned to Egypt, 1973–1981
Oil field

> MAP ACTIVITY

READING THE MAP: Where did the United States become involved diplomatically or militarily in the Middle East between 1948 and 1989?

CONNECTIONS: What role did U.S. foreign policy regarding the Middle East and events in Israel play in provoking the 1973 Arab oil embargo against the United States? What precipitated the taking of U.S. hostages in Iran in 1979?

ideals to strategic and security considerations, invoking no sanctions against repressive governments in Iran, South Korea, and the Philippines.

Carter's human rights principles faced another test when a popular movement overthrew an oppressive dictatorship in Nicaragua. U.S. officials were uneasy about the leftist Sandinistas who led the rebellion and had ties to Cuba. Once they assumed power in 1979, however, Carter recognized the new government and sent economic aid, signaling that the way a government treated its citizens was as important as how anti-Communist and friendly to American interests it was.

Applying moral principles to relations with Panama, Carter sped up negotiations over control of the Panama Canal and in 1977 signed a treaty providing for Panama's takeover of the canal in 2000. Supporters viewed the treaty as restitution for the U.S. seizure of Panamanian territory in 1903. Opponents insisted on retaining the vital waterway. "We bought it, we paid for it, it's ours," claimed Ronald Reagan during the presidential primaries of 1976. It took a massive effort by the administration to get Senate ratification of the **Panama Canal treaty**.

Seeking to promote peace in the Middle East, Carter seized on the courage of Egyptian president Anwar Sadat, the first Arab leader to risk his political

Panama Canal treaty

▶ 1977 agreement that returned control of the Panama Canal from the United States to Panama in 2000. To pass the treaty, President Carter overcame stiff opposition in the Senate from conservatives who regarded control of the canal as vital to America's interests.

CHAPTER LOCATOR | How did the Nixon presidency reflect the rise of postwar conservatism? | Why did the "outsider" presidency of Jimmy Carter fail to gain broad support?

career by talking directly with Israeli officials. In 1979, Carter invited Sadat and Israeli prime minister Menachem Begin to Camp David, Maryland, where he applied his tenacious diplomacy for thirteen days. These talks led to the **Camp David accords**, whereby Egypt became the first Arab state to recognize Israel, and Israel agreed to gradual withdrawal from the Sinai Peninsula, which it had seized in the 1967 Six-Day War (**Map 30.2**). Although the issues of Palestinian self-determination in other Israeli-occupied territories (the West Bank and Gaza) and the plight of Palestinian refugees remained unresolved, Carter had nurtured the first meaningful steps toward peace in the Middle East.

Camp David accords

▶ Agreements between Egypt and Israel reached at the 1979 talks hosted by President Carter at Camp David. In the accords, Egypt became the first Arab state to recognize Israel, and Israel agreed to gradual withdrawal from the Sinai Peninsula.

The Cold War Intensifies

Consistent with his human rights approach, Carter preferred to pursue national security through nonmilitary means and initially sought accommodation with the nation's Cold War enemies. Following up on Nixon's initiatives, in 1979 he formally recognized the People's Republic of China. That same year, he and Soviet premier Leonid Brezhnev signed a second strategic arms reduction treaty.

Yet that same year, Carter decided to pursue a military buildup when the Soviet Union invaded neighboring Afghanistan, whose recently installed Communist government was threatened by Muslim opposition (see Map 30.2). Carter imposed economic sanctions on the Soviet Union, barred U.S. participation in the 1980 Summer Olympic Games in Moscow, and obtained legislation requiring all nineteen-year-old men to register for the draft.

Claiming that Soviet actions jeopardized oil supplies from the Middle East, the president announced the "Carter Doctrine," threatening the use of any means necessary to prevent an outside force from gaining control of the Persian Gulf. His human rights policy fell by the wayside as the United States stepped up aid to the military dictatorship in Afghanistan's neighbor, Pakistan, and the CIA funneled secret aid through Pakistan to the Afghan rebels. Finally, Carter called for hefty increases in defense spending.

Events in Iran also encouraged this hard-line approach. Generous U.S. arms and aid had not enabled the shah to crush Iranian dissidents who still resented the CIA's role in the overthrow of the Mossadegh government in 1953 (see chapter 27), condemned the shah's brutal attempts to silence opposition, and detested his adoption of Western culture and values. These grievances erupted into a revolution in 1979 that forced the shah out of Iran and brought to power Shiite Islamic fundamentalists led by Ayatollah Ruholla Khomeini, whom the shah had exiled in 1964.

Carter's decision to allow the shah into the United States for medical treatment enraged Iranians, who believed that the United States would restore the shah to power as it had done in 1953. On November 4, 1979, a crowd broke into the U.S. Embassy in Iran's capital, Teheran, and seized sixty-six U.S. diplomats, CIA officers, citizens, and military attachés. Refusing the captors' demands that the shah be returned to Iran for trial, Carter froze Iranian assets in U.S. banks and placed an embargo on Iranian oil. In April 1980, he sent a small military operation into Iran, but the rescue mission failed.

The disastrous rescue attempt and scenes of blindfolded U.S. citizens paraded before TV cameras fed Americans' feelings of impotence, simmering since the defeat in Vietnam. These frustrations in turn increased support for a

What conservative goals were realized in the Reagan administration? | What strategies did liberals use to fight the conservative turn? | How did Ronald Reagan's foreign policy affect the Cold War? | Conclusion: What was the long-term impact of the conservative turn?

✓ LearningCurve
Check what you know.
bedfordstmartins.com
/roarkunderstanding

Iran hostage crisis
▶ Crisis that began in 1979 after the deposed shah of Iran was allowed into the United States following the Iranian revolution. Iranians broke into the U.S. Embassy in Teheran and took sixty-six Americans hostage. The hostage crisis contributed to President Carter's defeat in the 1980 presidential election.

more militaristic foreign policy. Opposition to Soviet-American détente, combined with the Soviet invasion of Afghanistan, nullified the thaw in superpower relations that had begun in the 1960s. The Iran hostage crisis dominated the news during the 1980 presidential campaign and contributed to Carter's defeat. Iran freed the hostages the day he left office, but relations with the United States remained tense.

> **QUICK REVIEW**

How did Carter implement his commitment to human rights, and why did human rights give way to other priorities?

CHAPTER LOCATOR | How did the Nixon presidency reflect the rise of postwar conservatism? | Why did the "outsider" presidency of Jimmy Carter fail to gain broad support?

CHAPTER 30
912 THE CONSERVATIVE TURN

What conservative goals were realized in the Reagan administration?

Ronald Reagan Addresses Religious Conservatives Reagan's victory in 1980 helped to reshape the Republican Party by attracting millions of evangelical Christians. In his 1983 address to the National Association of Evangelicals, Reagan called the Soviet Union an "evil empire" and appealed to religious conservatives with strong words about abortion and prayer in the schools, rejoicing that "America is in the midst of a spiritual awakening and a moral renewal." Ronald Reagan Presidential Library.

THE ELECTION OF RONALD REAGAN in 1980 marked the most important turning point in politics since Franklin D. Roosevelt's election in 1932. Reagan's victory established conservatism's dominance in the Republican Party, while Democrats searched for voter support by moving toward the right. The United States was not alone in this political shift. Conservatives rose to power in Britain, West Germany, Canada, and Sweden, while socialist and social democratic governments elsewhere trimmed their welfare states.

The Reagan administration embraced the conservative Christian values of the New Right, but it left its most important mark on the economy: victory over inflation, deregulation of industry, enormous tax cuts, and a staggering federal budget deficit. Popular culture celebrated financial success and displaying wealth, but poverty increased and economic inequality grew. Although the Reagan era did not see a policy revolution comparable to that of the New Deal, it dealt a sharp blow to the liberalism that had informed American politics since the 1930s.

What conservative goals were realized in the Reagan administration?	What strategies did liberals use to fight the conservative turn?	How did Ronald Reagan's foreign policy affect the Cold War?	Conclusion: What was the long-term impact of the conservative turn?	✔ **LearningCurve** Check what you know. bedfordstmartins.com /roarkunderstanding

> CHRONOLOGY

1979
- Moral Majority is founded.

1980
- Ronald Reagan is elected president.

1981
- Economic Recovery Tax Act.

1983
- Family Research Council is founded.

1984
- Reagan is reelected president.

New (Christian) Right
▶ Politically active religious conservatives who became particularly vocal in the 1980s. The New Right criticized feminism, opposed abortion and homosexuality, and promoted "family values" and military preparedness.

Appealing to the New Right and Beyond

Sixty-nine-year-old Ronald Reagan was the oldest candidate ever nominated for the presidency. Coming first to national attention as a movie actor, he initially shared the politics of his staunchly Democratic father but moved to the right in the 1940s and 1950s. He campaigned for Barry Goldwater in 1964.

Reagan's political career took off when he was elected governor of California in 1966. He ran as a conservative, but in office he displayed flexibility, approving a major tax increase, a strong water pollution bill, and a liberal abortion law. Displaying similar agility in the 1980 presidential campaign, he softened earlier attacks on programs such as Social Security and chose the moderate George H. W. Bush as his running mate.

Reagan's campaign capitalized on the economic recession and the international challenges symbolized by the Americans held hostage in Iran. Repeatedly, Reagan asked voters, "Are you better off now than you were four years ago?" He promised to "take government off the backs of the people" and to restore Americans' morale and other nations' respect. Reagan won the election, while Republicans took control of the Senate for the first time since the 1950s.

While the economy and the Iran hostage crisis sealed Reagan's victory, he also benefited from the burgeoning grassroots conservative movements. Reagan's support from religious conservatives, predominantly Protestants, constituted a relatively new phenomenon in politics known as the **New Right** or **New Christian Right**.

> **The Reagan Coalition**

- Free-market advocates
- Militant anti-Communists
- Fundamentalist Christians
- White southerners
- Reagan Democrats: white working-class Democrats who were disenchanted with the policies of the Democratic Party

During the 1970s, evangelical and fundamentalist Christianity claimed thousands of new adherents. Evangelical ministers such as Pat Robertson preached to huge television audiences, attacking feminism, abortion, and homosexuality. They called for the restoration of old-fashioned "family values." A considerable number of Catholics shared the fundamentalists' goal of a return to "Christian values."

Conservatives created political organizations such as the Moral Majority, founded by the Reverend Jerry Falwell in 1979, to fight "left-wing, social welfare bills, . . . pornography, homosexuality, [and] the advocacy of immorality in school textbooks." Dr. James Dobson, a clinical psychologist with a popular Christian talk show, founded the Family Research Council in 1983 to lobby Congress for measures to curb abortion, divorce, homosexuality, and single motherhood. The publications and think tanks of more traditional conservatives, who stressed limited government at home and militant anticommunism abroad, likewise flourished, while the monthly *Phyllis Schlafly Report* merged the sentiments of the old and new right.

CHAPTER LOCATOR | How did the Nixon presidency reflect the rise of postwar conservatism? | Why did the "outsider" presidency of Jimmy Carter fail to gain broad support?

Reagan spoke for the New Right on such issues as abortion and school prayer, but he did not push hard for so-called moral or social policies. Instead, his major achievements fulfilled goals of the older right—strengthening the nation's anti-Communist posture as well as reducing taxes and government restraints on free enterprise. "In the present crisis," Reagan declared, "government is not the solution to our problem, government is the problem."

Reagan was extraordinarily popular, appealing even to Americans who opposed his policies but warmed to his optimism, confidence, and easygoing humor. Ignoring the darker moments of the American past, he presented a version of history that Americans could feel good about.

Unleashing Free Enterprise

Reagan's first domestic objective was a massive tax cut. To justify tax cuts in the face of a large budget deficit, Reagan relied on a new theory called **supply-side economics**, which held that cutting taxes would actually increase revenue by enabling businesses to expand, encouraging individuals to work harder because they could keep more of their earnings (especially the wealthy who enjoyed the greatest tax savings), and increasing the production of goods and services—the supply—which in turn would boost demand. Reagan promised that the economy would grow so much that the government would recoup the lost taxes, but instead it incurred a galloping deficit.

In the summer of 1981, Congress passed the **Economic Recovery Tax Act**, the largest tax reduction in U.S. history. Rates were cut from 14 percent to 11 percent for the lowest-income individuals and from 70 percent to 50 percent for the wealthiest, who also benefited from reduced levies on corporations, capital gains, gifts, and inheritances. A second measure, the Tax Reform Act of 1986, cut taxes still further. Although the 1986 law narrowed loopholes used primarily by the wealthy, affluent Americans saved far more on their tax bills than did average tax-payers, and the distribution of wealth tipped further in favor of the rich. Carter had confined deregulation to particular industries, such as air transportation and banking, while increasing health, safety, and environmental regulations. The Reagan administration, by contrast, pursued across-the-board deregulation. It declined to enforce the Sherman Antitrust Act (see chapter 18), which limited monopolies, against an unprecedented number of business mergers and takeovers. Reagan also loosened regulations protecting employee health and safety, and he weakened labor unions. When members of the Professional Air Traffic Controllers Organization—one of the few unions to support him in 1980—struck in 1981, Reagan fired them, destroying the union and intimidating organized labor.

Reagan blamed environmental laws for the nation's sluggish economic growth and targeted them for deregulation. His first secretary of the interior, James Watt, declared, "We will mine more, drill more, cut more timber," and released federal lands to private exploitation. Meanwhile, the head of the Environmental Protection Agency relaxed enforcement of air and water pollution standards. Of environmentalists, Reagan wisecracked, "I don't think they'll be happy until the White House looks like a bird's nest," but their numbers grew in opposition to his policies. Popular support for environmental protection forced several officials to resign and blocked full realization of Reagan's deregulatory goals.

supply-side economics
▶ Economic theory claiming that tax cuts for individuals (especially the wealthy) and businesses encourage investment and production (supply) and stimulate consumption (demand) because individuals can keep more of their earnings. Despite promises to the contrary, under President Reagan supply-side economics created a massive federal budget deficit.

Economic Recovery Tax Act
▶ Legislation passed by Congress in 1981 that authorized the largest reduction in taxes in the nation's history. The tax cuts disproportionately benefited affluent Americans and widened the distribution of wealth in favor of the rich.

What conservative goals were realized in the **Reagan administration?** | What strategies did liberals use to fight the conservative turn? | How did Ronald Reagan's foreign policy affect the Cold War? | Conclusion: What was the long-term impact of the conservative turn? | ✔ LearningCurve Check what you know. bedfordstmartins.com /roarkunderstanding

915

Deregulation of the banking industry, begun under Carter with bipartisan support, created a crisis in the savings and loan industry. Some of the newly deregulated savings and loan institutions (S&Ls) extended enormous loans to real estate developers and invested in other high-yield but risky ventures. S&L owners reaped lavish profits, and their depositors enjoyed high interest rates. When real estate values began to plunge, hundreds of S&Ls went bankrupt. After Congress voted to bail out the S&L industry in 1989, American taxpayers bore the burden of the largest financial scandal in U.S. history, estimated at more than $100 billion.

The S&L crisis deepened the federal deficit. Reagan cut funds for food stamps, job training, student aid, and other social welfare programs, and hundreds of thousands of people lost benefits. Yet increases in defense spending far exceeded the budget cuts, the deficit soared, and the nation's debt tripled to $2.3 trillion, consuming one-seventh of all federal expenditures. Despite Reagan's antigovernment rhetoric, the number of federal employees increased from 2.9 million to 3.1 million during his presidency.

It took the severest recession since the 1930s to squeeze inflation out of the U.S. economy. Unemployment approached 11 percent late in 1982, and record numbers of banks and businesses closed. The threat of unemployment further undermined organized labor, forcing unions to make concessions that management insisted were necessary for industry's survival. In 1983, the economy recovered and entered a period of unprecedented growth.

That economic upswing and Reagan's own popularity posed a formidable challenge to the Democrats in the 1984 election. They nominated Carter's vice president, Walter F. Mondale, to head the ticket, but even his precedent-breaking move in choosing a woman as his running mate—New York representative Geraldine A. Ferraro—did not save the Democrats from a humiliating defeat. Reagan charged his opponents with concentrating on America's failures, while he emphasized success and possibility. Democrats, he claimed, "see an America where every day is April 15th [the deadline for income tax returns] . . . we see an America where every day is the Fourth of July." Reagan was reelected in a landslide victory, winning 59 percent of the popular vote and every state but Mondale's Minnesota.

Winners and Losers in a Flourishing Economy

After the economy took off in 1983, some Americans won great fortunes. Popular culture celebrated making money and displaying wealth. Books by business wizards topped best seller lists, the press described lavish million-dollar parties, and a new television show, *Lifestyles of the Rich and Famous,* drew large audiences. College students listed making money as their primary ambition.

Many of the newly wealthy got rich from moving assets around rather than from producing goods, making money by manipulating debt and restructuring corporations through mergers and takeovers. Notable exceptions included Steve Jobs, who invented the Apple computer in his garage; Bill Gates, who transformed the software industry; and Liz Claiborne, who created a billion-dollar fashion enterprise. Most financial wizards operated within the law, but greed sometimes led to criminal convictions.

Older industries faced increasing international pressures, as German and Japanese corporations overtook U.S. manufacturing in steel, automobiles, and

CHAPTER LOCATOR | How did the Nixon presidency reflect the rise of postwar conservatism? | Why did the "outsider" presidency of Jimmy Carter fail to gain broad support?

916 CHAPTER 30
THE CONSERVATIVE TURN

electronics. International competition forced the collapse of some older companies, while others moved factories and jobs abroad to be closer to foreign markets or to benefit from the low wages in countries such as Mexico and Korea. Service industries expanded and created new jobs at home, but at substantially lower wages.

The weakening of organized labor combined with the decline in manufacturing to erode the position of blue-collar workers. Chicago steelworker Ike Mazo, who contemplated the $6-an-hour jobs available to him, fumed, "It's an attack on the living standards of workers." Increasingly, a second income was needed to stave off economic decline. By 1990, nearly 60 percent of married women with young children worked outside the home. Yet even with two incomes, families struggled. Speaking of her children, Mazo's wife confessed, "I worry about their future every day. Will we be able to put them through college?"

In keeping with conservative philosophy, Reagan adhered to trickle-down economics, insisting that a booming economy would benefit everyone. Average personal income did rise during his tenure, but the trend toward greater economic inequality that had begun in the 1970s intensified in the 1980s, encouraged in part by his tax policies.

> ## Economic Inequality in the 1980s

- The number of full-time workers earning wages below the poverty level rose from 12 percent to 18 percent of all workers.
- The average $10,000 gap between men's and women's annual earnings made survival harder for the nearly 20 percent of families headed by women.
- The percentage of Americans living in poverty increased from 11.7 to 13.5, the highest poverty rate in the industrialized world.
- The economic boom bypassed racial minorities, female-headed families, and children.
- One in five children lived in poverty.

QUICK REVIEW <

Why did economic inequality increase during the Reagan administration?

| What conservative goals were realized in the Reagan administration? | What strategies did liberals use to fight the conservative turn? | How did Ronald Reagan's foreign policy affect the Cold War? | Conclusion: What was the long-term impact of the conservative turn? | ✓ LearningCurve Check what you know. bedfordstmartins.com /roarkunderstanding |

What strategies did liberals use to fight the conservative turn?

After the *Roe v. Wade* decision in 1973, several states enacted restrictions on abortion. In 1989, the Supreme Court upheld a Missouri law prohibiting public employees from performing abortions except to save a woman's life. The law also banned abortions in public buildings and required physicians to perform viability tests on the fetus after twenty weeks. Here, activists on both sides rally before the Supreme Court. AP Images/Ron Edmonds.

THE RISE OF CONSERVATISM put liberal social movements on the defensive, as the government moved away from the national commitment to equal opportunity undertaken in the 1960s and the president's federal court appointments reflected that shift. Feminists and minority groups fought to keep protections they had recently won, and the gay and lesbian rights movement grew.

Battles in the Courts and Congress

Ronald Reagan agreed with conservatives that the nation had moved too far in guaranteeing rights to minority groups. Crying "reverse discrimination," conservatives maintained that affirmative action unfairly hurt whites. Instead, they called for "color-blind" policies, ignoring statistics showing that minorities and white women still lagged far behind white men in opportunities and income.

Intense mobilization by civil rights groups, educational leaders, labor, and even corporate America prevented the administration from abandoning affirmative action, and the Supreme Court upheld important antidiscrimination policies. Moreover, against Reagan's wishes, Congress extended the Voting Rights Act with veto-proof majorities. The administration did, however, limit civil rights enforcement by appointing conservatives to the Justice Department, the Civil Rights Commission, and other agencies as well as by slashing their budgets.

CHAPTER LOCATOR | How did the Nixon presidency reflect the rise of postwar conservatism? | Why did the "outsider" presidency of Jimmy Carter fail to gain broad support?

918 CHAPTER 30
THE CONSERVATIVE TURN

Congress stepped in to defend antidiscrimination programs after the Justice Department, in the case of *Grove City v. Bell* (1984), persuaded the Supreme Court to severely weaken Title IX of the Education Amendments Act of 1972, a key law promoting equal opportunity in education. In 1988, Congress passed the Civil Rights Restoration Act over Reagan's veto, reversing the administration's victory in *Grove City* and banning government funding of any organization that practiced discrimination on the basis of race, color, national origin, sex, disability, or age.

The *Grove City* decision reflected a rightward movement in the federal judiciary, on which liberals had counted as a powerful ally. With the opportunity to appoint half of the 761 federal court judges and three new Supreme Court justices, President Reagan encouraged this trend by carefully selecting conservative candidates. The full impact of these appointments became clear after Reagan left office, as the Court allowed states to impose restrictions that weakened access to abortion for poor and rural women, reduced protections against employment discrimination, and whittled down legal safeguards against the death penalty.

> CHRONOLOGY

1981
– Researchers discover AIDS virus.
– Sandra Day O'Connor becomes first woman Supreme Court justice.

1984
– Retirement Equity Act is passed.

1988
– Civil Rights Restoration Act is passed over Reagan's veto.

Feminism on the Defensive

A signal achievement of the New Right was capturing the Republican Party's position on women's rights. For the first time in its history, the party took an explicitly antifeminist tone, opposing both the **Equal Rights Amendment (ERA)** and abortion rights, key goals of women's rights activists. When the time limit for ratification of the ERA ran out in 1982, feminists suffered defeat on a central objective (see chapter 28).

Cast on the defensive, feminists focused more on women's economic and family problems, where they found some common ground with the Reagan administration. The Child Support Enforcement Amendments Act helped single and divorced mothers collect court-ordered child support payments from absent fathers. The Retirement Equity Act of 1984 benefited divorced and older women by strengthening their claims to their husbands' pensions and enabling women to qualify more easily for private retirement pensions.

The Reagan administration had its own concerns about women, specifically about the gender gap in voting—women's tendency to support liberal and Democratic candidates in larger numbers than men did. Reagan appointed three women to cabinet posts and, in 1981, selected the first woman, Sandra Day O'Connor, a moderate conservative, for the Supreme Court, despite the Christian Right's objection to her support of abortion. But these actions accompanied a general decline in the number of women and minorities in high-level government positions. And with higher poverty rates than men, women suffered most from Reagan's cuts in social programs.

Although Supreme Court decisions placed restrictions on women's ability to obtain abortions, feminists fought successfully to retain the basic principles of *Roe v. Wade*. Moreover, they won a key decision from the Supreme

Equal Rights Amendment (ERA)
▶ Constitutional amendment passed by Congress in 1972 that would require equal treatment of men and women under federal and state law. Facing fierce opposition from the New Right and the Republican Party, the ERA was defeated as time ran out for state ratification in 1982.

Ratified the ERA
Did not ratify the ERA
Ratified and then voted to rescind ratification

The Fight for the Equal Rights Amendment

What conservative goals were realized in the Reagan administration?

What strategies did liberals use to fight the conservative turn?

How did Ronald Reagan's foreign policy affect the Cold War?

Conclusion: What was the long-term impact of the conservative turn?

✓ LearningCurve
Check what you know.
bedfordstmartins.com/roarkunderstanding

Court ruling that sexual harassment in the workplace constituted sex discrimination. Feminists also made some gains at the state level in such areas as pay equity, rape, and domestic violence.

The Gay and Lesbian Rights Movement

In contrast to feminism and other social movements, gay and lesbian rights activism grew during the 1980s, galvanized in part by the discovery in 1981 of a devastating disease, acquired immune deficiency syndrome (AIDS). Because initially the disease disproportionately affected male homosexuals in the United States, activists mobilized to promote public funding for AIDS education, prevention, and treatment.

The gay and lesbian rights movement helped closeted homosexuals "come out," and their visibility increased awareness, if not always acceptance, of homosexuality among the larger population. Beginning with the election of Elaine Noble to the Massachusetts legislature in 1974, several openly gay politicians won offices ranging from mayor to member of Congress, and the Democrats began to include gay rights in their party platforms. Activists organized gay rights marches throughout the country.

Popular attitudes about homosexuality moved toward greater tolerance but remained complex, leading to uneven changes in policies. Dozens of cities banned job discrimination against homosexuals, and beginning with Wisconsin in 1982, eleven states made sexual orientation a protected category under civil rights laws. Local governments and large corporations began to offer health insurance and other benefits to same-sex domestic partners.

Yet a strong countermovement challenged the drive for gay rights. The Christian Right targeted gays and lesbians as symbols of national immorality, and they succeeded in overturning some homosexual rights measures. Many states removed antisodomy laws from the books, but in 1986 the Supreme Court upheld the constitutionality of such laws. Until the Court reversed that opinion in 2003, more than a dozen states retained statutes that left homosexuals vulnerable to criminal charges for private consensual behavior.

Gay Pride Parades

Since June 1970, when gays and lesbians marched in New York City on the first anniversary of Stonewall (see chapter 28), annual gay pride parades have taken place throughout the United States. According to history professor Robert Dawidoff, the parades are not about "flaunting private things in public," as some people have charged, but a way for gay men and lesbians to express "pride . . . in having survived the thousand petty harassments and reminders of a special status we neither seek nor merit." Friends and families of homosexuals participate in the parades, as this sign from a parade in Los Angeles indicates. © Bettmann/Corbis.

> **QUICK REVIEW**

What gains and setbacks did minorities, feminists, and gays and lesbians experience during the Reagan years?

CHAPTER LOCATOR | How did the Nixon presidency reflect the rise of postwar conservatism? | Why did the "outsider" presidency of Jimmy Carter fail to gain broad support?

How did Ronald Reagan's foreign policy affect the Cold War?

The Fireside Summit This photograph captures the warmth that developed between President Ronald Reagan and Soviet leader Mikhail Gorbachev at their first meeting in Geneva in November 1985. Although the meeting did not produce any key agreements, the two men began to appreciate each other's concerns and to build trust, launching a relationship that would lead to nuclear arms reductions and the end of the Cold War. Ronald Reagan Presidential Library.

RONALD REAGAN ACCELERATED Jimmy Carter's arms buildup and harshly censured the Soviet Union, calling it "an evil empire." Yet despite the new aggressiveness—or, as some argued, because of it—Reagan presided over the most impressive thaw in superpower conflict since the Cold War had begun. On the periphery of the Cold War, however, Reagan practiced militant anticommunism, assisting antileftist movements in Asia, Africa, and Central America. He also dispatched troops to the Middle East and the Caribbean.

Militarization and Interventions Abroad

Reagan expanded the military with new bombers and missiles, an enhanced nuclear force in Europe, a larger navy, and a rapid-deployment force. Throughout Reagan's presidency, defense spending averaged $216 billion a year, up from $158 billion in the Carter years and higher even than in the Vietnam era.

Reagan startled many of his own advisers in March 1983 by announcing plans for research on the **Strategic Defense Initiative (SDI)**. Immediately dubbed "Star

Strategic Defense Initiative (SDI)

▶ Project launched by President Reagan to deploy lasers in space that would destroy enemy missiles before they could reach their targets. The Soviets protested that it violated the 1972 Antiballistic Missile Treaty. The project cost billions of dollars without producing a working system.

| What conservative goals were realized in the Reagan administration? | What strategies did liberals use to fight the conservative turn? | **How did Ronald Reagan's foreign policy affect the Cold War?** | Conclusion: What was the long-term impact of the conservative turn? | ☑ **LearningCurve** Check what you know. bedfordstmartins.com /roarkunderstanding |

1983
– Terrorist bomb kills 241 U.S. Marines in Beirut, Lebanon.
– Reagan announces Strategic Defense Initiative ("Star Wars").

1986
– Iran-Contra scandal.

1987
– Intermediate-range nuclear forces (INF) agreement is signed.

Wars" by critics who doubted its feasibility, the project would deploy lasers in space to destroy enemy missiles before they could reach their targets. Such a defense would allow the United States to strike first and not fear retaliation. The Soviets reacted angrily because SDI violated the 1972 Antiballistic Missile Treaty and because they would have to make huge investments to develop their own Star Wars technology. Subsequent administrations continued to spend billions on SDI research without producing a working system.

Reagan justified the military buildup and SDI as a means to negotiate with the Soviets from a position of strength, but he provoked an outburst of pleas to halt the arms race. In 1982, a rally demanding a freeze on additional nuclear weapons drew 700,000 people in New York City. That same year, the National Conference of Catholic Bishops issued a strong call for nuclear disarmament. Hundreds of thousands demonstrated across Europe, stimulated by fears of new U.S. missiles scheduled for deployment there in 1983.

The U.S. military buildup was impotent before the growing threat of terrorism by non-state organizations that sought political objectives by attacking civilian populations. Terrorism had a long history throughout the world, but in the 1970s and 1980s Americans saw it escalate in the Middle East, used by Palestinians after the Israeli occupation of the West Bank and by other groups hostile to Western policies. The terrorist organization Hezbollah, composed of Shiite Muslims and backed by Iran and Syria, arose in Lebanon in 1982 after Israeli forces invaded that country to stop the Palestine Liberation Organization from using sanctuaries in Lebanon to launch attacks on Israel.

Reagan's effort to stabilize Lebanon by sending 2,000 Marines to join an international peacekeeping mission failed. In April 1983, a suicide attack on the U.S. Embassy in Beirut killed 63 people, and in October a Hezbollah fighter drove a bomb-filled truck into a U.S. barracks there, killing 241 Marines. The attack prompted the withdrawal of U.S. troops, and Lebanon remained in chaos, while incidents of murder, kidnapping, and hijacking by various Middle Eastern extremist groups continued.

Following a Cold War pattern begun under Eisenhower, the Reagan administration sought to contain leftist movements across the globe. In October 1983, 5,000 U.S. troops invaded Grenada, a small Caribbean nation where Marxists had staged a successful coup. In Asia, the United States quietly aided the Afghan rebels' war against Afghanistan's Soviet-backed government. In the African nation of Angola, the United States armed

Attack on the Marine Barracks in Beirut

On October 23, 1983, members of Islamic Jihad, an anti-Israel, anti-Western, Iran-sponsored terrorist group, attacked U.S. troops stationed in Lebanon by exploding a car bomb outside the Marine compound near the Beirut airport. The Reagan administration withdrew from Lebanon, called "a thousand-year-old hornet's nest" by one official. Here military personnel search for and remove bodies of their 241 dead comrades. © Bettmann/Corbis.

CHAPTER LOCATOR | How did the Nixon presidency reflect the rise of postwar conservatism? | Why did the "outsider" presidency of Jimmy Carter fail to gain broad support?

CHAPTER 30
922 THE CONSERVATIVE TURN

rebel forces against the government supported by the Soviet Union and Cuba. Reagan also sided with the South African government, which was brutally suppressing black protest against apartheid, forcing Congress to override his veto in order to impose economic sanctions against South Africa.

Administration officials were most fearful of left-wing movements in Central America, which Reagan claimed could "destabilize the entire region from the Panama Canal to Mexico." When a leftist uprising occurred in El Salvador in 1981, the United States sent money and military advisers to prop up the authoritarian government. In neighboring Nicaragua, the administration secretly aided the Contras, an armed coalition seeking to unseat the left-wing Sandinistas, who had toppled a long-standing dictatorship.

El Salvador and Nicaragua

The Iran-Contra Scandal

Fearing another Vietnam, many Americans opposed aligning the United States with reactionary forces not supported by the majority of Nicaraguans. Congress repeatedly instructed the president to stop aiding the Contras, but the administration continued to secretly provide them with weapons and training. The Reagan administration also helped wreck the Nicaraguan economy. With support for his government undermined, Nicaragua's president, Daniel Ortega, agreed to a political settlement, and when he was defeated by a coalition of all the opposition groups, he stepped aside.

Secret aid to the Contras was part of a larger project that came to be known as the **Iran-Contra scandal**. It began in 1985 when officials of the National Security Council and CIA covertly arranged to sell arms to Iran, then in the midst of an eight-year war with neighboring Iraq, even while the United States openly supplied Iraq with funds and weapons. The purpose was to get Iran to pressure Hezbollah to release American hostages being held in Lebanon. Funds from the arms sales were then channeled through Swiss bank accounts to aid the Nicaraguan Contras. Over the objections of his secretary of state and secretary of defense, Reagan approved the arms sales, but the three subsequently denied knowing that the proceeds were diverted to the Contras.

When news of the affair surfaced in November 1986, the Reagan administration faced serious charges. The president's aides had defied Congress's express ban on military aid for the Contras. Investigations by an independent prosecutor appointed by Reagan led to a trial in which seven individuals pleaded guilty or were convicted of lying to Congress and destroying evidence. One felony conviction was later overturned on a technicality, and President George H. W. Bush pardoned the other six officials in December 1992. The independent prosecutor's final report found no evidence that Reagan had broken the law, but it concluded that he had known about the diversion of funds to the Contras and had "knowingly participated or at least acquiesced" in covering up the scandal.

Iran-Contra scandal

▶ Reagan administration scandal that involved the sale of arms to Iran, in exchange for Iran's efforts to secure the release of hostages held in Lebanon, and the redirection of the proceeds of those sales to the Nicaraguan Contras.

A Thaw in Soviet-American Relations

A momentous reduction in Cold War tensions soon overshadowed the Iran-Contra scandal. The new Soviet-American accord depended both on Reagan's flexibility

| What conservative goals were realized in the Reagan administration? | What strategies did liberals use to fight the conservative turn? | **How did Ronald Reagan's foreign policy affect the Cold War?** | Conclusion: What was the long-term impact of the conservative turn? | ✓ LearningCurve Check what you know. bedfordstmartins.com /roarkunderstanding |

923

and profound desire to end the possibility of nuclear war and on an innovative Soviet head of state who recognized that his country's domestic problems demanded an easing of Cold War antagonism. Mikhail Gorbachev assumed power in 1985 determined to revitalize the Soviet economy, which was incapable of delivering basic consumer goods. Hoping to stimulate production and streamline distribution, Gorbachev introduced some elements of free enterprise and proclaimed a new era of *glasnost* (greater freedom of expression), eventually allowing contested elections and challenges to Communist rule.

Concerns about immense defense budgets moved both Reagan and Gorbachev to the negotiating table. Enormous military expenditures stood between the Soviet premier and his goal of economic revival. With growing popular support for arms reductions, Reagan made disarmament a major goal in his last years in office and readily responded when Gorbachev took the initiative. The two leaders met four times between 1985 and 1988. Although Reagan's insistence on proceeding with SDI nearly killed the talks, by December 1987 the superpowers had completed an **intermediate-range nuclear forces (INF) agreement**. It eliminated all short- and medium-range missiles from Europe and provided for on-site inspection for the first time. This was also the first time that either nation had agreed to eliminate weapons already in place.

In 1988, Gorbachev further reduced tensions by announcing a gradual withdrawal from Afghanistan, which had become the Soviet equivalent of America's Vietnam. In addition, the Soviet Union, the United States, and Cuba agreed on a political settlement of the civil war in Angola. In the Middle East, both superpowers supported a cease-fire and peace talks in the eight-year war between Iran and Iraq. Within three years, the Cold War that had defined the world for nearly half a century would be history.

intermediate-range nuclear forces (INF) agreement

▶ Nuclear disarmament agreement reached between the United States and the Soviet Union in 1987, signifying a major thaw in the Cold War. The treaty eliminated all short- and medium-range missiles from Europe and provided for on-site inspection for the first time.

> **QUICK REVIEW**

How did anticommunism shape Reagan's foreign policy?

CHAPTER LOCATOR | How did the Nixon presidency reflect the rise of postwar conservatism? | Why did the "outsider" presidency of Jimmy Carter fail to gain broad support?

924 CHAPTER 30 THE CONSERVATIVE TURN

Conclusion: What was the long-term impact of the conservative turn?

"OURS WAS THE FIRST REVOLUTION in the history of mankind that truly reversed the course of government," boasted Ronald Reagan in his farewell address in 1989. The word *revolution* exaggerated the change, but his administration did mark the slowdown or reversal of expanding federal budgets for domestic programs and regulations that had taken off in the 1930s. Although he did not deliver on the social or moral issues dear to the heart of the New Right, Reagan used his skills as "the Great Communicator" to cultivate antigovernment sentiment and undermine the liberal assumptions of the New Deal.

Antigovernment sentiment grew along with the backlash against the reforms of the 1960s and the conduct of the Vietnam War. Watergate and other lawbreaking by Nixon administration officials further disillusioned Americans. Presidents Ford and Carter restored morality to the White House, but neither could solve the gravest economic problems since the Great Depression—slow economic growth, stagflation, and an increasing trade deficit. Even the Democrat Carter gave higher priority to fiscal austerity than to social reform, and he began the government's retreat from regulation of key industries.

A new conservative movement helped Reagan win the presidency and flourished during his administration. Reagan's tax cuts, combined with hefty increases in defense spending, created a federal deficit crisis that justified cuts in social welfare spending, made new federal initiatives unthinkable, and burdened the country for years to come. These policies also contributed to a widening income gap between the rich and the poor, weighing especially heavily on minorities, female-headed families, and children. Many Americans continued to support specific federal programs—especially those, such as Social Security and Medicare, that reached beyond the poor—but public sentiment about the government in general had taken a U-turn from the Roosevelt era. Instead of seeing the government as a helpful and problem-solving institution, many believed that not only was it ineffective at solving national problems but it also often made things worse. As Reagan appointed new justices, the Supreme Court retreated from liberalism, curbing the government's authority to protect individual rights and regulate the economy.

With the economic recovery that set in after 1982 and his optimistic rhetoric, Reagan lifted the confidence of Americans about their nation and its promise— confidence that had eroded with the economic and foreign policy blows of the 1970s. Beginning his presidency with harsh rhetoric against the Soviet Union and a huge military buildup, he left office having helped move the two superpowers to the highest level of cooperation since the Cold War began. Although that accord was not welcomed by strong anti-Communist conservatives, it signaled developments that would transform American-Soviet relations—and the world—in the next decade.

What conservative goals were realized in the Reagan administration?

What strategies did liberals use to fight the conservative turn?

How did Ronald Reagan's foreign policy affect the Cold War?

Conclusion: What was the long-term impact of the conservative turn?

☑ LearningCurve
Check what you know.
bedfordstmartins.com
/roarkunderstanding

CHAPTER 30 STUDY GUIDE

 STEP 1 **GET STARTED ONLINE**

 ✓ **LearningCurve** ■ bedfordstmartins.com/roarkunderstanding

Now that you've read the chapter, make it stick by completing the LearningCurve activity.

STEP 2 **EXPLAIN WHY IT MATTERS**

Put your reading into practice. Identify each term below, and then explain why it matters in U.S. history.

TERM	WHO OR WHAT & WHEN	WHY IT MATTERS
Watergate (p. 901)		
National Energy Act of 1978 (p. 907)		
Panama Canal treaty (p. 910)		
Camp David accords (p. 911)		
Iran hostage crisis (p. 912)		
New (Christian) Right (p. 914)		
supply-side economics (p. 915)		
Economic Recovery Tax Act (p. 915)		
Equal Rights Amendment (ERA) (p. 919)		
Strategic Defense Initiative (SDI) (p. 921)		
Iran-Contra scandal (p. 923)		
intermediate-range nuclear forces (INF) agreement (p. 924)		

 STEP 3 **MOVE BEYOND THE BASICS**

To demonstrate a more advanced understanding, describe the key conservative strategies and policies of the 1970s and 1980s. Whom did they benefit? What was the ultimate result of their implementation?

Conservative strategy/policy	Who benefited?	Results
Nixon's "southern strategy"		
Supply-side economics		
Reagan's tax and environmental policies		
Strategic Defense Initiative (SDI)		

PUT IT ALL TOGETHER

Now, take a step back and try to explain the big picture. Remember to use specific examples from the chapter in your answers.

THE RISE OF CONSERVATISM

▶ What aspects of Nixon's domestic policy appealed to the conservative movement and why?

▶ What specific conservative goals were fulfilled during the presidency of Ronald Reagan?

LIBERALISM

▶ Should Jimmy Carter be considered a liberal? Why or why not?

▶ What tactics did liberal groups use to resist the conservative turn? How successful were they?

U.S. FOREIGN POLICY

▶ What were the major currents of Jimmy Carter's foreign policy agenda?

▶ How and why did U.S. foreign policy change during Reagan's presidency?

LOOKING BACKWARD, LOOKING AHEAD

▶ How did U.S. foreign policy evolve from the 1950s through the 1980s?

▶ In what way does the domestic legacy of the 1970s and 1980s continue to shape contemporary American society?

> IN YOUR OWN WORDS

Imagine that you must give an oral report to the class answering the following question: What were the effects of America's move to the political right on American society and on U.S. foreign policy? What would be the most important points to include and why?

 Do it online at the Student Site ▪ **bedfordstmartins.com/roarkunderstanding**

31

FACING THE PROMISES AND CHALLENGES OF GLOBALIZATION

SINCE 1989

> How have globalization and international terrorism changed the focus of U.S. domestic and foreign policy since the end of the Cold War? Chapter 31 explores the changing nature of American politics and foreign policy from 1989 to the present. It examines the end of the Cold War during the presidency of George H. W. Bush; the domestic and foreign policies of the Clinton administration; the George W. Bush administration's departures from previous U.S. policy in the wake of the September 11, 2001, terrorist attacks; and the first term of Barack Obama.

**LearningCurve**
bedfordstmartins.com/roarkunderstanding
After reading the chapter, use LearningCurve to
retain what you've read.

Nike store, Chongqing, China. A man walks past a Nike factory store in Chongqing, China, in January 2011. Imagine China via AP Images.

> How did the United States respond to the end of the Cold War and tensions in the Middle East?

> How did President Clinton seek a middle ground in American politics?

> How did President Clinton respond to the challenges of globalization?

> How did President George W. Bush change American politics and foreign policy?

> What obstacles stood in the way of President Obama's reform agenda?

> Conclusion: How have Americans debated the role of the government?

How did the United States respond to the end of the Cold War and tensions in the Middle East?

The Gulf War This soldier arriving in Saudi Arabia in September 1990 was part of the massive military buildup in the Persian Gulf area before the U.S.-led coalition drove Iraqi forces out of Kuwait. For the first time, women served in combat-support positions. More than 33,000 women were stationed throughout the area; eleven died, and two were held as prisoners. Among their duties were piloting planes and helicopters, directing artillery, and fighting fires. © Bettmann/Corbis.

VICE PRESIDENT GEORGE H. W. BUSH announced his bid for the presidency in 1988, declaring, "We don't need radical new directions." As president, Bush proposed few domestic initiatives, but he signed key environmental and disability rights legislation.

More dramatic changes swept through the world, and Bush confronted situations that did not fit the free-world-versus-communism framework of the Cold War years. Most Americans approved of Bush's handling of the disintegration of the Soviet Union and its hold over Eastern Europe as well as his response to Iraq's invasion of neighboring Kuwait. But voters' concern over a sluggish economy limited him to one term as president.

Gridlock in Government

The son of a wealthy New England senator, George Herbert Walker Bush fought in World War II, served in Congress during the 1960s, and headed the CIA during the Nixon and Ford years. When Ronald Reagan tapped him for second place on

CHAPTER LOCATOR | How did the United States respond to the end of the Cold War and tensions in the Middle East? | How did President Clinton seek a middle ground in American politics?

930 CHAPTER 31
FACING THE PROMISES AND CHALLENGES OF GLOBALIZATION

the Republican ticket in 1980, Bush adjusted his more moderate positions to fit Reagan's conservative agenda. At the end of Reagan's second term, Republicans rewarded Bush with the presidential nomination.

Several candidates competed for the Democratic nomination in 1988. The Reverend Jesse Jackson—a civil rights leader whose Rainbow Coalition campaign centered on the needs of minorities, women, the working class, and the poor—made an impressive bid, winning several primaries and seven million votes. But the centrist candidate, Massachusetts governor Michael Dukakis, won the nomination. On election day, Bush won 54 percent of the vote, but the Democrats gained seats in Congress.

President Bush promised "a kinder, gentler nation" and was more inclined than Reagan to approve government activity in the private sphere. For example, Bush approved the **Clean Air Act of 1990**, the strongest, most comprehensive environmental law in history.

Some forty million Americans benefited when Bush signed another regulatory measure in 1990, the **Americans with Disabilities Act**, banning discrimination and requiring that private businesses and public facilities be accessible to people with disabilities. Disability advocate Cynthia Jones, feeling a breeze stirring over the White House lawn at the signing ceremony, said, "It was kind of like a new breath of air was sweeping across America. . . . People knew they had rights. That was wonderful." Yet Bush also needed to satisfy party conservatives to whom he had pledged, "Read my lips: No new taxes." Bush vetoed thirty-six bills, including those extending unemployment benefits, raising taxes, and mandating family and medical leave for workers. Press reports increasingly used the words *stalemate*, *gridlock*, and *divided government*.

Continuing a trend begun during the Reagan years, some states compensated for this paralysis with their own innovations. States passed bills to establish parental leave policies, improve food labeling, and protect the environment. Dozens of cities passed ordinances requiring businesses receiving tax abatements or other city benefits to pay wages well above the federal minimum wage. And in 1999, California passed a much tougher gun control bill than reformers had been able to get through Congress.

Clean Air Act of 1990

▶ Environmental legislation signed by President George H. W. Bush. The legislation was the strongest and most comprehensive environmental law in the nation's history.

Americans with Disabilities Act

▶ Legislation signed by President George H. W. Bush in 1990 that banned discrimination against the disabled. The law also required handicapped accessibility in public facilities and private businesses.

Bush and Taxes

Running for president in 1988, George H. W. Bush appealed to conservatives, avowing, "Read my lips: No new taxes." Yet when the federal budget deficit he inherited grew even larger, Bush agreed to both budget cuts and tax increases, outraging many Republicans. Here, conservative cartoonist Scott Stantis likens Bush to Pinocchio, whose nose grew when he lied. Scott Stantis/Copley News Service.

How did President Clinton respond to the challenges of globalization?

How did President George W. Bush change American politics and foreign policy?

What obstacles stood in the way of President Obama's reform agenda?

Conclusion: How have Americans debated the role of the government?

✓ **LearningCurve**
Check what you know.
bedfordstmartins.com /roarkunderstanding

> CHRONOLOGY

1988
- George H. W. Bush is elected president.

1989
- Communism collapses in Eastern Europe.
- United States invades Panama.

1990
- Americans with Disabilities Act.

1991
- Persian Gulf War.

1992
- William Jefferson "Bill" Clinton is elected president.

The huge federal budget deficit inherited from the Reagan administration impelled Bush in 1990 to abandon his "no new taxes" pledge, outraging conservatives. The new law modestly raised taxes on high-income Americans and increased levies on gasoline, cigarettes, alcohol, and luxury items, while leaving intact most of Reagan's massive tax reductions. Neither the new revenues nor controls on spending curbed the deficit, which was boosted by rising costs for Social Security, Medicare, Medicaid, and natural disasters.

Like Reagan, Bush created a more conservative Supreme Court. His first nominee was a moderate, but in 1991, when the only African American on the Court, Justice Thurgood Marshall, retired, Bush set off a national controversy by nominating Clarence Thomas, a conservative black appeals court judge who had opposed affirmative action as head of the Equal Employment Opportunity Commission (EEOC) under Reagan. Charging that Thomas would not protect minority rights, civil rights groups and other liberal organizations fought the nomination. Then Anita Hill, a black law professor and former EEOC employee, accused Thomas of sexual harassment. Thomas angrily denied the charges, and Hill's testimony failed to sway the Senate, which voted narrowly to confirm Thomas. The hearings angered many women, who noted that only two women sat in the Senate. They denounced the male senators for not taking sexual harassment seriously.

Going to War in Central America and the Persian Gulf

President Bush won greater support for his actions abroad. In Central America, the United States had depended on Panamanian dictator Manuel Noriega for helping the Contras in Nicaragua and providing the CIA with information about Communist activities in the region. But in 1989, after an American grand jury indicted Noriega for drug trafficking and after his troops killed an American Marine, Bush ordered 25,000 military personnel into Panama. In Operation Just Cause, U.S. forces quickly overcame Noriega's troops, sustaining 23 deaths, while hundreds of Panamanians, including many civilians, died. General Colin Powell noted that "our euphoria over our victory in Just Cause was not universal." Both the United Nations and the Organization of American States censured the unilateral action taken by the United States.

By contrast, Bush's second military engagement rested solidly on international approval. Viewing Iran as America's major enemy in the Middle East, U.S. officials had quietly assisted the Iraqi dictator Saddam Hussein in the Iran-Iraq war, which began in 1980 and ended inconclusively in 1988. In August 1990, Hussein sent troops into the small, oil-rich country of Kuwait (**Map 31.1**), and the invasion soon neared the Saudi Arabian border, threatening the world's largest oil reserves. President Bush quickly ordered a massive mobilization of American forces and assembled an international coalition to stand up to Iraq. He invoked principles of national self-determination and international law, but long-standing interests in Middle Eastern oil also drove the U.S. response.

Reflecting the easing of Cold War tensions, the Soviet Union voted for a UN embargo on Iraqi oil and authorization for using force if Iraq did not withdraw

CHAPTER LOCATOR | How did the United States respond to the end of the Cold War and tensions in the Middle East? | How did President Clinton seek a middle ground in American politics?

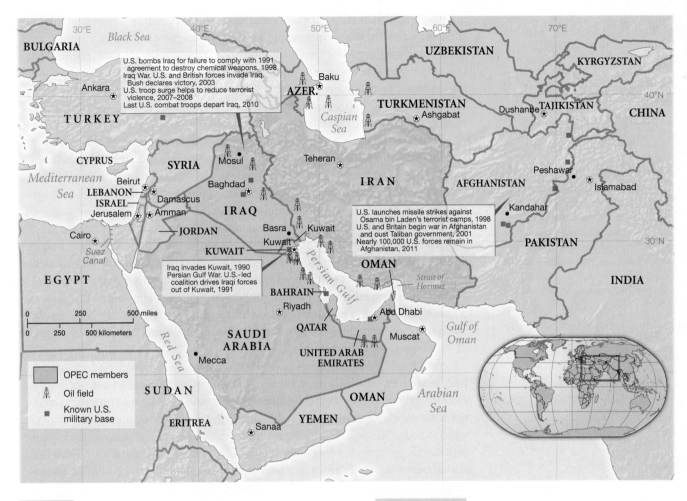

Map labels (selected):

BULGARIA · Black Sea · TURKEY · Ankara · CYPRUS · Mediterranean Sea · Beirut · LEBANON · ISRAEL · Damascus · Jerusalem · Amman · Cairo · Suez Canal · EGYPT · Red Sea · Mecca · SUDAN · ERITREA · Sanaa · YEMEN

SYRIA · Mosul · Baghdad · IRAQ · JORDAN · Basra · Kuwait · KUWAIT · Riyadh · SAUDI ARABIA · QATAR · BAHRAIN · Persian Gulf · UNITED ARAB EMIRATES · Abu Dhabi · OMAN · Muscat · Gulf of Oman · Arabian Sea · Strait of Hormuz

Baku · AZER. · Caspian Sea · Teheran · IRAN · Kandahar · OMAN

UZBEKISTAN · KYRGYZSTAN · TURKMENISTAN · Ashgabat · Dushanbe · TAJIKISTAN · CHINA · Peshawar · AFGHANISTAN · Islamabad · PAKISTAN · INDIA

Text box (Iraq, upper):
U.S. bombs Iraq for failure to comply with 1991 agreement to destroy chemical weapons, 1998
Iraq War. U.S. and British forces invade Iraq. Bush declares victory, 2003
U.S. troop surge helps to reduce terrorist violence, 2007–2008
Last U.S. combat troops depart Iraq, 2010

Text box (Afghanistan):
U.S. launches missile strikes against Osama bin Laden's terrorist camps, 1998
U.S. and Britain begin war in Afghanistan and oust Taliban government, 2001
Nearly 100,000 U.S. forces remain in Afghanistan, 2011

Text box (Kuwait):
Iraq invades Kuwait, 1990
Persian Gulf War. U.S.-led coalition drives Iraqi forces out of Kuwait, 1991

Scale: 0 250 500 miles / 0 250 500 kilometers

Legend:
OPEC members
Oil field
Known U.S. military base

MAP 31.1 ■ Events in the Middle East, 1989–2011

During the Persian Gulf War of 1991, the twenty-two-member Arab League supported the war to liberate Kuwait, and after September 11, 2001, it also approved of U.S. military operations in Afghanistan. Yet, except for the countries where the United States had military bases — Bahrain, Kuwait, Qatar, and Saudi Arabia — no Arab country supported the American invasion and occupation of Iraq in 2003. Arab hostility toward the United States also reflected the deterioration of Israeli-Palestinian relations after 1999, as Arabs charged that the United States allowed Israel to deny Palestinians land and liberty.

> MAP ACTIVITY

READING THE MAP: In what countries are the sources of oil located? In what countries does the United States have military bases?

CONNECTIONS: What conditions prompted the U.S. military interventions in Iraq and Afghanistan in 1991, 2001, and 2003? What were the U.S. goals in each of these interventions? To what extent were those goals realized?

from Kuwait by January 15, 1991. By then, the United States had deployed more than 400,000 soldiers to Saudi Arabia, joined by 265,000 troops from two dozen other nations, including several Arab states. "The community of nations has resolutely gathered to condemn and repel lawless aggression," Bush announced. "With few exceptions, the world now stands as one."

With Iraqi forces still in Kuwait, in January 1991 Bush asked Congress to approve war. Considerable sentiment favored waiting to see if the embargo and other means would force Hussein to back down, a position that Colin Powell

How did President Clinton respond to the challenges of globalization?

How did President George W. Bush change American politics and foreign policy?

What obstacles stood in the way of President Obama's reform agenda?

Conclusion: How have Americans debated the role of the government?

✔ LearningCurve
Check what you know.
bedfordstmartins.com /roarkunderstanding

933

quietly urged within the administration. Congress debated for three days and then authorized war by a margin of five votes in the Senate and sixty-seven in the House, with most Democrats in opposition. On January 17, 1991, the U.S.-led coalition launched Operation Desert Storm, a forty-day bombing campaign against Iraqi military targets, power plants, oil refineries, and transportation networks. Having severely crippled Iraq by air, the coalition then stormed into Kuwait, forcing Iraqi troops to withdraw (see Map 31.1).

"By God, we've kicked the Vietnam syndrome once and for all," President Bush exulted on March 1. Most Americans found no moral ambiguity in the **Persian Gulf War** and took pride in the display of military prowess. The United States stood at the apex of global leadership, steering a coalition in which Arab nations fought beside their former colonial rulers.

Some Americans criticized the Bush administration for ending the war without deposing Saddam Hussein. But Bush pointed to the limited UN mandate and to Middle Eastern leaders' concerns that an invasion of Iraq would destabilize the region. His secretary of defense, Richard Cheney, doubted that coalition forces could secure a stable government to replace Hussein and considered the price of a long occupation too high. Instead, administration officials counted on Hussein's pledges not to rearm or develop weapons of mass destruction, secured by a system of UN inspections to contain him.

Yet Middle Eastern stability remained elusive. Israel, which had endured Iraqi missile attacks, was more secure, but the Israeli-Palestinian conflict seethed. Despite military losses, Saddam Hussein remained in power and turned his war machine on Iraqi Kurds and Shiite Muslims whom the United States had encouraged to rebel. Hussein also found ways to conceal arms from UN weapons inspectors before he threw the inspectors out in 1998. Finally, the decision to keep U.S. troops based in Saudi Arabia, the holy land of Islam, fueled the hatred and determination of Muslim extremists like Osama bin Laden.

The Cold War Ends

Soviet support in the Persian Gulf War marked a momentous change in superpower relations. The progressive forces that Mikhail Gorbachev had encouraged in the Communist world (see chapter 30) swept through Eastern Europe in 1989, where popular uprisings demanded an end to state repression and inefficient economic bureaucracies. Communist governments toppled like dominoes (**Map 31.2**), virtually without bloodshed, because Gorbachev refused to prop them up with Soviet armies. East Germany opened its border with West Germany, and in November 1989 ecstatic Germans danced on the Berlin Wall.

Unification of East and West Germany sped to completion in 1990. Soon Poland, Hungary, and other former iron curtain countries lined up to join NATO. Although U.S. military forces remained in Europe as part of NATO, Europe no longer depended on the United States for its security. Its economic clout also grew as Western Europe formed a common economic market in 1992. Inspired by the liberation of Eastern Europe, republics within the Soviet Union soon sought their own independence. In December 1991, Boris Yeltsin, president of the Russian Republic, announced that Russia and eleven other republics had formed a new entity, the Commonwealth of Independent States, and other former Soviet states declared

Persian Gulf War

▶ 1991 war between Iraq and a U.S.-led international coalition. The war was sparked by the 1990 Iraqi invasion of Kuwait. A forty-day bombing campaign against Iraq, followed by coalition troops storming into Kuwait, brought a quick coalition victory.

CHAPTER LOCATOR | How did the United States respond to the end of the Cold War and tensions in the Middle East? | How did President Clinton seek a middle ground in American politics?

934 CHAPTER 31 FACING THE PROMISES AND CHALLENGES OF GLOBALIZATION

Berlin Wall falls, Nov. 1989
East and West Germany
reunified, Oct . 1990

Solidarity Party wins
elections, June 1989

Communist leadership ousted, Nov. 1989
Vaclav Havel named president, Dec. 1989
Splits into the Czech Republic and Slovakia, 1993

Gorbachev comes to power, 1985
Moscow coup fails and USSR
dissolves, Aug. 1991

Free elections sweep non-
Communists into power, April 1990

Communist dictator overthrown and
executed, Dec.1989
Salvation Front wins elections, May 1990

Dissolves in civil war, 1991
Truce, 1995

Communist leader ousted, Nov. 1989
Free elections held, Aug. 1990

Republics of the former Soviet Union

Commonwealth of Independent States

Other Communist regimes overthrown
since 1989

MAP 31.2 ■ Events in Eastern Europe, 1989–1995

The overthrow of Communist governments throughout Eastern
Europe and the splintering of the Soviet Union into more than a
dozen separate nations were the most momentous changes in
world history since World War II.

> MAP ACTIVITY

READING THE MAP: Which country was the first to overthrow its Communist government? Which was the last? In which nations did elections
usher in a change in government?

CONNECTIONS: What problems did Mikhail Gorbachev try to solve, and
how did he try to solve them? What policy launched by Ronald Reagan
contributed to Soviet dilemmas (see chapter 30)? Did this policy create
any problems in the United States?

their independence. With nothing left to govern, Gorbachev resigned. The Soviet
Union had dissolved, and with it the Cold War conflict that had defined U.S. foreign
policy for decades.

Colin Powell joked that he was "running out of villains. I'm down to Castro
and Kim Il Sung," the North Korean dictator who, along with China's leaders,
resisted the liberalizing tides sweeping the world. In 1989, Chinese soldiers
killed hundreds of pro-democracy demonstrators in Beijing, and the Communist
government arrested some ten thousand reformers. North Korea remained a
Communist dictatorship, committed to developing nuclear weapons.

| How did President Clinton respond to the challenges of globalization? | How did President George W. Bush change American politics and foreign policy? | What obstacles stood in the way of President Obama's reform agenda? | Conclusion: How have Americans debated the role of the government? | ✓ LearningCurve Check what you know. bedfordstmartins.com /roarkunderstanding |

Fall of the Berlin Wall

After 1961, the Berlin Wall stood as the prime symbol of the Cold War and the iron grip of communism over Eastern Europe and the Soviet Union. More than four hundred Eastern Europeans were killed trying to flee to the West. After Communist authorities opened the wall on November 9, 1989, permitting free travel between East and West Germany, Berliners from both sides gathered at the wall to celebrate.
Eric Bouvet/Gamma Press Images.

> VISUAL ACTIVITY

READING THE IMAGE: What does the image tell you about the revolutions in Eastern Europe in 1989?
CONNECTIONS: What were the major factors that made possible the dismantling of the Berlin Wall?

"The post–Cold War world is decidedly not post-nuclear," declared one U.S. official. In 1990, the United States and the Soviet Union signed the Strategic Arms Reduction Talks treaty, which cut about 30 percent of each superpower's nuclear arsenal. And in 1996, the UN General Assembly overwhelmingly approved a total nuclear test ban treaty. Yet India and Pakistan, hostile neighbors, refused to sign the treaty, and both exploded atomic devices in 1998. Moreover, the Republican-controlled U.S. Senate defeated ratification of the treaty. The potential for rogue nations and terrorist groups to develop nuclear weapons posed an ongoing threat.

The 1992 Election

In March 1991, Bush's chances for reelection in 1992 looked golden. The Gulf War victory catapulted his approval rating to 88 percent, causing the most prominent Democrats to opt out of the presidential race. But that did not deter William Jefferson "Bill" Clinton, who at age forty-five had served as governor of Arkansas for twelve years. Like Carter in 1976, Clinton and his running mate, Tennessee

CHAPTER LOCATOR | How did the United States respond to the end of the Cold War and tensions in the Middle East? | How did President Clinton seek a middle ground in American politics?

CHAPTER 31
936 FACING THE PROMISES AND CHALLENGES OF GLOBALIZATION

senator Albert Gore Jr., presented themselves as "New Democrats" and sought to rid the party of its liberal image.

Clinton promised to work for the "forgotten middle class," who "do the work, pay the taxes, raise the kids, and play by the rules." He promised a tax cut for the middle class, pledged to reinvigorate government and the economy, and vowed "to put an end to welfare as we know it." Bush was vulnerable to an unemployment rate of 7 percent and to a challenge from self-made Texas billionaire H. Ross Perot, whose third-party organization revealed Americans' frustrations with government and the major parties. Clinton won 43 percent of the popular vote, Bush 38 percent, and Perot 19 percent—the strongest third-party finish in eighty years. By casting nearly two-thirds of their votes against Bush, voters suggested a mandate for change but not the direction that change should take.

QUICK REVIEW <

How did George H. W. Bush respond to threats to U.S. interests as the Cold War came to an end?

| How did President Clinton respond to the challenges of globalization? | How did President George W. Bush change American politics and foreign policy? | What obstacles stood in the way of President Obama's reform agenda? | Conclusion: How have Americans debated the role of the government? | ✓ LearningCurve Check what you know. bedfordstmartins.com /roarkunderstanding |

How did President Clinton seek a middle ground in American politics?

Clinton's Appointments

President Clinton broke new ground by appointing women to offices traditionally considered to be male territory. Janet Reno served as attorney general, Laura Tyson as chair of the President's Council of Economic Advisers, Sheila Widnall as secretary of the air force, and Madeleine Albright as secretary of state. Here, Albright (left) and Reno (second from right) applaud Clinton's 1999 State of the Union address. AP Images/Doug Mills.

BILL CLINTON'S ASSERTION that "the era of big government is over" reflected the Democratic Party's move to the right that had begun with Jimmy Carter. Clinton did not completely abandon liberal principles. He extended benefits for the working poor; delivered incremental reforms to feminists, environmentalists, and other groups; and spoke out in favor of affirmative action and gay rights. Yet his administration restricted welfare benefits and attended more to the concerns of middle-class Americans than to the needs of the disadvantaged.

Clinton's eight-year presidency witnessed the longest economic boom in history and ended with a budget surplus. Although various factors generated the prosperity, many Americans identified Clinton with the buoyant economy, elected him to a second term, and supported him even when his reckless sexual behavior led to impeachment. Clinton was not convicted, but the scandal crippled his leadership in his last years in office.

Clinton's Reforms

Clinton wanted to restore confidence in government as a force for good while not alienating antigovernment voters. The huge budget deficit that he inherited—$4.4 trillion in 1993—precluded substantial federal initiatives. Moreover, Clinton

CHAPTER LOCATOR | How did the United States respond to the end of the Cold War and tensions in the Middle East? | **How did President Clinton seek a middle ground in American politics?**

938 CHAPTER 31 FACING THE PROMISES AND CHALLENGES OF GLOBALIZATION

failed to win a majority of the popular vote in both 1992 and 1996, and the Republicans controlled Congress after 1994. Throughout his presidency, Clinton was burdened by investigations into past financial activities and private indiscretions.

Despite these obstacles, Clinton achieved a number of incremental reforms. He issued executive orders easing restrictions on abortion and signed several bills that Republicans had previously blocked. Most significantly, Clinton pushed through a substantial increase in the **Earned Income Tax Credit (EITC)** for low-wage earners. Begun in 1975, the EITC gave tax breaks to people who worked full-time at meager wages or, if they owed no taxes, a subsidy to lift their family income above the poverty line. By 2003, some fifteen million low-income families were benefiting from the EITC, almost half of them minorities. One expert called it "the largest antipoverty program since the Great Society."

Earned Income Tax Credit (EITC)

▸ Federal antipoverty program initiated in 1975 that assisted the working poor by giving tax breaks to low-income, full-time workers or a subsidy to those who owed no taxes. President Bill Clinton pushed through a significant increase in the program in 1993.

> **Liberal Reforms under President Clinton**

- Family and Medical Leave Act of 1993
- Violence against Women Act of 1994
- Stricter air pollution controls and greater protection for national forests and parks
- A minimum-wage increase
- Expansion of aid for college students
- Expansion of the Earned Income Tax Credit

Shortly before Clinton took office, the economy had begun to rebound. Economic expansion, along with spending cuts, tax increases, and declining unemployment, produced in 1998 the first budget surplus since 1969. Despite a substantial tax cut in 1997 that reduced levies on estates and capital gains and that provided tax credits for families with children and for higher education, the surplus grew. Clinton failed, however, to provide universal health insurance and to curb skyrocketing medical costs. Under the direction of First Lady Hillary Rodham Clinton and with little congressional consultation, the administration proposed a complicated plan that drew criticism from all sides. Liberals wanted a single-payer plan similar to Medicare, while conservatives charged that the proposal would increase taxes and government interference in medical decisions. Congress enacted smaller reforms, such as underwriting health care for 5 million uninsured children, yet 40 million Americans remained uninsured.

Pledging to change the face of government to one that "looked like America," Clinton built on the gradual progress women and minorities had made since the 1960s. For example, African Americans and women had become mayors in major cities from New York to San Francisco. Virginia had elected the first black governor since Reconstruction, and Florida the first Latino. Clinton's cabinet appointments included six women, three African Americans, two Latinos, and an Asian American. Clinton's judicial appointments had a similar cast, and in 1993 he named the second woman to the Supreme Court, Ruth Bader Ginsburg, whose arguments as an attorney had won key women's rights rulings from that Court.

> **CHRONOLOGY**

1993
- President Clinton institutes a "don't ask, don't tell" policy for gays in the military.

1995
- Bombing of federal building in Oklahoma City.

1996
- Personal Responsibility and Work Opportunity Reconciliation Act.
- President Clinton is reelected.

1999
- Senate trial fails to approve impeachment of Clinton.

How did President Clinton respond to the challenges of globalization?

How did President George W. Bush change American politics and foreign policy?

What obstacles stood in the way of President Obama's reform agenda?

Conclusion: How have Americans debated the role of the government?

✓ LearningCurve
Check what you know.
bedfordstmartins.com
/roarkunderstanding

Accommodating the Right

The 1994 midterm elections swept away the Democratic majorities in Congress and helped push Clinton to the right. Led by Representative Newt Gingrich of Georgia, Republicans claimed the 1994 election as a mandate for their "contract with America," a conservative platform to end "government that is too big, too intrusive, and too easy with the public's money" and to elect "a Congress that respects the values and shares the faith of the American family."

The most extreme antigovernment sentiment developed far from Washington in the form of grassroots armed militias that stockpiled weapons, celebrated white Christian supremacy, and reflected conservatives' hostility to such diverse institutions as taxes and the United Nations. The militia movement grew after passage of new gun control legislation and after government agents stormed the headquarters of an armed religious cult in Waco, Texas, in April 1993, killing more than 80. On the second anniversary of that event, militia sympathizers bombed a federal building in Oklahoma City, taking 169 lives in the worst terrorist attack in the nation's history up to that point.

"don't ask, don't tell" policy

▶ Military policy announced by President Clinton in 1993 that barred officials from inquiring into the sexual orientation of military personnel but permitted the dismissal of personnel who admitted to being gay or engaged in homosexual behavior.

Clinton bowed to conservative views on gay and lesbian rights, backing away from his promise to lift the ban on gays in the military. Although many other nations welcomed homosexual soldiers, U.S. military leaders and key legislators objected to the proposal, and Clinton reverted to a **"don't ask, don't tell" policy** in 1993. Officials could not ask military personnel about their sexuality, but soldiers who said they were gay or who engaged in homosexual behavior could be dismissed. In 1996, Clinton signed the Defense of Marriage Act, prohibiting the federal government from recognizing state-licensed marriages between same-sex couples.

Nonetheless, attitudes and practices relating to homosexuality became more tolerant. By 2006, a majority of the five hundred largest companies provided health benefits to same-sex domestic partners and included sexual orientation in their nondiscrimination policies. A majority of states banned discrimination in public employment, and many of those laws extended to private employment, housing, and education. By 2012, gay marriage was legal in nine states and the District of Columbia. Several more states recognized civil unions and domestic partnerships, extending to same-sex couples rights available to married couples in such areas as inheritance, taxation, and medical decisions.

Clinton's efforts to dissociate his party from liberalism were apparent in his handling of the New Deal program Aid to Families with Dependent Children (AFDC), popularly called welfare. Public sentiment about poverty had shifted. Instead of blaming poverty on external circumstances, such as lack of adequate jobs, more people blamed the poor themselves and welfare programs that trapped the poor in cycles of dependency. Many questioned why they should subsidize poor mothers when so many women worked outside the home. Defenders of AFDC doubted that the economy could provide sufficient jobs at decent wages.

Personal Responsibility and Work Opportunity Reconciliation Act

▶ Legislation signed by President Clinton in 1996 that replaced Aid to Families with Dependent Children with Temporary Assistance for Needy Families, which provided grants to the states to assist the poor and limited welfare payments to two years, with a lifetime maximum of five years.

After vetoing two welfare bills, Clinton signed a less punitive measure as the 1996 election approached. The **Personal Responsibility and Work Opportunity Reconciliation Act** replaced AFDC with Temporary Assistance for Needy Families, which provided grants to the states to assist the poor. It limited welfare payments to two years, with a lifetime maximum of five years.

CHAPTER LOCATOR | How did the United States respond to the end of the Cold War and tensions in the Middle East? | **How did President Clinton seek a middle ground in American politics?**

940 CHAPTER 31
FACING THE PROMISES AND CHALLENGES OF GLOBALIZATION

Clinton's signature on the new law denied Republicans a partisan issue in the 1996 presidential campaign. The Republican Party also moved to the center, nominating Kansan Robert Dole, a World War II hero and former Senate majority leader. Clinton won 49 percent of the votes; 41 percent went to Dole and 9 percent to third-party candidate Ross Perot. Voters sent a Republican majority back to Congress.

In 1999, Clinton and Congress further deregulated the financial industry by repealing key aspects of the Glass-Steagall Act, passed during the New Deal to avoid another Great Depression. The Financial Services Modernization Act ended the separation between banking, securities, and insurance services, allowing financial institutions to engage in all three, practices that leading economists would link to the severe financial meltdown of 2008.

Impeaching the President

Clinton's magnetism, his ability to capture the middle ground, and the nation's economic resurgence enabled him to survive scandals and impeachment. Early in his presidency, charges related to firings of White House staff, political use of FBI records, and "Whitewater"—the nickname for real estate investments that the Clintons had made in Arkansas—led to an official investigation by an independent prosecutor.

In January 1998, the independent prosecutor, Kenneth Starr, began to investigate a charge that Clinton had had sexual relations with a twenty-one-year-old White House intern and then lied about it to a federal grand jury. After vehemently denying the charge, Clinton subsequently bowed to the mounting evidence against

| How did President Clinton respond to the challenges of globalization? | How did President George W. Bush change American politics and foreign policy? | What obstacles stood in the way of President Obama's reform agenda? | Conclusion: How have Americans debated the role of the government? | ✓ LearningCurve Check what you know. bedfordstmartins.com /roarkunderstanding |

941

him. Starr prepared a case for the House of Representatives, which in December 1998 voted to impeach the president for perjury and obstruction of justice. Clinton became the second president (after Andrew Johnson, in 1868) to be impeached by the House and tried by the Senate.

The Senate trial took place in early 1999. Most Americans condemned the president's behavior but approved of the job he was doing and opposed his removal from office. Some saw Starr as a fanatic invading individuals' privacy. One man said, "Let him get a divorce from his wife. Don't take him out of office and disrupt the country." Those favoring removal insisted that the president must set a high moral standard and that lying to a grand jury, even over a private matter, was a serious offense. With a two-thirds majority needed for conviction, the Senate voted 45 to 55 on the perjury count and 50 to 50 on the obstruction of justice count. A majority, including some Republicans, seemed to agree with a Clinton supporter that the president's behavior, though "indefensible, outrageous, unforgivable, shameless," did not warrant his removal from office. The investigation that led up to impeachment ended in 2000 when the independent prosecutor reported insufficient evidence of illegalities related to the Whitewater land deals.

The Booming Economy of the 1990s

Clinton's ability to weather impeachment owed much to the prosperous economy, which in 1991 began a period of tremendous expansion. Clinton's policies also contributed to the boom. He made deficit reduction a priority, and in exchange the Federal Reserve Board and bond market traders encouraged economic expansion by lowering interest rates. Businesses also prospered because they had lowered their costs through restructuring and laying off workers. Economic problems in Europe and Asia helped American firms become more competitive in the international market. And the computer revolution and the application of information technology boosted productivity.

> ### > The Booming Economy of the 1990s

- Gross domestic product grew by more than one-third.
- Thirteen million new jobs were created.
- Inflation remained in check.
- Unemployment dropped to 4 percent.
- The stock market soared.

People at all income levels benefited from the economic boom, but income inequality, rising since the 1970s, endured **(Figure 31.1)**. The growing use of computer technology increased demand for highly skilled workers, while the movement of manufacturing jobs abroad diminished opportunities and wages for the less skilled. Moreover, deregulation and the continuing decline of unions hurt lower-skilled workers, tax cuts favored the better-off, and the minimum wage failed to keep up with inflation.

CHAPTER LOCATOR | How did the United States respond to the end of the Cold War and tensions in the Middle East? | **How did President Clinton seek a middle ground in American politics?**

942   CHAPTER 31
FACING THE PROMISES AND CHALLENGES OF GLOBALIZATION

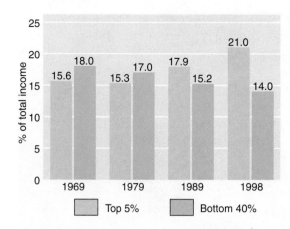

FIGURE 31.1 ■ The Growth of Inequality: Changes in Family Income, 1969–1998

For most of the post–World War II period, income increased for all groups on the economic ladder. But after 1979, the income of the poorest families actually declined, while the income of the richest 20 percent of the population grew substantially. Adapted from the *New York Times*, 1989.

Although more minorities than ever attained middle-class status, people of color overall remained lowest on the economic ladder. For instance, in 1999 the median income for white households surpassed $45,000, but it stood at only $29,423 and $33,676 for African American and Latino households, respectively. In 2000, poverty afflicted more than 20 percent of African Americans and Latinos, in contrast to 7.5 percent of whites.

QUICK REVIEW <

What policies of the Clinton administration moved the Democratic Party to the right?

| How did President Clinton respond to the challenges of globalization? | How did President George W. Bush change American politics and foreign policy? | What obstacles stood in the way of President Obama's reform agenda? | Conclusion: How have Americans debated the role of the government? | ✓ LearningCurve Check what you know. bedfordstmartins.com /roarkunderstanding |

How did President Clinton respond to the challenges of globalization?

U.S. Troops in Kosovo

In 1999, American troops joined a NATO peacekeeping unit in the former Yugoslav province of Kosovo after a U.S.-led NATO bombing campaign forced the Serbian army to withdraw. The NATO soldiers were dispatched to monitor the departure of Serbian troops, assist the return of ethnic Albanians who had fled the Serbian army, and reestablish civil governments. Here, an ethnic Albanian boy walks beside Specialist Brent Baldwin from Jonesville, Michigan, as he patrols the town of Gnjilane in southeast Kosovo in May 2000. Wide World Photos, Inc.

AMERICA'S ECONOMIC SUCCESS in the 1990s was linked to its dominance in the world economy, which was undergoing tremendous transformations in a process called globalization—the growing integration and interdependence of national citizens and economies. President Clinton lowered a number of trade barriers, despite critics who emphasized the economic deprivation and environmental devastation that often resulted. Debates likewise arose over the large numbers of immigrants entering the United States.

Clinton agreed with George H. W. Bush that the United States must retain its supreme position in the world. He took military action in Somalia, Haiti, the Middle East, and eastern Europe, and he pushed hard to ease the conflict between Israel and the Palestinians. Clinton also strove to safeguard American interests from terrorist attacks around the world, a challenge in many ways more difficult than combating communism.

CHAPTER LOCATOR | How did the United States respond to the end of the Cold War and tensions in the Middle East? | How did President Clinton seek a middle ground in American politics?

Defining America's Place in a New World Order

In 1991, President George H. W. Bush declared a "new world order" emerging from the ashes of the Cold War. As the sole superpower, the United States was determined to let no nation challenge its military superiority or global leadership, spending five times more on defense than did its nearest competitor, China. Yet policymakers struggled to define guiding principles for deciding when and how to use the nation's military and diplomatic power in a post–Cold War world.

Africa, where civil wars and extreme human suffering rarely evoked a strong American response, was a case in point. In 1992, guided largely by humanitarianism, President Bush had attached U.S. forces to a UN operation in the northern African country of Somalia, where famine and civil war raged. In 1993, President Clinton allowed that humanitarian mission to turn into "nation building"—an effort to establish a stable government—and eighteen U.S. soldiers were killed. After Americans saw film of a soldier's corpse dragged through the streets, the outcry suggested that most citizens were unwilling to sacrifice lives when no vital interest seemed threatened. Indeed, both the United States and the United Nations stood by in 1994 when more than half a million people were massacred in a brutal civil war in Rwanda.

As always, the United States was more inclined to use force nearer its borders. In 1994, after a military coup overthrew Jean-Bertrand Aristide, Haiti's democratically elected president, Clinton persuaded the United Nations to impose economic sanctions on Haiti and to authorize military intervention. Hours before U.S. forces were to invade, Haitian military leaders promised to step down. U.S. forces landed peacefully, and Aristide was restored to power, but Haiti continued to face grave economic challenges and political instability.

In eastern Europe, the collapse of communism ignited a severe crisis. During the Cold War, the Communist government of Yugoslavia had held together a federation of six republics. After the Communists were swept out in 1989, ruthless leaders exploited ethnic differences to bolster their power. Yugoslavia splintered into separate states and fell into civil war.

The Serbian aggression under President Slobodan Milosevic against Bosnian Muslims, which included rape, torture, and mass killings, in particular, horrified much of the world, but European and U.S. leaders hesitated to use military force. Finally, in 1995, Clinton ordered U.S. fliers to join NATO forces in intensive bombing of Serbian military concentrations. That effort and successful offensives by the Croatian and Bosnian armies forced Milosevic to the bargaining table, where representatives from Serbia, Croatia, and Bosnia hammered out a peace treaty.

In 1998, new fighting broke out in the southern Serbian province of Kosovo, where ethnic Albanians, who constituted 90 percent of the population, demanded independence. The Serbian army retaliated, driving out one-third of Kosovo's 1.8 million Albanian Muslims. In 1999, NATO launched a U.S.-led bombing

> CHRONOLOGY

1993
- Israel and Palestine Liberation Organization (PLO) sign peace accords.
- North American Free Trade Agreement (NAFTA).

1994
- United States sends troops to Haiti.
- General Agreement on Tariffs and Trade establishes World Trade Organization.

1995
- United States, with NATO, bombs Serbia.

1998
- United States bombs terrorist sites in Afghanistan and Sudan.

1998–2000
- United States bombs Iraq.

Breakup of Yugoslavia

AUSTRIA · HUNGARY · SLOVENIA · CROATIA · Vojvodina Province · ROMANIA · BOSNIA-HERZEGOVINA · SERBIA · Adriatic Sea · ITALY · MONTENEGRO · BULGARIA · KOSOVO · MACEDONIA · ALBANIA · GREECE

0 · 100 · 200 miles
0 · 100 · 200 kilometers

— Yugoslavia 1945–1991

| How did President Clinton respond to the challenges of globalization? | How did President George W. Bush change American politics and foreign policy? | What obstacles stood in the way of President Obama's reform agenda? | Conclusion: How have Americans debated the role of the government? | ✓ **LearningCurve** Check what you know. bedfordstmartins.com /roarkunderstanding |

Israel and PLO sign accords, 1993
Israel and Jordan sign peace treaty, 1994
Progress of Israeli-Palestinian negotiations
halts and violence escalates, 2000
Israel withdraws from Gaza, 2005
Israel at war with Hezbollah in Lebanon, 2006
Israel invades Gaza, 2008

Events in Israel since 1989

attack on Serbian military and government targets that, after three months, forced Milosevic to agree to a settlement. Serbians voted Milosevic out of office in October 2000, and he died in 2006 while on trial for genocide by a UN war crimes tribunal.

Elsewhere, Clinton deployed U.S. power when he could send missiles rather than soldiers, and he was prepared to act without international support or UN sanction. In August 1998, bombings at the U.S. embassies in Kenya and Tanzania killed 12 Americans and more than 250 Africans. Clinton retaliated with missile attacks on terrorist training camps in Afghanistan and facilities in Sudan controlled by Osama bin Laden, a Saudi-born millionaire who financed the Islamic-extremist terrorist network linked to the embassy attacks. Clinton also launched air strikes against Iraq in 1993 when a plot to assassinate former president Bush was uncovered, in 1996 after Saddam Hussein attacked the Kurds in northern Iraq, and repeatedly between 1998 and 2000 after Hussein expelled UN weapons inspectors. Whereas Bush had acted in the Gulf War with the support of an international force that included Arab states, Clinton acted unilaterally and in the face of Arab opposition.

To defuse the Israeli-Palestinian conflict, Clinton used diplomatic rather than military power. In 1993, Norwegian diplomats had brokered an agreement between Yasir Arafat, head of the Palestine Liberation Organization (PLO), and Yitzhak Rabin, Israeli prime minister, to recognize the existence of each other's states. Israel agreed to withdraw from the Gaza Strip and Jericho, allowing for Palestinian self-government there. In July 1994, Clinton presided over another turning point as Rabin and King Hussein of Jordan signed a declaration of peace. Yet difficult issues remained, especially control of Jerusalem and the presence of more than 200,000 Israeli settlers in the West Bank, the land seized by Israel in 1967, where 3 million Palestinians were determined to establish their own state. Continuing violence between Israelis and Palestinians strengthened anti-American sentiment among Arabs, who saw the United States as Israel's ally.

Debates over Globalization

North American Free Trade Agreement (NAFTA)

▶ 1993 treaty that eliminated all tariffs and trade barriers among the United States, Canada, and Mexico. NAFTA was supported by President Clinton, a minority of Democrats, and a majority of Republicans.

World Trade Organization

▶ International economic body established in 1994 through the General Agreement in Tariffs and Trade to enforce substantial tariff and import quota reductions. Many corporations welcomed these trade barrier reductions, but critics linked them to job loss and the weakening of unions.

Building on efforts by Reagan and Bush, Clinton sought to speed up the growth of a "global marketplace" with new measures to ease restrictions on international commerce. Although the process of globalization was centuries old, new communications technologies such as the Internet and cell phones connected nations, corporations, and individuals at much greater speed and much less cost than ever before. To advance globalization, in 1993 Clinton won congressional approval of the **North American Free Trade Agreement (NAFTA)**, which eliminated all tariffs and trade barriers among the United States, Canada, and Mexico, in the face of opposition from organized labor and others fearing loss of jobs and industries to Mexico. A majority of Democrats opposed NAFTA, but Republican support ensured approval. In 1994, the Senate ratified the General Agreement on Tariffs and Trade, establishing the **World Trade Organization** to enforce substantial tariff and import quota reductions among some 135 member nations. And in 2005, Clinton's successor, George W. Bush, lowered more trade barriers with the passage of the Central American–Dominican Republic Free Trade Agreement.

CHAPTER LOCATOR | How did the United States respond to the end of the Cold War and tensions in the Middle East? | How did President Clinton seek a middle ground in American politics?

CHAPTER 31
946 FACING THE PROMISES AND CHALLENGES OF GLOBALIZATION

The free trade issue was intensely contested. Much of corporate America welcomed the elimination of trade barriers. "Ideally, you'd have every plant you own on a barge," remarked Jack Welch, CEO of General Electric. Critics linked globalization to the loss of jobs, the weakening of unions, and the growing gap between rich and poor. Demanding "fair trade" rather than simply free trade, critics wanted treaties to require decent wage and labor standards. Environmentalists wanted countries seeking increased commerce with the United States to reduce pollution and prevent the destruction of endangered species.

Globalization controversies often centered on relationships between the United States, which dominated the world's industrial core, and developing nations on the periphery, whose cheap labor and lax environmental standards caught investors' eyes. United Students against Sweatshops, for example, attacked the international conglomerate Nike, which paid Chinese workers $1.50 to produce a pair of shoes selling for more than $100 in the United States. Yet leaders of developing nations actively sought foreign investment, because wages deemed pitiful by Americans often provided their impoverished people a much better living than they could otherwise obtain. At the same time, developing countries often pointed to American hypocrisy in advocating free trade in industry while heavily subsidizing the U.S. agricultural sector. "When countries like America, Britain and France subsidize their farmers," complained a grower in Uganda, "we get hurt."

Whereas globalization's cheerleaders pointed to the cheap consumer goods available to Americans and argued that everyone would benefit in the long run, critics focused on the short-term victims. American businessman George Soros conceded that international trade and investments generated wealth, "but they cannot take care of other social needs, such as the preservation of peace, alleviation of poverty, protection of the environment, labor conditions, or human rights." In 2000, President Clinton responded to such criticism by ordering an environmental impact review before the signing of any trade agreement. Beyond the United States, officials from the World Bank and the International Monetary Fund, along with representatives from wealthy economies, promised to provide poor nations more debt relief and a greater voice in decisions about loans and grants. According to World Bank president James D. Wolfensohn, "Our challenge is to make globalization an instrument of opportunity and inclusion—not fear."

The Internationalization of the United States

The United States experienced the dynamic forces of globalization within its own borders. Already in the 1980s, Japanese, European, and Middle Eastern investors had purchased U.S. stocks and bonds, real estate, and corporations. Local communities welcomed foreign capital, and states competed to recruit foreign automobile plants. By 2002, the paychecks of nearly four million American workers came from foreign-owned companies, such as Honda and BMW.

Globalization was also transforming American society, as the United States experienced a tremendous surge of immigration, part of a worldwide trend that counted some 214 million immigrants across the globe in 2010. The promise of economic opportunity, as always, lured immigrants to America, and the Immigration and Nationality Act of 1965 enabled them to come. The law allowed close relatives of U.S. citizens to enter above the annual ceiling of 270,000 immigrants, thus creating

How did President Clinton respond to the challenges of globalization?

How did President George W. Bush change American politics and foreign policy?

What obstacles stood in the way of President Obama's reform agenda?

Conclusion: How have Americans debated the role of the government?

✓ LearningCurve
Check what you know.
bedfordstmartins.com
/roarkunderstanding

947

family migration chains. Moreover, during the Cold War, U.S. immigration policy was generous to refugees from communism, welcoming more than 800,000 Cubans and more than 600,000 Vietnamese, Laotians, and Cambodians.

> ### Globalization and American Demography

- By 2006, the 35.7 million immigrants in the United States constituted 12.4 percent of the population.
- By the 1980s, the vast majority of immigrants came from Asia, Latin America, and the Caribbean.
- By 2004, 41 million Latinos constituted — at 14 percent — the largest minority group in the nation.

The racial composition of the new immigration heightened the long-standing wariness of native-born Americans toward newcomers. Pressure for more restrictive policies stemmed from beliefs that immigrants took jobs from the native-born, suppressed wages by accepting low pay, strained the capability of social services, or eroded the dominant culture and language. Americans expressed particular hostility toward immigrants who were in the country illegally—an estimated 12 million in 2008—even though the economy depended on their cheap labor.

The new immigration was once again making America an international, interracial society. The largest numbers of immigrants flocked to California, New York, Texas, Florida, New Jersey, and Illinois, but new immigrants dispersed

Immigrant Labor Large commercial farms depended on Latino workers, who constituted more than 45 percent of agricultural labor in 2002. The dependence of agriculture and service industries on immigrant labor helped block movements for greater immigration restrictions. The workers here are harvesting strawberries near Carlsbad, California. In 2002, the median weekly pay for migrant farmworkers was $300. Sandy Huffaker/Getty Images.

CHAPTER LOCATOR | How did the United States respond to the end of the Cold War and tensions in the Middle East? | How did President Clinton seek a middle ground in American politics?

CHAPTER 31
948   FACING THE PROMISES AND CHALLENGES OF GLOBALIZATION

throughout the country. Taquerias, sushi bars, and Vietnamese restaurants appeared in southeastern and midwestern towns; cable TV companies added Spanish-language stations; and the international sport of soccer soared in popularity. Mixed marriages displayed the growing fusion of cultures, recognized in 2000 on Census Bureau forms, where Americans could check more than one racial category. Like their predecessors, the majority of post-1965 immigrants were unskilled and poor. They took the lowest-paying jobs, constituting nearly half of all farmworkers and housekeepers. They also performed other work that employers maintained native-born Americans would not do. Yet a significant number of immigrants were highly skilled workers, sought after by burgeoning high-tech industries. By 2006, nearly one-third of all software developers were foreign-born, as were 28 percent of all physicians.

QUICK REVIEW <

What key issues surrounding globalization did the United States face in the 1990s?

| How did President Clinton respond to the challenges of globalization? | How did President George W. Bush change American politics and foreign policy? | What obstacles stood in the way of President Obama's reform agenda? | Conclusion: How have Americans debated the role of the government? | ✓ LearningCurve Check what you know. bedfordstmartins.com /roarkunderstanding |

949

How did President George W. Bush change American politics and foreign policy?

9/11

The magnitude of the destruction and loss of lives in the 9/11 attacks made Americans feel more vulnerable than they had since the Cold War ended. The attacks also affected people around the world, who streamed to U.S. embassies or expressed their shock and sympathy in other ways. Steve Ludlum/The New York Times/Redux.

ALTHOUGH FAILING TO CAPTURE a plurality of the popular vote in 2000, George W. Bush made his mark in domestic policy with key legislation to improve public school education, subsidize prescription drugs for elderly citizens, and greatly reduce taxes for the wealthy. The tax cuts, along with spending on new international and domestic crises, turned the substantial budget surplus that Bush had inherited into the largest deficit in the nation's history, and a financial crisis near the end of his presidency sent the economy into a recession.

As Islamist terrorism replaced communism as the primary threat to U.S. security, the Bush administration launched a war in Afghanistan in 2001 and adopted a policy of unilateralism and preemption by going to war against Iraq in 2003. Bush

CHAPTER LOCATOR | How did the United States respond to the end of the Cold War and tensions in the Middle East? | How did President Clinton seek a middle ground in American politics?

won reelection in 2004, but stability in Iraq and Afghanistan remained elusive, and he confronted serious foreign and domestic crises in his second term. Democrats capitalized on widespread dissatisfaction with his administration to gain control of Congress in 2006 and the White House in 2008.

The Disputed Election of 2000

George W. Bush won the Republican nomination after a series of richly funded, hard-fought primaries. The oldest son of former president George H. W. Bush, he had served as governor of Texas since 1994. Inexperienced in national and international affairs, Bush chose for his running mate a seasoned official, Richard B. Cheney, who had served in three previous Republican administrations. Many observers predicted that the thriving economy would give the Democratic contender, Vice President Al Gore, the edge, and he did surpass Bush by more than half a million votes. Once the polls closed, however, it became clear that Florida's 25 electoral college votes would decide the presidency. Bush's tiny margin in Florida prompted an automatic recount of the votes, which eventually gave him an edge of 537 votes in that state.

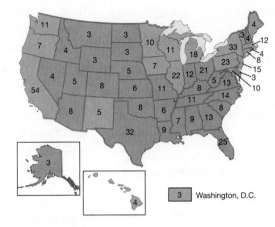

Candidate	Electoral Vote	Popular Vote	Percent of Popular Vote
George W. Bush (Republican)	271	50,456,062	47.8
Al Gore (Democrat)	267	50,996,862	48.4
Ralph Nader (Green Party)	0	2,858,843	2.7
Patrick J. Buchanan (Reform Party)	0	438,760	0.4

MAP 31.3 ■ The Election of 2000

Meanwhile, the Democrats asked for hand-counting of Florida ballots in several heavily Democratic counties where machine errors and confusing ballots may have left thousands of Gore votes unrecorded. The Republicans, in turn, went to court to try to stop the hand-counts. The outcome of the 2000 election hung in the balance for weeks as cases went all the way to the Supreme Court. Finally, a bitterly divided Court ruled five to four against further recounts. While critics charged partisanship, noting that the conservative justices had abandoned their custom of favoring state over federal authority, Gore conceded the presidency to Bush. For the first time since 1888, a president who failed to win the popular vote took office (**Map 31.3**). Despite the lack of a popular mandate, the Bush administration set out to make dramatic policy changes.

The Domestic Policies of a "Compassionate Conservative"

Bush had promised to govern as a "compassionate conservative." A devout born-again Christian, he immediately established the White House Office of Faith-Based and Community Initiatives to encourage religious groups to participate in government programs aimed at prison inmates, the unemployed, and others. The religious right praised the initiatives, but others charged that they violated the constitutional separation of church and state. Federal courts ruled in several dozen cases that faith ministries were using government funds to indoctrinate the people they served.

Bush's fiscal policies were more compassionate toward the rich than toward average Americans. In 2001, he signed a bill reducing taxes over the next ten years

How did President Clinton respond to the challenges of globalization?	**How did President George W. Bush change American politics and foreign policy?**	What obstacles stood in the way of President Obama's reform agenda?	Conclusion: How have Americans debated the role of the government?	☑ LearningCurve Check what you know. bedfordstmartins.com /roarkunderstanding

951

> CHRONOLOGY

2000
- George W. Bush is elected president.

2001
- Terrorists attack World Trade Center and Pentagon.
- U.S.-led coalition drives Taliban government out of Afghanistan.
- USA Patriot Act.
- $1.35 trillion tax cut.

2002
- No Child Left Behind Act.
- Department of Homeland Security is established.

2003
- United States attacks Iraq.
- Prescription drug coverage is added to Medicare.

2004
- George W. Bush is reelected president.

2005
- Hurricane Katrina.

2007
- Bush begins troop surge in Iraq.

No Child Left Behind Act

▶ 2002 legislation championed by President George W. Bush that expanded the role of the federal government in public education. The law required every school to meet annual testing standards, penalized failing schools, and allowed parents to transfer their children out of such schools.

by $1.35 trillion. A 2003 tax law slashed another $320 billion. The laws heavily favored the rich by reducing income taxes, phasing out estate taxes, and cutting tax rates on capital gains and dividends. They also provided benefits for married couples and families with children and offered tax deductions for college expenses.

The tax cuts contributed to a mushrooming federal deficit—the highest in U.S. history. In 2009, the deficit surpassed $1 trillion as the government struggled to combat a recession. By then, the national debt had risen to $9.6 trillion, making the United States increasingly dependent on China and other foreign investors, who held more than half of the debt.

Bush used executive powers to weaken environmental protection as part of his larger goals of reducing government regulation, promoting economic growth, and increasing energy production. The administration opened millions of wilderness acres to mining, oil, and timber industries and relaxed standards under the Clean Air and Clean Water Acts. To worldwide dismay, the administration withdrew from the Kyoto Protocol on global warming, signed in 1997 by 178 nations to reduce greenhouse gas emissions.

Conservatives hailed Bush's two appointments to the Supreme Court. In 2005, John Roberts, who had served in the Reagan and George H. W. Bush administrations, was named chief justice. Bush then replaced the moderate Sandra Day O'Connor with Samuel A. Alito, a staunch conservative who won confirmation by a narrow margin. While the Court stood up to the administration in rulings on the rights of accused terrorists, it tilted right on cases concerning abortion, gun control, sex discrimination in employment, campaign financing, and regulation of business.

In contrast to the partisan conflict over judicial appointments and tax and environmental policy, Bush won bipartisan support for the **No Child Left Behind Act** of 2002, marking the first substantial expansion of the federal government in public education since the 1960s. Promising to end, in Bush's words, "the story of children being just shuffled through the system," the law required every school to meet annual testing standards, penalized failing schools, and allowed parents to transfer their children out of such schools. As states struggled to finance the new standards, school officials began to criticize the one-size-fits-all approach, and they pointed to family and community impoverishment as sources of student deficiencies.

The Bush administration's second effort to co-opt Democratic Party issues constituted what the president hailed as "the greatest advance in health care coverage for America's seniors" since Medicare became law in 1965. In 2003, Bush signed a bill authorizing prescription drug benefits for the elderly and also expanding the role of private insurers in the Medicare system. Most Democrats opposed the legislation, charging that it subsidized private insurers with federal funds, banned imports of low-priced drugs, and prohibited the government from negotiating with drug companies to reduce prices. The law was a boon to the elderly, but medical costs overall continued to soar, and the number of uninsured Americans surpassed forty million in 2008.

One domestic undertaking of the Bush administration found little approval anywhere: its handling of Hurricane Katrina, which in August 2005 devastated the coasts of Alabama, Louisiana, and Mississippi and ultimately resulted in some fifteen hundred deaths. The catastrophe that ensued when the levees in

CHAPTER LOCATOR | How did the United States respond to the end of the Cold War and tensions in the Middle East? | How did President Clinton seek a middle ground in American politics?

Residents of the poverty-stricken Lower Ninth Ward of New Orleans cry for help after floods submerged 80 percent of the city in the wake of Hurricane Katrina in August 2005. The boat was useless to these people because it had lost its motor. Some residents waited as long as five days to be rescued. A historian of the disaster wrote, "Americans were not used to seeing their country in ruins, their people in want." Wide World Photos, Inc.

New Orleans broke, flooding 80 percent of the city, shook a deeply rooted assumption held by Americans: that government owed its citizens protection from natural disasters. New Orleans residents who were too old, too poor, or too sick to flee the flooding spent anguished days waiting on rooftops for help; wading in filthy, toxic water; and enduring the heat, disorder, and lack of basic necessities at the convention center and Superdome, where they had been told to go for safety and protection. "How can we save the world if we can't save our own people?" wondered one Louisianan. Thousands of volunteers rushed to help, and millions more opened their pocketbooks to aid the victims. Yet the immense private generosity and the superb response of a few groups, such as the U.S. Coast Guard and the Louisiana Department of Wildlife and Fisheries, could not make up for the feeling that the nation had failed some of its citizens when they needed it most. Since so many of Katrina's hardest-hit victims were poor and black, the disaster also highlighted the injustices and deprivations remaining in American society.

| How did President Clinton respond to the challenges of globalization? | **How did President George W. Bush change American politics and foreign policy?** | What obstacles stood in the way of President Obama's reform agenda? | Conclusion: How have Americans debated the role of the government? | ✔️ **LearningCurve** Check what you know. bedfordstmartins.com /roarkunderstanding |

953

The Globalization of Terrorism

The response to Hurricane Katrina contrasted sharply with the government's decisive reaction to the horror that had unfolded four years earlier on the morning of September 11, 2001. Nineteen terrorists hijacked four planes and flew two of them into the twin towers of New York City's World Trade Center and one into the Pentagon near Washington, D.C.; the fourth crashed in a field in Pennsylvania. The attacks took nearly 2,800 lives, including U.S. citizens and people from ninety countries.

The hijackers belonged to Osama bin Laden's Al Qaeda international terrorist network. Organized from Afghanistan, where the radical Muslim Taliban government harbored Al Qaeda, the attacks reflected Islamic extremists' rage at the spread of Western culture and values into the Muslim world. The attacks also demonstrated their opposition to the 1991 Persian Gulf War against Iraq and the stationing of American troops in Saudi Arabia. Bin Laden sought to rid the Middle East of Western influence and install puritanical Muslim control.

The 9/11 terrorists and others who came after them ranged from poor to middle-class; some lived in Middle Eastern homelands governed by undemocratic and corrupt governments, others in Western cities where they felt alienated and despised. All saw the West, especially the United States, as the evil source of their humiliation and the supporter of Israel's oppression of Palestinian Muslims.

In the wake of the September 11 attacks, President Bush sought a global alliance against terrorism and won at least verbal support from most governments. On October 11, the United States and Britain began bombing Afghanistan, and American special forces aided the Northern Alliance, the Taliban government's main opposition. By December, the Taliban government was destroyed, but bin Laden eluded capture, continuing to direct Al Qaeda forces throughout the world, until U.S. special forces killed him in Pakistan in 2011. Afghans elected a new national government, but the Taliban remained strong in large parts of the country, continued to challenge U.S. and NATO troops, and contributed to economic instability and insecurity.

After the September 11 attacks, anti-immigrant sentiment revived throughout the United States, and anyone appearing to be Middle Eastern or practicing Islam often aroused suspicion. Authorities arrested more than a thousand Arabs and Muslims, and a Justice Department study later reported that many people with no connection to terrorism spent months in jail, denied their rights. "I think America overreacted . . . by singling out Arab-named men like myself," said Shanaz Mohammed, who was jailed for eight months for an immigration violation.

USA Patriot Act

▶ 2001 law that gave the government new powers to monitor suspected terrorists and their associates, including the ability to access personal information. Critics charged that it represented an unwarranted abridgment of civil rights.

Afghanistan

In October 2001, Congress passed the **USA Patriot Act**, which gave the government new powers to monitor suspected terrorists and their associates, including the ability to access personal information. It soon provoked calls for revision from both conservatives and liberals. Kathleen MacKenzie, a councilwoman in Ann Arbor, Michigan, explained why the

CHAPTER LOCATOR | How did the United States respond to the end of the Cold War and tensions in the Middle East? | How did President Clinton seek a middle ground in American politics?

CHAPTER 31
954 FACING THE PROMISES AND CHALLENGES OF GLOBALIZATION

council opposed the Patriot Act: "As concerned as we were about national safety, we felt that giving up [rights] was too high a price to pay." A security official countered, "If you don't violate someone's human rights some of the time, you probably aren't doing your job."

Insisting that presidential powers were virtually limitless in times of national crisis, Bush stretched his authority as commander in chief until he met resistance from the courts and Congress. The United States detained more than seven hundred prisoners captured in Afghanistan and taken to the U.S. military base at Guantánamo, Cuba, where, until the courts acted, they had no rights and some were tortured. Although President Barack Obama promised to close the detention camp, more than one hundred prisoners remained there in 2012. The government also sought to protect Americans from future terrorist attacks through the greatest reorganization of the executive branch since 1948. In November 2002, Congress authorized the new Department of Homeland Security, combining 170,000 federal employees from twenty-two agencies responsible for various aspects of domestic security. Chief among the department's duties were intelligence analysis; immigration and border security; chemical, biological, and nuclear countermeasures; and emergency preparedness and response.

Unilateralism, Preemption, and the Iraq War

The Bush administration sought collective action against the Taliban, but on most other international issues it adopted a go-it-alone approach. In addition to withdrawing from the Kyoto Protocol on global warming and violating international rules about the treatment of military prisoners, it scrapped the 1972 Antiballistic Missile Treaty in order to develop the space-based Strategic Defense Initiative first proposed by Ronald Reagan. Bush also withdrew the United States from the United Nations' International Criminal Court, and he rejected an agreement to enforce bans on biological weapons—an agreement signed by all of America's European allies.

Nowhere was the policy of unilateralism more striking than in a new war against Iraq, a war endorsed by Vice President Dick Cheney and Secretary of Defense Donald H. Rumsfeld, but not by Colin Powell, who was then secretary of state. Addressing West Point graduates in June 2002, President Bush proclaimed a new security strategy based not on containment but on preemption: "Traditional concepts of deterrence will not work against a terrorist enemy whose avowed tactics are wanton destruction and the targeting of innocents; whose so-called soldiers seek martyrdom in death and whose most potent protection is statelessness." Because nuclear, chemical, and biological weapons enabled "even weak states and small groups [to] attain a catastrophic power to strike great nations," the United States had to "be ready for preemptive action." The president's claim that the United States had the right to start a war was at odds with international law and with many Americans' understanding of their nation's ideals. It distressed most of America's great-power allies.

Nonetheless, the Bush administration soon applied the doctrine of preemption to Iraq, whose dictator, Saddam Hussein, appeared to be violating UN resolutions from the 1991 Gulf War restricting Iraqi development of nuclear, chemical, and biological weapons. In November 2002, the United States persuaded the UN

How did President Clinton respond to the challenges of globalization?

How did President George W. Bush change American politics and foreign policy?

What obstacles stood in the way of President Obama's reform agenda?

Conclusion: How have Americans debated the role of the government?

✓ LearningCurve Check what you know. bedfordstmartins.com /roarkunderstanding

955

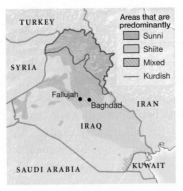

Iraq

Security Council to pass a resolution demanding that Iraq disarm or face "serious consequences." When Iraq failed to comply fully with new UN inspections, the Bush administration decided on war. Making claims (subsequently refuted) that Hussein had links to Al Qaeda and harbored terrorists and that Iraq possessed weapons of mass destruction, the president insisted that the threat was immediate and great enough to justify preemptive action. Despite opposition from the Arab world and most major nations—including France, Germany, China, and Russia—the United States and Britain invaded Iraq on March 19, 2003, supported by some thirty nations (see Map 31.1). Coalition forces won an easy victory, and Bush declared the end of the **Iraq War** on May 1. Saddam Hussein remained at large until December 2003.

Chaos followed the quick victory. Damage from U.S. bombing and widespread looting resulting from the failure of U.S. troops to secure order and provide basic necessities left Iraqis wondering how much they had gained. "With Saddam there was tyranny, but at least you had a salary to put food on your family's table," said a young father. A Baghdad hospital worker complained, "They can take our oil, but at least they should let us have electricity and water." Five years after the invasion, continuing violence had caused 2 million to flee their country and displaced 1.9 million within Iraq.

The administration had not planned adequately for the occupation and failed to send sufficient troops to Iraq. The 140,000 American forces there came under attack almost daily from remnants of the former Hussein regime, religious extremists, and hundreds of foreign terrorists now entering the chaotic country. Seeking to divide Iraqis and undermine the occupation, terrorists launched deadly assaults resulting in the death of tens of thousands of Iraqis. By the end of the Iraq War, nearly 4,500 U.S. soldiers had lost their lives, and many returned home grievously wounded.

The war became an issue in the presidential campaign of 2004. Massachusetts senator John Kerry, the Democratic nominee, criticized Bush's unilateralist foreign policy and the administration's conduct of the war. A slim majority of voters, however, indicated their belief that Bush would better protect American security than Kerry. The president eked out a 286 to 252 victory in the electoral college, winning 50.7 percent of the popular and carrying Republican majorities into Congress.

In June 2004, the United States transferred sovereignty to an interim Iraqi government, and in January 2005 Iraqis elected a national assembly, which then had to organize a government satisfactory to Iraq's three major groups—Sunnis, Shiites, and Kurds. Violence escalated against government officials, Iraqi civilians, and occupation forces. A nineteen-year-old Iraqi confined to his house by his parents, who feared their son could be killed or lured into terrorist activities, said, "If I'm killed, it doesn't even matter because I'm dead right now." In 2006, a majority of Americans told pollsters that the Iraq War was a mistake.

By 2006, Bush's conduct of the war faced criticism that crossed party lines and included military leaders. Critics acknowledged that the United States had felled a brutal dictator, but coalition forces were not large enough or adequately

Iraq War

▶ War launched by the United States, Britain, and several smaller countries in March 2003 against the government of Iraqi dictator Saddam Hussein. The decision to go to war was based on claims (subsequently refuted) that Hussein's government had links to Al Qaeda, harbored terrorists, and possessed weapons of mass destruction.

CHAPTER LOCATOR | How did the United States respond to the end of the Cold War and tensions in the Middle East? | How did President Clinton seek a middle ground in American politics?

CHAPTER 31

956 FACING THE PROMISES AND CHALLENGES OF GLOBALIZATION

prepared for the turmoil that followed. Nor did they find the weapons of mass destruction or links to Osama bin Laden that administration officials had insisted made the war necessary. Rather, in the chaos brought on by the invasion, more than a thousand terrorists entered Iraq—the place, according to one expert, "for fundamentalists to go . . . to stick it to the West."

The war and occupation exacted a steep price in American and Iraqi lives, dollars, U.S. relations with other great powers, and the nation's reputation in the world, especially among Arab nations. Revelations of prisoner abuse in the Abu Ghraib prison in Iraq and in the Guantánamo detention camp housing captives from the war in Afghanistan further tarnished the image of the United States. Anti-Americanism around the world rose to its highest point in history. The budget deficit swelled, and resources were diverted to Iraq from other national security challenges, including the stabilization of Afghanistan, the elimination of bin Laden and Al Qaeda, and the threats posed by North Korea's and Iran's pursuit of nuclear weapons.

Voters registered their dissatisfaction in 2006, when Democrats captured both houses of Congress for the first time since 1994. The Bush administration displayed more willingness to work with other nations in dealing with Iraq, Iran, and North Korea. In 2007, it began a troop surge in Iraq, increasing U.S. forces there to 160,000. The surge, along with actions by Iraqi leaders, contributed to a significant reduction in violence, and the administration began planning for the withdrawal of U.S. forces, which was completed at the end of 2011.

QUICK REVIEW

What impact did the terrorist attacks on September 11, 2001, have on U.S. foreign and domestic policy?

How did President Clinton respond to the challenges of globalization?

How did President George W. Bush change American politics and foreign policy?

What obstacles stood in the way of President Obama's reform agenda?

Conclusion: How have Americans debated the role of the government?

☑ LearningCurve
Check what you know.
bedfordstmartins.com
/roarkunderstanding

957

What obstacles stood in the way of President Obama's reform agenda?

Health Care Reform In March 2010, President Obama signed the Patient Protection and Affordable Care Act, sometimes called "Obamacare," as congressional leaders and others look on. At the signing were Marcelas Owens (left), whose mother died after she lost her job and her health insurance, and former Michigan congressman John Dingell (right, seated), who first introduced national health insurance in the 1940s. The Supreme Court upheld the controversial measure in June 2012. AP/Wide World Photos

DESPITE THE IMPROVING SITUATION IN IRAQ, President Bush's approval ratings sank on the eve of the 2008 elections. The Republicans nominated Senator John McCain of Arizona, a Vietnam War hero, who chose as his running mate Alaska governor Sarah Palin, the second woman to run for vice president on a major party ticket. Even more historic changes occurred in the Democratic Party when, for the first time, an African American and a woman were the top two contenders. In hard-fought primary battles, Illinois senator Barack Obama edged out New York senator and former First Lady Hillary Rodham Clinton for the nomination.

Born to a white mother and a Kenyan father and raised in Hawai'i and Indonesia, Obama served in the Illinois senate and won election to the U.S. Senate in 2004. At the age of forty-seven, he won the Democratic nomination with brilliant grassroots and Internet organizing and by appealing to deep-seated longings for a new kind of politics and racial reconciliation. He won 53 percent of the popular vote and defeated McCain 365 to 173 in the electoral college to become the first African American president, while Democrats increased their majorities in the House and Senate.

Obama hoped to work across party lines as he pursued reforms in health care, education, the environment, and immigration policy, but he confronted a severe economic crisis. A recession had struck in late 2007, fueled by a breakdown in financial institutions that had accumulated trillions of dollars of bad debt, much of

CHAPTER LOCATOR | How did the United States respond to the end of the Cold War and tensions in the Middle East? | How did President Clinton seek a middle ground in American politics?

CHAPTER 31
958 FACING THE PROMISES AND CHALLENGES OF GLOBALIZATION

it from risky home mortgages. As the recession spread to other parts of the world, home mortgage foreclosures skyrocketed, major companies went bankrupt, and unemployment rose to 9.8 percent in late 2010, the highest rate in more than twenty-five years.

The crisis was so severe that Congress passed the Bush administration's $700 billion Troubled Asset Relief Program in 2008 to inject credit into the economy and shore up banks as well as other businesses. Obama followed with the American Recovery and Reinvestment Act of 2009, $787 billion worth of spending and tax cuts to stimulate the economy and relieve unemployment. He also arranged a federal bailout of General Motors and Chrysler, saving an estimated one million jobs related to the automobile industry. Finally, to address the conditions that triggered the financial crisis, Congress expanded governmental regulation with the Wall Street Reform and Consumer Protection Act in 2010.

Obama's judicial appointments increased the number of women on the Supreme Court to three, including the first ever Latina justice. His greatest domestic achievement was passage of a health care reform bill, the **Patient Protection and Affordable Care Act** of 2010, which represented the largest expansion of government since the Great Society.

> ### > The Patient Protection and Affordable Care Act of 2010

- Required nearly all Americans to carry health insurance and provided subsidies to those in need
- Encouraged businesses to offer coverage to employees
- Imposed new regulations on insurance companies to protect their customers
- Contained provisions to limit health care costs

Republicans had previously endorsed key elements of the measure, but not a single one voted for it. In the face of widespread opposition to what critics called "Obamacare," the Supreme Court upheld its constitutionality by a five-to-four vote, as the United States became the last of the industrialized democracies to underwrite health care for all its citizens.

In foreign affairs, Obama reached out to Muslim nations, recommitted the United States to multilateralism, and worked to contain the proliferation of nuclear weapons. He continued the Bush administration's plan to withdraw from Iraq, and the last troops departed in 2011, although Iraq continued to endure terrorist violence. Even though corruption permeated Afghanistan's government and a majority of Americans opposed the war there, which by 2011 had taken more than 2,000 American lives, Obama dispatched 50,000 more military personnel, promising that the United States would fully withdraw by 2014. In May 2011, U.S. special forces killed Osama bin Laden, who was hiding in Pakistan.

Voters were more concerned with domestic issues when they issued a sharp rebuke to Obama in the 2010 midterm elections, turning over the House to the Republicans and cutting into the Democratic majority in the Senate. Although the stock market had rebounded, nearly 10 percent of American workers were unemployed, the federal deficit that Obama had inherited from the Bush administration soared to $1.4 trillion, and a vocal minority of mostly older and white voters expressed their fury at what they considered an overreaching government by

> CHRONOLOGY

2008
- Worst financial crisis since the Great Depression.
- Barack Obama is elected president.

2009
- American Recovery and Reinvestment Act.

2010
- Patient Protection and Affordable Care Act.
- Wall Street Reform and Consumer Protection Act.
- United States ends combat operations in Iraq and increases troops in Afghanistan.

2011
- Osama bin Laden is killed.

Patient Protection and Affordable Care Act
▶ Sweeping 2010 health care reform bill that established nearly universal health insurance by providing subsidies and compelling larger business to offer coverage to employees. Championed by President Barack Obama, the act also imposed new regulations on insurance companies and contained provisions to limit health care costs.

How did President Clinton respond to the challenges of globalization?

How did President George W. Bush change American politics and foreign policy?

What obstacles stood in the way of President Obama's reform agenda?

Conclusion: How have Americans debated the role of the government?

✓ LearningCurve
Check what you know.
bedfordstmartins.com
/roarkunderstanding

959

Candidate	Electoral Vote	Popular Vote	Percent of Popular Vote
Barack Obama (Democrat)	332	65,899,660	51.1
Mitt Romney (Republican)	206	60,932,152	47.2

MAP 31.4 ■ The Election of 2012

joining grassroots movements that took the name the Tea Party revolt. As one Tea Party supporter put it, "The government is taking over everything—I want my freedom back."

The intensely polarized political environment complicated Obama's efforts to reduce unemployment and cut the enormous federal debt. It also thwarted his efforts to reform environmental and immigration policy. With Congress blocking him at every turn, Obama used his executive authority to stiffen requirements on motor vehicle emissions, to temporarily protect young illegal immigrants from deportation, and to end discrimination against gays in the military.

Obama carried the burden of a nearly 8 percent unemployment rate into the 2012 election, in which he faced Republican Mitt Romney, former governor of Massachusetts and the first Mormon to be nominated for the presidency. With the electorate deeply divided over the role of the federal government, Obama won easily in the electoral college, with 332 votes to Romney's 206, and he captured 51 percent of the popular vote to Romney's 47 percent (**Map 31.4**). The Democrats made small gains in Congress, but Republicans still controlled the House, and government remained divided as the nation continued to struggle to reduce unemployment and deal with a staggering national deficit and debt. Abroad, Obama faced nuclear ambitions in Iran and North Korea, along with intensified instability in the Middle East, where U.S. support of democratic revolutions also risked strengthening Muslim extremists.

> **QUICK REVIEW**

What were the successes and failures of President Obama's first term as president?

CHAPTER LOCATOR | How did the United States respond to the end of the Cold War and tensions in the Middle East? | How did President Clinton seek a middle ground in American politics?

Conclusion: How have Americans debated the role of the government?

C

COLIN POWELL REFERRED to the unfinished nature of the American promise when he declared that the question of America's role in the world "isn't answered yet." The end of the Cold War, the rise of international terrorism, and the George W. Bush administration's doctrines of preemption and unilateralism sparked new debates over the long-standing question of U.S. actions beyond its borders.

Americans had also debated for more than two centuries what responsibilities the government should shoulder and what was best left to private enterprise, families, churches, and other voluntary institutions. Far more than most industrialized democracies, the United States had relied on individual or private rather than collective or public solutions. In the twentieth century, Americans significantly enlarged the federal government's powers, but since the 1960s fewer people trusted in government's ability to improve people's lives, even as a poverty rate of 20 percent among children continued and a growing gap between rich and poor intensified.

The see-sawing of control of the government between Republicans and Democrats from 1989 to 2010 reflected ongoing debate over government's role in domestic affairs. The first Bush administration's civil rights measure for people with disabilities and Bill Clinton's incremental reforms both built on a tradition that sought to realize the American promise of justice and well-being. Those who mobilized against the ravages of globalization worked internationally for what earlier reformers had sought for the domestic population: protection of individual rights, curbs on capitalism and assistance for its victims, and fiscal policies that placed greater responsibility on those best able to pay. Even the second Bush administration, which sought to limit government's reach, supported the No Child Left Behind Act, the Medicare prescription drug program, and a gigantic bail-out of failing businesses when the financial crisis hit the economy in 2008. The controversy over Obama's efforts to stimulate the economy and to reform health care and the financial industry replayed America's long-standing debate about the government's appropriate role.

The United States became more embedded in the global economy as products, information, and people crossed borders with amazing speed and frequency. New waves of immigration altered the face of the American population. Globalization also contributed to the threat of deadly terrorism within America's own borders. In response to those dangers, the second Bush administration launched wars in Afghanistan and Iraq. Obama ended the Iraq War in 2011, but he pursued terrorists aggressively and continued the war in Afghanistan. Both administrations sought to maintain U.S. preeminence in the world, but debate continued about how best to use that power.

| How did President Clinton respond to the challenges of globalization? | How did President George W. Bush change American politics and foreign policy? | What obstacles stood in the way of President Obama's reform agenda? | Conclusion: How have Americans debated the role of the government? | ✔ LearningCurve Check what you know. bedfordstmartins.com /roarkunderstanding |

CHAPTER 31 STUDY GUIDE

GET STARTED ONLINE

 LearningCurve ▪ bedfordstmartins.com/roarkunderstanding

Now that you've read the chapter, make it stick by completing the LearningCurve activity.

EXPLAIN WHY IT MATTERS

Put your reading into practice. Identify each term below, and then explain why it matters in U.S. history.

TERM	WHO OR WHAT & WHEN	WHY IT MATTERS
Clean Air Act of 1990 (p. 931)		
Americans with Disabilities Act (p. 931)		
Persian Gulf War (p. 934)		
Earned Income Tax Credit (EITC) (p. 939)		
"don't ask, don't tell" policy (p. 940)		
Personal Responsibility and Work Opportunity Reconciliation Act (p. 940)		
North American Free Trade Agreement (NAFTA) (p. 946)		
World Trade Organization (p. 946)		
No Child Left Behind Act (p. 952)		
USA Patriot Act (p. 954)		
Iraq War (p. 956)		
Patient Protection and Affordable Care Act (p. 959)		

MOVE BEYOND THE BASICS

To demonstrate a more advanced understanding, analyze the impact of some of the key events and developments of the 1990s and 2000s on the United States and the global community. Which events or developments are still having an impact today? In what way?

Event/development	Impact
End of the Cold War	
Booming economy of the 1990s	
Free trade and globalization	
Attacks of September 11, 2001	
Iraq War	

PUT IT ALL TOGETHER

Now, take a step back and try to explain the big picture. Remember to use specific examples from the chapter in your answers.

THE END OF THE COLD WAR

▶ How did U.S. foreign policy change after the fall of communism in Eastern Europe and the Soviet Union?

▶ How did U.S. economic policy change after 1992?

DOMESTIC REFORM

▶ How did domestic reforms of the Clinton administration affect lower-income people in the United States?

▶ Why have the reforms of the Obama administration created intense disagreement among lawmakers and U.S. citizens?

THE POST-9/11 WORLD

▶ How were international relations between the United States and other nations affected by the events of September 11, 2001?

▶ How did 9/11 affect Americans in the decade that followed?

LOOKING BACKWARD, LOOKING AHEAD

▶ Compare and contrast the place of the United States in the world in 1900 and in 2013.

▶ Defend or refute the following statement: In fifty years' time, the United States will still be the most powerful nation in the world.

> ## IN YOUR OWN WORDS

Imagine that you must give an oral report to the class answering the following question: **How have globalization and international terrorism changed the focus of U.S. domestic and foreign policy since the end of the Cold War?** What would be the most important points to include and why?

 Do it online at the Student Site ■ **bedfordstmartins.com/roarkunderstanding**

APPENDIX I

DOCUMENTS

THE DECLARATION OF INDEPENDENCE

In Congress, July 4, 1776,

THE UNANIMOUS DECLARATION OF THE THIRTEEN
UNITED STATES OF AMERICA

When in the course of human events, it becomes necessary for one people to dissolve the political bands which have connected them with another, and to assume, among the powers of the earth, the separate and equal station to which the laws of nature and of nature's God entitle them, a decent respect to the opinions of mankind requires that they should declare the causes which impel them to the separation.

We hold these truths to be self-evident, that all men are created equal; that they are endowed by their Creator with certain unalienable rights; that among these, are life, liberty, and the pursuit of happiness. That, to secure these rights, governments are instituted among men, deriving their just powers from the consent of the governed; that, whenever any form of government becomes destructive of these ends, it is the right of the people to alter or to abolish it, and to institute a new government, laying its foundation on such principles, and organizing its powers in such form, as to them shall seem most likely to effect their safety and happiness. Prudence, indeed, will dictate that governments long established, should not be changed for light and transient causes; and, accordingly, all experience hath shown, that mankind are more disposed to suffer, while evils are sufferable, than to right themselves by abolishing the forms to which they are accustomed. But, when a long train of abuses and usurpations, pursuing invariably the same object, evinces a design to reduce them under absolute despotism, it is their right, it is their duty, to throw off such government and to provide new guards for their future security. Such has been the patient sufferance of these colonies, and such is now the necessity which constrains them to alter their former systems of government. The history of the present King of Great Britain is a history of repeated injuries and usurpations, all having, in direct object, the establishment of an absolute tyranny over these States. To prove this, let facts be submitted to a candid world: He has refused his assent to laws the most wholesome and necessary for the public good.

He has forbidden his governors to pass laws of immediate and pressing importance, unless suspended in their operation till his assent should be obtained; and, when so suspended, he has utterly neglected to attend to them.

He has refused to pass other laws for the accommodation of large districts of people, unless those people would relinquish the right of representation in the legislature; a right inestimable to them, and formidable to tyrants only.

He has called together legislative bodies at places unusual, uncomfortable, and distant from the depository of their public records, for the sole purpose of fatiguing them into compliance with his measures.

He has dissolved representative houses repeatedly for opposing, with manly firmness, his invasions on the rights of the people.

He has refused, for a long time after such dissolutions, to cause others to be elected; whereby the legislative powers, incapable of annihilation, have returned to the people at large for their exercise; the state remaining in the mean-time exposed to all the danger of invasion from without, and convulsions within.

He has endeavoured to prevent the population of these States; for that purpose, obstructing the laws for naturalization of foreigners, refusing to pass others to encourage their migration hither, and raising the conditions of new appropriations of lands.

He has obstructed the administration of justice, by refusing his assent to laws for establishing judiciary powers.

He has made judges dependent on his will alone, for the tenure of their offices, and the amount and payment of their salaries.

He has erected a multitude of new offices, and sent hither swarms of officers to harass our people, and eat out their substance.

He has kept among us, in times of peace, standing armies, without the consent of our legislature.

He has affected to render the military independent of, and superior to, the civil power.

He has combined, with others, to subject us to a jurisdiction foreign to our Constitution, and unacknowledged by our laws; giving his assent to their acts of pretended legislation:

For quartering large bodies of armed troops among us:

For protecting them by a mock trial, from punishment, for any murders which they should commit on the inhabitants of these States:

For cutting off our trade with all parts of the world:

For imposing taxes on us without our consent:

For depriving us, in many cases, of the benefit of trial by jury:

For transporting us beyond seas to be tried for pretended offences:

For abolishing the free system of English laws in a neighboring province, establishing therein an arbitrary government, and enlarging its boundaries, so as to render it at once an example and fit instrument for introducing the same absolute rule into these colonies:

For taking away our charters, abolishing our most valuable laws, and altering, fundamentally, the powers of our governments:

For suspending our own legislatures, and declaring themselves invested with power to legislate for us in all cases whatsoever.

He has abdicated government here, by declaring us out of his protection, and waging war against us.

He has plundered our seas, ravaged our coasts, burnt our towns, and destroyed the lives of our people.

He is, at this time, transporting large armies of foreign mercenaries to complete the works of death, desolation, and tyranny, already begun, with circumstances of cruelty and perfidy scarcely paralleled in the most barbarous ages, and totally unworthy the head of a civilized nation.

He has constrained our fellow citizens, taken captive on the high seas, to bear arms against their country, to become the executioners of their friends, and brethren, or to fall themselves by their hands.

He has excited domestic insurrections amongst us, and has endeavored to bring on the inhabitants of our frontiers, the merciless Indian savages, whose known rule of warfare is an undistinguished destruction of all ages, sexes, and conditions.

In every stage of these oppressions, we have petitioned for redress; in the most humble terms; our repeated petitions have been answered only by repeated injury. A prince, whose character is thus marked by every act which may define a tyrant, is unfit to be the ruler of a free people.

Nor have we been wanting in attention to our British brethren. We have warned them, from time to time, of attempts made by their legislature to extend an unwarrantable jurisdiction over us. We have reminded them of the circumstances of our emigration and settlement here. We have appealed to their native justice and magnanimity, and we have conjured them, by the ties of our common kindred, to disavow these usurpations, which would inevitably interrupt our connections and correspondence. They, too, have been deaf to the voice of justice and consanguinity. We must, therefore, acquiesce in the necessity which denounces our separation, and hold them as we hold the rest of mankind, enemies in war, in peace, friends.

We, therefore, the representatives of the United States of America, in general Congress assembled, appealing to the Supreme Judge of the world for the rectitude of our intentions, do, in the name, and by authority of the good people of these colonies, solemnly publish and declare, that these united colonies are, and of right ought to be, free and independent states: that they are absolved from all allegiance to the British Crown, and that all political connection between them and the state of Great Britain is, and ought to be, totally dissolved; and that, as free and independent states, they have full power to levy war, conclude peace, contract alliances, establish commerce, and to do all other acts and things which independent states may of right do. And, for the support of this declaration, with a firm reliance on the protection of Divine Providence, we mutually pledge to each other our lives, our fortunes, and our sacred honor.

The foregoing Declaration was, by order of Congress, engrossed, and signed by the following members:

JOHN HANCOCK

New Hampshire
Josiah Bartlett
William Whipple
Matthew Thornton

Massachusetts Bay
Samuel Adams
John Adams
Robert Treat Paine
Elbridge Gerry

Rhode Island
Stephen Hopkins
William Ellery

Connecticut
Roger Sherman
Samuel Huntington
William Williams
Oliver Wolcott

New York
William Floyd
Phillip Livingston
Francis Lewis
Lewis Morris

New Jersey
Richard Stockton
John Witherspoon
Francis Hopkinson
John Hart
Abraham Clark

Pennsylvania
Robert Morris
Benjamin Rush
Benjamin Franklin
John Morton
George Clymer
James Smith

George Taylor
James Wilson
George Ross

Delaware
Caesar Rodney
George Read
Thomas M'Kean

Maryland
Samuel Chase
William Paca
Thomas Stone
Charles Carroll, of
    Carrollton

North Carolina
William Hooper
Joseph Hewes
John Penn

South Carolina
Edward Rutledge
Thomas Heyward, Jr.
Thomas Lynch, Jr.
Arthur Middleton

Virginia
George Wythe
Richard Henry Lee
Thomas Jefferson
Benjamin Harrison
Thomas Nelson, Jr.
Francis Lightfoot Lee
Carter Braxton

Georgia
Button Gwinnett
Lyman Hall
George Walton

Resolved, That copies of the Declaration be sent to the several assemblies, conventions, and committees, or councils of safety, and to the several commanding officers of the continental troops; that it be proclaimed in each of the United States, at the head of the army.

THE CONSTITUTION OF THE UNITED STATES*

Agreed to by Philadelphia Convention, September 17, 1787. Implemented March 4, 1789.

Preamble

We the people of the United States, in order to form a more perfect union, establish justice, insure domestic tranquility, provide for the common defense, promote the general welfare, and secure the blessings of liberty to ourselves and our posterity, do ordain and establish this Constitution for the United States of America.

Article I

Section 1 All legislative powers herein granted shall be vested in a Congress of the United States, which shall consist of a Senate and a House of Representatives.

Section 2 The House of Representatives shall be composed of members chosen every second year by the people of the several States, and the electors in each State shall have the qualifications requisite for electors of the most numerous branch of the State Legislature.

No person shall be a Representative who shall not have attained to the age of twenty-five years, and been seven years a citizen of the United States, and who shall not, when elected, be an inhabitant of that State in which he shall be chosen.

Representatives and direct taxes shall be apportioned among the several States which may be included within this Union, according to their respective numbers, *which shall be determined by adding to the whole number of free persons, including those bound to service for a term of years and excluding Indians not taxed, three-fifths of all other persons.* The actual enumeration shall be made within three years after the first meeting of the Congress of the United States, and within every subsequent term of ten years, in such manner as they shall by law direct. The number of Representatives shall not exceed one for every thirty thousand, but each State shall have at least one Representative; *and until such enumeration shall be made, the State of New Hampshire shall be entitled to choose three, Massachusetts eight, Rhode Island and Providence Plantations one, Connecticut five, New York six, New Jersey four, Pennsylvania eight, Delaware one, Maryland six, Virginia ten, North Carolina five, South Carolina five, and Georgia three.*

When vacancies happen in the representation from any State, the Executive authority thereof shall issue writs of election to fill such vacancies.

The House of Representatives shall choose their Speaker and other officers; and shall have the sole power of impeachment.

Section 3 The Senate of the United States shall be composed of two Senators from each State, *chosen by the legislature thereof*, for six years; and each Senator shall have one vote.

Immediately after they shall be assembled in consequence of the first election, they shall be divided as equally as may be into three classes. The seats of the Senators of the first class shall be vacated at the expiration of the second year, of the second class at the expiration of the fourth year, and of the third class at the expiration of the sixth year, so that one-third may be chosen every second year; and if vacancies happen by resignation or otherwise, during the recess of the legislature of any State, the Executive thereof may make temporary appointments until the next meeting of the legislature, which shall then fill such vacancies.

No person shall be a Senator who shall not have attained to the age of thirty years, and been nine years a citizen of the United States, and who shall not, when elected, be an inhabitant of that State for which he shall be chosen.

The Vice-President of the United States shall be President of the Senate, but shall have no vote, unless they be equally divided.

The Senate shall choose their other officers, and also a President *pro tempore*, in the absence of the Vice-President, or when he shall exercise the office of President of the United States.

The Senate shall have the sole power to try all impeachments. When sitting for that purpose, they shall be on oath or affirmation. When the President of the United States is tried, the Chief Justice shall preside: and no person shall be convicted without the concurrence of two-thirds of the members present.

Judgment in cases of impeachment shall not extend further than to removal from the office, and disqualification to hold and enjoy any office of honor, trust or profit under the United States: but the party convicted shall nevertheless be liable and subject to indictment, trial, judgment and punishment, according to law.

Section 4 The times, places and manner of holding elections for Senators and Representatives shall be prescribed in each State by the legislature thereof; but the Congress may at any time by law make or alter such regulations, except as to the places of choosing Senators.

The Congress shall assemble at least once in every year, and such meeting *shall be on the first Monday in December, unless they shall by law appoint a different day.*

Section 5 Each house shall be the judge of the elections, returns and qualifications of its own members, and a majority of each shall constitute a quorum to do business; but a smaller number may adjourn from day to day, and may be authorized to compel the attendance of absent members, in such manner, and under such penalties, as each house may provide.

Each house may determine the rules of its proceedings, punish its members for disorderly behavior, and with the concurrence of two-thirds, expel a member.

Each house shall keep a journal of its proceedings, and from time to time publish the same, excepting such parts as may in their judgment require secrecy; and the yeas and nays of the members of either house on any question shall, at the desire of one-fifth of those present, be entered on the journal.

Neither house, during the session of Congress, shall, without the consent of the other, adjourn for more than three days, nor to any other place than that in which the two houses shall be sitting.

Section 6 The Senators and Representatives shall receive a compensation for their services, to be ascertained by law and paid out of the treasury of the United States. They shall in all cases except treason, felony and breach of the peace, be privileged from arrest during their attendance at the session of their respective houses, and in going to and returning from the same; and for any speech or debate in either house, they shall not be questioned in any other place.

No Senator or Representative shall, during the time for which he was elected, be appointed to any civil office under the authority of the United States, which shall have been created, or the emoluments whereof shall have been increased, during such time; and no person holding any office under the United States shall be a member of either house during his continuance in office.

Section 7 All bills for raising revenue shall originate in the House of Representatives; but the Senate may propose or concur with amendments as on other bills.

Every bill which shall have passed the House of Representatives and the Senate, shall, before it become a law, be presented to the President of the United States; if he approve he shall sign it, but if not he shall return it with objections to that house in which it shall have originated, who shall enter the objections at large on their journal, and proceed to reconsider it. If after such reconsideration two-thirds of that house shall agree to pass the bill, it shall be sent, together with the objections, to the other house, by which it shall likewise be reconsidered, and, if approved by two-thirds of that house, it shall become a law. But in all such cases the votes of both houses shall be determined by yeas and nays, and the names of the persons voting for and against the bill shall be entered on the journal of each house respectively. If any bill shall not be returned by the President within ten days (Sundays excepted) after it shall have been presented to him, the same shall be a law, in like manner as if he had signed it, unless the Congress by their adjournment prevent its return, in which case it shall not be a law.

Every order, resolution, or vote to which the concurrence of the Senate and House of Representatives may be necessary (except on a question of adjournment) shall be presented to the President of the United States; and before the same shall take effect, shall be approved by him, or being disapproved by him, shall be repassed by two-thirds of the Senate and House of Representatives, according to the rules and limitations prescribed in the case of a bill.

Section 8 The Congress shall have power

To lay and collect taxes, duties, imposts, and excises, to pay the debts and provide for the common defense and general welfare of the United States; but all duties, imposts and excises shall be uniform throughout the United States;

To borrow money on the credit of the United States;

To regulate commerce with foreign nations, and among the several States, and with the Indian tribes;

To establish an uniform rule of naturalization, and uniform laws on the subject of bankruptcies throughout the United States;

To coin money, regulate the value thereof, and of foreign coin, and fix the standard of weights and measures;

To provide for the punishment of counterfeiting the securities and current coin of the United States;

To establish post offices and post roads;

To promote the progress of science and useful arts by securing for limited times to authors and inventors the exclusive right to their respective writings and discoveries;

To constitute tribunals inferior to the Supreme Court;

To define and punish piracies and felonies committed on the high seas and offences against the law of nations;

To declare war, grant letters of marque and reprisal, and make rules concerning captures on land and water;

To raise and support armies, but no appropriation of money to that use shall be for a longer term than two years;

To provide and maintain a navy;

To make rules for the government and regulation of the land and naval forces;

To provide for calling forth the militia to execute the laws of the Union, suppress insurrections and repel invasions;

To provide for organizing, arming, and disciplining the militia, and for governing such part of them as may be employed in the service of the United States, reserving to the States respectively the appointment of the officers, and the authority of training the militia according to the discipline prescribed by Congress;

To exercise exclusive legislation in all cases whatsoever, over such district (not exceeding ten miles square) as may, by cession of particular States, and the acceptance of Congress, become the seat of the government of the United States, and to exercise like authority over all places purchased by the consent of the legislature of the State, in which the same shall be, for erection of forts, magazines, arsenals, dock-yards, and other needful buildings; — and

To make all laws which shall be necessary and proper for carrying into execution the foregoing powers, and all other powers vested by this Constitution in the government of the United States, or in any department or officer thereof.

Section 9 *The migration or importation of such persons as any of the States now existing shall think proper to admit shall not be prohibited by the Congress prior to the year one thousand eight hundred and eight; but a tax or duty may be imposed on such importation, not exceeding ten dollars for each person.*

The privilege of the writ of habeas corpus shall not be suspended, unless when in cases of rebellion or invasion the public safety may require it.

No bill of attainder or ex post facto law shall be passed.

No capitation, or other direct, tax shall be laid, unless in proportion to the census or enumeration herein before directed to be taken.

No tax or duty shall be laid on articles exported from any State.

No preference shall be given by any regulation of commerce or revenue to the ports of one State over those of another; nor shall vessels bound to, or from, one State be obliged to enter, clear, or pay duties in another.

No money shall be drawn from the treasury, but in consequence of appropriations made by law; and a regular statement and account of the receipts and expenditures of all public money shall be published from time to time.

No title of nobility shall be granted by the United States: and no person holding any office of profit or trust under them, shall, without the consent of the Congress, accept of any present, emolument, office, or title, of any kind whatever, from any king, prince, or foreign state.

Section 10 No State shall enter into any treaty, alliance, or confederation; grant letters of marque and reprisal; coin money; emit bills of credit; make anything but gold and silver coin a tender in payment of debts; pass any bill of attainder, ex post facto law, or law impairing the obligation of contracts, or grant any title of nobility.

No State shall, without the consent of Congress, lay any imposts or duties on imports or exports, except what may be absolutely necessary for executing its inspection laws: and the net produce of all duties and imposts, laid by any State on imports or exports, shall be for the use of the treasury of the United States; and all such laws shall be subject to the revision and control of the Congress.

No State shall, without the consent of Congress, lay any duty of tonnage, keep troops, or ships of war in time of peace, enter into any agreement or compact with another State, or with a foreign power, or engage in war, unless actually invaded, or in such imminent danger as will not admit of delay.

Article II

Section 1 The executive power shall be vested in a President of the United States of America. He shall hold his office during the term of four years, and, together with the Vice-President, chosen for the same term, be elected as follows:

Each State shall appoint, in such manner as the legislature thereof may direct, a number of electors, equal to the whole number of Senators and Representatives to which the State may be entitled in the Congress; but no Senator or Representative, or person holding an office of trust or profit under the United States, shall be appointed an elector.

The electors shall meet in their respective States, and vote by ballot for two persons, of whom one at least shall not be an inhabitant of the same State with themselves. And they shall make a list of all the persons voted for, and of the number of votes for each; which list they shall sign and certify, and transmit sealed to the seat of government of the United States, directed to the President of the Senate. The President of the Senate shall, in the presence of the Senate and House of Representatives, open all the certificates, and the votes shall then be counted. The person having the greatest number of votes shall be the President, if such number be a majority of the whole number of electors appointed; and if there be more than one who have such majority, and have an equal number of votes, then the House of Representatives shall immediately choose by ballot one of them for President; and if no person have a majority, then from the five highest on the list said house shall in like manner choose the President. But in choosing the President the votes shall be taken by States, the representation from each State having one vote; a quorum for this purpose shall consist of a member or members from two-thirds of the States, and a majority of all the States shall be necessary to a choice. In every case, after the choice of the President, the person having the greatest number of votes of the electors shall be the Vice-President. But if there should remain two or more who have equal votes, the Senate shall choose from them by ballot the Vice-President.

The Congress may determine the time of choosing the electors, and the day on which they shall give their votes; which day shall be the same throughout the United States.

No person except a natural-born citizen, *or a citizen of the United States at the time of the adoption of this Constitution,* shall be eligible to the office of President; neither shall any person be eligible to that office who shall not have attained to the age of thirty-five years, and been fourteen years a resident within the United States.

In cases of the removal of the President from office or of his death, resignation, or inability to discharge the powers and duties of the said office, the same shall devolve on the Vice-President, and the Congress may by law provide for the case of removal, death, resignation, or inability, both of the President and Vice-President, declaring what officer shall then act as President, and such officer shall act accordingly, until the disability be removed, or a President shall be elected.

The President shall, at stated times, receive for his services a compensation, which shall neither be increased nor diminished during the period for which he shall have been elected, and he shall not receive within that period any other emolument from the United States, or any of them.

Before he enter on the execution of his office, he shall take the following oath or affirmation: — "I do solemnly swear (or affirm) that I will faithfully execute the office of the President of the United States, and will to the best of my ability preserve, protect and defend the Constitution of the United States."

Section 2 The President shall be commander in chief of the army and navy of the United States, and of the militia of the several States, when called into the actual service of the United States; he may require the opinion, in writing, of the principal officer in each of the executive departments, upon any subject relating to the duties of their respective offices, and he shall have power to grant reprieves and pardons for offenses against the United States, except in cases of impeachment.

He shall have power, by and with the advice and consent of the Senate, to make treaties, provided two-thirds of the Senators present concur; and he shall nominate, and by and with the advice and consent of the Senate, shall appoint ambassadors, other public ministers and consuls, judges of the Supreme Court, and all other officers of the United States, whose appointments are not herein otherwise provided for, and which shall be established by law: but Congress may by law vest the appointment of such inferior officers, as they think proper, in the President alone, in the courts of law, or in the heads of departments.

The President shall have power to fill up all vacancies that may happen during the recess of the Senate, by granting commissions which shall expire at the end of their next session.

Section 3 He shall from time to time give to the Congress information of the state of the Union, and recommend to their consideration such measures as he shall judge necessary and expedient; he may, on extraordinary occasions, convene both houses, or either of them, and in case of disagreement between them, with respect to the time of adjournment, he may adjourn them to such time as he shall think proper; he shall receive ambassadors and other public ministers; he shall take care that the laws be faithfully executed, and shall commission all the officers of the United States.

Section 4 The President, Vice-President and all civil officers of the United States shall be removed from office on impeachment for, and on conviction of, treason, bribery, or other high crimes and misdemeanors.

Article III

Section 1 The judicial power of the United States shall be vested in one Supreme Court, and in such inferior courts as the Congress may from time to time ordain and establish. The judges, both of the Supreme and inferior courts, shall hold their offices during good behavior, and shall, at stated times, receive for their services a compensation which shall not be diminished during their continuance in office.

Section 2 The judicial power shall extend to all cases, in law and equity, arising under this Constitution, the laws of the United States, and treaties made, or which shall be made, under their authority;—to all cases affecting ambassadors, other public ministers and consuls;—to all cases of admiralty and maritime jurisdiction;—to controversies to which the United States shall be a party;—to controversies between two or more States;—between a State and citizens of another State;—*between citizens of different States*;—between citizens of the same State claiming lands under grants of different States, and between a State, or the citizens thereof, and foreign states, citizens or subjects.

In all cases affecting ambassadors, other public ministers and consuls, and those in which a State shall be party, the Supreme Court shall have original jurisdiction. In all the other cases before mentioned, the Supreme Court shall have appellate jurisdiction, both as to law and fact, with such exceptions, and under such regulations, as the Congress shall make.

The trial of all crimes, except in cases of impeachment, shall be by jury; and such trial shall be held in the State where said crimes shall have been committed; but when not committed within any State, the trial shall be at such place or places as the Congress may by Law have directed.

Section 3 Treason against the United States shall consist only in levying war against them, or in adhering to their enemies, giving them aid and comfort. No person shall be convicted of treason unless on the testimony of two witnesses to the same overt act, or on confession in open court.

The Congress shall have power to declare the punishment of treason, but no attainder of treason shall work corruption of blood, or forfeiture except during the life of the person attainted.

Article IV

Section 1 Full faith and credit shall be given in each State to the public acts, records, and judicial proceedings of every other State. And the Congress may by general laws prescribe the manner in which such acts, records, and proceedings shall be proved, and the effect thereof.

Section 2 The citizens of each State shall be entitled to all privileges and immunities of citizens in the several States.

A person charged in any State with treason, felony, or other crime, who shall flee from justice, and be found in another State, shall on demand of the executive authority of the State from which he fled, be delivered up, to be removed to the State having jurisdiction of the crime.

No Person held to service or labor in one State, under the laws thereof, escaping into another, shall, in consequence of any law or regulation therein, be discharged from such service or labor, but shall be delivered up on claim of the party to whom such service or labor may be due.

Section 3 New States may be admitted by the Congress into this Union; but no new State shall be formed or erected within the jurisdiction of any other State; nor any State be formed by the junction of two or more States, or parts of States, without the consent of the legislatures of the States concerned as well as of the Congress.

The Congress shall have power to dispose of and make all needful rules and regulations respecting the territory or other property belonging to the United States; and nothing in this Constitution shall be so construed as to prejudice any claims of the United States, or of any particular State.

Section 4 The United States shall guarantee to every State in this Union a republican form of government, and shall protect each of them against invasion; and on application of the legislature, or of the executive (when the legislature cannot be convened), against domestic violence.

Article V

The Congress, whenever two-thirds of both houses shall deem it necessary, shall propose amendments to this Constitution, or, on the application of the legislatures of two-thirds of the several States, shall call a convention for proposing amendments, which, in either case, shall be valid to all intents and purposes, as part of this Constitution, when ratified by the legislatures of three-fourths of the several States, or by conventions in three-fourths thereof, as the one or the other mode of ratification may be proposed by the Congress; provided *that no amendments which may be made prior to the year one thousand eight hundred and eight shall in any manner affect the first and fourth clauses in the ninth section of the first article; and that no State, without its consent, shall be deprived of its equal suffrage in the Senate.*

Article VI

All debts contracted and engagements entered into, before the adoption of this Constitution, shall be as valid against the United States under this Constitution, as under the Confederation.

This Constitution, and the laws of the United States which shall be made in pursuance thereof; and all treaties made, or which shall be made, under the authority of the United States, shall be the supreme law of the land; and the judges in every State shall be bound thereby, anything in the Constitution or laws of any State to the contrary notwithstanding.

The Senators and Representatives before mentioned, and the members of the several State legislatures, and all executive and judicial officers, both of the United States and of the several States, shall be bound by oath or affirmation to support this Constitution; but no religious test shall ever be required as a qualification to any office or public trust under the United States.

Article VII

The ratification of the conventions of nine States shall be sufficient for the establishment of this Constitution between the States so ratifying the same.

Done in convention by the unanimous consent of the States present, the seventeenth day of September in the year of our Lord one thousand seven hundred and eighty-seven and of the Independence of the United States of America the twelfth. In witness whereof we have hereunto subscribed our names.

GEORGE WASHINGTON
PRESIDENT AND DEPUTY FROM VIRGINIA

New Hampshire
John Langdon
Nicholas Gilman

Massachusetts
Nathaniel Gorham
Rufus King

Connecticut
William Samuel Johnson
Roger Sherman

New York
Alexander Hamilton

New Jersey
William Livingston
David Brearley

William Paterson
Jonathan Dayton

Pennsylvania
Benjamin Franklin
Thomas Mifflin
Robert Morris
George Clymer
Thomas FitzSimons
Jared Ingersoll
James Wilson
Gouverneur Morris

Delaware
George Read
Gunning Bedford, Jr.
John Dickinson

Richard Bassett
Jacob Broom

Maryland
James McHenry
Daniel of St. Thomas
 Jenifer
Daniel Carroll

Virginia
John Blair
James Madison, Jr.

North Carolina
William Blount
Richard Dobbs Spaight
Hugh Williamson

South Carolina
John Rutledge
Charles Cotesworth
 Pinckney
Charles Pinckney
Pierce Butler

Georgia
William Few
Abraham Baldwin

AMENDMENTS TO THE CONSTITUTION WITH ANNOTATIONS
(including the six unratified amendments)

Amendment I

Congress shall make no law respecting an establishment of religion, or prohibiting the free exercise thereof; or abridging the freedom of speech, or of the press; or the right of the people peaceably to assemble, and to petition the government for a redress of grievances.

Amendment II

A well-regulated militia being necessary to the security of a free State, the right of the people to keep and bear arms shall not be infringed.

Amendment III

No soldier shall, in time of peace, be quartered in any house without the consent of the owner, nor in time of war, but in a manner to be prescribed by law.

Amendment IV

The right of the people to be secure in their persons, houses, papers, and effects, against unreasonable searches and seizures, shall not be violated, and no warrants shall issue but upon probable cause, supported by oath or affirmation, and particularly describing the place to be searched, and the persons or things to be seized.

Amendment V

No person shall be held to answer for a capital, or otherwise infamous crime, unless on a presentment or indictment of a grand jury, except in cases arising in the land or naval forces, or in the militia, when in actual service in time of war or public danger; nor shall any person be subject for the same offence to be twice put in jeopardy of life or limb; nor shall be compelled in any criminal case to be a witness against himself, nor be deprived of life, liberty, or property, without due process of law; nor shall private property be taken for public use without just compensation.

Amendment VI

In all criminal prosecutions, the accused shall enjoy the right to a speedy and public trial, by an impartial jury of the State and district wherein the crime shall have been committed, which district shall have been previously ascertained by law, and to be informed of the nature and cause of the accusation; to be confronted with the witnesses against him; to have compulsory process for obtaining witnesses in his favor, and to have the assistance of counsel for his defence.

Amendment VII

In suits at common law, where the value in controversy shall exceed twenty dollars, the right of trial by jury shall be preserved, and no fact tried by a jury shall be otherwise reexamined in any court of the United States, than according to the rules of the common law.

Amendment VIII

Excessive bail shall not be required, nor excessive fines imposed, nor cruel and unusual punishments inflicted.

Amendment IX

The enumeration in the Constitution, of certain rights, shall not be construed to deny or disparage others retained by the people.

Amendment X

The powers not delegated to the United States by the Constitution, nor prohibited by it to the States, are reserved to the States respectively, or to the people.

Unratified Amendment

Reapportionment Amendment (proposed by Congress September 25, 1789, along with the Bill of Rights)

After the first enumeration required by the first article of the Constitution, there shall be one Representative for every thirty thousand, until the number shall amount to one hundred, after which the proportion shall be so regulated by Congress, that there shall be not less than one hundred Representatives, nor less than one Representative for every forty thousand persons, until the number of Representatives shall amount to two hundred; after which the proportion shall be so regulated by Congress, that there shall not be less than two hundred Representatives, nor more than one Representative for every fifty thousand persons.

Amendment XI

[Adopted 1798]

The judicial power of the United States shall not be construed to extend to any suit in law or equity, commenced or prosecuted against one of the United States by citizens of another State, or by citizens or subjects of any foreign state.

Amendment XII

[Adopted 1804]

The electors shall meet in their respective States, and vote by ballot for President and Vice-President, one of whom, at least, shall not be an inhabitant of the same State with themselves; they shall name in their ballots the person voted for as President, and in distinct ballots the person voted for as Vice-President, and they shall make distinct lists of all persons voted for as President, and of all persons voted for as Vice-President, and of the number of votes for each, which lists they shall sign and certify, and transmit sealed to the seat of government of the United States, directed to the President of the Senate; — the President of the Senate shall, in the presence of the Senate and House of Representatives, open all the certificates and the votes shall then be counted; — the person having the greatest number of votes for President shall be the President, if such number be a majority of the whole number of electors appointed; and if no person have such majority, then from the persons having the highest numbers not exceeding three on the list of those voted for as President, the House of Representatives shall choose immediately, by ballot, the President. But in choosing the President, the votes shall be taken by States, the representation from each State having one vote; a quorum for this purpose shall consist of a member or members from two-thirds of the States, and a majority of all the States shall be necessary to a choice. And if the House of Representatives shall not choose a President whenever the right of choice shall devolve upon them, *before the fourth day of March* next following, then the Vice-President shall act as President, as in the case of the death or other constitutional disability of the President.

The person having the greatest number of votes as Vice-President shall be the Vice-President, if such number be a majority of the whole number of electors appointed; and if no person have a majority, then from the two highest numbers on the list the Senate shall choose the Vice-President; a quorum for the purpose shall consist of two-thirds of the whole number of Senators, and a majority of the whole number shall be necessary to a choice. But no person constitutionally ineligible to the office of President shall be eligible to that of Vice-President of the United States.

Unratified Amendment

Titles of Nobility Amendment (proposed by Congress May 1, 1810)

If any citizen of the United States shall accept, claim, receive or retain any title of nobility or honor or shall, without the consent of Congress, accept and retain any present, pension, office or emolument of any kind whatever, from any emperor, king, prince or foreign power, such person shall cease to be a citizen of the United States, and shall be incapable of holding any office of trust or profit under them or either of them.

Unratified Amendment

Corwin Amendment (proposed by Congress March 2, 1861)

No amendment shall be made to the Constitution which will authorize or give to Congress the power to abolish or interfere, within any State, with the domestic institutions thereof,

including that of persons held to labor or service by the laws of said State.

Amendment XIII

[Adopted 1865]

Section 1 Neither slavery nor involuntary servitude, except as a punishment for crime whereof the party shall have been duly convicted, shall exist within the United States, or any place subject to their jurisdiction.

Section 2 Congress shall have power to enforce this article by appropriate legislation.

Amendment XIV

[Adopted 1868]

Section 1 All persons born or naturalized in the United States, and subject to the jurisdiction thereof, are citizens of the United States and of the State wherein they reside. No State shall make or enforce any law which shall abridge the privileges or immunities of citizens of the United States; nor shall any State deprive any person of life, liberty, or property, without due process of law; nor deny to any person within its jurisdiction the equal protection of the laws.

Section 2 Representatives shall be appointed among the several States according to their respective numbers, counting the whole number of persons in each State, excluding Indians not taxed. But when the right to vote at any election for the choice of Electors for President and Vice-President of the United States, Representatives in Congress, the executive and judicial officers of a State, or the members of the legislature thereof, is denied to any of the male inhabitants of such State, being twenty-one years of age and citizens of the United States, or in any way abridged, except for participation in rebellion, or other crime, the basis of representation therein shall be reduced in the proportion which the number of such male citizens shall bear to the whole number of male citizens twenty-one years of age in such State.

Section 3 No person shall be a Senator or Representative in Congress, or Elector of President and Vice-President, or hold any office, civil or military, under the United States, or under any State, who, having previously taken an oath, as a member of Congress, or as an officer of the United States, or as a member of any State legislature, or as an executive or judicial officer of any State, to support the Constitution of the United States, shall have engaged in insurrection or rebellion against the same, or given aid or comfort to the enemies thereof. Congress may, by a vote of two-thirds of each house, remove such disability.

Section 4 The validity of the public debt of the United States, authorized by law, including debts incurred for payment of pensions and bounties for services in suppressing insurrection or rebellion, shall not be questioned. But neither the United States nor any State shall assume or pay any debt or obligation incurred in aid of insurrection or rebellion against the United States, or any claim for the loss or emancipation of any slave;

but all such debts, obligations, and claims shall be held illegal and void.

Section 5 The Congress shall have power to enforce, by appropriate legislation, the provisions of this article.

Amendment XV

[Adopted 1870]

Section 1 The right of citizens of the United States to vote shall not be denied or abridged by the United States or by any State on account of race, color, or previous condition of servitude.

Section 2 The Congress shall have power to enforce this article by appropriate legislation.

Amendment XVI

[Adopted 1913]

The Congress shall have power to lay and collect taxes on incomes, from whatever source derived, without apportionment among the several States, and without regard to any census or enumeration.

Amendment XVII

[Adopted 1913]

Section 1 The Senate of the United States shall be composed of two Senators from each State, elected by the people thereof, for six years; and each Senator shall have one vote. The electors in each State shall have the qualifications requisite for electors of [voters for] the most numerous branch of the State legislatures.

Section 2 When vacancies happen in the representation of any State in the Senate, the executive authority of such State shall issue writs of election to fill such vacancies: Provided, that the Legislature of any State may empower the executive thereof to make temporary appointments until the people fill the vacancies by election as the Legislature may direct.

Section 3 This amendment shall not be so construed as to affect the election or term of any Senator chosen before it becomes valid as part of the Constitution.

Amendment XVIII

[Adopted 1919; repealed 1933 by Amendment XXI]

Section 1 After one year from the ratification of this article the manufacture, sale, or transportation of intoxicating liquors within, the importation thereof into, or the exportation thereof from the United States and all territory subject to the jurisdiction thereof, for beverage purposes, is hereby prohibited.

Section 2 The Congress and the several States shall have concurrent power to enforce this article by appropriate legislation.

Section 3 This article shall be inoperative unless it shall have been ratified as an amendment to the Constitution by the legislatures of the several States, as provided by the Constitution, within seven years from the date of the submission thereof to the States by the Congress.

Amendment XIX

[Adopted 1920]

Section 1 The right of citizens of the United States to vote shall not be denied or abridged by the United States or by any State on account of sex.

Section 2 Congress shall have the power to enforce this article by appropriate legislation.

Unratified Amendment

Child Labor Amendment (proposed by Congress June 2, 1924)

Section 1 The Congress shall have power to limit, regulate, and prohibit the labor of persons under eighteen years of age.

Section 2 The power of the several States is unimpaired by this article except that the operation of State laws shall be suspended to the extent necessary to give effect to legislation enacted by Congress.

Amendment XX

[Adopted 1933]

Section 1 The terms of the President and Vice-President shall end at noon on the 20th day of January, and the terms of Senators and Representatives at noon on the 3rd day of January, of the years in which such terms would have ended if this article had not been ratified; and the terms of their successors shall then begin.

Section 2 The Congress shall assemble at least once in every year, and such meeting shall begin at noon on the 3rd day of January, unless they shall by law appoint a different day.

Section 3 If, at the time fixed for the beginning of the term of the President, the President-elect shall have died, the Vice-President-elect shall become President. If a President shall not have been chosen before the time fixed for the beginning of his term, or if the President-elect shall have failed to qualify, then the Vice-President-elect shall act as President until a President shall have qualified; and the Congress may by law provide for the case wherein neither a President-elect nor a Vice-President-elect shall have qualified, declaring who shall then act as President, or the manner in which one who is to act shall be selected, and such person shall act accordingly until a President or Vice-President shall have qualified.

Section 4 The Congress may by law provide for the case of the death of any of the persons from whom the House of Representatives may choose a President whenever the right of choice shall have devolved upon them, and for the case of the death of any of the persons from whom the Senate may choose a Vice-President whenever the right of choice shall have devolved upon them.

Section 5 Sections 1 and 2 shall take effect on the 15th day of October following the ratification of this article.

Section 6 This article shall be inoperative unless it shall have been ratified as an amendment to the Constitution by the Legislatures of three-fourths of the several States within seven years from the date of its submission.

Amendment XXI

[Adopted 1933]

Section 1 The eighteenth article of amendment to the Constitution of the United States is hereby repealed.

Section 2 The transportation or importation into any State, Territory, or Possession of the United States for delivery or use therein of intoxicating liquors, in violation of the laws thereof, is hereby prohibited.

Section 3 This article shall be inoperative unless it shall have been ratified as an amendment to the Constitution by conventions in the several States, as provided in the Constitution, within seven years from the date of the submission thereof to the States by the Congress.

Amendment XXII

[Adopted 1951]

Section 1 No person shall be elected to the office of the President more than twice, and no person who has held the office of President, or acted as President, for more than two years of a term to which some other person was elected President shall be elected to the office of President more than once. But this article shall not apply to any person holding the office of President when this Article was proposed by the Congress, and shall not prevent any person who may be holding the office of President, or acting as President, during the term within which this Article becomes operative from holding the office of President or acting as President during the remainder of such term.

Section 2 This article shall be inoperative unless it shall have been ratified as an amendment to the Constitution by the legislatures of three-fourths of the several States within seven years from the date of its submission to the States by the Congress.

Amendment XXIII

[Adopted 1961]

Section 1 The District constituting the seat of Government of the United States shall appoint in such manner as the Congress may direct: A number of electors of President and Vice-President equal to the whole number of Senators and Representatives in Congress to which the District would be entitled if it were a State, but in no event more than the least populous State; they shall be in addition to those appointed by the States, but they shall be considered for the purposes of the election of President and Vice-President, to be electors appointed by a State; and they shall meet in the District

and perform such duties as provided by the twelfth article of amendment.

Section 2 The Congress shall have the power to enforce this article by appropriate legislation.

Amendment XXIV

[Adopted 1964]

Section 1 The right of citizens of the United States to vote in any primary or other election for President or Vice-President, for electors for President or Vice-President, or for Senator or Representative in Congress, shall not be denied or abridged by the United States or any State by reason of failure to pay any poll tax or other tax.

Amendment XXV

[Adopted 1967]

Section 1 In case of the removal of the President from office or of his death or resignation, the Vice-President shall become President.

Section 2 Whenever there is a vacancy in the office of the Vice-President, the President shall nominate a Vice-President who shall take office upon confirmation by a majority vote of both Houses of Congress.

Section 3 Whenever the President transmits to the President pro tempore of the Senate and the Speaker of the House of Representatives his written declaration that he is unable to discharge the powers and duties of his office, and until he transmits to them a written declaration to the contrary, such powers and duties shall be discharged by the Vice-President as Acting President.

Section 4 Whenever the Vice-President and a majority of either the principal officers of the executive departments or of such other body as Congress may by law provide, transmit to the President pro tempore of the Senate and the Speaker of the House of Representatives their written declaration that the President is unable to discharge the powers and duties of his office, the Vice-President shall immediately assume the powers and duties of the office as Acting President.

Thereafter, when the President transmits to the President pro tempore of the Senate and the Speaker of the House of Representatives his written declaration that no inability exists, he shall resume the powers and duties of his office unless the Vice-President and a majority of either the principal officers of the executive department[s] or of such other body as Congress may by law provide, transmit within four days to the President pro tempore of the Senate and the Speaker of the House of Representatives their written declaration that the President is unable to discharge the powers and duties of his office. Thereupon Congress shall decide the issue, assembling within forty-eight hours for that purpose if not in session. If the Congress, within twenty-one days after receipt of the latter written declaration, or, if Congress is not in session, within twenty-one days after

Congress is required to assemble, determines by two-thirds vote of both Houses that the President is unable to discharge the powers and duties of his office, the Vice-President shall continue to discharge the same as Acting President; otherwise, the President shall resume the powers and duties of his office.

Amendment XXVI

[Adopted 1971]

Section 1 The right of citizens of the United States, who are eighteen years of age or older, to vote shall not be denied or abridged by the United States or by any State on account of age.

Section 2 The Congress shall have power to enforce this article by appropriate legislation.

Unratified Amendment

Equal Rights Amendment (proposed by Congress March 22, 1972; seven-year deadline for ratification extended to June 30, 1982)

Section 1 Equality of rights under the law shall not be denied or abridged by the United States or by any State on account of sex.

Section 2 The Congress shall have the power to enforce, by appropriate legislation, the provisions of this article.

Section 3 This amendment shall take effect two years after the date of ratification.

Unratified Amendment

D.C. Statehood Amendment (proposed by Congress August 22, 1978)

Section 1 For purposes of representation in the Congress, election of the President and Vice-President, and article V of this Constitution, the District constituting the seat of government of the United States shall be treated as though it were a State.

Section 2 The exercise of the rights and powers conferred under this article shall be by the people of the District constituting the seat of government, and as shall be provided by Congress.

Section 3 The twenty-third article of amendment to the Constitution of the United States is hereby repealed.

Section 4 This article shall be inoperative, unless it shall have been ratified as an amendment to the Constitution by the legislatures of three-fourths of the several states within seven years from the date of its submission.

Amendment XXVII

[Adopted 1992]

No law, varying the compensation for the services of the Senators and Representatives, shall take effect, until an election of Representatives shall have intervened.

U.S. POLITICS AND GOVERNMENT

PRESIDENTIAL ELECTIONS

Year	Candidates	Parties	Popular Vote	Percentage of Popular Vote	Electoral Vote	Percentage of Voter Participation
1789	GEORGE WASHINGTON (Va.)*				69	
	John Adams				34	
	Others				35	
1792	GEORGE WASHINGTON (Va.)				132	
	John Adams				77	
	George Clinton				50	
	Others				5	
1796	JOHN ADAMS (Mass.)	Federalist			71	
	Thomas Jefferson	Democratic-Republican			68	
	Thomas Pinckney	Federalist			59	
	Aaron Burr	Dem.-Rep.			30	
	Others	—			48	
1800	THOMAS JEFFERSON (Va.)	Dem.-Rep.			73	
	Aaron Burr	Dem.-Rep.			73	
	John Adams	Federalist			65	
	C. C. Pinckney	Federalist			64	
	John Jay	Federalist			1	
1804	THOMAS JEFFERSON (Va.)	Dem.-Rep.			162	
	C. C. Pinckney	Federalist			14	
1808	JAMES MADISON (Va.)	Dem.-Rep.			122	
	C. C. Pinckney	Federalist			47	
	George Clinton	Dem.-Rep.			6	
1812	JAMES MADISON (Va.)	Dem.-Rep.			128	
	De Witt Clinton	Federalist			89	
1816	JAMES MONROE (Va.)	Dem.-Rep.			183	
	Rufus King	Federalist			34	
1820	JAMES MONROE (Va.)	Dem.-Rep.			231	
	John Quincy Adams	Dem.-Rep.			1	

*State of residence when elected president.

Year	Candidates	Parties	Popular Vote	Percentage of Popular Vote	Electoral Vote	Percentage of Voter Participation
1824	JOHN Q. ADAMS (Mass.)	Dem.-Rep.	108,740	30.5	84	26.9
	Andrew Jackson	Dem.-Rep.	153,544	43.1	99	
	William H. Crawford	Dem.-Rep.	46,618	13.1	41	
	Henry Clay	Dem.-Rep.	47,136	13.2	37	
1828	ANDREW JACKSON (Tenn.)	Democratic	647,286	56.0	178	57.6
	John Quincy Adams	National Republican	508,064	44.0	83	
1832	ANDREW JACKSON (Tenn.)	Democratic	687,502	55.0	219	55.4
	Henry Clay	National Republican	530,189	42.4	49	
	John Floyd	Independent			11	
	William Wirt	Anti-Mason	33,108	2.6	7	
1836	MARTIN VAN BUREN (N.Y.)	Democratic	765,483	50.9	170	57.8
	W. H. Harrison	Whig			73	
	Hugh L. White	Whig	739,795	49.1	26	
	Daniel Webster	Whig			14	
	W. P. Mangum	Independent			11	
1840	WILLIAM H. HARRISON (Ohio)	Whig	1,274,624	53.1	234	78.0
	Martin Van Buren	Democratic	1,127,781	46.9	60	
	J. G. Birney	Liberty	7,069		—	
1844	JAMES K. POLK (Tenn.)	Democratic	1,338,464	49.6	170	78.9
	Henry Clay	Whig	1,300,097	48.1	105	
	J. G. Birney	Liberty	62,300	2.3	—	
1848	ZACHARY TAYLOR (La.)	Whig	1,360,099	47.4	163	72.7
	Lewis Cass	Democratic	1,220,544	42.5	127	
	Martin Van Buren	Free-Soil	291,263	10.1	—	
1852	FRANKLIN PIERCE (N.H.)	Democratic	1,601,117	50.9	254	69.6
	Winfield Scott	Whig	1,385,453	44.1	42	
	John P. Hale	Free-Soil	155,825	5.0	—	
1856	JAMES BUCHANAN (Pa.)	Democratic	1,832,995	45.3	174	78.9
	John C. Frémont	Republican	1,339,932	33.1	114	
	Millard Fillmore	American	871,731	21.6	8	
1860	ABRAHAM LINCOLN (Ill.)	Republican	1,866,452	39.8	180	81.2
	Stephen A. Douglas	Democratic	1,375,157	29.4	12	
	John C. Breckinridge	Democratic	847,953	18.1	72	
	John Bell	Union	590,631	12.6	39	
1864	ABRAHAM LINCOLN (Ill.)	Republican	2,213,665	55.1	212	73.8
	George B. McClellan	Democratic	1,805,237	44.9	21	
1868	ULYSSES S. GRANT (Ill.)	Republican	3,012,833	52.7	214	78.1
	Horatio Seymour	Democratic	2,703,249	47.3	80	

Year	Candidates	Parties	Popular Vote	Percentage of Popular Vote	Electoral Vote	Percentage of Voter Participation
1872	ULYSSES S. GRANT (Ill.)	Republican	3,597,132	55.6	286	71.3
	Horace Greeley	Democratic; Liberal Republican	2,834,125	43.9	66	
1876	RUTHERFORD B. HAYES (Ohio)	Republican	4,036,298	48.0	185	81.8
	Samuel J. Tilden	Democratic	4,288,590	51.0	184	
1880	JAMES A. GARFIELD (Ohio)	Republican	4,454,416	48.5	214	79.4
	Winfield S. Hancock	Democratic	4,444,952	48.1	155	
1884	GROVER CLEVELAND (N.Y.)	Democratic	4,874,986	48.5	219	77.5
	James G. Blaine	Republican	4,851,981	48.3	182	
1888	BENJAMIN HARRISON (Ind.)	Republican	5,439,853	47.9	233	79.3
	Grover Cleveland	Democratic	5,540,309	48.6	168	
1892	GROVER CLEVELAND (N.Y.)	Democratic	5,555,426	46.1	277	74.7
	Benjamin Harrison	Republican	5,182,690	43.0	145	
	James B. Weaver	People's	1,029,846	8.5	22	
1896	WILLIAM McKINLEY (Ohio)	Republican	7,104,779	51.1	271	79.3
	William J. Bryan	Democratic-People's	6,502,925	47.7	176	
1900	WILLIAM McKINLEY (Ohio)	Republican	7,207,923	51.7	292	73.2
	William J. Bryan	Dem.-Populist	6,358,133	45.5	155	
1904	THEODORE ROOSEVELT (N.Y.)	Republican	7,623,486	57.9	336	65.2
	Alton B. Parker	Democratic	5,077,911	37.6	140	
	Eugene V. Debs	Socialist	402,283	3.0	—	
1908	WILLIAM H. TAFT (Ohio)	Republican	7,678,908	51.6	321	65.4
	William J. Bryan	Democratic	6,409,104	43.1	162	
	Eugene V. Debs	Socialist	420,793	2.8	—	
1912	WOODROW WILSON (N.J.)	Democratic	6,293,454	41.9	435	58.8
	Theodore Roosevelt	Progressive	4,119,538	27.4	88	
	William H. Taft	Republican	3,484,980	23.2	8	
	Eugene V. Debs	Socialist	900,672	6.1	—	
1916	WOODROW WILSON (N.J.)	Democratic	9,129,606	49.4	277	61.6
	Charles E. Hughes	Republican	8,538,221	46.2	254	
	A. L. Benson	Socialist	585,113	3.2	—	
1920	WARREN G. HARDING (Ohio)	Republican	16,143,407	60.5	404	49.2
	James M. Cox	Democratic	9,130,328	34.2	127	
	Eugene V. Debs	Socialist	919,799	3.4	—	
1924	CALVIN COOLIDGE (Mass.)	Republican	15,725,016	54.0	382	48.9
	John W. Davis	Democratic	8,386,503	28.8	136	
	Robert M. La Follette	Progressive	4,822,856	16.6	13	

Year	Candidates	Parties	Popular Vote	Percentage of Popular Vote	Electoral Vote	Percentage of Voter Participation
1928	HERBERT HOOVER (Calif.)	Republican	21,391,381	57.4	444	56.9
	Alfred E. Smith	Democratic	15,016,443	40.3	87	
	Norman Thomas	Socialist	881,951	2.3	—	
	William Z. Foster	Communist	102,991	0.3	—	
1932	FRANKLIN D. ROOSEVELT (N.Y.)	Democratic	22,821,857	57.4	472	56.9
	Herbert Hoover	Republican	15,761,841	39.7	59	
	Norman Thomas	Socialist	881,951	2.2	—	
1936	FRANKLIN D. ROOSEVELT (N.Y.)	Democratic	27,751,597	60.8	523	61.0
	Alfred M. Landon	Republican	16,679,583	36.5	8	
	William Lemke	Union	882,479	1.9	—	
1940	FRANKLIN D. ROOSEVELT (N.Y.)	Democratic	27,244,160	54.8	449	62.5
	Wendell Willkie	Republican	22,305,198	44.8	82	
1944	FRANKLIN D. ROOSEVELT (N.Y.)	Democratic	25,602,504	53.5	432	55.9
	Thomas E. Dewey	Republican	22,006,285	46.0	99	
1948	HARRY S. TRUMAN (Mo.)	Democratic	24,105,695	49.5	303	53.0
	Thomas E. Dewey	Republican	21,969,170	45.1	189	
	J. Strom Thurmond	States'-Rights Democratic	1,169,021	2.4	38	
	Henry A. Wallace	Progressive	1,156,103	2.4	—	
1952	DWIGHT D. EISENHOWER (N.Y.)	Republican	33,936,252	55.1	442	63.3
	Adlai Stevenson	Democratic	27,314,992	44.4	89	
1956	DWIGHT D. EISENHOWER (N.Y.)	Republican	35,575,420	57.6	457	60.6
	Adlai Stevenson	Democratic	26,033,066	42.1	73	
	Other	—	—		1	
1960	JOHN F. KENNEDY (Mass.)	Democratic	34,227,096	49.9	303	62.8
	Richard M. Nixon	Republican	34,108,546	49.6	219	
	Other	—	—		15	
1964	LYNDON B. JOHNSON (Tex.)	Democratic	43,126,506	61.1	486	61.7
	Barry M. Goldwater	Republican	27,176,799	38.5	52	
1968	RICHARD M. NIXON (N.Y.)	Republican	31,770,237	43.4	301	60.9
	Hubert H. Humphrey	Democratic	31,270,533	42.7	191	
	George Wallace	American Indep.	9,906,141	13.5	46	
1972	RICHARD M. NIXON (N.Y.)	Republican	47,169,911	60.7	520	55.2
	George S. McGovern	Democratic	29,170,383	37.5	17	
	Other	—	—		1	
1976	JIMMY CARTER (Ga.)	Democratic	40,830,763	50.0	297	53.5
	Gerald R. Ford	Republican	39,147,793	48.0	240	
	Other	—	1,575,459	2.1	—	

Year	Candidates	Parties	Popular Vote	Percentage of Popular Vote	Electoral Vote	Percentage of Voter Participation
1980	RONALD REAGAN (Calif.)	Republican	43,901,812	51.0	489	54.0
	Jimmy Carter	Democratic	35,483,820	41.0	49	
	John B. Anderson	Independent	5,719,722	7.0	—	
	Ed Clark	Libertarian	921,188	1.1	—	
1984	RONALD REAGAN (Calif.)	Republican	54,455,075	59.0	525	53.1
	Walter Mondale	Democratic	37,577,185	41.0	13	
1988	GEORGE H. W. BUSH (Tex.)	Republican	47,946,422	54.0	426	50.2
	Michael S. Dukakis	Democratic	41,016,429	46.0	112	
1992	WILLIAM J. CLINTON (Ark.)	Democratic	44,908,254	43.0	370	55.9
	George H. W. Bush	Republican	39,102,282	38.0	168	
	H. Ross Perot	Independent	19,721,433	19.0	—	
1996	WILLIAM J. CLINTON (Ark.)	Democratic	47,401,185	49.2	379	49.0
	Robert Dole	Republican	39,197,469	40.7	159	
	H. Ross Perot	Independent	8,085,294	8.4	—	
2000	GEORGE W. BUSH (Tex.)	Republican	50,456,062	47.8	271	51.2
	Al Gore	Democratic	50,996,862	48.4	267	
	Ralph Nader	Green Party	2,858,843	2.7	—	
	Patrick J. Buchanan	—	438,760	0.4	—	
2004	GEORGE W. BUSH (Tex.)	Republican	61,872,711	50.7	286	60.3
	John F. Kerry	Democratic	58,894,584	48.3	252	
	Other	—	1,582,185	1.3	—	
2008	BARACK OBAMA (Ill.)	Democratic	69,456,897	52.9	365	56.8
	John McCain	Republican	59,934,314	45.7	173	
2012	BARACK OBAMA (Ill.)	Democratic	65,909,451	51.02	332	58
	Willard Mitt Romney	Republican	60,932,176	47.16	152	
	Other	—	2,350,895	1.82	—	

ADMISSION OF STATES TO THE UNION

State	Date of Admission	State	Date of Admission
Delaware	December 7, 1787	Virginia	June 25, 1788
Pennsylvania	December 12, 1787	New York	July 26, 1788
New Jersey	December 18, 1787	North Carolina	November 21, 1789
Georgia	January 2, 1788	Rhode Island	May 29, 1790
Connecticut	January 9, 1788	Vermont	March 4, 1791
Massachusetts	February 6, 1788	Kentucky	June 1, 1792
Maryland	April 28, 1788	Tennessee	June 1, 1796
South Carolina	May 23, 1788	Ohio	March 1, 1803
New Hampshire	June 21, 1788	Louisiana	April 30, 1812

State	Date of Admission	State	Date of Admission
Indiana	December 11, 1816	West Virginia	June 19, 1863
Mississippi	December 10, 1817	Nevada	October 31, 1864
Illinois	December 3, 1818	Nebraska	March 1, 1867
Alabama	December 14, 1819	Colorado	August 1, 1876
Maine	March 15, 1820	North Dakota	November 2, 1889
Missouri	August 10, 1821	South Dakota	November 2, 1889
Arkansas	June 15, 1836	Montana	November 8, 1889
Michigan	January 16, 1837	Washington	November 11, 1889
Florida	March 3, 1845	Idaho	July 3, 1890
Texas	December 29, 1845	Wyoming	July 10, 1890
Iowa	December 28, 1846	Utah	January 4, 1896
Wisconsin	May 29, 1848	Oklahoma	November 16, 1907
California	September 9, 1850	New Mexico	January 6, 1912
Minnesota	May 11, 1858	Arizona	February 14, 1912
Oregon	February 14, 1859	Alaska	January 3, 1959
Kansas	January 29, 1861	Hawaii	August 21, 1959

INDEX

Abenaki Indians, 19
Abington School District v. Schempp (1963), 843
ABMs. *See* Antiballistic missiles
Abolition and abolitionism, 313, 350(i), 351
    black leaders in, 317, 353–354
    "gag rule" and, 320
    Lincoln and, 440, 458–459
    reform and, 317–318
    violence against, 317(i), 318
    women and, 318, 470
Abortion and abortion rights, 859, 899, 901, 915, 918(i), 919, 939
Abstract expressionism, 826
Abu Ghraib prison abuse, 957
Abundance. *See also* Consumer(s); Prosperity; Wealth
    culture of, 804, 805(i), 822–823
Academies, for women, 282–283. *See also* Education
Accommodation
    by Indians, 491–492
    Washington, Booker T., and, 639
Acheson, Dean, 783, 784, 792
Acoma pueblo, revolt in, 17, *42*
Activism. *See also* Protest(s); Revolts and rebellions; specific individuals and movements
    African American civil rights, 844–850
    of antiwar movement, 841, 855, 881–882
    gay and lesbian, 855–856, 920
    Native American, 852
    of New Left and Counterculture, 854–855
    by women, 857–860
ADA. *See* Americans with Disabilities Act
Adams, Abigail, 175, 177–178, 178(i), 186, 212
Adams, Charles Francis, 395
Adams, John, 117, 160, 163, 254(i)
    Alien and Sedition Acts and, 256
    election of 1789 and, 236
    election of 1796 and, 253–254
    election of 1800 and, 256, 263, 263(m)
    France and, 250, 254–255
    midnight judges and, 264–265
    at Second Continental Congress, 174, 186
    on voting qualifications, 211
Adams, John Quincy
    election of 1824 and, 288, 289, 289(m)

election of 1828 and, 303–305, 305(m)
    presidency of, 290
Adams, Louisa Catherine, 288
Adams, Samuel, 152, 157, 174, 222
    in Confederation Congress, 209
Adams-Onís Treaty, 287–288
Adaptation
    environmental, 9
    human, 7
    Indian, 22
Addams, Jane, 612(i)
    First World War and, 659
    Hull House and, 613
    progressivism and, 641
    woman suffrage and, 616
Adding machine, 559
Adena culture, 17
Adultery, 826
Adventures of Ozzie and Harriet (TV program), 822(i)
Advertising
    in 1920s, 684, 707
    material goods and, 684
Advice to American Women (Graves), 313
Aerospace industry, 819
AFDC. *See* Aid to Families with Dependent Children
Affirmative action. *See also* African Americans; specific groups
    executive order for (1965), 847
    Nixon and, 864
    reverse discrimination and, 918
    for women, 847
Affluent society. *See* Wealth
Afghanistan
    bombings of, 954
    Bush, G. W., and, 950
    Clinton and, 946
    Obama and, 959
    Soviets and, 911, 924
    stabilization of, 957
    Taliban in, 954
    U.S. aid to rebels in, 922
AFL. *See* American Federation of Labor
Africa. *See also* African Americans; Slavery; specific locations
    acculturation of slaves from, 125, 126
    blacks returning to, 214
    human origins in, 6–7
    immigrants from, 112, 113(m), 123
    Italian fascism in, 746
    migration to New World from (1492–1700), 75(f)
    Nixon and, 887
    Portugal and, 31(m), 32–33
    slave's Christianity and, 375
    suffering in, 945
    third world and, 787

African Americans. *See also* Africa; Africans; Civil rights; Civil rights movement; Free blacks; Freedmen; Race and racism; Race riots; Rights; Slavery; Voting and voting rights
    in 1950s, 827–830
    as abolitionists, 317, 353–354
    accommodationism and, 639
    affirmative action for, 847
    antidraft riots and, 447
    in armed forces, 438(i), 441, 653, 670
    Attucks, Crispus, as, 160
    black codes and, 462(i), 463–464, 465
    black power and, 848–850
    as buffalo soldiers, 503
    Christianity of, 375
    churches of, 461, 475(m), 483
    in cities, 553, 554
    civil rights and, 827–830, 844–850
    in Civil War, 438–441, 438(i)
    Colfax massacre and, 480
    Colored Farmers' Alliance and, 581
    in Continental army, 181
    as cowboys, 509
    culture of, 127–128
    education for, 461, 471, 473, 475(m), 483, 639
    equal employment of, 764
    in First World War, 652, 653, 670
    after First World War, 667(i), 670–671
    in Great Depression, 703, 705–706, 706(i)
    Harlem Renaissance and, 689–690, 689(i)
    in higher education, 821
    incomes of, 943
    Jim Crow laws and, 531
    lynching and, 531–532, 553, 687
    in middle class, 865
    migration of, 667(i), 670–671, 693, 693(m), 764
    naming of, 128
    New Deal and, 723(i), 732–733, 732(i)
    "New Negro" and, 688–690, 689(i)
    Niagara movement and, 640
    People's Party and, 596
    political positions of, 939
    poverty of, 841
    as president, 958
    in Progressive Era, 639–640
    in Republican Party, 471–474, 473(f)
    after Revolution, 199–200
    Scottsboro Boys, 706
    Second World War and, 755(i), 763–764
    after Second World War, 792–793
    Sons of Liberty and, 155
    in Southern Congressional delegations (1865–1877), 473(f)
    student protests and (1968), 883
    terrorism against, 472, 478, 480
    in Vietnam War, 880

African Americans (continued)
  voting rights for, 457(i), 459, 463, 464,
    466, 467, 468, 468(m), 469–470, 471,
    472–473, 476, 476(i), 531, 848(m)
  in West, 503, 510
  women and, 465(i), 471(i), 474, 531–532,
    531(i), 558, 810
  in women's movement, 858
African Methodist Episcopal Church, 462
Africans. See also African Americans;
    Slavery
  mulattos in New Spain and, 47(i)
  as new Negroes, 126
  as slaves, 33, 46
Age
  of Vietnam soldiers, 879
  at voting, 285
Agencies. See Departments of government;
    Government (U.S.); specific agencies
Agent Orange, 875, 881, 892
Aggression
  by Axis powers (through 1941), 750(m)
  Japanese (through 1941), 752(m)
Agnew, Spiro T., 884, 902
Agrarianism
  Jefferson and, 264
  transformation of, 512
Agribusiness, 512
  water for, 819–820
Agricultural Adjustment Act (AAA), 721,
    723(i)
  first (1933), 721, 724
  second (1938), 737–738
Agricultural Marketing Act (1929), 700
Agricultural rural domain (global economic
    region), 549, 549(m)
Agriculture, 240–241. See also Crops;
    Farms and farming; Rural areas;
    specific crops
  in 1950s, 817–818, 818(i)
  of ancient Americans, 13, 16(i)
  commercial, 510–512, 511(f), 512(i)
  of Eastern Woodland peoples, 13, 15
  in Great Depression, 700, 701, 702, 703,
    707
  immigrant workers in, 948(i)
  income (1920–1940), 703(f), 704
  Japanese immigrants in, 505, 510
  labor for, 693(m), 694
  land policy and, 329
  migrant workers in, 510, 512, 853
  of Native American cultures, 15–17
  in New Deal, 717, 721, 734(i), 737–738
  in New England, 94, 115
  plantation, 459–460
  price supports for, 679
  railroads and, 540
  sharecropping system of, 510
  in South, 365–366, 365(m), 531, 541
  surplus products, 700, 701, 702
  of Taino, 35
  tariffs and, 539, 700
  technology and, 817–818
  in West, 541
Agriculture Department, creation of, 446
Aguinaldo, Emilio, 606
AIDS (acquired immune deficiency
    syndrome), 920
Aid to Families with Dependent Children
    (AFDC), 840, 940

AIM. See American Indian Movement
Air conditioning, 817(i), 819
Air controllers, strike by, 915
Air force
  in England, 749
  German, 78, 749, 751
  in Second World War, 749, 768
Airlines, deregulation of, 906
Air pollution, 526(i), 841, 863, 915
Alabama. See also Montgomery bus boycott
  black Congressmen in, 473
  civil rights movement and, 846–847
  conservative government in, 481(m)
  Indians in, 498
  military rule in, 468(m)
  readmission to union, 481(m)
  Redeemers in, 480
  secession and, 417, 418(m), 424
Alamo, battle of the, 341
Alaska, 337, 909
Alaskan Indians, 864
Albanians
  ethnic, 945–946
  Muslim, 945
Albany Congress, 144–146
Albany Plan of Union, 145, 146
Albright, Madeleine, 938(i)
Albuquerque, 42
Alcatraz, Indian seizure of, 851(i), 852
Alcohol and alcoholism. See also
    Temperance
  consumption of, 316
  First World War and, 658
  Indians and, 249, 338
  progressivism and, 614
  prohibition and, 685–687, 686(i)
Algeciras, Spain, conference in, 628
Algiers, 265, 266
Algonquian Indians, 19, 57
Ali, Muhammad, 882
Alien and Sedition Acts (1798), 255–256,
    310
Alien Land Law (California, 1913), 639
Aliens. See Illegal immigrants
Allen, Doris, 892
Allende, Salvador, 887
Alliance(s). See also specific alliances
  in First World War, 648–649, 649(m)
  with France, 193–194
  with Indians, 144
  NATO as, 786
  in Second World War, 751, 753, 760, 767,
    780, 780(i)
Allies (First World War), 648–649, 649(m),
    651, 653, 655, 657, 662–663, 665
  loans and, 680
  Paris Peace Conference and, 662–663,
    665
Allies (Second World War), 760, 761, 767(i)
  in European theater, 760–761, 768–770
  in Pacific theater, 759–760
  in UN, 770
  weapons produced by, 757, 757(f)
Allotment plan, in New Deal, 721, 724
Allotment policy, for Indian lands, 494, 496
Alphabet, Cherokee, 308
Al Qaeda, 954, 956
Altgeld, John Peter, 589
Amalgamated Association of Iron and Steel
    Workers, 563, 584, 585

Amalgamated Clothing Workers, 730
Amendments to Constitution. See also
    specific amendments
  Bill of Rights as, 238
America(s). See also Central America;
    Exploration; North America; South
    America; specific locations
  colonies in late 17th century, 103(m)
  Columbian exchange and, 38, 46
  European exploration of, 34–38
  mixed-race people in, 46, 47(i)
  naming of, 36
  origins of humans in, 6–9
  wealth from, 45, 45(f)
American Bell (telephone company), 524
American Civil Liberties Union (ACLU), 670
American Colonization Society, 317, 353
American Communist Party. See
    Communist Party
American dream, 683
American Equal Rights Association, 467
American Expeditionary Force (AEF), 653,
    654(m), 655
American Federation of Labor (AFL),
    563–564, 730. See also Labor unions;
    Strikes
  Coxey's Army and, 595
  in First World War, 658
  after First World War, 668
  in Great Depression, 705
  labor movement and, 565
  women workers and, 614
  working class and, 575
American GI Forum, 793, 854
American Indian Movement (AIM), 852
American Indians. See Native Americans
Americanization
  immigrants and, 553
  of Vietnam War, 878–879, 883
American Liberty League, 724, 730
American Medical Association, 688, 730
American Party. See Know-Nothing Party
American Psychiatric Association, gays
    classified by, 856
American Railway Union (ARU), Pullman
    strike and, 588–589
American Recovery and Reinvestment Act
    (2009), 959
American Red Cross, 447
American Revolution. See Revolutionary
    War (1775–1783)
American Sugar Refining Company, 540
American Sunday School Union, 315(i)
Americans with Disabilities Act (ADA,
    1990), 931
American System (Clay), 288
American system, of manufacturing, 329
American Telephone and Telegraph
    (AT&T), 524–525
American Temperance Society, 316
American Temperance Union, 316
American Tobacco Company, 531, 621
American Woman Suffrage Association
    (AWSA), 593
Ames, Adelbert, 480
Amusement parks, 566, 566(i), 567(i), 568
Anarchism, 564–565, 565(i)
  Sacco and Vanzetti trial and, 694
  unionism and, 586
Anasazi people, 17

Ancient Americans, 2–24. *See also* Archaic Indians; Native Americans; specific groups

Anderson, "Bloody Bill," 434

Anderson, Robert, 425

Andros, Edmund, 105

Angel Island immigration station, 553

Anglican Church. *See* Church of England

Anglo-American alliance, in Second World War, 751

Anglo-Americans
in California, 348, 349
in Mexican borderlands, 339, 340–341
in West, 503–504, 509

Anglo-Saxon, 692

Angola, 922–923, 924

Animals, in ancient Americas, 9, 12. *See also* Hunter-gatherer; Hunting; specific animals

Annapolis, meeting at (1786), 223

Annexation
Hawai'i and, 599
of Oregon, 343
of Texas, 342*(i)*, 343, 503
of Utah Territory, 339

Antebellum era, 453
immigration in (1840–1860), 334*(f)*
Mormons in, 339
politics of slavery in, 384–386
separate spheres in, 313*(i)*
southern society and culture in, 360, 361–387

Anthony, Susan B., 407, 532
advocacy by, 470*(i)*
Fourteenth Amendment and, 467
on "Negro first" strategy, 470

Anthracite coal strike (1902), 622

Anti-Americanism
Eisenhower policies and, 831
Iraq War and, 957

Antiballistic missiles (ABMs), 887

Antiballistic Missile Treaty (1972), 922

Anticommunism
in Cold War, 801
Eisenhower and, 807
Nixon and, 799, 898
Reagan and, 915
Truman and, 787, 795–796

Antidemocratic regimes, after First World War, 744

Antidiscrimination ordinance, for gays and lesbians, 856

Antidiscrimination programs, 919

Antietam, battle of (1862), 431*(i)*, **433**

Antifederalists, 227, **229**–230

Anti-German sentiment, during First World War, 660–661, 660*(i)*

Anti-immigrant sentiment, 693–694, 696

Anti-imperialism, 606

Antilynching legislation, 688

Antilynching movement, 531–532

Antinomian, 93–94

Antipoverty programs, 864
of Clinton, 939
of Johnson, L. B., 840

Anti-Saloon League, 614

Anti-Semitism. *See also* Jews and Judaism
in 1930s, 725
of Hitler, 746

Antislavery movement, 317–318, 386, 407. *See also* Abolition and abolitionism

Antisodomy laws, 920

Antitrust activities
holding companies and, 523
legislation, 528, 540
Roosevelt, T., and, 621
Taft and, 630
Wilson and, 634

Antiwar movement, in Vietnam War, 841, 855, 881–882, 889–890, 889*(i)*, 901

Antwerp, in Second World War, 770

Apache Indians, 21, 340, 343, 497, 497–498

Apartheid, in South Africa, 923

Apollo program, 872

Appalachian Mountains, colonial settlement and, 121, 149

Appeal . . . to Coloured Citizens of the World, An (Walker), 317

Appeasement, before Second World War, **748**–749

Appliances, 683*(f)*

Appomattox Court House, Virginia, Lee's surrender at (1865), 452

Apportionment, for voting, 285

Apprenticeship, laws in black codes, 464

Arabella (ship), 87

Arab-Israeli wars
Six-Day War (1967), 888
Yom Kippur War (1973), 862

Arab League, on U.S. in Afghanistan, 933*(m)*

Arab world. *See also* Arab-Israeli wars; Middle East; Persian Gulf War; specific locations
anti-immigrant sentiment and, 954
Clinton and, 946
Jews and, 664
Nasser and, 814
Nixon and, 888
Truman and, 788

Arafat, Yasir, 946

Arapaho Indians, 337, 494*(i)*, 498

Arbenz, Jacobo, 813

Arbitration, in strikes, 587, 589

Arbitration treaties, Taft and, 630

Archaeology and archaeologists, **4,** 5, 10*(i)*

Archaic Indians, 10, 12, 14*(t)*, 15

Architecture
Chicago school of, 570
skyscrapers and, 522, 543, 569–570, 569*(i)*
of World's Columbian Exposition, 572–574, 573*(i)*

Arctic National Wildlife Refuge, 909

Aristide, Jean-Bertrand, 945

Arizona, 16, 17, 343, 400, 400*(m)*
Indian reservation in, 497
mining in, 500, 501*(m)*

Arizona (ship), 753*(i)*

Ark (ship), 67

Arkansas, 270, 361, 414
farmers' alliances in, 581
Lincoln's Reconstruction plan and, 459
military rule in, 468*(m)*
readmission to Union, 481*(m)*
Redeemers in, 480
secession and, 424, 425, 426*(m)*

Armada (Spain), 85*(i)*

Armed forces. *See also* Continental army; Military; Militia; specific battles and wars

African Americans in, 438*(i)*, 441
in Civil War, 429–430, 438*(i)*, 441
desegregation of, 792–793
Indians and, 490, 492, 497, 499
Jefferson and, 264
Nazi, 751
in Second World War, 756–758
women in, 930*(i)*

Armed neutrality, 651

Armenian immigrants, 551

Armistead, William, 195*(i)*

Armistice
after First World War, 654*(i)*, 655, 663, 673
French–Nazi German, 749
after Korean War, 800

Arms and armaments. *See* Weapons; specific weapons

Arms race, 801, 811*(i)*, 815–816, 815*(i)*, 873–874, 873*(i)*. *See also* Disarmament
Eisenhower and, 811, 812
nuclear test ban treaty and, 874, 936

Army of Northern Virginia, 433

Army of the Potomac, 433, 450

Army of the Republic of Vietnam. *See* ARVN

Arnold, Benedict, 182, 197–198, 197*(i)*

Arsenal of democracy, U.S. as, 751, 758

Art(s). *See also* Literature; Poets and poetry; specific arts and artists; specific works
in 1950s, 826
in Harlem Renaissance, 689–690, 689*(i)*
Lost Generation and, 678, 685, 691

Arthur, Chester A., 535

Articles of Confederation (1781–1789), **206**–209. *See also* Constitution (U.S.)
amending of, 216
Congress under, 217
departments of government under, 209
economy and finances under, 207, 209, 220–221
equality and slavery under, 212–214
failure of, 215–222
representation under, 207, 224

Artifacts, 4, 5
of Archaic Indians, 10
Clovis, 9

Artisans, 556
slaves as, 373
Spanish, 45

Artist in His Museum, The (Peale), 261*(i)*

ARVN (Army of the Republic of Vietnam), 813, 874, 880, 889

Asia. *See also* specific locations
Columbus's search for, 35, 36
human origins in, 6–8
immigrants from, 504–505, 550–551, 553, 639, 694
land wars in, 800
Open Door policy in, 598*(i)*, 601, 627
Portugal and, 33
railroads in, 520*(f)*
sea route to, 33
before Second World War, 746
third world and, 787
trade with, 337

Asian Americans. *See also* specific groups
citizenship and, 504–505
New Deal and, 733
political appointments of, 939
in Progressive Era, 636

Asian people, McCarran-Walter Act and, 795
Aspirin Age, 678
Assassinations
    of Garfield, 535
    of Kennedy, John F., 838, 875
    of Kennedy, Robert F., 883–884
    of King, Martin Luther, Jr., 848
    of Lincoln, 452, 462
    of McKinley, 620
Assemblies. *See also* Legislatures; specific colonies and states
    colonial, 136, 154, 157
    before Revolution, 164
    in Virginia, 60
Assembly lines, 681–682
Assimilation
    immigrants and, 553
    of Indians, 308, 494–496, 495*(i)*, 733
Assumption, of state debts, 242, 243
Aswan Dam, 814
Atchison, David Rice, 408–409
Atlanta
    fall of (1864), 449*(m)*, 451, 452
    race riot in, 639
Atlanta Compromise, 639
Atlanta Constitution, 530
Atlantic Charter (1941), 751
Atlantic Ocean region
    Civil War in, 436
    colonial commerce and, 115, 131
    in Second World War, 759, 760
    slave trade and, 124*(m)*
    trade in, 116*(m)*
Atomic bomb
    in China, 893
    in India and Pakistan, 936
    in Second World War, 773–774
    Soviet, 785
Atomic power. *See* Nuclear energy
Attucks, Crispus, 160
Audiotapes, in Watergate scandal, 902
Augusta, Georgia, in Revolutionary War, 196
Auschwitz, Poland, concentration camp in, 766
Austin, Stephen F., 340
Australia, 550
    in Second World War, 759
Austria, 664
    Nazi Germany and, 748
Austria-Hungary, First World War and, 648, 649*(i)*, 664
Automobiles and automobile industry
    in 1920s, 677*(i)*, 678, 680–682, 681*(m)*, 682*(i)*
    in 1950s, 805*(i)*, 822
    Ford and, 678*(i)*, 680–681
    mass production in, 681
Aviation, Lindbergh and, 690–691
Axis powers (Second World War), 767–768, 775. *See also* Italy; Japan; Nazi Germany; Second World War; specific locations
    aggression through 1941, 750*(m)*
    weapons production by, 757*(f)*
Ayllón, Lucas Vázquez de, 41
Aztecs. *See* Mexica

Babbitt (Lewis), 691
Baby boom, 824, 824*(f)*
"Back to Africa" movement, 688
Bacon's Laws (1676), 71
***Bacon's Rebellion, 70**–71
Bad Heart Bull, Amos, 488*(i)*
Baer, George, 621
Bahrain, 933*(m)*
Baker, Ella, 845
Baker, Isaac Wallace, 349*(i)*
Baker v. Carr (1963), 842
Bakke case, 901
Balance of power
    First World War and, 648, 665
    naval, 680
Balboa, Vasco Núñez de, 37
Balch, Emily Greene, 659
Baldwin, Roger, 670
Balkan region, 664
"Ballad of Pretty Boy Floyd, The," 704–705
Ball courts
    of Hohokam peoples, 17
    Mexican, 17*(i)*
Baltimore (Lord), 67, 105
Baltimore, Maryland, 426
Baltimore and Ohio Railroad, 298, 561–562
"Banana republics," 601
Bancroft, Hubert Howe, 349
Bank(s) and banking. *See also* Bank of the United States; Federal Reserve Board; Panic(s)
    credit to foreign customers, 698
    deregulation and, 916
    failures of, 699, 703
    farmers and, 580–581, 582, 705
    in Great Depression, 699, 700, 703
    in New Deal, 718, 719*(f)*
    robberies, 704–705
    state-chartered, 300–301, 311
    Wilson and, 633–634
"Bank holiday" (1933), 718
Banknotes, 300–301, 311, 312, 542
Bank of the United States
    First, 243–244, 264
    Jackson and, 311–312
    Second, 301, 311–312
Bankruptcies
    of farmers (1920s), 679, 704, 705
    in Panic of 1819, 301
Banks, Dennis, 852
Bannock-Shoshoni Indians, 502
Baptists, 315, 374, 380, 461
    in colonies, 131
    women and, 282
Barbados, 72, **73**–75
    slavery and, 76, 125
Barbary Wars (1801–1805), 265–266
Barbed wire, 508
Barriers to trade, free trade and, 946–947
Barrios, in California, 504
Barry, Leonora, 563
Barter, by yeomen, 378–379
Barton, Clara, 447
Baruch, Bernard, 656–657
Baseball, 567, 690, 792
Bastogne, in Second World War, 770
Batista, Fulgencio, 813–814
Battle of Antietam (1862), 431*(i)*, **433**
Battle of Britain (1940), 749
Battle of the Bulge (1944–1945), 770

Battle of Bull Run (Manassas) (1861), **431**–432, 432*(m)*
Battle of Gettysburg (1863), 449–**450,** 449*(m)*, 450*(m)*
Battle of Shiloh (1862), 432*(m)*, **435**
Battles. *See* Wars and warfare; specific battles and wars
Bay of Pigs invasion (1961), **872,** 873
Bayonet rule, in South, 479, 481
Beals, Melba Patillo, 828
Beans, 16*(i)*
Bearden, Romare, 415*(i)*
Bear Flag Revolt, 341
Beat generation, 826, 855
Beaver furs. *See* Fur trade
Beecher family. *See also* Stowe, Harriet Beecher
    Catharine, 283
    Lyman, 316
Begin, Menachem, 911
Beirut, Marines killed in, 922, 922*(i)*
Belgium, in Second World War, 749
Bell, Alexander Graham, 524, 525
Bell, John, 416, 416*(m)*
Belleau Wood, battle at, 654–655, 654*(m)*
Benét, Stephen Vincent, 414
Benton, Thomas Hart (artist), 728*(i)*
Benton, Thomas Hart (Missouri senator), 337, 407
Berger, Victor, 669
Beringia (land bridge), **7**
Berkeley, California, free speech movement in, 854
Berkeley, William, 69, 69*(i)*, 70, 71
Berkman, Alexander, 586
Berlin, Germany, division and occupation of, 770, 785, 785*(m)*
Berlin, Treaty of (1899), 601, 601*(m)*
Berlin airlift, 785
Berlin Wall, 872, 936*(i)*
Bernard, Francis, 153, 157, 159
Berry, Chuck, 826
Bessemer, Henry, 521
Bethlehem, Pennsylvania, 118*(i)*
Bethune, Mary McLeod, 732, 732*(i)*
Bett, Mum. *See* Freeman, Elizabeth
Bibb, Henry, 353
Bible
    King James version of, 86
    school prayer and, 843
Bicameral legislature, 224
"Big Bonanza," 502
Big business. *See also* Business; Economy
    muckraking and, 623
    railroads as, 518–521, 519*(m)*, 520*(f)*
    regulation of, 624, 634
    Roosevelt, T., and, 622, 624
    steel, 521–522, 522*(f)*
    tariffs and, 629
"Big stick" foreign policy, of Roosevelt, T., 624–628, 626*(i)*, 627*(m)*, 628*(m)*, 647
Big Three, in Second World War, 770
"Billion Dollar Congress," 539
Bill of Rights (U.S.), 229, 230, 236, **237**–238. *See also* Amendments; Constitution (U.S.); specific Amendments
Bills of rights
    under Articles of Confederation, 212
    in state constitutions, 211

Bimetallism system, 541
Bin Laden, Osama, 934, 946, 954, 957, 959
Biological weapons, Bush, G. W., and, 955
"Birds of passage" (immigrants), 552
Birmingham, Alabama, 530
    children's crusade for civil rights in, 846
    civil rights movement in, 835*(i)*, 845
Birth control movement, 637–638, 687, 688
Birthrate. *See also* Baby boom
    in 1950s, 822, 824*(f)*
    in Great Depression, 704
    after Second World War, 791
Bishop Hill, 328*(i)*
Bison (buffalo), 337
    hunters of, 9, 12
    slaughter of, 338, 489, 491, 491*(i)*
Black codes, 462*(i)*, *463*–464, 465
Black Death, 30–*31*
Black Elk (Oglala holy man), 493
Blackfeet Indians, 21
Black Hawk (Sauk and Fox Indians), 308,
    429
Black Hawk War (1832), 308
Black Hills, Indians and, 488, *492*–493
Black Kettle (Cheyenne Indians), 490
Blacklist
    McCarthyism and, 796
    of union members, 587
Black Panthers, 850
Black power movement, 850
Blacks. *See also* Africa; African Americans;
    Africans; Free blacks; Freedmen;
    Slavery
    in Barbados, 75
Black Star Line, 688
Black suffrage, 285. *See also* African
    Americans; Voting and voting rights
    Congress and, 469
    Fifteenth Amendment and, 469–470
    Fourteenth Amendment and, 467
    Lincoln on, 459
    Military Reconstruction Acts and, 468,
        468*(m)*
    Republican party and, 471, 472–473
Black Thursday (October 24, 1929), 700
Black Tuesday (October 29, 1929), 700
Blaine, James G., 535, 536–537, 536*(i)*,
    537*(m)*, 539, 601
"Bleeding Kansas" (1850s), 408–*409,*
    409*(m)*
"Bleeding Sumner," 409
Blitzkrieg ("lightning war"), 748*(i)*, 749
Blockade runners, 436
Blockades
    of Berlin, 785
    in Civil War, 429, 436, 443
    in Cuban missile crisis, 873
    in First World War, 650, 650*(m)*, 651, 663
"Bloody Sunday" (Selma, 1965), 846–847
Bloomers (clothing), 352*(i)*
Blue Eagle campaign (NRA), 722
Blue Jacket (Shawnee Indians), 248
Boarding schools, for Indians, 494–496,
    495*(i)*
Board of Indian Commissioners, 496
Boleyn, Anne (England), 85
Bolshevik Revolution, 670
Bolsheviks and Bolshevism, 653. See *also*
    Communism; Soviet Union
    First World War and, 653, 668–669

Bombings. *See also* Atomic bomb
    of Afghanistan, 954
    atomic bombings of Japan, 768, 770,
        773–774, 773*(i)*
    domestic, after First World War, 669
    of Serbia, 945–946
    in Vietnam War, 876, 877, 877*(f)*, 878, 888,
        889, 890, 891
Bomb shelters, in 1950s, 816
Bonanza farms, 511
Bond, Julian, 902
Bonds
    during Civil War, 430
    government, 242
Bonfield, John (Blackjack), 565
Bonus Marchers, in Great Depression, **705**
Bookbinders' union, 614
Book of Mormon, The (Smith), 339
Boom and bust cycles, 301–302, 520
Boonesborough, Kentucky, 192
Bootblacks, 558
Booth, John Wilkes, 452, 462
Bootlegging, in prohibition, 686, 686*(i)*
Borah, William, 666*(i)*
Border(s). *See also* Boundaries
    of Louisiana Purchase, 268
    of Oregon, 343
    Venezuela–British Guiana dispute, 601
Borderlands
    Mexican, 339–341
    trade and conflict in, 134–135
Border states (Civil War)
    freedom for blacks and, 439
    secession and, 425–426, 426*(m)*
Boré, Étienne de, 366
Borrowing, in 1950s, 823
Bosch, Juan, 878
Bosnia, 945
Bossism, 571–572, 575
Boston, 87, 399. *See also* Massachusetts
    economy of, 115
    immigrants in, 552
    merchants in, 115–116
    school busing in, 900
    Stamp Act protests in, 152–153
    subway system in, 570
    wealth in, 117
Boston Common, 114*(i)*
Boston Massacre, 159–*160,* 159*(i)*
Boston police strike (1919), 668
Boston Port Act (1774), 163*(t)*
Boston Public Library, 570–571
Boston Tea Party, 162–163
Boston-to-Albany turnpike, 241
Boudry, Nancy, 373
Boundaries. *See also* Border(s)
    of Texas, 343–344
    western lands after Revolution and, 207
Bow, Clara, 690
Bowdoin, James, 222
Bowie, James, 341
Boxer Protocol (1901), 600
Boxer uprising (China), 598, *600*
Boxing, 690
Boycotts
    anti-British, 157–159, 165
    grape, 853*(i)*
    of Pullman cars, 607
    against segregation, 830
Boyer, LaNada, 852

Boys. *See* Men
Bozeman Trail, 489*(m)*, 492
Bracero program, 820
Braddock, Edward, 146, 147
Bradford, William, 86
Brady, Mathew, 413*(i)*, 431*(i)*
Brains Trust, in New Deal, 717
Branch, Jacob, 373
Branches of government, in Constitution,
    225–226. *See also* specific branches
Brandeis, Louis, 634
Brant, Joseph. *See* Thayendanegea (Joseph
    Brant)
Bray, Rosemary, 841
Brazil, 42, 72*(i)*, 124*(m)*
Brazos River, 340
Breckinridge, John C., 414–417, 416*(m)*
Br'er Rabbit and Br'er Fox stories, 375
Brezhnev, Leonid, 911
Briand, Aristide, 680
Bridges, 522, 543, 569
    Brooklyn, 547*(i)*, 570
    Williamsburg, 570
Briggs, Laura, 781
Bristol docks, tobacco at, 64*(i)*
Britain. *See* England (Britain)
British Empire, 102–106. *See also* Colonies
    and colonization; England (Britain);
    specific colonies
    colonial politics and trade in, 135–136
British Guiana, Venezuela and, 601
British North America. *See also* Colonies
    and colonization; England (Britain);
    Navigation Acts; North America;
    specific locations
    common elements in, 130–136
Brooke, Edward, 861*(i)*
Brooklyn Bridge, 547*(i)*, 570
Brooks, Preston, 409
Brotherhood of Sleeping Car Porters, 764
Brown, John, 415*(i)*
    Harpers Ferry raid by, 414
    Pottawatomie Creek killings by, 409,
        409*(m)*
Brown, Joseph E., 443
Brown, Oliver, 828
Brown, William Wells, 353
Brown power, 854
Brownsville (Brooklyn, New York), birth
    control clinic in, 638
Brown v. Board of Education (1954), 794,
    828, 842
Brunauer, Esther, 796
Bryan, William Jennings
    election of 1896 and, 596, 597, 597*(m)*,
        607
    election of 1904 and, 622
    election of 1908, 628
    Lusitania sinking and, 650
    Scopes trial and, 695
    as secretary of state, 647
    on U.S expansionism, 606
Bryce, James, 571
Bubonic plague (Black Death), 30–31
Buchanan, James, 407, 412, 418
Buchanan, Patrick J., 951*(m)*
Budget, federal, 916, 932, 938–939, 952,
    957, 959
Buena Vista, Mexico, battle at, 338*(m)*, 345
Buffalo. *See* Bison (buffalo)

Buffalo soldiers, 503
Buffalo Telegraph, 537
Bulgaria, communism in, 781
Bulge, Battle of the (1944–1945), 770
Bull Moose Party. *See* Progressive Party, of
  1912
Bull Run (Manassas)
  battle of (1861), **431**–432, 432*(m)*
  second battle of (1862), 433
"Bully pulpit," Roosevelt, T., and, 620,
  620*(i)*
Bunche, Ralph J., 792
Bundy, McGeorge, 876
Bunker Hill, battle of (1775), 175*(m),* **176**
Bureaucracy. *See* Departments of
  government; specific departments
Bureau of Corporations, 621
Bureau of Indian Affairs, 492, 498
  Indian relocation and, 809
  Indian takeover of, 852
Bureau of Refugees, Freedmen, and
  Abandoned Lands. *See* Freedmen's
  Bureau
Burger, Warren E., and Burger Court, 897*(i),*
  900–901
Burgoyne, John, 175, 190–191
Burial mounds, 17
  in Mississippi River region, 15
  of Woodland Indians, 13, 17–18
Burleson, Albert, 661
Burma, in Second World War, 753, 759, 771
Burnham, Daniel, 572, 573
Burns, Anthony, 399
Burnside, Ambrose, 433–434
Burr, Aaron, 254, 263, 263*(m)*
Bus boycott, in Montgomery, 830
Bush, George H. W., 931*(i)*
  election of 1980 and, 914
  election of 1988 and, 930
  election of 1992 and, 936
  foreign policy of, 945
  government under, 930–932
  Iran-Contra and, 923
  new world order and, 945
  Panama intervention by, 932
  Persian Gulf War and, 930*(i),* 932–934,
    933*(m)*
  taxation and, 931
Bush, George W., 950–957
  domestic policy of, 951–953
  election of 2000 and, 950, 951, 951*(m)*
  election of 2004 and, 956
  Iraq War and, 956–958
  recession of 2007 and, 958–959
  trade and, 946
Business. *See also* Big business;
  Corporations; Finance capitalism;
  Labor unions
  in 1920s, 678–680, 682
  in 1950s, 818
  city bosses and, 572
  civil service reform and, 536
  after First World War, 667–668
  foreign policy and, 598–599
  in Gilded Age, 518–522, 519*(m),* 520*(f),*
    522*(f),* 540
  Great Depression and, 700–701
  mechanization in, 557, 561, 575
  monopolies in, 521–523, 526, 540, 541*(i)*
  in New Deal, 723–724

in Progressive Era, 623–624
  regulation of trusts and, 634
  after Second World War, 791
  telephones and, 524–525
Business organization
  horizontal integration, 523
  vertical integration, 522
Busing, school, integration and, 900
Butler, Andrew P., 409
Butler, Benjamin F., 439
Butler, Nicholas Murray, 660
Byles, Mather, 188
Byrd, Harry F., 837*(m)*

Cabinet (presidential). *See* specific
  presidents and posts
Cabot, John, 36
Cabral, Pedro Álvars, 36
Cabrillo, Juan Rodríguez, 42
Cady, Elizabeth. *See* Stanton, Elizabeth Cady
Cahokia, 18, 22
Caldwell, John, 145*(i)*
Calhoun, John C., 320, 396
  election of 1824 and, 288, 290
  election of 1828 and, 305
  nullification and, 310–311
  on slavery, 363, 394, 410
  War of 1812 and, 276
California, 343. *See also* Los Angeles
  ancient peoples of, 12–13, 12*(m)*
  Chinese in, 348–349, 349*(i),* 504–505
  corporate ranches in, 512
  farming in, 392*(i)*
  gold rush in, 500
  gun control in, 931
  Hispanics in, 503–504
  housing discrimination banned in, 848
  Indians of, 21
  Ku Klux Klan in, 694
  land speculation in, 507
  manifest destiny and, 341
  Mexican-American War in, 345
  Mexican migration to, 341
  Mexicans in, 820–821
  Proposition 13 in, 899, 899*(i)*
  statehood for, 395
  woman suffrage and, 593
"California compromise" (Clay), 391*(i)*
California gold rush (1849–1852), **347**–349,
  348*(i),* 392
California Trail, 338*(m),* 341
Californios, 349, 503–504
Calley, William, 890
Calvinism, of Puritans, ***90***
Cambodia, 874
  Vietnam War and, 888–889, 889*(i),*
    889*(m),* 891
Camden, battle of (1780), 196*(m),* 197, 198
Campaigns (military). *See* specific battles
  and wars
Campaigns (political). *See also* Elections
  for 1828 election, 304
  campaign pins in (1884), 536*(i)*
  contributions to, 536
  television and, 825
Camp David accords, 911
Camp meetings, 315
Canada, 353, 549. *See also* New France;
  specific locations

agriculture in, 549
  English exploration of, 50*(t)*
  expansionists and, 276
  immigrants from, 550, 550*(m)*
  Indians fleeing to, 497
  loyalists in, 188
  Native Americans in, 19
  in NATO, 786
  in Seven Years' War, 146
  War of 1812 and, 276, 277, 277*(m)*
Canals, 297*(m)*
  Erie Canal, 296*(i),* 298
  Love Canal, 910
  Panama Canal, 625–626, 627*(m),* 905, 910
  Suez Canal, 760, 814
Canal Zone. *See* Panama Canal
Canary Islands, 35, 36
Cane Ridge, revival meeting at, 315
Cannon, Joseph, 624
Cantigny, battle at, 654–655
CAP. *See* Community Action Program
Cape of Good Hope, 33
Capital city, 240. *See also* Washington, D.C.
  location along Potomac, 243, 264
  in South, 243
Capitalism
  crony, 522
  finance, 526–527
  freewheeling, 518
  Great Depression and, 705
  in New Deal, 717, 725
  politics and, 528, 540
  regulation and, 540
  Roosevelt, F. D., and, 739
  Stalin on, 783
  welfare, 682
Capone, Alphonse (Big Al), 686–687
Caravel, 32, 35
Caribbean region. *See also* specific locations
  Columbus in, 35, 38
  Cortés in, 39–40
  people from, 852, 853
  Quasi-War in, 255
  Roosevelt, T., and, 625
  in Seven Years' War, 146
  slaves in, 124*(m)*
  Taft and, 630, 630*(m)*
  U.S. involvement in, 601, 647*(m),* 871*(m)*
Carleton, Guy, 200
Carlisle Indian School, 495
Carmel, California, mission in, 135*(i)*
Carmichael, Stokely, 850
Carnegie, Andrew
  criticism of, 526
  Gilded Age and, 518
  and gospel of wealth, 528
  Homestead strike and, 584–585, 587
  Morgan, J. P., and, 527
  social Darwinism and, 528
  steel industry and, 521–522
  workers, 550
Carney, Kate, 370
Carolina(s). *See also* North Carolina; South
  Carolina
  in 17th century, 74*(m)*
  charter for, 76
  Indians of, 20
  northern, 61
  settlement in, 121
  slavery in, 72, 76, 214

Carolina Grant, 74*(m)*
Carpetbaggers, 472
Carrier, Willis Haviland, 817*(i)*
Carson, Rachel, 862–863
Carter, James Earl, Jr. (Jimmy), 904
   deregulation by, 906, 915, 916
   domestic policy of, 905–909
   election of 1976 and, 904
   election of 1980 and, 912
   energy and, 906–908
   environment and, 907–909
   foreign policy of, 905, 911–912
   human rights and, 909–911
Carter, Rosalyn, 905
Carter Doctrine, 911
Cartier, Jacques, 50*(t)*
Cartography, 36
Casablanca meeting (1943), 761
Cash-and-carry policy, before Second World
   War, 746, 751
Cash crops. *See also* specific crops
   in South, 365–366, 365*(m)*
Cash register, 559
Cass, Lewis, 394, 395
Castro, Fidel, 872, 935. *See also* Cuba
   Bay of Pigs invasion and, 872
   CIA activities against, 813–814, 903
Casualties. *See also* specific wars and
   battles
   in Civil War, 431–432, 431*(i)*, 433, 434,
     435, 441, 450
   Soviet, in Second World War, 780–781
   in steamboat accidents, 298
Catholicism, 530, 537. *See also* Missions
   and missionaries; Protestant
   Reformation; Religion(s)
   in Canada, 114
   in colonies, 131
   Democratic Party and, 714
   in England, 84
   Luther and, 48–49
   in Maryland, 67
   vs. Protestantism, 405–406
   of Smith, Alfred, 696
   in Spanish colonies, 73
Catlin, George, 337
Catt, Carrie Chapman, 659
Cattell, James McKeen, 660
Cattle ranching, 508–510, 508*(m)*
Cattle trails, 508*(m)*
Cavalry, 490, 492, 493, 498, 499
Cayuga Indians, 20
CCC. *See* Civilian Conservation Corps
Cease and desist orders, 634
Censorship, mail, 320
Census
   of 1790, 243*(i)*
   of 1810, 275
Central America. *See also* America(s); Latin
   America; specific locations
   Native Americans in, 9
   United Fruit in, 601
   U.S. intervention in, 601
Central American-Dominican Republic Free
   Trade Agreement, 946
Central High School, Little Rock, 828, 829*(i)*
Centralia, Washington, IWW in, 669
Central Intelligence Agency (CIA), 787
   antiwar movement and, 882
   Chilean destabilization by, 887

Cuba and, 813–814, 872
Guatemala and, 813
illegal operations by, 903–904
Iran-Contra and, 923
Middle East and, 814
Central Pacific Railroad, 504, 505*(i)*
Central Park (New York City), 570
Central Powers (First World War), 649*(m)*
Century of Dishonor, A (Jackson), 496
Cerro Gordo, Mexico, battle at (1847), 346
Cession, of Indian land. *See* Land; Native
   Americans
Chaco Canyon, 17
Chamberlain, Neville, 748
Chamberlain, W. G., 336*(i)*
Chamberlain, Wilt, 861
Chamber of Commerce, 724, 730
Champlain, Lake, 146
Chancellorsville, battle at (1863), 449,
   449*(m)*
Chaplin, Charlie, 690
Chapultepec, battle of (1847), 346
Charles I (England), 67, 87, 94, 104
Charles I (Spain). *See* Charles V (Holy
   Roman Empire)
Charles II (England), 76, 99, 104, 105
Charles V (Holy Roman Empire), 49
Charleston, South Carolina (Charles Town),
   76, 196*(m)*
   in Civil War, 425
   in Revolutionary War, 196
Charlestown peninsula. *See* Bunker Hill,
   Battle of
Charter(s)
   for Bank of the United States, 301, 311
   for Carolina, 76
   of Massachusetts, 84, 87, 91, 105, 106
   of Virginia Company, 60
Charter of Privileges, in Pennsylvania, 101
Chase, Salmon P., 396, 429, 462, 469
Chattanooga, battle of (1863), 450,
   459*(m)*
Chavez, Cesar, 853, 853*(i)*
Cheney, Richard B.
   Iraq War and, 955
   Persian Gulf War and, 934
   as vice president, 951
Cherokee Indians, 192, 308–310, 434
   removal of, 490
Chesapeake (ship), 273
Chesapeake region. *See also* Maryland;
   South; Tobacco and tobacco
   industry; Virginia; specific locations
   black population in, 75
   colonies in, 54, 56–71, 62*(m)*
   English trade regulations in, 102–103
   government in, 60, 68*(i)*, 70
   Jamestown in, 57–58
   religion in, 66–67
   slavery in, 76–78, 123–129
   society and economy in, 68–71
   tobacco in, 60, 61–66, 69
Chesnut, James, 384*(i)*
Chesnut, Mary Boykin, 371, 385–386
Cheyenne Indians, 21, 337, 490, 492, 498
Chiang Kai-shek. *See* Jiang Jieshi (Chiang
   Kai-shek)
Chicago, 401
   African Americans in, 553, 671
   de facto segregation in, 848

Democratic National Convention in
   (1968), 884, 884*(i)*
gangsters in (1920s), 686–687
Great Fire of 1871 in, 570
Haymarket bombing in, 564–565, 565*(i)*
Hull House in, 613
immigrants in, 548, 552
migration from rural areas to, 548
skyscrapers in, 569*(i)*, 570
strikes in, 562
World's Columbian Exposition in,
   572–574, 573*(i)*
Chicago Bears (football team), 690
"Chicago school" of architecture, 570
Chicago Tribune, 464
   on 1948 election, 794
   on Pullman strike, 589
Chicano movement and Chicanos, ***853,*** 854
Chickasaw Indians, 20, 308, 310, 434, 490
Chiefdoms, 15, ***17***
Chief Joseph (Nez Percé chief), 497, 497*(i)*
Chief Justice. *See also* Supreme Court
   (U.S.); specific individuals
   Burger as, 897*(i)*, 900–901
   Jay as, 251
   Taney as, 410
   Warren as, 838, 842–843, 900
Child, Lydia Maria, 403*(i)*
Childbearing, birth control and, 637–638
Childbirth
   lifespan and, 114
   in New England, 95
   by slaves, 126
Child care, 791
   Nixon on, 901
Child labor, 533, 687
   Fair Labor Standards Act and, 738
   Keating-Owen Act and, 635
   in late 19th century, 558
   in mills, 530, 556
   in mines, 556
   progressivism and, 612
   women's clubs on, 533
Children. *See also* Child labor
   black codes, apprenticeship laws, and,
     464
   in civil rights campaign, 846*(i)*
   Continental army and, 181
   depression of 1890s and, 594
   education for, 314, 315*(i)*, 461, 471, 473,
     474, 475*(m)*, 483, 694
   of immigrants, 552
   Indian, 490, 494–496, 495*(i)*, 498, 499
   middle class, 567
   in New England, 88
   of planters, 370
   slave, 126, 371, 371*(i)*, 373
   working class, 557–558, 558*(i)*
Children's Bureau, 630
Children's crusade (1963), 846*(i)*
Child Support Enforcement Amendments
   Act, 919
Chile
   Carter and, 909
   CIA and, 887
China, 549, 549*(m)*. *See also* Korean War;
   Manchuria
   atomic bomb of, 893
   Boxer uprising in, 598
   Carter and, 911

China (continued)
  Communists vs. Nationalists in, 787
  immigrants from, 553
  investment by, 952
  Japan and, 753
  missionaries in, 599–600, 600(i)
  Nixon and, 887
  North Korea and, 797
  Open Door policy in, 598(i), 601, 627
  Portugal and, 33
  protests in (1989), 935
  Roosevelt, T., and, 628
  in Second World War, 771, 775
  Soviet Union and, 788
  trade, 598(i)
  UN and, 770
  Vietnam and, 891
Chinese Exclusion Act
  of 1882, 505, 553, 671
  of 1902, 639
Chinese immigrants, 694
  in California, 348–349, 349(i), 504–505,
    505(i)
  in cities, 553
  as cooks, 512
  as farm laborers, 510
  in mining, 502
  railroads and, 504, 505(i)
Chippewa Indians, 19, 219
Chiricahua Apache Indians, 497
Chisholm, Shirley, 901
Chisholm Trail, 508, 508(m)
Chivalry, in South, 370
Chivington, John M., 490
Choctaw Indians, 20, 308, 310, 434, 490
Cholera, 346, 348
"Christian guardianship" (paternalism),
  368
Christianity. See also Evangelicalism;
    Protestant Reformation; specific
    groups
  of African Americans, 375
  in colonies, 131
  Indian conversion to, 44, 59, 148, 308
  Protestant Reformation and, 48–49,
    84–85
  slaves and, 374–375
Christian Right. See New (Christian) Right
Chrysler Corporation, bankruptcy and,
  906, 959
Chumash people, 12, 14(t)
Churches. See also Religion(s); specific
    groups
  black, 461, 475(m), 483
  colonial, 131
  membership in, 315, 824
  New England government and, 90–92
  women and, 281–282
Churchill, Winston, 749. See also Second
    World War
  at Casablanca, 761
  iron curtain speech of, 782(m), 783
  at Teheran, 768
  at Yalta, 761
Church of England (Anglican), Puritans
  and, 66–67, 68(i), 86, 88, 92
Church of Jesus Christ of Latter-Day Saints.
  See Mormons
Churubusco, battle of (1847), 346
CIA. See Central Intelligence Agency

Cigarettes and cigarette industry, 531,
    681. See also Tobacco and tobacco
    industry
Cincinnati, Ohio, 567
CIO (Committee for Industrial
    Organization, Congress of Industrial
    Organizations), 730
Circumnavigation of globe, 37
Cisler, Lucinda, 859
Cities and towns, 728(i). See also Urban
    areas; specific locations
  in 1920s, 681, 692, 693(m)
  in 1950s, 819
  African Americans in, 553, 670–671, 764
  architecture of, 569–571, 569(i)
  automobile and, 681
  bosses (political) in, 571–572, 575
  electric lights in, 524(i), 525
  global migration and, 548–552, 548(i),
    549(m), 550(m), 551(f)
  in Great Depression, 703–704
  growth of, 543
  immigrants in, 550–557, 550(m)
  Indian relocation to, 809, 809(m)
  mass transit in, 554
  movement to, 548–552, 549(m), 692,
    693(m)
  neighborhoods in, 554
  in New England, 89
  poverty in, 554, 557
  progressivism and, 613–614, 618
  reforms in, 572
  segregation in, 554–555
  slaves employed in, 372
  social geography of, 554–555
  in South, 367
  transportation to, 298
Citizens and citizenship
  Asians and, 504, 505
  for Californios, 503
  Civil Rights Act of 1866 and, 465
  Fifteenth Amendment and, 469
  Fourteenth Amendment and, 466–467,
    479
  for free blacks, 410
  gender and, 531
  McCarran-Walter Act and, 795
  Native Americans and, 496, 694
  after Revolution, 210–214
  Supreme Court and, 479
  women and, 470
City upon a hill, Massachusetts Bay colony
  as, 88
Civil Defense Administration, 816
Civilian Conservation Corps (CCC), 719
Civil liberties
  First World War and, 656–658
  Red scare and, 669–670
  for women, 352
Civil rights. See also Civil rights movement;
    specific groups
  in 1950s, 827–830
  for African Americans, 792–793
  Eisenhower and, 828
  for Latinos, 852–854
  for Mexican Americans, 793–794
  Reagan and, 918
  during Reconstruction, 465, 473, 478
  after Second World War, 792–794
  sexual orientation and, 920

Truman and, 792–794, 795
Warren Court and, 842
Civil Rights Act. See also Title VII
  of 1866, 465
  of 1875, 478
  of 1957, 828
  of 1960, 828
  of 1964, 838–839, 840, 847, 858, 864, 899
  of 1968, 841, 848
Civil Rights Commission, 918
Civil rights movement, 844–850. See also
    Civil Rights Act; King, Martin Luther,
    Jr.; specific leaders and events
  freedom rides in (May, 1961), 845(m)
  protests during, 844–847
  after Second World War, 792
Civil Rights Restoration Act (1988), 919
Civil service, 478
  exams for, 534(i)
  Jackson's "spoils system" and, 206
Civil Service Commission, 536
  antigay policy of, 856
Civil service reform, 535–537, 536
Civil unions, 940
Civil war(s)
  in Guatemala, 813
  in Mexico, 671
  in Rwanda, 945
  in Spain, 746(m), 747
  Vietnam War as, 892
Civil War (U.S., 1861–1865), 424(i). See also
    Casualties; Reconstruction
  African Americans in, 438–441, 438(i)
  battles in (1861–1862), 431–435, 432(m),
    433(m), 434(m), 435(f)
  battles in (1863–1865), 448–452, 448(m),
    449(m), 451(f)
  diplomacy in, 436–437
  draft in, 441, 443–444
  in Eastern theater, 431–434, 431(i),
    448–451, 449(m), 450(m)
  effects of, 453
  emancipation and, 438–441
  events leading to, 392–402, 408–417
  financing of, 430
  Fort Sumter attack and, 424(i), 425
  home fronts during, 442–447
  Indians in, 433, 434
  Lee's surrender and, 452
  resources of North and South in, 427–428,
    427(i), 428(f)
  secession and, 417–418, 418(m), 424,
    425–426, 426(m)
  slavery and, 427, 437
  strategy in, 428–429, 434, 450
Civil Works Administration (CWA), 719
Claiborne, Liz, 916
Clamshell Alliance, 907–908
Clark, George Rogers, 192
Clark, William, 269–270
Classes. See also Hierarchies; specific
    classes
  conflict in Gilded Age, 528, 539
  in South, 364, 387
  voting rights and, 212
Clay, Edward W., 364(i)
Clay, Henry, 304, 306, 311
  American System of, 288
  "California compromise" of, 391(i)
  election of 1824 and, 288, 289, 289(m)

election of 1828 and, 304
election of 1844 and, 343
Missouri Compromise and, 286
on slavery in territories, 395, 397
War of 1812 and, 276
Clayton Antitrust Act (1914), 634
Clean Air Act
of 1970, 863, 952
of 1990, 931
Clean Water Act (1972), 863, 952
"Clear and present danger" test, 669
Clemenceau, Georges, 663
Clemens, Samuel Langhorne. *See* Twain, Mark
Clergy, in Chesapeake, 66–67
Clerical jobs, 818
women in, 559–560
Clermont (steamboat), 295(i), 298
Cleveland, Grover, 536(i)
election of 1884 and, 536–537, 537(m)
election of 1888 and, 538
election of 1892 and, 517(i), 538, 596(m)
election of 1896 and, 596
gold standard and, 542, 543
Hawai'i and, 599
on immigration restriction, 554
Monroe Doctrine and, 601
Pullman strike and, 589
tariff reform and, 539
Cleveland, Ohio, 548
migration to, 548, 554
progressive government in, 618
"Cliffs of the Upper Colorado," 487(i)
Climate, of ancient Americas, 9, 15
Clinton, DeWitt, 277
Clinton, Henry, 175, 196, 197
Clinton, Hillary Rodham, 939
election of 2008 and, 958
Clinton, William Jefferson (Bill), 936–949
appointments by, 938(i)
cabinet of, 938(i)
economy and, 937, 938–939, 942–943
election of 1992 and, 936–937
election of 1996 and, 941
foreign policy of, 944–949
globalization and, 947
impeachment of, 938, 941–942
right wing and, 940–941
Clodfelter, Mike, 880
Closed shops, 679
Clothing. *See also* Cotton and cotton industry; Garment industry; Textiles and textile industry
bathing outfits and, 566(i)
bloomers as, 352(i)
of flappers, 685(i), 688
homespun, 158
in Indian schools, 495, 495(i)
of slaves, 369
Clovis culture, 9
Clovis points, 8
Coal and coal industry, 330, 758
strikes against, 622, 705, 705(m)
Coalitions
in New Deal, 715
Reagan, 914
Cobb, Howard, 417
Cobb, Thomas R. R., 364
Cockran, Bourke, 606
Codex Mendoza, 23(i)

Coerced labor. *See* Slavery
Coercive (Intolerable) Acts (1773), **163**–165, 163(t), 166
Cold Harbor, battle of (1864), 449(m), 450
Cold War, 778, 779(i), **781.** *See also* Eastern Europe; Soviet Union; Vietnam War
beginning of, 780–783
Caribbean region in, 871(m)
Carter and, 911–912
consequences of, 801
détente in, 887
disarmament in, 887
end of, 934–936, 935(m)
as holy war, 824
Kennedy, J. F., and, 870–875
Korean War and, 797–800
Latin America and, 871(m)
Reagan and, 921–924
Sun Belt and, 819–821
Colfax, Schuyler, 477
Colfax massacre, 480
Collaboration, in Second World War, 749
Collective action, by Latinos, 854
Collective security, 680, 786
Colleges. *See* Higher education; Universities and colleges
Colleton, John, 76
Collier, John, 733
Colombia, Panama Canal and, 626
Colonialism. *See also* Colonies and colonization
third world and, 549, 549(m)
in West, 488–493, 496–499
Colonies and colonization. *See also* British North America; France; Native Americans; New France; New Spain; Revolutionary War; Spain; specific colonies and locations
in 17th century, 103(m)
in 18th century, 112–136
African Americans and, 317, 353
assemblies in, 136
Atlantic trade in 18th century, 116(m)
British North American, 130–136
in Chesapeake region, 56–71, 62(m)
English empire and, 102–106
European in New World, 43(m), 50
exports from, 132(f)
after First World War, 662, 665
French and English conflicts over, 106
governors in, 136
immigration to, 107
Indians and, 59–60, 134–135
as mark of national greatness, 648
middle colonies and, 98–101, 118–122
Monroe Doctrine and, 601
Navigation Acts and, 70
in New England, 86–97, 87(m), 114–117
northern, 82–106
population of, 112
Portuguese, 42
religions in, 131
Seven Years' War and, 143(m), 146–147
slavery in, 123–129
social and racial hierarchies in, 46
southern, 54–78, 123–129
Spanish, 39–46, 47(i), 73, 134–135
trade in, 59, 102–104
wedding tapestry from, 111(i)
women in, 65

Colonization policy, of Lincoln, 439
Colorado, 17, 343
manifest destiny and, 490
mining in, 500, 501(m)
Sand Creek massacre in (1864), 490
voting by women in, 592(i)
Colorado River, 487(i)
Color barriers, breaking, 792
Colored Farmers' Alliance, 581
Colt, William L., Mrs., 656(i)
Columbian exchange, 38, 46
"Columbia Patriot, A" (Mercy Otis Warren), 229
Columbia University, protests at, 883
Columbus, Christopher, 495(i)
explorations by, 34–36, 38
Comanche Indians, 21, 267, 337, 340, 343, 491–492, 496–497
Comanchería, 491–**492**
Combine (farm machine), 511
Coming of Age in Mississippi (Moody), 844(i)
Comintern, 668
Commander in chief, of Continental army, 175
Commerce. *See also* Trade
colonial, 94, 101, 115, 130–131
Hamilton on, 264
Commerce and Labor Department, 621
Commercial agriculture, 510–512, 511(f), 512(i)
Commercialization, of leisure, 566(i), 567–568
Committee for Industrial Organization (CIO), 730
Committee on Civil Rights (1946). *See* President's Committee on Civil Rights (1946)
Committee on Fair Employment Practices (1941), 764
Committee on Public Information (CPI), 660
Committees of correspondence, 162, 163, 165
Committees of public safety, 165
Commodity Credit Corporation, 721
Common economic market, in Europe, 934
Common laborers, 556
Common Sense (Paine), **176**–177
Commonwealth, New England families as, 88
Commonwealth of Independent States, 934–935
Communalism, 351
Communication(s)
globalization and, 946
railroads and, 521
telegraph and, 330
telephone and, 524–525
transportation and, 298
Communism. *See also* Cold War; Soviet Union
in China, 787
in Cuba, 813–814
in Czechoslovakia, 785
in Eastern Europe, 785, 934
after First World War, 668–670
Graham, Billy, on, 824
in Great Depression, 705, 706, 725, 734
immigration quotas and, 795
Iran and, 814

Communism (continued)
McCarthyism and, 795–796
in Middle East, 814
in Southeast Asia, 812, 891
in third world, 787
Truman Doctrine and, 783–784
in Vietnam, 882
Communist Party
Arbenz and, 813
in Great Depression, 725
McCarthyism and, 796
membership in, 707
Scottsboro Boys and, 706
unions and, 705
Communities
African American, 503
utopian, 351
yeomen, 379
Community Action Program (CAP), 839
Competition
antitrust laws and, 540
foreign, 539
Morgan and, 527
North vs. South, 530
in petroleum industry, 523
in railroad industry, 520, 521
social Darwinism and, 527–528
Compromise of 1850, 395–**397,** 396(m),
398–399
Compromise of 1877, 482
Compulsory free labor, 460
Computers, in 1990s, 942
Comstock, Anthony, 637
Comstock, Henry, 500
Comstock Lode (Nevada), 392, **500,** 500(i),
501–503
Concentration camps, in Holocaust, 766
Concentration policy, 338
Concord, battle at, 166–167, 167(m)
Condren, Don, 791
Conestoga Indians, 148
Coney Island, New York, 566(i), 568,
574
Confederate Congress, 443
Confederate States of America, 417,
424. *See also* Civil War (U.S.,
1861–1865)
"belligerent" status for, 436
bread riots in, 443
centralization in, 442–443
collapse of, 452
diplomacy and, 436–437
draft in, 443–444
emancipation of slaves and, 440
industry in, 429–430, 443
inflation in, 430, 443
mobilization of, 427–430
nationalism in, 444
resources of, 427–428, 428(f)
revenues of, 430, 443
secession and, 417–418, 418(m), 425–426,
426(m)
slavery in, 427
Confederation. *See* Articles of
Confederation
Confiscation Act
of 1861, 439, 459
of 1862, 440, 459
Conformity, in 1950s, 824
Congregational Church, in colonies, 131

Congress (U.S.), 225. *See also* Congressional
Reconstruction; Continental
Congress; House of Representatives;
Senate; specific acts
in 1950s, 806, 809–810
under Articles of Confederation, 217
"Billion Dollar," 539
conservation and, 624
Constitution on, 225–226
election of 1876 and, 481–482
Equal Rights Amendment of 1923 and, 687
ex-Confederates in, 464
farm prices and, 705
First World War and, 651, 659, 661
in Gilded Age, 534–535, 539, 541–542
home of, 209
on immigrants, 693–694
Indian reservation allotment and, 496
Indian schools funding by, 495
Johnson, L. B., and, 838–841
literacy tests approved by, 554
override of presidential vetoes, 464–465
Reconstruction and, 458, 459, 460, 462,
478, 483
Red scare and, 669
school busing and, 900
slavery and, 318, 395–397, 410, 439, 440
southern congressional delegations and,
473(f)
Taft and, 628, 629
Vietnam War and, 889
Wilmot Proviso and, 394
Congressional Reconstruction, 467–470
Congress of Industrial Organizations (CIO),
730
Congress of Racial Equality (CORE), 764,
831, 850
Conkling, Roscoe, 535
Connecticut, 94
emancipation in, 213
government of, 136
land sales in, 115
western lands of, 207
Conoco road map, 682(i)
Conquistadors, 41–42, 44
Conscription. *See* Draft (military)
Conservation. *See also* Environment
New Deal programs and, 719–721
Nixon and, 862
Roosevelt, T., and, 625(m)
Conservatives and conservatism. *See
also* Right wing (political); specific
politicians and movements
1969–1989, 896–925
Bush, G. W., and, 951–953
Great Depression and, 713
New Deal and, 736–737
Nixon and, 898–904
of Supreme Court, 526, 528
Consolidation, of business, 526, 527
Constitution(s). *See also* Constitution (U.S.)
of Cherokees, 308
Lecompton, 412
reconstruction, in South, 459, 463, 466(i),
468, 471, 472–473
state, 210–211
Constitution (U.S.), 223–226. *See also*
Amendments; Bill of Rights;
Supreme Court (U.S.); specific
Amendments

Antifederalists and, 227, 229–230
democracy vs. republicanism in, 225–226
Federalists and, 227–229
"general welfare" clause of, 244
judicial review of, 265
Korean War and, 798
ratification of, 227–230, 228(m), 237
slavery and, 392–393, 398
three-fifths clause and, 225
Constitutional conventions, 205(i),
222–226
suffrage reform and, 285
Constitutional Union Party, 414–417,
416(m)
Consumer(s)
in 1920s, 682(i), 683–684, 699
colonial, 115, 130–131
Johnson, L. B., and, 840
passive, 683
prices and farm income of (1865–1910),
580, 582(f)
after Second World War, 791
Consumer culture
in 1920s, 683–684, 699
in 1950s, 822–823, 825
advertising and, 682(i)
Columbian Exposition and, 574
in Gilded Age, 560
women in, 678, 688
Consumer goods, 681, 683, 818, 831
credit and, 699
production of (1920–1929), 678, 683(f)
Consumption
Great Depression and, 707
inequality of wealth and, 699
market expansion and, 684
mass production and, 684
Containment policy, 780, **783**
Eisenhower and, 811, 812–813
Korean War and, 798–799
Nixon and, 887
Reagan and, 922
six-pronged strategy for, 785
superpower global rivalry and, 787–788
Continental army, 175, 180–181, 180(i),
184. *See also* Revolutionary War
campaigns of 1777–1779 and, 190–197
Continental Association, 165
Continental Congress, 161, 165, 174,
175, 181. *See also* Articles of
Confederation; Congress (U.S.)
First, 164–165
prisoners of war and, 188
Second, 166
Shays's Rebellion and, 222
Continental drift, 6, 7(m)
Contraband of war, runaway slaves as,
439, 440(i)
Contraception. *See* Birth Control movement
Contract labor, freedmen and, 459–460
Contras, in Nicaragua, 923, 932
Conventions. *See* specific political parties
Conversion. *See* Christianity; Halfway
Covenant; Missions and
missionaries
Coode, John, 105
Cook, John F., 381(i)
Coolidge, Calvin
business and, 678, 679
election of 1924, 680

taxes cut by, 699
unions and, 668
Cooperatives, farmers', 581–582
Copperheads (Peace Democrats), 447
Copper mining, 501(m)
Coral Sea, Battle of (1942), 771
CORE. See Congress of Racial Equality
Corinth, Mississippi, in Civil War, 435
Corn (maize), 16(i), 57, 580
Cornplanter (Seneca Indians), 217
Cornstalk (Shawnee), 192
Cornwallis, Charles, 195(i), 196–197,
198–199
Coronado, Francisco Vásquez de, 41, 42
Coronado, Juan Rodríguez de, 41
Corporate liberalism, 624
Corporate profits, mass production and, 683
Corporations. See also Business
assembly line and management changes
in, 681–682
international competition with, 916–917
Supreme Court and, 526, 528, 540
taxes on, 731
"Corrupt bargain," 289, 304
Corruption
in city government, 571–572
in Gilded Age, 534–535
under Grant, 477, 477(i), 481
under Harding, 679
during Revolution, 191–192
in southern Republican governments,
474, 479
Cortés, Hernán, 39–41, 44, 346
Cosmetics, standards for, 840
Costa Rica, 601
Cotton and cotton industry, 76, 241, 360(i).
See also Cotton gin; Textiles and
textile industry
black women field workers in, 471(i)
Civil War and, 428, 436–437
cotton famine in, 436
cotton gin and, 366, 366(i)
European imports of (1860–1870), 437(f)
mills and, 366
panic of 1837 and, 321
sharecropping and, 474–475
slaves and, 361(m), 362
in South, 530
in Texas, 510, 511
yeomen farmers in, 378
Cotton belt, yeomen in, 377, 378(m)
Cotton Club, 689, 689(i)
Cotton gin, 241, 366, 366(i)
Cotton kingdom, 361–**362,** 361(m)
Coughlin, Charles, 725, 731
Counterculture, 855
Country-born slaves, 126
Coups. See also specific locations
in Chile, 887
against Diem, 875
in Iran, 814
Court-packing plan, of Roosevelt, F. D.,
735
Courts. See Judiciary; Supreme Court
(U.S.); specific cases
Covenant
of grace vs. covenant of works, 93
Puritan, 87, 88, 90
Covenant Chain, 144, 146
Covert operations, of CIA, 903–904

Cowboys
cattle ranching and, 509–510
industrial, 512
Cox, Archibald, 902
Cox, James M., 672, 672(m), 713
Coxey, Jacob S., 594(i), 595, 595(i)
Coxey's army, 594(i), **595,** 595(i), 607
Cradles (farm tool), 328(i)
Craft unions, 563–564
Crashes (financial). See Depressions
(financial); Panic(s)
Crater Lake National Park, 625(m)
Crawford, William H., 288, 289(m), 290
Crazy Horse (Sioux chief), 493, 495(i)
Credit. See also National debt
economic panics and, 301, 302, 321
Hamilton on, 242
sharecropping and, 474–475
Credit cards, 823
Creditor, U.S. as, 680
Creek Indians, 20, 246–247, 434, 490
removal of, 308, 310
Creek War (1813–1814), **278**
Creel, George, 660
Creoles, 46
Crime and criminals
in California gold rush, 348
in Great Depression, 704–705
Miranda ruling and, 843
during prohibition, 685–687
Crimes against humanity. See also War
crimes
by Nazis, 766
Criminal justice system, Warren Court and,
843
Cripple Creek
miners' strike (1894) in, 584, **587,** 607
mining in, 501(m), 502
Croatia, 945
Croatoan, discovery of word, 50(t)
Crocker, Charles, 505(i)
Crockett, Davy, 341
Crogman, William, 639
Croly, Jane Cunningham (Jennie June),
532–533
Cromwell, Oliver, 94
Cronkite, Walter, 882
Crook, George, 497, 498
Crop lien system, 474–475, 531, 581
Crops. See also Agriculture; Farms and
farming; specific crops
African, 128
of ancient Americans, 16(i)
in Carolina, 76
in Columbian exchange, 38
of Eastern Woodland peoples, 13
in New Deal, 721
in New England, 115
price decline for, 580, 582(f)
of South, 124, 365–366, 365(m)
specialization in, 818
tobacco as, 60, 61–66
of yeomen farmers, 378–379
"Cross of gold" speech, of Bryan, 596
Crow Dog, Mary, 852
Crow Indians, 21, 497
Crusade for Justice (Wells), 532
Cuba, 400. See also Castro, Fidel; Cuban
missile crisis
in 1930s, 745

Bay of Pigs invasion in, 872
CIA and, 813–814
England and, 146
Platt Amendment and, 605
Spain and, 39
Spanish-American War and, 602–604,
603(i), 604(m), 606
United States and, 287, 604–606, 647(m)
U.S. naval base in, 605
yellow journalism and, 602(i)
Cuban missile crisis, 873, 873(m)
Cuban revolution, 813–814
Cuffe, Paul and **John,** 213
Cullen, Countee, 690
Cult(s), in Waco, 940
Cult of domesticity, 566–567, 592
Cultural imperialism, 494–496, 495(i)
Culture(s). See also specific groups
in 1830s, 313–318
in 1950s, 822–826
African, 125, 126
African American, 127–128
Anasazi, 17
of Archaic Indians, 10
in British North America, 130–136
Clovis, 8–9
consumer, 682(i), 683–684
of Great Basin, 12
Hohokam, 16–17
hunting and gathering, 10
of Mesoamerica and South America,
23–24
of Mexica, 23–24
Native American, 11(m), 22, 494–496, 809
of New England, 114–117
of Pacific Ocean region, 12–13
of plain folk, 380
politics and, 529–533, 529(i)
slave, 127–128, 375
southern, 129, 362
Southwestern, 15–17
Spanish impact on Native American, 46,
47(i)
television and, 824–825
Woodland, 13–15, 17–18
of youth, 707
Cumberland River region, in Civil War, 435
Currency. See also Money
banknotes as, 300–301, 311, 312
gold standard for, 538(i), 541, 542
"In God We Trust" on, 824
Populist reforms and, 597
during Revolution, 175, 189
Curriculum
in Indian schools, 494–496
in women's academies, 283
Cushman, Belle, 560
Custer, George Armstrong, 493, 496
"Custer's Last Stand," 493
Custody rights, of women, 593
Customs. See also Duties; Taxation
tobacco and, 70
Czechoslovakia, 664
communism and, 781, 785
Second World War and, 748
Czolgosz, Leon, 620

Daguerreotypes, 299(i), 349(i)
Dakotas. See North Dakota; South Dakota
Dakota Sioux, 491–492

Dallas, 819
    Kennedy, J. F., assassination in, 838
Dallas, George M., 342(i)
Darley, Felix O. C., 377(i)
Darlington Agency (Indian Territory), 494(i)
Darrow, Clarence, 695
Darwin, Charles, 528, 695. See also Reform
    Darwinism; Social Darwinism
Daughters of Liberty, 156, 158
Davis, Henry Winter, 459
Davis, James J., 557
Davis, Jefferson, 395, 417, 424, 425, 429,
    444
Davis, John W., 679
Davis, Paula Wright, 353
Dawes, Charles, 680
Dawes, Henry, 496
Dawes Allotment Act (1887), *496,* 733
Dawes Plan, 680
D Day, 768–770
DDT, 863
Dean, John, 902
Death camps, Nazi, 766
Death penalty, 919
Death rate. See Mortality; Mortality rate
Debates
    Kennedy-Nixon, 837
    Lincoln-Douglas, 411–412
Debs, Eugene V.
    election of 1912 and, 632, 633(m)
    Espionage Act and, 661
    as progressive, 632
    Pullman strike and, 588–589, 590
    Socialist Party and, 632, 633, 633(m), 637
Debt. See also National debt; War debt
    under Articles of Confederation, 216
    Civil War, 539
    Confederate, 463, 473
    corporate, 301
    economic panics and, 301
    farm, 511, 531, 541, 698
    federal, 242, 312
    after First World War, 698
    manipulation and restructuring of,
        916
    Spanish, 49
    state, 531
Decatur, Stephen, 265, 265(i), 266
"Declaration of Dependence, A," 187
Declaration of Independence (1776), 174(i),
    178–*179,* 212
"Declaration on the Causes and Necessity
    of Taking Up Arms, A" (Jefferson),
    175
Declaratory Act (1766), *155*
Deep South. See also Slavery; South (U.S.
    region)
    slavery in, 214
Deere, John, 329
Defender (Chicago newspaper), 553
Defense, national security state and,
    785–787. See also National security
Defense industry, 819, 820(m)
Defense of Marriage Act (1996), 940
Defense spending. See also Military;
    specific wars
    Carter and, 911
    Kennedy, J. F., and, 782
    Korean War and, 800
    Reagan and, 921–922

after Second World War, 791
    in Sun Belt, 899
    Vietnam War and, 893
Deferments, in Vietnam War, 880
Deficit, in federal budget, 916, 932,
    938–939, 952, 957, 959
Deists, in colonies, 131–133
Delany, Martin R., 353
Delaware, 424, 425, 426(m). See also Middle
        colonies
    emancipation and, 213–214
    western lands of, 208
Delaware (Lenni Lenape) Indians, 187, 192,
    193(m), 249
    land cession by, 219
Delaware River, Washington at, 184
Demilitarization
    in Germany, 782
    in Korea, 800
Democracy
    Hitler on, 746
    popular sovereignty and, 394
    vs. republicanism, 225–226
Democratic National Convention
    of 1896, 596
    of 1960, 836
    of 1968, 884, 884(i)
Democratic Party, 402. See also Elections;
        specific presidents
    election of 1912, 631, 631(i)
    on emancipation of slaves, 440–441
    First World War and, 661
    free silver and, 596
    in Gilded Age, 530, 534–535, 539,
        541–542
    Klan and, 472
    in New York City, 571
    Peace Democrats in, 447, 451–452
    popular sovereignty and, 405
    progressive reform, 630, 635
    Roosevelt, F. D., and, 713
    South and, 385, 475, 478, 479–480, 480(f),
        483, 531, 539
    southern Republican state governments
        and, 473
    Union-supporting, 463
    Versailles treaty and, 666
    Watergate break-in and, 901–902
    white supremacy and, 479–480, 480(i)
Democratization, of higher education, 821
Democrats, 304, 305. See also Democratic
        Party
Demography, globalization and, 948
Demonstrations. See Civil rights entries;
        Protest(s); Revolts and rebellions;
        specific demonstrations
Dempsey, Jack, 690
Denby, Charles, 600
Denmark, in Second World War, 749
Departments of government. See also
        specific departments
    under Articles of Confederation, 209
Department stores, 560
Deportation
    of Mexican Americans, in Great
        Depression, 704
    during Red scare, 669
Depressions (financial), 520. See also Great
        Depression; Panic(s); Recessions
    in 1870s, 478, 541, 557, 561

in 1890s, 511, 526, 538, 542, 557, 575,
        595, 596, 598
Deregulation
    in 1990s, 942
    by Carter, 906, 915, 916
    by Reagan, 915–916
Desegregation. See also Segregation
    Nixon and, 864
Desertion, in Civil War, 443, 452
De Soto, Hernando, 41, 42
Détente policy, *886*–887, 904
Detroit
    alcohol business in, 686
    auto industry in, 681, 681(m)
    Great Depression and, 704
    race riots in, 764, 849
Detroit, Fort, 148, 192, 193(m)
Developing nations, 872. See also Third
        world; specific locations
    aid to, 787
    globalization and, 947
Dew, Thomas R., 364, 370
Dewey, George, 603(m)
Dewey, Thomas E., 765
Dias, Bartolomeu, 33
Díaz, Porfirio, 671
Dickens, Charles, 533
Dickinson, John, 157, 174, 176
Dickson, Alvin, 175
Dictators and dictatorships. See specific
        individuals and locations
Diem, Ngo Dinh, 813, 874
Dien Bien Phu, 812–813
Diet (food). See also Food(s)
    Columbian exchange and, 38
    in Great Depression, 703, 707
    of slaves, 369
Dingell, John, 958
Dinwiddie, Robert, 144
Diplomacy. See also Foreign policy; specific
        presidents, treaties, and locations
    in Civil War, 428, 436–437
    of Clinton, 946
    dollar diplomacy and, 630, 630(m), 647
    in First World War, 650
    King Cotton, 436–437
    Monroe Doctrine and, 601
    of Roosevelt, F. D., 745
Direct election of senators, 583
Direct primary, 618
Dirksen, Everett, 839
Disabled people, ADA and, 931
Disarmament, 887
    by Iraq, 957
    nuclear freeze demands and, 922
    Reagan and, 924
    Rush-Bagot treaty and, 279
    Washington Disarmament Conference
        and, 680
Discovery. See Exploration
Discovery (ship), 57
Discrimination. See also Civil rights; Civil
        rights movement; Integration; Race
        and racism; Segregation
    against African Americans, 353–354, 441,
        503, 531–532, 732–733, 847
    in armed forces, 757–758
    against Asians and Asian Americans,
        504–505, 733
    black codes and, 463

against Californios, 349
against Chinese, 348–349
Civil Rights Act (1964) and, 847
economic, 792
gender, 353, 535, 920
against Hispanic Americans, 733
homosexuals and, 920
in housing, 841, 848
immigrants and, 693–694
against Japanese Americans, 639, 733
Mexican Americans and, 503–504
during Reconstruction, 478–479
reverse, 918
during Second World War, 764
women and, 847
Disease. *See also* Medicine; specific conditions
during California gold rush, 348
in cities, 554
in Columbian exchange, 38, 46
Indians and, 40–41, 46, 135, 338, 341, 490, 498
in Mexican-American War, 346
in New England, 95
sexually transmitted, 613
in Virginia, 60
Disfranchisement. *See also* Voting and voting rights
of African Americans, 639
of women, 407
Disney, Walt, 744*(i)*
Dissent. *See also* Protest(s)
in 1950s, 825–826
First World War and, 656, 661, 673
in New England, 92–94
in North (Civil War), 447
Red scare and, 668
religious, 131
Dissidents, in Soviet Union and Eastern Europe, 887
District of Columbia, 318. *See also* Washington, D.C.
Diversity
in English colonies, 135
in middle colonies, 98, 100
in Pennsylvania, 100–101
in West, 348, 500, 503–505
Divorce, 281, 370
Dix, Dorothea, 446
Dixiecrats, 794
Dobson, James, 914
Dodge, Richard, 491*(i)*
Dole, Robert, 941
Dollar Decade, 678
Dollar diplomacy (Taft), 630, 630*(m)*, 647
"Domestic allotment plan" in New Deal, 721, 724
Domesticity
in 1950s, 823–824
cult of, 566–567, 592
women and, 314
Domestic partnerships, 920. *See also* Gays and lesbians; Homosexuals and homosexuality
Domestic policy. *See* specific presidents
Domestics (domestic servants), 370, 567. *See also* Servants
black women as, 670

Domestic slave trade, 362
Dominican Republic, 626, 628, 628*(m)*, 630, 630*(m)*
U.S. intervention in, 647, 876, 878, 878*(i)*
Dominion of New England, 105
Dominis, Lydia Kamakaeha. *See* Lili'uokalani
Domino theory, 812
Donelson, Fort, battle at, 432*(m)*, 435
Donnelly, Ignatius, 595
"Don't ask, don't tell" policy, 940
Double standard, of sexual behavior, 687
Double V campaign, 763–764
"Doughboys," 652*(i)*
"Doughfaces," northerners as, 400, 407
Douglas, Aaron, 690
Douglas, Helen Gahagan, 790, 791
Douglas, Stephen A., 425
Compromise of 1850 and, 397
debates with Lincoln, 411–412
election of 1860 and, 414–417, 416*(m)*
Freeport Doctrine of, 412
Kansas-Nebraska Act of, 401–402
on Lecompton constitution, 412
popular sovereignty and, 405, 407
Douglass, Frederick, 350*(i)*, 353, 396, 400, 439, 467
Dove (ship), 67
Downs, Frederick, 879, 891
Draft (military)
antidraft riots and, 447
Carter and, 911
in Civil War, 441, 443–444, 447
in First World War, 653
Dred Scott decision (*Dred Scott v. Sandford,* 1857), 409–411, **410**, 412
Drift and Mastery (Lippmann), 618
Drought
in Dust Bowl, 724–725, 725*(m)*
on Great Plains (1880s–1890s), 508
Drugs (legal). *See* Medicine (drugs)
Du Bois, W. E. B., 532, 640, 653, 688
Due process, 466
Dukakis, Michael, 931
Duke family, 531
Duke of York. *See* James II (England)
Dulles, John Foster, 811, 812, 813, 814
Dunkirk, 749
Dunmore (Lord), 167–168
Du Pont, 621
Duquesne, Fort, 146
Dürer, Albrecht, 49
Dust Bowl, in Great Depression, 724–725, 725*(m)*
Dutch. *See also* Netherlands
in borderlands, 134
East and West India companies of, 98
New Netherland colony of, 98
in Second World War, 753
Dutch East India Company, 98
Dutch East Indies. *See* East Indies
Dutch Reformed Church, 99
Duties. *See also* Tariffs; Taxation; specific acts
Embargo Act (1807) and, 273
on imports, 244
on tobacco, 70
Townshend, 157
Dynamic Sociology (Ward), 618
Dysentery, 346

Earned Income Tax Credit (EITC), 939
Earth
circumnavigation of, 37
Columbus on, 35
Earth Day (1970), 863, 863*(i)*
East (U.S. region)
Civil War in, 431–434, 431*(i)*, 432*(m)*, 433*(m)*, 448–451
immigrants in, 548
East (world region), search for routes to, 30
East Berlin, 785, 785*(m)*
Berlin Wall and, 872, 936*(i)*
Eastern Europe. *See also* Europe and Europeans; specific locations
Clinton and, 944
end of Cold War and, 934–936, 935*(m)*
events in (1989–2002), 935*(m)*
Marshall Plan and, 784
after Second World War, 781, 785
Soviet power in, 781
after Soviet Union, 945–946
Eastern Hemisphere, competition for trade in, 601
Eastern Woodland Indians, 13–15, 14*(t)*
East Germany, 782, 785, 872
Berlin Wall and, 836*(i)*, 872
end of communism in, 934
East Indies, 33. *See also* Dutch East India Company
Columbus and, 35
Dutch, 753, 759
Magellan and, 38
Portugal and, 42–44
in Second World War, 753
East River, 556
Eaton, William, 266
Eckford, Elizabeth, 829*(i)*
Economic inequality, 333–334, 917
Economic Opportunity Act (1964), 839, 840
Economic Recovery Tax Act (1981), *915*
Economics, trickle-down, 700–701, 917
Economy, 240–242. *See also* Depressions; Globalization; New Deal; Panic(s); Recessions; Tariffs; Trade; Wealth
in 1920s, 680, 683
in 1950s, 817–820, 823*(f)*
in 1990s, 942–943
under Articles of Confederation, 207, 209, 220–221
auto industry and, 680–681
banking and, 300–301
Bank War and, 311–312
boom and bust cycles in, 301–302
Bush, G. W., and, 951–952
business devices and, 518
Carter and, 905–906
in Chesapeake region, 68–69
in Civil War, 430, 445–446
Clinton and, 937, 938–939, 942–943
Eisenhower and, 807, 808, 810
after First World War, 667–668
Ford administration and, 904
free-labor, 333–334
global regions of world, 549, 549*(m)*
before Great Crash, 698–699
growth in, 328, 329–331
Hamilton and, 240
interdependence of, 360
in Japan, 788
Kennedy, J. F., and, 837

Economy (continued)
  Keynes and, 703, 736
  manifest destiny and, 337
  market revolution and, 294, 296–302
  national populations and (ca. 1938), 737(f)
  in New England, 94–95, 115–117
  in New Spain, 44
  Nixon and, 862, 901
  plantation, 340, 365–367
  railroads and, 330–331
  Reagan and, 913–917
  in Reconstruction South, 472–473
  in Revolutionary War, 189
  Roosevelt, F. D., and, 713, 728–729
  Second World War and, 758, 775
  after Second World War, 781, 789–792,
    823(f)
  in South, 530–531
  in southern colonies, 79
  in Spain, 49
  tariffs and, 538–540
Edenton ladies, politics and, 156(i)
Edison, Thomas Alva, 524, 525
Education. See also Academies; Higher
    education; School(s)
  for African Americans, 639, 732–733
  free-labor ideal and, 333
  for Indians, 494–496, 495(i)
  job-training as, 837
  Ku Klux Klan and, 694
  for Mexican Americans, 793
  for motherhood, 238–239
  NDEA and, 816
  No Child Left Behind Act and, 952
  plain folk and, 380
  in South, 370, 461, 471, 472, 473, 474,
    475(m), 483
  women and, 282–283, 370, 470
  of youth, 314
Education Amendments Act (1972), Title IX
    of, 859, 919
Edwards, Jay Dearborn, 360(i)
Edwards, Jonathan, 133
EEOC. See Equal Employment Opportunity
    Commission
Efficiency, 641, 681–682
Effigy
  of Oliver, 153
  Ozette whale, 13(i)
  Taino, 35(i)
Egypt
  Nasser in, 814
  Six-Day War and, 888
Eighteenth Amendment, 658
  implementation of, 685
  repeal of, 687
Eighth Amendment, 238
Eight-hour workday, 564–565, 583, 587, 630,
    635, 658, 668
Eighty-ninth Congress (1965–1966), 839
Einstein, Albert, 785
Eisenhower, Dwight D.
  arms race and, 811, 812
  civil rights and, 828–829
  containment policy and, 811
  D-Day invasion and, 768–770
  domestic policy of, 806–810
  economy and, 807, 808, 810
  election of 1952 and, 799, 825
  election of 1956 and, 809–810

  Korean War and, 799
  McCarthy and, 807
  "middle way" of, 806–810
  on military-industrial complex, 816
  modern Republicanism of, 806–808
  Native Americans and, 809
  in Second World War, 760
  television and, 825
  Truman's foreign policy compared with,
    788, 811–816, 831
  Vietnam and, 812–813
  welfare state and, 831
Eisenhower Doctrine, 814, 814(m)
EITC. See Earned Income Tax Credit
El-Alamein, Battle of (1942), 760
"Elect," Puritans as, 90
Elections. See also Voting and voting rights
  of 1789, 236
  of 1792, 246
  of 1796, 253–254
  of 1800, 256, 262–263, 263(m)
  of 1804, 272
  of 1808, 273
  of 1812, 277
  of 1816, 284
  of 1820, 284
  of 1824, 284, 288–289, 289(m)
  of 1828, 303–305, 305(m)
  of 1832, 301, 311
  of 1836, 320–321
  of 1840, 322
  of 1844, 342(i), 343
  of 1848, 394(i), 395, 395(m), 404(m)
  of 1852, 400, 403, 404(m)
  of 1854, 405–406
  of 1855, 405–406
  of 1856, 403, 403(i), 404(m), 407
  of 1860, 322, 404(m), 414–417, 416(m)
  of 1862, 441
  of 1864, 451–452
  of 1866, 467
  of 1868, 476–477, 476(m)
  of 1872, 477–478
  of 1874, 479
  of 1876, 481–482, 535
  of 1878, 541
  of 1880, 535
  of 1884, 536–537, 536(i), 537(m)
  of 1888, 538, 539
  of 1890, 539
  of 1892, 517(i), 538, 596, 596(m)
  of 1896, 595–597, 597(m)
  of 1900, 621, 637
  of 1904, 622, 628, 636(i)
  of 1908, 628
  of 1910, 630
  of 1912, 631, 631(i), 632–633
  of 1914, 634
  of 1916, 634, 635, 650–651
  of 1920, 665, 672, 672(m), 679, 713
  of 1924, 679–680
  of 1928, 695–696, 696(m)
  of 1932, 713–715, 714(m)
  of 1934, 727
  of 1936, 735
  of 1938, 738
  of 1940, 751
  of 1944, 765
  of 1948, 789(i), 792, 794, 794(m)
  of 1952, 799, 825

  of 1954, 806
  of 1956, 809–810
  of 1960, 837, 837(m)
  of 1964, 839, 877, 899
  of 1968, 861, 883–885
  of 1972, 898, 901
  of 1976, 903, 904
  of 1980, 912, 913, 914
  of 1984, 916
  of 1988, 930, 931
  of 1992, 936
  of 1994, 940
  of 1996, 941
  of 2000, 950, 951, 951(m)
  of 2004, 956
  of 2006, 957
  of 2008, 958
  of 2010, 959–960
  of 2012, 960, 960(m)
  of senators, 412, 535, 583
  state, 285
  television and, 825
  in Virginia, 70
  voter turnout, 529
Electoral college, 285
  in Constitution, 226
  election of 1796 and, 254
  election of 1824 and, 289, 289(m)
  election of 2000 and, 951, 951(m)
Electoral commission, for 1876 election,
    481–482
Electric industry, 525
Electricity, 570
  dangers of, 524(i)
  in rural areas, 525, 719–720
  in urban areas, 525
Electric streetcar, 554
Elementary and Secondary Education Act
    (ESEA, 1965), 840
Elevated trains, 522
Elites. See also Classes
  in Chesapeake, 69
  as grandees, 69(i), 71, 75, 78
  ratification of Constitution and, 229
  southern, 128–129, 370, 385
  of southern free blacks, 382–383
Elizabeth I (England), 85, 85(i)
Elkins Act (1903), 621, 622
Ellington, Duke, 689(i)
Ellis Island, 548(i), **554**
Ellison, William, 383
El Paso, 671(i)
El Salvador
  Carter and, 909
  Reagan and, 923, 923(m)
Emancipation
  gradual, 213, 320
  Lincoln and, 438–439
  as military necessity, 440
  in Northwest Territory, 220
  proponents and opponents of, 439
  in South, 381
  status of slaves as contraband and, 439
Emancipation Proclamation (1863), 438,
    440–441
Embargo
  against Japan, 753
  by Jefferson, 272
  on oil, 888, 911, 932–933
Embargo Act (1807), **273**

Emergency Banking Act (1933), 718
Emerson, Ralph Waldo, 351, 414
Emigrant aid societies, Kansas settlement
    and, 408
Emigration. *See* Immigrants and
    immigration; Migration
Eminent domain, 301
Empires. *See also* New France; New Spain;
    specific empires
    British, 102–106, 134, 134(m)
    Comanchería, 491–492
    Eastern North American zones of, 134(m)
    French, 106, 114, 134, 134(m)
    of Hitler, 749
    Incan, 41–42
    of Mexica, 24
    Portuguese, 33
    slave, 361(m), 362
    Spanish, 39–46, 73, 134–135, 134(m)
    of United States, 488, 604–606, 605(m)
Employment. *See also* Unemployment;
    Women; Workforce
    in 1990s, 942
    affirmative action and, 847
    of African Americans in Second World
      War, 764
    in auto industry, 681
    black codes limitations on, 464
    of free blacks, 382
    Great Society and, 841
    low wages, 522
    racial discrimination in, 847
    by railroads, 520
    seasonal, 557
    speculation and, 520
    Truman and, 790
    of women, 556, 556(i), 558, 559–560, 658,
      688, 704, 838
    youth, 314
Employment Act (1946), 790
Encomenderos, 44
Encomienda system, **44**–45
Energy. *See also* specific types and sources
    Carter and, 906–908
    consumption of, 909(f)
    Nixon and, 862
    nuclear, 907–909
England (Britain). *See also* British Empire;
    Colonies and colonization; First
    World War; Revolutionary War;
    Second World War; specific colonies
    Afghanistan bombing by, 954
    in American Revolution, 181–184, 183(m)
    appeasement of Hitler by, 748–749
    colonial exports to, 128
    colonies of, 57–78, 103(m)
    cotton from South and, 366, 428, 436
    empire of, 102–106, 134–135, 134(m)
    exploration by, 50, 50(t)
    France and, 106, 251, 272–273
    German occupation zone of, 782
    Glorious Revolution in, 105
    Hitler and, 749
    immigrants from, 112, 334(f), 550, 551
    India and, 787
    Indians and, 144, 192–193
    loyalists in, 188
    middle colonies of, 98–101
    Navigation Acts and, 70
    Oregon Country claims of, 337, 343

    Ottoman empire and, 664
    Puritans and, 67, 94
    railroads in, 520(f)
    Revolutionary War loss and, 201
    in Second World War, 749–751
    settlement house movement in, 612
    southern colonies of, 54–78
    southern strategy in Revolution,
      195–199
    Suez Canal and, 814
    Texas and, 342
    in UN, 770
    Venezuelan-British Guiana borders and,
      601
    War of 1812 and, 276–278
    West Indies and, 73–75, 74(m)
    women's rights in, 638
English Empire. *See* British Empire
English Reformation, **84**–85
Enlightenment, **133**–134
Enola Gay (airplane), 773(i)
Entertainment. *See also* Leisure; specific
    types
    in 1920s, 689–691, 689(i)
    commercialization of, 566(i), 567–568
    politics as, 529
Entrepreneurs, 300
Environment. *See also* Air pollution; Water
    pollution
    adaptation to, 9, 22
    Bush, G. W., and, 952
    Carter and, 907–909
    of Eastern Woodland peoples, 13
    fire in, 22
    Indians and, 9
    Johnson, L. B., and, 841
    Nixon and, 862–863
    Reagan and, 915
    steamboats and, 298
    in Sun Belt, 819–820
    trade and, 946
Environmental Protection Agency (EPA),
    863, 915
Epidemics. *See also* specific diseases
    Plains Indians and, 338
    Spanish influenza, 668, 669(i)
Equal Employment Opportunity
    Commission (EEOC), 854, 864, 932
Equality. *See also* Civil rights movement;
    Gender and gender issues; Slavery;
    specific rights and groups
    under Articles of Confederation, 212–214
    for women, 763
Equal protection, in Fourteenth
    Amendment, 466, 842–843
Equal rights. *See* Civil rights; Rights;
    specific groups
Equal Rights Amendment (ERA)
    of 1923, 687
    of 1972, 858, 859, **919**
Equiano, Olaudah, 125, 125(i), 133
Erie, Lake, 146, 278
Erie Canal, 296(i), **298**
Ervin, Samuel J., 902
Espionage. *See* Spies and spying
Espionage Act (1917), 661
Established church, Congregational, 131
Estates (land), in Hudson valley, 120
Ethiopia, Italian conquest of, 746
"Ethiopian Regiment," 168

Ethnic groups. *See also* specific groups
    in cities, 552–554
    in Pennsylvania, 100–101
    politics and, 530
Eugenics, birth control and, 688
Europe and Europeans. *See also* Colonies
    and colonization; First World War;
    Second World War; specific locations
    Civil War (U.S.) and, 428, 436–437
    common economic market and, 934
    cotton imports of (1860–1870), 437(f)
    division after Second World War, 782(m)
    exploration by, 30–46, 37(m)
    after First World War, 663–665, 664(m),
      698
    immigrants from, 112, 113(m), 548,
      550–552, 550(m), 551(f), 553–554, 693
    Indians and, 29(i)
    industrial nature of, 549, 549(m)
    Lost Generation in, 691
    migration to New World from
      (1492–1700), 75(f)
    Monroe Doctrine and, 288, 601
    New World colonies of, 43(m)
    North American influence of, 147(m)
    Roosevelt, T., and, 625, 628
    Second World War and, 760–761,
      768–770, 769(i)
    Seven Years' War and, 143(m)
    Spanish New World exploration and,
      48–50
    trade by, 30–32, 31(m)
European Recovery Plan. *See* Marshall Plan
Evangelicalism, 313, 315–316. *See also*
    Revivals and revivalism
    in 1950s, 824
    Reagan and, 913(i)
    reform and, 318, 350–351
    slaves and, 374–375
Evans, Hiram Wesley, 694
"Eve of Destruction," 855
Everett, Sarah, 339
Everett, Wesley, 669
Evers, Medgar, 792, 845
Evolution, 528, 695
*Exact View of the Late Battle at
    Charlestown, An, June 17th 1775,*
    177(i)
Exceptionalism, 488
Excise tax, 244
Executive. *See also* Presidency; President;
    specific presidents and departments
    under Articles of Confederation, 206, 209
    in Virginia Plan, 224
Executive Orders
    8802, 764
    9066, 756
    9835, 796
    desegregating armed services, 792–793
Executives (business), 559
Exodusters, 510
Expansion and expansionism. *See also*
    Imperialism; Monroe Doctrine; Open
    Door policy; Westward movement
    California and, 341
    of English colonies, 106
    as foreign policy, 598, 601
    Indian land cessions and, 248–250,
      249(m)
    slavery and, 400–402

Expansion and expansionism (continued)
  Spanish-American War and, 604,
    605–606, 605(m)
  Texas and, 340–341
  U.S. overseas through 1900, 605(m)
  War of 1812 and, 276
  in West, 336–341, 488–489, 489(m),
    506–512, 513
Expatriates, in 1920s, 691
Expertise, 618
Exploration. See also Colonies and
    colonization
  by Columbus, 34–36, 38
  by England (Britain), 50, 50(t)
  European, 30–46, 37(m), 50(t)
  by Lewis and Clark, 269–270
  by Portugal, 31(m), 32–33
  of space, 815, 872
  by Spain, 34–38, 39–46, 47(i)
Exports
  in 1930s, 745
  colonial, 128, 132(f)
  of cotton, 366
  embargo on, 273
  English, 103, 131
  from English colonies, 79
  during First World War, 650
  after First World War, 698
  in New England, 115
  southern crops as, 128, 365
  of tobacco, 61
  wheat as, 581(f)

Factionalism, 534, 535. See also Political
    parties; specific parties
Factories
  assembly-line production in, 681–682
  auto manufacturing, 680–682, 681(f)
  in New Deal, 717
  slaves in, 372
  women in, 299–300, 762, 763
Factory workers, 560
Fair Deal, 789, 794–795
Fair Labor Standards Act (1938), 738
Fair trade, 947
Faith, Luther on, 49
Faith ministries, 951
Fall, Albert, 679
Fallen Timbers, battle of (1794), 249, 274
Families
  birth control movement and, 637
  in depression of 1890s, 594
  farm, 580(i), 698
  female-headed, 841
  of freedmen, 460, 461, 461(i), 474, 475(m)
  in Great Depression, 698, 703–704
  Mexican, 345(i)
  Native American, 495
  Panic of 1837 and, 319(i)
  of pioneers, 336(i)
  of planters, 368(i), 370, 378
  Puritan immigrants as, 88
  in Second World War, 763
  separate spheres idea and, 313–314,
    313(i)
  of slaves, 126, 359(i), 374
  in working class, 557
  of yeomen, 378
Family economy, 557–558

Family law, 281. See also Law(s); Marriage
Family Research Council, 914
Family values, 914
Farewell address
  of Eisenhower, 816
  of Jackson, 310
  of Nixon, 902
  of Reagan, 925
  of Washington, 253
Farm Credit Act (FCA, 1933), 721
Farmers' Alliance, 580–581, 607
Farmers Friend Manufacturing Company,
    512(i)
Farms and farming, 240–241. See
    also Agriculture; Planters and
    plantations; Rural areas; Shays's
    Rebellion; Tenant farmers
  in 1920s, 682, 692, 693(m), 698
  in 1950s, 817–818
  agrarian revolt in, 580–582
  bankruptcies, 679, 704, 705
  in California, 392(i)
  in Civil War, 446
  commercial, 510–512, 511(f), 512(i)
  cooperatives and, 581–582
  debt of, 511, 531, 698
  First World War and, 657
  free silver issue and, 538, 541, 542
  in Great Depression, 703, 705, 706, 707
  implements for, 328(i), 329
  income decline and, 580–581, 582(f)
  Jefferson and, 264
  land for, 329
  mechanization of, 329
  Mexican rebellion and, 648
  migratory labor and, 510
  in New Deal, 717, 734(i)
  in New England, 115
  prohibition and, 686
  railroads and, 540
  sharecropping and, 474–475, 475(m), 510
  slaves and, 365, 372
  in South, 474–475, 475(m)
  tariffs and, 539
  tenant farmers and, 129, 379
  in West, 507–509, 510–512
  yeomen and, 68, 377–379, 377(i)
Farm Security Administration (FSA, 1937),
    737
Fascism. See also Italy; Mussolini, Benito;
    Nazi Germany
  after First World War, 746
  Hitler and, 739
  Roosevelt, F. D., on, 738
  in Spain, 747
Fathers, slave, 373. See also Families; Men
Faubus, Orval, 828
Faulkner, William, 691
FBI. See Federal Bureau of Investigation
Federal budget. See Deficit
Federal Bureau of Investigation (FBI)
  civil rights movement and, 846
  illegal activities by, 903–904
Federal Communications Commission, 825
Federal Deposit Insurance Corporation
  (FDIC), 718
Federal Election Campaign Act (1974), 903
Federal Emergency Relief Administration
  (FERA), 719
Federal government. See Government (U.S.)

Federalist Papers, The, 230
Federalists, 227–229, 253, 286, 323
  Bill of Rights and, 237
  collapse of, 284
  election of 1796 and, 253–254
  election of 1800 and, 262–263
  election of 1808 and, 273
  Jefferson and, 264–265
  Quasi-War and, 255, 256
  after War of 1812, 278–279
Federal Republic of Germany. See West
    Germany
Federal Reserve Act (1913), 633–634
Federal Reserve Board, 634
  Carter and, 906
  Clinton and, 942
Federal Trade Commission (FTC), 634, 679
Female academies, 282–283
Female-headed families, 841
Females. See Feminism and feminists;
    Women
Female suffrage. See Woman suffrage
Feme covert doctrine, 280–281
Feminine Mystique, The (Friedan), 823
Feminism and feminists, 857–860. See also
    Women; specific individuals
  birth control movement and, 637–638
  countermovement to, 859–860
  division in, 687
  ERA and, 687
  Reagan and, 919–920
Fences, ranching and, 508
Ferdinand (Spain), 35
Ferraro, Geraldine A., 916
Ferris, G. W. G., 573
Ferris wheel, 566(i), 573
Fetterman, William, 489(m), 492
Fictive kin, 127
Field hands, slaves as, 373
Fife and drum music, 181(i)
Fifteenth Amendment, 469–470
Figgins, J. D., 10(i)
Filipinos. See also Philippines
  as migrant workers, 510
  in Spanish-American War, 602
Fillmore, Millard, 397, 407
Films. See Movies
Finance capitalism, 526–527
Finances. See also Economy; Hamilton,
    Alexander
  under Articles of Confederation, 207, 209,
    220–221
  for Civil War, 430
  in New Deal, 718
  during Revolution, 189
Financial Services Modernization Act
  (1999), 941
Finland, 782(m)
Finney, Charles Grandison, 315, 316
Fire, Indian uses of, 22
Fire-eaters (radical Southerners), 396
Fireside chats, of Roosevelt, F. D., 718
First Amendment, 238, 843
  Pentagon Papers and, 890
First Bank of the United States, 243–244,
    264
First Congress, 237
First Continental Congress (1774), 164–165
First Lady. See specific individuals
First New Deal, 716–722

First South Carolina Infantry, 438(i)
First World War (1914–1918)
    African Americans and, 652, 653, 670
    alliances in, 648–649, 649(i)
    American Expeditionary Force in, 653–655, 654(m)
    armed forces in, 653–655
    armistice in, 654(i), 655, 663, 673
    casualties in, 650, 655, 673
    eastern front in, 653
    Europe after, 663–665, 664(m)
    events leading to, 648–649
    in France, 653–655, 654(m)
    home front during, 656–661, 656(i), 657(f), 659(m), 660(i)
    legacy of, 744
    patriotism during, 660–661
    peace after, 663–666
    Red Scare after, 668–670
    Russian withdrawal from, 652
    submarine warfare in, 650, 650(m), 651, 661, 673
    trench warfare in, 652(i), 653
    United States in, 651–655, 652(i), 654(m), 673
Fishing and fishing industry
    in New England, 95, 115
    in Pacific Northwest, 13
Fitzgerald, F. Scott, 691
Fitzhugh, George, 363
Five Civilized Tribes, 434, 490
Five-Power Naval Treaty (1922), 680
Flaming Youth, 678
Flappers, 677(i), 685, 685(i), 688
Flexible response policy, 872
Florida, 362
    election of 2000 and, 951
    expansionists and, 276
    Indians in, 73, 498
    Jackson in, 287
    military rule in, 468(m)
    readmission to union, 481(m)
    secession of, 417, 418(m), 424
    Spain and, 42, 73, 228
Folk music, 855
Folsom culture, Folsom point and, 10(i)
Food(s). See also Agriculture; Crops; Diet (food); Hunter-gatherer; Hunting; Plants; specific crops and foods
    African, 128
    in Confederacy, 430
    of Eastern Woodland peoples, 13
    in Jamestown, 57
    of Southwestern cultures, 15
    standards for, 840
Food Administration, in First World War, 657, 698
Food stamp program, 840, 862
Football, 690
Foote, Henry S., 396
Foraging, 9
Force Bill (1833), 311
Forced labor. See Slavery
Ford, Betty, 903(i)
Ford, Edsel, 678(i)
Ford, Gerald, 902, 903–904, 903(i)
Ford, Henry, 678(i), 680–681, 684, 705, 707
Ford's Theatre, Lincoln at, 452

Foreclosures
    on farms, 580
    in Great Depression, 704, 705, 706
Foreign aid
    in Cold War, 786–787
    to developing nations, 787
    Marshall Plan as, 780, 784, 784(i)
    to Pakistan and Afghan rebels, 911
    to South Korea, 797
    Truman Doctrine and, 783–784
Foreigners. See Immigrants and immigration
Foreign Miners' Tax Law (California, 1850), 348
Foreign policy. See also Cold War; Diplomacy; specific presidents and policies
    business and, 598–599
    disarmament and, 680
    isolationism and expansionism in, 598
    militarization of, 797
    Monroe Doctrine and, 288, 601
    multilateralism in, 959
    "New Look" in (Eisenhower), 812
    noninvolvement in 1930s as, 746–747
    president and, 226
    of Roosevelt, T., 624–628, 626(i), 627(m), 628(m)
    after Second World War, 781
    of Taft, 630
    Truman-Eisenhower comparison in, 788, 811–816, 831
    unilateralism in, 950, 955
    U.S. as world power and, 601
Forest reserves, 624, 625(m)
Forests
    in New England, 94
    steamboat fuel from, 298
Forrestal, James V., 781
Fort(s). See also specific forts
    in Ohio River region, 219
    along Oregon Trail, 338, 338(m)
    in Revolutionary War, 183(m)
Fortas, Abe, 838(i)
Fort Laramie. See Laramie, Fort
Fort Sill Reservation, 492
Fort Stanwix. See Stanwix, Fort
Fort Stanwix, Treaty of, 217, 219, 248
Fort Sumter. See Sumter, Fort
Fort Worth, 819
Forty-niners, 347, 349
Forty-second Street (movie), 704
Founding Fathers. See Constitution (U.S.); specific individuals
Fourier, Charles, 351
Fourierist phalanxes, 351
"Four-Minute Men," 660
Fourteen Points, 662–663, 666
Fourteenth Amendment, 466–467, 479
    ratification by southern states, 467, 473
    voting rights and, 467, 479, 842
"Fraggings," in Vietnam War, 890
Framers. See Constitution (U.S.)
France. See also First World War; French Revolution; New France; Second World War
    appeasement of Hitler and, 749
    colonies of, 134–135
    cotton from South and, 428
    England and, 251, 272–273

    English colonies and, 106, 142–144
    exploration by, 50
    German occupation zone of, 782
    Indochina and, 800
    Louisiana and, 268
    Morocco crisis and, 628
    Native Americans and, 144
    New England and, 114, 142
    Ottoman empire and, 664
    privateers from, 254–255
    railroads in, 520(f)
    Revolutionary War and, 178, 193–194, 194(i), 195, 198–199
    in Second World War, 749
    Spanish influenza epidemic in, 668
    Suez Canal and, 814
    in UN, 770
    Vichy government in, 749
    Vietnam and, 812–813
    West Indies and, 74(m)
Franchise, for adult males, 285. See also Voting and voting rights
Franciscans, in California, 341
Franco, Francisco, 747
Franklin, Benjamin, 122, 133, 147, 222, 224
    Albany Plan of Union and, 145
    on British taxation, 151
    Second Continental Congress and, 175
Franz Ferdinand (Archduke, Austria-Hungary), 648, 649(i)
Fredericksburg, battle of (1862), 433–434
Free blacks, 333, 381, 382. See also African Americans
    elite, 382
    enfranchisement of, 285
    as slaveholders, 383
    in South, 381–383
Freedmen, 457(i)
    black codes and, 462(i), 463–464
    education and, 461, 474, 475(m), 483
    as Exodusters, 510
    freedom and, 459–461
    land for, 460, 474–475, 475(m)
    in Republican Party, 471–474, 474(f)
    search for families by, 461
    sharecropping by, 474–475, 475(m)
    support for, 478–479
    voting rights for, 457(i), 463, 464, 466, 467, 468, 469, 471, 476, 476(f), 476(i)
Freedmen's Bureau, 460, 467, 469
Freedmen's Bureau Acts (1865 and 1866), 465
Freedom(s). See also Civil rights; Civil rights movement; specific rights and freedoms
    in 1790s, 253
    in Bill of Rights, 238
    of free blacks, 382
    of poor southern whites, 77–78
    religious, 93
    in state constitutions, 211
Freedom fighters (Hungary), 812
"Freedom papers," 381(i)
Freedom Rides, 845(m)
Free enterprise, Coolidge and, 679
Free labor, 393
    compulsory, 460
    Republican Party on, 406
    vs. slavery, 363, 459–460
    in West, 393

Free-labor ideal, 332, 333, 350
    economic inequality and, 333–334
    immigrants and, 334–335
Freeman, Elizabeth (Mum Bett), 213, 213(i)
Freemen
    in Chesapeake colonies, 69, 70, 71
    in Massachusetts, 91–92
Freeport Doctrine, 412
Free silver, 538, *541*–542, 541(i)
Free-soilers and free soil doctrine, 393, 394,
    396, 409
Free-Soil Party, 395, 400, 401
Free speech, 447, 669
    birth control and, 638
"Free speech" movement, 854
Free states, 286, 331(m), 395, 396(m),
    401(m), 406(m). *See also* specific
    states
Free trade, 646. *See also* Trade
    in 1930s, 745
    in 1941, 745
    agreements for, 946
    debate over, 947
Freewill Baptists, 282
Frémont, Jessie Benton, 403(i), 407
Frémont, John C., 341, 403(i), 407, 439
French and Indian War. *See* Seven Years'
    War
French Revolution, 250–251
Frick, Henry Clay, 585, 586, 586(i)
Friedan, Betty, 823, 858
Frobisher, Martin, 50(t)
Frontier
    Indians along, 192–193, 193(m)
    in Pennsylvania, 120
    in Revolutionary War, 199
    warfare along, 134
Frontier thesis (Turner), 488, 513
Frowne, Sadie, 557
"Fruit juices," 686
FTC. *See* Federal Trade Commission
Fuel Administration, 657
Fuels. *See also* Energy; Gasoline; Oil and
    oil industry
    alternative, 909
Fugitive Slave Act (1850), 396, 398–*399,*
    398(i)
Fugitive slaves, 78
    in Civil War, 439, 444
    Compromise of 1850 and, 398–399
    resistance by, 375–376
    underground railroad and, 354, 399
Full-employment legislation, 790
Fulton, Robert, 295(i), 298
Fundamental Constitutions of Carolina, 76
Fundamentalism, Protestant, 695
Fundamental Orders of Connecticut, 94
Fur trade, 94, 106, 120, 134, 142, 146, 337

Gabler, Mel and **Norma,** 899
Gabriel's rebellion (1800), 263
Gadsden, James, 400
Gadsden Purchase (1853), 400, 400(m)
Gage, Thomas, 163, 164, 166–167, 175
"Gag rule," in Congress, 320
Galloway, Joseph, 164
Gandhi, Mohandas (Mahatma), 853(i)
Gang system, of slave labor, 373
Garfield, James A., 467, 535

Garland, Hamlin, 573
Garment industry, 557
    Triangle Shirtwaist Company and,
        614–616, 615(i)
Garnet, Henry Highland, 353
Garrison, William Lloyd, 317, 396, 482
Garvey, Marcus, 688
Gary, Martin, 480
Gas. *See* Poison gas
Gasoline, shortages of, 907(i). *See also*
    Energy; Oil and oil industry
Gaspée (ship), 161, 162
Gates, Bill, 916
Gates, Horatio, 197, 198
Gates, Merrill, 496
Gatherers, hunters and, 10. *See also* Food;
    Plants
Gathering Corn in Virginia (Darley), 377(i)
GATT. *See* General Agreement on Tariffs
    and Trade
Gay Liberation Front, 856
Gay marriage, 940
Gays and lesbians. *See also* Homosexuals
    and homosexuality; Same-sex
    relationships
    gay rights protests and, 920
    organizing by, 855–856
    protecting rights of, 918
    in Second World War, 758
Gaza Strip, 888, 911, 946
Gender and gender issues. *See also* Men;
    Women; specific issues
    in 1950s, 821, 825–826
    in colonies, 65
    inequality of, 281
    in Iroquoian tribes, 20
    politics and, 531–533, 543
    separate spheres and, 313–314
    voting and, 919
    women in workplace and, 556, 556(i),
        558, 559–560
General Agreement on Tariffs and Trade
    (GATT), 946
General Assembly (UN), 770
General Court (Massachusetts), 91–92
General Electric (GE), 525, 527
General Federation of Women's Clubs
    (GFWC), 533
Generall Historie of Virginia (Smith), 55(i)
General Managers Association (GMA), 589,
    590
General Motors (GM), 730, 959
"General welfare" clause, 244
Geneva accords (1954), 813, 813(m)
Geneva meeting (1955), 815
Genocide, in Holocaust, 766, 775
"Gentlemen's Agreement" (1907), 628
Gentry, slaveholding, 129
Geographic mobility, free labor and, 334
Geographic regions, global, 549, 549(m)
Geographic revolution, 36–38
George III (England), 150, 156, 174, 179
Georgia, 124
    Cherokee removal and, 309–310
    Civil War in, 449(m), 450–451
    cotton field and worker in, 471(i)
    Indians of, 20, 247
    military rule in, 468(m)
    plantation, 475(m)
    readmission to union, 481(m)

Reconstruction taxation in, 480
Redeemers in, 480
Revolutionary War and, 195–196
secession and, 417, 418(m), 424, 463
slavery in, 214
German Americans, First World War and,
    660–661
Germany. *See also* East Germany; First
    World War; Nazi Germany; Second
    World War; West Germany
    American foreign policy and, 601
    Dawes Plan and, 680
    immigrants from, 112, 118–119, 123,
        332(i), 334(f), 335, 405, 550, 551
    Lusitania and, 646(i), 650, 650(m)
    manufacturing in, 916–917
    Morocco crisis and, 628
    Pago Pago and, 601
    Pennsylvania Dutch from, 118
    postwar zones in, 782
    printing in, 32
    railroads in, 520(f)
    reparations of, 680
    as republic, 655
    revolt in, 655
    after Second World War, 781
    U-boats of, 650, 655
    Venezuela confrontation and, 626
    war guilt assigned to, 665
Geronimo (Apache shaman), 495(i), 497–498
Gettysburg, battle of (1863), 449–*450,*
    449(m), 450(m)
Ghettos, Harlem, 689
Ghost Dance, 494(i), *498*–499
Gibbon, John, 493
GI Bill of Rights (1944), *764*–765, 775, 791
Gideon v. Wainright (1963), 838(i), 843
GI Forum. *See* American GI Forum
Gilbert, Humphrey, 50(t)
Gilded Age, 518
    cities in, 554–555, 555(i)
    consolidation in, 526, 527
    depression in, 520, 526, 538, 541, 542
    economy during, 538–542
    free silver issue in, 538, 541–542, 541(i)
    gender, race, and politics in, 531–532
    industry during, 518–524, 518(i), 522(f)
    materialism of, 513
    New South during, 530–531
    politics in, 534–535
    poverty in, 528
    presidency during, 622
    presidential politics in, 534, 535, 536–537
    regulation of railroads and trusts in, 540
    social Darwinism and, 527–528
    Supreme Court during, 526, 528, 540
    wealthy in, 521, 528, 554–555, 555(i)
    West in, 513
    women in, 529(i), 531–533, 532(i)
Gilded Age, The (Twain and Warner), 513
Gingrich, Newt, 940
Ginsberg, Allen, 826
Ginsburg, Ruth Bader, 939
Girls. *See* Women
Glasnost, 924
Glass-Steagall Banking Act (1933), 718, 941
Glenn, John H., 872
Global issues. *See* Economy; Immigrants
    and immigration; Imperialism;
    Migration; specific issues

Globalization
  debates over, 946–947
  economic, 946
  shipping and, 928
  of terrorism, 936, 954–955
  in United States, 947–949
  U.S. demography and, 948
Global markets, for western agriculture, 510, 511, 512
Global migration, growth of cities and, **548**–552, 548(i), 549(m), 550(m), 551(f)
Glorieta Pass, battle at (1862), 434, 434(m)
Glorious Revolution (England), 105
Gods and goddesses. *See also* Religion(s); specific deities and peoples
  Indian, 44
  of Taino people, 35
Godspeed (ship), 57
Golan Heights, 888
Gold. *See also* Gold standard
  from Americas, 45, 45(f)
  Indians and discovery of, 492–493
  from Peru, 42
  western mining for, 500, 501, 501(m)
Gold City, Nevada, 500(i)
Gold Diggers of 1933 (movie), 704
Golden Twenties, 678
Goldman, Emma, 669
Goldmark, Josephine, 616
Gold rush, in California, 347–349, 348(i), 392
Gold standard
  election of 1896 and, 596–597
  vs. free silver, 538(i), 541, 542
  Nixon and, 862
Goldwater, Barry M., 839, 898–899
Goliad, massacre at (1836), 341
Gompers, Samuel, 563, 564, 565, 637, 668
"Good immigrants," 694
Good neighbor policy, **745**
Goodwood, Thomas (Hehakaavita [Yellow Elk]), 495
Gorbachev, Mikhail
  end of Cold War and, 934, 935
  Reagan and, 921(i), 924
Gore, Albert, Jr., 937, 951, 951(m)
Gorgas, Josiah, 430
Gospel of wealth, 526, **528,** 613, 614
"Gospel of Wealth" (Carnegie), 528
Gould, Jay, 518, 520, 521
Gould and Curry mine, 502
Government. *See also* Chiefdoms; Conservatives and conservatism; Government (U.S.); Legislation; State(s); specific programs
  of Carolina, 76
  in Chesapeake region, 70
  by chiefdoms, 15, 17
  Eisenhower on, 807
  of Massachusetts, 86, 87
  by Mexica, 24
  of middle colonies, 98, 100
  of New England, 90–92, 104–106
  of Pennsylvania, 100, 101
  progressive, 618–619
  Puritan, 90–92
  role of, 961
  of Virginia, 60, 68(i)
  in Virginia and New Jersey plans, 224–225

Government (U.S.). *See also* Constitution (U.S.); Federal budget; Legislation; specific programs
  under Articles of Confederation, 209
  Bush, G. H. W., and, 930–932
  capital of, 240
  Civil War and, 445–446
  expansion under Roosevelt, F. D., 716
  spending in 1950s, 818
Governors. *See also* specific individuals
  colonial, 136
  salary payments to, 157, 162
Gradual emancipation, **213**
  in New York, 320
  in Pennsylvania, 213
Gradualism policy, of Washington, Booker T., 640
Grady, Henry, 530
Graham, Billy, 824
Grain, 511
  harvesting of, 328(i)
Grand Canyon National Park, 625(m)
Grandees, 69(i), 71, 75, 78. *See also* Elites
Grange, 540, 581
Grange, Harold (Red), 690
Grant, Ulysses S.
  in Civil War, 431, 434–435, 449(m), 450, 452
  corruption and, 477, 477(f), 481, 534
  election of 1868 and, 476–477, 476(m), 480(f)
  election of 1872 and, 477–478
  peace policy for Indians, 492
  presidency of, 476–478, 477(i)
  Reconstruction and, 476–477
  tariffs and, 599(f)
Grape boycott, 853(i)
Grapes of Wrath, The (Steinbeck), 725
Grasse (Comte de), 198
Grassroots conservatism, 899–900, 960
Graves, A. J. (Mrs.), 313
Gray, Martin, 480
Great American Desert, farmers in, 508
Great Awakening, **133**
  Second, 313, 315–316
Great Basin region, cultures of, 12, 14(t)
Great Britain. *See* England (Britain)
Great Compromise, 224–225
Great Depression (1930s). *See also* New Deal; Roosevelt, Franklin Delano; specific leaders and programs
  crash of 1929 and, 698–701, 699(i)
  economy during, 702–704, 702(i), 703(f)
  foreign affairs during, 745
  labor unions in, 729–730
  lifestyle in, 703–704
  migrant labor during, 724–725
  politics in, 725–728
  tariffs and, 698, 700
  unemployment in, 721–722
  working-class militancy in, 705–706
"Great Die Up," 510
Great East River Bridge. *See* Brooklyn Bridge
Greater East Asia Co-Prosperity Sphere, 752
Great Fire (Chicago, 1871), 570
Great Lakes region, 298
  Indians of, 19, 120, 148
Great Plains. *See also* Plains Indians
  bison and, 12, 14(t), 337, 489, 491, 491(i)
  drought in, 508

  dust storms in, 724–725
  farming in, 508
  Indians of, 20–21, 267, 270–271
Great Railroad Strike (1877), 561–563, 561(i), **562,** 562(m), 575, 587
Great Salt Lake, 339
Great Sioux Uprising (1862), 489(m), 492
Great Society, 836, 839–841, 865
  assessment of, 841
  Nixon and, 898
  Vietnam War and, 877, 891
Great Tenochtitlán (Rivera), 3(i)
"Great War." *See* First World War
Great White Fleet, 628
Greece, 664
  foreign aid to, 786
  after Second World War, 784, 784(i)
Greeley, Horace, 430, 478, 548
Green, William, 705
Greenback Labor Party, 541, 581
Green Berets, 873
Greenville, Treaty of (1795), 249, 250
Grenada, invasion of, 922
Grenville, George, 150–152, 150(i)
Griffith, D. W., 660(i)
Grimké sisters (Angelina and **Sarah),** 300, 318, 320
Grinnell, Julius S., 565
Gross national product (GNP)
  in 1950s, 823(f)
  Kennedy and, 837
  after Second World War, 775
Grosvenor, Thomas, 173(i)
Grosvenor and Salem (Trumbull), 173(i)
Grove City v. Bell (1984), 919
Guadalcanal, Battle of, 771
Guadalupe Hidalgo, Treaty of (1848), **346**–347, 503
Guadeloupe, 146
Guam, 604, 605, 759
Guantánamo, Cuba
  detention camp in, 955, 957
  U.S. base at, 605
Guatemala, 601, 813
Guerrilla war
  during Civil War, 426, 434
  with Filipino nationalists, 602
  in Kansas, 409
  in Revolutionary War, 198
  in Vietnam, 875
Guiteau, Charles, 535
Gulf of Mexico region. *See* Louisiana Purchase; New Orleans; specific locations
Gulf of Tonkin Resolution (1964), **877,** 889
Gulf War. *See* Persian Gulf War
"Gun Belt," 819
Gunboats, in Civil War, 435
Gun control, in California, 931
Gutenberg, Johannes, 32
Guthrie, Woody, 704, 733

Habeas corpus, Lincoln and, 425–426
Haires, Francis, 65
Haiti, 353
  intervention in, 647, 944, 945
  migration of planters from, 252
  Republic of, 251
Haitian Revolution, 251–**252**

Hakluyt, Richard, 57
Half Breeds, 535
Halfway Covenant, 96
Hamilton, Alexander, 240(i)
    Adams, John, and, 256
    on Bank of the United States, 243–244
    at constitutional convention, 223
    Constitution and, 229, 230
    economy and, 240
    election of 1796 and, 254
    election of 1800 and, 263
    Jefferson and, 264
    Report on Manufactures, 244
    Report on Public Credit, 242
    as treasury secretary, 240
Hamilton, Grant, 602(i)
Hammond, James Henry, 393
Hampton Institute (Indian boarding school),
    495, 495(i)
Hancock, John, 152
Hancock, Winfield Scott, 535
Hanna, Mark, 597, 604
Hanoi. *See* Vietnam; Vietnam War
Harding, Warren Gamaliel, 672, 679, 680
Hard money, 244, 321
Harlan County coal strike, 705, 705(m)
Harlem Renaissance, 689–690, 689(i)
Harmar, Josiah, 248
Harpers Ferry, Virginia, Brown's raid on
    (1859), 414
Harper's Weekly, 476(i), 491(i)
Harrington, Michael, 837
Harrison, Benjamin, 499, 539, 596(m)
Harrison, Carter, 565
Harrison, William Henry, 275–276, 321,
    342, 538, 539
Harrows, 511
Hartford, 94
Hartford Convention (1814), 278–*279*
Hartford Seminary, 283
Hawai'i. *See also* Pearl Harbor
    annexation and, 599
    in Second World War, 753, 753(i), 760
Hawks, in Vietnam War, 882–883
Hawley-Smoot tariff (1930), 700
Hay, John, 601, 602, 627
Hayes, Rutherford B.
    election of 1876 and, 481–482, 482(m),
        535
    Great Railroad Strike and, 562, 563
    presidency of, 535
Haymarket bombing, 561, *564*–565, 565(i)
Haywood, William Dudley (Big Bill), 637
Headright, 63, 65, 76
Head Start, 839
Health, Education, and Welfare,
    Department of, 807
Health and health care. *See also* Disease;
    Medicine; specific conditions
    Bush, G. W., and, 952
    Carter and, 906
    Clinton and, 939
    environmental illnesses and, 908
    Johnson, L. B., and, 840
    in New England, 95
    Obama and, 958(i), 959
    Truman and, 790, 795
Hearst, William Randolph, 602(i), 603
Hegemony, of U.S., 601
Hehakaavita (Yellow Elk), 495

Heidt, Wesley and Edward, 753(i)
Held, John, Jr., 677(i)
Helicopters, in Vietnam War, 876(i)
Helsinki accords (1975), *887*
Hemings, Sally, 262(i)
Hemingway, Ernest, 691
Hendrick (Mohawk Indians), 145, 145(i)
Hendricks, Thomas A., 478
Henry VIII (England), 84, 85
Henry, Fort, battle at, 432(m), 435
Henry, Patrick, 152, 162, 164, 224, 230
Henry Street settlement, 613
Henry the Navigator (Portugal), 32
Hepburn Act (1906), 623
Hernandez, Aileen, 858
Hernandez v. Texas (1954), *821*
Herndon, William, 411
Hessians, 182, 199
Hester Street (New York City), 552
Hezbollah, 922
Hickory Clubs, 304
Hierarchies
    in New Spain, 46
    social and political, 15
Higginson, Thomas W., 438(i)
Higher education, 314. *See also* Education;
    Universities and colleges; specific
    schools
    in 1950s, 817
    for African Americans, 791–792
    Clinton and, 939
    democratization of, 821
    after Second World War, 791–792
    for women, 282–283
Higher Education Act (1965), 840
"Higher law" doctrine, of Seward, 396–397,
    416
High schools, 570
High-tech industries, workers for, 949
Highways. *See* Roads and highways
Hill, Aaron (Mohawk Indians), 217
Hill, Anita, 932
Hillman, Sidney, 730
Hillsborough (Lord), 157
Hippies, 855
Hirohito (Japan), 753
Hiroshima, atomic bombing of, 773(i), 774
Hispanics and Hispanic Americans. *See
    also* Latinos/Latinas; specific groups
    migration of, 693, 693(m)
    New Deal and, 733
    in Southwest, 503–504
    use of term, 852
Hispaniola, Haitian Revolution and,
    251–252
History and *historians, 4*
    archaeology and, 4–5
    Turner's frontier thesis, 488, 513
"History of the Standard Oil Company"
    (Tarbell), 523–524
Hitler, Adolf, 739, 744, 748(i). *See also* Nazi
    Germany
    aggression through 1941, 750(m)
    anti-Semitism of, 746
    German rearmament and, 745
Hoboes, in Great Depression, 703
Ho Chi Minh, 812, 813, 874
Ho Chi Minh Trail, 874
Hohokam culture, 16–17
Holding companies, 523

Holland. *See* Dutch; Netherlands
Hollywood, California, 690
"Hollywood Ten," 796
Holmes, George F., 400
Holmes, Oliver Wendell, 669
Holocaust, 765–*766,* 765(i), 766(m)
Holy experiment, of Penn, 100
Home front
    in Civil War, 442–447
    in First World War, 656–661, 656(i), 657(f),
        659(m), 660(i)
    in Revolutionary War, 185–189, 187(m)
    in Second World War, 755–756, 762–765,
        762(i)
Homeland Security, Department of, 955
Homelessness
    in Chicago, 570, 573
    of children, 558
    in Great Depression, 703
Home rule, for South, 478, 479
Homespun cloth, 158
Homestead Act of 1862, 446, *506,* 507(m)
Homesteaders, 507–508, 507(m)
Homestead lockout, 584–587, *585,* 586(i),
    607
Homo erectus, 6
Homo sapiens, 6–7
Homosexuals and homosexuality. *See
    also* Gays and lesbians; Same-sex
    relationships
    immigration restrictions and, 795
    Kinsey on, 826
    in military, 940
    organizing by, 855–856
    in Second World War, 758
Honduras, 601
Hone, Philip, 321–322
Honor, in South, 369–370
Hood, John B., 451
Hooker, Thomas, 94
Hoover, Herbert, 698
    Bonus Marchers and, 705
    campaign poster, 697(i)
    crash of 1929 and, 700
    election of 1928 and, 695, 696, 696(m)
    as Food Administration head, 657, 689
    in Great Depression, 697, 700–701
    inauguration of, 679
    individualism and, 700–701
    on New Deal, 736
    as Secretary of Commerce, 678, 679,
        697(i)
Hoover, J. Edgar, 669
Hoovervilles, 704
Hopewell culture, 17–18
Hopi Indians, 17
Horizontal integration, 523
Horsecars, 570
Horses, 337
    Plains Indians and, 492
Horseshoe Bend, Battle of (1814), 278
Hostages, in Iran, 911–912
Hotchkiss rapid-fire guns, 499
Households
    appliances for, 683
    separate spheres in, 313–314
House of Burgesses, 60, 68(i), 70, 152
House of Representatives (U.S.), 225, 226,
    229. *See also* Congress (U.S.)
    election of 1800 and, 262–263

election of 1824 and, 284, 289(m)
presidential impeachment by, 469
Reconstruction and, 459, 464, 467, 479
House servants, slaves as, 373
**House Un-American Activities Committee
(HUAC), 796,** 799
Housewives. *See* Domesticity; Women
Housing
in 1950s, 819, 821
of African Americans, 128
Anasazi, 17
California ban on discrimination in, 848
in cities, 548
colonial, 117
discrimination in, 841, 848
federal government and, 839, 840, 841,
848, 862
of Iroquoian tribes, 20
low-income, 738, 841
in mill towns, 299
of Mogollon peoples, 16
public, 840
racism in, 819
after Second World War, 791
for slaves, 359(i), 369, 369(f), 372(i)
slums and, 548
sod houses, 507
Truman and, 789
urban renewal and, 837
working class, 554
Housing Act (1949), **794**–795
Houston, Sam, 341
Howe, Eleanor, 899
Howe, William, 175, 176, 182–184, 191, 196
How the Other Half Lives (Riis), 554–555,
555(i)
Hudson, Carrie, 373
Hudson, Henry, 98
Hudson River region, 120, 182, 187(m), 190,
197, 298
Huerta, Dolores, 853–854
Huerta, Victoriano, 647, 648
Hughes, Charles Evans, 650, 680
Hughes, Langston, 690
Huguenots, in colonies, 131
Hull House, 612(i), 613, 614
Human rights, Carter and, 909–911
Humans
migration into Americas, 6–9
of world and Western Hemisphere, 8(f)
Humphrey, Hubert H., 872, 884, 885
Hundred Days, 716
Hungary
communism and, 781
after First World War, 664
immigrants from, 550
revolt in (1956), 812
Hunger
in Great Depression, 701, 702, 705
in Jamestown, 57, 59
Hunter, David, 439–440
Hunter-gatherer, 10
Paleo-Indians as, 8–10
in Southwest, 15
Woodland peoples and, 18
Hunting
Archaic, 10
of bison, 12, 338
by Eastern Woodland peoples, 13
North American Indian, 22

Huron Indians, 148
Hurricane Katrina, 952–953
Hurston, Zora Neale, 690
Husbands. *See also* Men
in South, 370
Hussein (Jordan), 946
Hussein, Saddam, 932, 933–934, 955–956
in Persian Gulf War, 932
Hutchinson, Anne, 93–94
Hutchinson, Thomas, 151, 153, 163
Albany Plan of Union and, 145
Boston Tea Party and, 162–163
Hutchinson family, 158–159
Hydroelectricity, New Deal programs for,
720

Iberian Peninsula, 32. *See also* Portugal;
Spain
Muslim expulsion from, 32
ICBMs. *See* Intercontinental ballistic
missiles
Idaho
mining in, 500, 501(m)
voting rights for women in, 592(i)
Ideology, free-labor, 332–335
"I have a dream" speech (King), 845
Illegal immigrants, 820–821, 948
Illinois, Ku Klux Klan in, 694
Illiteracy, 380
Illness. *See* Disease
Illustrated Weekly, 586(i)
Immigrants and immigration. *See also*
Migration; Slavery; specific groups
from 1840–1860, 334(f)
in American Communist Party, 725
anti-immigrant sentiment and, 502,
693–694, 696
Asian, 502, 504–505, 505(i), 553
cities and, 332(i), 548–552, 548(i), 692
to colonies, 107, 112, 118–119
as domestic servants, 567
education for, 570
European, 548, 550–552, 550(m), 551(f),
553–554
free labor and, 334–335
globalization and, 947
global migration, urbanization, and,
548–552, 549(m)
Hispanic, 733
McCarran-Walter Act and, 795
Mexican, 671–672, 671(i)
in middle colonies, 118–119
mining and, 502
old and new immigration, 552
progressive social work and, 611(i)
Puritan, 84–85
quotas on, 693–694, 695, 795
racial composition of, 948–949
racism and, 552–554
restrictions on, 504–505, 554, 692,
693–694, 695
sentiment against, 954
source in 18th century, 112
South and, 367
in textile industry, 300
travel by, 551
voting and, 687
Immigration and Nationality Act (1965),
840, 947–948

Impartial Administration of Justice Act
(1774), 163(t)
Impeachment
of Clinton, 938, 941–942
of Johnson, A., 468–469, 942
of Nixon, 902
Imperialism, 488
cultural, 494–496, 495(i)
debate over, 604–606, 605(m)
First World War and, 648, 665
Indians and, 488–489, 494–496, 495(i)
in West, 488–496, 495(i)
Imperial presidency, 902
Imports
colonial goods as, 103
into colonies, 115
duties on, 244
of slaves, 125(t)
tariffs and, 599, 599(f)
Impressment, 272–**273**
in Civil War, 443
Inauguration
of Eisenhower (1953), 811
of Hoover (1929), 679
of Jackson, 305
of Jefferson (1801), 257
of Kennedy, 837, 870–871
of Polk, 343
of Reagan, 897(i)
of Roosevelt, T., 498
Incandescent light bulb, 525
Incan empire, 41–42
Income. *See also* Wages
in 1920s, 683, 684, 698–699
in 1950s, 822
of African Americans, 764, 943
agricultural, 703(f)
of Latinos, 943
manufacturing, 703(f)
national, 702
redistribution of, 841
rise in per capita, 683
Social Security as, 731
of whites, 943
Income tax, 446, 731
Sixteenth Amendment and, 630
state, 618
Incorporation laws, 301
Indentured servants, 51, 63–**65,** 68, 88, 119,
127. *See also* Slavery
Independence. *See also* Revolutionary War;
specific locations
for Philippines, 787
voting for, 178–179
Independent magazine, 557, 563
Independent treasury system, 322
India, 146
atomic bomb and, 936
England and, 787
railroads in, 520(f)
sea route to, 33
in Second World War, 753
Indian(s). *See also* Native Americans;
specific groups
named by Columbus, 35
Indiana
Ku Klux Klan in, 694
prohibition in, 686
Indian Citizen Day (1892), 495(i)
Indian Citizenship Act (1924), 694

Indian Claims Commission (1946), 809
Indian country. *See also* Indian Territory;
	Oklahoma; West
	in Ohio Valley, 190
	in Revolutionary War, 192–193
Indian policy. *See also* Native Americans
	allotment as, 494, 496
	assimilation as, 494–496, 495(i)
	concentration, 338
	removal of, 306, 308–310, 309(m), 488–490
	reservations and, 338, 488–490, 497
	in Virginia, 70
	under Washington, 247–248
Indian Relocation Program (1948), 809
Indian Removal Act of 1830, 308
Indian Reorganization Act (1934), 733
Indian Rights Association, 496
Indian Territory, 309(m), 310, 489(i),
	490–493, 496–499. *See also* Indian
	country
Indian wars, in West, 489, 491–493
Indies. *See* East Indies; West Indies;
	specific locations
Indigenous people. *See* Native Americans;
	specific groups
Indigo, 76, 124, 128
Individualism, 351, 369
	limits on, 700–701
	Nixon on, 898
Indochina, 800. *See also* Cambodia; Laos;
	Vietnam
Indonesia. *See also* Dutch East Indies; East
	Indies
	Portugal and, 33
Industrial core (global economic region),
	549, 549(m)
Industrial cowboys, 511–512
Industrial evolution, 328, 355
Industrialism
	bison herds and, 491
	urban, 500
	western commercial farming and,
		510–512, 511(f), 512(i)
	women activists and, 591
**Industrial Workers of the World (IWW),
	637,** 668, 669
Industry. *See also* specific industries
	bison slaughter and, 491
	Confederate, 443
	in First World War, 657–658, 657(f)
	in Gilded Age, 518–524, 518(i), 522(f),
		538–540, 543
	globalization and, 947
	Great Depression and, 700–701
	heavy, 818
	New Deal and, 721–722
	in North (Civil War), 427(i)
	production by, 818
	railroads and, 330
	in Second World War, 762–763
	service, 917
	in South, 366
	technology and, 818
Inequality. *See also* Equality
	economic, 333–334
	social Darwinism and, 527–528
	wealth and, 698–699
Infant Welfare Society, 611(i)
Inflation. *See also* Economy; Stagflation
	in 1830s, 312

	in 1990s, 942
	Carter and, 906
	in Civil War, 430, 443
	after First World War, 668
	Nixon and, 862
	in Second World War, 763
	after Second World War, 790
Influenza. *See* Spanish influenza epidemic
Inheritance
	partible, 115
	tax on, 731, 915
	by women, 281
In His Steps (Sheldon), 614
Initiative, 618, 619
Inoculation, against smallpox, 176
Installment buying, 684, 823
Insurance, national health, 906, 952
Integration. *See also* Segregation
	Freedom Rides and, 845(m)
	in Little Rock, 828
	of public schools, 354, 828, 829(i), 900
	after Second World War, 792
Intellectual thought. *See also* Education;
	Literature; specific works and
	individuals
	on slavery defense, 362–363
	transcendentalists and, 351
	utopians and, 351
Intelligence agencies, 786(i), 903–904. *See
	also* Central Intelligence Agency;
	Federal Bureau of Investigation
Intercontinental ballistic missiles (ICBMs),
	815
Interesting Narrative (Equiano), 125(i)
Interlocking directorates, 634
Intermarriage, 45, 308. *See also* Marriage
**Intermediate-range nuclear forces (INF)
	agreement, 924**
Internal taxation, 152. *See also* Taxation
International Criminal Court (UN), 955
Internationalism
	of Roosevelt, F. D., 745
	after Second World War, 770
	of Wilson, 680
Internationalization, of United States,
	947–949
International Ladies' Garment Workers
	Union (ILGWU), 615
International Monetary Fund, 947
Internment camps, for Japanese
	Americans, **756,** 756(m)
**Interstate Commerce Commission (ICC),
	540,** 622–623
**Interstate Highway and Defense System
	Act** (1956), **807**–808, 807(m), 819. *See
	also* Roads and highways
Intervention and interventionism. *See also*
	specific locations
	in Afghanistan, 959
	in Beirut, 922(i)
	by CIA, 787
	in Grenada, 922
	in Haiti, 944, 945
	in Latin America, 813–814, 872, 876, 932
	in Second World War, 748
Intolerable Acts. *See* Coercive (Intolerable)
	Acts
Inventions and inventors. *See also*
	Electricity; specific types
	from 1865–1899, 524(f)

Investment
	in Bank of the United States, 244
	foreign, in United States, 947
	after Second World War, 781
	by Southerners, 366
	in United States by China, 952
Iran. *See also* Iran hostage crisis
	CIA and, 814
	Hezbollah and, 922
	Nixon administration and, 888
	nuclear weapons and, 957
	revolution in (1979), 907, 907(i), 911
	Soviet Union and, 781
Iran-Contra scandal, Reagan and, **923**
Iran hostage crisis, 911–**912,** 914
Iran-Iraq war, 924, 932
Iraq. *See also* Iraq War (2003–2011)
	Kurds in, 934
	Paris Peace Conference (1919) and,
		664
	Persian Gulf War and, 932–934, 933(m)
Iraq War (2003–2011), 950, 955–957, **956**
	casualties in, 956
Ireland. *See also* Scots-Irish
	immigrants from, 296(i), 334, 334(f), 335,
		405, 502, 551, 552, 556
Irish Americans
	as domestic workers, 567
	in mining, 502
Iron and iron industry, 518, 521, 522, 522(f),
		530–531
	labor unions and, 563
	puddlers and, 557
Ironclad warships, 436
Iron curtain, 782(m), **783.** *See also* Soviet
	Union
Iroquois Confederacy, 144, 145, 191, 217
Iroquois Indians, 19, 20, 106, 193(m), 248
	at Albany Congress, 145, 146
	in middle colonies, 120
	in New England, 114
	during Revolution, 190
Irreconcilables, in Congress, 665, 666
"Irrepressible conflict" speech (Seward),
	416
Irrigation, 15, 339
Isabella (Spain), 35
Isham, Edward, 379
Islam. *See also* Muslims
	extremists and, 954
Islamic Jihad, 922(i)
Isolationism
	in 1920s, 680
	in 1930s, 745, 746, 747
	foreign policy and, 598
Israel
	since 1989, 946(m)
	Camp David accords and, 911
	Clinton and, 944
	Eisenhower and, 814
	Nixon and, 888
	Palestine and, 922
	Six-Day War and (1967), 888, 911
	state of (1948), 788, 788(m), 888
	Yom Kippur War and (1973), 862, 888
Isthmus of Panama, 37
Italy. *See also* First World War; Mussolini,
	Benito; Second World War
	CIA operations in, 787
	Ethiopia and, 746